Pittsburgh Series in Bibliography

WALT WHITMAN

Walt Whitman

A DESCRIPTIVE BIBLIOGRAPHY

Joel Myerson

UNIVERSITY OF PITTSBURGH PRESS
Pittsburgh and London
1993

The preparation of this volume was made possible (in part) by a grant from the Research Materials Program of the National Endowment for the Humanities, an independent Federal agency.

Published by the University of Pittsburgh Press, Pittsburgh, Pa., 15260

Manufactured in the United States of America
Printed on acid-free paper

Library of Congress Cataloging in Publication Data

Myerson, Joel.
    Walt Whitman : a descriptive bibliography / Joel Myerson.
      p. cm. — (Pittsburgh series in bibliography)
    Includes index.
    ISBN 0-8229-3739-5
    1. Whitman, Walt, 1819–1892–Bibliography. I. Title.
  II. Series.
  Z8971.5.M93 1993
  [PS3231]
  016.811′3—dc20   92-25927
                                     CIP

A CIP catalogue record for this book is available from the British Library.

Eurospan, London

For Harrison Hayford

Contents

Acknowledgments

IN COMPILING this bibliography I have incurred many debts of gratitude. Unhappily, I can only thank in a general way the many librarians who answered my questions about copies of Whitman's works at their institutions. I wish to express my thanks to the following institutions and their staffs for help in using their collections during my visits to them: American Antiquarian Society, Bolton Public Library (Bolton, England), Boston Public Library, Boston University (Alice and Rollo G. Silver Collection), British Library, Brown University, Cambridge University, Columbia University, Duke University (Gay Wilson Allen and Trent Collections), Dunedin Public Library (Dunedin, New Zealand), Harvard University Libraries (Houghton and Widener libraries), Library of Congress (Charles E. Feinberg and Carolyn Wells Houghton Collections), Massachusetts Historical Society, National Library of Scotland, New York Public Library (Oscar Lion and Berg Collections), New York University, Oxford University (Bodleian Library), Pierpont Morgan Library, Princeton University, Providence Athenaeum, John Rylands University Library of Manchester, Stanford University, Toronto Public Library, Trinity College (Dublin, Ireland), Tulane University, University of North Carolina, University of Pennsylvania, University of South Carolina, University of Texas (Humanities Research Center), University of Toronto, University of Virginia (Clifton Waller Barrett Library), Walt Whitman Association (Camden, New Jersey), and Yale University (Beinecke Library). Daniel Boice, Jens Holley, and the Interlibrary Loans staff at the University of South Carolina were of great assistance in obtaining books for me.

Many people have helped me in this project and I would especially like to thank the following: Gay Wilson Allen, Julius P. Barclay, Alice Lotvin Birney, Alan Brasher, Lawrence Buell, Kathryn Cain, David Chesnutt, Ken Craven, Rosemary Cullen, A. R. Darvall, M. Deas, Edward L. Doctoroff, Masako Dorrill, Peter Drummey, T. H. Dunne, Maggie Du Priest, Anthony Edwards, Rudolph Ellenbogen, Clark Evans, Ed Folsom, Claudia Funke, Cathie Gottlieb, Charles E. Greene, Jon Guillot,

J. Samuel Hammond, Robert Harris, Jo Hayford, Shirley Brice Heath, Cathy Henderson, Joan F. Higbee, Nigel Hobbs, Glenn Horowitz, Maxine James, James Kirkpatrick, John Lancaster, James Lewis, Nat Lewis, Erika C. D. Lindemann, Richard Lindemann, Jerome Loving, Bernard McTique, William Major, Patricia Middleton, Edwin Haviland Miller, Bettsy Mosimann, Tom Nicely, A. M. Northover, Morton D. Paley, Margit Resch, David W. Riley, G. Ross Roy, Christine Ruggere, Sukari Saloné, Patrick G. Scott, Rollo G. Silver, Jean Strachan, Anthony Szczsiul, G. Thomas Tanselle, John R. Turner, Daniel Traister, Peter VanWingen, Robert L. Volz, James L. W. West III, William White, Patricia C. Willis, Elizabeth Hall Witherell, and Georgianna Ziegler. William R. Cagle, Ezra Greenspan, Charles W. Mann, and Joseph McElrath all read an earlier version of this bibliography and made valuable suggestions. Information on copies at the Lilly Library was kindly supplied by Mr. Cagle, and at the Chapin Library by Mr. Volz. I am grateful to Jane Flanders for her skillful copyediting of this book.

The secondary bibliographies of Whitman by Scott Giantvalley and Donald D. Kummings were of great value to me and I thank them for their work. Professor Kummings also kindly supplied me with copies of hard-to-find materials.

All work on Whitman is indebted to Charles E. Feinberg, whose Whitman collection at the Library of Congress is the best one in the world. Mr. Feinberg's generosity has made scores of Whitman projects possible, including the collected edition of Whitman's writings now in progress. His collection has helped make this book possible.

Frederick A. Hetzel is responsible for starting and supporting the Pittsburgh Series in Bibliography. I am grateful to him for his support.

Matthew J. Bruccoli has been generous with his assistance, and this bibliography is much the better for it. We have argued about bibliography for twenty years now and I have learned more than just a little from him.

A grant from the National Endowment for the Humanities, Division of Research Programs, greatly facilitated the research and preparation of this book.

The University of South Carolina has provided material support for the preparation of this book. A grant from the Research and Productive Scholarship Committee financed my early work. I am grateful to Trevor Howard-Hill and Bert Dillon, chairs of the department of English, and Carol McGinnis Kay, Dean of the College of Humanities and

Social Sciences, for their help. I also wish to thank Armida Gilbert and Alfred G. Litton for being superb research assistants.

I am grateful to the following for permission to reproduce photographs of materials in their collections: Boston Public Library, Duke University, Dunedin Public Library, Library of Congress, Lilly Library of Indiana University, Missouri Historical Society, Princeton University, University of Pennsylvania, University of Texas, University of Virginia, and Yale University.

Harrison Hayford helped start me in my career, sold me my first rare book (and the beginnings of my own Whitman collection), and taught me how to buy books on extended credit. I dedicate this book to him as a small way of expressing my appreciation for many things over many years.

Greta has endured Whitman because I promised it was my last major author collection and my last bibliography. More than anyone, she has helped me in finishing this book, and my debt to her for love, friendship, and support is enormous.

Introduction

THIS DESCRIPTIVE BIBLIOGRAPHY of the works of Walt Whitman is limited to writings by Whitman. Writings about Whitman are not listed, except in cases where they include something by Whitman published for the first time, or in the *Appendix* listing principal works about Whitman.

FORMAT

Section A lists chronologically all books and pamphlets wholly by Whitman, including all printings of all editions in English and other languages through 1892, the year of Whitman's death, and all editions and reprintings in English through 1991. *Leaves of Grass* presents a unique case, and it is treated differently, as will be discussed below.

The numbering system for Section A indicates the edition and printing for each entry. Thus, for *Two Rivulets*, A 9.1.a indicates that this is the ninth title published by Whitman (A 9), and that the entry describes the first edition (1), first printing (a). For multivolume works, the number of the volume is added to the numbering system; thus, for *Correspondence*, A 41.II.1.a indicates that this is the forty-first Whitman title published (41), and that the entry describes the second volume (II), first edition (1), first printing (a). Issues are indicated by inferior numbers—thus A 3.1.a$_2$ is the second issue of the first printing of *Drum-Taps*. States are discussed within an entry.

Each initial entry begins with a facsimile of the title page (with its dimensions given) and, where relevant, the copyright page, then pagination information, information about illustrations when present, a collation of the gatherings, and the dimensions of the pages and thickness of the sheets.[1] A description of the contents is followed, when

---

1. Because Whitman published his own books, copies within a single printing were usually bound at various times, resulting in different trim sizes for different sized cas-

needed, by a listing of the contents and information about prior appearances in print. For poems in *Leaves of Grass* and its annexes, the "Index
to the Poems in *Leaves of Grass*" at the end of this book provides information about the publication histories of individual poems within the
various editions, printings, and issues of the book during Whitman's lifetime, as well as their first newspaper or magazine appearances. Information on typography and paper includes the dimensions of the printed
text, type of paper, number of lines per page, and running heads. Thus
$5'' \times 3''$ indicates the height and width of the area containing the text on a
page; $5'' (4\frac{1}{2}'') \times 3''$ indicates the height (first from the top of the running
head to the bottom of the last line of text, and second from the top of the
first line of text to the bottom of the last line of text) and width of the
printed area. All paper is white unless otherwise indicated. Binding
information includes cloth types, dimensions of stampings, and descriptions of flyleaves, endpapers, page trimming, and page-edge gilding or
staining. Flyleaves and endpapers are wove paper unless otherwise
indicated. All wrappers are wove paper unless otherwise indicated.
Dust jackets, when present, are wove paper unless otherwise indicated
and are fully described and usually reproduced.[2] Information on publication is drawn from Whitman's journals, letters, and unpublished manuscripts; publishers' records; copyright information (from both published and manuscript records of the Copyright Office); and contemporary book trade announcements. Locations are provided to identify the
libraries holding copies of each title described and examined. Notes
deal with information not discussed elsewhere in the entry.

Section B lists chronologically all collected editions of Whitman's
writings through 1991.

Section C lists chronologically all miscellaneous collections of Whitman's writings through 1991. Foreign-language editions published
through 1892, the year of Whitman's death, are also listed. Binding is
assumed to be cloth or boards unless otherwise indicated. Locations
are given for the copies examined.

---

ings. Also, some works were poorly bound (especially the 1860 *Leaves of Grass* [A 2.3]),
resulting in sprung gatherings that affect the measurement of sheet bulking. Both
factors make it hard—if not impossible—for a single measurement of page size or sheet
bulking to apply to all copies within a single printing; the reader should take all such
measurements to be approximate.

2. Exceptions are unprinted glassine dust jackets and dust jackets for the second or
subsequent volumes in a series, such as *Correspondence*.

Whitman revised and expanded *Leaves of Grass* from 1855 until his death in 1892, and the Section A entry for the book (A 2) concentrates on those complete editions with which Whitman was involved or which were published during his lifetime.[3]

Section D lists chronologically all titles in which material by Whitman appears for the first time in a book or pamphlet. Entries within a year are arranged alphabetically. Included are prose, poetry, and letters. All items are signed unless otherwise indicated. Previously published materials are so identified. The first printings only of these titles are described, but English editions and selected reprintings are also noted. Binding is assumed to be cloth or boards unless otherwise indicated. Locations are given for the copies examined.

Section E lists chronologically all first American and English publications in newspapers and magazines of material by Whitman through 1991. No attempt has been made to list contemporary accounts of Whitman's lectures or of interviews with him. Publications are prose unless otherwise indicated. When applicable, information on first book publication and first appearance in a book by Whitman is given.

Section F lists all proof copies, circulars, and broadsides of Whitman's poetry and prose published during his lifetime.

Section G lists, chronologically, reprinted prose and poetry by Whitman in books and pamphlets through 1892, the year of his death. Entries within a single year are arranged alphabetically. All items are signed unless otherwise indicated. Binding is cloth or boards unless otherwise indicated. Locations are given for the copies examined.

Section H lists alphabetically separate publications of individual poems and prose works through 1991. Binding is cloth or boards unless otherwise indicated. Locations are given for the copies examined.

Section I lists chronologically references to possible publications by Whitman that have not been dealt with elsewhere in the bibliography.

---

3. For example, had the type-facsimile of the 1855 *Leaves of Grass* produced by Thomas Mosher or the reset edition of that work done by Viking Press, both published in the twentieth-century, been added as separate editions of the 1855 *Leaves* immediately following the main entry for that edition, then all subsequent editions of *Leaves of Grass* would have lost their numbering in the contemporary sequence of events.

A case might be made for the inclusion of William Michael Rossetti's much-shortened edition of *Leaves of Grass* as *Poems* in 1868 (see C 1), but since Whitman was not responsible for the selections, I have decided to list it in Section C rather than give it the undeserved status of a Section A entry.

The "Index to the Poems in *Leaves of Grass*" provides information about the publication histories of individual poems within the various editions, printings, and issues of *Leaves of Grass*, as well as their first newspaper or magazine appearances.

An *Appendix* lists principal works about Whitman.

TERMS AND METHODS

Edition. All copies of a book printed from a single setting of type—including all reprintings from standing type, from plates, or by photo-offset processes.

Printing. All copies of a book printed at one time (without removing the type or plates from the press).

State. States occur only within single printings and are created by an alteration not affecting the conditions of publication or sale to *some* copies of a given printing (usually by stop-press correction or cancellation of leaves). For instance, the fourth issue of *Specimen Days in America* (A 11.2.a$_4$) has been located in four states, distinguished by the cancellation of various combinations of leaves in the integral publisher's advertisements at the end of the book. There must be two or more states.

Issue. Issues occur only within single printings and are created by an alteration affecting the conditions of publication or sale to *some* copies of a given printing. The most common way of creating an *issue* is with a cancel title leaf, but it is also possible to create an issue by printing a new first gathering with a different title page (bearing the imprint of a different publisher) or by placing the name of another publisher on the title page by using a rubber stamp.[4] For instance, when David McKay took over the sheets of *Leaves of Grass* from Rees Welsh in 1882, he sold them with a cancel title leaf bearing his imprint dated '1883' (see A 2.7.h$_2$). However, when he reprinted the book in 1883 with his own imprint on the title page and sent copies to Scotland

---

4. Beginning in 1867, Whitman added "annexes" to *Leaves of Grass* by binding in the sheets of his separately-published works (with original or cancel title leaves, or in new printings with the title pages reset as half titles) in a multivolumes-in-one format. I have treated these versions of *Leaves of Grass* (the general title Whitman gave *Leaves of Grass* and its annexes) as issues, since the different formats clearly affect the conditions of publication.

for sale, he reset the integral title page with the imprint of the publisher there, Wilson & McCormick (see A 2.7.j$_2$). There cannot be a first issue without a second.

Edition, printing, state, and *issue* have here been restricted to the sheets of the book.

Publisher's advertisements are described but the reader should be aware that they generally exist in three forms. First, they may be integral in the first or last gatherings of a book. In such cases, variants between the advertisements can be used to determine the printing history of the book, since the advertisements were printed in the same press run as the rest of the work. Second, advertisements may be printed on the endpapers of a book. No examples of this have been found for Whitman. The third form, inserted catalogues of publisher's advertisements, may indicate only binding and not printing histories. It can be stated unequivocally that the date on the inserted advertisements in a book has no direct bearing on the priority of a printing.

Dust jackets for Section A entries have been discussed in detail beause they are part of the original publication effort and sometimes provide information on how the book was marketed. There is, of course, no certainty that a jacket now on a book was always on it.

For binding-cloth designations, I have used the method proposed by G. Thomas Tanselle;[5] most of these cloth grains are illustrated in Jacob Blanck, ed., *Bibliography of American Literature* (New Haven: Yale University Press, 1955–1991).

Color specifications are based on the *ISCC-NBS Color Name Charts Illustrated with Centroid Colors* (National Bureau of Standards). Centroid numbers have not been assigned; instead, the general color designations have been used.[6]

The spines of bindings or dust jackets are printed horizontally un-

---

5. G. Thomas Tanselle, "The Specifications of Binding Cloth," *The Library*, 21 (September 1966), 246–247. The reader should also consult Tanselle's excellent "The Bibliographical Description of Patterns," *Studies in Bibliography*, 23 (1970), 72–102, which reproduces all of the cloth grains illustrated in the *BAL* plus additional ones.

6. See G. Thomas Tanselle, "A System of Color Indentification for Bibliographical Description," *Studies in Bibliography*, 20 (1967), 203–234, for a discussion of how this system can be fully employed. I feel, however, that the use of exact Centroid designations creates a false sense of precision, especially for nineteenth-century books. Oxidation, fading, wear, and nonuniform dyeing practices make precise color identification difficult, if not impossible. In any case, color identification by the Centroid system is inexact.

less otherwise indicated. The reader is to assume that vertically printed spines read from top to bottom unless otherwise indicated.

In the descriptions of title pages, bindings, and dust jackets, the color of the lettering is black unless otherwise indicated.

Pagination for reprintings of Section A, C, and H entries indicates the number of the last printed page in the book, exclusive of publisher's advertisements.

The term *royalty* cannot be applied to most of Whitman's works. Once he was paid a flat fee (with *Franklin Evans* [A 1]), but usually he paid for the printing of the books himself and sold them himself, or paid for the printing of the book and sold the finished sheets (with or without casings) to a bookseller for distribution. Information about Whitman's financial involvement with his books is given under the *Publication* rubric.

Some miscellaneous collections of Whitman's works have a publisher's imprint listing multiple geographical locations, usually cities in which the publisher had offices. In such cases, one to three cities are listed in this bibliography, but four or more are described with a *[&c.]* following the first city listed.

Copyright on Whitman's works prior to 1871 was registered with the clerks of the district courts of Massachusetts or New York in two stages: first, the book's title was given and entered into the copyright books, then a copy of the published work was deposited. Both these dates are given when available.

Publication information for books published by David McKay is drawn from manuscript records at the University of Pennsylvania and from Whitman's own notes at the Library of Congress. Information about *After All, Not to Create Only* (A 6) is drawn from the Roberts Brothers account books on deposit at the Houghton Library of Harvard University.

This bibliography makes use of deposit and inscribed copies to help determine publication dates. Dates given for copies at BC, BD, BE, BL, BO, and DLC are the dates written or stamped on the copies deposited for copyright at those institutions and are enclosed within single quotation marks. Dates given for copies at other collections indicate either the date the copy was received into the collection or a date written by a contemporary owner of the book. Whitman also inscribed many copies of his books; such presentation copies contemporaneous with the publication of a book are listed.

Some of Whitman's works were sold in series. When the series is identified in the work (such as on the title page or binding), it is italicized. When the series is not identified in the work but can be ascertained from contemporary book trade announcements, it is placed within quotation marks.

Attributions of Whitman's journalism are based primarily on William White's pioneering *Walt Whitman's Journalism: A Bibliography* (1969). When material is attributed to Whitman in works published before White's bibliography in 1969 but not included in it, I have indicated this fact by using the rubric "Not in White, *Journalism*." If items listed in White's bibliography were first attributed in print to Whitman by someone other than White, I have listed the place(s) in which the work was reprinted. When items were attributed to Whitman after the publication of White's bibliography, I have indicated the source. Thus, if a journalistic item appearing before Whitman's death is listed without any source for attribution or reprinting given, one may assume that it appears by virtue of its inclusion in White's bibliography.

Much bibliographical lore about Whitman derives from the early bibliographies by Frank Shay and by Carolyn Wells and Alfred F. Goldsmith, which provide little information about their sources. When information is supplied from these works, it is so indicated.

The volume of *Bibliography of American Literature* containing the section on Whitman was published after this bibliography went to press, and I have incorporated information from it selectively, such as collational information in Section A and titles in Section F. The *BAL* has a policy of not allowing scholars to view the bibliographical information it has assembled until after a volume is in print; for this reason, the editor of *BAL*, Michael Winship, and I were unable to share information about our respective work on Whitman.

Dates of letters, when not given in the printed source, are supplied on the authority of Edwin Haviland Miller's edition of Whitman's *Correspondence* (A 41) and its supplements.

This bibliography is based on evidence gathered from my personal inspection of multiple copies of Whitman's works in American, Canadian, British, Irish, and New Zealand libraries. For first English and American editions, only libraries holding copies that are bibliographically intact (not rebound or repaired) are listed. Exceptions are rebound copies containing nonbibliographical information, such as dated owners' inscriptions, which is mentioned in notes.[7] The symbols used for American libraries are those employed by the National Union Catalog; those for Canadian libraries are the same as those listed in *Symbols of Canadian Libraries,* 7th ed. (Ottawa: National Library of Canada, 1977), which are here preceded by *Ca.* The following are additional location symbols:

Blackwell's	Blackwell's Bookstore, Oxford, England
BBo	Bolton Public Library, Bolton, England
BC	Cambridge University, England
BD	Trinity College, Dublin
BE	National Library of Scotland, Edinburgh
BL	British Library, London
BMR	John Rylands University Library, Manchester, England
BO	Oxford University, England
InU-L	Lilly Library, Indiana University
JM	Collection of Joel Myerson
NN-B	Berg Collection, New York Public Library
NN-R	Rare Books Division, New York Public Library
NjCW	Walt Whitman Association, Camden, New Jersey
NzD	Dunedin Public Library, Dunedin, New Zealand

The following are abbreviations are used throughout:

Aurora	*Walt Whitman of the New York Aurora,* ed. Joseph Jay Rubin and Charles H. Brown. State College, Penn.: Bald Eagle Press, 1950.
BAL	*Bibliography of American Literature,* comp. Jacob Blanck, 9 vols. New Haven: Yale University Press, 1955–1991.
BIP	*Books in Print*
CBI	*Cumulative Book Index*
Civil War	*Walt Whitman and the Civil War,* ed. Charles I. Glicksberg. Philadelphia: University of Pennsylvania Press, 1933.

---

7. Because some Whitman titles are extremely scarce, I have listed locations for bibliographically defective or rebound copies in notes when fewer than five copies have been located.

Correspondence	*The Correspondence,* ed. Edwin Haviland Miller, 6 vols. New York: New York University Press, 1961–1977.
Daybooks	*Daybooks and Notebooks,* ed. William White, 3 vols. New York: New York University Press, 1978.
Early Poems and Fiction	*The Early Poems and the Fiction,* ed. Thomas L. Brasher. New York: New York University Press, 1963.
GF	*The Gathering of the Forces,* ed. Cleveland Rodgers and John Black, 2 vols. New York: Putnam's, 1920.
Half-Breed	*The Half-Breed and Other Stories,* ed. Thomas Ollive Mabbott. New York: Columbia University Press, 1927.
ISL	*I Sit and Look Out,* ed. Emory Holloway and Vernolian Schwarz. New York: Columbia University Press, 1932.
Notebooks	*Notebooks and Unpublished Prose Manuscripts,* ed. Edward F. Grier, 6 vols. New York: New York University Press, 1984.
NUC	National Union Catalog
NYD	*New York Dissected,* ed. Emory Holloway and Ralph Adimari. New York: Rufus Rockwell Wilson, 1936.
PW92	*Prose Works 1892,* ed. Floyd Stovall, 2 vols. New York: New York University Press, 1963–1964.
Reader's Edition	*Leaves of Grass: Comprehensive Reader's Edition,* ed. Harold W. Blodgett and Sculley Bradley. New York: New York University Press, 1965.
RLIN	Research Libraries Information Network (computer data base)
Schools	*Walt Whitman Looks at the Schools,* ed. Florence Bernstein Freedman. New York: King's Crown Press, 1950.
Shay	Frank Shay, *The Bibliography of Walt Whitman.* New York: Friedmans', 1920.

UPP	*Uncollected Poetry and Prose,* ed. Emory Holloway, 2 vols. Garden City, N.Y. Doubleday, Page, 1920.
Wells and Goldsmith	Carolyn Wells and Alfred F. Goldsmith, *A Concise Bibliography of the Works of Walt Whitman.* Boston: Houghton Mifflin, 1922.
White, *Journalism*	William White, *Walt Whitman's Journalism: A Bibliography.* Detroit: Wayne State University Press, 1969.
Whitman at Auction	Gloria A. Francis and Artem Lozynsky, *Whitman at Auction, 1899–1972.* Detroit: Bruccoli Clark/Gale, 1978.
WWWC	Horace Traubel, *With Walt Whitman in Camden,* 6 vols. Boston: Small, Maynard, 1906; New York: D. Appleton, 1908; New York: Mitchell Kennerley, 1914; Philadelphia: University of Pennsylvania Press, 1953; Carbondale: Southern Illinois University Press, 1964, 1982.

This bibliography is not an attempt to indicate the scarcity of Whitman's works and should not be taken as such. If there is only one location listed, it means that, of all the libraries I visted and corresponded with, only one had or reported having a copy with all the examined points intact; it does not mean that there is only one copy of that work in existence. For recent editions I have not listed as many locations as for earlier ones, where I have tried to be as comprehensive as possible.

A bibliography is outdated the day it goes to the printer. Addenda and corrigenda are earnestly solicited.

Edisto Beach, South Carolina
15 January 1992

WALT WHITMAN

A. Separate Publications

All books, pamphlets, or broadsides wholly or substantially by Whitman, including all printings of all editions in English through 1991, and all foreign-language editions through 1892, the year of Whitman's death, arranged chronologically.

A 1 FRANKLIN EVANS
1842

A 1.1
First edition, only printing (1842)

THE NEW WORLD.

PARK BENJAMIN,
EDITOR.

J. WINCHESTER,
PUBLISHER.

" No pent-up Utica contracts our powers; for the whole boundless continent is ours."

EXTRA SERIES.   OFFICE 30 ANN-STREET.   NUMBER 34

VOL. II....No. 10.   NEW-YORK, NOVEMBER, 1842.   PRICE 12½ CENTS.

Original Temperance Novel.

Entered according to Act of Congress, in the year 1842,
BY J. WINCHESTER,
In the Clerk's Office of the Southern District of New York.

FRANKLIN EVANS;

OR

THE INEBRIATE.

A TALE OF THE TIMES.

BY WALTER WHITMAN

INTRODUCTORY.

THE story I am going to tell you, reader, will be somewhat aside from the ordinary track of the novelist. It will not abound, either with profound reflections, or sentimental remarks. Yet its moral—for I flatter myself it has one, and one which it were well to engrave on the heart of each person who scans its pages—will be taught by its own incidents, and the current of the narrative.

Whatever of romance there may be—I leave it to any who have, in the course of their every-day walks, heard the histories of intemperate men, whether the events of the tale, strange as some of them may appear, have not had their counterpart in real life. If you who live in the city should go out among your neighbors and investigate what is being transacted there, you might come to behold things far more improbable. In fact, the following chapters contain but the account of a young man, thrown by circumstances amid the vortex of dissipation—a country youth, who came to our great emporium to seek his fortune—and what befell him there. So it is a plain story; yet as the grandest truths are sometimes plain enough to enter into the minds of children—it may be that the delineation I shall give will do benefit, and that educated men and women may not find the hour they spend in its perusal, altogether wasted.

And I would ask your belief when I assert that, what you are going to read is not a work of fiction, as the term is used. I narrate occurrences that have had a far more real existence, than in my fancy. There will be those who, as their eyes turn past line after line, will have their memories carried to matters which they have heard of before, or taken a part in themselves, and which, they know, are *real*.

Can I hope, that my story will do good? I entertain that hope Issued in the cheap and popular form you see, and wasted by every mail to all parts of this vast republic; the facilities which its publisher possesses, giving him the power of diffusing it more widely than any other establishment in the United States; the mighty and deep public opinion which, as a tide bears a ship upon its bosom, ever welcomes anything favorable to the Temperance Reform; its being written *for the mass*, though the writer hopes, not without some claim upon the approval of the more fastidious; and, as much as anything else, the fact that it is as a pioneer in this department of literature—all these will give "THE INEBRIATE," I feel confident, a more than ordinary share of patronage.

For youth, what can be more invaluable? It teaches sobriety, that virtue which every mother and father prays nightly, may be resident in the characters of their sons. It wars against Intemperance, that evil spirit which has levelled so many fair human forms before its horrible advances. Without being presumptuous, I would remind those who believe in the wholesome doctrines of abstinence, how the earlier teachers of piety used parables and fables, as the fit instruments whereby they might convey to men the beauty of the system they professed. In the resemblance, how reasonable it is to suppose that you can impress a lesson upon him whom you would influence to sobriety, in no better way than letting him read such a story as this.

It is usual for writers, upon presenting their works to the public, to bespeak indulgence for faults and deficiences. I am but too well aware that the critical eye will see some such in the following pages; yet my book is not written for the critics, but for THE PEOPLE; and while I think it best to leave it to the reader's own decision whether I have succeeded, I cannot help remarking, that I have the fullest confidence in the verdict's being favorable.

And, to conclude, may I hope that he who purchases this volume, will give to its author, and to its publisher also, the credit of being influenced not altogether by views of the profit to come from it? Whatever of those views may enter into our minds, we are not without a strong desire that the principles here inculcated will strike deep, and grow again, and bring forth good fruit. A prudent, sober, and temperate course of life cannot be too strongly taught to old and young; to the young, because the future years are before them—to the old, because it is their business to prepare for death. And though, as before remarked, the writer has abstained from thrusting the moral upon the reader, by dry and abstract disquisitions—preferring the more pleasant and quite as profitable method of letting the reader draw it himself from the occurrences—it is hoped that the New and Popular Reform now in the course of progress over the land, will find no trifling help from a " TALE OF THE TIMES."

A 1.1: Binding A: 11½″ × 7⅞″

[1] 2–31 [32]

[1]¹⁶. Sheets bulk ¹⁄₃₂″.

Contents: pp. 1–31: text; p. 32: advertisements for books, headed 'NEW WORKS IN PRESS.'.

Typography and paper: 10″ (9¾″) × 6⅜″; wove paper; double columns, 77 lines per column. Running heads: rectos: pp. 3–31: 'Evans. THE NEW WORLD. | [double rule]'; versos: pp. 2–30: 'THE NEW WORLD. Franklin. | [double rule]'.

Binding: Three styles have been noted:

Binding A: Head title. Untrimmed.

Binding B: Head title with medium yellowish brown wrappers. Front wrapper recto: '[all within a 10″ high × 6⅜″ wide × 1⁵⁄₁₆″ thick ornate printed border, with 'PARK BENJAMIN, EDITOR' within center at the top, and 'J. WINCHESTER, PRINTER, | 30 Ann-street, New-York.' within center at bottom] FRANKLIN EVANS, | OR | THE INEBRIATE. | [wavy rule] | A TALE OF THE TIMES. | [wavy rule] | BY A POPULAR AMERICAN AU-THOR. | [wavy rule] | [paragraph indent] "Oh, thou invisible spirit of wine, if thou hast no name to be known by, let | us call thee—Devil!' [flush right] Shakspere. | [wavy rule] | NEW-YORK: | J. WINCHESTER, 30 ANN-STREET. | [dotted rule] | [dotted rule] | 1842. | [rule] | [rule] | PRICE 12½ CENTS.'; front wrapper verso: advertisement for *Books for the People* series; spine: blank; back wrapper recto: advertisement for "Dr. Rush's Infallible Health Pills"; back wrapper verso: advertisements for *New World* and *Every Youth's Gazette*. All edges trimmed.

Binding C: Head title with pale pink or light orange-yellow wrappers. Front wrapper recto: '[all within a 9⅞″ high × 6³⁄₁₆″ wide × 1″ thick ornate printed border, with two fountains within each side, 'KNOWLEDGE IS POWER.' in ornate lettering within center at the top, and 'BOOKS FOR THE PEOPLE.' in ornate lettering within center at the bottom] [gothic] Copyright Edition. | [rule] | [rule] | THE MERCHANT'S CLERK, | IN NEW YORK; | OR THE | CAREER OF A YOUNG MAN FROM THE COUNTRY. | [rule] | BY WALTER WHITMAN, | AUTHOR OF "DEATH IN THE SCHOOLROOM," ETC. ETC. | [rule] | [rule] | [gothic] New-York: | J. WIN-CHESTER, 30 ANN STREET. | SUN OFFICE, CORNER OF FULTON AND NASSAU STS. | J. C. WADLEIGH, 459 BROADWAY; BRAINARD & CO., BOSTON; AND SOLD BY ALL | RESPECTABLE BOOKSELLERS AND PERIODICAL AGENTS THROUGHOUT THE | UNITED STATES. | [rule] | [rule] | PRICE 6¼ CENTS.'; front wrapper verso: advertisement for J. Winchester's publications; spine: blank; back wrapper recto: advertisement

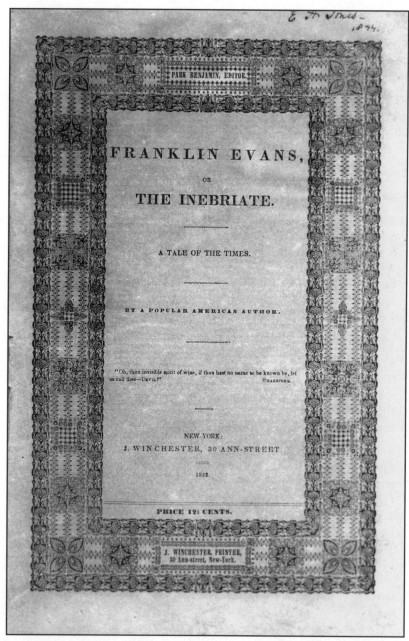

PARK BENJAMIN, EDITOR.

FRANKLIN EVANS,

OR

THE INEBRIATE.

A TALE OF THE TIMES.

BY A POPULAR AMERICAN AUTHOR.

"Oh, thou invisible spirit of wine, if thou hast no name to be known by, let
us call thee—DEVIL!"   SHAKSPERE.

NEW-YORK:
J. WINCHESTER, 30 ANN-STREET.

1842.

PRICE 12½ CENTS.

J. WINCHESTER, PRINTER,
30 Ann-street, New-York.

A 1.1: Binding B: 12⅜″ × 7⅞″

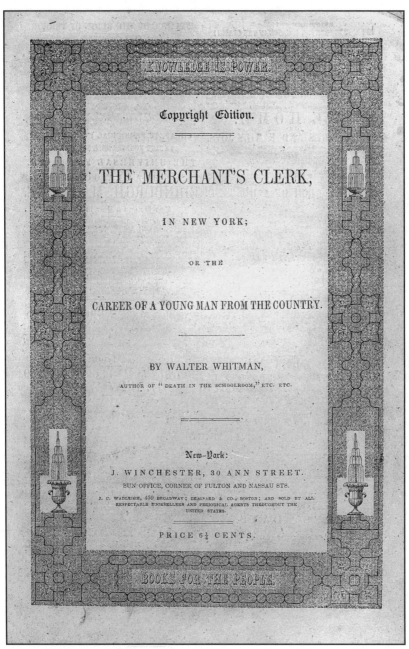

KNOWLEDGE IS POWER.

Copyright Edition.

THE MERCHANT'S CLERK,

IN NEW YORK;

OR THE

CAREER OF A YOUNG MAN FROM THE COUNTRY.

BY WALTER WHITMAN,

AUTHOR OF "DEATH IN THE SCHOOLROOM," ETC. ETC.

New-York:

J. WINCHESTER, 30 ANN STREET.

SUN-OFFICE, CORNER OF FULTON AND NASSAU STS.

J. C. WADLEIGH, 450 BROADWAY; BRAINARD & CO., BOSTON; AND SOLD BY ALL RESPECTABLE BOOKSELLERS AND PERIODICAL AGENTS THROUGHOUT THE UNITED STATES.

PRICE 6¼ CENTS.

BOOKS FOR THE PEOPLE.

A 1.1: Binding C: 12¼″ × 8⅜″

for Froissart's *Chronicles* and "Dr. Rush's Infallible Health Pills"; back wrapper verso: advertisement for *Books for the People* series. Untrimmed.

Printing: J. Winchester, New York (p. [1]).

Publication: Recalling this book, Whitman said that he had "finished" it in "three days of constant work," and that he had received "seventy five dollars cash down" for writing it, adding that "the book sold so well they sent me fifty dollars more in two or three weeks" (2 May, 15 September 1888, in *WWWC*, I, 93; II, 323).

Simultaneously in *The New World*, 2, no. 10; *The New World, Extra Series*, no. 24 (November 1842); and *Books for the People*. Prices: bindings A and B: 12½¢; binding C: 6¼¢. Copies inscribed by owners: binding B: ViU (1844). Announced for 23 November publication in *New World*, 5 (5 November 1842), 305. Reviewed in *New-York Daily Tribune*, 23 November 1842, p. 1. Advertised as *Franklin Evans; or the Merchant's Clerk: A Tale of the Times* in *New World*, 19 August 1843.

Locations: Binding A: CtY (2), DLC, JM, MBU, MH, NN-B, NN-R (2), NNC (2), NcD, PU (2), RPB, ScU, TxU, ViU; binding B: NjP, ViU; Binding C: NNPM, NjP.

Note one: Agnes Strickland's *The Letters of Mary Queen of Scots* in the *Books for the People* series is listed on the front wrapper verso of binding B for publication on 30 November, but on p. [32] is a "Postponement" announcement putting it back to 7 December from the earlier date. The book was published in *New World*, 2, nos. 13–14 (December 1842), and in the *Extra Series* of the same date as nos. 37–38. This evidence suggests that the wrappers were printed before the text, and makes it likely that copies with head titles were sold simultaneously with copies distributed in wrappers.

Note two: The back wrapper verso of binding C notes under the heading "Prices Reduced" that because the post office had decided to change the mailing charges for the *Books for the People* series from the lower newspaper rate to the higher periodical rate, "the proprietors of the New World have determined to take off an amount more than equivalent to the increased rate of postage."

Note three: According to Shay, "between 20,000 and 25,000 copies" were sold, which "netted the author about $200" (p. 14).

A 1.2
Franklin Evans or The Inebriate. New York: Random House, MDCCCCXXIX.

249 pp. Unprinted glassine dust jacket. Edited with an introduction by Emory Holloway. Printed by D. B. Updike at the Merrymount Press, Boston. DLC

copy received from the publisher 11 April 1930. Limited to 700 copies. Price, $10.00. *Locations:* BL, DLC, JM, PU.

Note: Some copies have a white paper label on the front pastedown endpaper stating that the copy was presented at the occasion of "the get-together in honor of collected books April twenty-sixth MDCCCCXXXII": JM, PU.

A 1.3
Franklin Evans or The Inebriate. New Haven: College & University Press, [1967].

187 pp. Cloth (with dust jacket) or wrappers. Edited with an introduction by Jean Downey. Cloth: *Masterworks of Literature Series;* paper: *Masterworks of Literature Series M-22.* Copyright 20 March 1967; A974084. Deposit copies: cloth: DLC ('FEB 12 1968'). Presentation copies: cloth: NcD (from Downey, 20 December 1967). Prices: cloth, $4.50; paper, $1.95. *Locations:* DLC, JM (both), NcD.

A 2 LEAVES OF GRASS

Listed below is a genealogy of the various editions, printings, issues, and states of *Leaves of Grass* published during Whitman's lifetime:

A 2.1   *First edition* (1855)

A 2.1.a₁   *Only printing, first issue:* Brooklyn, N.Y., 1855.

> *First state:* Copyright page bears no printing.
> *Second state:* Copyright information is printed on the copyright page.

A 2.1.a₂   *Only printing, second issue:* Brooklyn, N.Y., 1855; London: Wm. Horsell, [1855]. American sheets with a pasted label on the title page.

A 2.2   *Second edition* (1856)

A 2.2   *Only printing:* Brooklyn, N.Y., 1856.

A 2.3   *Third edition* (1860)

A 2.3.a₁   *First printing, first issue:* Boston: Thayer & Eldridge, 1860–61.

A 2.3.a₂   *First printing, second issue:* Boston: Thayer & Eldridge, 1860–61; London: Trübner, [1860]. American sheets with a pasted label on the title page.

A 2.3.b   *Second printing:* Boston: Thayer & Eldridge, 1860–61.

A 2.3.c   *Third printing:* Boston: Thayer & Eldridge, 1860–61 [i.e., New York: Richard Worthington, 1880(?)].

A 2.3.d–f   *Fourth through sixth printings:* Boston: Thayer & Eldridge, 1860–61 [i.e., New York: Richard Worthington, n.d.].

A 2.4   *Fourth edition* (1867)

A 2.4.a₁   *First printing, first issue:* New York, 1867. 338 + 72 + 24 + 36 pp.

A 2.4.a₂   *First printing, second issue:* New York, 1867 [i.e., 1868]. 338 + 36 pp.

A 2.4.a₃   *First printing, third issue:* New York, 1867 [i.e., 1868]. 338 pp.

A 2.5   *Fifth edition* (1871)

A 2.5.a₁   *First printing, first issue:* Washington, 1871. 384 pp.

A 2.5.a₂   *First printing, second issue:* Washington, 1871. 384 + 120 pp.

A 2.5.b₁   *Second printing, first issue:* Washington, 1872. 384 + 120 pp.

A 2.5.b₂   *Second printing, second issue:* Camden, 1876. 384 pp. "Author's Edition, With Portraits and Intercalations." Title leaf is a cancel.

A 2.5.c₁   *Third printing, first (false) issue:* Camden, 1876. "Author's Edition, With Portraits and Intercalations." Title leaf is a cancel.

A 2.5.c₂   *Third printing, second issue:* Camden, 1876. "Author's Edition, With Portraits from Life."

A 2.5.c₃   *Third printing, third issue:* Camden, 1876; London: Trübner, [1876]. American sheets with a pasted label on the title page.

A 2.6   *Sixth edition* (1871)

A 2.6   *Only printing:* Washington, 1872 [i.e., London: John Camden Hotten, 1873]. 384 + 120 + 14 pp.

A 2.7   *Seventh edition* (1881)

A 2.7.a₁   *First printing, first issue:* Boston: James R. Osgood, [1881].

> *First state:* Title page reads '1881—2'.
> *Second state:* Title page reads '1881—82'.

A 2.7.a₂   *First printing, second issue:* London: Trübner, 1881. Title leaf is a cancel.

A 2.7.b₁   *Second printing, first issue:* Boston: James R. Osgood, 1881–82.

A 2.7.b₂   *Second printing, second issue:* London: David Bogue, 1881. Title leaf is a cancel.

A 2.7.c₁   *Third printing, first issue:* Boston: James R. Osgood, 1881–82. "Third Edition."

A 2.7.c₂   *Third printing, second issue:* London: David Bogue, 1881 [i.e., 1882]. Title leaf is a cancel.

A 2.7.c₃   *Third printing, third issue:* Camden, N.J., 1882. "Author's Edition." Title leaf is a cancel.

A 2.7.d–g   *Fourth through seventh printings:* Philadelphia: Rees Welsh, 1882.

A 2.7.h₁   *Eighth printing, first issue:* Philadelphia: Rees Welsh, 1882.

A 2.7.h₂   *Eighth printing, second issue:* Philadelphia: David McKay, 1883. Title leaf is a cancel.

A 2.7.i   *Ninth printing:* Philadelphia: David McKay, 1882.

A 2.7.j₁   *Tenth printing, first issue:* Philadelphia: David McKay, 1883.

A 2.7.j₂   *Tenth printing, second issue:* Glasgow: Wilson & McCormick, 1883. Title leaf is integral.

A 2.7.j₃   *Tenth printing, third issue:* Glasgow: Wilson & McCormick, 1883. Title leaf is a cancel.

A 2.7.k₁   *Eleventh printing, first issue:* Philadelphia: David McKay, 1884. 382 pp.

A 2.7.k₂   *Eleventh printing, second issue:* Glasgow: Wilson & McCormick, 1884. Title leaf is a cancel.

A 2.7.k₃   *Eleventh printing, third issue:* Philadelphia: David McKay, 1884 [i.e., 1888]. 404 pp.

A 2.7.l₁   *Twelfth printing, first issue:* Philadelphia: David McKay, 1888. 404 pp.

A 2.7.l₂   *Twelfth printing, second issue:* Philadelphia: David McKay, 1891–'92. 438 pp. Known as the "Deathbed Edition." Title leaf is a cancel.

A 2.7.m   *Thirteenth printing: Complete Poems & Prose.* [Philadelphia: Ferguson Bros., 1888].

A 2.7.n   *Fourteenth printing:* [Philadelphia: Ferguson Bros., 1889]. 404 + 18 pp.

A 2.7.o   *Fifteenth printing:* Philadelphia: David McKay, 1891–'92. 438 pp.

A 2.8   *Eighth edition* (1886)

A 2.8.a   *First printing:* London and Newcastle-on-Tyne: Walter Scott, 1886.

A 2.8.b   *Second printing:* London and Newcastle-on-Tyne: Walter Scott, 1887.

A 2.8.c–e   *Third through fifth printings:* London: Walter Scott, [n.d.]

A 2.8.f   *Sixth printing:* London and New York: Walter Scott, [n.d.]

A 2.8.g   *Seventh printing:* London and Newcastle-on-Tyne: Walter Scott, [1902].

A 2.8.h   *Eighth printing:* London, Felling-on-Tyne, New York: Walter Scott, [1906].

A 2.8.i   *Ninth printing:* London, Felling-on-Tyne, New York: Walter Scott, [1911].

A 2 LEAVES OF GRASS
1855

A 2.1
First edition, only printing (1855)

Two issues have been noted:

A 2.1.a₁
First (American) issue (1855)

Leaves

of

Grass.

—•••—

Brooklyn, New York:
1855.

A 2.1.a₁: 11³⁄₁₆″ × 7⅝″

Frontispiece for A 2.1.a,

Two states of the copyright page have been noted:

First state:

Entered according to act of Congress in the year 1855,
by Walter Whitman in the Clerk's office
of the District Court of the United States
for the Southern District of New York.

The copyright page bears no printing; in both located copies, the copyright notice is written in Whitman's hand. *Locations:* RPAt (rebound), ViU (binding A). See *Note eleven*.

[i–iii] iv–xii [13] 14–56 [57] 58–64 [65] 66–95 [96]. Single leaf with Samuel Hollyer engraving of Whitman printed on verso, followed by protective tissue, is inserted before the title page; see *Notes one, two,* and *three*.

[1–12]⁴. Sheets bulk 7/32″.

Contents: p. i: title page; p. ii: blank; pp. iii–xii: preface; pp. 13–95: text; p. 96: blank.

Second state:

Copyright page: 'Entered according to Act of Congress in the year 1855, *by* WALTER WHITMAN, *in the Clerk's Office of the District Court of the* | *United States for the Southern District of New York.*'.

Contents are the same as in the first state, except: p. ii: copyright information.

Note: Two states of p. iv, col. 2, l. 4, have been noted: the first state reading is 'cities adn'; the second state reading is 'cities and' (see *BAL,* IX, 31).

Poems: ["I celebrate myself . . ."], ["Come closer to me . . ."], ["To think of time . . ."], ["I wander all night in my vision . . ."], ["The bodies of men and women engirth me . . ."], ["Sauntering the pavement or riding the country byroad here then are faces . . ."], ["A young man came to me with a message from his brother . . ."], ["Suddenly out of its stale and drowsy lair . . ."], ["Clear the way there Jonathan!"], ["There was a child went forth every day . . ."], ["Who learns my lesson complete?"], ["Great are the myths . . ."]. See "Index to the Poems in *Leaves of Grass*" for information about the publication histories of individual poems within the various editions, printings, and issues of *Leaves of Grass.*

Typography and paper: 9⅜″ (9⅛″) × 5⅞″; wove paper; 55 lines per page in double columns in preface; various lines per page (up to 45) in text. Running heads: rectos: pp. 15–95: 'Leaves of Grass.'; versos: pp. 14–94: 'Leaves of Grass.'.

Binding: Three styles have been noted:

Binding A: Dark olive-green AR cloth (coarse ribbed-morocco). Front cover: goldstamped triple-rule frame surrounding five blindstamped leaf-and-vine designs at top and bottom (the tip of the center ornament at the top has two leaves going to the right and one to the left, that of the center ornament at the bottom has two leaves going to the left and one to the right) with goldstamped '[rustic letters] Leaves of Grass.' in center; back cover: goldstamped triple-rule frame surrounding five blindstamped leaf-and-vine designs at top and bottom (the tip of the center ornament at the top has two leaves going to the right and one to the left, that of the center ornament at the bottom has two leaves going to the left and one to the right) with goldstamped '[rustic letters] Leaves of Grass.' in center; spine: goldstamped '[leaf-and-vine design] | [leaf-and-vine design] | [three lines in rustic letters] Leaves | *of* | Grass. | [leaf-and-vine design] | [leaf-and-vine design] | [leaf-and-vine design]'. No flyleaves; back flyleaf; front and back flyleaves; or front and double back flyleaves. Blue, red, yellow, black, and brown nonpareil marbled endpapers, coated on one side. All edges trimmed. All edges gilded. See *Notes four* and *eight*.

Binding B: Dark olive-green AR cloth (coarse ribbed-morocco). Front cover: blindstamped triple-rule frame surrounding five blindstamped leaf-and-vine designs at top and bottom (the tip of the center ornament at the top has two leaves going to the left and one to the right, that of the center ornament at the bottom has two leaves going to the right and one to the left)

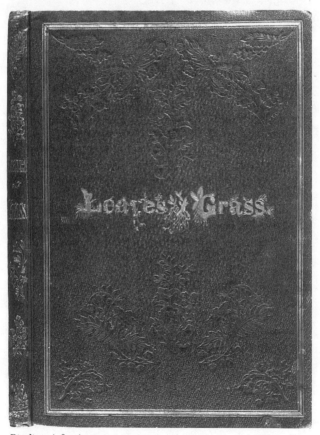

Binding A for A 2.1.a₁

with goldstamped '[rustic letters] Leaves of Grass.' in center; back cover: blindstamped triple-rule frame surrounding five blindstamped leaf-and-vine designs at top and bottom (the tip of the center ornament at the top has two leaves going to the left and one to the right, that of the center ornament at the bottom has two leaves going to the right and one to the left) with blindstamped '[rustic letters] Leaves of Grass.' in center; spine: goldstamped in rustic letters: 'Leaves | *of* | Grass.'. Front flyleaf; front and back flyleaves; or front flyleaf and triple back flyleaves. White or pale yellow endpapers. All edges trimmed. See *Notes four, seven,* and *eight.*

Binding C: Light yellowish green or pink wrappers. Front cover: 'Leaves of Grass.'; back and spine: blank. No flyleaves or double front flyleaves. Top and bottom edges trimmed, front edges uncut. See *Notes five, six, seven,* and *eight.*

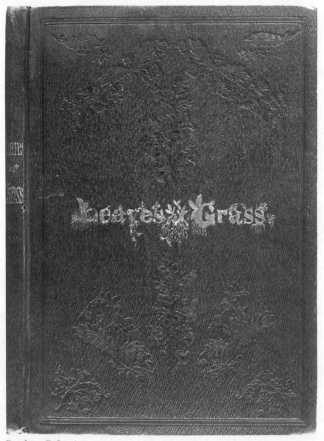

Binding B for A 2.1.a₁

Publication: There is no evidence to corroborate Whitman's statement in his open letter to Emerson (published in the 1856 *Leaves of Grass*), "I printed a thousand copies, and they readily sold" (p. 346). A statement from the binder shows that 795 copies were bound (see *Note eight*). On 31 March 1885, Whitman wrote "800 copies were struck off on a hand press by Andrew Rome, in whose job office the work was all done—the author himself setting some of the type" (*Correspondence*, VI, 30).

Announced for sale by Fowler and Wells in *New-York Daily Tribune*, 6 July

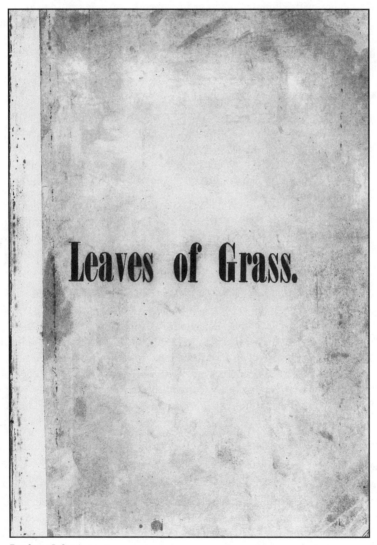

Binding C for A 2.1.a₁

1855, p. 1. Deposited for copyright: title, 15 May 1855; book, not given. Copyright renewed for 14 years from 15 May 1883, on 15 March 1883; 4808. According to *Life Illustrated,* copies "rapidly disappeared" after being placed on sale (n.s. 2 [16 August 1856], 124–125). Sold primarily by Fowler and Wells, Brooklyn. Deposit copies: binding A: DLC (second state; received at the Smithsonian 3 May 1856). RPAt copy (first state; rebound) ordered and received from a Providence bookseller on 9 October 1855. Presentation copies: binding C: RPB (second state; from Whitman, November 1855; identified as his desk copy, with clippings). Copies inscribed by owners (all second state): binding A: NNC (20 October 1855), MH (1855); binding B: CSt (13 February 1856). Prices: cloth, $2.00; wrappers, 75¢. As late as 14 June 1856, Fowler and Wells were selling copies in cloth for $1.25 and in wrappers for 75¢ ("Notes and Queries," *Life Illustrated,* n.s. 2:54).

Printing: Andrew and James Rome, Brooklyn.

Locations: Binding A: BBo, BE, CtY, DLC (3), InU-L, MB, MBU, MH (2), NN-B (4), NN-R (2), NNC (3), NNPM (2), NcD (2), NcU, NjCW, NjP, PU (2), RPB (2), ScU, TxU (3), ViU (4); binding B: BL, CSt, CtY (2), DLC (9), InU-L, JM, MH (2), NN-B (2), NN-R, NcD (2), NcU, NjCW, RPB, TxU (3), ViU (4); binding C: CtY, DLC, NN-R (spine repaired), ViU (see *Note five*).

Note one: Copies in binding A have the frontispiece on paper between .011″ and .012″ thick, with the Hollyer engraving of Whitman printed directly on the paper within a lightly embossed 8¾″ × 5¾″ frame. One copy has the Hollyer engraving printed directly on the paper without a lightly embossed frame (PU).

Note two: Copies in bindings B and C have the frontispiece printed on thin paper measuring 7¹¹⁄₁₆″ × 4¹³⁄₁₆″ (NN-R [B], TxU), 7⅞″ × 5⅛″ (CtY [C]), 7¾″ × 5″ (DLC [B], ViU [B]), 7⅞″ × 4¹⁵⁄₁₆″ (DLC [B]), 7 ¾″ × 5½″ (NjCW), 7¹³⁄₁₆″ × 4⅞″ (NcD), 7⅞″ × 4⅞″ (NN-B [2B]), 7⅝″ × 5″ (ViU [C]), or 7¾″ × 4¹³⁄₁₆″ (CtY [B], DLC [B], NN-R [C]), pasted within a heavily embossed frame measuring 8¾″ × 5 ¾″ on the same paper stock as the copies in binding A. Other copies in binding B have the engraving printed directly on the paper, as above. A copy in binding B at NN-B has the frontispiece printed directly on the recto, a binding error of no significance.

Note three: One copy has the Hollyer engraving on thin paper measuring 6⅝″ × 4¼″ pasted within a heavily embossed frame measuring 7¾″ × 4⅞″ (DLC [B]).

Note four: There is often significant slippage of the blocks used for the blindstamped leaf-and-vine designs of the front and back covers in bindings A and B, often as much as ¼″ variation from the bottoms of the second and fourth ornaments to the outer frame, and as much as ½″ variation in the distance between the second and fourth ornaments at the top of the front and back covers. This may be due to the casings being stamped at different times.

Note five: The copy in binding C at ViU has the light green paper wrappers pasted over boards, with a white paper shelfback; this is most likely a sophisticated copy.

Note six: Copies of the green and pink wrappers alone (measuring 8″ × 10″) were sold at the Bucke sale, 15–16 April 1936, items 156–161 (see *Whitman at Auction,* pp. 283–284). NjP has a light yellowish green front wrapper, measuring 9⅞″ × 7⅞″. NcD has light yellowish green conjugate front and back wrappers, measuring 9⅞″ × 8″ and 10″ × 8¹⁄₁₆″ (2 sets), and light pink conjugate front and back wrappers, measuring 10″ × 8¹⁄₁₆″ (3 sets). These wrappers were probably later trimmed by Whitman for use as writing paper.

Note seven: A four-leaf [1–2]² gathering is inserted in some copies in bindings B and C at the front, before the frontispiece (CtY [B], DLC [5B], NN-B [2B], NN-R [B, C], NcD, NjCW, RPB, TxU, ViU [C]). Wells and Goldsmith report copies with the advertisements at the back (p. 4); no copies have been located.

The contents of the inserted advertising gathering are: E. P. Whipple, review of Rufus W. Griswold's *The Poets and Poetry of America, North American Review,* January 1844 (p. 1); [Walt Whitman], "Walt Whitman, A Brooklyn Boy," *Brooklyn Daily Times,* 29 September 1855 (pp. 1–2 [E 1179]); [Walt Whitman], "Walt Whitman and His Poems," *United States Review,* September 1855 (pp. 2–4 [E 1178]); [Charles Eliot Norton], review of *Leaves of Grass, Putnam's Monthly Magazine,* September 1855 (pp. 4–5); [Walt Whitman], "An English and an American Poet," *American Phrenological Journal,* October 1855 (pp. 5–7 [E 1180]); "Have Great Poets Become Impossible?" *London Eclectic Review,* July 1850 (pp. 7–8); "Extracts from Letters and Reviews" (p. 8).

Galley proofs of the *Putnam's* review and the three reviews by Whitman, produced from different settings of type than here or in their original newspaper or magazine printings, have been noted (see F 26, F 88, F 91, and I 12).

Note eight: The binder's statement shows that 200 copies were bound in binding A in June 1855 and another 137 in July 1855; 169 copies were bound in binding B in December 1855 and another 93 in January 1856; 150 copies were bound in binding C in December 1855–January 1856; and 46 copies were bound in "Boards mounted" in July 1855—a total of 795 copies. This document is printed in William White, "The First (1855) 'Leaves of Grass': How Many Copies?" *Papers of the Bibliographical Society of America,* 57 (3d Quarter 1963), 352–354; the assignment of binding cloth types is mine.

Note nine: The following textual variant, due to mis-inking, is present in some copies in binding A:

15.10   city   ]   city I

(MB, NN-B, NNC, NjCW, NN-R).

Note ten: A copy at NNPM in binding A has a letter by Samuel Hollyer of 17 November 1897 laid in, stating, "[Whitman] presented me with the first copy of his book in token of his admiration" for Hollyer's work on the frontispiece; the "first copy" referred to is this one. But in a letter of 24 April 1903, Hollyer states that he had received for his work "one [copy] out of the first 12 which he [Whitman] had just fetched from the binders" (CtY).

Note eleven: A copy of the first state (without copyright page handwriting) in binding B (with the press notices inserted) is listed in Randall House catalogue XX, item 511, and again in Thomas Goldwasser Rare Books, Catalogue 1, n.s., item 158.

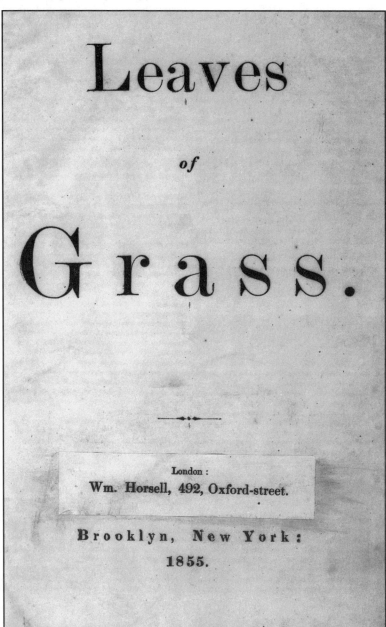

Leaves

of

Grass.

London :
Wm. Horsell, 492, Oxford-street.

Brooklyn, New York:
1855.

A 2.1.a₂: 11″ × 7⅝″

Paper label (measuring 4³⁄₁₆″ × 1³⁄₈″ [DLC] or 4⅛″ × 1¼″ [CtY] or 4³⁄₁₆″ × 1⁵⁄₁₆″ [NN-B] or 4¼″ × 1″ [NcD]) is pasted over the rule between the title and Brooklyn imprint (CtY, DLC, NN-B) or between the rule and Brooklyn imprint (NcD). The copyright page is the same as in the first issue, second state. The Hollyer engraving of Whitman, followed by protective tissue, serves as the frontispiece and is printed directly on paper .010″ thick within a lightly embossed 8¾″ × 5¾″ frame.

Binding: Same as in the first issue, binding A, except: no flyleaves.

Publication: Listed in *Publishers' Circular and Booksellers' Record*, 15 October 1855. Listed in the *English Catalogue* as an importation. Copies inscribed by owners: CtY (25 December 1856). Price, 7s.6d.

Locations: CtY, DLC, NN-B, NcD.

Note one: The reading at 15.10 is 'city' in the CtY, NN-B, and NcD copies; see A 2.1.a₁, *Note nine*.

Note two: For the distribution of copies of *Leaves of Grass* in England by a traveling bookseller, see Ernest Rhys's introduction to the Walter Scott edition of *Leaves of Grass* (A 2.8); *Autobiographical Notes of the Life of William Bell Scott*, ed. W. Minto, 2 vols. (New York: Harpers, 1892), II, 32; *WWWC*, III, 115–116. The Dixon-Scott-Rossetti copy referred to in these works is now at CtY.

Leaves

of

Grass.

BROOKLYN, NEW YORK,
1856.

A 2.2: 6⅛″ × 3¹³⁄₁₆″

[i–iii] iv [5] 6–100 [101] 102 [103] 104–120 [121] 122–139 [140] 141–160
[161] 162–166 [167] 168–179 [180] 181–201 [202] 203–205 [206] 207–210
[211] 212–222 [223] 224–239 [240] 241–243 [244] 245–248 [249] 250–251
[252] 253–254 [255] 256 [257] 258–261 [262] 263–264 [265] 266–267 [268]
269–270 [271] 272–274 [275] 276–278 [279] 280–281 [282] 283–285 [286]
287–301 [302] 303–308 [309] 310–312 [313] 314–315 [316] 317–321 [322]
323–331 [332] 333–342 [343–345] 346–358 [359] 360–384. Single leaf with
Samuel Hollyer engraving of Whitman printed on verso, followed by protective
tissue, is inserted before the title page.

$[1–32]^6$. Signed $[1]^{12}$ $2–16^{12}$. Sheets bulk 1⅛″.

Contents: p. i: title page; p. ii: copyright page; pp. iii–iv: contents; pp. 5–
342: text of poems; p. 343: half title 'LEAVES-DROPPINGS.'; p. 344: blank;
pp. 345–58: text, headed 'Correspondence.'; pp. 359–384: text, headed 'Opinions. 1855–6.'.

Poems: "Poem of Walt Whitman, an American," "Poem of Women," "Poem of
Salutation," "Poem of The Daily Work of The Workmen and Workwomen of
These States," "Broad-Axe Poem," "Poem of a Few Greatnesses," "Poem of The
Body," "Poem of Many In One," "Poem of Wonder at The Resurrection of
The Wheat," "Poem of You, Whoever You Are," "Sun-Down Poem," "Poem of
The Road," "Poem of Procreation," "Poem of The Poet," "Clef Poem," "Poem of
The Dead Young Men of Europe, The 72d and 73d Years of These States,"
"Poem of the Heart of The Son of Manhattan Island," "Poem of The Last Expla-
nation of Prudence," "Poem of The Singers, and of The Words of Poems," "Faith
Poem," "Liberty Poem for Asia, Africa, Europe, America, Australia, Cuba, and
The Archipelagoes of the Sea," "Poem of Apparitions in Boston, The 78th Year of
These States," "Poem of Remembrances for A Girl or A Boy of These States,"
"Poem of Perfect Miracles," "Poem of The Child That Went Forth, and Always
Goes Forth, Forever and Forever," "Night Poem," "Poem of Faces," "Bunch
Poem," "Lesson Poem," "Poem of the Propositions of Nakedness," "Poem of The
Sayers of The Words of The Earth," "Burial Poem"

Prose: "Correspondence (letter from Emerson to Whitman, 21 July 1855; letter from Whitman to Emerson, August 1856), "Opinions. 1855–6" (reviews of
Leaves of Grass from *London Weekly Dispatch, Brooklyn Daily Times* [by Whitman; see E 1179], *Christian Spiritualist, Putnam's Monthly Magazine, American Phrenological Journal* [by Whitman; see E 1180], *Critic* [London], *Examiner* [London], *London Leader,* and *Boston Intelligencer*). See "Index to the

Poems in *Leaves of Grass*" for information about the publication histories of individual poems within the various editions, printings, and issues of *Leaves of Grass*.

Typography and paper: 4⅞" (4½") × 2¾"; wove paper; various lines per page (up to 29). Running heads: rectos: pp. 7–99, 105–119, 123–159, 163–165, 169–209, 213–221, 225–247, 251–253, 259–263, 267–269, 273, 277, 281–307, 311, 315–341: 'LEAVES OF GRASS.'; pp. 347–357, 361–383: 'LEAVES-DROPPINGS.'; versos: pp. iv, 6–138, 142–178, 182–200, 204, 208–238, 242, 246–260, 264–266, 270–280, 284, 288–300, 304–314, 318–320, 324–330, 334–342: 'LEAVES OF GRASS.'; pp. 346–384: 'LEAVES-DROPPINGS.'.

Binding: Dark gray olive-green or dark grayish green A-like cloth (ribbed morocco). Front cover: blindstamped triple-rule frame with blindstamped 1⁵⁄₁₆" floral ornaments at top and bottom corners, with goldstamped 'Leaves | of | Grass' in center; back cover: same as the front cover, except: all blindstamped; spine: goldstamped 'Leaves | of | Grass | [leaf design] | Walt | Whitman | [leaf design] | I Greet You at the | Beginning of A | Great Career | R W Emerson'. Front flyleaf and back flyleaf with conjugate pasted under endpaper; or front and back flyleaves with conjugates pasted under endpapers; or double front flyleaves; or front and back flyleaves; or front flyleaf and double back flyleaves. Pale yellow endpapers. All edges trimmed; or all edges trimmed and speckle-stained red.

Printing: Fowler and Wells, New York.

Publication: According to John Burroughs, Fowler and Wells "printed and bound a batch of a thousand copies" which "soon sold" (*Notes on Walt Whitman* [D 5], p. 19). In his open letter to Emerson, printed in this edition, Whitman said "I stereotype, to print several thousand copies" of the book (p. 346). Listed on 16 August 1856 as "about to be issued. The author is still his own publisher, and . . . Fowler and Wells will again be his agents for the sale of the work" (*Life Illustrated*, n.s. 2 [16 August 1856], 124–125). Advertised for sale in *New-York Daily Tribune* on 12 September 1856. Reviewed in *Christian Examiner*, 61 (November 1856), 471–473; *New York Daily Times*, 13 November 1856, p. 2. Deposited for copyright: title: 11 September 1856; book, 11 September 1856. Copyright renewed for 14 years from 11 September 1884 on 31 July 1884; 15648. Deposit copies: DLC (received in Clerk's Office in New York 11 September 1856). Presentation copies: ViU (from Whitman, May 1857). Copies inscribed by owners: TxU (1857), DLC (30 May 1857). Price, $1.00.

Locations: BBo, BE, CSt, CtY (4), DLC (7), InU-L, JM, MB, MBU, MH (2), NN-R, NNC, NNPM, NcD, NcU, NjCW (3), NjP (2), NzD, PU (3), RPB, ScU, TxU (4), ViU (2).

Binding for A 2.2

Note one: A two-leaf gathering with advertisements for *Leaves of Grass* printed on the first page is inserted at the end.

Note two: A copy at CtY, bound in full leather and measuring 8⅜″ × 4″, contains a note by H. Buxton Forman of April 1895 that this copy was "found by R. M. Bucke, folded ready for binding, & is the only uncut copy he or I ever saw or heard of."

Note three: Whitman's sketch for the spine stamping of this book is at DLC (see illustration).

Whitman's drawing for the spine of A 2.2

A 2.3.a
Third edition, first printing (1860)

Two issues have been noted:

A 2.3.a₁
First (American) issue (1860)

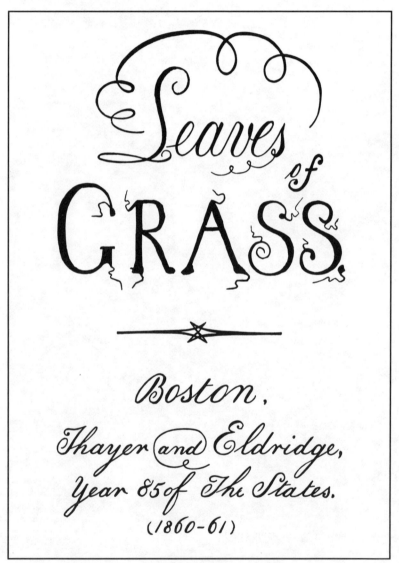

A 2.3.a₁: Binding A: 7¾" × 5⅛"; bindings B–E: 7½" × 4⅞"

```
Entered, according to Act of Congress, in the year 1860,
                     By WALT WHITMAN,
In the Clerk's Office of the District Court of the District of Massachusetts.



              ELECTROTYPED AT THE
         BOSTON STEREOTYPE FOUNDRY.



                 PRINTED BY
         GEORGE C. RAND & AVERY.
```

[i–ii] iii–iv 5–456. Single leaf with engraving of Whitman printed on verso, followed by a protective tissue, is inserted before the title page.

The frontispiece has been noted in three forms:

Form 1: Signed in plate 'Schoff' on a light brown background: binding A: CtY, DLC, InU-L, NN-B, RPB, ViU (2); binding B: JM, TxU, ViU; binding C: CtY (2), DLC (2), JM, MBU, MH (2), NN-B, NN-R, NcU, NjCW, PU (2), ScU, TxU; binding D: DLC (2), MB, NN-B, NN-R, TxU; binding E: DLC, JM, RPB (lacks spine).

Form 2: Signed in plate 'Schoff' on a plain white background: binding A: CtY.

Form 3: Signed in plate 'S. A. Schoff' on a plain white background: binding D: DLC (2), ViU.

Note: The engraving signed 'S. A. Schoff' was done later than those signed 'Schoff' and differs slightly from it; see illustrations.

[1]⁶ 2–38⁶ . Sheets bulk 1⅜″.

Contents: p. i: title page; p. ii: copyright page; pp. iii–iv: contents; pp. 5–456: text of poems.

Poems: "Proto-Leaf," "Walt Whitman," "*Apostrophe,*" "Chants Democratic. 1," "Chants Democratic. 2," "Chants Democratic. 3," "Chants Democratic. 4," "Chants Democratic. 5," "Chants Democratic. 6," "Chants Democratic. 7," "Chants Democratic. 8," "Chants Democratic. 9," "Chants Democratic. 10," "Chants Democratic. 11," "Chants Democratic. 12," "Chants Democratic. 13," "Chants Democratic. 14," "Chants Democratic. 15," "Chants Democratic. 16," "Chants Democratic. 17." "Chants Democratic. 18," "Chants Democratic. 19," "Chants Democratic. 20," "Chants Democratic. 21," "Leaves of Grass. 1" ["Elemental drifts!"], "Leaves of Grass. 2" ["Great are the myths . . ."], "Leaves of Grass. 3" ["A young man came to me with a message from his brother . . ."],

Form 3 of frontispiece for A 2.3.a₁

Form 2 of frontispiece for A 2.3.a₁

Form 1 of frontispiece for A 2.3.a₁

"Leaves of Grass. 4" ["Something startles me where I thought I was safest . . ."], "Leaves of Grass. 5" [All day I have walked the city . . ."], "Leaves of Grass. 6," "Leaves of Grass. 7," "Leaves of Grass. 8," "Leaves of Grass. 9," "Leaves of Grass. 10," "Leaves of Grass. 11," "Leaves of Grass. 12," "Leaves of Grass. 13," "Leaves of Grass. 14," "Leaves of Grass. 15," "Leaves of Grass. 16," "Leaves of Grass. 17," "Leaves of Grass. 18," "Leaves of Grass. 19," "Leaves of Grass. 20," "Leaves of Grass. 21," "Leaves of Grass. 22," "Leaves of Grass. 23," "Leaves of Grass. 24," "Salut au Monde!", "Poem of Joys," "A Word Out of The Sea," "Leaf of Faces," "Europe, The 72d and 73d Years of These States," "Thought" ["Of Public Opinion . . ."], "Enfans d'Adam. 1," "Enfans d'Adam. 2," "Enfans d'Adam. 3," "Enfans d'Adam. 4," "Enfans d'Adam. 5," "Enfans d'Adam. 6," "Enfans d'Adam. 7," "Enfans d'Adam. 8," "Enfans d'Adam. 9," "Enfans d'Adam. 10," "Enfans d'Adam. 11," "Enfans d'Adam. 12," "Enfans d'Adam. 13," "Enfans d'Adam. 14," "Enfans d'Adam. 15," "Poem of the Road," "To The Sayers of Words," "A Boston Ballad, The 78th Year of These States," "Calamus. 1," "Calamus. 2," "Calamus. 3," "Calamus. 4," "Calamus. 5," "Calamus. 6," "Calamus. 7," "Calamus. 8," "Calamus. 9," "Calamus. 10," "Calamus. 11," "Calamus. 12," "Calamus. 13," "Calamus. 14," "Calamus. 15," "Calamus. 16," "Calamus. 17," "Calamus. 18," "Calamus. 19," "Calamus. 20," "Calamus. 21," "Calamus. 22," "Calamus. 23," "Calamus. 24," "Calamus. 25," "Calamus. 26," "Calamus. 27," "Calamus. 28," "Calamus. 29," "Calamus. 30," "Calamus. 31," "Calamus. 32," "Calamus. 33," "Calamus. 34," "Calamus. 35," "Calamus. 36," "Calamus. 37," "Calamus. 38," "Calamus. 39," "Calamus. 40," "Calamus. 41," "Calamus. 42," "Calamus. 43," "Calamus. 44," "Calamus. 45," "Crossing Brooklyn Ferry," "Longings For Home," "To You, Whoever You Are," "To a Foiled Revolter or Revoltress," "To Him that was Crucified," "To One shortly To Die," "To a Common Prostitute," "To Rich Givers," "To a Pupil," "To The States, To Identify the 16th, 17th, or 18th Presidentiad," "To a Cantatrice," "Walt Whitman's Caution," "To a President," "To other Lands," "To Old Age," "To You" ["Let us twain walk aside from the rest . . ."], "To You" ["Stranger!"], "Mannahatta" ["I was asking for something specific and perfect for my city . . ."], "France, The 18th Year of These States," "Thoughts. 1" ["Of the visages of things . . ."], "Thoughts. 2" ["Of waters, forests, hills . . ."], "Thoughts. 3" ["Of persons arrived at high positions . . ."], "Thoughts. 4" ["Of ownership . . ."], "Thoughts. 5" ["As I sit with others . . ."], "Thoughts. 6" ["Of what I write from myself . . ."], "Thoughts. 7" ["Of obedience, faith, adhesiveness . . ."], "Unnamed Lands," "Kosmos," "A Hand-Mirror," "Beginners," "Tests," "Savantism," "Perfections," "Says," ["Debris"] ["He is wisest who has the most caution . . ."], ["Debris"] ["Any thing is as good as established . . ."], ["Debris"] ["What General has a good army in himself . . ."], ["Debris"] ["Have you learned lessons only of those who admired you . . ."], ["Debris"] ["Despairing cries float ceaselessly toward me . . ."], ["Debris"] ["I understand your anguish . . ."], ["Debris"] ["A thousand perfect men and women appear . . ."], ["Debris"] ["A mask . . ."], ["Debris"] ["One sweeps by . . ."], ["Debris"] ["Three old men slowly pass . . ."], ["Debris"] ["Women sit, or move to and fro . . ."], ["Debris"] ["What weeping face is that looking from the window?"], ["Debris"] ["I will take an egg out of the robin's nest in the orchard . . ."], ["Debris"] ["Behavior . . ."] ["Debris"] ["Not the pilot has charged himself to bring his ship into port . . ."], ["Debris"] ["I thought I was not alone . . ."], "Sleep-Chasings," "Burial," "To My Soul," "So long!". *Note:* The poems "To You, Whoever You Are" through the second "To You" form the cluster "Messenger Leaves." See "Index to the Poems in *Leaves of Grass*" for information about the publication histories of individual poems within the various editions, printings, and issues of *Leaves of Grass*.

Typography and paper: 6″ (5⅝″) × 3⁵⁄₁₆″; wove paper; various lines per page (up to 33). Running heads: rectos: pp. 7–9: 'PROTO-LEAF.'; pp. 11–21: 'LEAVES OF GRASS.'; pp. 25–27: 'WALT WHITMAN.'; pp. 29–103: 'LEAVES OF GRASS.'; pp. 107–141, 145–157, 161–181: 'CHANTS DEMOCRATIC.'; p. 183: 'LEAVES OF GRASS.'; pp. 185–187: 'CHANTS DEMOCRATIC.'; p. 189: 'LEAVES OF GRASS.'; p. 191: 'CHANTS DEMOCRATIC.'; pp. 193, 197–241: 'LEAVES OF GRASS.'; p. 245: 'SALUT AU MONDE!'; pp. 247–257: 'LEAVES OF GRASS.'; pp. 261–263: 'POEM OF JOYS.'; pp. 265–267: 'LEAVES OF GRASS.'; pp. 271–273: 'A WORD OUT OF THE SEA.'; pp. 275–281, 285, 289: 'LEAVES OF GRASS.'; pp. 291–299: 'ENFANS D'ADAM.'; pp. 301–305: 'LEAVES OF GRASS.'; pp. 307–311: 'ENFANS D'ADAM.'; p. 313: 'LEAVES OF GRASS.'; pp. 317–327: 'POEM OF THE ROAD.'; pp. 331–335: 'TO THE SAYERS OF WORDS.'; p. 339: 'LEAVES OF GRASS.'; pp. 343–353: 'CALAMUS.'; p. 355: 'LEAVES OF GRASS.'; pp. 357–363: 'CALAMUS.'; p. 365: 'LEAVES OF GRASS.'; pp. 367–371: 'CALAMUS.'; p. 373: 'LEAVES OF GRASS.'; pp. 375–377: 'CALAMUS.'; pp. 381–387: 'CROSSING BROOKLYN FERRY.'; pp. 393–403: 'MESSENGER LEAVES.'; p. 405: 'MANNAHATTA.'; p. 407: 'FRANCE.'; p. 409: 'LEAVES OF GRASS.'; p. 411: 'THOUGHTS.'; pp. 413–417: 'LEAVES OF GRASS.'; p. 419: 'SAYS.'; pp. 423–427: 'LEAVES OF GRASS.'; pp. 429–439: 'SLEEP-CHASINGS.'; pp. 441–447: 'BURIAL.'; p. 453: 'SO LONG.'; p. 455: 'LEAVES OF GRASS.'; versos: p. iv: 'CONTENTS.'; pp. 6–106: 'LEAVES OF GRASS.'; p. 108: 'CHANTS DEMOCRATIC.'; pp. 110–124, 128–180: 'LEAVES OF GRASS.'; p. 182: 'CHANTS DEMOCRATIC.'; pp. 184–186: 'LEAVES OF GRASS.'; p. 188: 'CHANTS DEMOCRATIC.'; p. 190: 'LEAVES OF GRASS.'; pp. 192–194: 'CHANTS DEMOCRATIC.'; pp. 196–276, 284–286: 'LEAVES OF GRASS.'; p. 288: 'ENFANS D'ADAM.'; pp. 290–300: 'LEAVES OF GRASS.'; pp. 302–304: 'ENFANS D'ADAM.'; pp. 306–310: 'LEAVES OF GRASS.'; pp. 312–314: 'ENFANS D'ADAM.'; pp. 316–352: 'LEAVES OF GRASS.'; p. 354: 'CALAMUS.'; pp. 356–362: 'LEAVES OF GRASS.'; p. 364: 'CALAMUS.'; pp. 366–370: 'LEAVES OF GRASS.'; pp. 372–374: 'CALAMUS.'; p. 376: 'LEAVES OF GRASS.'; p. 378: 'CALAMUS.'; pp. 380–396: 'LEAVES OF GRASS.'; pp. 398–400: 'MESSENGER LEAVES.'; p. 402: 'LEAVES OF GRASS.'; p. 410: 'THOUGHTS.'; pp. 414–416: 'LEAVES OF GRASS.'; p. 420: 'SAYS.'; pp. 422–424, 428–438, 442–456: 'LEAVES OF GRASS.';

Binding: Five styles have been noted, priority assumed:

Binding A: Light yellowish brown unprinted wrappers. Front and back flyleaves. No endpapers or pale yellow endpapers. Top edges trimmed, front and bottom edges uncut. See *Notes one* and *two.*

Binding B: Dark reddish orange coarse TR cloth (vertical wavy-grain); beveled edges. Front and back covers: blank; spine: goldstamped '[wavy rule] | [three lines in handprinted letters with ornate initial capitals in first and third lines] LEAVES | of | GRASS | [hand with butterfly]'. Front and back flyleaves. Gray endpapers. All edges trimmed.

Binding C: Same as binding B, except: front cover: blindstamped '[lettering in same format as spine] LEAVES | [drawing of globe with clouds] *of* | GRASS'; back cover: same as front cover, except: '[drawing of sunrise] *of*; front flyleaf or front and back flyleaves.

Binding D: Same as binding C, except: medium brown or dark reddish orange or grayish olive-green coarse TR cloth (vertical wavy-grain); or dark green or deep purplish red HC-like cloth (hexagon-grain); or dark reddish orange H cloth (fine diaper); or dark reddish orange BD cloth (bead-grain); spine: '[three lines goldstamped within a goldstamped single-rule frame curved at the top] [three lines in handprinted lettering with ornate initial capitals in first and third lines] LEAVES | OF | GRASS' | [blindstamped hand with butterfly in relief on blindstamped oval background, within blindstamped single-rule circular frame] | [two lines blindstamped within blindstamped oval single-rule frame, all in relief on blindstamped oval background] Walt | Whitman'; back flyleaf or front flyleaf or front and back flyleaves; gray endpapers or endpapers coated brown on one side.

Binding E: Medium brown A cloth (ribbed morocco). Front and back covers: blindstamped triple-rule frame surrounding double-rule frame, with inner frame intersecting and forming triangular designs, once at top and bottom and twice on sides; spine: goldstamped 'LEAVES | OF | GRASS.'. No flyleaves or front flyleaf. White endpapers. Top edges trimed, front and bottom edges rough trimmed. See *Note three.*

Printing: See copyright page.

Publication: Although Whitman had written on 20 [June] 1857, "I work now to bring out a third edition," nothing substantial was done until Thayer and Eldridge wrote him on 10 February 1860 that they "want[ed] to be the publisher of Walt. Whitman's poems—Leaves of Grass" (*Correspondence*, I, 44, 48n). On 27 February, they offered Whitman "10 per cent of the retail price for your copyright" (I, 48n). Whitman reported on 29 March, "my book is well under way" with about 120 pages "set up"; on 1 April, he was still "reading proof" (I, 49,

50); on 10 May, he announced, "The book is finished in all that makes the reading part, and is all through the press complete—It is electrotyped—." However, he was "just now in 'suspenders' on account of the engraving. I have about decided, though, to have 1000 copies printed from it, as it is—and then let Schoff, the engraver, finish it afterwards" (I, 52).

1,000 copies. Whitman wrote on 10 May, "[the] probability is that the book will be bound and ready, May 19" (*Correspondence*, I, 52), and sets of advance sheets state that publication was scheduled for that date (see *Notes one* and *two*). Review copies were distributed by 24 May (I, 48n). Announced as published in *New York Illustrated News*, 1 (5 May 1860), 394. Deposited for copyright: title, 14 May 1860; book, 24 May 1860. Reviewed in *Saturday Press* (New York), 19 May 1860, p. 2; *New York Times*, 19 May 1860, supplement, p. 1. The 16 June 1860 *New York Illustrated News* states that the book was selling well (p. 91). Presentation copies: binding C: MH (from Whitman, July 1860), TxU (from Whitman, July 1860); binding D: NN-B (from Eldridge, June 1860), DLC (from Whitman, August 1860). Copies inscribed by owners: binding C: DLC (1 August 1864); binding D: ViU (17 October 1860). Price, $1.25.

Locations: Binding A: CtY (lacks title page), CtY (lacks frontispiece), DLC, NN-B, RPB, ViU (2); binding B: JM, TxU, ViU; binding C: CtY (2), DLC (2), JM, MBU, MH (2), NN-B, NN-R, NNPM, NcU, NjCW, PU (2), ScU, TxU; binding D: DLC (4), MB, NN-B, NN-R, TxU, ViU; binding E: DLC, JM, RPB (lacks spine).

Note one: A copy at DLC in binding A has the following written on the front cover: 'Advance Sheets for the Editor— | Will be published May 19ᵗʰ | Bound Copy will be sent as | soon as ready—'.

Note two: A copy at CtY in binding A has an undated note from Thayer and Eldridge to the editor of the *New York Evening Post* on the front wrapper, stating that these are '*advance sheets*', that the book will be "formally published Saturday May 19ᵗʰ," and that "a fully bound copy will be sent you as soon as ready."

Note three: A note in a copy of binding E, probably by Caroline Wells Houghton, states that this is the "Large Paper" edition and "Probably a small edition sent to England" (DLC). A similar note is in Wells and Goldsmith (p. 9). The copy at RPB contains remnants of advertisements from British publications used in the casing, undoubtedly indicating that sheets were sent to England for binding there.

Note four: Whitman's marked copy of this edition (at NN-R), used for preparing the 1867 edition, is facsimiled in *Walt Whitman's Blue Book* (A 43).

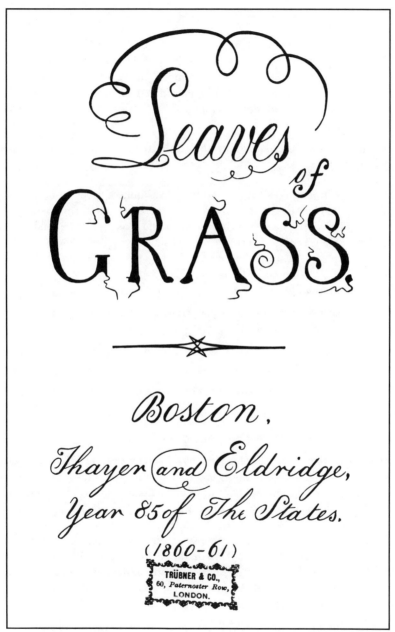

A 2.3.a₂: 7½″ × 4⅞″

Trübner imprint is on a paper label pasted on the title page. Frontispiece engraving is signed in plate 'Schoff' and is on a light brown background.

Binding: Dark reddish orange coarse TR cloth (vertical wavy-grain); beveled edges. Front cover: blindstamped '[handprinted letters with ornate initial capital] Leaves | [drawing of globe with clouds] *of* | GRASS'; back cover: blindstamped '[handprinted letters with ornate initial capital] 'Leaves | [drawing of sunrise] *of* | GRASS'; spine: goldstamped '[wavy rule] | [three lines in handprinted letters with ornate initial capitals in first and third lines] Leaves | of | GRASS | [hand with butterfly]'. Front and back flyleaves. Gray endpapers. All edges trimmed.

Publication: Listed in *Literary Gazette,* 7 July 1860.

Locations: BE, JM, NcD.

Note: Whitman later recalled that Trübner "was quite a friend of Leaves of Grass," but when his son took over the firm, he "beheaded me at short notice— quickly concluded that Leaves of Grass was not the book for him to handle" (6 November 1889, *WWWC,* VI, 116).

A 2.3.b
Third edition, second printing (1860)

Pagination, collation, contents, and typography and paper are the same as in the first printing. Sheets bulk 1½".

Frontispiece engraving is signed in plate 'S. A. Schoff' and is on a plain white background.

Binding: Two styles have been noted, priority assumed:

   Binding A: Same as in the first printing, first issue (A 2.3.a₁), binding C.

   Binding B: Same as in the first printing, first issue (A 2.3.a₁), binding D.

Publication: Thayer and Eldridge wrote Whitman on 14 June 1860, "the first edition is nearly all gone, and the second is all printed and ready for binding," and on the 29th, they reported that the second edition would sell out within a month (*Correspondence,* I, 48n). Unfortunately, the firm was beset by financial problems, and on 5 December 1860 Thayer wrote Whitman: "We go by the boards tomorrow or the next day." The plates were sold to Horace Wentworth of Boston by 6 February 1861 and when, on 16 November 1866 Wentworth wrote Whitman offering the plates for sale, the author threatened suit (I, 49n). For the further disposition of the plates, see *Publication* in A 2.3.c. Copies inscribed by owners: binding B: CtY (October 1860). Price, $1.25.

Locations: Binding A: BL, BO, RPB; binding B: BMR, CaOTU, CtY (2), DLC (6), JM, NN-B (2), NN-R, NNC, NcD, NjCW, NjP, PU (2), ScU, TxU, ViU (3).

A 2.3.c

Third edition, presumed third (first unauthorized) printing [1880?]

Title page is the same as in the first printing; copyright page lacks both Boston Stereotype Foundry and George C. Rand and Avery imprints (see illustration).

Entered, according to Act of Congress, in the year 1860,

By WALT WHITMAN,

In the Clerk's Office of the District Court of the District of Massachusetts.

Pagination is the same as in the first printing.

Frontispiece engraving has been noted in three forms, prioity undetermined:

Form 1: Signed in plate 'Schoff' on a light brown background: binding B: MBU.

Form 2: Signed in plate 'S A Schoff' on a light brown background: binding A: NN-B, NN-R (3), TxU (3).

Form 3: Signed in plate 'S A Schoff' on a plain white background: binding A: BMR, BO, DLC (2), JM (2), MBU, PU (3), RPB, ScU, TxU; binding B: CtY (2).

$[1-19]^{12}$. Signed $[1]^6$ $2-38^6$. Page size $7\frac{1}{2}'' \times 4 \frac{5}{8}''$. Sheets bulk $1\frac{1}{4}''$.

Contents: pp. i–iv, 5–436: same as in the first printing.

Typography and paper: Same as in the first printing.

Binding: Two styles have been noted, priority undetermined:

Binding A: Deep purplish red PB-like cloth (bubble-grain) or deep purplish red L cloth (morocco); beveled edges. Front cover: blindstamped '[three lines in handprinted lettering with ornate initial capitals] LEAVES | [drawing of globe and clouds] *of* | GRASS'; back cover: same as the front cover, except: '[drawing of sunrise] *of*;* spine: '[goldstamped within a goldstamped single-rule frame curved at the top] [three lines in handprinted lettering with ornate initial capitals in first and third lines] LEAVES | OF | GRASS' | [blindstamped hand with butterfly] | [two lines blindstamped within a blindstamped oval single-rule frame, all in relief on blindstamped background] Walt | Whitman'. Front and back flyleaves. Dark brown endpapers coated on one side; or light pink endpapers with light blue-veined pattern; or pale yellow endpapers; or yellow endpapers. All edges trimmed.

Binding B: Same as binding A, except: dark reddish orange PB-like cloth (bubble-grain); spine: '[blindstamped hand with butterfly within a blindstamped single-rule circular frame]' in center; gray endpapers.

Printing: Unknown.

Publication: In September 1879, a "Mr Williams" bought the plates for this edition at auction for $200 (*Correspondence,* III, 200). Richard Worthington then purchased the plates and wrote Whitman on the 29th, asking him to "complete" the book and offering him $250 for his work (III, 196n). Whitman refused the offer and thought no more about it until he found a copy of the piracy at a Philadelphia bookstore on 22 November 1880 and was told that "they procured it from Worthington, & had been so procuring it off & on, for nearly a year" (III, 198). Although Whitman threatened Worthington with legal action a number of times, he accepted $50 from Worthington in December 1880, $25 in August 1881 ("due me on back sales," which Whitman took after turning down Worthington's offer of $50 for a new printing of 500 copies), $44.50 in July 1882, and $24 in November 1885 (*Daybooks,* I, 214, 252; II, 371). Thomas Harned paid $209.75 on 12 July 1892 to purchase the plates used by Worthington (DLC). The inventory of Whitman's belongings made at his death lists an unspecified number of copies of the Worthington reprinting bound and in sheets (DLC). Listed in the *American Catalogue* for [1880]. Copies inscribed by owners: binding A: TxU (16 November 1880; SA Schoff, white); NN-R (13 November 1886; SA Schoff, light brown); NN-R (21 February 1888; SA Schoff, light brown). Price, $3.75.

Locations: Binding A: BMR, BO, DLC (2), JM (2), MBU, NN-B, NN-R (3), PU (3), RPB, ScU, TxU (2); binding B: CtY (2), MBU.

Note: According to Shay, "over ten thousand copies" were sold "within the next ten years" (p. 10).

A 2.3.d-e
Third edition, presumed fourth and fifth (second and third unauthorized) printings [n.d.]

Title and copyright pages are the same as in the third printing.

[i–iv] [i–ii] iii–iv 5–456 [457–458]. Single leaf with Schoff engraving, printed on verso, followed by a protective tissue, is inserted before title page; see collation.

Frontispiece engraving has been noted in three forms, priority undetermined:

Form 1: Signed in plate 'Schoff' on a light brown background: NcD.

Form 2: Signed in plate 'S A Schoff' on a light brown background: NN-R.

Form 3: Signed in plate 'S A Schoff' on a plain white background: CSt, JM (5), MH, NN-R, NNC (2), NNPM, NjCW (3), NjP (2), RPB, TxU (4), ViU.

[1–29]^8 (±1^2). Signed [1]^8 2^6 [3]^6 4–5^6 [6]^6 7–20^6 [21]^6 22–37^6 38^8. The frontispiece leaf is a cancel; leaf 29$_8$ is canceled or pasted under the rear pastedown endpaper. Page size 7⅜″ × 4 7/16″. Sheets bulk 19/32″ or 1 13/32″.

Contents: pp i–iv, 5–456: same as in the third printing; pp. 457–458: blank.

Typography and paper: Same as in the third printing, except: laid paper with horizontal chain lines 1¼″ apart.

Binding: Deep purplish red L cloth (morocco); beveled edges. Front cover: blindstamped '[three lines in handprinted lettering with ornate initial capitals] LEAVES | [drawing of globe and clouds] *of* | GRASS'; back cover: same as the front cover, except: '[drawing of sunrise] *of*;* spine: '[goldstamped within a goldstamped single-rule frame curved at the top] [three lines in handprinted lettering with ornate initial capitals in first and third lines] LEAVES | OF | GRASS' | [blindstamped hand with butterfly] | [two lines blindstamped within a blindstamped oval single-rule frame, all in relief on blindstamped background] Walt | Whitman'. White, yellow, pale yellow, or pale pink endpapers. All edges trimmed.

Publication: Copies inscribed by owners: JM (1892), TxU (1892), MH (1894), JM (February 1894), NjP (5 August 1896).

Locations: CSt, JM (5), MH, NN-R (2), NNC, NNPM, NcD, NcU, NjCW (3), NjP (2), RPB, TxU (4), ViU.

Note one: One copy lacks the frontispiece and has leaf 1$_1$ pasted under the front pastedown endpaper (NcD).

Note two: One copy has the frontispiece tipped to the title page and leaf 1$_1$ pasted under the front pastedown endpaper (NNC).

Note three: The NNPM copy has a comment by Laurens Maynard on the front endpaper about the publisher he calls "Slippery Dick" Worthington: "Whitman bought the plates from Worthington who also turned over to him what he guaranteed to be all of the books he had left. But upon his subsequent failure after Whitman's death a large number of this edition were found in his stock."

A 2.3.f
Third edition, presumed sixth (fourth unauthorized) printing [n.d.]

Title and copyright pages are the same as in the third printing.

[i–ii] iii–iv 5–456 [1–8]. Frontispiece engraving is signed in plate 'S A Schoff' and is on a plain white background.

[1–29]^8. Signed [1]^6 2^6 [3]^6 4–5^6 [6]^6 7–20^6 [21]^6 22–38^6 [39]^4 . Page size 7¼" × 4¾". Sheets bulk ¹⁵⁄₁₆".

Contents: pp. i–iv, 5–456: same as in the third printing; pp. 1–8: undated publisher's catalogue.

Typography and paper: Same as in the third printing.

Binding: Deep purplish red L cloth (morocco); beveled edges. Front cover: blindstamped '[three lines in handprinted lettering with ornate initial capitals] LEAVES | [drawing of globe and clouds] *of* | GRASS'; back cover: same as the front cover, except: '[drawing of sunrise] *of*; spine: '[three lines goldstamped in handprinted lettering over 2" blindstamped band at the top] LEAVES | OF | GRASS | [blindstamped hand with butterfly in middle] | [two lines blindstamped in handprinted lettering in relief over blindstamped ⅞" band at bottom] WALT | WHITMAN'. Front and back flyleaves. Pale yellow endpapers. All edges trimmed.

Publication: Presentation copies: BMR (from Traubel, November 1892), BBo (from Traubel, 29 November 1892). Copies inscribed by owners: JM (from Traubel, 15 December 1894), DLC (February 1897).

Locations: BBo, BMR, CtY, DLC (5), JM, MBU, MH, NN-R, NcD, NcU, NjCW, NjP, PU (4), RPB, TxU.

Note one: The books advertised in Worthington's catalogue were published between 1878 and 1892, making the latter date the earliest that this printing could have been done.

Note two: A copy at PU has this comment by Thomas Harned on the free front endpaper: "After Walt Whitman died I bought these plates and all unsold copies. . . . This is one of the copies."

A 2.4.a
Fourth edition, first printing (1867)

Three issues have been noted, priority of last two undetermined:

A 2.4.a₁
First issue (1867)

LEAVES

OF

GRASS.

⁓⁓⁓⁓

New-York.

⁓

1867.

A 2.4.a₁: Binding A: 7¾″ × 4⅝″; binding B: 7⁵/₁₆″ × 4⅜″

Leaves of Grass, Drum-Taps, Sequel to Drum-Taps, and "Songs Before Parting."

[i–iii] iv [5–7] 8–22 [23] 24–94 [95] 96–118 [119] 120–139 [140] 141–144 [145] 146–158 [159] 160–168 [169] 170–184 [185] 186–198 [199] 200–206 [207] 208–214 [215] 216–224 [225] 226–238 [239] 240–248 [249] 250 [251] 252–256 [257] 258–260 [261] 262–270 [271] 272–284 [285] 286–290 [291] 292–314 [315] 316–318 [319] 320–330 [331] 332–338 [339–340] [i–iii] iv 5–72 [1–3] 4–24 [1–3] 4–21 [22] 23–32 [33] 34–36

[a]² A–E¹² E–M¹² [1–4]¹² [1]¹² 2⁶. Signature 'E' is repeated (but the gathering is signed F² on leaf 5ʳ). Blank binder's leaves are inserted after pp. iv (contents), second p. 72, and third p. 24. Sheets bulk ¹⁵⁄₁₆″.

Contents: p. i: title page; p. ii: copyright page; pp. iii–iv: contents; p. 5: inscriptions; p. 6: blank; pp. 7–338: text of *Leaves of Grass;* pp. 339–340: blank; p. i: *Drum-Taps* title page; p. ii: copyright page; pp. iii–iv: contents; pp. 5–72: text of *Drum-Taps* (A 3.1.a₁); p. 1: *Sequel to Drum-Taps* title page; p. 2: contents; pp. 3–24: text of *Sequel to Drum-Taps* (A 3.1.a₂); p. 1: 'LEAVES OF GRASS. | SONGS | BEFORE PARTING.'; p. 2: contents; pp. 3–36: text of *Songs Before Parting.*

Poems: Leaves of Grass: "Inscription," "Starting from Paumanok," "Walt Whitman," "To the Garden, the World," "From Pent-up Aching Rivers," "I Sing the Body Electric," "A Woman Waits for Me," "Spontaneous Me," "One Hour to Madness and Joy," "We Two—How Long we were Fool'd," "Native Moments," "Once I pass'd through a Populous City," "Facing West from California's Shores," "Ages and Ages, Returning at Intervals," "O Hymen! O Hymenee," "I am He that Aches with Love," "As Adam, Early in the Morning," "Excelsior," "In Paths Untrodden," "Scented Herbage of My Breast," "Whoever you are, Holding me now in Hand," "These I, Singing in Spring," "A Song," "Not Heaving from my Ribb'd Breast only," "Of the Terrible Doubt of Appearances," "Recorders Ages Hence," "When I Heard at the Close of Day," "Are you the New Person Drawn Toward me?", "Roots and Leaves Themselves Alone," "Not Heat Flames up and Consumes," "Trickle Drops," "Of Him I Love Day and Night," "City of Orgies," "Behold this Swarthy Face," "I saw in Louisiana a Live-Oak Growing," "That Music Always Round Me," "To a Stranger," "This Moment, Yearning and

Thoughtful," "I Hear it was Charged Against Me," "The Prairie-Grass Dividing," "We Two Boys Together Clinging," "O Living Always—Always Dying!", "When I Peruse the Conquer'd Fame," "A Glimpse," "A Promise to California," "Here, Sailor!", "Here the Frailest Leaves of Me," "What Think you I take my Pen in Hand?", "No Labor-Saving Machine," "I Dreamed in a Dream," "To the East and to the West," "Earth! My Likeness!", "A Leaf for Hand in Hand," "Fast Anchor'd, Eternal, O Love," "Sometimes with One I Love," "That Shadow, my Likeness," "Among the Multitude," "To a Western Boy," "O you whom I Often and Silently Come," "Full of Life, Now," "Salut au Monde!", "What Place is Besieged?", "Leaves of Grass. 1" ["There was a child went forth every day . . ."], "Leaves of Grass. 2" ["Myself and mine gymnastic ever . . ."], "Leaves of Grass. 3" ["Who learns my lesson complete?"], "Leaves of Grass. 4" ["Whoever you are . . ."], "Beginners," "Tests," "Perfections," "Song of the Broad-Axe," "With Antecedents," "Savantism," "Crossing Brooklyn Ferry," "To a Foil'd Revolter or Revoltress," "To Get Betimes in Boston Town," "To a Common Prostitute," "To a Pupil," "To Rich Givers," "A Word Out of the Sea," "A Leaf of Faces," "Stronger Lessons," "Europe, The 72d and 73d Years of These States," "Thought" ["Of Public Opinion . . ."], "The Runner," "To The Sayer of Words," "Longings for Home," "To a President," "Walt Whitman's Caution," "To other Lands," "Song of the Open Road," "To the States, To Identify the 16th, 17th, or 18th Presidentiad," "To a certain Cantatrice," "To Workingmen," ["Debris"] ["He is wisest who has the most caution . . ."], "Leaves of Grass. 1" ["O hastening light!"], "Leaves of Grass. 2" ["Tears! tears! tears!"], "Leaves of Grass. 3" ["Aboard, at the ship's helm . . ."], "American Feuillage," "Mannahatta" ["I was asking for something specific and perfect for my city . . ."], "To You" ["Let us twain walk aside from the rest . . ."], "France, The 18th Year of These States," "A Hand-Mirror," "Thoughts. 1" ["Of the visages of things . . ."], "Thoughts. 2" ["Of waters, forests, hills . . ."], "Thoughts. 3" ["Of persons arrived at high positions . . ."], "Thoughts. 4" ["Of ownership . . ."], "Thoughts. 5" ["As I sit with others . . ."], "Thoughts. 6" ["Of what I write from myself . . ."], "Thoughts. 7" ["Of obedience . . ."], "To Him that was Crucified," "To Old Age," "To One Shortly to Die," "To You" ["Stranger!"], "Unnamed Lands," "Kosmos," "When I Read the Book," "Says," "Despairing Cries," "Picture" ["A thousand perfect men and women appear"], "Poems of Joy," "Respondez!", "The City Dead-House," "Leaflets," "Leaves of Grass. 1" ["Think of the Soul . . ."], "Leaves of Grass. 2" ["Unfolded out of the folds of the woman . . ."], "Leaves of Grass. 3" ["Night on the prairies . . ."], "Leaves of Grass. 4" ["The world below the brine . . ."], "Leaves of Grass. 5" ["I sit and look out upon all the sorrows of the world . . ."], "Visor'd," "Not the Pilot," "As if a Phantom Caress'd Me," "Picture" ["Women sit, or move to and fro"], "Great are the Myths," "Now List to my Morning's Romanza," "Burial," "This Compost!", "I hear America Singing," "Manhattan's Streets I Saunter'd, Pondering," "I was Looking a Long While," "The Indications," "Leaves of Grass. 1" ["On the beach at night alone . . ."], "Leaves of Grass. 2" ["To oratists . . ."],

"Leaves of Grass. 3" ["Laws for Creations . . ."], "Leaves of Grass. 4" ["Poets to come!"], "Me Imperturbe," "Sleep-Chasings," "Elemental Drifts," "Miracles," "You Felons on Trial in Courts," "Mediums," "Now Lift me Close." *Note:* The poems "To the Garden, the World" through "Full of Life, Now" form the cluster "Calamus." *Songs Before Parting:* "As I sat Alone by Blue Ontario's Shore," "Leaves of Grass. 1" ["O me, man of slack faith so long!"], "Leaves of Grass. 2" ["Forms, qualities, lives . . ."], "Leaves of Grass. 3" ["Now I make a leaf of Voices . . ."], "Leaves of Grass. 4" [What am I . . ."], "Leaves of Grass. 5" [Locations and times . . ."], "Thoughts. 1" ["Of these years I sing . . ."], "Thoughts. 2" ["Of seeds dropping into the ground . . ."], "As Nearing Departure," "As I Walk, Solitary, Unattended," "Song at Sunset," "To a Historian," "Assurances," "So Long!". See "Index to the Poems in *Leaves of Grass*" for information about the publication histories of individual poems within the various editions, printings, and issues of *Leaves of Grass*.

Typography and paper: 5⁷⁄₁₆″ (5⅛″) × 3³⁄₁₆″; wove paper; various lines per page (up to 38). Running heads: rectos: pp. 9–21: 'STARTING FROM PAUMANOK.'; pp. 25–93: 'WALT WHITMAN.'; pp. 97–117: 'CHILDREN OF ADAM.'; pp. 121–143: 'CALAMUS.'; pp. 147–157: 'SALUT AU MONDE!'; pp. 161–167: 'LEAVES OF GRASS.'; pp. 171–181: 'SONG OF THE BROAD-AXE.'; p. 183: 'LEAVES OF GRASS.'; pp. 187–191: 'CROSSING BROOKLYN FERRY.'; pp. 193–197: 'LEAVES OF GRASS.'; pp. 201–205: "A WORD OUT OF THE SEA.'; pp. 209–211: 'A LEAF OF FACES.'; p. 213: 'EUROPE.'; pp. 217–221: 'TO THE SAYERS OF WORDS.'; p. 223: 'LEAVES OF GRASS.'; pp. 227–237: 'SONG OF THE OPEN ROAD.'; pp. 241–247: 'TO WORKINGMEN.'; pp. 253–255: 'AMERICAN FEUILLAGE.'; p. 259: 'LEAVES OF GRASS.'; p. 263: 'THOUGHTS.'; pp. 265–269: 'LEAVES OF GRASS.'; pp. 273–279: 'POEMS OF JOY.'; pp. 281–283: 'RESPONDEZ.'; pp. 287–289: 'LEAVES OF GRASS.'; p. 293: 'GREAT ARE THE MYTHS.'; pp. 295–297: 'MORNING ROMANZA.'; pp. 299–305: 'BURIAL.'; pp. 307–313, 317: 'LEAVES OF GRASS.'; pp. 321–329: 'SLEEP-CHASINGS.'; p. 333: 'ELEMENTAL DRIFTS.'; pp. 335–337: 'LEAVES OF GRASS.'; pp. i–iii, 5–71, 1–23: the same as in *Drum-Taps* and *Sequel to Drum-Taps* (A 4.1.a₂); pp. 5–31, 35: 'SONGS BEFORE PARTING.'; versos: p. iv: 'CONTENTS.'; pp. 8–338: 'LEAVES OF GRASS.'; pp. ii–iv, 6–72, 2–24: the same as in *Drum-Taps* and *Sequel to Drum-Taps* (A 4.1.a₂); pp. 4–20, 24–36: 'LEAVES OF GRASS.'.

Printing: See copyright page.

Binding: Two styles have been noted:

Binding A: Unprinted light gray yellowish brown wrappers; spine: blank or with white paper label with 'LEAVES | *of* | GRASS | *Complete.*' and with '1867 Edn.' handwritten at bottom. White endpapers. All edges trimmed; or top and bottom edges trimmed, front edges rough trimmed.

Binding B: Half black leather with red, orange, blue, and white nonpareil marbled paper-covered sides; half black leather with medium reddish brown coarse C cloth (sand-grain) sides; half dark green leather with medium brown coarse C cloth (sand-grain) sides; or half blackish red leather with medium reddish brown coarse C cloth (sand-grain) sides. Spine: gold-stamped printing with blindstamped rules: '[double rule] | [double rule] | [ornate 'L'] LEAVES | *of* | [ornate 'G'] GRASS | [double rule] | [double rule] | ED'N. 1867. | [double rule] | [double rule]'. No flyleaves; back flyleaf; or front and back flyleaves. Red, blue, yellow, and black nonpareil marbled end-papers, coated on one side; yellow endpapers, coated on one side; or yellow endpapers. All edges trimmed. Front and bottom edges or all edges stained red in nonpareil marbled pattern; or all edges speckle-stained dark red.

Publication: On 1 August 1866, Whitman wrote, "I have obtained leave of absence, & am coming to New York, principally to bring out a new & much better edition" (*Correspondence,* I, 282). His progress reports over the next two months show the book was "being printed—gets along rather slowly" on 25 August; on the next day Chapin "engages to have the composition & presswork done in from two to three weeks"; and by 10 September the book was "a little more than half done" (I, 283, 284, 286). On 16 October, he wrote his mother, assuming that she had received her copy, and on the 20th he noted it was "just now out," selling for $3.00 (I, 288; V, 289).

Whitman wrote on 20 February 1867 that "a small edition has just been published" (I, 314). On 13 October 1867, he noted that the bookbinder who is "custodian of the sheets" has "failed" (I, 344). A month later, he wrote to a New York bookseller that he assumes a binder in that city has "100 copies, just bound" (I, 350). On 19 February 1868, Whitman sent a check to a New York binder in payment for binding 90 copies, adding that he wanted to know "how many of the deficient signatures of 'Drum-Taps' etc., I will require to finish up the edition" (II, 18). On 4 February 1874, Whitman wrote that a New York bookseller should have 24 copies still in stock (II, 273).

Reviewed in *Commonwealth* (Boston), 10 November 1866. Deposit copy: DLC ('22 May 1867'; rebound; dated by the office of the district court of New York 17 November 1866). Presentation copies: binding B (all from Whitman): NN-B (to O'Connor, 11 October 1866), MH (20 October 1866; rebound), DLC (26 September 1868), DLC (March 1869). Copies inscribed by owners: binding B: TxU (14 January 1867; spine defective), TxU (December 1867), DLC (26 September 1868).

Locations: Binding A: DLC (2), TxU (spine defective; lacks back wrapper); binding B: BO, CtY (2), DLC (3), InU-L (2), MH, NN-B (2), NN-R (2), NNC, NcD (2), NjCW, NzD, PU, RPB (2), TxU (2), ViU.

Note one: The contents page lists *Drum-Taps* and "Songs Before Parting" with the comment, "See Table of Contents prefixed."

Note two: The page number for p. 140 is present (MH, PU) or is not present (all other copies).

Note three: There is (BMR, MBU [both rebound]) or is not (all other copies) inking to the right of the page number on p. 64 in *Leaves of Grass*.

Note four: One copy is in unprinted pale orange-yellow stiff paper wrappers with unprinted gray reddish orange paper shelfback, measuring 7¾" × 45⁄8", without flyleaves or endpapers, and with top and bottom edges trimmed and front edges rough trimmed, with an undated inscription from Whitman to Ellen O'Connor (NN-B).

Note five: The leaf with the Hollyer engraving printed on the verso has been noted in some copies in binding B after p. 22 (MH) or after p. 28 (DLC [3]).

Note six: A set of unsewn, uncut sheets, measuring 83⁄8" × 5", is at DLC.

A 2.4.a₂
Presumed second issue (1867) [i.e., 1868]

New York: [William E. Chapin], 1867.

Leaves of Grass and "Songs Before Parting."

[i–iii] . . . 332–338 [339–340] [1–3] . . . 34–36

[a]² A-E¹² E-M¹² [1]¹² 2⁶. Signature 'E' is repeated (but the gathering is signed F² on leaf 5ʳ). Page size 77⁄16" × 4 3⁄8". Sheets bulk ¾".

Contents: pp. i–iv, 5–340: same as in *Leaves of Grass* in the first issue; pp. 1–36: same as in "Songs Before Parting" in the first issue.

Typography and paper: pp. i–iv, 5–340: same as in *Leaves of Grass* in the first issue; pp. 1–36: same as in *Songs Before Parting* in the first issue.

Binding: Half black leather with red, orange, blue, and white nonpareil marbled paper covered sides. Spine: goldstamped printing with blindstamped rules: '[double rule] | [double rule] | [ornate 'L'] 'Leaves | of | [ornate 'G'] Grass. | [double rule] | [double rule] | [double rule]'. No flyleaves; or front and back flyleaves. Endpapers marbled on one side the same as the covers. All edges trimmed. All edges stained in blue, red, and white nonpariel pattern.

Publication: On 13 August 1868, Whitman wrote that "the new edition" is "already fixed" (*Correspondence*, II, 39). On 27 September, he was "having fixed up, & bound, (partly printed too,) the remainings of Leaves of Grass, edition 1867—as there are none on hand, & there is a small demand" (II, 48).

And on 9 October, he wrote, "I am having finished about 225 copies of Leaves of Grass bound up, to supply orders. Those copies form all that is left of the old editions" (II, 58). Deposit copies: BL ('8 DE70'; rebound).

Locations: CtY (2), DLC (2), JM, NcU, PU, TxU, ViU.

Note one: The contents page lists *Drum-Taps* and "Songs Before Parting" with the comment, "See Table of Contents prefixed."

Note two: The page number for p. 140 is present (ScU [rebound]) or is not present (all other copies).

Note three: There is (JM, PU) or is not (all other copies) inking to the right of the page number on p. 64.

Note four: One copy has been rebound in dark green C cloth (sand-grain), with the front cover goldstamped 'WALT WHITMAN.', the back cover blank, and the spine goldstamped 'LEAVES | OF | GRASS | 1867.' (MWA).

A 2.4.a₃
Presumed third issue (1867) [i.e., 1868]

New York: [William E. Chapin], 1867.

Leaves of Grass only.

[i–iii] . . . 332–338 [339–340]

[a]² A-E¹² E-M¹² . Signature 'E' is repeated (but the gathering is signed F² on leaf 5ʳ). Page size 7⁷⁄₁₆″ × 4⅜″. Sheets bulk 2¹⁄₃₂″.

Contents: p. i–iv, 5–340: same as in *Leaves of Grass* in the first issue.

Typography and paper: pp. i–iv, 5–338: same as in *Leaves of Grass* in the first issue.

Binding: Half black leather with red, yellow, blue, and white nonpareil marbled paper-covered sides. Spine: goldstamped printing with blindstamped rules: '[double rule] | [double rule] | [ornate 'L'] LEAVES | *of* | [ornate 'G'] GRASS | [double rule] | [double rule] | [double rule]'. Endpapers marbled on one side the same as the covers. All edges trimmed. All edges marbled red and yellow in nonpareil pattern.

Locations: CtY, DLC.

Note one: The contents page lists *Drum-Taps* and "Songs Before Parting" with the comment, "See Table of Contents prefixed."

Note two: The page number for p. 140 is not present.

Note three: There is no inking to the right of the page number on p. 64.

Note four: Rebound copies are at DLC and NN-R.

Note five: *BAL* "doubts that these sheets were, in fact, issued separately" (IX, 34).

Note six: Wells and Goldsmith report an issue composed of *Leaves of Grass, Drum-Taps,* and *Sequel to Drum-Taps* (p. 15); no copies have been located.

A 2.5.a
Fifth edition, first printing (1871)

Two issues have been noted:

A 2.5.a₁
First issue (1871)

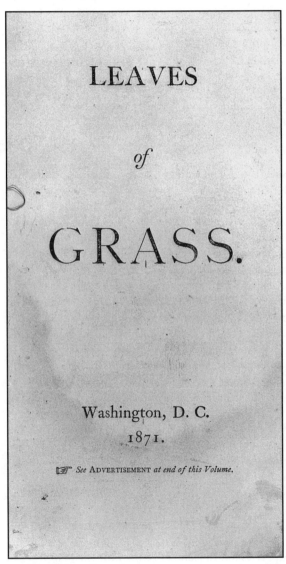

A 2.5.a₁: 8⅛″ × 5″

Leaves of Grass only.

[i–iii] iv–vi [7] 8–12 [13] 14–28 [29] 30–96 [97] 98–120 [121] 122–144 [145]
146–158 [159] 160–164 [165] 166–176 [177] 178–188 [189] 190 [191] 192–
200 [201] 202–208 [209] 210–218 [219] 220–230 [231] 232–238 [239] 240–
242 [243] 244–248 [249] 250–252 [253] 254–260 [261] 262–298 [299] 300–
308 [309] 310–340 [341] 342–348 [349] 350–360 [361] 362 [363] 364–369
[370] 371–372 [373] 374–384

[1–2]¹² 3¹² [4]¹² 5–16¹². Sheets bulk ⅞″.

Poems: "One's Self I Sing," "As I Ponder'd in Silence," "In Cabin'd Ships at
Sea," "To Foreign Lands," "To a Historian," "For Him I Sing," "When I Read
the Book," "Beginning my Studies," "To Thee, Old Cause!", "Starting from Pau-
manok, "The Ship Starting," "Unfolded Out Of The Folds," "To You"
["Stranger!"], "Walt Whitman," "Laws for Creations," "Visor'd," "To the Garden, the World," "From Pent-up Aching Rivers," "I Sing the Body Electric," "A
Woman Waits for Me," "Spontaneous Me," "One Hour to Madness and Joy,"
"We Two—How long We were Fool'd," "Out of the Rolling Ocean, the Crowd,"
"Native Moments," "Once I pass'd through a Populous City," "Facing West
from California's Shores," "Ages and Ages, Returning At Intervals," "O Hy-
men! O Hymenee!", "As Adam, Early in the Morning," "I Heard You, Solemn-
sweet Pipes of the Organ," "I Am He That Aches With Love," "To Him that was
Crucified," "Perfections," "In Paths Untrodden," "Scented Herbage of My
Breast," "Whoever you are, Holding me now in Hand," "These I, Singing in
Spring," "A Song," "Not Heaving from my Ribb'd Breast only," "Of the Terrible
Doubt of Appearances," "The Base of all Metaphysics," "Recorders Ages
Hence," "When I heard at the Close of the Day," "Are You the New Person
drawn toward Me?", "Roots and Leaves Themselves Alone," "Not Heat Flames
up and Consumes," "Trickle Drops," "City of Orgies," "Behold this Swarthy
Face," "I saw in Louisiana a Live-Oak Growing," "To A Stranger," "This Mo-
ment, Yearning and Thoughtful," "I Hear it was Charged Against Me," "The
Prairie-Grass Dividing," "We Two Boys Together Clinging," "A Promise to
California," "Here the Frailest Leaves of Me," "When I Peruse the Conquer'd
Fame," "What Think You I take my Pen in Hand?", "A Glimpse," "No Labor-
Saving Machine," "A Leaf For Hand In Hand," "To the East and to the West,"
"Earth! My Likeness!", "I Dream'd in a Dream," "Fast Anchor'd, Eternal, O

Love!", "Sometimes with One I Love," "That Shadow, my Likeness," "Among the Multitude," "To a Western Boy," "O you whom I Often and Silently Come," "Full of Life, Now," "Salut Au Monde!", "A Child's Amaze," "The Runner," "Beautiful Women," "Mother and Babe," "Thought" ["Of obedience . . ."], "American Feuillage," "Song of the Broad-Axe," "Song of the Open Road," "I Sit and Look Out," "Me Imperturbe," "As I Lay with my Head in your Lap, Camerado," "Crossing Brooklyn Ferry," "With Antecedents," "Now List to my Morning's Romanza," "The Indications," "Poets to Come," "I hear America Singing," "The City Dead-House," "A Farm Picture," "Carol of Occupations," "Thoughts" ["Of ownership . . ."], "The Sleepers," "Carol of Words," "Ah Poverties, Wincings, and Sulky Retreats," "A Boston Ballad. (1854.)," "Year of Meteors. (1859–60.)," "A Broadway Pageant. Reception Japanese Embassy, June, 1860," "Suggestions," "Great are the Myths," "Thought" ["Of persons arrived at high positions . . ."], "There was a Child went Forth," "Longings for Home," "Think of the Soul," "You Felons on Trial in Courts," "To a Common Prostitute," "I was Looking a Long While," "To a President," "To the States, To Identify the 16th, 17th, or 18th Presidentiad," "Drum-Taps" (prefaced by the poem *["Aroused and Angry"])*, "1861," "Beat! Beat! Drums!", "From Paumanok Starting I Fly like a Bird," "Rise, O Days, from your Fathomless Deeps," "City of Ships," "The Centenarian's Story," "An Army Corps on the March," "Cavalry Crossing a Ford," "Bivouac on a Mountain Side," "By the Bivouac's Fitful Flame," "Come Up from the Fields, Father," "Vigil Strange I Kept on the Field one Night," "A March in the Ranks hard-prest, and the Road Unknown," "A Sight in Camp in the Day-break Grey and Dim," "Not the Pilot," "As Toilsome I Wander'd Virginia's Woods," "Year that Trembled and Reel'd Beneath Me," "The Dresser," "Long, too long, O Land," "Give Me the Splendid Silent Sun," "Dirge for Two Veterans," "Over the Carnage Rose Prophetic a Voice," "The Artilleryman's Vision," "I Saw Old General at Bay," "O Tan-Faced Prairie-Boy," "Look Down Fair Moon," "Reconciliation," "Spirit whose Work is Done," "How Solemn, as One by One," "Not Youth Pertains to Me," "To the Leaven'd Soil They Trod," "Faces," "Manhattan's Streets I Saunter'd, Pondering," "All is Truth," "Voices," "As I sat Alone by Blue Ontario's Shore," "Pioneers! O Pioneers!", "Respondez!", "Turn O Libertad," "Adieu to a Soldier," "As I Walk These Broad, Majestic Days," "Weave In, Weave In, My Hardy Life," "Race of Veterans," "O Sun of Real Peace," "This Compost," "Unnamed Lands," "Mannahatta" ["I was asking for something specific and perfect for my city . . ."], "Old Ireland," "To Oratists," "Solid, Ironical, Rolling Orb," "Bathed in War's Perfume," "Delicate Cluster," "Song of the Banner at Day-Break," "Ethiopia Saluting the Colors," "Lo! Victress on the Peaks!", "World, Take Good Notice," "Thick-Sprinkled Bunting," "A Hand-Mirror," "Germs," "O Me! O Life!", "Thoughts" ["Of Public Opinion . . ."], "Beginners," "Still Though The One I Sing," "To A Foil'd European Revolutionaire," "France, The 18th Year of These States," "Europe, The 72d and 73d Year of These States," "Walt Whit-

man's Caution," "To a Certain Cantatrice," "To You" ["Whoever you are . . ."],
"As the Time Draws Nigh," "Years of the Modern," "Thoughts" ["Of these
years I sing . . ."], "Song at Sunset," "When I Heard the Learn'd Astronomer,"
"To Rich Givers," "Thought" ["Of what I write from myself . . ."], "So Long!"
Note: The poems "One's Self I Sing" through "The Ship Starting" form the
cluster "Inscriptions"; the poems "To the Garden the World" through "I Am He
That Aches With Love" form the cluster "Children of Adam"; the poems "In
Paths Untrodden" through "Full of Life, Now" form the cluster "Calamus"; the
poems "I Sit and Look Out" and "Me Imperturbe" form the cluster "Leaves of
Grass"; the poems "Now List to my Morning's Romanza" through "I hear
America Singing" form the cluster "The Answerer"; the poems "A Boston
Ballad. (1854.)" and "Year of Meteors. (1859–60.)" form the cluster "Leaves of
Grass"; the poems "There was a Child went Forth" through "To the States, to
Identify the 16th, 17th, or 18th Presidentiad" form the cluster "Leaves of
Grass"; the poems "Drum-Taps" through "To the Leaven'd Soil They Trod"
form the cluster "Drum-Taps"; the poems "Faces" through "Voices" form the
cluster "Leaves of Grass"; the poems "As I sat Alone by Blue Ontario's Shore"
through "O Sun of Real Peace" form the cluster "Marches Now the War is
Over"; the poems "This Compost" through Solid, Ironical, Rolling Orb" form
the cluster "Leaves of Grass"; the poems "Bathed in War's Perfume" through
"Thick-Sprinkled Bunting" form the cluster "Bathed in War's Perfume"; the
poems "O Me! O Life!" through "Beginners" form the cluster "Leaves of
Grass"; the poems "Still Though The One I Sing" through "To a Certain
Cantatrice" form the cluster "Songs of Insurrection"; the poems "As the Time
Draws Nigh" through "So Long!" form the cluster "Songs of Parting." See
"Index to the Poems in *Leaves of Grass*" for information about the publication
histories of individual poems within the various editions, printings, and issues
of *Leaves of Grass.*

Contents: p. i: title page; p. ii: copyright page; pp. iii–vi: contents; pp. 7–
384: text of *Leaves of Grass.*

Typography and paper: 5⅝″ (5⁵⁄₁₆″) × 3³⁄₁₆″; wove paper; various lines per
page (up to 41). Running heads: rectos: p. v: 'CONTENTS.'; pp. 9–11: 'INSCRIP-
TIONS.'; pp. 15–27: 'STARTING FROM PAUMANOK'; pp. 31–95: 'WALT WHIT-
MAN.'; pp. 99–119: 'CHILDREN OF ADAM.'; pp. 123–143: 'CALAMUS.'; pp. 147–
157: 'SALUT AU MONDE!'; pp. 161–163: 'AMERICAN FEUILLAGE.'; pp. 167–
175: 'SONG OF THE BROAD-AXE.'; pp. 179–187: 'SONG OF THE OPEN ROAD.'; pp.
193–197: 'CROSSING BROOKLYN FERRY.'; p. 199: 'LEAVES OF GRASS.'; pp. 203–
207: 'THE ANSWERER.'; pp. 211–217: 'CAROL OF OCCUPATIONS.'; pp. 221–229:
'THE SLEEPERS.'; pp. 233–237: 'CAROL OF WORDS.'; p. 241: 'A BOSTON BAL-
LAD.'; pp. 245–247: 'A BROADWAY PAGEANT.'; p. 251: 'GREAT ARE THE
MYTHS.'; pp. 255–259: 'LEAVES OF GRASS.'; pp. 263–297: 'DRUM-TAPS.'; pp.
301–307: 'LEAVES OF GRASS.'; pp. 311–339: 'MARCHES NOW THE WAR IS

Over.'; pp. 343–347: 'Leaves of Grass.'; pp. 351–355: 'Song of the Banner at Day-break.'; pp. 357–359: 'Bathed in War's Perfume.'; pp. 365–369: 'Songs of Insurrection.'; p. 371: 'Leaves of Grass.'; pp. 375–383: 'Songs of Parting.'; versos: pp. iv–vi: 'Contents.'; pp. 8–368, 372–384: 'Leaves of Grass.'.

Binding: Three styles have been noted, priority undetermined:

Binding A: Light yellow-green coated stiff wrappers. Front cover: '[flush right] Price, $2.50 | LEAVES | *of* | Grass | Washington, D. C. | 1871. | New-York: J. S. REDFIELD, Publisher, 140 Fulton St., (up stairs.)'; back cover: advertisements for *Leaves of Grass, Passage to India,* and *Democratic Vistas,* listing sales agents in Washington, New York, Boston, Brooklyn, and London; spine: blank. White endpapers. Top edges rough trimmed, front and bottom edges uncut.

Binding B: Same as binding A, except: spine: white paper label with '[double rule] | LEAVES | *of* | GRASS | *Complete.* | [double rule]'.

Binding C: Same as binding A, except: spine: vertically: 'Leaves of Grass.—1871.'; no flyleaves; issued uncut.

Printing: See copyright page.

Publication: On 9 October 1868, after the last set of sheets from the 1867 edition were bound, Whitman announced, "there will be no more in the market till I have my new & improved edition set up & stereotyped, which it is my present plan to do the ensuing winter at my leisure in Washington" (*Correspondence*, II, 58). As usual, Whitman's estimate proved optimistic, and it was not until 21 July 1870 that he again mentions a "new edition of my book" which "will be printed this fall" (II, 100). By 24 September he was in New York "electrotyping" the book, of which he was "just delivered" on 10 October (II, 113, 116).

Listed in *American Literary Gazette and Publishers' Circular,* 1 November 1870. Deposited for copyright: title, 27 September 1870; book, 8 November 1870; 2257. Deposit copies: DLC ('1870'; rebound). Reviewed in *New York Times,* 11 November 1870, p. 2. Deposit copies: BL ('22 JY 82'; rebound). Presentation copies: binding A: DLC (from Whitman, 1871). Copies inscribed by owners: binding A: CtY (noted as received from Whitman in November 1871); binding B: DLC (March 1871). Price, $2.50.

Locations: Binding A: DLC, ViU; binding B: DLC; binding C: CtY (spine repaired), DLC (3), PU.

Note: Redfield originally sent copies to Sampson Low for sale in England but, after Redfield went out of business, on 28 March 1873 they transferred this account to Whitman; it was not closed until 18 February 1876 (*Correspon-*

Back wrapper for A 2.5.a₁

Price, $2.50.

LEAVES

of

GRASS.

Washington, D. C.
1871.

NEW-YORK: J. S. REDFIELD, PUBLISHER, 140 Fulton St., (up stairs.)

Front wrapper for A 2.5.a₁

dence, II, 118n; *Daybooks*, I, 17). Trübner also sold the book from at least late 1873 on (*Correspondence*, II, 263). Whitman had sent 100 copies to England for sale (as he wrote on 4 February 1874), and 41 copies were on hand on 31 December 1872 (II, 273, 273n).

A 2.5.a₂
Second issue (1871)

Washington [New York: J. S. Redfield], 1871.

Leaves of Grass and *Passage to India.*

[i–iii] . . . 374–384 [i–iii] iv [5] 6–16 [17] 18–24 [25] 26–30 [31] 32–42 [43] 44–52 [53] 54–62 [63] 64–70 [71] 72–86 [87] 88–116 [117] 118–120

[1–2]¹² 3¹² [4]¹² 5–16¹² [1]¹² 2–5¹². Sheets bulk 1¼″.

Contents: pp. i–384: same as in *Leaves of Grass* in the first issue; p. i: title page of *Passage to India;* p. ii: copyright page; pp. iii–iv: contents; pp. 5–120: text of *Passage to India* (A 5).

Typography and paper: Running heads: rectos: pp. v–383: same as in *Leaves of Grass* in the first issue; pp. 7–15: 'Passage to India.'; pp. 19–23: 'Proud Music of the Storm.'; pp. 27–29: 'Ashes of Soldiers.'; pp. 33–39: 'President Lincoln's Burial Hymn.'; p. 41: 'Memories of President Lincoln.'; pp. 45–51: 'Poem of Joys.'; pp. 55–59: 'To Think of Time.'; p. 61: 'Chanting the Square Deific.'; pp. 65–69: 'Whispers of Heavenly Death.'; pp. 73–85: 'Sea-Shore Memories.'; pp. 89–113: 'Leaves of Grass.'; p. 115: 'Passage to India.'; p. 119: 'Now Finale to the Shore.'; versos: pp. iv–vi: 'Contents.'; pp. 8–368, 372–384: 'Leaves of Grass.'; p. iv: 'Contents.'; pp. 6–16: 'Leaves of Grass.'; pp. 18–40: 'Passage to India.'; p. 42: 'Memories of President Lincoln.'; pp. 44–118: 'Passage to India.'; p. 120: 'Now Finale to the Shore.'.

Binding: Shelfback of unprinted light yellow-brown paper; or dark reddish brown or gray reddish brown P cloth (pebble-grain); or dark gray reddish brown HC cloth (hexagon-grain) over light yellow-green stiff wrappers, which have been covered with green, blue, and yellow Spanish marbled paper. Spine: paper label: '[double rule] | LEAVES | of | GRASS | *Complete.* | *ED'N 1871–2.* | [double rule]'. White endpapers. Top edges rough trimmed, front and bottom edges uncut; or all edges trimmed.

Publication: Presentation copies (all from Whitman): CtY (1871, with a letter from Whitman of 28 July 1871 inserted), CtY (July 1871), MH (November 1871), NN-B (from Whitman, 1871).

Locations: CtY (2), DLC (2), InU-L, MH, NN-B, TxU, ViU.

Note: Some copies have a sheet advertising *Leaves of Grass, Passage to India,* and *Democratic Vistas* pasted to the rear pastedown endpaper (CtY [2], DLC [2], MH, NN-B, TxU). This advertisement was originally printed with the spine label on a single leaf measuring 4¾″ × 6¹³⁄₁₆″ (ViU; see illustration).

ADVERTISEMENT.

Walt Whitman's Books.

Leaves of Grass—*complete,* -   **$3 00**
Passage to India—*separate,* -   **1 00**
Democratic Vistas, - - - - **75**

☞ Can be obtained of the author -- address at Washington, D. C.

NEW YORK:
  J. S. REDFIELD, 140 Fulton St.
  B. F. FELT, 91 Mercer St.
WASHINGTON:
  PHILP & SOLOMON, Pennsylvania Ave.
LONDON:
  TRUBNER, 8 and 60 Paternoster Row.

LEAVES *of* **GRASS** *Complete.* *ED'N 1871-2.*

Sheet with advertisement and spine label for A 2.5.a₂

A 2.5.b
Fifth edition, second printing (1872)

Two issues have been noted:

A 2.5.b₁
First issue (1872)

LEAVES

of

GRASS.

Washington, D. C.
1872.

A 2.5.b₁: 8″ × 5″

Leaves of Grass and *Passage to India*. Copyright page is the same as in the first printing.

[i–iii] . . . 374–384 [i–iii] . . . 118–120

$[1-2]^{12}\ 3^{12}\ [4]^{12}\ 5-16^{12}\ [1]^{12}\ 2-5^{12}$. See *Note two*. Sheets bulk 1¼″.

Contents and typography and paper are the same as in the first printing, second issue (A 2.5.a₂).

Binding: Very dark yellowish green V cloth (smooth). Front and back covers: blank; spine: goldstamped '*LEAVES* | *of* | *GRASS* | *Complete*'. Front and back flyleaves. Gray wove endpapers. Top edges uncut, front and bottom edges rough trimmed; or all edges trimmed.

Printing: See copyright page.

Publication: On 2 February 1872, Whitman returned to New York "to bring out a new edition of my Poems," which he said was "under way" on the 23d (*Correspondence*, V, 294; II, 166). On 15 March, he announced: "I have got out my new edition, from the same plates as the last, only all bound in One Vol.—neatly done in green cloth, vellum" (II, 168). Eight days later, J. S. Redfield accepted 496 copies for sale; and in his will, dated 23 October, Whitman refers to 500 copies at Redfield's (II, 118n). As late as 8 February 1874, Whitman confirmed that this printing "consisted of 500 copies" (II, 275). On 4 February 1874, Whitman wrote a New York bookseller that 168 copies should be in his stock, which, with about 25 more shipped from another dealer, meant *"there are, positively, no other copies in existence, & of course none in the market"* (II, 273).

   Listed in *Publishers' and Stationers' Weekly Trade Circular*, 29 February 1872. Advertised in *Publishers' Weekly*, 4 April 1874. Deposit copies: BL ('25JY72'; rebound). Presentation copies: NN-B (from Whitman, April 1872). Copies inscribed by owners: BO (8 January 1873), NcU (1 July 1873). A presentation copy from Whitman, dated April 1872, was sold at the William F. Gable sale, 5–6 November 1923, item 889 (see *Whitman at Auction*, p. 82). Price, $1.50.

Locations: BO, CSt, CtY, DLC (3), InU-L, JM (2), MH, NN-B, NN-R, NNC, NcD (2), NcU, NjCW, PU, ScU, TxU (2), ViU (2).

Note one: The title page to *Passage to India* reads: '*LEAVES OF GRASS.* | PASSAGE | *to* | INDIA. | [five lines of verse] | Washington, D.C. | 1872.'.

Note two: The following textual alterations first appear in this printing of *Leaves of Grass:*

   88.31–32   measured. | [line space] | I   ]   measured. I
   99.20   as it is;   ]   as to is

234.27	they.] they
291.9	For] (For
291.12	them.] them.)
303.24	² After] After
304.10	⁵ Not] Not
345.30	summer air,] summer-air,
367.4	¹ SUDDENLY,] SUDDENLY,
374.17	broken;] broken

Note three: The *Passage to India* annex has been noted in two forms: the first has sheets from the 1871 printing with a cancel 1872 title leaf; the second is a new printing, with textual alterations and an integral 1872 title leaf. The following textual alterations first appear in this printing of *Passage to India*:

iv.28	["Lessons" not present]] ["Lessons" listed in contents]
14.5	achiev'd,] achiev'd.
19.8	Art with] Art, with
43.7	Death;] Death.
64.2	2] [not present]
93.14	13] 14
105.11	States;] States
114.21–29	["To You" present]] ["To You" not present]
115.23	6] [not present]
115.34	sun, or star by night,] Sun, or star by night:
116.27–31	["Lessons" not present]] ["Lessons" present]

Copies with the first format of the *Passage to India* annex (1871 sheets with a cancel 1872 title leaf) are at BO, DLC (3), NN-B, NcU, ViU (2).

Leaves

OF

GRASS.

COME, said my Soul,
Such verses for my Body let us write, (for we are one,)
That should I after death invisibly return,
Or, long, long hence, in other spheres,
There to some group of mates the chants resuming,
(Tallying Earth's soil, trees, winds, tumultuous waves,)
Ever with pleased smile I may keep on,
Ever and ever yet the verses owning—as, first, I here and
    now,
Signing for Soul and Body, set to them my name,

Walt Whitman

AUTHOR'S EDITION,
With Portraits and Intercalations.

CAMDEN. NEW JERSEY.

1876.

A 2.5.b₂: 7½″ × 4½″

Leaves of Grass only.

[i–iii] . . . 374–384. Electrotyping notice is not present on the copyright page. Single leaf with the Samuel Hollyer engraving of Whitman printed on verso is inserted after p. 28; single leaf with W. J. Linton engraving of G. C. Potter photograph of Whitman printed on verso is inserted after p. 284.

[1–2]¹² (±1₁) 3¹² [4]¹² 5–16¹². Title leaf is a cancel. Slip listing four intercalary poems and two portraits pasted in contents; slips containing printed poems pasted on pp. 207, 247, 359, 369; slip containing revised title pasted on p. 285. Sheets bulk ⅞″.

vi   CONTENTS.

	PAGE
LEAVES OF GRASS.	
This Compost	341
Unnamed Lands	343
Mannahatta	345
Old Ireland	346
To Oratists	347
Solid, Ironical, Rolling Orb	348
BATHED IN WAR'S PERFUME.	
Bathed in War's Perfume	349
Delicate Cluster	349
Song of the Banner at Day-Break	350
Ethiopia Saluting the Colors	357
Lo! Victress on the Peaks	358
World, Take Good Notice	358
Thick-Sprinkled Bunting	359
A Hand-Mirror	360
Germs	360
LEAVES OF GRASS.	
O Me! O Life!	361
Thoughts	361
Beginners	362
SONGS OF INSURRECTION.	
Still, though the One I sing	363
To a foil'd European Revolutionaire	363
France, the 18th year of These States	365
Europe, the 72d and 73d years of These States	367
Walt Whitman's Caution	369
To a Certain Cantatrice	369
LEAVES OF GRASS.	
To You	370
SONGS OF PARTING.	
As the Time Draws Nigh	373
Years of the Modern	373
Thoughts	375
Song at Sunset	377
When I heard the Learn'd Astronomer	380
To Rich Givers	380
Thought	380
So Long	381

INTERCALATIONS.

As in a Swoon	page	207
The Beauty of the Ship	"	247
When the Full-Grown Poet Came	"	359
After an Interval	"	369

PORTRAITS.—Facing page 29, Daguerreotyped from life, July, 1854, by Gabe Harrison, Brooklyn, and drawn on steel by Kae, N. Y. Facing page 285, Photo'd from life, Washington, 1871, by Geo. C. Potter, and drawn on wood by W. J. Linton.

Contents page for A 2.5.b₂, showing intercalated material

I HEAR AMERICA SINGING.

I HEAR America singing, the varied carols I hear;
Those of mechanics—each one singing his, as it should be, blithe and strong;
The carpenter singing his, as he measures his plank or beam,
The mason singing his, as he makes ready for work, or leaves off work;
The boatman singing what belongs to him in his boat—the deck-hand singing on the steamboat deck;
The shoemaker singing as he sits on his bench—the hatter singing as he stands;
The wood-cutter's song—the ploughboy's, on his way in the morning, or at the noon intermission, or at sundown;
The delicious singing of the mother—or of the young wife at work—or of the girl sewing or washing—Each singing what belongs to her, and to none else;
The day what belongs to the day—At night, the party of young fellows, robust, friendly,
Singing, with open mouths, their strong melodious songs.

AS IN A SWOON.

As in a swoon, one instant,
Another sun, ineffable, full-dazzles me,
And all the orbs I knew—and brighter, unknown orbs;
One instant of the future land, Heaven's land.
Intercalation.

Page 207 of A 2.5.b_2, showing intercalated poem

The box-lid is but perceptibly open'd—nevertheless the perfume pours copiously out of the whole box.

8

13 Young Libertad!
With the venerable Asia, the all-mother,
Be considerate with her, now and ever, hot Libertad—for you are all;
Bend your proud neck to the long-off mother, now sending messages over the archipelagoes to you;
Bend your proud neck low for once, young Libertad.

9

14 Were the children straying westward so long? so wide the tramping?
Were the precedent dim ages debouching westward from Paradise so long?
Were the centuries steadily footing it that way, all the while unknown, for you, for reasons?

15 They are justified—they are accomplish'd—they shall now be turn'd the other way also, to travel toward you thence;
They shall now also march obediently eastward, for your sake, Libertad.

THE BEAUTY OF THE SHIP.

WHEN, staunchly entering port,
After long ventures, hauling up, worn and old,
Batter'd by sea and wind, torn by many a fight,
With the original sails all gone, replaced, or mended,
I only saw, at last, the beauty of the Ship.
Intercalation.

Page 247 of A 2.5.b_2, showing intercalated poem

THE WOUND-DRESSER.

1

An old man bending, I come, among new faces,
Years looking backward, resuming, in answer to children,
Come tell us, old man, as from young men and maidens that love me;
Years hence of these scenes, of those furious passions, these chances,
Of unsurpass'd heroes, (was one side so brave? the other was equally brave;)
Now be witness again—paint the mightiest armies of earth;
Of those armies so rapid, so wondrous, what saw you to tell us?
What stays with you latest and deepest? of curious panics,
Of hard-fought engagements, or sieges tremendous, what deepest remains?

2

' O maidens and young men I love, and that love me,
What you ask of my days, those the strangest and sudden your talking recalls;
Soldier alert I arrive, after a long march, cover'd with sweat and dust;
In the nick of time I come, plunge in the fight, loudly shout in the rush of successful charge;
Enter the captur'd works . . . yet lo! like a swift-running river, they fade;
Pass and are gone, they fade—I dwell not on soldiers' perils or soldiers' joys;
(Both I remember well—many the hardships, few the joys, yet I was content.)

' But in silence, in dreams' projections,
While the world of gain and appearance and mirth goes on,

Page 285 of A 2.5.b_2, showing intercalated poem title

Walt Whitman's Caution.

TO The States, or any one of them, or any city of The
    States, *Resist much, obey little*;
Once unquestioning obedience, once fully enslaved;
Once fully enslaved, no nation, state, city, of this earth,
    ever afterward resumes its liberty.

———

To a Certain Cantatrice.

HERE, take this gift!
I was reserving it for some hero, speaker, or General,
One who should serve the good old cause, the great
    Idea, the progress and freedom of the race;
Some brave confronter of despots—some daring rebel;
—But I see that what I was reserving, belongs to you
    just as much as to any.

———

AFTER AN INTERVAL.

(*Nov. 22, 1875. midnight.—Saturn and Mars in conjunction.*)

AFTER an interval, reading, here in the midnight,
With the great stars looking on—all the stars of Orion
    looking,
And the silent Pleiades—and the duo looking of Saturn and
    ruddy Mars;
Pondering, reading my own songs, after a long interval,
    (sorrow and death familiar now,)
Ere closing the book, what pride! what joy! to find them,
Standing so well the test of death and night!
And the duo of Saturn and Mars!

    Intercalation.

Page 369 of A 2.5.b₂, showing intercalated
poem

Thick-Sprinkled Bunting.

THICK-SPRINKLED bunting! Flag of stars!
Long yet your road, fateful flag!—long yet your road,
    and lined with bloody death!
For the prize I see at issue, at last is the world!
All its ships and shores I see, interwoven with your
    threads, greedy banner!
—Dream'd again the flags of kings, highest borne, to
    flaunt unrival'd?
O hasten, flag of man! O with sure and steady step,
    passing highest flags of kings,
Walk supreme to the heavens, mighty symbol—run up
    above them all,
Flag of stars! thick-sprinkled bunting!

———

WHEN THE FULL-GROWN POET CAME.

WHEN the full-grown Poet came,
Out spake pleas'd NATURE, (the round impassive Globe,
    with all its shows of Day and Night,) saying,
    He is mine;
But out spake too the SOUL of Man, proud, jealous and
    unreconciled, *Nay, he is mine alone*;
—Then the full-grown Poet stood between the Two, and took
    each by the hand;
And to-day and ever so stands, as Blender, Uniter, tightly
    holding hands,
Which he will never release until he reconciles the Two,
And wholly and joyously blends them.

    Intercalation.

Page 359 of A 2.5.b₂, showing intercalated
poem

Binding: Two styles have been noted:

Binding A: Half light brown leather with deep orange S cloth (diagonally fine-ribbed) sides; edges beveled. Spine: goldstamped '[row of vertical lines] | [double rule] | [dark blue leather label with two lines] *CENTENNIAL* | *Ed'n*—1876. | [double rule] | [floral design] | [double rule] | [row of vertical lines] | [triple rule] | [very deep red leather label with three lines] LEAVES | OF | GRASS | [triple rule] | [row of vertical lines] | [double rule] | [floral design] | [double rule] | [row of vertical lines] | [double rule] | [dark blue leather label with one line] WALT WHITMAN | [double rule] | [floral design] | [double rule] | [row of vertical lines] | [double rule] | [floral design] | [double rule] | [dark blue leather label with one line] *Portraits.* | [double rule] | [row of vertical lines]'. Front flyleaf and double back flyleaves. Very light yellow-green stiff endpapers embossed with leaves on one side. All edges trimmed; or top edges trimmed, front and bottom edges uncut. All edges gilded or top edges gilded. See *Note four.*

Binding B: Half cream leather with light brown, yellow, and red shell-like marbled paper-covered sides. Spine: blindstamped boxes and bands with two dark green leather labels with goldstamped '*LEAVES | of | GRASS*' and '*ED'N*—1876'. Front flyleaf and double back flyleaves. Very light yellow-green stiff endpapers embossed with flowers on one side. Uncut. See *Note eight.*

Printing: Bound by James Arnold, Philadelphia.

Publication: Whitman began plans for the book by ordering "1000 impressions of the cut, my head" from the engraver W. J. Linton on 24 February 1875, receiving them on 28 March (*Correspondence,* II, 323, 326). On 2 March, he wrote that if "practicable," he would "bring out a Vol. the coming summer" in what he later called "its permanent form" (II, 325; 7 May, II, 332). He reported on 26 November that the book was "getting ready," and on 17 December that it was "nearly ready," with "only 100 copies issued" (II, 343, 344). By 26 January 1876 it was "about got ready," and on 4 March Whitman wrote a friend that he had sent him copies "two or three days" ago (III, 20, 26). By 20 June he could wrote that these copies "have become exhausted" (III, 51). But the inventory of Whitman's belongings made after his death lists five signed copies and "several boxes" ("uncounted") of unsigned copies of this issue (DLC).

100 copies. *Centennial Edition.* Deposited for copyright: title, 5 February 1876; book, 21 March 1876; 1585. Announced as published in the 2 January 1876 *New York Herald.* Announced for publication soon in an edition limited to 100 copies in *Springfield Daily Republican,* 18 January 1876, pp. 4–5. Whitman reviewed the book anonymously in the *New-York Daily Tribune,* 19

February 1876, p. 4 (E 2551), and *Camden New Republic,* 11 March 1876 (E 2552). Deposit copies: binding B: DLC (not dated). Inscribed copies: binding A: ViU (from Whitman, 2 March 1876). Price, $5.00.

Locations: Binding A: CtY, DLC (3), NN-B, NN-R, NNC, PU, TxU (2), ViU (2); binding B: DLC, RPB.

Note one: The intercalated material was printed on the recto of a single leaf (DLC, MB, ViU).

Note two: A single leaf, with advertisements for Whitman's books printed on the recto (see illustration), is inserted between the back flyleaves.

Note three: All located copies are signed by Whitman on the title page.

Note four: The goldstamping on the spine of copies in binding A is erratic, resulting in the rules appearing in various combinations on or off the leather labels. For ease of reporting, only the lettering on the leather labels is given in the description.

Note five: A blue silk ribbon marker is present in copies in binding A.

Note six: Copies in binding A were sold in England for £1 by Whitman, with his friends serving as agents (see W. M. Rossetti's printed circular, dated 20 May 1876 [PU]).

Note seven: The following textual alteration first appears in this issue:

Title   ["Come, said my soul" present]   ]   [not present]

The following readings are present in the intercalations:

vi.40–48   ["As in a Swoon," "The Beauty of the Ship," "When the Full-Grown Poet Came," "After an Interval" listed on paste-in] [paragraph] PORTRAITS.—Facing page 29, Daguerreotyped from life, July, 1854, by | Gabe Harrison, Brooklyn, and drawn on steel by Rae, N. Y. | [paragraph] Facing page 285, Photo'd from life, Washington, 1871, by Geo. C. Potter | and drawn on wood by W. J. Linton [on same paste-in as above]

207.25–29   ["As in a Swoon" pasted in]

247.25–30   ["The Beauty of the Ship" pasted in]

285.1   ["THE WOUND-DRESSER." title pasted in]

359.16–28   ["When the Full-Grown Poet Came" pasted in]

369.17–28   ["After an Interval" pasted in]

Both Shay (p. 25) and Wells and Goldsmith (p. 21) report copies with "To a Man-of-War Bird" and "A Death Sonnet for Custer" pasted in. The slips for these poems are almost certainly clippings of their newspaper appearances

Binding A for A 2.5.b$_2$

(see E 2555 and E 2556) and not true intercalations like the others, which were printed specially by Whitman.

Note eight: *BAL* argues that copies in binding B (used in the third printing, first issue [A 2.5.c$_1$]) seem "likely" to be "recased" (IX, 39).

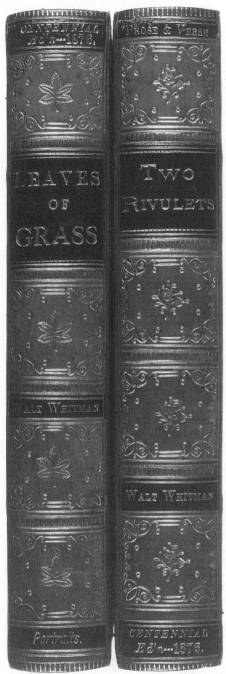

Binding A for A 2.5.b₂ and binding B for
A 9.1.a, sold as a set

Advertisement in A 2.5.b₂

THE BEAUTY OF THE SHIP.

WHEN, staunchly entering port,
After long ventures, hauling up, worn and old,
Batter'd by sea and wind, torn by many a fight,
With the original sails all gone, replaced, or mended,
I only saw, at last, the beauty of the Ship.

Intercalation.

AS IN A SWOON.

As in a swoon, one instant,
Another sun, ineffable, full-dazzles me,
And all the orbs I knew—and brighter, unknown orbs;
One instant of the future land, Heaven's land.

Intercalation.

AFTER AN INTERVAL.

(Nov. 22, 1875, midnight—Saturn and Mars in conjunction.)

AFTER an interval, reading, here in the midnight,
With the great stars looking on—all the stars of Orion looking,
And the silent Pleiades—and the duo looking of Saturn and ruddy Mars;
Pondering, reading my own songs, after a long interval,
(Sorrow and death familiar now,)
Ere closing the book, what pride! what joy! to find them,
Standing so well the test of death and night!
And the duo of Saturn and Mars!

Intercalation.

WHEN THE FULL-GROWN POET CAME.

WHEN the full-grown poet came,
Out spake pleased NATURE, (the round impassive Globe, with all its shows of Day and Night,) saying,
He is mine;
But out spake too the SOUL of Man, proud, jealous and unreconciled, *Nay, he is mine alone;*
—Then the full-grown Poet stood between the Two, and took each by the hand;
And to-day and ever so stands, as Blender, Uniter, tightly holding hands,
Which he will never release until he reconciles the Two,
And wholly and joyously blends them.

Intercalation.

THE WOUND-DRESSER.

PORTRAITS—Facing page 29, Daguerreotyped from life, July, 1854, by Gabe Harrison, Brooklyn, and drawn on steel by Mac, N. Y. Facing page 305, Photo'd from life, Washington, 1871, by Geo. C. Potter, and drawn on wood by W. J. Linton.

Sheet with intercalated material used in A 2.5.b₂

A 2.5.c
Fifth edition, third printing (1876)

Three issues have been noted:

A 2.5.c₁
First (false) issue (1876)

Leaves

OF

G R A S S.

COME, said my Soul,
Such verses for my Body let us write, (for we are one,)
That should I after death invisibly return,
Or, long, long hence, in other spheres,
There to some group of mates the chants resuming,
(Tallying Earth's soil, trees, winds, tumultuous waves,)
Ever with pleased smile I may keep on,
Ever and ever yet the verses owning—as, first, I here and now,
Signing for Soul and Body, set to them my name,

Walt Whitman

AUTHOR'S EDITION,
With Portraits from life.

CAMDEN, NEW JERSEY.

1876.

A 2.5.c₁: 7⅝″ × 4⅝″

> *Entered according to Act of Congress, in the year 1876, by*
> **WALT WHITMAN,**
> *In the Office of the Librarian of Congress, at Washington.*
>
> Electrotyped by SMITH & McDOUGAL, 82 Beekman Street, New York.

Title leaf is a cancel. The title page has been reset and a notice of electrotyping has been added to the copyright page; see illustration. The most likely explanation for this false issue is that copies of the first gathering were printed with the reset contents pages but with the title page reading "With Portraits and Intercalations" and the copyright page lacking the electrotyping notice erroneously retained. When this was noticed, the title and copyright pages were corrected for the remainder of the printing and cancel title leaves replaced the erroneous title leaves on copies already run off. A rebound copy has been noted with the earlier forms of the title and copyright pages, but with the reset contents pages (Magnum Opus Rare Books). *Locations:* BL (rebound), NcD.

A 2.5.c₂
Second (American) issue (1876)

Title leaf is integral. Title and copyright pages are the same as in the first issue.

[i–iii] . . . 374–384. Single leaf with the Samuel Hollyer engraving of Whitman printed on verso is inserted after p. 28; single leaf of coated paper with W. J. Linton engraving of G. C. Potter photograph of Whitman printed on verso is inserted after p. 284.

[1–2]¹² 3¹² [4]¹² 5–16¹². Sheets bulk ⅞".

Contents: Previously intercalated material is now printed in the contents and on pp. 207, 247, 285, 359, 369.

Binding: Half cream leather with red, black, and green shell marbled paper-covered sides. Spine: blindstamped '[row of vertical rules] | [double rule] | [double rule] | [double rule] | [double rule] | [coarse diaperlike pattern] | [double rule] | [double rule] | [row of vertical rules]' with light brown or dark reddish brown leather label after second double rule with goldstamped '[double rule] | *LEAVES* | OF | *GRASS* | Ed'n 1876 | [double rule]'. Double front and back flyleaves; or triple front and double back flyleaves. Endpapers coated yellow on one side. All edges trimmed.

Printing: Electrotyped by Smith and McDougal, New York; printed by Samuel W. Green, New York; bound by James Arnold, Philadelphia.

Binding for A 2.5.c₂

Publication: On 4[?] May 1876, Whitman wrote the printer Samuel W. Green to order 600 copies "with corrections," to be ready for the binder, James Arnold of Philadelphia, on the 24th (*Correspondence*, III, 43; *Daybooks*, I, 13–14). Whitman began receiving copies from the bindery on 1 September and started to send off copies on the fourth (*Correspondence,* III, 55, 56; but a letter of 30 August mentions that he is sending a copy [VI, 15]). On 10 December 1881, Whitman stated that between 100 and 200 copies were "on hand" and as late as 28 May 1886 he sold 20 copies (III, 256; *Daybooks,* II, 386). Deposit copies: BL ('14DE76'; rebound), BL ('4 JY88'; rebound). Price, $5.00.

Locations: BBo (3), BMR, CtY (3), DLC (14), InU-L, JM (2), MBU, MH (3), NN-B (2), NN-R (2), NNC, NNPM, NcD, NcU, NjCW (3), NjP, NzD, PU (4), ScU, TxU (7), ViU.

Note one: A single leaf, with advertisements for Whitman's books printed on the recto (see illlustration), is inserted between the back flyleaves.

Note two: The title page is signed by Whitman in some copies: BBo (2), CtY, DLC (13), MH (3), NN-B (2), NN-R, NNPM, NcD, NjCW, NjP, NzD, PU (4), TxU (5), ViU.

Advertisement in A 2.5.c₂

Note three: A copy was sold with a note by Traubel that "W. W. himself did some typographical work on this 1876 edn. in the office of the New Republican, Camden, New Jersey" (T. B. Mosher sale, 10–11 May 1948, item 474; see *Whitman at Auction*, p. 398).

Note four: Material that appeared in intercalations in A 2.5.b₂ is now printed as follows:

iv.52	["As in a Swoon" listed]
v.2	["The Beauty of the Ship" listed]
vi.16	["When the Full-Grown Poet Came" listed]
vi.30	["After an Interval" listed]
vi.42–45	["portraits" information printed]
207.25–29	["As in a Swoon" printed]
247.25–30	["The Beauty of the Ship" printed]
285.1	["THE WOUND-DRESSER." title printed]
359.16–28	["When the Full-Grown Poet Came" printed]
369.17–28	["After an Interval" printed]

The following textual alterations first appear in this printing:

v.34	The Wound-Dresser]	The Dresser
vi.42	by Gabe]	by | Gabe [in intercalation]
vi.43	McRae]	Rae [in intercalation]
vi.44	Photograph'd]	Photo'd [in intercalation]
vi.44	G.]	C. [in intercalation]
7.8	Muse]	muse
8.1	Genius]	genius
53.18	Reality,]	reality,
53.20	Science!]	science!
251.30	it is]	is it

A 2.5.c₃
Third (English) issue [1876]

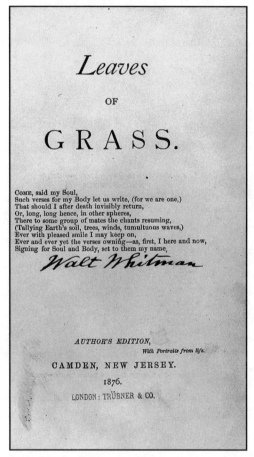

A 2.5.c₃: 7⅝″ × 4⅝″

The Trübner imprint is rubberstamped in black.

Binding: Same as in the second issue, except: double front and back flyleaves.

Publication: Trübner distributed the book in England, reporting on 8 November 1877 that 10 copies had been sold, and on 10 July 1880 that all copies were gone and ordering 10 more (*Correspondence*, III, 137n, 193n). The only located copy was originally presented by Edward Dowden to the Trinity College Library in Dublin in 1881.

Location: TxU.

A 2.6
Sixth (English) edition, only printing (1872) [i.e., 1873]

LEAVES

of

GRASS.

Washington, D. C.
1872.

A 2.6: Binding A: 7⅝″ × 4¹¹⁄₁₆″; binding B: 7⅞″ × 4⅞″

Entered according to Act of Congress, in the year 1871, by
WALT WHITMAN,
In the Office of the Librarian of Congress, at Washington.

〜〜〜〜〜〜〜〜〜〜〜〜〜〜〜〜〜〜〜〜〜〜〜〜〜

Electrotyped by SMITH & McDOUGAL, 82 Beekman Street, New York.

Leaves of Grass, Passage to India, and *After All, Not to Create Only.* Published by John Camden Hotten.

[i–ii] [i–iii] . . . 374–384 [i–iii] . . . 118–120 [1–3] 4–14

[1–2]² [3–34]⁸. Sheets bulk 15⁄16″.

Contents: pp. i–ii: blank; p. i: title page; p. ii: copyright page; pp. iii–vi: contents; pp. 7–384: text of *Leaves of Grass;* p. i: title page; p. ii: copyright page; pp. iii–iv: contents; pp. 5–120: text of *Passage to India* (A 5); p. i: title page; p. ii: copyright page; pp. 3–16: text of *After All, Not to Create Only* (A 6).

Typography and paper: Same as in the fifth edition. Running heads: rectos: pp. v–383, 7–119: same as in *Leaves of Grass* and *Passage to India* in the fifth edition; pp. 5–13: 'AMERICAN INSTITUTE POEM.'; versos: pp. iv–384, iv–120: same as in *Leaves of Grass* and *Passage to India* in the fifth edition; pp. 4–12: 'WALT WHITMAN'S'; p. 14: 'WALT WHITMAN'S A. INSTITUTE POEM.'.

Binding: Two styles have been noted, priority undetermined:

Binding A: Very purplish blue or dark reddish orange LG cloth (smooth morocco); or very purplish blue or dark yellowish green or dark red S cloth (diagonal fine-ribbed); or dark reddish orange HT cloth (dot-and-line grain). Front cover: blackstamped triple-rule frame surrounding double-rule frame with ornate intersections in corners; back cover: the same as the front cover, except: all blindstamped; spine: goldstamped '[triple rule] | [ornate band] | LEAVES | OF | GRASS | BY | WALT WHITMAN | [rule with ornament in center] | [blades of grass design] | COMPLETE | [ornate band] | [triple rule]'. No flyleaves or back flyleaf. Cream endpapers coated on one side or pale yellow endpapers coated on one side. All edges rough trimmed.

Binding B: Very dark yellowish green V cloth (smooth). Front and back covers: blank; spine: goldstamped '*LEAVES | of | GRASS | Complete*'. Front and back flyleaves; or back flyleaf. Light green endpapers. Top edges uncut, front and bottom edges rough trimmed; or all edges trimmed.

Printing: Billing, London.

Binding A for A 2.6

Publication: 500 copies ordered from the printer on 6 March 1873. Hotten's ledgers show 206 copies were delivered and 106 were bound (see *Note two*). Listed in the *English Catalogue* as an importation by Hotten. Advertised in *Athenæum,* 14 June 1873. Copies inscribed by owners: binding A: NN-R (February 1875); binding B: NN-R (24 October 1875). Price, 9s.

Locations: Binding A: BL, BMR, BO, CSt, CtY, DLC (3), JM (2), NN-R (2), NNC, NjCW, NjP, PU (2), RPB, TxU (2), ViU (2); binding B: BMR, CtY, NN-R (2), NNPM, PU, ViU.

Note one: The title page to the *Passage to India* annex reads: 'LEAVES OF GRASS. | PASSAGE | *to* | INDIA. | [five lines of verse] | Washington, D.C. | 1872.'. The textual readings are those of the 1872 reprinting.

Note two: This type facsimile was published by John Camden Hotten of London. There are different textual readings, line breaks, copyright date ('1871'), and ornaments between the poems (see illustrations) that distinguish it from the American edition. Hotten's anonymous piracy was no doubt due to British censorship laws, which he probably thought he could avoid more easily by posing as the distributor of the book rather than as the publisher of it. For a full discussion, see Morton D. Paley, "John Camden Hotten and the First British Editions of Walt Whitman—'A Nice Milky Cocoa-Nut,'" *Publishing History,* 6 (1979), 5–35.

Note three: H. Buxton Forman wrote the following note, dated 1 January 1876, in his copy: "This edition of 'Leaves of Grass,' purporting to be printed in New York, was in reality printed in London,—one of the many meaningless swindles of the late John Hotten" (NN-R [A]).

Top reproduction

FAST ANCHOR'D, ETERNAL, O LOVE!

FAST-ANCHOR'D, eternal, O love! O woman I love!
O bride! O wife! more resistless than I can tell, the
    thought of you!
—Then separate, as disembodied, or another born,
Ethereal, the last athletic reality, my consolation;
I ascend—I float in the regions of your love, O man,
O sharer of my roving life.

Sometimes with One I Love.

SOMETIMES with one I love, I fill myself with rage, for
    fear I effuse unreturn'd love;
But now I think there is no unreturn'd love—the pay is
    certain, one way or another;
(I loved a certain person ardently, and my love was not
    return'd;
Yet out of that, I have written these songs.)

That Shadow, my Likeness.

THAT shadow, my likeness, that goes to and fro, seeking
    a livelihood, chattering, chaffering;
How often I find myself standing and looking at it where
    it fits;
How often I question and doubt whether that is really
    me;
—But in these, and among my lovers, and caroling my
    songs,
O I never doubt whether that is really me.

Page 142 for A 2.6, showing ornaments separating the
poems (compare with illustration for same page in A 2.5.a₁)

Bottom reproduction

FAST ANCHOR'D, ETERNAL, O LOVE!

FAST-ANCHOR'D, eternal, O love! O woman I love!
O bride! O wife! more resistless than I can tell, the
    thought of you!
—Then separate, as disembodied, or another born,
Ethereal, the last athletic reality, my consolation;
I ascend—I float in the regions of your love, O man,
O sharer of my roving life.

Sometimes with One I Love.

SOMETIMES with one I love, I fill myself with rage, for
    fear I effuse unreturn'd love;
But now I think there is no unreturn'd love—the pay
    is certain, one way or another;
(I loved a certain person ardently, and my love was
    not return'd;
Yet out of that, I have written these songs.)

That Shadow, my Likeness.

THAT shadow, my likeness, that goes to and fro, seek-
    ing a livelihood, chattering, chaffering;
How often I find myself standing and looking at it
    where it fits;
How often I question and doubt whether that is really
    me;
—But in these, and among my lovers, and caroling my
    songs,
O I never doubt whether that is really me.

Page 142 for A 2.5.a₁, showing ornaments separating the
poems (compare with illustration for same page in A 2.6)

A 2.7.a
Seventh edition, first printing [1881]

Two issues have been noted:

A 2.7.a₁
First (American) issue [1881]

Two states have been noted:

First state:

LEAVES

of

GRASS

BOSTON
JAMES R. OSGOOD AND COMPANY
1881–2

A 2.7.a₁: First state: 7⅜″ × 4¹³⁄₁₆″

The date on the title page is '1881—2'.

Second state:

LEAVES

of

GRASS

BOSTON
JAMES R. OSGOOD AND COMPANY
1881–82

A 2.7.a₁: Second state: 7⅜″ × 4¹³⁄₁₆″

The date on the title page is '1881—82'.

[1–2] 3–382 [383–384]. Single leaf with Samuel Hollyer engraving of Whitman printed on verso, followed by protective tissue, is inserted after p. 28.

[1–16]¹² . Sheets bulk 1″.

Contents: p. 1: title page; p. 2: copyright page; pp. 3–8: contents; pp. 9–382:
text; pp. 383–384: blank.

Poems: "One's-Self I Sing," "As I Ponder'd in Silence," "In Cabin'd Ships At
Sea," "To Foreign Lands," "To a Historian," "To Thee Old Cause," "Eidolons,"
"For Him I Sing," "When I Read the Book," "Beginning My Studies," "Begin-
ners," "To The States," "On Journeys Through The States," "To a Certain
Cantatrice," "Me Imperturbe," "Savantism," "The Ship Starting," "I Hear America Singing," "What Place is Besieged?", "Still Though the One I Sing," "Shut
not Your Doors," "Poets to Come," "To You" ["Stranger"], "Thou Reader," "Start-
ing From Paumanok," "Song of Myself," "To the Garden the World," "From
Pent-up Aching Rivers," "I Sing the Body Electric," "A Woman Waits for Me,"
"Spontaneous Me," "One Hour to Madness and Joy," "Out of the Rolling Ocean
the Crowd," "Ages and Ages Returning at Intervals," "We Two, How Long We
were Fool'd," "O Hymen! O Hymenee!", "I am He that Aches with Love,"
"Native Moments," "Once I Pass'd through a Populous City," "I Heard You
Solemn-Sweet Pipes of the Organ," "Facing West from California's Shores,"
"As Adam Early in the Morning," "In Paths Untrodden," "Scented Herbage of
My Breast," "Whoever You are Holding Me Now in Hand," "For You O Democ-
racy," "These I Singing in Spring," "Not Heaving from my Ribb'd Breast Only,"
"Of the Terrible Doubt of Appearances," "The Base of All Metaphysics," "Re-
corders Ages Hence," "When I Heard at the Close of the Day," "Are You the
New Person Drawn toward Me?", "Roots and Leaves Themselves Alone," "Not
Heat Flames up and Consumes," "Trickle Drops," "City of Orgies," "Behold
This Swarthy Face," "I Saw in Louisiana a Live-Oak Growing," "To a
Stranger," "This Moment Yearning and Thoughtful," "I Hear It was Charged
against Me," "The Prairie-Grass Dividing," "When I Peruse the Conquer'd
Fame," "We Two Boys together Clinging," "A Promise to California," "Here the
Frailest Leaves of Me," "No Labor-Saving Machine," "A Glimpse," "A Leaf for

Hand in Hand," "Earth, My Likeness," "I Dream'd in a Dream," "What Think You I Take My Pen in Hand?", "To the East and to the West," "Sometimes with One I Love," "To a Western Boy," "Fast-Anchor'd Eternal O Love," "Among the Multitude," "O You whom I Often and Silently Come," "That Shadow My Likeness," "Full of Life now," "Salut au Monde!", "Song of the Open Road," "Crossing Brooklyn Ferry," "Song of the Answerer," "Our Old Feuillage," "A Song of Joys," "Song of the Broad-Axe," "Song of the Exposition," "Song of the Redwood-Tree," "A Song for Occupations," "A Song of the Rolling Earth," "Youth, Day, Old Age and Night," "Song of the Universal," "Pioneers! O Pioneers!", "To You" ["Whoever you are . . ."], "France, The 18th Year of these States," "Myself and Mine," "Year of Meteors. (1859–60.)," "With Antecedents," "A Broadway Pageant," "Out of the Cradle Endlessly Rocking," "As I Ebb'd with the Ocean of Life," "Tears," "To the Man-of-War-Bird," "Aboard at a Ship's Helm," "On the Beach at Night," "The World Below the Brine," "On the Beach at Night Alone," "Song for All Seas, All Ships," "Patroling Barnegat," "After the Sea-Ship," "A Boston Ballad. (1854.)," "Europe, The 72d and 73d Years of These States," "A Hand-Mirror," "Gods," "Germs," "Thoughts" ['Of ownership . . ."], "When I Heard the Learn'd Astronomer," "Perfections," "O Me! O Life!", "To a President," "I Sit and Look Out," "To Rich Givers," "The Dalliance of the Eagles," "Roaming in Thought," "A Farm Picture," "A Child's Amaze," "The Runner," "Beautiful Women," "Mother and Babe," "Thought" ["Of obedience . . ."], "Visor'd," "Thought" ["Of Justice . . ."], "Gliding O'er All," "Hast Never Come to Thee an Hour," "Thought" ["Of Equality . . ."], "To Old Age," "Locations and Times," "Offerings," "To the States, To Identify the 16th, 17th, or 18th Presidentiad," "First O Songs for a Prelude," "Eighteen Sixty-One," "Beat! Beat! Drums!", "From Paumanok Starting I Fly like a Bird," "Song of the Banner at Daybreak," "Rise O Days from Your Fathomless Deeps," "Virginia—the West," "City of Ships," "The Centenarian's Story," "Cavalry Crossing a Ford," "Bivouac on a Mountain Side," "An Army Corps on the March," "By the Bivouac's Fitful Flame," "Come Up from the Fields Father," "Vigil Strange I Kept on the Field One Night," "A March in the Ranks Hard-Prest, and the Road Unknown," "A Sight in Camp in the Daybreak Gray and Dim," "As Toilsome I Wander'd Virginia's Woods," "Not the Pilot," "Year that Trembled and Reel'd Beneath Me," "The Wound-Dresser," "Long, too Long America," "Give Me the Splendid Silent Sun," "Dirge for Two Veterans," "Over the Carnage Rose Prophetic a Voice," "I Saw Old General at Bay," "The Artilleryman's Vision," "Ethiopia Saluting the Colors," "Not Youth Pertains to Me," "Race of Veterans," "World Take Good Notice," "O Tan-Faced Prairie-Boy," "Look Down Fair Moon," "Reconciliation," "How Solemn as One by One," "As I Lay with My Head in Your Lap Camerado," "Delicate Cluster," "To a Certain Civilian," "Lo, Victress on the Peaks," "Spirit Whose Work is Done," "Adieu to a Soldier," "Turn O Libertad," "To the Leaven'd Soil They Trod," "When Lilacs Last in the Dooryard Bloom'd," "O Captain, My Captain," "Hush'd be the

Camps To-day," "The Dust was Once the Man," "By Blue Ontario's Shore,"
"Reversals," "As Consequent, Etc.," "The Return of the Heroes," "There Was a
Child Went Forth," "Old Ireland," "The City Dead-House," "This Compost,"
"To a Foil'd Revolutionaire," "Unnamed Lands," "Song of Prudence," "The
Singer in the Prison," "Warble for Lilac-Time," "Outlines for a Tomb," "Out
from Behind This Mask," "Vocalism," "To Him That was Crucified," "You
Felons on Trial in Courts," "Laws for Creations," "To a Common Prostitute," "I
was Looking a Long While," "Thought" ["Of persons arrived at high posi-
tions . . ."], "Miracles," "Sparkles From the Wheel," "To a Pupil," "Unfolded
Out of the Folds," "What am I After All," "Kosmos," "Others may Praise What
They Like," "Who Learns My Lesson Complete?", "Tests," "The Torch," "O
Star of France. 1870–71," "The Ox-Tamer," "An Old Man's Thought of
School," "Wandering at Morn," "Italian Music in Dakota," "With All Thy Gifts,"
"My Picture-Gallery," "The Prairie States," "Proud Music of the Storm," "Pas-
sage to India," "Prayer of Columbus," "The Sleepers," "Transpositions," "To
Think of Time," "Darest Thou Now O Soul," "Whispers of Heavenly Death,"
"Chanting the Square Deific," "Of Him I Love Day and Night," "Yet, Yet, Ye
Downcast Hours," "As if a Phantom Caress'd Me," "Assurances," "Quicksand
Years," "That Music Always Round Me," "What Ship Puzzled at Sea," "A Noise-
less Patient Spider," "O Living Always, Always Dying," "To One Shortly to Die,"
"Night on the Prairies," "Thought" ["As I sit with others at a great feast . . ."],
"The Last Invocation," "As I Watch'd the Ploughman Ploughing," "Pensive and
Faltering," "Thou Mother with Thy Equal Brood," "A Paumanok Picture," "Thou
Orb Aloft Full-Dazzling," "Faces," "The Mystic Trumpeter," "To a Locomotive in
Winter," "O Magnet-South," "Mannahatta" ["I was asking for something spe-
cific and perfect for my city . . ."], "All is Truth," "A Riddle Song," "Excelsior,"
"Ah Poverties, Wincings, and Sulky Retreats," "Thoughts" ["Of public opin-
ion . . ."], "Mediums," "Weave in, My Hardy Life," "Spain, 1873–74," "By Broad
Potomac's Shore," "From Far Dakota's Canons. June 25, 1876," "Old War-
Dreams," "Thick-Sprinkled Bunting," "What Best I See in Thee," "Spirit That
Form'd This Scene," "As I Walk These Broad Majestic Days," "A Clear Mid-
night," "As the Time Draws Nigh," "Years of the Modern," "Ashes of Soldiers,"
"Thoughts" ["Of these years I sing . . ."], "Song at Sunset," "As at Thy Portals
Also Death," "My Legacy," "Pensive on Her Dead Gazing," "Camps of Green,"
"The Sobbing of the Bells," "As They Draw to a Close," "Joy, Shipmate, Joy,"
"The Untold Want," "Portals," "These Carols," "Now Finale to the Shore," "So
Long!" *Note:* The poems "One's-Self I Sing" through "Thou Reader" form the
cluster "Inscriptions"; the poems "To the Garden the World" through "As Adam
Early in the Morning" form the cluster "Children of Adam"; the poems "In Paths
Untrodden" through "Full of Life now" form the cluster "Calamus"; the poems
"Song of the Universal" through "With Antecedents" form the cluster "Birds of
Passage"; the poems "Out of the Cradle Endlessly Rocking" through "After the
Sea-Ship" form the cluster "Sea-Drift"; the poems "A Boston Ballad. (1854.)"

through "To the States, to Identify the 16th, 17th, or 18th Presidentiad" form the cluster "By the Roadside"; the poems "First O Songs for a Prelude" through "To the Leaven'd Soil They Trod" form the cluster "Drum-Taps"; the poems "When Lilacs Last in the Dooryard Bloom'd" through "The Dust was Once the Man" form the cluster "Memories of President Lincoln"; the poems "As Consequent, Etc." through "The Prairie States" form the cluster "Autumn Rivulets"; the poems "Darest Thou Now O Soul" through "Pensive and Faltering" form the cluster "Whispers of Heavenly Death"; the poems "Thou Orb Aloft Full-Dazzling" through "A Clear Midnight" form the cluster "From Noon to Starry Night"; the poems "As the Time Draws Nigh" through "So Long!" form the cluster "Songs of Parting." See "Index to the Poems in *Leaves of Grass*" for information about the publication histories of individual poems within the various editions, printings, and issues of *Leaves of Grass*.

Typography and paper: 6⅜″ (6″) × 3⅝″; wove paper; various lines per page (up to 45). Running heads: rectos: pp. 5–7: '*CONTENTS.*'; pp. 11–17: '*INSCRIP-TIONS.*'; pp. 19–27: '*STARTING FROM PAUMANOK.*'; pp. 29–77: '*SONG OF MY-SELF.*'; pp. 79–93: '*CHILDREN OF ADAM.*'; pp. 95–111: '*CALAMUS.*'; pp. 113–119: '*SALUT AU MONDE!*'; pp. 121–127: '*SONG OF THE OPEN ROAD.*'; pp. 129–133: '*CROSSING BROOKLYN FERRY.*'; pp. 135–137: '*SONG OF THE ANSWERER.*'; pp. 139–141: '*OUR OLD FEUILLAGE.*'; pp. 143–147: '*A SONG OF JOYS.*'; pp. 149–155: '*SONG OF THE BROAD-AXE.*'; pp. 157–163: '*SONG OF THE EXPOSITION.*'; pp. 165–167: '*SONG OF THE REDWOOD-TREE.*'; pp. 169–175: '*A SONG FOR OCCUPA-TIONS.*'; pp. 177–179: '*A SONG OF THE ROLLING EARTH.*'; pp. 181–191: '*BIRDS OF PASSAGE.*'; pp. 193–195: '*A BROADWAY PAGEANT.*'; pp. 197–207: '*SEA-DRIFT.*'; pp. 209–217: '*BY THE ROADSIDE.*'; pp. 219–253: '*DRUM-TAPS.*'; pp. 255–263: '*MEMORIES OF PRESIDENT LINCOLN.*'; pp. 265–275: '*BY BLUE ON-TARIO'S SHORE.*'; pp. 277–309: '*AUTUMN RIVULETS.*'; pp. 311–313: '*PROUD MUSIC OF THE STORM.*'; pp. 315–321: '*PASSAGE TO INDIA.*'; p. 323: '*PRAYER OF COLUMBUS.*'; pp. 325–331: '*THE SLEEPERS.*'; pp. 333–337: '*TO THINK OF TIME.*'; pp. 339–345: '*WHISPERS OF HEAVENLY DEATH.*'; pp. 347–351: '*THOU MOTHER WITH THY EQUAL BROOD.*'; pp. 353–369: '*FROM NOON TO STARRY NIGHT.*'; pp. 371–381: '*SONGS OF PARTING.*'; versos: pp. 4–8: '*CONTENTS.*'; pp. 10–382: '*LEAVES OF GRASS.*'.

Binding: Two styles have been noted:

Binding A: Slightly orange-yellow or medium olive-brown S cloth (diagonal fine-ribbed). Front cover: goldstamped: single-rule frame around facsimile signature at top; back cover: blank; spine: goldstamped '[six lines over blades of grass design] [three lines in ornate capitals] LEAVES | OF | GRASS | [rule] | WALT WHITMAN | [rule] | [hand with butterfly] | JAMES R. OSGOOD & Co.'. Wove or laid flyleaves. Light blue vein-pattern endpapers. All edges trimmed.

Binding B: Half light brown leather with red, blue, and yellow shell marbled paper-covered sides. Spine: seven goldstamped boxes with floral designs inside six of them, one box (second from top) with a dark red leather
label with goldstamped '[ornate band] | [rule] | LEAVES | OF | GRASS | [rule]
| [ornate band]'. Front flyleaf. Endpapers marbled the same as the covers. All
edges trimmed. All edges marbled the same as the covers.

Printing: See copyright page.

Publication: On 26 April 1881, John Boyle O'Reilly wrote to Whitman that
"James R Osgood wants to see the material for your complete book" (*Correspondence,* III, 224n). Whitman wrote Osgood on 8 May offering a book of "about
400 pages," and the firm responded on the 12th that they wanted to see "the
copy" for the book in order to "give you our views" (III, 224, 225n). Whitman
replied eight days later that he was "fixing up the copy, which I will send on to
you in a few days—perhaps it will be a week" (III, 225). But after Osgood
wrote on the 23d asking for the copy "*this* week," Whitman replied three days
later that he would send it at once, and he did send 527 pages of "copy" on the
27th (III, 226n, 226; *Daybooks,* I, 241). On the 31st, Osgood wrote Whitman
that they would be "glad to publish the book," and offered a 10% royalty
(*Correspondence,* III, 226n). Whitman replied on 1 June by countering with a
royalty of 25¢ per copy if the book was priced at $2.00, or 30¢ for a $2.50 retail
price, and Osgood accepted on the third (III, 227, 227n). Whitman confirmed
the agreement the next day, suggesting a "plain green muslin binding," with
the Gutekunst photograph as a frontispiece (III, 228). The contract, signed on
1 October, gave Whitman the copyright and a 25¢ royalty on a $2.00 retail
price and named Osgood as the sole publisher of the book for ten years
(*Daybooks,* I, 263; printed in full, 263n).

On 16 June, Whitman wrote Osgood that he had "finished my copy which is
now ready to put at hand" (*Correspondence,* III, 230). Osgood sent sample
pages on the 10th and Whitman announced on the 17th that the book would
"probably be out before winter" (III, 230n, 231). In Boston to see the book
through press, by 6 July Whitman was "busy five or six hours yet every day" on
it, and on the 22d he "spent the forenoon" at Rand, Avery's printing office,
"outlining matters of type, size of page, & other details" (III, 233; *Daybooks,* I,
254). Although the book was announced in the *Critic* for 13 August, the "first
batch of page-proof" did not arrive until the 24th (I, 256n). On the 15th, "less
than 2000 impressions" were "struck off" of the plate of the Hollyer engraving
(*Correspondence,* III, 243). Three days later, the book was "almost finished—I
am on the last pages of the proof—will be in the stores ab't last of October" (III,
244). Whitman finished reading proof on 30 September and noted, "the printing of my book is finished" on 10 October (*Daybooks,* I, 263; *Correspondence,*
III, 248; Whitman later gave the dates for when the book was "Set up, cast &

printed" as "Aug: 22–Sept: 29—'1881" [*Daybooks,* I, 264n]). On 23 October, he noted that "it is all ready, & will be delivered & for sale 4th Nov."; he began sending out copies on 9 November (*Correspondence,* III, 249, 252). He also "advised Osgood to sell "250 tru-calf (or half-calf) binding for holiday sales," but the plan was apparently not carried out (*Daybooks,* I, 268). On 25 October 1881, Whitman wrote to a friend that he had sent him a circular advertising the book a week ago (III, 251).

1,010 copies printed 4 October 1881. Sales were initially good and Benjamin Ticknor of the firm wrote Whitman on 14 November 1881: "The first edition is all gone & we are binding up the second" (III, 253n). On 25 January 1882, Dr. John Johnston wrote Whitman, quoting a note from Osgood, who had "printed three editions, 2000 copies in all" (III, 276–277n). On 13 April, Osgood paid Whitman $405.50 in royalties (the equivalent of 1,622 copies at 25¢ each) (III, 273n). Although the *Springfield Republican* of 23 May 1882 reported that 1,600 copies had been sold, Whitman wrote a friend on 7 May that "I think [some?] 3000 must have been published" (III, 276).

Accounts of Whitman seeing the book through press appeared in the *Boston Daily Globe,* 24 August 1881, p. 2, and *Boston Pilot,* 44 (27 August 1881), 5. Deposited for copyright: title, 7 October 1881; book, 7 November 1881; 15514. Reviewed in *Boston Sunday Herald,* 30 October 1881, p. 3. Deposit copies: second state: binding A: DLC ('NOV 7 1881'; rebound), DLC ('NOV 7 1881'). Presentation copies: second state: binding A: DLC (from Whitman, November 1881); binding B: DLC (from J. R. Osgood to John Lane, 26 April 1899). Copies inscribed by owners: second state: binding A: TxU (November 1881), NN-R (26 November 1881). Price, $2.00.

Locations: First state: binding A: CtY, JM, NN-R, TxU; second state: binding A: BL, BMR, BO, CtY, DLC (5), InU-L, JM (2), MB, NN-B (2), NN-R, NNPM, NcD, NjCW, NjP, PU, RPB (2), ScU, TxU (4), ViU; binding B: DLC.

Note one: An eight-page advertising brochure has been noted: p. 1: quotations from critics and reviewers (printed in black and red); p. 2: discussions of *Leaves of Grass* from the 24 August 1881 *Boston Globe* and an unidentified newspaper of October 1881; pp. 3–8: contents pages from *Leaves of Grass* (CtY, DLC). Proofs of this brochure, with instructions to the printer to print 1,000 copies, are at CtY.

Note two: A broadside advertising circular, printed on both sides, is at DLC.

Note three: Also advertised in half calf for $4.00 and tree calf for $5.00; no copies have been located, although binding B may be publisher's half calf.

Note four: A note in the DLC copy in binding B (second state) by Charles Feinberg calls this the large paper presentation binding.

A 2.7.a₂
Second (English) issue (1881)

LEAVES

of

GRASS

————

LONDON

TRÜBNER & CO., LUDGATE HILL

1881

A 2.7.a₂: 7⅜″ × 4¹³⁄₁₆″

[i–ii] [1–2] 3–382 [383–384]. Single leaf with Samuel Hollyer engraving of Whitman printed on verso, followed by a protective tissue, is inserted after p. 28.

[1]¹² (−1₁, +1₁.₂) [2–16]¹² . A two-leaf gathering, with the half title, advertisements, and title leaves, is pasted to the stub of leaf 1₁.

Contents: Same as in the first issue, except: p. i: '*LEAVES of GRASS*'; p. ii: Trübner advertisement for Whitman's books; p. 1: English title page; p. 2: blank.

Binding: Dark grayish olive-green S cloth (diagonal fine-ribbed). Front and back covers: blindstamped '[double rule] | [band of flowers] | [double rule]' at top and blindstamped '[double rule] | [band of thistles and dots] | [double rule]' at bottom; spine: goldstamped '[double rule] | [band of flowers] | [double rule] | LEAVES | OF | GRASS | [rule] | WALT | WHITMAN | TRÜBNER & Cᵒ | [double rule] | [band of thistles and dots] | [double rule]'. Light brown floral-pattern endpapers printed on one side. Top edges trimmed, front and bottom edges uncut. Top edges gilded.

Publication: Whitman wrote to Trübner, who was to serve as the British distributor, on 5 October that he was sending them copies to secure British copyright, and on 1 November he returned the copyright form to them (*Correspondence,* III, 247; *Daybooks,* I, 270). However, they declined and David Bogue agreed to take up the book (8 December 1881, *Correspondence,* V, 314–315; *Daybooks,* I, 276).

Listed as published on 31 October in *Athenæum,* 5 November 1881. Deposit copies: BL ('31OC87'). Price, 7s.6d.

Location: BL.

A 2.7.b
First edition, second printing [1881]

Two issues have been noted:

A 2.7.b₁
First (American) issue [1881]

Boston: James R. Osgood, 1881–82.

Copies of the first printing, second state, and the second printing have not been differentiated. 508 copies printed 8 November 1881.

A 2.7.b₂
Second (English) issue (1881)

LEAVES OF GRASS

BY

WALT WHITMAN.

AUTHOR'S COPYRIGHT EDITION.

LONDON:

DAVID BOGUE 3, ST. MARTIN'S PLACE,

TRAFALGAR SQUARE, W. C.

1881.

A 2.7.b₂: 7¾″ × 5″

[i–ii] [1–2] 3–382 [383–384]. Single leaf with Samuel Hollyer engraving of Whitman printed on verso, followed by a protective tissue, is inserted after p. 28 (NcD [A]) or between half title and title (all other copies).

[1]¹² (−1₁, +1₁.₂) [2–16]¹². A two-leaf gathering, with the half title and title leaves, is pasted to the stub of leaf 1₁.

Contents: Same as in the first issue, except: p. i: 'LEAVES OF GRASS.'; p. ii: blank; p. 1: English title page; p. 2: blank.

Binding: Four styles have been noted, priority undetermined:

Binding A: Medium olive S cloth (diagonal fine-ribbed). A band of four blackstamped rules runs across the top of the covers and spine; a band of seven blackstamped rules runs across the bottom of the covers and spine. Front cover: goldstamped within bands: '[top left] Leaves of Grass | [bottom right] Walt Whitman'; back cover: bands; spine: goldstamped within bands: 'Leaves | of | Grass | Walt | Whitman | [intersecting 'D' and 'B']'. No flyleaves. Gray endpapers. Top edges trimmed, front and bottom edges uncut. Top edges gilded.

Binding B: Same as binding A, except: light olive S cloth (diagonal fine-ribbed); the title and Whitman's name are centered on the front cover; light blue vein-pattern endpapers.

Binding C: Same as binding A, except: medium olive or light olive S cloth (diagonal fine-ribbed); a band of eight blackstamped rules runs across the top of the covers and spine; a band of eleven blackstamped rules runs across the bottom of the covers and spine; the spine has '[intersecting 'D' and 'B' within single-rule frame]'; light blue or gray vein-pattern endpapers.

Binding D: Same as binding A, except: light olive S cloth (diagonal fine-ribbed); a band of eight blackstamped rules runs across the top of the covers and spine; a band of eleven blackstamped rules runs across the bottom of the covers and spine; the title and Whitman's name are centered on the front cover; the spine has '[intersecting 'D' and 'B' within single-rule frame]'; light blue vein-pattern endpapers.

Publication: After Trübner declined to serve as the British distributor, David Bogue agreed to take up the book (8 December 1881, *Correspondence,* V, 314–315; *Daybooks,* I, 276). Whitman wrote Bogue on 14 December and asked him to "have a little circular printed" for distribution to his friends (*Correspondence,* III, 257; see *Note*). Although Mrs. Gilchrist reported to Whitman on 8 May 1882 that Bogue's sales were "progressing satisfactorily," the firm evidently had financial troubles, and on 24 November she wrote Whitman: "I fear you will be a loser by Bogue's bankruptcy" (III, 272n). Osgood wrote Whitman on 13 April 1882, in settling the firm's account with him, that 400 copies had been sent to England, "which we assume to be sold, but the sale of which is uncertain" (copy, PU).

Listed in *Athenæum,* 12 November 1881. *Author's Copyright Edition.* Price, 4s.

Locations: Binding A: NcD; binding B: ViU; binding C: CtY, DLC (2), JM, NN-R, NcD, PU; binding D: InU-L, TxU.

Note one: A copy of the first issue in binding A contains a four-page flier inserted between the front endpapers, done as a facsimile of a handwritten letter from David Bogue, 4 January 1882, stating 'Dear Sir | I am requested by | M͇ Walt Whitman to inform | you that the new and unabridged | edition of his "Leaves of Grass" is | now published' for 4s. Also tipped in is a note of 14 December 1881 from Whitman to Bogue asking for him to make an announcement that a new edition is out 'with your place as the London agency & depository' (TxU).

A 2.7.c
First edition, third printing [1882]

Three issues have been noted:

A 2.7.c₁
First (American) issue [1882]

LEAVES

of

GRASS

THIRD EDITION

BOSTON
JAMES R. OSGOOD AND COMPANY
1881–82

A 2.7.c₁: 7⅜″ × 4¹³⁄₁₆″

[1–2] 3–382 [383–384]. Single leaf with Samuel Hollyer engraving of Whitman printed on verso, followed by protective tissue, is inserted after p. 28.

[1–16]¹² . Sheets bulk ⅞".

Contents and typography and paper are the same as in the first printing.

Binding: Medium olive-brown or slightly orange-yellow S cloth (diagonal fine-ribbed). Front cover: goldstamped: single-rule frame around facsimile signature at top; back cover: blank; spine: goldstamped '[six lines over blades of grass design] [three lines in ornate capitals] LEAVES | OF | GRASS | [rule] | WALT WHITMAN | [rule] | [hand with butterfly] | JAMES R. OSGOOD & Co.'. Wove or laid flyleaves. Light blue vein-pattern endpapers. All edges trimmed.

Publication: 510 copies printed 17 December 1881. Deposit copy: BL ('17 JY 82'). Copies inscribed by owners: NNC (25 December 1881), MH (29 March 1882).

Locations: BL, CtY, DLC (3), JM, MBU, MH, NN-B, NNC, NcD, NjCW, PU (2), RPB, TxU (2), ViU.

A 2.7.c₂
Second (English) issue (1881) [i.e., 1882]

London: David Bogue, 1881.

Title page is the same as in the second printing, second issue (A 2.7.b₂). Page size 7¾" × 5".

[i–ii] [1–2] 3–382 [383–384]. Single leaf with Samuel Hollyer engraving of Whitman printed on verso is inserted between the half title and title leaves (BMR, BO, JM, RPB) or is not present (MBU).

[1]¹² (−1₁, +1₁.₂) [2–16]¹². Title leaf is a cancel, with a two-leaf gathering pasted to the stub of leaf 1₁.

Contents: Same as in the first state, except: p. i: 'LEAVES OF GRASS.'; p. ii: blank; p. 1: English title page; p. 2: blank.

Binding: Light olive S cloth (diagonal fine-ribbed). A band of eight black-stamped rules runs across the top of the covers and spine and a band of 11 blackstamped rules runs across the bottom of the covers and spine. Front cover: goldstamped within bands: '[top left] Leaves of Grass | [bottom right] Walt Whitman'; back cover: bands; spine: goldstamped within bands: 'Leaves | of | Grass | Walt | Whitman | [intersecting 'D' and 'B' within single-rule frame]'. No flyleaves or front flyleaf. Light blue vein-pattern endpapers. Top edges trimmed, front and bottom edges uncut. Top edges gilded.

Publication: *Author's Copyright Edition*. Price, 4s.

Locations: BMR, BO, JM, MBU, RPB.

A 2.7.c₃
Third (American) issue (1882)

LEAVES

of

GRASS

COME, said my Soul,
Such verses for my Body let us write, (for we are one,)
That should I after death invisibly return,
Or, long, long hence, in other spheres,
'There to some group of mates the chants resuming,
(Tallying Earth's soil, trees, winds, tumultuous waves.)
Ever with pleased smile I may keep on,
Ever and ever yet the verses owning — as, first, I here and now,
Signing for Soul and Body, set to them my name,

Walt Whitman

AUTHOR'S EDITION
CAMDEN, NEW JERSEY
1882

A 2.7.c₃: 7¾″ × 4⅞″

Copyright page: 'COPYRIGHT 1881 | BY WALT WHITMAN | *All rights reserved*'.

[1–2] 3–382 [383–384]. Single leaf with Samuel Hollyer engraving of Whitman printed on verso, followed by protective tissue, is inserted after p. 28; single leaf, with W. J. Linton engraving of Whitman printed on the recto, followed by a protective tissue, is inserted after p. 296.

[1]¹² (±1₁) [2–16]¹² . Title leaf is a cancel.

Binding: Dark green S cloth (diagonal fine-ribbed); edges beveled. Front and back covers: blank; spine: goldstamped '[two lines in script] Author's | Edition | [ornate 'L'] LEAVES | *of* | [ornate 'G'] GRASS | [four lines in script] complete | Autograph | & portraits | 1882'. Front and back flyleaves. Yellow endpapers coated on one side. Top edges trimmed, front and bottom edges rough trimmed; or all edges trimmed. Top edges gilded.

Printing: Cancel title leaf by Rand, Avery, Boston; bound by James Arnold, Philadelphia.

Publication: On 1 March 1882, the district attorney labeled the book "obscene literature" and asked for its "withdrawal . . . from circulation" (*Daybooks,* II, 285–286n; and see *Correspondence,* III, 267ff). Osgood expressed their concern to Whitman ("We are . . . naturally reluctant to be identified with any legal proceedings in a matter of this nature") and asked him to make changes (*Daybooks,* II, 285n). Whitman agreed to revise some lines but refused to delete entire poems. The district attorney would not agree to Whitman's revisions, and Osgood wrote Whitman on 10 April, that "there seems no alternative for us but to decline to further circulate the book," and they made arrangements to give the plates to Whitman (*Correspondence,* III, 273n). On 17 May the transfer was completed: Whitman received the plates, portraits, and dies; received "225 copies (more or less), in sheets"; and was paid $100 in cash (*Daybooks,* II, 289n).

On 19 May 1882, Whitman ordered "new titles" for 225 copies from the printer Rand, Avery (*Correspondence,* III, 280). Henry H. Clark of the firm sent "proof" of the title page to Whitman on 22 May (NjP), which Whitman marked and he instructed them to "print 250 copies," noting, "I have 225 copies here in sheets to be bound here & these titles are for them" (NjP). On 8 June, he sent "corrections" to Rand, Avery and "ordered 1000 copies printed," but, perhaps fearing legal action against them, the firm refused (III, 280n; Whitman did pay them for something, either the corrections or the new title pages, on 24 July [*Daybooks,* II, 297]).

Author's Edition. Presentation copies (all from Whitman): CtY (19 June 1882), DLC (8 November 1883), TxU (27 February 1884), MH (19 July 1884), NN-R (1 January 1885), DLC (11 June 1885). Price, $3.00.

Locations: CtY (4), DLC (6), InU-L, MBU, MH, NN-B (3), NN-R, NNC, NNPM, NjCW, PU, RPB, ScU, TxU (2), ViU (2).

Note one: The title page is signed by Whitman in all located copies.

Note two: An advertising card has been noted (measuring 3⅞″ × 2 ³⁄₁₆″) printed on the recto of brilliant green paper covered cardboard stock, probably written by Whitman, reading '[ornate 'T'] *THE price of Walt Whitman's Poems, "LEAVES OF GRASS," (complete, latest, special edition, | with autograph), is $3 a copy. Address him, 328 Mickle Street,* Camden, New–Jersey. Send p.o. | *order. He also sells his prose book, "SPECIMEN | DAYS AND COLLECT," at $2 a copy.*' (CtY).

A 2.7.d–g
Seventh edition, fourth through seventh printings (1882)

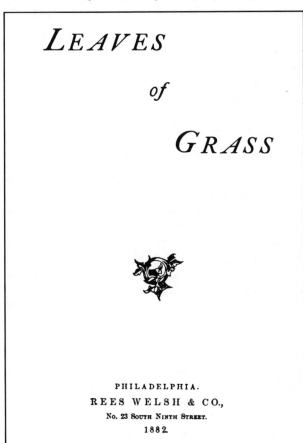

LEAVES

of

GRASS

PHILADELPHIA.
REES WELSH & CO.,
No. 23 SOUTH NINTH STREET.
1882.

A 2.7.d: 7⅜″ × 4¹³⁄₁₆″

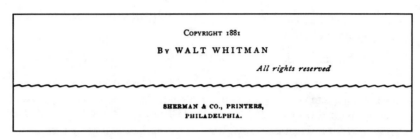

Copies of the fourth through seventh printings have not been differentiated.

[1–2] 3–382 [383–384]. Single leaf with Samuel Hollyer engraving of Whitman printed on verso, followed by protective tissue, is inserted after p. 28.

[1–16]¹² . Sheets bulk 1″.

Contents and typography and paper are the same as in the first printing.

Binding: Slightly orange-yellow or medium olive-brown S cloth (diagonal fine-ribbed). Front cover: goldstamped: single-rule frame around facsimile signature at top; back cover: blank; spine: goldstamped '[six lines over blades of grass design] [three lines in ornate capitals] LEAVES | OF | GRASS | [rule] | WALT WHITMAN | [rule] | [hand with butterfly] | REES WELSH & CO.'. Front and back flyleaves. Light blue vein-pattern endpapers; or light green leaf-and-vine design endpapers printed on one side. All edges trimmed.

Printing: 'SHERMAN & CO., PRINTERS, | PHILADELPHIA.' (p. [2]).

Publication: On 5 June 1882, David McKay of the firm of Rees Welsh wrote Whitman to inquire about publishing his book (PU). On the 17th Whitman agreed to meet with the firm, and three days later he wrote them with his terms (*Correspondence,* III, 291). He was to receive a 35¢ royalty on a $2.00 retail price for each copy sold if his plates were used; Rees Welsh could purchase the plates from Whitman for $400 and, thereafter, the royalty would be reduced to 25¢ (III, 292). Rees Welsh agreed to the first set of terms and signed a contract with Whitman on 22 July for two years and two months (PU). Whitman's suggestion of a special edition "for holiday presents in handsome binding, (say half calf, gilt)," to sell at $5.00, with him receiving 87½¢ royalty, was written into the contract but apparently never acted upon (*Correspondence,* III, 292). The contract also gave Whitman the right "to personally sell or dispose of" the 1876 *Centennial Edition* and the 1882 *Author's Edition* of *Leaves of Grass.* Finally, the contract obligated Rees Welsh to "furnish Desk room for Walt Whitman personally in their store without charge so long as they publish his books."

Printing was begun at Sherman and Company by 9 June; on the 29th Whitman wrote that the book would be "in the market in ten or twelve days," and on 19 July he wrote that the book *"looks well"* (III, 296; V, 316; III, 297). He continued that it was "announced ready by 17th (being pretty cautious printed only 1000) began to come in from the bindery late that day—Early this fornoon *they were all clean'd out—hadn't a copy left—*are hurrying up their second batch" (III, 297–298). Elsewhere, Whitman noted that copies had arrived on the 18th and by the "morning of 20th" they were "all exhausted—not a copy left" (*Daybooks*, II, 297).

On 21 July Whitman noted that a "2d & larger" printing would be ready "ab't 26th or 7th" (*Correspondence*, III, 298). Although he wrote on 3 August that the book would be "launch'd to-day," on the sixth he wrote that publication had been delayed until the fourth; when the books "commenced coming in at noon" they started selling and "by noon next day" 500 copies had sold (III, 300). On the 13th he summed up the activity to a friend: "a cautious 1000" were "exhausted in a day—the second came in ab't five days ago, & is now nearly gone—a third is ordered," and on the 27th he noted that Rees Welsh were "now paying out their third edition" (III, 301, 302).

On 8 October, Whitman noted: "Four Phil: editions" had been "issued & sold within the last three months—they are now on the fifth" (II, 309). McKay's royalty statement to Whitman of 1 December 1882 shows 4,900 copies printed and 3,118 sold, plus 947 for "Editor's" (PU). These figures presumably include between 4000 and 4500 copies printed by Rees Welsh.

The edition was described as sold out in the *Press* (Philadelphia), 22 July 1882, p. 4, and as sold out within two days of publication in *Foote's Health Monthly*, 7 (September 1882), 13. An advertising flier at MB states, "Since July 20, Five Large Editions have been Sold." Presentation copies: DLC (from Whitman, 17 November 1882). Copies inscribed by owners: NjP (19 August 1882). Price, $2.00.

Locations: BBo, BO, CSt, CtY, DLC (5), JM (3), MB, MBU, MH, NN-B, NN-R (2), NNC (2), NcD (3), NcU, NjCW (4), NjP, PU (6), RPB (5), ScU, TxU (4), ViU (2).

Note one: Some copies have "Walt Whitman's Books" (see illustration) tipped to the free front endpaper recto (CtY, DLC, JM, MH, NjP, RPB, ViU).

Note two: Some copies have a slip tipped to the free front endpaper recto, reading 'READY IN SEPTEMBER. | WHITMAN'S PROSE WORKS. | Specimen Days and Collect, Price $2.00. | [ornate rule] | Leaves of Grass, Price $2.00.' (DLC, MB, NjCW, TxU, ViU).

Note three: Also advertised in half calf for $4.00 and tree calf for $5.00; no copies have been located.

Note four: A broadside advertising poster for Rees Welsh, measuring 29¼″ × 24″, printed in black and green, is at NNC.

Advertising slip for "Walt Whitman's Books"

Note five: The following textual alterations first appear in this printing:

19.9	one, the] one the
21.2	finalè] finale
28.14	See, in] See in
28.17	See, on] See. on
29.8	MYSELF.] MYSELF,
64.26	Enough!] Enough
107.8	seaboard,] seaboard
218.11	books, politics] books politics
293.31	lilac-time, (returning in reminiscence,)] lilac-time,
294.27	lilac-time, returning in reminiscence.] lilac-time.
309.36	what if] what of
346.30	go] go,
366.29	ambuscade, the craft, the fatal environment,] ambuscade, the slaughter and environment
376.35	companions] compaions
377.3	after you,] after you.
382.4	preparing.] repairing.

A 2.7.h
Seventh edition, eighth printing (1882)

Two issues have been noted:

A 2.7.h$_1$
First issue (1882)

Philadelphia: Rees Welsh, 1882.

Copies of the fourth through seventh printings (see A 2.7.d–g) have not been differentiated from copies of the eighth printing.

A 2.7.h$_2$
Second issue (1883)

Philadelphia: David McKay, 1883.

[1–2] 3–382 [383–384]. Single leaf with Samuel Hollyer engraving of Whitman printed on verso, followed by protective tissue, is inserted after p. 28.

[1]^{12} ($\pm$1$_1$) [2–16]^{12} . Title leaf is a cancel.

Binding: Medium olive-brown or slightly orange-yellow S cloth (diagonal fine-ribbed). Front cover: goldstamped: single-rule frame around facsimile signature at top; back cover: blank; spine: goldstamped '[six lines over blades of grass design] [three lines in ornate capitals] LEAVES | OF | GRASS | [rule] | WALT WHITMAN | [rule] | [hand with butterfly] | DAVID MÇKAY'. Front and back flyleaves. Light green leaf-and-vine design endpapers printed on one side; or light blue vein-pattern endpapers. All edges trimmed.

Publication: For David McKay's purchase of Rees Welsh, see A 2.7.i below. Presumably, McKay placed his cancel title leaf on unbound sheets left over from Rees Welsh.

Locations: JM, NN-R, PU, TxU.

A 2.7.i
Seventh edition, ninth printing (1882)

LEAVES

of

GRASS

PHILADELPHIA.

DAVID McKAY,

No. 23 SOUTH NINTH STREET.

1882.

A 2.7.i: 8⅜″ × 4¹¹⁄₁₆″

[1–2] 3–382 [383–384]. Single leaf with Samuel Hollyer engraving of Whitman printed on verso, followed by protective tissue, is inserted after p. 28.

[1–16]¹² . Sheets bulk 1″.

Contents and typography and paper are the same as in the first printing.

Binding: Medium olive-brown S cloth (diagonal fine-ribbed). Front cover: goldstamped: single-rule frame around facsimile signature at top; back cover: blank; spine: goldstamped '[six lines over blades of grass design] [three lines in ornate capitals] LEAVES | OF | GRASS | [rule] | WALT WHITMAN | [rule] | [hand with butterfly] | DAVID MÇKAY'. Front and back flyleaves. Light green leaf and vine design endpapers printed on one side. All edges trimmed.

Printing: See copyright page.

Publication: Whitman changed publishers when, as he announced on 12 November 1882, David McKay "formally bo't out & assumed" the business of Rees Welsh (*Correspondence,* III, 314); a notice to this effect appeared in *Publishers' Weekly,* 7 October 1882. McKay immediately prepared a printing under his imprint, and on 10 December Whitman sent a friend a "full set loose leaves" (III, 318n). Advertised in *New-York Daily Tribune,* 11 November 1882. McKay's royalty statement to Whitman of 1 December 1882 shows 4,900 copies had been printed by that date, presumably between 500 and 1,000 with his imprint (PU).

Locations: CaOTP, DLC (2), InU-L, JM (2), NjP, NzD, PU, TxU (2).

A 2.7.j
Seventh edition, tenth printing (1883)

Three issues have been noted:

A 2.7.j₁
First (American) issue (1883)

Philadelphia: David McKay, 1883.

[1–2] 3–382 [383–384]. Single leaf with Samuel Hollyer engraving printed on verso, followed by protective tissue, is inserted after p. 28.

[1–16]¹² . Page size 7⅜″ × 5″. Sheets bulk ²⁵⁄₃₂″.

Contents and typography and paper are the same as in the first printing.

Binding: Slightly orange-yellow S cloth (diagonal fine-ribbed). Front cover: goldstamped: single-rule frame around facsimile signature at top; back cover: blank; spine: goldstamped '[six lines over blades of grass design] [three lines in ornate capitals] LEAVES | OF | GRASS | [rule] | WALT WHITMAN | [rule] | [hand with butterfly] | DAVID MϾKAY'. Front and back flyleaves. Light green leaf-and-vine design endpapers printed on one side. All edges trimmed.

Printing: 'SHERMAN & CO., PRINTERS, | PHILADELPHIA.' (p. [2]).

Publication: McKay's royalty statement to Whitman of 1 June 1883 shows 500 copies had been printed by that date, 400 of which were for sale in America (PU).

Locations: CtY, NcD, PU.

A 2.7.j₂
Second (Scottish) issue (1883)

LEAVES

of

GRASS

GLASGOW
WILSON & McCORMICK, Saint Vincent Street
1883

A 2.7.j₂: 8⅜″ × 5″

Two states have been noted:

First state: [1–2] 3–382 [383–384]. Single leaf with Samuel Hollyer engraving printed on verso, followed by protective tissue, is inserted before the title page.

$[1-16]^{12}$. Title leaf is integral.

Contents: Same as in the first issue, except: p. 1: Scottish title page; p. 2: blank.

Second state: [1–2] 3–382. Single leaf with Samuel Hollyer engraving printed on verso, followed by protective tissue, is inserted before the title page.

$[1-16]^{12}$ (-16_{12}). Title leaf is integral.

Contents: Same as in the first issue, except: p. 1: Scottish title page; p. 2: blank; pp. 383–384 (blank pages) are canceled.

Binding: Dark orange-yellow S cloth (diagonal fine-ribbed). Front cover: goldstamped facsimile signature; back cover: blank; spine: goldstamped '[double rule] | [three lines in ornate capitals] | LEAVES | OF | GRASS | [rule] | WALT WHITMAN | [rule] | WILSON & MᶜCORMICK | [double rule]'. Endpapers coated and printed with a brown geometric or a floral pattern on one side; or white wove endpapers. Top and front edges rough trimmed, bottom edges trimmed.

Publication: Whitman noted on 27 June 1883 that Wilson and McCormick had issued the book, a copy of which he received on 20 July (*Correspondence,* III, 344; *Daybooks,* II, 316). F. W. Wilson of the firm wrote Whitman on 27 February 1884 that sales were "going very well here" (*Correspondence,* III, 328n). McKay's royalty statement to Whitman of 1 June 1883 shows that of the 500 copies printed, 100 were "for export" (PU). Whitman received 17½¢ each for copies sent abroad.

Announced in *Publishers' Circular and Booksellers' Record,* 15 May 1883. Price, 10s.6d.

Locations: First state: CtY, DLC, ScU, TxU, ViU; second state: NzD.

A 2.7.j₃
Third (Scottish) issue (1884)

Glasgow: Wilson & McCormick, 1884.

[i–ii] [1–2] 3–382 [383–386]. Single leaf with Samuel Hollyer engraving of Whitman printed on verso is inserted before title page.

$[1]^{12}$ $(-1_1, +1_{1.2})$ $[2-16]^{12}$ (16_{12+1}). Title leaf is a cancel, with a two-leaf gathering pasted to the stub of leaf 1_1.

Contents: Same as in the first issue, except: p. i: *'LEAVES OF GRASS';* p. ii: blank; p. 1: Scottish title page; p. 2: 'COPYRIGHT 1881 | BY WALT WHITMAN | *All rights reserved.';* p. 385: Wilson and McCormick advertisement for *Specimen Days;* p. 386: blank.

Binding: Dark orange-yellow S cloth (diagonal fine-ribbed). Front cover: goldstamped facsimile signature; back cover: blank; spine: goldstamped '[double rule] | [three lines in rustic lettering] LEAVES | OF | GRASS | [rule] | WALT WHITMAN | [rule] | WILSON & MСCORMICK | [double rule]'. Endpapers coated and printed on one side with a brown geometric pattern design. Top edges rough trimmed, front and bottom edges trimmed.

Publication: McKay's royalty statement to Whitman of 1 December 1883 shows 200 sets of sheets "for exportation," with Whitman receiving 17 ½¢ each (half his royalty) from McKay (PU). Advertised in *Publishers' Circular and Booksellers' Record,* 1 October 1884. Price, 10s.6d.

Locations: BMR, JM, NN-R.

A 2.7.k
Seventh edition, eleventh printing (1884)

Three issues have been noted:

A 2.7.k₁
First (American) issue (1884)

Philadelphia: David McKay, 1884.

[1–2] 3–382 [383–384]. Single leaf with Samuel Hollyer engraving of Whitman printed on verso is inserted after p. 28 (bindings A and B) or before the title page, followed by a protective tissue (bindings C and D).

[1–16]¹² . Page size 8¼″ × 5¼″. Sheets bulk 1″.

Contents and typography and paper are the same as in the first printing.

Binding: Four styles have been noted, priority assumed:

Binding A: Medium olive-brown or slightly orange-yellow S cloth (diagonal fine-ribbed). Front cover: goldstamped: single-rule frame around facsimile signature at top; back cover: blank; spine: goldstamped '[six lines over blades of grass design] [three lines in ornate capitals] LEAVES | OF | GRASS | [rule] | WALT WHITMAN | [rule] | [hand with butterfly] | DAVID MСKAY'. Front and back flyleaves with conjugate leaves pasted under endpapers; back flyleaf; or front flyleaf. Light gray or light blue vein-patterned endpapers. Issued with front and bottom edges uncut. Top edges gilded.

Binding B: Dark orange-yellow V cloth (smooth). Front cover: gold-stamped facsimile signature; back cover: blindstamped facsimile signature; spine: goldstamped '[double rule] | [three lines in rustic lettering] LEAVES | OF | GRASS | [double rule]'. Light green floral pattern endpapers printed on one side. All edges trimmed.

Binding C: Black or medium bluish green V cloth (smooth). A band of six blackstamped rules runs across the top of the covers and spine; a band of eight blackstamped rules runs across the bottom of the covers and spine. Front cover: goldstamped within the bands: '[top left] Leaves of Grass | [bottom right] Walt Whitman'; back cover: blank; spine: goldstamped within the bands: 'Leaves | of | Grass | Walt | Whitman | PUTNAM'S SONS'. No flyleaves. Light green floral pattern endpapers printed on one side. All edges trimmed. Top edges gilded. See *Note two*.

Binding D: Same as binding C, except: medium yellowish green V cloth (smooth); spine has goldstamped 'PUTNAM'. See *Note two*.

Printing: 'SHERMAN & CO., PRINTERS, | PHILADELPHIA.' (p. [2]).

Publication: McKay's royalty statement to Whitman of 1 December 1884 shows 2,400 copies had been printed (PU). Deposit copies: binding A: BL ('14 AP 87').

Locations: Binding A: BL, CSt, CtY, DLC, JM, MH, NN-R, NNC, NcD, NcU, PU, RPB, TxU (3), ViU; binding B: CSt, TxU; binding C: DLC, RPB; binding D: BE, CtY, DLC (2), JM, NN-R, NjCW, NjP, PU.

Note one: One copy in binding A has sheets measuring 7⅜″ × 4⅞″, front and back flyleaves, yellow endpapers, and all edges trimmed, probably a trial binding (CtY).

Note two: Bindings C and D were probably used for sale in England since it is similar to those bindings used by David Bogue in 1881 (see A 2.7.b₂, A 2.7.c₂). The copy at PU in binding D has the stamp of a Bolton, England, bookseller and a handwritten price of 10s.6d.

Note three: A bound copy, with sheets measuring 8⅜″ × 5 ¾″, with all edges trimmed, possibly of unbound sheets, is at CtY.

Note four: Shay reports copies with the McKay imprint dated '1885' (p. 26); no copies have been located.

A 2.7.k₂
Second (Scottish) issue (1884)

Glasgow: Wilson & McCormick, 1884.

Two states have been noted:

First state: [1–2] 3–382 [383–384]. Single leaf with Samuel Hollyer engraving of Whitman, printed on verso, followed by protective tissue, is inserted before the title page.

[1]^{12} ($\pm$1$_1$) [2–16]^{12} . Title leaf is a cancel. Page size 8 ⅜″ X 5″.

Contents: Same as in the first issue, except: p. 1: Scottish title page; p. 2: 'COPYRIGHT 1881 | BY WALT WHITMAN | *All rights reserved*'.

Second state: [1–2] 3–382 [383–386]. Single leaf with Samuel Hollyer engraving of Whitman, printed on verso, followed by protective tissue, is inserted before the title page.

[1]^{12} ($\pm$1$_1$) [2–16]^{12} (16$_{12+1}$). Title leaf is a cancel.

Contents: Same as in the first issue, except: p. 1: Scottish title page; p. 2: 'COPYRIGHT 1881 | BY WALT WHITMAN | *All rights reserved*'; p. 385: Wilson and McCormick advertisement for *Specimen Days;* p. 386: blank.

Binding: Deep yellowish brown or dark orange-yellow S cloth (diagonal fine-ribbed). Front cover: goldstamped facsimile signature; back cover: blank; spine: goldstamped '[double rule] | [three lines in rustic lettering] LEAVES | OF | GRASS | [rule] | WALT WHITMAN | [rule] | WILSON & M^{C}CORMICK | [double rule]'. No flyleaves. White wove endpapers or endpapers coated and printed with a brown patterned design on one side. Top edges rough trimmed, front and bottom edges trimmed; or top and bottom edges rough trimmed, front edges trimmed.

Publication: Advertised in *Publishers' Circular and Booksellers' Record*, 1 October 1884. Deposit copies: BO ('MAY1886'). Price, 10s.6d.

Locations: First state: BBo, BO, DLC, NcD, PU, RPB, TxU; second state: CSt.

Note one: Some copies of the first state have a 12-page undated publisher's catalogue inserted at the back (BBo, DLC, NcD, PU, RPB, TxU).

A 2.7.k$_3$
Third (American) issue (1884) [i.e., 1888]

Philadelphia: David McKay, 1884.

Leaves of Grass and "Sands at Seventy."

[1–2] 3–382 [383] 384–404 [405–406]. Single leaf with Samuel Hollyer engraving of Whitman printed on verso, followed by protective tissue, is inserted before the title page (RPB) or after p. 28 (all other copies).

[1–16]¹² (–16₁₂) [18–19]⁶ . Sheets bulk 1¼″.

Contents: p. 1: title page; p. 2: copyright page; pp. 3–8: contents; pp. 4–382: text of *Leaves of Grass;* p. 383: 'ANNEX | TO PRECEDING PAGES. | SANDS AT SEVENTY. | Copyright, 1888, by WALT WHITMAN. | (See "NOVEMBER BOUGHS.")'; p. 384: contents; pp. 385–404: text of "Sands at Seventy"; pp. 405–406: blank.

Poems: "Mannahatta" ["My city's fit and noble name resumed . . ."], "Paumanok," "From Montauk Point," "To Those Who've Fail'd," "A Carol Closing Sixty-Nine," "The Bravest Soldiers," "A Font of Type," "As I Sit Writing Here," "My Canary Bird," "Queries to My Seventieth Year," "The Wallabout Martyrs," "The First Dandelion," "America," "Memories," "To-day and Thee," "After the Dazzle of Day," "Abraham Lincoln, born Feb. 12, 1809," "Out of May's Shows Selected," "Halcyon Days," "The Pilot in the Mist," "Had I the Choice," "You Tides With Ceaseless Swell," "Last of Ebb, and Daylight Waning," "And Yet Not You Alone," "Proudly the Flood Comes In," "By That Long Scan of Waves," "Then Last of All," "Election Day, November, 1884," "With Husky-Haughty Lips, O Sea," "Death of General Grant," "Red Jacket (from Aloft.)," "Washington's Monument, February, 1885," "Of That Blithe Throat of Thine," "Broadway," "To Get the Final Lilt of Songs," "Old Salt Kossabone," "The Dead Tenor," "Continuities," "Yonnondio," "Life," "Going Somewhere," "Small the Theme of My Chant," "True Conquerors," "The United States to Old World Critics," "The Calming Thought of All," "Thanks in Old Age," "Life and Death," "The Voice of the Rain," "Soon Shall the Winter's Foil Be Here," "While Not the Past Forgetting," "The Dying Veteran," "Stronger Lessons," "A Prairie Sunset," "Twenty Years," "Orange Buds by Mail From Florida," "Twilight," "You Lingering Sparse Leaves of Me," "Not Meagre, Latent Boughs Alone," "The Dead Emperor," "As the Greek's Signal Flame," "The Dismantled Ship," "Now Precedent Songs, Farewell," "An Evening Lull," "Old Age's Lambent Peaks," "After the Supper and Talk." *Note:* The poems "The Pilot in the Mist" through "Then Last of All" form the cluster "Fancies at Navesink." See "Index to the Poems in *Leaves of Grass*" for information about the publication histories of individual poems within the various editions, printings, and issues of *Leaves of Grass.*

Typography and paper: The same as in the first printing, except: running heads: rectos: pp. 385–403: '*SANDS AT SEVENTY.*'; versos: pp. 386–404: '*SANDS AT SEVENTY.*'.

Binding: Dark orange-yellow or or slightly orange-yellow or medium olive-brown S cloth (diagonal fine-ribbed). Front cover: goldstamped: single-rule frame around facsimile signature at top; back cover: blank; spine: goldstamped '[six lines over blades of grass design] [three lines in ornate capitals] LEAVES | OF | GRASS | [rule] | WALT WHITMAN | [rule] | [hand with butterfly] |

DAVID • MC • KAY'. Front and back flyleaves. Pale blue, pale gray, pale green, or pale pink endpapers; or light blue-vein patterned endpapers. Top edges trimmed; front and bottom edges rough trimmed or uncut. Top edges gilded.

Printing: 'SHERMAN & CO., PRINTERS, | PHILADELPHIA.' (p. [2]).

Publication: McKay had 941 sets of unbound sheets on hand on 1 March 1888 and undoubtedly added the "Sands at Seventy" annex to them in binding when the 1888 reprinting (see A 2.7.l) was completed in October, selling this issue and the new printing simultaneously (royalty statement, PU). Presentation copies: DLC (from Whitman, 31 October 1890).

Locations: CtY, DLC (3), InU-L, JM (3), MB, MBU, NN-R, NjCW, PU (2), RPB (2), ScU.

Note: BAL notes that "Sands at Seventy" is "printed from the slightly altered duplicate set of plates for this section of *November Boughs*" (IX, 50).

A 2.7.l
Seventh edition, twelfth printing (1888)

Two issues have been noted:

A 2.7.l₁
First issue (1888)

Philadelphia: David McKay, 1888.

Leaves of Grass and "Sands at Seventy."

[1–2] 3–8 [9] 10–382 [383] 384–404 [405–406]. Single leaf with Samuel Hollyer engraving of Whitman printed on verso, followed by protective tissue, is inserted after p. 28.

[1–16]¹² (–16₁₂) [18–19]⁶ . Page size 8⅜" × 5⅜". Sheets bulk 1¼".

Contents: p. 1: title page; p. 2: copyright page; pp. 3–8: contents; pp. 4–382: text of *Leaves of Grass;* p. 383: half title; p. 384: contents; pp. 385–404: text of "Sands at Seventy"; pp. 405–406: blank.

Typography and paper: Same as in the eleventh printing, third issue (A 2.7.k₃).

Binding: Light olive-brown or medium olive-brown or slightly orange-yellow S cloth (diagonal fine-ribbed). Front cover: goldstamped: single-rule frame around facsimile signature at top; back cover: blank; spine: goldstamped '[six lines over blades of grass design] [three lines in ornate capitals] LEAVES | OF | GRASS | [rule] | WALT WHITMAN | [rule] | [hand with butterfly] | • DAVID • MC • KAY • '. Front and back flyleaves. Pale blue, pale yellow, or white endpapers. Top edges trimmed, front and bottom edges uncut. Top edges gilded.

Printing: 'SHERMAN & CO., PRINTERS, | PHILADELPHIA.' (p. [2]).

Publication: On 23 June 1888, Whitman wrote that he had "proof pages" of "Sands at Seventy," and he wrote Bucke on 2 July that " 'Sands' is intended as an 'Annex,' " to "follow L of G. consecutively paged," and that it was now in proof *(Correspondence,* IV, 180–181). Whitman received a copy on 19 December *(WWWC,* III, 336). On 20 December, he announced that the book was "out," priced at $2.00 (IV, 251). McKay's royalty statement to Whitman of 8 October 1888 shows 1,400 copies had been printed, but he told Whitman that 2,200 were done (PU; 10 October 1888, in *WWWC,* II, 460). Price, $2.00.

Locations: DLC, JM (4), NN-R, NcD, NjCW, NjP, RPB, ScU, TxU, ViU.

Note: Between 1882 and 20 October 1891, Rees Welsh and David McKay sold 6,414 copies of *Leaves of Grass,* bringing Whitman a royalty at 35¢ each of $2,244.90. In addition, 400 sets of sheets were sold at 17½¢ each for export, bringing Whitman an additional $70.00.

A 2.7.l₂
Second issue (1892)

Leaves of Grass

Including

    SANDS AT SEVENTY... *1st Annex*,
    GOOD-BYE MY FANCY... *2d Annex*,
    A BACKWARD GLANCE O'ER TRAVEL'D ROADS,
    and Portrait from Life.

COME, said my Soul,
Such verses for my Body let us write, (for we are one,)
That should I after death invisibly return,
Or, long, long hence, in other spheres,
There to some group of mates the chants resuming,
(Tallying Earth's soil, trees, winds, tumultuous waves,)
Ever with pleas'd smile I may keep on,
Ever and ever yet the verses owning—as, first, I here and now,
Signing for Soul and Body, set to them my name,

Walt-Whitman

PHILADELPHIA
DAVID McKAY, PUBLISHER
23 SOUTH NINTH STREET
1891-'2

A 2.7.l₂: 8⅜″ × 5⅝″

COPYRIGHTS, &c.

———

1st ed'n 1855, Brooklyn (N. Y., South District)—renew'd (1883) 14 yrs.
2d ed'n 1856, Brooklyn—renew'd (1884) 14 yrs.
3d ed'n 1860, Boston, Thayer & Eldridge Pub'rs.
4th ed'n 1867, N. Y., So. Dist.: Pub'd New York.
5th ed'n 1871, Washington, D. C.
6th ed'n 1876—Centennial issue—inc'd'g Two RIVULETS: two vols.
7th ed'n 1881, Boston, Mass.: Osgood Pub.: [This includes in the present
     vol. pages 1 to 382.]
8th ed'n 1882, Philadelphia: McKay Pub'r.
Sands at Seventy: Annex, 1888—November Boughs—Philadelphia.
A Backward Glance, &c.: November Boughs, 1888—Philadelphia.
Good-Bye my Fancy: 2d Annex, 1891—Philadelphia.

                    Library of Congress . . . . . Copyright Office, Washington.
      No. 18382 W.
          To wit: Be it remembered . . . That on the 19th day of May, *anno Domini*, 1891, Walt
      Whitman, of Camden, N. J., has deposited in this office the title of a Book, the title or descrip-
      tion of which is in the following words, to wit:
                    GOOD-BYE MY FANCY,
                 2d Annex to Leaves of Grass.
                    Philadelphia . . . David McKay . . . 1891.
      The right whereof he claims as author, in conformity with the laws of the United States
      respecting copyrights.
                    A. R. SPOFFORD,
                       Librarian of Congress.

      [Which last-named copyright (holding good to 1919—then, on application,
      continued 14 years further) expires May 19, 1933.]

                         ———

          ☞ As there are now several editions of L. of G., different texts and
      dates, I wish to say that I prefer and recommend this present one, complete,
      for future printing, if there should be any; a copy and fac-simile, indeed, of
      the text of these 438 pages. The subsequent adjusting interval which is so
      important to form'd and launch'd work, books especially, has pass'd; and
      waiting till fully after that, I have given (pages 423-438) my concluding
      words.   W. W.

Leaves of Grass, "Sands at Seventy," *Good-Bye My Fancy,* and "A Backward Glance O'er Travelled Roads."

[1–2] 3–8 [9] . . . [383] 384–423 [424] 425–438 [439–440]. Single leaf with Samuel Hollyer engraving of Whitman printed on verso, followed by protective tissue, is inserted after p. 28.

[1]¹² (±1₁, ±1₄) [2–16]¹² (–16₁₂) [17–18]⁶ (–18₆) [19]¹² [20]⁶. The title leaf and the last general contents leaf (pp. 7–8) are cancels (see *Note five*). Sheets bulk 1⅜″.

Contents: p. 1: title page; p. 2: copyright page; pp. 3–8: contents; pp. 9–382: text of *Leaves of Grass;* p. 383: half title; p. 384: contents; pp. 385–404: text of "Sands at Seventy"; p. 405: '2D ANNEX. | GOOD-BY MY FANCY. | Copyright, 1891, by WALT WHITMAN.'; p. 406: contents; pp. 407–422: texts of poems; p. 423: 'A | BACKWARD GLANCE | O'ER | TRAVEL'D ROADS.'; p. 424: 'Copyright, 1888, by WALT WHITMAN. | See "November Boughs." '; pp. 425–438: text of "A Backward Glance O'er Travel'd Roads"; pp. 439–440: blank.

Poems and Prose: "Prefatory Note to 2d Annex" (includes the poem ["Last Droplets . . ."]), "Sail Out for Good, Eidólon Yacht," "Lingering Last Drops," "Good-Bye my Fancy," "On, on the Same, ye Jocund Twain," "My 71st Year," "Apparitions," "The Pallid Wreath," "An Ended Day," "Old Age's Ship & Crafty Death's," "To the Pending Year," "Shakespere-Bacon's Cipher," "Long, Long Hence," "Bravo, Paris Exposition!", "Interpolation Sounds," "To the Sun-set Breeze," "Old Chants," "A Christmas Greeting," "Sounds of the Winter," "A Twilight Song," "When the Full-grown Poet Came," "Osceola," "A Voice from Death," "A Persian Lesson," "The Commonplace," " 'The Rounded Catalogue Divine Complete,' " "Mirages," "L. of G.'s Purport," "The Unexpress'd," "Grand is the Seen," "Unseen Buds," "Good-Bye my Fancy"; "A Backward Glance O'er Travel'd Roads" (prose). See "Index to the Poems in *Leaves of Grass*" for information about the publication histories of individual poems within the various editions, printings, and issues of *Leaves of Grass*.

Typography and paper: Same as the first issue, except: rectos: pp. 411–421: '*GOOD-BYE MY FANCY.*'; pp. 427–437: '*O'ER TRAVEL'D ROADS.*'; versos: p. 408: '*PREFACE NOTE TO 2d ANNEX.*'; pp. 410–422: '*GOOD-BYE MY FANCY.*'; pp. 426–436: '*A BACKWARD GLANCE*'; p. 438: '*A BACKWARD GLANCE O'ER TRAVEL'D ROADS.*'.

Binding: Four styles have been noted:

Binding A: Unprinted medium brown wrappers with yellow paper label on spine: '[double rule] | Walt Whitman's | LEAVES | OF | [ornate lettering] Grass | Complete | 1892 | [double rule]'. Front flyleaf or no flyleaves. Wove endpapers. Issued uncut. See *Note one*.

Binding B: Unprinted stiff light gray wrappers with black vein-pattern over stiff endpapers with yellow paper label on spine: '[double rule] | Walt Whitman's | LEAVES | OF | [ornate lettering] Grass | Complete | 1892 | [double rule]'. No flyleaves or back flyleaf. White endpapers. Issued uncut. See *Note two*.

Binding C: Slightly orange-yellow S cloth (diagonal fine-ribbed). Front cover: goldstamped: single-rule frame around facsimile signature at top; back cover: blank; spine: goldstamped '[six lines over blades of grass design] [three lines in ornate capitals] LEAVES | OF | GRASS | [rule] | WALT WHITMAN | [rule] | [hand with butterfly] | DAVID • Mc • KAY • '. Front and back flyleaves. Pale yellow endpapers. Top edges trimmed, front and bottom edges uncut. Top edges gilded.

Binding D: Dark green V cloth (smooth). Front and back covers: blank; spine: goldstamped '*LEAVES | of | GRASS | Complete | 1892.* | [facsimile signature] | [ornate lettering] D McKay'. No flyleaves; or flyleaves; or front and back flyleaves with conjugates pasted under endpapers; or front flyleaf

Binding B for A 2.7.l₂

and double back flyleaves with conjugate pasted under endpaper. Pale yellow endpapers. Top edges trimmed, front and bottom edges uncut. Top edges plain or gilded.

Printing: Unknown.

Publication: On 18 June 1890, Whitman announced: "I shall put in order a last little 6 or 8 page annex (the second) of my *Leaves of Grass*—& that will probably be the finish" (*Correspondence,* V, 54). He worked on the annex during the rest of the year: on 6 August he "bother[ed] (scribble, transpose, add, dawdle)" at it; on 3 November he was "leisurely cooking" it up; on 1 December, he was "shaping" it (V, 68, 112, 126). Although he was "a little fretted" at his progress on 10 February 1891, on the 19th he wrote "copy is to go to printers in three days," and on the 22d he reported that the printers would begin "to-morrow" (V, 163, 167, 168). By 30 April, he stated that 20 pages of "Good-bye" would go into the annex (V, 196). On 4 September he reported: "Intend to finish out (bind) L of G with 'Good Bye' & Last of all 'Backward Glance' & shall then let it go as *completed*" (V, 239). On the 15th he estimated the length as 438 pages, and the next day said the book would "probably" be ready in "two or three weeks" (V, 243). Although a letter of 20 September was written on a proof of the title page, the book was "not yet" out by 20 October (V, 245, 255). On 6 December, he sent Bucke the "first copy (rude, flimsy cover; but good paper, print & stitching)"; four days later he told Bucke he would send another copy with "heavier covers" and that "the regular forthcoming cloth b'd ed'n will be in new *green* & stamp" (V, 270, 271). The inventory of Whitman's belongings made after his death lists 15 copies of this issue "bound in gray paper" (DLC).

Known as the "Deathbed Edition" because Whitman's impending death forced him to "create" copies of his final "edition" of *Leaves of Grass* from the 1888 sheets with cancel title and contents leaves and with the annexes added. A copy at NN-B in binding A is inscribed from Whitman to Bucke, 6 December 1891, as the "first copy completed." A copy at DLC in binding B is inscribed (undated) from Whitman to Traubel and noted as received 8–10 December 1891 by Traubel. A copy at NN-B in binding B (lacking the spine label) is inscribed by Whitman 11 December 1891. Presentation copies (all from Trau- bel, acting for Whitman): MH (7 January 1892; rebound); binding B: NjP (3 January 1892), DLC (7 January 1892), NNC (7 January 1892), TxU (7 Janu- ary 1892), InU-L (8 January 1892), NN-B (8 January 1892), DLC (11 January 1892), DLC (14 January 1892; 2 copies), DLC (January 1892), NN-R (Janu- ary 1892; 2 copies). Copies inscribed by owners: NN-B (31 January 1892). The BBo copy (binding B) has an undated inscription by Whitman. Not for sale.

Locations: Binding A: CtY, DLC, InU-L, NN-B, NN-R; binding B: BBo, BL, BMR (lacks spine label), CtY, CtY (lacks spine label), DLC (10), InU-L, MB, MH, NN-B (3), NN-B (lacks spine label), NN-R (2), NNC (lacks front wrap- per), NNPM (lacks spine label), NjP, PU (lacks spine label), RPB (lacks spine label), TxU (2); binding C: NN-B, NjCW; binding D: DLC, JM, NN-R.

Note one: A copy in binding A is inscribed by Traubel 'The rejected cover | Dec 1891' (NN-R). Also inserted is a letter from Anne Montgomery Traubel, dated 4 October 1927, stating that when Traubel brought the only three copies in this binding home to her, she said, "They look like Philadelphia brown stone front houses." When Traubel repeated this to Whitman, he replied, "Look respectable, eh?" But note that five copies in this binding have been located.

Note two: A copy in binding B has inserted a letter from Traubel, dated 25 February 1908, stating that the book is "one of the hundred copies of the Leaves sent out by W[hitman]. to his closer personal friends just before his death" (NN-R). Traubel continues that Whitman signed a few copies, but then gave the remainder to Traubel for signing. Other copies in binding B contain similar notes (DLC, NNPM).

Note three: Prior to the onset of Whitman's final illness in December 1891, he apparently thought of making this a limited edition. DLC has drafts in Whitman's hand of an advertisement for the book (noting "less than 200 copies pub'd"), priced at $5.00, and for a title page dated "1892" (see illustration).

Note four: Whitman's nurse reports that "fifty copies" bound "in Manila paper covers" were prepared, and that the "last words" Whitman wrote were a printed advertisement for the book (Elizabeth Leavitt Keller, *Walt Whitman in Mickle Street* [New York: Mitchell Kennerley, 1921], pp. 168–170; the advertisement is pasted onto the facsimile of Whitman's letter of 6–7 February 1892 to John H. Johnston [see F 42]).

Note five: The last leaf of the general contents in the 1888 sheets (pp. 7–8, ending with "So Long" listed as appearing on pp. 380–382) is canceled, and the last leaf of the contents in the 1891 sheets (listing "Sands at Seventy," *Good-Bye My Fancy,* and "A Backward Glance O'er Travel'd Roads" as being present) is tipped to the stub.

Note six: BAL examines only the NN-B copy in binding C, which it says "appears to have been recased and . . . it is sophisticated" (IX, 53).

Note seven: BAL reports a copy bound the same as binding D, except: facsimile signature is not present (IX, 53).

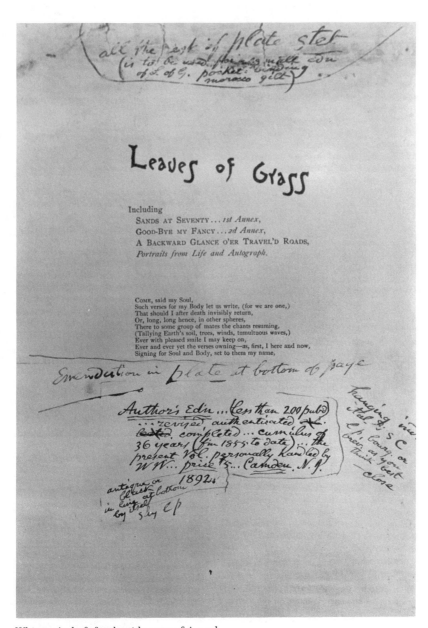

Whitman's draft for the title page of A 2.7.l₂

LEAVES

of

GRASS

COME, said my Soul,
Such verses for my Body let us write, (for we are one,)
That should I after death invisibly return,
Or, long, long hence, in other spheres,
There to some group of mates the chants resuming,
(Tallying Earth's soil, trees, winds, tumultuous waves,)
Ever with pleased smile I may keep on,
Ever and ever yet the verses owning — as, first, I here and now,
Signing for Soul and Body, set to them my name,

Walt Whitman

A 2.7.m: 10¼″ × 6½″

Leaves of Grass, Specimen Days & Collect, and *November Boughs.*

[i–ii] [1–2] 3–8 [9] 10–382 [i–ii] iii–vi 7–374 [1–2] 3–140 [1] 2 [141–142]. Leaves of coated paper with the illustrated *Complete Poems & Prose* title page printed on the recto, W. J. Linton engraving of G. C. Potter photograph of Whitman printed on the recto, and photograph of Whitman in his seventieth year (followed by a protective tissue) printed on the verso, are inserted before the "Note at Beginning," after the first p. 296, and before the *November Boughs* title page; a single leaf with the Samuel Hollyer engraving of Whitman printed on the verso is inserted after the first p. 28.

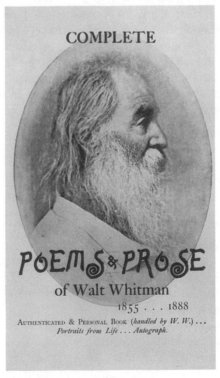

Illustrated title page for A 2.7.m

Edition: Six Hundred.
Number One Hundred Twenty-Eight.

Sample statement of limitation for A 2.7.m

[1]^8 (1$_{1+1}$) [2–24]^8 (–24$_8$) [1]^8 (±1$_1$) [2–22]^8 23–25^4 (–25$_4$) [1]^8 (±1$_1$) 2–3^8 [4]^8 5–9^8 (9$_{7+1}$, –9$_8$). The leaf containing "Note at Beginning" is tipped in; the final leaves of *Leaves of Grass* (blank leaf), *Specimen Days* (containing a two-page advertisement for David McKay), and *November Boughs* (blank leaf) are cancelled; the title leaves of *Specimen Days & Collect* and *November Boughs* are cancels; the leaf containing "Note at End" is tipped in. *Specimen Days* is falsely signed the same as in A 11.1.a. Sheets bulk 1⅝".

Contents: p. i: 'NOTE AT BEGINNING.'; p. ii: blank; p. 1: *Leaves of Grass* title page; p. 2: copyright page; pp. 3–8: contents; pp. 9–382: text of *Leaves of Grass;* p. i: '[three lines in handprinted lettering] Specimen | Days | & collect'; p. ii: copyright page; pp. iii–vi: contents; pp. 7–374: text of *Specimen Days & Collect;* p. 1: '[two lines in handprinted lettering] November [concentric circle design] | [concentric circle design] Boughs'; p. 2: copyright page; pp. 3–4: contents; pp. 5–140: text of *November Boughs;* pp. 1–2: 'NOTE AT END.', signed 'W. W., *Nov.* 13, '88.'; pp. 141–142: blank.

Typography and paper: Size of printed text and number of lines per page the same as in A 2.7.a, A 11.1.a, and A 12.1.a; all wove paper. Running heads: rectos: pp. 5–381: same as in A 2.7.a; pp. v–373: same as in A 11.1.a; pp. 7–139: same as in A 12.1.a; versos: pp. 4–382: same as in A 2.7.a; pp. iv–374: same as in A 11.1.a; pp. 4–140: same as in A 12.1.a.; p. 2: '*NOTE AT END.*'

Binding: Three styles have been noted, priority assumed:

Binding A: Half very dark green coarse HT cloth (dot-and-line grain) or very dark green C cloth (sand-grain) with green, yellow, and brown or green and yellow stormontlike marbled paper-covered sides; or half very dark C cloth (sand-grain) with brown, yellow, green, and black peacocklike marbled paper-covered sides. Spine: paper label: '[double rule] | [lettering slants from right to left] WALT WHITMAN | [ornate 'C'] COMPLETE | Poems & Prose | [rule] | [flush left] Leaves of Grass | [flush left] Specimen Days | [flush right] *and Collect* | [flush left] November Boughs | [two lines flush right] *with Sands at Seventy* | *Annex to L. of G.* | [rule] | [flush left] Portraits from Life, &

NOTE AT BEGINNING.

The following volume contains

LEAVES OF GRASS, SANDS AT SEVENTY, *in November Boughs*,

SPECIMEN DAYS AND COLLECT . . . . and

NOVEMBER BOUGHS,

Revised, corrected, &c., down to date.

(When I had got this volume well under way, I was quite suddenly prostrated by illness—paralysis, continued yet—which will have to serve as excuse for many faults both of omission and commission in it.)

But I would not let this volume well under way, I was quite suddenly prostrated by illness—paralysis, continued yet—which will have to serve as excuse for many faults both of omission and commission in it.)

But I would not let this volume slip away without attempting to arrest in a special printed book (as much in spirit as letter, and may-be for the future more than the present,) some few specimens—even vital throbs, breaths—as representations of it all—from my point of view, and right from the midst of it, jotted at the time.

There is a tally-stamp and stage-result of periods and nations, elusive, at second or third hand, often escaping the historian of matter-of-fact—in some sort the nation's spiritual formative ferment or chaos—the getting in of its essence, formulating identity—a law of it, and significant part of its progress. (Of the best of events and facts, even the most important, there are finally not the events and facts only, but something flashing out and fluctuating like tuft-flames or eiddlons, from all.) My going up and down amidst these years, and the impromptu jottings of their sights and thoughts, of war and peace, have been in accordance with that law, and probably a result of it. . . . In certain respects, (emotionality, passions, spirituality, the invisible trend,) I therefore launch forth the divisions of the following book as not only a consequence of that period and its influences, but in one sort a History of America, the past 35 years, after the rest, after the adjuncts of that history have been studied and attended to.

"Note at Beginning" in A 2.7.m

NOTE AT END
of Complete Poems and Prose.

As I conclude—and (to get typographical correctness,) after running my eyes diligently through the three big divisions of the preceding volume—the interrogative wonder-fancy rises in me whether (if it be not too arrogant to even state it,) the 33 years of my current time, 1855-1888, with their aggregate of our New World doings and people, have not, indeed, created and formulated the foregoing leaves—forcing their utterance as the pages stand—coming actually from the direct urge and developments of those years, and not from any individual epic or lyrical attempts whatever, or from my pen or voice, or any body's special voice. Out of that supposition, the book might assume to be consider'd an autochthonic record and expression, freely render'd, of and out of these 30 to 35 years—of the soul and evolution of America—and of course, by reflection, not ours only, but more or less of the common people of the world. . . : Seems to me I may dare to claim a deep native tap-root for the book, too, in some sort. I came on the stage too late for personally knowing much of even the lingering Revolutionary worthies—the men of '76. Yet, as a little boy, I have been press'd tightly and lovingly to the breast of Lafayette, (Brooklyn, 1825,) and have talk'd with old Aaron Burr, and also with those who knew Washington and his surroundings, and with original Jeffersonians, and more than one very old soldier and sailor. And in my own day and maturity, my eyes have seen, and ears heard, Lincoln, Grant and Emerson, and my hands have been grasp'd by their hands. Though in a different field and range from most of theirs, I give the foregoing pages as perfectly legitimate, resultant, evolutionary and consistent with them. If these lines should ever reach some reader of a far off future age, let him take them as a missive sent from Abraham Lincoln's fateful age. . . . Repeating, parrot-like, what in the preceding divisions has been already said, and must serve as a great reason-why of this whole book—1st, That the main part about pronounc'd events and shows, (poems and persons also,) is the point of view from which they are view'd and estimated—and 2d, That I cannot let my momentous, stormy, peculiar Era

"Note at End" in A 2.7.m

---

of peace and war, these States, these years, slip away without arresting some of its specimen events—even its vital breaths—to be portray'd and inscribed from out of the midst of it, from its own days and nights—not so much in themselves, (statistically and descriptively our times are copiously noted and memorandized with an industrial zeal)—but to give from them here their flame-like results in imaginative and spiritual suggestiveness—as they present themselves to me, at any rate, from the point of view afflided to.

Then a few additional words yet to this hurried farewell note. In another sense than the warp crossing the woof, and knitted in, the book is probably a sort of autobiography; an element I have not attempted to specially restrain or erase. As alluded to at beginning, I had about got the volume well started by the printers, when a sixth recurrent attack of my war-paralysis fell upon me. It has proved the most serious and continued of the whole. I am now uttering *November Boughs*, and printing this book, in my 70th year. To get out the collection—mainly the born results of health, flush life, buoyancy, and happy out-door volition—and to prepare the *Boughs*—have beguiled my invalid months (the past summer and fall. ("Are we to be beaten down in our old age?" says one white-hair'd (fellow remonstratingly to another in a budget of letters I read last night.) . . . Then I have wanted to leave something markedly *personal*. I have put my name with pen-and-ink with my own hand in the present volume. And from engraved or photo'd portraits taken from life, I have selected some, of different stages, which please me best, (or at any rate displease me least,) and bequeath them at a venture to you, reader, with my love.

W. W. *Nov.* 13. '88.

"Note at End" in A 2.7.m

| *Autograph* | Ed'n 1888—'9 | [double rule]'. Front flyleaf or double front flyleaves. White endpapers. Issued uncut. See *Note four*.

Binding B: Dark green leather shelfback with dark green L cloth (morocco) sides. Spine: goldstamped '[rule] | [design] | [rule] | [three lines on dark reddish brown leather label within goldstamped single-rule frame] WALT WHITMAN'S | COMPLETE | WORKS | [rule] | [design] | [rule] | [on very dark green leather label within goldstamped single-rule frame] POEMS & PROSE | [rule] | [design] | [rule] | [design] | [rule] | EDITION 1889 | [rule]'. Flyleaves. Green, pink, and gray stormontlike marbled endpapers. Top edges trimmed, front and bottom edges uncut. Top edges gilded. See *Publication*.

Binding C: Medium brown buckram; front and back covers: blank; spine: goldstamped 'WALT | WHITMAN'. No flyleaves. White endpapers. All edges trimmed. Top edges gilded. See *Note five*.

Spine label of
binding A for
A 2.7.m

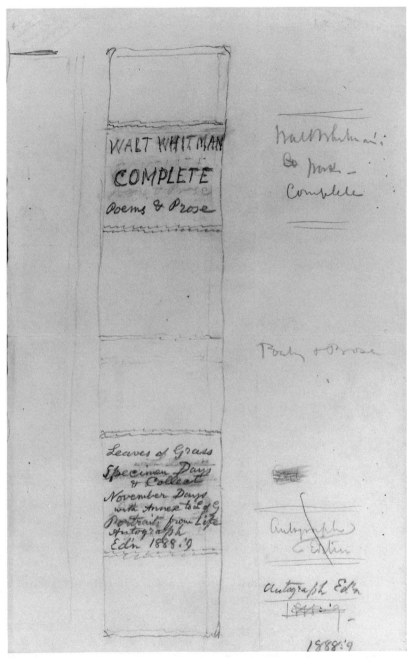

Whitman's draft of the spine label for binding A for A 2.7.m

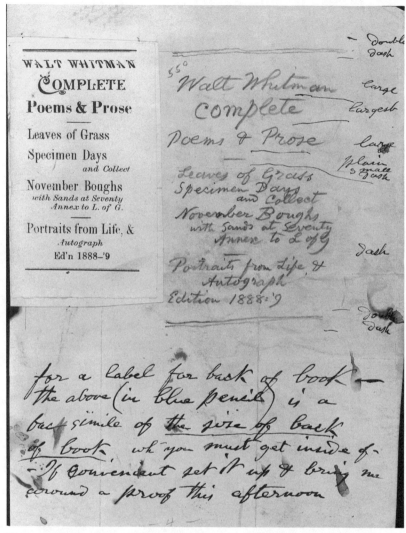

Whitman's instructions to the printer for the spine label for binding A of A 2.7.m

Printing: '[wavy rule] | FERGUSON BROS. & CO., | PRINTERS, PHILA-DELPHIA. | [wavy rule]' (first p. ii).

Publication: As early as 26 August 1886, Whitman thought "of bringing out a complete budget of *all* [his] writing in one book," which he described as "a revised ed'n of complete writings" on 17 August 1887 (*Correspondence*, IV, 46, 117). On 25 May 1888, he had received McKay's permission to use the plates of *Specimen Days* in "my *complete works edition*" of "500 or 600 copies"

(*Daybooks*, II, 461). By 14 August, he had "the design of making a 900 page Vol. of my *complete works*," and on 2 September he wrote that "a large Vol. comprising all my stuff begun" (*Correspondence*, IV, 200, 204). Progress was rapid: on the 13th the book was "nearly done" and on the 19th it was "going through the presses"; on 1 October it was "all printed & the sheets are at the binder's" and by the sixth, Whitman announced it would be out in "a month" (IV, 211, 213, 217, 219). However, Whitman's work was not completed. On the ninth he began signing the first of the 600 "poetic motto" title pages, and on 10 November he "finished the little beginning & end Notes" and sent them to the printer (IV, 221, 233). On 27 November, he received a "paper-bound specimen" from the binder (IV, 239).

There was much discussion about the bindings for this book. When Whitman received his "paper-bound specimen" on 27 November 1888, he desired 50 copies "bound in good strong paper covers—w'd it do in some handsome *marble* paper?", and he ordered spine labels to be printed (IV, 240). By mistake, the binder sent over a copy on 1 December "finished with green cloth and marbleized paper," which Whitman accepted as "inspiration" (*WWWC*, III, 212). On 4 December, he ordered 150 copies "bound in the style I like" from Frederick Oldach, enclosing 100 labels (50 had been sent earlier), and pointing out that the copyright notice had been left off from *Specimen Days* (*Correspondence*, IV, 242). On the next day, he announced that "the cheap form" was being bound; four copies were delivered on the 10th and the remainder on the 14th (IV, 242; *WWWC*, III, 274, 295).

On 8–9 January 1889, Whitman met with McKay to "try to fix on some style—(calf or more likely half-calf)—for the better binding of the big book" (*Correspondence*, IV, 266). On 23–24 January, Whitman examined "the costlier binding specimen copy" which Traubel had brought him, which he described thus: "dark green, half calf, gilt top, rough bottom & front," with the "back lettering simply 'Walt Whitman's Complete Works,'" then half way down 'Poems and Prose' and then at bottom 'Edition 1889.'" This binding would cost Whitman $1.24 (IV, 274–275). On the 29th, Whitman ordered 50 copies of this "fine binding" from Oldach, and on 4–5 February he sold copies to McKay for $4.00 each (IV, 277, 281).

On 23–24 March 1889, Whitman offered to sell McKay "the sheets entire with autograph & plates" for $3.33 each, "he to bind them," but McKay declined and Whitman decided to "fall back on supplying the first (boards) binding only" (IV, 309; *Daybooks*, II, 487).

On 21 October 1890, Whitman sold 50 sets of sheets to McKay (II, 573). On 5 November he ordered another 150 copies, to be bound "in the same style as formerly," from Oldach, and promised to "furnish you with back labels" (*Correspondence*, V, 113–114). On the eighth, Whitman reported: "am having 100 complete works bound up same style as the first (boards) with printed booklabel & ab't 200 folded in sheets . . . tied & stored away" (V, 115). On the 12th, he reported that he had "got rid of 300" (V, 116). On 31 March 1891, he noted that Oldach had 190 copies left in sheets (*Daybooks*, II, 591). On 17 November 1891, Oldach wrote Traubel that he still had 80 sets of sheets on hand (DLC), and on 13 March 1893 Oldach was paid for binding 88 copies (DLC).

On 25 April 1890, the first sales to England (in binding A) were made, with 100 copies sent for sale there (*Correspondence*, V, 42). Another 50 copies were sent to England in August or September 1890, and 50 in both October and November 1891; these were unbound sheets (V, 76, 90; *Daybooks*, II, 582, 605). Listed by Putnam in *Publishers' Circular and Booksellers' Record*, 1 October 1890.

Limited to 600 numbered copies, signed by Whitman on the *Leaves of Grass* title page. Reviewed in *Boston Herald*, 3 January 1889, p. 4. Presentation copies (all from Whitman): unbound sheets: DLC (27 September 1888; see *Note three*); binding A: NN-B (21 December 1888), ViU (21 December 1888), DLC (to Bucke, 21 December 1888), DLC (to Kennedy, 21 December 1888), DLC (31 December 1888), DLC (to Traubel, December 1888), NN-B (to O'Connor, 3 March 1889), DLC (3 March 1889), ViU (to Stedman, 11 March 1889), DLC (17 March 1889), MH (23 March 1889), DLC (26 March 1889), DLC (28 March 1889), RPB (April 1889), DLC (31 May 1889), NjCW (14 June 1889), NN-R (21 June 1889), TxU (20 September 1889), TxU (10 October 1889), NjCW (29 January 1890), TxU (22 May 1890), DLC (August 1890); binding B: DLC (to Traubel, 10 February 1889), DLC (to Bucke, 8 March 1889), DLC (21 March 1889). Price, $6.00. Whitman also sold copies with "four portraits extra on loose sheets" for $6.50 (6 January 1889, *Correspondence*, IV, 264).

Locations: Binding A: BBo, CSt, CtY, DLC (13), JM, MH, NN-B (3), NN-R, NNPM, NjCW (4), PU (3), RPB, TxU (3), ViU (3); binding B: BMR, CtY, DLC (3), RPB; binding C: BMR, BO, CtY, DLC, InU-L, JM, MBU, NNC, NcD, ScU, TxU.

Note one: The title page is signed by Whitman in all located copies.

Note two: The statement of limitation information is on the back of the "Note at Beginning" page (binding A: DLC [7], JM, MH, NN-B, NN-R, NjCW [2], PU, TxU [3]; binding B: BMR, CtY, DLC [2]; binding C: TxU); on the copyright page (binding C: BMR, BO, CtY, JM, NNC, NcD); not present (all other copies). Copies sent out before 14 February 1889 were unnumbered; the statement of limitation on other copies was written by Horace Traubel (see *WWWC*, IV, 143).

Note three: A set of unbound, unsewn, and uncut gatherings, measuring 10¼″ × 65⁄8″, with only the Linton engraving present, the final leaves of *Leaves of Grass* and *Specimen Days* integral, and the title leaves of *Specimen Days* and *November Boughs* canceled with the new half title leaves laid in, is at DLC (inscribed from Whitman to Traubel, 27 September 1888).

Note four: A copy in binding A, without any statement of limitation, inscribed to Louisa Whitman, and a note (not in Whitman's hand) "The first one given away, or looked at even by himself on its return from Publishers" is at ViU.

Note five: A copy at CtY in binding C has this note on the free front end-paper: "The binding on this was made only for England."

Note six: A copy at DLC had been privately bound for Whitman (dated by him 7 December 1888) in half dark brown leather with dark brown morroco-grain cloth sides; spine: blindstamped rules and six boxes, the second having goldstamped 'WALT WHITMAN'S | COMPLETE | WORKS' and the fourth having goldstamped 'POEMS & PROSE' (see *WWWC*, III, 501–502).

Note seven: A broadside advertising circular, printed on the recto, is at DLC.

Note eight: Whitman's design for the spine label and his instructions to the printer are at CtY.

Note nine: The following textual alterations first appear in this printing of *Leaves of Grass:*

19.9	dawn] dusk	
26.32	traveler,] traveller,	
31.29	me to] to me	
55.18	guess'd] guessed	
58.2	plate glass,] plate-glass,	
139.42	sweep-seines, the] sweep-seines. the	
170.30	are, if] are if	
197.37	next,] next	
235.1	begins and goes against us, behold] begins, and goes against us behold	
235.20	person a] person, a	
287.30	garroté,] garrote,	
314.29	throbbings,] thobbings,	
376.9	finalés] finales	
380.3	Now land] Now, land	

The following textual alterations first appear in this printing of *Specimen Days & Collect:*

16.43–44	Judge	Murphy,] Alden	Spooner,
83.12	vistas!] vistas.	
84.25	after 2] after 3	
93.19–20	de-	scription] de-	scription,
101.40	Antares-neck'd.] Aretus-neck'd.	
108.16	"S.] S.	
108.37	"I] I	

108.43   children."]   children.
121.25   good time,]   good-time,
122.23   return'd]   reflected
124.3   depart]   return
124.7   winter, also]   winter, have
146.35   near or toward]   considerably over
154.14   heavy]   pitch'd
180.21   amid]   in the
184.11   knowledge,]   knowledge;
264.3   newspapers]   newpapapers
281.52   me.]   me
295.23   reminiscence,]   reminiscenes,
318.35   a main]   another

A 2.7.n
Seventh edition, fourteenth printing (1889)

Leaves of Grass

with SANDS AT SEVENTY

& A BACKWARD GLANCE O'ER TRAVEL'D ROADS.

MAY 31, 1889.

To-day, finishing my 70th year, the fancy comes for celebrating it by a special, complete, final utterance, in one handy volume, of L. of G., with their Annex, and Backward Glance—and for stamping and sprinkling all with portraits and facial photos, such as they actually were, taken from life, different stages. Doubtless, anyhow, the volume is more A PERSON *than a book. And for testimony to all, (and good measure,) I here with pen and ink append my name:*

Walt Whitman

PORTRAITS FROM LIFE.   AUTOGRAPH.   SPECIAL ED'N.

(300 copies only printed—$5 each.)

A 2.7.n: 7″ × 4½″

Leaves of Grass, "Sands at Seventy," and "A Backward Glance O'er Travelled Roads."

[1–2] 3–8 [9] 10–382 [383] 384–404 [1–2] 3–18 [19–20]. Frontispiece of stiff paper with original photograph of Whitman with butterfly pasted on verso. Single leaf with Hollyer engraving of Whitman printed on verso, followed by protective tissue, is inserted after p. 28; single leaves of coated paper with photograph of Whitman with hat printed on recto, head and shoulders photograph of Whitman by Gutekunst printed on recto (followed by protective tissue), W. J. Linton engraving of G. C. Potter photograph of Whitman printed on recto, and photograph of Whitman seated with cane printed on verso are inserted after pp. 132, 214, 296, 382.

[1–25]⁸ [26–28]⁴ . Sheets bulk ⅝″.

Contents: p. 1: title page; p. 2: copyright page; pp. 3–8: contents; pp. 9–382: text of *Leaves of Grass;* p. 383: half title; p. 384: contents; pp. 385–404: text of "Sands at Seventy"; p. 1: half title; p. 2: copyright page; pp. 3–18: text of "A Backward Glance O'er Travel'd Roads"; pp. 19–20: blank.

Typography and paper: Same as the first printing, except: rectos: pp. 387–403: 'SANDS AT SEVENTY.'; pp. 7–17: 'O'ER TRAVEL'D ROADS.'; versos: pp. 386–404: 'SANDS AT SEVENTY.'; pp. 6–16: 'A BACKWARD GLANCE'; p. 18: 'A BACKWARD GLANCE O'ER TRAVEL'D ROADS.'.

Binding: Three styles have been noted, priority of last two assumed:

Binding A: Black leather over flexible boards with tongued flap on rear folding over to fit under raised band on front; back cover opens to form bellows pocket, with tongue part lined in green morocco-pattern leather. Front cover: blank; back cover: goldstamped '[handprinted letters on slight downward slant] Leaves of Grass | WITH [ornate 'A'] SANDS AT [ornate 'V'] SEVENTY | AND A [ornate 'K'] BACKWARD [ornate 'A'] GLANCE | O'ER | [ornate 'A' and 'V'] TRAVEL'D [ornate 'R'] ROADS. | [facsimile signature]'; spine: blank. No flyleaves or laid double front and back flyleaves. Red, pink, black, white, and yellow antique spot marbled endpapers; or black, white and green spotlike marbled endpapers. All edges trimmed. All edges gilded.

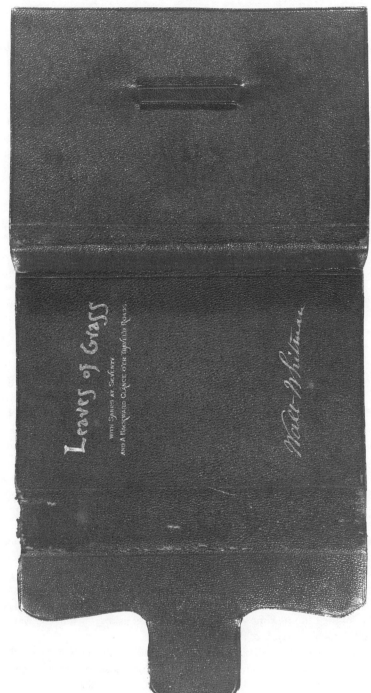

Binding A for A 2.7.n

Binding B: Same as binding A, except: the back cover has a bellowslike pocket (with accordian flaps on sides but not connected at bottom); double front and back flyleaves.

Binding C: Black leather over flexible boards; front cover: same as the back cover in binding A; back cover: blank; spine: blank. No bellows pocket. Double laid back flyleaves; or front and double back flyleaves; or double front and back flyleaves. Red, pink, black, white, and yellow antique spot marbled endpapers. All edges trimmed. Top edges gilded or all edges gilded. See *Publication* and *Note five.*

Printing: See copyright page.

Publication: Whitman wrote on 19–20 February 1889 that he had "a fancy, contemplation, of a small special edition of L of G with Annex & 'Backward Glance,' all bound in pocket-book style pretty well, probably morocco, edges cut pretty close" (*Correspondence,* IV, 293). By 12 March, he had decided to use "Oxford Bible paper" (*WWWC,* IV, 328). On 23–24 March, he was planning a book of "ab't 420 pp" which would sell for $5.00, adding on the 26th that there would be 300 copies (*Correspondence,* IV, 309; *Daybooks,* II, 488). He paid the binder, Frederick Oldach, on 26 March and was "going to print" on the 28th (*Correspondence,* IV, 311, 313). The "printed sheets" were at the binder's by 11–12 May (IV, 336). On the 16th, Whitman approved a binding with a "tongue or tuck-flap" and a "paper pocket" (IV, 338). He received 100 copies on 29 May and noted it was "out" on his birthday, the 31st (*Daybooks,* II, 495, 513). By 8 August 1891, 175 copies were still on hand (*Daybooks,* II, 597). The inventory of Whitman's belongings made after his death lists signed copies of this printing, "not counted" (DLC).

There was some discussion about the binding for this book. On 1 June 1889 Whitman sent a copy in binding A to Bucke. On the 16th, Bucke wrote Horace Traubel that, while he was "charmed" with the book, he wanted "a copy exactly like the one I have except that the *flap,* and of course the *tuck* on the front cover be left off and the letters on cover and be put on front instead of back cover" (William White, "Whitman's *Leaves of Grass:* Notes on the Pocketbook [1889] Edition," *Studies in Bibliography,* 18 [1965], 280–281). On 3 July, Whitman ordered from Oldach 20 copies (in binding B or C) to be bound according to Bucke's wishes (DLC), and on 2 August, he sent two copies to Bucke "of the little new morocco bound ed'n" and asked: "is that the way you wanted?" (*Correspondence,* IV, 361).

Limited to 300 copies. DLC has a copy in Binding A inscribed as one of the "first copies from the binder, May, 1889." DLC has a set of unbound gatherings (see *Note three*) received from Whitman by Traubel on 9 May 1889. Presentation copies (all from Whitman): binding A: JM (to Harned, 31 May 1889), NN-R (to Traubel, 31 May 1889), PU (31 May 1889), TxU (to Louisa

Whitman, 31 May 1889), TxU (31 May 1889), DLC (to Kennedy, 13 October 1889), ViU (12 November 1889), ScU (10 December 1889), DLC (28 August 1890); binding C: DLC (2 August 1889), DLC (9 May 1891). Copies inscribed by owners: binding A: NN-R (6 March 1890); binding B: NN-R (16 September 1891). Price, $5.00.

Locations:　Binding A: BBo, BMR, CtY, DLC (6), JM, NN-B, NN-R (2), NNC, NcD, NjCW (2), NjP, PU, ScU, TxU (4), ViU; binding B: DLC (2), NN-R, RPB, ViU; binding C: CtY, DLC (6), InU-L, MBU, MH, NN-R, NNC, NNPM, NcD, ViU.

Note one:　All located copies are signed by Whitman on the title page.

Note two:　An uncut set of the first gathering, signed by Whitman, with pages measuring 9⅛″ × 5½″ and 8″ × 4¹⁵⁄₁₆″, is at RPB.

Note three:　Three sets of unbound, unsewn, and uncut gatherings, measuring 9⅛″ X 5⅝″, are at DLC (one set received from Whitman by Traubel on 9 May 1889).

Note four:　A copy at DLC, marked by Whitman "sample proof vol: to see if the picts: are put in right," is dated "early June '89", and is in a binding the same as binding A but lacking the bellows pocket.

Note five:　A copy is at NNPM in binding C with 'LEAVES | OF | GRASS | WHITMAN | 1889' goldstamped on the spine, undoubtedly at a later date.

Note six:　The following textual alterations first appear in this printing:

114.21	Nagasaki	]	Nagusaki
185.15	suns	]	sons
6.33	*mèlée*	]	*m lée*
11.3	least	]	last

A 2.7.0
Seventh edition, fifteenth printing (1892)

Philadelphia: David McKay, 1891–92. Title page has "23 South Ninth Street" for publisher's address.

Leaves of Grass, "Sands at Seventy," *Good-Bye My Fancy,* and "A Backward Glance O'er Travelled Roads."

[1–2] 3–8 [9] . . . [383] 384–423 [424] 425–438 [439–440]. Single leaf with Hollyer engraving of Whitman printed on verso, followed by protective tissue, is inserted after p. 28. The leaf with pp. 439–440 (blank pages) may be pasted under the rear endpaper in some copies.

[1–27]⁸ [28]⁴. Page size: 8¼″ × 5⅜″; sheets bulk 1⁹⁄₃₂″.

Contents: Same as in the seventh edition, twelfth printing, second issue (A 2.7.l₂).

Binding: Dark green V cloth (smooth). Front and back covers: blank; spine: goldstamped '*LEAVES | of | GRASS | Complete | 1892.* | [facsimile signature] | [ornate] D McKay'. No flyleaves; or flyleaves; or front and back flyleaves with conjugates pasted under endpapers. Pale yellow or white or white laid endpapers. Top edges trimmed, front and bottom edges uncut. Top edges gilded.

Publication: McKay's royalty statement of 13 October 1892 shows 2,000 copies printed (DLC). Reviewed in *Poet-Lore,* 4 (May 1892), 286–287. Deposit copies: BL ('8 NO93'). Presentation copies: BMR (from Traubel, 9 July 1892). Copies inscribed by owners: NcD (May 1892), MBU (December 1893). Price, $2.00. Listed as an importation by Gay & Bird in *Bookseller,* April 1892. Listed in *English Catalogue* for October 1892 at 10s.6d.

Locations: BBo, BL, BMR, BO, CaOTP, CtY (2), DLC, JM, MBU, NN-B, NNC, NcD (2), NjP, NzD, PU, RPB, ScU, TxU, ViU.

Note: *BAL* reports a copy at DLC in a binding that lacks the facsimile signature (IX, 53).

A 2.8.a
Eighth (English) edition, first printing (1886)

𝕷𝖊𝖆𝖛𝖊𝖘 𝖔𝖋 𝕲𝖗𝖆𝖘𝖘.

THE POEMS

OF

WALT WHITMAN

[SELECTED]

WITH INTRODUCTION

BY ERNEST RHYS.

LONDON:

Walter Scott, 24 Warwick Lane Paternoster Row,

AND NEWCASTLE-ON-TYNE.

1886.

A 2.8.a: 5⅝″ × 4″; the frame, 'THE POEMS', 'WALT WHITMAN', and 'Walter . . . Row,' are in red [i–iii] iv–vii [viii–ix] x–xxxix [xl] [1] 2–10 [11] 12–26 [27] 28–43 [44] 45–97 [98] 99–114 [115] 116–133 [134] 135–144 [145] 146–192 [193] 194–205 [206] 207–224 [225] 226–259 [260] 261–277 [278] 279–290 [291] 292–300 [301] 302–318 [319–320]. Single leaf with photograph of Whitman printed on verso is inserted before the title page.

[a]⁸ b⁸ c⁴ 301–320⁸ . Sheets bulk ⅝″.

Contents: p. i: title page; p. ii: blank; pp. iii–vii: contents; p. viii: poem by Richard Watson Gilder from November 1881 *Century Magazine;* pp. ix–xxxix: "Walt Whitman," signed 'ERNEST RHYS. | CHELSEA, 1886.'; p. xl: engraving of two cherubs; pp. 1–318: text; p. 319: advertisement for *Canterbury Poets;* p. 320: advertisement for *Camelot Classics.*

Poems: Same as the 1881 American edition, in approximately the same order, except "Vocalism" has been retitled "Voices" and the following poems have beem omitted: "Eidolons," "For Him I Sing," "To The States," "On Journeys Through The States," "To a Certain Cantatrice," "Savantism," "Song of Myself," "To the Garden the World," "From Pent-up Aching Rivers," "I Sing the Body Electric," "A Woman Waits for Me," "Spontaneous Me," "One Hour to Madness and Joy," "Out of the Rolling Ocean the Crowd," "Ages and Ages Returning at Intervals," "We Two, How Long We were Fool'd," "O Hymen! O Hymenee!", "I am He that Aches with Love," "Native Moments," "Once I Pass'd through a Populous City," "I Heard You Solemn-Sweet Pipes of the Organ," "Facing West from California's Shores," "As Adam Early in the Morning," "Scented Herbage of My Breast," "Whoever You are Holding Me Now in Hand," "Not Heaving from my Ribb'd Breast Only," "Not Heat Flames up and Consumes," "Trickle Drops," "City of Orgies," "Behold This Swarthy Face," "We Two Boys together Clinging," "A Promise to California," "Here the Frailest Leaves of Me," "Earth, My Like- ness," "To a Western Boy," "Salut au Monde!", "Our Old Feuillage," "Song of the Exposition," "A Song for Occupations," "A Song of the Rolling Earth," "Year of Meteors. (1859–60.)," "A Broadway Pageant," "Tears," "On the Beach at Night," "A Hand-Mirror," "Gods," "Germs," "Thoughts" ["Of ownership . . ."], "Visor'd," "Locations and Times," "Offerings," "To the States, To Identify the 16th, 17th, or 18th Presidentiad," "The Centenarian's Story," "World Take Good Notice," "Reversals," "The Singer in the Prison," "Outlines for a Tomb," "Out from Be- hind This Mask," "To Him That was Crucified," "You Felons on Trial in Courts," "Laws for Creations," "To a Common Prostitute," "I was Looking a Long While," "Thought" ["Of persons arrived at high positions . . ."], "What am I After All," "Others may Praise What They Like," "The Ox-Tamer," "Wandering at Morn," "Italian Music in Dakota," "Passage to India," "The Sleepers," "Transpositions," "Chanting the Square Deific," "Of Him I Love Day and Night," "That Music Always Round Me," "What Ship Puzzled at Sea," "A Noiseless Patient Spider," "O Living Always, Always Dying," "To One Shortly to Die," "Night on the Prairies," "A Paumanok Picture," "Faces," "The Mystic Trumpeter," "To a Locomotive in Winter," "All is Truth," "Ah Poverties, Wincings, and Sulky Retreats," "Thoughts" ["Of public opinion . . ."], "Mediums," "Weave in, My Hardy Life," "Spain, 1873–74," "By Broad Potomac's Shore," "From Far Dakota's Canons. June 25, 1876," "Spirit That Form'd This Scene," "Portals," "These Carols."

Typography and paper: 4⅛″ (3⅞″) × 2¹³⁄₁₆″; all within 4½″ × 3″ single-rule red frame; wove paper; introduction: 33 lines per page; text: various lines per page (up to 35). Running heads: rectos: p. vii: 'CONTENTS.'; pp. xi–xxxix: 'IN CABIN'D SHIPS AT SEA.'; p. 5: 'BEGINNING MY STUDIES.'; p. 7: 'I HEAR AMERICA SINGING.'; p. 9: 'POETS TO COME.'; pp. 13–25: 'STARTING FROM PAUMANOK.'; pp. 29–43: 'CALAMUS.'; pp. 45–55: 'SONG OF THE OPEN ROAD.'; pp. 57–63: 'CROSSING BROOKLYN FERRY.'; pp. 65–67: 'SONG OF THE ANSWERER.'; pp. 69–77: 'A SONG OF JOYS.'; pp. 79–89: 'SONG OF THE BROAD-AXE.'; pp. 91–95: 'SONG OF THE REDWOOD-TREE.'; p. 97: 'OLD AGE AND NIGHT.'; p. 99: 'SONG OF THE UNIVERSAL.';pp. 101–105: 'PIONEERS! O PIONEERS!'; p. 107: 'TO YOU.'; p. 109: 'FRANCE.'; p. 111: 'MYSELF AND MINE.'; p. 113: 'ANTECEDENTS.'; pp. 117–121: 'OUT OF THE CRADLE.'; pp. 123–125: 'AS I EBB'D WITH THE OCEAN.';p. 127: 'ABOARD AT SHIP'S HELM.'; p. 129: 'THE WORLD BELOW THE BRINE.'; p. 131: 'SONG FOR ALL SEAS.'; p. 133: 'AFTER THE SEA-SHIP.'; p. 135: 'A BOSTON BALLAD.'; p. 137: 'EUROPE.'; p. 139: 'O ME! O LIFE!'; p. 141: 'DALLIANCE OF THE EAGLES.'; p. 143: 'GLIDING O'ER ALL.'; p. 147: 'FIRST O SONGS.'; p. 149: 'BEAT! BEAT! DRUMS!'; pp. 151–157: 'SONG OF THE BANNER.'; p. 159: 'RISE O DAYS.'; p. 161: 'VIRGINIA—THE WEST.'; p. 163: 'BIVOUAC ON A MOUNTAIN SIDE.'; p. 165: 'COME UP FROM THE FIELDS.';p. 167: 'VIGIL STRANGE I KEPT.'; p. 169: 'A MARCH IN THE RANKS.'; p. 171: 'AS TOILSOME I WANDER'D.'; pp. 173–175: 'THE WOUND-DRESSER.'; p. 177: 'GIVE ME THE SPLENDID SON.'; p. 179: 'DIRGE FOR TWO VETERANS.'; p. 181: 'OVER THE CARNAGE.'; p. 183: 'THE ARTIL-LERYMAN'S VISION.'; p. 185: 'O TAN-FACED PRAIRIE-BOY.'; p. 187: 'AS I LAY WITH MY HEAD.'; p. 189: 'SPIRIT WHOSE WORK IS DONE.'; p. 191: 'TURN O LIBERTAD.'; pp. 195–203: 'WHEN LILACS BLOOM'D.'; p. 205: 'THIS DUST WAS ONCE.'; pp. 207–223: 'BY BLUE ONTARIO'S SHORE.'; pp. 227–231: 'THE RETURN OF THE HEROES.'; p. 233: 'THERE WAS A CHILD.'; p. 235: 'OLD IRELAND.'; pp. 237–239: 'THIS COMPOST.'; p. 241: 'UNNAMED LANDS.'; pp. 243–245: 'SONG OF PRUDENCE.'; p. 247: 'VOICES.'; p. 249: 'MIRACLES.'; p. 251: 'UNFOLDED OUT OF THE FOLDS.'; p. 253: 'WHO LEARNS MY LESSON.'; p. 255: 'O STAR OF FRANCE.'; p. 257: 'AN OLD MAN'S THOUGHT.'; p. 259: 'THE PRAIRIE STATES.'; pp. 261–265: 'PROUD MUSIC OF THE STORM.'; pp. 267–269: 'PRAYER OF COLUMBUS.'; pp. 271–277: 'TO THINK OF TIME.'; p. 279: 'YET, YET, YE DOWNCAST HOURS.'; p. 281: 'QUICKSAND YEARS.'; p. 283: 'PENSIVE AND FALTER-

ING.'; pp. 285–289: *'THOU MOTHER.'*; p. 293: *'O MAGNET-SOUTH.'*; p. 295:
'A RIDDLE SONG.'; p. 297: *'OLD WAR-DREAMS.'*; p. 299: *'AS I WALK THESE
DAYS.'*; p. 303: *'ASHES OF SOLDIERS.'*; p. 305: *'THOUGHTS.'*; pp. 307–309:
'SONG AT SUNSET.'; p. 311: *'PENSIVE ON HER DEAD GAZING.'*; p. 313:
'THE SOBBING OF THE BELLS.'; pp. 315–317: *'SO LONG!'*; versos: p. vi:
'CONTENTS.'; pp. x–xxxviii: *'WALT WHITMAN.'*; pp. 2–42, 46–96, 98–132,
136–258, 262–278, 280–318: *'LEAVES OF GRASS.'*.

Binding: Three styles have been noted, priority assumed:

> *Binding A:*   Blackish blue B cloth (linen). Front and back covers: blank;
> spine: white paper label with '[all within a single-rule red frame] The Poems
> of | WALT | WHITMAN. | With | Prefatory Notice. | Edited by | ERNEST
> RHYS.'. Laid or wove endpapers. Issued uncut.

> *Binding B:*   Same as binding A, except: 'ERNEST RHYS'.

> *Binding C:*   Medium yellow-brown S cloth (diagonal fine-ribbed). Front
> cover: blackstamped '[two lines in gothic] The Canterbury | Poets | [birds and
> flowers] | [goldstamped background with raised single-rule frame around
> 'WHITMAN', both in relief and within an ornate blackstamped frame]'; back
> cover: blindstamped triple-rule frame with floretlike design in each corner;
> spine: blackstamped '[triple rule] | [dome and rule] | [goldstamped rule] | [rule]
> | [goldstamped background with two lines in gothic 'Whitman's | Poems' in
> relief] | [rule] | [goldstamped rule] | [vine design] | [rule] | [flowers and vines
> design] | [rule] | WALTER | SCOTT. | [triple rule]'. No flyleaves. Dark brown
> endpapers coated on one side. All edges trimmed. All edges stained red.

Printing: *'Printed by* WALTER SCOTT, *Felling, Newcastle-on-Tyne'* (p. 318).

Publication: On 7 July 1885, Ernest Rhys, acting on behalf of Walter Scott,
proposed a one-shilling edition of Whitman's verse in the *Canterbury Poets*
series (*Correspondence,* III, 407n). Whitman received £10.10s. on 9 September and wrote on 9 November to give his permission for sale in England only
(*Daybooks,* II, 372; *Correspondence,* III, 407). On 4 March 1886, Whitman
received a presentation copy from Rhys, with another three copies received on
the 18th (IV, 22–23n; *Daybooks,* II, 381). Rhys wrote on 22 May to report that
8,000 copies had been sold and a second edition planned (*Correspondence,* IV,
23n). On 25–29 September, Rhys again wrote Whitman and enclosed a payment from Scott; Whitman endorsed his letter with "the little English selection . . . is out since, & the whole edition (10,000) sold" (III, 407n).
    The Canterbury Poets. Listed in *Publishers' Circular and Booksellers' Rec-
ord,* 15 March 1886. Deposit copies: binding C: BL ('15JY86'), BO ('26AUG
86'). Presentation copies: binding A: DLC (from Rhys to Whitman, 1 March
1886), PU (from Rhys to W. M. Rossetti, 1 March 1886). DLC has a copy in

Binding C for A 2.8.a

binding A which includes a letter from Whitman, 20 June 1886, sent with the book. Price, 1s.

Locations: Binding A: CSt, DLC (2), JM, NN-R, NzD, PU, TxU; binding B: BBo, JM; binding C: BE, BO, BL, CSt, CtY, JM, NN-R.

Note one: One copy in binding A has a four-page undated publisher's catalogue inserted at the back (NN-R).

Note two: Also advertised in red roan for 2s.2d. and in silk plush for 4s.6d.; no copies have been located.

A 2.8.b
Eighth (English) edition, second printing (1887)

London and Newcastle-on-Tyne: Walter Scott, 1887.

No series identification or *The Canterbury Poets.*

Locations: JM, NN-R, RPB, ViU; *Canterbury:* NzD, NN-R, RPB.

A 2.8.c
Presumed third printing [n.d.]

[ornate 'P'] | POEMS OF WALT WHIT- | MAN (FROM 'LEAVES | OF GRASS'), WITH INTRO- | DUCTION BY ERNEST RHYS. | LONDON: | WALTER SCOTT, LIMITED, | 24 WARWICK LANE.

The Canterbury Poets. Printing: 'THE WALTER SCOTT PRESS, NEW-CASTLE-ON-TYNE.' (p. 318).

Locations: BBo, BMR, CtY (2).

A 2.8.d
Presumed fourth printing [n.d.]

[ornate 'P'] . . . LONDON: | WALTER SCOTT, 24 WARWICK LANE, | PA-TERNOSTER ROW.

No series identification. Printing: 'THE WALTER SCOTT PRESS, NEW-CASTLE-ON-TYNE.' (p. 318).

Location: TxU.

A 2.8.e
Presumed fifth printing [n.d.]

[ornate 'P'] . . . LONDON: | WALTER SCOTT, LIMITED, | PATERNOSTER SQUARE.

The Canterbury Poets. Printing: 'THE WALTER SCOTT PRESS, NEWCASTLE-ON-TYNE.' (p. 318). Copies inscribed by owners: JM (30 July 1900).

Locations: JM (2), NcD, TxU.

A 2.8.f
Presumed sixth printing [n.d.]

[ornate 'P'] . . . LONDON: | WALTER SCOTT, LIMITED, | PATERNOSTER SQUARE. | NEW YORK: 3 EAST FOURTEENTH STREET.

The Canterbury Poets. Printing: 'THE WALTER SCOTT PRESS, NEWCASTLE-ON-TYNE.' (p. 318). Copies inscribed by owners: JM (3 June 1896).

Locations: JM, NzD, TxU.

A 2.8.g
Presumed seventh printing [1902]

[ornate 'P'] . . . RHYS. | THE WALTER SCOTT PUBLISHING CO., LTD., | LONDON AND NEWCASTLE-ON-TYNE.

The Canterbury Poets. Printing: 'THE WALTER SCOTT PUBLISHING CO., LTD., NEWCASTLE-ON-TYNE. | 10–02' (p. 318); publisher's code probably represents October 1902 printing date.

Location: BMR.

A 2.8.h
Presumed eighth printing [1906]

[ornate 'P'] . . . RHYS. | THE WALTER SCOTT PUBLISHING CO., LTD., | LONDON AND FELLING-ON-TYNE. | NEW YORK: 3 EAST 14TH STREET.

No series; *The Canterbury Poets;* or *Photogravure Edition* of *The Canterbury Poets.* RPB copy *(Canterbury)* received 5 November 1907. Printing: 'THE WALTER SCOTT PUBLISHING CO., LIMITED, FELLING-ON-TYNE. | I–06' (p. 318); publisher's code probably represents January 1906 printing date.

Locations: JM; *Canterbury:* RPB, TxU; *Photogravure:* JM.

A 2.8.i
Presumed ninth printing [1911]

[ornate 'P'] . . . STREET.

The Canterbury Poets. Printing: 'THE WALTER SCOTT PUBLISHING CO., LIMITED, FELLING-ON-TYNE. | I–II' (p. 318); publisher's code probably represents January 1911 printing date.

Locations: CtY, JM, PU, TxU.

A 3 DRUM-TAPS
1865

A 3.1.a
First edition, first printing (1865)

Three issues have been noted:

A 3.1.a$_1$
First issue (1865)

WALT   WHITMAN'S

DRUM-TAPS.

New-York.

—

1865.

A 3.1.a$_1$: 7$^{1}/_{16}''$ × 4$^{3}/_{8}''$

[i–iii] iv 5–72

[1–3]¹² . Signed [A]⁶ B–F⁶ . Sheets bulk 5/32″.

Contents: p. i: title page; p. ii: copyright page; pp. iii–iv: contents; pp. 5–72: text.

Poems: "Drum-Taps," "Shut not your Doors to me proud Libraries," "Cavalry Crossing a Ford," "Song of the Banner at Day-Break," "By the Bivouac's fitful flame," "1861," "From Paumanok starting I fly like a bird," "Beginning my studies," "The Centenarian's Story," "Pioneers! O Pioneers!", "Quicksand years that whirl me I know not whither," "The Dresser," "When I heard the learn'd Astronomer," "Rise O Days from Your fathomless Deeps," "A child's amaze," "Beat! Beat! Drums!", "Come Up from the Fields Father," "City of Ships," "Mother and Babe," "Vigil strange I Kept on the field one night," "Bathed in War's Perfume," "A march in the ranks hard-prest, and the road unknown," "Long, too long, O land," "A sight in camp in the day-break Grey and dim," "A Farm Picture," "Give Me the Splendid Silent Sun," "Over the carnage rose prophetic a voice," "Did you ask dulcet rhymes from me?", "Year of Meteors. (1859–60.)," "The Torch," "Years of the unperform'd," "Year that Trembled and Reel'd Beneath Me," "The Veteran's Vision," "O Tan-Face Prairie-Boy," "Camps of Green," "As toilsome I wander'd Virginia's woods," "Hymn of Dead Soldiers," "The Ship," "A Broadway Pageant. (Reception Japanese Embassy, June 16, 1860.)," "Flags of Stars, Thick-Sprinkled Bunting," "Old Ireland," "Look Down Fair Moon," "Out of the rolling ocean, the crowd," "World, Take Good Notice," "I Saw Old General at Bay," "Others May Praise What They Like," "Solid, Ironical, Rolling Orb," "Hush'd be the Camps To-Day," "Weave in, Weave in, My Hardy Life," "Turn O Libertad," "Bivouac on a Mountain Side," "Pensive on Her Dead Gazing, I Heard the Mother of All," "Not Youth Pertains to Me." See "Index to the Poems in *Leaves of Grass*" for information about the publication histories of individual poems within the various editions, printings, and issues of *Leaves of Grass*.

Typography and paper: 59/16″ (53/16″)×3⅛″; wove paper; various lines per page (up to 40). Running heads: rectos: p. 7: 'DRUM-TAPS.'; pp. 11–15: 'BANNER AT DAY-BREAK.'; p. 17: 'DRUM-TAPS.'; pp. 21–23: 'THE CENTENARIAN'S STORY.'; pp. 27–29: 'PIONEERS! O PIONEERS!'; p. 33: 'THE DRESSER.'; p. 37: 'RISE, O DAYS!'; pp. 41–59, 63–71: 'DRUM-TAPS.'; versos: p. iv: 'CONTENTS.'; pp. 6–72: 'DRUM-TAPS.'.

Binding: Dark grayish red or deep yellowish brown C cloth (sand-grain). Front cover: blindstamped triple-rule frame surrounding goldstamped double-rule circular frame around four lines in relief on goldstamped horizontal ribbed background in center: '[floral rule] | DRUM | TAPS. | [floral rule]'; back cover: same as the front cover, except: all blindstamped; spine: blank. Front and back flyleaves. White endpapers. All edges trimmed. All edges plain or speckle-stained red.

Printing: Peter Eckler, Philadelphia.

Publication: Whitman had earlier planned this book as *Banner at Day-Break,* which Thayer and Eldridge advertised in October and November 1860, but the failure of the firm soon after publication of the 1860 *Leaves of Grass* ended plans for publication (see David Goodale, "Walt Whitman's 'Banner at Day-Break,' 1860," *Huntington Library Quarterly,* 26 [November 1962], 105–110). On 31 March 1863, Whitman referred to "the little MS book, 'Drum Taps,' " and on 17 November, he decided "I must bring [it] out" (*Correspondence,* I, 86, 185). By 10 April 1864, he had made plans to "try to print" the book, which his brother confirmed in a letter to their mother about Walt's plans of "publishing a small book this Spring" (I, 210, 210n). By 5 July, Whitman proclaimed, "I intend to move heaven & earth to publish my 'Drum Taps' as soon as I am able to go around," and by the 24th he had concluded to bring it out himself in "an edition of 500" (I, 236, 239). Matters proceeded slowly: on 11 September it "was not yet begun to be printed"; indeed, by 6 January 1865 "perfect copy" was still being "made for the printers," and he supposed it "may come out this winter" (I, 240, 246). On 1 April, a contract was signed calling for 500 copies to be printed, and Peter Eckler gave Whitman a receipt for "payment in advance" (DLC). The book was "now to press" on 26 April and planned for delivery at the binder's in a few days (I, 261n). On 2 May, Whitman sent Eckler "a copy of each of the printed sheets," reminded him that he had already paid "for binding the first 100" (I, 260), and the next day wrote him, "Deliver the sheets to A. Simpson, Spruce Street . . . If you have the plates of the two cancelled pages, I wish you would take these impressions of each page & enclose to me" (VI, 4).

500 copies. Advertised as published that day in *New-York Daily Tribune,* 28 October 1865, p. 2. Reviewed in *Watson's Weekly Art Journal,* 4 November 1865, pp. 34–35. A copy at DLC contains an inserted note by Whitman, dated 20 December 1865, to "send copy Drum Taps to Congressional Library." Presentation copies (all from Whitman): NN-B (to William O'Connor, 28 May 1865), NN-B (to Ellen O'Connor, 28 May 1865), DLC (12 July 1865), NjP (1865). Price, $1.00. Listed in the *English Catalogue* as an importation at 5s.

Locations: BE, BL, CSt, CtY (2), DLC (4), InU-L, MB, MH (2), NN-B (3), NN-R, NNC, NcD, NjP, PU, RPB, TxU, ViU.

Note one: A set of unbound sheets, measuring 8⅛″ × 4⅞″, with each gathering stapled and all punched through with three holes, and with top edges trimmed and front and bottom edges uncut, is at NN-B.

Note two: A copy, bound in three-quarter leather with sheets measuring 7⅝″ × 4⁹⁄₁₆″, with all edges trimmed, possibly prepared from unbound sheets, is at CtY.

Note three: Whitman wrote an advertising placard used for this book; see F 23.

A 3.1.a₂
Second issue (1865)

Drum-Taps and *Sequel to Drum-Taps*

Title page for *Sequel* in A 3.1.a₂

[i–iii] iv 5–72 [1–3] 4–24

[1–4]¹² . Signed [A]⁶ B–F⁶ [G]¹² . A blank binder's leaf is inserted after p. 72. Sheets bulk 7/32″.

Contents: pp. i–72: *Drum-Taps;* p. 1: title page for *Sequel;* p. 2: contents; pp. 3–24: text of *Sequel.*

Poems: The additional poems are "When Lilacs Last in the Door-Yard Bloom'd," "Race of Veterans," "O Captain! My Captain!", "Spirit whose Work is Done," "Chanting the Square Deific," "I heard you, Solemn-sweet Pipes of the Organ," "Not My Enemies Ever Invade Me," "O Me! O Life!", "Ah Poverties, Wincings, and Sulky Retreats," "As I Lay with My Head in Your Lap, Camerado," "This Day, O Soul," "In Clouds Descending, in Midnight Sleep," "An Army on the March," "Dirge for Two Veterans," "How Solemn, as One by One," "Lo! Victress on the Peaks!", "Reconciliation," "To the Leaven'd Soil They Trod." See "Index to the Poems in *Leaves of Grass*" for information about the publication histories of individual poems within the various editions, printings, and issues of *Leaves of Grass.*

Typography and paper: pp. 1–72: same as in *Drum-Taps;* pp. 1–24: 5½″ (5¼″)×3³⁄₁₆″; wove paper; various lines per page (up to 33); running heads: rectos: pp. 5–23: 'SEQUEL TO DRUM-TAPS.'; versos: pp. 4–24: 'SEQUEL TO DRUM-TAPS'.

Binding: Same as in the first issue, except: front and back flyleaves with conjugates pasted under endpapers; all edges speckle-stained red.

Printing: 'GIBSON BROTHERS, PRINTERS.' (*Sequel*, p. [2]).

Publication: Whitman began plans for publishing the *Sequel* soon after Abraham Lincoln's death on 15 April 1865. The printing was done by Gibson Brothers, who gave Whitman a receipt for preparing 1,000 copies on 2 October 1865 (DLC). On 15 October, Whitman wrote, "I have made an addition to the little book 'Drum Taps,' & will send you one of the perfect copies soon" (*Correspondence,* I, 269). Five days later he wrote that the book would be bound shortly and "next week be put in the hands of a New York publisher" (I, 270). Abraham Simpson wrote Whitman on 20 October, acknowledging $50 on account for binding 300 copies, and again on 1 November, billing him for binding 500 copies (I, 270–271n). On 26 August 1866, Whitman reported seeing Huntington (of the firm Bunce and Huntington) in New York, and he reported that the book "sold somewhat better than I anticipated" (I, 284). But as late as 4 February 1874, he wrote that a New York bookseller should have nine copies in stock (II, 273).

   1,000 copies. Deposited for copyright: title: 26 April 1865; book, 24 October 1865. Reviewed in *North American Review,* 104 (January 1867), 301–303.

Deposit copies: DLC ('May 26 1866'), BL ('15 JY 67'). Copies inscribed by owners: TxU (14 February 1866), NNPM (by Peter Doyle as received from Whitman in May 1867). Price, $1.00.

Locations: BL, CtY (3), DLC (5), JM, MB, MBU, MH (2), NN-R, NNPM (2), NcD (2), NcU, NjP, NzD, ScU, TxU (5), ViU.

Note one: One copy has a printed sheet from Bunce and Huntington to reviewers pasted to the front endpapers (CtY).

Note two: A set of unbound and uncut sheets, measuring 8¼″×4¾″, sewn with a ribbon, is at NN-B.

Note three: A copy bound in half leather, with sheets measuring 7⅞″ × 4⁹⁄₁₆″, with all edges trimmed, possibly prepared from unbound sheets, is at NN-B.

Note four: A broadside advertising circular, printed on the recto, is at DLC.

A 3.1.a₃
Third issue (1867)

Drum-Taps and *Sequel to Drum-Taps* combined with *Leaves of Grass* and "Songs Before Parting" in four-volumes-in-one format; see A 2.4.a₁.

A 3.1.b
Walt Whitman's Drum-Taps (1865) and Sequel to Drum-Taps (1865–6). Gainesville, Fla.: Scholars' Facsimiles & Reprints, 1959.

Facsimile reprinting. Edited with an introduction by F. De Wolfe Miller. Deposit copies: BO ('6JUN1959'), BE ('20 OC 1959'). Presentation copies: TxU (from the publisher, 2 January 1959). Price, $6.00. *Locations:* BE, BO, ScU, TxU.

Note: Includes manuscript facsimiles, being the first publication of ["Unveil thy bosom, faithful tune"] and ["Thou West that gave'st him to us"], opposite pp. xxiv, xlii. These two items were reprinted in Harold W. Blodgett, "A Poet's Hero," *Symposium,* 1 (Spring 1962), 29.

A 3.2
Second (English) edition, only printing (1915)

DRUM-TAPS

BY

WALT   WHITMAN

LONDON
CHATTO & WINDUS
1915

A 3.2: 6⅜″ × 4¾″

Three states have been noted, priority assumed:

First state:

[i–vi] 1–12 [13–16] [16a–16b] 17–72

[1]^{12} 2–4^8 5^4 . Sheets bulk ¼″.

Contents: p. i: half title, 'DRUM-TAPS'; p. ii: blank; p. iii: title page; p. iv: blank; p. v: 'NOTE' that the introduction is reprinted from the 1 April 1915 *Times Literary Supplement* [by Walter de la Mare]; p. vi: blank; pp. 1–12: introduction; pp. 13–14: blank; pp. 15–16: contents; pp. 16a–16b: blank; pp. 1–72: text.

Second state:

[i–vi] 1–12 [13–16] 17–72

[1]^{12} (−1$_{10}$) 2–4^8 5^4 .

Contents: pp. i–vi, 1–16, 17–72: same as in the first state.

Third state:

[i–x] 1–12 17–72

[a]^6 (−a$_5$) [1]^6 2–4^8 5^4 . See *Note one*.

Contents: pp. i–ii: blank; p. iii: half title; p. iv: blank; p. v: title page; p. vi: blank; pp. vii–viii: contents; p. ix: 'NOTE'; p. x: blank; pp. 1–12: introduction; pp. 1–72: text.

Typography and paper: 4⅞″ (4¹¹⁄₁₆″)×3¹¹⁄₁₆″; wove paper; introduction: 30 lines per page; poems: various lines per page (up to 30). Running heads: rectos: pp. 3–11: 'INTRODUCTION'; p. 19: 'SONGS FOR A PRELUDE'; p. 21: 'BEAT! BEAT! DRUMS'; pp. 23–29: 'SONG OF THE BANNER AT DAYBREAK'; pp. 31–33: 'RISE O DAYS FROM YOUR FATHOMLESS DEEPS'; p. 35: 'CITY OF SHIPS'; pp. 37–39: 'THE CENTENARIAN'S STORY'; p. 41: 'CAVALRY CROSS-ING A FORD'; p. 43: 'BY THE BIVOUAC'S FITFUL FLAME'; p. 45: 'COME UP FROM THE FIELDS FATHER'; p. 47: 'A MARCH IN THE RANKS HARD-PREST'; p. 49: 'A SIGHT IN CAMP IN THE DAYBREAK'; p. 51: 'YEAR THAT TREMBLED AND REEL'D BENEATH ME'; p. 53: 'THE WOUND-DRESSER'; p. 55: 'LONG, TOO LONG AMERICA'; p. 57: 'GIVE ME THE SPLENDID SI-LENT SUN'; p. 59: 'OVER THE CARNAGE ROSE PROPHETIC A VOICE'; p. 61: 'I SAW OLD GENERAL AT BAY'; p. 63: 'ETHIOPIA SALUTING THE COL-OURS'; p. 65: 'O TAN-FACED PRAIRIE-BOY'; p. 67: 'DELICATE CLUS-TERED'; p. 69: 'SPIRIT WHOSE WORK IS DONE'; p. 71: 'TURN O LIBERTAD'; versos: pp. 2–12: 'INTRODUCTION'; pp. 18–72: 'DRUM-TAPS'.

Binding: Slightly orange FL cloth (dotted-line-ribbed) shelfback with paper-covered sides. Front and back covers: orange and white large circular ornaments and swords on black background; spine: blackstamped 'DRUM | TAPS | • | CHATTO & | WINDUS'. White endpapers. Top and front edges trimmed, bottom edges rough trimmed. Top edges plain or stained yellow or stained orange.

Dust jacket: Three styles have been noted:

Jacket A: Coated white paper. Front cover: 'GREAT WAR POEMS | [within drawing of drumhead] DRUM-TAPS | By WALT WHITMAN'; back cover: advertisement for Chatto & Windus' poetry publications; spine: vertically: 'DRUM-TAPS By WALT WHITMAN 1/– net'; flaps: blank.

Jacket B: Same as jacket A, except: spine: a paper label with '1s.6d. NET' is pasted over '1/– net'.

Jacket C: White wove paper. Front cover: '[all within a double-rule frame] DRUM-TAPS | BY | WALT WHITMAN | ONE SHILLING AND SIXPENCE NET'; back cover: blank; spine: vertically: 'DRUM-TAPS BY WALT WHITMAN 1s. 6d. NET'; front and back flaps: blank. See *Note two.*

Printing: 'BILLING AND SONS LTD., PRINTERS, GUILDFORD, ENGLAND' (p. 72).

Publication: Reviewed in *Conservator,* 26 (January 1916), 171. Published November 1915. Deposit copies: First state: BL ('3 NOV 15'), BC ('DE 2 1915'), BE ('2 DEC 1915'), BO ('3 12 15'). Copies inscribed by owners: first state: CtY (25 December 1915), RPB (11 February 1916). Price, 1s.

Locations: First state: BBo (dj A), BC, BE, BL, BMR, BO (dj A), CtY, DLC (dj C), JM, JM (dj A), JM (dj B), MBU (dj A), NcU, NzD, PU, RPB; second state: NN-R, TxU; third state: TxU (dj C).

Note one: The third state may be the result of a binding error in which the sheets of the first gathering were redistributed into two six-leaf gatherings, with the sheets of the first gathering then shuffled.

Note two: In the printing on the spine in dust jacket C, the title is $^3/_{16}''$ high, the author $^1/_8''$ high, and 'BY' and 'NET' $^3/_{32}''$ high.

A 3.3.a–b
Drum Taps. New York: Grosset & Dunlap, [1936].

139 pp. Boxed. J. J. Little & Ives imprint on copyright page. *Cameo Classics.* Price, 69¢. Undated reprinting in *Cameo Classics* without the Little and Ives imprint on the copyright page. *Locations:* JM (1936), ScU (1936), NcD (n.d.).

GREAT WAR POEMS

DRUM-TAPS

By WALT WHITMAN

DRUM-TAPS By WALT WHITMAN 1/- net

RECENT POETRY

PUBLISHED BY CHATTO & WINDUS

The Celestial Aftermath
By CYRIL SCOTT. 5s. net. Also a limited edition, large paper vellum, £1 1s. net.

Songs to Save a Soul
By IRENE RUTHERFORD McLEOD
Fourth Edition - - 2s. 6d. net.

Tid'apa (What *Does* it Matter?)
By GILBERT FRANKAU, Author of
"One of Us" - - 2s. 6d. net.

ALSO PUBLISHED IN THE ST. MARTIN'S LIBRARY
Cloth 2s. net. Leather 3s. net.

POEMS BY WALT WHITMAN
Selected and Edited by WILLIAM MICHAEL ROSSETTI
WITH A PORTRAIT

Dust jacket A for A 3.2

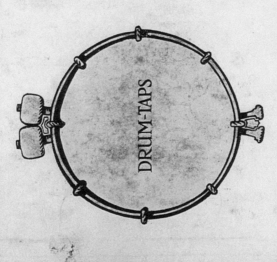

GREAT WAR POEMS

DRUM-TAPS   By WALT WHITMAN

DRUM-TAPS

By WALT WHITMAN

1s. 6d. net

RECENT POETRY

PUBLISHED BY CHATTO & WINDUS

The Celestial Aftermath

By CYRIL SCOTT. 5s. net. Also a limited edition, large paper vellum, £1 1s. net.

Songs to Save a Soul

By IRENE RUTHERFORD McLEOD
Fourth Edition   -   -   2s. 6d. net.

Tid'apa (What *Does* it Matter?)

By GILBERT FRANKAU, Author of "One of Us"   -   -   2s. 6d. net.

ALSO PUBLISHED IN THE ST. MARTIN'S LIBRARY

Cloth 2s. net. *Leather* 3s. net.

POEMS BY WALT WHITMAN

Selected and Edited by WILLIAM MICHAEL ROSSETTI
WITH A PORTRAIT

Dust jacket B for A 3.2

Dust jacket C for A 3.2

A 3.3.c
New York: Somerset, [1959?].

Leatherette. Dust jacket. *Somerset Classics*. Price, $1.00. *Locations:* JM, RPB.

A 3.4
Drum-Taps. New York: Thomas Y. Crowell Co., [n.d.].

63 pp. Miniature book. Limp leather. Sold with Kipling's *Recessional* and *In Flanders Field*. Copies inscribed by owners: RPB (December 1922). *Location:* RPB.

A 4 DEMOCRATIC VISTAS
1871

A 4.1.a
First edition, first printing (1871)

Two issues have been noted:

A 4.1.a₁
First issue (1871)

MEMORANDA.

DEMOCRATIC

VISTAS.

Washington, D. C.
1871.

☞ *See* ADVERTISEMENT *at end of this Volume.*

A 4.1.a₁: 8⅛″ × 5″

> Entered according to Act of Congress, in the year 1870, by
> *WALT WHITMAN,*
> In the Office of the Librarian of Congress, at Washington.
>
> Electrotyped by SMITH & McDOUGAL, 82 Beekman Street, New York.

[1–3] 4–78 [79] 80–84

$[1-2]^{12}$ 3^{12} 4^{6} . Sheets bulk 5/32″.

Contents: p. 1: title page; p. 2: copyright page; pp. 3–78: text; pp. 79–84: "General Notes."

Typography and paper: 5⅝″ (5⅜″)×3¼″; wove paper; various lines per page (up to 41). Running heads: rectos: pp. 5–77: '*DEMOCRATIC VISTAS.*'; pp. 81–83: '*GENERAL NOTES.*'; versos: pp. 4–84: '*DEMOCRATIC VISTAS.*'.

Binding: Light yellow-green coated stiff wrappers. Front cover: '[flush right] Price, 75 Cents. | Democratic | VISTAS. | Washington, D.C. | 1871. | NEW-YORK: J. S. REDFIELD, PUBLISHER, 140 Fulton St., (up stairs.)'; back cover: advertisement for *Leaves of Grass, Passage to India* and *Democratic Vistas,* listing sales agents in Washington, New York, Boston, Brooklyn, and London; spine: blank. White endpapers or no endpapers. Issued uncut.

Printing: See copyright page.

Publication: Whitman wrote on 13 August 1868, "I am working at my leisure on my little book" (*Correspondence,* II, 39). On 21 July 1870 he wrote that the book would be "printed this fall" and on 10 October he said he was "just delivered" of it (II, 100, 116). J. S. Redfield printed at least 500 copies, the amount Whitman said was at the firm in his will, dated 23 October 1872 (II, 118n). Although Whitman wrote a New York bookseller on 4 February 1874 that he should have 86 copies in stock, sales thereafter were slow: Whitman still had copies in stock on 6 January 1889, and the inventory of Whitman's belongings made after his death lists four copies of this edition (II, 274; IV, 264; DLC).

Listed in *American Literary Gazette and Publishers' Circular,* 1 November 1870. Reviewed in *New York Times,* 11 November 1870, p. 2. Deposited for copyright: title, 27 September 1870; book, 8 November 1870; 2259. Deposit copies: BL ('25AP72'; rebound with wrappers). Presentation copies (all from Whitman): MH (February 1871; rebound with wrappers), MH (November 1871; rebound with wrappers), CtY (1871), DLC (1871). Copies inscribed by owners: NcD (March 1871). Price, 75¢. Advertised for sale by Trübner in 1881 for 4s.

Back wrapper for A 4.1.a₁

Front wrapper for A 4.1.a₁

Locations: BBo, BMR, BO, CSt, CtY (3), DLC (8), JM, MBU, NN-R (2), NNC, NNPM, NcD, NcU, NjCW, NjP, PU, RPB, TxU (8), ViU (3).

Note one: A set of unbound, unsewn, and trimmed gatherings, measuring 8⅛″ × 4⅞″, is at DLC.

Note two: A set of unbound, unsewn, and trimmed gatherings, measuring 8⅛″ × 4⅞″, with p. 1 (title page) reading 'DEMOCRATIC | VISTAS', is at DLC. This was probably for use in the second printing of *Two Rivulets* (see A 9.1.b).

Note three: Redfield sent copies to Sampson Low for sale in England (on 31 December 1872 there were 48 copies in stock), but after he went out of business, the account was transferred to Whitman's name by 28 March 1873 and it was closed by 18 February 1876 (II, 273n, 118n; *Daybooks*, I, 17). Trübner also distributed the book, reporting 61 copies in stock on 31 May 1878 and closing the account by 20 October 1888 with the sale of 39 copies (*Correspondence*, III, 137n; IV, 235n).

Note four: Incorporates "Democracy" and "Personalism" from the December 1867 and May 1868 *Galaxy Magazine* (E 2504, E 2505).

A 4.1.a$_2$
Second issue (1876)

Combined with other works in *Two Rivulets;* see A 9.1.a.

A 4.1.b
First edition, second printing (1876)

Combined with other works in *Two Rivulets;* see A 9.1.b. The title page is reset as a half title page.

A 4.2
Second (Danish) edition, only printing (1874)

Demokratiske Fremblik. | Af | Walt Whitman. | Oversat efter den amerikanske Original | af | Rudolf Schmidt. | [double short rule] | Kjøbenhavn. | Karl Schønbergs Forlag. | 1874.

132 pp. Wrappers. *Locations:* DLC (2), TxU.

Note: Whitman acknowledged receiving copies of this on 4 March 1874 (*Correspondence*, II, 282).

A 4.3.a
Third (English) edition, first printing (1888)

Two issues have been noted:

A 4.3.a₁
First issue (1888)

D EMOCRATIC VISTAS, AND
OTHER PAPERS.   BY

WALT WHITMAN.

[Published by arrangement with the Author.]

LONDON
WALTER SCOTT, 24 WARWICK LANE
TORONTO : W. J. GAGE & CO.
1888

A 4.3.a₁: 7″ × 4¾″

[i–viii] 1–83 [84] 85–94 [95] 96–99 [100] 101–105 [106] 107–108 [109] 110–112 [113] 114–124 [125] 126–129 [130] 131–139 [140] 141 [142] 143–173 [174] 175 [176]

[a]⁴ 1–11⁸ . Sheets bulk ½″.

Contents: p. i: '[gothic] The Camelot Series | EDITED BY ERNEST RHYS | DEMOCRATIC VISTAS.'; p. ii: blank; p. iii: title page; p. iv: blank; p. v: contents; p. vi: blank; pp. vii–viii: preface, signed 'CAMDEN, NEW JERSEY, | *April* 1888.'; pp. 1–84: text of *Democratic Vistas;* pp. 85–175: texts of other works; p. 176: blank.

Prose: "Preface," *Democratic Vistas*, "My Book and I," "A Backward Glance on My Own Road," "Our Eminent Visitors (Past, Present, and Future)," "A Thought on Shakespeare," "What Lurks Behind Shakespeare's Historical Plays," "Robert Burns as Poet and Person," "A Word About Tennyson," " 'How I Made a Book,' " "Five Thousand Poems," "Notes Left Over" (the same as the American edition, with the addition of "Darwinism—[Then Furthermore.]" from *Collect*), "A Letter" [20 December 1881 to John Fitzgerald Lee].

Typography and paper: 5⅜″ (5⅛″)×3⁵⁄₁₆″; wove paper; 33 lines per page. Running heads: rectos: pp. 3–83: 'DEMOCRATIC VISTAS.'; pp. 85–93: 'MY BOOK AND I.'; pp. 97–99: 'A BACKWARD GLANCE.'; pp. 101–105: 'OUR EMINENT VISTORS.'; p. 107: 'A THOUGHT ON SHAKSPERE.'; p. 111: 'SHAKSPERE'S HISTORICAL PLAYS.'; pp. 115–123: 'ROBERT BURNS.'; pp. 127–129: 'A WORD ABOUT TENNYSON.'; pp. 131–139: "HOW I MADE A BOOK."; p. 141: 'FIVE THOUSAND POEMS.'; pp. 143–173: 'NOTES LEFT OVER.'; p. 175: 'A LETTER.'; versos: p. viii: 'PREFACE.'; pp. 2–82: 'DEMO-CRATIC VISTAS.'; pp. 86–94: 'MY BOOK AND I.'; pp. 96–98: 'A BACKWARD GLANCE.'; pp. 102–104: 'OUR EMINENT VISTORS.'; p. 108: 'A THOUGHT ON SHAKSPERE.'; pp. 110–112: 'SHAKSPERE'S HISTORICAL PLAYS.'; pp. 114–124: 'ROBERT BURNS.'; pp. 126–128: 'A WORD ABOUT TENNYSON.'; pp. 132–138: "HOW I MADE A BOOK."; pp. 144–172: 'NOTES LEFT OVER.'.

Binding: Two styles have been noted, priority undetermined:

Binding A: Very red B cloth (linen). Front cover: blackstamped '[two lines in upper left corner] The Camelot Series. | [ornate headdress design] | [bottom right corner] [urn and dish]'; back cover: blank; spine: '[three lines blackstamped] [double rule] | [dotted line] | [six lines goldstamped] [rule] | Democratic Vistas | and other papers | [rule] | Walt Whitman | [rule] | [eight lines blackstamped] CAMELOT | SERIES | [urn] | [double rule] | WALTER SCOTT | [double rule]'. No flyleaves. White endpapers. All edges trimmed.

Binding B: Dark bluish gray or grayish blue B cloth (linen). Front and back covers: blank; spine: white paper label '[all within a red single-ruled

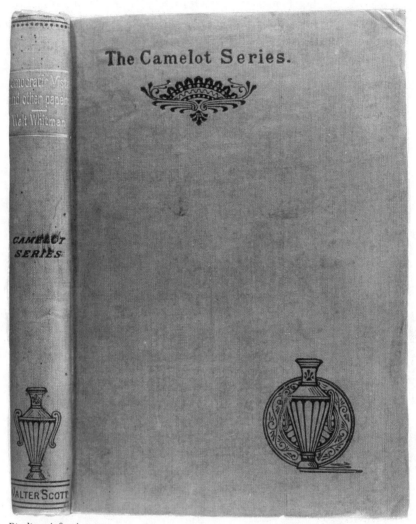

Binding A for A 4.3.a₁

frame] Camelot Series | [rule] | DEMOCRATIC | VISTAS | AND | OTHER
PAPERS | [rule] | WALT WHITMAN'. All edges rough trimmed; or top
edges trimmed, front and bottom edges uncut.

Printing: 'Printed by WALTER SCOTT, *Felling, Newcastle-on-Tyne.*' (p. 175).

Publication: On 2 February 1887, Whitman sent Ernest Rhys a copy of
Specimen Days & Collect (A 11) "with emendations" and suggested printing
"all up to page 200" as one book and "then another Vol. of the matter from page

203 to 338 (including 'My Book & I' which I send) & call it *'Democratic Vistas and other papers' By Walt Whitman"* (*Correspondence*, VI, 36). On the eighth, he sent Rhys "some additional newer matter" (VI, 44). And on the 11th, he wrote Rhys with suggestions for deleting material and his terms: a payment of ten guineas or £10.10s. ("same as my other vols") and 10 copies *"bound in roan."* He added that he had already been billed for 50 copies and wanted this amount deducted from the cash payment (VI, 44–45). On 17 January 1888 Whitman sent Rhys "the 'Preface' proof" (VI, 47).

The Camelot Series. Announced for publication for 25 May on an advertising slip pasted in a copy in binding A (JM). Whitman received 50 copies on 26 June 1888 (*WWWC*, I, 384, 410). Reviewed in *Academy*, 33 (30 June 1888), 441–442. Deposit copies: BL ('26MY88'; rebound); binding A: BC ('3 OCT 1888'), BO ('3–NOV.1888'). Copies inscribed by owners: binding B: PU (2 June 1888), BBo (4 June 1888), JM (28 June 1888). Price, 1s.

Locations: Binding A: BC, BE, BO, CtY, JM (2), NcD, RPB, ViU; binding B: BBo, BMR, CtY, DLC (2), JM (4), NN-R, NNC, PU (2).

Note one: All located copies have an undated eight-page publisher's catalogue, with *Democratic Vistas* the last title listed on p. [2], bound in at the back.

Note two: A copy in "half brown polished morocco," inscribed from Whitman to Bucke, and described as "apparently one of the copies which the editor had specially bound to send to Whitman for presentation," was sold at the Bucke sale, 15–16 April 1936, item 292 (see *Whitman at Auction*, p. 357). On the back of a 16 June 1888 letter written to him, Whitman noted that he had received "four copies" in "gold top, bound gold marbled paper, half leather" (DLC). These copies may be in the same binding as binding C for the first issue of *Specimen Days in America* (A 11.2.a₁).

Note three: Wells and Goldsmith report copies in "brown paper wrappers" (p. 31); no copy has been located. Copies were advertised for sale in red roan and in half calf at 3s.; no copies have been located.

A 4.3.a₂
Second issue (1888)

PROSE WRITINGS

of

WALT WHITMAN

———

LONDON
WALTER SCOTT
24 WARWICK LANE, PATERNOSTER ROW
——
1888

(All rights reserved.)

A 4.3.a₂: 7″ × 4¾″

[a–d] [iii–v] . . . 14–312 [i–vi] . . . [176]

[a]² [b]⁸ 273–291⁸ (–291₅₋₈) [a]⁴ (–a₁) 1–11⁸. Sheets bulk 1½″.

Contents: p. a: 'PROSE WRITINGS | OF | WALT WHITMAN'; p. b: blank; p. c: title page; p. d: blank; pp. [iii–v] . . . 14–312: the same as the first issue of *Specimen Days in America* (A 11.2.a₁), with half title page but without advertisements; pp. [i–vi] . . . [176]: same as the first issue of *Democratic Vistas, and Other Papers* (A 4.3.a₁).

Typography and paper: Same as in the first issues of both books.

Binding: Dark olive-green buckram; edges beveled. Front cover: black-stamped ornate bands in upper and lower right-hand corners, with 2½″ black-stamped strap design with two goldstamped screwlike designs inside each, extending 1¾″ from the spine; back cover: same as the front cover, except the bands are in the upper and lower left-hand corners; spine: goldstamped '[double rule] | [floral design] | [double rule] | Walter Scott's | Victoria Library | [double rule] | [cross and dot design] | [double rule] | [leaf design] | [double rule] | [rule] | WALT WHITMAN | SPECIMEN DAYS | [short rule] | DEMOCRATIC VISTAS | [rule] | [double rule] | [flower and cross design] | [double rule] | [boxes design] | [double rule] | [double rule] | [floral design] | [double rule]'. White endpapers. All edges trimmed. All edges gilded.

Publication: Victoria Library.

Location: NzD.

Note: An undated eight-page catalogue of Walter Scott's publications is inserted at the back.

A 4.3.a₃
Third issue [not before 1892]

Title and copyright pages are the same as in the first issue.

[i–vi] . . . [176]

[a]⁴ (–a₁) 1–11⁸ . The *Camelot Series* half title page is canceled.

Contents: pp. iii–176: same as in the first issue.

Binding: Eight styles have been noted, priority undetermined:

Binding A: Dark reddish orange B cloth (linen). Front cover: blindstamped: single-rule frame with ornamental rectangular design in center; back cover: blank; spine: blindstamped rules with goldstamped lettering: '[rule] | Democratic | Vistas | Whitman | [goldstamped circular publisher's device with 'SCOTT LIBRARY']'. White endpapers. Top and front edges trimmed, bottom edges rough trimmed.

Binding B: Dark olive-green S cloth (diagonal fine-ribbed). Front cover: goldstamped 'THE | Scott | Library' in upper left, with three parallel vertical lines 1¼″ from spine, and 1″ high triangles of ornamental design with triple parallel lines at bottom in top and bottom right corners; back cover: blank; spine: goldstamped 'Democratic Vistas | and other papers | Walt Whitman | Walter Scott'. Wove or laid endpapers. All edges trimmed; or top edges trimmed, front and bottom edges uncut. Top edges gilded.

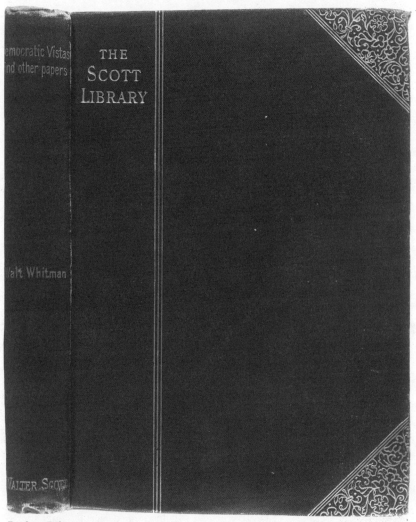

Binding B for A 4.3.a₃

Binding C: Same as binding B, except: spine: goldstamped 'Democratic . . .
papers | by | WALT WHITMAN | . . . '; front and bottom edges uncut.

Binding D: Same as binding B, except: spine: goldstamped 'Democratic . . .
Whitman | WALTER SCOTT | PUBLISHING CO., LTD.'; no flyleaves; wove
endpapers.

Binding E: Dark olive S cloth (diagonal fine-ribbed). Front cover: '[gold-
stamped frame with two goldstamped leaf-and-vine designs coming out
from the top and one out from the bottom, surrounding a goldstamped leaf-
and-vine design on a black background, surrounding a goldstamped frame
with 'DEMOCRATIC' in center] | VISTAS | [blue-, gold-, and blackstamped
picture of wilderness scene]'; back cover: blank; spine: '[goldstamped-
blackstamped-goldstamped rules] | [ten lines goldstamped] [leaf-and-vine de-
sign] | [ornate band] | [rule] | Democratic Vistas | and other papers | [rule] | Walt
Whitman | [rule] | [ornate band] | [leaf-and-vine design] | [blue-, gold-, and
blackstamped picture of wilderness scene] | [three lines blackstamped] [rule]
| WALTER SCOTT | [rule] | [goldstamped rule] | [blackstamped rule]'. Olive
floral pattern endpapers printed on side. All edges trimmed. All edges gilded.

Binding F: Deep red B cloth (linen). Front cover: blindstamped: single-
rule frame with rectangular design in center surrounding 'WS | PC'; back
cover: blank; spine: goldstamped 'Democratic | Vistas | Etc. | Whitman |
[circular publisher's device with 'SCOTT LIBRARY']'. Laid endpapers. All
edges trimmed.

Binding G: Dark olive-green S cloth (diagonal fine-ribbed) shelfback with
light blue, dark blue, and gold silk brocade-covered boards. Front cover:
cloth with goldstamped 'T', short rules pattern, and leaf-and-vine design
extending ⅞″ from spine, with cloth with goldstamped leaf-and-vine design
extending 1¼″ in at top and bottom right corners in an irregular shape; back
cover: same as the front, except the cloth corners are at the top and bottom
left; spine: goldstamped pattern the same as the shelfback extending on the
covers, with goldstamped '[rule] | Democratic Vistas | and other papers |
[rule] | Walt Whitman | [rule]' at top. Endpapers of black floral pattern silk
brocade printed on one side. All edges trimmed. All edges gilded. See *Notes
three* and *four.*

Binding H: Very deep red S cloth (diagonal fine-ribbed) shelfback with
gold silk brocade-covered boards. Front cover: cloth with goldstamped leaf-
and-vine design with single goldstamped rule at right, extending 1⅛″ from
spine, with ⅜″ high unstamped cloth triangles at the top and bottom right
edges, with black printed pattern of cherubs and flowers and vines; back
cover: same as the front, except: the cloth triangles are at the top and bottom
left; spine: goldstamped pattern the same as the shelfback extending on to

Binding E for A 4.3.a₃

the cover, with goldstamped 'Democratic Vistas | and other papers | [rule] | Walt Whitman' at top. All edges trimmed. All edges gilded.

Publication: *Scott Library,* no. 23. The title of the *Camelot Series* was changed to the *Scott Library* in February 1892 (see *Bookseller,* 4 February 1892, p. 164). Volumes in the *Scott Library* were first reviewed in the *Athenæum,* 16 April 1892; *Democratic Vistas* was first advertised in the *Scott Library* in the *Bookseller,* 6 August 1892, p. 763. Copies inscribed by owners:

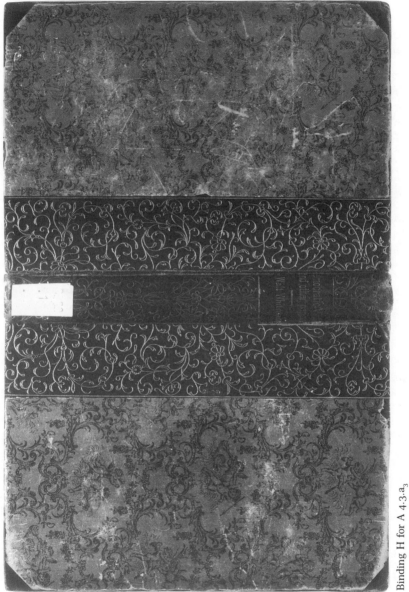

Binding H for A 4.3.a$_3$

binding G: MB (September 1898). Prices: bindings A-F: 1s.; bindings G and H: 4s.

Locations: Binding A: JM; binding B: DLC, JM (2), NNC, NcD, NjP, ViU; binding C: JM; binding D: NzD; binding E: NcD; binding F: NcD, RPB, TxU; binding G: MB; binding H: NjP.

Note one: Copies have an undated 16-page publisher's catalogue inserted at the back, advertising the first 74 volumes in the *Scott Library* (JM [C]) or the first 78 volumes (DLC [B]) or the first 81 volumes (NcD [B]) or the first 83 volumes (JM [B], MB [G], NNC [B], NzD [D], ViU [B]) or the first 113 volumes (JM [B], NjP [B]) or the first 121 volumes (JM [A]) or the first 125 volumes (RPB [F], TxU [F]).

Note two: The only located copy in binding G has a Toronto bookseller's name on the free front endpaper (MB).

Note three: An unbound set of stitched sheets, measuring 6¾″×4⅞″, with top edges trimmed, front and bottom edges uncut, and top edges gilded, is at NcD.

Note four: Copies in binding G were sold as a two-volume set with *Specimen Days in America* (A 11.2.a₄) in a triangular half box (advertised as a "shell case") covered with the same silk brocade as in binding G, priced at 4s. *Location:* MB.

Note five: Advertisements have been noted for a two-volume 'EMERSON | WHITMAN' set bound in silk brocade in a "shell case" for 4s. or bound in roan in a roan case for 6s. The Emerson title is *Selected Essays of Ralph Waldo Emerson;* the Whitman title may be either *Democratic Vistas* or *Specimen Days*.

Note six: Binding G is similar to that used in binding B in the fourth issue of *Specimen Days in America* (see illustration at A 11.2.a₄).

A 4.3.b
Second printing [n.d.]

DEMOCRATIC VISTAS, AND | OTHER PAPERS. BY WALT | WHITMAN. | [*Published by arrangement with the Author.*] | THE WALTER SCOTT PUBLISHING CO., LTD. | LONDON AND FELLING-ON-TYNE. | NEW YORK: 3 EAST 14TH STREET.

The Scott Library, no. 23.

Locations: BBo, CSt, JM.

A 4.3.c
Democratic Vistas, and Other Papers. St. Clair Shores, Mich.: Scholarly Press,
1970.

83 pp. Facsimile reprinting of *Democratic Vistas* only from the second printing
of the English edition (A 4.3.b). Price, $7.50. *Location:* ScCC.

A 4.4
Democratic Vistas and Other Papers. London: George Routledge & Sons; New
York: E. P. Dutton, [1906].

186 pp. Cloth (with dust jacket); or cloth or leather over flexible boards. *The
New Universal Library* and *The Works of Walt Whitman,* vol. 2. Deposit
copies: BL ('28 AP 1906'), BE ('2 OCT 1906'), BO ('8 10 1906'). Copies inscribed by owners: RPB (25 December 1907). *Locations:* BE, BL, BO, JM,
RPB, TxU.

Note: Copies have Routledge's imprint on the spine (BE, BL, BO, JM, RPB)
or with no publisher's imprint (TxU).

A 4.5
First Japanese edition (1948)

Democratic Vistas. Osaka: Kyoiku Tosho Co., 1948.

142 pp. English text on pp. 1–85. Self wrappers. Introduction and notes by K.
Ishibashi. *Standard Authors Series 8. Location:* NcD.

A 4.6.a–b
Democratic Vistas. New York: Liberal Arts Press, 1949.

69 pp. Wrappers. Edited with an introduction by John Valente. *The Little
Library of Liberal Arts,* no. 9. Copyright 1 April 1949; A31481. Deposit copy:
DLC ('APR –5 1949'). Price, 40¢. Reprinted in wrappers in 1949 in *The Li-
brary of Liberal Arts. Locations: Little Library of Liberal Arts:* DLC, JM;
Library of Liberal Arts: TxU.

A 5 PASSAGE TO INDIA
1871

A 5.1.a
First edition, first printing (1871)

Three issues have been noted:

A 5.1.a₁
First issue (1871)

LEAVES OF GRASS.

PASSAGE

to

INDIA.

Gliding o'er all, through all,
Through Nature, Time, and Space,
As a Ship on the waters advancing,
The Voyage of the Soul—not Life alone,
Death—many Deaths, I sing.

Washington, D. C.
1871.

☞ *See* ADVERTISEMENT *at end of this Volume.*

A 5.1.a₁: 8⅛″ × 5″

[i–iii] iv [5] 6–16 [17] 18–24 [25] 26–30 [31] 32–42 [43] 44–52 [53] 54–62 [63] 64–70 [71] 72–86 [87] 88–116 [117] 118–120

[1]¹² 2–5¹². Sheets bulk ¼″.

Contents: p. i: title page; p. ii: copyright page; pp. iii–iv: contents; pp. 5–120: texts of poems.

Poems: "Passage to India," "Thought," "O Living Always—Always Dying!", "Proud Music of the Storm" (prefaced by the poem [*"Again a verse for the sake of you"*]), "Ashes of Soldiers," "In Midnight Sleep," "Camps of Green," "To a Certain Civilian," "Pensive on Her Dead Gazing, I Heard the Mother of All," "When Lilacs Last in the Door-Yard Bloom'd," "O Captain! My Captain!", "Hushed be the Camps To-Day," "This Dust was Once the Man," "Poem of Joys," "To Think of Time," "Chanting the Square Deific," "Whispers of Heavenly Death," "Darest Thou Now, O Soul," "Of Him I Love Day and Night," "Assurances," "Yet, Yet, Ye Downcast Hours," "Quicksand Years," "That Music Always Round Me," "As If a Phantom Caress'd Me," "Here, Sailor!", "A Noiseless, Patient Spider," "The Last Invocation," "As I Watch'd the Ploughman Ploughing," "Pensive and Faltering," "Out of the Cradle Endlessly Rocking," "Elemental Drifts," "Tears," "Aboard, at a Ship's Helm," "On the Beach, at Night," "The World Below the Brine," "On the Beach at Night Alone," "A Carol for Harvest, for 1867," "The Singer in the Prison," "Warble for Lilac-Time," "Who Learns My Lesson Complete?", "Thought" ["Of Justice . . ."], "Myself and Mine," "To Old Age," "Miracles," "Sparkles from the Wheel," "Excelsior," "Mediums," "Kosmos," "To a Pupil," "What Am I, After All," "Others May Praise What They Like," "Brother of All, with Generous Hand," "Night on the Prairies," "On Journeys Through the States," "Savantism," "Locations and Times," "Thought" ["Of Equality . . ."], "Offerings," "Tests," "The Torch," "Gods," "To One Shortly to Die," "Lessons," "Now Finale to the Shore," "Shut Not Your Doors, &c.," "Thought" ["As they draw to a close . . ."], "The Untold Want," "Portals," "These Carols," "This Day, O Soul," "What Place is Besieged?", "To the Reader at Parting," "Joy, Shipmate, Joy!" *Note:* The poems "Ashes of Soldiers" through "Pensive on Her Dead Gazing, I Heard the Mother of All" form the cluster "Ashes of Soldiers"; the poems "Whispers of Heavenly Death" through "Pensive and Faltering" form the cluster "Whispers of Heavenly Death"; the poems "Out of the Cradle Endlessly Rocking" through "On the Beach at Night Alone" form the cluster "Sea-Shore Memories"; the poems "A Carol for Harvest, for 1867" through "To One Shortly to Die" form the cluster "Leaves of Grass"; the poems "Now Finale to the Shore" through "Joy, Shipmate, Joy!" form the cluster "Now Finale to the Shore." See "Index to the Poems in *Leaves of Grass*" for information about the publication histories of individual poems within the various editions, printings, and issues of *Leaves of Grass*.

Typography and paper: 5⅝" (5⅝₁₆")×3³⁄₁₆"; wove paper; various lines per page (up to 41). Running heads: rectos: pp. 7–15: 'PASSAGE TO INDIA.'; pp. 19–23: 'PROUD MUSIC OF THE STORM.'; pp. 27–29: 'ASHES OF SOLDIERS.'; pp. 33–39: 'PRESIDENT LINCOLN'S BURIAL HYMN.'; p. 41: 'MEMORIES OF PRESIDENT LINCOLN.'; pp. 45–51: 'POEM OF JOYS.'; pp. 55–59: 'TO THINK OF TIME.'; p. 61: 'CHANTING THE SQUARE DEIFIC.'; pp. 65–69: 'WHISPERS OF HEAVENLY DEATH.'; pp. 73–85: 'SEA-SHORE MEMORIES.'; pp. 89–113: 'LEAVES OF GRASS.'; p. 115: 'PASSAGE TO INDIA.'; p. 119: 'NOW FINALE TO THE SHORE.'; versos: p. iv: 'CONTENTS.'; pp. 6–16: 'LEAVES OF GRASS.'; pp. 18–40: 'PASSAGE TO INDIA.'; p. 42: 'MEMORIES OF PRESIDENT LINCOLN.'; pp. 44–118: 'PASSAGE TO INDIA.'; p. 120: 'NOW FINALE TO THE SHORE.'.

Binding: Light yellow-green coated stiff wrappers. Front cover: '[flush right] Price, $1.00. | PASSAGE | *to* | INDIA. | Washington, D. C. | 1871. | NEW-YORK: J. S. REDFIELD, PUBLISHER, 140 Fulton Street, (up stairs.)'; back cover: advertisement for *Leaves of Grass, Passage to India,* and *Democratic Vistas,* listing sales agents in Washington, New York, Boston, Brooklyn, and London; spine: vertically: 'PASSAGE TO INDIA.'. White endpapers. Issued uncut.

Printing: See copyright page.

Publication: On 15 March 1870 Whitman asked the printers Andrew and Thomas Rome if the manuscript of the book had arrived safely "last week" (*Correspondence,* II, 94). Whitman announced on 10 October 1870 that he was "just delivered" of the book (II, 116). On 4 February 1874, he wrote a New York bookseller that he should have 18 copies in stock. The inventory of Whitman's belongings made after his death lists nine copies of this edition (DLC).

Deposited for copyright: title, 27 September 1870; book, 8 November 1870; 2258. Listed in *American Literary Gazette and Publishers' Circular,* 1 November 1870. Reviewed in *New York Times,* 11 November 1870, p. 2. Deposit copies: BL ('25AP72'; rebound). Presentation copies: ViU (from Whitman, 4 January 1871). Copies inscribed by owners: TxU (H. Buxton Forman, 22 December 1870). Price, $1.00.

Locations: BBo, BL, CSt, CtY, DLC (4), MBU, MH, NN-R, NNC, NNPM, NcD, TxU (4), ViU.

Back wrapper for A 5.1.a₁

Price, $1.00.

PASSAGE

to

INDIA.

Washington, D. C.
1871.

NEW-YORK: J. S. REDFIELD, PUBLISHER, 140 Fulton St., (up stairs.)

Front wrapper for A 5.1.a₁

Note one: A set of unbound and uncut gatherings, measuring 8 1/6″ × 5″, is at DLC.

Note two: A set of unbound and sewn gatherings, measuring 8⅛″×4⅞″, with the top edges rough trimmed and the front and bottom edges uncut, is at DLC. The last gathering lacks leaves 5_{1-3}, 5_{10-12} (pp. 99–102, 114–120), and the title page reads 'PASSAGE | to | INDIA. | [five lines of verse]'; the other lines are present, but have been canceled in ink. This may have been used as a proof copy for an issue of *Leaves of Grass* or a printing of *Two Rivulets* containing *Passage to India.*

Note three: The book was sold by Trübner in England; as early as 27 December 1873, Whitman was asking the firm for an account of sales (II, 263).

Note four: Sets of proofs in two sheets, measuring 20″×14 ⅝″, are at CtY and MH.

A5.1.a₂
Second issue (1871)

Combined with *Leaves of Grass* in two-volumes-in-one format; see A 2.5.a₂.

A5.1.a₃
Third issue (1872)

Combined with *Leaves of Grass* in two-volumes-in-one format, with cancel title leaf; see A 2.5.b₁.

A5.1.b
First edition, second printing (1872)

Two issues have been noted:

A 5.1.b₁
First issue (1872)

Combined with *Leaves of Grass* in two-volumes-in-one format; see A 2.5.b₁.

Note: Textual alterations are present in this printing; see A 2.5.b₁, *Note three.*

A5.1.b₂
Second issue (1876)

Combined with other works in *Two Rivulets;* see A 9.1.a.

A 5.1.c
First edition, third printing (1876)

Combined with other works in *Two Rivulets;* see A 9.1.b.

A 5.1.d
New York: Haskell House, 1969.

Facsimile reprinting. Advertised as in "Studies in Walt Whitman Series," no. 28. DLC copy received from the publisher 17 November 1969. Price, $9.95. *Locations:* DLC, ScU.

A 5.1.e
New York: Gordon, [n.d.].

Facsimile reprinting listed in *BIP* (1971) for $6.00. *Not seen.*

A 5.2
Second edition, only printing (1872) [i.e., 1873]

Combined with *Leaves of Grass* and *After All, Not to Create Only* in three-volumes-in-one format; see A 2.6.

A 6 AFTER ALL, NOT TO CREATE ONLY
   1871

A 6.1
First edition, only printing [*1871*]

[*PROOFS*—Office American Institute, New York.]

After all, Not to Create only.

[*Recited by* Walt Whitman, *on invitation of Directors American Institute, on Opening of their 40th Annual Exhibition, New York, noon, September 7, 1871.*]

1.

A FTER all, not to create only, or found only,
    But to bring, perhaps from afar, what is already founded,
To give it our own identity, average, limitless, free ;
To fill the gross, the torpid bulk with vital religious fire ;
Not to repel or destroy, so much as accept, fuse, rehabilitate :
To obey, as well as command—to follow, more than to lead ;
These also are the lessons of our New World ;
—While how little the New, after all—how much the Old, Old
    World !

Long, long, long, has the grass been growing,
Long and long has the rain been falling,
Long has the globe been rolling round.

2.

Come, Muse, migrate from Greece and Ionia ;
Cross out, please, those immensely overpaid accounts,
That matter of Troy, and Achilles' wrath, and Eneas', Odysseus'
    wanderings ;
Placard "*Removed*" and "*To Let*" on the rocks of your snowy
    Parnassus :
Repeat at Jerusalem—place the notice high on Jaffa's gate, and
    on Mount Moriah :
The same on the walls of your Gothic European Cathedrals, and
    German, French and Spanish Castles ;
For know a better, fresher, busier sphere—a wide, untried do-
    main awaits, demands you.

A 6.1: 11″ × 8½″

[1] 2–11

Loose sheets, printed on recto only. Sheets bulk ⅟₃₂″.

Contents: pp. 1–11: text.

Typography and paper: 89⁄16″ × 5⅟16″; wove paper; various lines per page (up to 37).

Binding: Head title. Unbound single sheets. All edges trimmed.

Printing: 'PEARSON, PRINTER, WASHINGTON.' (p. 11).

Publication: Not for sale.

Locations: CtY, DLC (2), MH, NN-R, NNC, NNPM, RPB, ScU, TxU (2), ViU (2).

Note one: Some copies have a blank page of the same paper stock as the text at the end, with all pages stitched together (DLC [2], MH, TxU).

Note two: A set of yellow wrappers, measuring 8½″ × 11″, on which "Piece for Am Institute" and "15 copies Aug 5 '71 to Lycett & one extra" is written by Whitman, is at DLC.

A 6.2
Second edition, only printing (1871)

AFTER ALL, NOT TO CREATE ONLY.

Recited by WALT WHITMAN *on Invitation of Managers American Institute, on Opening their 40th Annual Exhibition, New York, noon, September* 7, 1871.

QUI · LEGIT · REGIT

BOSTON:

ROBERTS BROTHERS.

1871.

A 6.2: 7⅞″ × 5″

Entered according to Act of Congress, in the year 1871, by

WALT WHITMAN,

In the Office of the Librarian of Congress at Washington.

CAMBRIDGE:
PRESS OF JOHN WILSON AND SON.

[i–v] vi–vii [viii] [9] 10–24 [25–28]

[1]¹⁴ . Sheets bulk ³⁄₃₂″.

Contents: p. i: 'WALT WHITMAN'S | *AMERICAN INSTITUTE* | POEM.'; p. ii: blank; p. iii: title page; p. iv: copyright page; pp. v–vii: information about the American Institute; p. viii: blank; pp. 9–24: text; pp. 25–26: blank; p. 27: report of Whitman's lecture from the 11 September *Washington Chronicle;* p. 28: resolution of thanks to Whitman from the American Institute.

Typography and paper: 5³⁄₄″ (5½″)×3⁵⁄₁₆″; wove paper; various lines per page (up to 52 for prose, 31 for poetry). Running heads: rectos: pp. 11–23: '*AMERI-CAN INSTITUTE POEM.*'; versos: pp. 10–22: '*WALT WHITMAN'S*'; p. 24: '*WALT WHITMAN'S A. INSTITUTE POEM.*'.

Binding: Two styles have been noted:

Binding A: Dark grayish red or dark green or strong green or reddish orange or medium reddish brown FL cloth (dotted-line-ribbed) covered flexible boards. Front cover: goldstamped '[curved above center ornament] WALT WHITMAN'S | [double-rule circular frame around next three lines, which are in relief on goldstamped radii background] AFTER ALL | NOT TO | CREATE ONLY. | [curved under center ornament] AMERICAN INSTITUTE POEM.'; back cover and spine: blank. Dark brown endpapers coated on one side. All edges trimmed.

Binding B: Dark grayish green S cloth (fine-ribbed); or medium reddish brown or dark green FL cloth (dotted-line-ribbed); beveled edges. Front cover: same as binding A; back cover and spine: blank. Front and back flyleaves; or double front and triple back flyleaves; or triple front and back flyleaves; or front and back flyleaves gathered in fours (see *Note one*) and back flyleaf. White endpapers or endpapers coated brown on one side. All edges trimmed. Top edges plain or gilded. See *Note two.*

Printing: See copyright page.

Publication: On 17 September 1871, Whitman wrote Roberts Brothers that he was sending "the copy" of the poem, adding that it would be "plain sailing" through the press, and asking for "revised proofs" (*Correspondence,* II, 139). The Roberts Brothers records indicate that 2,000 copies were made from stereotyped plates by John Wilson and Son, with printing completed by 24 October (MH). Whitman wrote on 23–24 January 1872 that he had "just got some nice copies" of the book from Boston (II, 156). On 8 February 1874, he wrote to a New York bookseller that he should have two copies of the book in stock (II, 274).

2,000 copies published 24 October 1871; approximately 300 copies were still in sheets in 1889 (see *Note two*). Binding A listed in *American Literary Gazette and Publishers' Circular,* 15 November 1871. Deposited for copyright: title, 3 November 1871; book, 6 November 1871; 10445. Deposit copies: binding A: BL ('7 MY74'). MB copy (rebound) received 3 November 1871. Price, 30¢. Listed in the *English Catalogue* as an importation at 1s.6d.

Locations: Binding A: BL, BMR, BO, CSt, CtY (2), DLC (5), JM (2), MBU (2), MH (3), NN-R, NNC, NNPM, NcD, NjP (2), PU (2), RPB (3), ScU, TxU (5), ViU (2); binding B: BBo, CaOTP, CtY (2), DLC (3), InU-L, MB, NN-R, NcD, NcU, NjCW, NzD, PU (2), TxU (4), ViU.

Note one: In some copies in binding B, the front and back flyleaves and endpapers are gatherings of four, with leaf 1_1 under the front pastedown endpaper, leaf 1_2 the front pastedown endpaper, leaf 1_3 the free front endpaper, and leaf 1_4 the front flyleaf; and leaf 1_1 the back flyleaf, leaf 1_2 the back free endpaper, leaf 1_3 the back pastedown endpaper, and leaf 1_4 under the back pastedown endpaper.

Note two: On 1 May 1889, Whitman noted that David McKay had "the remnant (about 300) . . . which he proposes to bind up and sell as a first edition . . . in solid covers," and Whitman received such a copy on 7 October (*WWWC,* V, 112; VI, 48).

Note three: Whitman said of the front cover: "This is my design—I conceived it" (7 October 1889, in *WWWC,* VI, 48).

A 6.3
Third edition, only printing (1872) [i.e., 1873]

Combined with *Leaves of Grass* and *Passage to India* in three-volumes-in-one format; see A 2.6.

A7 AS A STRONG BIRD ON PINIONS FREE
1872

A7.1.a
Only edition, first printing (1872)

Three issues have been noted:

A 7.1.a₁
First (American) issue (1872)

LEAVES OF GRASS.

As a Strong Bird on

Pinions Free.

AND OTHER POEMS.

WASHINGTON, D. C.
1872.

A 7.1.a₁: 8″ × 4⅝″

Entered, according to Act of Congress, in the year 1872, by

W A L T   W H I T M A N ,

in the Office of the Librarian of Congress, at Washington.

S. W. GREEN, Printer, 16 and 18 Jacob Street, New-York.

[i–v] vi–x [xi–xiv] [1] 2–7 [8] 9–12 [13] 14 [15–18] 1–8 [9–10]

$[1–3]^6 (+3_4) [4]^2$. Sheets bulk ⅛″.

Contents: p. i: title page; p. ii: copyright page; p. iii: contents; p. iv: blank; pp. v–x: "Preface," signed 'Washington, D. C., May 31, 1872.'; p. xi: "One Song, America, Before I Go"; p. xii: blank; p. xiii: "Souvenirs of Democracy"; p. xiv: blank; pp. 1–7: "As a Strong Bird on Pinions Free"; pp. 8–12: "The Mystic Trumpeter"; pp. 13–14: "O Star of France!"; p. 15: "Virginia—The West"; p. 16: "By Broad Potomac's Shore"; pp. 17–18: blank; pp. 1–8: advertisements for Whitman's books; pp. 9–10: blank.

Poems: "One Song, America, Before I Go," "Souvenirs of Democracy," "As a Strong Bird on Pinions Free," "The Mystic Trumpeter," "O Star of France!", "Virginia—The West," "By Broad Potomac's Shore." See "Index to the Poems in *Leaves of Grass*" for information about the publication histories of individual poems within the various editions, printings, and issues of *Leaves of Grass*.

Typography and paper: 5¾″ (5⁷⁄₁₆″)×3⁵⁄₁₆″; wove paper; preface: 37 lines per page; text, various lines per page (up to 37); advertisements, various lines per page. Running heads: rectos: pp. vii–ix: *'PREFACE.'*; pp. 3–7: *'ON PINIONS FREE'*; pp. 9–11: *'THE MYSTIC TRUMPETER.'*; pp. 1–7: *'ADVERTISEMENT.'*; versos: pp. vi–x: *'PREFACE.'*; pp. 2–6: *'AS A STRONG BIRD'*; pp. 10–12: *'THE MYSTIC TRUMPETER.'*; p. 14: *'O STAR OF FRANCE.'*; pp. 2–8: *'ADVERTISEMENT.'*.

Binding: Very dark green V cloth (smooth). Front cover: goldstamped '*As a Strong Bird | on Pinions Free'*; back cover and spine: blank. Front flyleaf with conjugate pasted under front pastedown endpaper and back flyleaf; or double front flyleaves and back flyleaf. Gray or light green endpapers. All edges trimmed or top edges trimmed, front and bottom edges rough trimmed.

Printing: See copyright page.

Publication: On 14 June 1872, twelve days before Whitman was scheduled to delivered this poem at Dartmouth College, he wrote: "I shall print my College Poem in a small book" (*Correspondence*, II, 177). On 12 July, Samuel W. Green signed a receipt acknowledging 572 copies were in stock, and in Whitman's will, dated 23 October 1872, he notes that J. S. Redfield had 400 copies (II, 275n, 118n). Whitman wrote to a New York bookseller on 8 February 1874 that he should have "[?]94" copies of the book in stock and noted that he himself had "somewhere between 300 & 350" copies "bound & ready"; on 8 February, he stated the the number in hand in New York was "perhaps 350" (II, 273; V, 297). The numerous presentation copies from the late 1880s suggest a slow sale for this book. The inventory of Whitman's belongings made after his death lists 57 copies of this book (DLC).

Deposited for copyright: title, 13 July 1872; book, 26 August 1872; 7521. Price, 50¢.

Locations: BBo, BL, BMR, BO, CSt, CtY (2), DLC (14), InU-L, JM, MB, MBU, MH, NN-B (5), NN-R (2), NNC, NNPM, NcD (2), NcU, NjP, NzD, PU (2), RPB, ScU, TxU (4), ViU (3).

Note: The prose commentary on *Leaves of Grass* in the "Advertisement" (pp. 1–4) is attributed to Whitman in Herbert Bergman, "Walt Whitman: Self Advertiser," *Bulletin of the New York Public Library*, 74 (December 1970), 634–639. Earlier, William Rosco Thayer had attributed p. 3 of the advertisements to Whitman ("Personal Recollections of Walt Whitman," *Scribner's Magazine*, 65 [June 1919], 674–687).

LEAVES OF GRASS.

As a Strong Bird on

Pinions Free.

AND OTHER POEMS.

WASHINGTON, D. C.
1872.
LONDON
TRÜBNER & C? 57 & 59 LUDGATE HILL.

A 7.1.a₂: 8″ × 4⅝″

The Trübner imprint is rubberstamped in black.

Binding: Same as in the first issue, except: front flyleaf with conjugate pasted under front pastedown endpaper; gray endpapers; top and bottom edges trimmed, front edges rough trimmed.

Publication: The book was sold by Trübner in England; as early as 27 December 1873, Whitman was asking the firm for an account of sales (II, 263).

Location: TxU.

A 7.1.a₃
Third issue (1876)

Combined with other works in *Two Rivulets;* see A 9.1.a.

A 7.1.b
Only edition, second printing (1876)

Combined with other works in *Two Rivulets;* see A 9.1.b.

A 7.1.c
New York: Gordon, [n.d.].

Facsimile reprinting listed in *BIP* (1972–1984) for $9.95. *Not seen.*

A 8 MEMORANDA DURING THE WAR
1876

A 8.1.a
Only edition, first printing (1876)

Three issues have been noted:

A 8.1.a₁
First issue (1876)

MEMORANDA

During the War.

BY WALT WHITMAN.

——

Author's Publication.
CAMDEN, NEW JERSEY
1875—'76.

A 8.1.a₁: 7⅝″ × 4⅝″

> *Entered according to Act of Congress, in the year* 1875, *by*
> *WALT WHITMAN,*
> *In the Office of the Librarian of Congress at Washington.*
>
> NEW REPUBLIC PRINT.
> Federal St., Camden

Combined with other works in *Two Rivulets;* see A 9.1.a.

[1–3] 4–58 [59] 60–68

[1]⁴ 2–8⁴ [9]² . Sheets bulk ³⁄₁₆″.

Contents: p. 1: title page; p. 2: copyright page; pp. 3–58: text; pp. 59–68: notes.

Typography and paper: text: 6″ (5¹³⁄₁₆″)×3⁵⁄₁₆″; 50 lines per page; notes: 6⅛″ (5¹⁵⁄₁₆″)×3⁵⁄₁₆″; 71 lines per page; wove paper. Running heads: rectos: pp. 5–57: 'DURING THE WAR.'; pp. 61–67: 'NOTES.'; versos: pp. 4–56: 'MEMORANDA'; p. 58: 'MEMORANDA, &c.'; pp. 60–68: 'NOTES.'.

Binding: See *Two Rivulets* (A 9.1.a).

Printing: See copyright page.

Publication: Whitman had written to James Redpath about this book, then called *Memoranda of a Year,* on 21 October 1863, but nothing came of his proposal (*Correspondence,* I, 171–172; see also *WWWC,* IV, 415–418). Whitman announced on 31 July 1875: "I am printing a little book, my War-Hospital *Memoranda* of ten & twelve years since" (*Correspondence,* II, 337). On 2 December 1875, Bonsall and Carse of the New Republic Printing Office gave Whitman a receipt for $400 on account for printing the book (DLC). Whitman wrote on 4 March that the "extra copies . . . not being ready bound, at present, I will send by mail," and on 20 April, Bonsall and Carse gave Whitman a receipt for his payment in full for printing the book (III, 27; DLC). Manuscript notations by Whitman state that 1,000 copies were printed, and that 750 copies were bound by James Arnold of Phildelphia (DLC; *Daybooks,* I, 13–14).

100 copies bound in *Two Rivulets,* which was placed on sale in March 1876.

Locations: See *Two Rivulets* (A 9.1.a).

A 8.1.a₂
Second issue (1876)

Title page is the same as in the first issue. Inserted before the title page are leaves with "Remembrance Copy," Samuel Hollyer engraving printed on verso, W. J. Linton engraving on coated paper printed on recto or verso, and a blank binder's leaf; see *Notes two, three, four, five* and *six*.

Pagination, collation, contents, and typography and paper are the same as in the first issue. Page size: 7¹¹⁄₁₆″×4⅞″.

Binding: Dark purplish red C cloth (sand-grain). Front cover: all within a blindstamped triple-rule frame: goldstamped 'WALT | WHITMAN'S | MEMO-RANDA | OF THE WAR | Written on the Spot | in 1863–'65.'; back cover: blindstamped triple-rule frame; spine: blank. Back flyleaf. Light green stiff endpapers embossed with pattern of flowers on one side. All edges trimmed. All edges gilded.

Printing: Bound by James Arnold, Philadelphia.

Publication: Not sold earlier than April 1876, the date on the verso of the "Remembrance Page." Extracts were printed in *Cincinnati Commercial*, 16 February 1876, and *New York Daily Tribune* and *Philadelphia Press*, both 19 February. On 24 February, the *Philadelphia Times* announced that the book would be out "in about two weeks." Price, $1.50. Originally sold in England for 6s. by Whitman, with friends acting as his agents (see W. M. Rossetti's printed circular, dated 20 May 1876 [PU]). Advertised for sale by Trübner in 1881 in the firm's *Leaves of Grass* at 7s.6d.

Locations: CtY (3), DLC (11), MBU (2), NN-B, NN-R, NNC (2), NcD (2), NjCW, NjP (2), PU, RPB, ScU, TxU, ViU.

Note one: Sets of unbound, unsewn, and uncut gatherings, measuring 8³⁄₁₆″ × 5⅜″, lacking the "Remembrance Page," both pictures, and the advertise-ments in the back, are at DLC and NN-R.

Note two: Most copies are signed by Whitman on the "Remembrance Page" but some are unsigned (CtY, DLC, RPB, TxU).

Note three: The "Remembrance Page" is not present in some copies (MBU, NcD, NjCW, ScU).

Note four: The blank binder's leaf is not present in some copies (CtY, NjCW, TxU).

Note five: There are no pictures present in some copies (DLC, NjCW, ScU).

Note six: The "Remembrance Page," blank binder's leaf, and both pictures are not present in some copies (DLC, MBU, NN-R, NNC, NjP, ViU).

Remembrance Copy.

TO

From

~~~~~~~~~~~~

PERSONAL—NOTE.

Dear Friend :

I do not hesitate to briefly precede your Remembrance-Copy with some biographical facts of myself, I know you will like to have—also, to bind in, for your eye and thought, the little Portraits that follow.

I was born May 31, 1819, in my father's farm-house, at West Hills, L. I., New York State. My parents' folks mostly farmers and sailors—on my father's side, of English—on my mother's, (Van Velsor's,) from Hollandic immigration.

We moved to Brooklyn while I was still a little one in frocks—and there in B. I grew up out of the frocks—then, as child and boy, went to the public schools—then to work in a printing office.†

When only sixteen or seventeen years old, and for two years afterward, I went to teaching country schools down in Queens and Suffolk counties, Long Island, and "boarded round." Then, returning to New York, worked as printer and writer, (with an occasional shy at "poetry.")‡

‡ The picture in shirt-sleeves was daguerreotyped from life, one hot day in August 1855, by my friend Gabriel Harrison, in Fulton St, Brooklyn—and here drawn on steel by McRae:—(was a very faithful and characteristic likeness, at the time.) The final that follows was photographed from life, Washington, 1872, by Geo. C. Potter, here drawn on wood by W. J. Linton.

† There was first and last, a large family of children; (I was the second.) Beside those mentioned above, were my elder brother Jesse, my dear sister Mary, my brother Andrew, and then my youngest brother Edward, (always badly crippled—as I now am of late years.)

"Remembrance Copy" page (recto) for A 8.1.a₂

~~~~~~~~~~~~

PERSONAL—NOTE.

1848–'9.—About this time went off on a leisurely journey and working expedition (my brother Jeff with me,) through all the Middle States, and down the Ohio and Mississippi rivers. Lived a while in New Orleans, and worked there. After a time, plodded back northward, up the Mississippi, the Missouri, &c., and around to, and by way of the great lakes, Michigan, Huron and Erie, to Niagara falls and lower Canada—finally returning through Central New York, and down the Hudson.

1851–'54.—Occupied in house-building in Brooklyn. (For a little of the first part of that time in printing a daily and weekly paper.)

1855.—Lost my dear father, this year, by death.... Commenced putting *Leaves of Grass* to press, for good—after many MS. doings and undoings—(I had great trouble in leaving out the stock "poetical" touches—but succeeded at last.)

1862.—In December of this year went down to the field of War in Virginia. My brother George, reported badly wounded, in the Fredericksburgh fight. (For 1863 and '64, see my *Memoranda* following.)

1865 to '71.—Had a place as clerk (till '74) in the Attorney General's Office, Washington.

(New York and Brooklyn seem more like *home*, as I was born near, and brought up in them, and lived, man and boy, for 30 years. But I lived some years in Washington, and have visited most of the Western and E. stern cities.)

1872.—Took a two months' trip through the New England States, up the Connecticut valley, Vermont, the Adirondack region—and to Burlington, to see my dear sister Hannah once more. Returning, had a pleasant day-trip down Lake Champlain—and, the next day, down the Hudson.

1873.—This year lost, by death, my dear, dear mother—and, just before, my sister Martha—(the two best and sweetest women I have ever seen or known, or ever expect to see.)

Same year, paralyzed. Quit work at Washington, and moved to Camden, New Jersey—where I now (April, 1876) write these lines.

W. W.

"Remembrance Copy" page (verso) for A 8.1.a₂

Note seven: A single leaf, with advertisements for Whitman's books (the same as those in the *Centennial Edition* of the 1876 *Leaves of Grass* [A 2.5.b₂]) printed on the recto, is inserted after the back flyleaf in some copies (CtY [3], DLC [9], MBU [2], NN-B, NN-R, NNC [2], NcD, NjP [2], PU, RPB, TxU, ViU).

Note eight: A bound and trimmed copy at DLC (lacking the "Remembrance Page," pictures, and advertisement) has a note by Traubel on the front flyleaf that the "unbound sheets of this book were received . . . by Walt Whitman" and given by him to Traubel "to be thrown away."

Note nine: A copy at NNPM, bound in half leather, measuring 8 ³⁄₁₆″×5⅜″ (lacking the "Remembrance Page," pictures, and advertisement), has a comment by Laurens Maynard on the front flyleaf that "unbound sheets of this book were rescued" by Whitman and given by him to Traubel "to be thrown away." Since he says that Traubel had "discovered" only "3 sets of sheets," Maynard concludes that copies in publisher's binding of *Memoranda During the War* are scarce due to Whitman's having "[e]conomised on printing & paper" by binding the remaining sheets as part of *Two Rivulets*.

Note ten: Wells and Goldsmith state that it is "improbable that more than 100 copies were issued" (pp. 19–20).

Note eleven: Much of the text of this book was incorporated into *Specimen Days* (A 11), pp. 21–81.

A 8.1.a₃
Third issue (1876)

Combined with other works in *Two Rivulets;* see A 9.1.b.

A 8.1.b
Walt Whitman's Memoranda During the War   Death of Abraham Lincoln.
Bloomington: Indiana University Press, 1962.

48, [v], 68, [xiv], 14 pp. Facsimile reprinting. Boards. Clear plastic dust jacket imprinted on flaps. Boxed. Edited with an introduction by Roy P. Basler. Published 19 April 1962. Reviewed in *Times Literary Supplement,* 2 November 1962, p. 840. Copyright 10 May 1962; A565711. Deposit copies: DLC ('MAY 28 1962'), BO ('–5APR1963'), BL ('15 APR 64'). DLC copy received from the publisher 16 April 1962. Price, $6.95. *Locations:* BL, BO, CaOTU, DLC (2), JM.

Note: One copy has an errata slip tipped in after the copyright page (CaOTU).

A 8.1.c
Walt Whitman's Memoranda During the War   Death of Abraham Lincoln.
Westport, Conn.: Greenwood, [1972].

Facsimile reprinting of A 8.1.b. Price, $9.00. *Location:* MBU.

A 8.1.d
Memoranda During the War. Boston: Applewood, 1990.

Facsimile reprinting of A 8.1.a$_2$. Wrappers. Price, $6.95. *Location:* JM.

A 9 TWO RIVULETS
1876

A 9.1.a
Only edition, first printing (1876)

For the Eternal Ocean bound,
These ripples, passing surges, streams of Death and Life.

TWO

RIVULETS

Including DEMOCRATIC VISTAS, CENTENNIAL
SONGS, *and* PASSAGE TO INDIA.

AUTHOR'S EDITION.
CAMDEN, NEW JERSEY.
1876.

A 9.1.a: 7⅝″ × 4⅝″

> *Entered according to Act of Congress, in the year* 1875, *by*
> **WALT WHITMAN,**
> *In the Office of the Librarian of Congress at Washington.*
>
> NEW REPUBLIC PRINT.
> Federal St., Camden.

[1–5] 6–14 [15] 16–32 [1–3] 4–78 [79] 80–84 [1–3] 4–18 [i–v] vi–x [xi–xiv] [1] 2–7 [8] 9–12 [13] 14 [15–16] [1–3] 4–58 [59] 60–68 [i–iii] iv [5] 6–16 [17] 18–24 [25] 26–30 [31] 32–42 [43] 44–52 [53] 54–62 [63] 64–70 [71] 72–86 [87] 88–116 [117] 118–120. Single leaf with sepia photograph of Whitman by G.F.E. Pearsall pasted on recto is inserted before the title page; see *Notes two* and *three*.

$[1]^4 2-3^4 [4]^4 [1-2]^{12} 3^{12} 4^6 [4a]^4 5^4 [6]^1 [1-2]^6 [3]^6 (-3_{4-6}) [1]^4 2-8^4 [9]^2 [1]^{12} 2-5^{12}$. Blank binder's leaves are inserted after *Two Rivulets, Democratic Vistas, Centennial Songs, As a Strong Bird on Pinions Free,* and *Memoranda During the War.* Sheets bulk ⅞″.

Contents: p. 1: title page; p. 2: copyright page; pp. 3–4: contents; pp. 5–14: preface; pp. 15–32: text of *Two Rivulets;* p. 1: half title for *Democratic Vistas;* p. 2: copyright page; pp. 3–78: text; pp. 79–84: "General Notes"; p. 1: half title for *Centennial Songs;* p. 2: copyright page; pp. 3–18: text; p. i: half title for *As a Strong Bird on Pinions Free;* p. ii: copyright page; p. iii: contents; p. iv: blank; pp. v–x: preface; p. xi: text of "One Song, America, Before I Go"; p. xii: blank; p. xiii: text of "Souvenirs of Democracy" with facsimile signature; p. xiv: blank; pp. 1–16: text; p. i: half title of *Memoranda During the War;* p. 2: copyright page; pp. 3–58: text; pp. 59–68: notes; p. i: half title of *Passage to India;* p. ii: copyright page; pp. iii–iv: contents; pp. 5–120: text. See *Note one* for information on half title pages.

Poems and Prose: Two Rivulets: "Two Rivulets," "Or From That Sea of Time," "Eidólons," "Spain, 1873–'74," "Prayer of Columbus," "Out from Behind this Mask," "To a Locomotive in Winter," "The Ox Tamer," "Wandering at Morn," "An Old Man's Thought of School," "With All Thy Gifts," "From My Last Years," "In Former Songs," "After the Sea-Ship"; *Democratic Vistas* (see A 4); *Centennial Songs—1876:* "Song of the Exposition," "Song of the Redwood-Tree," "Song of the Universal," "Song for All Seas, All Ships"; *As a Strong Bird on Pinions Free* (A 7); *Memoranda During the War* (A 8); *Passage to India* (A 5). See "Index to the Poems in *Leaves of Grass*" for information about the publication histories of individual poems within the various editions, printings, and issues of *Leaves of Grass.*

Typography and paper: *Two Rivulets:* 6¹⁄₁₆″ (5¹³⁄₁₆″) X 3⁵⁄₁₆″; various lines per page (up to 50 for prose, 53 for poems); *Democratic Vistas:* see A 4; *Centennial Songs:*   6¹⁄₁₆″ (5¹³⁄₁₆″)×3⁵⁄₁₆″; various lines per page (up to 45); *As a Strong Bird on Pinions Free:* see A 7; poems: 5¹³⁄₁₆″ (5⁹⁄₁₆″)×3⁵⁄₁₆″; various lines per page (up to 36); *Memoranda During the War:* see A 8; notes: 6¹⁄₈″ (5¹⁵⁄₁₆″) × 3⁵⁄₁₆″; 71 lines per page; *Passage to India:* see A 5; all parts on wove paper. Running heads: rectos: pp. 7–13: '*Preface.*'; pp. 17–31: '*Two Rivulets.*'; pp. 5–83: see A 4; pp. 5–11: '*SONG OF THE E×POSITION.*'; p. 13: '*SONG OF THE REDWOOD-TREE.*'; p. 15: '*CENTENNIAL SONGS.*'; p. 17: '*SONG OF THE UNIVERSAL.*'; pp. vii–11: see A 7; pp. 5–57: see A 8; pp. 7–119: see A 5; versos: pp. 6–14: '*Preface.*'; pp. 16–32: '*Two Rivulets.*'; pp. 4–84: see A 3; pp. 4–16: '*CENTENNIAL SONGS.*'; p. 18: '*SONG FOR ALL SEAS.*'; pp. vi–14: see A 7; pp. 4–68: see A 8; p. iv–120: see A 5.

Binding: Two styles have been noted:

Binding A: Quarter black leather with tan, red, green, and black shell-like marbled paper covered sides. Spine: '[six lines goldstamped] [double rule] | [double rule] | TWO | RIVULETS | [four lines blindstamped] [double rule] | [double rule] | [goldstamped] WHITMAN | [five lines blindstamped] [double rule] | [rule] | [double rule]'. Front and back flyleaves. White endpapers. All edges trimmed. All edges plain or speckle-stained red.

Binding B: Half light brown leather with deep orange S cloth (diagonal fine-ribbed) sides; edges beveled. Spine: goldstamped '[row of vertical lines] | [double rule] | [dark blue leather label with one line] Prose & Verse | [double rule] | [floral design] | [double rule] | [row of vertical lines] | [double rule] | [rule] | [very deep red leather label with two lines] Two | Rivulets | [rule] | [double rule] | [row of vertical lines] | [double rule] | [floral design] | [double rule] | [row of vertical lines] | [double rule] | [floral design] | [double rule] | [row of vertical lines] | [double rule] | [dark blue leather label with one line] Walt Whitman | [double rule] | [floral design] | [double rule] | [double rule] | [dark blue leather label with two lines] *CENTENNIAL* | *Ed'n* —1876. | [double rule] | [row of vertical lines]'. Front flyleaf and double or triple back flyleaves. Light green stiff endpapers embossed with a pattern of flowers or a coarse diaperlike pattern on one side. All edges trimmed. All edges gilded.

Printing: See copyright page. Bound by James Arnold, Philadelphia.

Publication: On 2 May 1875, Whitman announced: "I shall . . . bring out a volume this summer, partly as my contribution to our National Centennial. It is to be called *"Two Rivulets"*— (i.e. two flowing chains of prose and verse, emanating the real and ideal)[.] it will embody much that I had previously written & that you know, but about one third, as I guess, that is fresh" (*Correspondence,* V, 301). Five days later Whitman said, "[the book] is now being put

Binding B for A 9.1.a

into type" (II, 332). On 8 July he noted that he was "leisurely preparing" the book (II, 338). Publication appeared imminent for some time: on 26 November it was "getting ready"; on 17 December it was "nearly ready"; and on 26 January it was "about got ready" (II, 343, 344; III, 20–21). Whitman planned for "only 100 copies [to be] issued" (II, 344). On 4 March 1876, Whitman wrote a friend that he had sent him copies "two or three days" ago (III, 26).

100 copies. *Centennial Edition.* Whitman applied for copyright on 20 De-

cember 1875 (*Correspondence,* II, 345). Copyright 13576. Deposit copies: binding A: DLC ('1875'). Announced as published in *New York Herald,* 2 January 1876. Announced for publication soon in an edition of 100 copies in *Springfield Daily Republican,* 18 January 1876, pp. 4–5. Prepublication extracts were included in *London Daily News,* 11 March 1876, pp. 5–6. Whitman reviewed the book anonymously in *New York Daily Tribune,* 19 February 1876, p. 4 (E 2551), and *Camden New Republic,* 11 March 1876 (E 2552). Reviewed in *Academy,* 9 (24 June 1876), 602–603. Price, $5.00.

Locations: Binding A: DLC, JM (lacks frontispiece); binding B: CtY, DLC (4), MH, NN-B, NN-R, PU, TxU, ViU.

Note one: The following half title pages are present for each section:

(1) '[flush right] *Memoranda.* | DEMOCRATIC | VISTAS. | Washington, D. C. | 1871. | [hand pointing to the right] *See* Advertisement *at the end of this Volume.*' with the last line (binding B: CtY, DLC [3], MH, NN-B, NN-R, PU, TxU, ViU) or the first and last three lines (binding A: DLC, JM) abraded in some copies.

(2) '[two lines in ornate capitals] *CENTENNIAL* | *SONGS—1876.* | Song of the Exposition. | Song of the Redwood-Tree. | Song of the Universal. | Song for All Seas.';

(3) '[flush right] *Leaves of Grass.* | *As a Strong Bird on* | *Pinions Free.* | *AND OTHER POEMS.* | Washington, D. C. | 1872.' with the first line (binding B: DLC) or the first and last two lines (binding A: DLC, JM) abraded in some copies;

(4) 'MEMORANDA | [ornate letters] *During the War.* | *BY WALT WHITMAN.* | [ornate rule] | *Author's Publication.* | CAMDEN, NEW JERSEY | 1875—'76.';

(5) '*Leaves of Grass.* | PASSAGE | *to* | INDIA. | [five lines of verse] | Washington, D. C. | 1872.' with the first line (binding B: DLC) or the first and last two lines (binding A: DLC, JM) abraded in some copies.

BAL notes that "most" sheets of *As a Strong Bird on Pinions Free* have "Advertisement.' abraded in the contents, and that most sheets of *Passage to India* have the heading '*Leaves of Grass.*' abraded on pp. 5, 17, 25, 31, 43, 53, 71, 117 (IX, 40).

Note two: The frontispiece photograph is signed by Whitman 'Walt Whitman born May 31 1819' in all located copies.

Note three: On the sheet on which the frontispiece photograph is mounted is printed: '*Photo'd from life, Sept., '72, Brooklyn, N.Y.* | *by G. F. E. Pearsall, Fulton St.*'.

Photo'd from life, Sept., '72, Brooklyn, N. Y.
by G. F. E. Pearsall, Fulton St.

Frontispiece for A 9.1.a

Note four: The goldstamping on the spine in binding B is erratic, resulting in the rules appearing in various combinations on or off the leather labels. For ease of reporting, only the lettering on the leather labels is given in the description.

Note five: A single leaf, with advertisements for Whitman's books printed on the recto (see illustration at A 2.5.b₂), is inserted between the back flyleaves. The copy at NN-R lacks the advertisment but has the top four lines and the wavy rules around them pasted to the copyright page.

Note six: Whitman's marked copy that was to serve as printer's copy for the English edition is at TxU.

Note seven: A blue silk ribbon marker was originally bound in all copies in binding B.

Note eight: Copies in the *Centennial Edition* binding were originally sold in England for £1 by Whitman, with his friends acting as agents (see W. M. Rossetti's printed circular, dated 20 May 1876 [PU]). Trübner distributed the book in England, reporting on 8 November 1877 that 10 copies had been sold, and on 10 July 1880 that all copies were gone and ordering five more (*Correspondence*, III, 137n, 193n).

Note nine: Whitman has written in a copy at CtY in binding B the information under the frontispiece, crossed out the first and fourth through sixth lines of the *Democratic Vistas* half title page and the first and last two lines of the *Passage to India* half title page, and added instructions to himself and to the printer throughout.

A 9.1.b
Only edition, second printing (1876)

Title page is the same as in the first printing.

This printing is composed of the first printing sheets of *Two Rivulets, Centennial Songs,* and *Memoranda During the War,* with the other works printed from revised plates.

Pagination is the same as in the first printing, except: a blank binder's leaf is not present after *As a Strong Bird on Pinions Free.*

Collation is the same as in the first printing, except: *As a Strong Bird on Pinions Free* collates [1]¹² [2]⁴.

Contents and typography and paper are the same as in the first printing. See *Note one* for information on half title pages.

Binding: Two styles have been noted, priority undetermined:

Binding A: Half cream leather with red, green, black, and white shell marbled paper-covered sides. Spine: blindstamped '[row of vertical lines] | [double rule] | [double rule] | [double rule] | [double rule] | [coarse diaperlike pattern] | [double rule] | [double rule] | [row of vertical lines]' with light brown leather label after second double rule with goldstamped '[double rule] | TWO | *Rivulets* | *Prose & Verse* | [double rule]'. Double front and back flyleaves; or single front and double back flyleaves. Endpapers coated yellow on one side. All edges trimmed.

Binding B: Same as binding A, except: spine label has '*Verse.*'; single back flyleaf or double back flyleaves; white endpapers.

Printing: A copy at PU in binding A has a comment by Harned on the free front endpaper: "Much of the matter in this book was set up by Walt Whitman at the printing office of the 'Post' in Camden." The editor of the *Post,* Harry Bonsall, "extended to him all the facilities of a printing establishment."

Publication: An undated manuscript note by Whitman states that 800 copies were printed, probably of both printings (DLC). On 26 June 1876, Whitman noted that the stock of the first printing had "become exhausted," and he planned to reprint another 650 copies (*Correspondence,* III, 51). On 1 September, he began "to receive from the bindery" (James Arnold of Philadelphia) the first of 600 copies, and he started sending books to friends on the fourth (III, 55, 56; but a letter of 30 August mentions that he is sending a copy [VI, 15]; *Daybooks,* I, 13–14). On 10 December 1881, Whitman stated that between 100 and 200 copies were "on hand" and he sold 20 copies as late as 28 May 1886 (*Correspondence,* III, 256; *Daybooks,* II, 386). The inventory of Whitman's belongings made after his death lists five signed copies of this work and "several boxes" ("not counted") of unsigned copies (DLC). Presentation copies: binding A: DLC (from Whitman, July 1878). Price, $5.00.

Locations: Binding A: BBo, BMR, CSt, CaOTU, CtY (3), DLC (12), InU-L (2), JM (2), MB, MBU (3), MH (2), NN-B (2), NN-R (3), NcD (3), NcU, NjCW (3), PU, RPB (2), ScU, TxU (8), ViU (3); binding B: BO, DLC (2), MH, ViU.

Note one: The following half title pages are present for each section:

(1) 'DEMOCRATIC | VISTAS.';
(2) '[two lines in ornate capitals] *CENTENNIAL | SONGS—1876.* | Song of the Exposition. | Song of the Redwood-Tree. | Song of the Universal. | Song for All Seas.';
(3) '*As a Strong Bird on | Pinions Free. | AND OTHER POEMS.*';
(4) 'MEMORANDA | [ornate letters] *During the War.* | BY WALT WHITMAN. | [ornate rule] | *Author's Publication.* | CAMDEN, NEW JERSEY | 1875—'76.';
(5) 'PASSAGE | *to* | INDIA. | [five lines of verse]'.

Binding A for A 9.1.b

A copy in binding A at PU contains two half titles that differ from those above: (3) '[flush right] *Leaves of Grass.* | *As a Strong Bird on* | *Pinions Free.* | *AND OTHER POEMS.*' with the first line abraded; and (5) '[flush right] *Leaves of Grass.* | PASSAGE | *to* | INDIA. | [five lines of verse]' with the first line abraded. This may be a trial copy prepared for Whitman.

Note two: The frontispiece photograph may be signed by Whitman 'Walt Whitman born May 31 1819' (binding A: BBo, CaOTU, CtY [2], DLC [8], InU-L [2], MBU, MH, NN-B, NN-R, NcD [2], NjCW [2], RPB, TxU [4], ViU [2]; binding B: BO, DLC [2], MH, ViU); or 'Walt Whitman 1880' (binding A: ScU); or 'Walt Whitman 1881' (binding A: MBU); or 'Walt Whitman' (binding A: JM); or be unsigned (binding A: BMR, CSt, CtY, DLC [3], JM, MB, NN-B, NN-R, NcD, PU, RPB, TxU, ViU); or be absent (binding A: DLC, MH, NN-R, NcU, NjCW, TxU [3]).

Note three: On the sheet on which the frontispiece photograph is mounted is printed: '*Photo'd from life, Sept., '72, Brooklyn, N.Y.* | *by G. F. E. Pearsall, Fulton St.* | *(Printed by C. F. Spieler, Phila.)*'.

Note four: A single leaf, with advertisements for Whitman's books printed on the recto (see illustration at A 2.5.c$_1$), is inserted between the back flyleaves.

Note five: A copy at ViU in binding A has a comment on the front endpaper by Traubel, dated July 1904, that "W. W. always autographed the portrait in the copies of this Ed^n Which went out during his lifetime."

Note six: A number of copies have been located inscribed by one of Whitman's literary executors with a note that the copy was found in Whitman's room at his death.

Note seven: The following textual alterations first appear in this printing of *Democratic Vistas:*

7.35	far back]	far-back
14.39	women]	woman
22.25	get]	got
24.37	Spiritual, shall fully appear.]	Spiritual, the aspirational, shall fully | appear.
36.19	Poets]	poets
64.31	is I]	is, I
72.21	price.]	price
76.39	(the |	(of
81.30	Cervantes']	Cervantes

The following textual alterations first appear in this printing of *As a Strong Bird on Pinions Free:*

Photo'd from life, Sept., '72, Brooklyn, N. Y.
by G. F. E. Pearsall, Fulton St.
(Printed by C. F. Spieler, Phila.)

Frontispiece for A 9.1.b

iii.10   [not present]] ADVERTISEMENT.
ix.26   living] lusty
2.13   Modern. . . . . Out] Modern. . : . . Out
2.23   (And yet,] And yet,
2.33   thee.)] thee.

The top part of the colon at 2.13 has been abraded and the parentheses added by hand at 2.23 and 2.33 in some copies.

The following textual alterations first appear in this printing of *Passage to India:*

iv.26   ["To You" listed in contents]] ["To You" not listed in contents]
5.1   [not present]] *LEAVES OF GRASS.*
17.1   [not present]] *LEAVES OF GRASS.*
21.6   lustrous] lustrious
25.1   [not present]] *LEAVES OF GRASS.*
31.1   [not present]] *LEAVES OF GRASS.*
43.1   [not present]] *LEAVES OF GRASS.*
53.1   [not present]] *LEAVES OF GRASS.*
63.1   [not present]] *LEAVES OF GRASS.*
71.1   [not present]] *LEAVES OF GRASS.*
87.4–10   [In all . . . promptly solve.]] [not present]
102.12   the rest,] my mother,
108.1   [above title] [right-pointing hand] *To any . . . anywhere.*] [not present]
117.1   [not present]] *LEAVES OF GRASS.*

A 9. 1.c
Two Rivulets. [Norwood, Penn.]: Norwood Editions, 1979.

Facsimile reprinting of the second printing. Introduction by Gay Wilson Allen. MH copy received 27 June 1980. Price, $65.00. *Locations:* MH, ScU.

Note: Listed in *BIP* (1980) as a publication by Folcroft Library Editions of Folcroft, Penn., for $50.00. No copies have been located.

A 10 LEAVES OF GRASS PREFACE
1881

A 10.1.a
Only edition, presumed first printing (1881)

LEAVES OF GRASS

BY

WALT WHITMAN:

PREFACE

TO THE

ORIGINAL EDITION, 1855.

LONDON:
TRÜBNER & CO.
1881.

A 10.1.a: 9¾" × 6"

[1–3] 4–31 [32]

[1]^8 2^8 . Sheets bulk ³⁄₃₂″.

Contents: p. 1: title page; p. 2: blank; pp. 3–31: text; p. 32: advertisement for Whitman's books.

Typography and paper: 5⅞″×3½″; laid paper watermarked 'HODGKINSON & C⁰', with vertical chain lines 1¼″ apart; 31 lines per page.

Binding: Unsewn gatherings laid into light greenish blue wrappers: front cover recto: '[ornate initial capital] LEAVES OF GRASS. | [rule] | BY | WALT WHITMAN. | PREFACE TO THE ORIGINAL EDITION, 1855. | [floral design] | LONDON: | TRÜBNER & CO.'; front cover verso: advertisement for *Leaves of Grass Preface* and John Macleay Peacock's *Poems;* back cover recto and verso: advertisement for *Papers for the Times;* spine: blank. Top edges trimmed, front and bottom edges uncut.

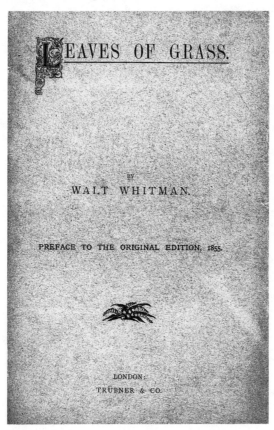

Wrapper for A 10.1.a

Printing: 'HAY, NISBET & Co., Printers, 38 Stockwell Street, Glasgow.' (p. [32]).

Publication: Probably limited to 25 copies; see *Note.* Advertised in 1881 Trübner *Leaves of Grass* as "A few copies have been printed on large paper." Price, 4s.

Locations: BMR, NN-R, TxU (spine repaired).

Note: A copy of the second printing at MBU has the following manuscript notation at the bottom of p. [32]: "Printed for me at the Press of Hay Nisbet & Co, Glasgow, 1881 500 copies Demy 8vo 25 L.P. copies W. Lewin."

A 10.1.b
Only edition, presumed second printing (1881)

Title page, pagination, collation, and contents are the same as in the first printing. Page size 8¾″×5½″. Sheets bulk 3⁄32″.

Typography and paper: Same as in the presumed first printing, except: wove paper.

Binding: Two styles have been noted, priority undetermined:

Binding A: Cover title. Uncut.

Binding B: Light greenish blue paper wrappers printed the same as the wrappers in the presumed first printing. Issued uncut.

Printing: Same as in the presumed first printing.

Publication: Limited to 500 copies. Price, 1s.6d.

Locations: Binding A: BMR, NjP; binding B: CtY, DLC (5), InU-L, JM, MBU, MH, NcD, PU, ScU, TxU (3), ViU (2).

Note one: A one-leaf advertising flier from Trübner, printed on recto, for the trade printing, is at NN-R.

Note two: A one-leaf subscription form from Walter Lewin, printed on recto, for the trade printing, is at NN-R.

A 11 SPECIMEN DAYS & COLLECT
1882

A 11.1.a
First edition, first printing (1882)

Specimen

Days

& collect

By WALT WHITMAN,

Author of " LEAVES OF GRASS."

PHILADELPHIA:

R E E S   W E L S H   &   C O.,

No. 23 SOUTH NINTH STREET.

1882–'83.

A 11.1.a: Binding A: 8½″ × 5⅜″; binding B: 7⅜″ × 4⅞″; binding C: 8⅜″ × 5⅜″

[i–ii] iii–vi 7–376

Two sequences of the illustrations have been noted:

Sequence A:

Single leaf of coated paper with sepia photograph of Whitman and butterfly printed on recto, preceded by a protective tissue, is inserted after p. 122. Noted with bindings A and B only.

Sequence B:

Leaves of plain paper with photographs of Whitman's mother, printed on verso, of Whitman's father, printed on recto, and of Whitman in a broad-brimmed hat (by Gutekunst), printed on recto, all with protective tissues, are inserted after pp. 10, 20, and 198; of coated paper with sepia photograph of Whitman and butterfly, printed on recto, preceded by a protective tissue; is inserted after p. 122. Noted with binding C only.

[1–15]^{12} [16]^6 [17]^2. Signed [1]^8 2^4 3^8 4^4 5^8 6^4 7^8 8^4 9^8 10^4 11^8 12^4 13^8 14^4 15^8 16^4 17^8 18^4 19^8 20^4 21^8 22^4 23^8 24^4 25^8 26^4 27^8 28^4 29^8 30^4 31^8. Sheets bulk 3^1⁄$_{32}$″.

Contents: p. i: title page; p. ii: copyright page; pp. iii–vi: contents; pp. 7–200: '*Specimen Days*'; p. 201: 'COLLECT.'; pp. 202–374: '*Collect;*' pp. 375–376: Rees Welsh advertisement for *Leaves of Grass*.

Poems and Prose: Specimen Days: "A Happy Hour's Command," "Answer to an Insisting Friend," "Genealogy—Van Velsor and Whitman," "The Old Whitman and Van Velsor Cemeteries," "The Maternal Homestead," "Two Old Family Interiors," "Paumanok, and My Life on It as Child and Young Man," "My First Reading—Lafayette," "Printing Office—Old Brooklyn," "Growth—Health—Work," "My Passion for Ferries," "Broadway Sights," "Omnibus Jaunts and Drivers," "Plays and Operas Too," "Through Eight Years," "Sources of Character—Results—1860," "Opening of the Secession War," "National Uprising and Volunteering," "Contemptuous Feeling," "Battle of Bull Run, July, 1861," "The Stupor Passes—Something Else Begins," "Down at the Front," "After First Fredericksburg," "Back to Washington," "Fifty Hours Left Wounded on the Field," "Hospital Scenes and Persons," "Patent-Office Hospital," "The White House by Moonlight," "An Army Hospital Ward," "A Connecticut Case," "Two Brooklyn Boys," "A Secesh Brave," "The Wounded from Chancellorsville," "A Night Battle, Over a Week Since," "Unnamed Remains the Bravest Soldier," "Some Specimen Cases," "My Preparations for Visits," "Ambulance Processions," "Bad Wounds—The Young," "The Most Inspiriting of All War's Shows," "Battle of Gettysburg," "A Cavalry Camp," "A New York Soldier," "Home-Made Music," "Abraham Lincoln," "Heated Term," "Soldiers and Talks," "Death of a Wisconsin Offier," "Hospitals Ensemble," "A Silent Night Ramble," "Spiritual Characters Among the Soldiers," "Cattle Droves About Washington," "Hospital Perplexity," "Down at the Front," "Paying the Bounties," "Rumors, Changes, &c.," "Virginia," "Summer of 1864," "A New Army Organization Fit for America," "Death of a Hero," "Hospital Scenes—Incidents," "A Yankee Soldier," "Union Prisoners South," "Deserters," "A Glimpse of War's Hell-Scenes," "Gifts—Money—Discrimination," "Items from My Note Books," "A Case from Second Bull Run," "Army Surgeons—Aid Deficiencies," "The Blue Everywhere," "A Model Hospital," "Boys in the Army," "Burial of a Lady Nurse," "Female Nurses for Soldiers," "Southern Escapees," "The Capitol by Gas-Light," "The Inauguration," "Attitude of Foreign Governments During the War," "The Weather—Does It Sympathize with These Times?", "Inauguration Ball," "Scene at the Capitol," "A Yankee Antique," "Wounds and Diseases," "Death of President Lincoln," "Sherman's Army's Jubilation—Its Sudden Stoppage," "No Good Portrait of Lincoln," "Releas'd Union Prisoners from South," "Death of a Pennsylvania Soldier," "The Armies Returning," "The Grand Review," "Western Soldiers," "A Soldier on Lincoln," "Two Brothers, One South, One North," "Some Sad Cases Yet," "Calhoun's Real Monument," "Hospitals Closing," "Typical Soldiers," " 'Convulsiveness,' " "Three Years Summ'd Up," "The Million Dead, Too, Summ'd Up," "The Real War Will Never Get in the Books," "An Interregnum Paragraph," "New Themes Entered Upon," "Entering a Long Farm-Lane," "To the Spring and Brook," "An Early Summer Reveille," "Birds Migrating at Midnight," "Bumble-Bees," "Cedar-Apples," "Summer Sights and Indolencies," "Sundown Perfume—Quail-Notes—The Hermit-Thrush," "A July Afternoon by the Pond," "Locusts and Katydids," "The Lesson of a Tree," "Autumn Side-Bits," "The Sky—Days and Nights—Happiness," "Colors—A Contrast," "November 8, '76," "Crows and Crows," "A Winter Day on the Sea-Beach," "Sea-Shore Fancies," "In Memory of Thomas Paine," "A Two Hours' Ice-Sail," "Spring Overtures—Recreations," "One of the Human Kinks," "An Afternoon Scene," "The Gates Opening," "The Common Earth, the Soil," "Birds and Birds and Birds," "Full-Starr'd Nights," "Mulleins and Mulleins," "Distant Sounds," "A Sun-Bath—Nakedness," "The Oaks and I," "A Quinette," "The First Frost—Mems," "Three Young Men's Deaths," "February Days," "A Meadow Lark," "Sundown Lights," "Thoughts Under an Oak—A Dream," "Clover and Hay Perfume," "An Unknown," "Bird-Whistling," "Horse-Mint," "Three of Us," "Death of William Cullen Bryant," "Jaunt Up the Hudson," "Happiness and Raspberries," "A Specimen Tramp Family," "Manhattan from the Bay," "Hu-

America—Shakspere—The Future," "A Memorandum at a Venture," "Death of Abraham Lincoln. Lecture *deliver'd in New York, April 14, 1879—in Philadelphia, '80—in Boston, '81*," "Two Letters" [17 March 1876 to William Michael Rossetti and 20 December 1881 to John Fitzgerald Lee], "Notes Left Over" ("Nationality—[And Yet.], "Emerson's Books, [The Shadows of Them.]," "Ventures, on an Old Theme," "British Literature," " 'Society,' " "The Tramp and Strike Questions," "Democracy in the New World," "Foundation Stages—Then Others," "General Suffrage, Elections, &c.," "Who Gets the Plunder?", "Friendship, [The Real Article.]," "Lacks and Wants Yet," "Rulers Strictly Out of the Masses," "Monuments—The Past and Present," "Little or Nothing New, After All," "A Lincoln Reminiscence," "Freedom," "Book-Classes—America's Literature," "Our Real Culmination," "An American Problem," "The Last Collective Compaction"); *Collect. (Appendix.) Pieces in Early Youth. 1834–'42:* "Dough-Face Song," "Death in the School-Room. *(A Fact.)*," "One Wicked Impulse!", "The Last Loyalist," "Wild Frank's Return," "The Boy Lover," "The Child and the Profligate," "Lingave's Temptation," "Little Jane," "Dumb Kate," "Talk to an Art-Union," "Blood-Money," "Wounded in the House of Friends," "Sailing the Mississippi at Midnight."

Typography and paper: 6¼" (6")×3¹¹⁄₁₆"; wove paper; 45 lines per page. Running heads: rectos: p. v: *'CONTENTS.';* pp. 9–199: *'SPECIMEN DAYS.';* pp. 205–257: *'DEMOCRATIC VISTAS.';* pp. 259–261: *'ORIGINS OF ATTEMPTED SECESSION.';* pp. 263–273: *'PREFACE, 1855.';* pp. 275–279: *'PREFACE, 1872.';* pp. 281–287: *'PREFACE, 1876.';* pp. 289–301: *'POETRY TO-DAY IN AMERICA, &C.';* pp. 303–305: *'A MEMORANDUM AT A VENTURE.';* pp. 307–313: *'DEATH OF ABRAHAM LINCOLN.';* p. 315: *'TWO LETTERS.';* pp. 317–337: *'NOTES LEFT OVER.';* pp. 341–373: *'PIECES IN EARLY YOUTH.';* versos: pp. iv–vi: *'CONTENTS.';* pp. 8–200: *'SPECIMEN DAYS.';* pp. 204–338: *'COLLECT.';* pp. 340–374: *'COLLECT—(Appendix).'.*

Binding: Three styles have been noted, priority undetermined:

Binding A: Unprinted grayish yellow wrappers. White endpapers. Top edges rough trimmed, front and bottom edges uncut.

Binding B: Slightly orange-yellow S cloth (diagonal fine-ribbed). Front cover: goldstamped: single-rule frame around facsimile signature at top; back cover: blank; spine: goldstamped '[four lines in handprinted lettering similar to title page] Specimen | Days | & | collect | [hand with butterfly] | REES WELSH & CO.'. Front and back flyleaves. Light blue vein-pattern endpapers. All edges trimmed.

Binding C: Same as binding B, except: Large Paper format with top edges trimmed, front and bottom edges uncut; top edges gilded.

Printing: Sherman and Company, Philadelphia.

Publication: Whitman first planned what would become *Specimen Days &
Collect* in 1863, when, on 12 October, he wrote the publisher James Redpath:
"Do you want to print a little 30 or 50ct book about the scenes, war, camp,
hospitals &c (especially the &c.)" (*Correspondence, I,* 164). Although Whitman described the book further in a letter of 21 October, nothing came of this
plan (I, 171–172).

When James R. Osgood expressed interest in *Leaves of Grass* in 1882,
Whitman also proposed that they publish another book, "*Specimen Days &
Thoughts*" (III, 269). The firm declined committing to two books by Whitman
at once and, as the censorship battle emerged, nothing more was said of the
book. However, on 20 June 1882, Whitman wrote Rees Welsh (the new publisher of *Leaves of Grass*) to propose the book ("now mostly in MS") at a 22¢
royalty on a $2.00 retail price, and offered to make them exclusive publishers
of it for five years (III, 292). David McKay of Rees Welsh replied the next day
and asked to see the manuscript (PU). Whitman was considering a book of
"about 380 pages" (*Correspondence,* V, 316). Rees Welsh agreed to these
terms for a book of "from 350 to 400 pages" and signed a contract on the 22d
for five years and two months, with Whitman to receive 25 copies from the first
1,000 printed and 12 copies from each succeeding 1,000 printed (PU). On 9
July Whitman wrote that the production process would begin "in about a
week" (*Correspondence,* III, 296). Sherman and Company "commenced type-
setting" on the 19th and on 27 August Whitman noted, "[it] will be all finished
the coming week & the book out ten days afterward" (III, 298, 302). On 3
September it was "all in type & receiving the finishing touches—is to be on the
market the 15th" (III, 303). Whitman wrote on 10 September that it was
"finished," with sheets to go to the binder on the 19th, but not until the 30th
did he call the book "done" (V, 317; III, 305; *Daybooks,* II, 301).

Whitman wrote on 8 October that the first printing was "exhausted in less
than a week" and that the book was "now on the *second*" (*Correspondence,* III,
309). Both the *Critic* of 21 October 1882 and the *Academy* of 18 November
1882 noted that the book had sold out before publication. On 12 November,
David McKay "formally bo't out & assumed" the business of Rees Welsh (this
was announced in *Publishers' Weekly,* 7 October 1882), and his royalty statement to Whitman of 1 December showed that 1,000 copies had been printed
and 925 sold (III, 314; PU).

An advertising slip pasted in a copy in binding B (MB) states that the book
would be ready in September. Extracts appeared in the 10 September *Springfield Republican.* An advertising flier at MB states that the book would be ready
on 15 September. Whitman noted that publication was on 1 October (*Daybooks,* II, 301). Reviewed in *New York Tribune,* 14 October 1882, p. 6. Deposited for copyright: title, 20 September 1882; book, 5 October 1882; 15514.
Deposit copy: binding B: DLC ('OCT 5 1882'). Presentation copies (all from
Whitman): binding B: TxU (4 July 1883); binding C: TxU (1882), ViU (to

Louisa Whitman, 5 October 1882), NjCW (December 1882; lacks spine). Copies inscribed by owners: binding B: BL (22 October 1882), TxU (26 October 1882), CaOTU (11 November 1882). MB copy (rebound) received 25 January 1883. Prices: binding B: $2.00; binding C: $3.00. Listed in the *English Catalogue* as an importation by Trübner in 1883 at 9s., and by Simpkin, as a "New edition" in 1883 at 10s.6d. Reviewed in *Academy*, 22 (18 November 1882), 357–359.

Locations: Binding A: DLC (2), NN-B; binding B: BL, BMR, BO, CSt, CaOTU, CtY, DLC (4), InU-L, JM (2), MB, MBU, MH, NN-B (2), NN-R (2), NNC, NNPM, NcD (2), NcU, NjCW, NjP, PU (2), RPB, TxU (9), ViU (2); binding C: DLC (5), NjCW, PU, TxU (2), ViU.

Note one: A copy at DLC in binding A has Whitman's notes on the title page to delete the comma after his name, the period after 'GRASS", and the Rees Welsh imprint; on p. 376 to change the ordering information in the advertisement from Rees Welsh to David McKay; and for stamping on the front cover and spine. This was probably used as a proof copy for McKay (see A 11.1.b₁).

Note two: A copy at NN-B in binding A is inscribed by Whitman 14 March 1887, and has Rees Welsh's name crossed out on p. 376 and McKay's name inserted in Whitman's hand.

Note three: Inserted in a DLC copy of binding C is a postcard from Whitman, dated 6 November 1882, to the recipient of this volume, sending the book and charging $3.00 for it.

Note four: A broadside advertising circular, printed on the recto, is at DLC.

Note five: An advertising card has been noted (measuring 3⅞"×2³⁄₁₆") printed on the recto of brilliant green paper-covered cardboard stock, probably written by Whitman, reading '[ornate 'T'] THE *price of Walt Whitman's Poems, "LEAVES OF GRASS," (complete, latest, special edition,* | *with autograph), is $3 a copy. Address him, 328 Mickle Street, Camden, New-Jersey. Send p. o.* | *order. He also sells his prose book, "SPECIMEN* | *DAYS AND COLLECT," at $2 a copy.*' (CtY).

Note six: One copy has "Walt Whitman's Books" tipped to the free front endpaper recto (NN-B [B]; see illustration at A 2.7.d–g).

Note seven: A set of sewn, uncut gatherings, measuring 8½"×5¼", lacking the title leaf, is at DLC.

A 11.1.b
First edition, second printing (1882)

Two issues have been noted:

A 11.1.b₁
First issue (1882)

Specimen
Days
& collect

By WALT WHITMAN,

Author of " LEAVES OF GRASS."

PHILADELPHIA:
DAVID McKAY,
No. 23 SOUTH NINTH STREET.
1882–'83.

A 11.1.b₁: 7⅜″ × 4⅞″

[i–ii] iii–vi 7–376 [377–378]

[1–15]¹² [16]¹⁰ . Leaf 16₁₀ is either canceled or pasted under the back endpaper. Signed the same as in the first printing. Sheets bulk 3¹/₃₂″.

Contents: Same as in the first printing, except: pp. 377–378: blank.

Typography and paper: Same as in the first printing.

Binding: Three styles have been noted, priority of the last two undetermined:

> *Binding A:*   Medium olive-brown S cloth (diagonal fine-ribbed). Front cover: goldstamped: single-rule frame around facsimile signature at top; back cover: blank; spine: goldstamped '[four lines in handprinted lettering similar to title page] Specimen | Days | & | collect | [hand with butterfly] | DAVID MꟼKAY'. Front flyleaf. Light green floral-pattern endpapers printed on one side. All edges trimmed. See *Note two.*

> *Binding B:*   Same as binding A, except: slightly orange-yellow S cloth (diagonal fine-ribbed); goldstamped at the foot of the spine is 'Dᴀ-ᴠɪᴅ • Mᴄ • Kᴀʏ • '; front and back flyleaves. See *Note two.*

> *Binding C:*   Same as binding A, except: slightly orange-yellow S cloth (diagonal fine-ribbed); light blue hair-vein endpapers; goldstamped at the foot of the spine is 'DAVID Mᶜ KAY'.

Publication: On 12 November 1882, David McKay announced that he had "formally bo't out & assumed" the business of Rees Welsh (*Correspondence,* III, 314); a formal notice to that effect had appeared in *Publishers' Weekly,* 7 October 1882. McKay's royalty statement to Whitman of 1 June 1883 shows that an additional 1,172 copies had been printed by that date (PU). McKay sold 394 copies of the second printing by 20 October 1891 (royalty statement, PU). Advertised in *New-York Daily Tribune,* 11 November 1882. Presentation copies: binding A: DLC (from Whitman, 3 November 1884). Copies inscribed by owners: binding A: RPB (13 December 1882). Price, $2.00. Listed as an importation by Trübner at 9s. in *Athenæum,* 27 January 1883.

Locations: Binding A: BE, DLC (6), JM, MB, NN-B, NN-R (2), NcD (2), NcU, NzD, RPB, ScU (2), TxU (2); binding B: CtY, JM, ScU, ViU; binding C: CtY, PU.

Note one: The advertisement for *Leaves of Grass* on pp. 375–376 lists Rees Welsh as the publisher.

Note two: Copies in binding A are identical to the earliest form of McKay's bindings for *Leaves of Grass,* which he also took over from Rees Welsh and published simultaneously with *Specimen Days.* Copies in binding B are identical to the later form of McKay's binding for *Leaves of Grass* used in 1884 and

1888. Of the 1,172 copies printed by 1 June 1883, 460 were apparently bound at once and 172 were left in sheets on that date; this number had dwindled to 134 by 1 March 1888. These remaining sheets were probably bound before the next printing, done before 8 October 1888 (royalty statements, PU).

Note three: A broadside advertising poster for McKay, measuring 20½″ × 17¾″, printed in black and orange, is at NNC.

A 11.1.b₂
Second issue (1888)

By WALT WHITMAN,

Author of "LEAVES OF GRASS."

PHILADELPHIA:

DAVID McKAY,

No. 23 SOUTH NINTH STREET.

1882–'88.

A 11.1.b₂: 7⅜″ × 4⅞″

$[1]^{12} (\pm 1_1) [2-15]^{12} [16]^{10}$. Title leaf is a cancel. Leaf 16_{10} may be pasted under the rear endpaper. Single leaf of coated paper with sepia photograph of Whitman and butterfly printed on verso is inserted after p. 122.

Binding: Slightly orange-yellow S cloth (diagonal fine-ribbed). Front cover: goldstamped: single-rule frame around facsimile signature at top; back cover: blank; spine: goldstamped '[four lines in handprinted lettering similar to title page] Specimen | Days | & | collect | [hand with butterfly] | DAVID • Mc • KAY • '. Front flyleaf. Light blue vein-pattern endpapers printed on one side. All edges trimmed.

Publication: Copies inscribed by owners: TxU (25 December 1889).

Locations: JM, MH, TxU.

Note one: The advertisement for *Leaves of Grass* on pp. 375–376 lists Rees Welsh as the publisher.

Note two: A copy at DLC measures 8½"×5¾", bulks 1 ⅜", and is bound in green, pink, yellow, and red Spanish marbled paper wrappers, edges uncut, in 476 pp. It includes the texts of *Specimen Days* and pp. 39–140 ("Our Eminent Visitors" through "George Fox and Shakespeare") of *November Boughs,* along with the contents page from *Complete Prose Works* (1892) tipped in and the material listed after *November Boughs* crossed out. *November Boughs* has been repaginated and 'NOVEMBER BOUGHS.' appears at the head of the text on p. 375.

Note three: McKay's royalty statement to Whitman of 8 October 1888 shows 1,000 copies printed by that date and left in sheets (these may have included the ones used in *Complete Poems & Prose* [see A 11.1.d]). No copies of *Specimen Days* with an '1888' date on the title page have been located. His subsequent royalty statements through 20 October 1891 indicate that no copies were bound or sold. McKay's royalty statement of 6 April 1892 shows 1,160 copies still in stock, but his statement of 30 September 1898 shows only 47 copies in stock (DLC).

A 11.1.c
Third (American) printing for Scottish sale (1883)

Specimen

Days

& collect

By WALT WHITMAN

Author of "LEAVES OF GRASS"

GLASGOW

WILSON & McCORMICK, Saint Vincent Street

1883

A 11.1.c: 8¼″ × 5″

Two states have been noted:

First state:

[a–b] [i–ii] iii–vi 7–376 [377–378]. Single leaf of coated paper with sepia photograph of Whitman and butterfly printed on verso is inserted before the title page.

[a]^1 [1–15]^{12} [16]^8 (16$_{8+1}$). The half title and the leaf containing the Wilson & McCormick advertisement for *Leaves of Grass* are tipped in.

Contents: p. a: '*Specimen Days | and Collect*'; p. b: blank; p. i: Scottish title page; p. ii: blank; pp. iii–376: same as in the first issue; p. 377: Wilson & McCormick advertisement for *Leaves of Grass;* p. 378: blank.

Second state:

[a–b] [i–ii] iii–vi 7–374 [375–376]. Single leaf of coated paper with sepia photograph of Whitman and butterfly printed on verso is inserted before the title page.

[a]^1 [1–15]^{12} [16]^8 (–16$_8$, 16$_{7+1}$). The leaf containing the David McKay advertisement for *Leaves of Grass* has been canceled; the half title and the leaf containing the Wilson & McCormick advertisement for *Leaves of Grass* are tipped in.

Contents: p. a: '*Specimen Days | and Collect*'; p. b: blank; p. i: Scottish title page; p. ii: blank; pp. iii–374: same as in the first state; p. 375: Wilson & McCormick advertisement for *Leaves of Grass;* p. 376: blank.

Binding: Two styles have been noted, priority assumed:

Binding A: Medium olive-brown or slightly orange-yellow S cloth (diagonal fine-ribbed). Front cover: goldstamped facsimile signature in center; back cover: blindstamped facsimile signature in center; spine: goldstamped '[double rule] | *Specimen | Days | BY | Walt Whitman* | [double rule]'. Light brown endpapers coated and printed with a dark brown geometric pattern on one side. Top and bottom edges trimmed, front edges rough trimmed; or all edges trimmed.

Binding B: Slightly orange-yellow S cloth (diagonal fine-ribbed). Front cover: goldstamped facsimile signature in center; back cover: blank; spine: goldstamped '[double rule] | [four lines in handwriting similar to title page] Specimen | Days | & | collect | [rule] | WALT WHITMAN | [rule] | WILSON & MＣCORMICK | [double rule]'. Light brown endpapers coated and printed with a dark brown geometric pattern on one side; or light brown floral design endpapers. Issued uncut.

Publication: On 11 January 1883, Whitman wrote that the book had been "republished in Scotland," and on 27 June, he noted that Wilson and McCormick were the publishers and that sales were "somewhat sluggish yet" (*Correspondence*, III, 323, 344). Advertised for "next week" by Wilson & Mc-

Cormick in *Publishers' Circular and Booksellers' Record,* 15 February 1883.
BAL reports advertisements by Trübner, Alexander Gardner, and Simpkin,
Marshall (IX, 45). Deposit copies: second state: BO ('16OCT1885'). McKay's
royalty statement to Whitman of 1 June 1883 shows 500 copies for "exportation" (PU). Whitman received 11¢ each for copies sent abroad. Price, 10s.6d.

Locations: First state: binding A: BMR, DLC, JM, NNC, NcD (2), NzD;
second state: binding A: BO; binding B: BBo, BMR, CSt, CtY, DLC (2), JM
(2), NN-B, NN-R, NcU, NzD, PU (2), RPB (2), ViU.

Note: The following textual alterations first appear in this printing:

71.6	seen]	seem
149.40	are in]	are on
167.35	*and in*]	*in ana*
174.23	century]	century,
175.40	at any reconstruct,]	it, any reconstruct
176.15	continuous-immutable]	unseen but immutable
178.24	see]	saw
197.42	motion;]	emotion;
199.29	by my own life-afternoon now]	by own life's afternoon having
200.28	certainly]	morbidly
209.top	*VISTAS.*]	*VISTA*
210.1	(namely.]	namely,
258.19	*some*]	*same*
259.38	forming of]	forming, of
288.1	SHAK–]	SHAK
321.37	attribute]	attributes
372.2	*(A Brooklyn fragment.)*]	*(Extracts—1839—Long Island.)*
[376]	[advertisement lists David McKay]]	[advertisement lists Rees Welsh]

Note three: Between 1882 and 20 October 1891, Rees Welsh and McKay sold
1,319 copies of *Specimen Days* bringing Whitman a royalty (at 22¢ each) of
$290.18. Another 500 sets of sheets were sold for export sale, bringing Whit-
man an additional royalty (at 11¢ each) of $55.00.

A 11.1.d
First edition, fourth printing (1888)

Combined with other works in *Complete Poems & Prose;* see A 2.7.m, where a
list of variant readings between the third and fourth printings is given.

Note: A set of the sheets of *Specimen Days* used in *Complete Poems & Prose*
(with the plates reimposed to make gatherings of eights), has the advertise-

ment on pp. 375–376 listing McKay as the publisher (DLC); this sheet is canceled in all bound copies of the book.

A 11.2.a
Second (English) edition, first printing (1887)

Four issues have been noted:

A 11.2.a₁
First issue (1887)

SPECIMEN DAYS

IN AMERICA

BY WALT WHITMAN

NEWLY REVISED BY THE AUTHOR, WITH FRESH PREFACE
AND ADDITIONAL NOTE

———•———

LONDON
WALTER SCOTT, 24 WARWICK LANE
PATERNOSTER ROW
1887

A 11.2.a₁: 6⅞″ × 4½″

[i–v] vi–x [xi–xii] [13] 14–312 [313–320]

[a]⁸ 273–291⁸. Sheets bulk ¹³⁄₁₆″.

Contents: p. i: '[gothic] The Camelot Series | EDITED BY ERNEST RHYS. | SPECIMEN DAYS IN AMERICA.'; p. ii: blank; p. iii: title page; p. iv: blank; pp. v–x: contents; pp. xi–xii: Whitman's 'PREFACE. TO THE READER IN THE BRITISH ISLES.'; pp. 13–309: texts; pp. 310–312: 'ADDITIONAL NOTE. *Written* 1887 *for the English Edition*.'; pp. 313–320: advertisements for Scott's publications.

Prose: "Preface. To the Reader in the British Isles," text of *Specimen Days* only, "Additional Note. *Written* 1887 *for the English Edition*."

Typography and paper: 5⅜″ (5⅛″)×3⁵⁄₁₆″; wove paper; 33 lines per page. Running heads: rectos: pp. vii–ix: '*CONTENTS*.'; pp. 15–311: '*IN AMER-ICA*.'; versos: pp. vi–x: '*CONTENTS*.'; pp. 14–312: '*SPECIMEN DAYS*'.

Binding: Three styles have been noted, priority undetermined:

Binding A: Very red B cloth (linen). Front cover: blackstamped '[two lines in upper left corner] The Camelot Series. | [ornate headress design] | [bottom right corner] [urn and dish]'; back cover: blank; spine: '[three lines black-stamped] [double rule] | [dotted line] | [six lines goldstamped] [rule] | Speci-men Days | in America | [rule] | Walt Whitman | [rule] | [eight lines black-stamped] *CAMELOT* | *SERIES* | [urn] | [double rule] | WALTER SCOTT | [double rule]'. White laid endpapers. Issued uncut. See *Note three*.

Binding B: Blackish blue B cloth (linen). Front and back covers: blank; spine: white paper label with '[all within a single-rule red frame] | Camelot Series | [rule] | SPECIMEN | DAYS IN | AMERICA | [rule] | BY | WALT WHITMAN'. White wove or laid endpapers. Issued uncut.

Binding C: Reddish brown leather shelfback with dark yellow S cloth (di-agonal fine-ribbed) sides. Front and back covers: blank; spine: goldstamped '[double rule] | [design] | [double rule] | Specimen Days | in America | [rule] | Walt Whitman | [double rule] | [design] | [double rule] | [design] | [double rule] | [design] | [double rule] | design] | [double rule]'. Red nonpareil mar-bled endpapers. All edges trimmed. Top edges gilded.

Printing: '*Printed by* WALTER SCOTT, *Felling, Newcastle-on-Tyne*' (p. 312).

Publication: On 13 October 1886, Whitman wrote to Ernest Rhys, who was acting on behalf on Walter Scott: "I am willing you should print 'Specimen Days' in your series" (*Correspondence,* IV, 52). Rhys replied on 19 January 1887 that Scott would pay ten guineas (£10.10s.) for the book (IV, 52n). On 2 February, Whitman sent Rhys a copy "with emendations" and put forward a plan: "My notion would be for you to print a Vol. including all to page 200, and call it '*Specimen Days in America—By Walt Whitman*' " (VI, 36). On 8 March, he sent to Rhys "a little Preface" that "might make two pages" (VI, 38). He received payment from Scott on 14 March (*Daybooks*, II, 413). On 11 May, Whitman asked Rhys to send him 50 copies, "two or three of them in y'r good leather binding," and on 17 June, Whitman received "56 and 5" copies (*Correspondence*, VI, 40; *Daybooks*, II, 427). Rhys reported on the 24th that the book was in the bookstores (*Correspondence*, IV, 98n).

Extracts were printed in *Pall Mall Gazette*, 27 April 1887. Reviewed in *Academy*, 4 June 1887. Deposit copies: BL ('4JU87'; rebound); binding A: BO ('12JUN.88'), BC ('18 JUL 88'). Copies inscribed by owners: binding A: JM (1 August 1887); binding B: TxU (June 1887), BBo (July 1887), TxU (29 July 1887), DLC (16 September 1887), CSt (21 September 1887), TxU (20 February 1888). MB copy (binding B) received 5 July 1898. Prices: bindings A and B: 1s.; binding C: 3s.

Locations: Binding A: BC, BO, CaOTU, JM (4), MH, NcD, RPB, TxU (2), ViU; binding B: BBo, BMR, CSt, CtY (2), DLC (2), JM (4), MB, MBU, NcD (3), NjP, PU, RPB, ScU, TxU (5), ViU; binding C: NjCW.

Note one: Also advertised in red roan at 4s.; *BAL* notes having seen a copy in "leather" (IX, 47), which may be of this binding.

Note two: A copy of the first edition, second printing (A 11.1.b), at TxU is bound in full leather with binding B (olive) bound in at end, with a two-page manuscript inscription by H. Buxton Forman, dated 10 January 1892: "This is the copy prepared by Walt Whitman and sent to Ernest Rhys for publication in England. . . . The 'fresh preface and additional note' which appear in the Camelot book were sent separately to Rhys written upon four quarto leaves, with instructions that the note should follow page 200."

Note three: Binding A is similar to that used in binding A of the first issue of *Democratic Vistas, and Other Papers* (see illustration at A 4.3.a₁).

A 11.2.a₂
Presumed second issue (1888)

Combined with *Democratic Vistas, and Other Papers* in two-volumes-in-one format as *Prose Writings of Walt Whitman;* see A 4.3.a₂.

A 11.2.a₃
Presumed third (Canadian) issue (1888)

SPECIMEN DAYS

IN AMERICA

By WALT WHITMAN

NEWLY REVISED BY THE AUTHOR, WITH FRESH PREFACE
AND ADDITIONAL NOTE

———•———

TORONTO:

W. J. GAGE & CO.

1888.

A 11.2.a₃: 6⅝″ × 4⅝″

[i–v] . . . 14–312

Binding is too tight to permit collation.

Contents: Same as pp. i–312 in the first printing, first issue.

Typography and paper: Same as in the first printing.

Binding: Very dark red leather shelfback with dark red, gold, black, and white Spanish marbled paper sides. Spine: goldstamped 'SPECIMEN | DAYS | IN AMERICA | [rule] | WHITMAN'. Flyleaves. Marbled endpapers the same as the covers. Top and bottom edges trimmed, front edges rough trimmed. Top edges gilded.

Printing: 'Printed by WALTER SCOTT, *Felling, Newcastle-on-Tyne*' (p. 312).

Location: JM.

A 11.2.a₄
Fourth issue [not before 1892]

Title and copyright pages are the same as in the first issue.

Four states have been noted, priority undetermined:

First state:

[iii–v] . . . 14–312 [313–314]

[a]^8 ($-a_1$) 273–291^8 ($-291_{5-6,8}$). See *Note one.*

Contents: pp. iii–xi, 13–312: same as in the first issue; pp. 313–314: advertisements for Scott's publications.

Second state:

[iii–v] . . . 14–312 [313–316]

[a]^8 ($-a_1$) 273–291^8 (-291_{5-6}). See *Note two.*

Contents: pp. iii–xi, 13–312: same as in the first issue; pp. 313–316: advertisements for Scott's publications.

Third state:

[iii–v] . . . 14–312 [313–314]

[a]^8 ($-a_1$) 273–291^8 (-291_{5-7}). See *Note three.*

Contents: pp. iii–xi, 13–312: same as in the first issue; pp. 313–314: advertisements for Scott's publications.

Fourth state:

[iii–v] . . . 14–312

[a]^8 (–a$_1$) 273–291^8 (–291$_{5-8}$). See *Note four.*

Contents: pp. iii–xi, 13–312: same as in the first issue.

Binding: Three styles have been noted, priority undetermined:

> *Binding A:*   Dark olive-green S cloth (diagonal fine-ribbed). Front cover: goldstamped 'THE | Scott | Library' in upper left, with three parallel vertical lines 1¼″ from spine, and 1″ high triangles of ornamental design with triple parallel lines at bottom in top and bottom right corners; back cover: blank; spine: goldstamped 'Specimen Days | in America | Walt Whitman | Walter Scott'. Laid or wove endpapers. All edges trimmed. Top edges gilded. See *Note eight.*

> *Binding B:*   Dark olive-green S cloth (diagonal fine-ribbed) shelfback with light blue, dark blue, and gold silk brocade-covered boards. Front cover: cloth with goldstamped 'T', short rules pattern, and leaf-and-vine design extending ⅞″ from spine, with cloth with goldstamped leaf-and-vine design extending 1¼″ in at top and bottom right corners in an irregular shape; back cover: same as the front, except the cloth corners are at the top and bottom left; spine: goldstamped pattern the same as the shelfback extending on the covers, with goldstamped '[rule] | Specimen Days | in America [[rule] | Walt Whitman | [rule]' at top. Front and back endpapers of silk brocade with black floral pattern on one side. All edges trimmed. All edges gilded.

> *Binding C:*   Very deep red S cloth (diagonal fine-ribbed) shelfback with silk brocade-covered boards. Front cover: cloth with goldstamped leaf-and-vine design with single goldstamped rule at right, extending 1⅛″ from spine, with ⅜″ high unstamped cloth triangles at the top and bottom edges, with black printed pattern of cherubs and flowers and vines on gold silk brocade background; back cover: same as the front, except: the cloth triangles are at the top and bottom left; spine: goldstamped pattern the same as the shelfback extending on to the cover, with goldstamped '[rule] | Specimen Days | in America | [rule] | Walt Whitman | [rule]' at top. All edges trimmed. All edges gilded. See *Note eight.*

Publication: *The Scott Library,* no. 22. The title of the *Camelot Series* was changed to the *Scott Library* in February 1892 (see *Bookseller,* 4 February 1892, p. 164). Volumes in the *Scott Library* were first reviewed in the *Athenæum,* 16 April 1892; *Specimen Days in America* was first advertised in the *Scott Library* in the *Publishers' Circular and Booksellers' Record,* 2 April 1892, p. 295. Prices: binding A: 1s.6d.; bindings B–C: 4s.

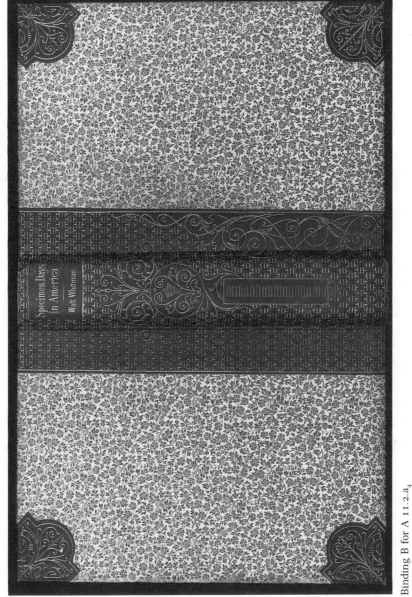

Binding B for A 11.2.a₄

Locations: First state: binding A: RPB; second state: binding A: CtY, NN-R, PU (2); binding B: MB; third state: binding A: JM; fourth state: binding A: NzD, PU; binding C: FPeU.

Note one: In the first state, the leaves containing the *Camelot Series* half title and all the advertisements except *For a Song's Sake* (p. 313) and *Gladys the Singer* (p. 314) have been canceled.

Note two: In the second state, the leaves containing the *Camelot Series* half title and all the advertisements except *For a Song's Sake* (p. 313), *Gladys the Singer* (p. 314), *The Land of the Vikings* (p. 315), and *Conduct and Duty* (p. 316) have been canceled.

Note three: In the third state, the leaves containing the *Camelot Series* half title and all the advertisements except *The Land of the Vikings* (p. 313) and *Conduct and Duty* (p. 314) have been canceled.

Note four: In the fourth state, the leaves containing the *Camelot Series* half title and all the advertisements have been canceled.

Note five: Some copies have an undated 16-page catalogue of Scott's publications inserted at the back advertising the first 76 volumes in the *Scott Library* (CtY, PU [both state 2, binding A]) or the first 81 volumes (JM [state 3, binding A], MB [state 2, binding B], NN-R [state 2, binding A], PU [state 2, binding A], RPB [state 1, binding A]) or the first 100 volumes (PU [state 4, binding A]) or the first 103 volumes (NzD [state 4, binding A]).

Note six: Copies in the second state in binding B were sold as a two-volume set with *Democratic Vistas, and Other Papers* (A 4.2.a³) in a triangular half-box (advertised as a "shell case") covered with the same silk brocade as in binding B, priced at 4s. *Location:*   MB.

Note seven: Advertisements have been noted for a two-volume 'EMERSON | WHITMAN' set bound in silk brocade in a "shell case" for 4s. or bound in roan in a roan case for 6s. The Emerson title is *Selected Essays of Ralph Waldo Emerson;* the Whitman title may be either *Specimen Days* or *Democratic Vistas.*

Note eight: Binding A is similar to that used in binding B of the second issue of *Democratic Vistas, and Other Papers,* and binding C is similar to that used in binding H of the second issue of *Democratic Vistas, and Other Papers* (see illustrations at A 5.3.a₄).

A 11.2.b
Second printing [1902]

Specimen Days in America. | By Walt Whitman. | REVISED BY THE AUTHOR, | WITH FRESH PREFACE AND | ADDITIONAL NOTE. | THE

WALTER SCOTT PUBLISHING CO., LTD., | LONDON AND NEW-CASTLE-ON-TYNE.

The Camelot Series or *The Scott Library,* no. 22. Printing: 'THE WALTER SCOTT PUBLISHING CO., LTD., NEWCASTLE-ON-TYNE. | 11-02' (p. 312); publisher's code probably indicates November 1902 printing date.

Locations: *Camelot:* CSt, RPB, TxU; *Scott:* BBo, CaOTU, CtY, NcU, PU, ScU.

A 11.3.a
Specimen Days in America. London: George Routledge & Sons; New York: E. P. Dutton, [1906].

317 pp. Cloth (with dust jacket); leather; leather over flexible boards; or cloth over flexible boards. *The New Universal Library* and *The Works of Walt Whitman,* vol. 1. Published March 1906. Deposit copies: BL ('28 AP 1906'), BO ('27 8 1906'). Prices: cloth, 1s; leather, 2s. *Locations:* BL, BO, JM, TxU.

Note: Copies have been noted with Routledge's imprint on the spine (BL, BO, JM) or with no publisher's imprint (TxU).

A 11.3.b
London: Humphrey Milford, Oxford University Press, [1931].

Dust jacket. *The World's Classics,* no. 371. Published September 1931. Deposit copies: BL ('7 OCT 31'), BO ('12OCT1931'), BC ('15 OC 1931'), BE ('19 OCT 1931'). Prices: 2s. or 80¢. *Locations:* BC, BE, BL, BO, MBU.

A 11.4
Specimen Days, Democratic Vistas, and Other Prose. Garden City, N.Y.: Doubleday, Doran, [1935].

370 pp. Dust jacket. Edited with an introduction by Louise Pound. *Doubleday-Doran Series in Literature.* Copyright A83447; received 1 June 1935. Published 20 May 1935. Deposit copy: DLC ('JUN –1 1935'). Price, $1.00. *Locations:* DLC, JM.

A 11.5
Walt Whitman in Camden. Camden, N.J.: Haddon Craftsmen, 1938.

45 pp. Burlap. Boxed. Introduction by Christopher Morley. Photographs by Arnold Genthe. Published 19 December 1938. Copyright A125241; received, 23 December 1938. Deposit copies: DLC ('DEC 23 1938'; 2 copies). MH copy received 18 February 1939. Limited to 1,100 copies. Price, $10.00. *Locations:* DLC (2), JM, MH, TxU.

Note: Some copies have a printed Christmas greeting from the Haddon Craftsmen tipped in (JM, TxU).

A 11.6
Specimen Days. [New York]: New American Library, [1961].

[271] pp. Wrappers. Foreword by Richard Chase. *A Signet Classic CP 104.* Copyright 6 December 1961; A546432. Published December 1961. Price, 60¢. *Locations:* JM, NcU.

A 11.7.a
Specimen Days. Boston: David R. Godine, 1971.

197 pp. Dust jacket. Boxed. Edited by Lance Hidy. Introduction by Alfred Kazin. Deposit copy: BO ('29JAN1973'). Reviewed in *Library Journal,* 96 (15 November 1971), 3761. Copyright 7 July 1971; A278719. Limited to 1,250 copies printed on laid paper with facsimile signature watermark. Price, $35.00. *Locations:* BO, CtY, JM, TxU.

Note: Some copies have a label pasted at the bottom of the back flap (over the information that copies can be ordered from Godine or Small Publishers' Company) containing the information that copies can be ordered from Godine or Barre Publishers (CtY, TxU).

A 11.7.b
Boston: David R. Godine, 1971.

Cloth (with dust jacket) or wrappers. MH copy (cloth) received 12 September 1972. 2,500 copies bound in cloth and 2,500 in wrappers. Prices: cloth, $25.00; paper, $10.00. *Locations:* MH, JM (both).

A 11.8
Specimen Days in America. London: Folio Society, 1979.

253 pp. Boxed. Introduction by Gavin Ewart. Deposit copies: BL ('16 AUG 79'), BO ('28FEB1980'), BE ('4 AP 80'). Price, £6.95. *Locations:* BE, BL, BO, JM.

A 12 NOVEMBER BOUGHS
1888

A 12.1.a
Only edition, first printing (1888)

Two issues have been noted:

A 12.1.a₁
First (American) issue (1888)

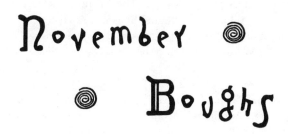

BY WALT WHITMAN

PHILADELPHIA
DAVID McKAY, 23 South Ninth Street
1888

A 12.1.a₁: Bindings A–B: 9″×6″; Bindings C–F: 8 ⅞″×6″

Copyright page: '[short rule] | Copyright, 1888, by WALT WHITMAN. | [short rule]'.

[1–2] 3–140 [141–144]. Inserted leaf of coated paper, with photograph of Whitman in his seventieth year, printed on verso, followed by protective tissue, is positioned before the title page.

[1]⁸ 2–3⁸ [4]⁸ 5–9⁸ (9₆₊₁, –9₈). Single leaf with advertisements is tipped to the verso of leaf 9₆; leaf 9₈ is canceled. Sheets bulk ¹⁵⁄₃₂″.

Contents: p. 1: title page; p. 2: copyright page; pp. 3–4: contents; pp. 5–18: "A Backward Glance O'er Travel'd Roads"; pp. 19–38: "Sands at Seventy"; pp. 39–42: "Our Eminent Visitors"; pp. 43–46: "The Bible as Poetry"; pp. 47–49: "Father Taylor (and Oratory.)"; pp. 50–51: "The Spanish Element in Our Nationality"; pp. 52–54: "What Lurks Behind Shakspere's Historical Plays?"; pp. 55–56: "A Thought on Shakspere"; pp. 57–64: "Robert Burns as Poet and Person"; pp. 65–67: "A Word About Tennyson"; pp. 68–72: "Slang in America"; pp. 73–75: "An Indian Bureau Reminiscence"; pp. 76–79: "Some Diary Notes at Random"; pp. 80–85: "Some War Memoranda"; p. 86: "Five Thousand Poems"; pp. 87–92: "The Old Bowery"; pp. 93–96: "Notes to Late English Books"; pp. 97–99: "Abraham Lincoln"; pp. 100–104: "New Orleans in 1848"; pp. 105–108: "Small Memoranda"; pp. 109–117: "Last of the War Cases"; p. 118: "Portrait in Old Age"; pp. 119–140: "Elias Hicks"; p. 141: advertisements for Whitman books published by McKay; pp. 142–144: blank.

Typography and paper: 6¼″ (6″)×3⅝″; wove paper; 45 lines per page. Running heads: rectos: pp. 7–17: 'O'ER TRAVEL'D ROADS.'; pp. 21–37: 'SANDS AT SEVENTY.'; p. 41: 'OUR EMINENT VISITORS.'; p. 45: 'THE BIBLE AS POETRY.'; p. 49: 'FATHER TAYLOR (AND ORATORY.)'; p. 51: 'THE SPANISH ELEMENT IN OUR NATIONALITY.'; p. 53: 'WHAT LURKS BEHIND SHAKSPERE'S PLAYS?'; pp. 59–63: 'ROBERT BURNS AS POET AND PERSON.'; p. 67: 'A WORD ABOUT TENNYSON.'; pp. 69–71: 'SLANG IN AMERICA.'; p. 75: 'AN INDIAN BUREAU REMINISCENCE.'; pp. 77–79: 'SOME DIARY NOTES AT RANDOM.'; pp. 81–85: 'SOME WAR MEMORANDA.'; pp. 89–91: 'THE OLD BOWERY.'; p. 95: 'NOTES TO LATE ENGLISH BOOKS.'; p. 99: 'ABRAHAM LINCOLN.'; pp. 101–103: 'NEW ORLEANS IN 1848.'; p. 107: 'SMALL MEMORANDA.'; pp. 111–117: 'LAST OF THE WAR CASES.'; pp. 121–139: 'ELIAS HICKS.'; versos: p. 4: 'CONTENTS.'; pp. 6–16: 'A BACKWARD GLANCE.'; p. 18: 'A BACKWARD GLANCE O'ER TRAVEL'D ROADS.'; pp. 20–38: 'SANDS AT SEVENTY.'; pp. 40–42: 'OUR EMINENT VISITORS.'; pp. 44–46: 'THE BIBLE AS POETRY.'; p. 48: 'FATHER TAYLOR (AND ORATORY.)'; p. 54: 'WHAT LURKS BEHIND SHAKSPERE'S PLAYS?'; p. 56: 'A THOUGHT ON SHAKSPERE.'; pp. 58–64: 'ROBERT BURNS AS POET AND PERSON.'; p. 66: 'A WORD ABOUT TENNYSON.'; pp. 70–72: 'SLANG IN AMERICA.'; p. 74: 'AN INDIAN BUREAU REMINISCENCE.'; p. 78: 'SOME

DIARY NOTES AT RANDOM.'; pp. 82–84: 'SOME WAR MEMORANDA.'; pp. 88–92: 'THE OLD BOWERY.'; pp. 94–96: 'NOTES TO LATE ENGLISH BOOKS.'; p. 98: 'ABRAHAM LINCOLN.'; pp. 102–104: 'NEW ORLEANS IN 1848.'; pp. 106–108: 'SMALL MEMORANDA.'; pp. 110–116: 'LAST OF THE WAR CASES.'; p. 118: 'PORTRAIT IN OLD AGE.'; pp. 120–140: 'ELIAS HICKS.'.

Binding: Six styles have been noted, priority of the first two and the last four undetermined.

Binding A: Presentation binding: very deep red V cloth (smooth) over flexible boards. Front cover: goldstamped 'WALT WHITMAN'S | NOVEMBER BOUGHS | [ornate rule]'; spine: goldstamped from bottom to top 'NOVEMBER BOUGHS' [measuring 4½"]. Front flyleaf. Wove endpapers. Top edges rough trimmed, front and bottom edges uncut. See *Note three.*

Binding B: Presentation binding the same as binding A, except: front cover: goldstamped 'WALT WHITMAN'S | [flush left] NOVEMBER | [flush right] BOUGHS'; issued uncut. See *Note three.*

Binding C: Very deep red V cloth (smooth); beveled edges. Front cover: goldstamped at top '[handlettered] November [concentric circle design] | [concentric circle design] [handlettered] Boughs | [facsimile signature]' with goldstamped ornate 'D McKay' at bottom right; back cover: blank; spine: goldstamped from bottom to top: '[ornate letters] NOVEMBER BOUGHS' [measuring 4 ⁵⁄₁₆"]. Front flyleaf. White wove or white coated endpapers. All edges trimmed. Top edges gilded.

Binding D: Same as binding C, except: edges not beveled; no flyleaves or laid front flyleaf; laid front and wove back endpapers; all edges trimmed, or top edges trimmed and front and bottom edges rough trimmed.

Binding E: Same as binding C, except: the spine has goldstamped horizontal triple rules at the top and bottom; wove or laid front flyleaf, or double front flyleaves placed between front endpapers, or front and back flyleaves; white laid front and wove back endpapers, or white endpapers; top and front edges trimmed, bottom edges rough trimmed; or all edges trimmed, top edges plain or gilded.

Binding F: Very deep red V cloth (smooth); beveled edges. Front cover: goldstamped at top in plain lettering 'NOVEMBER | BOUGHS | [facsimile signature]'; back cover: blank; spine: goldstamped in plain lettering from bottom to top: 'NOVEMBER BOUGHS' [measuring 4½"]. Front flyleaf. White endpapers. Top and bottom edges trimmed, front edges rough trimmed. Top edges gilded.

Printing: Ferguson Brothers, Philadelphia.

Publication: Whitman wrote on 16 March 1886 that he planned to "scoop up what I have (poems and prose) of the last MSS since 1881 and '2, & put in probably 200 page book (or somewhat less) to be called perhaps *November Boughs*" (*Correspondence*, IV, 22; also substantially repeated on 26 August 1886, IV, 46). By 24 March 1887 Whitman was "think[ing] of pub.," and on 14 June he announced: "I want to have [it] out before '87 closes" (IV, 77, 100). He was still "gathering" material for the book by 17 August, and on 22 September, replying to someone who had sent him $5.00 for a copy, he noted that it was still "contemplated" though "not printed yet" (IV, 117, 123). After another hiatus, Whitman stated on 8 April 1888: "I feel lately as if I sh'd make a start in putting [the book] in type making perhaps 150 to less than 200 pp." (IV, 160).

Preparations began in earnest on 22 May 1888, when Whitman wrote: "I want to have printed (stereotyped) a book of (probably) 160 to 200 pages." His "copy" was "ready—it is all printed matter—(or nearly all)—is all plain sailing—you could commence next Monday" (*Correspondence*, IV, 171). By the 25th, he was negotiating with the Philadelphia printer George Ferguson to set type (*WWWC*, I, 205). He later suggested printing 1,000 copies, with pictures of Elias Hicks and "my own bust" (7 July 1888, *Correspondence*, IV, 182–183). Over the next four months, Whitman sent regular bulletins to friends about the progress of the book, concluding on 19 September that it was "all done printed & press'd & waits the binding" (*Daybooks*, II, 464, 471; see *Correspondence*, IV, 173, 178, 179, 182, 188, 189, 192, 193, 195, 197, 198, 200, 202, 211, 213). To help sales, Whitman wanted a price of $1.25, "or better still $1" (IV, 200).

Even though a notice of the book, with extracts from the Hicks article, appeared in the 17 September *New York Herald,* publication was delayed because Whitman considered himself "obligated not to print" the book until after the appearance of the October *Century Magazine* containing his "Army and Hospital Cases" (which had been "accepted & paid" two years ago) and which would be reprinted in *November Boughs* (IV, 194). He did apply for copyright on 11 September and received it on the 22d (*Daybooks*, II, 471; McKay sent two copies to the Librarian of Congress for copyright on 23 November 1890 [II, 577]). On 22 September, he wrote: "I expect to get a specimen copy . . . from the binder this evening" (*Correspondence*, IV, 214; for his receipt of them on that date, see *WWWC*, II, 360). The *Century* came out on 1 October and Whitman declared "now the coast is clear": the book was "all printed & the sheets are at the binder's" (*Correspondence*, IV, 217). On 6 October, he wrote Bucke that he should have received his copy, which he mailed, along with others, on the seventh (IV, 218–219; *Daybooks*, II, 474).

There was some discussion about the binding. Earlier, Bucke had suggested that "a good idea would be to print a hundred or two hundred copies on good (and large) paper, bind them nicely and sell them *yourself* for $5. or even $10. with autograph, by & by publish through McKay or another" (*Correspondence,*

IV, 194–195n). When Horace Traubel had arrived with a specimen copy, "bound for sample," on 22 September, Whitman gave "an order or two changing the lettering on the cover, &c." (IV, 214). On 9 October, Whitman reported that McKay "wants a different binding," considering the "binding I have" to be "coarse & cheap," to which Whitman assented, "very likely." Whitman agreed with McKay, but "at his seeing [to] & expense" (IV, 221). On 22 October 1888, Whitman ordered the binder Frederick Oldach to proceed with binding the books with the casings McKay had wanted (and would pay for), "except for 100 copies wh' I will pay you" (IV, 225). On the next day, Whitman announced that the book "comes out in two or three days" (IV, 226). That same day, McKay agreed to purchase 950 copies for $313.50, with Whitman receiving an additional 50 books "for editor's copies"; in return, McKay had the right to reprint the book for three years, with Whitman receiving a 12¢ royalty on each copy sold (memorandum written by Whitman and signed by McKay, PU). Yet according to Whitman, the printing was 1,100 copies (with 950 for McKay, 50 for review, and 100 for Whitman) (*Correspondence*, IV, 228).

By 16–17 February 1889, Whitman stated that "over 700 have been sold" (*Correspondence*, IV, 291). The inventory of Whitman's belongings made after his death shows bound copies and copies in sheets "not counted" (DLC). As late as February–April 1896, Oldach was still binding copies (see receipts, DLC).

Deposited for copyright: title, 12 September 1888; book: 24 November 1890; 25926. Deposit copies: binding C: DLC ('NOV 24 1890'); binding E: BL ('6SE89'). Reviewed (in "flexible dark red covers") in *Boston Evening Transcript*, 17 October 1888, p. 5. A copy in binding B has inserted in it a letter from Traubel, dated 15 October 1888, stating, "I despatch a copy *November Boughs* this mail" (DLC). Presentation copies (all from Whitman): binding A: DLC (to Traubel, 22 September 1888), CtY (to Louisa Whitman, October 1888); binding B: DLC (to Bucke, 4 October 1888), DLC (6 October 1888), JM (to Harned, 6 October 1888), NN-B (to O'Connor, 7 October 1888), CtY (13 October 1888), CtY (17 October 1888), DLC (to his sister Mary E. Van Nostrand, 22 October 1888), DLC (26 October 1888), DLC (October 1888; 4 copies), ViU (to Stedman, October 1888), TxU (10 November 1888), TxU (7 December 1888), DLC (4 January 1889), NN-B (6 January 1889), DLC (20 April 1889), DLC (23 September 1889), TxU (22 May 1890); binding D: RPB (19 December 1889); binding E: NN-R (28 October 1888), DLC (25 December 1888), PU (31 January 1889). Copies inscribed by owners: binding C: PU (25 December 1891); binding E: CSt (January 1891). Prices: bindings A and B: not for sale; bindings C–F: $1.25.

Locations: Binding A: CtY, DLC; binding B: CtY (2), DLC (15), JM, NN-B (2), PU, TxU (3), ViU; binding C: CaOTP, InU-L, JM, MB, NN-R, PU, TxU (2), ViU; binding D: BMR, CtY, JM, MH, RPB; binding E: BL, CSt, CaOTU,

DLC (2), JM, MBU, NN-B, NN-R (2), NNC, NNPM, NcD, NjCW, NjP (3), PU (2), RPB, ScU, TxU (3); binding F: MBU.

Note one: A set of unbound, unsewn, and uncut gatherings, measuring 9¼″ × 6¹⁄₁₆″, inscribed by Whitman to Traubel, 10 September 1888, without the frontispiece or inserted advertisement, is at DLC.

Note two: A copy at ViU in binding B has a comment by Traubel, 21 May 1911, on the front flyleaf, stating "bound in rejected cover. At first sure that this cover was the one he wished Walt got more & more skeptical till he adopted the stiffer boards afterwards."

Note three: Oldach bound only 100 copies in flexible boards, after which, at Traubel's suggestion, stiff boards were used and the lettering from the title page was copied on the front cover (6 October 1888, in *WWWC*, II, 440 [though on 15 October the figure is given as 65 (see II, 483)], 441).

Note four: A set of final page proofs, on wove paper measuring 11¼″×7⅞″, with a paper label on which Whitman has written 'Proof plates   printed sheets | *Nov: Boughs* | 140 pp. complete | [flush left] Oct: 1 '88' is at CtY.

November Boughs

BY WALT WHITMAN.

ALEXANDER GARDNER,
Publisher to Her Majesty the Queen,
PAISLEY; AND PATERNOSTER ROW, LONDON.
1889

A 12.1.a₂: 9″×6″

[1–2] 3–140. Inserted leaf of coated paper, with photograph of Whitman in his seventieth year, printed on verso, followed by protective tissue, is positioned before the title page.

$[1]^8 (\pm 1_1) 2–3^8 [4]^8 5–9^8 (–9_{7–8})$. Title leaf is a cancel.

Contents: p. i: Scottish title page; p. ii: blank; pp. 3–140: same as in the first issue.

Binding: Very deep red V cloth (smooth); beveled edges. Front cover: goldstamped '[handlettered] November [concentric circle design] | [concentric circle design] [handlettered] Boughs | [facsimile signature]'; back cover: blank; spine: goldstamped from bottom to top '[triple horizontal rules] | [ornate letters] NOVEMBER BOUGHS' [measuring 49⁄16″] | [triple horizontal rules]'. White endpapers or endpapers coated black on one side. All edges trimmed. Top edges gilded.

Publication: On 19 November 1888, Whitman noted that an order for 250 copies had arrived from Scotland, and by 3–4 December he had received a proof of the Scottish title page (*Correspondence*, IV, 235, 241). McKay sent 250 copies "in sheets" to Scotland on 17 November 1888 (*WWWC*, III, 113). Copies inscribed by owners: BBo (2 January 1888 [i.e., 1889]), PU (2 January 1889), PU (January 1889). Listed in *Athenæum*, 22 December 1888. Reviewed in *Pall Mall Gazette*, 25 January 1889, p. 3. Deposit copies: BL ('14MY89'), BO ('4–JUN.89'). Price, 7s.6d.

Locations: BBo (2), BE, BL, BO, CtY, DLC (2), JM, NN-R, NcD, NcU, NzD (2), PU (3), TxU, ViU.

A 12.1.b
Only edition, second printing (1888)

Combined with other works into *Complete Poems & Prose;* see A 2.7.m.

Note: Duplicate plates for "Sands at Seventy" (pp. 19–38) were repaged 385–404 and used as the first annex to copies of *Leaves of Grass* published in 1888 and later (see A 2.7.l₁).

A 12.1.c
Only edition, third printing (1888) [i.e., 1891]

The title page is the same as in the first printing, bearing the date '1888'.

[1–2] 3–140 [141–142]

$[1]^8 2–3^8 [4]^8 5–9^8$. Leaf 9₈ is pasted under the rear pastedown endpaper. Page size: 9⅛″×6⅛″. Sheets bulk ½″.

Contents: Same as in the first printing, except: p. 141: advertisements for Whitman books published by McKay; p. 142: blank.

Typography and paper: Same as in the first printing, except: laid paper with vertical chain lines 13/16″ apart.

Binding: Very deep green V cloth (smooth); beveled edges. Front cover: goldstamped at top: '[handlettered] November [concentric circle design] | [concentric circle design] [handlettered] Boughs | [facsimile signature]'; back cover: blank; spine: goldstamped from bottom to top: '[ornate letters] NOVEMBER BOUGHS'. Laid or wove front flyleaf or no flyleaves. White wove or laid endpapers; or white wove front endpapers and laid back endpapers. Issued with front and bottom edges uncut. Top edges gilded. See *Note one.*

Printing: Ferguson Brothers, Philadelphia.

Publication: On 19[?] May 1891, Whitman acknowledged an order from McKay for 400 copies and reserved for himself "100 the little double vol: | N B & G B bound (as to be made)"; this would leave McKay 300 copies of *November Boughs/Good-Bye, My Fancy* in sheets, for which he was to pay Whitman 40¢ a set (*Correspondence,* VI, 56). On 22 May, he wrote the printer George Ferguson: "If the paper is bo't & any commencem't made in printing the 400 'Nov: Boughs' all right—If nothing, *stop it* & wait for further orders" (V, 202). Sometime in May, Whitman received a bill from Ferguson for printing 400 copies (*Daybooks,* II, 581). Whitman's plans for a one-volume edition of *November Boughs* and *Good-Bye My Fancy* for distribution to his friends ended with his death, but his executors most likely carried out his wishes by binding up sheets from the 1891 printings of each book in green cloth in a large-paper format. Not for sale.

Locations: BBo, BL, BO, CaOTU, CtY, DLC (7), InU-L, JM (2), MB, MH (2), NN-B, NNC, NcD (2), NcU, NjCW (4), PU (3), RPB, ScU, TxU (4), ViU.

Note one: The copy at RPB has a note in Traubel's hand that this "edition" was made by Whitman "for his personal friends & never put upon the market." Likewise, a copy at DLC has a note in Traubel's hand: "Whitman's private edition. Made only for his friends. Never put on the market." The copy at CtY has a similar note.

Note two: Sets of unbound, unsewn, and uncut gatherings, measuring 9⅝″ × 6⅜″, are at DLC (inscribed by Whitman to Traubel, 25 May 1891) and CtY (inscribed by Whitman, 1891).

Note three: A set of proof sheets with Whitman's label designating them "first proof sheets" is at NNC.

Note four: The following textual alterations first appear in this printing:

6.33   *mèlée*]   *m lée*
11.3   least]   last

Note five: The corrected plates for "A Backward Glance O'er Travel'd Roads" (pp. 5–18) were used to print the final pages of the 1889 *Leaves of Grass* (A 2.7.n); they were repaginated 425–438 and used to print the final section in the 1891–1892 *Leaves of Grass* (see A 2.7.l₂ and A 2.7.o).

Note six: The plates for pp. 39–140 were repaginated 375–476 and used in *Complete Prose Works* (C 6).

A 13 GOOD-BYE MY FANCY
1891

A 13
Only edition, only printing (1891)

Good-Bye

My Fancy

2D ANNEX TO LEAVES OF GRASS

PHILADELPHIA
DAVID McKAY, PUBLISHER
23 SOUTH NINTH STREET
1891

A 13: Binding A: 8⅞″×5¾″; Bindings B–C: 9½″ X 6¼″

Copyright page: 'COPYRIGHT 1891 | BY WALT WHITMAN | *All rights reserved*'.

[1–2] 3–66. Inserted leaf of coated paper, with photograph of Whitman in 1891, printed on verso, followed by a protective tissue, is positioned before the title page; see below. This leaf is not present in some copies.

[1]^8 2–3^8 [4]^8 (4$_{8+1}$). Sheets bulk 7/32".

The frontispiece has been noted in three styles, priority undetermined:

> *Style 1:*   No caption under photograph.

> *Style 2:*   Caption under photograph in facsimile of Whitman's script: 'Walt Whitman | 1891'.

> *Style 3:*   Caption under photograph in facsimile of Whitman's script: 'Walt Whitman | [two lines within a pair of parentheses] sculptor's profile | May 1891'.

Contents: p. 1: title page; p. 2: copyright page; pp. 3–4: contents; pp. 5–6: "Preface Note to 2d Annex"; pp. 7–20: "Good-Bye My Fancy"; pp. 21–23: "An Old Man's Rejoinder"; pp. 24–28: "Old Poets"; pp. 29–34: "American National Literature"; pp. 35–36: "Gathering the Corn"; pp. 37–38: "A Death-Bouquet"; pp. 39–44: "Some Laggards Yet"; pp. 45–66: "Memoranda."

Poems and Prose: "Prefatory Note to 2d Annex," "Sail Out for Good, Eidólon Yacht," "Lingering Last Drops," "Good-Bye my Fancy," "On, on the Same, ye Jocund Twain," "My 71st Year," "Apparitions," "The Pallid Wreath," "An Ended Day," "Old Age's Ship & Crafty Death's," "To the Pending Year," "Shakespere–Bacon's Cipher," "Long, Long Hence," "Bravo, Paris Exposition!", "Interpolation Sounds," "To the Sun-set Breeze," "Old Chants," "A Christmas Greeting," "Sounds of the Winter," "A Twilight Song," "When the Full-grown Poet Came," "Osceola," "A Voice from Death," "A Persian Lesson," "The Commonplace," " 'The Rounded Catalogue Divine Complete,' " "Mirages," "L. of G.'s Purport," "The Unexpress'd," "Grand is the Seen," "Unseen Buds," "Good-Bye my Fancy," "An Old Man's Rejoinder," "Old Poets" (includes "Ship Ahoy!" and "For Queen Victoria's Birthday"), "American National Literature," "Gathering the Corn," "A Death-Bouquet," "Some Laggards Yet" ("The Perfect Human Voice," "Shakspere for America," " 'Unassail'd Renown,' " "Inscription for a Little Book on Giordano Bruno," "Splinters," "Health, [Old Style.]," "Gay-Heartedness," "As in a Swoon," "L. of G.," "After the Argument," "For Us Two, Reader Dear"), "Memoranda" (includes "A World's Show," "New York—The Bay—The Old Name," "A Sick Spell," "To the Present Only," " 'Intestinal Agitation,' " " 'Walt Whitman's Last "Public," ' " "Ingersoll's Speech," "Feeling Fairly," "Old Brooklyn Days," "Two Questions," "Preface" [to O'Connor's *Three Tales*], "An Engineer's Obituary," "Old Actors, Singers, Shows, &c., in New York," "Some Personal and Old-

Age Jottings," "Out in the Open Again," "America's Bulk Average," "Last Saved Items"). See "Index to the Poems in *Leaves of Grass*" for information about the publication histories of individual poems within the various editions, printings, and issues of *Leaves of Grass*.

Typography and paper: 6¼″ (6″)×3⅝″; laid paper with vertical chain lines ¹³⁄₁₆″ apart; 45 lines per page. Running heads: rectos: pp. 9–19, 23–27, 31–33, 41–43, 47–65: 'GOOD-BYE MY FANCY.'; versos: p. 4: 'CONTENTS.'; p. 6: 'PREFACE NOTE TO 2d ANNEX.'; pp. 8–22, 26–66: 'GOOD-BYE MY FANCY.'.

Binding: Three styles have been noted, priority assumed:

Binding A: Very deep red V cloth (smooth); beveled edges. Front cover: goldstamped '[two lines in handlettering] Good-Bye | My Fancy | [facsimile signature]' and goldstamped ornate 'D McKay' at bottom right; back cover: blank; spine: goldstamped from bottom to top 'GOOD-BYE MY FANCY' (see *Note one*). No flyleaves; wove or laid flyleaves; wove or laid front flyleaves; laid front and wove back fyleaves; or wove front and laid back flyleaves. White endpapers. All edges trimmed. Top edges gilded.

Binding B: Very deep red V cloth (smooth); beveled edges. Front cover: goldstamped '[two lines in handlettering] Good-Bye | My Fancy | [facsimile signature]'; back cover: blank; spine: goldstamped from bottom to top 'GOOD-BYE MY FANCY'. White coated flyleaves. White coated endpapers. Top edges plain or gilded. See *Note two*.

Binding C: Same as binding B, except: very deep green V cloth (smooth); wove flyleaves, or laid front and wove back flyleaves, or front flyleaf of coated white paper and laid back flyleaf; white coated or wove or laid endpapers; top edges trimmed, front and bottom edges uncut; top edges gilded or stained red. See *Note three*.

Printing: Ferguson Brothers, Philadelphia.

Publication: On 5 September 1890, Whitman announced his plans for "an appendix to November Boughs"; by 3 November this had become "a collected appendix," and nine days later he wrote, "Shall call my little 2d annex 'Good Bye my Fancy' after a little piece in it," and he felt he could "possibly print it Spring or before" (*Correspondence*, V, 80, 112–113, 116). Work progressed slowly: on 1–2 January 1891, Whitman was "putting some little licks" in on the book, and on 18 May he called the proofs "essentially done & pass'd in" (V, 193). On 14 May he sent a set of unbound sheets to Bucke; he also sent unbound sheets on 17 May to six other people, and a set of "stitched sheets unb'd" to another person on the 20th (V, 193, 200; *Daybooks*, II, 594; *Correspondence*, V, 201). He wrote Ferguson on 22 May that the "*press work*" was "first rate" (V, 202).

Whitman applied for copyright on 18 May 1891 (VI, 56). The next day, he acknowledged an order from McKay for 1,000 copies and reserved for himself 100 bound volumes and 50 copies in sheets, plus "100 the little double vol: | N B & G B bound (as to be made)"; this would leave McKay 300 copies of *November Boughs/Good-Bye My Fancy* in sheets, for which he was to pay Whitman 40¢ a set, as well as 30¢ a set for the sheets of *Good-Bye My Fancy* (VI, 56). On 15 May, Whitman received a bill from Ferguson for typesetting and printing 1,000 copies (DLC). The inventory of Whitman's belongings made after his death shows bound copies and copies in sheets of this book "not counted" (DLC). Frederick Oldach was still binding copies as late as February–March 1896 (see receipts, DLC). Whitman's plans for a one-volume edition of *Good-Bye My Fancy* and *November Boughs* for distribution to his friends ended with his death, but his executors most likely carried out his wishes by binding up sheets from the 1891 printings of each book in green cloth in a large-paper format.

1,000 copies. Announced in *Critic*, n.s. 14 (29 November 1890), 282. Listed in *Publishers' Weekly*, 8 August 1891. Reviewed in *New-York Tribune*, 16 August 1891, p. 14; *Pall Mall Gazette*, 12 December 1891, p. 3. Copyright: title, 19 May 1891; book, not listed; 18382; renewed, 15 January 1919; 13180. Deposit copy: binding A: BL ('16 AP 92'). Presentation copies (all from Whitman): binding A: DLC (to Traubel, 20 June 1891), CtY (13 August 1891), BBo (21 October 1891), DLC (21 October 1891; 2 copies). Copies inscribed by owners: binding A: NNPM (14 July 1891). Prices: binding A: $1.00; bindings B and C: not for sale. Listed in the *English Catalogue* for September 1891 at 5s.

Locations: Binding A: BBo (2), BE, BL, BMR (3), CSt, CtY (3), DLC (4), JM (4), MB (2), MBU, MH, NN-B (3), NN-R (3), NNC, NNPM, NcD (2), NjP, PU (3), RPB (2), TxU (6), ViU; binding B: DLC, InU-L, ViU; binding C: BL, CaOTP, CaOTU, DLC (5), JM (2), MB, MBU, MH, NN-R, NcD, NcU, NjCW, PU (3), ScU, TxU (2).

Note one: There was significant slippage in the die used for stamping the spines of copies in binding A: copies have been noted with 'GOOD-BYE MY FANCY' measuring 4⁷⁄₁₆″ (BBo, BMR, CtY, DLC, MB, MBU, NN-R, NNC, NNPM, PU, RPB, TxU), 4½″ (BL, JM, NN-B [2], NjP, PU, TxU), 4⅝″ (CSt, NcD, PU, TxU [2]), 4¹³⁄₁₆″ (BE, BL, BMR, DLC, RPB, TxU), 4⅞″ (BBo, BMR, DLC, JM [2], NcD, TxU, ViU), or 4¹⁵⁄₁₆″ (CtY [2], DLC, JM, MB, NN-B, NN-R [2]).

Note two: A copy at DLC in binding B has been noted inscribed by Traubel with his comment that "Whitman produced this edⁿ for the use of his friends— as a greeting from him to them. It was never put on the market."

Note three: A copy at DLC in binding B has an inscription by Traubel with his comment: "This copy . . . is taken from an edition made by W. W. only for his friends & never put on sale."

Note four: Sets of unbound, stitched, and uncut gatherings, measuring 9⅝″×6⁵⁄₁₆″, with a single leaf pasted to leaf 4₈, are at MH (inscribed by Whitman, 20 May 1891), BBo (noted by John Johnston as received from Whitman on 28 May 1891), TxU (inscribed by Whitman, 29 May 1891), NN-B (inscribed by Whitman, 29 August 1891), NNC (inscribed by Whitman, 1891), DLC (2), MBU, and NN-B. Another set at DLC has this note by Harned: "*First* copy of first Edition of Walt Whitman's last book. The publisher submitted this for approval *unbound*. Afterwards he gave it to me."

Note five: Sets of unbound, unsewn, and uncut gatherings, measuring 9⅝″×6⁵⁄₁₆″, with a single leaf pasted to leaf 4₈, are at CtY (inscribed by Whitman, 13 May 1891) and DLC (inscribed by Whitman, 13 May 1891).

Note six: The 8 August 1891 *Academy* noted that Bucke was in England "making arrangements" for publication, and that the book would be "issued" by "Messrs. Reeves & Turner of Fleet-street, the publishers of William Morris and James Thomson" (40:114). A letter from Reeves and Turner of 17 August 1891 asking for 100 copies "In binding as issued" for their sale is at DLC. No copies with this publisher's imprint have been located.

Note seven: The plates for "Good-Bye My Fancy" (pp. 7–20) were repaginated 407–422 and used as the second annex to the 1891–1892 *Leaves of Grass* (see A 2.7.1₂ and A 2.7.0).

Note eight: The plates for pp. 21–66 were repaginated 477–522 and used in *Complete Prose Works* (C 6).

A 14 CALAMUS
1897

A 14.1.a
Only edition, first printing (1897)

CALAMUS ❧ A SERIES OF LETTERS WRITTEN
DURING THE YEARS 1868–1880 BY WALT
WHITMAN TO A YOUNG FRIEND (PETER DOYLE)
❧ EDITED WITH AN INTRODUCTION BY RICHARD
MAURICE BUCKE M.D. ONE OF WHITMAN'S
LITERARY EXECUTORS ❧ ❧ ❧ ❧ ❧ ❧ ❧ ❧

"Publish my name and hang up my picture as that of
   the tenderest lover,
The friend, the lover's portrait of whom his friend his
   lover was fondest,
Who was not proud of his songs but of the measureless
   ocean of love within him and freely poured it forth."
            Leaves of Grass (Ed'n 1892), p. 102.

PUBLISHED BY LAURENS MAYNARD AT 287 CONGRESS
STREET IN BOSTON MDCCCXCVII ❧ ❧ ❧ ❧ ❧

A 14.1.a: 7¾″×5½″

ENTERED ACCORDING TO THE ACT OF
CONGRESS IN THE YEAR 1897 BY
LAURENS MAYNARD, IN THE OFFICE
OF THE LIBRARIAN OF CONGRESS
AT WASHINGTON.

[i–iv] [i–ii] iii–viii 1–173 [174–176]. Inserted leaves of Japan paper, with a drawing of Whitman and Peter Doyle printed on the verso, a drawing of Whitman at age 72 printed on the recto, and a photograph of a manuscript page printed on the recto, are positioned before the title page and after pp. 32, 112.

[1]² [2]⁴ [3–13]⁸ . Sheets bulk ⅝″.

Contents: p. i: statement of limitation; pp. ii–iv: blank; p. i: title page; p. ii: copyright page; p. iii: Whitman's inscription in a copy of *Specimen Days* sent to Doyle; p. iv: lines from *Leaves of Grass;* p. v: passages on Doyle from John Addington Symonds' *Walt Whitman;* p. vi: lines from *Leaves of Grass;* p. vii: contents; p. viii: lines from *Leaves of Grass;* pp. 1–7: chronology of Whitman's life; p. 8: lines from *Leaves of Grass;* pp. 9–33: introduction; p. 34: lines from *Leaves of Grass;* pp. 35–51: "Letters of 1868"; p. 52: lines from *Leaves of Grass;* pp. 53–59: "Letters of 1869"; p. 60: lines from *Leaves of Grass;* pp. 61–79: "Letters of 1870"; pp. 81–86: "Letters of 1871"; pp. 87–98: "Letters of 1876–1880"; pp. 99–135: "Letters of 1873"; p. 136: lines from *Leaves of Grass;* pp. 137–157: "Letters of 1874"; p. 158: lines from *Leaves of Grass;* pp. 159–164: "Letters of 1875"; pp. 165–172: "Letters of 1876–1880"; p. 173: lines from *Leaves of Grass;* p. 174: blank; p. 175: printing information; p. 176: blank.

Typography and paper: 4⅞″ (4⅝″)×3⅜″; laid paper with horizontal chain lines 1¹⁄₁₆″ apart watermarked 'W KING ALTON MILLS'; 28 lines per page. Running heads: rectos: pp. 3–7: 'CHRONOLOGICAL NOTES'; pp. 11–19: 'INTRODUCTION'; pp. 21–33: 'INTERVIEW WITH PETER DOYLE'; pp. 37–51: 'LETTERS OF 1868'; pp. 55–59: 'LETTERS OF 1869'; pp. 63–79: 'LETTERS OF 1870'; pp. 83–85: 'LETTERS OF 1871'; pp. 89–97: 'LETTERS OF 1872'; pp. 101–135: 'LETTERS OF 1873'; pp. 139–157: 'LETTERS OF 1874'; pp. 161–163: 'LETTERS OF 1875'; pp. 167–171: 'LETTERS OF 1876–1880'; versos: pp. 2–6, 10–32, 36–50, 54–58, 62–78, 82–134, 138–156, 160–172: 'CALAMUS'.

Binding: Olive-gray paper-covered boards with white T cloth (bold-ribbed) shelfback. Front and back covers: blank; spine: white paper label with green printing: '[double rule] | CALAMUS | [rule] | LETTERS | TO | PETER DOYLE | [rule] | WALT | WHITMAN | [leaf design] | [double rule]'. Laid endpapers. Top edges rough trimmed, front and bottom edges uncut.

Dust jacket: Unprinted glassine.

Box: Dark yellow-green YR cloth (coarse linen) covered box open at one end.

Printing: 'DONE INTO TYPES AND PRINTED | FOR LAURENS MAY-NARD AT THE | CO-OPERATIVE PRESS CAMBRIDGE | U. S. A. MAY MDCCCXCVII.' (p. [175]).

Publication: Limited to 35 numbered copies signed by Bucke, 25 of which are for sale. Bucke wrote Laurens Maynard on 15 May 1897 that he had "signed" and mailed the "printed sheets," presumably referring to the statement of limitation page (NNPM). Published 30 April 1897. Bucke wrote Laurens Maynard on 30 May 1897 that he had received two copies of the book "yesterday"; presumably, one copy was the limited printing (NNPM). Copyright: 26469; book received, 10 June 1897. Deposit copies: DLC ('JUN 10 1897'). Presentation copies: ScU (from Bucke, 7 June 1897). MB copy received from the publisher 19 July 1897. Price, $5.00.

Locations: CtY (2), DLC (3), DLC (box, dj), JM, MB, NN-R (2), NNPM, NcD, PU, RPB, ScU, TxU, ViU.

OF THIS EDITION THIRTY-FIVE LARGE-PAPER COPIES

(OF WHICH TWENTY-FIVE ARE FOR SALE) HAVE BEEN

PRINTED ON ALTON MILLS PAPER, CONTAINING AN

EXTRA PORTRAIT, AND WITH THE ILLUSTRATIONS ON

JAPAN PAPER.

THIS IS NUMBER   *25*   OF THE LARGE-PAPER

EDITION.

Statement of limitation for A 14.1.a

Note one: Some copies are also signed by Peter Doyle on the limitation page (NN-R, TxU).

Note two: A four-page flier for the book, advertising both the large paper and trade printings, is at NNPM and TxU.

A 14.1.b
Only edition, second printing (1897)

Three issues have been noted:

A 14.1.b₁
First (American) issue (1897)

Boston: Laurens Maynard, MDCCCXCVII.

[i–ii] iii–viii 1–173 [174–176]. Inserted leaves of Japan paper, with a drawing of Whitman and Peter Doyle printed on verso and a photograph of a manuscript page printed on recto, are positioned before the title page and after p. 112.

[1]⁴ [2–12]⁸ . Page size 7″×4⅞″. Sheets bulk ⅝″.

Contents: Same as pp. i–viii, 1–[176] of the first printing, except: pp. 174–175: blank; p. 176: printing information.

Typography and paper: Same as the first printing, except: laid paper with vertical chain lines 1¼″ apart, unwatermarked.

Binding: Dark yellow-green T-like cloth (bold-ribbed). Front and back covers: blindstamped single-rule frame; spine: '[blindstamped rule] | [10 lines goldstamped] CALAMUS | [rule] | LETTERS | TO | PETER DOYLE | [rule] | WALT | WHITMAN | [leaf design] | MAYNARD | [blindstamped rule]'. Laid front flyleaf. White endpapers. All edges trimmed.

Printing: Same as the first printing, p. [176].

Publication: A postcard dated 4 May from the publisher announcing that the book's publication has been delayed until "about" 20 May is at MB. Bucke wrote Laurens Maynard on 30 May 1897 that he had received two copies of the book "yesterday"; presumably, one copy was the trade printing (NNPM). Noticed in *Time and the Hour*, 22 May 1897. Deposit copies: BL ('8 SE97'). Copies inscribed by owners: CSt (June 1897), MB (June 1897). A copy inscribed by Laurens Maynard, 25 June 1897, was sold at the Swann Galleries, 21 March 1957, item 254 (see *Whitman at Auction*, p. 407). MB copy received from the publisher 19 July 1897. Price, $1.00. Listed in the *English Catalogue* as an importation in July 1897 at 5s. Listed as an importation by Gay & Bird in the *Athenæum*, 7 August 1897.

Locations: BL, BMR, BO, CSt, CaOTP, CtY, DLC (2), JM, MB (2), MBU, NN-B (2), NNC, NNPM, NcD (2), NcU, NjCW, PU, RPB, ScU, TxU (2), ViU (2).

A 14.1.b₂
Second (American) issue (1897)

C ALAMUS ❧ A SERIES OF LETTERS WRITTEN
DURING THE YEARS 1868–1880 BY WALT
WHITMAN TO A YOUNG FRIEND (PETER DOYLE)
❧ EDITED WITH AN INTRODUCTION BY RICHARD
MAURICE BUCKE M.D. ONE OF WHITMAN'S
LITERARY EXECUTORS ❧ ❧ ❧ ❧ ❧ ❧ ❧ ❧

"Publish my name and hang up my picture as that of
the tenderest lover,
The friend, the lover's portrait of whom his friend his
lover was fondest,
Who was not proud of his songs but of the measureless
ocean of love within him and freely poured it forth."
Leaves of Grass (Ed'n 1892), p. 102.

BOSTON : SMALL, MAYNARD & COMPANY : MDCCCXCVII

A 14.1.b₂: 7″×4⅞″

[1]⁴ (±1₁) [2–12]⁸. Title leaf is a cancel.

Binding: Two styles have been noted, priority undetermined:

    Binding A: Same as in the first issue, except: goldstamped at the bottom of the spine is 'SMALL | MAYNARD | & COMPANY | [blindstamped rule]'; front flyleaf.

    Binding B: Same as binding A, except: front and back covers are blank; no flyleaves.

Publication: Price, $1.00.

Locations: Binding A: RPB, ViU; binding B: JM, NjP.

A 14.1.b₃
Third (English) issue (1898)

CALAMUS ❧ A SERIES OF LETTERS WRITTEN DURING THE YEARS 1868–1880 BY WALT WHITMAN TO A YOUNG FRIEND (PETER DOYLE) ❧EDITED WITH AN INTRODUCTION BY RICHARD MAURICE BUCKE M.D. ONE OF WHITMAN'S LITERARY EXECUTORS ❧ ❧ ❧ ❧ ❧ ❧ ❧ ❧

"Publish my name and hang up my picture as that of
the tenderest lover,
The friend, the lover's portrait of whom his friend his
lover was fondest,
Who was not proud of his songs but of the measureless
ocean of love within him and freely poured it forth."
Leaves of Grass (Ed'n 1892), p. 102.

LONDON : G. P. PUTNAM'S SONS ❧ BOSTON : SMALL, MAYNARD & COMPANY. MDCCCXCVIII ❧ ❧ ❧

A 14.1.b₃: 7″×4⅞″

[1]⁴ (±1₁) [2–12]⁸. Title leaf is a cancel.

Contents: Same as in the first issue, except: p. i: English title page.

Binding: Same as in the first issue, binding A.

Publication: Announced in the *Bookseller,* October 1898.

Location: PU.

A 14.1.c₁
[Folcroft, Penn.]: Folcroft Library Editions, 1972.

Facsimile reprinting of the English issue (A 14.1.b₃). Deposit copy: DLC for CIP ('3AUG1972'). Price, $25.00. *Locations:* DLC, ScU.

A 14.1.c₂
[Norwood, Penn.]: Norwood Editions, 1974.

Title leaf is inserted. Deposit copy: DLC for CIP ('20 MAY 1976' but received 11 June 1975). Limited to 100 copies. *Location:* DLC.

A 14.1.c₃
[Norwood, Penn.]: Norwood Editions, 1977.

Title leaf is inserted. *Location:* NbWayS.

A 14.1.c₄
[Philadelphia]: Richard West, 1978.

Title leaf is inserted. Deposit copy: DLC for CIP ('APR 7 1978'). Limited to 100 copies. Price, $25.00. *Location:* DLC.

Note: Listed in *NUC* (1973–1977) as a 1978 publication by Norwood Editions for $20.00. No copies have been located.

A 15 THE WOUND DRESSER
1898

A 15.1.a
Only edition, first printing (1898)

THE

WOUND DRESSER

A Series of Letters
Written from the Hospitals in Washington
During the War of the Rebellion

By

WALT WHITMAN

Edited by
RICHARD MAURICE BUCKE, M.D.
One of Whitman's Literary Executors

SCIRE
QVOD
SCIENDVM

Boston
SMALL, MAYNARD & COMPANY
1898

A 15.1.a: 7¾″×5″

Copyright page: 'Copyright, 1897, by Small, Maynard & Company'.

[i–vi] [i–vi] vii–viii [ix–x] 1–19 [20] 21–141 [142] 143–201 [203–204]. Inserted leaves of Japan paper, with Gardner photograph of Whitman in 1863 printed on verso, manuscript facsimile printed on recto and verso, and daguerreotype of Whitman's mother printed on verso, all followed by protective tissues, are positioned before the title page and after pp. 46, 92.

[a]^8 1–6^8 7^8 8–12^8 [13]^6. Sheets bulk $^{25}/_{32}''$.

Contents: pp. i–vi: blank; p. i: half title, 'THE WOUND DRESSER'; p. ii: statement of limitation; p. iii: title page; p. iv: copyright page; p. v: lines from "The Wound Dresser"; p. vi: blank; pp. vii–viii: preface; p. ix: contents; p. x: blank; pp. 1–10: "The Great Army of the Wounded"; pp. 11–19: "Life Among Fifty Thousand Soldiers"; p. 20: blank; pp. 21–46: "Hospital Visits"; pp. 47–141: "Letters of 1862–3"; pp. 143–200: "Letters of 1864"; p. 201: lines from Whitman; p. 202: blank; p. 203: printing information; p. 204: blank.

Prose: Reprints E 2483, E 2485, E 2492, E 2775.

Typography and paper: 5⅝″ (5⁵⁄₁₆″)×3⅜″; laid paper with horizontal chain lines 1¹⁄₁₆″ apart, watermarked 'W KING ALTON MILLS'; 32 lines per page. Running heads: rectos: pp. 3–9: 'The Great Army of the Wounded'; pp. 13–19: 'Life among Fifty Thousand Soldiers'; pp. 23–45: 'Hospital Visits'; pp. 49–141: 'Letters of 1862–3'; pp. 145–199: 'Letters of 1864'; versos: p. viii: 'Preface'; pp. 2–18, 22–140, 144–200: 'The Wound Dresser'.

Binding: Dark red buckram. Front and back covers: blank; spine: white paper label with '[rule] | *The* | *Wound* | *Dresser* | [design | *Walt* | *Whitman* | [rule] | *BOSTON,* 1898 | [rule]'. Laid endpapers. Top edges rough trimmed, front and bottom edges uncut.

Dust jacket: Unprinted glassine.

Box: Unprinted white paper covered box open at one end.

Printing: 'Printed by John Wilson and Son, at the Univer- | sity Press, Cambridge, U.S.A., in December, 1897' (p. [203]).

Publication: Limited to 60 numbered copies signed by Bucke, of which 50 are for sale. Bucke wrote Laurens Maynard on 15 May 1897, "When we get this book *[Calamus] launched* if it seems likely to do well we must then turn our attention to the Letters from 'Hospital to Mother' " (NNPM). Copies inscribed by owners: DLC (1 April 1898). MB copy received from the publisher 24 August 1898. Price, $5.00.

Locations: CtY, DLC, DLC (box, dj), MB, NNC, NcD, RPB (2), ScU, TxU, ViU.

Of this edition sixty copies (of which fifty are for sale) have been printed on Alton Mills paper, with the illustrations on Japan paper, and containing a facsimile of one of the letters.

This is number 55

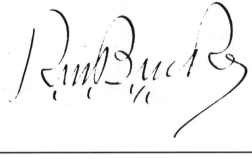

Statement of limitation for A 15.1.a

Note one: The publisher's device on the title page is centered.

Note two: A duplicate spine label is inserted after p. [202] (CtY, DLC, MB, RPB) or p. [204] (DLC, NNC, NcD, RPB, ScU, TxU, ViU).

Note three: A four-page advertising brochure for both the limited and trade printings is at JM, PU, and ViU.

Note four: A copy that has not been numbered is at TxU.

A 15.1.b
Only edition, second printing (1898)

Three issues have been noted:

A 15.1.b₁
First (American) issue (1898)

THE

WOUND DRESSER

A Series of Letters
Written from the Hospitals in Washington
During the War of the Rebellion

By

WALT WHITMAN

Edited by
RICHARD MAURICE BUCKE, M.D.
One of Whitman's Literary Executors

SCIRE
QVOD
SCIENDVM

Boston
SMALL, MAYNARD & COMPANY
1898

A 15.1.b₁: 7½″×5″

Pagination is the same as in the first printing, except: inserted leaves of wove paper, with Gardner photograph of Whitman in 1863 and daguerreotype of Whitman's mother, printed on versos, are positioned before the title page and after p. 46.

Collation is the same as in the first printing. Sheets bulk $^{21}/_{32}''$.

Contents: Same as in the first printing, except: second p. ii: blank.

Typography and paper: Same as in the first printing, except: laid paper with vertical chain lines $^{13}/_{16}''$ apart, unwatermarked.

Binding: Deep red S cloth (diagonal fine-ribbed). Front cover: goldstamped within a blindstamped single-rule frame: '[floral band] THE [floral band] | WOUND [solid triangle] DRESSER | [floral design] WALT [solid triangle] WHITMAN [floral design]'; back cover: blindstamped single-rule frame; spine: goldstamped '[leaf] THE [leaf] | WOUND | DRESSER | WHITMAN | [leaf] SMALL [leaf] | MAYNARD | & COMPANY'. Laid white endpapers. Top edges trimmed, front and bottom edges rough trimmed. Top edges gilded.

Printing: Same as in the first printing.

Publication: Published 11 December 1897. Listed in *Publishers' Weekly*, 5 February 1898. Copyright: 69032; book received, 6 January 1898. Deposit copies: DLC ('JAN 6 1898'). Copies inscribed by owners: MB (January 1898). MB copy received from the publisher 24 August 1898. Price, $1.50.

Locations: CSt, CtY, DLC (2), JM, MB (2), NNC, NNPM, NcD, NjCW, NjP, PU, RPB, ScU, TxU, ViU.

Note one: The publisher's device on the title page is to the left of center. A copy at NNPM has a comment by Laurens Maynard on the front endpaper that the "device on the title page printed out of centre—by error of locking up page— This error was corrected in all but a few copies by an inserted cancel title page."

Note two: A copy at PU has a comment by Harned on the front endpaper: "One of the first few copies struck off—sent me in advance by the publishers."

Note three: A copy without the frontispiece is at TxU.

A 15.1.b$_2$
Second (American) issue (1898)

Boston: Small, Maynard, 1898.

[a]^8 ($\pm$a$_5$) 1–6^8 7^8 8–12^8 [13]^6. Title leaf is a cancel.

Publication: Deposit copies: BL ('19AU98'). Presentation copies: MBU (from publisher, 5 February 1898), DLC (from Bucke, 18 January 1898), TxU (from

Bucke, 14 February 1898). Copies inscribed by owners: DLC (14 January 1898). Price, $1.50.

Locations: CaOTU, CtY, DLC (2), JM, MBU, NcD, TxU (4), ViU.

Note: The publisher's device on the title page is centered.

A 15.1.b₃
Third (English) issue (1898)

THE

WOUND DRESSER

A Series of Letters
Written from the Hospitals in Washington
During the War of the Rebellion

By

WALT WHITMAN

Edited by
RICHARD MAURICE BUCKE, M.D.
One of Whitman's Literary Executors

SCIRE
QVOD
SCIENDVM

Boston: SMALL, MAYNARD & COMPANY
London: G. P. PUTNAM'S SONS

1898

A 15.1.b₃: 7½″×5″

> *Copyright, 1898, by Small, Maynard & Company,*
> *for the United States of America.*
>
> *Printed by the University Press, Cambridge,*
> *Mass., U.S.A.*

Pagination is the same as in the first issue, except: inserted leaves may be of Japan (NcU) or wove (all other copies) paper.

[a]^8 ($\pm$a$_5$) 1–6^8 7^8 8–12^8 [13]^6. Title leaf is a cancel.

Contents: Same as in the first issue, except: second p. iii: English title page; second p. iv: English copyright page.

Binding: Same as in the first issue.

Publication: Published April 1898. Listed in the *Athenæum*, 2 April 1898. Deposit copies: BL ('25OC98'). Copies inscribed by owners: BE (10 May 1898). Price, 6s.

Locations: BE, BL, BMR, NN-R, NNC, NcU, ViU.

Note: The publisher's device on the title page is centered.

A 15.1.c
[New York]: Bodley Press, 1949.

200 pp. Facsimile reprinting. Dust jacket. Introduction by Oscar Cargill. Reviewed in *New York Times Book Review*, 7 August 1949, p. 6. Copyright 14 February 1949; A30566. Deposit copy: DLC ('FEB 15 1949'). Copies inscribed by owners: BMR (4 April 1949). Price, $3.00. *Locations:* BMR, DLC, JM.

A 15.1.d₁
[Folcroft, Penn.]: Folcroft Library Editions, 1975.

Facsimile reprinting of the second printing, first issue (A 15.1.b₁). Deposit copy: DLC for CIP ('MAR 22 1976'). Limited to 100 copies. Price, $35.00. *Locations:* DLC, ScU.

A 15.1.d₂
[Norwood, Penn.]: Norwood Editions, 1978.

Title leaf is inserted. Deposit copy: DLC for CIP ('MAY 22 1978'). Limited to 100 copies. Price, $30.00. *Location:* DLC.

A 16 WALT WHITMAN AT HOME
    1898

A 16.1.a
Only edition, first printing (1898)

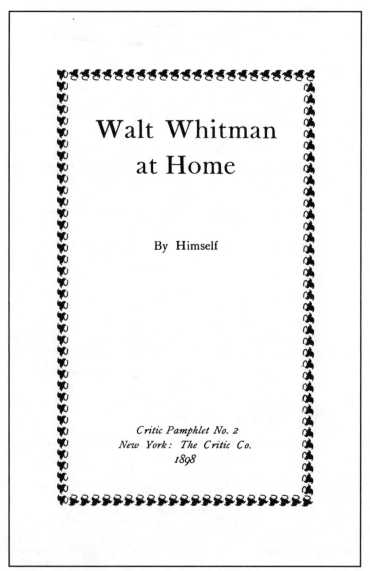

A 16.1.a: 7⁷⁄₁₆″×4¹³⁄₁₆″

[1–6] 7–14 [15–16] 17–20 [21–28]

[1]¹⁴. Sheets bulk ³⁄₃₂″. The conjugate leaves 1₃ (pp. 5–6) and 1₁₂ (pp. 23–24) are coated paper.

Contents: p. 1: cover title; p. 2: table of contents; p. 3: title page; p. 4: copyright page; p. 5: blank; p. 6: photograph of Whitman at home, dated 24 October 1891; pp. 7–14: "Walt Whitman in Camden" [from 28 February 1885 *Critic*]; p. 15: manuscript facsimile from "Walt Whitman in Camden"; p. 16: blank; pp. 17–20: "A Visit to Whitman's Shanty" by "J[eannette]. L. G[ilder]." [from 28 November 1891 *Critic*]; p. 21: manuscript facsimile of "Spirit that form'd this scene"; pp. 22–24: blank; p. 25: advertisement for *Critic Pamphlets;* p. 26: advertisement for *Critic Leaflets;* p. 27: advertisements for *Critic, Essays from the Critic,* and *Authors at Home;* p. 28: '[all flush right in red] "Walt | Whitman | at | Home" | By | Himself'.

Typography and paper: 5⁷⁄₁₆″×2½″; laid paper with vertical chain lines 1⅛″ apart, watermarked 'RUISDAEL'; 33 lines per page. No running heads.

Binding: Cover title: front: '[all flush left in red] "Walt | Whitman | at | Home" | By | Himself'; back: '[all flush right in red] "Walt | Whitman | at | Home" | By | Himself'. All edges rough trimmed.

Printing: Unknown.

Publication: *Critic Pamphlet,* no. 2. Noted in *Publishers' Weekly,* 19 March 1898; listed in *Publishers' Weekly,* 14 May 1898. Copyright: 28025; book received, 5 May 1898. Copies inscribed by owners: PU (14 January 1899). Price, 50¢.

Locations: CtY, MB, MH, PU, TxU (2).

Note: Reprints "Walt Whitman in Camden" by "George Selwyn" from *Critic,* 28 February 1885 (E 2636), and *Authors at Home* (D 16).

A 16.1.b
Folcroft, Penn.: Folcroft Library Editions, 1973.

Facsimile reprinting. Listed in *BIP* (1973) for $6.50. *Not seen.*

A 16.1.c
[Folcroft, Penn.]: Folcroft Library Editions, 1976.

Facsimile reprinting. *Location:* ScCleU.

A 16.1.d
Philadelphia: Richard West, 1978.

Facsimile reprinting. Listed in *Walt Whitman Review,* 25 (June 1979), 82–83. Price, $7.50. *Not seen.*

A 17 NOTES AND FRAGMENTS
1899

A 17.1.a
Only edition, first printing (1899)

NOTES AND FRAGMENTS: LEFT BY WALT
WHITMAN AND NOW EDITED BY DR. RICHARD
MAURICE BUCKE, ONE OF HIS LITERARY EX-
ECUTORS.

" *Waifs from the deep cast high and dry.*"
—Leaves of Grass, p. 278.

PRINTED
FOR PRIVATE DISTRIBUTION ONLY.
1899.

A 17.1.a: Binding A: 11$^{15}\!/_{16}$″×8⅞″; Binding B: 11 $^1\!/_{16}$″×7⅝″

[i–v] vi [vii–viii] [9] 10–53 [54–55] 56–74 [75] 76–149 [150–151] 152–179 [180–181] 182–192 [193] 194–211 [212]

[1–27]⁴. Leaf 27₃ is the free back endpaper; leaf 27₄ is the pastedown back endpaper. Sheets bulk ²³⁄₃₂″. The copy in binding A has inserted mounted photographs of Bucke (signed by him) on the verso before the half title page, the Gutekunst photo of Whitman in a broad-brimmed hat on white paper (signed in blue pencil by Whitman) on the verso before the title page, and of Bucke on the recto after p. 212.

Contents: p. i: half title, 'NOTES AND FRAGMENTS.'; p. ii: printing information; p. iii: title page; p. iv: statement of limitation; pp. v–vi: "Editor's Preface"; p. vii: contents; p. viii: '"*A Trail of Drift and Debris.*" | —LEAVES OF GRASS, p. 203.'; pp. 9–53: "First Drafts and Rejected Lines and Passages, Mostly very Fragmentary, from 'Leaves of Grass,' Largely Antecedent to the 1855 Edition"; p. 54: blank; pp. 55–74: "Notes on the Meaning and Intention of 'Leaves of Grass' "; pp. 75–149: "Memoranda from Books and from His Own Reflections— Indicating the Poet's Reading and Thought Prefatory to Writing 'Leaves of Grass' "; p. 150: blank; pp. 151–179: "Shorter Notes, Isolated Words, Brief Sentences, Memoranda, Suggestive Expressions, Names and Dates"; p. 180: blank; pp. 181–192: "Notes on English History"; pp. 193–211: "List of Certain Magazine and Newspaper Articles Studied and Preserved by Walt Whitman and Found in His Scrapbooks and Among His Papers"; p. 212: blank.

Typography and paper: 9⅛″ (8⅝″)×6″; laid paper with horizontal chain lines 1¹⁄₁₆″ apart; preface: 45 lines per page; text: various lines per page (up to 42). Running heads: rectos: pp. 11–53: 'Leaves of Grass—First Drafts.'; pp. 57–73: 'Meaning and Intention of Leaves of Grass.'; pp. 77–149: 'Prepatory Reading and Thought.'; pp. 153–179: 'Shorter Notes, Isolated Words, Etc.'; pp. 183–191: 'Notes on English History.'; pp. 195–211: 'Magazine and Newspaper Articles.'; versos: p. vi: 'Notes and Fragments.'; pp. 10–52: 'Leaves of Grass—First Drafts.'; pp. 56–74: 'Meaning and Intention of Leaves of Grass.'; pp. 76–148: 'Prepatory Reading and Thought.'; pp. 152–178: 'Shorter Notes, Isolated Words, Etc.'; pp. 182–192: 'Notes on English History.'; pp. 194–210: 'Magazine and Newspaper Articles.'.

Binding: Two styles have been noted:

Binding A: White V cloth (smooth). Front and back covers: blank; spine: goldstamped '[double rule] | [double rule] | [six lines on a dark green leather label] NOTES | AND | FRAGMENTS | [rule] | WALT | WHITMAN | [double rule] | 1899 | [double rule]'. Laid front endpapers; for back endpapers, see collation above. Top edges trimmed, front and bottom edges rough trimmed. Top edges gilded. See *Note one*.

Binding B: Very dark greenish blue A cloth (ribbed morocco). Front cover: all within a blindstamped triple-rule frame with fifteen circular designs in each corner: goldstamped at a 45° angle from bottom to top '[ornate capital] NOTES [rule under next word] and | [ornate capital] Fragments.'; back cover: the same as the front cover, except: all blindstamped; spine: goldstamped '[double rule] | Notes | and | Fragments | [double rule] | [double rule] | WALT. | WHITMAN | [double rule] | [double rule] | Dr. R. M. Bucke | [double rule]'. Laid front endpapers; for back endpapers, see collation above. All edges trimmed.

Printing: 'PRINTED FOR THE EDITOR BY | A. TALBOT & CO., LONDON, ONTARIO, CANADA.' (p. ii).

Publication: Limited to 225 numbered copies, signed by Bucke. Bucke wrote to H. Buxton Forman on 29 May 1899 that the book was "in the printer's hands," and on 19 July 1899, that "I mail you today" a copy of the book (NN-R). Reviewed in *Conservator,* 10 (September 1899), 108–109. Copies inscribed by owners: CtY (by Harned, July 1899), NjP (10 August 1899). MB copy received 7 October 1899 from Small, Maynard. Prices: available directly from Bucke for $5.00 (Canadian); distributed in the United States by Small, Maynard at $10.00.

THIS BOOK IS PRINTED FROM THE TYPE, AND ITS ISSUE LIMITED TO TWO HUNDRED AND TWENTY-FIVE COPIES.   THIS IS No. *69*

Statement of limitation for A 17.1.a

Locations: Binding A: DLC; binding B: BE, BL, BMR, BO, CSt, CaOTP, CtY (3), DLC (3), JM, MB, NN-R, NNC, NNPM, NcD, NjCW (2), NjP, PU, RPB, TxU (4).

Note one: The only located copy in binding A has on the limitation page, after 'THIS IS', the following in Bucke's hand: 'one of | three special copies and | is not included in the | two hundred and twenty five | mentioned above | R. M. Bucke | 8 Nov. 1899' (DLC).

Note two: A four-page prospectus, printed on pp. 1 and 3, with a clip-off coupon on p. 3 for ordering directly from Bucke, is at DLC.

Note three: A copy at TxU has a mimeographed typescript letter from Bucke, dated 11 May 1899, "To Subscribers," stating, "I have not enough subscriptions to cover the cost of producing the book, nevertheless, I shall begin printing next week and will issue copies as soon as possible. Shall limit the issue to 200 copies and shall number each."

Note four: A copy at TxU has a printed form, dated 22 July 1899 in Bucke's hand, stating that the copy was mailed "this day."

Note five: Copies of a broadside circular, printed on the recto only, headed 'JUST OUT===JULY, 1889.', stating that "most of the impression is sold" but that 35 of "the copies that are left" are available from Bucke, are at NN-R and TxU.

Note six: A copy at CtY has a note by Harned, 15 April 1917, on the free front endpaper, that as of July 1899 only five copies were left.

Note seven: A 34-leaf combination manuscript and typescript prepared by Bucke for a second edition was sold at the Bucke sale, 13 May 1935, item 115 *(Whitman at Auction,* p. 216).

A 17.1.b₁
[Folcroft, Penn.]: Folcroft Library Editions, 1972.

Facsimile reprinting. Deposit copy: DLC for CIP ('20 JUN 1972'). Price, $20.00. *Locations:* DLC, CaOTU.

A 17.1.b₂
[Norwood, Penn.]: Norwood Editions, 1972.

Title leaf is inserted. *Location:* CtNbT.

A 17.1.b₃
[Norwood, Penn.]: Norwood Editions, 1977.

Title leaf is inserted, Price, $22.50. *Locations:* CtNbT, PPT.

Note one: The 1972 Folcroft title leaf is present in the CtNbT copy.

Note two: Listed in RLIN and *NUC* (1973–1977) as a 1975 publication by Norwood Editions for $22.50, and in *NUC* (1978) as a 1977 publication by Richard West of Philadelphia for $22.45. No copies have been located.

A 18 LETTERS WRITTEN . . . TO HIS MOTHER
1902

A 18.1.a
Only edition, first printing (1902)

LETTERS WRITTEN BY

WALT WHITMAN TO HIS MOTHER

FROM 1866 TO 1872

TOGETHER WITH CERTAIN PAPERS PREPARED
FROM MATERIAL NOW FIRST UTILIZED

EDITED BY

THOMAS B. HARNED

ONE OF WHITMAN'S LITERARY EXECUTORS

G. P. PUTNAM'S SONS
NEW YORK AND LONDON
The Knickerbocker Press
1902
[1]

A 18.1.a: 9″×6³⁄₁₆″

Copyright page: 'COPYRIGHT, 1902, BY | THOMAS B. HARNED'.

1 [2] 3–132

[1–16]⁴ [17]². Signed [a]⁴ 12⁸ 13⁸ 14⁸ 17⁸ *[sic]* 16⁸ 17⁸ 18⁸ 19⁶ in the form 'VOL. VIII—12.' and so on. Sheets bulk 11/32″.

Contents: p. 1: title page; p. 2: copyright page; pp. 3–4: "Prefatory Note" by Harned; pp. 5–75: texts of letters; pp. 76–92: "Whitman and Oratory" by Harned; pp. 93–106: "Walt Whitman and Physique" by Harned (see E 2783); pp. 107–132: "Walt Whitman and His Second Boston Publishers."

Typography and paper: 6¹³/₁₆″ (6⅜″)×4″; laid paper with vertical chain lines ¹³/₁₆″ apart; 29 lines per page. Running heads (all in gothic): rectos: pp. 7–75: 'Whitman to His Mother'; pp. 77–91: 'Whitman and Oratory'; pp. 93–105: 'Whitman and Physique'; pp. 109–131: 'His Second Boston Publishers'; versos: p. 4: 'Prefatory Note'; pp. 6–74: 'Whitman to His Mother'; pp. 78–92: 'Whitman and Oratory'; pp. 94–106: 'Whitman and Physique'; pp. 108–132: 'His Second Boston Publishers'.

Binding: Three styles have been noted, priority undetermined:

Binding A: Light grayish olive-green wrappers. Front cover: the same as the title page; back cover: unknown; spine: blank. Top edges trimmed, front and bottom edges rough trimmed. See *Note.*

Binding B: Dark grayish green wrappers (white on inside). Front cover: pasted light grayish olive-green paper label, the same as in binding A, except: 'LETTERS . . . UTILIZED' only; back cover and spine: blank. Top edges trimmed, front and bottom edges uncut.

Binding C: Light grayish olive-green wrappers. Front cover: the same as in binding A, except: 'LETTERS . . . EXECUTORS' only; back cover and spine: blank. Top edges trimmed, front and bottom edges rough trimmed.

Printing: Knickerbocker Press, New York.

Publication: Copyright 44637; received 27 October 1902. Deposit copies: binding A: DLC ('OCT 25 1902'; 2 copies). The ViU copy (binding B) has the following note, dated 12 November 1902, written by Harned across the front cover: "This book is one of twelve copies only printed for Copyright purposes. None others will be printed separately. It is to form part of the 8th Volume of the Definitive Edition of Whitman." A copy at DLC (binding C) has the following undated note by Harned on the front wrapper: "Only five copies of this book were printed—for the purpose of Copyright." The CtY copy (binding C) has an undated note by Harned on the front wrapper, stating that "a few copies [were] printed to comply with the Copyright Law." Not for sale.

Locations: Binding A: DLC (3); binding B: ViU; binding C: CtY, DLC, NN-B.

Note: All located copies of binding A lack the back wrapper; two have been rebound with the front wrapper bound in at the rear.

A 18.1.b
Only edition, second printing (1936)

Letters Written By Walt Whitman

To His Mother

1866 — 1872

With An

Introductory Note

by

Rollo G. Silver

1936

Alfred F. Goldsmith
At the Sign of the Sparrow
New York

A 18.1.b: 8¼″×5¹⁄₁₆″

Copyright page: 'Copyright 1936 | New York | Alfred F. Goldsmith'.

[i–vi] 1–71 [72]

[1–5]^8 (–1$_1$). The stub of canceled leaf 1$_1$ is pasted to the free front endpaper. A slip with the statement of limitation, printed on the recto, is pasted to p. i. Sheets bulk ³⁄₁₆″.

Contents: p. i: blank; p. ii: drawing of Whitman's birthplace; p. iii: title page; p. iv: copyright page; pp. v–vi: introduction by Rollo G. Silver; pp. 1–71: text; p. 72: blank.

Typography and paper: 6″ (5⅝″)×3½″; wove paper; 29 lines per page. Running heads: rectos: pp. 3–71: '[gothic] Whitman to His Mother'; versos: pp. 2–70: '[gothic] Whitman to His Mother'.

Binding: Medium blue paper covered boards. Front cover: white paper label with 'WALT WHITMAN'S LETTERS | TO HIS MOTHER | 1866—1872'; back cover: blank; spine: white paper label with vertical 'WALT WHITMAN'S LETTERS TO HIS MOTHER'. White endpapers. All edges trimmed.

Printing: Unknown.

Publication: Limited to 325 numbered copies. Published 30 October 1936. Copyright A100845; received, 31 October 1936. Deposit copies: DLC ('OCT 31 1936'), BL ('1 MAR 37'). NN-R copy received 10 December 1936. Price, $2.50.

Locations: BL, CSt, CtY, DLC (3), JM (2), MB, MBU, MH, NN-R (2), NNC, NcD, NcU, NjCW, NjP, PU (3), ScU, TxU (3), ViU.

Note one: The slip containing the statement of limitation may be missing (JM), marked "out of series" (TxU), marked with a dash instead of a number (TxU), or lacking a number (DLC, NjCW),

Note two: A photoreduction from the plates of the *Complete Writings* (B 4).

A 18.1.c$_1$
[Folcroft, Penn.]: Folcroft Library Editions, 1977.

Facsimile reprinting of the second printing. Deposit copy: DLC for CIP ('DEC 2 1977'). Limited to 100 copies. Price, $17.50. *Location:* DLC.

A 18.1.c$_2$
[Philadelphia]: Richard West, 1979.

Title leaf is inserted. *Location:* MChB.

Note: Listed in *NUC* (1978:150) as a 1978 publication by Norwood Editions of Norwood, Penn., for $15.00. No copies have been located.

A 19 AN AMERICAN PRIMER
1904

A 19.1.a
Only edition, first printing (1904)

Two issues have been noted:

A 19.1.a₁
First (American) issue (1904)

AN
AMERICAN PRIMER
BY WALT WHITMAN
WITH FACSIMILES OF
THE ORIGINAL MANUSCRIPT
EDITED BY
HORACE TRAUBEL

SCIRE QVOD
SCIENDVM

BOSTON
SMALL, MAYNARD & COMPANY
MCMIV

A 19.1.a₁: Binding A: 9⅝″×6″; Binding B: 9¼″ X 5¾″

COPYRIGHT, 1904, BY
HORACE TRAUBEL

———

Entered at Stationers' Hall

〜〜〜

Published November, 1904

〜〜〜

THE UNIVERSITY PRESS, CAMBRIDGE, U.S A.

[i–vi] [i–iv] v–ix [x–xviii] 1–35 [36–40]

[a]^8 [b]^4 1–2^8 3^4. In some copies, leaf a₁ is the front pastedown endpaper and leaf a₂ is the front free endpaper; pagination is affected accordingly. Inserted leaf with an engraving of Whitman printed on verso, followed by a protective tissue, is pasted to leaf a₄ (facing title page). Sheets bulk ¼″.

Contents: pp. i–v: blank; p. vi: statement of limitation; p. i: half title, 'AN AMERICAN PRIMER'; p. ii: blank; p. iii: title page; p. iv: copyright page; pp. v–ix: foreword by Horace Traubel; p. x: blank; p. xi: 'SOME FACSIMILES OF THE ORIGINAL MANUSCRIPT'; p. xii: blank; p. xiii: photograph of manuscript page on pale yellow background; p. xiv: blank; p. xv: photograph of manuscript page on pale green background; p. xvi: blank; p. xvii: photograph of manuscript page on light green background; p. xviii: blank; pp. 1–35: text; pp. 36–40: blank.

Typography and paper: 5¾″ (5⁷⁄₁₆″)×3⁵⁄₁₆″; second gathering (illustrations) on wove paper, and all other gatherings on wove paper watermarked '[script] U S A Old Stratford'; 28 lines per page. Running heads: rectos: vii–ix: 'FORE-WORD'; pp. 3–35: 'AN AMERICAN PRIMER'; versos: pp. vi–viii: 'FORE-WORD'; pp. 2–34: 'AN AMERICAN PRIMER'.

Binding: Two styles have been noted:

Binding A: Dark grayish green paper-covered boards with white vellum shelfback and ¼″ high vellum triangles at the outside corners. Front cover: goldstamped: leaf and flower design with scroll in center imprinted 'SCIRE • QVOD | • SCIENDVM • '; back cover: blank; spine: goldstamped from bottom to top 'AN AMERICAN PRIMER—WALT WHITMAN'. For front endpaper, see collation above; back white endpaper. Issued uncut.

Binding B: Medium greenish blue V cloth (smooth). Front cover: blu-estamped: leaf-and-flower design with scroll in center imprinted 'SCIRE • QVOD | • SCIENDVM •'; back cover: blank; spine: bluestamped from bottom to top: 'AN AMERICAN PRIMER—WALT WHITMAN'. For front endpaper, see collation above; back white endpaper. All edges trimmed.

Dust jacket: Unprinted glassine (with binding A).

Printing: See copyright page.

Publication: Limited to 500 copies. Printed November 1904. Advertised as "now issued" in *Publishers' Weekly*, 26 November 1904; listed in *Publishers' Weekly*, 17 December 1904. Copyright 102654; received, 28 November 1904; renewed: 30 November 1931; R16657. Published 17 December 1904. Deposit copies: binding A: DLC ('NOV 28 1904'). Presentation copies: binding A: PU (from Harned, 1 January 1905). RPB copy (binding B; no frontispiece) received 1 December 1909. MB copy (binding A) received 2 December 1904. Copies inscribed by owners: binding A: MBU (10 January 1905); binding B: NcD (1 February 1910; frontispiece), RPB (11 June 1910; frontispiece). Prices: binding A: $2.50; binding B, $2.00.

Locations: Binding A: BMR, CtY, DLC (2), DLC (dj), JM, MB, MBU, NNPM, NcD, PU, RPB, ScU, ViU; binding B: DLC, JM, MBU, NN-R, NcD, NjP, PU, RPB (2), TxU (3), ViU.

Note one: Revised from the *Atlantic Monthly Magazine,* April 1904 (E 2786).

Note two: The portrait is not present in some copies in binding B (DLC, JM, NjP, RPB).

Note three: Shay reports that "few were sold" in binding A (p. 39).

Note four: Published simultaneously with *Walt Whitman's Diary in Canada* (A 20).

A 19.1.a₂
Second (English) issue (1904)

AN
AMERICAN PRIMER
BY WALT WHITMAN

WITH FACSIMILES OF
THE ORIGINAL MANUSCRIPT

EDITED BY
HORACE TRAUBEL

G. P. PUTNAM'S SONS
24 BEDFORD STREET, STRAND
LONDON
1904

A 19.1.a₂: 9⅝″×6″

Copyright page: 'COPYRIGHT, 1904 | G. P. PUTNAM'S SONS'.

[a]^8 ($\pm$a$_5$) [b]^4 1–2^8 3^4 . Title leaf is a cancel.

Contents: Same as the American issue, except: second p. iii: English title page; p. iv: English copyright page.

Binding: Unprinted dark gray wrappers. Uncut.

Publication: A printed receipt from Stationers' Hall, dated 5 December 1904, acknowledges registering the book for copyright (DLC). Deposit copies: BL ('31 DE 1904'), BO ('28 1 1905'), BC ('3 FE 1905'), BD ('Feb. 1905'; rebound).

Locations: BC, BE, BL, BO.

Note: Possibly used for English copyright purposes only and therefore not for sale.

A 19.1.b$_1$
Folcroft, Penn.: Folcroft Press, [1969].

Facsimile reprinting of the first issue. Price, $10.00. *Location:* MdU-BC.

A 19.1.b$_2$
[Folcroft, Penn.]: Folcroft Library Editions, 1977.

Title leaf is inserted. Deposit copy: DLC for CIP ('DEC 12 1977'). Limited to 100 copies. Price, $12.50. *Location:* DLC.

A 19.1.b$_3$
[Norwood, Penn.]: Norwood Editions, 1977.

Title leaf is inserted. *Location:* TxWB.

Note: Listed in RLIN and *NUC* (1978:149) as a 1978 publication by Norwood Editions. No copies have been located.

A 19.1.c
San Francisco: City Lights Books, [1970].

Facsimile reprinting of the first issue. Wrappers. Published January 1970. Price, $1.50. *Locations:* JM, RPB.

A 19.1.d
[Philadelphia]: Richard West, 1980.

Facsimile reprinting of the first issue. Limited to 150 copies. *Locations:* RPB, ScU.

A 19.1.e
[Stevens Point, Wis.]: Holy Cow! Press, 1987.

Facsimile reprinting of the first issue. Cloth or wrappers. Afterword by Gay Wilson Allen. Published January 1987. Deposit copies: paper and cloth: DLC ('JUN 22 1987'). Prices: cloth, $13.00; paper, $5.95. *Locations:* DLC (both), JM (both).

A 19.1.f
New York: Gordon, [n.d.].

Facsimile reprinting listed in *BIP* (1972–1984) for $11.00. *Not seen.*

A 20 DIARY IN CANADA
1904

A 20.1.a
Only edition, first printing (1904)

Two issues have been noted:

A 20.1.a₁
First (American) issue (1904)

WALT WHITMAN'S
DIARY IN CANADA
WITH EXTRACTS FROM
OTHER OF HIS DIARIES AND
LITERARY NOTE–BOOKS
EDITED BY
WILLIAM SLOANE KENNEDY

SCIRE QVOD
SCIENDVM

BOSTON
SMALL, MAYNARD & COMPANY
MCMIV

A 20.1.a₁: 9⅝″×6⅛″

COPYRIGHT, 1904, BY
WILLIAM SLOANE KENNEDY

Entered at Stationers' Hall

Published November, 1904

THE UNIVERSITY PRESS, CAMBRIDGE, U.S.A.

[i–iv] [i–iv] v–vi 1–45 [46–48] 49–73 [74–78]. In some copies, leaf 1₁ is the front pastedown endpaper and leaf 1₂ is the front free endpaper; pagination is affected accordingly.

[1–5]⁸ [6]⁴ . Signed [a]⁵ 1–4⁸ 5⁷ . Frontispiece photograph of Whitman in 1880 printed on verso, followed by a protective tissue, is pasted to leaf a₃ (facing title page). Sheets bulk 11⁄32″.

Contents: pp. i–iii: blank; p. iv: statement of limitation; p. i: half title, 'WALT WHITMAN'S | DIARY IN CANADA'; p. ii: blank; p. iii: title page; p. iv: copyright page; pp. v–vi: "Editor's Preface," signed 'W. S. K. | BELMONT, MASS., | November, 1904.'; pp. 1–45: "Walt Whitman's Diary in Canada"; p. 46: blank; p. 47: 'FROM OTHER JOURNALS OF | WALT WHITMAN'; p. 48: blank; pp. 49–65: "From Other Journals of Walt Whitman"; pp. 66–73: "Personal Memoranda, Notes and Jottings"; pp. 74–78: blank.

Typography and paper: 5¾″ (5⁷⁄16″)×3³⁄16″; wove paper watermarked '*Old Stratford* [ornate capitals] USA'; 28 lines per page. Running heads: rectos: pp. 3–45: 'DIARY IN CANADA'; pp. 51–73: 'WALT WHITMAN'; versos: p. vi: 'EDITOR'S PREFACE'; pp. 2–44: 'WALT WHITMAN'S'; pp. 50–64, 68–72: 'JOURNALS OF'.

Binding: Dark greenish gray paper-covered boards with white vellum shelf-back and ¼″ high vellum triangles at the outside corners. Front cover: goldstamped: leaf and flower design with scroll in center imprinted 'SCIRE • QVOD | • SCIENDVM •'; back cover: blank; spine: goldstamped from bottom to top 'WALT WHITMAN'S DIARY IN CANADA'. No flyleaves; or front flyleaf pasted in center of endpapers. White endpapers the same as the text. Top edges rough trimmed, front and bottom edges uncut.

Dust jacket: Unprinted glassine.

Printing: See copyright page.

Publication: Limited to 500 copies. Copyright 102653; received, 28 November 1904. Published 17 December 1904. Noted in *Publishers' Weekly*, 26 November 1904; listed in *Publishers' Weekly*, 17 December 1904. Deposit copies: DLC ('NOV 28 1904'; rebound), BL ('17 AP 1905'). Presentation copies: CtY (from Kennedy, 16 June 1905). MB copy received 2 December 1904. Price, $2.50.

Locations: BL, BMR (dj), CSt, CtY (2, dj), JM (2), MB, MBU, NN-R (2), NNC, NNPM, NcD (2), NjCW (2), NjP, PU, RPB (2), ScU, TxU (4), ViU (2).

Note one: Shay reports that "few were sold" and "the balance" were "bound up in light blue cloth, some without portrait" (p. 39); no copies have been located. Because these two bindings were used for *An American Primer* (A 19), Shay may have assumed that the same was true for this book.

Note two: Published simultaneously with *An American Primer* (A 19).

A 20.1.a₂
Second (English) issue (1904)

WALT WHITMAN'S
DIARY IN CANADA
WITH EXTRACTS FROM
OTHER OF HIS DIARIES AND
LITERARY NOTE–BOOKS
EDITED BY
WILLIAM SLOANE KENNEDY

G. P. PUTNAM'S SONS
24 BEDFORD STREET, STRAND
LONDON
1904

A 20.1.a₂: 9⅝″×6⅛″

Copyright page: 'COPYRIGHT, 1904 | G. P. PUTNAM'S SONS'.

$[1-5]^8 (\pm 1_4) [6]^4$. Title leaf is a cancel.

Contents: Same as in the first issue, except: second p. iii: English title page; p. iv: English copyright page.

Binding: Unprinted dark gray wrappers. Uncut.

Publication: Deposit copies: BL ('31 DE 1904'; rebound), BO ('28 1 1905'), BC ('3 FE 1905'), BD ('Feb. 1905'; rebound).

Locations: BC, BE, BO.

Note: Possibly used for English copyright purposes only and therefore not for sale.

A 20.1.b
[Folcroft, Penn.]: Folcroft Press, [1970].

Facsimile reprinting of the first issue. Deposit copy: DLC for CIP ('2AUG1972').
Location: DLC.

A 20.1.c
[Norwood, Penn.: Norwood Editions, 1977].

Facsimile reprinting of the first issue. Price, $15.00. *Location:*   ScCleU.

A21 LAFAYETTE IN BROOKLYN
1905

A21.1.a
Only edition, first printing (1905)

LAFAYETTE IN BROOKLYN

BY

WALT WHITMAN

WITH AN INTRODUCTION
BY
JOHN BURROUGHS

GEORGE D. SMITH
NEW YORK
1905

A 21.1.a: 8¹¹⁄₁₆″ × 5¾″

```
┌──────────────────────────────────────────────────────────────────┐
│                                                                    │
│                         Copyright, 1905                            │
│                       BY GEORGE D. SMITH                           │
│                                                                    │
│  ~~~~~~~~~~~~~~~~~~~~~~~~~~~~~~~~~~~~~~~~~~~~~~~~~~~~~~~~~~~~~~~~~~~  │
│                                                                    │
│                     THE LITERARY COLLECTOR PRESS                   │
│                        GREENWICH, CONNECTICUT                      │
│                                                                    │
└──────────────────────────────────────────────────────────────────┘
```

[1–32]. Inserted leaf of Japan paper, with a photograph of Whitman printed on verso, is positioned before the title page; inserted leaves, on Japan paper, with a foldout photograph of a manuscript page and a painting of Lafayette, printed on rectos, are positioned after pp. 20, 26.

[1–4]⁴ . Sheets bulk ³⁄₃₂″.

Contents: pp. 1–2: blank; p. 3: half title, 'LAFAYETTE IN BROOKLYN'; p. 4: statement of limitation; p. 5: title page; p. 6: copyright page; p. 7: contents; p. 8: list of illustrations; p. 9: information about Whitman's lecture and manuscript; p. 10: blank; p. 11: 'INTRODUCTION | BY | JOHN BURROUGHS'; p. 12: blank; pp. 13–17: introduction; p. 18: blank; p. 19: 'LAFAYETTE IN BROOKLYN | BY | WALT WHITMAN'; p. 20: blank; p. 21: information about Whitman's lecture; p. 22: blank; pp. 23–27: text; p. 28: blank; p. 29: notes; pp. 30–32: blank.

Typography and paper: 4¾″ (4⁷⁄₁₆″)×2½″; vellum; 23 lines per page. Running heads: rectos: pp. 15–17: 'INTRODUCTION'; pp. 25–27: 'WALT WHITMAN'; versos: pp. 14–16: 'INTRODUCTION'; pp. 24–26: 'LAFAYETTE IN BROOKLYN'.

Binding: Light gray paper-covered boards with light gray V cloth (smooth) shelfback. Front cover: white paper label with 'LAFAYETTE | IN | BROOK-LYN | BY | WALT WHITMAN | 1904'; back cover: blank; spine: white paper label with 'LAFAYETTE IN BROOKLYN—WHITMAN' from bottom to top. Vellum endpapers. Uncut.

Printing: See copyright page.

Publication: Listed in *Publishers Weekly,* 18 February 1905. Limited to 250 numbered copies signed by George D. Smith, of which 15 are on Imperial Japanese Vellum and 235 on American Handmade Paper. Published 18 February 1905. Presentation copies: BMR (from Smith, 3 February 1905). Price, $7.50.

Locations: BMR, CtY, DLC, NN-R.

A 21.1.b
Only edition, second printing (1905)

New York: George D. Smith, 1905.

> *Of this book 250 copies have been printed
> at the Literary Collector Press, as follows:
> 15 copies on Imperial Japanese Vellum, and
> 235 copies on American Hand Made Paper.*
>
> 95
>
> *Geo. D. Smith*

Statement of limitation for A 21.1.a

Pagination, collation, and contents are the same as in the first printing. Page size 8½″×5½″. Sheets bulk ⅛″.

Typography and paper: Same as in the first printing, except: wove paper.

Binding: Same as in the first printing, except: all in light gray paper-covered boards; white endpapers.

Printing: Same as in the first printing.

Publication: Limited to 250 numbered copies signed by George D. Smith, of which 15 are on Imperial Japanese Vellum and 235 on American Handmade Paper. Copyright A110818; received, 7 March 1905. Published 18 February 1905, but a letter from Smith to Beverly Chew, dated 21 January 1905, says, "I have just published" this book, a copy of which is sent with the letter (CSt). Deposit copies: DLC ('MAR 7 1905'), BL ('22 MY 1905'). Presentation copies: PU (from the publisher, 12 December 1905). NN-R copy received 27 February 1905. Price, $2.50.

Locations: BL, CSt, CtY, DLC (3), JM (2), MB, MBU, NN-R, NNC, NcD, NcU, NjP, PU, RPB, ScU, TxU (4), ViU (2).

A 21.1.c₁
[Folcroft, Penn.:] Folcroft Library Editions, 1973.

Facsimile reprinting. Deposit copy: DLC for CIP ('2– JAN 1973'). Limited to 100 copies. Price, $15.00. *Locations:* DLC, ScU.

A 21.1.c₂
Norwood, Penn.: Norwood Editions, 1978.

Title leaf is inserted. DLC copy (now at FPeU) received for CIP data 15 November 1978. Limited to 100 copies. Price, $15.00. *Location:* FPeU.

Note: Listed in *BIP* (1973) as a publication by Richard West of Philadelphia for $10.00. No copies have been located.

A 22 CRITICISM AN ESSAY
1913

A 22.1.a
First edition, first printing (1913)

CRITICISM

AN ESSAY

BY

WALT WHITMAN

NEWARK NEW JERSEY

THE CARTERET BOOK CLUB

1913

A 22.1.a: 7⁵⁄₁₆″ × 5″

Copyright page: 'Copyright 1913 by THE CARTERET BOOK CLUB'.

[1–22]

[1–4]⁴. Leaf 1₁ is pasted under leaf 1₂, which is the front pastedown endpaper; leaf 1₃ is the front free endpaper; leaf 4₃ is pasted under leaf 4₄, which is the back pastedown endpaper. Sheets bulk 1/16″.

Contents: pp. 1–2: blank (see collation above); p. 3: half title, 'CRITICISM'; p. 4: blank; p. 5: title page; p. 6: copyright page; p. 7: information about essay; p. 8: blank; pp. 9–17: text; p. 18: blank; p. 19: statement of limitation; pp. 20–22: blank (see collation above).

Typography and paper: 4⅞″×3″; laid paper with vertical chain lines 1 1/16″ apart, watermarked with a shield design; 18 lines per page.

Binding: Light olive-gray laid paper-covered boards. Front cover: white paper label with 'CRITICISM | AN ESSAY | BY | WALT WHITMAN'; back cover and spine: blank. For flyleaves and endpapers, see collation above. Top edges trimmed, front and bottom edges rough trimmed.

Box: Light olive-gray laid paper-covered slipcase, open at one end. White paper label on side with 'CRITICISM | AN ESSAY | BY | WALT WHITMAN'.

Printing: Marion Press (p. [19]).

Publication: Limited to 100 numbered copies. Printed May 1913. Copyright A351276; received, 7 August 1913. Published 17 July 1913. Listed in *Publishers Weekly,* 29 November 1913. Deposit copies: DLC ('AUG 7 1913'; 2 copies).

The Marion Press certifies that only one hundred copies of "Criticism, an Essay by Walt Whitman," have been printed from type, on Italian handmade paper, in the month of May 1913.

This copy is number 8 0

Statement of limitation for A 22.1.a

Locations: CtY (box), DLC (3; 1 box), MB (box), MBU (box), NNC, NcD (box), NjP (box), ScU (box), TxU (box), ViU (box).

A 22.1.b
New York: Gordon, [n.d.].

Facsimile reprinting listed in *Books in Print* (1972) for $7.95. *Not seen.*

A 22.1.c
Philadelphia: Richard West, [n.d.].

Facsimile reprinting listed in *BIP* (1973) for $7.75. *Not seen.*

A 22.2
Second edition, only printing (1924)

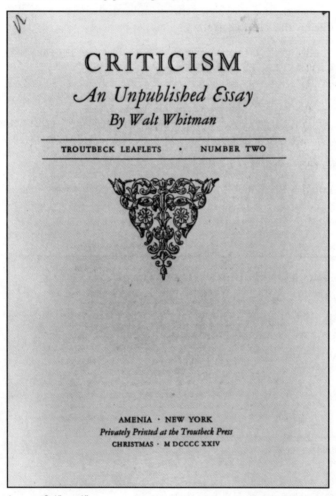

A 22.2: 8¾"×5½"

[1–12]

[1]⁶ . Sheets bulk ⅟₃₂″.

Contents: p. 1: title page; p. 2: statement of limitation; pp. 3–4: "Prefatory Note"; p. 5: 'CRITICISM'; p. 6: blank; pp. 7–10: text; pp. 11–12: blank.

Typography and paper: 5¹¹⁄₁₆″×3⅝″; laid paper with vertical chain lines 1⅟₁₆″ apart, watermarked '[script] RIVES [roman] (FRANCE)'; introduction: various lines per page; text: 28 lines per page.

Binding: Grayish yellow-green wrappers; front cover: '[ornate lettering] CRITICISM | *An Unpublished Essay* | *By Walt Whitman* | [rule] | TROUTBECK LEAFLETS • NUMBER TWO | [rule] | [triangular leaf-and-flower design]'; front cover verso, back cover recto and verso: blank. Top edges rough trimmed, front and bottom edges untrimmed.

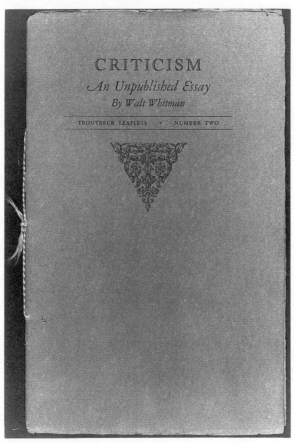

Wrapper for A 22.2

Printing: See statement of limitation.

Publication: Limited to 200 copies. *Troutbeck Leaflets Number Two.* Printed Christmas 1924. Deposit copies: BL ('10 JA 1925'). MB copy received from Spingarn 23 December 1924. DLC copy received from Spingarn 2 January 1925.

> *Of this second number of Troutbeck Leaflets,*
> *two hundred copies have been printed as a*
> *Christmas Greeting to the friends of*
> *Amy E. and J. E.Spingarn*

Statement of limitation for A 22.2

Locations: BL, CtY (2), DLC, JM, MB, NNC, PU, RPB, TxU (2).

Note: Edited by J. E. Spingarn.

A 23 THE GATHERING OF THE FORCES
1920

A 23.1.a
Only edition, first printing (1920)

THE GATHERING OF THE FORCES

BY

WALT WHITMAN

EDITORIALS, ESSAYS, LITERARY AND DRAMATIC REVIEWS
AND OTHER MATERIAL WRITTEN BY WALT WHITMAN
AS EDITOR OF THE BROOKLYN DAILY EAGLE IN
1846 AND 1847

EDITED BY

CLEVELAND RODGERS AND JOHN BLACK

WITH A FOREWORD AND A SKETCH OF WHITMAN'S LIFE AND WORK
DURING TWO UNKNOWN YEARS

IN TWO VOLUMES

VOLUME ONE

ILLUSTRATIONS IN PHOTOGRAVURE

G. P. PUTNAM'S SONS
NEW YORK AND LONDON
The Knickerbocker Press
1920

A 23.1.a: Binding A: $9\frac{5}{16}'' \times 5\frac{3}{4}''$; Bindings B–C: $9'' \times 5\frac{1}{2}''$

Volume I: [i–ii] [i–iv] v–lxi [lxii] lxiii [lxiv] 1 [2] 3–93 [94] 95 [96] 97–177 [178] 179–272. Inserted leaves with Kurtz drawing of Whitman printed on verso, followed by a leaf of transparent paper with caption printed on recto, is positioned before the title page; inserted leaves with photographs of Whitman's birthplace, the schoolhouse where Whitman taught, printed on rectos, both followed by a leaf of transparent paper with caption printed on verso, are positioned after pp. 74, 124; inserted leaf of transparent paper with foldout facsimile of manuscript page printed on recto, followed by a leaf of transparent paper with caption printed on verso, is positioned after p. 206.

Volume II: [i–iv] [i–ii] iii–xi [xii] xiii [xiv] 1 [2] 3–83 [84] 85 [86] 87–233 [234] 235 [236] 237–365 [366] 367 [368] 369–394 [395–396]. Inserted leaf with photograph of Whitman in 1849 printed on verso, followed by a leaf of transparent paper with caption printed on recto, is positioned before the title page; inserted leaves with photographs of a group of pilgrims at Whitman's birthplace, William Henry Sutton, Whitman's home on Myrtle Street in Brooklyn, and the Hollyer engraving of Whitman, printed on rectos, all preceded by a leaf of transparent paper with caption printed on verso, are positioned after pp. 98, 202, 242, 314.

Volume I: [a]^1 [b–e]^8 1–17^8. Sheets bulk 1$^1\!/_{16}$".

Volume II: [a]^1 [b]^8 1–24^8 25^6. Sheets bulk 1$^5\!/_{32}$".

Contents: Vol. I: p. i: statement of limitation; p. ii: blank; p. i: half title, 'The Gathering of the Forces'; p. ii: blank; p. iii: title page; p. iv: copyright page; pp. v–x: foreword; pp. xi–liii: "Whitman's Life and Work 1846–1847"; p. liv: acknowledgments; pp. lv–lxi: contents; p. lxii: blank; p. lxiii: list of illustrations; p. lxiv: blank; p. 1: 'Part I | DEMOCRACY'; p. 2: blank; pp. 3–93: texts; p. 94: blank; p. 95: 'Part II | HUMANITY'; p. 96: blank; pp. 97–176: texts; p. 177: 'Part III | SLAVERY AND THE MEXICAN WAR'; p. 178: blank; pp.

179–272: texts; Vol. II: p. i: statement of limitation, same as in vol. I; p. ii: blank; p. iii: half title, same as in vol. I; p. iv: blank; p. i: title page, same as in vol. I, except: 'VOLUME TWO'; p. ii: copyright page, same as in vol. I; pp. iii–xi: contents; p. xii: blank; p. xiii: list of illustrations; p. xiv: blank; p. 1: 'Part IV | POLITICS'; p. 2: blank; pp. 3–83: texts; p. 84: blank; p. 85: 'Part V | ESSAYS, PERSONALITIES, SHORT | EDITORIALS'; p. 86: blank; pp. 87–233: texts; p. 234: blank; p. 235: 'Part VI | LITERATURE, BOOK REVIEWS, | DRAMA, ETC.'; p. 236: blank; pp. 237–365: texts; p. 366: blank; p. 367: 'Part VII | TWO SHORT STORIES | *[Not Included in Whitman's Published Works]*'; p. 368: blank; pp. 369–386: texts; pp. 387–394: index; pp. 395–396: blank.

Prose: Reprints E 28, E 142, E 151, E 163, E 234, E 240, E 243, E 249, E 257, E 266, E 267, E 271, E 274, E 275, E 280, E 282, E 288, E 291, E 315, E 334, E 337, E 365, E 369, E 371, E 376, E 379, E 381, E 383, E 387, E 391, E 393, E 395, E 398, E 401–404, E 404, E 407, E 409, E 410, E 414–416, E 419, E 422, E 423, E 427–433, E 438, E 439, E 447, E 448, E 452–454, E 458, E 463–465, E 471–473, E 476, E 477, E 480, E 481, E 484, E 485, E 487, E 490, E 492, E 495, E 496, E 498, E 499, E 506, E 508, E 512, E 515–519, E 521–524, E 528–534, E 538, E 541, E 545, E 547, E 548, E 551, E 553, E 558–E 566, E 568, E 570–572, E 578, E 579, E 583, E 586, E 588, E 590, E 596, E 597, E 604, E 607, E 608, E 610, E 613, E 618–622, E 624, E 627, E 631, E 633, E 636, E 639, E 642, E 643, E 645, E 648–650, E 652, E 654–656, E 658, E 660, E 661, E 663–666, E 672–674, E 680, E 682, E 687–691, E 693, E 695, E 696, E 698–700, E 705, E 708, E 710, E 711, E 714, E 717, E 719, E 722–728, E 730–732, E 737, E 742, E 743, E 746, E 749, E 751, E 752, E 755, E 756, E 762, E 766–768, E 773, E 777, E 783, E 784, E 788, E 789, E 791, E 792, E 794, E 797, E 798, E 801–803, E 807, E 811, E 814, E 815, E 818, E 819, E 822, E 823, E 825, E 828, E 830–835, E 837–839, E 842–844, E 850, E 852–855, E 858, E 863, E 867, E 870–873, E 875, E 878, E 880, E 886–890, E 896, E 898, E 899, E 903, E 905, E 906, E 909, E 911, E 918, E 919, E 923, E 924, E 931, E 932, E 934, E 940, E 941, E 944, E 945, E 947, E 948, E 950, E 954, E 961, E 969, E 972, E 976, E 978, E 979, E 983, E 984, E 986, E 988–990, E 994, E 996, E 997, E 1001, E 1008, E 1013, E 1019–1022, E 1027, E 1030, E 1033, E 1034, E 1036, E 1037, E 1048, E 1049, E 1053–1055, E 1060, E 1062, E 1063, E 1066, E 2812.

Typography and paper: 6″ (5½″)×3⅜″; wove paper watermarked '[curved] WARREN'S | OLDE STYLE'; introduction and texts: 25 lines per page; index: double columns, 48 lines per column. All running heads are between thick-thin and thin rules. Running heads: vol. I: rectos: pp. vii–ix: 'FOREWORD'; pp. xiii–liii: 'WHITMAN'S LIFE AND WORK'; p. lvii–lxi: 'CONTENTS'; pp. 5–27: 'AMERICAN DEMOCRACY'; pp. 31–49: 'EUROPE AND AMERICA'; pp. 53–73: 'GOVERNMENT'; pp. 77–93: 'PATRIOTISM'; pp. 99–109: 'HANGING'; pp. 111–115: 'PRISON REFORM'; pp. 117–119: 'UNFORTUNATES';

pp. 123–147: 'EDUCATION, CHILDREN'; pp. 149–157: 'LABOR, FEMALE LABOR'; pp. 161–165: 'EMIGRANTS'; pp. 167–175: 'ENGLAND'S OPPRESSION OF IRELAND'; pp. 181–227: 'THE EXTENSION OF SLAVERY'; pp. 231–239: 'THE UNION OF STATES'; pp. 241–265: 'WAR WITH MEXICO'; pp. 269–271: 'THE OREGON BOUNDARY DISPUTE'; versos: pp. vi–x: 'FOREWORD'; pp. xii–lii: 'WALT WHITMAN'; pp. lvi–lx: 'CONTENTS'; pp. 4–92, 98–146, 168–176, 180–238, 242–272: 'WALT WHITMAN'; vol. II: rectos: v–xi: 'CONTENTS'; pp. 5–23: 'POLITICAL CONTROVERSIES'; pp. 27–45: 'TWO LOCAL POLITICAL CAMPAIGNS'; pp. 47–57: 'CIVIL INTERESTS'; pp. 59–69: 'FREE TRADE'; pp. 71–83: 'THE CURRENCY SYSTEM'; pp. 89–177: 'GENERAL ESSAYS'; pp. 179–197: 'PERSONALITIES OF THE TIME'; pp. 201–209: 'THE ART OF HEALTH'; pp. 211–221: 'SHORT EDITORIALS'; pp. 225–233: 'WHITMAN AS A PARAGRAPHER'; pp. 239–277: 'AMERICAN LITERATURE'; pp. 279–307: 'WHITMAN'S BOOK REVIEWS'; pp. 311–343: 'WHITMAN AS A DRAMATIC CRITIC'; pp. 347–359: 'THE MUSIC LOVER'; pp. 361–365: 'COMMENT ON ART'; pp. 371–375: 'THE LOVE OF ERIS'; pp. 379–385: 'A LEGEND OF LIFE AND LOVE'; pp. 389–393: 'INDEX'; versos: pp. iv–x: 'CONTENTS'; pp. 4–44, 48–56, 60–82, 88–176, 180–208, 212–232, 238–276, 280–358, 362–364, 370–386: 'WALT WHITMAN'; pp. 388–394: 'INDEX'.

Binding: Three styles have been noted; priority of the last two undetermined:

Binding A: Light gray paper-covered boards. Front and back covers: gold-stamped circular double-rule frame surrounding stylized 'WW', in center; spine: leather label with goldstamped '[double rule] | THE | GATHERING | OF THE | FORCES | 1846–1847 | [rule] | WALT WHITMAN | [single-rule circular frame around '1' (or '2')] | [double rule]'. Light brown endpapers with drawing of stone and tablet marking Whitman's birthplace printed in brown on the front and back pastedown endpapers. All edges rough trimmed.

Binding B: Grayish olive buckram. Front and back covers: blank; spine: blackstamped '[double rule] | THE | GATHERING | OF THE | FORCES | 1846–1847 | [rule] | WALT WHITMAN | [single-rule circular frame around '1' (or '2')] | [double rule] | PUTNAM'. Endpapers are the same as in binding A. All edges trimmed.

Binding C: Light blue V cloth (smooth). Front and back covers: black-stamped: circular double-rule frame surrounding stylized 'WW', in center; spine: blackstamped 'THE | GATHERING | OF THE | FORCES | 1846–1847 | [rule] | WALT WHITMAN | [single-rule circular frame around '1' (or '2')] | PUTNAM'. Endpapers are the same as in binding A. All edges rough trimmed.

Dust jackets: Light gray paper. Front cover: circular double-rule frame surrounding stylized 'WW', in center; back cover: blank; spine: '[double rule] |

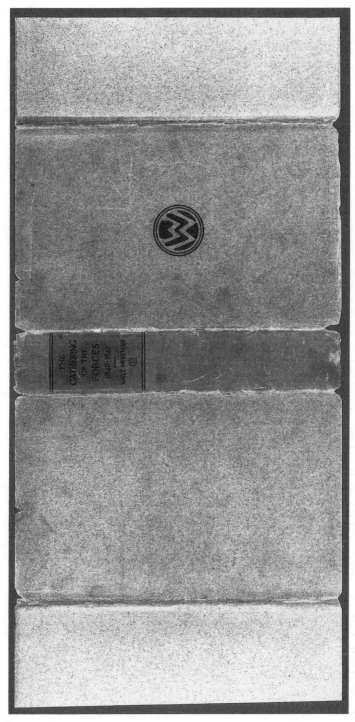

THE
GATHERING
OF THE
FORCES
1846-1847
—
WALT WHITMAN
②

Dust jacket for A 23.1.a

LIMITED LETTERPRESS EDITION, PRINTED
FROM TYPE

This is one of 1250 sets, each in two
volumes issued in the Autumn of 1920.
No other edition will be issued.

G. P. Putnam's Sons

Statement of limitation for A 23.1.a

THE | GATHERING | OF THE | FORCES | 1846–1847 | [rule] | WALT
WHITMAN | [single-rule circular frame around '1' (or '2')] | [double rule]';
front and back flaps: blank.

Printing: See copyright page.

Publication: Limited to 1,250 sets. Reviewed in *New York Sun,* 24 December
1920, p. 7; *Times Literary Supplement,* 10 February 1921, p. 88. Copyright
A608265; received 7 February 1921. Published 10 December 1920. Deposit
copies: DLC ('FEB –7 1921'; vol. I rebound); binding A: BL ('19 JAN 21'),
DLC ('FEB –7 1921'; vol. II), BE ('22 FEB 1921'), BO ('FEB1921'). Presentation copies: binding A: TxU (from Black, 17 December 1920). Copies inscribed by owners: binding A: TxU (January 1921). MB set received 16 December 1920. Price, $15.00 the set. Listed in the *English Catalogue* as an
importation in February 1921 at 90s. Listed as an importation by Putnam in
the *Bookseller,* March 1921.

Locations: Binding A: BE, BL, BMR (dj), BO, CSt, CaOTU, CtY (dj), DLC,
DLC (II), InU-L (dj), JM, JM (dj), MB, MBU, NNC (2), NcD, NjCW (I), PU,
PU (dj), RPB, ScU, TxU (6; 4dj), ViU (2; 2dj); binding B: MBU, PU; binding
C: JM.

Note: Bindings B and C are undoubtedly remainder bindings and were probably sold without dust jackets.

A 23.1.b
Philadelphia: Richard West, [n.d.].

Facsimile reprinting in 2 vols. listed in *BIP* (1974–1980) for $100.00. *Not
seen.*

A 24 THE UNCOLLECTED POETRY AND PROSE
1921

A 24.1.a
Only edition, first printing (1921)

Three issues have been noted:

A 24.1.a₁
First (American) issue (1921)

THE
UNCOLLECTED POETRY
AND PROSE OF
WALT WHITMAN

MUCH OF WHICH HAS BEEN
BUT RECENTLY DISCOVERED
WITH
VARIOUS EARLY MANUSCRIPTS
NOW FIRST PUBLISHED

COLLECTED AND EDITED BY
E M O R Y H O L L O W A Y
PROFESSOR OF ENGLISH IN ADELPHI COLLEGE

ILLUSTRATED

—

IN TWO VOLUMES
VOLUME
ONE

GARDEN CITY, N. Y., AND TORONTO
DOUBLEDAY, PAGE & COMPANY
1921

A 24.1.a₁ : 8¼″×5½″; first four lines and publisher's device are in orange

Vol. I: [i–viii] ix–xv [xvi] xvii–xx [xxi–xxii] xxiii–xcii [i–ii] 1–264 [265–268]. Inserted leaf of coated paper, with Gutekunst photograph of Whitman in 1889, printed on verso, is positioned before the title page; inserted leaves of coated paper, with photographs of a 14 June 1842 letter and drawings from Whitman's notebook, printed on rectos, are positioned after pp. 84, 194.

Vol. II: [iii–vi] vii–viii [ix–x] [i–ii] 1–321 [322–324] 325–351 [352]. Inserted leaf of coated paper with photograph of Whitman in 1840 printed on verso is positioned before the title page; inserted leaf of coated paper with a photograph of pages from Whitman's notebooks printed on recto is inserted after p. 70.

Vol. I: [1–22]^8 (1_{1+1}) [23]^4. The title leaf is tipped to the recto of leaf 1_2 (dedication page). Sheets bulk 1⅛".

Vol. II: [a]^1 [1–22]^8 [23]^4. The title leaf is tipped to the recto of leaf 1_1 (dedication page). Sheets bulk 1⅛".

Contents: Vol. I: p. i: half title, 'THE | UNCOLLECTED POETRY AND PROSE | OF | WALT WHITMAN'; p. ii: blank; p. iii: title page [book title and publisher's device in red]; p. iv: copyright page; p. v: dedication; p. vi: blank; p. vii: '*A vast batch left to oblivion.* | —WHITMAN'; p. viii: blank; pp. ix–xv: preface; p. xvi: blank; pp. xvii–xx: contents to vol. I; pp. xxi: list of illustrations in vol. I; p. xxii: blank; pp. xxiii–lx: biographical introduction; pp. lxi–xcii: critical introduction; p. i: half title, the same as p. i; p. ii: blank; pp. 1–31: poems; pp. 32–264: shorter prose works; p. 265: printer's imprint and information; pp. 266–268: blank; vol. II: p. iii: title page, same as in vol. I, except: 'VOLUME | TWO'; p. iv: copyright page, same as in vol. I; p. v: dedication page, same as in vol. I; p. vi: blank; pp. vii–viii: contents of vol. II; p. ix: list of illustrations in vol. II; p. x: blank; p. i: half title, same as in vol. I; p. ii: blank; pp. 1–62: shorter prose works; pp. 63–102: manuscripts; pp. 103–321: longer prose publications; p. 322: blank; p. 323: 'SUBJECT INDEX'; p. 324: blank; pp. 325–351: subject index; p. 352: printer's imprint and information, same as in vol. I.

Poetry and Prose: Reprints E 1, E 3–5, E 7, E 12–19, E 22–24, E 26–28, E 33–36, E 40, E 42, E 151, E 157, E 159, E 163, E 165, E 172, E 196, E 197, E 203, E 234, E 235, E 242, E 257, E 266, E 275, E 288, E 358, E 360, E 364, E

371, E 396, E 403, E 415, E 452, E 477, E 519, E 533, E 539, E 565, E 578, E 580, E 581, E 585, E 597, E 598, E 605, E 607, E 617, E 624, E 644, E 645, E 653, E 655, E 662, E 665, E 718, E 746, E 750, E 758, E 761, E 762, E 777, E 790, E 821, E 833, E 835, E 842, E 844, E 848, E 851, E 854, E 861, E 876, E 877, E 895, E 906, E 915, E 918, E 927, E 932, E 948, E 957–959, E 967, E 976, E 995, E 1004, E 1009, E 1021, E 1026, E 1036, E 1062, E 1067, E 1068, E 1070, E 1073–1075, E 1079, E 1080, E 1082, E 1090, E 1099, E 1107–1109, E 1111, E 1114, E 1116, E 1119, E 1121, E 1125–1127, E 1159, E 1162, E 1165, E 1169–1174, E 1176, E 1177, E 1240, E 1262, E 1304, E 1405, E 1772, E 1812, E 1828, E 1879, E 2141, E 2444–2446, E 2450, E 2452, E 2454–2463, E 2466, E 2468, E 2470, E 2474–2477, E 2479–2481, E 2485, E 2487, E 2488, E 2490, E 2530, E 2531, E 2545, E 2636, E 2756, E 2768.

Typography and paper: 6⅝″ (6⅜″)×4¹³⁄₁₆″; wove paper; 42 lines per page. Running heads: vol. I: rectos: pp. xi–xv: 'PREFACE'; p. xix: 'CONTENTS'; pp. xxv–lix: 'INTRODUCTION: BIOGRAPHICAL'; pp. lxiii–xci: 'INTRODUCTION: CRITICAL'; pp. 2–263: 'PROSE OF WALT WHITMAN'; versos: pp. x–xiv: 'PREFACE'; pp. xviii–xx: 'CONTENTS'; pp. xxiv–lx: 'INTRODUCTION: BIOGRAPHICAL'; pp. lxii–xcii: 'INTRODUCTION: CRITICAL'; pp. 2–30, 34–264: 'THE UNCOLLECTED POETRY AND'; vol. II: rectos: pp. 3–61, 65–101, 105–321: 'PROSE OF WALT WHITMAN'; pp. 327–351: 'INDEX'; versos: p. viii: 'CONTENTS'; pp. 2–60: 'THE UNCOLLECTED POETRY AND'; p. 62: 'POETRY AND PROSE OF WALT WHITMAN'; pp. 64–100: 'THE UNCOLLECTED POETRY AND'; p. 102: 'POETRY AND PROSE OF WALT WHITMAN'; pp. 104–220, 224–320: 'THE UNCOLLECTED POETRY AND'; pp. 326–350: 'INDEX'.

Binding: Dark grayish green T cloth (bold-ribbed). Front cover: blind-stamped single-rule frame; back cover: blank; spine: white paper label with green printing: '[all within double-rule frame] [leaf] THE UN- | COLLECTED | POETRY | AND | PROSE | OF | WALT | WHITMAN | BY | EMORY | HOLLOWAY | [rule] | VOLUME | I [II]' at top, and blindstamped 'DOUBLE-DAY | PAGE & CO.' at bottom. White wove endpapers. Top edges trimmed, front edges rough trimmed, bottom edges uncut.

Dust jacket: Cream coated paper. Front and back covers: blank; spine: 'The | [orange] UNCOLLECTED | Poetry and | Prose of | WALT | WHITMAN | [orange double rule] | *Edited by* | EMORY | HOLLOWAY | VOL. I [II] | [two lines to the left of orange publisher's device] *The Country | Life Press* | [orange rule] | DOUBLEDAY | PAGE & CO.'; front and back flaps: blank.

Box: Cream coated paper-covered box open at one end. Pasted completely over front and rear of box are cream coated papers with '[ornate band] | [orange rule] | [oval picture of Whitman] | [orange] THE UNCOLLECTED | POETRY AND PROSE | *of* | WALT WHITMAN | [orange leaf design] | *Edited by EMORY*

Dust jacket for A 24.1.a,

HOLLOWAY | [15-line description of book and blurb by Thomas B. Harned]' on one side and '[ornate band] . . . HOLLOWAY | [13 lines from Holloway's introduction]' on the other side.

Printing: '[drawing of building within thick-thin circular frame] | THE COUNTRY LIFE PRESS | GARDEN CITY, N.Y.' (I, [265]; II, [352]).

Publication: Listed in *Publishers Weekly,* 12 November 1921. Reviewed in *New York Times Book Review,* 25 December 1921, p. 8. Copyright A627747; received 16 November 1921. Published 24 October 1921. Deposit copies: DLC ('NOV 16 1921'; vol. I rebound). Presentation copies: RPB (from Holloway,

October 1921), ViU (from Holloway, October 1921). Copies inscribed by owners: TxU (October 1921). MB set (rebound) received 27 October 1921. Price, $7.50 the set.

Locations: CaOTU, CtY (dj; box), DLC, DLC (II), JM, MBU (dj, box), NcU, NjCW, NjP, PU (2), RPB, ScU (II), TxU, TxU (dj), ViU (2).

A 24.1.a₂
Second (English) issue (1921)

THE UNCOLLECTED
POETRY AND PROSE
OF
WALT WHITMAN

BY
EMORY HOLLOWAY

LONDON
CURTIS BROWN, LTD.
1921

A 24.1.a₂: 8¼″×5½″

Vol. I: [1–22]⁸ (1₁₊₁) [23]⁴. The title leaf is tipped to the recto of leaf 1₂ (dedication page).

Vol. II: [a]¹ [1–22]⁸ [23]⁴. The title leaf is tipped to the recto of leaf 1₁ (dedication page).

Contents: Same as in the first issue, except: vol. I: p. iii: English title page; p. iv: copyright page; vol. II: p. iii: English title page; p. iv: English copyright page.

Binding: Same as in the first issue.

Publication: Reviewed in *London Morning Post*, 2 March 1922. Deposit copies: BL ('3 NOV 21'), BE ('15 NOV 1921'), BO ('NOV1921').

Locations: BE, BL, BO.

A 24.1.a₃
Third (English) issue (1922)

THE
UNCOLLECTED POETRY
AND PROSE OF
WALT WHITMAN

MUCH OF WHICH HAS BEEN
BUT RECENTLY DISCOVERED
WITH
VARIOUS EARLY MANUSCRIPTS
NOW FIRST PUBLISHED

COLLECTED AND EDITED BY
EMORY HOLLOWAY
PROFESSOR OF ENGLISH IN ADELPHI COLLEGE

ILLUSTRATED

—

IN TWO VOLUMES

VOLUME
ONE

LONDON: WILLIAM HEINEMANN

A 24.1.a₃: 8¼″×5½″; first four lines are in red

Vol. I: $[1-22]^8 (1_{1+1}) [23]^4$. The title leaf is tipped to the recto of leaf 1_2 (dedication page).

Vol. II: $[a]^1 [1-22]^8 [23]^4$. The title leaf is tipped to the recto of leaf 1_1 (dedication page).

Contents: Same as in the first issue, except: vol I: p. iii: English title page; p. iv: blank; vol. II: p. iii: English title page; p. iv: blank.

Binding: Very deep red S cloth (diagonal fine-ribbed). Front cover: blind-stamped double-ruled frame; back cover: blank; spine: paper label with '[double rule] | THE | UNCOLLECTED | POETRY AND | PROSE OF | WALT | WHITMAN | I [II] | HEINEMANN | [double rule]'. White endpapers. All edges trimmed.

Publication: Listed in the *English Catalogue* for March 1922 at 30s. the set. Deposit copies: BL ('2 MAR 22'), BE ('13 MAR 1922'), BO ('MAR1922').

Locations: BBo, BE, BL, BMR, BO, InU-L.

A 24.1.b–c
New York: Peter Smith, 1932.

2 vols. Facsimile reprinting of the first issue. DLC set (vol. II rebound) received 5 June 1933. Price, $7.50 the set. Reprinted with Gloucester, Mass., imprint in 2 vols. in 1972. *Locations:;* DLC (1932), JM (both).

A25 THE HALF-BREED AND OTHER STORIES
1927

A25.1.a
Only edition, first printing (1927)

THE
HALF-BREED
and other stories by
WALT WHITMAN
Now first collected by
Thomas Ollive Mabbott
Woodcuts by
Allen Lewis

Columbia University
Press·New York·1927

A25.1.a: 9¼"×6½"

Two states have been noted:

First state:

Illustrations on thin Japanlike paper, printed on recto and signed by the artist, are pasted to blank pp. iv, 43, 51, 93, and 111 at the top and in the gutter.

Second state:

Illustrations are printed directly on pp. iv, 43, 51, 93, 111.

[i–ii] [i–x] [11] 12–19 [20–21] 22–42 [43] 44–50 [51] 52–76 [77–81] 82–85 [86–89] 90–92 [93] 94–97 [98–101] 102–104 [105–109] 110 [111] 112–113 [114–116] 117–129 [130–134]

[1–4]⁸ [5]⁴ [6–9]⁸. Sheets bulk ½".

Contents: pp. i–ii: blank; p. i: '[leaf] SHORT | STORIES | BY [leaf] WALT | WHITMAN | [three circular ornaments] | WOODCUTS [leaf] BY | ALLEN [leaf] LEWIS'; pp. ii–iv: blank [p. iv: illustration]; p. v: title page; p. vi: blank; p. vii: contents; p. viii: blank; p. ix: dedication to Cleveland Rodgers; p. x: blank; pp. 11–19: introduction, signed 'T. O. M. | *December 31, 1926*'; p. 20: blank; p. 21: all within a decorated border '[two crosslike designs] | THE | HALF- | BREED | A Tale of the | Western Frontier | [drawing of Indian's head] | Arrow-Tip'; p. 22: blank; pp. 23–76: text [pp. 43, 51: illustration]; p. 77: drawing; p. 78: blank; p. 79: all within a decorative border 'SHIRVAL | A TALE OF | JERUSA- | LEM | [leaf design]'; p. 80: blank; pp. 81–85: text; p. 86: blank; p. 87: all within a triple-rule frame '[drawing of ship] | RICHARD | PARKER'S | WIDOW | [two ornaments]'; p. 88: blank; pp. 89–97: text [p. 93: illustration]; p. 98: blank; p. 99: all within a frame of locomotives, railroad cars, and houses '[leaf design] | [two leaf designs] | [two leaf designs] | SOME | FACT- | ROMANCES'; p. 100: blank; pp. 101–104: text; p. 105: drawing; p. 106: blank; p. 107: all within flower-and-vine design border: triple-rule frame surrounding 'MY | BOYS | AND | GIRLS'; p. 108: blank; pp. 109–113: text [p. 111: illustration]; p. 114: blank; p. 115: 'NOTES | [ornament]'; p. 116: blank; pp. 117–129: notes; p. 130: blank; p. 131: statement of limitation and printer's information; pp. 132–134: blank.

Prose: Reprints E 169, E 174–176, E 205.

Typography and paper: 6¼"×4¼"; wove paper watermarked 'RIVES | FRANCE'; introduction and text: 33 lines per page; notes, double columns, 39 lines per column, and normal column width, 37 lines per page.

Binding: Light yellowish brown B cloth (linen) shelfback with paper-covered sides. Front cover: gray-and-white patterned background (see illustration) with: all within a triple-ruled frame, corners not connected: '[leaf] SHORT | STORIES | BY [leaf] WALT | WHITMAN | [three ornaments] | WOODCUTS

[leaf] BY | ALLEN [leaf] LEWIS'; back cover: gray-and-white patterned background with: all within a triple-ruled frame, corners not connected: '[leaf] COLUMBIA | UNIVERSITY | [ornament] PRESS [ornament] | [crown] | [open book, with '17 | 18' on verso, and '54 | 93' on recto] | [scroll]'; spine: white paper label with vertical '[all within a triple–rule frame, corners not connected] STORIES • BY • W • W • '. White endpapers. Top edges trimmed, front and bottom edges rough trimmed. Top edges stained gray or gilded.

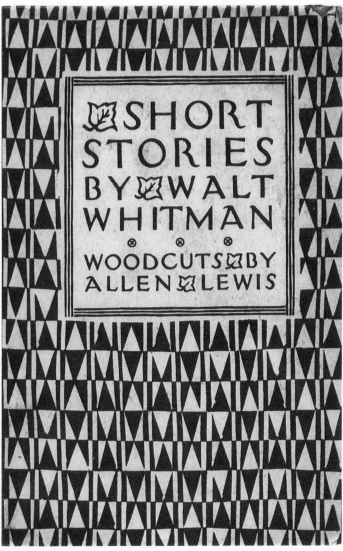

Binding for A 25.1.a

Dust jacket: Unprinted glassine.

Printing: See illustration.

This book has been published and copyrighted by the Columbia University Press. The type was set by hand at the Strawberry-Hill Press, and the book was printed by them in the month of February, nineteen hundred and twenty-seven. One hundred and fifty-five copies are printed on hand-made paper. In the first thirty the illustrations are proofs pulled direct from the wood blocks and signed by the artist.

This is number . 21 . .

Statement of limitation for A 25.1.a

Publication: Printed February 1927. Limited to 155 numbered copies; in "the first thirty the illustrations are proofs pulled direct from the woodblocks and signed by the artist" (p. [131]; see illustration). Sold by subscription. Price, $25.00.

Locations: First state: CtY, DLC, JM, NcD, NjP, TxU (dj); second state: JM, NcU, RPB.

Note: A four-page advertising flier is at CtY, NcD, and TxU.

A 25.1.b
Second printing (1927)

Title page is the same as in the first printing.

Pagination, collation, and binding are the same as in the first printing. Page size: 9″×6¼″.

Contents: Same as in the first printing, second state, except: p. vii: dedication to Cleveland Rodgers; p. ix: contents.

Typography and paper: Same as in the second printing, except: wove paper watermarked '[script] Made in U. S. A. Old Stratford'.

Dust jacket: Unprinted glassine.

Printing: See illustration.

Publication: Printed February 1927. Unknown number of copies in trade printing. Listed in *Publishers Weekly,* 26 March 1927. Reviewed in *Saturday Review of Literature,* 3 (28 May 1927), 869. Copyright A967704; received, 28

> This book has been published and copyrighted by the Columbia University Press. The type was set by hand at the Strawberry-Hill Press, and the book was printed by them in the month of February, nineteen hundred and twenty-seven. One hundred and fifty-five copies are printed on hand-made paper. In the first thirty the illustrations are proofs pulled direct from the wood blocks and signed by the artist.

Statement of limitation for A 25.1.b

February 1927. Published 26 February 1927. Deposit copies: DLC ('FEB28'27'), BL ('28 MAY 27'), BO ('15 JUN 1927'). Presentation copies: ScU (from Mabbott, 27 April 1927). Copies inscribed by owners: RPB (4 April 1927). CaOTU copy received 13 April 1927. Price, $4.50. Listed in the *English Catalogue* as an importation by Oxford University Press for May 1927 at 23s. Listed in *Bookseller,* 27 May 1927.

Locations: BL, BO, CSt, CaOTP, CaOTU, CtY, DLC, InU-L, JM, MBU, MH, NNC, NcU, NcD, NjCW (2), NjP, PU, RPB, ScU, TxU (3), ViU.

Note one: Because the statement of limitation is present in copies of the trade printing (except for the line on which the number of the copy was written), copies of the trade printing are sometimes described as "unnumbered" or "out of series" copies of the limited printing(s) of 155 copies.

Note two: Some copies have 'PRINTED IN U.S.A.' stamped in blue ink at the bottom of p. 131 (statement of limitation) (BL, BO).

A 25.1.c
[Folcroft, Penn.]: Folcroft Library Editions, 1972.

Facsimile reprinting of the second printing (A 25.1.b). Deposit copy: DLC for CIP ('24 AUG 1972'). Price, $20.00. *Location:* DLC.

Note: Listed in *NUC* (1978:150) as a 1978 publication by Norwood Editions of Norwood, Penn., for $20.00. No copies have been located.

A 26 PICTURES
1927

A 26.1.a
Only edition, first printing (1927)

PICTURES

An Unpublished Poem

OF

Walt Whitman

With an Introduction and Notes
by Emory Holloway

NEW YORK : THE JUNE HOUSE

London : Faber & Gwyer, Ltd.

1927

A 26.1.a: 8¹⁄₁₆″×5″; drawing of house is in green

Copyright page: 'PRINTED IN THE UNITED STATES OF AMERICA'.

[1–7] 8–11 [12–13] 14–28 [29] 30–37 [38–40]

[1–5]⁴. Sheets bulk ⅛″.

Contents: p. 1: half title, 'PICTURES'; p. 2: blank; p. 3: title page [drawing of house in green]; p. 4: copyright page; p. 5: acknowledgment of reprinting "with slight changes" from *Southwest Review;* p. 6: blank; pp. 7–11: introduction, signed 'Emory Holloway | *Brooklyn, March, 1927';* p. 12: statement that superscript numbers in text refer to notes at the end of the book; pp. 13–28: text; pp. 29–37: notes; p. 38: blank; p. 39: statement of limitation and printing information; p. 40: blank.

Typography and paper: 5¾″ (5⁷⁄₁₆″)×3³⁄₁₆″; wove paper watermarked '100% BR RAG | READING | 1924'; various lines per page (up to 24). Running heads: rectos: pp. 9–11: 'INTRODUCTION'; pp. 15–27: 'PICTURES'; pp. 31–37: 'NOTES'; versos: pp. 8–10: 'INTRODUCTION'; pp. 14–28: 'PICTURES'; pp. 30–36: 'NOTES'.

Binding: Boards covered with white paper with very light blue vein pattern. Front and back covers: blank; spine: light green paper label with from bottom to top: ' *'PICTURES'* '. White endpapers. Top edges trimmed, front and bottom edges rough trimmed.

Dust jacket: Unprinted glassine.

Printing: Handset and printed by Earl Widtman of the Press of M. J. Widtman, Utica, New York, April–August 1927 (p. [39]).

Publication: Limited to 700 copies, 350 of which are for sale in the United States by James Wells and 350 for sale in England by Faber and Gwyer. Advertised in a June House flier (see *Note one*) as 'in preparation' for 15 September publication. Deposit copies: BL ('17 FEB 28'), BE ('4 MAY 1928'), BO ('MAY 4 1928'). Presentation copies: DLC (from Goldsmith, 22 November 1927), TxU (with presentation slip from Alfred Goldsmith [see *Note two*], 22 November 1927; 2 copies). Copies inscribed by owners: TxU (13 December 1927), RPB (25 December 1927). Price, $4.00. Listed in the *English Catalogue* for December 1927 at 17s.6d.

Locations: BBo (dj), BE, BL, BMR, BO, CSt, CaOTP, CtY, DLC, InU-L, JM (dj), MBU, MH, NNC (dj), NcD, NcU, NjCW, NjP, PU (5), RPB (2), TxU (5), ViU (dj).

Note one: A broadside advertising flier, dated 15 August, printed on both sides, for *Pictures* and *Out of the Cradle Endlessly Rocking* (H 48), is at CSt.

THIS *first edition of "Pictures" by Walt Whitman consists of seven hundred copies, three hundred and fifty of which are to be sold in the United States by James Wells and three hundred and fifty in England by Faber & Gwyer, Ltd. Vignette of the June House from a wood-engraving by Leon Underwood. Typography etc., by James Hendrickson.*

Printed for The June House, the type being set by hand, by Earl Widtman at the Press of M. J. Widtman, Utica, New York, April— August, 1927.

Statement of limitation for A 26.1.a

Note two: Some copies have a slip tipped to p. [39] stating that '25 copies were withdrawn for presentation to Henry Goldsmith numbered and signed by him.', and with a presentation inscription by him (DLC, TxU [2]). The RPB copy has the slip but is unnumbered and unsigned. A PU copy has the slip, unnumbered but signed and tipped to the free front endpaper.

Note three: Revised from *Southwest Review*, July 1925 (E 2818).

A 26.1.b
[Folcroft, Penn.]: Folcroft Press, [1969].

Facsimile reprinting. Price, $20.00. *Location:* MBU.

A 26.1.c₁
[Folcroft, Penn.]: Folcroft Library Editions, 1977.

Limited to 100 copies. Deposit copy: DLC for CIP ('DEC 1 1977'). Price, $10.00. *Location:* DLC.

A 26.1.c₂
[Norwood, Penn.]: Norwood Editions, 1978.

Title leaf is inserted. Limited to 100 copies. Price, $10.00. *Location:* RPB.

Note: Listed in *BIP* (1973) as a publication by Richard West of Philadelphia for $7.95. No copies have been located.

A 27 THE EIGHTEENTH PRESIDENCY!
1928

A 27.1.a
First edition, only printing [1928]

Two issues have been noted:

A 27.1.a₁
First issue [1928]

A 27.1.a₁: 9⅞″×6½″

[1–3] 4 [5] 6–31 [32]

[1–2]⁸. Sheets bulk ³⁄₃₂″.

Contents: p. 1: title page; p. 2: blank; pp. 3–4: introduction (in French) by Jean Catel; pp. 5–31: text; p. 32: printing information.

Typography and paper: 6¹⁄₁₆″×3¹⁵⁄₁₆″; laid paper with horizontal chain lines 1⅛″ apart; 31 lines per page.

Binding: Grayish yellow-brown stiff wrappers. Front cover recto: 'WALT WHITMAN | THE EIGHTEENTH PRESIDENCY! | Voice of Walt Whitman to each Young | Man in the Nation, North, South, | East, and West.'; front cover verso, back cover recto and verso, and spine: blank. Issued uncut. Stapled.

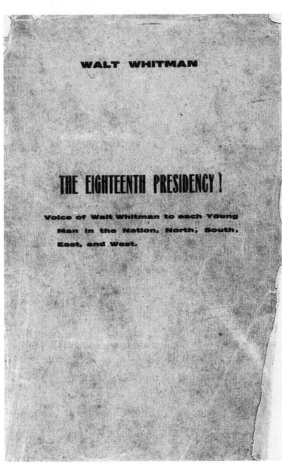

Wrapper for A 27.1.a₁

Printing: Causse, Graille, and Castelnau, Montpellier (p. [32]).

Publication: Printed January 1928. An undated postcard from Catel states, "They are a limited edition (300)" (NN-R).

Locations: JM, MBU, NN-R (2), RPB.

Note: First published in French translation in *Navire d'Argent,* March 1926 (E 2821).

A 27.1.a₂
Second issue [1930?]

THE EIGHTEENTH PRESIDENCY !

Voice of Walt Whitman to each Young
Man in the Nation, North, South,
East, and West.

EDITION « TAMBOUR », 3, RUE BERTHOLLET, PARIS

A 27.1.a₂: 9⅞″×6½″

Title page has a label pasted at the bottom: 'Edition "TAMBOUR", 3, rue Berthollet, PARIS'.

Binding: Same as in the first issue.

Publication: Deposit copies: BL ('14 FEB 31'; rebound with wrappers). Presentation copies: PU (from Catel, January 1930). RPB copy received 17 April 1930. DLC copy received 13 February 1931.

Locations: BBo, BMR, CSt, CtY, DLC, NjP, PU, RPB, ScU, TxU (2), ViU (2).

A 27.2
Second edition, only printing [1956]

WALT WHITMAN

THE
EIGHTEENTH
PRESIDENCY!

A CRITICAL TEXT EDITED BY

EDWARD F. GRIER

UNIVERSITY OF KANSAS PRESS
LAWRENCE, KANSAS

A 27.2: 8⅝16″×5⅝16″

[i–x] 1–47 [48–50]

[1–2]^8 [3]^6 [4]^8. Sheets bulk ¾6″.

Contents: p. i: half title, 'THE | EIGHTEENTH | PRESIDENCY!'; p. ii: blank; p. iii: title page; p. iv: copyright page; pp. v–vii: preface; p. viii: blank; p. ix: contents; p. x: blank; pp. 1–18: introduction; pp. 19–44: text; pp. 45–47: notes; pp. 48–50: blank.

Typography and paper: 6⁷⁄₁₆″ (6¼″)×3¹¹⁄₁₆″; wove paper; 32 lines per page. Running heads: rectos: pp. 3–17: 'INTRODUCTION'; pp. 21–43: 'THE EIGHTEENTH PRESIDENCY!'; p. 47: 'NOTES'; versos: pp. 2–18: 'INTRODUCTION'; pp. 20–44: 'THE EIGHTEENTH PRESIDENCY!'; p. 46: 'NOTES'.

Binding: Dark green buckram. Front and back covers: blank; spine: gold-stamped vertically 'GRIER WHITMAN: THE EIGHTEENTH PRESIDENCY! KANSAS'. White endpapers. All edges trimmed.

Dust jacket: Medium orange paper printed in dark brown. Front cover: 'WALT WHITMAN | [three lines within an irregular decorated border] THE | EIGHTEENTH | PRESIDENCY! | A CRITICAL TEXT EDITED BY | EDWARD F. GRIER'; back cover: description of two books from the press; spine: vertically: 'GRIER WHITMAN: THE EIGHTEENTH PRESIDENCY! KANSAS'; front flap: 21–line description of book and price in lower right corner; back flap: 20–line description of book and editor.

Printing: Division of Printing of Kansas Department of Administration.

Publication: 1,513 copies. Copyright 28 September 1956; A269352. Deposit copies: DLC ('DEC 10 1956'), DLC ('JAN 25 1957'), BO ('16JUL1957'). MBU copy has a note by Rollo G. Silver that the publication date was 28 September. Reviewed in *Detroit News*, 8 October 1956, p. 22. NjP copy received 23 October 1956. Price, $2.00. Listed in *CBI* as distributed in Canada by Burns and McEachern at $2.75.

Locations: BO, CSt (dj), DLC (2), InU-L (dj), JM (dj), MBU (dj), MH, NcD, NcD (dj), NjP (2), PU (dj), RPB, TxU (dj), ViU (2).

$2.00

Walt Whitman's tract *The Eighteenth Presidency!* was written during the political campaign of 1856. Though it may have been sent out to some editors in the form of proof sheets, apparently it was not published during the nineteenth century. With the hope of saving the Union from the political bungling which threatened a sectional split, its author appeals to the principles of the Constitution and the Declaration of Independence, incidentally proposing a nonpartisan political youth movement. This limited edition, of special interest to students and collectors, is issued a hundred years after the date of composition. It offers the first critical text, noting changes made by Whitman in previously unstudied proof sheets. The thoughtful Introduction shows the relationship of the tract to contemporary events, to Whitman's political thought, and to his poetry. Explanatory notes are included.

The editor, Edward F. Grier, who took his Ph.D. degree at the University of Pennsylvania, has made a special study of American life and literature, and is the author of articles in that field. In 1953 he was awarded a Ford Fellowship in order to investigate courses in American civilization, and in 1956 received a Fulbright Grant to lecture on American literature at the Universities of Lyons and Clermont-Ferrand, France. He is a member of the Department of English at the University of Kansas, where he is Chairman of the Major in American Civilization, and has also taught at Dartmouth College and Indiana University.

WALT WHITMAN

THE
EIGHTEENTH
PRESIDENCY!

A CRITICAL TEXT EDITED BY

EDWARD F. GRIER

GRIER WHITMAN: THE EIGHTEENTH PRESIDENCY! KANSAS

OTHER RECENT PUBLICATIONS

The Early Masters of English Fiction, by Alan D. McKillop

A discussion of the essential contributions to the novel form of Defoe, Richardson, Fielding, Smollett, Sterne; without neglecting recent scholarly examination of these writers, the author, known for his books on eighteenth-century English literature, aims at a balanced critical judgment. ————— $5.00

Selected Essays of Ludvig Holberg, translated and edited with an Introduction and Notes, by P. M. Mitchell

Holberg, "the father of Scandinavian literature," known chiefly as a dramatist, also achieved distinction as an essayist and historian. This volume make accessible to English readers representative essays, chosen for their intrinsic interest, their revelation of the author's views, and their relevance for students of English literature and history. The editor and translator is a member of the Department of Germanic Languages and Literatures at the University of Kansas ————— $3.50

UNIVERSITY OF KANSAS PRESS
LAWRENCE, KANSAS

Dust jacket for A 27.2

A 28 WALT WHITMAN'S WORKSHOP
1928

A 28.1.a
Only edition, first printing (1928)

WALT WHITMAN'S WORKSHOP.

A COLLECTION
OF UNPUBLISHED MANUSCRIPTS.

EDITED WITH AN INTRODUCTION AND NOTES

BY

CLIFTON JOSEPH FURNESS.

CAMBRIDGE:

HARVARD UNIVERSITY PRESS.

1928.

A 28.1.a: 10⁹⁄₁₆″×8″

[i–ix] x [xi–xiv] [1–3] 4–24 [25–27] 28–32 [33] 34–38 [39] 40–53 [54] 55–64 [65] 66–68 [69–71] 72–73 [74] 75–84 [85–87] 88–91 [92] 93–113 [114–117] 118–137 [138–141] 142–149 [150] 151–154 [155–157] 158–162 [163] 164 [165–167] 168 [169] 170 [171] 172 [173] 174 [175–179] 180 [181] 182 [183–185] 186–265 [266]. Inserted leaf of coated paper with Sarony photograph of Whitman printed on the verso is positioned before the title page; inserted leaves of coated paper, with photographs of the earliest known picture of Whitman, manuscript page of "My Task," manuscript scraps by Whitman, "Oratory" manuscript notebook entries, manuscript page of "Religion" lecture, front wrapper from 1855 *Leaves of Grass,* manuscript page of the 1864 introduction of *Leaves of Grass,* manuscript page from "Inscription" to *Leaves of Grass,* untitled manuscript page, manuscript page from "Introduction to the London Edition," manuscript page from "To the Reader" of *Leaves of Grass,* manuscript page from the 1861 introduction to *Leaves of Grass,* manuscript page from the introduction to *Leaves of Grass,* manuscript page from "Inscription" to *Leaves of Grass,* manuscript page from "A Starry Midnight," and manuscript letter of 22 December 1881 to T.W.H. Rolleston, all printed on the rectos, are positioned after pp. 8, 24, 30, 34, 38, 118, 126, 130, 134, 150, 166, 168, 170, 172, 174, 252.

[1–16]^8 [17]^4 [18]^8. Sheets bulk 3¹/₃₂″.

Contents: p. i: half title, 'WALT WHITMAN'S WORKSHOP'; p. ii: 'LONDON: HUMPHREY MILFORD, | OXFORD UNIVERSITY PRESS.'; p. iii: title page; p. iv: copyright page; p. v: dedication; p. vi: blank; p. vii: lines from Whitman's manuscripts; p. viii: blank; pp. ix–x: preface, signed 'C. J. F. | BOSTON, MASSACHUSETTS, | *August* 8, 1928.'; p. xi: contents; p. xii: blank; p. xiii: list of illustrations; p. xiv: blank; p. 1: 'INTRODUCTION.'; p. 2: blank; pp. 3–24: introduction; p. 25: 'I | NOTES FOR LECTURES.'; p. 26: blank; pp. 27–68: texts; p. 69: 'II | ANTI–SLAVERY NOTES.'; p. 70: blank; pp. 71–84: texts; p. 85: 'III | THE EIGHTEENTH PRESIDENCY!'; p. 86: blank; pp. 87–113: texts; p. 114: blank; p. 115: 'IV | INTRODUCTIONS INTENDED FOR | AMERICAN EDITIONS OF | "LEAVES OF GRASS." '; p. 116: blank; pp. 117–137: texts; p. 138: blank; p. 139: 'V | INTRODUCTION TO THE | LON-

DON EDITION.'; p. 140: blank; pp. 141–154: text; p. 155: 'VI | TO THE FOREIGN READER.'; p. 156: blank; pp. 157–164: text; p. 165: 'APPEN-DIX.'; p. 166: blank; pp. 167–175: texts; p. 176: blank; p. 177: 'NOTES.'; p. 178: blank; pp. 179–180: list of abbreviations; pp. 181–182: "Notes on the Format of this Book"; p. 183: "Notes on the Illustrations"; p. 184: "Notes on the Mottoes"; pp. 185–265: notes; p. 266: blank.

Poems and Prose: "Notes on Lecturing and Oratory," "Notes for Lectures on Religion," "Notes for Lectures on Democracy and 'Adhesiveness,'" "Notes for Lectures on Literature," "Anti-Slavery Notes," "The Eighteenth Presidency!", "Introductions Intended for American Editions of 'Leaves of Grass,'" "Introduction to the London Edition [of *Leaves of Grass*]," "To the Foreign Reader," "*To the Reader* At the Entrance of Leaves of Grass," "Inscription *at the entrance of Leaves of Grass*," "A Starry Midnight" (poem).

Typography and paper: 7⅛″ (6⅞″)×4⅝″; wove paper; text: 28 lines per page; notes: 42 lines per page. Running heads: rectos: pp. 5–23: 'INTRODUC-TION.'; pp. 29–31, 35–37, 41–63, 67: 'NOTES FOR LECTURES.'; pp. 73–83: 'ANTI-SLAVERY NOTES.'; pp. 89–113: 'THE EIGHTEENTH PRESI-DENCY.'; pp. 119–137: 'AMERICAN EDITIONS.'; pp. 143–153: 'THE LON-DON EDITION.'; pp. 159–161: 'TO THE FOREIGN READER.'; pp. 187–265: 'NOTES.'; versos: p. x: 'PREFACE.'; pp. 4–24, 28–52, 56–68, 72, 76–84, 88–90, 94–112, 118–136, 142–148, 152–154, 158–164: 'WALT WHIT-MAN'S WORKSHOP.'; pp. 168–174: 'APPENDIX.'; p. 180: 'ABBREVIA-TIONS.'; pp. 182, 186–264: 'NOTES.'.

Binding: Dark gray laid paper-covered boards with black V cloth (smooth) shelfback. Front and back covers: blank; spine: '[blindstamped double rule] | [six lines goldstamped] WALT | WHITMAN'S | WORK- | SHOP | [rule] | FURNESS | [blindstamped double rule] | [blindstamped double rule] | [blind-stamped double rule] | [goldstamped publisher's device] | [blindstamped dou-ble rule]'. White endpapers. All edges rough trimmed.

Dust jacket: Light orange-yellow paper. Front cover: '[two lines in red] WALT WHITMAN'S | WORKSHOP. | A COLLECTION | OF UNPUB-LISHED MANUSCRIPTS. | EDITED WITH AN INTRODUCTION AND NOTES | BY | CLIFTON JOSEPH FURNESS.'; back cover: advertisements for books from the press, with first line and bottom two lines in red; spine: 'WALT | WHITMAN'S | WORKSHOP | [rule] | FURNESS | [red Harvard seal] | HARVARD'; front flap: '$7.50'; back flap: blank.

Printing: See copyright page.

Publication: Limited to 750 copies. A letter from Furness of 30 July 1928 states that "I am now reading proof" (NzD). Published 7 November 1928. Reviewed in *New York Evening Post*, 1 December 1928, sec. 3, p. 8; *Times*

WALT WHITMAN'S WORKSHOP.

A COLLECTION
OF UNPUBLISHED MANUSCRIPTS.

EDITED WITH AN INTRODUCTION AND NOTES

BY

CLIFTON JOSEPH FURNESS.

WALT WHITMAN'S WORKSHOP

FURNESS

HARVARD

American Literature and Art

FOLK-SONGS OF THE SOUTH
Edited by John H. Cox

ON THE TRAIL OF NEGRO FOLK-SONGS
By Dorothy Scarborough

AMERICAN NEGRO FOLK-SONGS
By Newman I. White

SOUTH CAROLINA BALLADS
By Reed Smith

SONGS AND BALLADS OF THE MAINE LUMBERJACKS
Edited by Roland P. Gray

BALLADS AND SONGS OF THE BRANDYWINE
Edited by Frank Brinkley

BALLADS AND SEA-SONGS FROM NOVA SCOTIA
Collected by W. Roy Mackenzie

THE NOVELTY OF VERMONT
By John E. Pomeroy

WILLIAM DEAN HOWELLS
By Oscar W. Firkins

PRUNES AND PRISM
By Clarissa Hall Grasmere

BRUCE ROGERS: DESIGNER OF BOOKS
By Frederic Warde

GREEK AND ROMAN SCULPTURE IN AMERICAN MUSEUMS
By Gisela M. Richter

A HISTORY OF EUROPEAN AND AMERICAN SCULPTURE
By Chandler R. Post

THE OLD FARMER AND HIS ALMANACK
By G. L. Kittredge

INCREASE MATHER
By Kenneth B. Murdock

COTTON MATHER
By Barrett Wendell

HARVARD UNIVERSITY PRESS
CAMBRIDGE, MASSACHUSETTS

Dust jacket for A 28.1.a

Literary Supplement, 21 February 1929, p. 136. Copyright A1680; received, 12 November 1928. Deposit copies: DLC ('NOV 12 1928'), BL ('18 JAN 29'), BO ('18FEB1929'), BE ('11 JUL 1929'). Presentation copies: NN-R (from Furness, 14 November 1928). MH copy (rebound) received 9 November 1928. Price, $7.50. Listed in *English Catalogue* as an importation by Oxford University Press for January 1929 at 30s. Listed in *Bookseller,* 2 February 1929.

Locations: BE, BL, BMR, BMR (dj), BO, CSt, CtY, DLC (2), JM (dj), MB, MBU (dj), MH, NN-R (dj), NNC, NcD, NjCW, NjP (2), NzD (dj), RPB, TxU (6; 4dj), ViU (2; 2dj).

A 28.1.b
New York: Russell & Russell, 1964.

Facsimile reprinting. ScU copy received 6 February 1964. Price, $10.00. *Locations:* MB, ScU.

A 29 A CHILD'S REMINISCENCE
1930

A 29
Only edition, only printing (1930)

A Child's Reminiscence

by

WALT WHITMAN

COLLECTED BY
THOMAS O. MABBOTT *and* ROLLO G. SILVER
With an Introduction and Notes

1930
UNIVERSITY OF WASHINGTON BOOK STORE
Seattle

A 29: 12½″×9⅜″; 'UQW' is in green

Copyright page: 'COPYRIGHT, 1930, BY GLENN HUGHES | PRINTED IN THE UNITED STATES OF AMERICA'.

[i–iv] [1–10] 11–44

[1–3]⁸. Sheets bulk 7⁄32″.

Contents: pp. i–ii: blank; p. iii: 'UNIVERSITY OF WASHINGTON QUAR-TOS | EDITED BY GLENN HUGHES | I | A CHILD'S REMINISCENCE"; p. iv: statement of limitation; p. 1: title page; p. 2: copyright page; p. 3: dedication; p. 4: blank; pp. 5–7: introduction, signed 'THOMAS OLLIVE MABBOTT. | *Hunter College of the City of New York, October 7, 1930.';* p. 8: acknowledgments; p. 9: half title, 'A CHILD'S REMINISCENCE'; p. 10: "Walt Whitman's Poem"; pp. 11–18: "A Child's Reminiscence"; pp. 19–21: "All About a Mocking Bird"; pp. 22–28: "Walt Whitman"; pp. 29–31: facsimile advertisements for *Leaves of Grass* and *Leaves of Grass Imprints;* pp. 32–35: article by George S. Phillips from *New York Illustrated News;* p. 36: facsimile advertisement for *Leaves of Grass Imprints;* pp. 37–40: "Walt Whitman's New Poem" from *Cincinnati Commercial;* pp. 41–43: notes; p. 44: "Additional Whitman Items in the *New York Saturday Press.*"

Poetry and Prose: Reprints E 2434, E 2437, E2438.

Typography and paper: 7¹⁵⁄₁₆″×5⁷⁄₁₆″; wove paper watermarked '[drawing of unicorn] | UNICORN | 100% RAG'; various lines per page (up to 41).

Binding: Paper-covered boards with dark orange-yellow B cloth (linen) shelfback. Front and back covers: black and white printed design (see illustration); spine: vertically: 'A CHILD'S REMINISCENCE [inverted triangle of three dots] WHITMAN'. Endpapers of the same paper as the text. Top edges trimmed, front edges rough trimmed, bottom edges untrimmed.

Dust jacket: Unprinted glassine.

Printing: Unknown.

Publication: *University of Washington Quartos I.* Limited to 475 numbered copies. Published 10 November 1930. Listed in *Publishers Weekly,* 6 December 1930. Reviewed in *New York Times,* 7 December 1930, sec. 2, p. 3. Copyright A34151; received, 30 January 1931. Deposit copies: DLC ('JAN 30 1931'; 2 copies), BL ('10 JAN 31'; inscribed from the editors, 3 December 1930), BO ('–7APR1933'). RPB copy received 4 December 1930. Prices: $5.00 or 7s.6d.

Locations: BE, BL, BO, CSt, CtY, DLC (2), JM, MB, NN-R (2), NcD, NjP, RPB, ScU, TxU (2).

Note: A four-page advertising flier (printed on the same size pages as the text) is at CSt (received 12 November 1930).

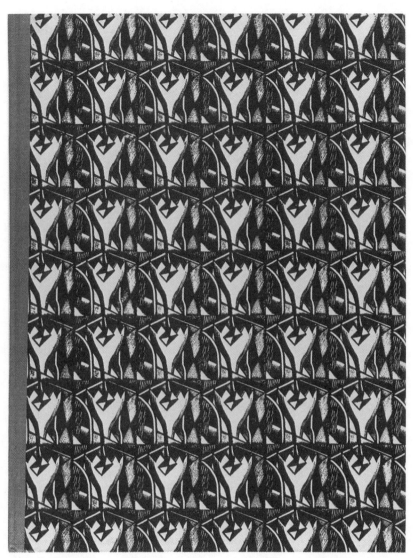

Binding for A 29

Of this book four hundred and seventy-five copies have been printed, and the type destroyed. This copy is number *75*

Statement of limitation for A 29

A 30 I SIT AND LOOK OUT
1932

A 30.1.a
Only edition, first printing (1932)

I SIT AND LOOK OUT

EDITORIALS FROM THE BROOKLYN DAILY TIMES

BY WALT WHITMAN

SELECTED AND EDITED BY

EMORY HOLLOWAY · VERNOLIAN SCHWARZ

NEW YORK   M · CM · XXXII

COLUMBIA   UNIVERSITY   PRESS

A 30.1.a: 9″×6″

OF THESE WRITINGS OF WALT WHITMAN
ONE THOUSAND COPIES WERE PRINTED BY
THE TORCH PRESS, CEDAR RAPIDS, IOWA
UNITED STATES OF AMERICA

COPYRIGHT
COLUMBIA UNIVERSITY PRESS
1932

[i–ii] [i–ix] x–xii [1–2] 3–30 [31–32] 33–175 [176–178] 179–198 [199–200] 201–232 [233–234] 235–248 [249–254]. Inserted leaf with Schoff engraving of Whitman printed on verso is positioned before the title page.

[1–16]^8 [17]^6. Sheets bulk $^{23}/_{32}$″.

Contents: pp. i–ii: blank; p. i: half title, 'I SIT AND LOOK OUT'; p. ii: blank; p. iii: title page; p. iv: copyright page; p. v: dedication; p. vi: "I Sit and Look Out" from *Leaves of Grass;* p. vii: acknowledgments; p. viii: blank; pp. ix–xii: contents; p. 1: 'INTRODUCTION'; p. 2: blank; pp. 3–30: introduction; p. 31: 'EDITORIALS'; p. 32: blank; pp. 33–175: texts; p. 176: blank; p. 177: 'APPENDICES'; p. 178: blank; pp. 179–185: "Articles of Possible Whitman Authorship"; pp. 186–188: "Reviews of Whitman's Poetry"; pp. 189–196: "Chronological List of Whitman Editorials"; pp. 197–198: "Whitman's Reviews of Magazines and Books"; p. 199: 'NOTES'; p. 200: blank; pp. 201–232: notes; p. 233: 'INDEX'; p. 234: blank; pp. 235–248: index; p. 249: list of Whitman books by Emory Holloway; p. 250: blank; p. 251: press imprint and note that Oxford University is its foreign agent; pp. 253–254: blank.

Prose: Reprints E 1194, E 1195, E 1197, E 1199, E 1202, E 1204, E 1206, E 1214, E 1225, E 1226, E 1231, E 1239, E 1243, E 1249, E 1256, E 1270, E 1271, E 1283, E 1288, E 1291, E 1294, E 1311, E 1312, E 1325, E 1334, E 1340, E 1342, E 1347, E 1357, E 1359, E 1381, E 1390, E 1399, E 1414, E 1425, E 1426, E 1435, E 1443, E 1453, E 1461, E 1464, E 1476, E 1485, E 1502, E 1515, E 1549, E 1588, E 1589, E 1593, E 1609, E 1621, E 1622, E 1625, E 1627, E 1639, E 1643, E 1644, E 1652, E 1657, E 1666, E 1670, E 1688, E 1689, E 1696, E 1699, E 1719, E 1722, E 1748, E 1749, E 1751–1753, E 1764, E 1765, E 1776, E 1790, E 1802, E 1804, E 1806, E 1815, E 1830, E 1834, E 1865, E 1867, E 1868, E 1890, E 1891, E 1908, E 1912, E 1914, E 1921, E 1933, E 1935, E 1940, E 1941, E 1950, E 1961, E 1970, E 1973, E 1979, E 2003, E 2004, E 2007, E 2010, E 2017, E 2025, E 2036, E 2044, E 2064, E 2067, E 2078, E 2084, E 2089, E 2097, E 2102, E 2116, E 2131, E 2135, E 2148, E 2166, E 2188, E 2201, E 2230, E 2261, E 2281, E 2293, E 2333, E 2359, E 2406, E 2412, E 2416, E 2433.

Typography and paper: 7″ (6⁷⁄₁₆″)×4¼″; wove paper; introduction and text: 34 lines per page; notes: 47 lines per page; index: 48 lines per page. Running heads: rectos: p. xi: 'CONTENTS'; pp. 5–29: 'INTRODUCTION'; pp. 35–39: 'THE PRESS'; pp. 43–49: 'REFORM'; pp. 53–55: 'EDUCATION—LECTURES'; pp. 59–61: 'HOLIDAYS'; pp. 63–69: 'LITERARY NOTES AND REVIEWS'; pp. 73–85: 'RELIGION—HUMANITARIANISM'; pp. 87–89: 'SLAVERY'; pp. 93–99: 'NATIONAL POLITICS'; pp. 101–109: 'THE WEATHER—SPORTS—PUBLIC HEALTH'; pp. 113–121: 'WOMEN—SEX—MARRIAGE'; pp. 125–155: 'CIVIC INTEREST AND CITY SCENES'; pp. 157–163: 'FOREIGN AFFAIRS'; pp. 165–175: 'MISCELLANEOUS EDITORIALS'; pp. 181–187, 191–195: 'APPENDICES'; pp. 203–231: 'NOTES'; pp. 237–247: 'INDEX'; versos: pp. x–xii: 'CONTENTS'; pp. 4–30: 'INTRODUCTION'; pp. 34–40: 'THE PRESS'; pp. 44–50: 'REFORM'; pp. 52–56: 'EDUCATION—LECTURES'; pp. 58–60: 'HOLIDAYS'; pp. 64–70: 'LITERARY NOTES AND REVIEWS'; pp. 72–84: 'RELIGION—HUMANITARIANISM'; pp. 88–90: 'SLAVERY'; pp. 92–98: 'NATIONAL POLITICS'; pp. 102–110: 'THE WEATHER—SPORTS—PUBLIC HEALTH'; pp. 112–122: 'WOMEN—SEX—MARRIAGE'; pp. 124–154: 'CIVIC INTEREST AND CITY SCENES'; pp. 158–162: 'FOREIGN AFFAIRS'; pp. 166–174: 'MISCELLANEOUS EDITORIALS'; pp. 180–184, 188–198: 'APPENDICES'; pp. 202–232: 'NOTES'; pp. 236–248: 'INDEX'.

Binding: Six styles have been noted, priority undetermined:

Binding A: Dark yellowish green buckram. Front cover: blindstamped single-rule frame with goldstamped publisher's device of crown-book-scroll within single-rule circular frame, in center; back cover: blank; spine: goldstamped '[double rule] | WALT | WHITMAN | [double rule] | I SIT | AND | LOOK | OUT | [double rule] | [double rule] | EDITORIALS | SELECTED BY | HOLLOWAY | AND | SCHWARZ | [double rule] | [double rule] | [cross] [crown] [cross] | COLUMBIA | UNIVERSITY | [cross] PRESS [cross] | [double rule]'. White endpapers. All edges trimmed. Top edges speckle-stained green.

Binding B: Same as binding A, except: publisher's device and circular frame on the front cover are blindstamped.

Binding C: Same as binding A, except: dark grayish green coarse V cloth (smooth); front cover has blindstamped single-rule frame only; spine is silverstamped; cream endpapers; top edges plain.

Binding D: Gray reddish orange buckram. Front and back covers: blank; spine: blackstamped '[double rule] | WALT | WHITMAN | [double rule] | I SIT | AND | LOOK | OUT | [double rule] | [double rule] | EDITORIALS | SELECTED BY | HOLLOWAY | AND | SCHWARZ | [double rule]'. White or very pale yellow endpapers. All edges trimmed.

Binding E: Gray reddish orange horizontal T cloth (fine-ribbed). Front and back covers: blank; spine: blackstamped '[double rule] | WALT | WHITMAN | [double rule] | I SIT | AND | LOOK | OUT | [double rule] | COLUMBIA | UNIVERSITY | PRESS'. White endpapers. All edges trimmed.

Binding F: Medium yellowish green V cloth (smooth). Front and back covers: blank; spine: silverstamped '[double rule] | WALT | WHITMAN | [double rule] | | I SIT | AND | LOOK | OUT | [double rule] | EDITORIALS | SELECTED BY | HOLLOWAY | AND | SCHWARZ | [cross] [crown] [cross] | COLUMBIA | UNIVERSITY | [cross] PRESS [cross] | [double rule]'. Cream endpapers. All edges trimmed. Top edges speckle-stained green.

Dust jacket: Two styles have been noted.

Jacket A: Light gray paper printed in green. Front cover: '[three lines in script] I Sit | and | Look Out | *by Walt Whitman* | EDITORIALS FROM THE BROOKLYN DAILY TIMES | SELECTED AND EDITED BY | EMORY HOLLOWAY AND VERNOLIAN SCHWARZ'; back cover: 14-line blurb for *The Half-Breed;* spine: bottom to top '[five words in script] I Sit and Look Out   *Walt Whitman';* front flap: price at top right corner and 25-line description of book; back flap: blank.

Jacket B: Light blue laid paper with chain lines 1″ apart, printed in brown. Front cover: '[four lines within single-rule window-and-shutters frame] I SIT AND | LOOK OUT | *By* | WALT WHITMAN | UNPUBLISHED EDITORIALS FROM THE | DAILY TIMES | OF BROOKLYN | SELECTED AND EDITED | *By* | EMORY HOLLOWAY & VERNOLIAN SCHWARZ'; back cover: 19-line blurb for *An Anthology of American Poetry, 1630–1941*, ed. Alfred Kreymborg, within dotted-line frame; spine: '[double rule] | WALT | WHITMAN | [rule] | I SIT | AND | LOOK | OUT | [rule] | EDITED | BY | HOLLOWAY | AND | SCHWARZ | [double rule] | [rule] | COLUMBIA'; front flap: 20-line description of book; back flap: blank.

Printing: See copyright page.

Publication: Limited to 1,000 copies. Published 31 May 1932. Listed in *Publishers Weekly*, 28 May 1932. Reviewed in *New York Times Book Review*, 5 June 1932, p. 2. Copyright A52248; received, 1 June 1932; renewed, 16 March 1960; R255656. Deposit copies: binding A: DLC ('JUN –1 1932'), BL ('31 MAY 32'), BO ('27JUN1932'), BE ('18 AUG 1932'). ViU copy (binding A) purchased 13 June 1932. CaOTU copy (binding B) received 2 December 1941; MH copy (binding D) received 20 June 1975. Presentation copies (all from Holloway): binding A: ViU (dj A; 11 May 1932), RPB (18 May 1932), TxU (31 May 1932). Copies inscribed by owners: binding A: BO (1 June 1932). NN-R copy (binding A, dj A) received 3 June 1932. Price, $3.50. Listed

$3.50

Although Walt Whitman's newspaper work had great influence upon his philosophy and his poetry, it is only in the past ten years that scholars have attempted anything like a comprehensive investigation of his journalistic career.

Two Brooklyn papers edited by Whitman still require examination: the Free-Soil *Brooklyn Freeman* with which Whitman was identified in 1848-49, a short-lived journal of which, unfortunately, no file or copy appears to have survived, and *The Brooklyn Daily Times*, from which only a very few of the editorials Whitman wrote have hitherto been reprinted. The present volume attempts to fill that gap in the *Times* records, as far as is possible.

Whitman was thirty-eight when he went to the *Times*. His opinions on reform, the press, education, books, religion, slavery, national politics, sports, women, civic questions, international affairs show a degree of maturity that makes them valuable documents for both Whitman students and historians of the period.

I Sit and Look Out

by Walt Whitman

EDITORIALS FROM THE BROOKLYN DAILY TIMES
SELECTED AND EDITED BY
EMORY HOLLOWAY AND VERNOLIAN SCHWARZ

I Sit and Look Out   Walt Whitman

Walt Whitman

THE HALF-BREED

AND OTHER STORIES NOW FIRST COLLECTED
BY THOMAS OLLIVE MABBOTT

A short novel and four sketches from the period of Whitman's apprenticeship in newspaper and magazine work which preceded the production of LEAVES OF GRASS, now first issued in book form. They are otherwise available only in the files of rare periodicals.

Illustrated with woodcuts by Allen Lewis. Limited Edition of 115 copies. Large 8vo, $15.00. Regular Edition, Small 8vo, $4.50.

COLUMBIA UNIVERSITY PRESS

Dust jacket A for A 30.1.a

I SIT AND LOOK OUT

By

WALT WHITMAN

UNPUBLISHED EDITORIALS FROM THE

DAILY TIMES

OF BROOKLYN

SELECTED AND EDITED

By

EMORY HOLLOWAY & VERNOLIAN SCHWARZ

COLUMBIA

WALT WHITMAN

I SIT AND LOOK OUT

EDITED BY

HOLLOWAY AND SCHWARZ

Dust jacket B for A 30.1.a

in the *English Catalogue* as an importation by Oxford University Press for June 1932 at 17s.6d.

Locations: Binding A: BBo, BE, BL, BO, CSt, CaOTP (dj A), DLC, MB, MBU (dj A), MH, NN-R (dj A), NN-R (dj A), RPB, TxU, TxU (dj A), ViU, ViU (dj A); binding B: JM (dj A), NNC, NcD (dj A); binding C: CSt, CaOTU, CtY (dj A); binding D: JM (dj B), MH, NcD (dj B), PU, PU (dj B), TxU (dj B), ViU (dj B); binding E: JM (dj B), TxU (dj B); binding F: NjCW.

Note one: The bottom right-hand corner of the front flap in dust jacket A is torn off in all located copies.

Note two: Dust jacket A has been located with copies in bindings A, B, and C.

Note three: Dust jacket B has been located with copies in bindings D and E.

A 30.1.b
New York: AMS Press, 1966.

Facsimile reprinting. Price, $14.00. *Locations:* NcU, ScU.

A 31 WALT WHITMAN AND THE CIVIL WAR
1933

A 31.1.a
Only edition, first printing (1933)

Two issues have been noted:

A 31.1.a₁
First issue (1933)

> # Walt
> # Whitman
>
> ## AND THE CIVIL WAR
>
> *A COLLECTION OF ORIGINAL
> ARTICLES AND MANUSCRIPTS*
>
> *Edited by*
> **CHARLES I. GLICKSBERG**
>
> UNIVERSITY OF PENNSYLVANIA PRESS
>
> **Philadelphia 1933**

A 31.1.a₁: 9″×6″

[i–vi] vii–xii 1–11 [12–14] 15–83 [84] 85–89 [90] 91–119 [120] 121–128 [129–130] 131–169 [170] 171–181 [182] 183–201 [202–204]. Inserted leaves of coated paper, with photographs of manuscript pages from Whitman's notebook and "The Artilleryman's Vision," printed on rectos, are positioned after pp. 80, 122; inserted leaves of coated paper, with photographs of manuscript pages from "Quicksand Years," printed on versos, are positioned after pp. 124, 126.

[1–13]⁸ [14]⁴. Sheets bulk ¹⁹⁄₃₂″.

Contents: p. i: half title, 'WALT WHITMAN AND THE CIVIL WAR'; p. ii: blank; p. iii: title page; p. iv: copyright page; p. v: dedication; p. vi: blank; pp. vii–viii: preface, signed 'C. I. G. | Philadelphia | October 15, 1932'; pp. ix–x: contents; p. xi: list of illustrations; p. xii: list of abbreviations; pp. 1–11: introduction; p. 12: blank; p. 13: 'Part I | ORIGINAL WRITINGS'; p. 14: blank; pp. 15–83: texts; p. 84: blank; pp. 85–89: texts; p. 90: blank; pp. 91–119: texts; p. 120: blank; pp. 121–128: poems; p. 129: 'Part II | MANUSCRIPT MATERIAL'; p. 130: blank; pp. 131–169: texts; p. 170: blank; pp. 171–181: texts; p. 182: blank; pp. 183–192: appendix; pp. 193–201: index; pp. 202–204: blank.

Poetry and Prose: Reprints E 2464, E 2465, E 2467, E 2469, E 2471–2473, E 2493, E 2497.

Typography and paper: 6¹⁵⁄₁₆″ (6⁷⁄₁₆″)×4″; wove paper watermarked '[curved] WARREN'S | OLDE STYLE'; text: 17 lines per page; index: double columns, 48 lines per column. Running heads: rectos: pp. 3–11: 'Introduction'; pp. 17–61: 'City Photographs'; pp. 65–83: 'New York City Veterans'; pp. 87–89: 'Return of a Brooklyn Veteran'; pp. 93–119: 'Letters'; pp. 123–127: 'Poems'; pp. 133–139: 'Diary for 1863'; p. 143: 'War Memoranda'; pp. 147–159: 'Hospital Cases'; pp. 163–165: 'Literary Jottings'; p. 169: 'Hospital Mismanagement'; p. 175: 'Lincoln and Whitman'; pp. 179–181: 'Exchange of George Whitman'; pp. 185–191: 'Appendix'; pp. 195–201: 'Index'; versos: p. viii: 'Preface'; p. x: 'Contents'; pp. 2–10, 16–82, 86–88, 92–118, 122–128, 132–168, 172–180, 184–192: 'Walt Whitman and the Civil War'; pp. 194–200: 'Index'.

Binding: Light grayish brown V cloth (smooth). Front and back covers: three blackstamped rules extending across entire cover; spine: '[rule extending over to connect with rules of front and back covers] | [vertical] Walt Whitman | [rule extending over to connect with rules of front and back covers] | [vertical] and the Civil War | [rule extending over to connect with rules of front and back covers] | [horizontal] GLICKSBERG'. White endpapers. All edges trimmed.

Dust jacket: Medium yellowish pink laid paper with horizontal chain lines 1 ¹⁄₁₆″ apart. Front cover: '[photograph of Whitman] | Walt Whitman | AND THE CIVIL WAR'; back cover: description of other books from the press; spine: '[vertical] Walt Whitman and the Civil War | [horizontal] GLICKS-BERG'; front flap: 42-line description of book, price, and photo credit for jacket; back flap: blank.

Printing: Unknown.

Publication: Published 10 March 1933. Listed in *Publishers Weekly*, 18 March 1933. Reviewed in *New York Herald-Tribune Books*, 10 (8 October 1933), 15. Copyright A60582; received, 14 March 1933. Deposit copies: DLC ('MAY 14 1933'; rebound), BL ('13 APR 33'), BO ('30MAY1933'), BE ('16 OCT 1933'). Copies inscribed by owners: NjCW (March 1933). PU copy (rebound) received 10 March 1933. Price, $2.50. Listed in the *English Catalogue* as an importation by Oxford University Press for April 1933 at 10s.6d.

Locations: BE, BL, BMR (dj), BO, CSt, CaOTU, CtY (dj), JM (dj), MBU (dj), NN-R (dj), NcD (dj), NcU, NjCW (2), NjP (dj), RPB, TxU (dj), ViU.

What was Walt Whitman doing in 1862? This year which has long been a puzzle of obscurity to Whitman biographers is now explained by the publication in this volume of recently discovered articles written by Whitman under a pseudonym for the New York Leader. Entitled "City Photographs" and signed by a name derived from family associations these articles are not only of greatest importance as vigorous examples of Whitman's journal, but dispel forever the accusation that he was idle, and uninterested in the Civil War at its beginning. In his descriptions of The Broadway Hospital he is revealed as already playing the part of comforter to sick and wounded soldiers which he later assumed at the front.

This book also contains two hitherto unidentified articles on the "Fifty-first New York Ci y Veterans" with whose Whitman's brother, George, was enlisted. In addition, unpublished manuscript material relating to the Civil War from the Harned Collection in the Library of Congress is presented. This includes a number of letters, a few manu script poems, the diary for 1863, war memoranda, cases of soldiers, literary jottings, notes on hospital mismanagement, incidents and anecdotes; landsketches, a chapter on George Whitman's imprisonment, and an appendix of newspaper clippings. A book of vivid interest and of the utmost significance as an explanation of the effect of war on America's great poet.

$2.50

Photograph on cover in the Collection of Alfred Goldsmith

Walt Whitman
AND THE CIVIL WAR

GLICKSBERG

Walt Whitman and the Civil War

American Literature
By
Arthur Hobson Quinn

THE SOUL OF AMERICA

From the *NEW YORK TIMES*: "Mr. Quinn, who is a member of the English faculty of the University of Pennsylvania, author and editor of many works and man of letters, studies the birth of the American character in the fusion of races with which our Colonies began, recounts the gifts to the making of the national soul brought by those several groups and estimates the influence exerted by each of them and by later waves of migration on the development and strengthening of the national character that followed the achievement of nationhood and accompanied the conquering of the western lands.

"To his discussion of all these matters Mr. Quinn brings a richly equipped mind, a sane and sympathetic temper, and a very skilful pen. It is a constant pleasure to read his smoothly flowing, beautiful English that is, nevertheless, virile with strength and vigor. One of his outstanding qualities is the sureness of his recognition of those factors of national and individual spirit that are of fundamental and lasting consequence. That insight is discoverable, to mention only one of its manifestations, in his discussion and estimates of the comparative value of the works of important American authors all through our history. "It is good, wholesome, exhilarating, reassuring reading for these present days."

Other Titles

KATE CHOPIN AND HER CREOLE STORIES
By Daniel S. Rankin
Illustrated, $3.00

OLD DRURY OF PHILADELPHIA
By Reese D. James
Illustrated, $6.00

THE INGENIOUS DR. FRANKLIN
By Nathan Goodman
Illustrated, $3.00

PROPOSALS RELATING TO THE EDUCATION OF YOUTH IN PENSILVANIA
By Benjamin Franklin
$2.50

GEORGE HENRY BOKER
By Edwin S. Bradley
Illustrated, $4.00

SONNETS & NYDIA
By George Henry Boker
$2.00 each

JAMES NELSON BARKER
By Paul H. Musser
$3.00

Descriptive Circulars on Request

UNIVERSITY OF PENNSYLVANIA PRESS : PHILADELPHIA

Dust jacket for A 31.1.a₁

A31.1.a₂
Second issue (1933)

WALT WHITMAN
AND THE CIVIL WAR

———————

A THESIS

IN ENGLISH

PRESENTED TO THE FACULTY OF THE GRADUATE SCHOOL OF THE
UNIVERSITY OF PENNSYLVANIA IN PARTIAL FULFILLMENT
OF THE REQUIREMENTS FOR THE DEGREE
OF DOCTOR OF PHILOSOPHY

CHARLES I. GLICKSBERG

PHILADELPHIA

1933

A 31.1.a₂: 9″×6″

Pagination and collation are the same as in the first issue.

Contents: Same as the first issue, except: p. iii: dissertation title page.

UNIVERSITY OF PENNSYLVANIA

———

WALT WHITMAN
AND THE CIVIL WAR

CHARLES I. GLICKSBERG

A THESIS

IN ENGLISH

PRESENTED TO THE FACULTY OF THE GRADUATE SCHOOL IN
PARTIAL FULFILLMENT OF THE REQUIREMENTS FOR
THE DEGREE OF DOCTOR OF PHILOSOPHY

PHILADELPHIA
1933

Wrapper for A 31.1.a$_2$

Binding: Light gray yellowish brown stiff wrappers with light blue hair-vein pattern. Front cover: 'UNIVERSITY OF PENNSYLVANIA | [rule] | WALT WHITMAN | AND THE CIVIL WAR | CHARLES I. GLICKSBERG | A THE-SIS | IN ENGLISH | PRESENTED TO THE FACULTY OF THE GRADU-ATE SCHOOL IN | PARTIAL FULFILLMENT OF THE REQUIREMENTS FOR | THE DEGREE OF DOCTOR OF PHILOSOPHY | PHILADELPHIA | 1933'; back cover: blank; spine: unknown. All edges trimmed. All edges plain or speckle-stained black.

Publication: PU copies received 16 March 1933. DLC copy received 21 March 1933. MB copy received 5 April 1933. Not for sale.

Locations: DLC (bound), MB (bound, lacks back wrapper), MH (bound), PU (2; bound, lack back wrapper, lack pp. 203–204).

Note: The university press probably made a stop-press substitution of the dissertation title page so that the author could use such copies to fulfill his dissertation requirements.

A 31.1.b
New York: A. S. Barnes, [1963].

Facsimile reprinting of the first issue. Wrappers. *A Perpetua Book P–4081.* Price, $1.95. *Locations:* JM, NjCW.

A 32 NEW YORK DISSECTED
1936

A 32.1.a
Only edition, first printing (1936)

Two issues have been noted:

A 32.1.a₁
First issue (1936)

New York Dissected

By

Walt Whitman

*A Sheaf of Recently Discovered
Newspaper Articles by
the Author of*
LEAVES OF GRASS

Introduction and Notes by
Emory Holloway and
Ralph Adimari

Illustrated from Old Prints
and Photographs

New York
Rufus Rockwell Wilson, Inc.
1936

A 32.1.a₁: 9″×6″

Copyright, 1936, by
Emory Holloway and Ralph Adimari

PRINTED IN THE UNITED STATES OF AMERICA

[i–x] xi–xiii [xiv–xvi] 1–14 [15–16] 17–23 [24–26] 27–40 [41–42] 43–48 [49–50] 51–65 [66–68] 69–73 [74–76] 77–84 [85–86] 87–102 [103–104] 105–114 [115–116] 117–124 [125–126] 127–132 [133–134] 135–142 [143–144] 145–176 [177–178] 179–187 [188–190] 191–196 [197–198] 199–245 [246–248] 249–257 [258]. Inserted leaf of coated paper with drawing of Whitman from 2 June 1880 *New York Illustrated News* printed on verso, is positioned before the title page; inserted leaves of coated paper, with painting of Henry Abbott, engraving of the Astor House, portrait of Charles Anderson Dana, engraving of Baron John William Spolasco, engraving of Robert Bonner, engraving of William Cullen Bryant, and drawing of "Fanny Fern" printed on rectos, are positioned after pp. 32, 64, 96, 128, 160, 192, 224.

[1–17]⁸ (17₈₊₁). Sheets bulk ¹⁵⁄₁₆″.

Contents: p. i: half title, 'New York Dissected'; p. ii: blank; p. iii: statement of limitation; p. iv: blank; p. v: title page; p. vi: copyright page; p. vii: line from *Leaves of Grass;* p. viii: blank; p. ix: acknowledgments; p. x: blank; pp. xi–xii: contents; p. xiii: list of illustrations; p. xiv: blank; p. xv: 'Life Begins at Thirty-Five'; p. xvi: blank; pp. 1–14: text; p. 15: 'The Opera'; p. 16: blank; pp. 17–23: text; p. 24: blank; p. 25: 'One of the Lessons Bordering Broadway | The Egyptian Museum'; p. 26: blank; pp. 27–40: text; p. 41: 'Christmas at "Grace" '; p. 42: blank; pp. 43–48: text; p. 49: 'America's Mightiest Inheritance'; p. 50: blank; pp. 51–65: text; p. 66: blank; p. 67: 'Voltaire'; p. 68: blank; pp. 69–73: text; p. 74: blank; p. 75: 'New York Dissected | I. *New York Amuses Itself— The Fourth of July';* p. 76: blank; pp. 77–84: text; p. 85: 'New York Dissected | II. *Wicked Architecture. Decent Homes for Working-Men';* p. 86: blank; pp. 87–102: text; p. 103: 'New York Dissected | III. *The Slave Trade';* p. 104: blank; pp. 105–114: text; p. 115: 'New York Dissected | IV. *Broadway';* p. 116: blank; pp. 117–124: texts; p. 125: 'New York Dissected | V. *Street Yarn';* p. 126: blank; pp. 127–132: text; p. 133: 'New York Dissected | VI. *Advice to Strangers';* p. 134: blank; pp. 135–142: text; p. 143: 'Reviews of *Leaves of Grass';* p. 144: blank; pp. 145–176: texts; p. 177: 'Imitators of *Leaves of Grass';* p. 178: blank; pp. 179–187: texts; p. 188: blank; p. 189: 'Appendix'; p. 190: blank; pp. 191–196: texts; p. 197: 'Notes'; p. 198: blank; pp. 199–245: notes; p. 246: blank; p. 247: 'Index'; p. 248: blank; pp. 249–257: index; p. 258: blank.

Prose: Reprints E 1181–1193.

Typography and paper: 6⅝″ (6⅜″)×4″; wove paper watermarked 'Blue |
Hill | Text'; introduction and texts: 33 lines per page; index: double columns,
57 lines per column. Running heads: rectos: pp. 3–13: 'Life Begins at Thirty-
Five'; pp. 19–23: 'The Opera'; pp. 29–39: 'The Egyptian Museum'; pp. 45–47:
'Christmas at "Grace" '; pp. 53–65: 'America's Mightiest Inheritance'; pp. 71–
73: 'Voltaire'; pp. 79–83: 'New York Amuses Itself'; pp. 89–101: 'Wicked
Architecture'; pp. 107–113: 'The Slave Trade'; pp. 119–123: 'Broadway'; pp.
129–131: 'Street Yarn'; pp. 137–141: 'Advice to Strangers'; pp. 147–169, 173–
175: 'Reviews of *Leaves of Grass*'; pp. 185–187: 'Imitators of *Leaves of Grass*';
pp. 193–195: 'Appendix'; pp. 201–245: 'Notes'; pp. 251–257: 'Index'; versos:
p. xii: 'Contents'; pp. 2–14, 18–22, 28–40, 44–48, 52–64, 70–72, 78–84, 88–
102, 106–114, 118–124, 128–132, 136–142, 146–160, 164, 168–170, 176,
180–186, 192–196: 'New York Dissected'; pp. 200–244: 'Notes'; pp. 250–256:
'Index'.

Binding: Dark green or mottled medium yellowish buckram. Front cover:
goldstamped 'New York Dissected | Walt Whitman'; back cover: blank; spine:
goldstamped 'New York | Dissected | Walt | Whitman | Rufus Rockwell | Wil-
son, Inc.'. White endpapers. All edges trimmed.

Dust jacket: Two styles have been noted:

Jacket A: Unprinted glassine.

Jacket B: White paper coated on one side. Front: all printed in red on a
brilliant yellow background: '[six rules extending over to spine] | NEW
YORK | DISSECTED | *by* | WALT WHITMAN | *A sheaf of recently discov-
ered newspaper* | *articles by the author of* | *Leaves of Grass* | EDITION
LIMITED TO 750 COPIES | [six rules extending over to spine]'; back: all in
red on a white background: '[all within a single-rule frame] FOR VICTORY |
[statue of Minuteman to the left of next seven lines] BUY | UNITED |
STATES | WAR | BONDS | AND | STAMPS | [rule]'; spine: all printed in red
on a brilliant yellow background: '[six rules extending over to front] | New
York | Dissected | by | WALT WHITMAN | [six rules extending over to
front]'; front flap: 34-line description of book in red; back flap: blank.

Printing: Unknown.

Publication: Limited to 750 numbered copies. Published 20 April 1936. Copy-
right A93995; received, 4 May 1936. Deposit copies: DLC ('MAY –4 1936').
Copies inscribed by owners: TxU (1936). RPB copy received 4 May 1936.
NNPM copy received from Adamari May 1936. Price, $6.00.

Locations: BO, CSt, CaOTP, CtY (2), DLC, JM, MB, MBU, NNC (2),
NNPM, NcD, NcU, NjP, PU (dj B), RPB, ScU, TxU (3; 1dj A), ViU (3).

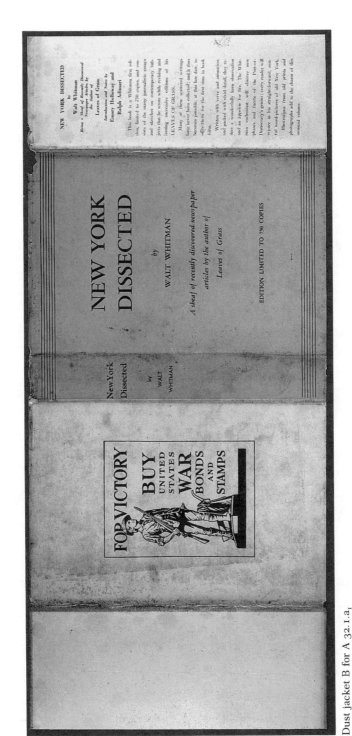

Dust jacket B for A 32.1.a₁

This, the first edition

of

New York Dissected

is limited to 750 numbered
copies

This copy is
No.

424

Statement of limitation for A 32.1.a₁

A 32.1.a₂
Second issue [n.d.]

Pagination is the same as in the first issue, except: [iii–x] . . . [258].

$[1–17]^8 (-1_2) (17_{8+1})$. Leaf 1_2, containing the statement of limitation, has been cancelled.

Contents: Same as in the first issue, pp. i–ii, v–[258].

Binding: Same as in the first issue.

Dust jacket: The only located dust jacket is the same as dust jacket A in the first issue.

Publication: Deposit copy: BL ('30 NOV 60').

Locations: BL, BMR, InU-L (dj), JM, MBU, NjCW, TxU.

A 32.1.b₁
[Folcroft, Penn.]: Folcroft Library Editions, 1972.

Facsimile reprinting of the first issue. Deposit copy: DLC for CIP ('19 NOV 1974'). Limited to 100 copies. Price, $20.00. *Locations:* DLC, ScU.

A 32.1.b₂

[Norwood, Penn.]: Norwood Editions, 1976.

Title leaf is inserted. Deposit copy: DLC for CIP ('AUG 19 1977'). Limited to 100 copies. Price, $27.50. *Location:* DLC.

A 32.1.b₃

[Norwood, Penn.]: Norwood Editions, 1977.

Title leaf is inserted. *Location:* WU.

A 32.1.b₄

[Folcroft, Penn.]: Folcroft Library Editions, 1978.

Title leaf is inserted. *Location:* CaBVaSM.

Note: Listed in RLIN as a 1977 publication by Richard West of Philadelphia. No copies have been located.

A 33 A WHITMAN MANUSCRIPT FROM THE . . . BENDER
COLLECTION . . .
1939

A 33
Only edition, only printing (1939)

A
Whitman Manuscript

FROM

THE ALBERT M. BENDER COLLECTION

OF MILLS COLLEGE

THE BIBLIOPHILE SOCIETY OF MILLS COLLEGE · MCMXXXIX

A 33: 9½″×6⅞″; reclining figure is in red

Copyright page: 'Copyright 1939 by The Bibliophile Society • Mills College'.

[1–10] 11–13 [14] 15–19 [20] 21 [22–28]

[1–4]⁴. Leaf 1₁ is the front pastedown endpaper; leaf 1₂ is the free front endpaper. Sheets bulk ¹⁄₁₆″.

Contents: pp. 1–3: blank; p. 4: facsimile of "Waves in the Vessel's Wake"; p. 5: title page; p. 6: copyright page; p. 7: *'To* | ALBERT M. BENDER'; p. 8: information on Bibliophile Society of Mills College; p. 9: contents; p. 10: blank; pp. 11–12: "Foreword" by Oscar Lewis; p. 13: text of "After the Sea–Ship"; p. 14: blank; pp. 15–18: "Whitman's Revisions" by Sidney L. Gulick, Jr.; p. 19: text of "Waves in the Vessel's Wake"; p. 20: blank; p. 21: "Readings of Canceled Words"; p. 22: blank; p. 23: [ornate numerals] 175 | copies | printed at the Eucalyptus Press, Mills College, | in the month of January, 1939'; pp. 24–28: blank.

Typography and paper: 6″×4½″; pale gray wove paper watermarked '[star] ARAK [star] | W & A'; various lines per page (up to 27). No running heads.

Binding: Two styles have been noted, priority assumed.

Binding A: Gray, brownish orange, and white patterned paper-covered boards (see illustration) with gold V cloth (smooth) shelfback. See collation for front endpapers; back endpapers of the same paper as the text. Top and front edges trimmed, bottom edges deckle edged.

Binding B: Gray, brownish orange, and white; or orange and white; or light orange, brown, white, and gray patterned paper-covered boards (see illustration) with gold V cloth (smooth) shelfback. Front cover has paper label (1¼″×3¼″) printed in brownish orange with '[rule around top, right side, and bottom] *A Walt Whitman Manuscript* | FROM THE ALBERT M. BENDER | COLLECTION OF MILLS COLLEGE'. See collation for front endpapers; back endpapers of the same paper as the text. Top and front edges trimmed, bottom edges deckle edged.

Printing: Printed by the Eucalyptus Press, Mills College (p. 23).

Publication: Limited to 175 copies. Published 30 January 1939. Copyright A127313; received, 9 March 1939. NN-R copy (binding B) received 22 February 1939. DLC copy (binding B) received 4 November 1939. Price, $1.10.

Locations: Binding A: JM (2), TxU; binding B: CSt, CaOTU, CtY (2), DLC (2), MBU, NN-R, NcD, NcU, NjP, PU, RPB, ViU (3).

Note: Copies in binding A may in fact be binding B copies on which the paper label was not pasted on the front cover.

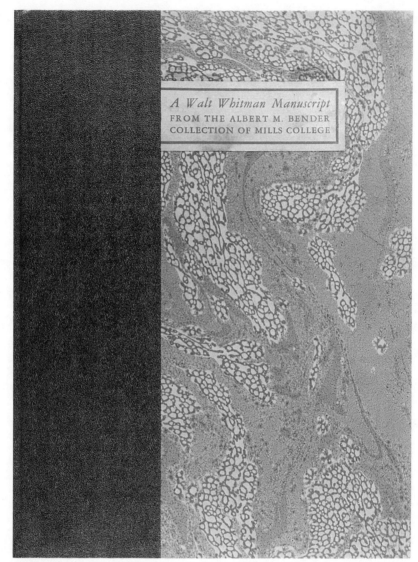

A Walt Whitman Manuscript
FROM THE ALBERT M. BENDER
COLLECTION OF MILLS COLLEGE

Binding B for A 33

175
copies
printed at the Eucalyptus Press, Mills College,
in the month of January, 1939

Statement of limitation for A 33

A 34 WALT WHITMAN'S BACKWARD GLANCES
1947

A 34.1.a
Only edition, first printing (1947)

Walt Whitman's

BACKWARD GLANCES

A BACKWARD GLANCE O'ER TRAVEL'D ROADS
And Two Contributory Essays
Hitherto Uncollected

———◆———

Edited with an Introduction on the Evolution
of the Text by
SCULLEY BRADLEY
and
JOHN A. STEVENSON

———◆———

Philadelphia:
UNIVERSITY OF PENNSYLVANIA PRESS
1947

A 34.1.a: 10⁵⁄₁₆″×6⅞″

[i–ii] [i–iv] v–viii [ix–x] 1–13 [14] 15–22 [23–24] [24a–t] 25–51 [52]. Inserted leaf with photograph of Whitman in 1868 printed on verso is positioned before the title page.

[1]^6 [2–3]^{10} [4]^6 [5]^8. Sheets bulk ¼″.

Contents:　pp. i–ii: blank; p. i: half title, 'WALT WHITMAN'S | BACKWARD GLANCES'; p. ii: blank; p. iii: title page; p. iv: copyright page; p. v: "To Thee Old Cause" from "Inscriptions" in *Leaves of Grass;* p. vi: "To Foreign Lands" from "Inscriptions" in *Leaves of Grass;* pp. vii–viii: preface, dated *'Philadelphia, December 1946';* p. ix: contents; p. x: blank; pp. 1–13: introduction; p. 14: chart showing the evolution of *A Backward Glance;* pp. 15–16: "A Note on the Texts"; pp. 17–22: "A Backward Glance on My Own Road"; p. 23: 'Facsimile of Manuscript of | A BACKWARD GLANCE ON MY OWN ROAD'; p. 24: blank; pp. 24a–t: facsimile of the manuscript; pp. 25–33: "How 'Leaves of Grass' Was Made"; p. 34: section 46 of "Song of Myself"; pp. 35–51: "A Backward Glance O'er Travel'd Roads"; p. 52: blank.

Typography and paper:　7^{11}/₁₆″ (7^7/₁₆″)×5″; wove paper; 41 lines per page. Running heads: rectos: pp. 3–13, 19–22, 27–33, 37–51: 'BACKWARD GLANCES'; versos: p. viii: 'PREFACE'; pp. 2–12: 'WALT WHITMAN'S'; p. 16: 'WALT WHITMAN'S BACKWARD GLANCES'; pp. 18–22, 26–32, 36–50: 'WALT WHITMAN'S'.

Binding:　Dark green fine B cloth (linen). Front and back covers: blind-stamped triple-rule frame; spine: goldstamped vertically: '[leaf design] | WALT WHITMAN'S BACKWARD GLANCES [leaf design] Bradley *and* Stevenson [leaf design]'. White endpapers. All edges trimmed.

Dust jacket:　Light yellowish green laid paper with vertical chain lines 1″ apart, printed in green. Front cover: 'Walt Whitman's | BACKWARD GLANCES | A BACKWARD GLANCE O'ER TRAVEL'D ROADS | And Two Contributory Essays | Hitherto Uncollected | [rule] | *Edited with an Introduction on the Evolution* | *of the Text by* | SCULLEY BRADLEY | *and* | JOHN A. STEVENSON | [rule] | UNIVERSITY OF PENNSYLVANIA PRESS'; back cover: blank; spine: vertically: 'WALT WHITMAN'S BACKWARD GLANCES: Bradley *and* Steven-

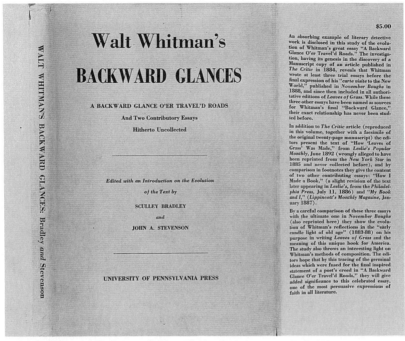

WALT WHITMAN'S BACKWARD GLANCES: Bradley and Stevenson

Walt Whitman's

BACKWARD GLANCES

A BACKWARD GLANCE O'ER TRAVEL'D ROADS

And Two Contributory Essays

Hitherto Uncollected

Edited with an Introduction on the Evolution

of the Text by

SCULLEY BRADLEY

and

JOHN A. STEVENSON

UNIVERSITY OF PENNSYLVANIA PRESS

$5.00

An absorbing example of literary detective work is disclosed in this study of the evolution of Whitman's great essay "A Backward Glance O'er Travel'd Roads." The investigation, having its genesis in the discovery of a Manuscript copy of an article published in *The Critic* in 1884, reveals that Whitman wrote at least three trial essays before the final expression of his "*carte visite* to the New World," published in *November Boughs* in 1888, and since then included in all authoritative editions of *Grass*. While these three other essays have been named as sources for Whitman's final "Backward Glance," their exact relationship has never been studied before.

In addition to *The Critic* article (reproduced in this volume, together with a facsimile of the original twenty-page manuscript) the editors present the text of "How 'Leaves of Grass' Was Made," from *Leslie's Popular Monthly*, June 1892 (wrongly alleged to have been reprinted from the *New York Star* in 1885 and never collected before), and by comparison in footnotes they give the content of two other contributing essays: "How I Made a Book," (a slight revision of the text later appearing in *Leslie's*, from the *Philadelphia Press*, July 11, 1886) and "My Book and I," (*Lippincott's Monthly Magazine*, January 1887).

By a careful comparison of these three essays with the ultimate one in *November Boughs* (also reprinted here) they show the evolution of Whitman's reflections in the "early candle light of old age" (1883-88) on his purpose in writing *Leaves of Grass* and the meaning of this unique book for America. The study also throws an interesting light on Whitman's methods of composition. The editors hope that by this tracing of the germinal ideas which were fused for the final inspired statement of a poet's creed in "A Backward Glance O'er Travel'd Roads," they will give added significance to this celebrated essay, one of the most persuasive expressions of faith in all literature.

Dust jacket for A 34.1.a

son'; front flap: 47-line description of book with price in upper right corner; back flap: blank.

Printing: Unknown.

Publication: Listed in *Publishers Weekly*, 7 June 1947. Copyright 28 May 1947; A13630. Deposit copies: DLC ('MAY 31 1947'), BL ('11 AUG 47'), BO ('4 SEP 1947'), BE ('6 NOV 1947'). Presentation copies: TxU (from Stevenson, 20 May 1947). Copies inscribed by owners: DLC (30 May 1947). PU copy received 23 May 1947. Price, $5.00. Listed in *CBI* as distributed in England by Oxford University Press at 27s.6d.

Locations: BE, BL, BO, CSt (dj), CtY, DLC (dj), JM (dj), MB, MBU, MH (2), NN-R, NNC (dj), NcD, NcU, NjCW (dj), NjP, PU (3; 3dj), RPB, ScU, TxU (3; 2dj), ViU.

A 34.1.b
Freeport, N.Y.: Books for Libraries Press, [1968].

Reduced format facsimile reprinting. *Essay Index Reprint Series*. DLC copy received from the publisher 6 January 1969. Price, $6.50. *Locations:*   DLC, ScU.

A 35 WALT WHITMAN OF THE NEW YORK AURORA
1950

A 35.1.a
Only edition, first printing (1950)

Walt
Whitman
of the New York **Aurora**
EDITOR AT TWENTY-TWO

A Collection of Recently Discovered Writings
edited by

JOSEPH JAY RUBIN

CHARLES H. BROWN

BALD EAGLE PRESS
State College, Pennsylvania
1950

A 35.1.a: 9¾₁₆″×5¹³⁄₁₆″

> ## Copyright 1950 by Bald Eagle Press
>
> Printed in the United States of America
> *by*
> ### THE CARROLLTOWN NEWS
> CARROLLTOWN, PENNSYLVANIA
>
> ## Designed by Frances Boldereff

[i–vii] viii [ix–xii] [1] 2–13 [14–17] 18–54 [55–57] 58–83 [84–87] 88–101 [102–105] 106–122 [123–125] 126–135 [136–137] 138–147 [148]

[1–10]^8. Sheets bulk $^{17}\!/_{32}$″.

Contents: p. i: half title, ornate letters 'WALT WHITMAN | of the | New York Aurora'; p. ii: blank; p. iii: title page; p. iv: copyright page; p. v: acknowledgments; p. vi: blank; pp. vii–viii: preface by W. L. Werner; pp. ix–xii: contents; pp. 1–13: introduction; p. 14: blank; p. 15: ' "*New York | is a great place | . . . . | a mighty world | in itself*" '; p. 16: drawing of a donkey in man's clothes; pp. 17–54: texts; p. 55: ' "*We never intend | to mince | matters | . . . . | to stop | for | honeyed words*" '; p. 56: blank; pp. 57–83: texts; p. 84: blank; p. 85: ' "*Government | is at best | but a necessary | evil*" '; p. 86: blank; pp. 87–101: texts; p. 102: blank; p. 103: ' "*In writing, it is | occasionally | requisite | to have ideas*" '; p. 104: blank; pp. 105–122: texts; p. 123: ' "*We determined | to perpetrate | a few paragraphs | of sentiment*" '; p. 124: blank; pp. 125–135: texts; p. 136: blank; pp. 137–147: notes; p. 148: index.

Poetry and Prose: Reprints E 46, E 49–51, E 53–57, E 59–63, E 66, E 68–80, E 82–86, E 90–96, E 98–110, E 112–119, E 121–129, E 131–140, E 142–147.

Typography and paper: 7⅛″ (6¾″)×4″; wove paper watermarked '[curved] WARREN'S | OLDE STYLE'; introduction and text: 43 lines per page; notes: 53 lines per page. Running heads: rectos: p. xi: '[ornate letters] Contents'; pp. 3–13: 'INTRODUCTION'; pp. 19–53, 59–83, 89–101, 107–121, 127–135: titles of articles; p. 139: 'NOTES • PART I'; p. 141: 'NOTES • PART II'; p. 143: 'NOTES • PART III'; p. 145: 'NOTES • PART IV'; p. 147: 'NOTES • PART V'; versos: p. viii: 'PREFACE'; pp. x–xii: '[ornate letters] Contents'; pp. 2–12: 'INTRODUCTION'; pp. 18–54: 'PART I'; pp. 58–82: 'PART II'; pp. 88–100: 'PART III'; pp. 106–122: 'PART IV'; pp. 126–134: 'PART V'; pp. 138–140: 'NOTES • PART I'; p. 142: 'NOTES • PART II'; pp. 144–146: 'NOTES • PART IV'.

Binding: Medium yellow V cloth (smooth) stamped in brown. Front cover: bottom left: '[rules-bars-and-bullets design] | *Walt* | *Whitman* | [rules-bars-and-bullets design]'; back cover: blank; spine: '[rules-bars-and-bullets design] | WALT | WHITMAN | of | the | New York | Aurora | [rule-bar-and-bullet design] | BALD | EAGLE'. White endpapers. All edges trimmed.

Dust jacket: Unprinted light brown paper.

Printing: See copyright page.

Publication: Listed in *Publishers Weekly*, 22 July 1950. Reviewed in *New York Times Book Review*, 19 November 1950, p. 44. Copyright 20 July 1950; A45877. Deposit copies: DLC ('AUG –4 1950'), BE ('14 SP 1951'), BO ('24JAN1952'), BL ('28 MAY 54'). NjP copy (rebound) received 1 September 1950. Price, $4.00.

Locations: BE, BL, BO, CSt, DLC, JM, MB, MBU, MH, NNC, NcD, NjCW, PU, RPB, ScU, TxU (dj), ViU (3).

A 35.1.b
Westport, Conn.: Greenwood, [1972].

Facsimile reprinting. *Location:* CSt.

A 36 WALT WHITMAN LOOKS AT THE SCHOOLS
1950

A 36.1.a
Only edition, only printing (1950)

Two issues have been noted:

A 36.1.a₁
First issue (1950)

WALT WHITMAN

LOOKS AT THE SCHOOLS

FLORENCE BERNSTEIN FREEDMAN

1950 · KING'S CROWN PRESS
COLUMBIA UNIVERSITY · NEW YORK

A 36.1.a₁: 8″×5⅜″

[i–ii] [i–vii] viii [ix] x–xii [xiii–xiv] [1–3] 4–13 [14] 15–24 [25] 26–34 [35] 36–61 [62–65] 66–96 [97] 98–212 [213] 214–217 [218] 219 [220–221] 222–259 [260–261] 262–272 [273] 274–278 [279–280]. Inserted leaf of coated paper with photograph of manuscript school book recording Whitman's visits printed on recto and verso is positioned after p. 32.

[1–16]⁸ [17]⁴ [18–19]⁸. Sheets bulk ²¹⁄₃₂″.

Contents: pp. i–ii: blank; p. i: half title, 'Walt Whitman Looks at the Schools'; p. ii: blank; p. iii: title page; p. iv: copyright page; p. v: dedication; p. vi: blank; pp. vii–viii: preface, signed 'FLORENCE B. FREEDMAN | New York City | July, 1950'; pp. ix–xii: contents; pp. xiii–xiv: epigraphs from *Brooklyn Daily Eagle* and *Leaves of Grass;* p. 1: half title, same as p. i; p. 2: blank; pp. 3–61: texts; p. 62: blank; p. 63: 'Articles on Schools and the | Education of Youth | in the | Brooklyn "Evening Star" | and the | Brooklyn "Daily Eagle" '; p. 64: note on the texts; pp. 65–212: texts; pp. 213–217: Appendix A; pp. 218–219: Appendix B; p. 220: blank; pp. 221–259: notes; p. 260: blank; pp. 261–272: bibliography; pp. 273–278: index; pp. 279–280: blank.

Prose: Reprints E 180, E 184, E 187, E 191, E 192, E 195, E 201, E 202, E 207, E 211, E 212, E 215, E 220, E 224, E 226–229, E 231, E 236, E 245, E 247, E 248, E 250, E 251, E 272, E 273, E 288, E 292, E 293, E 300, E 301, E 308, E 319, E 321, E 322, E 328, E 332, E 341, E 343, E 345, E 363, E 366, E 370, E 373, E 378, E 382, E 392, E 408, E 418, E 424, E 428, E 435, E 459–461, E 479, E 482, E 495, E 520, E 537, E 546, E 569, E 582, E 587, E 592, E 593, E 595, E 605, E 626, E 630, E 638, E 645, E 651, E 659, E 678, E 679, E 681, E 683, E 685, E 701, E 702, E 704, E 722, E 739–741, E 744, E 745, E 757, E 771–774, E 778, E 779, E 782, E 785, E 786, E 796, E 798–800, E 804,

E 810, E 812, E 813, E 826, E 827, E 836, E 839, E 841, E 845–848, E 864, E 865, E 869, E 900, E 901, E 904, E 935, E 949, E 962, E 963, E 970, E 971, E 973, E 977, E 980, E 992, E 1000, E 1006, E 1007, E 1018, E 1028, E 1029, E 1031, E 1044, E 1061, E 1064, E 1065.

Typography and paper: 6¼″ (6″)×4″; wove paper watermarked '[curved] WARREN'S | OLDE STYLE'; introduction, text, and bibliography: 33 lines per page; notes: 35 lines per page; index: double columns, 41 lines per page. Running heads: rectos: p. xi: '*Contents*'; pp. 5–13: ' "*Who Would Presume to Teach Here*" '; pp. 15–23: '"*Go-befores and Embryons*" '; pp. 27–33: '"*To Girlhood, Boyhood Look*" '; pp. 37–61: '"*The Reporter's Lead Flies Swiftly*" '; pp. 67–79: '*September, 1845, to March, 1846*'; pp. 99–211: '*March, 1846, to January, 1848*'; pp. 215–217: '*Other Articles in the "Star"* '; p. 219: '*Related Articles in the "Eagle"* '; pp. 223–259: '*Notes*'; pp. 263–271: '*Bibliography*'; pp. 275–277: '*Index*'; versos: p. viii: '*Preface*'; pp. x–xii: '*Contents*'; pp. 4–12: ' "*Who Would Presume to Teach Here*" '; pp. 16–24: '"*Go-befores and Embryons*" '; pp. 26–34: '"*To Girlhood, Boyhood Look*" '; pp. 36–60: '"*The Reporter's Lead Flies Swiftly*" '; pp. 66–96: '*Brooklyn "Evening Star"* '; pp. 98–212: '*Brooklyn "Daily Eagle"* '; pp. 214–216: '*Other Articles in the "Star"* '; pp. 222–258: '*Notes*'; pp. 262–272: '*Bibliography*'; pp. 274–278: '*Index*'.

Binding: Greenish gray V cloth (smooth) stamped in green. Front cover: 'WALT WHITMAN | LOOKS AT THE SCHOOLS | FLORENCE BERNSTEIN FREEDMAN'; back cover: blank; spine: vertically: 'Freedman WALT WHITMAN LOOKS AT THE SCHOOLS | [three horizontal lines] King's | Crown | Press'. White endpapers. All edges trimmed.

Printing: Unknown.

Publication: 800 copies. Published 21 December 1950. Listed in *Publishers Weekly*, 30 December 1950. Copyright 21 December 1950; A50920. Deposit copies: DLC ('DEC 15 1950'), BL ('21 FEB 51'), BE ('28 MAY 1951'). NjP copy received 2 January 1951. Price, $3.50.

Locations: BE, BL, CSt, DLC, JM, MBU, MH, NN-R, NcD, NcU, NjCW (2), NjP, RPB, ScU, TxU, ViU (3).

A 36.1.a₂
Second issue (1950)

WALT WHITMAN

LOOKS AT THE SCHOOLS

FLORENCE BERNSTEIN FREEDMAN

*Submitted in partial fulfillment of
the requirements for the degree of
Doctor of Philosophy in the Faculty
of Philosophy, Columbia University*

1950 · KING'S CROWN PRESS
COLUMBIA UNIVERSITY · NEW YORK

A 36.1.a₂: 8″×5⅜″

Pagination, collation, and binding are the same as in the first issue.

Contents: Same as in the first issue, except: p. iii: dissertation title page.

Publication: DLC copy stamped '3/13/51' and received 15 March 1951. Not for sale.

Locations: DLC, NNC.

Note: The university press probably made a stop-press substitution of the dissertation title page so that the author could use such copies to fulfill her dissertation requirements.

A 37 WHITMAN'S MANUSCRIPTS   LEAVES OF GRASS (1860)
1955

A 37.1.a
Only edition, first printing [1955]

Whitman's Manuscripts

Leaves of Grass

(1860)

A PARALLEL TEXT

Edited with Notes and Introduction

By

Fredson Bowers

THE UNIVERSITY OF CHICAGO PRESS

A 37.1.a: 9½"×6⅝"

Library of Congress Catalog Number: 55-7313

THE UNIVERSITY OF CHICAGO PRESS, CHICAGO 37
Cambridge University Press, London, N.W. 1, England
The University of Toronto Press, Toronto 5, Canada

Copyright 1955 by The University of Chicago. All rights reserved.
Copyright 1955 under the International Copyright Union
Published 1955. Composed and printed by THE WILLIAM BYRD
PRESS, INC., Richmond, Virginia, U.S.A.

[i–vi] vii–ix [x] xi–xx [xxi–xxii] xxiii–lxxiv [1] 2–56 [57] 58–264 [265–266]. Inserted two-leaf gathering (with picture of Whitman in 1860 on p. 1, and photographs of manuscript pages of "Premonition," "Enfans d'Adam," and "Calamus" on pp. 2–4) is positioned after the copyright page.

[1–5]¹⁶ [6]¹⁰ [7–11]¹⁶. Sheets bulk ¹⁵⁄₁₆″.

Contents: p. i: 'Whitman's Manuscripts | [double rule] | *Leaves of Grass* | (1860)'; p. ii: blank; p. iii: title page; p. iv: copyright page; p. v: dedication; p. vi: blank; pp. vii–ix: foreword, signed 'F. B. | CHARLOTTESVILLE, VIRGINIA | 15 October 1954'; p. x: blank; pp. xi–xii: contents; pp. xiii–xviii: "The Valentine-Barrett Manuscripts"; pp. xix–xx: Rome sales list of Whitman manuscripts; p. xxi: *'Introduction'*; p. xxii: blank; pp. xxiii–lxxiv: introduction; p. 1: *'The Texts'*; pp. 2–56: texts; p. 57: blank; pp. 58–260: texts; pp. 261–264: index of first lines; pp. 265–266: blank.

Poems: "Premonition," "Calamus" cluster, "Enfans d'Adam" cluster, "Proto-Leaf," "Chants Democratic," "Leaves of Grass" cluster, "Messenger Leaves" cluster, "Mannahatta" ["I was asking for something specific and perfect for my city . . ."], "Poem of Joys," "France," "Unnamed Lands," "Kosmos," "A Hand-Mirror," "Savantism," "Says," "To My Soul," "So Long!," "Sparkles from the Wheel," "Fables," "To an Exclusive."

Typography and paper: 7⅜″ (7¹⁄₁₆″)×4¹³⁄₁₆″; wove paper watermarked '[curved] WARREN'S | OLDE STYLE'; introduction and texts: various lines per page (up to 39); index: 44 lines per page. Running heads: rectos: p. ix: *'FORE-WORD'*; pp. xiii–xvii: *'TABLE OF MANUSCRIPTS'*; pp. xxv–xxxi: *'THE VALENTINE-BARRETT MANUSCRIPTS'*; pp. xxxiii–xlix: *'THE GROWTH OF THE THIRD EDITION'*; p. li–lxi: *'PREMONITION'*; pp. lxiii–lxiv: *'CALAMUS AND ENFANS D'ADAM'*; pp. 3–35: *'PROTO-LEAF'*; pp. 37–39: *'APPENDIX I'*; pp. 41–55: *'APPENDIX II'*; pp. 59–65: *'ENFANS D'ADAM'*; pp. 67–123: *'CALA-MUS'*; pp. 125–169: *'CHANTS DEMOCRATIC'*; pp. 171–183: *'LEAVES OF GRASS'*; pp. 185–193: *'MESSENGER LEAVES'*; pp. 195–197: *'MAN-NAHATTA'*; pp. 199–215: *'POEM OF JOYS'*; pp. 217–219: *'FRANCE'*; pp. 221–223: *'UNNAMED LANDS'*; p. 225: *'KOSMOS'*; p. 227: *'A HAND-MIRROR'*; p.

229: 'SAVANTISM'; pp. 231–233: 'SAYS'; p. 235: 'TO MY SOUL'; pp. 237–247: 'SO LONG!'; pp. 249–253: 'APPENDIX II'; p. 255: 'SPARKLES FROM THE WHEEL'; p. 257: 'FABLES'; p. 259: 'TO AN EXCLUSIVE'; p. 263: 'FIRST-LINE INDEX'; versos: p. viii: 'FOREWORD'; p. xii: 'WHITMAN MANUSCRIPTS'; pp. xiv–xviii: 'TABLE OF MANUSCRIPTS'; p. xx: 'ROME SALES LIST'; pp. xxiv–lxxiv: 'INTRODUCTION'; pp. 2–258: 'WHITMAN MANUSCRIPTS'; p. 260: 'WHITMAN'S LIST FOR THE THIRD EDITION'; pp. 262–264: 'FIRST-LINE INDEX'.

Binding: Dark bluish green B cloth (linen). Front and back covers: blank; spine: '[horizontal] BOWERS | [two parallel vertical lines] Whitman's Manuscripts | *Leaves of Grass (1860)* | [horizontal] [publisher's device]'. White endpapers. All edges trimmed. Top edges stained blue.

Dust jacket: Black spine with light blue sides and white flaps. Front cover: '[green, from bottom to top on black background where it meets the light blue] A PARALLEL TEXT | [white blades of grass design on black and light blue backgrounds] | [script with white 'W' on black background] Whitman's Manuscripts | [four lines in green] [first five letters on black background] LEAVES OF GRASS • 1860 | [first word on black background] edited by Fredson Bowers | WALT WHITMAN REVEALED IN | THE ART OF MAKING POETRY'; back cover: white blades of grass design on light blue background; spine: '[horizontal] [white] BOWERS | [vertical] [white script] Whitman's Manuscripts [green] LEAVES OF GRASS • 1860 | [two horizontal lines in white] [publisher's device] | CHICAGO'; front flap: 25-line description of book with price in upper right-hand corner; back flap: 24-line description of book and editor.

Printing: See copyright page.

Publication: 1,000 copies. Published 4 July 1955. Listed in *Publishers Weekly*, 9 July 1955. Copyright 4 July 1955; A197424. Deposit copies: DLC ('JUL –7 1955'), BL ('12 OCT 55'), BO ('1 NOV1955'), BE ('7 NO 1955'). NjP copy received 23 August 1955. Price, $12.50. Listed in the *English Catalogue* as an importation by Cambridge University Press at 94s.

Locations: BE, BL, BO, CSt (dj), CaOTU, DLC, JM (dj), MBU (dj), MH, NcD (dj), NcU, NjCW (dj), NjP, RPB, TxU (dj), ViU (2; 2dj).

A 37.1.b
Chicago and London: University of Chicago Press, [1965].

Copyright page: '*Second Impression 1965*'. *Location:* JM.

A 37.1.c
Chicago and London: University of Chicago Press, [1969].

Copyright page: '*Third Impression 1969*'. *Location:* JM.

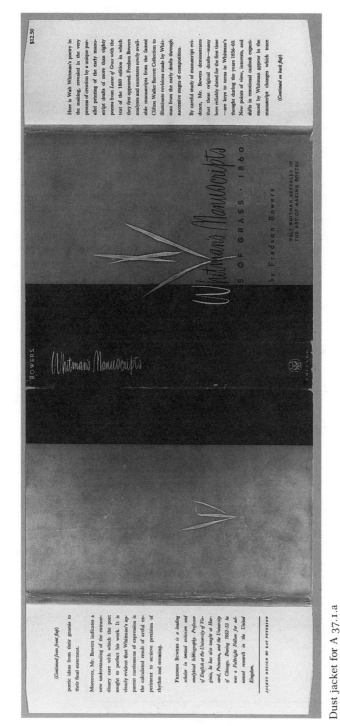

$12.50

Here is Walt Whitman's poetry in the making, revealed in the very process of creation by a unique parallel printing of the early manuscript drafts of more than eighty poems from *Leaves of Grass* with the text of the 1860 edition in which they first appeared. Fredson Bowers analyzes and annotates newly available manuscripts from the famed Clifton Waller Barrett Collection to illuminate revisions made by Whitman from the early drafts through successive stages of composition.

By careful study of manuscript evidence, Mr. Bowers demonstrates that these original drafts—many here reliably dated for the first time—are keys to turns in Whitman's thought during the years 1856–60. New points of view, interests, and shifts in emotional outlook experienced by Whitman appear in the manuscript changes which trace

(Continued on back flap)

BOWERS

Whitman's Manuscripts

Whitmans Manuscripts
S OF GRASS · 1860

by Fredson Bowers

WALT WHITMAN REVEALED IN
THE ART OF MAKING POETRY

CHICAGO

(Continued from front flap)

poetic ideas from their genesis to their final statement.

Moreover, Mr. Bowers indicates a new understanding of the extraordinary care with which the poet sought to perfect his work. It is clearly evident that Whitman's apparent carelessness of expression is the calculated result of artful experiment to achieve precision of rhythm and meaning.

Fredson Bowers is a leading scholar in textual criticism and analytical bibliography. Professor of English at the University of Virginia, he has also taught at Harvard, Princeton, and the University of Chicago. During 1952–53 he was a Fulbright Fellow for advanced research in the United Kingdom.

JACKET DESIGN BY RAY PEFFERSON

Dust jacket for A 37.1.a

A 38 AN 1855–56 NOTEBOOK
1959

A 38.1.a
Only edition, first printing [1959]

Four issues have been noted:

A 38.1.a₁
First issue [1959]

Walt Whitman

AN 1855-56 NOTEBOOK

TOWARD

THE SECOND EDITION OF

LEAVES OF GRASS

INTRODUCTION AND NOTES BY
HAROLD W. BLODGETT

With a Foreword by CHARLES E. FEINBERG
Additional Notes by WILLIAM WHITE

SOUTHERN ILLINOIS UNIVERSITY PRESS

CARBONDALE

A 38.1.a₁: 10¼″×6¹⁵⁄₁₆″; four-line title and rules are in green [i–iv] v–x [1–2] 3–20 [21–22] 23–41 [42–46]

[1–7]⁴. Sheets bulk ³⁄₁₆″.

Contents: p. i: half title, 'WALT WHITMAN: AN 1855–56 NOTEBOOK'; p. ii: blank; p. iii: title page; p. iv: copyright page; pp. v–vi: "Foreword" by Charles E. Feinberg; pp. vii–x: "Introduction" by Harold W. Blodgett; p. 1: 'WALT WHITMAN: AN 1855–56 NOTEBOOK'; p. 2: blank; pp. 3–20: text; p. 21: 'ILLUSTRATIONS'; p. 22: blank; pp. 23–30: illustrations; pp. 31–41: notes; p. 42: blank; p. 43: printing information and statement of limitation; pp. 44–46: blank.

Typography and paper: 7″×4⁵⁄₁₆″; gatherings one through four and six and seven are on laid paper with horizontal chain lines 1¹⁄₁₆″ apart, watermarked 'Arches'; gathering 5 (illustrations) is on wove paper; foreword and introduction, 27 lines per page; text, 24 lines per page; notes, 34 lines per page. No running heads.

Binding: Medium green buckram with dark reddish orange leather shelfback. Front cover: goldstamped facsimile signature; back cover: blank; spine: goldstamped vertically: 'WALT WHITMAN: AN 1855–56 NOTEBOOK'. White laid endpapers. Top edges trimmed, front and bottom edges rough trimmed. Top edges gilded.

Box: Slipcase open at one end containing text and portfolio boxes. Both slipcase and text boxes are covered in green paper, with green, brown, and gold peacocklike marbled paper pasted over front and back. Portfolio box is similar, but shaped like a casing with three folding flaps inside (see *Publication*).

Printing: Composed and printed by Clarke & Way, New York. Collotypes by Meriden Gravure, Meriden, Connecticut. Bound by Russell-Rutter Company, New York.

Publication: Limited to 50 numbered copies signed by Feinberg, each accompanied by a portfolio with "fourteen original items of Whitman memorabilia." See illustration for contents of copies numbered I to XVIII. Published February 1959. Listed in published copyright catalogue: 25 March 1959; A389210. Price, $125.00.

Locations: NjWC (box), ViU (box).

The text of WALT WHITMAN: AN 1855–56 NOTEBOOK, was composed
in Monotype Scotch and printed by Clarke & Way, Inc., New York.
The collotypes were made by the Meriden Gravure Company, Meriden,
Connecticut. The book was bound by the Russell-Rutter Company, New
York. The format was designed by Andor Braun.

This edition, printed on mould made Arches paper, has been limited to
fifty copies. To accompany this edition, fifty portfolios of fourteen original items of Whitman memorabilia have been made up.

The copies numbered I to XVIII have included with them the following
fourteen collectors' items:

> Engraving of Whitman, 1860; wood engraving by W. J. Linton, 1875; photograph
> of Whitman by G. F. E. Pearsall, 1872; proof of "Remembrance Copy" page, 1875–76;
> proof of title page of Centennial Edition, 1876; proof of intercalations used in Centennial
> Edition, 1876; ticket for Whitman's lecture "Death of Abraham Lincoln," 1880; photo-
> graph of Whitman by F. Gutekunst, 1880; proof of double title label for *Complete Poems &
> Prose,* 1888–89; handbill advertising Ingersoll lecture on "Liberty and Literature," 1890;
> reproduction of photograph of Whitman by F. Gutekunst; printed Whitman envelope,
> 1891; announcement label of the 1892 edition of *Leaves of Grass;* prospectus of *Leaves of
> Grass* 1860 facsimile reprint proposed by Horace Traubel.

This copy is number

VIII

And is here signed by

Statement of limitation for A 38.1.a₁

Note one:　A two-page mimeographed flier is at NcD, giving the publication
date as 15 February; stating the prepublication price is $100.00, after which it
goes up to $125.00; and announcing that the limitation is 25 copies, but if
"additional collectors' material becomes available" it may be possible to prepare
"a few more copies."

Note two:　Revised from *Walt Whitman Newsletter,* December 1956 (E
2871).

A 38.1.a₂
Second issue [1959]

Same as the first issue, except: the statement of limitation reads: 'The copies
numbered XIX to XXV' and 'Engraving of Whitman, 1860; proof of title page

signature *Notes* on *[sic] Walt Whitman,* | *As Poet and Person,* by John Bur-
roughs, 1871; wood engraving by W. J. Linton, 1875; | photograph of Whitman
by G. F. E. Pearsall, 1872; proof of "Remembrance Copy" page, | 1875–76;
proof of title page of Centennial Edition, 1876; proof of intercalations used in |
Centennial Edition, 1876; photograph of Whitman by F. Gutekunst, 1880;
proof of dou- | ble title label for *Complete Poems & Prose,* 1888–89; handbill
advertising Ingersoll lecture on "Liberty and Literature," 1890; reproduction of
photograph of Whitman by F. | Gutekunst; printed Whitman envelope, 1891;
announcement label of the 1892 edition of | *Leaves of Grass;* prospectus of
Leaves of Grass 1860 facsimile reprint proposed by Horace | Traubel.'.

Publication: NjP copy received 3 April 1959.

Locations: NjP (box), RPB (box).

A 38.1.a$_3$
Third issue [1959]

Same as the first issue, except: the statement of limitation reads: 'The copies
numbered XXVI to XXXVIII' and 'Engraving of Whitman, 1860; wood engrav-
ing by W. J. Linton, 1873; photograph | of Whitman by G. F. E. Pearsall,
1872; proof of title page of Centennial Edition, 1876; | proof of intercalations
used in Centennial Edition, 1876; proof of double title label for | *Complete
Poems & Prose,* 1888–89; handbill advertising Ingersoll lecture on "Liberty
and | Literature," 1890; printed Whitman envelope, 1891; prospectus of
Leaves of Grass 1860 fac- | simile reprint proposed by Horace Traubel; an-
nouncement label for the 1892 edition of | *Leaves of Grass;* Graveside issue,
Conservator, 1892; proof of "Remembrance Copy" page, | 1875–76; photo-
graph of Whitman by Edy Bros., 1880; proof of advertisement and *Leaves* | *of
Grass* label, 1872.'.

Locations: DLC (box), InU-L (box), NcD (box).

A 38.1.a$_4$
Fourth issue [1959]

Same as the first issue, except: the statement of limitation reads: 'The copies
numbered XXXIX to L' and 'Engraving of Whitman, 1860; wood engraving by
W. J. Linton, 1875; photograph | of Whitman by G. F. E. Pearsall, 1872; proof
of title page of Centennial Edition, 1876; | proof of intercalations used in
Centennial Edition, 1876; proof of double title label for *Com-* | *plete Poems &
Prose,* 1888–89; handbill advertising Ingersoll lecture on "Liberty and Litera-* |
ture," 1890; printed Whitman envelope, 1891; prospectus of *Leaves of Grass*
facsimile | reprint proposed by Horace Traubel; announcement label for the
1892 edition of *Leaves of* | *Grass;* Graveside issue, Conservator, 1892; *Old Age*

Echoes proof sheet, 1890; photograph | of Whitman by Edy Bros., 1890; proof of advertisement and *Leaves of Grass* label, 1872.'.

Location: NcD (box).

A 38.1.b
Only edition, second printing [1959]

Carbondale: Southern Illinois University Press, [1959]. Four-line title and rules are in green.

Pagination and collation are the same as in the first printing. Page size 10¹⁄₁₆″×6¹¹⁄₁₆″. Sheets bulk ³⁄₁₆″.

Contents: Same as in the first printing, except: statement of limitation is different (see illustration).

Typography and paper: Same as in the first printing, except: gatherings one through four and six and seven are on laid paper with vertical chain lines 1″ apart and are watermarked 'CURTIS RAG'.

Binding: Medium green buckram. Front cover: goldstamped facsimile signature; back cover: blank; spine: goldstamped vertically: 'WALT WHITMAN: AN 1855–56 NOTEBOOK'. Very light brown endpapers. All edges trimmed. Top edges stained light brown.

Box: Slipcase open at one end. Front and back covered in green or white paper; top, bottom, and spine covered in dark bluish gray paper.

Printing: Same as in the first printing.

Publication: Limited to 500 numbered copies signed by Feinberg. Published February 1959. Listed in *Publishers Weekly,* 11 May 1959. Copyright 25 March 1959; A389210. Deposit copies: DLC ('APR 20 1959'), BL ('15 FEB 60'). A second DLC copy received from the publisher 10 April 1959. Price, $8.50.

Locations: BL, BMR (box), BO (box), CtY (box), DLC (2), JM (box), MB, MBU, MH, NN-R (box), NcU, PU, RPB (box), ScU (box), TxU, ViU (box), ViU (box).

The text of WALT WHITMAN: AN 1855–56 NOTEBOOK, was composed in Monotype Scotch and printed by Clarke & Way, Inc., New York. The collotypes were made by the Meriden Gravure Company, Meriden, Connecticut. The book was bound by the Russell-Rutter Company, New York. The format was designed by Andor Braun.

This edition, printed on Curtis Rag paper, has been limited to five hundred copies numbered 1 to 500.

This copy is number

63

And is here signed by

Charles B Feinberg

Statement of limitation for A 38.1.b

A 39 KENTUCKY
1960

A 39
Only edition, only printing [1960]

"KENTUCKY"–WALT WHITMAN'S
UNCOMPLETED POEM

Fragments Edited with a Commentary

By Harry R. Warfel

KEEPSAKE NUMBER 8
UNIVERSITY OF KENTUCKY
LIBRARY ASSOCIATES
1960

Cover title for A 39: 11″×8⁷⁄₁₆″

[1–16]

[1]⁸. Sheets bulk ⅟₃₂″.

Contents: p. 1: cover title; p. 2: blank; p. 3: text; p. 4: blank; pp. 5–7: "Commentary on 'Kentucky,' Walt Whitman's Uncompleted Poem" by Warfel; p. 8: "Note on the Manuscripts"; pp. 9–14: facsimiles of the manuscripts; pp. 15–16: blank.

Typography and paper: 8⁵⁄₁₆″×5″; wove paper; 45 lines per page.

Binding: Cover title. All edges trimmed.

Printing: Unknown.

Publication: Presentation copies: CSt (from Warfel, August 1961). MB copy received 6 November 1961.

Locations: BL, CSt, DLC, JM, MB, MBU, MH, NjP, RPB, TxU, ViU (2).

Note: See *Walt Whitman Newsletter,* June 1958 (E 2880), and *Prairie Schooner,* Fall 1958 (E 2882) for earlier publication.

A 40 THE PEOPLE AND JOHN QUINCY ADAMS
1961

A 40.1
First edition, only printing (1961)

THE PEOPLE AND
JOHN QUINCY ADAMS
BY WALT WHITMAN

⟦ WITH A NOTE BY WILLIAM WHITE ⟧

PRIVATELY PRINTED BY THE ORIOLE PRESS

BERKELEY HEIGHTS ⁄ NEW JERSEY

1 9 6 1

A 40.1: 8″×5⅛″; first two lines, bird's head, and date are in green

Copyright page: 'COPYRIGHT 1961 BY THE ORIOLE PRESS | PRINTED IN THE UNITED STATES OF AMERICA'.

[1–6] 7 [8] 9 [10] 11 [12] 13 [14] 15 [16] 17 [18] 19 [20] 21 [22–24]

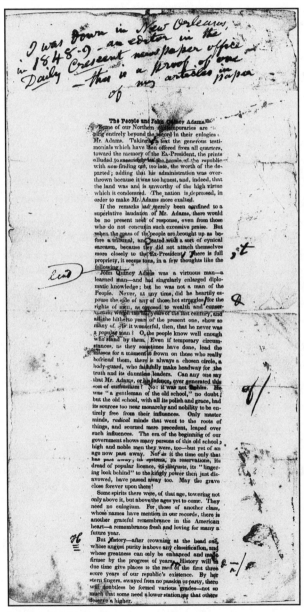

Frontispiece for A 40.1

[1]¹² . An inserted leaf (11½"×5¹⁄₁₆"), folded once, with a facsimile of a newspaper clipping printed on verso, is positioned facing the title page. Sheets bulk 1⁄16".

Contents: p. 1: green 'THE PEOPLE AND JOHN QUINCY ADAMS | BY WALT WHITMAN | [rule] | [device]'; p. 2: blank; p. 3: title page; p. 4: copyright page; p. 5: text of unpublished manuscript, beginning "Remember, statesman, in all you do"; p. 6: blank; pp. 7–13: "Whitman in New Orleans" signed 'WILLIAM WHITE | Wayne State University | *31 May 1961*' [pp. 8, 10, 12 are blank]; p. 14: blank; pp. 15–21: text [pp. 16, 18, 20 are blank]; p. 22: blank; p. 23: colophon and statement of limitation; p. 24: blank.

Typography and paper: 5³⁄₁₆"×2¹¹⁄₁₆" (introduction); 5³⁄₁₆" (5")×2¹¹⁄₁₆" (text); wove paper watermarked 'STRATHMORE PASTELLE'; 24 lines per page. Running heads: rectos: pp. 17–21: 'THE PEOPLE AND JOHN QUINCY ADAMS'; versos: none.

Binding: Three styles have been noted, priority undetermined:

Binding A: Grayish yellow-green laid paper, watermarked '*MADE IN* FRANCE [ornate lettering] INGRES D'ARCHES' with horizontal chain lines 1¹⁄₁₆" apart, wrapped around stiff covers and pasted to insides of front and back edges. Front cover: green 'THE PEOPLE AND | JOHN QUINCY ADAMS | BY WALT WHITMAN | [stylized bird's head within circular frame]'; back cover and flaps: blank. Wraparound endpapers. Top and bottom edges trimmed, front edges deckle edged.

Binding B: Same as binding A, except: watermarked 'M B M' with vertical chain lines 1¹⁄₁₆" apart.

Binding C: Same as binding A, except: watermarked with a floral pattern.

Dust jacket: Unprinted glassine noted with bindings B and C.

Printing: See statement of limitation.

Publication: Limited to 100 numbered copies signed by Charles E. Feinberg. Reviewed in *Walt Whitman Review,* 8 (March 1962), 19–20. Copyright 14 June 1961; A512263. Deposit copy: binding B: BL ('30 AUG 61'). Presentation copies (both from Feinberg): binding A: NNPM (20 June 1961); binding B: NjP (20 June 1961). Not for sale.

Locations: Binding A: DLC, InU-L, NNPM, PU, RPB, ViU; binding B: BL, NNC (dj), NjP (dj), TxU; binding C: CtY (dj).

A 40.2
Second edition, only printing (1962)

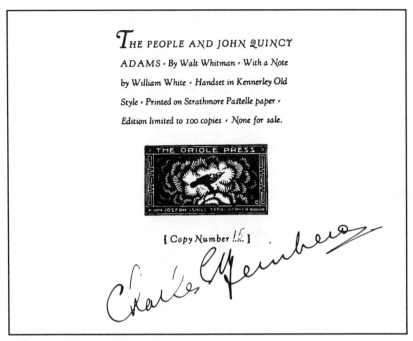

THE PEOPLE AND JOHN QUINCY

ADAMS · By Walt Whitman · With a Note

by William White · Handset in Kennerley Old

Style · Printed on Strathmore Pastelle paper ·

Edition limited to 100 copies · None for sale.

[Copy Number 15]

Statement of limitation for A 40.1

[two lines in red] | THE PEOPLE AND | JOHN QUINCY ADAMS | BY WALT WHITMAN | EDITED BY WILLIAM WHITE | [red engraving of Whitman] | PUBLISHED BY THE ORIOLE PRESS | BERKELEY HEIGHTS / NEW JERSEY / U.S.A. | • 1962 •

[1–24]

[1]¹². A leaf with a facsimile of a newspaper clipping printed on verso is positioned facing the title page. Page size 11″×5 ³⁄₁₆″. Sheets bulk ¹⁄₁₆″.

Contents: pp. 1–2: blank; p. 3: '[two lines in red] THE PEOPLE & JOHN QUINCY ADAMS | BY WALT WHITMAN [leaf design]'; p. 4: blank; p. 5: title page; p. 6: 'COPYRIGHT 1961 BY THE ORIOLE PRESS'; p. 7: text of unpublished manuscript, beginning "Remember, statesman, in all you do"; p. 8: blank; pp. 9–13: "Whitman in New Orleans" signed 'WILLIAM WHITE | Wayne State University | 24 *February 1962*' [pp. 10, 12 are blank]; p. 14: blank; pp. 15–19: text [pp. 16, 18 are blank]; p. 20: blank; p. 21: colophon and statement of limitation; pp. 22–24: blank.

Typography and paper: 7½″ (7¼″)×3⁵⁄₁₆″; wove paper; 33 lines per page. Running heads: rectos: pp. 11–13: '[red] WHITMAN IN NEW ORLEANS [leaf design]'; pp. 17–19: '[red] THE PEOPLE AND JOHN QUINCY ADAMS [leaf design]'; versos: none.

Binding: Cream paper wrapped around cardboard covers, pasted to insides of front and back edges, with '[three lines in red] THE PEOPLE AND | JOHN QUINCY ADAMS | BY WALT WHITMAN | [gray engraving of Whitman]' at top of front cover. Wraparound endpapers. Top and bottom edges trimmed, front edges deckle edged.

Dust jacket: Unprinted pinkish orange-yellow paper.

Printing: Same as in the first edition.

Publication: Limited to 75 numbered copies. Completed Summer 1962. Not for sale.

Locations: CaOTU, JM, NN-R, NcU.

A 41 THE CORRESPONDENCE
1961–1977

A 41.I.1.a
Only edition, first printing (1961)

WALT WHITMAN

The Correspondence

VOLUME I: 1842 – 1867

Edited by Edwin Haviland Miller

 NEW YORK UNIVERSITY PRESS 1961

A 41.I.1.a: 10″×7″; second line and publisher's device are in red [i–vii] viii–x [xi–xii] [1] 2–18 [19] 20 [21] 22 [23–24] 25–244 [244a–l] 245–356 [357] 358–363 [364] 365–370 [371] 372–379 [380] 381–382 [383–384] 385–394 [395–396]. Leaves with photographs of Whitman and manuscript facsimiles are inserted before the title page and between pp. 244 and 245 (a gathering of six).

[1–11]^{16} [12]^{12} [13]^{16}. Sheets bulk 1$^{3}\!/_{16}$″.

Contents: p. i: 'The Collected Writings of Walt Whitman'; p. ii: blank; p. iii: title page; p. iv: copyright page; p. v: list of general editors and advisory editorial board; p. vi: acknowledgment to Charles E. Feinberg; pp. vii–x: 'Preface' by Miller, dated '*December 1, 1960*'; p. xi: 'CONTENTS'; p. xii: blank; pp. 1–8: 'Introduction'; pp. 19–20: 'A LIST OF WHITMAN'S CORRESPONDENTS'; pp. 21–22: 'ABBREVIATIONS'; p. 23: 'The Correspondence of Walt Whitman | VOLUME I: 1842–1867'; p. 24: blank; pp. 25–244: text; pp. 244a–l: photographs and manuscript facsimiles; pp. 245–356: text; pp. 357–363: 'Appendix A | A LIST OF MANUSCRIPT SOURCES AND | PRINTED APPEARANCES'; pp. 364–370: 'Appendix B | A CHECK LIST OF WHITMAN'S LOST LETTERS'; pp. 371–379: 'Appendix C | A CALENDAR OF LETTERS WRITTEN | TO WALT WHITMAN'; pp. 380–382: 'Appendix D | CHRONOLOGY | OF WALT WHITMAN'S LIFE AND WORK'; p. 383: 'Index'; p. 384: blank; pp. 385–394: 'Index'; p. 395: blank; p. 396: colophon.

Typography and paper: 8⅝″ (8$^{3}\!/_{16}$″) × 4⅞″; wove paper watermarked with publisher's logo and 'NYU' monogram; 41 lines per page (text). Running heads: rectos: pp. ix–x: 'PREFACE'; pp. 3–17: 'INTRODUCTION'; pp. 29–35, 37–303, 307–355: 'LETTER [number]: [date]'; pp. 359–363: 'SOURCES'; pp. 365–369: 'WHITMAN'S LOST LETTERS'; pp. 373–379: 'LETTERS WRITTEN TO WHITMAN'; p. 381: 'A WHITMAN CHRONOLOGY'; pp. 387–393: 'INDEX'; versos: p. viii: 'PREFACE'; pp. 2–18: 'INTRODUCTION'; pp. 20–22, 26–36, 38–44, 48–54, 60, 64–190, 194–244, 248–270, 274–362, 366–378: 'THE COLLECTED WRITINGS OF WALT WHITMAN'; pp. 386–394: 'INDEX'.

Binding: Light medium gray V cloth (smooth) with dark red buckram shelfback. Front: shelfback extends 2¾″ onto front, with goldstamped 'W' above 'W'; back: shelfback extends 2¾″ onto back; spine: goldstamped with first five lines on medium bluish green rectangular background: 'WHITMAN |

[rule] | THE | CORRESPONDENCE | 1842–1867 | EDITED BY | Edwin Haviland | Miller | [goldstamped arch and medium bluish green tree publisher's logo within medium bluish green single-rule rectangular frame with rounded corners]'. Medium gray endpapers. All edges trimmed. Top edges stained medium bluish green.

Dust jacket: Very light gray paper with light blue hair-vein pattern. Front: red 'THE COLLECTED WRITINGS OF WALT WHITMAN' printed from bottom to top, dividing the first line after 'THE' and the last line after the publisher's logo, with 'THE CORRESPONDENCE | OF WALT WHITMAN | [red] *VOLUME I:* [black] 1842–1867 | Edwin Haviland Miller, *Editor* | GAY WILSON ALLEN | [flush right] *General Editors* | SCULLEY BRADLEY | [publisher's logo] NEW YORK UNIVERSITY PRESS'; back: black and red 30-line description of the series, listing 14 volumes; spine: vertically: 'THE COLLECTED WRITINGS OF WALT WHITMAN | [red] THE CORRESPONDENCE [black] *VOLUME I:* [red] 1842–1867 [black] *MILLER*' with horizontal '[red publisher's logo on two lines] N Y | U P' at bottom; front flap: black and red 46-line blurb for book and the series; back flap: 26-line blurb for book and description of the editor.

Printing: Printed at the Kingsport Press, Kingsport, Tenn.; bound by Quinn and Bodin.

Publication: 3,500 copies. Reviewed in *New York Times Book Review,* 2 July 1961, p. 5; *John O'London's,* 5 (6 July 1961), 12. Copyright 20 June 1961; A509744. Deposit copies: BL ('30 JAN 62'), BO ('27FEB1963'), BE ('10 AU 1964'). DLC copy received from the publisher 26 June 1961. Copies inscribed by owners: ViU (16 July 1961). NjP copy received 26 June 1961. Price, $10.00.

Locations: BE, BL, BO, CaOTU, CtY (dj), DLC, InU-L (dj), JM (dj), MB, MBU, NN-R, NNC, NcU, NjCW, NjP, PU (2; dj), RPB, ViU.

Note: Three sizes of lettering are used on the second vertical line of the dust jacket spine: the book's title is the largest, the editor's name is smaller, and the volume information is the smallest.

A41.I.1.b
Second printing (1961)

New York: New York University Press, 1961.

One-piece binding with title page all in black.

Location: TxU.

A41.II.1.a
Only edition, first printing (1961)

$10.00

THE COLLECTED WRITINGS OF WALT WHITMAN
Gay Wilson Allen and Sculley Bradley
General Editors

The Correspondence of Walt Whitman
Volume I: 1842-1867
Edwin Haviland Miller, Editor

This is the first time the correspondence of America's foremost poet has been systematically presented in its entirety without excisions and deletions. For almost seventy years Whitman's letters have been printed sporadically in books and journals, some of which are not easily accessible. Moreover, the editorial procedures of many early compilers prevented faith's texts. This type of unsystematic publication constitutes an injustice to America's greatest poet, as well as a serious inconvenience to readers and scholars. It is no longer tolerable, when large quantities of Whitman material are available in major collections, both public and private, that the letters should be printed without clarifying annotation. New York University Press, in an effort to remedy such situations as this, has undertaken the publication of THE COLLECTED WRITINGS OF WALT WHITMAN in fourteen volumes, each containing a chronology of the life of Walt Whitman compiled by Gay Wilson Allen. Extensive data have been corrected and reliance identified. Approximately sixty per cent of the letters now collected appear in print for the first time.

The Correspondence of Walt Whitman: 1842-1867 includes the poet's correspondence during the Civil War, when he was in Washington, D. C., caring, wounded, and helping soldiers. In tender, moving letters to his mother, he described the suffering and sorrow he encountered in Washington hospitals; he wrote to parents of soldiers and offered hope—or consolation at the loss of an unsung hero. Soldiers who recovered and left the hospitals often wrote to Walt, and he replied with friendly advice and paternal solicitude. As Whitman himself admitted, rarely was his heart so engaged as in these hospital scenes of the war. Known, too, like his greatest poems, reflect the characteristic themes—love and death.

In discussing letter-writing on various occasions Whitman made his own views clear: simplicity and naturalness were his guides. "I like letters to be personal—very

continued on back flap

THE COLLECTED WRITINGS OF WALT WHITMAN

THE CORRESPONDENCE OF WALT WHITMAN

VOLUME I: 1842-1867

Edwin Haviland Miller, Editor

GAY WILSON ALLEN
SCULLEY BRADLEY
General Editors

NEW YORK UNIVERSITY PRESS

THE COLLECTED WRITINGS OF WALT WHITMAN
THE CORRESPONDENCE   VOLUME I: 1842-1867   MILLER

THE COLLECTED WRITINGS OF WALT WHITMAN
IN FOURTEEN VOLUMES
GAY WILSON ALLEN and SCULLEY BRADLEY
General Editors

Advisory Editorial Board

Professor Roger Asselineau, the University of Paris • Professor Harold W. Blodgett, Union College • Charles E. Feinberg • Professor Clarence Gohdes, Duke University • Professor Emeritus Emory Holloway, Queens College • Professor Rollo G. Silver, Simmons College • Professor Floyd Stovall, the University of Virginia

Volumes in Preparation

VOLUME III: THE CORRESPONDENCE OF WALT WHITMAN
edited by Edwin Haviland Miller, New York University
VOLUME IV: THE CORRESPONDENCE OF WALT WHITMAN
edited by Edwin Haviland Miller, New York University

LEAVES OF GRASS: A Variorum Edition (two volumes)
edited by Sculley Bradley and Harold W. Blodgett

LEAVES OF GRASS: Reader's Edition
edited by Sculley Bradley and Harold W. Blodgett

THE PROSE WORKS OF WALT WHITMAN (two volumes)
edited by Floyd Stovall

BIBLIOGRAPHY
edited by William White, Wayne State University

NOTEBOOKS, DIARIES, AND PROSE FRAGMENTS (two volumes)
edited by Edward Grier and William White, University of Kansas

FICTION AND EARLY POEMS
edited by Thomas Brasher, San Marcos State College

JOURNALISTIC WRITINGS
edited by Herbert Bergman, Michigan State University

NEW YORK UNIVERSITY PRESS WASHINGTON SQUARE, NEW YORK 3

continued from front flap

personal—and then stop.' To his mother Whitman was considerate, loving, tactfully suggesting and guiding. To the soldiers whom he nursed and watched depart from the hospitals he was simultaneously a father or brother and comrade. To Peter Doyle, the young Washington motorman, he poured his affection without fear or restraint. To Emerson and Thoreau he wrote as an equal.

Dr. Miller, the editor of the present volume (and subsequent volumes of The Correspondence of Walt Whitman), has utilized hundreds of Whitman documents and thousands of letters written in the past. Thus he has been successful in many cases to establish the people mentioned in the letters as well as to shed light on previously obscure points about Whitman expositions in addition to the chronology, a list of manuscript sources by letter and by collection, a check list of lost letters, and a calendar of the correspondence directed to Whitman.

About the Editor: EDWIN HAVILAND MILLER earned his Ph.D. at Harvard. He is the author of The Professional Writer in Elizabethan England and a regular contributor to scholarly and literary journals. Dr. Miller is an associate professor of English at New York University.

Dust jacket for A 41.1.1.a

Two states have been noted:

First state:

The title page is the same as in vol. I, except: 'VOLUME II: 1868–1875'.

[i–vii] viii [ix–x] [1] 2–7 [8] 9–10 [11] 12 [12a–b] 13–244 [244a–h] 245–349 [350] 351–359 [360] 361–364 [365] 366–373 [374] 375–376 [377–378] 379–387 [388]. Leaves with photographs of Whitman and manuscript facsimiles are inserted before the title page and between pp. 244 and 245 (a gathering of four).

[1–11]^{16} [12]^8 [13]^{16}. Page size: 10″×7″. Sheets bulk 1³⁄₁₆″.

Contents: p. i: 'The Collected Writings of Walt Whitman'; p. ii: blank; p. iii: title page; p. iv: copyright page; p. v: list of general editors and advisory editorial board; p. vi: acknowledgment to Charles E. Feinberg; pp. vii–viii: 'Preface'; p. ix: 'CONTENTS'; p. x: blank; pp. 1–7: 'Introduction'; pp. 8–10: 'A LIST OF WHITMAN'S CORRESPONDENTS'; pp. 11–12: 'ABBREVIATIONS'; p. 12a: blank; p. 12b: 'The Correspondence of Walt Whitman | VOLUME II: 1868–1875'; pp. 13–244: text; pp. 244a–h: photographs and manuscript facsimiles; pp. 245–349: text; pp. 350–359: 'Appendix A | A LIST OF MANUSCRIPT SOURCES AND | PRINTED APPEARANCES'; pp. 360–364: 'Appendix B | A CHECK LIST OF WHITMAN'S LOST LETTERS'; pp. 365–373: 'Appendix C | A CALENDAR OF LETTERS WRITTEN | TO WALT WHITMAN'; pp. 374–376: 'Appendix D | CHRONOLOGY | OF WALT WHITMAN'S LIFE AND WORK'; p. 377: 'Index'; p. 378: blank; pp. 379–387: 'Index'; p. 388: colophon.

Second state:

[1]^{16} (±1$_{12}$) [2–11]^{16} [12]^8 [13]^{16}.

Contents: Same as in the first state, except: p. 12a: 'The Correspondence of Walt Whitman | VOLUME II: 1868–1875'; p 12b: blank.

Typography and paper: Same as in vol. I. Running heads are the same as in vol. I, except on different sequences of pages.

Binding: Same as in vol. I, except: spine: goldstamped '1868–1875'.

Dust jacket: Same as in vol. I, except: front: '[red] VOLUME II: [black] 1868–1875'; spine: '[black] VOLUME II: [red] 1868–1875'; back flap: 52-line blurb for book and description of the editor.

Printing: Printed at the Kingsport Press, Kingsport, Tenn.; bound by Quinn and Bodin.

Publication: 3,500 copies. Reviewed in *New York Times Book Review*, 2 July 1961, p. 5; *John O'London's*, 5 (6 July 1961), 12. Copyright 20 June 1961;

A509743. Deposit copies: DLC ('JUN 26 1961'), BL ('30 JAN 62'), BO ('27FEB1963'), BE ('10 AU 1964'). Copies inscribed by owners: ViU (16 July 1961). NjP copy received 26 June 1961. Price, $10.00.

Locations: BE, BL, BO, CaOTU, CtY (dj), DLC, InU-L (dj), JM (dj), MB, MBU, MH, NN-R, NNC, NcU, NjCW, NjP, PU (2; dj), RPB, ViU.

A 41.II.1.b
Second printing (1961)

New York: New York University Press, 1961.

One-piece binding with title page all in black.

Location: TxU.

A 41.III
Only edition, only printing (1964)

The title page is the same as in vol. I, except: 'VOLUME III: 1876–1885'.

[i–ii] [i–vii] viii–ix [x–xii] 1–9 [10] 11–13 [14] 15 [16–19] 20–73 [74] 75–105 [106] 107–145 [146] 147–171 [172] 173–202 [202a–l] [203] 204–262 [263] 264–321 [322] 323–360 [361] 362–384 [385] 386–417 [418] 419–429 [430] 431–439 [440] 441–453 [454] 455–456 [457] 458–473 [474]. Leaves with photographs of Whitman and manuscript facsimiles are inserted before the title page and between pp. 202 and 203 (a gathering of six).

[1–5]^{16} [6]^{20} [7–15]^{16}. Page size: 10″ × 7″. Sheets bulk 1⅜″.

Contents: pp. i–ii: blank; p. i: 'The Collected Writings of Walt Whitman'; p. ii: blank; p. iii: title page; p. iv: copyright page; p. v: list of general editors and advisory editorial board; p. vi: acknowledgment to Charles E. Feinberg; pp. vii–ix: 'Preface'; p. x: blank; p. xi: 'CONTENTS'; p. xii: blank; pp. 1–9: 'Introduction'; pp. 10–13: 'A LIST OF WHITMAN'S CORRESPONDENTS'; pp. 14–15: 'ABBREVIATIONS'; p. 16: blank; p. 17: 'The Correspondence of Walt Whitman | VOLUME III: 1876–1885'; pp. 19–202: text; pp. 202a–l: photographs and manuscript facsimiles; pp. 203–417: text; pp. 418–429: 'Appendix A | A LIST OF MANUSCRIPT SOURCES AND | PRINTED APPEAR-ANCES'; pp. 430–439: 'Appendix B | A CHECK LIST OF WHITMAN'S LOST | LETTERS'; pp. 440–453: 'Appendix C | A CALENDAR OF LETTERS WRIT-TEN | TO WALT WHITMAN'; pp. 454–456: 'Appendix D | CHRONOLOGY | OF WALT WHITMAN'S LIFE AND WORK'; p. 457: 'Index'; pp. 458–473: 'Index'; p. 474: colophon.

Typography and paper: Same as in vol. I. Running heads are the same as in vol. I, except on different sequences of pages.

Binding: Same as in vol. I, except: spine: goldstamped '1876–1885'.

Dust jacket: Same as in vol. I, except: front: '[red] *VOLUME III* [black] 1876–1885'; back: black and red 34-line description of the series, listing 15 volumes; spine: '[black] *VOLUME III*: [red] 1876–1885'; front flap: black and red 36-line blurb for book; back flap: 16-line blurb for book and description of the editor.

Printing: Printed at the Kingsport Press, Kingsport, Tenn.; bound by Quinn and Bodin.

Publication: 3,500 copies. Copyright 8 April 1964; A698046. Listed in *Publishers Weekly,* 6 April 1964. Deposit copies: DLC ('APR 10 1964'), BL ('APR 64'), BO ('20MAY1964'), BE ('10 AU 1964'). Copies inscribed by owners: ViU (6 August 1964). NjP copy received 24 March 1964. Price, $10.00. Sold in Canada as an importation by Ryerson for $12.50.

Locations: BE, BL, BO, CaOTU, CtY (dj), DLC, InU-L (dj), JM (dj), MB, MBU, MH, NN-R, NcU, NjCW, NjP, PU (2; dj), RPB, TxU, ViU.

A41.IV
Only edition, only printing (1969)

The title page is the same as in vol. I, except: 'VOLUME IV: 1886–1889'.

[i–vii] viii [ix–x] [1] 2–12 [13–15] 16–61 [62] 63–138 [139] 140–259 [260] 261–278 [278a–l] 279–410 [411] 412–423 [424] 425–427 [428] 429–441 [442] 443–444 [445–446] 447–458 [459–460]. Leaves with photographs of Whitman and manuscript facsimiles are inserted before the title page and between pp. 278 and 279 (a gathering of six).

[1–13]^{16} [14]^{12} [15]^{16}. Page size: 10″×7″. Sheets bulk 1⁵⁄₁₆″.

Contents: p. i: 'The Collected Writings of Walt Whitman'; p. ii: blank; p. iii: title page; p. iv: copyright page; p. v: list of general editors and advisory editorial board; p. vi: acknowledgment to Charles E. Feinberg; pp. vii–viii: 'Preface'; p. ix: 'CONTENTS'; p. x: blank; pp. 1–6: 'Introduction'; pp. 7–10: 'A LIST OF WHITMAN'S CORRESPONDENTS'; pp. 11–12: 'ABBREVIATIONS'; p. 13: 'The Correspondence of Walt Whitman | VOLUME IV: 1886–1888'; p. 14: blank; pp. 15–278: text; pp. 278a–l: photographs and manuscript facsimiles; pp. 279–410: text; pp. 411–423: 'Appendix A | A LIST OF MANUSCRIPT SOURCES AND | PRINTED APPEARANCES'; pp. 424–427: 'Appendix B | A CHECK LIST OF WHITMAN'S LOST | LETTERS'; pp. 428–441: 'Appendix C | A CALENDAR OF LETTERS WRITTEN | TO WALT WHITMAN'; pp. 442–444: 'Appendix D | CHRONOLOGY | OF WALT WHITMAN'S LIFE AND WORK'; p. 445: 'Index'; p. 446: blank; pp. 447–458: 'Index'; p. 459: colophon; p. 460: blank.

Typography and paper: Same as in vol. I. Running heads are the same as in vol. I, except on different sequences of pages.

Binding: Same as in vol. I, except: spine: goldstamped '1886–1889'.

Dust jacket: Same as in vol. I, except: front: '[red] *VOLUME IV* [black] 1886–1889'; back: black and red 33-line description of the series, listing 17 volumes; spine: '[black] *VOLUME IV* [red] 1886–1889'; front flap: black and red 36–line blurb for book; back flap: 17-line blurb for book and description of the editor.

Printing: Printed at the Kingsport Press, Kingsport, Tenn.; bound by Quinn and Bodin.

Publication: 3,100 copies. Copyright 30 June 1969; A106994. Deposit copies: DLC ('NOV –3 1969'), BL ('SEP 69'), BO ('29SEP1969'), BE ('14 OC 1969'). NjP copy received 13 August 1969. Price, $12.50.

Locations: BE, BL, BO, CaOTU, CtY (dj), DLC, InU-L (dj), JM (dj), MB, MBU, MH, NN-R, NcU, NjCW, NjP, PU (dj), RPB, TxU, ViU.

Note one: In the table of contents, '1889' is listed beside the page number given for the start of the section of 1888 letters, and '1888' is listed beside the page number given for the start of the section of 1889 letters.

Note two: The inclusive dates on the half title (p. 13) are incorrectly given as through 1888.

Note three: A set of unsewn folded and gathered signatures laid into a casing is at DLC.

A41.V
Only edition, only printing (1969)

The title page is the same as in vol. I, except: 'VOLUME V: 1890–1892'.

[i–vii] viii–ix [x–xii] [1] 2–8 [9] 10–11 [12] 13 [14–16] 17–212 [212a–h] 213–321 [322] 323–330 [331] 332 [333] 334–349 [350] 351–352 [353–355] 356–365 [366–372]. Leaves with photographs of Whitman and manuscript facsimiles are inserted before the title page and between pp. 212 and 213 (a gathering of four).

[1–12]^{16} . Page size: 10″×7″. Sheets bulk 1 ⅛″.

Contents: p. i: 'The Collected Writings of Walt Whitman'; p. ii: blank; p. iii: title page; p. iv: copyright page; p. v: list of general editors and advisory editorial board; p. vi: acknowledgment to Charles E. Feinberg; pp. vii–ix: 'Preface', dated *'May 1, 1968'*; p. x: blank; p. xi: 'CONTENTS'; p. xii: blank; pp. 1–8: 'Introduction'; pp. 9–11: 'A LIST OF WHITMAN'S CORRESPON-

DENTS'; pp. 12–13: 'ABBREVIATIONS'; p. 14: blank; p. 15: 'The Correspondence of Walt Whitman | VOLUME V: 1889–1892'; p. 16: blank; pp. 17–212: text; pp. 212a–h: photographs and manuscript facsimiles; pp. 213–321: text; pp. 322–330: 'Appendix A | A LIST OF MANUSCRIPT SOURCES AND | PRINTED APPEARANCES'; pp. 331–332: 'Appendix B | A CHECK LIST OF WHITMAN'S LOST | LETTERS'; pp. 333–349: 'Appendix C | A CALENDAR OF LETTERS WRITTEN | TO WALT WHITMAN'; pp. 350–352: 'Appendix D | CHRONOLOGY | OF WALT WHITMAN'S LIFE AND WORK'; p. 353: 'Index'; p. 354: blank; pp. 355–365: 'Index'; p. 366: blank; p. 367: colophon; p. 368–372: blank.

Typography and paper: Same as in vol. I. Running heads are the same as in vol. I, except on different sequences of pages.

Binding: Same as in vol. I, except: spine: goldstamped '1890–1892'.

Dust jacket: Same as in vol. I, except: front: '[red] *VOLUME V* [black] 1890–1892'; back: black and red 33-line description of the series, listing 17 volumes; spine: '[black] *VOLUME V* [red] 1890–1892'; front flap: black and red 36-line blurb for book; back flap: 17-line blurb for book and description of the editor.

Printing: Printed at the Kingsport Press, Kingsport, Tenn.; bound by Quinn and Bodin.

Publication: 3,100 copies. Copyright 30 June 1969; A98277. Deposit copies: DLC ('OCT –3 1969'), BL ('SEP 69'), BO ('29SEP1969'), BE ('14 OC 1969'). Copies inscribed by owners: ViU (2 September 1969). NjP copy received 13 August 1969. Price, $12.50.

Locations: BE, BL, BO, CaOTU, CtY (dj), DLC, InU-L (dj), JM (dj), MB, MBU, MH, NN-R, NcU, NjCW, NjP, PU (dj), RPB, TxU, ViU.

Note: A set of unsewn folded and gathered signatures, inscribed by Miller 2 May 1969, is at DLC.

A41.VI
Only edition, only printing (1977)

[flush right] WALT WHITMAN | [flush left] The Correspondence | [two lines flush right] VOLUME VI: A SUPPLEMENT | *with a* COMPOSITE INDEX | [centered] *Edited by* Edwin Haviland Miller | [publisher's logo placed over first letters in line below] | [flush right] NEW YORK UNIVERSITY PRESS   1977

[i–vii] viii [ix–xi] xii–xxii [xxiii] xxiv–xxxvi [xxxvii] xxxviii [xxxix] xl [xli–xlviii] [1–3] 4–62 [63] 64–65 [66] 67 [68] 69 [70] 71–72 [73] 74–78 [79] 80–124 [125–128]

$[1–3]^{16}$ $[4]^{8}$ $[5–6]^{16}$. Page size: 10″×7″. Sheets bulk ½″.

Contents: p. i: 'The Collected Writings of Walt Whitman'; p. ii: frontispiece; p. iii: title page; p. iv: copyright page; p. v: list of general editors and advisory editorial board; p. vi: blank; pp. vii–viii: 'Preface'; p. ix: 'CONTENTS'; p. x: blank; pp. xi–xxii: 'Introduction'; pp. xxiii–xxxvi: 'Appendix | NOTES TO TABLES 1 AND 2'; pp. xxxvii–xxxviii: 'A LIST OF WHITMAN'S CORRESPONDENTS'; pp. xxxix–xl: 'ABBREVIATIONS'; p. xli: 'ILLUSTRATIONS'; pp. xlii–xlvii: photographs; p. xlviii: blank; p. 1: 'The Correspondence of Walt Whitman | VOLUME VI: A Supplement *with a* composite Index'; p. 2: blank; pp. 3–62: text; pp. 63–65: 'Appendix A | A LIST OF MANUSCRIPT SOURCES | AND PRINTED APPEARANCES'; pp. 66–67: 'Appendix B | A CHECK LIST OF WHITMAN'S | LOST LETTERS'; pp. 68–69: 'Appendix C | A CALENDAR OF LETTERS WRITTEN | TO WALT WHITMAN'; pp. 70–72: 'Appendix D | CHRONOLOGY | OF WALT WHITMAN'S LIFE AND WORK'; pp. 73–78: 'Appendix E | A LIST OF CORRECTIONS AND | ADDITIONS TO VOLUMES I–V'; pp. 79–124: 'Composite Index To Volumes I–VI'; pp. 125–128: blank.

Typography and paper: Same as in vol. I. Running heads are the same as in vol. I, except on different sequences of pages and in a smaller size font.

Binding: Deep red buckram. Front: goldstamped 'W' above 'W'; back: blank; spine: goldstamped, with the first three lines on a medium bluish green rectangular background: 'WHITMAN | THE CORRESPONDENCE | VOLUME VI | A SUPPLEMENT *with a* COMPOSITE INDEX | *Edited by* Edwin Haviland Miller', with a horizontal goldstamped arch and medium bluish green tree within a medium bluish green single-rule rectangular frame with rounded corners at the bottom. Medium gray endpapers. All edges trimmed. Top edges stained medium bluish green.

Dust jacket: Gray paper. Front: red 'THE COLLECTED WRITINGS OF WALT WHITMAN' printed from bottom to top, dividing the second line after 'THE' and the last line after the publisher's logo, with 'A Supplement to | THE CORRESPONDENCE | OF WALT WHITMAN | with a COMPOSITE INDEX | [red] *VOLUME VI* | Edwin Haviland Miller, *Editor* | GAY WILSON ALLEN | [flush right] *General Editors* | SCULLEY BRADLEY | [publisher's logo] NEW YORK UNIVERSITY PRESS'; back: black and red 37-line description of the series, listing 18 volumes; spine: 'THE COLLECTED WRITINGS OF WALT WHITMAN | [red] THE CORRESPONDENCE [black] *VOLUME VI* [red] SUPPLEMENT AND INDEX' with a horizontal '[red publisher's logo on two lines] N   Y | U   P' at bottom; front flap: black and red 47-line blurb for book and the series; back flap: 42-line blurb for book and description of the editor.

Printing: Printed at the Kingsport Press, Kingsport, Tenn.; bound by Quinn and Bodin.

Publication: 1,500 copies. Copyright 16 August 1977; A908108. Deposit copies: DLC ('AUG 29 1977'), BL ('FEB 82'), BO ('18 JAN 1982'). Copies inscribed by owners: ViU (21 October 1977). NjP copy received 22 September 1977. Price, $19.50.

Locations: BL, BO, CaOTU, CtY (dj), DLC (dj), JM (dj), MB, MBU, MH, NcU, NjP, RPB, TxU, ViU.

Note: Three sizes of lettering are used on the second vertical line of the dust jacket spine: the book's title is the largest, the editor's name is smaller, and the volume information is the smallest.

A 41.2
Selected Letters of Walt Whitman. Iowa City: University of Iowa Press, [1990].

320 pp. Cloth (with dust jacket) or wrappers. Edited by Edwin Haviland Miller. 512 copies bound in cloth and 2,118 in wrappers. Prices: cloth, $39.95; wrappers, $16.50. *Locations:*   JM, NjP.

A 42 THE EARLY POEMS AND THE FICTION
1963

A 42.1.a
Only edition, first printing (1963)

WALT WHITMAN

The Early Poems
and the Fiction

Edited by Thomas L. Brasher

 NEW YORK UNIVERSITY PRESS 1963

A 42.1.a: 10″×7″; title and publisher's device are in red

[i–vii] viii–ix [x–xi] xii–xiii [xiv–xv] xvi–xviii [xix] x [xxi–xxii] [1–2] 3–52 [53–54] 55–109 [109a–h] 110–334 [335] 336–339 [340] 341–343 [344–346] 347–352 [353–354]. Leaves with manuscript facsimiles are inserted before the title page and between pp. 109 and 110 (a gathering of four).

[1–8]¹⁶ [9]¹² [10–12]¹⁶. Sheets bulk 1⅛″.

Contents: p. i: 'The Collected Writings of Walt Whitman'; p. ii: blank; p. iii: title page; p. iv: copyright page; p. v: list of general editors and advisory editorial board; p. vi: acknowledgment to Charles E. Feinberg; pp. vii–ix: 'Preface' by Brasher, dated *'April 10, 1962'*; p. x: blank; pp. xi–xiii: 'CONTENTS'; p. xiv: blank; pp. xv–xviii: 'Introduction'; pp. xix–xx: 'A NOTE ON THE TEXT'; pp. xxi–xxii: 'ABBREVIATIONS'; p. 1: 'Walt Whitman | The Early Poems and the Fiction | THE POEMS'; p. 2: blank; pp. 3–52: texts of poems; p. 53: 'Walt Whitman | The Early Poems and the Fiction | THE FICTION'; pp. 54–109: texts of fiction; pp. 109a–h: photographs of works; pp. 110–334: texts of fiction; pp. 335–339: 'Appendix A | PUBLICATION HISTORY OF WHITMAN'S | FICTION'; p. 340: blank; pp. 341–343: 'Appendix B | CHRONOLOGY | OF WALT WHITMAN'S LIFE AND WORK'; p. 344: blank; p. 345: 'Index'; p. 346: blank; pp. 347–352: 'Index'; p. 353: blank; p. 354: colophon.

Poems and Prose: *Poems:* "Young Grimes," "The Inca's Daughter," "The Love That Is Hereafter," "The Spanish Lady," "The Columbian's Song," "The Winding-Up," "Each Has His Grief," "The Punishment of Pride," "Ambition," "The Death and Burial of McDonald Clarke. A Parody," "Time to Come," "Death of the Nature-Lover," "The Play-Ground," "Ode," "The House of Friends," "Resurgemus," "Sailing the Mississippi at Midnight," "Dough-Face Song," "Blood-Money," "New Year's Day, 1848," "Isle of La Belle Riviere"; *Prose:* "Death in the School-Room," "Wild Frank's Return," "The Child and the Profligate," "Bervance: or, Father and Son," "The Tomb Blossoms," "The Last of the Sacred Army," "The Last Loyalist," "Reuben's Last Wish," "A Legend of Life and Love," "The Angel of Tears," *Franklin Evans,* "The Death of Wind-Foot," "Little Jane," "The Madman," "The Love of Eris: A Spirit Record," "My Boys and Girls," "Dumb Kate," "The Little Sleighers," "The Half-Breed: A Tale of the Western Frontier," "Shirval: A Tale of Jerusalem," "Richard Parker's Widow," "The Boy Lover," "One Wicked Impulse!", "Some Fact-Romances," "The Shadow and the Light of a Young Man's Soul," "Lingave's Temptation."

Typography and paper: 8⅜″ (8″)×4⅞″; wove paper watermarked with publisher's logo and 'NYU' monogram; 41 lines per page (text). Running heads: rectos: p. ix: 'PREFACE'; p. xi: 'CONTENTS'; p. xvii: 'INTRODUCTION'; pp. 5–51, 55–333: 'THE EARLY POEMS AND THE FICTION'; pp. 337–339: 'PUBLICATION HISTORY OF WHITMAN'S FICTION'; p. 343: 'THE COLLECTED WRITINGS OF WALT WHITMAN'; pp. 349–351: 'INDEX'; versos: p. viii: 'PREFACE'; p. xii: 'CONTENTS'; pp. xvi–xviii: 'INTRODUCTION'; p. xx: 'A NOTE ON THE TEXT'; p. xxii: 'ABBREVIATIONS'; pp. 4–52, 56–338: 'THE COLLECTED WRITINGS OF WALT WHITMAN'; p. 342: 'A WHITMAN CHRONOLOGY": pp. 348–352: 'INDEX'.

Binding: Light medium gray B cloth (linen) with dark red buckram shelfback. Front: shelfback extends 2¾″ onto front, with goldstamped 'W' above 'W'; back: shelfback extends 2¾″ onto back; spine: goldstamped, with first five lines on medium bluish green rectangular background: 'WHITMAN | [rule] | EARLY POEMS | AND | FICTION | EDITED BY | Thomas Brasher | [goldstamped arch and medium bluish green tree publisher's logo within medium bluish green single-rule rectangluar frame with rounded corners]'. Medium gray endpapers. All edges trimmed. Top edges stained very light green.

Dust jacket: Very light gray paper with light blue hair-vein pattern. Front: red 'THE COLLECTED WRITINGS OF WALT WHITMAN' printed from bottom to top, dividing the first line after 'THE' and the last line after the publisher's logo, with 'THE EARLY POEMS | AND THE FICTION | Thomas L. Brasher, *Editor* | GAY WILSON ALLEN | [flush right] *General Editors* | SCULLEY BRADLEY | [publisher's logo] NEW YORK UNIVERSITY PRESS'; back: black and red 32-line description of the series, listing 15 volumes; spine: vertically: 'THE COLLECTED WRITINGS OF WALT WHITMAN | [red] THE EARLY POEMS AND THE FICTION [black] BRASHER' with a horizontal '[red publisher's logo on two lines] N Y | U P' at bottom; front flap: black and red 37-line blurb for book and description of editor; back flap: black and red 25-line blurb for vols. 1 and 2 of *Correspondence*.

Printing: Printed at the Kingsport Press, Kingsport, Tenn.; bound by Quinn and Bodin.

Publication: 3,500 copies. Published 24 April 1963. Listed in *Publishers Weekly*, 13 May 1963. Reviewed in *Library Journal*, 88 (15 May 1963), 2011. Copyright 24 April 1963; A621787. Deposit copies: DLC ('APR 26 1963'), BO ('21 JUN1963'), BE ('10 AU 1964'). Copies inscribed by owners: ViU (11 April 1963). ScU copy received 3 May 1963. Price, $10.00. Sold as an importation in Canada by Ryerson at $12.50.

Locations: BE, BL, BO, CaOTU, CtY (dj), DLC, InU-L, MB, MH, NcU, NjCW, NjP (2), PU (2; dj), RPB, ScU, ViU.

THE COLLECTED WRITINGS OF WALT WHITMAN
Gay Wilson Allen and Sculley Bradley
General Editors

The Early Poems and the Fiction
edited by Thomas L. Brasher

By 1855, before Walter Whitman had become Walt Whitman, the great poet of *Leaves of Grass*, he had published at least twenty-four pieces of fiction and nineteen poems. With the exception of a single poem, which became part of *Leaves of Grass*, and a few stories and poems first collected in 1892 in *Specimen Days and Collect* and later included in the 1892 edition of *Complete Prose Works*, these early pieces have been scattered among several posthumous collections, most of them now out of print. The situation is a natural result of the difficult task of searching out and identifying pieces which Walter Whitman wrote but which Walt Whitman did not include in his collected work.

Whitman's early fiction and poetry appeared—and often reappeared—in some twenty magazines and newspapers. Professor Brasher has for the first time collected and collated all known versions of this early work and thereby established a definitive text. This volume brings together Whitman's early efforts in a scrupulously annotated and ordered whole, which will be of interest to the intelligent general reader and of inestimable value to the scholar.

About the editor
A professor of English at Southwest Texas State College, San Marcos, Thomas L. Brasher's interest in Whitman goes back at least a decade. He is a frequent contributor of Whitmaniana to the periodicals.

See back flap for comments on *The Collected Writings of Walt Whitman.*

THE COLLECTED WRITINGS OF WALT WHITMAN

THE EARLY POEMS AND THE FICTION

Thomas L. Brasher, *Editor*

**GAY WILSON ALLEN
SCULLEY BRADLEY** *General Editors*

NEW YORK UNIVERSITY PRESS

THE COLLECTED WRITINGS OF WALT WHITMAN
THE EARLY POEMS AND THE FICTION *BRASHER*

THE COLLECTED WRITINGS OF WALT WHITMAN
IN FIFTEEN VOLUMES
GAY WILSON ALLEN AND SCULLEY BRADLEY
General Editors

Advisory Editorial Board
Professor Roger Asselineau, the University of Paris • Professor Harold W. Blodgett, Union College • Charles E. Feinberg • Professor Clarence Gohdes, Duke University • Professor Emeritus Emory Holloway, Queens College • Professor Rollo G. Silver, Simmons College • Professor Floyd Stovall, the University of Virginia

Already Published

THE CORRESPONDENCE, edited by Edwin Haviland Miller
Volume I: 1842-1867
Volume II: 1868-1875

THE EARLY POEMS AND THE FICTION, edited by Thomas L. Brasher

PROSE WORKS 1892, edited by Floyd Stovall
Volume I, Specimen Days

Volumes in Preparation

LEAVES OF GRASS: Reader's Edition, edited by Harold W. Blodgett and Sculley Bradley

PROSE WORKS 1892, edited by Floyd Stovall
Volume II, "Democratic Vistas," Prefaces, and Essays

A VARIORUM EDITION OF LEAVES OF GRASS (in two volumes), edited by Sculley Bradley and Harold W. Blodgett

THE CORRESPONDENCE (Volumes III, IV, and V), edited by Edwin Haviland Miller

NOTEBOOKS, DIARIES, AND MISCELLANY (in two volumes), edited by Edward Grier and William White

JOURNALISTIC WRITINGS, edited by Herbert Bergman

BIBLIOGRAPHY, edited by William White

NEW YORK UNIVERSITY PRESS   WASHINGTON SQUARE, NEW YORK 3

Some comments on
THE COLLECTED WRITINGS OF WALT WHITMAN
THE CORRESPONDENCE OF WALT WHITMAN
edited by Edwin Haviland Miller
Volume I: 1842-1867
Volume II: 1868-1875

The participants in this enterprise, both editors and publisher, are to be congratulated for doing something about the notorious fact that virtually none of the great American authors is represented in a collected and definitive edition, or, for that matter, in a uniform, up-to-date edition of any kind. . . . Edwin Miller . . . has done an estimable job with these first two volumes.
—Richard Chase, *The New York Times*

. . . these letters of Whitman signalize the most important event of the year in American literary scholarship. . . . A completely admirable job of editing, printing, and binding, these letters (and no doubt the volumes to follow) are indispensable for the serious student of American literature.
—*Library Journal*

Mr. Miller's volumes are models of professional competence.
—Perry Miller, *The Christian Science Monitor*

Dust jacket for A 42.1.a

A 42.1.b
Second printing (1963)

New York: New York University Press, 1963. Title page is all in black.

Pagination is the same as in the first printing; the manuscript facsimiles are now printed on integral leaves.

$[1-12]^{16}$. Sheets bulk 1⅛″.

Contents: Same as in the first printing, except: p. ii: manuscript facsimile; pp. 353–354: blank.

Typography and paper: Same as in the first printing, except: paper is not watermarked.

Binding: Deep red buckram. Front: goldstamped 'W' above 'W'; back: blank; spine: goldstamped, with first five lines on dark bluish green rectangular background: 'WHITMAN | [rule] | EARLY POEMS | AND | FICTION | EDITED BY | Thomas Brasher | [goldstamped arch and dark bluish green tree publisher's logo within dark bluish green single-rule rectangluar frame with rounded corners]'. Medium gray endpapers. All edges trimmed. Top edges stained very light green.

Location: JM.

A 43 WALT WHITMAN'S BLUE BOOK
1968

A 43
Only edition, only printing (1968)

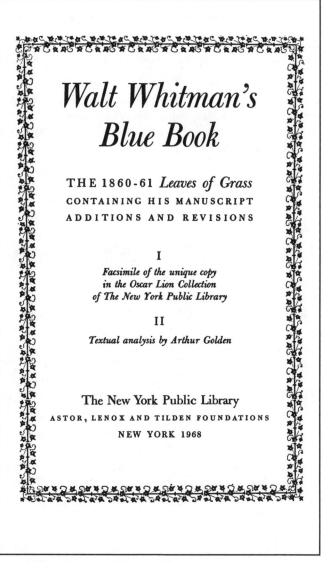

Walt Whitman's
Blue Book

THE 1860-61 *Leaves of Grass*
CONTAINING HIS MANUSCRIPT
ADDITIONS AND REVISIONS

I

*Facsimile of the unique copy
in the Oscar Lion Collection
of The New York Public Library*

II

Textual analysis by Arthur Golden

The New York Public Library
ASTOR, LENOX AND TILDEN FOUNDATIONS
NEW YORK 1968

A 43: 8⅜″×5⅜″; ornate frame is in blue

Vol. I: [i–viii 1–468]. Slips of various sizes with photographs of the manuscript printed on both sides are tipped onto pp. 11 (two slips), 114, 115, 120, 175 (two slips), and 455.

Vol. II: [i–xii] xiii–lxi [lxii] lxiii–lxv [lxvi] [1–410] 411–428. Inserted leaf of coated paper, with photograph of Whitman's memoranda when he resigned from the Department of the Interior, printed on recto, with a typeset transcription printed on verso, is positioned after p. lviii.

Vol. I: $[1]^4 [2]^{10} [3]^6 [4]^{10} [5]^6 [6]^{10} [7]^6 [8]^{10} [9]^6 [10]^{10} [11]^6 [12]^{10} [13]^6 [14]^{10} [15]^6$ $[16]^{10} [17]^6 [18]^{10} [19]^6 [20]^{10} [21]^6 [22]^{10} [23]^6 [24]^{10} [25]^6 [26]^{10} [27]^6 [28]^{10} [29]^6$ $[30]^{10}$. Sheets bulk $1\frac{3}{32}''$.

Vol. II: $[1–31]^8$. Sheets bulk $1\frac{17}{32}''$.

Contents: Vol. I: pp. i–ii: blank; p. iii: '*Volume I* | FACSIMILE'; p. iv: blank; p. v: title page; p. vi: copyright page; p. vii: 'FACSIMILE | *of Whitman's Blue Book* | *in the Oscar Lion Collection* | *The New York Public Library*'; p. viii: blank; pp. 1–468: facsimile; Vol. II: pp. i–ii: blank; p. iii: '*Volume II* | TEXTUAL ANALYSIS'; p. iv: blank; p. v: title page, the same as in vol. I; p. vi: copyright page, the same as in vol. I; p. vii: dedication; p. viii: blank; pp. ix–x: acknowledgments; p. xi: contents; p. xii: blank; pp. xiii–lxi: introduction; p. lxii: blank; pp. lxiii–lxiv: "A Note on the Textual Analysis"; p. lxv: "Key to Symbols & Abbreviations"; p. lxvi: blank; p. 1: 'TEXTUAL ANALYSIS | *by Arthur Golden*'; p. 2: blank; pp. 3–407: textual anaylsis; p. 408: blank; p. 409: 'APPENDICES'; p. 410: blank; pp. 411–420: appendices; pp. 421–428: index of titles.

Typography and paper: Vol. I: text on wove paper; facsimiles on coated paper. Vol. II: $6\frac{5}{16}'' (6\frac{1}{16}'') \times 4\frac{11}{16}''$; wove paper; introduction: 34 lines per page; textual analysis: various lines per page (up to 34); appendices: various lines per page (up to 43); index: various lines per page (up to 44). Running heads: rectos (all running heads on rectos except the first one and the last two are followed by '[[page number of facsimile in vol. I]': pp. xv–lxi: 'INTRODUCTION'; pp. 5–33: 'PROTO–LEAF'; pp. 35–101: 'WALT WHITMAN'; pp. 103–207: 'CHANTS DEMOCRATIC'; pp. 211–259: 'LEAVES OF GRASS'; p. 263: 'SALUT AU MONDE!'; pp. 265–269: 'POEM OF JOYS'; pp. 271–283: 'A WORD OUT OF THE SEA; p. 285: 'LEAF OF FACES'; p. 287: 'THOUGHT'; pp. 289–313: 'ENFANS

D'ADAM'; pp. 315–319: 'POEM OF THE ROAD'; pp. 321–323: 'TO THE SAYERS OF WORDS'; p. 325: 'A BOSTON BALLAD'; pp. 327–367: 'CALAMUS'; p. 369: 'LONG-INGS FOR HOME'; pp. 373–377: 'MESSENGER LEAVES'; p. 381: 'FRANCE'; p. 383: 'THOUGHTS'; p. 385: 'PERFECTIONS'; p. 387: 'SAYS'; pp. 389–393: 'DEBRIS'; p. 397: 'BURIAL'; pp. 399–401: 'TO MY SOUL'; pp. 403–409: 'SO LONG!'; pp. 413, 419: 'APPENDICES'; pp. 423–427: 'INDEX'; versos: p. x: 'ACKNOWLEDGMENTS'; pp. xiv–lx: 'INTRODUCTION'; pp. 4–102, 106–286, 290–312, 316–324, 328–366, 370–380, 390–408: '[page number of facsimile]] LEAVES OF GRASS'; pp. 412–420: 'APPENDICES'; pp. 422–428: 'INDEX'.

Binding: Deep blue B cloth (linen). Vol. I: front and back covers: blank; spine: goldstamped *'Walt | Whitman's | Blue Book* | I | Facsimile | The New York | Public Library'. Light blue laid endpapers. All edges trimmed. Vol. II: front and back covers: blank; spine: goldstamped the same as vol. I, except: 'II | Textual Analysis | GOLDEN'. Light blue endpapers; back free endpaper has foldout with "Keys to Symbols & Abbreviations" printed on recto; back paste-down endpaper has "Key" also printed on it. All edges trimmed.

Box: Deep blue B cloth (linen) with light blue laid paper pasted over sides and back, open at one end. Front: *'Walt Whitman's Blue Book* | [Schoff engrav-ing of Whitman] | [nine-line description of book]'; back: 29-line description of book; spine: *'Walt Whitman's | Blue Book* | THE 1860–61 *Leaves of Grass* | CONTAINING HIS MANUSCRIPT | ADDITIONS AND REVISIONS | [leaf-and-vine design] | Facsimile of the unique copy in | the Oscar Lion Collection of | The New York Public Library | with Textual Analysis by | Arthur Golden | THE NEW YORK PUBLIC LIBRARY'.

Printing: See copyright page.

Publication: 1,500 copies. Announced as published "yesterday" in *New York Times,* 30 March 1968, p. 35. Reviewed in *Saturday Review,* 51 (18 May 1968), 59; *Times Literary Supplement,* 15 August 1968, p. 867. Copyright 29 March 1968; A999372. Deposit copies: BL ('MAY 68'), BO ('16JAN1969'). NjP copy received 5 April 1968. DLC copy received from the publisher 15 April 1968. Price: $25.00 before publication, $30.00 thereafter.

Locations: BE, BL (box), BO (box), CSt (box), CaOTU, CtY (box), DLC, JM (box), MBU, MH, NN-R (box), NNC (box), NcD (box), NcU, NjCW, NjCW (box), NjP (2), PU (box), RPB (box), ScU, TxU, ViU.

Note one: A four-page advertising flier, with a facsimile of p. 126 from the 1860 edition, is at CtY.

Note two: Horace Traubel had announced a similar project earlier, planning to print 500 copies for a price of $10.00. In a four-page brochure, *A Leaves of Grass Reprint* (Philadelphia: Horace Traubel, 1902), he facsimiles p. 105 from the 1860 edition (JM, MBU).

A 44 WALT WHITMAN'S AUTOGRAPH REVISION OF THE
ANALYSIS OF LEAVES OF GRASS
1974

A 44
Only edition, only printing (1974)

WALT WHITMAN

Walt Whitman's Autograph Revision

of the Analysis of Leaves of Grass

(FOR DR. R. M. BUCKE'S WALT WHITMAN)

Introductory Essay by
QUENTIN ANDERSON

Text Notes by
STEPHEN RAILTON

———

With thirty-five facsimile pages
of the manuscript

NEW YORK
NEW YORK UNIVERSITY PRESS
1974

A 44: 11″×7⅝″

[1–6] 7–9 [10] 11–30 [31] 32–42 [43] 44–127 [128] 129–191 [192]. See *Note one.*

[1–12]⁸. Sheets bulk 9⁄16″.

Contents: p. 1: 'WALT WHITMAN | [leaf design] | WALT WHITMAN'S AUTOGRAPH REVISION | OF THE ANALYSIS OF LEAVES OF GRASS | FOR DR. R. M. BUCKE'S WALT WHITMAN'; p. 2: 1872 photograph of Whitman; p. 3: title page; p. 4: copyright page; p. 5: contents; p. 6: photograph of a manuscript page; pp. 7–9: foreword by Daniel Maggin; p. 10: engraving of Whitman in 1870; pp. 11–52: "Whitman's New Man" by Quentin Anderson [p. 30: photograph of Whitman with butterfly in 1889; p. 43: photograph of Whitman in 1891]; pp. 53–63: "Whitman's Indicative Words" by Galway Kinnell; pp. 64–185: photographs of Bucke's *Walt Whitman* and the manuscript [p. 105: 1873 photograph of Whitman; p. 128: Hollyer engraving of Whitman]; pp. 186–188: "Note on the Text" by Stephen Railton; pp. 189–191: appendices; p. 192: printing and binding information.

Typography and paper: 8³⁄16″ (7⅞″) × 5³⁄16″; wove paper; text: 38 lines per page. Running heads: rectos: p. 9: 'FOREWORD'; pp. 13–29, 33–41, 45–51: 'WHITMAN'S NEW MAN'; pp. 55–63: 'WHITMAN'S INDICATIVE WORDS'; p. 187: 'NOTE ON THE TEXT'; p. 191: "APPENDICES'; versos: p. 8: 'FOREWORD'; pp. 12–52: 'WHITMAN'S NEW MAN'; pp. 54–62: 'WHITMAN'S INDICA-TIVE WORDS'; p. 188: 'NOTE ON THE TEXT'; p. 190: 'APPENDICES'.

Binding: Two styles have been noted, priority assumed:

Binding A: Dark green V cloth (smooth). Front cover: goldstamped '[all within double-rule frame] 'WALT WHITMAN | [leaf design] | WALT WHIT-MAN'S AUTOGRAPH REVISION | OF THE ANALYSIS OF LEAVES OF GRASS | (FOR DR. R. M. BUCKE'S WALT WHITMAN)'; back cover: blank; spine: goldstamped vertically: '[two lines parallel] WALT WHITMAN | AUTOGRAPH REVISION OF R. M. BUCKE | *New York University Press* | [horizontal] [publisher's device]'. White endpapers. All edges trimmed.

Binding B: Same as binding A, except: double-rule goldstamped frame on front cover is not present.

Dust jacket: Unprinted glassine.

Printing: 'SET IN TYPE BY THE STINEHOUR PRESS | PRINTED BY THE MERIDEN GRAVURE COMPANY | AND BOUND AT THE NEW HAMPSHIRE BINDERY' (p. [192]).

Publication: Reviewed in *Library Journal,* 99 (1 December 1974), 3134. Copyright 1 July 1974; A684115. Deposit copy: binding B: DLC ('NOV −7 1975'). ViU copy (binding B) received 21 July 1975. NjP copy (binding A) received 1 August 1975. Price, $15.00.

Locations: Binding A: JM (dj), NN-R, NjP, TxU (dj); binding B: BE, CaOTU, DLC, JM (dj), MB, NcD, PU, ScU, ViU.

Note one: The photographs of both Whitman's manuscript and Bucke's book have commentary printed in either or both side margins.

Note two: For information about Bucke's 1883 *Walt Whitman* and reprintings of it, see D 13.

A 45 DAYBOOKS AND NOTEBOOKS
1978

A 45.I
Only edition, only printing (1978)

WALT WHITMAN

Daybooks and Notebooks

VOLUME I: DAYBOOKS
1876–November 1881

Edited by William White

 NEW YORK UNIVERSITY PRESS 1978

A 45.I: 10"×7"

© 1977 BY NEW YORK UNIVERSITY PRESS

LIBRARY OF CONGRESS CATALOG CARD NUMBER: 75-27382

MANUFACTURED IN THE UNITED STATES OF AMERICA

ISBN: 0-8147-9167-0-Vol. I

[i–vii] viii [ix–xi] xii–xix [xx–xxi] xxii–xxiv [xxv] xxvi–xxvii [xxviii–xxx] 1–4 [5] 6–7 [8] 9–10 [11] 12–17 [18] 19–154 [155] 156–179 [180] 181–188 [189] 190–235 [236] 237–254 [255] 256–258 [259] 260–268 [269] 270–278 [279–282]

$[1-8]^{16}$ $[9]^{12}$ $[10]^{16}$. Sheets bulk ⅞".

Contents: p. i: 'The Collected Writings of Walt Whitman'; p. ii: Center for Editions of American Authors "An Approved Text" seal; p. iii: title page; p. iv: copyright page; p. v: list of general editors and advisory editorial board; p. vi: acknowledgments to Charles E. Feinberg and the National Endowment for the Humanities; pp. vii–viii: 'Preface' by White, dated '31 May 1976'; p. ix: 'CONTENTS'; p. x: blank; pp. xi–xix: 'Introduction'; p. xx: blank; pp. xxi–xxiv: 'Editorial Statement'; pp. xxv–xxvii: 'CHRONOLOGY | OF WALT WHITMAN'S LIFE AND WORK'; p. xxviii: blank; p. xxix: 'The Collected Writings of Walt Whitman'; p. xxx: blank; pp. 1–278: texts (with manuscript facsimiles on pp. 5, 8, 11, 18, 155, 180, 189, 236, 255, 259, 269); pp. 279–282: blank.

Typography and paper: 8⅜" (8")×4⅞"; wove paper; 41 lines per page (text). Running heads: rectos (all at right): pp. xiii–xix: 'INTRODUCTION'; p. xxiii: 'EDITORIAL STATEMENT' p. xxvii: 'CHRONOLOGY'; pp. 3, 7–9, 13–153, 157–187, 191–253, 257, 261–267, 271–277: 'DAYBOOKS, 1876–1891'; versos (all at left): p. vii: 'PREFACE'; pp. xii–xviii: 'INTRODUCTION'; pp. xxii–xxiv: 'EDITORIAL STATEMENT'; p. xxvi: 'CHRONOLOGY'; pp. 2–6, 10–16, 20–178, 182–234, 238–278: 'THE COLLECTED WRITINGS OF WALT WHITMAN'.

Binding: Deep red buckram. Front: goldstamped 'W' above 'W'; back: blank; spine: goldstamped, with first six lines on dark bluish green rectangular background: 'WHITMAN | [rule] | DAYBOOKS | AND | NOTEBOOKS | 1876–1881 | EDITED BY | William | White | [goldstamped arch and dark bluish green tree publisher's logo within dark bluish green single-rule rectangular frame with rounded corners]'. Medium gray endpapers. All edges trimmed. Top edges stained very light green.

Dust jacket: Very light gray paper with light blue hair-vein pattern. Front: red 'THE COLLECTED WRITINGS OF WALT WHITMAN' printed from bottom to top, dividing the last line after the publisher's logo, with 'DAYBOOKS | AND | NOTEBOOKS | [red] *VOLUME I:* 1876–1881 | [black] William White, *Editor* |

Dust jacket for A 45.I

THE COLLECTED WRITINGS OF WALT WHITMAN

DAYBOOKS AND NOTEBOOKS

VOLUME I: 1876-1881

William White, *Editor*

GAY WILSON ALLEN
SCULLEY BRADLEY
General Editors

NEW YORK UNIVERSITY PRESS

THE COLLECTED WRITINGS OF WALT WHITMAN
DAYBOOKS AND NOTEBOOKS VOLUME I: 1876-1881 WHITE

THE COLLECTED WRITINGS OF WALT WHITMAN
Gay Wilson Allen and Sculley Bradley
General Editors

WALT WHITMAN:
DAYBOOKS AND NOTEBOOKS
Edited by William White

This three-volume collection of Walt Whitman's Daybooks makes available for the first time these important sources for reference on the poet's daily activities. The sixteen-year record of the DAYBOOKS supplements the biographical information provided in the six volumes of Whitman's *Correspondence,* and outlines the terms of the poet's life which gave rise to his many letters and literary reminiscences. Often referred to as his *Commonplace Books,* Whitman's DAYBOOKS have been consulted by scholars for years and very brief excerpts have appeared in print from time to time. However, this is the first publication of the material in its entirety exactly as Whitman left it. The DAYBOOKS record the poet's daily activities, functioning as an account book, diary, journal, commonplace book and notebook all in one.

When Whitman first began to keep them, the Daybooks were a personal record of predominantly business matters—an account book. As with all of his editions, with two brief exceptions, he was not only the author but the publisher of his works; he was likewise his own business manager, shipper, and promoter. Whatever records he kept, of his sales and distribution, of printing and binding figures, of poetry and prose he sent to newspapers and magazines (their acceptance or rejection, payment for them, and their appearance), tax bills, water bills, subscription to daily papers, of payments for the keep of his brother Edward, his own board and room when he lived with his brother George, of letters received, those to whom he sent and when he came home: these and a whole variety of other things he entered on the right-hand pages.

(Continued on back flap)

(Continued from front flap)

In early September 1876, the Daybooks began to serve the poet as a diary as well as business account. From this date, they chronicle the poet's activities, literary and social, his friendships, his habits, his health and the weather, his trips, his finances, his visits and correspondence. As such, they are an invaluable reference for the Whitman scholar.

In this edition, Whitman's daily entries are fully annotated for identification, background, and relationship to his correspondence and other writings. Volume I consists of the Daybooks, 1876-November 1881. Volume II concludes the Daybooks with entries from December, 1881 through 1891. In addition to the Daybooks, Professor White has collected, in Volume III, Whitman's *Diary in Canada, Words,* a hitherto unpublished dictionary compiled by Whitman for his own use; *The Primer of Words,* miscellaneous journals, autobiographical notes, other notebooks and fragments of interest to the Whitman scholar; and an index. Like the DAYBOOKS, the Canadian diary, the journals and notes, and the two works on language *Words* and *The Primer of Words,* were not published during their author's lifetime, because they were never finished.

This edition of the Daybooks is their first publication complete, as Whitman wrote them, and has the authority of being included in the definitive series *The Collected Writings of Walt Whitman,* published by New York University Press. As such, this treasury of information on the great American poet will be a major aid to further studies of Whitman.

About the Editor

WILLIAM WHITE is Professor and Director of the Journalism Program at Oakland University and Adjunct Professor of American Studies at Wayne State University.

Jacket Design by Andor Braun

THE COLLECTED WRITINGS OF WALT WHITMAN
Gay Wilson Allen and Sculley Bradley
General Editors

Advisory Editorial Board

Professor Roger Asselineau, *The University of Paris* • Professor Harold W. Blodgett, *Union College* • Professor Charles E. Feinberg • Professor Clarence Gohdes, *Duke University* • Professor Rollo G. Silver, *Simmons College* • Professor Floyd Stovall, *The University of Virginia*

Volumes Published

LEAVES OF GRASS: Reader's Comprehensive Edition
edited by Harold W. Blodgett and Sculley Bradley
768 pages. ISBN: 0-8147-0040-9

PROSE WORKS 1892, *edited by Floyd Stovall*
Volume I: *Specimen Days.* 358 pages. ISBN: 0-8147-0442-5
Volume II: *Collect and Other Prose.* 445 pages. ISBN: 0-8147-0443-3

THE CORRESPONDENCE OF WALT WHITMAN
edited by Edwin Haviland Miller
Volume I: 1842-1867. 394 pages. ISBN: 0-8147-0455-2
Volume II: 1868-1875. 387 pages. ISBN: 0-8147-0456-0
Volume III: 1876-1885. 473 pages. ISBN: 0-8147-0457-9
Volume IV: 1886-1889. 458 pages. ISBN: 0-8147-0458-7
Volume V: 1890-1892. 365 pages. ISBN: 0-8147-0459-5
Volume VI: Supplement. 124 pages. ISBN: 0-8147-5415-5

THE EARLY POEMS AND THE FICTION, *edited by Thomas L. Brasher*
352 pages. ISBN: 0-8147-0441-7

WALT WHITMAN: DAYBOOKS AND NOTEBOOKS, *edited by William White*
900 pages-3 volumes
Volume I: ISBN: 0-8147-9167-0
Volume II: ISBN: 0-8147-9176-X
Volume III: ISBN: 0-8147-9177-8

Volumes in Preparation

LEAVES OF GRASS: A VARIORUM EDITION
edited by Sculley Bradley, Harold W. Blodgett and William White
900 pages-3 volumes

WALT WHITMAN: UNPUBLISHED NOTEBOOKS AND PROSE MANUSCRIPTS
edited by Edward F. Grier
900 pages-5 volumes

NEW YORK UNIVERSITY PRESS   WASHINGTON SQUARE, NEW YORK, N.Y. 10003   ISBN: 0-8147-9167-0

GAY WILSON ALLEN | [flush right] *General Editors* | SCULLEY BRADLEY |
[publisher's logo] NEW YORK UNIVERSITY PRESS'; back: black and red 40-
line description of the series, listing 19 volumes; spine: vertically: 'THE COL-
LECTED WRITINGS OF WALT WHITMAN | [red] DAYBOOKS AND NOTE-
BOOKS [black] *VOLUME I:* [red] 1876–1881 [black] *WHITE*' with a horizontal
'[red publisher's logo on two lines] N   Y | U   P' at bottom; front flap: black and
red 45-line blurb for book; back flap: 42-line blurb for book and description of the
editor.

Printing: Printed at the Kingsport Press, Kingsport, Tenn.; bound by Quinn
and Bodin.

Publication: 524 copies. Published 31 December 1977. Copyright Tx9–570;
received, 20 March 1978. Deposit copies: DLC ('JAN 23 1978'), BO ('–1 NOV
1978'), BL ('FEB 82'). CaOTU copy received 27 April 1978. Price, $75.00 the set.

Locations: BE, BL, BO, CaOTU, CtY (dj), DLC, InU-L (dj), JM, JM (dj),
MBU, MH, NcU, NjP, PU, RPB, ScU, TxU, ViU (dj).

Note: Three sizes of lettering are used on the second vertical line of the dust
jacket spine: the book's title is the largest, the editor's name is smaller, and the
volume information is the smallest.

A 45.II
Only edition, only printing (1978)

Title page is the same as in vol. I, except: 'VOLUME II: DAYBOOKS, | Decem-
ber 1881–1891'.

[i–x] 279–289 [290] 291–609 [610–612]

$[1–8]^{16}$ $[9]^8$ $[10]^4$ $[11–12]^{16}$. Page size: 10"×7". Sheets bulk 1".

Contents: p. i: 'The Collected Writings of Walt Whitman'; p. ii: Center for
Editions of American Authors "An Approved Text" seal; p. iii: title page; p. iv:
copyright page; p. v: list of general editors and advisory editorial board; p. vi:
acknowledgments to Charles E. Feinberg and the National Endowment for the
Humanities; p. vii: 'CONTENTS'; p. viii: blank; p. ix: 'The Collected Writings
of Walt Whitman'; p. x: blank; pp. 279–609: texts (with manuscript facsimile
on p. 290); pp. 610–612: blank.

Typography and paper: Same as in vol. I, except: running heads: rectos (all
at right): pp. 279–609: 'DAYBOOKS, 1876–1891'; versos (all at left): pp. 280–
288, 292–608: 'THE COLLECTED WRITINGS OF WALT WHITMAN'.

Binding: Same as in vol. I, except: spine: goldstamped '1881–1891'.

Dust jacket: Same as in vol. I, except: front: '*II:* 1881–1891'; back: ISBN
number is 0-8147-9176-X; spine: '*II:* [red] 1881–1891'.

Printing: Same as for vol. I.

Publication: See vol. I.

Locations: BE, BL, BO, CaOTU, CtY (dj), DLC, InU-L (dj), JM, JM (dj), MBU, MH, NcU, NjP, PU, RPB, ScU, TxU, ViU (dj).

A 45.III
Only edition, only printing (1978)

Title page is the same as in vol. I, except: 'VOLUME III: DIARY IN CANADA, | NOTEBOOKS, INDEX'.

[i–x] [611] 612–654 [655] 656–657 [658] 659–662 [663] 664–730 [731] 732–757 [758–759] 760–825 [826–828] 829–869 [870–872]

[1–6]^{16} [7]^8 [8–9]^{16}. Page size: 10"×7". Sheets bulk 13⁄16".

Contents: p. i: 'The Collected Writings of Walt Whitman'; p. ii: Center for Editions of American Authors "An Approved Text" seal; p. iii: title page; p. iv: copyright page; p. v: list of general editors and advisory editorial board; p. vi: acknowledgments to Charles E. Feinberg and the National Endowment for the Humanities; p. vii: 'CONTENTS'; p. viii: blank; p. ix: 'The Collected Writings of Walt Whitman'; p. x: blank; pp. 611–828: texts (with manuscript facsimiles on pp. 663, 731); p. 826: blank; p. 827: 'INDEX'; pp. 828–869: 'Index'; pp. 870–872: blank.

Typography and paper: Same as in vol. I, except: running heads: rectos (all at right): pp. 613–653: 'DIARY IN CANADA'; p. 657: 'MISCELLANEOUS JOURNALS'; pp. 659–661: 'AUTOBIOGRAPHICAL NOTES'; pp. 665–727: 'WORDS'; pp. 729, 733–757: 'THE PRIMER OF WORDS'; pp. 761–825: 'OTHER NOTEBOOKS, &c. ON WORDS'; pp. 829–869: 'INDEX'; versos (all at left): pp. 612–656, 660–756, 760–824: 'THE COLLECTED WRITINGS OF WALT WHITMAN'; pp. 830–868: 'INDEX'.

Binding: Same as in vol. I, except: spine: goldstamped 'WHITMAN | [rule] | DIARY IN | CANADA | NOTEBOOKS | INDEX'.

Dust jacket: Same as in vol. I, except: front: '[three lines in red] *VOLUME III:* DIARY IN CANADA | NOTEBOOKS | INDEX'; back: ISBN number is 0-8147-9177-8; spine: *'III:* [two lines in red] DIARY IN CANADA | NOTEBOOKS INDEX'.

Printing: Same as for vol. I.

Publication: See vol. I.

Locations: BE, BL, BO, CaOTU, CtY (dj), DLC, InU-L (dj), JM, JM (dj), MBU, MH, NcU, NjP, PU, RPB, ScU, TxU, ViU (dj).

A 46 NOTEBOOKS AND UNPUBLISHED PROSE
   MANUSCRIPTS
   1984

A 46.I
Only edition, only printing (1984)

WALT WHITMAN

Notebooks and Unpublished Prose Manuscripts

VOLUME I: FAMILY NOTES AND AUTOBIOGRAPHY
BROOKLYN AND NEW YORK

Edited by Edward F. Grier

 NEW YORK UNIVERSITY PRESS 1984

A 46.I: 10″×7″

© 1984 BY NEW YORK UNIVERSITY

Library of Congress Cataloging in Publication Data
Whitman, Walt, 1819–1892.
  Notebooks and unpublished prose manuscripts.

  (The Collected Writings of Walt Whitman)
  Bibliography: p.
  Includes index.
    1. Whitman, Walt, 1819–1892—Diaries. 2. Poets,
American—19th century—Biography. I. Grier, Edward F.
II. Title. III. Series: Whitman, Walt, 1819–1892. Works.
1961.
PS3231.A36 1984   818'.303 [B] 83-24415
ISBN 0-8147-2991-6 vol. I.
ISBN 0-8147-2992-4 vol. II.
ISBN 0-8147-2993-2 vol. III
ISBN 0-8147-2994-0 vol. IV
ISBN 0-8147-2995-9 vol. V
ISBN 0-8147-2996-7 vol. VI
ISBN 0-8147-2989-4 (set)

MANUFACTURED IN THE UNITED STATES OF AMERICA

CLOTHBOUND EDITIONS OF NEW YORK UNIVERSITY PRESS BOOKS
ARE SMYTH-SEWN AND PRINTED ON PERMANENT AND DURABLE ACID-FREE PAPER.

[i–ii] [i–vii] viii [ix] x–xi [xii–xiii] xiv–xx [xxi] xxii–xxiii [xxiv–xxv] xxvi–xxviii [xxix] xxx–lviii [lix] lx [lxi–lxii] [1–2] 3–41 [42] 43–245 [245a–h] 246–476 [477–480]

[1–15]^{16} [16]^4 [17–18]^{16}. Sheets bulk 1 $^{15}/_{16}''$.

Contents: pp. i–ii: blank; p. i: 'The Collected Writings of Walt Whitman'; p. ii: manuscript facsimile; p. iii: title page; p. iv: copyright page; p. v: list of general editors and advisory editorial board; p. vi: acknowledgments to the National Endowment for the Humanities and the Center for Scholarly Editions "An Approved Edition" seal; p. vii–viii: 'CONTENTS'; pp. ix–xi: 'Preface'; p. xii: blank; pp. xiii–xv: 'Introduction'; pp. xxi–xxiii: 'ABBREVIATIONS'; p. xxiv: blank; pp. xxv–xxvii: 'CHRONOLOGY | OF WALT WHITMAN'S LIFE AND WORK'; pp. xxix–lviii: 'LIST OF TITLES'; pp. lix–lx: 'LIST OF ILLUS-TRATIONS'; p. lxi: 'The Collected Writings of Walt Whitman'; p. lxii: blank; pp. 1: 'The Manuscripts'; p. 2: blank; pp. 3–245: texts; pp. 245a–h: manuscript facsimiles; pp. 246–276: texts; pp. 477–480: blank.

Typography and paper: 8$^5/_{16}''$ (7⅞'')×5'', wove paper; 44 lines per page (text). Running heads: rectos (all at right): p. xi: 'PREFACE'; pp. xv–xix: 'INTRO-DUCTION'; p. xxiii: 'ABBREVIATIONS'; p. xxvii: 'CHRONOLOGY'; pp. xxxi–lviii: 'LIST OF TITLES'; pp. 5–475: 'NOTEBOOKS AND UNPUB-

LISHED PROSE MANUSCRIPTS'; versos (all at left): p. viii: 'CONTENTS';
p. x: 'PREFACE'; pp. iv–xx: 'INTRODUCTION'; p. xxii: 'ABBREVIATIONS';
p. xxvi–xxviii: 'CHRONOLOGY'; pp. xxx–lviii: 'LIST OF TITLES'; p. lx:
'LIST OF ILLUSTRATIONS'; pp. 4–40, 44–476: 'THE COLLECTED WRIT-
INGS OF WALT WHITMAN'.

Binding: Slightly red B cloth (linen). Front: goldstamped 'W' above 'W';
back: goldstamped at bottom right: 'ISBN 0-8147-2989-4 {SET}'; spine:
goldstamped, with first six lines on deep bluish green rectangular background:
'WHITMAN | [rule] | NOTEBOOKS AND | UNPUBLISHED PROSE | MANU-
SCRIPTS | VOLUME I | EDITED BY | Edward F. Grier | [goldstamped arch
and deep bluish green tree publisher's logo within deep bluish green single-
rule rectangluar frame with rounded corners]'. Medium gray endpapers. All
edges trimmed. Top edges stained deep bluish green.

Printing: Printed and bound by Vail-Ballou.

Publication: 1,000 copies. Published 29 August 1984. Deposit copies: DLC
('AUG 17 1984'), BL ('27 SEP 84'), BO ('7NOV1984'). Copies inscribed by
owners: ViU (15 September 1984). CaOTU copy received 15 January 1985.
Price, $345.00 the set.

Locations: BL, BMR, BO, CaOTU, DLC, JM, NcU, NjP, RPB, ViU.

A 46.II
Only edition, only printing (1984)

Title page is the same as in vol. I, except: 'VOLUME II: WASHINGTON'.

[i–ii] [i–vii] viii [ix–x] 477–682 [683] 684–700 [700a–h] 701–734 [735] 736–
890 [891] 892–934 [935–936]

[1–15]^{16}. Page size 10"×7". Sheets bulk 1⅝".

Contents: pp. i–ii: blank; p. i: 'The Collected Writings of Walt Whitman'; p.
ii: blank; p. iii: title page; p. iv: copyright page; p. v: list of general editors and
advisory editorial board; p. vi: acknowledgments to the National Endowment
for the Humanities and the Center for Scholarly Editions "An Approved Edition" seal; p. vii–viii: 'CONTENTS'; p. ix: 'The Collected Writings of Walt
Whitman'; p. x: blank; pp. 477–700: texts; pp. 700a–h: manuscript facsimiles; pp. 701–934: texts; pp. 935–936: blank.

Typography and paper: Same as in vol, I: except: running heads: rectos
(all at right): pp. 479–681, 685–733, 737–889, 893–933: 'NOTEBOOKS
AND UNPUBLISHED PROSE MANUSCRIPTS'; versos (all at left): p. viii:
'CONTENTS'; pp. 478–934: 'THE COLLECTED WRITINGS OF WALT
WHITMAN'.

Binding: Same as in vol. I, except: 'VOLUME II'.

Printing: Same as in vol. I.

Publication: See vol. I.

Locations: BL, BMR, BO, CaOTU, DLC, JM, NcU, NjP, RPB, ViU.

A 46.III
Only edition, only printing (1984)

Title page is the same as in vol. I, except: 'VOLUME III: CAMDEN'.

[i–vii] viii [ix–x] [935] 936–1110 [1110a–d] 1111–1172 [1173] 1174–1279 [1280] 1281–1288

[1–10]^{16} [11]^8 [12]^{16} . Page size 10"×7". Sheets bulk 1¼".

Contents: p. i: 'The Collected Writings of Walt Whitman'; p. ii: blank; p. iii: title page; p. iv: copyright page; p. v: list of general editors and advisory editorial board; p. vi: acknowledgments to the National Endowment for the Humanities and the Center for Scholarly Editions "An Approved Edition" seal; p. vii–viii: 'CONTENTS'; p. ix: 'The Collected Writings of Walt Whitman'; p. x: blank; pp. 935–1110: texts; pp. 1110a–c: manuscript facsimiles; p. 1110d: blank; pp. 1111–1288: texts.

Typography and paper: Same as in vol, I: except: running heads: rectos (all at right): pp. 937–1171, 1175–1287: 'NOTEBOOKS AND UNPUBLISHED PROSE MANUSCRIPTS'; versos (all at left): p. viii: 'CONTENTS'; pp. 936–1278, 1282–1288: 'THE COLLECTED WRITINGS OF WALT WHITMAN'.

Binding: Same as in vol. I, except: 'VOLUME III'.

Printing: Same as in vol. I.

Publication: See vol. I.

Locations: BL, BMR, BO, CaOTU, DLC, JM, NcU, NjP, RPB, ViU.

A 46.IV
Only edition, only printing (1984)

Title page is the same as in vol. I, except: 'VOLUME IV: NOTES'.

[i–vii] viii [ix–x] [1289–1290] 1291–1425 [1426] 1427–1435 [1435a–b] 1436–1547 [1548] 1549–1583 [1584] 1585–1612

[1–9]^{16} [10]^8 [11]^{16}. Page size 10"×7". Sheets bulk 1³⁄₁₆".

Contents: p. i: 'The Collected Writings of Walt Whitman'; p. ii: blank; p. iii: title page; p. iv: copyright page; p. v: list of general editors and advisory editorial board; p. vi: acknowledgments to the National Endowment for the Humanities and the Center for Scholarly Editions "An Approved Edition" seal; p. vii–viii: 'CONTENTS'; p. ix: 'The Collected Writings of Walt Whitman'; p. x: blank; p. 1289: 'Notes'; pp. 1290: blank; p. 1291: '[double rule] | I. Proposed Poems.'; pp. 1292–1425: texts; p. 1426: blank; p. 1427: '[double rule] | II. Explanations.'; pp. 1428–1435: texts; pp. 1435a–b: manuscript facsimiles; pp. 1436–1547: texts; p. 1548: blank; p. 1549: '[double rule] | III. Attempts to Define the Poet's Role and | Tradition.'; pp. 1550–1583: texts; p. 1584: blank; p. 1585: '[double rule] | IV. Needs of American Literature.'; pp. 1586–1612: texts.

Typography and paper: Same as in vol. I: except: running heads: rectos (all at right): pp. 1293–1443, 1447–1611: 'NOTEBOOKS AND UNPUBLISHED PROSE MANUSCRIPTS'; versos (all at left): p. viii: 'CONTENTS'; pp. 1292–1424, 1428–1546, 1550–1582, 1586–1612: 'THE COLLECTED WRITINGS OF WALT WHITMAN'.

Binding: Same as in vol. I, except: 'VOLUME IV'.

Printing: Same as in vol. I.

Publication: See vol. I.

Locations: BL, BMR, BO, CaOTU, DLC, JM, NcU, NjP, RPB, ViU.

A 46.V
Only edition, only printing (1984)

Title page is the same as in vol. I, except: 'VOLUME V: NOTES'.

[i–vii] viii [ix–x] 1613–1709 [1710] 1711–1735 [1736] 1737–1779 [1779a–b] 1780–1809 [1810] 1811–2003 [2004]

[1–11]^{16} [12]^{10} [13]^{16}. Page size 10"×7". Sheets bulk 1⁷⁄₁₆".

Contents: p. i: 'The Collected Writings of Walt Whitman'; p. ii: blank; p. iii: title page; p. iv: copyright page; p. v: list of general editors and advisory editorial board; p. vi: acknowledgments to the National Endowment for the Humanities and the Center for Scholarly Editions "An Approved Edition" seal; p. vii–viii: 'CONTENTS'; p. ix: 'The Collected Writings of Walt Whitman'; p. x: blank; p. 1613: '[double rule] | V. Study Projects.'; pp. 1614–1620: texts; p. 1621: '[double rule] | VI. Words.'; pp. 1622–1709: texts; p. 1710: blank; p. 1711: '[double rule] | VII. American Writers.'; pp. 1712–1735: texts; p. 1736: blank; p. 1737: '[double rule] | VIII. English Writers.'; pp. 1738–1779: texts; pp. 1779a–b: manuscript facsimiles; pp. 1780–1809: texts; p. 1810: blank; p. 1811: '[double rule] | IX. German, French, Italian, Spanish, | Scandinavian and Classical Writers.'; pp. 1812–1892: texts; p. 1893: '[double rule] | X. English

History.'; pp. 1894–1914: texts; p. 1915: '[double rule] | XI. World History.'; pp. 1916–1930: texts; p. 1931: '[double rule] | XII. United States Geography.'; pp. 1932–1968: texts; p. 1969: '[double rule] | XIII. World Geography.'; pp. 1970–2003: texts; p. 2004: blank.

Typography and paper: Same as in vol. I: except: running heads: rectos (all at right): pp. 1615–1619, 1623–1891, 1895–1913, 1917–1929, 1933–1967, 1971–2003: 'NOTEBOOKS AND UNPUBLISHED PROSE MANUSCRIPTS'; versos (all at left): p. viii: 'CONTENTS'; pp. 1614–1708, 1712–1734, 1738–1808, 1812–2002: 'THE COLLECTED WRITINGS OF WALT WHITMAN'.

Binding: Same as in vol. I, except: 'VOLUME V'.

Printing: Same as in vol. I.

Publication: See vol. I.

Locations: BL, BMR, BO, CaOTU, DLC, JM, NcU, NjP, RPB, ViU.

A 46.VI
Only edition, only printing (1984)

Title page is the same as in vol. I, except: 'VOLUME VI: NOTES AND IN-DEX'.

[i–vii] viii [ix–x] 2005–2039 [2040] 2041–2107 [2108] 2109–2167 [2168] 2169–2199 [2200] 2201–2259 [2260–2262] 2263–2354

[1–9]^{16} [10]^{4} [11–12]^{16}. Page size 10″×7″. Sheets bulk 1¼″.

Contents: p. i: 'The Collected Writings of Walt Whitman'; p. ii: blank; p. iii: title page; p. iv: copyright page; p. v: list of general editors and advisory editorial board; p. vi: acknowledgments to the National Endowment for the Humanities and the Center for Scholarly Editions "An Approved Edition" seal; p. vii–viii: 'CONTENTS'; p. ix: 'The Collected Writings of Walt Whitman'; p. x: blank; p. 2005: '[double rule] | XV. Philosophy. | (See also Classical Writers, Section IX.)'; pp. 2006–2018: texts; p. 2019: '[double rule] | XVI. History of Religion.'; pp. 2020–2039: texts; p. 2040: blank; p. 2041: '[double rule] | XVII. Religion.'; pp. 2042–2107: texts; p. 2108: blank; p. 2109: '[double rule] | XVIII. American Politics.'; pp. 2110–2167: texts; p. 2168: blank; p. 2169: '[double rule] | XIX. Slavery.' pp. 2170–2199: texts; p. 2200: blank; p. 2201: '[double rule] | XX. Education.'; pp. 2202–2220: texts; p. 2221: '[double rule] | XXI. Oratory.'; pp. 2222–2244: texts; p. 2245: '[double rule] | XXII. Health.'; pp. 2246–2259: texts; p. 2260: blank; p. 2261: 'Index'; p. 2262: blank; pp. 2263–2354: 'Index'.

Typography and paper: Same as in vol. I: except: running heads: rectos (all at right): pp. 2007–2017, 2021–2219, 2223–2243, 2247–2259: 'NOTEBOOKS

AND UNPUBLISHED PROSE MANUSCRIPTS'; pp. 2265–2353: 'INDEX'; versos (all at left): p. viii: 'CONTENTS'; pp. 2006–2038, 2042–2106, 2110–2166, 2170–2198, 2202–2258: 'THE COLLECTED WRITINGS OF WALT WHITMAN'; pp. 2264–2354: 'INDEX'.

Binding: Same as in vol. I, except: 'VOLUME VI'.

Printing: Same as in vol. I.

Publication: See vol. I.

Locations: BL, BMR, BO, CaOTU, DLC, JM, NcU, NjP, RPB, ViU.

B. Collected Editions

All collected works of Whitman's writings through 1991, arranged chronologically.

B 1 *CENTENNIAL EDITION*
1876

Leaves of Grass and *Two Rivulets*. [Camden: Walt Whitman, 1876].

Whitman's first attempt at collecting his poetical and prose works; see A 2.5.b$_2$, A 2.5.c$_1$, and A 9.1.a for detailed information.

B 2 COMPLETE POEMS & PROSE
1888

Complete Poems & Prose. [Philadelphia: Ferguson Brothers, 1888].

Whitman's second attempt at collecting his poetical and prose works; see A 2.7.m for detailed information.

B 3 DAVID McKAY EDITION
1891–1892

Leaves of Grass and *Complete Prose Works*, 2 vols. Philadelphia: David McKay, 1891–1892, 1892.

Each volume was sold separately; see A 2.7.o, C 6, and C 8 for detailed information. Later published by Small, Maynard of Boston and D. Appleton and Mitchell Kennerley of New York.

B 4 COMPLETE WRITINGS
1902

The Complete Writings of Walt Whitman, 10 vols. New York and London: G. P. Putnam's Sons, [1902].

1,342 sets sold as six distinct "editions." All copies have works half title page stating *"The Complete Writings of Walt Whitman."* Each "edition" has a half

415

title page bearing the name of the "edition" and the statement of limitation information. Listed by title only ("edition" not specified) in the *English Catalogue* for November 1902 at 25s. per volume.

1. *Leaves of Grass*, vol. I. 294 pp.

2. *Leaves of Grass*, vol. II. 323 pp.

3. *Leaves of Grass*, vol. III. 318 pp.

4. *Complete Prose Works*, vol. I. 324 pp. Contains *Specimen Days*.

5. *Complete Prose Works*, vol. II. 301 pp. Contains *Specimen Days* and *Collect*.

6. *Complete Prose Works*, vol. III. 297 pp. Contains *Collect, November Boughs*, and *Good-Bye My Fancy*.

7. *Complete Prose Works*, vol. IV. 282 pp. Contains *Good-Bye My Fancy* and *Wound Dresser*.

8. *Complete Prose Works*, vol. V. 300 pp. Contains *Calamus, Letters Written . . . to His Mother*, and three articles by Thomas B. Harned: "Walt Whitman and Oratory," "Walt Whitman and Physique" (see E 2783), and "Walt Whitman and His Second Boston Publishers."

9. *Complete Prose Works*, vol. VI. 230 pp. Contains *Notes and Fragments*.

10. *Complete Prose Works*, vol. VII. 309 pp. Contains *Notes and Fragments* and two contributions by Oscar Lovell Triggs: "The Growth of 'Leaves of Grass' " and "Bibliography of Walt Whitman."

The following "editions" have been noted, priority assumed:

(1) *Author's Autograph Edition*. Limited to 10 numbered sets on Japan vellum, signed by the publisher, with a page of Whitman's manuscript and a notarized statement dated 19 May 1902 about the manuscript tipped in. Full leather. *Location:* NcD.

(2) *Author's Manuscript Edition*. Limited to 32 numbered sets on Whatman paper, signed by the publisher, with a page of Whitman's manuscript and a notarized statement dated 19 May 1902 (DLC, MH, NjP, TxU) or 3 January 1907 (NN-R) about the manuscript tipped in. Full leather. *Locations:* DLC, MH, NN-R, NjP, TxU (bound in 20 volumes).

(3) *The Connoisseur's Camden Edition*. Limited to 200 numbered sets signed (in print) by the publisher. Full leather. *Location:* PU.

(4) *Paumanok Edition*. Limited to 300 numbered sets on Ruisdael handmade paper, signed (in print) by the publisher. Half or three-quarter leather with marbled paper-covered boards; or full leather; or dark green

or dark red buckram with paper label on spine: "Paumanok Edition"; or light brown buckram with goldstamping on spine. *Locations:* BMR, CtY, JM, MBU, NN-R, PU, RPB, TxU.

(5) *The Collector's Camden Edition.* Limited to 300 numbered sets, signed (in print) by the publisher. Gray paper-covered boards with goldstamped vellum shelfback and "Camden Edition" on spine. *Locations:* CSt, RPB.

(6) *The Book-Lover's Camden Edition.* Limited to 500 numbered sets, signed (in print) by the publisher. Gray paper-covered boards with goldstamped vellum shelfback and "Camden Edition" on spine; or full leather. Gray-green linen dust jackets with green 'WRITINGS | OF | [floral design] WALT [floral design] | WHITMAN' on the spine in the same style as in the shelfback. Copyright 44134–44137; received, 24 October 1902; 48124–48128; received 12 December 1902. Deposit copies: DLC ('OCT 24 1902'), BL ('19 DE 1902'; rebound), BE ('2JAN1903'), BO ('7 1 1903'). Listed in the *American Catalogue* for 6 December 1902 at $60.00 in half vellum. *Locations:* BE, BO (dj), DLC, JM, MB, NNC, NcD, NcU, PU.

Note one: A salesman's dummy copy for the *Author's Manuscript Edition,* without binding or dust jacket samples, is at ViU.

Note two: A salesman's dummy copy for the *Paumanok Edition,* with samples of gray printed dust jackets but not bindings, is at DLC.

Note three: Salesman's dummy copies for the *Camden Edition,* with a stated limitation of 1,000 sets on Old Stratford Linen paper and with samples of goldstamped vellum and leather shelfbacks, listing prices of $60 for sets in quarter vellum, $100 for three-quarter levant, and $200 for full levant, are at DLC, NjP, and RPB.

Note four: The set of the *Paumanok Edition* at NN-R has a note by Harned, dated April 1917, on the front flyleaf to vol. I: "About 1300 sets were published and sold at prices ranging from $60 to $1000 the set."

Note five: Issue with inserted title leaf in 10 volumes: *The Complete Writings of Walt Whitman.* New York: Henry W. Knight, [1902]. No works half title. *National Edition.* Limited to 500 numbered sets. Reviewed in *Boston Evening Transcript,* 26 November 1902, p. 9. *Location:* IaAS (rebound).

Note six: Shay reports that the Lamb Publishing Company printed 1,000 sets from these plates as the "National Edition" (p. 38); Wells and Goldsmith also list Lamb (p. 44) but delete the entry in an "Errata" page.

Note seven: Reprinted: Grosse Point, Mich.: Scholarly Press, [1968], 10 vols., with no indication of which "edition" was used. DLC copy received from the publisher 4 November 1969. Price, $110.00. *Locations:* DLC, MBU, ViU.

B 5 COMPLETE POETRY AND PROSE
1948

The Complete Poetry and Prose of Walt Whitman, 2 vols. New York: Pelligrini & Cudahy, [1948].

482, 538 pp. Boxed. Edited with an introduction by Malcolm Cowley. *American Classics Series*. Reviewed in *New Republic*, 119 (25 October 1948), 23–24. Copyright 21 September 1948; A25943; renewed, 21 October 1975; R616234. Deposit copies: DLC ('OCT –8 1948') (vol. II rebound). Price, $8.50. Listed in *CBI* as distributed in Canada by McLeod at $10.50. *Locations:* JM, TxU.

Note one: Reprinted: Garden City, N.Y.: Garden City Books, [1954]. Combined in two-volumes-in-one format. Dust jacket. Advertised as in "World Famous Classics." Reviewed in *New York Times Book Review*, 16 May 1954, p. 18. MB copy received 28 December 1954. Price, $3.95. *Locations:* MB, RPB.

Note two: Reprinted in two volumes as *The Works of Walt Whitman:* New York: Funk & Wagnalls, [1968]. Dust jacket. Deposit copies: DLC ('JAN –9 1969'). DLC copies received from the publisher: vol. I, 27 November 1968; vol. II, 4 December 1968. Price, $7.95 per volume. *Locations:* DLC, JM.

Note three: Reprinted in two volumes as *The Works of Walt Whitman:* [New York]: Minerva Press, [1969]. Wrappers. *Minerva Press M–83, M–84.* Price, $2.95 per volume. *Location:* JM.

B 6 COLLECTED WRITINGS
1961–

The Collected Writings of Walt Whitman, ed. Gay Wilson Allen and Sculley Bradley, 22 vols. to date. New York: New York University Press, 1961–   .

Works half title. Volumes are not numbered sequentially. List below is in order of publication.

Correspondence, ed. Edwin Haviland Miller, 6 vols. 1961–1977. See A 41 for details.

The Early Poems and the Fiction, ed. Thomas L. Brasher. 1963. See A 42 for details.

Prose Works 1892, ed. Floyd Stovall, 2 vols. 1963–1964. See C 113 for details.

Leaves of Grass: Comprehensive Reader's Edition, ed. Harold W. Blodgett and Sculley Bradley. 1965. See C 119 for details.

Daybooks and Notebooks, ed. William White, 3 vols. 1978. See A 45 for details.

Leaves of Grass: A Textual Variorum of the Printed Poems, ed. Sculley Bradley, Harold W. Blodgett, Arthur Golden, and William White, 3 vols. 1980. See C 154 for details.

Notebooks and Unpublished Prose Manuscripts, ed. Edward F. Grier, 6 vols. 1984. See A 46 for details.

B 7 COMPLETE POETRY AND COLLECTED PROSE
1982

Complete Poetry and Collected Prose. [New York: Literary Classics of the United States, 1982].

1380 pp. Cloth with dust jacket for trade sales; cloth in slipcase for subscription sales. Edited by Justin Kaplan. *Library of America.* Published 6 May 1982. Deposit copies: DLC ('JUN 4 1982'). Prices: trade, $25.00; subscription, $19.95. Distributed to the trade by Viking Press. *Locations:* BL, DLC, JM. Reprintings with undated title pages have been noted: 'Third printing, July 1982' (deposit copy: BO ['21 JAN 1983']); 'Fourth Printing' (deposit copies: BL ['15 MAY 84'], BO ['24 MAY 1984'], BE ['6 JY 84']); 'Fifth Printing'; 'Sixth Printing'. *Locations:* ViU (3d), BO (3d, 4th), BE (4th), BL (4th), TxU (5th), ScU (6th).

Note: Copies of the fourth printing have a label pasted on the copyright page stating, 'Published outside North America by the Press Syndicate | of the University of Cambridge | [press' address] | ISBN 0-521-26215-1' (BE, BL, BO).

C. Miscellaneous Collections

All miscellaneous collections of Whitman's writings through 1991, arranged chronologically. Included are anthologies, topical studies, and editions of *Leaves of Grass* done after Whitman's death in 1892.

C 1.1
Poems. London: John Camden Hotten, 1868.

xii, 403 pp. Cloth (for information on binding variations, see *BAL*, IX, 35). Edited with an introduction by William Michael Rossetti. 1,500 copies printed; 1,000 copies bound on 28 February 1868 and 500 copies bound on 26 October 1873. Published 5 February 1868. Reviewed in *Academia* (London), 21 March 1868, p. 279; *London Review,* 16 (21 March 1868), 289. Whitman received six copies on 21 December 1886 (*Correspondence,* IV, 59). He was promised 1s. or 25¢ royalty for each copy sold in America, but never received any payment from Hotten. Deposit copies: BL (rebound) ('3 MA68'). Presentation copies: PU (from Rossetti, March 1868). Copies inscribed by owners: TxU (March 1868). Price, 7s.6d. *Locations:* JM, TxU.

Note one: The manuscript for Rossetti's introduction and his marked page proofs are at NNPM. He received £25 for his work.

Note two: On 24 July 1867, Whitman sent Moncure Daniel Conway "a copy of my Poems, prepared with care for the printers, with reference to republication in England" (*Correspondence,* I, 332). This copy, made up from two sets of sheets from the 1867 *Leaves of Grass* along with some sheets from *Drum-Taps,* is at NN-B.

Note three: For a full discussion of this edition, see Morton D. Paley, "John Camden Hotten and the First British Editions of Walt Whitman—'A Nice Milky Cocoa-Nut,' " *Publishing History,* 6 (1979), 5–35.

C 1.2.a–c
London: Chatto and Windus, 1886.

xii, 320 pp. Deposit copies: BL ('24JU86'), BO ('14AUG86'). Whitman received copies on 21 December 1886 (see *Correspondence,* IV, 59). Presentation copies: DLC (28 July 1886). Copies inscribed by owners: CtY (6 November 1886). Price, 6s. Reprinted in 1892, 1895. *Locations:* BL (1886), BO (1886), CtY (1886), DLC (1886), JM (1886), TxU (1892), BMR (1895), NcD (1895).

423

C 1.2.d–e
London: Chatto & Windus, 1901.

Reprinted in 1908. *Locations:* JM (both).

C 1.2.f–h
London: Chatto & Windus, 1910.

Cloth (with dust jacket) or leather. *Fine-Paper Edition;* or *Fine-Paper Edition* and *St. Martin's Library.* Published March 1910. Deposit copies: BO ('22 7 1910'), BE ('18 JUL 1910'). Copies inscribed by owners: RPB (11 June 1910). Prices: cloth, 2s.; leather, 3s. Reprinted in cloth or leather in 1911, 1920. *Locations:* BE (1910), BO (1910), RPB (1910), BBo (1911), JM (1911), NcD (1920).

C 1.2.i$_1$
London: Chatto & Windus, 1926.

Cloth or flexible leather boards. *Fine Paper Edition. Locations:* CSt, JM.

C 1.2.i$_2$
New York: Albert & Charles Boni, 1925.

Title leaf is a cancel. *Fine Paper Edition.* Advertised as in "American Library." Presentation copies: NjCW (from the publisher, 31 May 1926). Copies inscribed by owners: RPB (13 November 1925). Price, $1.50. *Locations:* NjCW, JM, RPB.

C 1.2.j
London: Chatto & Windus, [1945].

Listed in the *English Catalogue* for January 1945 at 6s. *Not seen.*

C 2.1.a
Canti Scleti. Milano: Edoardo Sonzogno, Editore, 1887.

[104] pp. Cloth or wrappers. Translated into Italian with an introduction by Luigi Gamberale. *Biblioteca Universale,* vol. 169. MB copy (wrappers) received 24 October 1887. *Location:* MB.

C 2.1.b
Milano: Società Editrice Sonzogno, [1908].

Cloth or wrappers. *Location:* BMR.

C 2.2.a
Milano: Casa Editrice Sonzogno, [1890].

128 pp. Cloth or wrappers. *Biblioteca Universale*, no. 198. *Location:* MiDW.

C 2.2.b
Milano: Edoardo Sonzogno, Editrice, 1891.

Cloth or wrappers. *Locations:* BMR, NIC.

C 2.2.c
Milano: Società Editrice Sonzogno, 1895.

Cloth or wrappers. *Location:* RPB.

C 3
Gems from Walt Whitman. Philadelphia: David McKay, 1889.

58 pp. Dust jacket. Edited with an introduction by Elizabeth Porter Gould. Reviewed in *Critic*, n.s. 13 (15 March 1890), 126. Deposited for copyright: title, 20 June 1889; book, 15 December 1890; 19027. Whitman received a copy on 12 October 1889 (*Correspondence*, IV, 382). MB has the editor's copy, marked by her "received . . . from the publisher immediately after its publication, in November 1889." Presentation copies: MB (from Gould, November 1889). Price, 50¢. Listed in the *English Catalogue* at 2s.6d. *Locations:* BL, JM, MB (2).

C 4
Grashalme. Zurich: Verlags-Magazin (J. Schabelitz), 1889.

[181] pp. Cloth or wrappers. Edited by Karl Knortz and T.W.H. Rolleston. Whitman received "first proofs" on 10 September 1888 and copies by 25 February 1889 (*Correspondence*, IV, 207, 295). Deposit copies: BL (rebound with wrappers, '21SE89'). Presentation copies: DLC (from Rolleston, February 1889). *Locations:* cloth: CSt; wrappers: DLC (5), NcD.

C 5.1.a$_1$
Autobiographia or The Story of a Life. New York: Charles L. Webster, 1892.

205 pp. Cloth or half leather. *Fiction, Fact, and Fancy Series*. Reviewed in *Dial*, 13 (16 October 1892), 249. Deposited for copyright: title, 25 August 1892; book, 29 September 1892; 34882. Deposit copies: DLC ('SEP 29 1892'), BL ('8 JU 93'). Price, 75¢. *Locations:* BL, DLC, JM.

Note one: A set of galley proofs is at DLC.

Note two: A copy in "publisher's polished half-calf," inscribed from David McKay to John Lane, was in Waiting for Godot Books, Catalogue 18.

Note three: Webster's royalty statement of 17 April 1893 shows 1,300 copies were printed, with 1,000 bound in cloth and 30 in half calf, the remainder being unbound (DLC).

Note four: Some copies have David McKay's imprint stamped at the foot of spine (CtY, NcD [2], TxU).

Note five: McKay's royalty statement of 31 March 1896 shows 2,035 copies "received"; 1,316 were still in stock on 29 December 1911 (DLC).

C 5.1.a$_2$
New York: Charles L. Webster; London: G. P. Putnam's Sons, 1892.

Title leaf is a cancel. Leaf with series information has been canceled. Published November 1893. Deposit copies: BL ('11NO92'), BO ('4–.DEC.93'). Price, 4s. *Locations:* BL, BO, NcD.

Note: Webster's royalty statement of 17 April 1893 shows 250 sets of sheets were sent to England for sale (DLC).

C 5.1.a$_3$
Philadelphia: David McKay, [n.d.].

Combined with *Selected Poems* in two-volumes-in-one format; see C 7.1.a$_3$. Spine title: '*Selections from Whitman Poetry and Prose*'. Both title leaves are cancels. Publisher's address 1022 Market Street. Copies inscribed by owners: RPB (3 December 1900). *Locations:* JM, RPB.

Note: McKay moved to his location on Market Street in October 1896.

C 5.1.b$_1$
[Folcroft, Penn.]: Folcroft Library Editions, 1972.

Facsimile reprinting of New York and London issue (C 5.1.a$_2$). Deposit copies: DLC for CIP ('08SEP1972'). Price, $20.00. *Locations:* DLC, ScU.

Note: Listed in ARLN and *NUC* (1973–1977) as a 1976 publication by Norwood Editions of Norwood, Penn., for $25.00. No copies have been located.

C 5.1.b$_2$
[Norwood, Penn.]: Norwood Editions, 1977.

Title leaf is inserted. *Location:* CLSU.

C 5.1.b$_3$
[Norwood, Penn.]: Norwood Editions, 1978.

Title leaf is inserted. *Location:* ScCleU.

C 5.1.c
Philadelphia: Richard West, 1977.

Facsimile reprinting listed in *NUC* (1978:149) and in *Walt Whitman Review,* 25 (June 1979), 82, for $30.00. *Not seen.*

C 5.1.d
[N.p.]: Arden Library, 1979.

Facsimile reprinting listed in *NUC* (1979–1984) for $30.00. *Not seen.*

C 5.1.e
New York: Gordon, [n.d.].

Facsimile reprinting listed in *BIP* (1972–1984) for $11.00. *Not seen.*

C 6.1.a–b
Complete Prose Works. Philadelphia: David McKay, 1892.

522 pp. *Specimen Days, November Boughs,* and *Good-Bye My Fancy.* Cloth or half leather. Deposit copies: BL ('8NO93'). Publisher's address 23 South Ninth Street. Copies inscribed by owners: CSt (25 December 1892). Reprinted in 1897. *Locations:* BL (1892), CSt (1892), JM (both).

Note one: McKay's royalty statement of 13 October 1892 shows that 232 copies had been sold and 802 were still in stock, and the firm's royalty statement of 30 September 1898 shows that 1,160 copies were still in stock (both, DLC).

Note two: BAL notes, "The sheets of *Specimen Days* are a reissue, with cancel title-page, of sheets printed before those used in *Complete Poems & Prose,* 1888, for they do not have the corrections and alterations to the text made in the latter" (IX, 91–92).

C 6.1.c
Prose Works. Philadelphia: David McKay, [n.d.].

476 pp. *Specimen Days* and *November Boughs.* Publisher's address 604–8 South Washington Square. Copies inscribed by owners: MB (1918). *Locations:* JM, MB.

Note: McKay moved to his location on Washington Square in November 1904.

C 6.2.a₁
Complete Prose Works. Boston: Small, Maynard, 1898.

527 pp. *Specimen Days, November Boughs,* and *Good-Bye My Fancy*. Cloth or half leather. *Large Paper Edition*. Frontispiece of Schoff engraving of Whitman, photograph of Whitman's birthplace after p. 6; manuscript facsimile on Homer after p. 176; 1855 daguerreotype of Whitman after p. 334; photograph of Mickle Street house after p. 434; engraving of Elias Hicks after p. 456; photograph of Whitman's tomb after p. 508; 1891 Eakins photo of Whitman after p. 524. Limited to 60 copies on handmade paper in the United States and 30 in England, both signed and numbered by the publisher. MB copy received 24 August 1898 from the publisher. *Locations:* MB, ScU.

Note: First book appearance of "Walt Whitman's Last" (pp. 526–527); see E 2763.

C 6.2.a₂
Boston: Small, Maynard; London: G. P. Putnam's Sons, 1898.

Title leaf is integral. Cloth or full leather. *Large Paper Edition*. Listed in the *English Catalogue* for April 1898. *Locations:* PU, ViU.

Note: The American and English issues differ only in their title pages, making it likely that the English issue is the American sheets with a reset first gathering.

C 6.2.b₁
Boston: Small, Maynard, 1898.

527 pp. The photographs after pp. 334 and 524 are omitted. MB copy received 24 August 1898 from the publisher. *Locations:* JM, MB.

C 6.2.b₂
Boston: Small, Maynard; London: G. P. Putnam's Sons, 1898.

Title leaf is a cancel. Deposit copies: BL ('28AP98'). *Locations:* BL, JM.

C 6.2.c
Boston: Small, Maynard; London: G. P. Putnam's Sons, 1898.

Title leaf is integral. Rubberstamped in blue on the copyright page is 'MADE AND PRINTED | IN GREAT BRITAIN.'. *Location:* CtY.

C 6.2.d–e
Boston: Small, Maynard, 1901.

Reprinted 1907. Copies inscribed by owners: JM (25 December 1907). *Locations:* NcD (1901), JM (both), PU (1907).

C 6.2.f$_1$
New York: D. Appleton, 1908.

Publisher's code '(1)' on p. 527. *Locations:* DLC, RPB.

Note: A typed note (by Carolyn Wells Houghton?) in the DLC copy states "The whole edition was destroyed by fire before distribution. Very few copies were saved."

C 6.2.f$_2$
New York: D. Appleton, 1908.

White paper label on front pastedown endpaper: '[publisher's device] | *This book is | now published by | Mitchell Kennerley*'. *Location:* ScU.

C 6.2.g
New York and London: D. Appleton, 1909.

Publisher's code '(1)' on p. 527. Listed in the *American Catalogue* for 26 June 1909; in the *English Catalogue* for October 1909 at 5s. *Locations:* JM, NcU.

C 6.2.h$_1$
New York and London: D. Appleton, 1910.

Publisher's code '(2)' on p. 527. *Location:* JM (2).

C 6.2.h$_2$
New York and London: D. Appleton, 1910.

White paper label on front pastedown endpaper: '[publisher's device] | *This book is | now published by | Mitchell Kennerley*'. *Location:* Collection of Matthew J. Bruccoli.

C 6.2.i
London and New York: D. Appleton, 1911.

Publisher's code '(2)' on p. 527. *Location:* JM.

C 6.2.j
New York: Mitchell Kennerley, MCMXIV.

Dust jacket. Publisher's code '(2)' on p. 527. Advertised as in "Library Edition" in cloth for $1.75 and as in "Popular Edition" in paper for $1.25. Copies inscribed by owners: JM (February 1915). *Locations:* JM (2), RPB.

Note: Some copies have bindings goldstamped at the foot of the spine 'DOUBLEDAY | PAGE & CO.' (CtY, TxU [inscribed by owner, 1921]).

C 6.2.k$_1$
London and New York: D. Appleton, [1920].

Publisher's code '(2)' on p. 527. *Location:* JM.

C 6.2.k$_2$
London: D. Appleton, 1920.

Title leaf is a cancel. Publisher's code '(2)' on p. 527. *Locations:* BMR, RPB.

C 7.1.a$_1$
Selected Poems. New York: Charles L. Webster, 1892.

179 pp. Cloth or half leather. Edited by Arthur Stedman. *Fiction, Fact, and Fancy Series.* Reviewed in *New York Daily Tribune,* 26 April 1892, p. 8. Deposited for copyright: title, 2 March 1892; book, 6 April 1892; 9482. Deposit copies: DLC ('APR 6 1892'), BL ('9 SE92'). Presentation copies: CtY (from the publisher, April 1892), DLC (from the publisher, April 1892; 2 copies). Price, 75¢. Listed in the *English Catalogue* for April 1892 as an importation by G. P. Putnam's Sons at 4s. *Locations:*   BL, CtY (2), DLC (2), JM (2), TxU, ViU.

Note one: The copy at MBU has an inserted manuscript draft of the title page by Whitman, on which he has written that he is to receive "$250 in advance in lump cash."

Note two: Some copies have a leaf inserted at the front stating that Webster's publications are also available from David McKay (BL, CtY [2], DLC [2], JM [2], TxU, ViU).

Note three: Some copies have David McKay's imprint at the foot of the spine (JM, TxU, ViU).

Note four: Webster's royalty statement of 31 May 1892 shows 3,001 copies printed, of which 2,034 were sold and 345 used as gifts or editorial copies (DLC).

C 7.1.a$_2$
Philadelphia: David McKay, [n.d.].

Title leaf is a cancel. Publisher's address 1022 Market Street. *Locations:* JM, RPB.

Note one: McKay's royalty statement of 31 March 1896 shows 2,478 copies "received"; 1,365 were still in stock on 29 December 1911 (both, DLC).

Note two: McKay moved to his location on Market Street in October 1896.

C 7.1.a₃
Philadelphia: David McKay, [n.d.].

Combined with *Autobiographia* in two-volumes-in-one format; see C 5.1.a₃.

C 8.1.a
Leaves of Grass. Philadelphia: David McKay, 1894.

438 pp. *Leaves of Grass,* "Sands at Seventy," *Good-Bye My Fancy,* and "A Backward Glance O'er Travel'd Roads." From the plates of the seventh edition, fifteenth printing (A 2.7.0). Publisher's address 23 South Ninth Street. Copies inscribed by owners: NNC (June 1894), MBU (1 September 1894). *Locations:* JM, MB, MBU, NNC.

Note: McKay's royalty statement of 3 April 1894 shows 900 copies printed (DLC).

C 8.1.b
Philadelphia: David McKay, [1896].

Copies inscribed by owners: CtY (5 June 1897). MB copy (rebound) received 29 April 1896. *Locations:* CtY (2), JM.

Note: McKay's royalty statement of 31 March 1896 shows 975 copies printed (DLC).

C 8.1.c₁
Philadelphia: David McKay, [1896].

Page size 7″×4½″. Wrappers with paper label on spine: '[thick-thin rule] | *Leaves* | *of* | *Grass* | *Complete* | *1892* | *Walt Whitman* | [thick-thin rule]' (DLC, JM, NjP, PU) or without label (NcD, RPB [2]), and with 'Printed in the United States' either present (RPB, JM) or not present (DLC, NcD, PU, RPB) on the back wrapper verso. Rubberstamped in blue on the copyright page in some copies is '*Printed in U.S.*' (DLC, NcD, RPB). In the July 1896 *Conservator,* J. W. Wallace wrote from England about "your American cheap edition . . . just about to be put upon our market" (VII, 75). According to 6 September 1897 *Bookman,* published in 1896 (VI, 81–82). DLC copy inscribed by Traubel, 7 April 1896, as "A first copy." Copies inscribed by owners: NcD (August 1896). Price, 50¢. *Locations:* DLC, JM, NcD, NjP, PU, RPB (2).

Note one: McKay's royalty statement of 30 September 1896 shows 3,000 copies printed and bound in wrappers (DLC).

Note two: One copy, bound in half leather, has rubberstamped in blue on the copyright page '*Printed in U.S.*' (JM).

C 8.1.c$_2$
Philadelphia: David McKay; Manchester: Labour Press Society, [n.d.].

Title leaf is a cancel. Wrappers with paper label imprinted with English price and without '*Printed in U.S.*' on back cover. Price, 2s.6d. *Location:* JM.

C 8.1.c$_3$
Philadelphia: David McKay, [n.d.].

Title leaf is a cancel. Wrappers with paper label on spine: '[thick-thin rule] | *Leaves | of | Grass | Complete | 1892 | Walt Whitman* | [thick-thin rule]'; back wrapper is blank. Publisher's address 1022 Market Street. Price, 50¢. *Location:* NN-R.

Note: McKay moved to his location on Market Street in October 1896.

C 8.1.d
Philadelphia: David McKay, [n.d.].

Page size 8¼"×5⅝". Copies inscribed by owners: TxU (6 March 1897). *Locations:* JM, TxU.

C 8.1.e
Philadelphia: David McKay, [n.d.].

Page size 7⅝"×5¼". Paper-covered boards. Copies inscribed by owners: JM (June 1898). *Locations:* JM, NjP.

C 8.1.f$_1$
Leaves of Grass. Boston: Small, Maynard, 1897.

446 pp. *Leaves of Grass,* "Sands at Seventy," *Good-Bye My Fancy, Old Age Echoes,* and "A Backward Glance O'er Travel'd Roads" (*Leaves of Grass* and *Good-Bye My Fancy* are reprinted from the McKay plates; the others are printed from new typesettings). Wrappers. *Popular Edition.* Deposit copies: DLC (rebound) ('OCT 6 1897'). Copies inscribed by owners: NN-B (28 October 1897). Price, 50¢. *Locations:* NjCW, NN-B.

Note: The "Old Age Echoes" section contains the first book publication of "To Soar in Freedom and in Fullness of Power" (p. 425), "Then Shall Perceive" (p. 425), "The Few Drops Known" (p. 425), "One Thought Ever at the Fore" (p. 425), "While Behind All Firm and Erect" (p. 426), "A Kiss to the Bride. Marriage of Nelly Grant, May 21, 1874" (p. 426), "Nay, Tell Me Not To-day the Publish'd Shame" (pp. 426–427), "Supplement Hours" (p. 427), "Of Many a Smutch'd Deed Reminiscent" (p. 427), "To Be at All" (pp. 427–428), "Death's Valley" (p. 428), "On the Same Picture" (p. 429), "A Thought of Columbus" (pp. 429–430).

C 8.1.f$_2$
London: G. P. Putnam's Sons; Boston: Small, Maynard, 1897.

Title leaf is integral. Cloth or wrappers or half leather. Deposit copies: BL ('25OC98'; rebound). Listed in the *English Catalogue* for October 1897 at 2s. A printed receipt from Stationers' Hall shows the book was registered for copyright on 4 November 1897 (DLC). *Locations:* BO, JM (5), PU.

Note one: One copy, in wrappers in *Popular Edition,* has the Hollyer frontispiece and 'LONDON AND | BOSTON 1900' at the foot of the spine (BMR).

C 8.1.g$_1$
Boston: Small, Maynard, 1897.

455 pp. (index added). Copyright 59932; received, 6 October 1897. Reviewed in 27 November 1897 *Literary World* (28:431–432). Copies inscribed by owners: CtY (February 1898). MB copy (rebound) received 20 March 1897. MB copy received 24 August 1898 from the publisher. *Locations:* CtY, JM.

C 8.1.g$_2$
London: G. P. Putnam's Sons; Boston: Small, Maynard, 1897.

Title leaf is a cancel. *Location:* RPB.

C 8.1.g$_3$
Boston: Small, Maynard; London: G. P. Putnam's Sons, 1898.

Title leaf is a cancel. Cloth or full leather. Deposit copy: BL ('14MH98'). *Locations:* BBo, BL, MBU, RPB.

C 8.1.h$_1$
Boston: Small, Maynard, 1898.

Cloth or half leather. *Large Paper Edition.* Frontispiece of Gutekunst photograph of Whitman in 1890; 1855 Hollyer engraving after p. 28; G. W. Waters 1877 painting of Whitman after p. 105; Gurney photograph of Whitman after p. 296; 1891 Eakins photograph of Whitman after p. 379; facsimile manuscript of "After the Supper and Talk" after p. 404; photograph of Mickle Street house after p. 434. Limited to 60 copies on handmade paper for sale in the United States and 30 in Great Britain, both numbered and signed by the publisher. MB copy received 24 August 1898 from the publisher. *Location:* MB, NcD.

C 8.1.h$_2$
Boston: Small, Maynard; London: G. P. Putnam's Sons, 1898.

Title leaf is integral. Cloth or full leather. *Large Paper Edition*. Photographs after pp. 105, 296, 379, 404, 434 are omitted. Listed in the *English Catalogue* for April 1898 at 9s. *Locations:* PU, RPB.

Note: The American and English issues differ only in their title pages, making it likely that the English issue is the American sheets with a reset first gathering.

C 8.1.i
Boston: Small, Maynard, 1899.

Locations: DLC, MH (2).

C 8.1.j–k
Boston: Small, Maynard, 1900.

446 pp. Page size 7½″×5″. Reprinted 1903. *Locations:* JM (1900), RPB (1900), TxU (1903).

C 8.1.l
London: G. P. Putnam's Sons; Boston: Small, Maynard, 1903.

446 pp. Title leaf is integral. Page size 7½″×5″. Cloth or leather-covered flexible boards or wrappers. Copies in wrappers in *Popular Edition* with 'LONDON AND | BOSTON 1900' (CtY, NN-R) or with 'LONDON AND | BOSTON 1904' (TxU) at foot of spine. *Locations:* CtY, JM (2), NN-R (2), TxU.

C 8.1.m
Boston: Small, Maynard, 1904.

455 pp. *Locations:* JM, TxU.

C 8.1.n
Boston: Small, Maynard, 1905.

446 pp. *Locations:* JM, NjCW.

C 8.1.o
Boston: Small, Maynard, 1907.

455 pp. *Locations:* JM (2), NNC.

C 8.1.p₁
New York: D. Appleton, 1908.

455 pp. Publisher's code '(1)' on p. 455. *Locations:* BL, DLC, JM.

Note: An inserted typed note (by Carolyn Wells Houghton?) states, "whole edition was destroyed by fire before distribution. Very few copies were saved" (DLC).

C 8.l.p₂
New York and London: D. Appleton, 1909.

Title leaf is a cancel. Listed in the *American Catalogue* for 3 July 1909 at $1.25 for cloth, $2.00 for de luxe edition; listed in the *English Catalogue* for October 1909 at 5s. *Location:*   RPB.

C 8.1.q
New York and London: D. Appleton, 1910.

Publisher's code '(2)' on p. 455. *Location:*   JM.

C 8.1.r
New York and London: D. Appleton, 1910.

Publisher's code '(3)' on p. 455. *Location:*   CSt.

C 8.1.s
London and New York: D. Appleton, 1911.

Publisher's code '(3)' on p. 455. *Locations:*   JM, ViLxW.

C 8.1.t
London and New York: D. Appleton, 1912.

Publisher's code '(3)' on p. 455. *Location:*   DLC.

C 8.1.u
New York and London: D. Appleton, 1912.

Publisher's code '(4)' on p. 455. Copies inscribed by owners: JM (3 May 1913). *Locations:*   JM, NjCW.

Note: Advertised by Mitchell Kennerley in cloth for $1.00 as in "Popular Edition" and in paper for 50¢ in *Conservator,* 23 (May 1912), 46.

C 8.1.v–y
New York: Mitchell Kennerley, MCMXIV.

Cloth with dust jacket or half leather or limp leather or leather over flexible boards or selfwrappers. Advertised as in "India Paper Edition" (leather) for $2.50, "Library Edition" (cloth) for $1.50, and "Popular Edition" (paper or cloth) for 60¢ or $1.00. Sheets bulk 1½″ (NcD, RPB) or 1⅛″ (BMR, CtY [3]) or ¹⁵⁄₃₂″

(RPB) or ⁵⁄₁₆″ (CtY, TxU). Publisher's code '(4)' on p. 455. Presentation copies: BMR (from Traubel, July 1914). Copies inscribed by owners: NcD (25 December 1914), CtY (⁵⁄₁₆″, 1915). *Locations:* BMR, CtY (4), NcD, RPB (2), TxU.

Note: A copy at CtY, bound in in half leather, with sheets bulking 1⅛″, has a note that "Mr Kennerley had 25 copies bound like this volume for Presentation."

C 9.1.a
Leaves of Grass. Philadelphia: David McKay, [1900].

496 pp. *Leaves of Grass,* "Gathered Leaves," and index. Publisher's address 1022 Market Street. Copyright page has Sherman Press imprint. Published 17 July 1900. Reviewed in *New York Times Saturday Review,* 10 November 1900, p. 772. Listed in *English Catalogue* for October 1900 at 6s. Price, $1.25. Copyright A18815; received, 19 July 1900. Deposit copies: DLC (rebound) ('JUL 19 1900'). Presentation copies: DLC (from Harned, 10 October 1900). *Locations:* DLC, JM.

C 9.1.b₁
Philadelphia: David McKay, [n.d.].

516 pp. Publisher's address Washington Square. Copies inscribed by owners: CtY (7 July 1906), TxU (21 September 1906). *Locations:* BL, BMR, CtY, JM (2), TxU (2).

Note: McKay moved to his location on Washington Square in November 1904.

C 9.1.b₂
Toronto: Musson, [n.d.].

Title leaf is inserted. *Locations:* CaOTU, JM.

C 9.1.b₃
London: Siegle, Hill, MCMVII.

Title leaf is a cancel. Cloth or half leather. Listed in the *English Catalogue* for February 1907 at 12s.6d. and for September 1907 at 7s.6d. Deposit copies: BL ('4 NO07'), BD ('Feb. 1908'), BE ('10 FEB 1908'), BO ('18 2 1909'); copies inscribed by owners: RPB (14 January 1908). *Locations:* BD, BE, BL, BO, NcD, RPB.

C 9.1.c
Philadelphia: David McKay, [n.d.].

526 pp. Cloth or half leather. *Locations:* CaOTP, NNC, NcU.

C9.1.d
Philadelphia: David McKay, [n.d.].

563 pp. *Locations:* CtY, JM.

C9.1.e–f
Philadelphia: David McKay, [n.d.].

567 pp. Dust jacket. Sheets bulk 1⅜″. Copies inscribed by owners: JM (4 October 1924). *Location:* JM (3). Later reprinting(s) bulk 1½″ and lack the Sherman Press imprint on the copyright page. *Locations:* JM, MBU (2).

Note: Some copies of the earlier printing have 'LONDON | LEOPOLD B. HILL' goldstamped at the foot of the spine (BL [deposit copy, '8 FEB 28'], JM [inscribed by owner, 21 March 1929]).

C9.1.g
Philadelphia: David McKay, [n.d.].

Sheets bulk ½″. Boxed. Advertised as in "Thin Paper Edition." Copies inscribed by owners: CtY (26 July 1945). *Locations:* CtY, ViU.

C9.1.h
Philadelphia: David McKay, [n.d.].

Sheets bulk ½″. Flexible leather-covered boards. Publisher's address 604–8 South Washington Square. Advertised as in "Thin Paper Edition." *Locations:* JM, NcD.

Note: McKay's royalty statement of 29 December 1911 shows 55 copies still in stock (DLC). The McKay firm advertised *Leaves of Grass* in *BIP* through 1960.

C10
Poems. London: "Review of Reviews" Office, [1895].

[i–ii], [1]–60, i, [ii–iv] pp.; also paginated [i–ii], 119–176, i, [ii–iv]. Wrappers. Edited by W. T. Stead. Simultaneously in *Penny Poets, XXVII,* and *Masterpiece Library, Vol. VII.* Price, 1s. Published in December 1895. *Locations:* JM (2), NcD.

Note one: Also in wrappers imprinted "London: Stead's Publishing House, [n.d.]" for 1s., containing advertisements for *Stead's Poets 27;* dated by *BAL* "*circa* 1925" (IX, 92) (RPB).

Note two: Cases were available for the 12 quarterly numbers in the *Penny Poets* series in seven styles, priced from 1s. to 10s.

C 11.1.a–b
Selections from the Prose and Poetry of Walt Whitman. Boston: Small, Maynard, 1898.

xliii, 257 pp. Edited with an introduction by Oscar Lovell Triggs. Reviewed in *Conservator,* 9 (April 1898), 28–29. Copyright 23593; received, 14 April 1898. Deposit copy: BL ('24 DEC 98'). Presentation copies: DLC (from the publisher, April 1898). Price, $1.25. Reprinted in 1906. *Locations:* BL (1898), DLC (1898), JM (both).

C 12.1.a₁
Leaves of Grass. New York and Boston: H. M. Caldwell, [1900].

88 pp. Cloth or flexible leather covered boards or limp leather. Title leaf is tipped in. No series identification or *Remarque Edition of Literary Masterpieces,* 20. Copyright A22458; received, 10 September 1900. Published 8 December 1900. RPB copy (no series) received 12 September 1905. Prices: cloth, 40¢; leather, 75¢; limp leather, $1.25. *Locations:* RPB, TxU; *Remarque Edition of Literary Masterpieces:* CtY, RPB.

C 12.1.a₂
London: Dean & Son, [n.d.].

Title leaf is tipped in. Cloth over flexible boards or limp suede with Caldwell's device on front. RPB copy received 20 March 1905. *Locations:* CtY, NzD, RPB.

C 12.1.a₃
London: George G. Harrap, [n.d.].

Title leaf and conjugate half title leaf are tipped in. Limp suede with Caldwell's device on front. Boxed. *The King's Treasury of Literary Masterpieces. Locations:* CtY, NzD, RPB.

C 12.1.b–c
Leaves of Grass. New York: Dodge, [1900].

Title leaf is tipped in. Leatherette or half leather with unprinted silk dust jacket. Publisher's address is 8th Ave. or 5th Ave. Advertised as in "Almanac Series" and "Cloister Craft Books." *Locations:* BL (8th Ave), CtY (8th Ave), NBuU (5th Ave).

C 13
Leaves of Grass. [N.p.]: Elder, [1901].

Listed in *CBI* (1902) in "Elder Impression Classics" in flexible leather at $1.00. *Not seen.*

C 14.1.a–b
Poems of Walt Whitman (Leaves of Grass). New York: Thomas Y. Crowell and
Company Publishers, [1902].

343 pp. Cloth or leather over flexible boards. Introduction by John Burroughs.
Astor Edition. Copyright 36237; received, 26 June 1902. Published 4 October
1902. Price, 60¢. *Locations:* JM, ViU. Undated reprinting with "Crowell &
Company" in imprint in cloth or leather over flexible boards as *Astor Edition* or
Gladstone Edition or with no series identification. Also advertised as in "Wood-
bine Edition." *Locations:* DLC, NcD; *Astor Edition:* JM, TxU; *Gladstone
Edition:* ViU.

C 14.2.a–b
Poems of Walt Whitman. New York: Thomas Y. Crowell & Company, [1902].

468 pp. Cloth or leather-covered flexible or padded boards. Introduction by
John Burroughs. No series identification or *Astor Edition* or *Gladstone Edi-
tion.* Copies inscribed by owners: CSt *(Astor, 8 July 1914). Locations:* MBU,
ScU; *Astor Edition:* CSt, JM, RPB; *Gladstone Edition:* RPB. Undated reprint-
ing with "Crowell Company" in imprint in cloth or flexible leather as *Astor
Edition* or *Gladstone Edition* or with no series identification. *Locations:* CtY;
Astor Edition: NcD; *Gladstone Edition:* JM, TxU.

C 14.3
The Poems of Walt Whitman (Leaves of Grass). New York: Thomas Y. Crowell
Company, [1927].

497 pp. Introduction by John Burroughs. Advertised as in "Laurel Series."
Location: CaOTP.

C 15
Leaves of Grass (Selected). London: Anthony Treherne, 1904.

xii, 260 pp. Page size 6⁷⁄₁₆″×4⁹⁄₁₆″. Cloth or leather-covered flexible boards with
'TREHERNE' on spine. Edited with an introduction by Harry Roberts. *The
Vagabond's Library,* vol. 1. Published June 1904. Deposit copies: cloth: BE
('8JUL1904'), BO ('11 7 1904'). Copies inscribed by owners: TxU (11 September 1904). Prices: cloth, 1s.6d.; leather, 2s.6d. *Locations:* BE, BO, DLC, TxU.

Note: Copies bound in cloth without the publisher's name on the spine, with
sheets measuring 7⅜″×4⅞″, are at CtY, JM.

C 16.1
Memories of President Lincoln and Other Lyrics of the War. Portland, Maine:
Thomas B. Mosher, MDCCCCIV.

41 pp. Printed on Japan vellum. Vellum-covered boards. Boxed. Foreword by Horace L. Traubel. Bibliographical note by Thomas Bird Mosher. Published 22 July 1905. DLC copy received 28 February 1905. Limited to 50 numbered copies, 40 of which are for sale. Price, $3.00. *Locations:* BL, DLC, MBU.

Note: Printed from the plates of *The Bibelot,* 10 (August 1904).

C 16.2.a
Memories of President Lincoln and Other Lyrics of the War. Portland, Maine: Thomas B. Mosher, MDCCCCVI.

43 pp. Printed on pure vellum. Unbound or in parchment-covered boards with box. Foreword by Horace L. Traubel. Limited to seven copies, signed by the publisher; advertised in *Memories of President Lincoln* (C 30) as limited to 10 copies. *Locations:* CtY, NcD.

C 16.2.b
Portland, Maine: Thomas B. Mosher, MDCCCCVI.

Printed on Japan vellum. Parchment-covered boards. Unprinted glassine dust jacket. Boxed. Published October 1906. Limited to 100 numbered copies. Price, $1.00. *Locations:* CtY (2), RPB.

C 16.2.c
Portland, Maine: Thomas B. Mosher, MDCCCCVI.

Printed on Van Gelder handmade paper. Boards. Unprinted glassine dust jacket. Boxed. Published October 1906. Limited to 950 copies. Listed in *CBI* as also including 25 copies on handmade paper; advertised in *Memories of President Lincoln* (C 30) as limited to 925 copies. Price, 50¢. *Locations:* BL, JM, ViU.

Note: The integral leaf with the statement of limitation has been reset for each printing.

C 16.2.d
Portland, Maine: Thomas B. Mosher, MDCCCCXII.

Boards. Boxed. Published May 1912. Limited to 950 copies on Van Gelder handmade paper. Price, $3.00. *Locations:* JM, PU.

C 17
Selected Poems of Walt Whitman. New York, London, Bombay: Longmans, Green, 1904.

Edited William Morton Payne. Advertised in "Wampum Library." *Not seen.*

C 18.1.a
Selected Poems of Walt Whitman. New York: Maynard, Merrill, [1904].

63 pp. Wrappers. Edited with an introduction and notes by Julian W. Abernethy. *Maynard's English Classics Series No.* 242. Copyright A101235; received, 30 November 1904. Published 1 December 1904. Deposit copy: DLC (rebound) ('NOV 30 1904'). Price, 12¢. *Locations:* NcD, TxU.

C 18.1.b
New York: Charles E. Merrill, [n.d.].

Wrappers. *Maynard's English Classics Series, No.* 242. Price, 12¢. *Locations:* NNC, TxU.

C 19.1.a
The Book of Heavenly Death. Portland, Maine: Thomas B. Mosher, MDCCCCV.

[103] pp. Printed on pure vellum. Unbound or in vellum wrappers with ties. Edited with an introduction by Horace Traubel. Copyright A114488; received, 27 April 1905; renewed, 21 May 1932; R19857. Published April 1905. Reviewed in *Conservator,* 16 (April 1905), 27. Limited to five numbered copies, signed by the publisher. *Locations:* DLC, ViU.

C 19.1.b
Portland, Maine: Thomas B. Mosher, MDCCCCV.

Printed on Japan vellum. Parchment-covered boards. Vellum dust jacket. Boxed. Limited to 50 numbered copies, signed by Mosher in some copies. Price, $3.00. *Locations:* DLC, NcD.

C 19.1.c
Portland, Maine: Thomas B. Mosher, MDCCCCV.

Printed on Van Gelder handmade paper. Boards. Dust jacket. Boxed. Deposit copies: DLC ('APR 27 1905'; 2 copies). Copies inscribed by owners: BMR (November 1905). Published April 1905. Limited to 500 copies. Price, $1.50. *Locations:* BL, BMR, DLC (3), JM.

Note: In all three printings, the integral leaf with the statement of limitation has been reset.

C 19.1.d
Portland, Maine: Thomas B. Mosher, MDCCCCVII.

Printed on Van Gelder handmade paper. Boards. Dust jacket. Boxed. Published August 1907. Presentation copies: DLC (from Mosher, 24 December 1907). Limited to 500 copies. Price, $1.50. *Locations:* DLC, RPB.

C 20

Leaves of Grass   A Selection. London: George Routledge & Sons; New York: E. P. Dutton, [1905].

60 pp. Self wrappers. *Broadway Booklets*. Published September 1905. Deposit copies: BL ('6 JA 1906'), BC ('AP 17.1906'), BO ('19 4 1906'). Copies inscribed by owners: RPB (8 July 1910). Price, 6d. *Locations:* BC, BL, BO, CtY, RPB.

C 21.1

Pearls from Walt Whitman. London: C. W. Daniel, [1905].

32 pp. Wrappers. Edited by F. E. Worland. Illustrated by S. W. Le Feaux. *Pearls from the Poets,* no. 6. Copies inscribed by owners: RPB (20 January 1914). *Locations:* BBo, NcD, RPB.

C 21.2

Pearls from Walt Whitman. London: C. W. Daniel, [n.d.].

34 pp. Wrappers. Edited by H. B. B[inns?]. *Pearls from the Poets,* no. 6. Copies inscribed by owners: RPB (January 1909). *Locations:* BMR, RPB.

C 22.1.a

A Little Book of Nature Thoughts. Portland, Maine: Thomas B. Mosher, MDCCCCVI.

[88] pp. Printed on vellum. Boards. Vellum wrappers. Boxed. Edited with a preface by Anne Montgomerie Traubel. Advertised as in "Vest Pocket Series." Published 16 March 1906. Reviewed in *Conservator,* 17 (May 1906), 43. Price, $1.00. *Locations:* DLC, NjP.

C 22.1.b

Portland, Maine: Thomas B. Mosher, MDCCCCVI.

Cloth or self wrappers or flexible leather-covered boards. Boxed. Presentation copies: DLC (from Annie Traubel, April 1906). Prices: cloth, 40¢; paper, 25¢; limp leather, 75¢. *Locations:* DLC, JM.

C 23

Selected Poems. Dublin: New Nation, 1907.

32 pp. Wrappers. Preface by Padraic Colum. *The New Nation Booklets Number One*. Price, 1d. *Locations:* BMR, DLC, NN-R.

Note: According to Wells and Goldsmith, this title is "very scarce, as most of the edition was destroyed" (p. 68).

C 24

Walt Whitman. Oxford: Clarendon Press, [1908].

32 pp. Cloth or wrappers. Edited with an introduction by A. T. Quiller-Couch. *Select English Classics*. Deposit copies: cloth: BL ('26NO08'), BC ('27 NO 1908'), BE ('27 NOV 1908'). Copies inscribed by owners: RPB (8 November 1913). Prices: cloth, 4d. or 25¢; wrappers, 3d. or 20¢. *Locations:* BC, BE, BL, CSt, RPB.

C 25.1.a–c

The Wisdom of Walt Whitman. New York: Brentano's, MCMVIII.

165 pp. Flexible leather. Boxed. Edited with an introduction by Laurens Maynard. Advertised as in "Wisdom Series." Copyright A217267; received, 27 October 1908. Published 18 September 1908. Deposit copies: DLC (rebound) ('OCT 27 1908'). Copies inscribed by owners: MBU (11 November 1908). Price, $1.00. *Locations:* JM, MBU. Reprinted in MCMXVII, MCMXXVI. *Locations:* JM (1917), TxU (1926).

C 25.1.d

[Folcroft, Penn.]: Folcroft Library Editions, 1979.

Facsimile reprinting of 1926 reprinting. Limited to 150 copies. *Location:* FU.

C 26

Leaves of Grass. London [&c]: Cassell, MCMIX.

468 pp. Cloth or leather over flexible boards. *The People's Library*, no. 89. Published April 1909. Deposit copies: BL (rebound) ('4 MY 09'), BC ('11 MY 1909'), BE ('11 MAY 1909'). Price, 1s.6d. *Locations:* BC, BE, JM (2), PU, RPB.

Note one: Some copies have '89' stamped on the spine (JM, RPB).

Note two: Some copies have advertisements at the end listing the first 100 volumes in *The People's Library* (BC, BE, JM, PU) or the first 120 volumes (JM).

C 27

Leaves of Grass (A Selection). London: Siegle, Hill, [1912].

128 pp. Limp suede. Advertised as in "Selected Series," no. 24. Published July 1912. Deposit copies: BL ('27 NOV 12'), BC ('FE 14 1913'), BO ('17 2 1913'). Copies inscribed by owners: RPB (10 August 1914). Price, 1s.6d. *Locations:* BC, BL, BO, CtY, RPB.

Note: Listed in the *English Catalogue* as published by L. B. Hill for August 1919 at 1s.6d.; as in "Value of Friendship Series" for May 1922 at 1s.; for September 1927 at 10s.6d. No copies have been located with a Hill imprint.

C 28.1.a–k

Leaves of Grass (1) & Democratic Vistas. London: J. M. Dent & Sons; New York: E. P. Dutton, [1912].

359 pp. Cloth or leather over flexible boards. Introduction by Horace Traubel. *Everyman's Library,* no. 573. Reviewed in *Poetry Review,* 3 (December 1913), 273–276. Deposit copies: BL ('26 FEB 12'), BE ('29 FEB 1912'). Copies inscribed by owners: TxU (August 1912). Prices: cloth, 50¢; leather, $1.00; library binding, 60¢. *Locations:* BE, BL, TxU. Reprinted in cloth or leather with undated title pages in 1914, 1916, 1919, 1921, 1925, 1927, 1930, 1935, 1939, 1943. *Locations:* JM (1914, 1919, 1925, 1930, 1939, 1943), CaOTP (1916), TxU (1927), DLC (1935).

C 29.1.a

A Little Book of Nature Thoughts. London: Siegle, Hill, [1912].

96 pp. Miniature book. Limp suede. Advertised as in "Langham Booklets," no. 123. Published June 1912. Deposit copies: BL ('27 NOV 12'), BC ('FE 14 1913'). Price, 1s. *Locations:* BC, BL, CtY, RPB.

C 29.1.b

London: Leopold B. Hill, [n.d.].

Copies inscribed by owners: NzD (1925). *Location:* NzD.

C 30.1.a

Memories of President Lincoln. Portland, Maine: Thomas B. Mosher, MDCCCCXII.

16 pp.; pp. 1–13 printed on rectos only. Printed on classic vellum. Vellum or paper dust jacket. Boxed. Introduction by Thomas B. Mosher. Printed September 1912. Published 20 September 1912. Copyright A327650; received, 1 November 1912. Limited to 10 numbered copies, signed by Mosher. *Locations:* NjP, TxU.

C 30.1.b

Portland, Maine: Thomas B. Mosher, MDCCCCXII.

Printed on Japan vellum. Vellum boards. Vellum or paper dust jacket. Limited to 50 numbered copies. *Locations:* NjP, RPB.

C 30.1.c

Portland, Maine: Thomas B. Mosher, MDCCCCXII.

Printed on Italian handmade paper. Boards. Dust jacket. Boxed. RPB copy received October 1912. Limited to 300 copies. *Locations:* NcD, RPB.

Note: The integral leaf with the statement of limitation has been reset for each printing.

C 31
The Rolling Earth. Boston and New York: Houghton Mifflin, 1912.

[223] pp. Dust jacket. Edited by Waldo R. Browne. Introduction by John Burroughs. Copyright A309562; received, 16 March 1912. Published 2 March 1912. Copies inscribed by owners: RPB (9 March 1912). Price, $1.00. *Locations:* JM, RPB.

C 32
Poems from Leaves of Grass. London: J. M. Dent & Sons; New York. E. P. Dutton, 1913.

260 pp. Cloth or half leather. Boxed. Illustrated by Margaret C. Cook. Dutton or Dent imprint on spine (see *Note one* below). Published October 1913. Deposit copies (all with Dent imprint on spine): BL ('20 OCT 13'), BC ('13 NO 1913'), BE ('13 NOV 1913'), BO ('17 11 1913'). Copies inscribed by owners: RPB (Dent; November 1913), TxU (Dutton; 25 December 1913). Prices: 21s. or $6.00. *Locations:* BC, BE, BL, BO, JM, PU, RPB, TxU.

Note one: Copies have Dent's imprint on the spine (BC, BE, BL, BO, JM, RPB) or Dutton's imprint on the spine (PU, TxU).

Note two: A four-page prospectus, with 10 plates, sent by Dent's Toronto office, is at RPB.

C 33.1.a
Leaves of Grass (Selected). London: Charles H. Kelly, [1914].

300 pp. Sheets bulk 15⁄16″. Dust jacket. Introduction by John Telford. *Every Age Library,* no. 20. Published July 1914. Deposit copies: BL ('27 JUL 14'), BC ('OC 13 1914'), BE ('13 OCT 1914'), BO ('13 10 1914'). Copies inscribed by owners: RPB (13 October 1914). Price, 10d. *Locations:* BC, BE, BL, BO, CtY, RPB.

Note: A copy in binding and dust jacket imprinted with 'SHARP' as publisher, priced at 1s.6d., is at JM.

C 33.1.b
London: Charles H. Kelly, [1914].

Sheets bulk 13⁄8″. Published September 1914. Deposit copies: BC ('FE 24 1915'), BE ('24 FEB 1915'). Price, 3s.6d. *Locations:* BC, BE, CSt.

C 34.1.a–d
Leaves of Grass. London: George G. Harrap, [1915].

263 pp. Dust jacket. *Harrap Library 19*. Published June 1915. Deposit copies: BL ('22 JUL 15'), BC ('MR 10 1916'), BE ('10 MAR 1916'), BO
('15MAR1916'). Price, 2s.6d. *Locations:* BC, BE, BL, BO, JM. Reprinted
with undated title page in April 1919. Copies inscribed by owners: JM (August 1919), RPB (2 December 1919). *Locations:* JM, RPB. Reprinted with
undated title page and London, Calcutta, Sydney imprint in May 1923. *Location:* JM. Reprinted with undated title page and London, Bombay, Sydney
imprint in July 1927. *Location:* JM.

C 35.1.a
Memories of President Lincoln. New York: Little Leather Library, [1916].

127 pp. Flexible leather. *Little Leather Library,* no. 42; or *Little Leather Library, Redcroft Edition;* or *Miniature Library*. Copies inscribed by owners:
RPB (*Leather,* 23 December 1916). *Locations: Little Leather Library:* RPB,
TxU; *Little Leather Library, Redcroft Edition:* JM, TxU; *Miniature Library:* DLC, RPB.

C 35.1.b
Chicago and Toronto: Shrewesbury, [n.d.].

Cloth or wrappers. *Locations:* JM, PU.

C 36.1.a₁
Sea Drift. New York: Hearst's International Library, [1916].

52 pp.; pp. 9–52 printed on rectos only. Leather over flexible boards. Unprinted glassine dust jacket. Boxed. Preface by George Goodchild. Printed by
Jarrold & Sons, London. *Miniature Classics*. Price, 75¢. *Locations:* NcD, ViU.

C 36.1.a₂
New York: Hearst's International Library, [n.d.].

Title leaf is a cancel. *Miniature Classics. Locations:* JM, TxU.

C 36.1.a₃
London: Jarrold & Sons, [1923].

Title leaf is a cancel. Cloth or cloth over flexible boards. Dust jacket. *Miniature
Classics*. Published September 1923. Copies inscribed by owners: RPB (February 1923). Advertised in cloth for 2s.; "leatherine," 2s.6d.; crushed morocco
and velvet calf, 5s. *Locations:* CtY, RPB.

C 37.1.a
Leaves of Grass. Garden City, N.Y.: Doubleday, Page, MCMXVII.

294, 323, 255 pp. Combined in three-volumes-in-one format. From the plates of *Complete Writings* (B 4). Cloth or leather. Dust jacket. Edited by Richard Maurice Bucke, Thomas B. Harned, and Horace L. Traubel. *Authorized Edition*. Also advertised as "Centenary Edition." Reviewed in *Conservator*, 28 (October 1917), 125. Copies inscribed by owners: NjP (29 October 1917). Prices: cloth, $1.25; leather, $3.00. *Locations:* NjP, JM.

Note: According to a note by Thomas Harned in a copy sent him by the publisher, "This book is issued for the purpose of driving the McKay (incomplete) Edition off the market" (NjP).

C 37.1.b₁
Garden City, N.Y.: Doubleday, Page, MCMXIX.

Copies inscribed by owners: JM (21 November 1919). *Location:* JM.

C 37.1.b₂
New York and London: D. Appleton, [1919].

Title leaf is integral. Cloth or half leather. *Centenary Edition*. Deposit copy: BL ('21JUN23'). Listed in the *English Catalogue* for November 1919 at 12s.6d. as an importation by Appleton. *Locations:* BL, BMR, JM (2).

C 37.1.c–e
Garden City, N.Y.: Doubleday, Page, MCMXX.

Reprinted MCMXXIII, MCMXXIV. *Locations:* JM (1920, 1924), NjCW (1923).

C 38.1.a–b
The Patriotic Poems of Walt Whitman. Garden City, N.Y.: Doubleday, Page, 1918.

194 pp. Cloth or leather over flexible boards. Published 22 March 1918. Reviewed in *New York Herald*, 20 April 1918, sec. 2, p. 10. Copyright A499449; received, 28 March 1918; renewed, 28 February 1946; R2372. Deposit copies: DLC ('MAR 28 1918'). Prices: cloth, $1.25; leather, $1.75. *Locations:* DLC, JM. Reprinted with Garden City and Toronto imprint in 1921. *Location:* NjCW.

Note: A salesman's dummy copy is at RPB.

C 39
Poems of Walt Whitman. [Boston: Old South Association, 1918].

16 pp. Head title. *Old South Leaflets,* no. 216. Advertised as in "General Series," vol. 9. Price, 5¢. *Locations:* RPB, TxU.

C 40.1.a
Leaves of Grass. Portland, Maine: Thomas Bird Mosher, William Francis
Gable, MDCCCCXIX.

[15], xii, 95 pp. Type facsimile of the 1855 edition. Printed on Japan vellum.
Vellum-covered boards goldstamped in partial facsimile of binding A of the
1855 edition. Dust jacket. Boxed. Contains facsimile of wrapper of 1855 edition on vellum. Introduction by Thomas Bird Mosher. Copyright A561097;
received, 22 December 1919. Published 19 December 1919. Price, $20.00.
According to a facsimile of a typed letter of 19 December 1919, distributed by
Mosher, he had been "badly delayed in getting out" this edition, "but at last it is
ready" (JM, RPB). Limited to 50 numbered copies, signed by Mosher. *Locations:* NcU, RPB.

Note one: An "Addenda" sheet, dated 14 July 1920, with information on the
pink and green wrappers of the 1855 edition and the sale of Moncure Daniel
Conway's copy of *Leaves of Grass,* along with a sheet with a facsimile of
Whitman's copy of Emerson's letter to him, is at RPB.

C 40.1.b
Portland, Maine: Thomas Bird Mosher, William Francis Gable, MDCCCCXIX.

Printed on Van Gelder handmade paper. Boards goldstamped in partial facsimile of binding A of the 1855 edition. Dust jacket. Contains facsimile of wrapper
of 1855 edition on white paper. Limited to 100 numbered copies. *Locations:* JM, RPB.

C 40.1.c
Portland, Maine: Thomas Bird Mosher, William Francis Gable, MDCCCCXIX.

Printed on Old Stratford wove paper. Green cloth in facsimile of binding A of
the 1855 edition. Dust jacket. Boxed. Contains facsimile of wrapper of 1855
edition on blue paper. Deposit copies: DLC ('DEC 22 1919'; 2 copies). Limited
to 250 copies. Price, $6.00. *Locations:* DLC (2), JM.

Note: The integral leaf with the statement of limitation has been reset in
each printing.

C 40.1.d
Portland, Maine: Thomas Bird Mosher, William Francis Gable, MDCCCCXX.

[16], xii, 95 pp. Printed on Old Stratford wove paper. Green cloth in facsimile of Binding A of the 1855 edition. Dust jacket. Contains facsimile of wrapper of 1855 edition on green paper. Deposit copies: BL ('5 JA 1921'). Copies inscribed by owners: NcD (11 August 1920). Limited to 500 copies. Price, $7.50. *Locations:* BL, JM, NcD.

Note: The integral leaf with the statement of limitation for the last two printings has been reset in each printing.

C41
Songs of Democracy. Philadelphia: David McKay, [1919].

186 pp. Dust jacket. Introduction by B. M. Copies inscribed by owners: RPB (January 1923). Price, $1.25. *Locations:* JM, RPB.

C42.1.a–g
Whitman's Poetical Works. Tokyo: Keiseisha, [1919].

64 pp. Wrappers. Selected by T. Arishima. Copies inscribed by owners: RPB (6 April 1923). *Location:* RPB. Latest reprinting is the seventh printing of [1922]. *Location:* JM.

C43.1.a–c
Leaves of Grass. London [&c]: Humphrey Milford, Oxford University Press, [1920].

392 pp. See *Note one* below for bindings. Dust jacket. Edited with an introduction by Ernest de Sélincourt. Simultaneously in *World's Classics*, CCXVIII, and *Pocket Edition*. Deposit copies: BL ('20 AUG 20'). DLC copy (rebound) received 2 December 1921. *Locations:* BL, BMR, JM, RPB (2), TxU. Reprinted with undated title pages in *World's Classics* in 1923; with London imprint only in 1929. *Locations:* JM (1923), NcD (1929).

Note one: Advertised as in "Pocket Edition" in limp cloth, limp sultan-red leather, Italian thin boards, and quarter vellum; and as in "Ordinary Edition" in cloth, limp sultan-red leather, limp lambskin, quarter vellum, half calf, whole calf, and tree calf.

Note two: Copies of the first printing have Milford's imprint on the spine (BMR, RPB, TxU) or the Oxford University Press imprint on the spine (JM, RPB).

C43.1.d
London: Oxford University Press, [1933].

Listed in the *English Catalogue* in *World's Classics* for October 1933 at 2s.6d. *Not seen.*

C 44
Twenty-Three Poems. London: Athenæum Literature Department, [1920].

52 pp. Wrappers. Edited by Gwen Williams. *Westminster Classics III*. Published September 1920. Deposit copies: BC ('JA29 1921'), BL ('29 JAN 21'), BO ('29.JAN.1921'), BE ('29 JAN 1921'). Copies inscribed by owners: RPB (29 March 1921). Price, 1s. *Locations:* BC, BE, BL, BO, NNC, RPB.

C 45.1.a–b
Leaves of Grass. New York: Boni and Liveright, [1921].

311 pp. Flexible cloth-covered boards. Dust jacket. Introduction by Carl Sandburg. *Modern Library* 97. Price, 95¢. *Location:* CtY. Undated reprinting as *Poems* in *Modern Library of the World's Best Books* 97. *Locations:* BL, JM, TxU.

C 45.1.c$_1$
Leaves of Grass. New York: Modern Library, [1921].

Flexible cloth-covered boards. Dust jacket. *Modern Library* 97. *Locations:* JM, PU. Undated reprinting as *Poems* in *Modern Library of the World's Best Books* 97. *Locations:* JM, TxU.

Note: Multiple undated reprintings.

C 45.1.c$_2$
Leaves of Grass. London: Hamish Hamilton, [1936].

Title leaf is a cancel; pp. [313–317], containing advertisements for books in the *Modern Library,* are canceled. Cloth-covered flexible boards. Dust jacket. *Modern Library*. Published December 1936. Deposit copies: BL ('3 FEB 37'), BO ('JUL 22 1937'), BC ('20 JY 1937'), BE ('22 JUL 1937'). Price, 3s.6d. *Locations:* BC, BE, BL, BO.

C 45.1.d
Leaves of Grass. New York: Carlton House, [n.d.].

Advertised as in "World's Greatest Literature" series. *Location:* NcD.

C 46.1.a
Walt Whitman's Poems. Girard, Kansas: Appeal to Reason, [1921].

92 pp. Wrappers or cover title. 'FIRST EDITION' is present on title page. *People's Pocket Series No. 73*. Price, 25¢. *Locations:* CSt, TxU.

C 46.1.b
Girard, Kansas: Appeal to Reason, [1921].

Wrappers. 'FIRST EDITION' is not present on title page. *People's Pocket Series No. 73*. DLC copy received 16 January 1924. Copies inscribed by owners: RPB (20 May 1921), NzD (10 June 1921). *Locations:* DLC, NzD, RPB.

C 46.2.a
Girard, Kansas: Appeal Publishing, [1922?].

90 pp. Wrappers (with Haldeman-Julius listed as publisher). *People's Pocket Series No. 73* on title page and *Ten Cent Pocket Series No. 73* on wrappers. *Location:* JM.

Note: "A Woman Waits for Me" (pp. 17–19) has been omitted.

C 46.2.b
Girard, Kansas: Haldeman-Julius, [1922].

Wrappers. *Ten Cent Pocket Series No. 73*. *Locations:* CtY, JM.

C 46.2.c
Girard, Kansas: Haldeman-Julius, [1923].

Wrappers. *Pocket Series No. 73*. *Location:* RPB.

C 46.3.a
Poems of Walt Whitman. Girard, Kansas: Haldeman-Julius, [1924].

96 pp. Wrappers. Edited with an introduction and notes by Nelson Antrim Crawford. *Little Blue Book No. 73*. Copyright A812392; received, 21 November 1924; renewed, 19 June 1952; R96428. Published 13 November 1924. *Locations:* JM, TxU.

C 46.3.b
Girard, Kansas: Haldeman-Julius, [1924].

Cover title (on different paper from the text). *Little Blue Book No. 73*. *Location:* TxU.

C 46.4
Best Poems of Walt Whitman. Girard, Kansas: Haldeman-Julius, [n.d.].

64 pp. Wrappers. *Little Blue Book No. 73*. *Location:* BMR.

C 47.1.a–d
Leaves of Grass (1850–1881). New York, Chicago, Boston: Charles Scribner's Sons, [1922].

504 pp. Dust jacket. Introduction by Stuart P. Sherman. Publisher's code 'A' on copyright page. *Modern Student's Library; or Modern Student's Library, American Division*. Published 27 January 1922. Copyright A654456; received, 31 January 1922. Copies inscribed by owners: RPB (21 February 1922). Price, $1.00. Listed in *CBI* as distributed in England by L. B. Hill at 1s. *Locations: Modern Student's Library:* RPB; *Modern Student's Library, American Division:* DLC, JM. Reprinted in both series with undated title pages in November 1929 (copyright page: 'B'), August 1931 ('C'), July 1936 ('D'). *Locations: Modern Student's Library:* JM ('D'), CSt ('D'); *Modern Student's Library, American Division:* DLC ('B'), NcD ('D').

Note: Rebound and sold in cloth by Darby Books (without their imprint or other information) for $40.00. *Location:* ScU (copyright page: 'D').

C 48.1.a
Prose Nature Notes. Girard, Kansas: Haldeman-Julius, [1922].

62 pp. Wrappers. *Ten Cent Pocket Series No. 299.* Copies inscribed by owners: RPB (25 September 1922). Price, 10¢. *Locations:* JM, RPB.

C 48.1.b
Girard, Kansas: Haldeman-Julius, [n.d.].

Wrappers. *Little Blue Book No. 299. Location:* NcD.

C 49.1.a
Memories of Lincoln. Girard, Kansas: Haldeman-Julius, [1923].

61 pp.; text on pp. 1–53. Wrappers. Forewords by Horace Traubel and John Burroughs. *Ten Cent Pocket Series No. 351.* DLC copy received 19 January 1924. *Locations:* DLC, PU.

C 49.1.b
Girard, Kansas: Haldeman-Julius, [n.d.].

Wrappers. *Ten Cent Pocket Series No. 351* on title page and *Little Blue Book No. 351* on wrappers. *Locations:* JM, PU.

C 50.1.a₁
Leaves of Grass. Garden City, N.Y.: Doubleday, Page, 1924.

728 pp. Page size 7⅝″×5⅛″. Cloth; or cloth- or leather-covered flexible boards. Dust jacket. Edited by Emory Holloway. *Inclusive Edition.* Published 28 November 1924. Reviewed in *Sun* (New York), 28 March 1925, p. 7. Copyright A814491; received, 2 January 1925; renewed, 30 November 1951; R86749.

Presentation copies: DLC (from Holloway, 4 December 1924). Prices: cloth, $3.00; leather, $5.00. *Locations:* DLC, NjCW, PU.

Note: A copy at CtY in boards with cloth shelfback, with sheets measuring 8¹⁄₁₆″×5½″, has a note that "this book is one of two large paper (uncut) copies published."

C 50.1.a$_2$
London: William Heinemann, 1924.

Title leaf is a cancel. Cloth-covered flexible boards. *Inclusive Edition.* Deposit copy: BL ('8 DEC24'). *Locations:* BL, JM.

C 50.1.b–d
Garden City, N.Y.: Doubleday, Page, 1925.

Reprinted in 1926, 1927. *Locations:* JM (all).

C 50.1.e–j
Garden City, N.Y.: Doubleday, Doran, 1928.

Reprinted in 1929, 1931, 1942, 1943, 1945. *Locations:* JM (1928, 1929, 1931), CSt (1942), PU (1943, 1945).

C 50.1.k–l
Garden City, N.Y.: Doubleday, 1946.

Reprinted in 1948. *Locations:* NcD (1946), ScU (1948).

C 51.1.a$_1$
Gerald Bullett. *Walt Whitman A Study and a Selection.* London: Grant Richards, 1924.

166 pp. Boards. Dust jacket. Printed at the Curwen Press. Reviewed in *New Statesman,* 24 (17 January 1925), 420–421. Deposit copies: BL ('4 DEC 24'), BE ('10 FEB 1925'). Copies inscribed by owners: RPB (26 January 1925). Limited to 750 copies for sale in England. Price, 15s. *Locations:* BE, BL, CtY, JM.

C 51.1.a$_2$
Philadelphia: J. B. Lippincott, 1925.

Title leaf is integral. Boards. Dust jacket. Presentation copies: NjCW (from the publisher, 26 March 1925). Limited to 780 numbered copies for sale in the United States. Price, $7.50. *Locations:* JM, NjCW.

C 51.1.b
[Folcroft, Penn.]: Folcroft Library Editions, 1976.

Facsimile reprinting of the second (Lippincott) issue. Deposit copies: DLC for
CIP ('DEC 22 76'). Limited to 100 copies. Price, $20.00. *Location:* DLC.

C 52.1.a–b
Leaves of Grass. Garden City, N.Y.: Doubleday, Page, 1926.

421 pp. Dust jacket. Edited with an introduction by Emory Holloway. Simultaneously in *Abridged Edition* and *Popular Authorized Edition*. Published 8
October 1926. Reviewed in *Saturday Review of Literature,* 3 (16 October
1926), 195. Copyright A967063; received, 1 November 1926. Deposit copies:
DLC ('NOV –1 1926'). Presentation copies: ViU (from Holloway, 4 November
1926). Copies inscribed by owners: TxU (October 1926). Price, $1.25. *Loca-
tions:* DLC, MBU, TxU, ViU. Reprinted 1927. *Location:* JM.

C 53
Two Prefaces. Garden City, N.Y.: Doubleday, Page, 1926.

67 pp. Dust jacket. Introduction by Christopher Morley. Reviewed in *Sewanee
Review,* 35 (January 1927), 124–125. Copyright A891799; received, 29 April
1926; renewed, 4 January 1954; R123576. Published 9 April 1926. Deposit
copies: DLC ('APR29'26'). Copies inscribed by owners: RPB (April 1926).
Price, $1.00. *Locations:* BL, DLC, JM, RPB.

Note: A set of unbound and unsewn sheets, lacking the title leaf, from
Chrisopher Morley's library, is at TxU.

C 54
Walt Whitman. London: Ernest Benn, [1926].

30 pp. Cover title. *Augustan Books of Modern Poetry*. Published February
1926. Deposit copies: BL ('19 MAR 26'), BC ('8AP 1926'), BE ('12 APR 1926').
Copies inscribed by owners: PU (December 1926). Price, 6d. *Locations:* BC,
BE, BL, JM, PU.

C 55
Walt Whitman. New York: Simon & Schuster, [1926].

31 pp. Cover title. Edited with an introduction by Louis Untermeyer. *Pamphlet
Poets*. RPB copy received 25 January 1927. Price, 25¢. *Locations:* JM, RPB.

C 56.1.a–b
Selections from Whitman. New York: Macmillan, 1927.

282 pp. Edited with an introduction by Zada Thornsburgh. *Macmillan Pocket Classics*. Copyright A972145; received, 23 March 1927. Published 22 March 1927. Deposit copies: DLC ('MAR23'27'), BL ('5 JUL 27'). Copies inscribed by owners: RPB (22 May 1927). Price, 48¢. Listed in the *English Catalogue* for June 1927 at 2s. *Locations:* BL, DLC, RPB. Reprinted in 1928. *Location:* JM.

C 57.1.a–d
Leaves of Grass. New York: Macmillan, MCMXXVIII.

505 pp. Cloth or half leather. Dust jacket. Edited with an introduction by John Valente. *Modern Readers' Series*. Published 13 November 1928. Copyright A616; received, 14 November 1928. Deposit copies: BL ('8 MAR 29'). Copies inscribed by owners: RPB (21 January 1929). Prices: cloth, 80¢; leather, $1.25. Listed in the *English Catalogue* for January 1929 at 5s. *Locations:* BL, RPB. Reprinted in MCMXXIX (November), MCMXXXI (August), MCMXXXVI (July). *Locations:* JM (1929), NjCW (1931), NcD (1936).

C 58.1.a
Rivulets of Prose. New York: Greenberg, MCMXXVIII.

226 pp. Unprinted glassine dust jacket. Boxed. Edited with an introduction by Carolyn Wells and Alfred F. Goldsmith. Deposit copies: DLC ('FEB 23 '28'). Presentation copies: MBU (from Goldsmith, 24 October 1928). Limited to 499 numbered copies. Price, $5.00. *Locations:* DLC, JM, MBU.

C 58.1.b
Freeport, N.Y.: Books for Libraries Press, [1969].

Essay Index Reprint Series. DLC copy received from the publisher 18 June 1969. Price, $8.75. *Locations:* DLC, ScU.

C 59
Leaves of Grass. New York: Limited Editions Club, 1929.

154 pp. Unprinted dust jacket. Boxed. Introduction by Carolyn Wells. Printed by William Edwin Rudge. Published 20 November 1929. Reviewed in *Bookman* (New York), 69 (May 1930), 327–328. Copyright 12 March 1930; A20234; renewed, 22 August 1957; R197953. Deposit copies: DLC ('MAR 12 1930'). The copy at NN-R has a presentation letter from the publisher, dated 26 November 1929, laid in, and "Office Copy" written on the limitation page instead of a number. Limited to 1,500 numbered copies, signed by the designer, Frederic Warde. Price, $10.00. *Locations:* BL, DLC, JM, NN-R.

C 60.1.a
Leaves of Grass. New York: Random House, 1930.

423 pp. Wood covers with leather shelfback. Boxed. Edited by Oscar Lewis (uncredited). Illustrated by Valenti Angelo. Printed by Edwin and Robert Grabhorn, San Francisco. NN-R copy received 1 December 1930. Limited to 400 numbered copies. Price, $100.00. *Locations:* BE, NN-R, NNC.

Note one: A copy at NNC, bound in full leather with "Out of Series" on the colophon page, has this note by Edwin Grabhorn: "This copy is for Bennett Cerf because I love him—sometimes."

Note two: Approximately 50 copies of loose text sheets were distributed in a specially printed wrapper "in remembrance of the dinner given by the Roxburghe Club of San Francisco to Frederic & Bertha Goudy October 5, 1931" (NN-R).

C 60.1.b
New York: Modern Library, [1940].

Dust jacket. No series identification; or *Modern Library;* or *Modern Library Giant G50*. Published February 1940. Deposit copy: BL ('2 JUL 48'). DLC copy received 9 April 1940. Price, $1.25. Listed in *CBI* as distributed in Canada by Macmillan at $1.49. *Locations:* BL, DLC, JM.

Note: Multiple undated reprintings.

C 60.1.c
Secaucus, N.J.: Longriver Press, [1976].

Leatherette. No illustrations. *Location:* JM.

C 60.1.d
A Facsimile Page from the Grabhorn Edition of The Leaves of Grass. [Kingston]: University of Rhode Island, 1977.

Unpaged (4 leaves); facsimile on p. 3. Wrappers. Limited to 100 numbered copies. *Location:* RPB.

C 61
One Precious Leaf from the First Edition   Leaves of Grass. By Walt Whitman. New York: [Bennett Book Studios], 1930.

Unpaged (8 leaves). Full leather. Boxed. Also contains "Walt Whitman's Monuments" by Guido Bruno, with text printed on rectos only. Limited to 47 numbered copies. *Locations:* NcD, RPB.

C 62.1.a–b
Leaves of Grass. New York: Aventine, [1931].

580 pp. Dust jacket. Boxed. *Aventine Classics,* no. 2. Colophon reads, 'THIS . . . J. J. LITTLE AND IVES COMPANY. THE BOOK IS SET | IN ESTIENNE TYPE, AND PRINTED ON AVENTINE PAPER' (p. [582]). DLC copy received 29 July 1932. Copies inscribed by owners: PU (February 1933). Price, $5.00. *Locations:* DLC, JM, PU. Reprinted with undated title page and colophon reading 'THIS . . . J. J. LITTLE AND IVES COMPANY'. Copies inscribed by owners: CtY (13 May 1936), NjCW (25 December 1936). *Locations:* BMR, CtY, JM, NjCW.

Note: Dust jackets have the imprint of the Aventine Press at the foot of the spine (CtY, JM, PU) or that of the Tudor Publishing Company at the foot of the spine (JM). The latter company apparently distributed this book after 1932.

C 63.1.a–b
Leaves of Grass. New York: Grosset & Dunlap, [1931].

537 pp. Dust jacket. *Universal Library.* Copies inscribed by owners: MB (2 October 1931). Price, $1.00. Undated reprinting in flexible leather, not in *Universal Library* series. *Locations:* MB (1931), JM (both).

C 63.1.c
[New York]: Literary Guild of America, [n.d.].

Introduction by Carl Van Doren. *Guild Classics. Locations:* NjP, RPB.

C 63.1.d
New York: Lowell Press, [n.d.].

World's Literary Masterpieces. Binding stamped 'SURREY PRESS' at foot of spine. *Locations:* JM, RPB.

C 63.1.e
New York: Harper & Brothers, [1950].

537 pp. Dust jacket. Introduction by Oscar Cargill. Publisher's code 'A-Z' on the copyright page, indicating January 1950 publication date. Copyright 15 February 1950; A41038. *Harper's Modern Classics.* Price, 95¢. *Locations:* MB, RPB.

C 64
Leaves of Grass. New York: Thomas Y. Crowell, [1933].

308 pp. Dust jacket. Boxed. Selected and illustrated by Charles Cullen. Introduction by Sherwood Anderson. Published 5 October 1933. Copyright A65567; received, 11 October 1933. Deposit copies: DLC (rebound) ('OCT 11 1933').

Presentation copies: TxU (from Cullen, 10 October 1933). Price, $3.50. *Locations:* JM, TxU.

C 65.1.a₁

Walt Whitman Representative Selections. New York [&c]: American Book Company, [1934].

426 pp. Edited with an introduction by Floyd Stovall. *American Writers Series.* Publisher's code on the copyright page: 'W. P. I.'. Copyright A70497; received, 3 March 1934. Published 28 February 1934. Deposit copies: DLC ('MAR–31934'), BL ('7 MAR 34'). Inscribed copies: CSt (November 1934). Price, $1.50. *Locations:* BL, CSt, DLC, JM.

C 65.1.a₂

New York [&c]: American Book Company, [1934].

'D. APPLETON–CENTURY COMPANY | Incorporated.' is stamped in red on the title page. Deposit copies: BC ('12 MR 1934'), BO ('MAR 14 1934'), BE ('15 MAR 1934'). *Locations:* BC, BE, BO.

C 65.2.a–f₁

New York [&c]: American Book Company, [1939].

lxvi, 480 pp. Edited with an introduction by Floyd Stovall. *American Writers Series.* Publisher's code on the copyright page: 'W. P. 2'. Copyright A134675; received, 8 December 1939. Published 30 November 1939. Deposit copies: DLC ('DEC –8 1939'). Price, $1.60. *Location:* DLC. Reprinted with undated title pages and copyright page readings of 'E. P. 2', 'E. P. 3', 'E. P. 4'. *Locations:* ViU (E. P. 2), JM (E. P. 3, E. P. 4).

C 65.2.f₂

[Folcroft, Penn.]: Folcroft Library Editions, 1970.

American Book Company sheets (E. P. 4) with Folcroft title leaf inserted. *Location:* NcDaD.

C 65.2.g

New York: Hill and Wang, [1961].

Wrappers. *American Century Series ACW42.* Copyright 24 October 1961; A530312. Published October 1961. DLC copy received from the publisher 31 October 1961. Price, $1.75. Listed in *CBI* as distributed in Canada by Copp for $2.15. *Locations:* DLC, JM. Reprinted with undated title page in wrappers in December 1966. *Location:* JM.

Note: A copy of the 1961 Hill and Wang sheets in a casing from Peter Smith, Gloucester, Mass., is at MB.

C 66
Leaves of Grass. Moscow: Co-operative Publishing Society of Foreign Workers in the U.S.S.R., 1936.

558 pp. Preface by D. S. Mirsky. *Library of English Classics.* 2,500 copies printed August 1936. *Location:* PU.

C 67.1.a$_1$
Leaves of Grass. New York: Heritage Press; London: Nonesuch Press, [1936].

527 pp. Edited by Emory Holloway. Illustrated by Rockwell Kent. Full leather. Boxed. Unprinted glassine dust jacket. Printed at the Lakeside Press. Limited to 1,000 copies signed by Kent. Statement of limitation on a single leaf tipped in at the back. NNC copy dated by Kent 16 October 1936. Price, $8.50. *Locations:* JM, NNC.

C 67.1.a$_2$
New York: Heritage Press; London: Nonesuch Press, [1936].

Boxed. Unprinted glassine dust jacket. Deposit copies: DLC ('DEC 16 1936'). Copies inscribed by owners: JM (25 December 1936). Price, $3.75. *Locations:* DLC, JM.

Note: A four-page flier (*Sandglass* 11n) is at JM and TxU.

C 67.1.b
New York: For the Members of the Heritage Club, [1937].

Boxed. *Location:* JM.

Note: A four-page flier (*Sandglass* 2A) is at JM.

C 67.1.c
New York: Heritage Reprints, [1943].

Cloth (with dust jacket) or full leather or half leather (with unprinted glassine dust jacket). Boxed. *Heritage Reprints.* Listed in *CBI* as distributed in Canada by Ambassador Books at $2.95. *Locations:* JM, TxU, ViU.

C 67.1.d
New York: Heritage Press, [1950].

Cloth or three-quarter leather. Boxed. MB copy received 24 May 1950. *Locations:* JM, MB.

Note: A four-page flier (*Sandglass* 6cx) is at JM.

C 67.1.e
Avon, Conn.: Heritage Press, [n.d.].

Boxed. *Location:* TxU.

C 67.1.f–g
Norwalk, Conn.: Easton Press, [1977].

Full leather. *100 Greatest Books Ever Written. Location:* JM. Reprinted in full leather with undated title page in *Greatest Books Ever Written* in 1977. *Location:* JM.

C 68.1.a–b
Complete Poetry & Selected Prose and Letters. London: Nonesuch Press, [1938].

1116 pp. Dust jacket. Edited with an introduction by Emory Holloway. *Nonesuch Library.* Copyright page: '*First edition March 1938*'. Published 31 March 1938. Deposit copies: BL ('4 APR 38'). Presentation copies: NN-R (from Holloway, 20 April 1939). Prices: 18s. or $3.50. Listed in *CBI* as distributed in England by Faber and Faber, and in Canada by Macmillan at $4.00. *Locations:* BL, JM, NN-R. Reprinted with undated title page and without first edition information on copyright page in 1938. Deposit copies: BE ('11 APR 1938'). NN-R copy received 31 March 1938. *Locations:* BE, BMR, NN-R.

Note: First publication of a number of letters.

C 68.1.c–d
London: Nonesuch Press; New York: Random House, [1938].

Published 12 July 1938. Dust jacket. *Random House One-Volume Series,* no. 16. Price, $3.50. *Location:* RPB. Undated reprinting. *Location:* JM.

C 68.1.e–k
London: Nonesuch Press, 1942.

Reprinted in 1944, 1947, 1949, 1964, 1967, 1971. *Locations:* MH (1964), CaOTU (1967), NcCuW (1971).

C 69
Leaves of Grass. New York: Columbia University Press for the Facsimile Text Society, M • CM • XXXIX.

95 pp. Facsimile reprinting of the 1855 edition. Unprinted dust jacket. Introduction by Clifton Joseph Furness. *Facsimile Text Society Publication No. 47.* Published 6 March 1939. Copyright A126319; received, 7 March 1939. De-

posit copies: DLC ('MAR −7 1939'). Presentation copies: RPB (from Furness, 28 February 1939). Price, $2.00. *Locations:* DLC, JM, RPB.

C 70
Leaves of Grass. Garden City, N.Y.: Doubleday, Doran, MCMXL.

[317] pp. Cloth or burlap. Boxed. Edited with an introduction by Christopher Morley. Illustrated by Lewis C. Daniel. Published 21 June 1940. Copyright A143637; 9 July 1940; renewed, 3 April 1968; R433077. Deposit copies: DLC (rebound) ('JUL −9 1940'). Presentation copies: DLC (from Daniel, July 1940), NN-R (from Daniel, July 1940). Price, $5.00. *Locations:* BL, DLC, JM, MBU (2), NN-R.

C 71.1.a
Leaves of Grass The Collected Poems of Walt Whitman. Garden City, N.Y.: Blue Ribbon Books, [1942].

505 pp. Cloth or leather. Edited by Emory Holloway. *Blue Ribbon Books.* Prices: cloth, $1.00; leather, $1.98. *Location:* GAE.

C 71.1.b
Leaves of Grass. Garden City, N.Y.: Halcyon House, 1942.

Leather-covered flexible boards. Boxed. *Blue Ribbon Books. Location:* NjCW.

C 71.1.c
New York: Book League of America, [1942].

Blue Ribbon Books. MB copy received 14 January 1943. *Locations:* JM, MB.

C 72.1.a
Leaves of Grass. New York: Limited Editions Club, 1942.

2 vols.: 123, 124–274 pp. Illustrated boards. Unprinted glassine dust jacket. Boxed. Introduction by Mark Van Doren. Photographs by Edward Weston. Published 25 November 1942. Copyright A169532; received, 12 December 1942; renewed, 18 November 1970; R495018. Deposit copies: DLC ('DEC 12 1942'). Limitation not specified in book; according to Ralph Geoffrey Newman and Glen Norman Wiche, *Great and Good Books: A Bibliographical Catalogue of The Limited Editions Club, 1929–1985* (Chicago: Ralph Geoffrey Newman, 1989), it was limited to 1,500 copies (item 141), signed and numbered by Weston. Price, $10.00. *Locations:* BL, DLC, NcD.

Note: The deposit copy at DLC has at the end of the colophon statement in vol. 2, after 'THIS COPY, WHICH IS NUMBER', the following embossed statement: 'THIS IS ONE OF 15 PRESENTATION COPIES OUT OF SERIES'.

C 72.1.b
[New York]: Paddington Press/Two Continents Publishing Group, [1976].

Combined in two-volumes-in-one format. Dust jacket. Introductions by Richard Ehrlich and Mark Van Doren. Copyright 28 April 1976; A779068. Deposit copies: DLC ('AUG –4 1976' but received 24 November 1975), BL ('5 MAY 76'), BO ('–3JUN1976'), BE ('24 JN 76'). Price, $19.95. *Locations:* BE, BL, BO, DLC, JM.

C 73
Leaves of Grass. Cleveland and New York: World, [1942].

303 pp. Dust jacket. Illustrated by S. Witkewitz. *Illustrated Editions E-18.* Published 6 April 1942. Copyright A163532; received, 13 April 1942. Deposit copies: DLC ('APR 13 1942'). Price, 59¢. *Locations:* DLC, JM.

C 74
The Selected Poems of Walt Whitman. New York: Published for the Classics Club by Walter J. Black, [1942].

357 pp. Introduction by Gordon S. Haight. *Classics Club Library.* Published 29 May 1942. Copyright A165071; received, 22 June 1942; renewed, 10 July 1969; R65090. Deposit copies: DLC ('JUN 22 1942'). Prices: 89¢; de luxe edition, $1.39. *Locations:* DLC, JM.

C 75.1.a–b
Leaves of Grass. New York: Penguin, [1943].

314 pp. Wrappers. *Penguin Books 523.* Published August 1943. A copy at NN-R has a presentation letter from the publisher, dated 20 September 1943, laid in. Copies inscribed by owners: CtY (17 November 1943). *Locations:* CtY, JM, NN-R. Reprinted in wrappers with undated title page in March 1944. *Location:* JM.

C 76
Leaves of Grass. Mount Vernon, N.Y.: Peter Pauper, [1943].

397 pp. Boards. Boxed. Illustrated by John Steuart Curry. Copyright 205461. NN-R copy received 23 September 1943. *Locations:* NN-R, PU.

C 77.1.a
Leaves of Grass. [New York: A. S. Barnes, 1944].

410 pp. Boards. Boxed. Introduction by Carl Sandburg. Illustrated by Boardman Robinson. *Illustrated Modern Library.* Published 25 September 1944. Copyright A184014; received, 4 November 1944. Deposit copy: DLC ('NOV –

4 1944'). MB copy (rebound) received 14 October 1944. Price, $2.50. Listed in *CBI* as distributed in Canada by Random House. *Locations:* DLC, JM.

C 77.1.b
[New York: Random House, n.d.].

Cloth or boards (with printed plastic dust jacket). *Illustrated Modern Library.* Deposit copies: BL ('2 JUL 48'). Copies inscribed by owners: RPB (June 1945). *Locations:* BL, JM, RPB.

C 77.1.c
New York: Carlton House, [n.d.].

Dust jacket. *Carlton House Classics. Location:* RPB.

C 77.1.d
New York: Modern Library, [n.d.].

Modern Library 97. Locations: JM, ScU.

Note: Numerous undated reprintings.

C 78.1.a
Walt Whitman   Poet of American Democracy. New York: International Publishers, [1944].

175 pp. Dust jacket (with prices of $1.50 or $2.00). Edited with an introduction by Samuel Sillen. Reviewed in *Nation*, 160 (24 February 1945), 215–220. Copyright A186881; received, 19 January 1945; renewed, 20 December 1971; R519827. Published 7 August 1944. Deposit copies: DLC ('JAN 19 1945'). MH copy received 5 October 1944. Price, $2.00. Listed in *CBI* as distributed in Canada by Progress Books at $2.75. *Locations:* BMR, DLC, JM, MH.

C 78.1.b
New York: International Publishers, [1955].

176 pp. Cloth (with dust jacket) or wrappers. Copyright 18 March 1955; A178295. Deposit copies: cloth: DLC ('MAR 14 1955'). Copies inscribed by owners: wrappers: RPB (2 August 1955). Prices: cloth, $2.50; wrappers, $1.25. *Locations:* DLC, JM, RPB.

C 79
Leaves of Grass. New York: Alfred A. Knopf, 1945.

549 pp. Dust jacket. Preface by Bernard Smith. Typographic and binding designs by W. A. Dwiggins. *Borzoi Books.* Published 22 November 1945.

Copyright A19200; received, 26 October 1945; renewed, 22 January 1973; R544471. Reviewed in *New York Times Book Review,* 24 February 1946, pp. 1, 36. Deposit copies: DLC ('OCT 26 1945'). Price, $2.00. *Locations:* DLC, JM.

C 80.1.a–b
Walt Whitman. New York: Viking, MCMXLV.

698 pp. Dust jacket. Edited with an introduction and notes by Mark Van Doren. *Viking Portable Library,* no. 11. Copyright 9 July 1945; A188994; renewed, 14 July 1972; R532343. Published July 1945. Deposit copies: DLC ('JUN 23 1945'). Price, $2.00. Listed in *CBI* as distributed in Canada by Macmillan at $2.75. *Locations:* DLC, JM. Reprinted in cloth in MCMXLV (August). *Location:* JM.

C 80.1.c
The Indispensable Walt Whitman. New York: Book Society, 1950.

Boxed. *Location:* JM.

C 80.1.d–q
Walt Whitman. New York: Viking, MCMLIII.

Cloth. Reprinted in August 1953. *Viking Portable Library,* no. 11. *Location:* JM. Reprinted in wrappers with undated title pages in January 1955, July 1958, July 1959, [unlocated reprinting], July 1962, December 1963, May 1965, June 1966, December 1967, February 1969, November 1969, [unlocated reprinting], April 1972. *Locations:* JM (1955, 1958, 1959, 1962, 1965, 1966, 1967, February 1969, November 1969, 1972), NcU (1963).

C 80.2.a–d
Walt Whitman. New York: Viking, [1974].

648 pp. Cloth or wrappers. Edited with an introduction and notes by Mark Van Doren. Revised with an introduction by Malcolm Cowley. Chronology and bibliographical checklist by Gay Wilson Allen. *Viking Portable Library P78.* Copyright 30 December 1973; A594370. Deposit copies: cloth: DLC ('DEC 20 1974'). Prices: cloth, $6.95; paper, $2.95. *Locations:* DLC, JM (both). Reprinted in wrappers with undated title pages in 1975, July 1976, and in cloth with copyright page reading 'h g f e d c b a'. *Locations:* JM (1976, 'h').

C 80.2.e–p
The Portable Walt Whitman. [Harmondsworth, England, and New York]: Penguin, [1977].

Wrappers. *Viking Portable Library.* Deposit copies: BL ('23 AUG 77'), BO ('8SEP1977'), BE ('22 SE 77'). Prices: £1.95 or $4.95. *Locations:* BE, BL, BO. Reprinted in wrappers with undated title pages in 1978, 1979 (deposit copies: BE ['3 AU 79']), 1981, 1982, 1983, 1984, 1985, and with copyright page readings '11 13 15 14 12 10', '13 15 14'. *Locations:* JM (1978, 1984, 1985, '10', '13'), BE (1979), BL (1979).

C 81

A Wartime Whitman. New York: Editions for the Armed Services, [1945].

96 pp., double columns. Wrappers. Edited with an introduction by William A. Aiken. *Armed Services Edition S-1.* Inscribed copy: JM (19 July 1945). Not for sale. *Locations:* JM, NcU.

C 82

I Hear the People Singing   Selected Poems of Walt Whitman. New York: International Publishers, [1946].

96 pp. Dust jacket. Introduction by Langston Hughes. Illustrated by Alexander Dobkin. *Young World Books.* Reviewed in *New York Times Book Review,* 28 July 1946, p. 12. Copyright 15 June 1946; A9148. Deposit copies: DLC ('DEC 14 1946'). Price, $1.75. Listed in *CBI* as distributed in Canada by Progress Books at $2.50. *Locations:* DLC, JM.

C 83.1.a

Whitman: His Immortal Leaves. [Kent, Wash.: John Victor, 1946].

84 pp. Edited with an introduction by Linden Dalberg. Introduction on "The Dance: Foundation of the Creative Arts" by Ted Shawn. Illustrated with photographs of the Ted Shawn dancers. *John Victor "Classic Abridgement."* Printed label states this is limited to 500 copies, 350 of which are signed and numbered by Ted Shawn. *Location:* ABAU.

C 83.1.b

[Kent, Wash.: John Victor, 1948].

Dust jacket. *John Victor "Classic Abridgement."* Copyright 3 May 1948; A23532. Deposit copy: DLC ('JUN 7– 1948'). In some copies, a printed label states this is limited to 500 copies, 350 of which are signed and numbered by Ted Shawn (JM, RPB). Price, $2.50. *Locations:* DLC, JM (2), RPB.

Note: This is undoubtedly the same work as the *Athletic Democracy* (Kent, Wash.: J. Victor, n.d.) listed in *BIP* (1950), no copies of which have been located.

C 84

Choix des Textes. [Paris]: GLM, [1947].

69 pp. Wrappers. Translated by Hélène Bokanowski. *Choix de Poèmes*. English and French on facing pages. Published May 1947. DLC copy received 9 November 1948. Limited to 625 numbered copies: 1–170 on vellum; 171–600 on verge; A–Z (25) on vellum signed by the translator. *Locations:* DLC, NcD.

C 85.1.a–g

Leaves of Grass. London: J. M. Dent and Sons; New York: E. P. Dutton, [1947].

468 pp. Dust jacket. Edited with an introduction and notes by Emory Holloway. *Everyman's Library,* no. 573. Published March 1947. Deposit copies: BL ('3 MAR 47'), BC ('3OC 1947'), BO ('3 OCT 1947'), BE ('14 OCT 1947'). MH copy received 25 March 1948. Prices: 4s. or $1.45. *Locations:* BC, BE, BL, BO, JM. Reprinted with undated title pages in 1949, 1950, 1957, 1961, 1968, 1971. *Locations:* OClW (1949), JM (1950), BL (1957), MoSpS (1961), NzD (1968), LNHT (1971).

C 86

Leaves of Grass. Mount Vernon, N.Y.: Peter Pauper, [1949?].

[174] pp. Boards. Boxed. Illustrated by John Steuart Curry. NN-R copy received 7 October 1953. Price, $2.00. *Locations:* JM, NN-R.

C 87.1.a–j

Leaves of Grass and Selected Prose. New York and Toronto: Rinehart, [1949].

568 pp. Wrappers. Edited with an introduction by Sculley Bradley. *Rinehart Editions 28*. Copyright 4 November 1949; A38537; renewed, 12 October 1977; R674247. Deposit copies: DLC ('NOV 29 1949'). Price, 75¢. *Locations:* DLC, JM. Reprinted in wrappers with undated title pages in July 1951, February 1953, [two unlocated reprintings], April 1957, May 1958, June 1959, February 1960; an undated reprinting has a San Francisco: Rinehart Press imprint. *Locations:* JM (all).

Note: The sixth and later reprintings have 576 pp.

C 87.1.k–l

New York: Holt, Rinehart and Winston, [1960].

Wrappers. Printed December 1960. *Location:* JM. Reprinted in wrappers with undated title page in October 1962. *Location:* JM.

C 87.1.m–t

New York [&c]: Holt, Rinehart and Winston, [1964].

Wrappers. Printed January 1964. *Location:* CaOTU. Reprinted in wrappers with undated title pages in June 1965, May 1966. *Locations:* OYesA (1965), PEdiS (1966). Undated reprintings in wrappers with copyright page readings '*16 17 18 19*', '*90123 68 191817*', '*2345 065 252423222120*'. *Locations:* JM (all).

C 88

The Poetry and Prose of Walt Whitman. New York: Simon and Schuster, 1949.

1224 pp. Dust jacket. Edited with an introduction by Louis Untermeyer. *Inner Sanctum Library of Living Literature.* Reviewed in *New York Times Book Review,* 1 January 1950, p. 10. Copyright A40055; received, 5 December 1949. Published 5 December 1949. Presentation copies: CtY (from Untermeyer, 2 December 1949). NjP copy (rebound) received 16 December 1949. Price, $5.00. Listed in *CBI* as distributed at Canada by Musson. *Locations:* CtY, JM.

Note: Sets of stitched uncorrected proof in two volumes are at CtY and NNC.

C 89

Leaves of Grass. Mount Vernon, N.Y.: Peter Pauper, [1950].

400 pp. Boards. Boxed. Illustrated by Boyd Hanna. NN-R copy received 4 January 1951. Limited to 1,100 numbered copies. Price, $27.50. *Locations:* JM, NN-R.

C 90.1.a–w

Leaves of Grass and Selected Prose. New York: Modern Library, [1950].

769 pp. Cloth (with dust jacket) or wrappers. Edited with an introduction by John Kouwenhoven. Cloth: *Modern Library of the World's Best Books 97;* wrappers: *Modern Library College Editions T40.* Copyright 26 September 1950; A49304; renewed, 17 October 1977; R674413. Deposit copies: wrappers: DLC ('NOV −3 1950'). Prices: cloth, $1.25; wrappers, 65¢. *Locations:* DLC, JM. Undated reprintings in wrappers with copyright page readings 'D', 'W'. *Locations:* ScU ('D'), ViU ('W').

C 90.2.a–b

New York: Modern Library, [1981].

763 pp. Wrappers. Edited with an introduction by Lawrence Buell. Enlarged photofacsimile edition. *Modern Library College Editions.* Copyright page: '9 8

7 6 5 4 3 2 1'. Deposit copy: DLC ('SEP 23 1981'). Price, $4.95. *Locations:* DLC, JM. Undated reprinting in wrappers with copyright page reading '9 8 7 6 5 4 3 2'. *Location:* JM.

C91
Selected Poems. [London]: Grey Walls, [1950].

64 pp. Boards. Dust jacket. Edited with an introduction by Stephen Spender. *Crown Classics.* Deposit copies: BL ('28 FEB 50'), BC ('14MR 1950'), BO ('14 MAR 1950'), BE ('29 MAR 1950'). DLC copy received 21 December 1950. Price, 3s.6d. Listed in *BIP* as distributed by the British Book Centre for 95¢. *Locations:* BC, BE, BL, BO, DLC, JM.

C92
Choix de Poèmes. Paris: Aubier, Éditions Montaigne, [1951].

354 pp. Wrappers. Translated with a preface by Pierre Messiaen. English and French on facing pages. *Collection Bilingue des Classiques Étrangers.* Completed May 1951. *Location:* NcD.

C93
The Best of Whitman. New York: Ronald Press, [1953].

478 pp. Dust jacket. Edited with an introduction and notes by Harold W. Blodgett. Copyright 1 April 1953; A85259. Deposit copies: DLC ('APR −6 1953'), BO ('26MAY1955'). Price, $2.75. *Locations:* BO, DLC.

C94.1.a–b
Leaves of Grass. Garden City, N.Y.: Doubleday, 1954.

682 pp. Dust jacket. Edited by Emory Holloway. *Inclusive Edition.* NjP copy received 19 November 1954. Price: $3.95. *Locations:* NjP, TxU. Undated reprinting. *Location:* JM.

C95.1.a
Leaves of Grass. [New York]: New American Library, [1954].

430 pp. Wrappers. Introduction by Sculley Bradley. *Mentor Book Ms117.* Published September 1954. Deposit copies: DLC ('SEP 21 1954'), BL ('28 DEC 55'). Copyright 25 August 1954; A153499. Price, 50¢. Listed in the *English Catalogue* as an importation by Muller for 14 November 1955 at 3s.6d. *Locations:* BL, DLC, JM.

C95.1.b–d
[New York]: New American Library, [1958].

Wrappers. Introduction by Gay Wilson Allen. *Mentor Book MD117*. Copyright 25 August 1958; A358591. Deposit copies: DLC ('OCT 13 1958'). Published August 1958. *Location:* DLC. Reprinted in wrappers with undated title pages in September 1959 and as *A Signet Classic CT23* in May 1960. *Location:* JM (1960).

C95.1.e–l
New York and Toronto: New American Library; London: New English Library, [n.d.].

431 pp. (with bibliography added). Undated reprintings in wrappers: *Signet Classic CT23* (copyright page: 'NINTH PRINTING'), *Signet Classic CQ456* ('ELEVENTH PRINTING'). *Locations:* NcD (9th), JM (11th).

C95.1.m–r
New York and Scarborough, Ontario: New American Library; London: New English Library, [n.d.].

Undated reprintings in wrappers: *Signet Classic CQ456* (copyright page: 'THIRTEENTH PRINTING', 'FOURTEENTH PRINTING', '15 16 17 18 19 20 21 22 23'); *Signet Classic CW1042* ('17 18 19 20 21 22 23 24'). *Locations:* JM (all).

C95.1.s–w
New York and Scarborough, Ontario: New American Library; London: New English Library, [1980].

432 pp. (with bibliography, copyright 1980, added). *Signet Classic CJ1395* (copyright page: '19 20 21 22 23 24 25'). *Location:* JM. Undated reprintings in wrappers with New York and Scarborough imprint as *Signet Classic CE1702* (copyright page: '20 21 22 23 24 25', '22 23 24 25', '23 24 25 26 27 28 29 30 31'). *Locations:* MB (20th), JM (22d, 23d).

Note: Also listed in *BIP* (1974–1975) as *Signet Classic CY818;* in *BIP* (1979–1980) as *Signet Classic CE1228;* and in *BIP* (1981–1982) as *Signet Classic CE1537*. No copies have been located.

C96
Leaves of Grass. Mount Vernon, N.Y.: Peter Pauper, [1955].

374 pp. Boards. Boxed. Illustrated by John Steuart Curry. Deposit copies: BL ('2 MAR 56' and '5 DEC 57'). Price, $4.50. Listed in *CBI* as distributed in England by Mayflower and Vision at 35s. *Locations:* BL (2), JM, NNC.

C97.1.a
Walt Whitman's Poems. New York: New York University Press, 1955.

280 pp. Dust jacket. Edited with an introduction by Gay Wilson Allen and Charles T. Davis. Copyright 27 May 1955; A197404. Deposit copies: DLC ('MAY 27 1955'). Price, $3.75. *Locations:* DLC, JM.

C 97.1.b
New York: Grove; London: John Calder, [1959].

Wrappers. *Evergreen Book E–161.* Deposit copies: BL ('27 JAN 60'), BE ('2 NO 60'), BO ('5NOV1960'). Prices: $1.95 or 14s.6d. Listed in *CBI* as distributed in Canada by McClelland at $2.15. *Locations:* BE, BL, BO, JM, NjP.

C 97.1.c
New York: New York University Press, [1968].

Cloth or wrappers. Price, $2.95. *Locations:* JM (both).

C 98
The Whitman Reader. New York: Pocket Books, [1955].

507 pp. Wrappers. Edited with an introduction by Maxwell Geismar. *Cardinal Giant GC–25.* Printed January 1955; published March 1955. Copyright 15 February 1955; A178176. Deposit copies: DLC ('FEB 14 1955'), BO ('13SEP1957'). Price, 50¢. *Locations:* BE, BO, DLC, JM.

C 99.1.a
Fragments from Walt Whitman. New York: Kurt H. Volk, 1956.

91 pp. Boards. Boxed. Unprinted glassine dust jacket. Edited with a preface by John L. Davenport. CaOTP copy has a presentation letter from Davenport dated 26 December 1956. *Locations:* CaOTP, JM, NjCW.

C 99.1.b
New York: Kindle Press, 1958.

Printed by the Peter Pauper Press, Mt. Vernon, N.Y. *Locations:* CaOTU, LNHT.

C 99.1.c
Keys to Walt Whitman. Key Biscayne, Fla.: Kindle Press, 1979.

Locations: NjCW, RPB.

C 100
Over the Carnage Rose Prophetic a Voice   The American Civil War in Prose and Verse. Bussum, The Netherlands: Paul Brand, [1957].

164 pp. Wrappers. Edited with an introduction by Oakleigh Ross Bush. DLC copy received 24 June 1958. Presentation copy: DLC (from editor, 1957). Price, 90¢. *Locations:* BL, DLC, MBU.

C 101
Walt Whitman's Poems Song of Myself By Blue Ontario's Shore. Tokyo: Kenkyusha, [1957].

115 pp. Wrappers. Dust jacket. Edited with an introduction and notes by William L. Moore. *Kenkyusha Pocket English Series,* no. 149. MBU copy received February 1957. *Locations:* BL, MBU, PU.

C 102
Poetry and Prose. Berlin: Seven Seas, [1958].

[550] pp. Wrappers. Edited with an introduction by Abe Capek. Simultaneously in *Seven Seas Books 7* and *Panther Book 7.* Deposit copies: BC ('25FE 1961'), BO ('25FEB1961'), BE ('–6 MR 61'). ViU copy purchased 21 May 1958. *Locations:* BC, BE, BO, JM, ViU.

C 103
Complete Poetry and Selected Prose. Boston: Houghton Mifflin, [1959].

516 pp. Cloth or wrappers. Edited with an introduction by James E. Miller, Jr. *Riverside Editions A34.* Copyright 19 May 1959; A391587. Deposit copies: wrappers: BO ('15DEC1960'). Prices: cloth, $3.00; wrappers, $1.15. *Locations:* BO, CaOTP, JM (both).

Note: Multiple undated reprintings in wrappers.

C 104.1.a₁
Walt Whitman's Leaves of Grass The First (1855) Edition. New York: Viking, 1959.

145 pp. Boxed. Unprinted glassine dust jacket. Edited with an introduction by Malcolm Cowley. Published 29 December 1959. Limited to 475 copies specially bound as a Christmas remembrance for the friends of the Viking Press; information on leaf tipped in at front of book. *Locations:* NNC, ViU.

C 104.1.a₂
New York: Viking, 1959.

Dust jacket. Published 29 December 1959. Reviewed in *New York Times Book Review,* 28 February 1960, p. 42. Copyright 28 December 1959; A424622. Deposit copies: DLC ('JAN 11 1960'). DLC copy received from the publisher

16 December 1959. Price, $5.00. Listed in *CBI* as distributed in Canada by Macmillan at $5.75. *Locations:* DLC (2), JM.

C 104.1.b₁
New York: Viking, 1960.

Copyright page: '*Second printing 1960*'. ViU copy received 19 September 1960. *Locations:* PU, ViU.

C 104.1.b₂
London: Secker & Warburg, [1960].

Title leaf is integral. Dust jacket. Copyright page: '*Printed in the United States of America*'. Reviewed in *Manchester Guardian*, 21 April 1961, p. 6. Deposit copies: BL ('16 FEB 61'), BO ('14APR1961'). Copies inscribed by owners: JM (September 1960). Price, 21s. *Locations:* BL, BO, JM, NNC.

C 104.1.c–r
New York: Viking, [1961].

Wrappers. *Compass Books C98*. Price, 95¢. Listed in *CBI* as distributed in Canada by Macmillan at $1.25. *Location:* JM. Reprinted in wrappers with undated title pages in July 1964, 1965, July 1966, June 1967, April 1968, 1968, March 1969, March 1970, November 1970, July 1971, 1972, 1972, June 1973, August 1974, 1975. *Locations:* ViW (1964), JM (1966, 1969, March 1970, November 1970, 1971, 1973), PU (1967), ScU (April 1968), NcD (1974).

C 104.1.s–cc
[Harmondsworth, England, and New York]: Penguin, [1976].

Wrappers. *Penguin Poets*. Deposit copies: DLC for CIP ('JUL 13 1976'), BL ('28 JUL 76'), BE ('–6 SE 76'). Price, $1.95. *Locations:* BE, BL, DLC. Reprinted in wrappers with undated title pages in 1977, 1977, 1978, 1980, 1981, 1982, 1983, 1984, 1985, 1985. *Locations:* JM (1977, 1977, 1981, 1982, 1983, 1985 [2d]), RPB (1980), MB (1985).

C 104.1.dd–hh
[Harmondsworth, England, and New York]: Penguin, [1986].

Wrappers. *Penguin Classics*. Price, $2.95. *Location:* JM. Reprinted in wrappers with undated title pages in 1987, 1987, 1988, and with copyright page reading '7 9 10 8 6'. *Location:* JM (1987 [2d], 1988, '6').

C 105.1.a–c
Whitman. [New York: Dell, 1959].

192 pp. Wrappers. Edited with an introduction by Leslie A. Fiedler. *Laurel Poetry Series LB121.* 51,000 copies printed March 1959; 1,250 sent to Canada for sale. Copyright 31 March 1959; A399018. Published March 1959. Deposit copy: DLC ('JUL –2 1959'). Copies inscribed by owners: ViU (18 May 1959). Price, 35¢. *Locations:* DLC, JM, ViU. Reprinted in wrappers with undated title pages in December 1960 (25,750 copies printed), March 1963. *Locations:* JM (1960), RPB (1963).

C 105.1.d–n
[New York: Dell, 1964].

Wrappers. *Laurel Poetry Series 9524.* Published February 1964. *Location:* JM. Reprinted in wrappers with undated title pages in October 1964, October 1965, September 1966, November 1967, April 1968, October 1969, October 1970, September 1971, August 1972, October 1973. *Locations:* JM (1964, 1966, 1967, 1968, 1972, 1973).

C 106
Leaves of Grass. Garden City, N.Y.: Doubleday, [1960].

153 pp. Wrappers. *Doubleday Dolphin Master C3.* Price, 95¢. Listed in *CBI* as distributed in England by Mayflower at 8s. *Locations:* JM, P.U.

C 107.1.a
Walt Whitman's Civil War. New York: Alfred A. Knopf, 1960.

[336] pp. Dust jacket. Edited with an introduction by Walter Lowenfels, with the assistance of Nan Braymer. *Borzoi Book.* Reviewed in *Newsweek,* 56 (21 November 1960), 111. Copyright 31 October 1960; A 473891. Published 21 November 1960. Deposit copies: DLC ('NOV –7 1960'), BL ('15 JAN 62'). DLC copy received from the publisher 24 October 1960. Price, $5.00. Listed in *CBI* as distributed in Canada by McClelland for $5.50. *Locations:* BL, DLC (2), JM.

Note: First publication of ["The Long, Long Solemn Trenches"] and ["There Rises in My Brain"] (pp. 13, 322).

C 107.1.b–c
New York: Alfred A. Knopf, 1961.

Published March 1961. *Location:* JM. Undated reprinting with copyright page reading 'W'. *Location:* NcU.

C 107.1.d
[New York: Da Capo, 1989].

Facsimile reprinting. Wrappers. *Da Capo Paperback*. Price, $13.95. *Location:* JM.

C 108
A Whitman Portrait. [New York: Spiral Press, 1960].

Unpaged (47 leaves), mostly printed on one side (recto or verso) only. Unprinted glassine dust jacket. Illustrated by Antonio Frasconi. Printed in fall 1960. Copyright 1 December 1960; K61128. Limited to 525 numbered copies, signed by Frasconi. *Locations:* DLC, NNC.

Note: The illustrations were reprinted in *Lines from Walt Whitman Overhead the Sun* (C 129) and the 1981 Franklin Library edition of *Leaves of Grass* (C 155).

C 109.1.a–c
Leaves of Grass. Ithaca, N.Y.: Cornell University Press, [1961].

467 pp. Facsimile reprinting of the 1860 edition. Wrappers. Introduction by Roy Harvey Pearce. *Great Seal Books*. Copyright 25 July 1961; A516101. Deposit copies: BL ('31 JAN 62'), BO ('21FEB1962'). DLC copy (rebound) received 8 October 1961. Price, $2.25. *Locations:* BL, BO, JM. Reprinted in wrappers with undated title pages and Ithaca and London imprint in *Cornell Paperbacks CP-95* in 1969, 1984. *Locations:* JM (both).

C 110.1.a
Selections from Leaves of Grass. New York: Crown, [1961].

115 pp. Edited with an introduction by Walter Lowenfels. Copyright 30 August 1961; A520095. *Locations:* JM, RPB.

Note: Sold with a set of four 12″ LP records, with readings by Dan O'Herlihy.

C 110.1.b–j
New York: Avenel Books, [n.d.].

Undated reprintings with the copyright page readings lacking codes and with 'i j k l m n o p', 'j k l m n o p'. *Locations:* JM (all).

C 111.1.a–b
Leaves of Grass. New Delhi: Eurasia Publishing House, 1962.

438 pp. Wrappers. Introduction by S. K. Kumar. *Location:* UU. Undated reprinting in wrappers with preliminary pages reset. *Location:* JM.

C 112

Leaves of Grass. [Lahore, India: Franklin, 1962].

Unpaged (90 leaves). Translated by Sheikh Niyaz Ahmad. English and Urdu on facing pages. *Publication Series Number 32. Location:* UU.

C 113.1.a

Prose Works 1892. Volume 1: Specimen Days; Volume 2: Collect and Other Prose. [New York]: New York University Press, 1963–1964.

2 vols: 358, 359–805 pp. Title page has book title and publisher's logo in red. Three-piece binding. Dust jacket. Edited with an introduction by Floyd Stovall. *The Collected Writings of Walt Whitman* (see B 6). Vol. 1 reviewed in *Library Journal,* 88 (15 May 1963), 2011. Copyright: vol. I: 24 April 1963; A621786; vol. II: 8 April 1964; A698498. Deposit copies: vol. 1: DLC ('APR 26 1963'), BO ('21 JUN1963'), BE ('10 AU 1964'); vol. 2: DLC ('APR 10 1964'), BL ('APR 64'), BO ('20MAY1964'), BE ('10 AU 1964'). Price, $10.00 per volume. Sold in Canada as an importation by Ryerson Press at $12.50 per volume. *Locations:* BE, BL, BO, DLC, JM.

C 113.1.b

[New York]: New York University Press, 1963–1964.

Title page all in black; one-piece binding. *Locations:* JM (I), TxU.

C 114.1.a

Walt Whitman's New York. New York: Macmillan; London: Collier-Macmillan, [1963].

188 pp. Dust jacket. Edited with an introduction by Henry M. Christman. Reviewed in *Library Journal,* 88 (15 November 1963), 4376. Copyright 11 November 1963; A659570. Deposit copies: BL ('15 FEB 67'). DLC copy received from the publisher 17 October 1963. Price, $4.50. *Locations:* BL, DLC, JM.

C 114.1.b

Freeport, N.Y.: Books for Libraries Press, [1972].

Facsimile reprinting. Deposit copies: DLC for CIP ('14 JUL 1972'). *Location:* DLC.

C 114.1.c

New York: New Amsterdam, [1989].

Facsimile reprinting. Wrappers. Price, $9.95. *Location:* JM.

C 115.1.a–b
Poems of Walt Whitman   Leaves of Grass. New York: Thomas Y. Crowell, [1964].

169 pp. Dust jacket. Edited with an introduction by Lawrence Clark Powell. Illustrated by John Ross and Clare Romano Ross. *Crowell Poets.* Reviewed in *Library Journal,* 90 (15 February 1965), 52. Copyright 23 September 1964; A735265. Deposit copies: DLC ('NOV 23 1964'). DLC copy received from the publisher, 6 October 1964. Price, $2.95. *Locations:* DLC, JM. Reprinted in wrappers with undated title page in *Apollo Editions A-312* for $1.95 in 1971. *Location:* RPB.

C 116
Walt Whitman's America. Cleveland and New York: World, [1964].

[111] pp. Dust jacket. Edited and illustrated by James Daugherty. Copyright 22 October 1964; A725488. Deposit copies: DLC ('NOV 19 1964'). Published 12 October 1964. DLC copy received from the publisher 16 October 1964. Price, $3.95. *Locations:* DLC, JM.

Note: A review copy, composed of loose folded and gathered signatures laid into the casing, with a letter from the publisher dated 14 September 1964, is at NcD.

C 117.1.a–b
Whitman's "Song of Myself"—Origin, Growth, Meaning. New York and Toronto: Dodd, Mead, 1964.

203 pp. Wrappers. Edited by James E. Miller, Jr. Copyright 12 May 1964; A695422. DLC copy (rebound) received from the publisher 20 May 1964. Price, $2.25. *Location:* JM. Reprinted in wrappers in 1971. *Locations:* JM, NcD.

C 118.1.a–b
Leaves of Grass. New York: Airmont, [1965].

383 pp. Wrappers. Introduction by Francis R. Gemme. *Airmont Classic CL91.* Copyright 24 December 1965; A897833. Price, 75¢. Published in Canada by the Ryerson Press. *Locations:* JM, NcD. Undated reprintings in wrappers have ISBN number on copyright page. Some sheets were bound and sold in *Cover Craft* series in illustrated cloth bindings by the Perfection Form Company. *Locations:* JM (both).

C 119.1.a$_1$
Leaves of Grass   Comprehensive Reader's Edition. [New York]: New York University Press, 1965.

768 pp. Title page has title and publisher's logo in red. Three-piece binding. Dust jacket. Edited with an introduction by Harold W. Blodgett and Sculley Bradley. *The Collected Writings of Walt Whitman* (B 6). Reviewed in *Antiquarian Bookman*, 35 (1 February 1965), 416. Copyright 12 February 1965; A742452. Deposit copies: DLC (rebound) ('FEB 18 1965'), BL ('MAR 65'), BO ('27MAR1965'). Sculley Bradley has written in his copy "Appeared on January 4, 1965" (PU). JM has ex libris copy received 8 February 1965. Price, $12.50. *Locations:* BL, BO, JM, PU.

Note: First book publication of the poems "A Song Duet. A Dialogue between Pleasure and the Soul" (pp. 676–677), "To the Poor——" (p. 677), "Pictures" (p. 678), "Broadway, 1861" (p. 678), ["I Too Am Drawn"] (p. 679), ["I Have Lived"] (p. 679), ["I Stand and Look"] (p. 679), "Of My Poems" (p. 680), "My Own Poems" (p. 680), "Of the Democratic Party" (p. 680), ["To What You Said"] (p. 681), ["While Some I So Deeply Loved"] (p. 681), "Reminiscences, 64" (p. 682), ["Disease and Death"] (p. 682), "Starry Union" (pp. 682–683), ["What the Word of Power"] (p. 683), "Last Words" (p. 684), ["Glad the Jaunts for the Known"] (p. 684), "Champagne in Ice" (pp. 684–685), "To the Soul" (p. 685), ["Two Little Buds"] (p. 685), ["Sunrise"] (p. 686), and various prose manuscript fragments (pp. 687–707).

C 119.1.a₂

[London]: University of London Press, [1965].

Title leaf is a cancel; the leaf following the title leaf is canceled, and a cancel leaf containing a list of titles in the edition in tipped on. Dust jacket. Reviewed in *Spectator*, 216 (25 March 1966), 365. Deposit copies: BL ('23 FEB 66'), BO ('3MAR1966'), BE ('11 MR 66'). Price, £4 4s. *Locations:* BE, BL, BO, NzD, RPB.

C 119.1.b

[New York]: New York University Press, 1965.

Title page all in black; one-piece binding. *Location:* TxU.

C 119.1.c–e

Leaves of Grass: Comphrehensive Reader's Edition. New York: W. W. Norton, [1965].

Cloth (with dust jacket) or wrappers. Copyright page: '1 2 3 4 5 6 7 8 9 0'. *Norton Library N430.* Prices: cloth, $7.50; paper, $2.95. *Locations:* JM, MB. Undated reprintings in wrappers with copyright page readings '2 3 4 5 6 7 8 9 0', '3 4 5 6 7 8 9 0'. *Locations:* ScU (2d), JM (3d).

C 119.2.a–j
Leaves of Grass. New York: W. W. Norton, [1973].

1008 pp. (additional secondary material). Cloth (with dust jacket) or wrappers. Copyright page: '1 2 3 4 5 6 7 8 9 0'. *Norton Critical Edition*. Reviewed in *Long Islander*, 27 September 1973, sec. I, p. 11. Copyright 25 June 1973; A621557. Deposit copies: cloth: BL ('15 JUL 74'). Presentation copies: wrappers: NcD (from Blodgett, 1 August 1973). Prices: cloth, $17.50 or £9.50; paper, $3.45. *Locations:* BL, JM (both), NcD. Undated reprintings in wrappers with New York and London imprint and copyright page readings '2 3 4 5 6 7 8 9 0'; '3 4 5 6 7 8 9 0' (received by MH, 28 September 1978); '7 8 9 0' (deposit copies: BO ['10DEC1981'], BE ['29 JA 82']); '0'. *Locations:* JM (2d), MH (3d), BE (7th), BO (7th), TxU (10th).

C 119.2.k
New Delhi: Prentice-Hall of India, 1986.

No publisher's code on the copyright page. Printed in India. *Location:* NNU.

C 120
Excerpts from Walt Whitman's Leaves of Grass. New York: Associated American Artists, MCMLXVI.

Unpaged (15 leaves). Unsewn sheets laid in wrappers. Slipcase. Edited by Sylvan Cole, Jr. Illustrated by Terry Haass. Printed in Paris. Limited to 173 numbered copies, signed by the artist: I–VI on Auvergne handmade rag paper with an extra suite of illustrations and one canceled copper plate; six collaborator's copies and ten artist's proofs on Auvergne; and 150 numbered copies on Rives paper. *Location:* DLC (Rives).

C 121
Leaves of Grass. [New York: Eakins Press, 1966].

95, [8] pp. Facsimile reprinting of 1855 edition with advertising supplement. Facsimile of binding B of the 1855 edition. Printed clear plastic dust jacket. Boxed. Deposit copy: BO ('–2MAY1967'). NcD copy presented from the publisher, 16 November 1966. Price, $12.50. *Locations:* BO, JM, NcD.

C 122
Selected Poems and Prose. [London]: Oxford University Press, 1966.

285 pp. Wrappers. Edited with an introduction by A. Norman Jeffares. *Classic American Texts*. Deposit copies: BL ('15 AUG 66'), BO ('22SEP1966'), BE ('30 SE 66'). DLC copy (rebound) received '6–FEB1967'. Prices: 21s. or $3.40. *Locations:* BE, BL, BO, JM, MB.

C 123
Walt Whitman's Complete Leaves of Grass. Tokyo: Taibundo, [1966].

1096 pp. Dust jacket. Boxed. Preface by Gay Wilson Allen. Introduction and annotations by William L. Moore. Illustrated by Kazuko Okamoto. Reviewed in *Times Literary Supplement,* 6 July 1967, p. 608. DLC copy received 'JUL 31 1968'. Price, $33.50. *Locations:* DLC, JM.

Note: Sold with a set of three 12″ records with readings by Moore and music by Kakusei Yamamoto (CSt).

C 124
Selections from Leaves of Grass. New York: Pyramid, [1967].

59 pp. Wrappers. *Little Pyramid Classic LP-25.* Published September 1967. Copyright 15 September 1967; A956442. Price, 35¢. *Locations:* JM, RPB.

C 125.1.a–g
A Choice of Whitman's Verse. London: Faber and Faber, [1968].

176 pp. Cloth (with dust jacket) or wrappers. Edited with an introduction by Donald Hall. Copies in wrappers in *Faber Paper Covered Editions.* Deposit copies: wrappers: BL ('12 FEB 68'); cloth: BO ('14MAR1968'). DLC copy (cloth) received '4–MAR1968'. Prices: cloth, 25s. or $4.95; paper, 9s.6d. or $2.95. *Locations:* BL, BO, DLC. Reprinted in cloth or wrappers with undated title page in 1971. *Location:* JM. Reprinted in cloth or wrappers with undated title pages and London and Boston imprint in 1979, 1985, 1987, 1989, 1990. *Locations:* JM (1979, 1985, 1987), Blackwell's (1989, 1990).

Note: Copies of the first printing in wrappers have a printed label on the front wrapper: 'TRANSATLANTIC | ARTS' (JM, NcD).

C 126
Leaves of Grass. San Francisco: Chandler, [1968].

95 pp. Facsimile reprinting of 1855 edition. Wrappers in photofacsimile of binding B of the 1855 edition. Introduction by Richard Bridgman. *Chandler Facsimile Editions in American Literature.* Copyright 8 July 1968; A35402. ViU copy received 26 December 1968. Price, $1.25. *Locations:* JM, ViU.

C 127
Leaves of Grass. Mount Vernon, N.Y.: Peter Pauper, [1968].

62 pp. Dust jacket. Illustrated by Mary Jane Gorton. Copyright 1 March 1968; A982632. Deposit copies: DLC ('APR –8 1968'). Price, $1.25. *Locations:* DLC, JM.

C 128.1.a–b
Leaves of Grass. [New York: Avon, 1969].

205 pp. Wrappers. Introduction by Francis Griffith. *Avon Library Book GS16.* Published June 1969. Price, 50¢. *Locations:* NcD, RPB. Reprinted in wrappers: [New York]: Avon Books, [1972]. Simultaneously in *Bard Poetry Series* and *Bard Books YS457.* Published June 1972. *Location:* JM.

C 129
Lines from Walt Whitman   Overhead the Sun. New York: Farrar, Straus and Giroux, [1969].

Unpaged (19 leaves). Dust jacket. Illustrated by Antonio Frasconi (reprinted from *A Whitman Portrait* [C 108]). Hand set at the Spiral Press. Reviewed in *New York Times Book Review,* 7 September 1969, p. 34. Copyright 15 August 1969; A93182. DLC copy received from the publisher 9 July 1969. Price, $4.95. *Locations:* DLC, JM.

Note: The illustrations were reprinted from this edition in the 1981 Franklin Library edition of *Leaves of Grass* (C 155).

C 130
Miracles   The Wonder of Life. Chicago, New York, San Francisco: Rand McNally, [1969].

Unpaged (13 leaves). Dust jacket. Illustrated by D. K. Stone. Copyright 6 October 1969; A107644. Published September 1969. DLC copy received from the publisher 23 October 1969. Price, $1.95. *Locations:* DLC, JM.

C 131
Poems. [Mindelheim, Bavaria]: Three Kings Press, [1969].

[30] pp. Cloth. Illustrated and printed by Melchior Mittl. Deposit copy: BO ('19JUN1969'). NN-R copy received 2 June 1969. Limited to 100 numbered copies, signed by Mittl. Price, $50.00. *Locations:* BO, NN-R.

C 132
Walt Whitman. [London]: Longmans, [1969].

28 pp. Wrappers. Edited by Leonard Clark. *Longman's Poetry Library. Location:* RPB.

C 133
Walt Whitman's Leaves of Grass   Selected Poetry and Prose. [Kansas City, Mo.]: Hallmark Editions, [1969].

61 pp. Dust jacket. Edited with an introduction by C. Merton Babcock. Illustrated by Jim Spanfeller. Copyright 1 August 1969; A104206. Deposit copies: DLC ('OCT 28 1969'). Price, $2.50. *Locations:* DLC, JM.

C 134

America the Beautiful In the words of Walt Whitman. [Waukesha, Wis.]: Country Beautiful Corporation, [1970].

98 pp. Dust jacket. Edited by Robert L. Polley. Copyright 30 October 1970; A207010. Deposit copies: DLC ('DEC –9 1970'), DLC ('JAN 18 1971'). Price, $7.95. Distributed by Rand McNally. *Locations:* DLC (2), JM.

C 135.1.a

Leaves of Grass   Selections. New York: Appleton-Century-Crofts, [1970].

174 pp. Wrappers. Edited with an introduction by Edwin Haviland Miller. *Crofts Classics.* Copyright 26 February 1970; A135396. Presentation copies: NcD (from Miller, 17 March 1970). Price, 75¢. *Locations:* JM, NcD.

C 135.1.b–c

Northbrook, Ill.: AHM Publishing, [n.d.].

Wrappers. Copyright page: 'Second Printing'. *Location:* JM. Also with undated title page, Arlington Heights, Ill., imprint, and copyright page reading 'Third Printing'. *Location:* NcD.

C 135.1.d–h

Arlington Heights, Ill.: Harlan Davidson, [n.d.].

Wrappers. Copyright page: '81 82 83 84 85CB10 9 8 7 6 5'. *Locations:* JM, ScU.

C 136.1.a

The Tenderest Lover   The Erotic Poetry of Walt Whitman. New York: Delacorte, [1970].

154 pp. Dust jacket. Edited with an introduction by Walter Lowenfels. Illustrated by J. K. Lambert. Copyright 23 October 1970; A198200. Deposit copies: DLC ('NOV –2 1970'). Price, $7.50. *Locations:* DLC, JM.

C 136.1.b–e

[New York: Dell, 1972].

Wrappers. *Delta Book.* Published October 1972. Price, $2.45. *Location:* RPB. Reprinted in wrappers with undated title pages and copyright page readings 'Second Printing', [unlocated reprinting], 'Fourth printing—June 1978'. *Locations:* JM (both).

C 137.1.a
The Illustrated Leaves of Grass. New York: Madison Square Press/Grosset &
Dunlap, [1971].

[192] pp. Dust jacket. Edited by Howard Chapnick. Introduction by William
Carlos Williams. *Black Star Book*. Copyright 28 June 1971; A267526. DLC copy
received from the publisher 20 July 1971. Price, $9.95. *Locations:* DLC, JM.

C 137.1.b–d
New York: Today Press/Grosset & Dunlap, [1976].

Wrappers. *Black Star Book*. Price, $6.95. *Location:* JM. Reprinted in wrap-
pers with undated title page and copyright page reading 'SECOND PRINT-
ING' in 1976. *Location:* JM. Reprinted in cloth or wrappers with Grosset &
Dunlap imprint only and undated title page in 1978. *Location:* JM.

C 138
Leaves of Grass (1855). [Hildesheim and New York: Olms Presse, 1971].

95 pp. Facsimile reprinting of the 1855 edition. Wrappers in photofacsimile of
binding B of the 1855 edition. Introduction (in German and English) by Karl
Adalbert on eight-leaf gathering included with copies. *Editiones Principes
Faksimiledrucke von Erstausgaben*. Deposit copies: BL ('15 OCT 71'). DLC
copy received '15 JUN1971'. Imported by Adler's Foreign Book Service for
$10.50. *Locations:* BL, DLC, JM.

C 139
Feuilles d'Herbe. [Paris]: Aubier-Flammarion, [1972].

511 pp. Wrappers. Translated with introduction and notes by Roger Asselineau. English and French on facing pages. *af 51*. *Locations:* CtY, NcD.

C 140
Miracles   Walt Whitman's Beautiful Celebration of Life. [Kansas City, Mo.]:
Hallmark Crown Editions, [1973].

Unpaged (26 leaves). Illustrated by Jim Hamil, Fred Klemushin, David R.
Miles, and Jim Paul. Copyright 10 October 1973; A510431. Deposit copies:
DLC ('MAR 18 1974'). Price, $4.00. *Locations:* DLC, JM.

C 141
*A Most Jubilant Song Inspired Writings About the Wonderful World Around
Us*. [Kansas City, Mo.]: Hallmark Crown Editions, [1973].

62 pp. Edited by Shifra Stein. Copyright 1 August 1973; A470822. DLC copy
received from the publisher 15 October 1973. Price, $6.00. *Location:* DLC.

C 142
Whitman. [Harmondsworth, England]: Penguin, [1973].

237 pp. Wrappers. Edited with an introduction by Robert Creeley. *Poet to Poet.*
Deposit copies: BL ('21 SEP 73'), BO ('5APR1977'). DLC copy received
'JUN111973'. Prices: 35p. or $1.95. *Locations:* BL, BO, DLC, JM.

Note: Copies sold in the United States either have a sticker with the dollar
price on the British wrappers (BL, BO, DLC) or are in wrappers imprinted with
the price in dollars (JM).

C 143.1.a–h
Select Poems. New Delhi: Rama Brothers, 1974.

Edited by Raghukul Tilak. *Not seen.* Reprinted in 1976, 1979, 1980, 1982,
1983, 1984. *Not seen.* Reprinted in wrappers with additional poems in 1986 as
'Eighth Edition' in 208 pp. *Location:* JM.

C 144
12 Poems of Walt Whitman. [Hyderabad, India: Mansoor Printing Press], 1974.

44 pp. Wrappers. Edited with an introduction, glossary, and notes by H. R.
Ghauri. *Location:* WaU.

C 145.1.a–i
The Complete Poems. [Harmondsworth, England]: Penguin Education, [1975].

892 pp. Wrappers. Edited with an introduction by Francis Murphy. *Penguin
English Poets.* Deposit copies: BL ('14 OCT 75'), BO ('23OCT1975'), BE ('–5
NO 75'). DLC copy received 'JAN261976'. Prices: £3.25 or $3.95. *Loca-
tions:* BE, BL, BO, DLC, JM. Reprinted in wrappers with undated title pages
and Penguin Books imprint in 1977, 1979, 1982, 1983, 1984. *Locations:* RPB
(1977), JM (1979, 1982, 1984). Reprintings in wrappers with undated title
pages and Penguin Books imprint in *Penguin Classics* in 1986, 1987, and with
copyright page reading '5 7 9 10 8 6'. *Locations:* JM (all).

C 146.1.a$_1$
Leaves of Grass. [Folcroft, Penn.]: Folcroft Library Editions, 1975.

384 pp. Facsimile reprinting of the 1856 edition. Introduction by Gay Wilson
Allen. Limited to 100 copies. Deposit copies: DLC for CIP ('NOV 14 1978' but
received 22 August 1975). Price, $75.00. *Location:* DLC.

C 146.1.a$_2$
[Norwood, Penn.]: Norwood Editions, 1976.

Title leaf is inserted. Price, $65.00. *Locations:* RPB, ScU.

C 147
Selected Poems of Walt Whitman. London: Heinemann; New York: Barnes & Noble, [1976].

145 pp. Cloth (with dust jacket) or wrappers. Edited with an introduction and notes by James Reeves and Martin Seymour-Smith. *Poetry Bookshelf*. Published in the United States on 15 February 1977. Deposit copies: cloth: BL ('15 OCT 76'), BO ('2DEC1976'), BE ('16 DE 76'), DLC for CIP ('DEC 28 '76'). Prices: cloth, £3.50 or $10.50; wrappers: £1.95. Distributed in the United States by Harper & Row. *Locations:* BE, BL, BO, DLC, JM.

Note: The frontispiece photograph is of James Russell Lowell.

C 148.1.a–b
Walt Whitman: Selected Poems. Bara Bazar, Bareilly [India]: Prakash Book Depot, [1976].

Edited with an introduction by A. N. Dwivedi. *Not seen*. Reprinted in 1980. *Not seen*.

C 148.2
Bara Bazar, Bareilly [India]: Prakash Book Depot, [1986].

364 pp. Wrappers. *Location:* JM.

C 149
Leaves of Grass   Foglie d'erba. [Milan]: Olivetti, [1977].

151 pp. Self wrappers. Unprinted glassine dust jacket. Boxed. Translated by Enzo Giachino. Edited by Giorgio Soavi. Illustrated by James McGarrell. English and Italian on facing pages. Also includes a separate pamphlet with 12 drawings by McGarrell (not for sale). *Locations:* JM, NcD.

C 150.1.a–b
Leaves of Grass. Franklin Center, Penn.: Franklin Library, [1979].

536 pp. Full leather. Copyright page: 'The Franklin Library'; colophon on p. [537]. *Location:* Collection of Ernest Castle. Undated reprinting in half leather with copyright page reading 'Franklin Mint Corporation' and p. [537] blank. *Location:* JM.

C 151
Selected Poems by Walt Whitman. [Sussex]: Snake River Press, [1979].

23 pp. Boards. Illustrated by Geofrey Trenaman. Limited to 20 numbered copies. *Location:* JM.

C 152

Selections from Song of Myself and other poems. Iowa City: [Inverted A] Press, 1979.

Unpaged (7 leaves). Illustrated by Barbara Henry. *Location:* JM.

C 153

City of Orgies & other poems. San Francisco: Live Oak Press, 1980.

Unpaged (31 leaves). Wrappers. Edited and illustrated by J. Lawrence Lembo. Deposit copy: DLC ('JUN 11 1980'). Limited to 1,000 copies, signed by Lembo. Price, $5.00. *Locations:* DLC, JM.

C 154

Leaves of Grass   A Textual Variorum of the Printed Poems. [New York]: New York University Press, 1980.

3 vols.: 272, 273–562, 563–779 pp. Dust jackets. Edited with an introduction by Sculley Bradley, Harold W. Blodgett, Arthur Golden, and William White. *The Collected Writings of Walt Whitman* (B 6). Deposit copies: DLC ('SEP 08 1980'), BL ('FEB 82'), BO ('18JAN1982'), BE ('18 MA 1982'). Price, $125.00 the set. *Locations:* BE, BL, BO, DLC, JM.

C 155

Leaves of Grass. Franklin Center, Penn.: Franklin Library, 1981.

513 pp. Full leather. Illustrations in black and white by Antonio Frasconi (reprinted from *Overhead the Sun* [C 129]). *100 Greatest Books of All Time.* DLC copy stamped 'gift publisher' and dated 'JAN 18 1983'. *Location:* DLC.

C 156

Leaves of Grass. Franklin Center, Penn.: Franklin Library, 1982.

[512] pp. Full leather. Illustrated by Liam Roberts. *100 Greatest Masterpieces of American Literature.* DLC copy stamped 'gift publisher' and dated 'JAN 18 1983'. *Locations:* DLC, NcD.

C 157.1.a–f

Leaves of Grass. Toronto [&c]: Bantam, [1983].

470 pp. Wrappers. Introduction by Justin Kaplan. *Bantam Classic.* Published July 1983. Deposit copies: DLC ('AUG –9 1983'; at NjWhiMi); BL ('1 NOV 83'), BE ('9 DE 83'). Prices: $2.95 or £2.50. *Locations:* BE, BL, JM, NjWhiMi. Undated reprinting in wrappers with copyright page reading 'OPM 14 13 12 11 10 9 8 7 6'. *Location:* JM.

C 158
Selected Poems of Walt Whitman. Franklin Center, Penn.: Franklin Library, 1983.

324 pp. Full leather. *Collector's Library of the World's Best-Loved Books.* DLC copy received from the publisher 'JAN 20 1984'. *Location:* DLC.

C 159
Ein Kosmos. [N.p.: Schwiftinger Galerie-Verlag, 1985].

115 pp. Wrappers. Dust jacket. Translated by Else and Hans Bestian. Illustrated by Eric Gand. English and German on facing pages. *Locations:* JM, NcD.

C 160
The Essential Whitman. New York: Ecco, [1987].

138 pp. Cloth (with dust jacket) or wrappers. Edited with an introduction by Galway Kinnell. *Essential Poets,* vol. 2. Published April 1987. Deposit copies: wrappers: DLC for CIP ('JUN 15 1987'); cloth: DLC ('JUL 17 1987'). Prices: cloth, $14.50; wrappers, $6.00. *Locations:* DLC (both), JM (both).

C 161.1.a
Walt Whitman. [London]: Aurum, [1987].

61 pp. Dust jacket. Edited with an introduction by Geoffrey Moore. *Illustrated Poets.* Price, £4.95. *Locations:* JM, RPB.

C 161.1.b
New York: Clarkson N. Potter, [1987].

Dust jacket. *Great American Poets.* Deposit copies: DLC for CIP ('NOV 12 1987'). Price, $6.95. *Locations:* DLC, JM.

C 162
Voyages   Poems by Walt Whitman. San Diego, New York, London: Harcourt Brace Jovanovich, [1988].

73 pp. Dust jacket. Edited by Lee Bennett Hopkins. Illustrated by Charles Mikolaycak. Price, $15.95. *Location:* JM.

C 163
The Call of the Open Road. New York: Limited Editions Club, 1989.

Full leather. Boxed. Illustrated by Aaron Siskind. Limited to 450 numbered copies, signed by the illustrator. Price, $1,200. Listed in Waiting for Godot Books, Catalogue 21, item 995. *Not seen.*

C 164
Leaves of Grass. Oxford and New York: Oxford University Press, [1990].

472 pp. Facsimile reprinting of the 1891–1892 text. Wrappers. Edited with an introduction by Jerome Loving. *World's Classics. Not seen.* Reprinted in wrappers with undated title page in 1990. *Location:* JM.

C 165
A Homage to Walt Whitman 1892–1992, 4 vols. [N.p.]: Contafil, [1991].

Each volume is a single sheet of stiff paper, fan-folded to make 12 pages, printed on pp. 3–11. Dust jackets. Boxed. Edited by Luigi Sampietro. Illustrated by Guido Villa. Limited to 499 numbered copies. Selections from "Song of Myself" (vols. I, II) and *Drum-Taps* (vol. III), and "Vigil Strange I Kept in the Field One Night" (vol. IV). Price, $20.00. *Location:* JM.

C 166
Selected Poems. New York: Dover, [1991].

119 pp. Wrappers. *Dover Thrift Editions*. Series editor, Stanley Applebaum. Price, $1.00. *Location:* JM.

Note: Also sold in a five-volume boxed set with poems by Shakespeare, Keats, Poe, and Dickinson (JM).

C 167
Wrenching Times. [Newtown, Powys, Wales]: Gwasg Gregynog, 1991.

72 pp. Edited by M. Wynn Thomas. Illustrated by Gaylord Schanilec. Selections from *Drum-Taps*. Limited to 450 numbered copies: 30 in a special binding, 400 in quarter leather, and 20 in unbound sheets. Prices: £200 in quarter leather; £150 in sheets. *Location:* Iall.

UNDATED EDITIONS

C 168
Individual Responsibilty. [N.p.]: Elder, [n.d.].

Listed in *CBI* (1912) in wrappers for 10¢. *Not seen.*

C 169
Leaves of Grass. New York, Boston: Books, Inc., [n.d.].

365 pp. Dust jacket. Simultaneously in *Art-Type Edition* and *World's Popular Classics* and *University Library of Classics,* C–71. Copies inscribed by own-

ers: JM (25 December 1941). Listed in *CBI* (1938–42) in "Duo-tone Classics" in leatherette at 50¢ and in "Registered Guild Library" at 39¢. *Locations:* JM, NcD.

C 170
Leaves of Grass. [N.p.]: Buccaneer Books, [n.d.].

350 pp. Listed in *BIP* (1984) for $19.95. *Not seen.*

C 171
Leaves of Grass. New York: Thomas Y. Crowell, [n.d.].

60 pp. Copies inscribed by owners: RPB (9 June 1921). *Locations:* PU, RPB.

C 172
Leaves of Grass. Garden City, N.Y.: International Collectors Library, [n.d.].

488 pp. Leatherette. Edited by Emory Holloway. *Location:* JM.

C 173
Leaves of Grass. Tokyo: Kenkyusha, [n.d.].

345 pp. Dust jacket. Edited with introduction and notes by Takeshi Funahashi. *Kenkyusha English Classics 98. Location:* TxU.

C 174
Selections from Walt Whitman. Leipzig: Otto Nemnich, [n.d.].

85 pp. Boards or wrappers. Introduction by Franz Rudolph. Introduction in German, text in English. *Boerner-Texte.* Copies inscribed by owners: RPB (1917). *Locations:* RPB, UU.

D. First Book and Pamphlet Appearances

Titles in which material by Whitman appears for the first time in a book or pamphlet, arranged chronologically. All items are credited to Whitman unless otherwise noted. Previously published items are so identified. The first printings only of these titles are described, but British editions, retitled reprintings, and selected reprintings are also noted.

D 1 VOICES FROM THE PRESS
1850

VOICES FROM THE PRESS; | A COLLECTION | OF | SKETCHES, ES-SAYS, AND POEMS, | BY | PRACTICAL PRINTERS. | EDITED BY | JAMES J. BRENTON. | NEW-YORK: | CHARLES B. NORTON, 71 CHAMBERS-STREET, | (IRVING HOUSE.) | 1850.

"The Tomb Blossoms," pp. 27–33. Signed "Walter Whitman." Fiction. *Reprint*. See E 35.

Location: JM.

D 2 THE AMERICAN HISTORICAL ANNUAL
1853

THE | AMERICAN | HISTORICAL ANNUAL. | ILLUSTRATED WITH NU-MEROUS ENGRAVINGS. | [wavy rule] | NEW-YORK: | PUBLISHED BY JOHN S. TAYLOR. | 143 NASSAU STREET. | 1853.

"Eris: A Spirit Record," pp. 99–102. Signed "Walter Whitman." Fiction. *Reprint*. See E 163.

Location: NNC.

Rambles among Words:

Their Poetry, History and Wisdom.

William Swinton.

Polonius.—What do you read, my lord?
Hamlet.—Words, words, words.
Hamlet.

New York:
CHARLES SCRIBNER, 124 GRAND STREET.
LONDON: SAMPSON LOW, SON & CO.
MDCCCLIX.

Title page for D3

[three lines in boldface] Rambles Among Words | [gothic] Their Poetry, History and Wisdom. | William Swinton. | Polonius.—What do you read, my lord? | Hamlet.—Words, words, words. | *Hamlet.* | [boldface] New York: | Charles Scribner, 125 Grand Street. | [boldface] London: Sampson Low, Son & Co. | MDCCCLIX.

302 pp.

Swinton was assisted by Whitman in preparing this book (see *Note one*).

Location: ViU.

Note one: For discussions of Whitman's role in this book, see C. Carroll Hollis, "Whitman and William Swinton: A Co-operative Friendship," *American Literature,* 30 (January 1959), 425–449; and James Perrin Warren, "Whitman as Ghostwriter: The Case of *Rambles Among Words," Walt Whitman Quarterly Review,* 2, no. 2 (Fall 1984), 22–30.

Note two: Reprinted: 'RAMBLES AMONG WORDS: | THEIR POETRY, HISTORY AND WISDOM. | BY | WILLIAM SWINTON | Polonius.—What do you read, my lord? | Hamlet.—Words, Words, Words. | *Hamlet.* | REVISED EDITION. | NEW YORK: | DION THOMAS, 142 NASSAU STREET. | 1864.' (KWiU).

Note three: Reprinted: 'RAMBLES AMONG WORDS: | [gothic] Their Poetry, History, and Wisdom. | BY | WILLIAM SWINTON, M.A., | AUTHOR OF "CAMPAIGNS OF THE ARMY OF THE POTOMAC," "DECISIVE BATTLES | OF THE WAR," "SCHOOL HISTORY OF THE UNITED STATES," | "WORD-ANALYSIS," ETC. | *Polonius.* What do you read, my lord? | *Hamlet.* Words, words, words. | Shakespeare. | *REVISED EDITION.* | NEW YORK AND CHICAGO: | IVISON, BLAKEMAN, TAYLOR, AND COMPANY. | 1872.' (ScRhW).

Note four: New edition (287 pp.): 'RAMBLES AMONG WORDS: | THEIR | POETRY, HISTORY, AND WISDOM. | BY | WILLIAM SWINTON. | LONDON AND GLASGOW: | RICHARD GRIFFIN AND COMPANY, | PUBLISHERS TO THE UNIVERSITY OF GLASGOW. | MDCCCLXI.' (MB).

Note five: Issue, with cancel title leaf: 'RAMBLES IN WORD LORE | THE | POETRY, HISTORY AND WISDOM | OF | WORDS | BY | WILLIAM SWINTON | LONDON | GRIFFIN, BOHN AND COMPANY | 1863' (CLU).

𝕷𝖊𝖆𝖛𝖊𝖘 𝖔𝖋 𝕲𝖗𝖆𝖘𝖘

IMPRINTS.

𝕬merican and 𝕰uropean 𝕮riticisms

ON

"LEAVES OF GRASS."

BOSTON:
THAYER AND ELDRIDGE.
1860.

Title page for D 4

[boldface gothic] Leaves of Grass | [boldface] IMPRINTS. | [rule] | [ornate letters] American and European Criticisms | ON | "LEAVES OF GRASS." | [rule] | BOSTON: | [boldface] THAYER AND ELDRIDGE. | 1860.

Wrappers (front wrapper dated 'June, 1860.').

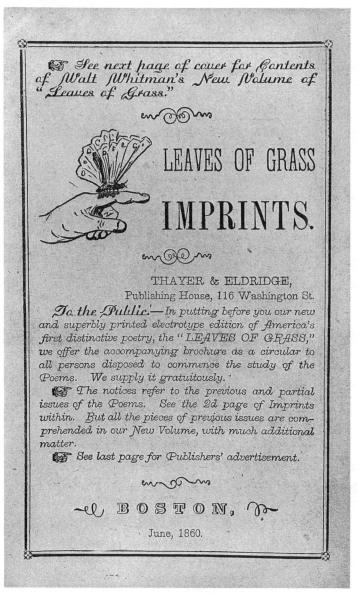

Front wrapper for D 4

Edited by Whitman.

["New Publications"] (from the 17 September 1856 *Brooklyn Daily Times*), pp. 49–50. *Reprint*. See E 1194.

Locations: DLC, BL.

Note: Whitman also contributed "Walt Whitman and His Poems" (E 1178), pp. 7–13; ["Walt Whitman, A Brooklyn Boy"] (E 1179), pp. 30–32; "An English and an American Poet" (E 1180), pp. 38–45. All three reviews were first collected in book form in the advertising supplement to the 1855 edition of *Leaves of Grass*

D5 NOTES ON WALT WHITMAN AS POET AND PERSON
1867

NOTES | ON | WALT WHITMAN, | As Poet and Person. | [rule] | [ornate initial capitals] By John Burroughs. | [rule] | *New York:* | AMERICAN NEWS COMPANY. | 1867.

108 pp. Whitman helped to write and edit this book (see *Note one*).

Location: PU.

Note one: According to Burroughs, the book "abounds in the marks of Whitman's hand," including "the whole" of chapter 21 and the "Biographical Notes [which] he enlarged and improved in the proof, from notes which he had given me verbally." Also, "the supplement to the last edition was entirely written by him" (Frederick P. Hier, Jr., "The End of a Literary Mystery," *American Mercury,* 1 [April 1924], 471–478, especially Burroughs' letters of 15 October and 6 November 1920 on pp. 475–476). See also Clara Barrus, *The Life and Letters of John Burroughs* (D 63), I, 126–129.

Note two: An uncut copy in unprinted wrappers is at NN-B.

Note three: See *BAL,* II, 434, for information on binding variants.

Note four: Reprinted in 126 pp. (pp. 109–126: "Supplementary Notes," dated "June, 1871"), with a new initial four-leaf gathering: 'NOTES . . . [rule] | *SECOND EDITION*. | [rule] | NEW YORK: | J. S. Redfield, 140 Fulton Street. | 1871.' (JM).

D6 POEMS BY WALT WHITMAN
1868

POEMS | BY | WALT WHITMAN. | SELECTED AND EDITED | BY | WIL-LIAM MICHAEL ROSSETTI. | Or si sa il nome, o per tristo o per buono, | E si sa pure al mondo ch'io ci sono. | MICHELANGELO. | [drawing of globe with clouds] | LONDON: | JOHN CAMDEN HOTTEN, PICCADILLY. | 1868.

Letter of [September? 1866] to Moncure D. Conway, pp. 17–18. *Reprint.* See E 2501.

Location: JM.

Note: For more information about this book, see C 1.

D7 BIRDS AND POETS
1877

[all within red single-rule frame with intersecting lines at each corner, surrounding black single-rule frame] [red] BIRDS AND POETS | [black] *WITH OTHER PAPERS* | BY | JOHN BURROUGHS | AUTHOR OF "WAKE-ROBIN" AND "WINTER SUNSHINE" | [drawing of bough] | [red] NEW YORK | [black] PUBLISHED BY HURD AND HOUGHTON | [gothic] Cambridge: The Riverside Press | 1877

"The Flight of the Eagle," pp. 213–262. See *Note one.*

Location: MB.

Note one: Burroughs later commented that p. 175 was "written by" Whitman and that "there are a few sentences scattered through it from his pencil" (see Burroughs' letter of 15 October 1920 in Frederick P. Hier, Jr., "The End of a Literary Mystery," *American Mercury,* 1 [April 1924], 475). A manuscript of this essay, with "emendations by Whitman" in "many paragraphs and one entire page," was sold at the Anderson Galleries, sale 2198, 25 November 1927 (see *Whitman at Auction,* p. 136).

Note two: Scottish edition in wrappers, with "The Flight of the Eagle" on pp. 243–310: 'BIRDS AND POETS | WITH OTHER PAPERS | BY | JOHN BUR-ROUGHS | [drawing of young man within ornate frame] | *Author's Edition* | EDINBURGH | DAVID DOUGLAS, CASTLE STREET | 1887' (JM).

D 8 CAMPAIGNS OF GENERAL CUSTER
1881

CAMPAIGNS | OF | GENERAL CUSTER | IN THE NORTH-WEST, | AND THE | FINAL SURRENDER | OF | SITTING BULL. | BY | JUDSON ELLI- OTT WALKER. | [rule] | ALL RIGHTS RESERVED. | [rule] | NEW YORK: | JENKINS & THOMAS, PRINTERS, | 8 Spruce Street. | [short rule] | 1881.

Wrappers.

"Custer's Last Rally," pp. 118–120.

Location: NjP.

Note: Whitman's comments were also printed on pp. [1]–2 of an eight-page undated (ca. 1882) pamphlet, with the head title: 'PRESS COMMENTS | — ON— | John Mulvany's Painting of | CUSTER'S LAST RALLY | [rule] | BY MR. WALT WHITMAN. | *[New York Tribune]* | [rule] | [37 lines of prose]" (ViU).

PRESS COMMENTS
—ON—

John Mulvany's Painting of

CUSTER'S LAST RALLY

BY MR. WALT WHITMAN.
[New York Tribune.]

I went to-day to see this just finished picture by John Mulvany, who has been out in far Montana on the spot at the forts, and among the frontiers-men, soldiers and Indians, for the last two or three years, on purpose to sketch it in from reality, or the best that could be got of it. I sat for over an hour before the picture, completely absorbed in the first view. A vast canvas, I should say twenty or twenty-two feet by twelve, all crowded, and yet not crowded, conveying such a vivid play of color, it takes a little time to get used to it. There are no tricks; there is no throwing of shades in masses; it is all at first painfully real, overwhelming, needs good nerves to look at it. Forty or fifty figures, perhaps more, in full finish and detail, life-size, in the mid-ground, with three times that number or more, through the rest—swarms upon swarms of savage Sioux in their war bonnets, fran-tic, mostly on ponies, driving through the back-ground through smoke, like a hurricane of demons. A dozen of the figures are wonderful. Altogether a Western, autochthonic phase of America, the frontiers, culminating typi-cal, deadly, heroic to the uttermost; nothing in the books like it, nothing in Homer, nothing in Shakespeare; more grim and sublime than either; all native, all our own, and all a fact. A great lot of muscular, tan-faced men brought to bay under terrible circumstances. Death a-hold of them, yet every man undaunted, not one losing his head, wringing out every cent of the pay before they sell their lives. Custer (his hair cut short) stands in the middle with dilated eye and extended arm, aiming a huge cavalry pistol. Captain Cook is there, par-tially wounded, blood on the white handkerchief around his head, but aiming his carbine cooly, half kneeling (his body was afterwards found close by Custer's). The slaughtered, or half slaughtered horses, for breast-works, make a peculiar feature. Two dead Indians, herculean, lie in the foreground clutching their Winchester rifles very characteristic. The many soldiers, their faces and attitudes, the carbines, the broad-brimmed Western hats; the powder smoke in puffs; the dying horses with their rolling eyes, almost human in their agony, the clouds of war-bonneted Sioux in the background, the figures of Custer and Cook, with, indeed, the whole scene, inexpressible, dreadful, yet with an attraction and beauty that will remain forever in my memory. With all its color and fierce action a certain Greek continence pervades it. A sunny sky and clear light develop all. There is almost an entire absence of the stock traits of European war pictures. The physiognomy of the work is realistic and Western.

First page for D 8 *(Note)*

D9 PEPACTON
1881

[all within red single-rule frame with intersecting lines at each corner, surrounding black single-rule frame] [red] PEPACTON | [black] BY | JOHN BURROUGHS | AUTHOR OF "WAKE ROBIN," "WINTER SUNSHINE," "BIRDS AND POETS," | AND "LOCUSTS AND WILD HONEY" | [drawing of bough] | [red] BOSTON | [black] HOUGHTON, MIFFLIN AND COMPANY | [gothic] The Riverside Press, Cambridge | 1881

"Nature and the Poets," pp. 93–129 (Whitman section on pp. 121–122). *Reprint*. See E 2575.

Location: MB.

Note: Scottish edition in wrappers, with "Nature and the Poets" on pp. 111–157 (Whitman section on pp. 148–151): 'PEPACTON | BY | JOHN BURROUGHS | [drawing of young man within ornate frame] | *Author's Edition* | EDINBURGH | DAVID DOUGLAS, CASTLE STREET | 1885' (JM).

D10 THE POETS' TRIBUTES TO GARFIELD
1881

THE | POETS' TRIBUTES | TO | GARFIELD | THE COLLECTION OF POEMS WRITTEN FOR THE | BOSTON DAILY GLOBE, AND MANY | SELECTIONS | [gothic] With Portrait and Biography | [rule] | CAMBRIDGE, MASS. | PUBLISHED BY MOSES KING | HARVARD SQUARE | 1881

80 pp. Cloth or wrappers.

"The Sobbing of the Bells. (Midnight, September 19–20.)," p. 71. Listed as *"From a forthcoming volume."* See E 2600.

Location: JM.

Note one: Reprinted in 168 pp., with Whitman's poem on the same page: 'THE . . . GARFIELD | [rule] | A COLLECTION OF MANY MEMORIAL POEMS | [gothic] With . . . SQUARE | 1882' (JM).

Note two: New edition, with Whitman's poem on p. 113: 'IN MEMORIAM. | Gems of Poetry and Song | ON | JAMES A. GARFIELD. | *WITH PORTRAIT AND EULOGY.* | [four lines of verse] | —LONGFELLOW. | COLUMBUS, O. | J. C. McClenahan & Company. | 1881.' (JM).

D 11 ESSAYS FROM "THE CRITIC"
1882

ESSAYS | FROM | "The Critic" | BY | [six lines, each to the right of the one before by a paragraph indentation] JOHN BURROUGHS | EDMUND C. STEDMAN | WALT WHITMAN | R. H. STODDARD | F. B. SANBORN | E. W. GOSSE | AND OTHERS | [publisher's device] | BOSTON | JAMES R. OSGOOD AND COMPANY | 1882

Edited by Jeannette L. Gilder.

"Death of Carlyle," pp. 31–37. See E 2590; A 11.
  "Death of Longfellow," pp. 41–45. See E 2603; A 11.

Location: TxU.

Note: Published 18 May 1882 (*BAL*, IX, 44); *Specimen Days & Collect,* which reprints both items, was published in September 1882.

D 12 IN MEMORIAM. RALPH WALDO EMERSON.
1882

[gothic] In Memoriam. | [rule] | RALPH WALDO EMERSON: | RECOLLECTIONS OF HIS VISITS TO ENGLAND | IN | 1833, 1847–8, 1872–3, | AND | EXTRACTS FROM UNPUBLISHED LETTERS. | BY | ALEXANDER IRELAND. | [three lines of verse] | [rule] | [nine lines of verse] | SAMUEL DANIEL (1562–1619). | LONDON: SIMPKIN, MARSHALL, & CO. | EDINBURGH: DAVID DOUGLAS. GLASGOW: DAVID M. MAIN. | MANCHESTER: J. E. CORNISH. | LIVERPOOL: J. CORNISH & SONS. BIRMINGHAM: CORNISH BROTHERS. | 1882.

"The Latest Glimpses of Emerson in His Home," pp. 113–115. *Reprint.* See E 2602.

Location: JM.

Note: New edition, with Whitman's contribution retitled "Latest Glimpses of Emerson" on pp. 296–299: 'RALPH WALDO EMERSON | HIS | LIFE, GENIUS, AND WRITINGS | A BIOGRAPHICAL SKETCH | TO WHICH ARE ADDED | *PERSONAL RECOLLECTIONS OF HIS VISITS TO ENGLAND | EXTRACTS FROM UNPUBLISHED LETTERS | AND MISCELLANEOUS CHARACTERISTIC RECORDS* | BY | ALEXANDER IRELAND | [gothic] Second Edition, Largely Augmented | THREE AUTOTYPE PORTRAITS | LONDON: SIMPKIN, MARSHALL, & CO. | 1882 | ALL RIGHTS RESERVED' (JM).

D 13 WALT WHITMAN
1883

WALT WHITMAN | BY | RICHARD MAURICE BUCKE, M.D. | Author of
"MAN'S MORAL NATURE." | PUBLISHED BY | DAVID McKAY, 23 SOUTH
NINTH STREET | PHILADELPHIA | 1883

236 pp. Cloth or wrappers.

Whitman helped to write and to edit this book; see *Walt Whitman's Autograph
Revision* (A 44).

Locations: DLC (both).

Note one: Uncut copies in unprinted wrappers are at DLC and NN-B.

Note two: Undated issue, with integral title leaf and no copyright notice:
'*WALT WHITMAN* | BY | RICHARD MAURICE BUCKE, M.D. | Author of
"MAN'S MORAL NATURE." | PUBLISHED FOR THE AUTHOR. | [rule] | *All
rights reserved.*' (DLC). *BAL* reports copies with "London: Trübner & Co."
handstamped below the title page imprint (IX, 46).

Note three: Issue, with McKay title page, with a slip tipped in and covering
the bottom half of the title page: '[flower] | GLASGOW | WILSON & Mc-
CORMICK, SAINT VINCENT STREET | 1882', with the '2' revised by hand to a '3'
(Howard S. Mott; see William White, "A Unique Copy of Bucke's *Walt Whitman?*", *Walt Whitman Review*, 25 [March 1979], 35–[36]).

Note four: Issue (in 255 pp.) with appendix and cancel title leaf: 'WALT
WHITMAN | BY | RICHARD MAURICE BUCKE, M.D. | TO WHICH IS
ADDED | *ENGLISH CRITICS ON WALT WHITMAN* | EDITED BY | ED-
WARD DOWDEN, LL.D. | PROFESSOR OF ENGLISH LITERATURE IN
THE UNIVERSITY OF DUBLIN | [flower] | GLASGOW | WILSON & Mc-
CORMICK, SAINT VINCENT STREET | 1884' (DLC).

Note five: Issue (in 255 pp.) with appendix and cancel title leaf: 'WALT . . . |
[flower] | ALEXANDER GARDNER | PAISLEY; AND 12 PATERNOSTER
ROW, LONDON' (BBo).

Note six: See also William White, "Variants of R. M. Bucke's *Walt Whitman*," *Serif*, 5 (December 1968), 25–29; Harold Jaffe, "Richard Maurice
Bucke's *Walt Whitman*," *Serif*, 7 (March 1970), 3–10; Howard Jaffe, "Bucke's
Walt Whitman: A Collaboration," *Walt Whitman Review*, 15 (September
1969), 190–194.

D 14 TRANSACTIONS OF THE BUFFALO HISTORICAL
SOCIETY
1885

TRANSACTIONS | OF THE | Buffalo Historical Society. | [rule] | [red]
RED JACKET. | [black] [peace pipe] | VOLUME III. | [rule with asterisk in
center] | BUFFALO: | PUBLISHED BY ORDER OF THE SOCIETY. | [rule] |
MDCCCLXXXV.

Wrappers.

"Red Jacket, (From Aloft.)," p. 105. *Reprint.* See E 2627.

Location: JM.

D 15 ANNE GILCHRIST   HER LIFE AND WRITINGS
1887

ANNE GILCHRIST | HER LIFE AND WRITINGS | EDITED BY | HERBERT
HARLAKENDEN GILCHRIST | With a Prefatory Notice by | William Michael
| Rossetti. | LONDON: | T. FISHER UNWIN | 1887

Letter of 3 December 1867 to William Michael Rossetti, pp. 179–182.
  Letter of 26 June 1876 to William Michael Rossetti, p. 225.
  Letter of [n.d.] to Anne Gilchrist, p. 252.
  Letter of 15 December 1885 to Herbert Gilchrist, p. 284.

Location: RPB.

D 16 AUTHORS AT HOME
1888

Authors at Home | *PERSONAL AND BIOGRAPHICAL SKETCHES OF* |
WELL-KNOWN AMERICAN WRITERS | EDITED BY | J. L. & J. B. Gilder |
[rule] | CASSELL & COMPANY, Limited | 104 & 106 FOURTH AVENUE,
NEW YORK

Copyright 1888.

"Walt Whitman in Camden" by "George Selwyn," pp. 335–342. *Reprint.* See E
2636.

Location: NcCU.

Note one: *BAL* reports a large paper printing with the copyright notice dated "1889" (IX, 415).

Note two: Reprinted as by "George Selwyn," with the Whitman piece on the same pages: 'Authors . . . [rule] | CASSELL PUBLISHING COMPANY | 104 & 106 Fourth Avenue' (JM).

Note three: Reprinted as by "George Selwyn," with the Whitman piece on the same pages: 'Authors . . . Gilder | [rule] | NEW YORK | A. WESSELS COMPANY | 1902' (ScU).

D 17 CAMDEN'S COMPLIMENT TO WALT WHITMAN
1889

Camden's Compliment | TO | WALT WHITMAN | *MAY 31, 1889* | Notes, Addresses, Letters, | Telegrams | EDITED BY | HORACE L. TRAUBEL | PHILADELPHIA | DAVID McKAY, Publisher | 23 South Ninth Street | 1889

"Autobiographic Note," p. 4.
  [Response at the dinner], p. 5.
  [Whitman's own advertisement for his books], p. 74.

Location: JM.

Note one: 1,000 copies printed, with Whitman receiving one of the first on 28 October 1889 (*Correspondence,* IV, 343, 390).

Note two: For Whitman's authorship of the advertisement, see *Correspondence,* IV, 404.

D 18 GIORDANO BRUNO
1890

Giordano Bruno: | PHILOSOPHER AND MARTYR. | TWO ADDRESSES. | BY | DANIEL G. BRINTON, M.D. | AND | THOMAS DAVIDSON, M.A. | [engraving of ornate tombstone] | PHILADELPHIA: | DAVID McKAY PUBLISHER, | No. 23 South Ninth Street. | 1890.

Cloth or wrappers.

Prefatory note, dated 24 February 1890, p. [iii]. *Reprint.* See E 2734.

Locations: CtY, TxCM.

D 19 LIBERTY IN LITERATURE
1890

LIBERTY IN LITERATURE | [rule] | TESTIMONIAL | TO | Walt Whitman |
BY | ROBERT G. INGERSOLL | [rule] | AN ADDRESS DELIVERED IN
PHILADELPHIA, OCT. 21, 1890 | WITH PORTRAIT OF WHITMAN | *"Let
us put wreaths on the brows of the living"* | AUTHORIZED EDITION | NEW
YORK | TRUTH SEEKER COMPANY | 28 Lafayette Place

77 pp. Cloth or wrappers.

"I bid you hail and farewell" comment by Whitman, p. 5.

Location: NcU.

Note one: Reprinted in wrappers with same title page in 86 pp. in [1892] (JM).

Note two: English edition in wrappers, with Whitman's comments on p. 2:
'*WREATHE THE LIVING BROWS.* | [rule] | AN ORATION | ON | WALT
WHITMAN | BY | COL. ROBERT G. INGERSOLL. | [rule with dot in center] |
LONDON: | PROGRESSIVE PUBLISHING COMPANY, 28 Stonecutter
Street, E.C. | [rule] | 1890' (RPB).

D 20 IDEALS OF LIFE
1892

IDEALS OF LIFE. | Human Perfection. How to Attain It. | A SYMPOSIUM | ON
| THE COMING MAN. | —BY— | [left] MEN OF SCIENCE, | [right] MEN OF
ACTION, | [left] MEN OF LETTERS, | [right] EMINENT WOMEN. | Edited by
Wallace Wood, M.D. | Professor of History of Art, University of the City of New
York. | *ILLUSTRATED.* | New York: | E. B. TREAT, 5 Cooper Union. | 1892.

Letter of [3 March 1891] to Wood titled "Avoid Threatening Dangers," pp.
389–390.
    "His Life's Philosophy," p. 394.

Location: CtY.

Note: Reprinted: Emory Holloway, "Whitman's Last Words," *American Literature,* 24 (November 1952), 367–369.

D 21 THE LIFE OF THOMAS PAINE
1892

THE | LIFE OF THOMAS PAINE | WITH A HISTORY OF HIS LITERARY,
POLITICAL | AND RELIGIOUS CAREER IN AMERICA | FRANCE, AND

ENGLAND | BY | MONCURE DANIEL CONWAY | AUTHOR OF "OMIT-TED CHAPTERS OF HISTORY DISCLOSED IN THE LIFE AND PAPERS OF | EDMUND RANDOLPH," "GEORGE WASHINGTON AND MOUNT VERNON," | "WASHINGTON'S 'RULES OF CIVILITY,' " ETC. | TO WHICH IS ADDED A SKETCH OF PAINE | BY WILLIAM COBBETT | (HITHERTO UNPUBLISHED) | [rule] | VOLUME I. [II.] | [rule] | G. P. PUTNAM'S SONS | NEW YORK   LONDON | 27 WEST TWENTY-THIRD STREET 24 BEDFORD STREET, STRAND | [gothic] The Knickerbocker Press | 1892

Interview with Sanborn, who "took down his words at the time" (II, 422–423).

Location: ScU.

D 22 THREE TALES
1892

THREE TALES | THE GHOST | THE BRAZEN ANDROID | THE CARPEN-TER | BY | WILLIAM DOUGLAS O'CONNOR | [publisher's device] | BOS-TON AND NEW YORK | HOUGHTON, MIFFLIN AND COMPANY | [gothic] The Riverside Press, Cambridge | 1892

"Preface," pp. [iii]–vii.

Location: JM.

D 23 APPLETON'S ANNUAL CYCLOPÆDIA
1893

APPLETON'S | ANNUAL CYCLOPÆDIA | AND | REGISTER OF IMPOR-TANT EVENTS | OF THE YEAR | 1892. | EMBRACING POLITICAL, MILI-TARY, AND ECCLESIASTICAL AFFAIRS; PUBLIC | DOCUMENTS; BIOG-RAPHY, STATISTICS, COMMERCE, FINANCE, LITERA- | TURE, SCI-ENCE, AGRICULTURE, AND MECHANICAL INDUSTRY. | NEW SE-RIES, VOL. XVII. | WHOLE SERIES, VOL. XXXII. | NEW YORK: | D. APPLE-TON AND COMPANY, | 1, 3, AND 5 BOND STREET. | 1893.

Biographical sketch by Whitman (in facsimile), after p. 795.

Location: ViU.

D 24 IN RE WALT WHITMAN
1893

IN RE WALT WHITMAN: EDITED BY HIS | [space] LITERARY EXECU-TORS, HORACE L. | [space] TRAUBEL, RICHARD MAURICE BUCKE, |

[space] THOMAS B. HARNED | [seven lines in italics from Lucretius] | *Published by the Editors through* | DAVID MCKAY | 23 SOUTH NINTH STREET | PHILADELPHIA | 1893

Limited to 1,000 copies.

"Letters in Sickness: Washington, 1873," pp. 73–92. Prose.
  "Immortality," pp. 349–351. Prose.
  [From Walt Whitman], pp. 200, 252, 412.
  Daniel Longaker, "The Last Sickness and the Death of Walt Whitman," pp. 393–411 [contains "A Crude Notion," p. 396].

Location: JM.

Note one: Advance copies in unprinted wrappers are at CtY and JM. In the CtY copy, the statement of limitation on the copyright page has been changed to read "5 left" of "50 *Copies.*"

Note two: Copies of a four-page advertising brochure are at CtY and JM, with two pages of contents (pp. ix–x) and a sample page of text (p. 31), with this title page: '[three lines in orange] In one volume, cloth, gilt top, Two Dollars Net. | Order through any bookseller. Or address Horace | L. Traubel, Camden, New Jersey. | IN RE . . . 1893'.

Note three: A four-page advertising brochure, printed with information about the book and for ordering it on pp. 1–3, is at NNC.

        D 25 WALT WHITMAN   A STUDY
              1893

[red] WALT WHITMAN | [black] A STUDY | BY | JOHN ADDINGTON SYMONDS | *WITH PORTRAIT AND FOUR ILLUSTRATIONS* | LONDON | [red] JOHN C. NIMMO | [black] 14 KING WILLIAM STREET, STRAND | MDCCCXCIII

Postcard of 30 March 1891 to John Addington Symonds, after p. xxviii (facsimile).

Location: JM.

Note one: Reprinted, with Whitman's letter in the same place, in a large paper format with the same title page, limited to 208 numbered copies (JM).

Note two: Reprinted, with Whitman's letter in the same place: '[red] WALT . . . *ILLUSTRATIONS* | New Edition | LONDON . . . STRAND | MDCCCXCVI' (NjCW).

D 26 A HISTORY OF THE CITY OF BROOKLYN
1894

A HISTORY | OF THE | CITY OF BROOKLYN | AND | KING'S COUNTY | BY | STEPHEN M. OSTRANDER, M.A. | LATE MEMBER OF THE HOLLAND SOCIETY, THE LONG ISLAND HISTORICAL | SOCIETY, AND THE SOCIETY OF OLD BROOKLYNITES | *EDITED, WITH INTRODUCTION AND NOTES, BY* | ALEXANDER BLACK | AUTHOR OF "THE STORY OF OHIO," ETC. | IN TWO VOLUMES | VOLUME I. [II.] | BROOKLYN | [gothic] Published by Subscription | 1894

Letter of 19 January 1885 to Charles M. Skinner, II, 89n, and in facsimile after p. 90. *Reprint.* See E 2770.

Location: TxU.

D 27 CONVERSATIONS WITH WALT WHITMAN
1895

Conversations with | Walt Whitman | BY | [ornate rule] SADAKICHI | Written in 1894 | PRICE, 50 CENTS | [ornate shield and vine design] | 1895 | E. P. COBY & CO., Publishers | NEW YORK

Wrappers.

Letter of [1886?] to Sadakichi Hartmann, p. 34.

Location: JM.

D 28 REMINISCENCES OF WALT WHITMAN
1896

REMINISCENCES | OF | WALT WHITMAN | WITH | *EXTRACTS FROM HIS LETTERS AND REMARKS | ON HIS WRITINGS* | By WILLIAM SLOANE KENNEDY | [rule] | "Who loves a Man may see his image here." | — J. R. Lowell. | [rule] | ALEXANDER GARDNER | [gothic] Publisher to Her Majesty the Queen | PAISLEY: and 26 PATERNOSTER SQUARE, LONDON | [rule] | 1896

Various letters.

Location: JM.

Note one: *BAL* reports copies with a slip reading "David McKay, Importer, Philadelphia" pasted to the title page (IX, 54).

Note two: A set of Gardner sheets in a David McKay casing is at JM.

D 29 WALT WHITMAN THE MAN
1896

WALT WHITMAN | THE MAN | BY | THOMAS DONALDSON | "What about my hundred pages that I am getting out about | you?"—THOMAS DONALDSON. | "Go on, Tom, go on—and God be with you."—WALT WHITMAN. | *At a birthday dinner at his house at Camden, N.J.,* | *May* 31, 1891. | [rule] | *ILLUSTRATIONS AND FACSIMILES* | [rule] | NEW YORK | FRANCIS P. HARPER | 1896

Various letters.

Location: JM.

Note one: English issue in wrappers with cancel title leaf: 'WALT . . . DON-ALDSON | LONDON | SUCKLING & GALLOWAY | 1896' (DLC).

Note two: English issue with cancel title leaf: 'WALT . . . *FACSIMILES* | [rule] | LONDON | GAY & BIRD | 1897 | *[All rights reserved]*' (BL).

D 30 WHITMAN A STUDY
1896

WHITMAN | *A STUDY* | BY | JOHN BURROUGHS | [publisher's device] | BOSTON AND NEW YORK | HOUGHTON, MIFFLIN AND COMPANY | [gothic] The Riverside Press, Cambridge | 1896

Various letters and manuscripts.

Location: JM.

Note one: English issue with integral title leaf in [1906]: 'WHITMAN | *A STUDY* | BY | JOHN BURROUGHS | A. P. WATT & SON | [gothic] Hastings House | NORFOLK STREET, STRAND | LONDON' (BL).

Note two: Undated reprinting in large paper format: 'WHITMAN . . . BUR-ROUGHS | [gothic] Wesminster | ARCHIBALD CONSTABLE & CO. | 2 WHITEHALL GARDENS' (JM).

D 31 ALFRED LORD TENNYSON A MEMOIR
1897

ALFRED LORD TENNYSON | A MEMOIR | BY HIS SON | I have lived my life, and that which I have done | May He within Himself make pure! | VOLUME I [II] | [gothic] New York | THE MACMILLAN COMPANY | LONDON: MAC-MILLAN & CO., LTD. | 1897 | *All rights reserved*

By Hallam Tennyson.

Letter of 2 September 1872 to Tennyson, II, 115.

Location: ScU.

D 32 THE CLOVER CLUB OF PHILADELPHIA
1897

[all but three letters and floral design in green] [drawing of woman in Grecian costume on pedestal to left] 1882–1897 | [red 'T'] The | [red 'C'] Clover | [red 'C'] Club | of | Philadelphia | By [triangular design] | MARY R. DEACON | [two red floral designs] | PHILADELPHIA: | Avil Printing Company | 1897

Letter of 2 December 1883 to [Moses P. Handy?], p. 140 (facsimile).

Location: MH.

D 33 SEXUAL INVERSION
1897

SEXUAL INVERSION | BY | HAVELOCK ELLIS | AND | JOHN ADDING-TON SYMONDS | LONDON | WILSON AND MACMILLAN, | 16, JOHN STREET, BEDFORD ROW, W.C. | 1897

Studies in the Psychology of Sex, vol. 1.

Letter of 19 August 1890 to John Addington Symonds, p. 19.

Location: MH.

D 34 DIARY NOTES OF A VISIT TO WALT WHITMAN
1898

DIARY NOTES OF | [red] A VISIT TO WALT WHITMAN | [black] *AND SOME OF HIS FRIENDS* | *IN 1890.* | WITH A SERIES OF ORIGINAL PHO-TOGRAPHS. | BY | *John Johnston, M.D. edin.,* | HONORARY SURGEON TO BOLTON INFIRMARY. | AUTHOR OF "MUSA MEDICA." | MANCHES-TER: | THE LABOUR PRESS LIMITED, | Arkwright Mills, Miller Street. | LONDON: | THE "CLARION OFFICE." 72, Fleet Street. | 1898.

Letter of 2 December 1890 to John H. Johnston, p. 147 (facsimile).

Location: BMR.

Note one:　One copy has a label tipped to the title page: 'AMERICAN EDI-
TION: | SMALL, MAYNARD & COMPANY, | 6 Beacon Street, Boston'
(JM).

Note two:　The letter is not present in the first edition: Johnston, *Notes of a
Visit to Walt Whitman, etc., in July, 1890* (Bolton: T. Brimelow, 1890).

Note three:　For a greatly revised edition, see D 51.

D 35 STANDARD RECITATIONS BY BEST AUTHORS
1898

[all within a double–rule frame with designs in each corner] No. 47 | [curved]
Standard Recitations | ——BY—— | BEST AUTHORS. | A CHOICE COL-
LECTION OF | [ornate lettering] Beautiful Compositions | Carefully Compiled
for | SCHOOL, LYCEUM, PARLOR, | AND OTHER ENTERTAINMENTS, |
——BY—— | *FRANCES P. SULLIVAN.* | [rule] | [at left] Issued Quarterly
March, 1898. [at right] Subscription, 50 Cents per Year. | [rule] | M. J. IVERS
& CO., | PUBLISHERS, | 379 PEARL STREET, N. Y. | Copyright 1898, by M.
J. Ivers & Co. | Entered at the Post Office, N. Y. as second class matter.

Wrappers.

"The Midnight Visitor," p. 37. *Reprint.* See E 2764.

Location:　RPB.

D 36 WALT WHITMAN　　DER DICHTER DER DEMOKRATIE
1899

[all on very light brown background] [ornate 'W' within a box extending for two
lines] ALT | HITMAN | Der Dichter der Demokratie | Von | Karl Knortz, |
Schulsuperintendent in Evansville (Indiana). | [fleur-de-leis] | II. Auflage. | Mit
den Beilagen: 1. Neue Uebersetzungen aus "Grashalme." | 2. Dreizehn Origi-
nalbriefe Whitman's. | [publisher's device] | Leipzig. | VERLAG VON FRIE-
DRICH FLEISCHER. | 1899.

Thirteen letters written between 14 November 1882 and 4 May 1889 to Karl
　Knortz, pp. [90]–95.

Location:　OClW.

Note:　Reprinted in Horst Frenz, "Walt Whitman's Letters to Karl Knortz,"
American Literature, 20 (May 1948), 155–163.

D 37 MEN AND MEMORIES
1901

[all within single-rule frame] [one line within single-rule frame] MEN AND MEMORIES | [six lines within single-rule frame] PERSONAL REMINIS-CENCES | BY | JOHN RUSSELL YOUNG | EDITED BY HIS WIFE | MAY D. RUSSELL YOUNG | [publisher's device] | [three lines within single-rule frame] F. TENNYSON NEELY | 114 Fifth Avenue 96 Queen Street | NEW YORK LONDON

Copyright 1901.

Letter of 24 October 1891 to J. R. Young, p. 90. *Reprint.* See E 2765.
  "A Font of Type," p. 107 (variant version). *Reprint.* See *Leaves of Grass* (1888).

Location: GU.

D 38 A HISTORY OF LONG ISLAND
1902

A HISTORY | OF | LONG ISLAND | From Its Earliest Settlement to the Present Time | [rule] | BY | PETER ROSS, LL.D. | [rule] | VOL. I [II] [III] | THE LEWIS PUBLISHING COMPANY | New York and Chicago | 1902

"Sons of Long Island," I, [iii]. Poem. *Reprint.* See E 403.

Location: OKentU.

D 39 MEDITATIONS OF AN AUTOGRAPH COLLECTOR
1902

[three lines in red] MEDITATIONS | OF AN | AUTOGRAPH COLLECTOR | [black] *by* | ADRIAN H. JOLINE | *"The undevout autograph collector is mad"* | —Young, N. T. ix. | ILLUSTRATED | [publisher's device] | NEW YORK AND LONDON | HARPER & BROTHERS | PUBLISHERS 1902

Published May 1902.

Letter of 6 February 1881 to Jeannette L. Gilder, p. 163.

Location: ScU.

D 40 GEORGE M. WILLIAMSON LIBRARY
1903

[all within a single-rule frame] *Catalogue of* | [three lines in red] *A Collection of Books Letters and* | *Manuscripts written by* | *Walt Whitman* | [black] *In the Library of* | *George M Williamson* | *Grand View on Hudson* | [hands holding book open] | [two lines in gothic] The Marion Press | Jamaica Queensborough New=York | *Dodd Mead & Company* | *Fifth-avenue and Thirtyfifth-street New-York*

Limited to 25 numbered copies on Japan paper and 102 numbered copies on plated paper. Printed January 1903. Unpaged.

Various manuscript facsimiles.

Locations: NN-B (Japan paper), PU (plated paper).

D 41 ROSSETTI PAPERS
1903

Rossetti Papers | 1862 to 1870 | A COMPILATION BY | WILLIAM MICHAEL ROSSETTI | C'est par là qu'ont passé des hommes disparus | Victor Hugo | LONDON | SANDS & CO | 12 BURLEIGH STREET, STRAND | 1903

Letters of 1 November 1867 to Moncure Daniel Conway (p. 275), 22 November 1867 and 3 December 1867 to William Michael Rossetti (pp. 283–284, 285–287).

Location: ScU.

D 42 AUTOBIOGRAPHY, MEMORIES AND EXPERIENCES OF MONCURE DANIEL CONWAY
1904

AUTOBIOGRAPHY | MEMORIES AND EXPERIENCES | OF | MONCURE DANIEL CONWAY | IN TWO VOLUMES | VOL. I [II] | [publisher's device] | BOSTON AND NEW YORK | HOUGHTON, MIFFLIN AND COMPANY | [gothic] The Riverside Press, Cambridge | 1904

Letter of 17 February 1868 to Conway (in four-page facsimile), following I, 218.

Location: JM.

Note one: English reprinting, with Whitman's letter following the same page: 'AUTOBIOGRAPHY | MEMORIES AND EXPERIENCES | OF | Moncure

Daniel Conway | WITH TWO PORTRAITS | VOL. I. [II.] | CASSELL and COMPANY, Limited | LONDON, PARIS, NEW YORK AND MELBOURNE. MCMIV | ALL RIGHTS RESERVED' (JM).

Note two: The facsimile is not present in the 1904 English edition, which has the same title page as the 1904 English reprinting.

D43 A LIFE OF WALT WHITMAN
1905

A LIFE OF | WALT WHITMAN | BY | HENRY BRYAN BINNS | WITH THIRTY–THREE ILLUSTRATIONS | METHUEN & CO. | 36 ESSEX STREET W.C. | LONDON

Copyright page: '*First Published in 1905*'.

Various letters.

Location: JM.

Note: American issue, with cancel title leaf: 'A . . . ILLUSTRATIONS. | NEW YORK | E. P. DUTTON & CO. | 1905' (ScU).

D44 PERSONAL REMINISCENCES OF HENRY IRVING
1906

PERSONAL | REMINISCENCES | OF | HENRY IRVING | BY | BRAM STOKER | [engraving of head] | VOLUME I [II] | [gothic] New York | THE MACMILLAN COMPANY | LONDON: MACMILLAN & CO., Ltd | 1906 | *All rights reserved*

Letter of 16 March 1876 to Stoker (in facsimile), following II, 196.

Location: ScU.

D45 WALT WHITMAN   HIS LIFE AND WORK
1906

[red] WALT WHITMAN | [black] HIS LIFE AND WORK | BY | BLISS PERRY | [three lines within a red frame] WITH ILLUSTRATIONS | [red rule] | [black] [Riverside Press device] | BOSTON AND NEW YORK | HOUGHTON, MIFF-

LIN AND COMPANY | [red gothic] The Riverside Press, Cambridge | [black] 1906

318 pp. Limited to 250 copies of uncut sheets with paper label on spine. Published October 1906.

Various letters and manuscripts.

Locations: JM, CaOTU.

Note one: An advance copy in unprinted greenish gray wrappers is at CtY.

Note two: English issue, with cancel title leaf, published October 1906: '[red] WALT . . . device] | [gothic] LONDON | ARCHIBALD CONSTABLE & CO., LTD. | BOSTON AND NEW YORK | HOUGHTON, MIFFLIN & CO. | 1906' (JM).

Note three: Reprinted in 1906 with same American title page and copyright page stating 'SECOND IMPRESSION' (ScU).

Note four: Undated reprinting, with copyright page stating 'THIRD IMPRESSION': '[red] WALT . . . Cambridge' (ScU).

Note five: Revised edition in 1908 (334 pp.), with copyright page stating 'FOURTH IMPRESSION': '[red] WALT . . . PERRY | [five lines within red rectangular frame] WITH ILLUSTRATIONS | [rule] | [Riverside Press device] | [rule] | SECOND EDITION, REVISED | BOSTON AND NEW YORK | HOUGHTON, MIFFLIN AND COMPANY | [red gothic] The Riverside Press, Cambridge' (ViU).

Note six: Revised edition reprinted: '[gothic] American Men of Letters | [rule] | WALT WHITMAN | BY | BLISS PERRY | [Riverside Press device] | BOSTON AND NEW YORK | HOUGHTON MIFFLIN COMPANY | [gothic] The Riverside Press Cambridge' (JM).

Note seven: Revised edition reprinted: 'RIVERSIDE POPULAR BIOGRAPHIES | [double rule] | WALT WHITMAN | BY | BLISS PERRY | [Riverside Press device] | BOSTON AND NEW YORK | HOUGHTON MIFFLIN COMPANY | [gothic] The Riverside Press Cambridge' (ViU).

D46 WITH WALT WHITMAN IN CAMDEN (VOL. I)
1906

WITH | WALT WHITMAN | IN CAMDEN | (March 28–July 14, 1888) | [rule] | HORACE TRAUBEL | [publisher's device] | BOSTON | SMALL, MAYNARD & COMPANY | 1906

Copyright page: *'Published February, 1906'.*

Location: TxU.

Note one: According to Traubel's wife, "The notes of the visits to Whitman were written on small bits of paper to fit into the pockets of [Traubel's] jacket, and were written in what he called 'condensed shorthand,' in the dim light of Whitman's room. Within the hour of the words spoken, the material was put into the complete form with which you are now familiar . . . There was no vacuum of time or emotion, thus preserving the vitality of the original conversation" (*WWWC*, IV, x).

Note two: Reprinted with same title page and copyright page reading *'Second edition, August, 1906'* (JM).

Note three: English issue of American sheets with integral title leaf: 'WITH . . . TRAUBEL | [Small, Maynard device] | LONDON: GAY & BIRD | BOSTON: SMALL, MAYNARD & COMPANY | 1906' (JM).

Note four: Reprinted: 'WITH . . . TRAUBEL | [Mitchell Kennerley device] | NEW YORK | MITCHELL KENNERLEY | 1915' (KMK).

Note five: Selections from the first five volumes of *With Walt Whitman in Camden* were published in 1973 as '[dotted-line rule] | Walt Whitman's | Camden Conversations | Selected and arranged with | an introduction by | WALTER TELLER | [ornate 'R'] | RUTGERS UNIVERSITY PRESS | *New Brunswick, New Jersey* | [dotted-line rule]' (JM).

D 47 WALT WHITMAN   L'HOMME ET SON ŒVRE
1908

LÉON BAZALGETTE | [rule] | Walt Whitman | L'Homme et son Œuvre | AVEC UN PORTRAIT ET UN AUTOGRAPHE | [winged helmet] | PARIS | SOCIÉTÉ DV MERCVRE DE FRANCE | XXVI, RVE DE CONDÉ, XXVI | [rule] | MCMVIII

Wrappers. Published 26 March 1908.

Frontispiece is manuscript facsimile of prose, beginning "I have had serious doubts."

Location: JM.

Note: Reprinted in wrappers, with facsimile as frontispiece: 'LÉON . . . [rule] | Walt Whitman | L'Homme . . . AUTOGRAPHE | DEUXIÈME ÉDITION | [winged helmet] . . . ' (DLC).

D 48 WITH WALT WHITMAN IN CAMDEN (VOL. II)
1908

WITH | WALT WHITMAN | IN CAMDEN | (July 16, 1888–October 31, 1888) | [rule] | HORACE TRAUBEL | [publisher's device] | NEW YORK | D. APPLE-TON AND COMPANY | 1908

Copyright page: '*Published February, 1908*'.

Conversations with Whitman.

Location: JM.

Note: Reprinted: 'WITH . . . TRAUBEL | [Mitchell Kennerley device] | NEW YORK | MITCHELL KENNERLEY | 1915' (ViU).

D 49 WITH WALT WHITMAN IN CAMDEN (VOL. III)
1914

WITH | WALT WHITMAN | IN CAMDEN | (March 28–July 14, 1888) | (November 1, 1888–January 20, 1889) | [rule] | HORACE TRAUBEL | [publisher's device] | NEW YORK | MITCHELL KENNERLEY | 1914

Despite title page information, this volume contains vol. III only.

Conversations with Whitman.

Location: JM.

Note: State, with cancel title leaf: 'WITH . . . CAMDEN | (November 1, 1888–January 20, 1889) | [rule] . . . ' (JM).

D 50 WALT WHITMAN AS MAN, POET AND FRIEND
1915

[all within a single-rule red frame, with a single vertical red rule parallel to the inside right edge] *WALT WHITMAN AS MAN, POET AND FRIEND* [between rule and right-hand frame] 5 | [red rule] | [black] [four lines in gothic] Walt Whitman | As Man, Poet and Friend | Being autograph pages from many pens, collected by | Charles N. Elliot | [publisher's device] | [two lines in gothic] Boston : Richard G. Badger | The Gorham Press

Limited to 500 numbered copies. Copyright 1915.

Letter of 26 February [1875] to Peter Doyle, pp. 82–83 (facsimile).

Location: JM.

D51 VISITS TO WALT WHITMAN IN 1890–1891
1917

VISITS TO | WALT WHITMAN | IN 1890–1891 | BY | TWO LANCASHIRE FRIENDS | J. JOHNSTON, M.D. | AND | J. W. WALLACE | WITH TWENTY ILLUSTRATIONS | LONDON: GEORGE ALLEN & UNWIN LTD. | RUSKIN HOUSE 40 MUSEUM STREET W.C. 1

Copyright page: '*First published in 1917*'.

Various letters.

Location: JM.

Note one: English reprinting, with the same title page as the first printing, and the copyright page stating '*Reprinted . . . February 1918*' (ScU).

Note two: English reprinting for American sale: 'VISITS . . . ILLUSTRATIONS | Published by EGMONT ARENS at the | *Washington Square Bookshop,* New York | 1918' (JM).

Note three: For an earlier edition, see D 34.

D52 THE LETTERS OF ANNE GILCHRIST AND WALT WHITMAN
1918

THE LETTERS | *OF* | ANNE GILCHRIST | *AND* | WALT WHITMAN | Edited | With an Introduction | BY | THOMAS B. HARNED | One of Walt Whitman's Literary Executors | [publisher's device] | Illustrated | GARDEN CITY   NEW YORK | DOUBLEDAY, PAGE & COMPANY | 1918

Various letters.

Location: JM.

Note one: English issue, with integral title leaf: 'THE . . . Executors | [acornlike design] | Illustrated | T. FISHER UNWIN, LTD. | LONDON   ADELPHI TERRACE' (JM).

Note two: Reprinted: 'THE . . . Executors | [publishers device] | Illustrated | GARDEN CITY   NEW YORK | DOUBLEDAY, PAGE & COMPANY | 1919' (JM).

D 53 FREDERICK LOCKER-SAMPSON
1920

Frederick Locker-Sampson | A CHARACTER SKETCH | WITH A SMALL
SELECTION FROM LETTERS ADDRESSED | TO HIM AND BIBLIO-
GRAPHICAL NOTES ON | A FEW OF THE BOOKS FORMERLY | IN THE
ROWFANT LIBRARY | [acorn device] | COMPOSED AND EDITED BY HIS
SON-IN-LAW | THE RIGHT HON. AUGUSTINE BIRRELL | HONORARY
FELLOW OF TRINITY HALL AND ONE OF THE BENCHERS | OF THE
INNER TEMPLE | LONDON | CONSTABLE AND COMPANY LIMITED |
1920

Letter of 26 May 1880 to Locker-Sampson, pp. 135–136.

Location: ScU.

D 54 THE LIFE OF WHITELAW REID
1921

THE LIFE OF | WHITELAW REID | BY | ROYAL CORTISSOZ | VOLUME I
[II] | JOURNALISM—WAR—POLITICS [POLITICS—DIPLOMACY] | NEW
YORK | CHARLES SCRIBNER'S SONS | 1921

Published March 1921.

Letter of 7 July 1876 to Whitelaw Reid, I, 312.

Location: ScU.

D 55 A MAGNIFICENT FARCE
1921

A MAGNIFICENT FARCE | AND OTHER DIVERSIONS | OF A BOOK-
COLLECTOR | BY | A. EDWARD NEWTON | AUTHOR OF | THE AMENI-
TIES OF BOOK-COLLECTING | [publisher's device] | WITH ILLUSTRA-
TIONS | BOSTON | THE ATLANTIC MONTHLY PRESS

Copyright 1921.

Manuscript statement about Richard Worthington, dated 26 November 1880,
    pp. 152–153.

Location: ScU.

D 56 NEWS HUNTING ON THREE CONTINENTS
1921

NEWS HUNTING | ON THREE CONTINENTS | *by* | JULIUS CHAMBERS, F.R.G.S. | *Author of "On a Margin," The Destiny of Doris," etc., etc.;* | *Formerly Managing Editor of the New York "Herald;"* | *Organizer and First Editor of the Paris "Herald;"* | *Managing Editor of the New York "World;"* | *Writer of Daily "Walks and Talks" for* | *Sixteen Years in the Brooklyn* | *"Daily Eagle"* | [publisher's device] | NEW YORK | MITCHELL KENNERLEY | MCMXXI

Letter of 3 July 1888 to James Gordon Bennett (in facsimile), p. 305.

Location: ScU.

D 57 THE LATEST THING AND OTHER THINGS
1922

THE LATEST THING | AND OTHER THINGS | By ALEXANDER BLACK | Author of "The Great Desire" "The Seventh Angel" Etc. | [publisher's device] | HARPER & BROTHERS PUBLISHERS | NEW YORK AND LONDON 1922

Letter of 12 May 1891 to Black, pp. 166–167.

Location: ScU.

Note: New edition in [1937], with Whitman's letter on p. 73 (and in partial facsimile following p. 74): '[ornate rule] | [ornate lettering] TIME AND CHANCE | *Adventures with People and Print* | *by* | Alexander Black | *With Illustrations by the Author* | [rule] | [publisher's device] | [rule] | FARRAR & RINEHART | INCORPORATED | *New York Toronto* | [ornate rule]' (ScU).

D 58 REMEMBERED YESTERDAYS
1923

[all within a triple-ruled frame] REMEMBERED | YESTERDAYS | BY | ROBERT UNDERWOOD JOHNSON | WITH ILLUSTRATIONS | [publisher's device] | BOSTON | LITTLE, BROWN, AND COMPANY | 1923

Published November 1923.

Letter of 29 October 1879 to Robert Underwood Johnson, p. 335.

Location: JM.

D 59 ET CETERA
1924

[all within a an ornate frame of human figures] | [red] ET CETERA | [black] A Collector's | Scrap-Book | [picture in red of man on horse] | [black] CHICAGO | PASCAL COVICI • *Publisher* | 1924

Edited by Charles Vincent Starrett. Limited to 625 numbered copies.

"Fragments" ["I too am drawn"], p. 193.
  "Broadway 1861" ["The flags now there,"], p. 195.

Location: ScU.

D 60 FRANCIS WILSON'S LIFE OF HIMSELF
1924

FRANCIS WILSON'S LIFE | OF | HIMSELF | WITH ILLUSTRATIONS | "I laugh for hope hath happy place with me" | [engraving of jester] | BOSTON AND NEW YORK | HOUGHTON MIFFLIN COMPANY | [gothic] The Riverside Press Cambridge | 1924

Facsimile of proof copy of "To the Sun-Set Breeze," inscribed by Whitman to Wilson in 1891, following p. 238.

Location: MH.

D 61 HOWELLS, JAMES, BRYANT AND OTHER ESSAYS
1924

HOWELLS, JAMES, BRYANT | AND OTHER ESSAYS | BY | WILLIAM LYON PHELPS | LAMPSON PROFESSOR OF ENGLISH LITERATURE | AT YALE | [gothic] New York | THE MACMILLAN COMPANY | 1924 | *All rights reserved*

Published March 1924.

Letter of 14 October 1880 to [Thomas Nicholson], pp. 31–32.

Location: ScU.

D 62 MEMOIRS OF AN EDITOR
1924

MEMOIRS | OF AN EDITOR | FIFTY YEARS OF AMERICAN JOURNAL-ISM | BY | EDWARD P. MITCHELL | FORMERLY EDITOR–IN–CHIEF OF

"THE SUN" OF NEW YORK | ILLUSTRATED | CHARLES SCRIBNER'S SONS | NEW YORK • LONDON | 1924

Letter of 20 November 1881 to Mitchell, p. 270 (and in facsimile).
  Manuscript on Abraham Lincoln, p. 271 (and in facsimile, p. 272).

Location: ScU.

D63 THE LIFE AND LETTERS OF JOHN BURROUGHS
1925

THE LIFE AND LETTERS | OF | [green] JOHN BURROUGHS | [black] BY | CLARA BARRUS | *Author of 'Our Friend John Buroughs,' 'John | Burroughs, Boy and Man,' etc.* | *With Illustrations* | VOLUME I [II] | [publisher's device] | BOSTON AND NEW YORK | HOUGHTON MIFFLIN COMPANY | [gothic] The Riverside Press Cambridge | 1925

Letter of [2] July 1866 to John Burroughs, I, 132.

Location: JM.

D64 THE FIGHT OF A BOOK FOR THE WORLD
1926

THE FIGHT OF A BOOK | FOR THE WORLD | A COMPANION VOLUME TO | LEAVES OF GRASS | BY | WILLIAM SLOANE KENNEDY | *Author of "Reminiscences of Walt Whitman," "The Real | John Burroughs," etc.* | *"Le fronde onde s' infronda tutto l' orto | dell' ortolano eterno."* | —DANTE, Par. xxvi, 64, 65. | THE STONECROFT PRESS | WEST YARMOUTH, MASS. | 1926

Whitman's will, pp. 289–291.

Location: JM.

Note: An earlier version of the manuscript of this book was commented on by Whitman; see *Correspondence,* IV, 33n.

D65 WHITMAN   AN INTERPRETATION IN NARRATIVE
1926

[double rule] | WHITMAN | *An Interpretation in Narrative* | [rule] | BY EM- ORY HOLLOWAY | [rule] | *Illustrated with portraits and facsimiles | of Whit- man's letters and diaries* | [publisher's device] | [rule] | *NEW YORK & LON- DON* | ALFRED • A • KNOPF | M *CMXXVI*

Various manuscripts.

Location: JM.

Note: English issue, with integral title leaf: '[double rule] . . . | [publisher's device] | [rule] | *LONDON* | ALFRED . . . ' (BMR).

D66 ABRAHAM LINCOLN AND WALT WHITMAN
1928

[all within a double-rule frame] Abraham Lincoln | *and* | Walt Whitman | *By* | William E. Barton | Author of *The Life of Abraham Lincoln,* | *The Women Lincoln Loved,* Etc. | Illustrated | INDIANAPOLIS | THE BOBBS-MERRILL COMPANY | PUBLISHERS

Copyright 1928.

Various letters and manuscripts.

Location: JM.

D67 WALT WHITMAN   LA NAISSANCE DU POÈTE
1929

BIBLIOTÈQUE DE LITTÉRATURE COMPARÉE | WALT WHITMAN | LA NAISSANCE DU POÈTE | PAR | JEAN CATEL | Arégé de L'Université | Docteur ès lettres | [drawing of man with bow] | LES EDITIONS RIEDER | 7, PLACE SAINT-SULPICE, PARIS | 1929

Wrappers.

Postcard of 5 January 1889 to Sylvester Baxter, following p. 304 (in facsimile).
  Reprint. See E 2820.

Location: JM.

D68 ROADSIDE MEETINGS
1930

ROADSIDE | MEETINGS | *By* | HAMLIN GARLAND | MEMBER OF THE AMERICAN ACADEMY | [drawing of mask, scroll, palette, and brush] | *Decorations by* | CONSTANCE GARLAND | *New York* | THE MACMILLAN COMPANY | 1930

Copyright page: 'Published September, 1930'.

Letter of [18 November 1888] to Hamlin Garland, p. 141.

Location: JM.

Note: English issue with cancel title leaf and copyright page reading: 'First published in 1931': 'ROADSIDE . . . GARLAND | JOHN LANE | THE BODLEY HEAD, LIMITED | VIGO STREET LONDON, W.' (BL).

D 69 COLLECTION OF WHITMANIANA IN THE REFERENCE LIBRARY, BOLTON
1931

COLLECTION | OF | WHITMANIANA | IN THE | REFERENCE LIBRARY | BOLTON | ARCHIBALD SPARKE, F.R.S.L., F.L.A., | CHIEF LIBRARIAN | PUBLISHED BY THE LIBRARIES COMMITTEE | 1931

Wrappers.

Letter of 3 August 1885 to Bessie and Isabella Ford (facsimile, facing p. 14); postcards of 28 May 1884 and 11 August 1885 to Bessie and Isabelle Ford (facsimiles, facing p. 15).

Location: MBU.

D 70 WHITMAN AND BURROUGHS   COMRADES
1931

Whitman and Burroughs | Comrades | BY CLARA BARRUS | WITH ILLUSTRATIONS | [boxed grass design] | *Boston and New York* | HOUGHTON MIFFLIN COMPANY | [gothic] The Riverside Press Cambridge | 1931

Copyright page: 'TWO HUNDRED AND FIFTY COPIES OF THIS FIRST | EDITION ARE BOUND UNCUT WITH PAPER LABEL'. Boxed.

Various letters.

Location: JM.

Note: Issue, with integral title leaf: 'Whitman . . . 1931' (ScU).

D 71 LETTERS OF WILLIAM MICHAEL ROSSETTI
1934

LETTERS OF | WILLIAM MICHAEL ROSSETTI | CONCERNING | *WHITMAN, BLAKE, AND SHELLEY* | TO | ANNE GILCHRIST | AND HER SON |

HERBERT GILCHRIST | WITH APPENDICES CONTAINING A LETTER |
TO PRESIDENT CLEVELAND | AND AN UNCOLLECTED | *WHITMAN* |
CIRCULAR | EDITED BY | CLARENCE GOHDES | AND | PAULL FRANK-
LIN BAUM | [publisher's device] | DUKE UNIVERSITY PRESS | DURHAM,
NORTH CAROLINA | 1934

Whitman's circular and letter of 30 May 1886 to William Michael Rossetti, pp.
 [184]–185. *Reprint*. See F 40.

Location: JM.

D 72 LEAVES OF MUSIC
1937

[all within a triple-rule frame] [two lines in ornate lettering] LEAVES | OF
MUSIC | BY | WALT WHITMAN | [leaf design] | *From the Collection of* | BELLA
C. LANDAUER | PRIVATELY PRINTED, 1937

Wrappers. Limited to 60 numbered copies.

Facsimile of manuscript book order by Whitman, 13 August 1867, p. [59].

Location: NhD.

D 73 A LINCOLN AND WHITMAN MISCELLANY
1938

[all ornate lettering] A | LINCOLN AND WHITMAN | MISCELLANY | By Carl
Sandburg | [drawing of eagle] | HOLIDAY PRESS | Chicago, 1938

Limited to 250 copies.

Letter of [27? April 1864] to J. P. Kirkwood, pp. 30–33.

Location: MH.

Note: Reprinted in 'CARL SANDBURG | [within single-rule frame] Lincoln
Collector | *The Story of Oliver R. Barrett's* | *Great Private Collection* | NEW
YORK | HARCOURT, BRACE AND COMPANY | 1950', pp. 322–323 (Sc).

D 74 WALT WHITMAN'S POSE
1938

Walt Whitman's Pose | [at right] *Esther Shephard* | Harcourt, Brace and Com-
pany New York

Copyright 1938. Copyright page: *'first edition'*.

Various letters.

Location: JM.

Note: English issue [1938]: 'Walt Whitman's Pose | [centered] *Esther Shephard* | LONDON | GEORGE G. HARRAP & CO., LTD. | BOMBAY & SYDNEY' (JM).

D 75 THE LETTERS OF RALPH WALDO EMERSON
1939

THE LETTERS OF | [two lines of ornate orange and black lettering] RALPH WALDO | EMERSON | [black] *IN SIX VOLUMES* | *EDITED BY* | RALPH L. RUSK | PROFESSOR OF ENGLISH IN | COLUMBIA UNIVERSITY | [orange horizontal brace] | [black] *VOLUME ONE [TWO] [THREE] [FOUR] [FIVE] [SIX]* | [orange horizontal brace] | [black] NEW YORK : MORNINGSIDE HEIGHTS | COLUMBIA UNIVERSITY PRESS | 1939

Letter of 29 December 1862 to Ralph Waldo Emerson, V, 302n.

Location: JM.

D 76 NOTABLES AND AUTOGRAPHS
1939

NOTABLES AND AUTOGRAPHS | *by* | ALEXANDER WILLIAM ARMOUR | PRIVATELY PRINTED FOR THE AUTHOR | BY PAUL OVERHAGE, INC. | NEW YORK CITY | 1939

Limited to 200 copies.

Postcard of 10 August [1886] to C. C. Buel of the *Century Magazine,* p. 180 (facsimile).

Location: JM.

D 77 THE RECORD BOOK OF THE SMITHTOWN DEBATING SOCIETY
1941

AN UNPUBLISHED | WHITMAN MANUSCRIPT | *The Record Book of the Smithtown Debating Society* | 1837–1838 | [manuscript facsimile] | BY KATH-

ERINE MOLINOFF | *Hunter College of the City of New York | Number One in a Series of Monographs | on Unpublished Whitman Material*

Cover title. Printed by the Comet Press, Brooklyn. Introduction by Oscar Cargill, dated 27 January 1941.

Record book kept by Whitman, pp. 8–13.

Location: DLC.

D78 SOME NOTES ON WHITMAN'S FAMILY
1941

Some Notes on | WHITMAN'S FAMILY | *Mary Elizabeth Whitman • Edward Whitman | Andrew and Jesse Whitman | Hannah Louisa Whitman |* [manuscript facsimile] | "*A Whitman Letter to Mary Elizabeth, with reference to* Hannah and Eddy." | BY | KATHERINE MOLINOFF | *Hunter College of the City of New York | Number Two in a Series of Mongraphs | on Unpublished Whitman Material*

Cover title. Copyright 1941. Printed by Comet Press, Brooklyn.

Letter of 28 November 1890 to Mary Elizabeth Van Nostrand, p. 8.

Location: DLC.

D79 WHITMAN'S TEACHING AT SMITHTOWN
1942

Whitman's Teaching | *at Smithtown, 1837–1838* | [ornate rule] | [photograph of schoolhouse] | PHOTOGRAPH ONE | *The Walt Whitman Schoolhouse at Smithtown Branch* | BY KATHERINE MOLINOFF | *Hunter College of the City of New York | Number Three in a Series of Monographs | on Unpublished Whitman Material*

Cover title. Copyright 1942. Printed by Comet Press, Brooklyn.

Various manuscripts.

Location: DLC.

D80 THE SHOCK OF RECOGNITION
1943

THE SHOCK | OF | RECOGNITION | [ornate rule] | THE DEVELOPMENT OF LITERATURE | IN THE UNITED STATES | RECORDED BY THE MEN

| WHO MADE IT | EDITED BY | EDMUND WILSON | [drawing] | DOUBLE-DAY, DORAN AND COMPANY, INC. | GARDEN CITY NEW YORK | 1943

Manuscript note on Emerson, p. 272.

Location: MH.

D 81 WALT WHITMAN   AN AMERICAN
1943

WALT WHITMAN | *an American* | [ornate rule] | A STUDY IN BIOGRAPHY | BY HENRY SEIDEL CANBY | *'Walt Whitman, an American, . . .* | *. . . of mighty Manhattan the son.'* | [publisher's device] | 1943 | HOUGHTON MIF-FLIN COMPANY • BOSTON

Various letters and manuscripts.

Location: JM.

Note: Reprinting in [1944?]: '[two lines in red] WALT WHITMAN | *an American* | [ornate rule] . . . CANBY | [two lines in red] *'Walt . . . son.'* | [publisher's device] | WITH ILLUSTRATIONS | LITERARY CLASSICS, INC. • NEW YORK | Distributed by | HOUGHTON MIFFLIN COMPANY • BOSTON' (BMR).

D 82 CATALOGUE OF THE . . . TRENT COLLECTION
1945

CATALOGUE OF THE | WHITMAN COLLECTION | IN THE DUKE UNI-VERSITY LIBRARY | BEING A PART OF THE | *TRENT COLLECTION* | GIVEN BY DR. AND MRS. JOSIAH C. TRENT | COMPILED BY | ELLEN FRANCES FREY | CURATOR OF RARE BOOKS | DURHAM, NORTH CAROLINA | DUKE UNIVERSITY LIBRARY | 1945

Wrappers.

Manuscript facsimiles.

Location: NcD.

D 83 SIDNEY LANIER LETTERS
1945

CENTENNIAL EDITION | VOLUME X | [red] SIDNEY LANIER | [black] LETTERS | 1878——1881 | [dotted rule] | APPENDICES, CALENDAR, AND

INDEX | EDITED BY | CHARLES R. ANDERSON AND AUBREY H. STARKE | BALTIMORE | THE JOHNS HOPKINS PRESS | 1945

The Centennial Edition of the Works of Sidney Lanier.

Postcard of 27 May 1878 to Sidney Lanier, pp. 40–41n.

Location: ScU.

D84 FAINT CLEWS AND INDIRECTIONS
1949

Faint Clews & Indirections | Manuscripts of | Walt Whitman *and* His Family | EDITED BY | CLARENCE GOHDES | AND | ROLLO G. SILVER | [publisher's device] | Duke University Press • Durham, N. C. | MCMXLIX

Various letters and manuscripts.

Location: JM.

D85 THE NEW STARS
1949

[rope with knots rule] | *The New Stars* | *LIFE AND LABOR IN OLD MISSOURI* | [rope with knots rule] | MANIE MORGAN | *as arranged by* | JENNIE A. MORGAN | *edited, with an introduction, by* | LOUIS FILLER | THE ANTIOCH PRESS – 1949 | [rope with knots rule]

Facsimile of letter of [n.d.] to Ben Smith, frontispiece.

Location: Sc.

D86 WHITMAN AND ROLLESTON   A CORRESPONDENCE
1951

Whitman and Rolleston | *A Correspondence* | Edited | with an introduction and notes | by | HORST FRENZ | INDIANA UNIVERSITY | Bloomington, Indiana | 1951

Wrappers. *Indiana University Publications, Humanities Series, No. 26.*

Various letters.

Location: JM.

Note: Irish issue in cloth or wrappers: 'Whitman and Rolleston | *A Correspondence* | Edited with an introduction and notes | by | HORST FRENZ | [publisher's device] | BROWNE AND NOLAN, LIMITED | The Richview Press, Dublin' (BL, DLC). The first gathering has been reprinted with a foreword by Roger McHugh.

D 87 WITH WALT WHITMAN IN CAMDEN (VOL. IV)
1953

WITH WALT WHITMAN | IN CAMDEN | *January 21 to April 7, 1889* | [thick-thin short rules] | BY | HORACE TRAUBEL | *Edited by* | SCULLEY BRADLEY | *Philadelphia* | University of Pennsylvania Press | LONDON: GEOFFREY CUMBERLEGE | OXFORD UNIVERSITY PRESS | 1953

Conversations with Whitman.

Location: NjCW.

Note: Reprinted: 'WITH | WALT WHITMAN | IN CAMDEN | January 21— April 7, 1889 | [rule] | HORACE TRAUBEL | *Edited by* | Sculley Bradley | SOUTHERN ILLINOIS | UNIVERSITY PRESS | 1959' (JM).

D 88 BERNARD O'DOWD
1954

Victor Kennedy and Nettle Palmer | [rule] | Bernard O'Dowd | [publisher's device] | MELBOURNE UNIVERSITY PRESS

Published 1954. Distributed in London and New York by Cambridge University Press.

Letter of [12] July 1890 to Bernard O'Dowd, p. 82.

Location: ViFreM.

D 89 L'ÉVOLUTION DE WALT WHITMAN
1954

ROGER ASSELINEAU | Maître de Conférences à l'Université de Clermont-Ferrand | Docteur ès lettres | L'ÉVOLUTION | DE | WALT WHITMAN | APRÈS LA PREMIÈRE ÉDITION DES FEUILLES D'HERBE | DIDIER | 4 et 6, rue de la Sorbonne | PARIS

Wrappers. Copyright 1954.

Letter.

Location: JM.

D 90 TEN NOTEBOOKS AND A CARDBOARD BUTTERFLY MISSING
1954

THE LIBRARY OF CONGRESS | [rule] | TEN NOTEBOOKS AND A CARD-BOARD BUTTERFLY | M I S S I N G | from the | Walt Whitman Papers | [rule] | WALT WHITMAN MANUSCRIPTS | in the | Library of Congress | Washington | 1954

Wrappers. Mimeographed.

Manuscript facsimiles, pp. 7, 9, 11, 13, 15, 17, 19, 21, 23–25, 29.

Location: JM.

Note: Preceded by *Notebooks and Other Pieces Missing from the Walt Whitman Papers* (Washington: Library of Congress, 1953); see John C. Broderick, "Whitman's Earliest Known Notebook: A Clarification," *PMLA,* 84 (October 1969), 1657. *Not seen.*

D 91 THE SOLITARY SINGER
1955

The Solitary Singer | A CRITICAL BIOGRAPHY OF | *WALT WHITMAN* | *by* | GAY WILSON ALLEN | THE MACMILLAN COMPANY • NEW YORK | *1955*

Copyright page: 'First Printing'.

Various letters.

Location: ScU.

D 92 WHITMAN'S CORRESPONDENCE   A CHECKLIST
1957

Walt Whitman's Correspondence | *A Checklist* | *By* | EDWIN H. MILLER | *and* | ROSALIND S. MILLER | New York | The New York Public Library | 1957

Wrappers.

Facsimile of letter of 31 October 1881 to Sylvester Baxter, p. [viii].

Location: JM.

D 93 THE T. E. HANLEY LIBRARY
1958

[all within a double-rule green ornate frame] *An Exhibition* | *on the occasion of the opening* | *of the* | T. E. HANLEY | LIBRARY | [University of Texas "75th Year" seal] | *The Research Center* | THE UNIVERSITY OF TEXAS | NOVEMBER 17, 1958

Cover title. Limited to 500 numbered copies.

"In Western Texas," back cover recto (in facsimile, back cover verso). Poem.

Location: JM.

D 94 THE TRANSATLANTIC SMITHS
1959

The Transatlantic Smiths | *by Robert Allerton Parker* [publisher's device] | [two lines at right] Random House | *New York*

Copyright 1959.

Letters of 20 June 1890 to Robert Pearsall Smith (p. 53) and 20 July 1885 to Mary Whitall Smith (pp. 59–60). *Reprint.* See E 2845.

Location: ScU.

Note: English issue with integral title leaf: 'A FAMILY | OF FRIENDS | *The Story of the Transatlantic Smiths* | *by* | Robert Allerton Parker | [drawing of Greek temple front] | Museum Press Limited' (ScU).

D 95 FAMILIAR BOOKS
1960

[all within an ornate green frame] FAMILIAR | BOOKS | *A Bibliographical Exhibit* | *for the Undergraduate* | ON THE OCCASION OF NATIONAL LIBRARY WEEK | [green University seal] | [black] *The Research Center* | THE UNIVERSITY OF TEXAS : APRIL 3, 1960

Wrappers. Limited to 300 copies.

Facsimile of "Now Precedent Songs, Farewell," p. [12]. Poem.

Location: KyU.

D 96 FREE AND LONESOME HEART
1960

Free and Lonesome | Heart | THE SECRET OF | WALT WHITMAN | By
EMORY HOLLOWAY | [publisher's device] | VANTAGE PRESS NEW YORK |
WASHINGTON HOLLYWOOD

Copyright 1960.

Various letters.

Location: JM.

D 97 WALT WHITMAN
1961

[first three lines flush right] GAY WILSON ALLEN | *Walt Whitman* | Ever-
green Profile Book 19 | GROVE PRESS, INC. EVERGREEN BOOKS LTD. |
NEW YORK LONDON

Wrappers. Copyright page: 'FIRST PUBLISHED IN THIS EDITION 1961'.

Letter of 17[?] September 1881 to Louisa Whitman (facsimile, p. 120) and
   postcard of 7 July 1889 to William Sloane Kennedy (facsimile, p. 124).

Location: JM.

D 98 WALT WHITMAN IN AUSTRALIA AND NEW ZEALAND
1964

[two lines underlined] WALT WHITMAN IN AUSTRALIA AND NEW ZEA-
LAND | A Record of His Reception | Collected and Edited by | A. L. McLeod |
[flush left] Wentworth Press [flush right] SYDNEY

Copyright 1964. Mimeographed. Distributed by Wentworth Press, Lock Haven,
Penn.

Letter of 15 March 1891 to Bernard O'Dowd, p. 37.

Location: TMM.

Note: Ten additional Whitman letters are reprinted from the June 1961 *Walt Whitman Review* (E 2906).

D 99 WITH WALT WHITMAN IN CAMDEN (VOL. V)
1964

WITH | WALT WHITMAN | IN CAMDEN | April 8—September 14, 1889 | [rule] | By HORACE TRAUBEL | *Edited by* | GERTRUDE TRAUBEL | SOUTHERN ILLINOIS UNIVERSITY PRESS | CARBONDALE, ILLINOIS

Copyright 1964.

Conversations with Whitman.

Location: JM.

D 100 WALT WHITMAN AT SOUTHOLD
1966

WALT WHITMAN | AT SOUTHOLD | [picture of schoolhouse] | The Locust Grove ("Sodom") School | by | KATHERINE MOLINOFF | C. W. POST COLLEGE OF LONG ISLAND UNIVERSITY | Brookville, New York | *Number Four in a Series of Monographs | on Unpublished Walt Whitman Material. | Part One*

Cover title. Copyright 1966.

Various manuscripts.

Location: DLC.

D 101 THE LETTERS OF JOHN ADDINGTON SYMONDS
1969

The Letters of | *John Addington Symonds* | *Volume* III | *1885–1893* | *edited by* | *Herbert M. Schueller* | *Wayne State University* | *&* | *Robert L. Peters* | *University of California, Irvine* | *Wayne State University Press, Detroit, 1969*

Letter of 29 July 1890 to John Addington Symonds, p. 484n.

Location: ScU.

D 102 POEMS IN MANUSCRIPT
1970

Poems in Manuscript | Selected and Introduced by James Thorpe | [library's device] | A facsimile reproduction of original manuscripts in the | HUNTINGTON LIBRARY, San Marino, California

Wrappers. Copyright 1970.

Facsimile of "To Him That Was Crucified," pp. 24–25.

Location: JM.

D 103 WHITMAN AS EDITOR OF THE BROOKLYN DAILY EAGLE
1970

[four lines in boldface to the right] whitman | as editor of | the brooklyn | daily eagle | [two lines flush left] *Thomas L. Brasher* | SOUTHWEST TEXAS STATE UNIVERSITY | [three lines to the right] *Detroit* | *Wayne State University Press* | *1970*

"Most, perhaps four-fifths, of the material I quote from the *Eagle* has not been reprinted elsewhere" (p. 15).

Location: JM.

D 104 WALT WHITMAN ON LONG ISLAND
1971

BERTHA H. FUNNELL | [vertical rule] | WALT WHITMAN | on | LONG ISLAND | [vertical rule] | Ira J. Friedman Division | KENNIKAT PRESS | Port Washington, New York/London

Copyright 1971.

Letter of 10 October 1850 to Carlos C. Stuart, following p. 50 (facsimile).

Location: ScU.

D 105 THE HISTORIC WHITMAN
1973

The Historic | WHITMAN | [rule] | JOSEPH JAY RUBIN | THE PENNSYLVANIA STATE UNIVERSITY PRESS | University Park and London

Copyright 1973.

"Letters from a Travelling Bachelor," pp. 311–354. *Reprint*. See E 1147–1156.

Location: JM.

D 106 OTHER PEOPLE'S MAIL
1973

[first three lines across two facing pages] [ornate lettering] Other People's Mail | LETTERS OF MEN AND WOMEN OF LETTERS | [slant-right lettering] Selected from the Henry W. and Albert A. Berg Collection of English and American Literature | [flush right] [leaf design] By Lola L. Szladits | [four lines flush left] THE NEW YORK PUBLIC LIBRARY | [slant-right lettering] Astor, Lenox and Tilden Foundations | & READEX BOOKS | [slant-right lettering] A Division of Readex Microprint Coporation

Copyright 1973. Cloth or wrappers.

Letter of [21 April 1863] to Thomas Sawyer, pp. 49–55 (in facsimile), pp. 52–55.

Location: JM.

D 107 THE FOREGROUND OF LEAVES OF GRASS
1974

The Foreground of | *Leaves of Grass* | by Floyd Stovall | University Press of Virginia | Charlottesville

Copyright page: '*First published 1974*'.

Prose piece on Emerson, p. 290.

Location: JM.

D 108 PAGES
1976

[light brown] Pages ['g' extending down into next line] | [black] THE WORLD OF BOOKS, WRITERS, AND WRITING | [light brown rule] | [black boldface] 1 | [light brown rule] | [black] MATTHEW J. BRUCCOLI | *Editorial Director* | C. E. FRAZER CLARK, JR. | *Managing Editor* | GALE RESEARCH COM-PANY • BOOK TOWER • DETROIT, MICHIGAN 48226 | [light brown rule]

Copyright 1976.

Various manuscript facsimiles in [William White], "Profile of a Book Collector: Charles E. Feinberg," pp. 272–289.

Location: JM.

D 109 AMERICAN LITERARY AUTOGRAPHS
1977

American | Literary Autographs | FROM WASHINGTON IRVING | TO HENRY JAMES | Herbert Cahoon, Thomas V. Lange, | Charles Ryskamp | DOVER PUBLICATIONS, INC., NEW YORK | *in association with* | THE PIERPONT MORGAN LIBRARY

Wrappers. Copyright 1977.

Fair copy of the introduction to the planned London edition of 1867, item 52 (2 pp. in facsimile).
    Sample page from a notebook, item 53 (1 p. in facsimile).
    "O Captain! My Captain!" (dated 27 April 1890), item 54 (1 p. in facsimile).

Location: JM.

D 110 WITH WALT WHITMAN IN CAMDEN (VOL. VI)
1982

WITH | WALT WHITMAN | IN CAMDEN | September 15, 1889—July 6, 1890 | 6 | [rule] | By HORACE TRAUBEL | *Edited by* | GERTRUDE TRAU-BEL | WILLIAM WHITE | SOUTHERN ILLINOIS UNIVERSITY PRESS | CARBONDALE AND EDWARDSVILLE

Copyright 1982.

Conversations with Whitman.

Location: JM.

D 111 THE CORRESPONDENCE OF WALT WHITMAN   A
SECOND SUPPLEMENT . . .
1991

THE CORRESPONDENCE OF | WALT WHITMAN | A Second Supplement with a Revised Calendar | of Letters Written to Whitman | Edited by | EDWIN

HAVILAND MILLER | Iowa City: | Walt Whitman Quarterly Review Press | 1991

Wrappers.

Various letters, pp. 9–42.

Location: JM.

Note: Published simultaneously as the Winter-Spring 1991 issue of the *Walt Whitman Quarterly Review* (E 3022).

D 112 WHITMAN IN HIS OWN TIME
1991

WRITERS IN THEIR OWN TIME: Volume I | WHITMAN IN | HIS OWN TIME: | *A Biographical Chronicle of His Life,* | *Drawn from Recollections,* | *Memoirs, and Interviews* | *by Friends and Associates* | Edited by | Joel Myerson | *University of South Carolina* | A Manly, Inc. Book | Omnigraphics, Inc. | Penobscot Building • Detroit, MI 48226

Copyright 1991.

Various manuscript facsimiles.

Location: JM.

E. First-Appearance Contributions to Magazines and Newspapers

First American and English publication in magazines and newspapers of material by Whitman through 1991, arranged chronologically. See the Introduction for a discussion of attributions of the nearly all anonomously published journalistic pieces.

E 1

"Effects of Lightning," *Long-Islander,* before 8 August 1838.

Reprinted in *Long Island Democrat,* 8 August 1838; *UPP,* I, 32; William White, "Walt Whitman's Earliest Extant Prose," *Walt Whitman Review,* 14 (September 1968), [142] (facsimile).

E 2

[Summer Produce and Fall Crops], *Long-Islander,* before 8 August 1838.

Reprinted in *Long Island Democrat,* 8 August 1838.

E 3

"Our Future Lot," *Long-Islander,* before 31 October 1838.

Poem. Reprinted in *Long Island Democrat,* 31 October 1838; *UPP,* I, 1–2; *Early Poems and Fiction,* pp. 28–29. Revised as "Time to Come" in *New York Aurora,* 9 April 1842 (E 112).

E 4

"Fame's Vanity," *Long Island Democrat,* 23 October 1839.

Poem. Reprinted in *UPP,* I, 4–5; *Early Poems and Fiction,* pp. 23–24. Revised as "Ambition" in *Brother Jonathan,* 29 January 1842 (E 36).

E 5

"My Departure," *Long Island Democrat,* 27 November 1839.

Poem. Reprinted in *UPP,* I, 5–6; *Early Poems and Fiction,* pp. 31–32. Revised as "Death of the Nature-Lover" in *Brother Jonathan,* 11 March 1843 (E 165).

E 6

"Greenwood Cemetery—Description and Reflections," *New York Christian Messenger,* before 7 December 1839.

Reprinted in *Rural Repository,* 7 December 1839, pp. 101–102.

E 7
"Young Grimes," *Long Island Democrat,* 1 January 1840.

Poem. Reprinted in *UPP,* I, 2–4 (dated '1839'); *Early Poems and Fiction,* pp. 3–4.

E 8
"From the Desk of a Schoolmaster," "Sun-Down Papers [No. 1]," *Hempstead Inquirer,* 29 February 1840.

E 9
"From the Desk of a Schoolmaster," "Sun-Down Papers [No. 2]," *Hempstead Inquirer,* 14 March 1840.

E 10
"From the Desk of a Schoolmaster," "Sun-Down Papers [No. 3]," *Hempstead Inquirer,* 28 March 1840.

E 11
"From the Desk of a Schoolmaster," "Sun-Down Papers [No. 4]," *Hempstead Inquirer,* 11 April 1840.

E 12
"From the Desk of a Schoolmaster," "Sun-Down Papers [No. 5]," *Hempstead Inquirer,* before 28 April 1840.

Reprinted in *Long Island Democrat,* 28 April 1840; *UPP,* I, 32–34.

E 13
"The Inca's Daughter," *Long Island Democrat,* 5 May 1840.

Poem. Reprinted in *UPP,* I, 8–9; *Early Poems and Fiction,* pp. 6–7.

E 14
"The Love That Is Hereafter," *Long Island Democrat,* 19 May 1840.

Poem. Reprinted in *UPP,* I, 9–10; *Early Poems and Fiction,* pp. 8–9.

E 15
"We All Shall Rest At Last," *Long Island Democrat,* 14 July 1840.

Poem. Reprinted in *UPP,* I, 10–11. Revised as "Each Has His Grief" in *New World,* 20 November 1841 (E 32).

E 16
"The Spanish Lady," *Long Island Democrat,* 4 August 1840.

Poem. Reprinted in *UPP,* I, 12–13; *Early Poems and Fiction,* pp. 10–11.

E 17
"From the Desk of a Schoolmaster," "Sun-Down Papers [No. 6]," *Hempstead Inquirer,* before 11 August 1840.

Reprinted in *Long Island Democrat,* 11 August 1840; *UPP,* I, 35–37.

E 18
"The End of All," *Long Island Democrat,* 22 September 1840.

Poem. Reprinted in *UPP,* I, 13–15. Revised as "The Winding-Up" in *Long Island Democrat,* 22 June 1841 (E 25).

E 19
"From the Desk of a Schoolmaster," "Sun-Down Papers [No. 7]," *Long Island Democrat,* 29 September 1840.

Reprinted in *UPP,* I, 37–39.

E 20
"A Card," *Long Island Democrat,* 6 October 1840.

Reprinted in Joseph Jay Rubin, "Whitman in 1840: A Discovery," *American Literature,* 9 (May 1937), 239–242.

E 21
"A Loco Foco Defeat," *Long Island Farmer,* 6 October 1840.

E 22
"From the Desk of a Schoolmaster," "Sun-Down Papers [No. 8]," *Long Island Democrat,* 20 October 1840.

Reprinted in *UPP,* I, 39–44.

E 23
"The Columbian's Song," *Long Island Democrat,* 27 October 1840.

Poem. Reprinted in *UPP,* I, 15–16; *Early Poems and Fiction,* pp. 12–13.

E 24
"From the Desk of a Schoolmaster," "Sun-Down Papers [No. 9]," *Long Island Democrat,* 28 November 1840.

Reprinted in *UPP,* I, 44–46.

E 25

"The Winding-Up," *Long Island Democrat,* 22 June 1841.

Signed "W. Whitman." Poem. Reprinted in *Early Poems and Fiction,* pp. 14–15. Revised version of "The End of All" in *Long Island Democrat,* 22 September 1840 (E 18).

E 26

"From the Desk of a Schoolmaster," "Sun-Down Papers [No. 9]," *Long Island Democrat,* 6 July 1841.

Reprinted in *UPP,* I, 46–48.

E 27

"From the Desk of a Schoolmaster," "Sun-Down Papers [No. 10]," *Long Island Farmer,* 20 July 1841.

Reprinted in *UPP,* I, 48–51.

E 28

[Report of Whitman's Speech in the Park in New York on 29 July 1841], *New Era,* 30 July 1841.

Reprinted in *Brooklyn Daily Eagle,* 6 April 1847; *GF,* II, 3–7; *UPP,* I, 51.

E 29

"Death in the School-Room (a Fact)," *United States Magazine, and Democratic Review,* 9 (August 1841), 177–181.

Fiction. Reprinted in *Long Island Farmer,* 10 August 1841; *New York Mirror,* 19 (21 August 1841), 266–267; *Ladies Garland,* 5 (September 1841), 73–75; *Maunch Corner Courier* [Maunch Corner, Penn.], 25 October 1841. Revised in *Brooklyn Daily Eagle,* 24 December 1847 (E 1046); reprinted in *Specimen Days* (A 11), pp. 340–344; *Early Poems and Fiction,* pp. 55–60.

E 30

"Wild Frank's Return," *United States Magazine, and Democratic Review,* 9 (November 1841), 476–482.

Fiction. Reprinted in *Long Island Farmer,* 11 January 1842. Revised in *Specimen Days* (A 11), pp. 353–357; *Early Poems and Fiction,* pp. 61–67.

E 31

"The Child's Champion," *New World,* 3 (20 November 1841), 321–322.

Fiction. Revised as "The Child and the Profligate" in *Columbian Magazine,* October 1844 (E 173); reprinted in *Brooklyn Daily Eagle,* 27–29 January 1847

(E 706); (revised) in *Specimen Days* (A 11), pp. 361–366; *Early Poems and Fiction*, pp. 68–79.

E 32
"Each Has His Grief," *New World*, 3 (20 November 1841), 1.

Signed "W. W." Poem. Reprinted in *Early Poems and Fiction*, pp. 16–17. Revised from "We All Shall Rest at Last" in *Long Island Democrat*, 14 July 1840 (E 15).

E 33
"Bervance: or, Father and Son," *United States Magazine, and Democratic Review*, 9 (December 1841), 560–568.

Signed "W. W." Fiction. Reprinted in *UPP*, I, 52–60; *Early Poems and Fiction*, pp. 80–87.

E 34
"The Punishment of Pride," *New World*, 3 (18 December 1841), 394.

Poem. Reprinted in *Conservator*, 12 (February 1902), 189; *UPP*, I, 17–19; *Early Poems and Fiction*, pp. 18–20.

E 35
"The Tomb Blossoms," *United States Magazine, and Democratic Review*, 10 (January 1842), 62–68.

Fiction. Reprinted in *Philadelphia Press*, 23 October 1892; *UPP*, I, 60–67. Revised in *Voices from the Press* (D 1), pp. 27–38; *Early Poems and Fiction*, pp. 88–94.

E 36
"Ambition," *Brother Jonathan*, 1 (29 January 1842), 5.

Poem. Reprinted in *UPP*, I, 19–20; *Early Poems and Fiction*, pp. 21–22. Revised version of "Fame's Vanity" in *Long Island Democrat*, 23 October 1839 (E 4).

E 37
"Walks in Broadway [No. 1]," *New York Aurora*, 23 February 1842.

E 38
"Walks in Broadway [No. 2]," *New York Aurora*, 24 February 1842.

E 39
"Walks in Broadway [No. 3]," *New York Aurora*, 25 February 1842.

E 40
"Boz and Democracy," *Brother Jonathan*, 1 (26 February 1842), 243–244.

Reprinted in *UPP*, I, 67–72.

E 41
"Walks in Broadway [No. 4]," *New York Aurora*, 26 February 1842.

E 42
"The Last of the Sacred Army," *United States Magazine, and Democratic Review*, 10 (March 1842), 259–264.

Fiction. Reprinted in *United States Magazine, and Democratic Review*, 29 (November 1851), 463–466; *UPP*, I, 72–78. Revised as Chapter 20 of *Franklin Evans, New World*, November 1842 (E 159); reprinted in *Early Poems and Fiction*, pp. 95–100.

E 43
"Walks in Broadway [No. 5]," *New York Aurora*, 1 March 1842.

E 44
"The System Must Stand," *New York Aurora*, 3 March 1842.

E 45
"Walks in Broadway [No. 6]," *New York Aurora*, 4 March 1842.

E 46
"Mr. Emerson's Lecture," *New York Aurora*, 7 March 1842.

Reprinted in *Aurora*, p. 105.

E 47
"Sectarianism and Our Public Schools," *New York Aurora*, 7 March 1842.

E 48
"The Free Schools," *New York Aurora*, 8 March 1842.

E 49
"Our City," *New York Aurora*, 8 March 1842.

Reprinted in *Aurora*, pp. 17–19.

E 50
[Death of McDonald Clarke], *New York Aurora*, 8 March 1842.

Reprinted in *Aurora*, pp. 105–108. Revised as "An Afternoon at Greenwood" in *Brooklyn Daily Eagle*, 13 June 1846 (E 381).

E 51
"How Bears the Wind," *New York Aurora,* 11 March 1842.

Reprinted in *Aurora,* pp. 87–89.

E 52
"Public Schools," *New York Aurora,* 11 March 1842.

E 53
[Hapless Afara!], *New York Aurora,* 12 March 1842.

Reprinted in *Aurora,* pp. 108–109.

E 54
"Life in New York," *New York Aurora,* 14 March 1842.

Reprinted in *Aurora,* pp. 19–20.

E 55
"A Peep Behind the Scenes," *New York Aurora,* 14 March 1842.

Reprinted in *Aurora,* pp. 89–90.

E 56
"Life in a New York Market," *New York Aurora,* 16 March 1842.

Reprinted in *Aurora,* pp. 20–22.

E 57
[The True Democratic Principle], *New York Aurora,* 16 March 1842.

Reprinted in *Aurora,* pp. 90–91.

E 58
"Cowardly Submission Worse than War," *New York Aurora,* 17 March 1842.

E 59
"Insult to American Citizenship," *New York Aurora,* 17 March 1842.

Reprinted in *Aurora,* pp. 57–58.

E 60
"The *Aurora* and the School Question," *New York Aurora,* 18 March 1842.

Reprinted in *Aurora,* pp. 58–59.

E 61
"The Death and Burial of McDonald Clarke. A Parody," *New York Aurora,* 18 March 1842.

Signed "W." Poem. Reprinted in *Aurora*, p. 135; *Early Poems and Fiction*, pp. 25–26.

E 62
"New York Boarding Houses," *New York Aurora*, 18 March 1842.

Reprinted in *Aurora*, pp. 22–24.

E 63
"About Silence," *New York Aurora*, 19 March 1842.

Reprinted in *Aurora*, pp. 125–126.

E 64
"Concerning the Misses Cushman," *New York Sunday Times*, 20 March 1842.

Listed in Herbert Bergman, "A Hitherto Unknown Whitman Story and a Possible Early Poem," *Walt Whitman Review*, 28 (March 1982), 6.

E 65
"A Ramble Up the Third Avenue," *New York Sunday Times*, 20 March 1842.

Listed in Herbert Bergman, "A Hitherto Unknown Whitman Story and a Possible Early Poem," *Walt Whitman Review*, 28 (March 1982), 6.

E 66
"The Last of Lively Frank." *New York Aurora*, 21 March 1842.

Reprinted in *Aurora*, pp. 24–25.

E 67
"Public Schools," *New York Aurora*, 21 March 1842.

E 68
"Park Theatre," *New York Aurora*, 22 March 1842.

Reprinted in *Aurora*, p. 110.

E 69
"Reform It Altogether," *New York Aurora*, 22 March 1842.

Reprinted in *Aurora*, p. 91.

E 70
"Americanism," *New York Aurora*, 23 March 1842.

Reprinted in *Aurora*, p. 92.

E 71
"An Hour in a Balcony," *New York Aurora*, 23 March 1842.

Reprinted in *Aurora*, pp. 26–27.

E 72
"Bamboozle and Benjamin," *New York Aurora*, 24 March 1842.

Reprinted in *Aurora*, pp. 110–111.

E 73
"Calhoun," *New York Aurora*, 24 March 1842.

Reprinted in *Aurora*, p. 93.

E 74
"The Clerk from the Country," *New York Aurora*, 24 March 1842.

Reprinted in *Aurora*, pp. 27–30.

E 75
"Flowers," *New York Aurora*, 24 March 1842.

Reprinted in *Aurora*, p. 30.

E 76
"Tammany in Trouble," *New York Aurora*, 24 March 1842.

Reprinted in *Aurora*, p. 60.

E 77
"The Penny Press," *New York Aurora*, 26 March 1842.

Reprinted in *Aurora*, pp. 111–112.

E 78
"Tammany's 'Family Jars,' " *New York Aurora*, 26 March 1842.

Reprinted in *Aurora*, p. 61.

E 79
"A Peep at the Israelites," *New York Aurora*, 28 March 1842.

Reprinted in *Aurora*, pp. 31–32.

E 80
"Yesterday," *New York Aurora*, 28 March 1842.

Reprinted in *Aurora*, pp. 30–31.

E 81
"Tyler's Message," *New York Aurora,* 28 March 1842.

E 82
"What's the Row," *New York Aurora,* 28 March 1842.

Reprinted in *Aurora,* pp. 93–94.

E 83
"Doings at the Synagogue," *New York Aurora,* 29 March 1842.

Reprinted in *Aurora,* pp. 33–34.

E 84
"The New York Press," *New York Aurora,* 29 March 1842.

Reprinted in *Aurora,* pp. 112–114.

E 85
"Organs of Democracy," *New York Aurora,* 29 March 1842.

Reprinted in *Aurora,* p. 62.

E 86
"A Peep in at Hudson's Rooms," *New York Aurora,* 29 March 1842.

Reprinted in *Aurora,* pp. 34–35.

E 87
"Prospects of War," *New York Aurora,* 29 March 1842.

E 88
"The Right of Search," *New York Aurora,* 29 March 1842.

E 89
"Geology and Scriptures," *New York Aurora,* 29 March 1842.

E 90
"The Benefit of Benevolence," *New York Aurora,* 30 March 1842.

Reprinted in *Aurora,* pp. 94–95.

E 91
"Centre Market Festival," *New York Aurora,* 30 March 1842.

Reprinted in *Aurora,* p. 35.

E 92
"Defining 'Our Position,' " *New York Aurora,* 30 March 1842.

Reprinted in *Aurora,* pp. 63–64.

E 93
"Temperance Among the Firemen!", *New York Aurora,* 30 March 1842.

Reprinted in *Aurora,* pp. 35–36.

E 94
"Dissensions of Tammany," *New York Aurora,* 1 April 1842.

Reprinted in *Aurora,* pp. 66–67.

E 95
[Guardians at the grave], *New York Aurora,* 1 April 1842.

Reprinted in *Aurora,* p. 39.

E 96
"Scenes of Last Night," *New York Aurora,* 1 April 1842.

Reprinted in *Aurora,* pp. 36–38. Revised as "A City Fire" in *Brooklyn Daily Eagle,* 24 February 1847 (E 761).

E 97
[Credo], *New York Aurora,* 1 April 1842.

E 98
" 'Black and White Slaves,' " *New York Aurora,* 2 April 1842.

Reprinted in *Aurora,* pp. 126–127.

E 99
"Dickens and Democracy," *New York Aurora,* 2 April 1842.

Reprinted in *Aurora,* pp. 114–116.

E 100
"The Park Meeting," *New York Aurora,* 2 April 1842.

Reprinted in *Aurora,* p. 40.

E 101
" 'Marble Time' in the Park," *New York Aurora,* 4 April 1842.

Reprinted in *Aurora,* pp. 42–44.

E 102
[A Disgraceful Proceeding], *New York Aurora,* 5 April 1842.

Reprinted in *Aurora,* pp. 41–42.

E 103
"The Fourth of April," *New York Aurora,* 5 April 1842.

Reprinted in *Aurora,* p. 95.

E 104
"Heart Rending," *New York Aurora,* 5 April 1842.

Reprinted in *Aurora,* p. 96.

E 105
[A Lazy Day], *New York Aurora,* 6 April 1842.

Reprinted in *Aurora,* pp. 44–45.

E 106
"Tammany Meeting Last Night," *New York Aurora,* 6 April 1842.

Reprinted in *Aurora,* pp. 65–66.

E 107
"A Word to Correspondents," *New York Aurora,* 6 April 1842.

Reprinted in *Aurora,* p. 116.

E 108
"The Mask Thrown Off," *New York Aurora,* 7 April 1842.

Reprinted in *Aurora,* pp. 67–68.

E 109
"Something Worth Perusal," *New York Aurora,* 7 April 1842.

Reprinted in *Aurora,* pp. 45–47.

E 110
"The Latest and Grandest Humbug," *New York Aurora,* 8 April 1842.

Reprinted in *Aurora,* pp. 96–97.

E 111
"The Bloody Sixth!", *New York Aurora,* 9 April 1842.

E 112
"Time to Come," *New York Aurora,* 9 April 1842.

Signed "Walter Whitman." Poem. Reprinted in *Aurora,* p. 134; *Early Poems and Fiction,* pp. 27–28. Revised from "Our Future Lot" in *Long Island Democrat,* 31 October 1838 (E 3).

E 113
"We," *New York Aurora,* 9 April 1842.

Reprinted in *Aurora,* pp. 116–117.

E 114
[Black–Hearted Deceit], *New York Aurora,* 11 April 1842.

Reprinted in *Aurora,* pp. 68–70.

E 115
"Tomorrow," *New York Aurora,* 11 April 1842.

Reprinted in *Aurora,* p. 70.

E 116
[Gross Political Chicanery], *New York Aurora,* 12 April 1842.

Reprinted in *Aurora,* pp. 71–72.

E 117
"Last Evening," *New York Aurora,* 12 April 1842.

Reprinted in *Aurora,* pp. 72–73.

E 118
"Playing in the Park," *New York Aurora,* 12 April 1842.

Reprinted in *Aurora,* p. 47.

E 119
[A Small Potato Arnold], *New York Aurora,* 12 April 1842.

Reprinted in *Aurora,* pp. 73–74.

E 120
"More Catholic Insolence!", *New York Aurora,* 12 April 1842.

E 121
"The House of Refuge," *New York Aurora,* 13 April 1842.

Reprinted in *Aurora,* pp. 49–50.

E 122
"Incidents of Last Night," *New York Aurora,* 13 April 1842.

Reprinted in *Aurora,* pp. 76–77.

E 123
"Result of the Election," *New York Aurora,* 13 April 1842.

Reprinted in *Aurora,* pp. 75–76.

E 124
"Sentiment and a Saunter," *New York Aurora,* 13 April 1842.

Reprinted in *Aurora,* pp. 48–49.

E 125
[A Higher Devotion Than Party], *New York Aurora,* 14 April 1842.

Reprinted in *Aurora,* p. 78.

E 126
"Over the Ocean," *New York Aurora,* 14 April 1842.

Reprinted in *Aurora,* pp. 127–128.

E 127
"Plots of the Jesuits!", *New York Aurora,* 14 April 1842.

Reprinted in *Aurora,* pp. 78–79.

E 128
"Italian Opera in New Orleans," *New York Aurora,* 15 April 1842.

Reprinted in *Aurora,* p. 118.

E 129
"The Late Riots," *New York Aurora,* 15 April 1842.

Reprinted in *Aurora,* pp. 79–80.

E 130
"Where Will Tammany Have to Stop?", *New York Aurora,* 15 April 1842.

E 131
"About Children," *New York Aurora,* 16 April 1842.

Reprinted in *Aurora,* pp. 50–52.

E 132
"The Catholic Rows Not Ended," *New York Aurora,* 16 April 1842.

Reprinted in *Aurora,* pp. 81–82.

E 133
[Native Americanism Repudiated], *New York Aurora,* 18 April 1842.

Reprinted in *Aurora,* pp. 82–83.

E 134
"Newspaperial Etiquette," *New York Aurora,* 18 April 1842.

Reprinted in *Aurora,* pp. 118–119.

E 135
"Old Land Marks," *New York Aurora,* 18 April 1842.

Reprinted in *Aurora,* pp. 98–99.

E 136
"The Schools' Holiday," *New York Aurora,* 18 April 1842.

Reprinted in *Aurora,* pp. 53–54.

E 137
"Snoring Made Music," *New York Aurora,* 18 April 1842.

Reprinted in *Aurora,* pp. 52–53.

E 138
"Horace Greeley," *New York Aurora,* 19 April 1842.

Reprinted in *Aurora,* p. 122.

E 139
[How to Write a Leader], *New York Aurora,* 19 April 1842.

Reprinted in *Aurora,* pp. 119–121.

E 140
"J. F. Cooper," *New York Aurora,* 19 April 1842.

Reprinted in *Aurora,* p. 121.

E 141
"The English Troubles in India, and Our Difficulties with Great Britain," *New York Aurora*, 19 April 1842.

E 142
[Legislation and Morality], *New York Aurora*, 20 April 1842.

Partially reprinted as "You Cannot Legislate Men into Virtue," *Brooklyn Daily Eagle*, 18 March 1846; reprinted in *GF*, I, 59–61; *Aurora*, pp. 99–100.

E 143
"Life and Love," *New York Aurora*, 20 April 1842.

Reprinted in *Aurora*, pp. 129–130.

E 144
"The Ocean," *New York Aurora*, 21 April 1842.

Reprinted in *Aurora*, pp. 130–131.

E 145
"Broadway Yesterday," *New York Aurora*, 22 April 1842.

Reprinted in *Aurora*, p. 54.

E 146
"Dreams," *New York Aurora*, 23 April 1842.

Reprinted in *Aurora*, pp. 132–133.

E 147
"Reform in Congress," *New York Aurora*, 23 April 1842.

Reprinted in *Aurora*, pp. 100–101.

E 148
"The Child–Ghost; a Story of the Last Loyalist," *United States Magazine, and Democratic Review*, 10 (May 1842), 451–459.

Fiction. Reprinted in *Concord Freeman*, 25 October 1844, p. 1. Revised as "The Last Loyalist" in *Specimen Days* (A 11), pp. 349–353; reprinted in *Early Poems and Fiction*, pp. 101–109.

E 149
"Reuben's Last Wish," *Washingtonian* (New York), 21 May 1842.

Fiction. Reprinted in *Early Poems and Fiction*, pp. 110–114.

E 150
"City Matters," *New York Evening Tattler*, 9 June 1842.

E 151
"A Legend of Life and Love," *United States Magazine, and Democratic Review*, 11 (July 1842), 83–86.

Fiction. Reprinted in *New-York Daily Tribune*, 6 July 1842; *Brother Jonathan*, 9 July 1842; *UPP*, I, 78–83. Revised in *Brooklyn Daily Eagle*, 11 June 1846 (E 377); reprinted in *GF*, II, 377–386; *Early Poems and Fiction*, pp. 115–119.

E 152
"An Hour at the Bath," *New York Evening Tattler*, 11 August 1842.

E 153
"Boz's Opinion of Us," *New York Evening Tattler*, 11 August 1842.

E 154
"No Turning Back," *New York Sunday Times*, 14 August 1842, p. 1.

Poem. Signed "Walter Whitman." Reprinted in Thomas Ollive Mabbott, "Walt Whitman Edits the *Sunday Times*, July, 1842–June, 1843," *American Literature*, 39 (March 1967), 100.

E 155
"Is Mesmerism True?", *New York Sunday Times*, 14 August 1842, p. 2.

Reprinted in Thomas Ollive Mabbott, "Walt Whitman Edits the *Sunday Times*, July, 1842–June, 1843," *American Literature*, 39 (March 1967), 101.

E 156
"Gad Correspondence," *New York Sunday Times*, 14 August 1842, p. 1.

Reprinted in Thomas Ollive Mabbott, "Walt Whitman Edits the *Sunday Times*, July, 1842–June, 1843," *American Literature*, 39 (March 1967), 101–102.

Note: Only scattered issues of the *New York Sunday Times* exist; there might be more contributions by Whitman in other issues.

E 157
"The Angel of Tears," *United States Magazine, and Democratic Review*, 11 (September 1842), 282–284.

Fiction. Reprinted in *UPP*, I, 83–86. Slightly revised in *Brooklyn Evening Star*, 28 February 1846 (E 232); *Early Poems and Fiction*, pp. 120–123.

E 158

"Queens County [Democratic Campaign]," *Plebian*, 14 October 1842.

Reprinted in Esther Shephard, "Walt Whitman's Whereabouts in the Winter of 1842–1843," *American Literature*, 29 (November 1957), 292.

E 159

"Franklin Evans; or The Inebriate. A Tale of the Times," *New World*, 2 (November 1842), 1–31.

Fiction. Incorporates "The Last of the Sacred Army" from the *United States Magazine, and Democratic Review*, March 1842 (E 42). Reprinted as *Franklin Evans: Knowledge as Power. The Merchant's Clerk, in New York; or Career as a Young Man from the Country* (A 1); *UPP*, II, 103–221; *Early Poems and Fiction*, pp. 126–239. Revised as "Fortunes of a Country-Boy; Incidents in Town—and his Adventures at the South. A Tale of Long Island" by "J. R. S." in *Brooklyn Daily Eagle*, 16–30 November 1846 (E 594).

Note: Two imbedded tales were reprinted seperately: (1) "The Death of Wind–Foot" (revised) in *American Review*, June 1845; *Massachusetts Ploughman*, 9 August 1845, p. 4; as "The Death of Wind-Foot. An Indian Story" in *Crystal Fount and Rechabite Recorder* (New York), 5 (18 October 1845), 81–84; (2) "Lady Jane" (revised) in *Brooklyn Daily Eagle*, 7 December 1846 (E 625).

E 160

"Our City Schools," *New York Sun*, 16 December 1842.

E 161

"Dangers to Country Youth in the City," *New York Sun*, 1 December 1842.

E 162

"The Madman," *Washingtonian and Organ* (New York), 28 January 1843.

Fiction. The first chapter in a serial; no more chapters have been located as no other issues of the periodical have been found. Reprinted in *Early Poems and Fiction*, pp. 240–243.

E 163

"Eris: A Spirit Record," *Columbian Magazine*, 1 (March 1843), 138–139.

Fiction. Reprinted in *American Historical Annual* (D 2), pp. 99–102; *UPP*, I, 86–89. Revised as "The Love of Eris: A Spirit Record" in *Brooklyn Daily Eagle*, 18 August 1846 (E 455); reprinted in *GF*, II, 369–376; *Early Poems and Fiction*, pp. 244–247.

E 164
"Boys and Girls," *Plebian,* 1 March 1843.

Reprinted in Esther Shephard, "Walt Whitman's Whereabouts in the Winter of 1842–1843," *American Literature,* 29 (November 1957), 294.

E 165
"Death of the Nature–Lover," *Brother Jonathan,* 4 (11 March 1843), 10.

Poem. Reprinted in *Conservator,* 12 (January 1905), 189; *UPP,* I, 7; *Early Poems and Fiction,* pp. 30–31. Revised from "My Departure" in *Long Island Democrat,* 27 November 1839 (E 5).

E 166
"Lesson of the Two Symbols," *Subterranean* (New York), 1, no. 1 (15 July 1843).

Poem. Reprinted in Elliott B. Gross, " 'Lesson of the Two Symbols': An Undiscovered Whitman Poem," *Walt Whitman Review,* 12 (December 1966), 77–80.

E 167
"The Fireman's Dream: With the Story of His Strange Companion. A Tale of Fantasie," *New York Sunday Times & Noah's Weekly Messenger,* 31 March 1844.

Fiction. Signed "Walter Whitman." Reprinted in Herbert Bergman, "A Hitherto Unknown Whitman Story and a Possible Early Poem," *Walt Whitman Review,* 28 (March 1982), 7–14.

E 168
"Tale of a Shirt: A Very Pathetic Ballad," *New York Sunday Times & Noah's Weekly Messenger,* 31 March 1844.

Signed "W." Poem. Reprinted in Herbert Bergman, "A Hitherto Unknown Whitman Story and a Possible Early Poem," *Walt Whitman Review,* 28 (March 1982), 14–15.

E 169
"My Boys and Girls," *Rover,* 3 (20 April 1844), 75.

Fiction. Reprinted in *Half-Breed,* pp. 109–113; *Early Poems and Fiction,* pp. 248–250.

E 170
"Dumb Kate.—An Early Death," *Columbian Magazine,* 1 (May 1844), 230–231.

Fiction. Revised in *Brooklyn Daily Eagle,* 13 July 1846 (E 417). Revised as "Dumb Kate" in *Specimen Days* (A 11), pp. 370–371; *Early Poems and Fiction,* pp. 251–253.

E 171
"A Visit to Greenwood Cemetery," *New York Sunday Times & Noah's Weekly Messenger,* 5 May 1844.

Listed in Herbert Bergman, "A Hitherto Unknown Whitman Story and a Possible Early Poem," *Walt Whitman Review,* 28 (March 1982), 6.

E 172
"The Little Sleighers. A Sketch of a Winter Morning on the Battery," *Columbian Magazine,* 2 (September 1844), 113–114.

Fiction. Reprinted in *UPP,* I, 90–92; *Early Poems and Fiction,* pp. 254–256.

E 173
"The Child and the Profligate," *Columbian Magazine,* 2 (October 1844), 149–153.

Revised from "The Child's Champion" in *New World,* 20 November 1841 (E 31).

E 174
"Shirval: A Tale of Jerusalem," *Aristidean,* 1 (March 1845), 12–15.

Fiction. Reprinted in *Half-Breed,* pp. 81–85; *Early Poems and Fiction,* pp. 292–295. Revised from manuscript in William White, "Shirval: A Tale of Jerusalem," *Daily Collegian* (Wayne State University), 28 February 1963, p. 8.

E 175
"Arrow-Tip," *Aristidean,* 1 (March 1845), 36–64.

Fiction. Revised as "The Half-Breed: A Tale of the Western Frontier" in *Brooklyn Daily Eagle,* 1–6, 8, 9 June 1846 (E 361); reprinted in *Half-Breed,* pp. 23–76; *Early Poems and Fiction,* pp. 257–291.

E 176
"Richard Parker's Widow," *Aristidean,* 1 (April 1845), 111–114.

Fiction. Reprinted in *Half-Breed,* pp. 89–97; *Early Poems and Fiction,* pp. 296–301.

E 177
"The Boy Lover," *American Review,* 1 (May 1845), 479–482.

Fiction. Reprinted in *Brooklyn Daily Eagle*, 4–5 January 1848; revised in *Specimen Days* (A 11), pp. 357–361; *Early Poems and Fiction*, pp. 302–308.

E 178

"Delightful Sights," *Broadway Journal*, 1 (31 May 1845), 347.

Reprinted in Burton R. Pollin, " 'Delightful Sights': A Possible Whitman Article in Poe's *Broadway Journal*," *Walt Whitman Review*, 15 (September 1969), 180–187.

E 179

"Revenge and Requital: A Tale of a Murderer Escaped," *United States Magazine, and Democratic Review*, 17 (July–August 1845), 105–111.

Fiction. Reprinted in *Weekly News* (New York), 16 August 1845. Revised as "One Wicked Impulse! (a tale of a Murderer escaped.)," *Brooklyn Daily Eagle*, 7–9 September 1846 (E 483). Revised as "One Wicked Impulse!", *Specimen Days* (A 11), pp. 348–349; reprinted in *Ellery Queen's Mystery Magazine*, 23 (January 1954), 92–100; *Early Poems and Fiction*, pp. 309–318.

E 180

"Brooklyn Schools and Teachers," *Brooklyn Evening Star*, 15 September 1845.

Reprinted in *Schools*, pp. 65–67.

E 181

"Our City's Pride and Beauty," *Brooklyn Evening Star*, 15 September 1845.

Signed "W."

E 182

"An Incident of Life in New York, Beneath the Surface," *Brooklyn Evening Star*, 30 September 1845.

Signed "W."

E 183

"The Cause and a Man," *Brooklyn Evening Star*, 2 October 1845.

Signed "W."

E 184

"Some Hints for County and Town," *Brooklyn Evening Star*, 2 October 1845.

Signed "W." Reprinted in *Schools*, pp. 67–68.

E 185
"Tours of Queen Victoria," *Brooklyn Evening Star*, 4 October 1845.

Signed "W."

E 186
"How to Avoid Dangerous Fires," *Brooklyn Evening Star*, 10 October 1845.

Signed "W."

E 187
"Some Hints to Apprentices and Youth," *Brooklyn Evening Star*, 10 October 1845.

Signed "W." Reprinted in *Schools*, pp. 69–70.

E 188
"Living Too High," *Brooklyn Evening Star*, 11 October 1845.

Signed "W."

E 189
"The Burlesque of Soldiery," *Brooklyn Evening Star*, 13 October 1845.

Signed "W."

E 190
"A Sign of Modern Improvement," *Brooklyn Evening Star*, 22 October 1845.

Signed "W."

E 191
"The Whip in Schools," *Brooklyn Evening Star*, 22 October 1845.

Signed "W." Reprinted in *Schools*, pp. 70–71. Revised as "The Rule of the Rod" in *Brooklyn Daily Eagle*, 8 October 1846 (E 520).

E 192
"Hints to the Young," *Brooklyn Evening Star*, 23 October 1845.

Signed "W." Reprinted in *Schools*, pp. 72–73.

E 193
"Niblo's Fair, Last Night," *Brooklyn Evening Star*, 24 October 1845.

Signed "W."

E 194
"A Suggestion—Brooklyn Amusements," *Brooklyn Evening Star*, 27 October 1845.

Signed "W."

E 195
"For the Star [Against Whipping]," *Brooklyn Evening Star*, 30 October 1845. Signed "W."

Reprinted in *Schools*, pp. 73–78.

E 196
"Tear Down and Build Over Again," *American Review*, 1 (November 1845), 536–538.

Reprinted in *UPP*, I, 92–97.

E 197
"A Dialogue [Against Capital Punishment]," *United States Magazine, and Democratic Review*, 17 (November 1845), 360–364.

Reprinted in *UPP*, I, 97–103.

E 198
"Church Folks of the Modern Times," *Brooklyn Evening Star*, 3 November 1845.

Signed "W."

E 199
"Corrections," *Brooklyn Evening Star*, 4 November 1845.

Signed "W."

E 200
"American Music, New and True!", *Brooklyn Evening Star*, 5 November 1845.

Signed "W."

E 201
"Winning Ways and Whipping Ways," *Brooklyn Evening Star*, 8 November 1845.

Signed "W." Reprinted in *Schools*, pp. 78–79.

E 202

"Hints to Apprentices, &c.," *Brooklyn Evening Star*, 12 November 1845.

Signed "W." Reprinted in *Brooklyn Daily Eagle*, 29 July 1846; *Schools*, pp. 79–80.

E 203

"Heart-Music and Art-Music," *Brooklyn Evening Star*, 14 November 1845.

Signed "W." Reprinted as "Art-Singing and Heart-Singing," *Broadway Journal*, 2 (29 November 1845), 318–319; *UPP*, I, 104–106. Revised as "Music That *Is* Music," *Brooklyn Daily Eagle*, 4 December 1846 (E 619).

E 204

"The Oratorio of St. Paul," *Brooklyn Evening Star*, 28 November 1845.

Signed "W."

E 205

"Some Fact–Romances," *Aristidean*, 1 (December 1845), 444–449.

Fiction. Partially reprinted in *Half-Breed*, p. 101. Various sections reprinted: (1) revised as "A Fact-Romance of Long Island," *Brooklyn Daily Eagle*, 16 December 1846 (E 644); (2) revised as "The Old Black Widow," *Brooklyn Daily Eagle*, 12 November 1846 (E 585); (3) reprinted in *Half-Breed*, pp. 102–103; (4) reprinted in Thomas Ollive Mabbott, "Walt Whitman and *The Aristidean*," *American Mercury*, 2 (June 1924), 206–207; *Half-Breed*, p. 104; (5) revised as "An Incident in Long Island Forty Years Ago," *Brooklyn Daily Eagle*, 24 December 1846 (E 662). All sections reprinted in *Early Poems and Fiction*, pp. 319–326.

E 206

"Anecdote of a Well Known Good Old Man," *Brooklyn Evening Star*, 6 December 1845.

Signed "W."

E 207

"Hints to the Young," *Brooklyn Evening Star*, 6 December 1845.

Signed "W." Reprinted in *Schools*, pp. 81–82.

E 208

"Hark! The Murder's Doing," *Brooklyn Evening Star*, 13 December 1845.

Reprinted in Emory Holloway, "More Light on Whitman," *American Mercury*, 1 (February 1924), 185.

E 209

"Some Calm Hints on an Important Contingency," *Brooklyn Evening Star*, 17 December 1845.

Signed "W." Reprinted in Emory Holloway, "More Light on Whitman," *American Mercury*, 1 (February 1924), 187.

E 210

"Letters from New York," *Brooklyn Evening Star*, 29 December 1845.

Reprinted in Emory Holloway, "More Light on Whitman," *American Mercury*, 1 (February 1924), 183–189.

E 211

"Educating the Young—Brooklyn Schools—Effect of Music on Children," *Brooklyn Evening Star*, 7 January 1846.

Signed "W." Reprinted in *Schools*, pp. 82–85. Revised as "Brooklyn Schools—Music" in *Brooklyn Daily Eagle*, 5 September 1846 (E 482).

E 212

"Hints to the Young—Manners," *Brooklyn Evening Star*, 8 January 1846.

Signed "W." Reprinted in *Schools*, pp. 85–86.

E 213

"Coercing of Juries," *Brooklyn Evening Star*, 12 January 1846.

Signed "W."

E 214

"True American Singing," *Brooklyn Evening Star*, 13 January 1846.

Signed "W."

E 215

"Hints to the Young—A Gem of Character," *Brooklyn Evening Star*, 16 January 1846.

Signed "W." Reprinted in *Brooklyn Daily Eagle*, 12 February 1847; *Schools*, pp. 86–88.

E 216

[Long Island], *Brooklyn Evening Star*, 23 January 1846.

Signed "W."

E 217
"Bitter Spite Toward Long Island," *Brooklyn Evening Star,* 28 January 1846.

E 218
"A Great American Publishing House," *Brooklyn Evening Star,* 30 January 1846.

Signed "W."

E 219
"Books Worth Reading [Lyman Blanchard, *Sketches; Dr. Cheever and Capital Punishment;* Thomas Carlyle, *The Letters and Speeches of Oliver Cromwell*]," *Brooklyn Evening Star,* 31 January 1846.

Signed "W." Partially reprinted in Joseph Jay Rubin, "Whitman and Carlyle: 1846," *Modern Language Notes,* 53 (May 1938), 370–371 (Carlyle).

E 220
"Public Schools," *Brooklyn Evening Star,* 3 February 1846.

Reprinted in *Schools,* p. 88.

E 221
" 'State' of Long Island," *Brooklyn Evening Star,* 3 February 1846.

E 222
"Commerce and Trade of Brooklyn," *Brooklyn Evening Star,* 5 February 1846.

E 223
"Books of Worth [Heinrich Zschokke, *Tales*]," *Brooklyn Evening Star,* 9 February 1846.

Reprinted in Florence B. Freedman, "Walt Whitman and Heinrich Zschokke: A Further Note," *American Literature,* 15 (May 1943), 181–182.

E 224
"Are Your Children Taught Singing?" *Brooklyn Evening Star,* 9 February 1846.

Reprinted in *Schools,* pp. 88–89.

E 225
"Long Island," *Brooklyn Evening Star,* 11 February 1846.

E 226
"A Pure Pleasure," *Brooklyn Evening Star*, 14 February 1846.

Reprinted in *Schools*, p. 89.

E 227
"The Lash in Schools," *Brooklyn Evening Star*, 16 February 1846.

Reprinted in *Schools*, pp. 89–90.

E 228
"An Evening at a Children's Concert," *Brooklyn Evening Star*, 20 February 1846.

Reprinted in *Schools*, pp. 90–92.

E 229
"Miss Peck's Case," *Brooklyn Evening Star*, 21 February 1846.

Reprinted in *Schools*, pp. 92–93.

E 230
"Books and Bookstores," *Brooklyn Evening Star*, 21 February 1846.

E 231
"Some Plain Hints to Plain Folks," *Brooklyn Evening Star*, 25 February 1846.

Reprinted in *Schools*, pp. 93–94.

E 232
"The Angel of Tears," *Brooklyn Evening Star*, 28 February 1846.

Revision of "The Angel of Tears" in *United States Magazine, and Democratic Review*, September 1842 (E 157).

E 233
"Mr. Marsh's Family," *Brooklyn Evening Star*, 3 March 1846.

E 234
[Review of John Keats, *Poetical Works*], *Brooklyn Daily Eagle*, 5 March 1846.

Reprinted in *GF*, II, 303–304; *UPP*, I, 133.

E 235
[Review of Francois Guizot, *History of the English Revolution of 1640*], *Brooklyn Daily Eagle,* 5 March 1846.

Reprinted in *UPP,* I, 132. Not in White, *Journalism.*

E 236
"Something About Children," *Brooklyn Evening Star,* 6 March 1846.

Reprinted in *Schools,* pp. 95–96.

E 237
[The Oregon Question], *Brooklyn Daily Eagle,* 9 March 1846.

E 238
"The Fairy Book," *Brooklyn Daily Eagle,* 9 March 1846.

E 239
"An Hour Among Shipping," *Brooklyn Daily Eagle,* 9 March 1846.

E 240
"Splendid Churches [No. 1]," *Brooklyn Daily Eagle,* 9 March 1846.

Reprinted in *GF,* II, 91–93.

E 241
[The Oregon Question], *Brooklyn Daily Eagle,* 9 March 1846.

E 242
[Review of William Gilmore Simms, *The Wigwam and the Cabin*], *Brooklyn Daily Eagle,* 9 March 1846.

Reprinted in *UPP,* I, 136. Not in White, *Journalism.*

E 243
"Boz and His New Paper," *Brooklyn Daily Eagle,* 10 March 1846.

Reprinted in *GF,* II, 256–257.

E 244
[President Polk], *Brooklyn Daily Eagle,* 10 March 1846.

E 245
[Reason with Students], *Brooklyn Daily Eagle,* 10 March 1846.

Reprinted in *Schools,* p. 97.

E 246
"Professor Fowler," *Brooklyn Daily Eagle,* 11 March 1846.

Reprinted in Thomas L. Brasher, "Whitman's Conversion to Phrenology," *Walt Whitman Newsletter,* 4 (June 1958), 96.

E 247
[Books Provided in New York City Schools], *Brooklyn Daily Eagle,* 12 March 1846.

Reprinted in *Schools,* p. 97.

E 248
"Polishing the 'Common People,' " *Brooklyn Daily Eagle,* 12 March 1846.

Reprinted in *Schools,* pp. 97–99.

E 249
[John Bull's Blustering about Oregon], *Brooklyn Daily Eagle,* 13 March 1846.

Reprinted in *GF,* I, 267–269.

E 250
[School Attendance], *Brooklyn Daily Eagle,* 13 March 1846.

Reprinted in *Schools,* p. 99.

E 251
"Normal School," *Brooklyn Daily Eagle,* 14 March 1846.

Reprinted in *Schools,* p. 99.

E 252
"Pretty Patriots," *Brooklyn Daily Eagle,* 16 March 1846.

E 253
" 'The Crushed Heart,' " *Brooklyn Daily Eagle,* 16 March 1846.

E 254
"Freedom of the Press," *Brooklyn Daily Eagle,* 16 March 1846.

E 255
"Work for the Convention," *Brooklyn Daily Eagle,* 17 March 1846.

E 256
"The Wrongs of Women," *Brooklyn Daily Eagle,* 17 March 1846.

E 257
"Slavery—and the Slave Trade," *Brooklyn Daily Eagle*, 18 March 1846.

Reprinted in *GF*, I, 187–191; *UPP*, I, 106–108.

E 258
"Clean the Streets," *Brooklyn Daily Eagle*, 18 March 1846.

E 259
"An Independent Treasury—How It Will Affect the Working Man," *Brooklyn Daily Eagle*, 19 March 1846.

E 260
"The Height of the 'Great Argument,' " *Brooklyn Daily Eagle*, 19 March 1846.

E 261
" 'The State of Long Island,' " *Brooklyn Daily Eagle*, 21 March 1846.

E 262
"Some Plain Paragraphs, for Plain People," *Brooklyn Daily Eagle*, 21 March 1846.

E 263
"Late Publications," *Brooklyn Daily Eagle*, 21 March 1846.

E 264
"Mr. Calhoun's Speech," *Brooklyn Daily Eagle*, 21 March 1846.

E 265
"Are We Never to Have Any Public Parks in Brooklyn," *Brooklyn Daily Eagle*, 23 March 1846.

Reprinted in "Editorials Written by Walt Whitman as Editor of the Eagle in 1846–47," *Brooklyn Daily Eagle*, 31 May 1919, Whitman sec., p. 6.

E 266
"Hurrah for Hanging!", *Brooklyn Daily Eagle*, 23 March 1846.

Reprinted in *GF*, I, 97–101; *UPP*, I, 108–110.

E 267
"Our Answer to a Reasonable Question," *Brooklyn Daily Eagle*, 24 March 1846.

Reprinted in *GF*, I, 104–107.

E 268
"Legislating for Morality," *Brooklyn Daily Eagle*, 24 March 1846.

E 269
"Illy Paid Labor in Brooklyn," *Brooklyn Daily Eagle*, 25 March 1846.

E 270
"Begin Life Well," *Brooklyn Daily Eagle*, 27 March 1846.

E 271
"Putting Down Immorality by Stress of Law," *Brooklyn Daily Eagle*, 27 March 1846.

Reprinted in *GF*, I, 62–65.

E 272
"Forming the Character," *Brooklyn Daily Eagle*, 28 March 1846.

Reprinted in *Schools*, p. 100.

E 273
"Educate Your Young Folk," *Brooklyn Daily Eagle*, 29 March 1846.

Reprinted in *Schools*, pp. 100–101.

E 274
"Splendid Churches [No. 2]," *Brooklyn Daily Eagle*, 30 March 1846.

Reprinted in *GF*, II, 93–96.

E 275
" 'Motley's Your Only Wear!' A Chapter for the First of April," *Brooklyn Daily Eagle*, 1 April 1846.

Reprinted in *GF*, II, 96–101; *UPP*, I, 110–113.

E 276
"Work for the Convention—No Debts, and Small Outlays," *Brooklyn Daily Eagle*, 2 April 1846.

E 277
"Gen. Cass's Speech," *Brooklyn Daily Eagle*, 2 April 1846.

E 278
"A Plan to Extinguish the Feudal Tenures," *Brooklyn Daily Eagle*, 2 April 1846.

E 279
"Oppress Not the Hireling!", *Brooklyn Daily Eagle,* 3 April 1846.

E 280
[John Jacob Astor], *Brooklyn Daily Eagle,* 3 April 1846.

Reprinted in *GF,* II, 231.

E 281
"Music for the Natural Ear," *Brooklyn Daily Eagle,* 3 April 1846.

Partially reprinted in Thomas L. Brasher, "Whitman's Conversion to Opera," *Walt Whitman Newsletter,* 4 (December 1958), 109.

E 282
"Duties of Government," *Brooklyn Daily Eagle,* 4 April 1846.

Reprinted in *GF,* I, 55–57.

E 283
"A Truly Noble Reform [Sub-Teasury Bill]," *Brooklyn Daily Eagle,* 4 April 1846.

E 284
"Another Speech from Gen. Cass," *Brooklyn Daily Eagle,* 4 April 1846.

E 285
"Mrs. Bodine's Case," *Brooklyn Daily Eagle,* 4 April 1846.

E 286
"Government Patronage of Men of Letters," *Brooklyn Daily Eagle,* 6 April 1846.

Reprinted in Theodore A. Zunder, "Walt Whitman and Nathaniel Hawthorne," *Modern Language Notes,* 47 (May 1932), 314–316.

E 287
"The 'Desert' Last Night," *Brooklyn Daily Eagle,* 7 April 1846.

E 288
"Something About the Children of Early Spring," *Brooklyn Daily Eagle,* 9 April 1846.

Reprinted in *GF,* I, 145–147; *UPP,* I, 113–114; as "Something About Children" in *Schools,* pp. 101–102.

E 289
"The Charity by Which 1000 Miles Gets Much Cash, and Home None," *Brooklyn Daily Eagle,* 10 April 1846.

E 290
"Money That Is *Not* Money," *Brooklyn Daily Eagle,* 10 April 1846.

E 291
[Daniel Webster], *Brooklyn Daily Eagle,* 11 April 1846.

Partially reprinted in *GF,* II, 181–184.

E 292
"A Fearful Fact," *Brooklyn Daily Eagle,* 13 April 1846.

Reprinted in *Schools,* p. 102.

E 293
" 'Stupid Dull Boy,' " *Brooklyn Daily Eagle,* 13 April 1846.

Reprinted in *Schools,* pp. 102–103.

E 294
"Most Atrocious Bribery!", *Brooklyn Daily Eagle,* 13 April 1846.

E 295
"Literary News, Notices, &c., Works of Art, &c.," *Brooklyn Daily Eagle,* 15 April 1846.

E 296
"Doings To-day in the U. S. Senate," *Brooklyn Daily Eagle,* 16 April 1846.

E 297
"Is Not Medicine Itself a Frequent Cause of Sickness?", *Brooklyn Daily Eagle,* 16 April 1846.

E 298
" 'Breakfast at 6,' " *Brooklyn Daily Eagle,* 16 April 1846.

E 299
[Editorial], *Brooklyn Daily Eagle,* 17 April 1846.

Reprinted in Thomas L. Brasher, "Whitman on the 'Attrocious Practice of Publishing Private Letters,' " *Walt Whitman Newsletter,* 3 (December 1957), 63.

E 300
"Teachers and Their Pay," *Brooklyn Daily Eagle*, 16 April 1846.

Reprinted in *Schools*, pp. 103–104.

E 301
"Mr. Bradbury's Concert at the N.Y. Tabernacle To-morrow Night," *Brooklyn Daily Eagle*, 16 April 1846.

Reprinted in *Schools*, pp. 104–105.

E 302
"Is It Right to Dance?" *Brooklyn Daily Eagle*, 17 April 1846.

E 303
"A Contemptible Trick," *Brooklyn Daily Eagle*, 18 April 1846.

E 304
"How Long, O Albany Papers," *Brooklyn Daily Eagle*, 18 April 1846.

E 305
" 'Mr. Sub-Treasury Note,' " *Brooklyn Daily Eagle*, 18 April 1846.

E 306
"A Great Day in the House of Representatives," *Brooklyn Daily Eagle*, 20 April 1846.

E 307
"Snags and Quicksands," *Brooklyn Daily Eagle*, 21 April 1846.

E 308
[Mr. Berteau's School], *Brooklyn Daily Eagle*, 21 April 1846.

Reprinted in *Schools*, p. 105.

E 309
"Farmers!", *Brooklyn Daily Eagle*, 23 April 1846.

E 310
"A 'Rouser' Let It Be!", *Brooklyn Daily Eagle*, 24 April 1846.

E 311
"Naval Reform. The Attrocious Practice of Flogging Seamen," *Brooklyn Daily Eagle*, 24 April 1846.

E 312
"Is It Not the Brooklyn Laborers," *Brooklyn Daily Eagle,* 24 April 1846.

E 313
"The English Complain," *Brooklyn Daily Eagle,* 24 April 1846.

E 314
"Land Free to Settlers on It!", *Brooklyn Daily Eagle,* 24 April 1846.

E 315
"How to Write for Newspapers," *Brooklyn Daily Eagle,* 24 April 1846.

Reprinted in *GF,* II, 274–275.

E 316
"We Are to Give the 'Notice,' " *Brooklyn Daily Eagle,* 25 April 1846.

E 317
"The Single District System," *Brooklyn Daily Eagle,* 27 April 1846.

E 318
[Religious Sentiment], *Brooklyn Daily Eagle,* 27 April 1846.

E 319
"Brooklyn Female Academy," *Brooklyn Daily Eagle,* 27 April 1846.

Reprinted in *Schools,* p. 105.

E 320
"Come Along!", *Brooklyn Daily Eagle,* 30 April 1846.

E 321
"The Orphan's College," *Brooklyn Daily Eagle,* 1 May 1846.

Reprinted in *Schools,* p. 105.

E 322
"Brooklyn Schools," *Brooklyn Daily Eagle,* 2 May 1846.

Reprinted in *Schools,* pp. 105–106.

E 323
"Relief to a Class Who Much Need It, Lunatics and Idiots," *Brooklyn Daily Eagle,* 2 May 1846.

E 324
"Prolific in Crime," *Brooklyn Daily Eagle,* 4 May 1846.

E 325
"Democratic Young Men," *Brooklyn Daily Eagle,* 6 May 1846.

E 326
"The Foot of Fulton Street," *Brooklyn Daily Eagle,* 6 May 1846.

E 327
" 'Let Young People . . . ,' " *Brooklyn Daily Eagle,* 6 May 1846.

E 328
"Noble Charity," *Brooklyn Daily Eagle,* 6 May 1846.

Reprinted in *Schools,* p. 106.

E 329
"An Injudicious Decision," *Brooklyn Daily Eagle,* 7 May 1846.

E 330
"Cheap Postage in Danger," *Brooklyn Daily Eagle,* 8 May 1846.

E 331
"Quarter Deck Rule," *Brooklyn Daily Eagle,* 8 May 1846.

E 332
"An Hour at a Brooklyn School," *Brooklyn Daily Eagle,* 9 May 1846.

Reprinted in *Schools,* pp. 106–108.

E 333
"Adjournment of Congress," *Brooklyn Daily Eagle,* 9 May 1846.

E 334
[The Mexican War Justified], *Brooklyn Daily Eagle,* 11 May 1846.

Reprinted in *GF,* I, 240–242.

E 335
"An Asylum for Idiots," *Brooklyn Daily Eagle,* 12 May 1846.

E 336
"Will the Senate Bar the Appropriations?", *Brooklyn Daily Eagle,* 13 May 1846.

E 337
"Mr. Calhoun," *Brooklyn Daily Eagle,* 14 May 1846.

Reprinted in *GF*, II, 191–192.

E 338
"Mr. Judson," *Brooklyn Daily Eagle,* 16 May 1846.

E 339
"To-morrow's Election," *Brooklyn Daily Eagle,* 18 May 1846.

E 340
"Literary Notices—Young People's Magazine," *Brooklyn Daily Eagle,* 19 May 1846.

E 341
"Free Schools of the Highest Order," *Brooklyn Daily Eagle,* 20 May 1846.

Reprinted in *Schools,* pp. 108–109.

E 342
" 'Home League' of Traitors," *Brooklyn Daily Eagle,* 20 May 1846.

E 343
"The Sunday Schools," *Brooklyn Daily Eagle,* 21 May 1846.

Reprinted in *Schools,* pp. 109–110.

E 344
[The *Brooklyn Advertiser*], *Brooklyn Daily Eagle,* 22 May 1846.

E 345
"A Cheap Good Library," *Brooklyn Daily Eagle,* 22 May 1846.

Reprinted in *Schools,* p. 110.

E 346
"No News, To-day," *Brooklyn Daily Eagle,* 23 May 1846.

E 347
"Something About Mexico," *Brooklyn Daily Eagle,* 23 May 1846.

E 348
"Barnum on Europe," *Brooklyn Daily Eagle,* 26 May 1846.

Reprinted in Theodore A. Zunder, "Whitman Interviews Barnum," *Modern Language Notes,* 48 (January 1933), 40.

E 349
" 'Annexation' of Mexico," *Brooklyn Daily Eagle,* 26 May 1846.

E 350
"Some Afternoon Gossip," *Brooklyn Daily Eagle,* 27 May 1846.

E 351
"Senator Benton," *Brooklyn Daily Eagle,* 28 May 1846.

E 352
"Delicate Nerves," *Brooklyn Daily Eagle,* 28 May 1846.

E 353
[The *Brooklyn Advertiser*], *Brooklyn Daily Eagle,* 28 May 1846.

E 354
"A Simile," *Brooklyn Daily Eagle,* 29 May 1846.

E 355
"A Reform," *Brooklyn Daily Eagle,* 29 May 1846.

E 356
"Daniel Webster," *Brooklyn Daily Eagle,* 30 May 1846.

E 357
"Oregon 'Notice' in England," *Brooklyn Daily Eagle,* 30 May 1846.

E 358
"Ourselves and the *Eagle,*" *Brooklyn Daily Eagle,* 1 June 1846.

Reprinted in *UPP,* I, 114–117.

E 359
"Innovations in Medicine—Physic *vs.* Health, &c.," *Brooklyn Daily Eagle,* 1 June 1846.

E 360
"The Play-Ground," *Brooklyn Daily Eagle,* 1 June 1846.

Signed "W." Poem. Reprinted in *UPP,* I, 21; *Early Poems and Fiction,* p. 33.

E 361
"The Half–Breed: A Tale of the Western Frontier," *Brooklyn Daily Eagle*, 1–6, 8, 9 June 1846.

Revised from "Arrow-Tip" in *Aristidean*, March 1845 (E 175).

E 362
"A Fable," *Brooklyn Daily Eagle*, 3 June 1846.

E 363
[Frequent Holidays], *Brooklyn Daily Eagle*, 3 June 1846.

Reprinted in *Schools*, pp. 110–111.

E 364
"A Pleasant Morning," *Brooklyn Daily Eagle*, 3 June 1846.

Reprinted in *UPP*, I, 117.

E 365
" 'Art of Health,' " *Brooklyn Daily Eagle*, 4 June 1846.

Reprinted in *GF*, II, 199–200.

E 366
"Our Public Schools," *Brooklyn Daily Eagle*, 4 June 1846.

Reprinted in *Schools*, p. 111.

E 367
"Professional Compliments," *Brooklyn Daily Eagle*, 4 June 1846.

E 368
"Accidental Sudden Deaths," *Brooklyn Daily Eagle*, 5 June 1846.

E 369
"Annexation," *Brooklyn Daily Eagle*, 6 June 1846.

Reprinted in *GF*, I, 242–244.

E 370
[Board of Education], *Brooklyn Daily Eagle*, 6 June 1846.

Reprinted in *Schools*, pp. 111–112.

E 371
"Andrew Jackson," *Brooklyn Daily Eagle*, 8 June 1846.

Reprinted in *GF*, II, 178–179; *UPP*, I, 117–118.

E 372
"City Intelligence—Fort Greene," *Brooklyn Daily Eagle*, 8 June 1846.

E 373
"An Afternoon at the Blind Asylum," *Brooklyn Daily Eagle*, 9 June 1846.

Reprinted in *Schools*, pp. 112–114.

E 374
"How About Oregon," *Brooklyn Daily Eagle*, 10 June 1846.

E 375
"Iowa," *Brooklyn Daily Eagle*, 10 June 1846.

E 376
"Bathing—Cleanliness—Personal Beauty," *Brooklyn Daily Eagle*, 10 June 1846.

Reprinted in *GF*, II, 201–207.

E 377
"A Legend of Life and Love," *Brooklyn Daily Eagle*, 11 June 1846.

Revised from *United States Magazine, and Democratic Review*, July 1842 (E 151).

E 378
"City Intelligence. The Whip in Schools," *Brooklyn Daily Eagle*, 12 June 1846.

Reprinted in *Schools*, pp. 114–117.

E 379
[Female Taste], *Brooklyn Daily Eagle*, 12 June 1846.

Reprinted in *GF*, II, 230.

E 380
[Re *New York Tribune*], *Brooklyn Daily Eagle*, 12 June 1846.

E 381
"An Afternoon at Greenwood," *Brooklyn Daily Eagle*, 13 June 1846.

Reprinted in *GF*, II, 105–113. Revised from *New York Aurora*, 8 March 1842 (E 50).

E 382
"Government of Children," *Brooklyn Daily Eagle*, 13 June 1846.

Reprinted in *Schools*, pp. 117–119.

E 383
"Very Excellent News [on the Oregon Treaty]," *Brooklyn Daily Eagle*, 15 June 1846.

Reprinted in *GF*, I, 270.

E 384
"Effect of the Oregon Treaty on the Mexican War," *Brooklyn Daily Eagle*, 16 June 1846.

E 385
"A Glance Ahead!", *Brooklyn Daily Eagle*, 17 June 1846.

E 386
"A Drive Out of Brooklyn," *Brooklyn Daily Eagle*, 18 June 1846.

E 387
" 'Our Flag is There!' " *Brooklyn Daily Eagle*, 19 June 1846.

Reprinted in "Editorials Written by Walt Whitman as Editor of the Eagle in 1846–47," *Brooklyn Daily Eagle*, 31 May 1919, Whitman sec., p. 11; *GF*, I, 270–271.

E 388
"Templeton the Singer," *Brooklyn Daily Eagle*, 19 June 1846.

E 389
"Peace with England!", *Brooklyn Daily Eagle*, 20 June 1846.

E 390
"Miserable Taste," *Brooklyn Daily Eagle*, 22 June 1846.

E 391
"The Age," *Brooklyn Daily Eagle*, 23 June 1846.

Reprinted in *GF*, I, 22–23.

E 392
"City Intelligence: Visit to the Orphan Asylum," *Brooklyn Daily Eagle*, 24 June 1846.

Reprinted in *Schools*, pp. 119–123.

E 393
"Hurrah for Choking Human Lives!", *Brooklyn Daily Eagle*, 24 June 1846.

Reprinted in *GF*, I, 107–108.

E 394
"A Day with Children," *Brooklyn Daily Eagle*, 25 June 1846.

E 395
"The New World and the Old," *Brooklyn Daily Eagle*, 26 June 1846.

Reprinted in "Editorials Written by Walt Whitman as Editor of the Eagle in 1846–47," *Brooklyn Daily Eagle*, 31 May 1919, Whitman sec., p. 11; *GF*, I, 15–18.

E 396
"East Long Island," *Brooklyn Daily Eagle*, 27 June 1846.

Reprinted in *UPP*, I, 118–121.

E 397
"City Intelligence—Lost Children," *Brooklyn Daily Eagle*, 29 June 1846.

E 398
"More Stars for the Spangled Banner," *Brooklyn Daily Eagle*, 29 June 1846.

Reprinted in "Editorials Written by Walt Whitman as Editor of the Eagle in 1846–47," *Brooklyn Daily Eagle*, 31 May 1919, Whitman sec., p. 11; *GF*, I, 244–246.

E 399
"Prisons," *Brooklyn Daily Eagle*, 30 June 1846.

E 400
"The Wandering Jew," *Brooklyn Daily Eagle*, 1 July 1846.

E 401
"God's Children's Property," *Brooklyn Daily Eagle*, 2 July 1846.

Reprinted in *GF*, II, 217–219.

E 402
"Visit to Plumbe's Gallery," *Brooklyn Daily Eagle*, 2 July 1846.

Reprinted in *GF*, II, 113–117.

E 403
"Ode: To be sung on Fort Greene; 4th of July, 1846," *Brooklyn Daily Eagle*, 2 July 1846.

Signed "Walter Whitman." Poem. Reprinted in Peter Ross, *A History of Long Island* (D 38), I, [iii]; *GF*, I, 75–76; *UPP*, I, 22–23; *Early Poems and Fiction*, pp. 34–35.

E 404
"Nominal Piety," *Brooklyn Daily Eagle*, 3 July 1846.

Reprinted in *GF*, I, 65–67.

E 405
"Love of Country!", *Brooklyn Daily Eagle*, 3 July 1846.

Reprinted in "Editorials Written by Walt Whitman as Editor of the Eagle in 1846–47," *Brooklyn Daily Eagle*, 31 May 1919, Whitman sec., p. 6.

E 406
"Just Verdicts, Doubtless," *Brooklyn Daily Eagle*, 6 July 1846.

E 407
"Our Territory on the Pacific," *Brooklyn Daily Eagle*, 7 July 1846.

Reprinted in *GF*, I, 246–247.

E 408
"How to Be a Man," *Brooklyn Daily Eagle*, 8 July 1846.

Reprinted in *Schools*, p. 123.

E 409
"Last Evening Upon Fort Greene," *Brooklyn Daily Eagle*, 8 July 1846.

Reprinted in *GF*, II, 118–121.

E 410
[Fort Greene Park, Brooklyn], *Brooklyn Daily Eagle*, 9 July 1846.

Reprinted in *GF*, II, 46–50.

E 411
"Cut Away!", *Brooklyn Daily Eagle,* 9 July 1846.

E 412
"Brooklyn Trees," *Brooklyn Daily Eagle,* 10 July 1846.

Reprinted in "Editorials Written by Walt Whitman as Editor of the Eagle in 1846–47," *Brooklyn Daily Eagle,* 31 May 1919, Whitman sec., p. 6. Not in White, *Journalism.*

E 413
"A Tale of the Wrongs of Women," *Brooklyn Daily Eagle,* 10 July 1846.

E 414
"A Thought [on Protective Tariff]," *Brooklyn Daily Eagle,* 10 July 1846.

Reprinted in *GF,* II, 70–71.

E 415
" 'Home Literature,' " *Brooklyn Daily Eagle,* 11 July 1846.

Reprinted in *GF,* II, 242–245; *UPP,* I, 121–123.

E 416
"Emigrants—Speed them West!", *Brooklyn Daily Eagle,* 13 July 1846.

Reprinted in *GF,* I, 164–165.

E 417
"Dumb Kate.—An Early Death," *Brooklyn Daily Eagle,* 13 July 1846.

Revised from May 1844 *Columbian Magazine* (E 170).

E 418
"The Country School House," *Brooklyn Daily Eagle,* 14 July 1846.

Reprinted in *Schools,* pp. 123–125.

E 419
"Promotion from the Ranks," *Brooklyn Daily Eagle,* 14 July 1846.

Reprinted in *GF,* II, 213–215.

E 420
"The Poor's Birthright," *Brooklyn Daily Eagle,* 14 July 1846.

E 421
"A Word for the 54-40's," *Brooklyn Daily Eagle,* 14 July 1846.

Reprinted in "Editorials Written by Walt Whitman as Editor of the Eagle in 1846–47," *Brooklyn Daily Eagle,* 31 May 1919, Whitman sec., p. 6. Not in White, *Journalism.*

E 422
"Old Mrs. [Alexander] Hamilton," *Brooklyn Daily Eagle,* 15 July 1846.

Reprinted in *GF,* II, 192–194.

E 423
"American Munificence and English Pomp," *Brooklyn Daily Eagle,* 16 July 1846.

Reprinted in *GF,* I, 38–40.

E 424
"Maxims for School Teachers," *Brooklyn Daily Eagle,* 17 July 1846.

Reprinted in *Schools,* pp. 125–126.

E 425
"Its 'Moral Effect,' " *Brooklyn Daily Eagle,* 17 July 1846.

E 426
"The Blind," *Brooklyn Daily Eagle,* 17 July 1846.

Reprinted in "Editorials Written by Walt Whitman as Editor of the Eagle in 1846–47," *Brooklyn Daily Eagle,* 31 May 1919, Whitman sec., p. 6. Not in White, *Journalism.*

E 427
"That Indian Gallery," *Brooklyn Daily Eagle,* 22 July 1846.

Reprinted in *GF,* II, 361–363.

E 428
"Brooklyn Young Men.—Athletic Exercises," *Brooklyn Daily Eagle,* 23 July 1846.

Reprinted in *GF,* II, 207–209; *Schools,* pp. 126–127.

E 429
"A Great Evil Avoided," *Brooklyn Daily Eagle,* 24 July 1846.

Reprinted in *GF,* I, 271–272.

E 430
"Women," *Brooklyn Daily Eagle*, 24 July 1846.

Reprinted in *GF*, II, 87–91.

E 431
"Swing Open the Doors!", *Brooklyn Daily Eagle*, 28 July 1846.

Reprinted in *GF*, I, 9–11.

E 432
"Ireland," *Brooklyn Daily Eagle*, 30 July 1846.

Reprinted in *GF*, I, 106.

E 433
"The Poor Wretches," *Brooklyn Daily Eagle*, 1 August 1846.

Reprinted in *GF*, I, 117–120.

E 434
"A Word to Our 'Native' Friends," *Brooklyn Daily Eagle*, 4 August 1846.

E 435
"A Thought [on an Unweeded Human Garden]," *Brooklyn Daily Eagle*, 5 August 1846.

Reprinted in *Schools*, p. 128.

E 436
"The First Session of the Twenty-Ninth Congress," *Brooklyn Daily Eagle*, 6 August 1846.

E 437
"No Slavery in Oregon," *Brooklyn Daily Eagle*, 7 August 1846.

E 438
"Honor to Him Who Has Been True to His Conscience and Country!", *Brooklyn Daily Eagle*, 7 August 1846.

Reprinted in *GF*, II, 175–177.

E 439
[Whitman Would Banish the Word 'Foreigners'], *Brooklyn Daily Eagle*, 8 August 1846.

Reprinted in *GF*, II, 15–17.

E 440
"Literary Notices," *Brooklyn Daily Eagle,* 10 August 1846.

E 441
"Sue's New Work," *Brooklyn Daily Eagle,* 10 August 1846.

E 442
" 'Injustice' to Ireland," *Brooklyn Daily Eagle,* 11 August 1846.

E 443
[A Hospital], *Brooklyn Daily Eagle,* 11 August 1846.

E 444
[The Episcopal Church], *Brooklyn Daily Eagle,* 12 August 1846.

E 445
[Templeton], *Brooklyn Daily Eagle,* 12 August 1846.

E 446
"Literary Notices," *Brooklyn Daily Eagle,* 13 August 1846.

E 447
[Charlotte Cushman], *Brooklyn Daily Eagle,* 13 August 1846.

Reprinted in *GF,* II, 344.

E 448
"About Acting," *Brooklyn Daily Eagle,* 14 August 1846.

Reprinted in *GF,* II, 325–327.

E 449
" 'Philanthropy,' " *Brooklyn Daily Eagle,* 14 August 1846.

Reprinted in "Editorials Written by Walt Whitman as Editor of the Eagle in 1846–47," *Brooklyn Daily Eagle,* 31 May 1919, Whitman sec., p. 6.

E 450
"Something We Love to Record," *Brooklyn Daily Eagle,* 15 August 1846.

E 451
"The Stage," *Brooklyn Daily Eagle,* 17 August 1846.

E 452
"Miss Bremer's Novels," *Brooklyn Daily Eagle,* 18 August 1846.

Reprinted in *GF,* II, 266–270; *UPP,* I, 128.

E 453
"Quin Was Right!", *Brooklyn Daily Eagle,* 18 August 1846.

Reprinted in *GF,* II, 224.

E 454
"Yes You Have!", *Brooklyn Daily Eagle,* 18 August 1846.

Reprinted in *GF,* II, 223.

E 455
"The Love of Eris: A Spirit Record," *Brooklyn Daily Eagle,* 18 August 1846.

Revised from "Eris: A Spirit Record" in *Columbian Magazine,* March 1843 (E 163).

E 456
"The Independent Treasury," *Brooklyn Daily Eagle,* 19 August 1846.

E 457
"Female Labor," *Brooklyn Daily Eagle,* 19 August 1846.

E 458
"Dramatics; and the True Secret of Acting," *Brooklyn Daily Eagle,* 20 August 1846.

Reprinted in *GF,* II, 321–325.

E 459
"Literary Notices.—Illustrated Botany, for August," *Brooklyn Daily Eagle,* 20 August 1846.

Reprinted in *Schools,* pp. 128–129.

E 460
"City Intelligence.—The Public Schools of Brooklyn and of the County," *Brooklyn Daily Eagle,* 21 August 1846.

Reprinted in *Schools,* pp. 129–130.

E 461
"Learning, &c.," *Brooklyn Daily Eagle,* 21 August 1846.

Reprinted in *Schools,* pp. 131–133.

E 462
[The *Brooklyn Star* and the *Brooklyn Advertiser*], *Brooklyn Daily Eagle*, 24 August 1846.

E 463
"The Drama," *Brooklyn Daily Eagle*, 25 August 1846.

Reprinted in *GF*, II, 340–341.

E 464
[Editorial Dinner], *Brooklyn Daily Eagle*, 26 August 1846.

Reprinted in *GF*, II, 231–232.

E 465
"We Must Laugh at This, Though We Respect Mr. Clay," *Brooklyn Daily Eagle*, 26 August 1846.

Reprinted in *GF*, II, 197–198.

E 466
"Facts for Working Folk," *Brooklyn Daily Eagle*, 26 August 1846.

E 467
"Literary Notices," *Brooklyn Daily Eagle*, 26 August 1846.

E 468
"More About the 'Operations of the British in India,' " *Brooklyn Daily Eagle*, 26 August 1846.

E 469
"The *Brooklyn Advertiser*," *Brooklyn Daily Eagle*, 26 August 1846.

E 470
"A Reminiscence," *Brooklyn Daily Eagle*, 27 August 1846.

Reprinted in "Editorials Written by Walt Whitman as Editor of the Eagle in 1846–47," *Brooklyn Daily Eagle*, 31 May 1919, Whitman sec., p. 6.

E 471
"More Hottentot Ignorance!", *Brooklyn Daily Eagle*, 27 August 1846.

Reprinted in *GF*, II, 224.

E 472
"Yankee Impertinence," *Brooklyn Daily Eagle*, 28 August 1846.

Reprinted in *GF*, II, 277.

E 473
"A Visit to a Camp, Etc.," *Brooklyn Daily Eagle*, 29 August 1846.

Reprinted in *GF*, II, 121–126.

E 474
"The Principles We Fight For," *Brooklyn Daily Eagle,* 29 August 1846.

E 475
"Literary Notices [Charles Burdett, *The Convict's Child*]," *Brooklyn Daily Eagle,* 31 August 1846.

E 476
"Acting . . . The Keans," *Brooklyn Daily Eagle*, 1 September 1846.

Reprinted in *GF*, II, 327–330.

E 477
"Mr. Bryant," *Brooklyn Daily Eagle*, 1 September 1846.

Reprinted in *GF*, II, 260–262; *UPP*, I, 128–129.

E 478
"Ion, Last Night," *Brooklyn Daily Eagle,* 2 September 1846.

E 479
"Flogging in Schools," *Brooklyn Daily Eagle,* 3 September 1846.

Reprinted in *Schools*, pp. 133–134.

E 480
"What is Best for Workingmen?", *Brooklyn Daily Eagle*, 3 September 1846.

Reprinted in *GF*, II, 67–69.

E 481
"Honest Opinions Forever [of the Stage]," *Brooklyn Daily Eagle*, 4 September 1846.

Reprinted in *GF*, II, 318–321.

E 482
"Brooklyn Schools—Music," *Brooklyn Daily Eagle*, 5 September 1846.

Revised from *Brooklyn Daily Eagle*, 7 January 1846 (E 211). Reprinted in *Schools*, pp. 134–136.

E 483
"One Wicked Impulse! (a tale of a Murderer escaped.)," *Brooklyn Daily Eagle*, 7–9 September 1846.

Revised from "Revenge and Requital: A Tale of a Murderer Escaped" in *United States Magazine, and Democratic Review*, July–August 1845 (E 179).

E 484
"Mr. [George] Bancroft," *Brooklyn Daily Eagle*, 8 September 1846.

Reprinted in *GF*, II, 194–196.

E 485
[On Samuel Lover], *Brooklyn Daily Eagle*, 8 September 1846.

Reprinted in *GF*, II, 277.

E 486
"Political Women," *Brooklyn Daily Eagle*, 8 September 1846.

E 487
"Orthodox But Sanguinary," *Brooklyn Daily Eagle*, 9 September 1846.

Reprinted in *GF*, I, 101–104.

E 488
"The Morning News," *Brooklyn Daily Eagle*, 9 September 1846.

E 489
"Something for the Ladies' Reading [Against 'Tight Lacing']," *Brooklyn Daily Eagle*, 11 September 1846.

E 490
"Servants," *Brooklyn Daily Eagle*, 16 September 1846.

Reprinted in *GF*, I, 154–156. Not in White, *Journalism*.

E 491
" 'Any Education . . . ,' " *Brooklyn Daily Eagle*, 16 September 1846.

E 492
"Authors," *Brooklyn Daily Eagle*, 17 September 1846.

Reprinted in *GF*, II, 255–256.

E 493
" 'Foreign' Prejudices," *Brooklyn Daily Eagle,* 18 September 1846.

E 494
" 'Political Women,' " *Brooklyn Daily Eagle*, 18 September 1846.

E 495
"School Officers' Duties," *Brooklyn Daily Eagle*, 19 September 1846.

Reprinted in *GF*, I, 142–144; *Schools*, pp. 137–138.

E 496
"Vocal Concerts, by Children," *Brooklyn Daily Eagle*, 19 September 1846.

Reprinted in *GF*, II, 358.

E 497
"What's the Matter with the Lamps?", *Brooklyn Daily Eagle*, 21 September 1846.

E 498
"The Pen," *Brooklyn Daily Eagle*, 22 September 1846.

Reprinted in *GF*, II, 245–248.

E 499
[Washington Irving], *Brooklyn Daily Eagle*, 22 September 1846.

Reprinted in *GF*, II, 275.

E 500
"Gayety of Americans," *Brooklyn Daily Eagle*, 23 September 1846.

Reprinted in "Editorials Written by Walt Whitman as Editor of the Eagle in 1846–47," *Brooklyn Daily Eagle*, 31 May 1919, Whitman sec., p. 6.

E 501
"The Literary World," *Brooklyn Daily Eagle*, 24 September 1846.

E 502
"Our Fortune Under Our Own Control," *Brooklyn Daily Eagle,* 25 September 1846.

E 503
"Petty Criticism," *Brooklyn Daily Eagle,* 25 September 1846.

E 504
"Minor Moralities," *Brooklyn Daily Eagle,* 25 September 1846.

E 505
"The Literary World," *Brooklyn Daily Eagle,* 26 September 1846.

E 506
"Claims of the Democratic Party at the Next Election," *Brooklyn Daily Eagle,* 28 September 1846.

Reprinted in *GF,* II, 25–27.

E 507
"American Editing and Editors," *Brooklyn Daily Eagle,* 29 September 1846.

E 508
"The Literary World [Alexander Dumas, *The Count of Monte-Cristo*]," *Brooklyn Daily Eagle,* 30 September 1846.

Reprinted in *GF,* II, 299–300.

E 509
"The 'Irish,' &c.," *Brooklyn Daily Eagle,* 30 September 1846.

E 510
"Mrs. Mowatt," *Brooklyn Daily Eagle,* 30 September 1846.

E 511
"Political Neutrality 'Showed Up,' " *Brooklyn Daily Eagle,* 1 October 1846.

E 512
"Do Such Energies Require 'Protection'?", *Brooklyn Daily Eagle,* 1 October 1846.

Reprinted in *GF,* II, 69–70.

E 513
"A Peaceful Conquest!", *Brooklyn Daily Eagle,* 2 October 1846.

E 514
"The Literary World," *Brooklyn Daily Eagle,* 5 October 1846.

E 515
"Nativism," *Brooklyn Daily Eagle*, 5 October 1846.

Reprinted in *GF*, I, 19–22.

E 516
"What We Thought at the Institute Fair, This Morning," *Brooklyn Daily Eagle*, 6 October 1846.

Reprinted in *GF*, II, 59–61.

E 517
"As a Very Average Proof [Theatrical Criticism]," *Brooklyn Daily Eagle*, 7 October 1846.

Reprinted in *GF*, II, 341–342.

E 518
"Indulgent Nature," *Brooklyn Daily Eagle*, 7 October 1846.

Reprinted in *GF*, II, 219–220.

E 519
"Baron von Raumer," *Brooklyn Daily Eagle*, 8 October 1846.

Reprinted in *GF*, II, 262–263; partially reprinted in *UPP*, I, 134–135.

E 520
"The Rule of the Rod," *Brooklyn Daily Eagle*, 8 October 1846.

Reprinted in *Schools,* pp. 138–139. Revised from "The Whip in Schools" in *Brooklyn Evening Star*, 22 October 1845 (E 191).

E 521
"An Indigent Official," *Brooklyn Daily Eagle*, 8 October 1846.

Reprinted in *GF*, II, 127–130.

E 522
"Progress," *Brooklyn Daily Eagle*, 8 October 1846.

Reprinted in *GF*, I, 12–14.

E 523
"Mr. Burke, The Violinist," *Brooklyn Daily Eagle*, 9 October 1846.

Reprinted in *GF*, II, 352–353.

E 524
" 'Yankee Doodle' Come," *Brooklyn Daily Eagle,* 9 October 1846.

Reprinted in *GF*, II, 271–272.

E 525
"The Union vs. Fanaticism," *Brooklyn Daily Eagle,* 9 October 1846.

E 526
"Our Charming Weather," *Brooklyn Daily Eagle,* 9 October 1846.

E 527
[Protection], *Brooklyn Daily Eagle,* 10 October 1846.

E 528
[The *Boston Post*], *Brooklyn Daily Eagle,* 10 October 1846.

Reprinted in *GF*, II, 277.

E 529
"The Literary World [Henry Wadsworth Longfellow, *Poems*]," *Brooklyn Daily Eagle,* 12 October 1846.

Reprinted in *GF*, II, 297–298.

E 530
"The New Violinist [Camillo Sivori]," *Brooklyn Daily Eagle,* 13 October 1846.

Reprinted in *GF*, II, 354–355.

E 531
"The Victory," *Brooklyn Daily Eagle,* 13 October 1846.

Reprinted in *GF*, I, 247–248.

E 532
"General Taylor," *Brooklyn Daily Eagle,* 14 October 1846.

Reprinted in *GF*, II, 188–191.

E 533
"The Literary World [Thomas Carlyle, *Heroes and Hero Worship*]," *Brooklyn Daily Eagle,* 17 October 1846.

Reprinted in *GF*, II, 290–291; *UPP*, I, 129.

E 534
" 'Sartor Resartus.' By Thomas Carlyle," *Brooklyn Daily Eagle*, 17 October 1846.

Reprinted in *GF*, II, 291.

E 535
"Pennsylvania and Ohio," *Brooklyn Daily Eagle*, 17 October 1846.

E 536
"Prohibition of Liquor-Vending, &c.," *Brooklyn Daily Eagle*, 17 October 1846.

E 537
"Local Intelligence: &c.—Ventilation of Domestic Rooms, Public Schools, Steamboat Cabins, and Our New City Hall," *Brooklyn Daily Eagle*, 19 October 1846.

Partially reprinted in *Schools*, pp. 139–140.

E 538
"Free Exhibitions of Works of Art," *Brooklyn Daily Eagle*, 21 October 1846.

Reprinted in *GF,* II, 360–361.

E 539
"Holy Bible—Illuminated," *Brooklyn Daily Eagle*, 21 October 1846.

Reprinted in *UPP*, I, 127.

E 540
"Death of Thomas Clarkson," *Brooklyn Daily Eagle*, 22 October 1846.

E 541
"Preparation [for Coming Elections]," *Brooklyn Daily Eagle*, 23 October 1846.

Reprinted in *GF*, II, 27–28.

E 542
"Political Truths in the West," *Brooklyn Daily Eagle*, 24 October 1846.

E 543
"Licenses, &c.," *Brooklyn Daily Eagle*, 26 October 1846.

E 544
"The Bugles Are Sounding," *Brooklyn Daily Eagle*, 26 October 1846.

E 545
[Whittier Nearly Killed], *Brooklyn Daily Eagle,* 26 October 1846.

Reprinted in *GF,* II, 275–276.

E 546
"Phonography," *Brooklyn Daily Eagle,* 27 October 1846.

Reprinted in *Schools,* pp. 140–141.

E 547
[The *Brooklyn Advertiser*], *Brooklyn Daily Eagle,* 28 October 1846.

Reprinted in *GF,* II, 24.

E 548
"$100 Reward," *Brooklyn Daily Eagle,* 28 October 1846.

Reprinted in *GF,* II, 28–29.

E 549
"A Word to Long Islanders!", *Brooklyn Daily Eagle,* 28 October 1846.

Continued in the 2 November issue (E 556).

E 550
"Free Trade Men!", *Brooklyn Daily Eagle,* 28 October 1846.

Continued in the 2 November issue (E 557).

E 551
["The Natives"], *Brooklyn Daily Eagle,* 29 October 1846.

Reprinted in *GF,* II, 230–231.

E 552
"Why Do So Many . . . ," *Brooklyn Daily Eagle,* 29 October 1846.

E 553
"Cutting Down Those Wages," *Brooklyn Daily Eagle,* 30 October 1846.

Reprinted in *GF,* I, 156–157.

E 554
"Notices of New Books," *Brooklyn Daily Eagle,* 30 October 1846.

E 555
"Mass Meeting of the Democratic Republicans of the County of Kings," *Brooklyn Daily Eagle,* 30 October 1846.

Signed "Walter Whitman, Secretary." Reprinted in William White, "Walter Whitman: Kings County Democratic Secretary," *Walt Whitman Review,* 17 (September 1971), 92–98.

E 556
"A Word to Long Islanders!", *Brooklyn Daily Eagle,* 2 November 1846.

Concluded from the 28 October issue (E 549).

E 557
"Free Trade Men!", *Brooklyn Daily Eagle,* 2 November 1846.

Concluded from the 28 October issue (E 550).

E 558
"Action [in the Election]," *Brooklyn Daily Eagle,* 2 November 1846.

Reprinted in *GF,* II, 34.

E 559
"Close Up Your Ranks!", *Brooklyn Daily Eagle,* 2 November 1846.

Reprinted in *GF,* II, 31–33.

E 560
"Fear Avaunt!", *Brooklyn Daily Eagle,* 2 November 1846.

Reprinted in *GF,* II, 33.

E 561
"Some Last Words," *Brooklyn Daily Eagle,* 2 November 1846.

Reprinted in *GF,* II, 29–31.

E 562
"A Single Vote," *Brooklyn Daily Eagle,* 3 November 1846.

Reprinted in *GF,* II, 34–35.

E 563
[And Then It Rained], *Brooklyn Daily Eagle,* 4 November 1846.

Reprinted in *GF,* II, 36.

E 564
" 'Dombey and Son.' By Charles Dickens," *Brooklyn Daily Eagle,* 5 November 1846.

Reprinted in *GF,* II, 295.

E 565
"Morbid Appetite for Money," *Brooklyn Daily Eagle,* 5 November 1846.

Reprinted in *GF,* II, 130–136; *UPP,* I, 123–125.

E 566
"Our Defeat in the State," *Brooklyn Daily Eagle,* 5 November 1846.

Reprinted in *GF,* II, 37.

E 567
"Notices of New Books," *Brooklyn Daily Eagle,* 5 November 1846.

E 568
" 'O, That Odious Law!' ", *Brooklyn Daily Eagle,* 6 November 1846.

Reprinted in *GF,* II, 76–78.

E 569
"Self-Advancement, &c.," *Brooklyn Daily Eagle,* 6 November 1846.

Reprinted in *Schools,* pp. 141–144.

E 570
"Indian Life and Customs. A True Subject for American Antiquarian Research," *Brooklyn Daily Eagle,* 7 November 1846.

Reprinted in *GF,* II, 136–140.

E 571
" 'It Is Well,' " *Brooklyn Daily Eagle,* 7 November 1846.

Reprinted in *GF,* II, 37–39.

E 572
"Perpetuity of the Democratic Spirit," *Brooklyn Daily Eagle,* 7 November 1846.

Reprinted in *GF,* 1, 6–9.

E 573
[Miss Northall's Concert], *Brooklyn Daily Eagle,* 7 November 1846.

E 574
"Slavery in Louisiana," *Brooklyn Daily Eagle*, 7 November 1846.

E 575
[Rent Collecting Season], *Brooklyn Daily Eagle*, 7 November 1846.

E 576
"Initiatory Moves," *Brooklyn Daily Eagle*, 9 November 1846.

E 577
"Liberty in France," *Brooklyn Daily Eagle*, 9 November 1846.

E 578
"Criticism—New Books," *Brooklyn Daily Eagle*, 9 November 1846.

Reprinted in *GF*, II, 278–280; *UPP*, I, 125–126.

E 579
"The 'Domestic Circle,' " *Brooklyn Daily Eagle*, 9 November 1846.

Reprinted in *GF*, II, 216–217.

E 580
"Working-Women," *Brooklyn Daily Eagle*, 9 November 1846.

Reprinted in *UPP*, I, 137.

E 581
[Review of Margaret Fuller, *Papers on Literature and Art*], *Brooklyn Daily Eagle*, 9 November 1846.

Reprinted in *UPP*, I, 132. Not in White, *Journalism*.

E 582
"Free Night Schools," *Brooklyn Daily Eagle*, 10 November 1846.

Reprinted in *Schools*, p. 144.

E 583
"A Development of Court-Life in Europe.—The Two Royal Marriages," *Brooklyn Daily Eagle*, 10 November 1846.

Reprinted in *GF*, I, 33–38.

E 584
"Don't Be Frightened, Democrats!", *Brooklyn Daily Eagle*, 10 November 1846.

E 585
"The Old Black Widow," *Brooklyn Daily Eagle,* 12 November 1846.

Reprinted in *UPP,* I, 138–139. Revised from "Some Fact-Romances" in *Aristidean,* December 1845 (E 205).

E 586
"Case of People *vs.* Paper," *Brooklyn Daily Eagle,* 12 November 1846.

Reprinted in *GF,* II, 78–83.

E 587
"Boys in the Streets.—Vacant Time and How to Spend It," *Brooklyn Daily Eagle,* 13 November 1846.

Reprinted in *Schools,* pp. 144–146.

E 588
"Force in Government," *Brooklyn Daily Eagle,* 13 November 1846.

Reprinted in *GF,* I, 54–55.

E 589
"Death of a Truly Good Man [Thomas Clarkson]," *Brooklyn Daily Eagle,* 13 November 1846.

E 590
"Abetting the Enemy," *Brooklyn Daily Eagle,* 16 November 1846.

Reprinted in *GF,* I, 248–250.

E 591
"Children," *Brooklyn Daily Eagle,* 16 November 1846.

E 592
"Notices of New Books [J. L. Blake, *History of the American Revolution;* J. G. Spurzheim, *Phrenology, or the Doctrine of the Mental Phenomena*]," *Brooklyn Daily Eagle,* 16 November 1846.

Reprinted in *Schools,* p. 146 (Blake), and in Edward Hungerford, "Walt Whitman and His Chart of Bumps," *American Literature,* 2 (January 1931), 357 (Spurzheim).

E 593
"Sabbath-School Education," *Brooklyn Daily Eagle,* 16 November 1846.

Reprinted in *Schools,* pp. 146–147.

E 594
"Fortunes of a Country-Boy; Incidents in Town—and His Adventures at the South. A Tale of Long Island," *Brooklyn Daily Eagle,* 16–30 November 1846.

Revision of "Franklin Evans; or The Inebriate. A Tale of the Times" from *New World,* November 1842 (E 159).

E 595
"Absurdities in School Government," *Brooklyn Daily Eagle,* 17 November 1846.

Reprinted in *Schools,* p. 147.

E 596
"One of the Bold and True [Captain James Lawrence]," *Brooklyn Daily Eagle,* 18 November 1846.

Reprinted in *GF,* I, 86–89.

E 597
"Incidents in the Life of the World-Famed Man: 'The Autobiography of Goethe—Truth and Poetry: from My Life.' From the German, by Parke Godwin," *Brooklyn Daily Eagle,* 19 November 1846.

Reprinted in *GF,* II, 294–295; *UPP,* I, 139–141.

E 598
"Matters Which Were Seen and Done in an Afternoon Ramble," *Brooklyn Daily Eagle,* 19 November 1846.

Reprinted in *UPP,* I, 141–144.

E 599
" 'Teachers Should Always . . . ,' " *Brooklyn Daily Eagle,* 20 November 1846.

E 600
[Contentment], *Brooklyn Daily Eagle,* 20 November 1846.

E 601
"The Hanging To-day," *Brooklyn Daily Eagle,* 20 November 1846.

E 602
["Yankee-Doodle"], *Brooklyn Daily Eagle,* 20 November 1846.

E 603
"New Publications," *Brooklyn Daily Eagle,* 20 November 1846.

E604
"About Pictures, &c.," *Brooklyn Daily Eagle,* 21 November 1846.

Reprinted in *GF,* II, 363–365.

E605
"Education—Schools, etc.," *Brooklyn Daily Eagle,* 23 November 1846.

Reprinted in *UPP,* I, 144–146; *Schools,* pp. 147–149.

E606
"Harry Langdon. A Tale [review]," *Brooklyn Daily Eagle,* 23 November 1846.

E607
" 'The French Revolution,' A History. By Thomas Carlyle," *Brooklyn Daily Eagle,* 23 November 1846.

Reprinted in *GF,* II, 292–293; *UPP,* I, 130.

E608
"American Futurity," *Brooklyn Daily Eagle,* 24 November 1846.

Reprinted in *GF,* I, 27–28.

E609
"The Twenty-fifth of November, 1783," *Brooklyn Daily Eagle,* 24 November 1846.

E610
[Thanksgiving Day], *Brooklyn Daily Eagle,* 25 November 1846.

Reprinted in *GF,* II, 221–222.

E611
"Coleman's Juvenile Publications," *Brooklyn Daily Eagle,* 27 November 1846.

E612
"That Omnibus Monopoly," *Brooklyn Daily Eagle,* 1 December 1846.

E613
[Writers' Small Pay], *Brooklyn Daily Eagle,* 2 December 1846.

Reprinted in *GF,* II, 276.

E614
"The Independent Treasury," *Brooklyn Daily Eagle,* 2 December 1846.

E 615
"Values," *Brooklyn Daily Eagle*, 2 December 1846.

E 616
"Notices of New Works," *Brooklyn Daily Eagle*, 2 December 1846.

E 617
"Travels by the Way-Side in Europe [review of Bayard Taylor, *Views Afoot*]," *Brooklyn Daily Eagle*, 4 December 1846.

Partially reprinted in *UPP*, 1, 136.

E 618
"Sixty-Three Years Since—The 4th of Dec., 1783," *Brooklyn Daily Eagle*, 4 December 1846.

Reprinted in *GF*, I, 76–80.

E 619
"Music That *Is* Music," *Brooklyn Daily Eagle*, 4 December 1846.

Reprinted in *GF*, II, 346–349. Revised from *Brooklyn Evening Star*, 14 November 1845 (E 203).

E 620
["Abolition" Extremism Denounced], *Brooklyn Daily Eagle*, 5 December 1846.

Reprinted in *GF*, I, 191–193.

E 621
"The Command of the American Army in Mexico," *Brooklyn Daily Eagle*, 5 December 1846.

Reprinted in *GF*, I, 250–252.

E 622
"The Queen of England," *Brooklyn Daily Eagle*, 5 December 1846.

Reprinted in *GF*, II, 140–143.

E 623
[Liberty], *Brooklyn Daily Eagle*, 5 December 1846.

E 624
"Literary English Characters of the Past Century—Dr. Johnson [review of the *Life* by James Boswell]," *Brooklyn Daily Eagle*, 7 December 1846.

Reprinted in *GF*, II, 280–283; *UPP*, I, 127–128.

E 625
"Lady Jane," *Brooklyn Daily Eagle,* 7 December 1846.

Revision of a chapter from "Franklin Evans; or The Inebriate. A Tale of the Times" in *New World,* November 1842 (E 159).

E 626
"Free Night Schools," *Brooklyn Daily Eagle,* 8 December 1846.

Reprinted in *Schools,* p. 150.

E 627
" 'That' Oil," *Brooklyn Daily Eagle,* 8 December 1846.

Reprinted in *GF,* II, 55.

E 628
"New York City, &c.," *Brooklyn Daily Eagle,* 8 December 1846.

E 629
"Re-election of Mr. Calhoun to the Senate," *Brooklyn Daily Eagle,* 10 December 1846.

E 630
" 'Lessons in Physiology,' " *Brooklyn Daily Eagle,* 10 December 1846.

Reprinted in *Schools,* p. 150.

E 631
"Autobiography of a Brooklyn Lamp (A Serial Tale)," *Brooklyn Daily Eagle,* 11 December 1846.

Reprinted in *GF,* II, 55–56.

E 632
"The Departed Soldier, and Other Tales [review]," *Brooklyn Daily Eagle,* 11 December 1846.

E 633
"Autobiography of a Brooklyn Lamp," *Brooklyn Daily Eagle,* 12 December 1846.

Reprinted in *GF,* II, 56.

E 634
"Notices of New Books," *Brooklyn Daily Eagle,* 12 December 1846.

E 635
[Cromwell and the Puritans], *Brooklyn Daily Eagle*, 12 December 1846.

E 636
"Make a Black Mark for It!", *Brooklyn Daily Eagle,* 14 December 1846.

Reprinted in *GF,* II, 57.

E 637
"The Viennoise Children," *Brooklyn Daily Eagle,* 14 December 1846.

E 638
"Works of History, for General Reading [review of J. Frost, *Beauties of English History* and *Beauties of French History;* Marcius Wilson, *A History of the United States*]," *Brooklyn Daily Eagle,* 14 December 1846.

Reprinted in *Schools,* pp. 150–151.

E 639
"John Quincy Adams," *Brooklyn Daily Eagle,* 15 December 1846.

Reprinted in *GF*, II, 198.

E 640
"Isms," *Brooklyn Daily Eagle,* 15 December 1846.

E 641
"Books for Youth," *Brooklyn Daily Eagle,* 15 December 1846.

E 642
"Don't Be So 'Mortal Genteel!' ", *Brooklyn Daily Eagle,* 16 December 1846.

Reprinted in *GF*, II, 355–356.

E 643
["The Most Bloodless" War Ever Known], *Brooklyn Daily Eagle,* 16 December 1846.

Reprinted in *GF,* I, 252–254.

E 644
"A Fact-Romance of Long Island," *Brooklyn Daily Eagle,* 16 December 1846.

Reprinted in *UPP,* I, 146–147. Revised from "Some Fact-Romances" in *Aristidean,* December 1845 (E 205).

E 645
"A Few Words to the Young Men of Brooklyn," *Brooklyn Daily Eagle*, 17 December 1846.

Reprinted in *GF*, I, 133–135; *UPP*, I, 148–149; *Schools*, pp. 151–152.

E 646
"The Effect of This Horrible 'Free Trade' Tariff on Mechanics' Wages," *Brooklyn Daily Eagle*, 17 December 1846.

E 647
"Startling!", *Brooklyn Daily Eagle*, 18 December 1846.

E 648
[Poe Ill, Destitute], *Brooklyn Daily Eagle*, 18 December 1846.

Reprinted in *GF*, II, 276.

E 649
[The Passing of Revolutionary Veterans], *Brooklyn Daily Eagle*, 18 December 1846.

Reprinted in *GF*, I, 92–93.

E 650
"The Republic of Cracow 'Extinguished,' " *Brooklyn Daily Eagle*, 19 December 1846.

Reprinted in *GF*, I, 47–49.

E 651
"School Arithmetic," *Brooklyn Daily Eagle*, 21 December 1846.

Reprinted in *Schools*, pp. 152–153.

E 652
"Set Down Your Feet, Democrats!", *Brooklyn Daily Eagle*, 21 December 1846.

Reprinted in *GF*, I, 194.

E 653
'Books Just Published [review of Izaac Walton, *The Lives of Dr. John Donne . . .*]," *Brooklyn Daily Eagle*, 21 December 1846.

Partially reprinted in *UPP*, I, 137.

E 654
"Health and Prosperity Go With Him [Henry Clay]," *Brooklyn Daily Eagle*, 22 December 1846.

Reprinted in *GF*, II, 196–197.

E 655
" 'Important Announcement,' " *Brooklyn Daily Eagle*, 22 December 1846.

Reprinted in *GF*, II, 342–343; *UPP*, I, 149.

E 656
" 'No License,' " *Brooklyn Daily Eagle*, 22 December 1846.

Reprinted in *GF*, I, 70–72.

E 657
"Theatricals," *Brooklyn Daily Eagle*, 22 December 1846.

E 658
"Altruism," *Brooklyn Daily Eagle*, 23 December 1846.

Reprinted in *GF*, II, 359.

E 659
"For the Boys," *Brooklyn Daily Eagle*, 23 December 1846.

Reprinted in *Schools*, p. 153.

E 660
"Will We Never Have Any Better State of Things?", *Brooklyn Daily Eagle*, 23 December 1846.

Reprinted in *GF*, II, 229.

E 661
" 'A Merry Christmas' Wishes the *Eagle* to Its Readers (in Advance)," *Brooklyn Daily Eagle*, 24 December 1846.

Reprinted in *GF*, II, 215–216.

E 662
"An Incident of Long Island Forty Years Ago," *Brooklyn Daily Eagle*, 24 December 1846.

Reprinted in *UPP*, I, 149–151. Revised from "Some Fact-Romances" in *Aristidean*, December 1845 (E 205).

E 663
" 'The Gladiator'—Mr. Forrest—Acting," *Brooklyn Daily Eagle*, 26 December 1846.

Reprinted in *GF*, II, 330–334.

E 664
" 'Robinson Crusoe,' " *Brooklyn Daily Eagle*, 26 December 1846.

Reprinted in *GF*, II, 308.

E 665
"The West," *Brooklyn Daily Eagle*, 26 December 1846.

Reprinted in *GF*, I, 26–27; *UPP*, I, 151–152.

E 666
"A Funeral by Moonlight," *Brooklyn Daily Eagle*, 28 December 1846.

Reprinted in *GF*, II, 144–146.

E 667
"Sign–Posts of the Times," *Brooklyn Daily Eagle*, 28 December 1846.

E 668
" 'That' Ruin," *Brooklyn Daily Eagle*, 28 December 1846.

E 669
"A Paragraph for the English Abolitionists," *Brooklyn Daily Eagle*, 29 December 1846.

E 670
[Book Notices], *Brooklyn Daily Eagle*, 30 December 1846.

E 671
" 'Hallowed from Innovation . . . ,' " *Brooklyn Daily Eagle*, 30 December 1846.

E 672
"Government," *Brooklyn Daily Eagle*, 2 January 1847.

Reprinted in *GF*, I, 53–54.

E 673
"True Yankee Talent.—A Word About Fostering Precocity in Children," *Brooklyn Daily Eagle*, 4 January 1847.

Reprinted in *GF*, II, 356–358.

E 674
"The War," *Brooklyn Daily Eagle*, 4 January 1847.

Reprinted in *GF*, I, 254–255.

E 675
"Death of Owen Flood," *Brooklyn Daily Eagle*, 4 January 1847.

E 676
[Viennoise Children], *Brooklyn Daily Eagle*, 4 January 1847.

E 677
"Slavery in New American Territory," *Brooklyn Daily Eagle*, 5 January 1847.

E 678
"Another School Officer Proposed," *Brooklyn Daily Eagle*, 6 January 1847.

Reprinted in *Schools*, p. 153.

E 679
"High School in Brooklyn," *Brooklyn Daily Eagle*, 6 January 1847.

Reprinted in *Schools*, p. 153.

E 680
" 'In the Twinkling of an Eye'—Mr. [Governor] Young's First Message," *Brooklyn Daily Eagle*, 6 January 1847.

Reprinted in *GF*, II, 228.

E 681
"Scraps of Education," *Brooklyn Daily Eagle*, 7 January 1847.

Reprinted in *Schools*, p. 154.

E 682
[Jackson's 1815 Victory], *Brooklyn Daily Eagle*, 8 January 1847.

Reprinted in *GF*, I, 93.

E 683
[School Tax], *Brooklyn Daily Eagle*, 9 January 1847.

Reprinted in *Schools*, p. 154.

E 684
"Monkeyism in Brooklyn," *Brooklyn Daily Eagle*, 12 January 1847.

E 685
[Schooling in Sparta], *Brooklyn Daily Eagle,* 13 January 1847.

Reprinted in *Schools,* p. 155.

E 686
"To Be Pitied," *Brooklyn Daily Eagle,* 13 January 1847.

E 687
"The Fools of the Nineteenth Century Trying to Kill the Goose That Lays Their Golden Eggs," *Brooklyn Daily Eagle,* 14 January 1847.

Reprinted in *GF,* II, 72–76.

E 688
[Horace Greeley "Burnt in Effigy"], *Brooklyn Daily Eagle,* 14 January 1847.

Reprinted in *GF,* II, 252.

E 689
[*Brooklyn Advertiser* Brainless], *Brooklyn Daily Eagle,* 15 January 1847.

Reprinted in *GF,* II, 24.

E 690
"New Reading, but the Same Meaning [*Brooklyn Advertiser*]," *Brooklyn Daily Eagle,* 15 January 1847.

Reprinted in *GF,* II, 24.

E 691
"Pay of Soldiers," *Brooklyn Daily Eagle,* 15 January 1847.

Reprinted in *GF,* II, 229–230.

E 692
["Goethe Avers . . ."], *Brooklyn Daily Eagle,* 15 January 1847.

E 693
"Democratic Doctrine," *Brooklyn Daily Eagle,* 16 January 1847.

Reprinted in *GF,* I, 194–196.

E 694
[Italian Opera], *Brooklyn Daily Eagle,* 16 January 1847.

Partially reprinted in Thomas L. Brasher, "Whitman's Conversion to Opera," *Walt Whitman Newsletter*, 4 (December 1958), 109–110.

E 695
[*Brooklyn Advertiser* and "Loco-focos"], *Brooklyn Daily Eagle*, 18 January 1847.

Reprinted in *GF*, II, 23–24.

E 696
"Egotism [*Brooklyn Advertiser*]," *Brooklyn Daily Eagle*, 18 January 1847.

Reprinted in *GF*, II, 23.

E 697
"Lately Published Books," *Brooklyn Daily Eagle*, 20 January 1847.

E 698
" 'Tis More Than Sixty Years Since!", *Brooklyn Daily Eagle*, 20 January 1847.

Reprinted in *GF*, I, 91.

E 699
"The Law of Blood.—Shall Russ Be Hung?", *Brooklyn Daily Eagle*, 21 January 1847.

Reprinted in *GF*, I, 109–110.

E 700
"The Latest Raw Head and Bloody Bones," *Brooklyn Daily Eagle*, 22 January 1847.

Reprinted in *GF*, I, 159–164.

E 701
"Night Schools for Brooklyn Apprentices and Other Youth.—Shall We Not Establish Them Yet?", *Brooklyn Daily Eagle*, 23 January 1847.

Reprinted in *Schools*, pp. 155–157.

E 702
"Books Just Published [*The Lives of Christopher Columbus and Americus Vespucius*]," *Brooklyn Daily Eagle*, 25 January 1847.

Reprinted in *Schools*, pp. 157–158.

E 703
"Arrival of the Hibernia," *Brooklyn Daily Eagle,* 25 January 1847.

E 704
"Free Evening Schools for Brooklyn Youth—A Word to the Common Council and to the Board of Education," *Brooklyn Daily Eagle,* 27 January 1847.

Reprinted in *Schools,* pp. 158–159.

E 705
"More Radicalism in the Pope," *Brooklyn Daily Eagle,* 27 January 1847.

Reprinted in *GF,* I, 50.

E 706
"The Child and the Profligate," *Brooklyn Daily Eagle,* 27–29 January 1847.

Revision of "The Child's Champion" in *New World,* 20 November 1841 (E 31).

E 707
[Book Notice], *Brooklyn Daily Eagle,* 28 January 1847.

E 708
"The Intemperance of Temperance," *Brooklyn Daily Eagle,* 29 January 1847.

Reprinted in *GF,* I, 67–69.

E 709
"The Poor in Brooklyn," *Brooklyn Daily Eagle,* 29 January 1847.

E 710
"The Sewing-Women of Brooklyn and New York," *Brooklyn Daily Eagle,* 29 January 1847.

Reprinted in *GF,* I, 148–151.

E 711
" 'The World is Governed Too Much,' " *Brooklyn Daily Eagle,* 29 January 1847.

Reprinted in *GF,* II, 343.

E 712
[Launching of the Ship *Washington*], *Brooklyn Daily Eagle,* 30 January 1847.

Reprinted in Thomas L. Brasher, "Whitman and Emma Willard's 'Rocked in the Cradle of the Deep,' " *Walt Whitman Newsletter,* 4 (March 1958), 78.

E 713
"Books Just Published," *Brooklyn Daily Eagle,* 1 February 1847.

E 714
[Poe's Wife Dead], *Brooklyn Daily Eagle,* 1 February 1847.

Reprinted in *GF,* II, 276–277.

E 715
" 'Wellman's Publications . . . ,' " *Brooklyn Daily Eagle,* 1 February 1847.

E 716
[An "Outrage"], *Brooklyn Daily Eagle,* 1 February 1847.

E 717
"One of the Results of the New Excise Law," *Brooklyn Daily Eagle,* 2 February 1847.

Reprinted in *GF,* I, 72–73.

E 718
[Review of Mary Howitt, *Ballads*], *Brooklyn Daily Eagle,* 2 February 1847.

Reprinted in *UPP,* I, 133. Not in White, *Journalism.*

E 719
"The Most Emphatic Expression of Opinion on an Important Subject Ever Given by the Empire State!", *Brooklyn Daily Eagle,* 3 February 1847.

Reprinted in *GF,* I, 197–198.

E 720
"Public Opinion," *Brooklyn Daily Eagle,* 3 February 1847.

E 721
[The *Brooklyn Advertiser*], *Brooklyn Daily Eagle,* 4 February 1847.

E 722
"Free Seminaries of Brooklyn—the Concord St. School—the York St. School—the Middagh St. School," *Brooklyn Daily Eagle,* 4 February 1847.

Partially reprinted in *GF,* I, 136–141; *Schools,* pp. 159–163.

E 723
[Get Married], *Brooklyn Daily Eagle,* 4 February 1847.

Reprinted in *GF,* II, 233.

E 724
[Devils' Feast], *Brooklyn Daily Eagle,* 5 February 1847.

Reprinted in *GF,* II, 232–233.

E 725
"More [*Brooklyn Advertiser*] Egotism," *Brooklyn Daily Eagle,* 5 February 1847.

Reprinted in *GF,* II, 23.

E 726
"More Terrible Tractoration!", *Brooklyn Daily Eagle,* 5 February 1847.

Reprinted in *GF,* II, 20–21.

E 727
"A Plea for the Stricken Ones!", *Brooklyn Daily Eagle,* 5 February 1847.

Reprinted in *GF,* I, 172–173.

E 728
"The Next Blessing to God's Blessing.—Shall It Be Jeopardized?", *Brooklyn Daily Eagle,* 6 February 1847.

Reprinted in *GF,* I, 229–234.

E 729
"Course of Brooklyn Whiggery Toward the Relief for Ireland Movement," *Brooklyn Daily Eagle,* 6 February 1847.

E 730
[Ridiculous *Brooklyn Advertiser*], *Brooklyn Daily Eagle,* 7 February 1847.

Reprinted in *GF,* II, 22–23.

E 731
"The Foreign Press on the American President," *Brooklyn Daily Eagle,* 8 February 1847.

Reprinted in *GF,* I, 31–33.

E 732
"Miserable State of the Stage.—Why Can't We Have Something Worth the Name of American Drama!", *Brooklyn Daily Eagle,* 8 February 1847.

Reprinted in *GF,* II, 310–314.

E 733
[The *Brooklyn Advertiser*], *Brooklyn Daily Eagle*, 8 February 1847.

E 734
"*Daniel Denniston* and the *Cumberland Statesman*," *Brooklyn Daily Eagle*, 8 February 1847.

E 735
"Points of Wish and Belief in the Two Parties Illustrated by the Leaders of the Democratic and American Reviews for February.—The Mexican War," *Brooklyn Daily Eagle*, 10 February 1847.

E 736
[Houses], *Brooklyn Daily Eagle*, 10 February 1847.

E 737
"Independent American Literature," *Brooklyn Daily Eagle*, 10 February 1847.

Reprinted in *GF*, II, 237–241.

E 738
"A Paragraph for Children," *Brooklyn Daily Eagle*, 10 February 1847.

E 739
"What Sort of Books Can Be Admitted in School Libraries," *Brooklyn Daily Eagle*, 10 February 1847.

Reprinted in *Schools*, pp. 163–164.

E 740
"A Daniel Come to Judgment!", *Brooklyn Daily Eagle*, 10 February 1847.

Reprinted in *Schools*, p. 164.

E 741
"Phonography," *Brooklyn Daily Eagle*, 10 February 1847.

Reprinted in *Schools*, p. 165.

E 742
"Why Don't Their Charity Begin at Home?", *Brooklyn Daily Eagle*, 10 February 1847.

Reprinted in *GF*, I, 42–44.

E 743
"Abroad," *Brooklyn Daily Eagle*, 11 February 1847.

Reprinted in *GF*, I, 29–31.

E 744
"State of the Common Schools," *Brooklyn Daily Eagle*, 11 February 1847.

Reprinted in *Schools*, pp. 165–166.

E 745
"Brooklyn Public Schools.—Statistics and Suggestions," *Brooklyn Daily Eagle*, 12 February 1847.

Reprinted in *Schools*, pp. 166–167.

E 746
"Why Do Theatres Languish? And How Shall the American Stage Be Resuscitated?", *Brooklyn Daily Eagle*, 12 February 1847.

Reprinted in *GF*, II, 314–318; *UPP*, I, 152–154.

E 747
[Italian Opera], *Brooklyn Daily Eagle*, 13 February 1847.

Partially reprinted in Thomas L. Brasher, "Whitman's Conversion to Opera," *Walt Whitman Newsletter*, 4 (December 1958), 109–110.

E 748
"Children of Father Type," *Brooklyn Daily Eagle*, 13 February 1847.

E 749
"Peace With Mexico," *Brooklyn Daily Eagle*, 13 February 1847.

Reprinted in *GF*, I, 255–256.

E 750
[Charles Lamb], *Brooklyn Daily Eagle*, 13 February 1847.

Partially reprinted in *UPP*, I, 133. Not in White, *Journalism*.

E 751
"One of the Sacredest Rights of an American Citizen Outraged—Punishment of an Editor for Daring to Speak His Mind," *Brooklyn Daily Eagle*, 15 February 1847.

Reprinted in *GF*, II, 248–252.

E 752
[Dull Day], *Brooklyn Daily Eagle*, 16 February 1847.

Reprinted in *GF*, II, 232.

E 753
[The Park Theatre], *Brooklyn Daily Eagle*, 16 February 1847.

E 754
"Indeed a Literary Banquet," *Brooklyn Daily Eagle*, 17 February 1847.

E 755
"Slavery in New Territory," *Brooklyn Daily Eagle*, 17 February 1847.

Reprinted in *GF*, I, 198–199.

E 756
"Women Should Possess Their Own," *Brooklyn Daily Eagle*, 18 February 1847.

Reprinted in *GF*, I, 73–74.

E 757
[Free Night Schools?], *Brooklyn Daily Eagle*, 19 February 1847.

Reprinted in *Schools*, p. 167.

E 758
[Review of Samuel Taylor Coleridge, *Letters, Conversations, and Recollections*, and Martin Farquhar Tupper, *Probabilities*], *Brooklyn Daily Eagle*, 20 February 1847.

Reprinted in *UPP*, I, 131, 136. Not in White, *Journalism*.

E 759
"The Reason Why We Have Our Flag Flying To-day," *Brooklyn Daily Eagle*, 22 February 1847.

E 760
"Public Feeling in Criminal Trials," *Brooklyn Daily Eagle*, 22 February 1847.

E 761
"A City Fire," *Brooklyn Daily Eagle*, 24 February 1847.

Reprinted in *UPP*, I, 154–156. Revised from *New York Aurora*, 1 April 1842 (E 96).

E 762
"What an Idea!", *Brooklyn Daily Eagle,* 24 February 1847.

Reprinted in *GF,* I, 234–235; *UPP,* I, 156.

E 763
"The Brooklyn Eagle on the Rio Grande," *Brooklyn Daily Eagle,* 25 February 1847.

E 764
"Will You Not Spend an Hour To-night at the Irish Relief Meeting, at the Brooklyn Institute?", *Brooklyn Daily Eagle,* 26 February 1847.

E 765
"Reading," *Brooklyn Daily Eagle,* 26 February 1847.

E 766
"Tone of the American Press.—Personality," *Brooklyn Daily Eagle,* 26 February 1847.

Reprinted in *GF,* II, 253–255.

E 767
"The Union Now and Forever!", *Brooklyn Daily Eagle,* 26 February 1847.

Reprinted in *GF,* I, 235–238.

E 768
"A Little Paragraph With a Big Moral," *Brooklyn Daily Eagle,* 1 March 1847.

Reprinted in *GF,* I, 158.

E 769
"Viennoise Children," *Brooklyn Daily Eagle,* 1 March 1847.

E 770
"How About the Doings in Congress?", *Brooklyn Daily Eagle,* 2 March 1847.

E 771
"The Fireside Friend, or Female Student, . . . by Mrs. Phelps," *Brooklyn Daily Eagle,* 4 March 1847.

Reprinted in *Schools,* p. 169.

E 772
"Flora's Festivals . . . Edited by Wm. E. Bradbury," *Brooklyn Daily Eagle*, 4 March 1847.

Reprinted in *Schools*, p. 169.

E 773
"An Hour in One of the Brooklyn Public Schools. Something More About Education and Teachers," *Brooklyn Daily Eagle*, 4 March 1847.

Reprinted in *GF*, I, 121–133; *Schools*, pp. 169–176.

E 774
"Lately Published Works [Marcius Wilson, *American History* . . .]," *Brooklyn Daily Eagle*, 4 March 1847.

Reprinted in *Schools*, p. 168.

E 775
"Loss of the Wilmot Proviso," *Brooklyn Daily Eagle*, 4 March 1847.

E 776
"Scenes in Nature," *Brooklyn Daily Eagle*, 4 March 1847.

E 777
" 'Woman, and Her Diseases, from the Cradle to the Grave.' By Edward H. Dixon, M.D. [review]," *Brooklyn Daily Eagle*, 4 March 1847.

Reprinted in *GF*, II, 305–306; *UPP*, I, 131.

E 778
"Don't Be Miserly in Such Matters!", *Brooklyn Daily Eagle*, 5 March 1847.

Reprinted in *Schools*, pp. 177–178.

E 779
"Mrs. C. A. Steuart's Elementary School," *Brooklyn Daily Eagle*, 5 March 1847.

Reprinted in *Schools*, pp. 176–177.

E 780
"The New Opera," *Brooklyn Daily Eagle*, 6 March 1847.

Partially reprinted in Thomas L. Brasher, "Whitman's Conversion to Opera," *Walt Whitman Newsletter*, 4 (December 1958), 109–110.

E 781
"Our Indian Articles," *Brooklyn Daily Eagle*, 8 March 1847.

E 782
"Lighting the Light," *Brooklyn Daily Eagle*, 8 March 1847.

Reprinted in *Schools*, pp. 178–179.

E 783
"The Poor of Scotland," *Brooklyn Daily Eagle*, 8 March 1847.

Reprinted in *GF*, I, 176.

E 784
"Honor to Literature!", *Brooklyn Daily Eagle*, 9 March 1847.

Reprinted in *GF*, II, 257–259.

E 785
"Education—Brooklyn Teachers and the Taught. Public School No. 6," *Brooklyn Daily Eagle*, 10 March 1847.

Reprinted in *Schools*, pp. 180–183.

E 786
"Something About Physiology and Phrenology," *Brooklyn Daily Eagle*, 10 March 1847.

Reprinted in Edward Hungerford, "Walt Whitman and His Chart of Bumps," *American Literature*, 2 (January 1931), 358; *Schools*, pp. 179–180.

E 787
" 'Dunigan's Home Library,' " *Brooklyn Daily Eagle*, 10 March 1847.

E 788
"The Opinions of Washington and Jefferson on an Important Point," *Brooklyn Daily Eagle*, 11 March 1847.

Reprinted in *GF*, I, 199–200.

E 789
" 'The Life of Christ,' in the Words of the Evangelists," *Brooklyn Daily Eagle*, 12 March 1847.

Reprinted in *GF*, II, 305.

E 790
[Review of Washington Irving, *Life and Voyages of Christopher Columbus*], *Brooklyn Daily Eagle*, 12 March 1847.

Reprinted in *UPP*, I, 133. Not in White, *Journalism*.

E 791
"Shall We Promulgate the Noble Temperance Reform, by Moral Means, or by Stringent Laws?", *Brooklyn Daily Eagle*, 13 March 1847.

Reprinted in *GF*, I, 69–70.

E 792
[Singers Hutchinsons], *Brooklyn Daily Eagle*, 13 March 1847.

Reprinted in *GF*, II, 359.

E 793
"Andrew Jackson," *Brooklyn Daily Eagle*, 15 March 1847.

E 794
"Hazlitt's 'Napoleon,' " *Brooklyn Daily Eagle*, 15 March 1847.

Reprinted in *GF*, II, 284–287.

E 795
"The Toils of a Newspaper," *Brooklyn Daily Eagle*, 16 March 1847.

E 796
"A Book for American Young Men [Edward Everett, *Practical Education and Useful Knowledge*]," *Brooklyn Daily Eagle*, 18 March 1847.

Reprinted in *Schools*, p. 183.

E 797
"The Ward Meetings Tonight.—Parties in Brooklyn," *Brooklyn Daily Eagle*, 18 March 1847.

Reprinted in *GF*, II, 39–41.

E 798
"Political Knolwedge," *Brooklyn Daily Eagle*, 19 March 1847.

Reprinted in *GF*, I, 57–58; *Schools*, pp. 184–186.

E 799
"Rules for Governing Children," *Brooklyn Daily Eagle*, 19 March 1847.

Reprinted in *Schools*, pp. 183–184.

E 800
"Brooklyn Public School, 4th District," *Brooklyn Daily Eagle*, 19 March 1847.

Reprinted in *Schools*, p. 184.

E 801
"That Observatory in Brooklyn Which We Must Have," *Brooklyn Daily Eagle*, 20 March 1847.

Reprinted in *GF*, II, 146–149.

E 802
[Opera at Palmo's], *Brooklyn Daily Eagle*, 20 March 1847.

Reprinted in *GF*, II, 359.

E 803
[Thirtieth Congress], *Brooklyn Daily Eagle*, 20 March 1847.

Reprinted in *GF*, I, 93.

E 804
"Works for Schools and for Young People [Francis T. Russell, *Russell's Juvenile Speaker*, and *Zumpt's Latin Grammar* by Charles A. Anthon]," *Brooklyn Daily Eagle*, 20 March 1847.

Reprinted in *GF*, II, 307; *Schools*, pp. 186–187 (versions differ).

E 805
"The Italian Opera and the Press," *Brooklyn Daily Eagle*, 20 March 1847.

E 806
"Beauties of Residing in New York City: By One Who Knows 'Em," *Brooklyn Daily Eagle*, 22 March 1847.

E 807
"[Part One of] 'Dombey and Son' [review]," *Brooklyn Daily Eagle*, 22 March 1847.

Reprinted in *GF*, II, 296.

E 808
"Combe's Physiology," *Brooklyn Daily Eagle*, 23 March 1847.

E 809
" 'The Barber of Seville,' " *Brooklyn Daily Eagle*, 23 March 1847.

Reprinted in *GF*, II, 349–351.

E 810
"Teaching Teachers," *Brooklyn Daily Eagle*, 24 March 1847.

Reprinted in *Schools*, p. 187.

E 811
" 'Improved Presses,' " *Brooklyn Daily Eagle*, 25 March 1847.

Reprinted in *GF*, II, 228.

E 812
"*The Constitutional History of England* . . . By Henry Hallam . . . ," *Brooklyn Daily Eagle*, 27 March 1847.

Reprinted in *Schools*, pp. 187–188.

E 813
[Schoolmaster Useful but Despised], *Brooklyn Daily Eagle*, 27 March 1847.

Reprinted in *Schools*, p. 188.

E 814
"Mind Your Steps," *Brooklyn Daily Eagle*, 29 March 1847.

Reprinted in *GF*, II, 274.

E 815
"One of the Last Relics of Bigotry," *Brooklyn Daily Eagle*, 29 March 1847.

Reprinted in *GF*, II, 275.

E 816
"Arts and Sciences in Kings County," *Brooklyn Daily Eagle*, 29 March 1847.

E 817
[Notice of Francis Liber, *Great Events*], *Brooklyn Daily Eagle*, 29 March 1847.

E 818
"The King's Highway. By G. P. R. James," *Brooklyn Daily Eagle*, 2 April 1847.

Reprinted in *GF*, II, 304.

E 819
" 'Marriage: Its History and Ceremonies, Etc.' By L. N. Fowler," *Brooklyn Daily Eagle*, 2 April 1847.

Reprinted in *GF*, II, 304.

E 820
"Warmth of Affection and Manner Toward Children," *Brooklyn Daily Eagle*, 2 April 1847.

E 821
[Review of William Hazlitt, *Napoleon Bonaparte*], *Brooklyn Daily Eagle*, 2 April 1847.

Reprinted in *UPP*, I, 133. Not in White, *Journalism*.

E 822
"Where the Great Stretch of Power Must Be Wielded," *Brooklyn Daily Eagle*, 2 April 1847.

Reprinted in *GF*, I, 25–26.

E 823
"Honor to the Hero! The Battle of Buena Vista—Bright Among the Brightest Emanations of American Glory," *Brooklyn Daily Eagle*, 3 April 1847.

Reprinted in *GF*, I, 80–83.

E 824
"Washington Park," *Brooklyn Daily Eagle*, 5 April 1847.

E 825
"Clean the Streets! Clean the Streets! Clean the Streets!", *Brooklyn Daily Eagle*, 7 April 1847.

Reprinted in *GF*, II, 55.

E 826
"Maxims," *Brooklyn Daily Eagle*, 7 April 1847.

Reprinted in *Schools*, pp. 188–189.

E 827
"American Biography," *Brooklyn Daily Eagle*, 8 April 1847.

Reprinted in *Schools*, p. 189.

E 828
"Signs," *Brooklyn Daily Eagle*, 9 April 1847.

Reprinted in *GF*, II, 41–42.

E 829
"A Word to Boys," *Brooklyn Daily Eagle*, 9 April 1847.

E 830
"Nothing But the Whole Ticket," *Brooklyn Daily Eagle*, 13 April 1847.

Reprinted in *GF*, II, 42–43.

E 831
" 'Diana of Meridor.' By Alexander Dumas," *Brooklyn Daily Eagle*, 14 April 1847.

Reprinted in *GF*, II, 300.

E 832
["Perfectly Serene" in the Face of Defeat], *Brooklyn Daily Eagle*, 14 April 1847.

Reprinted in *GF*, II, 43–45.

E 833
" 'Sylvandire.' By Alexander Dumas," *Brooklyn Daily Eagle*, 14 April 1847.

Reprinted in *GF*, II, 300; *UPP*, I, 132.

E 834
"Thomson's 'Seasons,' " *Brooklyn Daily Eagle*, 14 April 1847.

Reprinted in *GF*, II, 300–301.

E 835
" 'Past and Present, and Chartism.' By Thomas Carlyle," *Brooklyn Daily Eagle*, 14 April 1847.

Reprinted in *GF*, II, 293; *UPP*, I, 130 (dated '23 November 1846').

E 836
"Evening Schools," *Brooklyn Daily Eagle,* 15 April 1847.

Reprinted in *Schools,* p. 190.

E 837
"An Emanation of Brooklyn Patriotism—Meeting of Citizens in front of the Eagle Office to Testify Their Sense of Our Brilliant Victories in the South–West," *Brooklyn Daily Eagle,* 16 April 1847.

Reprinted in *GF,* I, 83–86.

E 838
[Stark Democracy's Destructiveness], *Brooklyn Daily Eagle,* 16 April 1847.

Reprinted in *GF,* II, 12–15.

E 839
"Flogging in Our Brooklyn Schools," *Brooklyn Daily Eagle,* 17 April 1847.

Reprinted in *GF,* I, 144–145; *Schools,* pp. 190–191.

E 840
"Fort Greene Park," *Brooklyn Daily Eagle,* 17 April 1847.

E 841
"Brooklyn Schools," *Brooklyn Daily Eagle,* 19 April 1847.

Reprinted in *Schools,* pp. 191–192.

E 842
"Dramatic Affairs, and Actors," *Brooklyn Daily Eagle,* 19 April 1847.

Reprinted in *GF,* II, 334–337; *UPP,* I, 156–158.

E 843
"Our New Press," *Brooklyn Daily Eagle,* 19 April 1847.

Reprinted in *GF,* II, 227.

E 844
[The Democratic Spirit], *Brooklyn Daily Eagle,* 20 April 1847.

Reprinted in *GF,* I, 3–6; *UPP,* I, 159–160.

E 845
"Brooklyn Schools," *Brooklyn Daily Eagle*, 20 April 1847.

Reprinted in *Schools*, p. 193.

E 846
"Play Grounds," *Brooklyn Daily Eagle*, 20 April 1847.

Reprinted in *Schools*, p. 193.

E 847
"Schools and Legislatures," *Brooklyn Daily Eagle*, 20 April 1847.

Reprinted in *Schools*, pp. 193–194.

E 848
"Book World [Francis Wayland, *The Pursuit of Knowledge Under Difficulties . . .* , and Jules Michelet, *History of France*]," *Brooklyn Daily Eagle*, 22 April 1847.

Partially reprinted in *UPP*, I, 134 (Michelet); *Schools*, pp. 194–195 (Wayland).

E 849
"The Home Treasury," *Brooklyn Daily Eagle*, 22 April 1847.

E 850
"New States: Shall They Be Slave or Free?", *Brooklyn Daily Eagle*, 22 April 1847.

Reprinted in *GF*, I, 200–202.

E 851
"The Ambition to 'Make a Show' in Dress.—Hints to Brooklyn Young Women and Men," *Brooklyn Daily Eagle*, 23 April 1847.

Reprinted in *UPP*, I, 162–163.

E 852
"Mr. Webster: The Great Bribed," *Brooklyn Daily Eagle*, 23 April 1847.

Reprinted in *GF*, II, 184–185.

E 853
"Reminiscences of the Slave Trade," *Brooklyn Daily Eagle*, 24 April 1847.

Reprinted in *GF*, II, 223.

E 854
"Anti–Democratic Bearing of Scott's Novels," *Brooklyn Daily Eagle*, 26 April 1847.

Reprinted in *GF*, II, 264–266; *UPP*, I, 163–164.

E 855
"Rights of Southern Freemen as Well as Northern Freemen.—Mr. Calhoun's Speech," *Brooklyn Daily Eagle*, 27 April 1847.

Reprinted in *GF*, I, 203–208.

E 856
"Serious Works," *Brooklyn Daily Eagle*, 30 April 1847.

E 857
[Book Notice], *Brooklyn Daily Eagle*, 3 May 1847.

E 858
"Encouragement to the Democrat," *Brooklyn Daily Eagle*, 3 May 1847.

Reprinted in *GF*, I, 24–25.

E 859
"Paley's Natural Theology," *Brooklyn Daily Eagle*, 4 May 1847.

E 860
" 'The Things Which We Have Learned . . . ,' " *Brooklyn Daily Eagle*, 5 May 1847.

E 861
[Notice of Herman Melville, *Omoo*], *Brooklyn Daily Eagle*, 5 May 1847.

Partially reprinted in *UPP*, I, 134; reprinted in John Howard Birss, "Whitman and Herman Melville," *Notes and Queries*, 164 (22 April 1933), 280.

E 862
[Notices of (Charles Burdett), *Arthur Martin*], *Brooklyn Daily Eagle*, 11 May 1847.

E 863
"Vulgar and Brutal Affair," *Brooklyn Daily Eagle*, 12 May 1847.

Reprinted in *GF*, II, 226–227.

E 864
"Brooklyn Normal Institute," *Brooklyn Daily Eagle,* 15 May 1847.

Reprinted in *Schools,* p. 195.

E 865
"Books Lately Published [*Story on the Constitution*]," *Brooklyn Daily Eagle,* 17 May 1847.

Reprinted in *Schools,* pp. 195–196.

E 866
" 'Minor Morals . . . ' [Maxims of Washington]," *Brooklyn Daily Eagle,* 17 May 1847.

E 867
"How Matters Are Going On, Abroad," *Brooklyn Daily Eagle,* 18 May 1847.

Reprinted in *GF,* I, 44–45.

E 868
[Notice of Eugène Sue, *Martin the Foundling*], *Brooklyn Daily Eagle,* 18 May 1847.

E 869
"Brooklyn Sunday School Children," *Brooklyn Daily Eagle,* 19 May 1847.

Reprinted in *Schools,* p. 196.

E 870
"Liberality, Indeed!", *Brooklyn Daily Eagle,* 20 May 1847.

Reprinted in *GF,* I, 158.

E 871
[Review of Mrs. Fanny Butler Kemble, *Year of Consolation*], *Brooklyn Daily Eagle,* 20 May 1847.

Reprinted in *GF,* II, 302.

E 872
[Colonel Jefferson Davis], *Brooklyn Daily Eagle,* 22 May 1847.

Reprinted in *GF,* II, 197.

E 873
"Disunion," *Brooklyn Daily Eagle*, 22 May 1847.

Reprinted in *GF*, I, 238–239.

E 874
"Lectures to Young Men, Etc. [review]," *Brooklyn Daily Eagle*, 28 May 1847.

E 875
"Mournful Matter!", *Brooklyn Daily Eagle*, 28 May 1847.

Reprinted in *GF*, II, 65–67.

E 876
" 'Self–Culture'—[William Ellery] Channing," *Brooklyn Daily Eagle*, 28 May 1847.

Reprinted in *UPP*, I, 130 (dated '28 June').

E 877
[Reviews of Eugéne Sue, *Martin the Foundling*, and Alexander Dumas, *Memoirs of a Physician*], *Brooklyn Daily Eagle*, 31 May 1847.

Partially reprinted in *UPP*, I, 132 (Dumas).

E 878
"The City of Dirt," *Brooklyn Daily Eagle*, 1 June 1847.

Partially reprinted in *GF*, II, 52–53.

E 879
"Young Men for Office," *Brooklyn Daily Eagle*, 2 June 1847.

E 880
"Paucity of News," *Brooklyn Daily Eagle*, 6 June 1847.

Reprinted in *GF*, II, 225.

E 881
"Religious Volumes," *Brooklyn Daily Eagle*, 7 June 1847.

E 882
"Fort Greene Park," *Brooklyn Daily Eagle*, 11 June 1847.

E 883
"New and Racy Work [William Howett, *Homes and Haunts of the Most Eminent British Poets*]," *Brooklyn Daily Eagle*, 11 June 1847.

E 884
[Royal Family Residing in Brooklyn?], *Brooklyn Daily Eagle,* 14 June 1847.

E 885
[Book World], *Brooklyn Daily Eagle,* 14 June 1847.

E 886
[Review of Schiller, *Homage of the Arts,* trans. Charles T. Brooks], *Brooklyn Daily Eagle,* 16 June 1847.

Reprinted in *GF*, II, 303.

E 887
"Ireland and England.—Eccentricity of English Charity," *Brooklyn Daily Eagle,* 17 June 1847.

Reprinted in *GF*, I, 170–171.

E 888
"Received with Thanks," *Brooklyn Daily Eagle,* 17 June 1847.

Reprinted in *GF*, II, 228.

E 889
"A Working Woman's Savings," *Brooklyn Daily Eagle,* 17 June 1847.

Reprinted in *GF*, I, 157–158.

E 890
"Lengths of Whig Partizanship. Infamous Charges!", *Brooklyn Daily Eagle,* 21 June 1847.

Reprinted in *GF*, I, 256–259.

E 891
"Book World," *Brooklyn Daily Eagle,* 21 June 1847.

E 892
"Honor to the Chief Magistrate of the United States!", *Brooklyn Daily Eagle,* 25 June 1847.

E 893
[Women's Annual Salary], *Brooklyn Daily Eagle,* 25 June 1847.

E 894
"The President in Brooklyn," *Brooklyn Daily Eagle,* 26 June 1847.

E 895
"Books [Review of *Autobiography of Goethe*]," *Brooklyn Daily Eagle*, 28 June 1847.

Reprinted in *UPP*, I, 132.

E 896
"The 'Law of Blood,'" *Brooklyn Daily Eagle*, 30 June 1847.

Reprinted in *GF*, I, 110–113.

E 897
"New Magazine [*Union Magazine*]," *Brooklyn Daily Eagle*, 30 June 1847.

E 898
"Independence Day," *Brooklyn Daily Eagle*, 3 July 1847.

Reprinted in *GF*, I, 89–91.

E 899
"More of the [*Brooklyn*] *Advertiser's* Logic," *Brooklyn Daily Eagle*, 6 July 1847.

Reprinted in *GF*, II, 21.

E 900
"Corporal Punishment in Schools," *Brooklyn Daily Eagle*, 7 July 1847.

Reprinted in *Schools*, p. 196.

E 901
"Brooklyn Schools," *Brooklyn Daily Eagle*, 9 July 1847.

Reprinted in *Schools*, pp. 197–200.

E 902
"Brooklyn Trees," *Brooklyn Daily Eagle*, 11 July 1847.

E 903
"We Have Proved the [*Brooklyn*] *Advertiser*," *Brooklyn Daily Eagle*, 12 July 1847.

Partially reprinted in *GF*, II, 19–20.

E 904
[Weeping Willow Sticks], *Brooklyn Daily Eagle*, 13 July 1847.

Reprinted in *Schools*, p. 200.

E 905
"Pleasant Two Hours' Jaunt.—East Brooklyn Stages," *Brooklyn Daily Eagle*, 13 July 1847.

Reprinted in *GF*, II, 149–151.

E 906
"Ride to Coney Island, and Clam-Bake There," *Brooklyn Daily Eagle*, 15 July 1847.

Reprinted in *GF*, II, 151–155; *UPP*, I, 164–166.

E 907
[Churches—Theatre], *Brooklyn Daily Eagle*, 16 July 1847.

E 908
"Paper Money," *Brooklyn Daily Eagle*, 20 July 1847.

E 909
[Common Words], *Brooklyn Daily Eagle*, 20 July 1847.

Reprinted in *GF*, II, 232.

E 910
" 'Be Very Careful . . . ,' " *Brooklyn Daily Eagle*, 20 July 1847.

E 911
" 'Dombey and Son' [review]," *Brooklyn Daily Eagle*, 20 July 1847.

Reprinted in *GF*, II, 296–297.

E 912
"Seventeen Hundred and Seventy-Six, Etc.," *Brooklyn Daily Eagle*, 22 July 1847.

E 913
"The Arabian Nights," *Brooklyn Daily Eagle*, 22 July 1847.

E 914
"The Alphabetical Drawing Book," *Brooklyn Daily Eagle*, 22 July 1847.

E 915
[Review of John Ruskin, *Modern Painters*], *Brooklyn Daily Eagle*, 22 July 1847.

Reprinted in *UPP*, I, 135. Not in White, *Journalism*.

E916
"Proceedings of the Repealers of Brooklyn," *Brooklyn Daily Eagle*, 23 July 1847.

E917
"A Nest of Cockney Blackguards," *Brooklyn Daily Eagle*, 23 July 1847.

E918
"New Light and Old," *Brooklyn Daily Eagle*, 26 July 1847.

Reprinted in *GF*, I, 51–53; *UPP*, I, 166–168.

E919
[England's "Doings" in India and China], *Brooklyn Daily Eagle*, 29 July 1847.

Reprinted in *GF*, I, 40–42.

E920
"Late Books," *Brooklyn Daily Eagle*, 29 July 1847.

E921
"Theatricals over the River," *Brooklyn Daily Eagle*, 4 August 1847.

E922
"The Good Genius, Etc.," *Brooklyn Daily Eagle*, 5 August 1847.

E923
"Mrs. [Anna] Bishop's Singing," *Brooklyn Daily Eagle*, 5 August 1847.

Partially reprinted in *GF*, II, 351–352.

E924
"What Makes a 'Gentleman' in the English Court," *Brooklyn Daily Eagle*, 7 August 1847.

Reprinted in *GF*, I, 45–46.

E925
"A Ridiculous Idea [Annex Cuba]," *Brooklyn Daily Eagle*, 9 August 1847.

E926
"Latest Issues in the Publishing World [Izaac Walton, *The Complete Angler*]," *Brooklyn Daily Eagle*, 9 August 1847.

E 927
[Review of Lamartine, *History of the Girondists*], *Brooklyn Daily Eagle*, 10 August 1847.

Partially reprinted in *UPP*, I, 133.

E 928
[Book Notices], *Brooklyn Daily Eagle*, 11 August 1847.

E 929
" 'The Stage' in Brooklyn," *Brooklyn Daily Eagle*, 12 August 1847.

E 930
"The 'Death Punishment' as in the French Revolution," *Brooklyn Daily Eagle*, 12 August 1847.

E 931
[Ladies' Slippers], *Brooklyn Daily Eagle*, 12 August 1847.

Reprinted in *GF*, II, 231 (dated '1846').

E 932
"Philosophy of Ferries," *Brooklyn Daily Eagle*, 13 August 1847.

Reprinted in *GF*, II, 159–166; *UPP*, I, 168–171.

E 933
"New Business for Governments," *Brooklyn Daily Eagle*, 13 August 1847.

E 934
"How We Went Down to Fort Hamilton—And Other Matters," *Brooklyn Daily Eagle*, 14 August 1847.

Reprinted in *GF*, II, 167–173.

E 935
[Teaching Too Much at a Time], *Brooklyn Daily Eagle*, 15 August 1847.

Reprinted in *Schools*, p. 200.

E 936
"Persian Poetry," *Brooklyn Daily Eagle*, 16 August 1847.

E 937
"Late Publications," *Brooklyn Daily Eagle*, 18 August 1847.

E 938
"The Second Fraud Perpetrated Upon Brooklyn (Long Island Rights and New York Governors)," *Brooklyn Daily Eagle,* 18 August 1847.

E 939
"The Second Fraud Perpetrated Upon Brooklyn (Long Island Rights and New York Governors)," *Brooklyn Daily Eagle,* 19 August 1847.

E 940
"Peaches and Courtesy," *Brooklyn Daily Eagle,* 19 August 1847.

Reprinted in *GF,* II, 226.

E 941
[Bad Axe-i-dent], *Brooklyn Daily Eagle,* 21 August 1847.

Reprinted in *GF,* II, 231 (dated '1846').

E 942
[Book Notice], *Brooklyn Daily Eagle,* 21 August 1847.

E 943
"Ballad of the Children's Wish," *Brooklyn Daily Eagle,* 25 August 1847.

E 944
"Condition of the Stage," *Brooklyn Daily Eagle,* 25 August 1847.

Reprinted in *GF,* II, 337–339.

E 945
"What the Defenders of the Gallows Say and an Answer Thereto," *Brooklyn Daily Eagle,* 26 August 1847.

Reprinted in *GF,* I, 113–116.

E 946
"The *Union Magazine,*" *Brooklyn Daily Eagle,* 27 August 1847.

E 947
"Today's Gloomy News [Death of Silas Wright]," *Brooklyn Daily Eagle,* 28 August 1847.

Reprinted in *GF,* II, 185–188.

E 948
"American Workingmen *versus* Slavery," *Brooklyn Daily Eagle*, 1 September
1847.

Reprinted in *GF*, I, 208–214; *UPP*, I, 171–174.

E 949
[School for Colored Pupils], *Brooklyn Daily Eagle*, 1 September 1847.

Reprinted in *Schools*, p. 200.

E 950
"Our Venerable Contemporary of the [*Brooklyn*] *Star*," *Brooklyn Daily Eagle*,
2 September 1847.

Reprinted in *GF*, II, 17–19.

E 951
[Country Schoolmaster], *Brooklyn Daily Eagle*, 2 September 1847.

E 952
"New Works from Harpers," *Brooklyn Daily Eagle*, 6 September 1847.

E 953
"Democratic Review," *Brooklyn Daily Eagle*, 7 September 1847.

E 954
"A Thought of Ours About Music in the United States," *Brooklyn Daily Eagle*,
8 September 1847.

Reprinted in *GF*, II, 345–346.

E 955
"Residence in Brooklyn," *Brooklyn Daily Eagle*, 14 September 1847.

E 956
"The [*Brooklyn*] Star and 'Credit,' " *Brooklyn Daily Eagle,* 14 September
1847.

E 957
"East Long Island Correspondence: Letter I," *Brooklyn Daily Eagle*, 16 September 1847.

Reprinted in *UPP*, I, 174–177.

E 958
"East Long Island Correspondence: Letter II," *Brooklyn Daily Eagle*, 18 September 1847.

Reprinted in *UPP*, I, 177–180.

E 959
"East Long Island Correspondence: Letter III," *Brooklyn Daily Eagle*, 20 September 1847.

Reprinted in *UPP*, I, 180–181.

E 960
"Disgraceful to the Profession of Editor!", *Brooklyn Daily Eagle*, 22 September 1847.

E 961
"When Will the War Be Ended?", *Brooklyn Daily Eagle*, 23 September 1847.

Reprinted in *GF*, I, 259–263.

E 962
"Brooklyn Schools and Teachers," *Brooklyn Daily Eagle*, 24 September 1847.

Reprinted in *Schools*, pp. 201–202.

E 963
"Educational Works Recently Published by the Harpers," *Brooklyn Daily Eagle*, 24 September 1847.

Reprinted in *Schools*, pp. 202–203.

E 964
"The Pocket versus the Mind," *Brooklyn Daily Eagle*, 24 September 1847.

E 965
"Tales and Sketches [review]," *Brooklyn Daily Eagle*, 27 September 1847.

E 966
"The Whip-Poor-Will [review]," *Brooklyn Daily Eagle*, 27 September 1847.

E 967
[Review of George Sand, *The Journeyman Joiner*], *Brooklyn Daily Eagle*, 27 September 1847.

Partially reprinted in *UPP*, I, 135. Not in White, *Journalism*.

E 968
[Book Notice], *Brooklyn Daily Eagle,* 28 September 1847.

E 969
"Hope for Ireland!", *Brooklyn Daily Eagle,* 29 September 1847.

Reprinted in *GF,* I, 173–174.

E 970
" 'The New *Juvenile Drawing* Book,' " *Brooklyn Daily Eagle,* 29 September 1847.

Reprinted in *Schools,* p. 204.

E 971
"Ventilation in Our Brooklyn School Rooms," *Brooklyn Daily Eagle,* 30 September 1847.

Reprinted in *Schools,* p. 204.

E 972
"Music at Midnight," *Brooklyn Daily Eagle,* 2 October 1847.

Reprinted in *GF,* II, 221.

E 973
"Something Which Every Youth Should Read," *Brooklyn Daily Eagle,* 2 October 1847.

Reprinted in *Schools,* pp. 204–206.

E 974
"The Happy Girl," *Brooklyn Daily Eagle,* 5 October 1847.

E 975
"Mr. James's Life of Henry IV of France," *Brooklyn Daily Eagle,* 9 October 1847.

E 976
"Late Publications [*The Arabian Nights*]," *Brooklyn Daily Eagle,* 11 October 1847.

Reprinted in *GF,* II, 306–307; partially reprinted in *UPP,* I, 126–127.

E 977
[Review of Jedediah Morse, *School Geography and Atlas*], *Brooklyn Daily Eagle,* 11 October 1847.

Reprinted in *Schools,* p. 206.

E 978
"The Same Subject [Fog] Continued," *Brooklyn Daily Eagle*, 15 October 1847.

Reprinted in *GF*, II, 225.

E 979
"Some Thoughts About This Matter of the Washington Monument," *Brooklyn Daily Eagle*, 17 October 1847.

Reprinted in *GF*, II, 102–105.

E 980
[Review of Samuel Breese, *Harper's Cerographic Map of the United States and Canada*], *Brooklyn Daily Eagle*, 20 October 1847.

Reprinted in *Schools*, pp. 206–207.

E 981
" 'The Parent Who Would . . . ,' " *Brooklyn Daily Eagle*, 20 October 1847.

E 982
"Idle Daughters," *Brooklyn Daily Eagle*, 25 October 1847.

E 983
[The Weather], *Brooklyn Daily Eagle*, 25 October 1847.

Reprinted in *GF*, II, 225.

E 984
"Real Question at Issue!", *Brooklyn Daily Eagle*, 28 October 1847.

Reprinted in *GF*, I, 214–217.

E 985
"The Circus," *Brooklyn Daily Eagle*, 30 October 1847.

E 986
"Some Reflections on the Past, and for the Future," *Brooklyn Daily Eagle*, 3 November 1847.

Reprinted in *GF*, I, 217–221.

E 987
[At the Park Theatre], *Brooklyn Daily Eagle*, 3 November 1847.

E 988
"Verdict of the Undaunted Democracy of the Empire State in Behalf of the Jeffersonian Ordinance," *Brooklyn Daily Eagle*, 4 November 1847.

Reprinted in *GF*, I, 221–225.

E 989
[A Defense of Whitman's Grammar], *Brooklyn Daily Eagle*, 5 November 1847.

Reprinted in *GF*, II, 7–12.

E 990
[Wit in the *Brooklyn Advertiser*], *Brooklyn Daily Eagle*, 5 November 1847.

Reprinted in *GF*, II, 22.

E 991
"Weather—Serenade—Mosquitos," *Brooklyn Daily Eagle*, 5 November 1847.

E 992
[*Coe's New Drawing Cards*], *Brooklyn Daily Eagle*, 8 November 1847.

Reprinted in *Schools*, p. 207.

E 993
" 'Even Yet One Must Laugh . . . ,' " *Brooklyn Daily Eagle*, 8 November 1847.

E 994
"A Question [on Politics] Answered," *Brooklyn Daily Eagle*, 8 November 1847.

Reprinted in *GF*, I, 225–226.

E 995
[Review of Theodore Sedgwick, *The American Citizen*], *Brooklyn Daily Eagle*, 8 November 1847.

Partially reprinted in *UPP*, I, 136. Not in White, *Journalism*.

E 996
"Oratorio of 'Elijah,' " *Brooklyn Daily Eagle*, 9 November 1847.

Partially reprinted in *GF*, II, 353–354.

E 997
"A Woman Hung," *Brooklyn Daily Eagle*, 10 November 1847.

Reprinted in *GF*, I, 116–117.

E 998
"Works of Dr. Chalmers," *Brooklyn Daily Eagle*, 11 November 1847.

E 999
"Reform in the Mode of Municipal Assessments," *Brooklyn Daily Eagle*, 12 November 1847.

E 1000
[Willow Branch], *Brooklyn Daily Eagle*, 12 November 1847.

Reprinted in *Schools*, p. 207.

E 1001
"Slavery in Delaware," *Brooklyn Daily Eagle*, 17 November 1847.

Reprinted in *GF*, I, 226.

E 1002
"Rally Round the Government!", *Brooklyn Daily Eagle*, 20 November 1847.

E 1003
"Another Son of Brooklyn! Death, in Mexico, of Francis Van Dyke, Jr.," *Brooklyn Daily Eagle*, 20 November 1847.

E 1004
[Review of George Smith, *Consular Cities of China*, and Henry Wadsworth Longfellow, *Poems*], *Brooklyn Daily Eagle*, 20 November 1847.

Partially reprinted in *UPP*, I, 133–134 (Longfellow).

E 1005
" 'Annexation of Mexico,' " *Brooklyn Daily Eagle*, 22 November 1847.

E 1006
[Review of (Daniel Pierce Thompson), *Locke Amsden, or the Schoolmaster*], *Brooklyn Daily Eagle*, 22 November 1847.

Reprinted in *Schools*, p. 208.

E 1007
"Schoolmasters and Printers," *Brooklyn Daily Eagle*, 24 November 1847.

Reprinted in *Schools*, p. 208.

E 1008
"To-morrow Is Set Apart," *Brooklyn Daily Eagle*, 24 November 1847.

Reprinted in *GF*, II, 173–175.

E 1009
"Thomson's 'Seasons,' " *Brooklyn Daily Eagle,* 24 November 1847.

Reprinted in *UPP,* I, 136.

E 1010
"Troubles in the Whig Camp," *Brooklyn Daily Eagle,* 26 November 1847.

E 1011
"The Broadway Theatre, New York," *Brooklyn Daily Eagle,* 26 November 1847.

E 1012
"Brooklyn No-Lights," *Brooklyn Daily Eagle,* 26 November 1847.

E 1013
"Bother Without Improvement," *Brooklyn Daily Eagle,* 26 November 1847.

Reprinted in *GF,* II, 53–54.

E 1014
"The World of Books," *Brooklyn Daily Eagle,* 26 November 1847.

E 1015
"A Place for the Musical Folk of Brooklyn," *Brooklyn Daily Eagle,* 30 November 1847.

E 1016
[Literary Notices], *Brooklyn Daily Eagle,* 1 December 1847.

E 1017
"Proper Lesson for the Sundays, Etc.," *Brooklyn Daily Eagle,* 1 December 1847.

E 1018
[Licking School Children], *Brooklyn Daily Eagle,* 2 December 1847.

Reprinted in *Schools,* pp. 208–209.

E 1019
"Mr. Gallatin's Plan of Settling Our Dispute With Mexico," *Brooklyn Daily Eagle,* 2 December 1847.

Partially reprinted in *GF,* I, 264–266.

E 1020
"Shall We Have That Monument!", *Brooklyn Daily Eagle,* 3 December 1847.

Partially reprinted in *GF,* II, 50–52.

E 1021
" 'Biographia Literaria'; Biographical Sketches of My Literary Life and Opinions. By Samuel Taylor Coleridge," *Brooklyn Daily Eagle,* 4 December 1847.

Reprinted in *GF,* II, 298–299; *UPP,* I, 131.

E 1022
"Shutting of Stores at 8 O'Clock p.m.—Junior Clerks," *Brooklyn Daily Eagle,* 4 December 1847.

Reprinted in *GF,* I, 152–154.

E 1023
"Little Loafers," *Brooklyn Daily Eagle,* 4 December 1847.

E 1024
" 'The Poetical Works of Oliver Goldsmith,' " *Brooklyn Daily Eagle,* 4 December 1847.

E 1025
"New Music—Jenny Lind's Songs," *Brooklyn Daily Eagle,* 6 December 1847.

E 1026
"Late Publications [review of Frederick von Schlegel, *The Philosophy of Life and Philosophy of Language*]," *Brooklyn Daily Eagle,* 7 December 1847.

Partially reprinted in *UPP,* I, 135.

E 1027
"A Foot and Boot Article," *Brooklyn Daily Eagle,* 8 December 1847.

Reprinted in *GF,* II, 155–159.

E 1028
[Review of Richard Green Parker, *Outlines of General History*], *Brooklyn Daily Eagle,* 8 December 1847.

Reprinted in *Schools,* p. 209.

E 1029
"Vocal Music in the Brooklyn Schools," *Brooklyn Daily Eagle*, 8 December 1847.

Reprinted in *Schools*, p. 209.

E 1030
"Cannot Brooklyn Too Say Something for Italy?", *Brooklyn Daily Eagle*, 9 December 1847.

Reprinted in *GF*, I, 175.

E 1031
"Free Evening Schools, in Brooklyn," *Brooklyn Daily Eagle*, 9 December 1847.

Reprinted in *Schools*, pp. 209–210.

E 1032
"Late Music from Atwill's," *Brooklyn Daily Eagle*, 9 December 1847.

E 1033
"What the Free-Traders Want," *Brooklyn Daily Eagle*, 10 December 1847.

Reprinted in *GF*, II, 61–65.

E 1034
"English Meanness," *Brooklyn Daily Eagle*, 13 December 1847.

Reprinted in *GF*, I, 46–47.

E 1035
"Condition of Our Brooklyn Streets," *Brooklyn Daily Eagle*, 14 December 1847.

E 1036
[Ralph Waldo Emerson], *Brooklyn Daily Eagle*, 15 December 1847.

Reprinted in *GF*, II, 270–271; partially reprinted in *UPP*, I, 132.

E 1037
"Broad Farce in Literature—'The *John-Donkey*,'" *Brooklyn Daily Eagle*, 17 December 1847.

Reprinted in *GF*, II, 272–273.

E 1038
"Rainbows for Children," *Brooklyn Daily Eagle*, 18 December 1847.

E 1039
"Simms' 'Views and Reviews, Etc.,' " *Brooklyn Daily Eagle,* 18 December 1847.

E 1040
"Prolific Legislation," *Brooklyn Daily Eagle,* 18 December 1847.

E 1041
"Late Publications," *Brooklyn Daily Eagle,* 18 December 1847.

E 1042
"Holiday Publications," *Brooklyn Daily Eagle,* 20 December 1847.

E 1043
"Theatricals in New York," *Brooklyn Daily Eagle,* 22 December 1847.

E 1044
[Young Men of Brooklyn, Look at This!], *Brooklyn Daily Eagle,* 22 December 1847.

Reprinted in *Schools,* pp. 210–211.

E 1045
"New and Beautiful Music," *Brooklyn Daily Eagle,* 23 December 1847.

E 1046
"Death in the School-Room (A Fact)," *Brooklyn Daily Eagle,* 24 December 1847.

Revised from *United States Magazine, and Democratic Review,* August 1841 (E 29).

E 1047
"Most Painful Accident in New York," *Brooklyn Daily Eagle,* 27 December 1847.

E 1048
"More and Worse Suffering in Ireland.—What Shall Be the Remedy?", *Brooklyn Daily Eagle,* 27 December 1847.

Reprinted in *GF,* I, 167–169.

E 1049
"A Vagrom Woman," *Brooklyn Daily Eagle,* 27 December 1847.

Reprinted in *GF,* I, 120.

E 1050
"Did O'Connell Do Evil or Good?", *Brooklyn Daily Eagle*, 29 December 1847.

E 1051
"Washington Park," *Brooklyn Daily Eagle*, 30 December 1847.

E 1052
"New Music," *Brooklyn Daily Eagle*, 31 December 1847.

E 1053
"New Year's Day," *Brooklyn Daily Eagle*, 31 December 1847.

Reprinted in *GF*, II, 211–213.

E 1054
"The Late Letter of Senator Cass," *Brooklyn Daily Eagle*, 3 January 1848.

Reprinted in *GF*, I, 227–228.

E 1055
"Ladies' Calls," *Brooklyn Daily Eagle*, 4 January 1848.

Reprinted in *GF*, II, 226.

E 1056
"About Newspapers," *Brooklyn Daily Eagle*, 6 January 1848.

E 1057
"A Word for the Theatre," *Brooklyn Daily Eagle*, 6 January 1848.

E 1058
[A Wife], *Brooklyn Daily Eagle*, 6 January 1848.

E 1059
"Disagreement Among Legislative Doctors," *Brooklyn Daily Eagle*, 7 January 1848.

E 1060
"Andrew Jackson [A Man of the People]," *Brooklyn Daily Eagle*, 8 January 1848.

Reprinted in *GF*, II, 180–181.

E 1061
[A Schoolmaster's Last Words], *Brooklyn Daily Eagle*, 8 January 1848.

Reprinted in *Schools*, p. 211.

E 1062
"Milton," *Brooklyn Daily Eagle*, 10 January 1848.

Reprinted in *GF*, II, 287–290; *UPP*, I, 134.

E 1063
"Ten Minutes in the Engine Room of a Brooklyn Ferry Boat," *Brooklyn Daily Eagle*, 10 January 1848.

Reprinted in *GF*, II, 210–211.

E 1064
"Children," *Brooklyn Daily Eagle*, 12 January 1848.

Reprinted in *Schools*, pp. 211–212.

E 1065
"School Superintendent for Brooklyn," *Brooklyn Daily Eagle*, 13 January 1848.

Reprinted in *Schools*, p. 212.

E 1066
[Brooklyn City Lamps], *Brooklyn Daily Eagle*, 14 January 1848.

Reprinted in *GF*, II, 54.

E 1067
"Excerpts from a Traveller's Note Book [1]: Crossing the Alleghanies," *New Orleans Daily Crescent*, 5 March 1848.

Reprinted in Emory Holloway, "Walt Whitman in New Orleans," *Yale Review*, 5 (October 1915), 168–171; *UPP*, I, 181–186.

E 1068
"Excerpts from a Traveller's Note Book [2]: Cincinnati and Louisville," *New Orleans Daily Crescent*, 6 March 1848.

Reprinted in *UPP*, I, 189–190.

E 1069
"Age Cannot Wither Her," *New Orleans Daily Crescent*, 6 March 1848.

E 1070
"Model Artists," *New Orleans Daily Crescent*, 6 March 1848.

Reprinted in *UPP*, I, 191.

E 1071
"Nothing," *New Orleans Daily Crescent,* 6 March 1848.

E 1072
"The Mississippi at Midnight," *New Orleans Daily Crescent,* 6 March 1848.

Poem. Reprinted in *Notes and Fragments* (A 17), pp. 41–42; Emory Holloway, "Walt Whitman in New Orleans," *Yale Review,* 5 (October 1915), 166–183; revised as "Sailing the Mississippi at Midnight" in *Specimen Days* (A 11), p. 374; reprinted (both versions) in *Early Poems and Fiction,* pp. 42–43.

E 1073
"Excerpts from a Traveller's Note Book [3]: Western Steamboats—The Ohio," *New Orleans Daily Crescent,* 10 March 1848.

Reprinted in *UPP,* I, 186–189.

E 1074
"The Habitants of Hotels," *New Orleans Daily Crescent,* 10 March 1848.

Reprinted in *UPP,* I, 193–195.

E 1075
"Hero Presidents," *New Orleans Daily Crescent,* 11 March 1848.

Reprinted in *UPP,* I, 195–198.

E 1076
"Mrs. Hunt," *New Orleans Daily Crescent,* 11 March 1848.

E 1077
"The Trist Treaty," *New Orleans Daily Crescent,* 11 March 1848.

E 1078
"Novelties in New Orleans," *New Orleans Daily Crescent,* 13 March 1848.

Reprinted in Emory Holloway, *Whitman* (D 65), pp. 50–52.

E 1079
"Sketches of the Sidewalks and Levees; With Glimpses into the New Orleans Bar (Rooms): Peter Funk, Esq.," *New Orleans Daily Crescent,* 13 March 1848.

Reprinted in *UPP,* I, 199–202.

E 1080
"A Question of Propriety," *New Orleans Daily Crescent,* 14 March 1848.

Reprinted in *UPP,* I, 191–193.

E 1081
" 'Old Fort Greene,'—Brooklyn, N.Y.," *New Orleans Daily Crescent,* 16 March 1848.

E 1082
"Sketches of the Sidewalks and Levees; With Glimpses into the New Orleans Bar (Rooms): Miss Dusky Grisette," *New Orleans Daily Crescent,* 16 March 1848.

Reprinted in Emory Holloway, "Walt Whitman in New Orleans," *Yale Review,* 5 (October 1915), 177–179; *UPP,* I, 202–205.

E 1083
"Mr. Edwin Forrest," *New Orleans Daily Crescent,* 17 March 1848.

E 1084
"Mr. Gliddon's Lectures," *New Orleans Daily Crescent,* 17 March 1848.

E 1085
"Orleans Theatre [on *Othello*]," *New Orleans Daily Crescent,* 18 March 1848.

E 1086
[On Works of Art], *New Orleans Daily Crescent,* 18 March 1848.

E 1087
"The Model Artistes," *New Orleans Daily Crescent,* 20 March 1848.

E 1088
"St. Charles Theatre—The Model Artists," *New Orleans Daily Crescent,* 22 March 1848.

E 1089
"St. Charles Theatre," *New Orleans Daily Crescent,* 23 March 1848.

E 1090
"Sketches of the Sidewalks and Levees; With Glimpses into the New Orleans Bar (Rooms): Daggerdraw Bowieknife, Esq.," *New Orleans Daily Crescent,* 23 March 1848.

Reprinted in *UPP,* I, 205–208.

E 1091
"Virtue *vs.* Vice," *New Orleans Daily Crescent,* 23 March 1848.

Reprinted in Emory Holloway, *Whitman* (D 65), p. 64.

E 1092
"Why Don't They Get Excited?" *New Orleans Daily Crescent,* 23 March 1848.

E 1093
"Make the Distinction," *New Orleans Daily Crescent,* 24 March 1848.

E 1094
"Lecture on Egypt—By Mr. Gliddon," *New Orleans Daily Crescent,* 24 March 1848.

E 1095
"Dr. Collyer's Model Artists," *New Orleans Daily Crescent,* 25 March 1848.

E 1096
"Mr. Edwin Forrest," *New Orleans Daily Crescent,* 25 March 1848.

E 1097
"Mr. Gliddon's Lectures," *New Orleans Daily Crescent,* 28 March 1848.

E 1098
"Important Questions," *New Orleans Daily Crescent,* 28 March 1848.

E 1099
"Sketches of the Sidewalks and Levees; With Glimpses into the New Orleans Bar (Rooms): John J. Jinglebrain," *New Orleans Daily Crescent,* 28 March 1848.

Reprinted in *UPP,* I, 208–210.

E 1100
"Vagrants! Vagrants! Vagrants!", *New Orleans Daily Crescent,* 28 March 1848.

E 1101
"Nauseating," *New Orleans Daily Crescent,* 29 March 1848.

E 1102
"Death of a Juvenile Model Artist," *New Orleans Daily Crescent,* 1 April 1848.

E 1103
"Mr. Gliddon's Lectures on Mummification," *New Orleans Daily Crescent,* 1 April 1848.

E 1104
"Who Shall Wear Motley?", *New Orleans Daily Crescent,* 3 April 1848.

E 1105
"Police News," *New Orleans Daily Crescent,* 3 April 1848.

E 1106
"Result of Prudishness," *New Orleans Daily Crescent,* 3 April 1848.

E 1107
"Sketches of the Sidewalks and Levees; With Glimpses into the New Orleans Bar (Rooms): Timothy Goujon, V. O. N. O. (Vendor of Oysters in New Orleans)," *New Orleans Daily Crescent,* 4 April 1848.

Reprinted in *UPP,* I, 211–213.

E 1108
"Death of Mr. Astor of New York," *New Orleans Daily Crescent,* 7 April 1848.

Reprinted in William Kernan Dart, "Walt Whitman in New Orleans," *Publications of the Louisiana Historical Society,* 7 (1915), 107–108 (dated '17 April'); *UPP,* I, 218–219.

E 1109
"University Studies," *New Orleans Daily Crescent,* 11 April 1848.

Reprinted in *UPP,* I, 220–221.

E 1110
"Sketches of the Sidewalks and Levees; With Glimpses into the New Orleans Bar (Rooms): Mrs. Giddy Gay Butterfly," *New Orleans Daily Crescent,* 12 April 1848.

Reprinted in William White, " 'Sketches of the Sidewalks and Levees; With Glimpses into the New Orleans Bar (Rooms): Mrs. Giddy Gay Butterfly,' " *Walt Whitman Newsletter,* 4 (September 1958), 87–90.

E 1111
"Sketches of the Sidewalks and Levees; With Glimpses into the New Orleans Bar (Rooms): Patrick McDray," *New Orleans Daily Crescent,* 18 April 1848.

Reprinted in *UPP,* I, 213–216.

E 1112
"A Deserving Actor," *New Orleans Daily Crescent*, 19 April 1848.

E 1113
"Vagrants," *New Orleans Daily Crescent*, 21 April 1848.

Reprinted in Emory Holloway, *Whitman* (D 65), p. 64.

E 1114
"The Old Cathedral," *New Orleans Daily Crescent*, 22 April 1848.

Reprinted in *UPP*, I, 221–222.

E 1115
"Return of a Slave," *New Orleans Daily Crescent*, 22 April 1848.

E 1116
"A Walk About Town," *New Orleans Daily Crescent*, 26 April 1848.

Signed "A Pedestrian." Reprinted in William Kernan Dart, "Walt Whitman in New Orleans," *Publications of the Louisiana Historical Society*, 7 (1915), 109–111; *UPP*, I, 223–224.

E 1117
"A Noble-Hearted Laborer!", *New Orleans Daily Crescent*, 1 May 1848.

E 1118
"Beautiful," *New Orleans Daily Crescent*, 2 May 1848.

E 1119
"Sketches of the Sidewalks and Levees; With Glimpses into the New Orleans Bar (Rooms): Samuel Sensitive," *New Orleans Daily Crescent*, 2 May 1848.

Reprinted in *UPP*, I, 216–218.

E 1120
"Dombey and Son Wound Up," *New Orleans Daily Crescent*, 6 May 1848.

E 1121
"General Taylor at the Theatre," *New Orleans Daily Crescent*, 9 May 1848.

Reprinted in William Kernan Dart, "Walt Whitman in New Orleans," *Publications of the Louisiana Historical Society*, 7 (1915), 106–107; *UPP*, I, 225.

E 1122
"Elizabeth," *New Orleans Daily Crescent*, 11 May 1848.

E 1123
"Isle of Cyprus," *New Orleans Daily Crescent*, 12 May 1848.

Reprinted in Emory Holloway, *Whitman* (D 65), pp. 62–64.

E 1124
"[Dombey and Son]," *New Orleans Daily Crescent*, 13 May 1848.

E 1125
"A Night at the Terpsichore Ball," *New Orleans Daily Crescent*, 18 May 1848.

Signed "You Know Who." Reprinted in Emory Holloway, "Walt Whitman in New Orleans," *Yale Review*, 5 (October 1915), 180–182; in *UPP*, I, 225–228.

E 1126
"Fourierism," *New Orleans Daily Crescent*, 20 May 1848.

Reprinted in *UPP*, I, 229.

E 1127
"The Shadow and the Light of a Young Man's Soul," *Union Magazine of Literature and Art*, 2 (June 1848), 280–281.

Fiction. Reprinted in *UPP*, I, 229–234; *Early Poems and Fiction*, pp. 327–330.

E 1128
" 'The Brooklyn Freeman,' 'The Daily Freeman,' " *Brooklyn Freeman*, 9 September 1848.

Note: The 9 September 1848 issue is the only one known to be extant.

E 1129
"Jefferson on the Non-Extension and Abolition of Slavery," *Brooklyn Freeman*, 9 September 1848.

E 1130
"How Things Have Been Managed in Kings County," *Brooklyn Freeman*, 9 September 1848.

E 1131
"Our Enmity to the South," *Brooklyn Freeman*, 9 September 1848.

E 1132
"[Martin] Van Buren's Last Best Letter," *Brooklyn Freeman*, 9 September 1848.

E 1133
"Vermont Election," *Brooklyn Freeman,* 9 September 1848.

E 1134
"Permanent Establishment of the Brooklyn Freeman," *Brooklyn Freeman,* 9 September 1848.

E 1135
"Read It [Van Buren's Letter] With Care," *Brooklyn Freeman,* 9 September 1848.

E 1136
"Separate Organization of the Free Soil Party in Brooklyn," *Brooklyn Freeman,* 9 September 1848.

E 1137
"Mass Meeting of the Brooklyn Free Soilers," *Brooklyn Freeman,* 9 September 1848.

E 1138
"General Taylor's Principles—A Clincher," *Brooklyn Freeman,* 9 September 1848.

E 1139
"A. C. Flagg," *Brooklyn Freeman,* 9 September 1848.

E 1140
"What Sort of a Man Has New-York Made President," *Brooklyn Freeman,* 9 September 1848.

E 1141
" 'Hunkerism,' " *Brooklyn Freeman,* 9 September 1848.

E 1142
"That Falsehood About Van Buren's Vote for Searching the Mails," *Brooklyn Freeman,* 9 September 1848.

E 1143
"Gen. Cass's Idea of 'Diffusing' Slavery," *Brooklyn Freeman,* 9 September 1848.

E 1144
"Arrival of the Hibernia," *Brooklyn Freeman,* 9 September 1848.

E 1145
"Liberty and Free Soil in Massachusetts," *Brooklyn Freeman,* 9 September 1848.

E 1146
[Twenty fillers and short paragraphs], *Brooklyn Freeman,* 9 September 1848.

E 1147
"Letters from a Travelling Bachelor. Number I," *New York Sunday Dispatch,* 14 October 1849.

Signed "Paumanok." Reprinted in Joseph Jay Rubin, *The Historic Whitman* (D 105), pp. 311–315.

E 1148
"Letters from a Travelling Bachelor. Number II," *New York Sunday Dispatch,* 21 October 1849.

Signed "Paumanok." Reprinted in Joseph Jay Rubin, *The Historic Whitman* (D 105), pp. 315–318.

E 1149
"Letters from a Travelling Bachelor. Number III," *New York Sunday Dispatch,* 28 October 1849.

Signed "Paumanok." Reprinted in Joseph Jay Rubin, *The Historic Whitman* (D 105), pp. 318–323.

E 1150
"Letters from a Travelling Bachelor. Number IV," *New York Sunday Dispatch,* 4 November 1849.

Signed "Paumanok." Reprinted in Joseph Jay Rubin, *The Historic Whitman* (D 105), pp. 324–329.

E 1151
"Letters from a Travelling Bachelor. Number V," *New York Sunday Dispatch,* 11 November 1849.

Signed "Paumanok." Reprinted in Joseph Jay Rubin, *The Historic Whitman* (D 105), pp. 329–334.

E 1152
"Letters from a Travelling Bachelor. Number VI," *New York Sunday Dispatch,* 18 November 1849.

Signed "Paumanok." Reprinted in Joseph Jay Rubin, *The Historic Whitman* (D 105), pp. 334–336.

E 1153
"Letters from a Travelling Bachelor. Number VII," *New York Sunday Dispatch,* 25 November 1849.

Signed "Paumanok." Reprinted in Joseph Jay Rubin, *The Historic Whitman* (D 105), pp. 336–341.

E 1154
"Letters from a Travelling Bachelor. Number IX," *New York Sunday Dispatch,* 16 December 1849.

Signed "Paumanok." Reprinted in Joseph Jay Rubin, *The Historic Whitman* (D 105), pp. 341–347.

Note: Letter Number VIII has not been located.

E 1155
"Letters from a Travelling Bachelor. Number X," *New York Sunday Dispatch,* 23 December 1849.

Signed "Paumanok." Reprinted in Joseph Jay Rubin, *The Historic Whitman* (D 105), pp. 347–352.

E 1156
"Letters from a Travelling Bachelor. Number XI," *New York Sunday Dispatch,* 6 January 1850.

Signed "Paumanok." Reprinted in Joseph Jay Rubin, *The Historic Whitman* (D 105), pp. 352–354.

E 1157
"Song for Certain Congressmen," *New York Evening Post,* 2 March 1850.

Signed "Paumanok." Poem. Revised as "Dough-Face Song" in *Specimen Days* (A 11), pp. 339–340; reprinted in *Early Poems and Fiction,* pp. 44–45.

E 1158
"Blood–Money," *New York Daily Tribune, Supplement,* 9 (22 March 1850), 1.

Signed "Paumanok." Poem. Reprinted in *New York Evening Post,* 30 April 1850; *Specimen Days* (A 11), pp. 372–373; revised in *Conservator,* 16 (October 1905), 122; *Early Poems and Fiction,* pp. 47–48.

E 1159
"Paragraph Sketches of Brooklynites: Rev. Henry Ward Beecher," *Brooklyn Daily Advertiser*, 25 May 1850.

Reprinted in *UPP*, I, 234–235.

E 1160
"Paragraph Sketches of Brooklynites [total of sixteen]," *Brooklyn Daily Advertiser*, 18 May–6 June 1850.

E 1161
"Church Sketches," *Brooklyn Daily Advertiser*, ca. 18 May–ca. 6 June 1850.

E 1162
"The House of Friends," *New York Daily Tribune*, 14 June 1850.

Poem. Reprinted in *UPP*, I, 25–27; *Early Poems and Fiction*, pp. 36–37. Revised as "Wounded in the House of Friends," *Specimen Days* (A 11), pp. 373–374.

E 1163
"Excursion to Greenport [1]," *Brooklyn Daily Advertiser*, 20 June 1850.

E 1164
"Excursion to Greenport [2]," *Brooklyn Daily Advertiser*, 21 June 1850.

E 1165
"Resurgemus," *New York Daily Tribune*, 21 June 1850.

Poem. Reprinted in *UPP*, I, 27–30; *Early Poems and Fiction*, pp. 38–40. Partially reprinted in "Art and Artists" in *Brooklyn Daily Advertiser*, 3 April 1851 (E 1171); *Brooklyn Daily Eagle*, 14 July 1900; *UPP*, I, 241–247. Revised as ["Suddenly out of its stale and drowsy lair"] in *Leaves of Grass* (1855), pp. 57–58; reprinted as "Poem of the Dead Young Men of Europe, the 72nd and 73rd Years of These States" in *Leaves of Grass* (1856), pp. 252–254; as "Europe, The 72nd and 73rd Years of These States" in *Leaves of Grass* (1860), pp. 283–285; *Early Poems and Fiction*, pp. 40–41.

E 1166
"Letter from New York," *National Era* (Washington), 4 (31 October 1850), 175.

Reprinted in Rollo G. Silver, "Whitman in 1850: Three Uncollected Articles," *American Literature*, 19 (January 1948), 302–317.

E 1167
"Letter from New York," *National Era* (Washington), 4 (14 November 1850), 181.

Reprinted in Rollo G. Silver, "Whitman in 1850: Three Uncollected Articles," *American Literature,* 19 (January 1948), 302–317.

E 1168
"Letter from New York," *National Era* (Washington), 4 (21 November 1850), 187.

Reprinted in Rollo G. Silver, "Whitman in 1850: Three Uncollected Articles," *American Literature,* 19 (January 1948), 302–317.

E 1169
"Something About Art and Brooklyn Artists," *New York Evening Post,* 1 February 1851.

Partially reprinted in *New York Evening Post Book Review,* 26 June 1920; *UPP,* I, 236–238.

E 1170
"A Letter from Brooklyn," *New York Evening Post,* 21 March 1851.

Reprinted in *UPP,* I, 239–241.

E 1171
"Art and Artists: Remarks of Walter Whitman, Before the Brooklyn Art Union, on the Evening of March 31, 1851," *Brooklyn Daily Advertiser,* 3 April 1851, p. 1.

Partially reprinted as "Talk to an Art-Union" in *Complete Prose Works* (C 6), p. 371; reprinted in full in *Brooklyn Daily Eagle,* 14 July 1900; *UPP,* I, 241–247. Includes "Resurgemus" from *New York Daily Tribune,* 21 June 1850 (E 1165).

E 1172
"Letters from Paumanok [No. 1]," *New York Evening Post,* 27 June 1851.

Signed "Paumanok." Reprinted in *UPP,* I, 247–249.

E 1173
"A Plea for Water," *Brooklyn Daily Advertiser,* 28 June 1851.

Reprinted in *UPP,* I, 254–255.

E 1174
"Letters from Paumanok [No. 2]," *New York Evening Post*, 28 June 1851.

Signed "Paumanok." Reprinted in *UPP*, I, 250–254.

E 1175
"Visit to the People's Bath and Wash House—A New Era," *Williamsburg Times*, 4 May 1852.

Listed in Joseph Jay Rubin, *The Historic Whitman* (D 105), p. 381.

E 1176
"Letters from Paumanok [No. 3]," *New York Evening Post*, 14 August 1851.

Signed "Paumanok." Reprinted in *UPP*, I, 255–259.

E 1177
"Sunday Restrictions," *Brooklyn Evening Star*, 20 October 1854.

Reprinted in *Conservator*, 14 (November 1903), 135; *UPP*, I, 259–264.

E 1178
"Walt Whitman and His Poems," *United States Review*, 5 (September 1855), 205–212.

Reprinted in *New York Evening Post*, 24 August 1855, p. 1; *Leaves of Grass Imprints* (D 4), pp. 7–13.

E 1179
"Walt Whitman a Brooklyn Boy. Leaves of Grass (A Volume of Poems Just Published)," *Brooklyn Daily Times*, 29 September 1855.

Reprinted in *Leaves of Grass* (1856), pp. 360–363; *Leaves of Grass Imprints* (D 4), pp. 30–32.

E 1180
"An English and an American Poet" [review of *Leaves of Grass* and Alfred, Lord Tennyson, *Maud*], *American Phrenological Journal*, 12 (October 1855), 90–91.

Reprinted in *Leaves of Grass* (1856), pp. 369–373; *Leaves of Grass Imprints* (D 4), pp. 38–45.

E 1181
"The Opera," *Life Illustrated*, 10 November 1855.

Signed "Mose Velsor, of Brooklyn." Reprinted in *NYD*, pp. 18–23.

E 1182
"One of the Lessons Boardering Broadway: The Egyptian Museum," *Life Illustrated*, 8 December 1855.

Reprinted in *NYD*, pp. 30–40.

E 1183
"Christmas at 'Grace,'" *Life Illustrated*, 26 January 1856.

Reprinted in *NYD*, pp. 46–48.

E 1184
"America's Mightiest Inheritance [The English Language]," *Life Illustrated*, 12 April 1856.

Signed. Reprinted in *NYD*, pp. 55–65.

E 1185
"Decent Homes for Working-Men," *Life Illustrated*, 12 April 1856.

Reprinted in *NYD*, pp. 98–102.

E 1186
"Voltaire," *Life Illustrated*, 10 May 1856.

Signed. Reprinted in *NYD*, pp. 7–73.

E 1187
"New York Dissected. [I.] New York Amuses Itself—The Fourth of July," *Life Illustrated*, 12 July 1856.

Reprinted in *NYD*, pp. 80–84.

E 1188
"New York Dissected. II. Wicked Architecture," *Life Illustrated*, 19 July 1856.

Reprinted in *NYD*, pp. 92–98.

E 1189
"New York Dissected. III. The Slave Trade," *Life Illustrated*, 2 August 1856.

Reprinted in *NYD*, pp. 108–114.

E 1190
"New York Dissected. IV. Broadway," *Life Illustrated*, 9 August 1856.

Reprinted in *NYD*, pp. 119–124.

E 1191
"New York Dissected. V. Street Yarn," *Life Illustrated,* 16 August 1856.

Reprinted in *NYD,* pp. 128–132.

E 1192
"New York Dissected. VI. Advice to Strangers," *Life Illustrated,* 23 August 1856.

Reprinted in *NYD,* pp. 136–142.

E 1193
"The Circus," *Life Illustrated,* 30 August 1856.

Reprinted in *NYD,* pp. 193–196.

E 1194
"New Publications: Leaves of Grass,—Brooklyn, N.Y." *Brooklyn Daily Times,* 17 December 1856.

Reprinted in *Leaves of Grass Imprints* (D 4), pp. 49–50; *ISL,* pp. 186–187.

E 1195
"The Lecture Season," *Brooklyn Daily Times,* 30 January 1857.

Reprinted in *ISL,* pp. 179–181, as of "possible Whitman authorship."

E 1196
"A New License System," *Brooklyn Daily Times,* 14 March 1857.

E 1197
[For Sunday Cars], *Brooklyn Daily Times,* 14 March 1857.

Reprinted in *ISL,* pp. 181–184, as of "possible Whitman authorship."

E 1198
[On the New York City Aldermen], *Brooklyn Daily Times,* 1 May 1857.

E 1199
"The First of May," *Brooklyn Daily Times,* 1 May 1857.

Reprinted in *ISL,* pp. 123–125.

E 1200
"What Injunctions May Effect," *Brooklyn Daily Times,* 2 May 1857.

E 1201
"The New Police Bill," *Brooklyn Daily Times*, 4 May 1857.

E 1202
"The Gas Question," *Brooklyn Daily Times*, 5 May 1857.

Reprinted in *ISL*, pp. 126–127.

E 1203
"The Religions of the Nations," *Brooklyn Daily Times*, 6 May 1857.

Listed in *ISL*.

E 1204
[Charles Dickens], *Brooklyn Daily Times*, 6 May 1857.

Reprinted in *ISL*, p. 62.

E 1205
"Consumption Incurable," *Brooklyn Daily Times*, 7 May 1857.

E 1206
"The Slave Trade [Cuba a Black Republic]," *Brooklyn Daily Times*, 7 May 1857.

Reprinted in *ISL*, pp. 86–87.

E 1207
"Brooklyn Mechanics—Sunday Cars," *Brooklyn Daily Times*, 9 May 1857.

E 1208
"The Fire Commissioners," *Brooklyn Daily Times*, 11 May 1857.

E 1209
"[Integrity of] Judge Davies," *Brooklyn Daily Times*, 11 May 1857.

Listed in *ISL*.

E 1210
"Unsettled Long Island Lands," *Brooklyn Daily Times*, 11 May 1857.

E 1211
"Graveyards and Waterworks," *Brooklyn Daily Times*, 12 May 1857.

Listed in *ISL*.

E 1212
"The Theatre Question," *Brooklyn Daily Times,* 13 May 1857.

Listed in *ISL.*

E 1213
"Our Relations with England," *Brooklyn Daily Times,* 13 May 1857.

E 1214
"Abolition Convention This Morning," *Brooklyn Daily Times,* 14 May 1857.

Reprinted in *ISL,* pp. 87–88.

E 1215
"The Navy Yard," *Brooklyn Daily Times,* 14 May 1857.

E 1216
"Effects of Arsenic Eating," *Brooklyn Daily Times,* 15 May 1857.

E 1217
"Independent and Party Papers," *Brooklyn Daily Times,* 16 May 1857.

Listed in *ISL.*

E 1218
"About China," *Brooklyn Daily Times,* 16 May 1857.

E 1219
"The City Railroad Yesterday," *Brooklyn Daily Times,* 18 May 1857.

E 1220
"Van Anden and His Elephant," *Brooklyn Daily Times,* 20 May 1857.

E 1221
"Two Mayors in a Dilemma," *Brooklyn Daily Times,* 20 May 1857.

E 1222
"California Wagon-Road," *Brooklyn Daily Times,* 21 May 1857.

E 1223
"Immigrant Changes," *Brooklyn Daily Times,* 22 May 1857.

E 1224
"The Police Contest," *Brooklyn Daily Times,* 22 May 1857.

E 1225
"Kansas and the Political Future," *Brooklyn Daily Times*, 23 May 1857.

Reprinted in *ISL*, pp. 91–92.

E 1226
"White Labor, versus Black Labor," *Brooklyn Daily Times*, 25 May 1857.

Reprinted in *ISL*, p. 88.

E 1227
"The Liquor Dealers' Association," *Brooklyn Daily Times*, 25 May 1857.

E 1228
"Crooking a Crash," *Brooklyn Daily Times*, 26 May 1857.

E 1229
"Whence Is City Power," *Brooklyn Daily Times*, 26 May 1857.

E 1230
"Patch Work Legislation," *Brooklyn Daily Times*, 27 May 1857.

E 1231
"A Word to the Ladies [Fashion Makes Marriage Impossible]," *Brooklyn Daily Times*, 28 May 1857.

Reprinted in *ISL*, pp. 111–112.

E 1232
"Nicaragua," *Brooklyn Daily Times*, 29 May 1857.

E 1233
"The Police and Burglaries," *Brooklyn Daily Times*, 29 May 1857.

E 1234
"Jackson's Hollow," *Brooklyn Daily Times*, 30 May 1857.

E 1235
"The First of June," *Brooklyn Daily Times*, 30 May 1857.

E 1236
"More 'Agitation,' " *Brooklyn Daily Times*, 30 May 1857.

E 1237
"Something for Barnum—Our Own Proposition," *Brooklyn Daily Times*, 1 June 1857.

E 1238
"A Humbug [The Reverend J. L. Hatch]," *Brooklyn Daily Times*, 1 June 1857.

E 1239
"Hot Weather Philosophy," *Brooklyn Daily Times*, 2 June 1857.

Reprinted in *ISL*, pp. 100–101.

E 1240
"Henry C. Murphy." *Brooklyn Daily Times*, 3 June 1857.

Reprinted as "[Reminiscences of Brooklyn]" in *UPP*, II, 1–5.

E 1241
"The Brooklyn Public Schools," *Brooklyn Daily Times*, 4 June 1857.

Listed in *ISL*.

E 1242
"The Doctors Persist but the Patient Dies," *Brooklyn Daily Times*, 5 June 1857.

E 1243
"Grand Buildings in New York City," *Brooklyn Daily Times*, 5 June 1857.

Reprinted in *ISL*, pp. 127–130.

E 1244
"Good for Governor Walker!", *Brooklyn Daily Times*, 6 June 1857.

E 1245
" 'Dead Heads,' " *Brooklyn Daily Times*, 6 June 1857.

E 1246
"Juvenile Burglars," *Brooklyn Daily Times*, 8 June 1857.

E 1247
"Sunday Cars in Brooklyn," *Brooklyn Daily Times*, 8 June 1857.

E 1248
"Brooklynites in Kansas," *Brooklyn Daily Times*, 9 June 1857.

E 1249
[Advice to the Farmer], *Brooklyn Daily Times*, 10 June 1857.

Reprinted in *ISL*, pp. 164–165.

E 1250
"New Publications [Henry C. Murphy's translation of the Voyages of D. P. de Vries; *Emerson's United States Magazine* for January–June 1857]," *Brooklyn Daily Times,* 10 June 1857.

E 1251
"Steam on Atlantic Street," *Brooklyn Daily Times,* 11 June 1857.

E 1252
"Religion," *Brooklyn Daily Times,* 11 June 1857.

Listed in *ISL.*

E 1253
"The Comet," *Brooklyn Daily Times,* 13 June 1857.

E 1254
"The Board of Health," *Brooklyn Daily Times,* 15 June 1857.

E 1255
"Alarmists [in New York Papers]," *Brooklyn Daily Times,* 15 June 1857.

Listed in *ISL.*

E 1256
"The Civil War in New York," *Brooklyn Daily Times,* 17 June 1857.

Reprinted in *ISL,* pp. 130–131.

E 1257
"Mayor Wood and His Defenders," *Brooklyn Daily Times,* 18 June 1857.

E 1258
"Is Brooklyn to Take Part in the Fight?", *Brooklyn Daily Times,* 18 June 1857.

E 1259
"The New York Disturbances," *Brooklyn Daily Times,* 19 June 1857.

E 1260
"The Newspaper Attache Nuisance," *Brooklyn Daily Times,* 19 June 1857.

E 1261
"Sundays and Newspaper Advertisements," *Brooklyn Daily Times,* 20 June 1857.

E 1262
"A Bad Subject [Prostitution] for a Newspaper Article," *Brooklyn Daily Times*, 20 June 1857.

Reprinted as "[On Vice]" in *UPP*, II, 5–8.

E 1263
"The License Law," *Brooklyn Daily Times*, 22 June 1857.

E 1264
"A True American [Governor Walker of Kansas]," *Brooklyn Daily Times*, 22 June 1857.

E 1265
"Rascally Plagiarism," *Brooklyn Daily Times*, 22 June 1857.

Listed in *ISL*.

E 1266
"An Expose from a Brooklyn Fire," *Brooklyn Daily Times*, 24 June 1857.

E 1267
"The Public Lands," *Brooklyn Daily Times*, 25 June 1857.

Listed in *ISL*.

E 1268
"Fire Department Troubles," *Brooklyn Daily Times*, 25 June 1857.

E 1269
"Enforcement of the New License Law," *Brooklyn Daily Times*, 26 June 1857.

E 1270
"Bathing," *Brooklyn Daily Times*, 27 June 1857.

Reprinted in *ISL*, pp. 101–102.

E 1271
"Sunday in the Sixteenth Ward," *Brooklyn Daily Times*, 27 June 1857.

Reprinted in *ISL*, pp. 131–132. Not in White, *Journalism*.

E 1272
"Conventions," *Brooklyn Daily Times*, 27 June 1857.

E 1273
"Of the Weather," *Brooklyn Daily Times*, 27 June 1857.

E 1274
"The Alleged Corruption in the Board of Health," *Brooklyn Daily Times*, 29 June 1857.

E 1275
"Book Notices ["Currer Bell" (Charlotte Bronte), *Jane Eyre;* Harper's Classical Library *Demosthenes;* George Borrow, *The Romany Rye*]," *Brooklyn Daily Times*, 29 June 1857.

E 1276
"The Shakers," *Harper's Monthly Magazine*, 15 (July 1857), 164–176.

Unsigned (later indexed as by B. J. Lossing). Reprinted in Charles I. Glicksberg, "A Whitman Discovery," *Colophon*, n.s. 1, no. 2 (Autumn 1935), 227–233. Not in White, *Journalism*.

E 1277
"Whipping in the Schools of Iowa," *Brooklyn Daily Times*, 30 June 1857.

Listed in *ISL*.

E 1278
"The Board of Health Corruption Case," *Brooklyn Daily Times*, 1 July 1857.

E 1279
"Magazine Notices [*London Quarterly Review, Blackwood's Magazine, Knickerbocker Magazine*]," *Brooklyn Daily Times*, 1 July 1857.

E 1280
"American Money Gone a Wool Cultivating," *Brooklyn Daily Times*, 2 July 1857.

E 1281
"Dead Milk Served Out by the Common Council," *Brooklyn Daily Times*, 2 July 1857.

E 1282
"The Old Cry," *Brooklyn Daily Times*, 2 July 1857.

E 1283
"The First Independence Days," *Brooklyn Daily Times*, 3 July 1857.

Reprinted in *ISL*, pp. 57–59.

E 1284
"Book Notices [William C. Prime, *Boat Life in Egypt and Nubia* and *Tent Life in the Holy Land*]," *Brooklyn Daily Times*, 3 July 1857.

E 1285
"Lawlessness in New York," *Brooklyn Daily Times*, 6 July 1857.

E 1286
"State Power—What Is the People's Power If That Is Not?", *Brooklyn Daily Times*, 7 July 1857.

E 1287
"Metropolitan Police Commission," *Brooklyn Daily Times*, 7 July 1857.

E 1288
" 'The Dead Rabbit Democracy,' " *Brooklyn Daily Times*, 8 July 1857.

Reprinted in *ISL*, pp. 92–94.

E 1289
"The Corruption Case," *Brooklyn Daily Times*, 8 July 1857.

E 1290
"William L. Marcy," *Brooklyn Daily Times*, 8 July 1857.

E 1291
"Free Academies at Public Cost," *Brooklyn Daily Times*, 9 July 1857.

Reprinted in *ISL*, pp. 53–54.

E 1292
"The Territories—Polygamy—and 'Domestic Institutions,' " *Brooklyn Daily Times*, 9 July 1857.

E 1293
"The Corruption Case Last Evening," *Brooklyn Daily Times*, 10 July 1857.

E 1294
"The Teachers,—Shall Not They Too Be Taught?", *Brooklyn Daily Times*, 10 July 1857.

Reprinted in *ISL*, pp. 54–55.

E 1295
"The Board of Health," *Brooklyn Daily Times*, 11 July 1857.

E 1296
"Health-Hints," *Brooklyn Daily Times*, 11 July 1857.

E 1297
"Sunday Excursionists," *Brooklyn Daily Times*, 13 July 1857.

E 1298
"A Case for the Board of Health," *Brooklyn Daily Times,* 13 July 1857.

E 1299
"The Heat," *Brooklyn Daily Times*, 13 July 1857.

E 1300
"No Fusion," *Brooklyn Daily Times*, 14 July 1857.

E 1301
"The Police and the Germans," *Brooklyn Daily Times*, 14 July 1857.

E 1302
"An Excursion to Sands Point," *Brooklyn Daily Times*, 15 July 1857.

Listed in *ISL*.

E 1303
"The Expulsion of Alderman Preston," *Brooklyn Daily Times*, 16 July 1857.

E 1304
"On the Old Subject—The Origin of It All," *Brooklyn Daily Times*, 17 July 1857.

Reprinted as "[Slavery]" in *UPP*, II, 8–10.

E 1305
"Democratic Papers," *Brooklyn Daily Times*, 17 July 1857.

E 1306
"These Splendid Nights," *Brooklyn Daily Times*, 17 July 1857.

E 1307
"[Capital Punishment] A Thought from an Occurrence of Yesterday," *Brooklyn Daily Times*, 18 July 1857.

E 1308
"Washington Park," *Brooklyn Daily Times*, 18 July 1857.

Listed in *ISL*.

E 1309
"Officers Bribed, in Brooklyn and Elsewhere—Plenty of Others Beside Preston," *Brooklyn Daily Times*, 20 July 1857.

E 1310
"Major Wood's Plottings," *Brooklyn Daily Times*, 20 July 1857.

E 1311
"The Nonsensical Arrests for Bathing," *Brooklyn Daily Times*, 20 July 1857.

Reprinted in *ISL*, pp. 103–104.

E 1312
"Outrages in Emigrant Ships," *Brooklyn Daily Times*, 21 July 1857.

Reprinted in *ISL*, pp. 112–113.

E 1313
"Give the City Cars, Night and Day," *Brooklyn Daily Times*, 21 July 1857.

E 1314
"Market Extortions—Causes—The Speculators—Could Not the Western Fashion Be Introduced Here?—Free Trade—'Market Car Company,' " *Brooklyn Daily Times*, 22 July 1857.

E 1315
"Book Notices [the author of 'Hope Leslie' (Catharine Maria Sedgwick), *Married or Single;* Margaret Oliphant, *The Athelings; or The Three Gifts*]," *Brooklyn Daily Times*, 22 July 1857.

E 1316
"Capital Punishment," *Brooklyn Daily Times*, 22 July 1857.

Listed in *ISL*. Not in White, *Journalism*.

E 1317
"The Police Board," *Brooklyn Daily Times*, 23 July 1857.

E 1318
"The Banquet to Mr. [Henry C.] Murphy," *Brooklyn Daily Times*, 24 July 1857.

E 1319
"Gen. Jackson's Bequest," *Brooklyn Daily Times*, 24 July 1857.

E 1320
"Husted's Cow Stables," *Brooklyn Daily Times*, 25 July 1857.

E 1321
"The August Magazines [*Harper's Monthly Magazine, Godey's Lady's Book, Harper's Story Books*]," *Brooklyn Daily Times*, 25 July 1857.

E 1322
"Would South Brooklyn Gain Anything by Not Having the L. I. R. R. Locomotives?", *Brooklyn Daily Times*, 27 July 1857.

E 1323
"The Season of Accidents," *Brooklyn Daily Times*, 27 July 1857.

E 1324
"Supposed Case of Yellow Fever," *Brooklyn Daily Times*, 27 July 1857.

E 1325
"Public Baths," *Brooklyn Daily Times*, 27 July 1857.

Reprinted in *ISL*, pp. 102–103. Not in White, *Journalism*.

E 1326
"The Yellow Fever Case," *Brooklyn Daily Times*, 28 July 1857.

E 1327
"Free Bathing—Accidents," *Brooklyn Daily Times*, 28 July 1857.

Listed in *ISL*.

E 1328
"Are Workpeople Injured by Labor Saving Machines?", *Brooklyn Daily Times*, 28 July 1857.

E 1329
"Is There a Yellow Fever Case Among Us?", *Brooklyn Daily Times*, 28 July 1857.

E 1330
"Our 'Health Wardens,'" *Brooklyn Daily Times*, 28 July 1857.

E 1331
"Democratic Discords and Harmonies," *Brooklyn Daily Times*, 29 July 1857.

E 1332
"Financial Prospects," *Brooklyn Daily Times,* 29 July 1857.

E 1333
"Is the Yellow Fever Among Us?", *Brooklyn Daily Times,* 30 July 1857.

E 1334
"Long Island Is a Great Place!", *Brooklyn Daily Times,* 30 July 1857.

Reprinted in *ISL,* pp. 165–168.

E 1335
"De Burg's Nuisance—The Green Bones—Animal Hair—Bottled Flesh—Cheap Smelling Salts—&c., &c.," *Brooklyn Daily Times,* 30 July 1857.

E 1336
"Magazine Notices [*Blackwood's Magazine, Knickerbocker Magazine*]," *Brooklyn Daily Times,* 30 July 1857.

E 1337
"What Is to Become of the Canadas?", *Brooklyn Daily Times,* 31 July 1857.

Listed in *ISL.*

E 1338
"Our Island," *Brooklyn Daily Times,* 31 July 1857.

Listed in *ISL.*

E 1339
"Prospects for a Grand Schrub Race for Sheriff Next Fall," *Brooklyn Daily Times,* 1 August 1857.

E 1340
"Trees in Our Streets," *Brooklyn Daily Times,* 1 August 1857.

Listed in *ISL* (dated '31 July').

E 1341
"About the Lawyers," *Brooklyn Daily Times,* 3 August 1857.

Listed in *ISL.*

E 1342
"An Hour Among the Porcelain Manufactories in Greenpoint—Where the Door–Plates and Knobs Come from—New Uses for Porcelain, &c., &c.," *Brooklyn Daily Times*, 3 August 1857.

Reprinted in *ISL*, pp. 132–138.

E 1343
"The City Finances," *Brooklyn Daily Times*, 4 August 1857.

E 1344
"What Are We Coming To?", *Brooklyn Daily Times*, 5 August 1857.

E 1345
"The Cunningham Conspiracy," *Brooklyn Daily Times*, 5 August 1857.

E 1346
"Book Notices [Fowler and Wells, *How to Do Business*]," *Brooklyn Daily Times*, 5 August 1857.

E 1347
"British Rule in India," *Brooklyn Daily Times*, 6 August 1857.

Reprinted in *ISL*, p. 156 (dated '1858').

E 1348
"A Word for the Police," *Brooklyn Daily Times*, 7 August 1857.

E 1349
"Suicides on the Increase," *Brooklyn Daily Times*, 8 August 1857.

E 1350
"Popular Absurdities," *Brooklyn Daily Times*, 10 August 1857.

E 1351
"Police Matters," *Brooklyn Daily Times*, 11 August 1857.

E 1352
"What the Country People Think," *Brooklyn Daily Times*, 11 August 1857.

E 1353
"Literary Notices [*Emerson's United States Magazine;* William R. Prince, *Address to the American Institute on . . . the Chinese Potato*]," *Brooklyn Daily Times*, 11 August 1857.

E 1354
"The House of Refuge," *Brooklyn Daily Times,* 12 August 1857.

E 1355
"Missouri To Be Free," *Brooklyn Daily Times,* 13 August 1857.

Listed in *ISL.*

E 1356
"The Cowstable Nuisance," *Brooklyn Daily Times,* 13 August 1857.

E 1357
"The Lady's Man," *Brooklyn Daily Times,* 13 August 1857.

Reprinted in *ISL,* pp. 168–169.

E 1358
"A Protest [Against Women's Wearing Apparel]," *Brooklyn Daily Times,* 13 August 1857.

E 1359
"The Weather," *Brooklyn Daily Times,* 13 August 1857.

Reprinted in *ISL,* p. 168.

E 1360
"Taking Time by the Forelock," *Brooklyn Daily Times,* 14 August 1857.

E 1361
"The Hottest Day," *Brooklyn Daily Times,* 14 August 1857.

Listed in *ISL.*

E 1362
"Spice [in Newspapers, Novels, Plays]," *Brooklyn Daily Times,* 14 August 1857.

E 1363
"Literary Intelligence [on T. B. Aldrich]," *Brooklyn Daily Times,* 14 August 1857.

E 1364
"Savants and Spiritualism," *Brooklyn Daily Times,* 15 August 1857.

E 1365
"Literary Notices [*Westminster Review, Arthur's Home Magazine*]," *Brooklyn Daily Times,* 15 August 1857.

E 1366

"A National Vice [Love of Excitement]," *Brooklyn Daily Times*, 17 August 1857.

E 1367

"Conflicting Jurisdiction—The N.Y. Judges," *Brooklyn Daily Times*, 18 August 1857.

E 1368

"All Work [With No Play Unhealthy]," *Brooklyn Daily Times*, 18 August 1857.

E 1369

"Cost of the New Police System," *Brooklyn Daily Times*, 19 August 1857.

E 1370

"Is There Room for a New Daily Paper in New York?", *Brooklyn Daily Times*, 20 August 1857.

E 1371

"Literary Notices [Mrs. Marsh, *The Rose of Ashurst;* Henry G. Liddell, *The History of Rome*]," *Brooklyn Daily Times*, 20 August 1857.

E 1372

"What the Joint Board Have Done," *Brooklyn Daily Times*, 21 August 1857.

E 1373

"The Water Works—Difficulties Ahead," *Brooklyn Daily Times*, 22 August 1857.

E 1374

" 'On Horror's Head, Horrors Accumulate,' " *Brooklyn Daily Times*, 22 August 1857.

E 1375

"What It [the Atlantic Cable] Will Effect," *Brooklyn Daily Times*, 24 August 1857.

E 1376

"The Water Works Difficulty," *Brooklyn Daily Times*, 25 August 1857.

E 1377

"Book and Magazine Notices [*Harper's Story Books;* John Bonner, *A Child's History of Greece;* R. T. Trail, *Family Gymnasium; Harper's Monthly Magazine*]," *Brooklyn Daily Times*, 25 August 1857.

E 1378
"The Turners' New Hall," *Brooklyn Daily Times*, 25 August 1857.

E 1379
"What Is It That Disgraces the Fire Department?", *Brooklyn Daily Times*, 26 August 1857.

E 1380
"The Recent Failures," *Brooklyn Daily Times*, 26 August 1857.

E 1381
"The Press and Its Power," *Brooklyn Daily Times*, 26 August 1857.

Reprinted in *ISL,* pp. 35–36.

E 1382
[On the Sheriffalty Election], *Brooklyn Daily Times*, 27 August 1857.

E 1383
"Fact vs. Speculation," *Brooklyn Daily Times*, 27 August 1857.

Listed in *ISL.*

E 1384
"The Atlantic Telegraph Cable," *Brooklyn Daily Times*, 28 August 1857.

E 1385
"Fifteenth Ward Politics," *Brooklyn Daily Times*, 29 August 1857.

E 1386
"On Exemption from Consumption," *Brooklyn Daily Times,* 29 August 1857.

E 1387
"The Traffic of Broadway," *Brooklyn Daily Times,* 29 August 1857.

E 1388
"The Courts—Expensive Delay," *Brooklyn Daily Times,* 31 August 1857.

E 1389
"Magazine Notices [*Knickerbocker Magazine, Mother's Magazine*]," *Brooklyn Daily Times,* 1 September 1857.

E 1390
"The Marriage Tie," *Brooklyn Daily Times,* 2 September 1857.

Reprinted in *ISL,* pp. 113–114.

E 1391
"The Primary Elections," *Brooklyn Daily Times,* 3 September 1857.

E 1392
"The Atlantic Telegraph Cable," *Brooklyn Daily Times,* 3 September 1857.

Listed in *ISL.*

E 1393
"The Circus and a Few Plain Words Concerning It," *Brooklyn Daily Times,* 3 September 1857.

E 1394
"[N. P.] Willis Visits [Washington] Irving," *Brooklyn Daily Times,* 3 September 1857.

E 1395
"The Juvenile House of Industry," *Brooklyn Daily Times,* 4 September 1857.

· Listed in *ISL.*

E 1396
"Obituary [Christina Metcalfe]," *Brooklyn Daily Times,* 4 September 1857.

E 1397
"Kings County Charitable Institutions," *Brooklyn Daily Times,* 5 September 1857.

E 1398
"New Publications [*Emerson's United States Magazine; Cosmopolitan Art Journal*]," *Brooklyn Daily Times,* 5 September 1857.

E 1399
"Literary Gossip: [Thomas Carlyle, T. B. Aldrich, Putnam's, R. W. Griswold], A Biographer Bitten [Elizabeth Gaskell], Alexander Smith Once More, [Douglas] Jerrold, Shakspeare and Mrs. Cowden Clark, The Grandson of His Grandfather [Henry Wadsworth Longfellow], [Nathaniel] Hawthorne," *Brooklyn Daily Times,* 5 September 1857.

Partially reprinted in *ISL,* pp. 62–63 (Griswold).

E 1400
"The Hotel System," *Brooklyn Daily Times,* 7 September 1857.

Listed in *ISL.*

E 1401
"Plagiarism," *Brooklyn Daily Times,* 7 September 1857.

E 1402
"Our State Banks—Unfounded Apprehensions," *Brooklyn Daily Times,* 8 September 1857.

E 1403
"Politics and Criminal Justice," *Brooklyn Daily Times,* 9 September 1857.

E 1404
"The Water Works," *Brooklyn Daily Times,* 9 September 1857.

E 1405
"Scenes in a Police Justice's Court Room," *Brooklyn Daily Times,* 9 September 1857.

Reprinted in *UPP,* II, 10–12.

E 1406
"The Police and Fire Telegraph," *Brooklyn Daily Times,* 10 September 1857.

E 1407
"State Politics—Gen. Sherman," *Brooklyn Daily Times,* 10 September 1857.

E 1408
"New Publications [*London Quarterly Review, Edinburgh Review, Blackwood's Magazine*]," *Brooklyn Daily Times,* 10 September 1857.

E 1409
"Adulteration Everywhere," *Brooklyn Daily Times,* 11 September 1857.

E 1410
"Worth Trying [Sensible and Systematised Economy]," *Brooklyn Daily Times,* 12 September 1857.

Listed in *ISL.*

E 1411
"The Contest in the 15th Ward," *Brooklyn Daily Times,* 14 September 1857.

E 1412
"New Publications [Henry Barth, *Travels and Discoveries in North and Central Africa; Guy Livingstone; or, 'Thorough'*; John S. C. Abbott, *History of King Philip*]," *Brooklyn Daily Times,* 14 September 1857.

E 1413
"The Revolt in India," *Brooklyn Daily Times*, 15 September 1857.

Listed in *ISL*.

E 1414
"Kissing a Profanation," *Brooklyn Daily Times*, 15 September 1857.

Reprinted in *ISL*, p. 114.

E 1415
"Lawyers and Litigation," *Brooklyn Daily Times*, 16 September 1857.

E 1416
"The Election in the 15th Ward," *Brooklyn Daily Times*, 16 September 1857.

E 1417
"Minie vs. Musket," *Brooklyn Daily Times*, 17 September 1857.

E 1418
"The Firemen's Demonstration in New-York," *Brooklyn Daily Times*, 17 September 1857.

E 1419
"Literary Gossip: [*Atlantic Monthly Magazine*], Mr. Thackeray's New Novel," *Brooklyn Daily Times*, 17 September 1857.

E 1420
"State and County Politics," *Brooklyn Daily Times*, 18 September 1857.

E 1421
"Thankful for Small Favors," *Brooklyn Daily Times*, 18 September 1857.

E 1422
"Literary Gossip [J. Parten, *The Life and Times of Aaron Burr*; Col. Benton, *Abridgement of the Debates in Congress*]," *Brooklyn Daily Times*, 18 September 1857.

E 1423
"Lectures and Lecturers," *Brooklyn Daily Times*, 19 September 1857.

E 1424
"Democratic County Convention," *Brooklyn Daily Times*, 21 September 1857.

E 1425
"Literary Gossip: Macaulay, A Poet [James Russell Lowell] Married, Gaillardet and the Tribune," *Brooklyn Daily Times*, 21 September 1857.

Partially reprinted in *ISL*, p. 63 ("A Poet Married").

E 1426
" 'One Touch of Nature,' " *Brooklyn Daily Times*, 22 September 1857.

Reprinted in *ISL*, pp. 71–72.

E 1427
"Political," *Brooklyn Daily Times*, 22 September 1857.

E 1428
"Board of Health," *Brooklyn Daily Times*, 22 September 1857.

E 1429
"Amateur Incendiarism," *Brooklyn Daily Times*, 23 September 1857.

E 1430
"The Sheriffalty," *Brooklyn Daily Times*, 23 September 1857.

E 1431
"Water Street Dance Houses," *Brooklyn Daily Times*, 23 September 1857.

E 1432
"Literary [Alexander Smith, *City Poems;* Edgar Allan Poe]," *Brooklyn Daily Times*, 23 September 1857.

E 1433
"The Board of Health," *Brooklyn Daily Times*, 24 September 1857.

E 1434
"New Publications [*Harper's Monthly Magazine, North British Review*]," *Brooklyn Daily Times*, 24 September 1857.

E 1435
"Our Daughters," *Brooklyn Daily Times*, 25 September 1857.

Reprinted in *ISL*, pp. 55–56.

E 1436
"Kansas," *Brooklyn Daily Times*, 26 September 1857.

E 1437
"The Democratic Assembly Nominations," *Brooklyn Daily Times*, 26 September 1857.

E 1438
"The Leading Journal [*New York Times*]," *Brooklyn Daily Times*, 28 September 1857.

E 1439
"The Hard Times," *Brooklyn Daily Times*, 28 September 1857.

E 1440
"The Legislature and the Ferries," *Brooklyn Daily Times*, 29 September 1857.

E 1441
"The Gloomiest Day," *Brooklyn Daily Times*, 29 September 1857.

Listed in *ISL*.

E 1442
"The Liquor Law," *Brooklyn Daily Times*, 30 September 1857.

E 1443
"The Cure," *Brooklyn Daily Times*, 30 September 1857.

Reprinted in *ISL*, pp. 42–43.

E 1444
"Debating Societies," *Brooklyn Daily Times*, 30 September 1857.

Listed in *ISL*.

E 1445
"Disagreeing Juries," *Brooklyn Daily Times*, 1 October 1857.

E 1446
"Whom Shall We Send to Albany This Winter?", *Brooklyn Daily Times*, 2 October 1857.

E 1447
[On Mormons], *Brooklyn Daily Times*, 2 October 1857.

E 1448
"The Water Works—Brooklyn City Bonds," *Brooklyn Daily Times*, 3 October 1857.

E 1449
"The Failure of the Farmer and Citizens Bank," *Brooklyn Daily Times*, 3 October 1857.

E 1450
"Savings Bank," *Brooklyn Daily Times*, 3 October 1857.

E 1451
"Policemen's Wages—A Reduction Called For," *Brooklyn Daily Times*, 5 October 1857.

E 1452
"Politics and the Police," *Brooklyn Daily Times*, 5 October 1857.

E 1453
"Our Pecuniary Difficulties," *Brooklyn Daily Times*, 5 October 1857.

Reprinted in *ISL*, pp. 169–170.

E 1454
"Valedictory Meeting at Public School No. 16," *Brooklyn Daily Times*, 5 October 1857.

E 1455
"The American Primaries," *Brooklyn Daily Times*, 6 October 1857.

E 1456
"Hard Times!", *Brooklyn Daily Times*, 7 October 1857.

E 1457
"The Pay of the Police," *Brooklyn Daily Times*, 7 October 1857.

E 1458
"Blackwood's Magazine," *Brooklyn Daily Times*, 7 October 1857.

E 1459
"The Fusion Accomplished," *Brooklyn Daily Times*, 8 October 1857.

E 1460
"Jury Duty," *Brooklyn Daily Times,* 9 October 1857.

E 1461
"Epicurean," *Brooklyn Daily Times,* 9 October 1857.

Reprinted in *ISL,* pp. 170–172.

E 1462
"Third Senatorial District," *Brooklyn Daily Times,* 9 October 1857.

E 1463
"Eureka! One Righteous Man [Barnabus H. Booth]," *Brooklyn Daily Times,* 10 October 1857.

E 1464
"Local Politics [No Allegiance to Party]," *Brooklyn Daily Times,* 12 October 1857.

Reprinted in *ISL,* pp. 36–37.

E 1465
"Spiritual Relief," *Brooklyn Daily Times,* 13 October 1857.

E 1466
"Drainage," *Brooklyn Daily Times,* 14 October 1857.

E 1467
[On 'Issachar Van Anden' of the *Brooklyn Daily Eagle*], *Brooklyn Daily Times,* 14 October 1857.

E 1468
"Financial Affairs," *Brooklyn Daily Times,* 14 October 1857.

E 1469
[On the Financial Crisis], *Brooklyn Daily Times,* 15 October 1857.

E 1470
[Unemployment in Newark], *Brooklyn Daily Times,* 16 October 1857.

E 1471
" 'The Partizan Press,' " *Brooklyn Daily Times,* 16 October 1857.

E 1472
"Leading Politicians," *Brooklyn Daily Times*, 17 October 1857.

E 1473
"The Moral of the Remsen Street Accident," *Brooklyn Daily Times*, 19 October 1857.

E 1474
"Political Movements," *Brooklyn Daily Times*, 20 October 1857.

E 1475
"The Truant Childrens Law," *Brooklyn Daily Times*, 21 October 1857.

E 1476
[Unemployment], *Brooklyn Daily Times*, 21 October 1857.

Reprinted in *ISL*, pp. 72–75.

E 1477
"The Democratic Meeting.—The Ferries," *Brooklyn Daily Times*, 22 October 1857.

E 1478
"All Humbug [on Unemployed Tailors]," *Brooklyn Daily Times*, 22 October 1857.

E 1479
"The Hard Times," *Brooklyn Daily Times*, 23 October 1857.

E 1480
"Harper's Magazine," *Brooklyn Daily Times*, 23 October 1857.

E 1481
"The Truant Home," *Brooklyn Daily Times*, 24 October 1857.

E 1482
"The Shrievalty—Is Mr. [Burdett] Stryker Eligible?" *Brooklyn Daily Times*, 24 October 1857.

E 1483
"The Shrievalty," *Brooklyn Daily Times*, 26 October 1857.

E 1484
"The Crisis—No Class Exempt," *Brooklyn Daily Times*, 26 October 1857.

E 1485
"The Atlantic Monthly, No. 1," *Brooklyn Daily Times*, 26 October 1857.

Reprinted in *ISL,* pp. 63–64.

E 1486
"Blackwood," *Brooklyn Daily Times*, 26 October 1857.

E 1487
"The Shrievalty Question," *Brooklyn Daily Times*, 27 October 1857.

E 1488
"The Arch Schemer [Mayor Fernando Wood of New York City]," *Brooklyn Daily Times*, 27 October 1857.

E 1489
"Williamsburgh Unpaid Assessments," *Brooklyn Daily Times*, 28 October 1857.

E 1490
"The Ferry Question," *Brooklyn Daily Times*, 28 October 1857.

E 1491
[On the Woman's Role], *Brooklyn Daily Times*, 28 October 1857.

E 1492
"The Shrievalty Question—A Tempest in a Teapot," *Brooklyn Daily Times*, 29 October 1857.

E 1493
"Conveniences to Reporters," *Brooklyn Daily Times*, 29 October 1857.

E 1494
[Modern Man Not Beyond the Ancients], *Brooklyn Daily Times*, 30 October 1857.

E 1495
"Harper's Weekly," *Brooklyn Daily Times*, 30 October 1857.

E 1496
"Political," *Brooklyn Daily Times*, 2 November 1857.

E 1497
"Depleting the Jail," *Brooklyn Daily Times*, 3 November 1857.

E 1498
"The Election Yesterday," *Brooklyn Daily Times*, 4 November 1857.

E 1499
"The City Railroad Company and Its Employees," *Brooklyn Daily Times*, 5 November 1857.

E 1500
"The Westminster Review," *Brooklyn Daily Times*, 5 November 1857.

E 1501
"A Transcendent Villain," *Brooklyn Daily Times*, 6 November 1857.

E 1502
"We Progress!", *Brooklyn Daily Times*, 7 November 1857.

Reprinted in *ISL*, p. 43.

E 1503
[Aggravations by the Unemployed], *Brooklyn Daily Times*, 7 November 1857.

E 1504
"Rotation in Office," *Brooklyn Daily Times*, 9 November 1857.

E 1505
" 'Moral Insanity' at the Flushing Lunatic Asylum," *Brooklyn Daily Times*, 9 November 1857.

E 1506
"Our Evening Schools," *Brooklyn Daily Times*, 9 November 1857.

E 1507
"A Useless Office [Ward Constable]," *Brooklyn Daily Times*, 10 November 1857.

E 1508
"Highway and Railroad Law," *Brooklyn Daily Times*, 11 November 1857.

E 1509
"The Metropolitan Police System," *Brooklyn Daily Times*, 11 November 1857.

E 1510
"The Common Council and Its Business," *Brooklyn Daily Times,* 12 November 1857.

E 1511
"What They Want [Education]," *Brooklyn Daily Times,* 12 November 1857.

E 1512
"Legalizing Vice," *Brooklyn Daily Times,* 13 November 1857.

Listed in *ISL.*

E 1513
"Secrecy vs. Opennness," *Brooklyn Daily Times,* 14 November 1857.

E 1514
"Rowdyism," *Brooklyn Daily Times,* 16 November 1857.

E 1515
[Ralph Waldo Emerson's "Brahma"], *Brooklyn Daily Times,* 16 November 1857.

Reprinted in *ISL,* p. 64.

E 1516
"The Unemployed," *Brooklyn Daily Times,* 17 November 1857.

E 1517
"Massacre of the Innocents," *Brooklyn Daily Times,* 18 November 1857.

E 1518
[The Poem "Nothing to Wear"], *Brooklyn Daily Times,* 18 November 1857.

E 1519
"Local News," *Brooklyn Daily Times,* 19 November 1857.

E 1520
"Taxation of Real Estate," *Brooklyn Daily Times,* 20 November 1857.

E 1521
"The Punishment of Crime," *Brooklyn Daily Times,* 21 November 1857.

E 1522
"Advice to Jones," *Brooklyn Daily Times,* 21 November 1857.

E 1523
"The Relief for the Unemployed," *Brooklyn Daily Times*, 23 November 1857.

E 1524
"New Publications [*Edinburgh Review*]," *Brooklyn Daily Times*, 23 November 1857.

E 1525
"Thanksgiving," *Brooklyn Daily Times*, 25 November 1857.

E 1526
"Yesterday [Thanksgiving]," *Brooklyn Daily Times*, 27 November 1857.

E 1527
"Curious Statistics," *Brooklyn Daily Times*, 28 November 1857.

E 1528
"A Fact for Mechanics [Laborers Pay the Most Taxes]," *Brooklyn Daily Times*, 28 November 1857.

E 1529
"A Chance for Small Capitalists," *Brooklyn Daily Times*, 30 November 1857.

E 1530
"A Substitute for Primaries," *Brooklyn Daily Times*, 30 November 1857.

E 1531
"National Topics," *Brooklyn Daily Times*, 1 December 1857.

E 1532
"The Industrial School Equestrian Exhibition," *Brooklyn Daily Times*, 1 December 1857.

E 1533
"Central American Affairs," *Brooklyn Daily Times*, 2 December 1857.

E 1534
"The New York Election," *Brooklyn Daily Times*, 2 December 1857.

E 1535
"The Sunday Cars and the Religious World," *Brooklyn Daily Times*, 3 December 1857.

E 1536
"How We Stand [Country Economically Sound]," *Brooklyn Daily Times,* 4 December 1857.

E 1537
"Plotting for the Succession [in the White House]," *Brooklyn Daily Times,* 5 December 1857.

E 1538
"The Officers of the House of Representatives," *Brooklyn Daily Times,* 7 December 1857.

E 1539
"The Long Islanders and the Water Works," *Brooklyn Daily Times,* 7 December 1857.

E 1540
"Why Fernando Wood Was Defeated," *Brooklyn Daily Times,* 7 December 1857.

E 1541
"Misdirected Economy," *Brooklyn Daily Times,* 8 December 1857.

E 1542
"The Jury System," *Brooklyn Daily Times,* 9 December 1857.

E 1543
"The Administration and the Demoractic Party," *Brooklyn Daily Times,* 10 December 1857.

E 1544
"Preposterous Figures [Social Statistics]," *Brooklyn Daily Times,* 10 December 1857.

E 1545
"Constables' Bills," *Brooklyn Daily Times,* 10 December 1857.

E 1546
"The President and the Senator [Douglas]," *Brooklyn Daily Times,* 11 December 1857.

E 1547
"New Publications [*London Quarterly Review, Arthur's Home Magazine*]," *Brooklyn Daily Times,* 11 December 1857.

E 1548
"Party Allegiance," *Brooklyn Daily Times,* 12 December 1857.

E 1549
"The Lecture Season," *Brooklyn Daily Times,* 12 December 1857.

Reprinted in *ISL,* pp. 51–52.

E 1550
"Greeley on Poetry," *Brooklyn Daily Times,* 12 December 1857.

E 1551
[Mrs. Horace Mann on Food and Morals], *Brooklyn Daily Times,* 12 December 1857.

E 1552
"Metallic and Paper Curency," *Brooklyn Daily Times,* 14 December 1857.

E 1553
"The Herald Editor and the President," *Brooklyn Daily Times,* 14 December 1857.

E 1554
"The British Magazines," *Brooklyn Daily Times,* 14 December 1857.

E 1555
"Godey's Lady's Book," *Brooklyn Daily Times,* 14 December 1857.

E 1556
"Northern and Southern Congressmen," *Brooklyn Daily Times,* 15 December 1857.

E 1557
" 'Washington Letter Writers,' " *Brooklyn Daily Times,* 16 December 1857.

E 1558
"New Publications [*The Poets of the Nineteenth Century,* ed. Robert Aris Willmott and Evert A. Duyckinck]," *Brooklyn Daily Times,* 16 December 1857.

E 1559
"What the Law Is For," *Brooklyn Daily Times,* 17 December 1857.

E 1560
"The Assessment Levy," *Brooklyn Daily Times,* 18 December 1857.

E 1561
"The Anticipated Schism in the Democratic Party," *Brooklyn Daily Times,* 18 December 1857.

E 1562
"The Ferries," *Brooklyn Daily Times,* 19 December 1857.

E 1563
"Police Matters," *Brooklyn Daily Times,* 19 December 1857.

E 1564
"Why Have the South 10th Street Ferry Reduced Their Rates?", *Brooklyn Daily Times,* 21 December 1857.

E 1565
"Law Making," *Brooklyn Daily Times,* 21 December 1857.

E 1566
"The Churches and the Poor," *Brooklyn Daily Times,* 21 December 1857.

E 1567
"The Ferry Question Again," *Brooklyn Daily Times,* 22 December 1857.

E 1568
"The Sewerage of the City," *Brooklyn Daily Times,* 23 December 1857.

E 1569
"New Publications [David Livingstone, *Missionary Travels and Researches in South America;* Mrs. L. H. Sigourney, *Howard's Journal; Merry's Museum*]," *Brooklyn Daily Times,* 23 December 1857.

E 1570
"Mr. Dayton and the Water Commissioners," *Brooklyn Daily Times,* 26 December 1857.

E 1571
"Christmas Day," *Brooklyn Daily Times,* 26 December 1857.

E 1572
"The Swill Milk Again," *Brooklyn Daily Times,* 28 December 1857.

E 1573
"The Atlantic Monthly," *Brooklyn Daily Times*, 28 December 1857.

E 1574
"The Capture of Gen. Walker," *Brooklyn Daily Times*, 29 December 1857.

E 1575
"The Next Presidency," *Brooklyn Daily Times*, 29 December 1857.

E 1576
"The Supervisors and the Sheriff," *Brooklyn Daily Times*, 30 December 1857.

E 1577
"Good Bye, Old Year!", *Brooklyn Daily Times*, 31 December 1857.

E 1578
[Old Christmas Song], *Brooklyn Daily Times*, 31 December 1857.

E 1579
"New Year's Day," *Brooklyn Daily Times*, 2 January 1858.

Listed in *ISL*.

E 1580
"The Sewerage of the Eastern District," *Brooklyn Daily Times*, 4 January 1858.

E 1581
"Governor's Message," *Brooklyn Daily Times*, 6 January 1858.

Listed in *ISL*.

E 1582
"The Metropolitan Police Act," *Brooklyn Daily Times*, 6 January 1858.

E 1583
"Death of Alderman [Charles C.] Fowler," *Brooklyn Daily Times*, 7 January 1858.

E 1584
"John M. Bernheisel, the Mormon Delegate," *Brooklyn Daily Times*, 8 January 1858.

E 1585
"The Metropolitan Police Law," *Brooklyn Daily Times,* 9 January 1858.

Listed in *ISL*.

E 1586
"Literary Notices [*Knickerbocker Magazine;* Leigh Richmond Dickinson, *Great Judgments*]," *Brooklyn Daily Times,* 9 January 1858.

E 1587
"Church Quarrels," *Brooklyn Daily Times,* 12 January 1858.

E 1588
"The Gem of the Antilles [Cuba]," *Brooklyn Daily Times,* 12 January 1858.

Reprinted in *ISL*, p. 157.

E 1589
"The Death Penalty," *Brooklyn Daily Times,* 13 January 1858.

Reprinted in *ISL*, pp. 46–47.

E 1590
"Magazine Notices [*Godey's Lady's Book, Merry's Museum*]," *Brooklyn Daily Times,* 13 January 1858.

E 1591
"A Daniel Come to Judgment," *Brooklyn Daily Times,* 14 January 1858.

E 1592
"What Williamsburgh Wants," *Brooklyn Daily Times,* 15 January 1858.

E 1593
"The Ferries," *Brooklyn Daily Times,* 16 January 1858.

Reprinted in *ISL*, pp. 138–140.

E 1594
"Paupers," *Brooklyn Daily Times,* 16 January 1858.

E 1595
"The Chief Engineership of the Eastern District," *Brooklyn Daily Times,* 16 January 1858.

E 1596
"The Historical Magazine," *Brooklyn Daily Times,* 16 January 1858.

E 1597
"The Sewerage of the Eastern District," *Brooklyn Daily Times,* 18 January 1858.

E 1598
"How to Hang Criminals," *Brooklyn Daily Times,* 18 January 1858.

E 1599
"Brooklyn's Benefactors," *Brooklyn Daily Times,* 19 January 1858.

E 1600
"The Fatal Conflagration," *Brooklyn Daily Times,* 20 January 1858.

E 1601
"The Two Coroners," *Brooklyn Daily Times,* 20 January 1858.

E 1602
"The Harbor," *Brooklyn Daily Times,* 21 January 1858.

E 1603
"Fire Department Ball," *Brooklyn Daily Times,* 21 January 1858.

E 1604
"Gas Companies and Consumers," *Brooklyn Daily Times,* 22 January 1858.

E 1605
"The Inquest [School-House Catastrophe]," *Brooklyn Daily Times,* 22 January 1858.

E 1606
"The Supposed Murder in Greene Street," *Brooklyn Daily Times,* 22 January 1858.

Reprinted in William White, "Walt Whitman Reports a Murder," *Quarterly Journal of the Book Club of Detroit,* 1, no. 4 (Summer 1968), 15–17.

E 1607
"The School Catastrophe," *Brooklyn Daily Times,* 22 January 1858.

E 1608
"Thackeray's New Novel [*The Virginians*]," *Brooklyn Daily Times,* 22 January 1858.

E 1609
"Liquor Legislation," *Brooklyn Daily Times*, 23 January 1858.

Reprinted in *ISL*, pp. 47–49.

E 1610
"The Board of Education," *Brooklyn Daily Times*, 23 January 1858.

E 1611
"Wanted a Critic," *Brooklyn Daily Times*, 25 January 1858.

Listed in *ISL*.

E 1612
"New Publications [Arthur Helps, *The Spanish Conquest in America, and Its Relation to the History, of Slavery and the Government of the Colonies; Debit and Credit,* trans. from Gustav Freytag; *The New York Almanac and Yearly Record for . . . 1858; Knickerbocker Magazine*]," *Brooklyn Daily Times*, 25 January 1858.

E 1613
"A Registry Law," *Brooklyn Daily Times*, 26 January 1858.

E 1614
[Duties of Public Officers], *Brooklyn Daily Times*, 26 January 1858.

E 1615
"The Police and the Fire Department," *Brooklyn Daily Times*, 27 January 1858.

E 1616
"The Supposed Murder in Greene Street, N.Y.," *Brooklyn Daily Times*, 27 January 1858.

Reprinted in William White, "Walt Whitman Reports a Murder," *Quarterly Journal of the Book Club of Detroit*, 1, no. 4 (Summer 1968), 17.

E 1617
"The Late School-House Tragedy," *Brooklyn Daily Times*, 28 January 1858.

E 1618
"The Jury Law," *Brooklyn Daily Times*, 28 January 1858.

E 1619
"Legislation for the City," *Brooklyn Daily Times*, 29 January 1858.

E 1620
[Fee System], *Brooklyn Daily Times*, 29 January 1858.

E 1621
"Professional Men," *Brooklyn Daily Times*, 30 January 1858.

Reprinted in *ISL*, pp. 33–35.

E 1622
"New Publications [*Atlantic Monthly Magazine*]," *Brooklyn Daily Times*, 30 January 1858.

Reprinted in *ISL*, pp. 64–66.

E 1623
"City Officials' Terms," *Brooklyn Daily Times*, 1 February 1858.

E 1624
"The Police.—Satan Rebuking Sin," *Brooklyn Daily Times*, 2 February 1858.

E 1625
"Testimonials and Presentations [to City Officials]," *Brooklyn Daily Times*, 3 February 1858.

Listed in *ISL* (dated '1 February').

E 1626
"Magazine Notices [*Blackwood's Magazine, The Scalpel*]," *Brooklyn Daily Times*, 3 February 1858.

E 1627
"What'll They Think," *Brooklyn Daily Times*, 4 February 1858.

Reprinted in *ISL*, p. 172.

E 1628
"The Ferriage Bill," *Brooklyn Daily Times*, 5 February 1858.

E 1629
"The City Railroad Company," *Brooklyn Daily Times*, 5 February 1858.

E 1630
"The Jersey Press," *Brooklyn Daily Times*, 5 February 1858.

E 1631
"The Inspectorship of the Fifth Precinct," *Brooklyn Daily Times*, 5 February 1858.

E 1632
"The Sunday Observance Question," *Brooklyn Daily Times*, 6 February 1858.

E 1633
"Congressional Manners," *Brooklyn Daily Times*, 6 February 1858.

E 1634
"Statistics of Health," *Brooklyn Daily Times*, 6 February 1858.

E 1635
"Mr. Beach's Ferry Bill," *Brooklyn Daily Times*, 8 February 1858.

E 1636
"The Assessment Laws," *Brooklyn Daily Times*, 9 February 1858.

E 1637
"The Financial Offices," *Brooklyn Daily Times*, 10 February 1858.

E 1638
"A Plagiarist [E. W. Andrews]," *Brooklyn Daily Times*, 10 February 1858.

E 1639
[Shakespeare's Women Characters], *Brooklyn Daily Times*, 10 February 1858.

Reprinted in *ISL*, p. 66.

E 1640
"A Step in the Right Direction [Police Replacing Constables in Court]," *Brooklyn Daily Times*, 11 February 1858.

E 1641
[Art in *Harper's Monthly Magazine*], *Brooklyn Daily Times*, 11 February 1858.

E 1642
"Alleged Municpal Corruption," *Brooklyn Daily Times*, 11 February 1858.

E 1643
"Prospects of the Slavery Question," *Brooklyn Daily Times,* 12 February 1858.

Reprinted in *ISL,* pp. 88–89.

E 1644
"The Royal Marriage," *Brooklyn Daily Times,* 12 February 1858.

Reprinted in *ISL,* pp. 157–158.

E 1645
"Diet and Digestion," *Brooklyn Daily Times,* 12 February 1858.

E 1646
"Time of Charter Elections," *Brooklyn Daily Times,* 13 February 1858.

E 1647
"The Normal School," *Brooklyn Daily Times,* 15 February 1858.

E 1648
"The Murder of Mr. Simonson [Inadequate Crimnal System]," *Brooklyn Daily Times,* 16 February 1858.

Listed in *ISL.*

E 1649
"The Legislature and the Board of Supervisors," *Brooklyn Daily Times,* 17 February 1858.

E 1650
[On the New Police Inspector of the Third Precinct], *Brooklyn Daily Times,* 17 February 1858.

E 1651
"Reporting Extraordinary [in the *Brooklyn Star*]," *Brooklyn Daily Times,* 17 February 1858.

E 1652
[On William Cullen Bryant], *Brooklyn Daily Times,* 17 February 1858.

Reprinted in *ISL,* pp. 66–67.

E 1653
"New Publications [*Westminster Review;* J. W. de Forest, *European Acquaintances;* George Eliot, *Scenes of Clerical Life*]," *Brooklyn Daily Times,* 18 February 1858.

E 1654
"Our Model Coroner," *Brooklyn Daily Times,* 20 February 1858.

E 1655
"The Fire Department," *Brooklyn Daily Times,* 20 February 1858.

E 1656
"The Board of Assessors," *Brooklyn Daily Times,* 20 February 1858.

E 1657
"Washington's Birthday," *Brooklyn Daily Times,* 22 February 1858.

Reprinted in *ISL,* pp. 59–60.

E 1658
"New Publications [Isaac Taylor, *The World of Man*]," *Brooklyn Daily Times,* 22 February 1858.

E 1659
"Steam on Atlantic Street," *Brooklyn Daily Times,* 23 February 1858.

E 1660
[The *New York Tribune* on Military and European Subjects], *Brooklyn Daily Times,* 23 February 1858.

Listed in *ISL.*

E 1661
"Amending the Metropolitan Police Act," *Brooklyn Daily Times,* 24 February 1858.

E 1662
"Percussion Coal Breaker," *Brooklyn Daily Times,* 24 February 1858.

E 1663
"Africa—Mungo Park—The Landers—Livingston," *Brooklyn Daily Times,* 25 February 1858.

Listed in *ISL.*

E 1664
"The Sunday Car Question Once More," *Brooklyn Daily Times,* 25 February 1858.

Listed in *ISL.*

E 1665
"Lola [Montez] at the Athenaeum," *Brooklyn Daily Times*, 25 February 1858.

E 1666
"More Miracles," *Brooklyn Daily Times*, 26 February 1858.

Reprinted in *ISL,* pp. 76–77.

E 1667
"Fire Commissioners," *Brooklyn Daily Times*, 26 February 1858.

E 1668
[On Judge Culver's Letter], *Brooklyn Daily Times*, 27 February 1858.

Listed in *ISL.*

E 1669
"Our Eleventh Volume [of the *Times*]," *Brooklyn Daily Times*, 1 March 1858.

E 1670
"The Revival Movement," *Brooklyn Daily Times*, 1 March 1858.

Reprinted in *ISL,* p. 77.

E 1671
"A Lesson for Lent," *Brooklyn Daily Times*, 1 March 1858.

E 1672
"Profits of the Ferries," *Brooklyn Daily Times*, 1 March 1858.

E 1673
"A Deacon in Trouble," *Brooklyn Daily Times*, 1 March 1858.

Listed in *ISL.*

E 1674
[Salaries], *Brooklyn Daily Times*, 2 March 1858.

E 1675
"A Double S," *Brooklyn Daily Times*, 2 March 1858.

E 1676
"The Landlord and Tenant Law," *Brooklyn Daily Times*, 3 March 1858.

E 1677
"New Publications [*Edinburgh Review, London Quarterly Review, Atlantic Monthly Magazine*]," *Brooklyn Daily Times*, 3 March 1858.

Listed in *ISL*.

E 1678
"The Ferries," *Brooklyn Daily Times*, 4 March 1858.

E 1679
"Rents," *Brooklyn Daily Times*, 4 March 1858.

E 1680
"Fashions for 1858," *Brooklyn Daily Times*, 4 March 1858.

Listed in *ISL*.

E 1681
"Lent," *Brooklyn Daily Times*, 6 March 1858.

Listed in *ISL*.

E 1682
"Politics and City Affairs," *Brooklyn Daily Times*, 6 March 1858.

E 1683
"Cartman, Take Notice," *Brooklyn Daily Times*, 6 March 1858.

E 1684
"New Publications [Thomas William Atkinson, *Oriental and Western Siberia*]," *Brooklyn Daily Times*, 6 March 1858.

E 1685
"The Williamsburgh Local Commission," *Brooklyn Daily Times*, 8 March 1858.

E 1686
"The Law's Delay," *Brooklyn Daily Times*, 8 March 1858.

E 1687
"New Publications [*Blackwood's Magazine*]," *Brooklyn Daily Times*, 8 March 1858.

E 1688
"The Temperance Movement," *Brooklyn Daily Times*, 10 March 1858.

Reprinted in *ISL*, p. 49.

E 1689
"A Revival Prayer Meeting," *Brooklyn Daily Times*, 11 March 1858.

Reprinted in *ISL*, pp. 77–79.

E 1690
"A Word to the Congressmen from the Vth," *Brooklyn Daily Times*, 12 March 1858.

E 1691
[Attack on the *(Brooklyn) Eagle*], *Brooklyn Daily Times*, 12 March 1858.

Listed in *ISL*.

E 1692
"Fire Department Matters," *Brooklyn Daily Times*, 12 March 1858.

E 1693
"The Common Council," *Brooklyn Daily Times*, 13 March 1858.

E 1694
"The Post Office," *Brooklyn Daily Times*, 15 March 1858.

E 1695
"New Publications [N. L. North, *Is Alcohol a Posion?*; *Sunday Legislation*; *Mr. Taylor on Lecompton*; *North British Review*]," *Brooklyn Daily Times*, 17 March 1858.

E 1696
[Political and Journalistic Garrulity], *Brooklyn Daily Times*, 17 March 1858.

Reprinted in *ISL*, p. 50.

E 1697
"The Rival Schools of Medicine," *Brooklyn Daily Times*, 18 March 1858.

Listed in *ISL*.

E 1698
"Mr. Hatch and Sunday Observance," *Brooklyn Daily Times*, 19 March 1858.

E 1699
[Brigham Young], *Brooklyn Daily Times,* 19 March 1858.

Reprinted in *ISL,* p. 173.

E 1700
"State Constitutions," *Brooklyn Daily Times,* 20 March 1858.

E 1701
"The Ferries," *Brooklyn Daily Times,* 20 March 1858.

E 1702
"Has Brooklyn No Water Rights?", *Brooklyn Daily Times,* 22 March 1858.

E 1703
"What We Pay for Schools," *Brooklyn Daily Times,* 23 March 1858.

Listed in *ISL.*

E 1704
"A Railroad President on His Muscle," *Brooklyn Daily Times,* 23 March 1858.

E 1705
"The Assessment Laws," *Brooklyn Daily Times,* 24 March 1858.

E 1706
"The President of the City Railroad and the *Eagle,*" *Brooklyn Daily Times,* 24 March 1858.

E 1707
" 'Sartaroe' [and a Forged Washington Irving Letter]," *Brooklyn Daily Times,* 24 March 1858.

E 1708
"The Railroads of the State," *Brooklyn Daily Times,* 25 March 1858.

E 1709
"All About Allsop," *Brooklyn Daily Times,* 26 March 1858.

E 1710
"Political: A Small Business," *Brooklyn Daily Times,* 29 March 1858.

E 1711
"The Revival," *Brooklyn Daily Times,* 29 March 1858.

E 1712
"Election Matters," *Brooklyn Daily Times,* 29 March 1858.

E 1713
"The Board of Supervisors at the County Buildings," *Brooklyn Daily Times,* 30 March 1858.

E 1714
"Political [Democratic City Convention]," *Brooklyn Daily Times,* 30 March 1858.

E 1715
"The Two Conventions," *Brooklyn Daily Times,* 31 March 1858.

E 1716
"Political," *Brooklyn Daily Times,* 31 March 1858.

E 1717
"The People and the Election," *Brooklyn Daily Times,* 1 April 1858.

E 1718
"Political," *Brooklyn Daily Times,* 1 April 1858.

E 1719
"Lecompton in the House," *Brooklyn Daily Times,* 2 April 1858.

Reprinted in *ISL,* pp. 94–95.

E 1720
"Political," *Brooklyn Daily Times,* 2 April 1858.

E 1721
"The Brooklyn State Arsenal," *Brooklyn Daily Times,* 3 April 1858.

E 1722
[Congratulations to Our Friend William Cauldwell], *Brooklyn Daily Times,* 3 April 1858.

Reprinted in *ISL,* p. 173.

E 1723
[One of Those Divine Days], *Brooklyn Daily Times,* 3 April 1858.

E 1724
"Political," *Brooklyn Daily Times,* 3 April 1858.

E 1725
"Punctuality," *Brooklyn Daily Times,* 3 April 1858.

E 1726
"The Colossal Fete at the Crystal Palace," *Brooklyn Daily Times,* 3 April 1858.

E 1727
[On a Man Who Loses His Temper], *Brooklyn Daily Times,* 5 April 1858.

Listed in *ISL.*

E 1728
"Blackwood's Magazine," *Brooklyn Daily Times,* 5 April 1858.

E 1729
"The Election," *Brooklyn Daily Times,* 6 April 1858.

Listed in *ISL.*

E 1730
[Removal of Balance Docks], *Brooklyn Daily Times,* 6 April 1858.

E 1731
[Get Rid of Coroner Connery], *Brooklyn Daily Times,* 6 April 1858.

E 1732
"The Election," *Brooklyn Daily Times,* 7 April 1858.

E 1733
"Real and Personal Property," *Brooklyn Daily Times,* 8 April 1858.

E 1734
"Harper's Magazine," *Brooklyn Daily Times,* 8 April 1858.

E 1735
"Common Council Meetings," *Brooklyn Daily Times,* 9 April 1858.

E 1736
"The Police and the Sabbath," *Brooklyn Daily Times,* 9 April 1858.

E 1737
"The Truant Home," *Brooklyn Daily Times,* 10 April 1858.

E 1738
"The Literature of the Insane," *Brooklyn Daily Times,* 10 April 1858.

E 1739
"Senator Spinola and the Police Commissioners," *Brooklyn Daily Times,* 10 April 1858.

E 1740
"The Common Council," *Brooklyn Daily Times,* 12 April 1858.

E 1741
"Regicide on a Small Scale," *Brooklyn Daily Times,* 12 April 1858.

E 1742
"Regular Nominations.—A Fair Confession," *Brooklyn Daily Times,* 13 April 1858.

E 1743
"Shall We Revolutionise the Fire Department of Brooklyn?", *Brooklyn Daily Times,* 14 April 1858.

E 1744
"About Railroads, Sundays, &c.," *Brooklyn Daily Times,* 14 April 1858.

E 1745
"The Ferries," *Brooklyn Daily Times,* 15 April 1858.

E 1746
"Brooklyn Misrepresented in Congress," *Brooklyn Daily Times,* 16 April 1858.

Listed in *ISL.*

E 1747
"Ald. Lowber's Fire Ordinance," *Brooklyn Daily Times,* 17 April 1858.

E 1748
"Brooklyn Parks," *Brooklyn Daily Times,* 17 April 1858.

Reprinted in *ISL,* pp. 140–141.

E 1749
"A Visit to the Water Works," *Brooklyn Daily Times,* 17 April 1858.

Reprinted in *ISL,* p. 140.

E 1750
"City Young Men—The Masses," *Brooklyn Daily Times,* 19 April 1858.

Listed in *ISL.*

E 1751
"A Moving Article," *Brooklyn Daily Times,* 19 April 1858.

Reprinted in *ISL,* pp. 125–126.

E 1752
"The Cant [of the Reformers]," *Brooklyn Daily Times,* 19 April 1858.

Reprinted in *ISL,* pp. 44–45.

E 1753
"A Little More Freedom," *Brooklyn Daily Times,* 20 April 1858.

Reprinted in *ISL,* pp. 141–142.

E 1754
"Adjournment of the Legislature," *Brooklyn Daily Times,* 20 April 1858.

E 1755
"England and France," *Brooklyn Daily Times,* 20 April 1858.

E 1756
"Portents for Dead Rabbits," *Brooklyn Daily Times,* 20 April 1858.

E 1757
"The Railroads and the Juries," *Brooklyn Daily Times,* 21 April 1858.

E 1758
"Public Morality, Old and New," *Brooklyn Daily Times,* 21 April 1858.

E 1759
"A Convention to Make a New State Constitution Again," *Brooklyn Daily Times,* 21 April 1858.

E 1760
[Literature at the South], *Brooklyn Daily Times,* 21 April 1858.

E 1761
"Thos. H. Benton," *Brooklyn Daily Times,* 21 April 1858.

Listed in *ISL.*

E 1762
"Don't Be Too Fast in Quashing the Old Fire Department," *Brooklyn Daily Times*, 22 April 1858.

E 1763
"One Side of the Registry Law Question," *Brooklyn Daily Times*, 22 April 1858.

E 1764
[Stephen A. Douglas], *Brooklyn Daily Times*, 22 April 1858.

Reprinted in *ISL*, p. 95.

E 1765
"Sneaking Politicians—Two Roads Before the Democratic Party—New Leading Men Wanted," *Brooklyn Daily Times*, 23 April 1858.

Reprinted in *ISL*, pp. 95–96.

E 1766
"More Trouble About Sunday," *Brooklyn Daily Times*, 23 April 1858.

E 1767
"Health—Nature's Aid—Consumption," *Brooklyn Daily Times*, 23 April 1858.

E 1768
"Public School Exhibitions—Their Tendencies, &c.," *Brooklyn Daily Times*, 23 April 1858.

E 1769
"Whipping the Devil Round the Stump," *Brooklyn Daily Times*, 24 April 1858.

E 1770
"The Rival Monthlies—Harper's and the Atlantic," *Brooklyn Daily Times*, 24 April 1858.

E 1771
"Free Homestead," *Brooklyn Daily Times*, 26 April 1858.

E 1772
"Long Island Schools and Schooling," *Brooklyn Daily Times*, 27 April 1858.

Reprinted in *UPP*, II, 13–15.

E 1773
"Yellow Fever," *Brooklyn Daily Times,* 27 April 1858.

E 1774
"Fire Department Election," *Brooklyn Daily Times,* 27 April 1858.

E 1775
"The Fire Department Question Still Under Debate," *Brooklyn Daily Times,* 28 April 1858.

E 1776
"A Suggestion for Consolidated Brooklyn," *Brooklyn Daily Times,* 29 April 1858.

Reprinted in *ISL,* pp. 142–144.

E 1777
"An Exursion Over the Whole Line of the Water Works," *Brooklyn Daily Times,* 30 April 1858.

E 1778
"Books and Readers," *Brooklyn Daily Times,* 30 April 1858.

E 1779
"Removal [of the *Times* to a New Office]," *Brooklyn Daily Times,* 1 May 1858.

E 1780
"Brooklyn is to Have a Paid Fire Department," *Brooklyn Daily Times,* 1 May 1858.

E 1781
"The Lecompton Conference Bill Has Passed," *Brooklyn Daily Times,* 1 May 1858.

E 1782
"Removal [of the *Times* to a New Office]," *Brooklyn Daily Times,* 2 May 1858.

E 1783
"The One Thing Wanted to Make the Brooklyn Water Works a Perfect Work," *Brooklyn Daily Times,* 3 May 1858.

E 1784
"New Publications [George Ticknor Curtis, *History of the Constitution of the United States; Blackwood's Magazine*]," *Brooklyn Daily Times,* 3 May 1858.

E 1785
"Common Council Appointments," *Brooklyn Daily Times*, 4 May 1858.

E 1786
"We Have Pitched Our Tent on a New Spot!", *Brooklyn Daily Times*, 5 May 1858.

E 1787
"New States," *Brooklyn Daily Times*, 5 May 1858.

E 1788
"Un-American Sunday Force Laws in the Eastern District," *Brooklyn Daily Times*, 5 May 1858.

Listed in *ISL*.

E 1789
"Cypress Hills Cemetery," *Brooklyn Daily Times*, 5 May 1858.

E 1790
"Prohibition of Colored Persons," *Brooklyn Daily Times*, 6 May 1858.

Reprinted in *ISL*, pp. 89–90.

E 1791
"12th Ward," *Brooklyn Daily Times*, 6 May 1858.

E 1792
"A Letter to the Republicans of Brooklyn, from Philadelphia," *Brooklyn Daily Times*, 6 May 1858.

E 1793
"Fires in Brooklyn," *Brooklyn Daily Times*, 6 May 1858.

E 1794
"The Speech–Making Season," *Brooklyn Daily Times*, 6 May 1858.

E 1795
"Women's Rights in the New Library," *Brooklyn Daily Times*, 8 May 1858.

E 1796
"What We Want [A Literary Association]," *Brooklyn Daily Times*, 10 May 1858.

Listed in *ISL*.

E 1797
"The Westminster Review for April," *Brooklyn Daily Times*, 10 May 1858.

E 1798
"Poor Devils," *Brooklyn Daily Times*, 10 May 1858.

E 1799
"Canada," *Brooklyn Daily Times*, 10 May 1858.

E 1800
"A Good Idea [Presidential Tour]," *Brooklyn Daily Times*, 10 May 1858.

E 1801
"The Old Fire Department of Brooklyn Yet Lives," *Brooklyn Daily Times*, 11 May 1858.

E 1802
"A City Sweet and Clean: The Brooklyn Sewerage," *Brooklyn Daily Times*, 12 May 1858.

Reprinted in *ISL*, pp. 144–145 (dated '13 May').

E 1803
"Abolitionists Around," *Brooklyn Daily Times*, 12 May 1858.

E 1804
"Living in Brooklyn," *Brooklyn Daily Times*, 13 May 1858.

Reprinted in *ISL*, pp. 145–146.

E 1805
"Swill Milk," *Brooklyn Daily Times*, 13 May 1858.

E 1806
"An American Translation of the Bible," *Brooklyn Daily Times*, 13 May 1858.

Reprinted in *ISL*, pp. 80–82.

E 1807
"Yesterday's Visit Over the Water Works," *Brooklyn Daily Times*, 14 May 1858.

E 1808
"Young Men's Unions," *Brooklyn Daily Times*, 14 May 1858.

E 1809
"Women's Rights—Free Love with a Vengeance," *Brooklyn Daily Times*, 14 May 1858.

E 1810
"Swill Milk," *Brooklyn Daily Times*, 14 May 1858.

E 1811
"A Hint to Mayor Powell," *Brooklyn Daily Times*, 15 May 1858.

E 1812
"Who Was Swedenborg?", *Brooklyn Daily Times*, 15 May 1858.

Reprinted in *UPP*, II, 16–18 (dated '15 June').

E 1813
"Harper's Magazine for June," *Brooklyn Daily Times*, 15 May 1858.

E 1814
"Amusements," *Brooklyn Daily Times*, 17 May 1858.

Listed in *ISL*.

E 1815
"A Woman in the Pulpit," *Brooklyn Daily Times*, 17 May 1858.

Reprinted in *ISL*, pp. 79–80.

E 1816
"H. W. Herbert—Lesson of a Morbid Life," *Brooklyn Daily Times*, 18 May 1858.

E 1817
"A New York Criticism on a Brooklyn Official," *Brooklyn Daily Times*, 19 May 1858.

E 1818
"New Constitutions—Every State to Its Fancy," *Brooklyn Daily Times*, 19 May 1858.

Listed in *ISL*.

E 1819
"Afternoon News, by Telegraph," *Brooklyn Daily Times*, 20 May 1858.

E 1820
"Topics This Morning," *Brooklyn Daily Times,* 20 May 1858.

E 1821
"Burial of Herbert—His Life More and More Opened Up," *Brooklyn Daily Times,* 20 May 1858.

E 1822
"More Reform—A Move Toward Direct Taxation," *Brooklyn Daily Times,* 20 May 1858.

E 1823
"Action of the Police Commissioners, on Sunday Laws," *Brooklyn Daily Times,* 21 May 1858.

E 1824
"This Morning's Topics," *Brooklyn Daily Times,* 21 May 1858.

E 1825
"Atlantic Monthly," *Brooklyn Daily Times,* 21 May 1858.

E 1826
"Free Homesteads," *Brooklyn Daily Times,* 21 May 1858.

E 1827
"Unhealthy Children in New York and Brooklyn," *Brooklyn Daily Times,* 22 May 1858.

Listed in *ISL.*

E 1828
"Capital Punishment," *Brooklyn Daily Times,* 22 May 1858.

Partially reprinted in *UPP,* II, 15–16. Not in White, *Journalism.*

E 1829
"Are We Resuming the Old Ways?" *Brooklyn Daily Times,* 22 May 1858.

E 1830
"A German Holiday," *Brooklyn Daily Times,* 24 May 1858.

Reprinted in *ISL,* p. 60.

E 1831
"National Conventions," *Brooklyn Daily Times,* 24 May 1858.

Listed in *ISL*. Not in White, *Journalism.*

E 1832
"Why Should Church Property Be Exempt from Taxation?", *Brooklyn Daily Times*, 26 May 1858.

Listed in *ISL*.

E 1833
"London Quarterly No. 206," *Brooklyn Daily Times*, 27 May 1858.

E 1834
"A Preacheress—Hicksite Quakers," *Brooklyn Daily Times*, 27 May 1858.

Reprinted in *ISL*, p. 80.

E 1835
"Old King Lear," *Brooklyn Daily Times*, 27 May 1858.

E 1836
"Blackwood's for May," *Brooklyn Daily Times*, 27 May 1858.

E 1837
"Judge Ingraham's Injunction—An Unfortunate Business," *Brooklyn Daily Times*, 28 May 1858.

E 1838
"The Eagle's Idea of a 'Friendly Joke' [Assault on Senator Sumner]," *Brooklyn Daily Times*, 28 May 1858.

Listed in *ISL*.

E 1839
"That Literary Institute for the Eastern District," *Brooklyn Daily Times*, 28 May 1858.

E 1840
"Can a Strict Party Man Be a Free man?" *Brooklyn Daily Times*, 31 May 1858.

E 1841
"Edinburgh Review for April," *Brooklyn Daily Times*, 31 May 1858.

E 1842
"No Free Homesteads Yet," *Brooklyn Daily Times*, 2 June 1858.

E 1843
"A Slop–Newspaper on Slop–Milk," *Brooklyn Daily Times*, 2 June 1858.

E 1844
"Something Like a Fight!", *Brooklyn Daily Times*, 3 June 1858.

E 1845
"Brooklyn Institutions," *Brooklyn Daily Times*, 4 June 1858.

E 1846
" 'Three Cheers for Williamsburgh,' " *Brooklyn Daily Times*, 4 June 1858.

E 1847
"Progress of the Brooklyn Reservoir," *Brooklyn Daily Times*, 5 June 1858.

Listed in *ISL*.

E 1848
"Lovers of Harmony, Attend!", *Brooklyn Daily Times*, 5 June 1858.

E 1849
"Signs in Europe," *Brooklyn Daily Times*, 7 June 1858.

Listed in *ISL*.

E 1850
"Three Young Men Drowned Yesterday, Off Greenpoint," *Brooklyn Daily Times*, 7 June 1858.

E 1851
"Historians and Ancient History," *Brooklyn Daily Times*, 8 June 1858.

E 1852
"Judge Culver's Case," *Brooklyn Daily Times*, 9 June 1858.

Listed in *ISL*.

E 1853
"Another Noble Institution for Brooklyn," *Brooklyn Daily Times*, 9 June 1858.

E 1854
"Plenty of Dimes," *Brooklyn Daily Times*, 10 June 1858.

E 1855
"Boy Drowned—A Brave Attempt to Rescue Him—Infamous Refusal," *Brooklyn Daily Times,* 10 June 1858.

E 1856
"Something Brooklyn is Free Of," *Brooklyn Daily Times,* 11 June 1858.

E 1857
"Topics This Morning," *Brooklyn Daily Times,* 11 June 1858.

E 1858
"Baseball—The Eastern District Against South Brooklyn," *Brooklyn Daily Times,* 11 June 1858.

E 1859
"About China, as Relates to Itself and to Us," *Brooklyn Daily Times,* 12 June 1858.

Listed in *ISL.*

E 1860
"Brigham and His Saints," *Brooklyn Daily Times,* 14 June 1858.

E 1861
"A Query [on Physical Education]," *Brooklyn Daily Times,* 14 June 1858.

Listed in *ISL.*

E 1862
"New Publications [Archibald Allison, *History of Europe from . . . 1789 to . . . 1815*]," *Brooklyn Daily Times,* 14 June 1858.

E 1863
"Common Council," *Brooklyn Daily Times,* 15 June 1858.

E 1864
"Our Public School Teachers," *Brooklyn Daily Times,* 16 June 1858.

Listed in *ISL.*

E 1865
"A Word of Explanation," *Brooklyn Daily Times,* 17 June 1858.

Reprinted *ISL*, pp. 37–38.

E 1866
"The Trial of Lally," *Brooklyn Daily Times*, 18 June 1858.

E 1867
"Base Ball," *Brooklyn Daily Times*, 18 June 1858.

Reprinted in *ISL*, pp. 106–108.

E 1868
"Into the Country," *Brooklyn Daily Times*, 19 June 1858.

Reprinted in *ISL*, pp. 104–105.

E 1869
"Which 'Pathy' Will You Have?", *Brooklyn Daily Times*, 19 June 1858.

E 1870
"The Verdict in the Case of Lally," *Brooklyn Daily Times*, 19 June 1858.

E 1871
" 'Harper' for July," *Brooklyn Daily Times*, 19 June 1858.

E 1872
"Hard to Please," *Brooklyn Daily Times*, 21 June 1858.

Listed in *ISL*.

E 1873
"Ferry Matters," *Brooklyn Daily Times*, 21 June 1858.

E 1874
"New Publications [Thomas W. Field, *Pear Culture; Atlantic Monthly*]," *Brooklyn Daily Times*, 21 June 1858.

E 1875
"The Common Council," *Brooklyn Daily Times*, 22 June 1858.

E 1876
"The Way Lives Are Wasted," *Brooklyn Daily Times*, 23 June 1858.

Listed in *ISL*.

E 1877
[Judge Culver], *Brooklyn Daily Times*, 23 June 1858.

E 1878
"The Sunday Question," *Brooklyn Daily Times,* 23 June 1858.

E 1879
"The Private Lives of Great Men," *Brooklyn Daily Times,* 23 June 1858.

Reprinted in *UPP,* II, 18–19.

E 1880
"Long Island Milk and Long Island Vegetables," *Brooklyn Daily Times,* 24 June 1858.

E 1881
"The Great Experiment [Atlantic Telegraph]," *Brooklyn Daily Times,* 24 June 1858.

E 1882
"The Board of Green Cloth," *Brooklyn Daily Times,* 24 June 1858.

E 1883
" 'Our Best Society,' " *Brooklyn Daily Times,* 25 June 1858.

E 1884
"Warm Weather Sermons," *Brooklyn Daily Times,* 26 June 1858.

E 1885
"Church Record—Something New," *Brooklyn Daily Times,* 26 June 1858.

E 1886
"Judge Culver's Case," *Brooklyn Daily Times,* 26 June 1858.

Listed in *ISL.*

E 1887
"New Publications [*Blackwood's*]," *Brooklyn Daily Times,* 26 June 1858.

E 1888
"The Health of the City," *Brooklyn Daily Times,* 28 June 1858.

E 1889
"Ninety–Five," *Brooklyn Daily Times,* 28 June 1858.

E 1890
[Frogs], *Brooklyn Daily Times,* 28 June 1858.

Reprinted in *ISL,* p. 173.

E 1891
"The Radicals in Council," *Brooklyn Daily Times,* 29 June 1858.

Reprinted in *ISL,* pp. 45–46.

E 1892
"The Common Council," *Brooklyn Daily Times,* 29 June 1858.

E 1893
"Picnics and Excursions," *Brooklyn Daily Times,* 30 June 1858.

Listed in *ISL.*

E 1894
[Mrs. Bennett's Town House], *Brooklyn Daily Times,* 2 July 1858.

Listed in *ISL.*

E 1895
"Our City Just 33 Years Since," *Brooklyn Daily Eagle,* 3 July 1858.

E 1896
" 'Freedom's Natal Day,' " *Brooklyn Daily Times,* 3 July 1858.

Listed in *ISL.*

E 1897
"Woman's Wrongs," *Brooklyn Daily Times,* 3 July 1858.

Listed in *ISL.*

E 1898
"The Monroe Obsequies," *Brooklyn Daily Times,* 3 July 1858.

E 1899
"Judge Culver's Council," *Brooklyn Daily Times,* 6 July 1858.

E 1900
"A Fitting Occasion for a Celebration and Ovation [Atlantic Cable]," *Brooklyn Daily Times,* 7 July 1858.

Listed in *ISL.*

E 1901
"Another National Anniversary Passed," *Brooklyn Daily Times,* 7 July 1858.

E 1902
"Judge Culver and His Traducers," *Brooklyn Daily Times,* 9 July 1858.

Listed in *ISL.*

E 1903
[Benefit for Miss Sewell], *Brooklyn Daily Times,* 9 July 1858.

Listed in *ISL.*

E 1904
"The Monroe Obsequies—The Finale," *Brooklyn Daily Times,* 9 July 1858.

E 1905
"Little Hope Left!", *Brooklyn Daily Times,* 10 July 1858.

E 1906
"The De Reviere Romance—Williamsburgh Interested in the Matter," *Brooklyn Daily Times,* 10 July 1858.

E 1907
"Base Ball," *Brooklyn Daily Times,* 10 July 1858.

E 1908
"Down Below," *Brooklyn Daily Times,* 12 July 1858.

Reprinted in *ISL,* pp. 82–83.

E 1909
"A Want to Be Supplied," *Brooklyn Daily Times,* 13 July 1858.

E 1910
"Clergymen's Salaries," *Brooklyn Daily Times,* 13 July 1858.

Listed in *ISL.*

E 1911
"Immaculate Property," *Brooklyn Daily Times,* 13 July 1858.

E 1912
"The Future of Brooklyn," *Brooklyn Daily Times,* 14 July 1858.

Reprinted in *ISL,* pp. 146–147.

E 1913
"De Burg," *Brooklyn Daily Times*, 14 July 1858.

E 1914
"More Gold [on the Frazer's River]," *Brooklyn Daily Times*, 15 July 1858.

Reprinted in *ISL*, p. 99.

E 1915
"The Suicide at Berlin Heights," *Brooklyn Daily Times*, 16 July 1858.

E 1916
[*Godey's Lady's Book*], *Brooklyn Daily Times*, 16 July 1858.

E 1917
"A Northern Pacific Railroad," *Brooklyn Daily Times*, 17 July 1858.

Listed in *ISL*.

E 1918
"Summer Resorts," *Brooklyn Daily Times*, 19 July 1858.

Listed in *ISL*.

E 1919
"Common Council Proceedings," *Brooklyn Daily Times*, 20 July 1858.

E 1920
"The Appetite for Scandal," *Brooklyn Daily Times*, 20 July 1858.

Listed in *ISL*.

E 1921
"The Press—Its Future," *Brooklyn Daily Times*, 21 July 1858.

Reprinted in *ISL*, pp. 38–39 (dated '31 July').

E 1922
"Better Than Gold," *Brooklyn Daily Times*, 22 July 1858.

E 1923
[Dickens Scandal], *Brooklyn Daily Times*, 22 July 1858.

E 1924
"Harper's Magazine," *Brooklyn Daily Times*, 22 July 1858.

E 1925
"The Public Health," *Brooklyn Daily Times*, 23 July 1858.

Listed in *ISL*.

E 1926
[Real Estate Sales Not Made Known], *Brooklyn Daily Times*, 23 July 1858.

E 1927
[Bulwer Scandal], *Brooklyn Daily Times*, 23 July 1858.

E 1928
"Broadway (Brooklyn) Railroad," *Brooklyn Daily Times*, 24 July 1858.

E 1929
"Judge Culver Explains His Motives," *Brooklyn Daily Times*, 24 July 1858.

Listed in *ISL*. Not in White, *Journalism*.

E 1930
"Rowdyism Rampant," *Brooklyn Daily Times*, 26 July 1858.

E 1931
"New Publications [*Cyclopedia of Commerce and Navigation,* ed. J. Smith Homans and J. Smith Homans, Jr.; *Selected Discourses from the French and German;* Henry Ward Beecher, *Life Thoughts;* (Charles Hatch Smith), *George Melville; The Darm*]," *Brooklyn Daily Times*, 26 July 1858.

E 1932
"Rational Enjoyment," *Brooklyn Daily Times*, 27 July 1858.

E 1933
"Public Baths," *Brooklyn Daily Times*, 27 July 1858.

Reprinted in *ISL*, pp. 102–103.

E 1934
"Blackwood," *Brooklyn Daily Times*, 27 July 1858.

E 1935
"What Is Music, Then?", *Brooklyn Daily Times*, 28 July 1858.

Reprinted in *ISL*, pp. 173–175.

E 1936
"The Frazer River Ferment," *Brooklyn Daily Times,* 28 July 1858.

E 1937
"The Last Day of the Condemned," *Brooklyn Daily Times,* 29 July 1858.

E 1938
"Divorce Cases," *Brooklyn Daily Times,* 29 July 1858.

Listed in *ISL.*

E 1939
"A Music Hall in Brooklyn," *Brooklyn Daily Times,* 30 July 1858.

E 1940
"Literary Scandal," *Brooklyn Daily Times,* 30 July 1858.

Reprinted in *ISL,* p. 67.

E 1941
"Manufacturing Presidents," *Brooklyn Daily Times,* 31 July 1858.

Reprinted in *ISL,* pp. 40–41.

E 1942
"The Saints Still Hostile," *Brooklyn Daily Times,* 31 July 1858.

E 1943
"Temporary Injunctions," *Brooklyn Daily Times,* 2 August 1858.

E 1944
"New Publications [Anthony Trollope, *Dr. Thorne;* Charles H. Haswell, *Mensuration and Practical Geometry; Abbott's Histories for Children*]," *Brooklyn Daily Times,* 2 August 1858.

E 1945
"The Colored Folk's Festival," *Brooklyn Daily Times,* 3 August 1858.

Listed in *ISL.*

E 1946
"The Sabbatarians, Here and Elsewhere," *Brooklyn Daily Times,* 4 August 1858.

E 1947
"The Cable Laid!", *Brooklyn Daily Times,* 6 August 1858.

Listed in *ISL.*

E 1948
"The Mammoth Cave, Kentucky, by Charles W. Wright," *Brooklyn Daily Times,* 6 August 1858.

E 1949
"Ferry Matters," *Brooklyn Daily Times,* 7 August 1858.

E 1950
"Honor to Cyrus W. Field," *Brooklyn Daily Times,* 9 August 1858.

Reprinted in *ISL,* pp. 158–159.

E 1951
"The [*Brooklyn*] Eagle Turned Critic," *Brooklyn Daily Times,* 9 August 1858.

E 1952
"New Publications [*The New American Cyclopaedia,* ed. George Ripley and Charles A. Dana]," *Brooklyn Daily Times,* 9 August 1858.

E 1953
"Manly Exercises," *Brooklyn Daily Times,* 10 August 1858.

Listed in *ISL.*

E 1954
"Walker Redivivus," *Brooklyn Daily Times,* 11 August 1858.

E 1955
"A Gossipy August Article," *Brooklyn Daily Times,* 12 August 1858.

Listed in *ISL.*

E 1956
"Prospects Ahead," *Brooklyn Daily Times,* 12 August 1858.

E 1957
"The Course of the Administration," *Brooklyn Daily Times,* 13 August 1858.

E 1958
"Steam on the Erie Canal," *Brooklyn Daily Times*, 13 August 1858.

Listed in *ISL*.

E 1959
[Summer Heats], *Brooklyn Daily Times*, 14 August 1858.

E 1960
"New Publications [Madame de B., *Memoirs of Rachel;* Catharine Sedgwick, *Life of Joseph Curtis*]," *Brooklyn Daily Times*, 14 August 1858.

E 1961
"Will Queen Victoria Ever Visit the United States?", *Brooklyn Daily Times*, 16 August 1858.

Reprinted in *ISL*, pp. 160–161.

E 1962
"The Press on the Atlantic Cable," *Brooklyn Daily Times*, 16 August 1858.

E 1963
"The British Quarterlies," *Brooklyn Daily Times*, 16 August 1858.

E 1964
"Harper's Magazine," *Brooklyn Daily Times*, 16 August 1858.

E 1965
"The Two Worlds United," *Brooklyn Daily Times*, 17 August 1858.

Listed in *ISL*.

E 1966
"Quite a Step Foward," *Brooklyn Daily Times*, 17 August 1858.

E 1967
"An Extraordinary Document," *Brooklyn Daily Times*, 18 August 1858.

E 1968
"A Thought out of the Grand Topic of the Day," *Brooklyn Daily Times*, 18 August 1858.

E 1969
"The Demonstration Yesterday," *Brooklyn Daily Times*, 19 August 1858.

Listed in *ISL*.

E 1970
"The Moral Effect of the Atlantic Cable," *Brooklyn Daily Times*, 20 August 1858.

Reprinted in *ISL*, pp. 159–160.

E 1971
"Our Late Little 'Cold Snap,' " *Brooklyn Daily Times*, 20 August 1858.

E 1972
"A Little More on the Same Subject [Atlantic Telegraph]," *Brooklyn Daily Times*, 21 August 1858.

E 1973
"Pugilism and Pugilists," *Brooklyn Daily Times*, 23 August 1858.

Reprinted in *ISL*, pp. 105–106.

E 1974
"Brooklyn Schools—Are They Doing as Well as Could Be Expected?", *Brooklyn Daily Times*, 24 August 1858.

E 1975
"The London Quarterly Review," *Brooklyn Daily Times*, 24 August 1858.

E 1976
"An Afternoon Aboard the Niagara," *Brooklyn Daily Times*, 25 August 1858.

Listed in *ISL*.

E 1977
"How About Business?", *Brooklyn Daily Times*, 26 August 1858.

E 1978
[Cyrus W. Field], *Brooklyn Daily Times*, 26 August 1858.

Listed in *ISL*.

E 1979
[Douglas, Lincoln, and Trumbull], *Brooklyn Daily Times*, 26 August 1858.

Reprinted in *ISL*, p. 96.

E 1980
"Dickens's Last Letter," *Brooklyn Daily Times*, 26 August 1858.

E 1981
"Yesterday's Great News—What It Suggests," *Brooklyn Daily Times*, 27 August 1858.

Listed in *ISL*.

E 1982
"A Female Preacher in Williamsburgh," *Brooklyn Daily Times*, 27 August 1858.

Listed in *ISL*.

E 1983
"New Publications: Blackwood," *Brooklyn Daily Times*, 27 August 1858.

E 1984
"The Water Works and the Common Council," *Brooklyn Daily Times*, 28 August 1858.

E 1985
"A Monster Grievance," *Brooklyn Daily Times*, 30 August 1858.

E 1986
"Newspaperdom Half a Century Ago," *Brooklyn Daily Times*, 30 August 1858.

Listed in *ISL*.

E 1987
"The County Charitable Institutions," *Brooklyn Daily Times*, 30 August 1858.

E 1988
"The 'Great Powers,' " *Brooklyn Daily Times*, 31 August 1858.

Listed in *ISL*.

E 1989
"The Celebration Yesterday," *Brooklyn Daily Times*, 2 September 1858.

E 1990
"Fun 'Out West,' " *Brooklyn Daily Times*, 3 September 1858.

Listed in *ISL*.

E 1991
"The Quarantine Outrage," *Brooklyn Daily Times*, 3 September 1858.

E 1992
[Domestic Misfortunes of Charles Dickens], *Brooklyn Daily Times,* 3 September 1858.

Listed in *ISL.*

E 1993
"A Nod Is as Good as a Wink, &c.," *Brooklyn Daily Times,* 4 September 1858.

E 1994
"Another Cable Wanted," *Brooklyn Daily Times,* 4 September 1858.

Listed in *ISL.*

E 1995
"Medical Quackery," *Brooklyn Daily Times,* 6 September 1858.

E 1996
[East New York], *Brooklyn Daily Times,* 6 September 1858.

E 1997
"A Sunday Prize Fight," *Brooklyn Daily Times,* 6 September 1858.

E 1998
"Woman in the Pulpit—Sermon by Mrs. Lydia Jenkins, Last Night," *Brooklyn Daily Times,* 6 September 1858.

E 1999
"The Projected Small Pox Hospital at Flatbush," *Brooklyn Daily Times,* 7 September 1858.

E 2000
"The Police and the Quarantine Burning," *Brooklyn Daily Times,* 7 September 1858.

E 2001
"North British Review," *Brooklyn Daily Times,* 7 September 1858.

E 2002
"Excursion to the Water Works," *Brooklyn Daily Times,* 8 September 1858.

E 2003
"Douglas and Buchanan," *Brooklyn Daily Times,* 8 September 1858.

Reprinted in *ISL,* p. 97.

E 2004
[Bohemianism in Literary Circles], *Brooklyn Daily Times*, 8 September 1858.

Reprinted in *ISL*, p. 67.

E 2005
"Excelsior Literary Association," *Brooklyn Daily Times*, 8 September 1858.

E 2006
"The 70th Regiment and the Navy Yard Officers," *Brooklyn Daily Times*, 9 September 1858.

E 2007
"The Spanish American Republics," *Brooklyn Daily Times*, 10 September 1858.

Reprinted in *ISL*, pp. 162–163.

E 2008
"The Conventions," *Brooklyn Daily Times*, 10 September 1858.

E 2009
[Dickens More Widely Read in America than England], *Brooklyn Daily Times*, 10 September 1858.

E 2010
"Criminal Abortions," *Brooklyn Daily Times*, 11 September 1858.

Reprinted in *ISL*, pp. 114–116.

E 2011
"Our Foreign Policy," *Brooklyn Daily Times*, 13 September 1858.

Listed in *ISL*.

E 2012
"The Finale of the Free Love Convention," *Brooklyn Daily Times*, 14 September 1858.

Listed in *ISL*.

E 2013
"Appealing to the People," *Brooklyn Daily Times*, 15 September 1858.

Listed in *ISL*.

E 2014
"The Divided Democracy," *Brooklyn Daily Times*, 17 September 1858.

E 2015
[Lectures and Concerts], *Brooklyn Daily Times,* 17 September 1858.

Listed in *ISL.*

E 2016
"The Conventions," *Brooklyn Daily Times,* 18 September 1858.

E 2017
"The Genius Irritable," *Brooklyn Daily Times,* 18 September 1858.

Reprinted in *ISL,* pp. 67–68.

E 2018
"Two American Sailors in a Spanish Dungeon," *Brooklyn Daily Times,* 20 September 1858.

E 2019
"Harper's Monthly Magazine," *Brooklyn Daily Times,* 20 September 1858.

E 2020
"A Curious Problem," *Brooklyn Daily Times,* 21 September 1858.

E 2021
"Senator Douglas," *Brooklyn Daily Times,* 21 September 1858.

Listed in *ISL.*

E 2022
"Literary [Herman Melville to Lecture]," *Brooklyn Daily Times,* 21 September 1858.

E 2023
"The Republicans of Kings County and the Local Press," *Brooklyn Daily Times,* 22 September 1858.

E 2024
"Local Politics," *Brooklyn Daily Times,* 23 September 1858.

E 2025
"How to Diminish Pauperism," *Brooklyn Daily Times,* 24 September 1858.

Reprinted in *ISL,* pp. 83–84.

E 2026
" 'The Hour and the Man,' " *Brooklyn Daily Times,* 24 September 1858.

E 2027
"The Cable Again," *Brooklyn Daily Times*, 25 September 1858.

E 2028
"The National Crime," *Brooklyn Daily Times*, 25 September 1858.

E 2029
"Adventures and Achievements of Americans, by Henry Howe," *Brooklyn Daily Times*, 25 September 1858.

E 2030
"The Water Works," *Brooklyn Daily Times*, 27 September 1858.

E 2031
"The Water Works and the Common Council," *Brooklyn Daily Times*, 28 September 1858.

E 2032
"Libraries for the Station Houses," *Brooklyn Daily Times*, 28 September 1858.

E 2033
"Fusion of the Opposition in Kings County," *Brooklyn Daily Times*, 29 September 1858.

E 2034
"The Quarantine—A Visit to the West Bank," *Brooklyn Daily Times*, 29 September 1858.

E 2035
"Fees Retained by Justices," *Brooklyn Daily Times*, 30 September 1858.

E 2036
"The Fall Regatta—A Sail in the Julia," *Brooklyn Daily Times*, 1 October 1858.

Reprinted in *ISL*, pp. 108–109.

E 2037
"The Firemen's Tournament at Albany," *Brooklyn Daily Times*, 1 October 1858.

E 2038
"Poetical," *Brooklyn Daily Times*, 1 October 1858.

E 2039
"Enlargement of the County Farm," *Brooklyn Daily Times,* 2 October 1858.

E 2040
"The Peck-Slip Ferry Lease—Who Shall Have It?", *Brooklyn Daily Times,* 4 October 1858.

E 2041
"What Constitutes Waste?", *Brooklyn Daily Times,* 4 October 1858.

E 2042
"The Public Schools," *Brooklyn Daily Times,* 5 October 1858.

E 2043
"How to Build up the City," *Brooklyn Daily Times,* 6 October 1858.

E 2044
"Burning of the Crystal Palace," *Brooklyn Daily Times,* 6 October 1858.

Reprinted in *ISL,* p. 147.

E 2045
"Human Nature Under an Unfavorable Aspect," *Brooklyn Daily Times,* 7 October 1858.

E 2046
"The Evergreens Cemetery," *Brooklyn Daily Times,* 7 October 1858.

E 2047
"The Police," *Brooklyn Daily Times,* 8 October 1858.

E 2048
"Our Foreign Policy and English Influence," *Brooklyn Daily Times,* 8 October 1858.

Listed in *ISL.*

E 2049
"Longfellow's New Poem," *Brooklyn Daily Times,* 8 October 1858.

Listed in *ISL.*

E 2050
"Four Tickets in the Field," *Brooklyn Daily Times,* 12 October 1858.

E 2051
"A Southside View of Brooklyn," *Brooklyn Daily Times*, 13 October 1858.

E 2052
"The Vth Congressional District—Shall We Re-elect Mr. Maclay?", *Brooklyn Daily Times*, 14 October 1858.

E 2053
"Godey's Lady's Book," *Brooklyn Daily Times*, 14 October 1858.

E 2054
"How to Beat Mr. Maclay," *Brooklyn Daily Times*, 15 October 1858.

E 2055
"Revision of the [State] Constitution," *Brooklyn Daily Times*, 16 October 1858.

Listed in *ISL*.

E 2056
"The 5th Congressional District," *Brooklyn Daily Times*, 16 October 1858.

E 2057
"What We Drink," *Brooklyn Daily Times*, 18 October 1858.

E 2058
"The Water Works," *Brooklyn Daily Times*, 18 October 1858.

E 2059
"Who Are Responsible for Bad Government?", *Brooklyn Daily Times*, 19 October 1858.

E 2060
"The Pulpit and the People," *Brooklyn Daily Times*, 20 October 1858.

Listed in *ISL*.

E 2061
"The Contest in Illinois," *Brooklyn Daily Times*, 20 October 1858.

Listed in *ISL*.

E 2062
"Fifth Congressional District—Reply to Mr. Warner," *Brooklyn Daily Times*, 21 October 1858.

E 2063
"Fifth Dist. American Congressional Convention," *Brooklyn Daily Times*, 22 October 1858.

E 2064
"The Prize Fight," *Brooklyn Daily Times*, 22 October 1858.

Reprinted in *ISL*, p. 106.

E 2065
"Under Which King, Bizonian?", *Brooklyn Daily Times*, 22 October 1858.

E 2066
"The Atlantic Monthly," *Brooklyn Daily Times*, 22 October 1858.

E 2067
"Our New Brooklyn Arsenal, and Its Reminiscences," *Brooklyn Daily Times*, 23 October 1858.

Reprinted in *ISL*, pp. 152–155.

E 2068
"The Contest in Illinois [Douglas and Lincoln]," *Brooklyn Daily Times*, 23 October 1858.

E 2069
"New Publication [(Samuel Adams Hammett), *Piney Woods Tavern, or Sam Slick in Texas*]," *Brooklyn Daily Times*, 23 October 1858.

E 2070
"The Yellow Fever in Brooklyn—A Secret Circular from Dr. Boyd—The Public to Be Kept in the Dark," *Brooklyn Daily Times*, 25 October 1858.

E 2071
"Fusion in the Congressional Districts," *Brooklyn Daily Times*, 26 October 1858.

E 2072
"Our Correspondents," *Brooklyn Daily Times*, 26 October 1858.

E 2073
"Irregular Nominations," *Brooklyn Daily Times*, 27 October 1858.

E 2074
"The Cable," *Brooklyn Daily Times,* 27 October 1858.

E 2075
"Can Americans and Republicans Consistently Vote for Mr. Hamilton?", *Brooklyn Daily Times,* 27 October 1858.

E 2076
"Political Terms and Expressions," *Brooklyn Daily Times,* 28 October 1858.

Listed in *ISL.*

E 2077
"Blackwood's Magazine," *Brooklyn Daily Times,* 29 October 1858.

E 2078
"Local Items [Anti-Lecomptonites]," *Brooklyn Daily Times,* 30 October 1858.

Reprinted in *ISL,* p. 175.

E 2079
"To the Voters of the Vth Congressional District," *Brooklyn Daily Times,* 1 November 1858.

E 2080
"The Duty of Citizens," *Brooklyn Daily Times,* 1 November 1858.

E 2081
"The State," *Brooklyn Daily Times,* 1 November 1858.

E 2082
"The Election," *Brooklyn Daily Times,* 2 November 1858.

Listed in *ISL.*

E 2083
"Enterprising Journalism," *Brooklyn Daily Times,* 2 November 1858.

E 2084
"New Publications [Thomas Carlyle, *History of Frederick II of Prussia;* Elias Loomis, *Elements of Natural Philosophy;* Charles C. B. Seymour, *Self-Made Man;* Henry Dawson, *Battles of the United States by Sea and Land;* Oliver

Wendell Holmes, *The Autocrat of the Breakfast Table*]," *Brooklyn Daily Times*, 2 November 1858.

Partially reprinted in *ISL*, p. 68 (Carlyle).

E 2085
"The [Election] Result," *Brooklyn Daily Times*, 3 November 1858.

E 2086
"Animal Heat," *Brooklyn Daily Times*, 4 November 1858.

E 2087
"The Election," *Brooklyn Daily Times*, 4 November 1858.

E 2088
"Public School Training," *Brooklyn Daily Times*, 5 November 1858.

E 2089
"Senator Douglas's Success in Illinois," *Brooklyn Daily Times*, 5 November 1858.

Reprinted in *ISL*, p. 98.

E 2090
"The Democratic Factions," *Brooklyn Daily Times*, 5 November 1858.

E 2091
"The Sewerage," *Brooklyn Daily Times*, 6 November 1858.

E 2092
"Land Telegraph to Europe," *Brooklyn Daily Times*, 6 November 1858.

E 2093
"The Water Works—A Celebration in Contemplation," *Brooklyn Daily Times*, 6 November 1858.

E 2094
"The Williamsburgh Local Improvement Commission," *Brooklyn Daily Times*, 8 November 1858.

E 2095
"Literary Intelligence Extraordinary [Carlyle's *Peter the Great* Reviewed in the *Brooklyn Eagle*]," *Brooklyn Daily Times*, 8 November 1858.

E 2096
"The Telegraph in Williamsburgh," *Brooklyn Daily Times*, 9 November 1858.

E 2097
"The Opera in Brooklyn?", *Brooklyn Daily Times*, 10 November 1858.

Reprinted in *ISL*, pp. 147–148.

E 2098
"The 14th Ward Election Case," *Brooklyn Daily Times*, 11 November 1858.

E 2099
"Broadway Railroad," *Brooklyn Daily Times*, 11 November 1858.

E 2100
"The Board of Education," *Brooklyn Daily Times*, 12 November 1858.

E 2101
"City Election Returns," *Brooklyn Daily Times*, 13 November 1858.

E 2102
"The Game of Chess," *Brooklyn Daily Times*, 13 November 1858.

Reprinted in *ISL*, pp. 109–110.

E 2103
"Judicial Salaries," *Brooklyn Daily Times*, 15 November 1858.

E 2104
"The Ferries," *Brooklyn Daily Times*, 15 November 1858.

E 2105
"The Common Council," *Brooklyn Daily Times*, 16 November 1858.

E 2106
"Thanksgiving Day," *Brooklyn Daily Times*, 17 November 1858.

Listed in *ISL*.

E 2107
"Music," *Brooklyn Daily Times*, 19 November 1858.

Listed in *ISL*.

E 2108
"Thanksgiving Day," *Brooklyn Daily Times,* 19 November 1858.

E 2109
"New Publications [William W. Sanger, *The History of Prostitution; Book of the Mormon*]," *Brooklyn Daily Times,* 19 November 1858.

E 2110
"The Ferries," *Brooklyn Daily Times,* 20 November 1858.

E 2111
"The Water Works," *Brooklyn Daily Times,* 20 November 1858.

E 2112
"Inequalities of Taxation," *Brooklyn Daily Times,* 23 November 1858.

E 2113
"Magazines, &c. [*Edinburgh Review; Atlantic Monthly; Ladies' Home Magazine*]," *Brooklyn Daily Times,* 23 November 1858.

E 2114
"England and France," *Brooklyn Daily Times,* 24 November 1858.

Listed in *ISL.*

E 2115
"The Ferries," *Brooklyn Daily Times,* 24 November 1858.

E 2116
"Why Douglas Succeeded," *Brooklyn Daily Times,* 24 November 1858.

Reprinted in *ISL,* pp. 98–99.

E 2117
"National Conventions," *Brooklyn Daily Times,* 25 November 1858.

E 2118
"The Board of Supervisors," *Brooklyn Daily Times,* 26 November 1858.

E 2119
"A Southerner on Slavery," *Brooklyn Daily Times,* 27 November 1858.

E 2120
"Common Council," *Brooklyn Daily Times,* 30 November 1858.

E 2121
"Parks for Brooklyn," *Brooklyn Daily Times,* 30 November 1858.

E 2122
"Municipal Legislation," *Brooklyn Daily Times,* 1 December 1858.

E 2123
"The Public Schools," *Brooklyn Daily Times,* 1 December 1858.

E 2124
"The Bright and Dark Sides," *Brooklyn Daily Times,* 2 December 1858.

E 2125
"Selling Real Estate," *Brooklyn Daily Times,* 3 December 1858.

E 2126
"Is This a Free Country?", *Brooklyn Daily Times,* 4 December 1858.

E 2127
"The Season and Its Prospects," *Brooklyn Daily Times,* 6 December 1858.

E 2128
"The Wallabout Bay Filling," *Brooklyn Daily Times,* 6 December 1858.

E 2129
"The Water Celebration," *Brooklyn Daily Times,* 6 December 1858.

E 2130
"The President's Message," *Brooklyn Daily Times,* 6 December 1858.

Listed in *ISL.* Not in White, *Jouralism.*

E 2131
"Saturday Night—'Items' Makes a Tour," *Brooklyn Daily Times,* 6 December 1858.

Reprinted in *ISL,* pp. 148–152.

E 2132
"The Common Council," *Brooklyn Daily Times,* 7 December 1858.

E 2133
"The City Government," *Brooklyn Daily Times,* 8 December 1858.

E 2134
"The New York City School Commissioners," *Brooklyn Daily Times*, 9 December 1858.

E 2135
[Dr. William Sanger's Work on Prostitution], *Brooklyn Daily Times*, 9 December 1858.

Reprinted in *ISL*, pp. 118–119 (dated '1859').

E 2136
"The Ferries," *Brooklyn Daily Times*, 10 December 1858.

E 2137
"Public School Education," *Brooklyn Daily Times*, 10 December 1858.

E 2138
"A New Way to Collect Debts," *Brooklyn Daily Times*, 11 December 1858.

Listed in *ISL*.

E 2139
"Dr. Sanger's Book," *Brooklyn Daily Times*, 11 December 1858.

E 2140
"The Ferries—A Suggestion," *Brooklyn Daily Times*, 13 December 1858.

E 2141
" 'The Sunday Papers,' " *Brooklyn Daily Times*, 13 December 1858.

Reprinted as "[Sensation Stories in Sunday Papers]," *UPP*, II, 19–21.

E 2142
"Common Council," *Brooklyn Daily Times*, 14 December 1858.

E 2143
"New Books [William Hickling Prescott, *Philip II of Spain*]," *Brooklyn Daily Times*, 14 December 1858.

E 2144
"Rev. Mr. Hatch and the Sunday Question," *Brooklyn Daily Times*, 15 December 1858.

E 2145
[Torquato Tasso's Pawn Ticket], *Brooklyn Daily Times*, 15 December 1858.

E 2146
"At the Chief's Office," *Brooklyn Daily Times,* 15 December 1858.

E 2147
"Our Political Machinery," *Brooklyn Daily Times,* 16 December 1858.

Listed in *ISL.*

E 2148
"Health Among Females," *Brooklyn Daily Times,* 17 December 1858.

Reprinted in *ISL,* pp. 116–117 (dated '17 October 1858').

E 2149
"Our 'Sick Man' [Mexico]," *Brooklyn Daily Times,* 18 December 1858.

E 2150
"The Ferry Sale," *Brooklyn Daily Times,* 20 December 1858.

E 2151
"New Publications [*Appleton's New American Cyclopaedia,* ed. George Ripley and Charles A. Dana]," *Brooklyn Daily Times,* 20 December 1858.

E 2152
"The New Gas Contract," *Brooklyn Daily Times,* 21 December 1858.

E 2153
"The Ferries," *Brooklyn Daily Times,* 22 December 1858.

E 2154
"The 5th Congressional District: Mr. Hamilton Elected a Member of Congress," *Brooklyn Daily Times,* 22 December 1858.

E 2155
"Hamilton vs. Maclay," *Brooklyn Daily Times,* 23 December 1858.

E 2156
[Exhibition at the Gymnasium], *Brooklyn Daily Times,* 23 December 1858.

E 2157
"To-morrow," *Brooklyn Daily Times,* 24 December 1858.

Listed in *ISL.*

E 2158
"The Temperance Question," *Brooklyn Daily Times*, 24 December 1858.

E 2159
"The Ferries," *Brooklyn Daily Times*, 24 December 1858.

E 2160
"Fifth Congressional District," *Brooklyn Daily Times*, 27 December 1858.

E 2161
"Christmas-Time," *Brooklyn Daily Times*, 27 December 1858.

E 2162
"Common Council," *Brooklyn Daily Times*, 28 December 1858.

E 2163
"Sleep, Health, and Mental Toil," *Brooklyn Daily Times*, 29 December 1858.

Listed in *ISL*.

E 2164
"The Atlantic Monthly," *Brooklyn Daily Times*, 29 December 1858.

Listed in *ISL*.

E 2165
"The Ferries," *Brooklyn Daily Times*, 30 December 1858.

E 2166
"The Old Year and the New," *Brooklyn Daily Times*, 31 December 1858.

Reprinted in *ISL*, pp. 60–61.

E 2167
"Rebuilding of [School House] No. 14," *Brooklyn Daily Times*, 31 December 1858.

E 2168
"Our Legislature," *Brooklyn Daily Times*, 3 January 1859.

E 2169
"New Year's Day—How It Was Celebrated—Accidents, Incidents, &c.," *Brooklyn Daily Times*, 3 January 1859.

E 2170
"Affairs at Albany," *Brooklyn Daily Times*, 4 January 1859.

E 2171
"A Small Business," *Brooklyn Daily Times*, 4 January 1859.

E 2172
"Eccentricities of Metropolitan Journalism," *Brooklyn Daily Times*, 5 January 1859.

E 2173
"The Troubles of a Modest Man," *Brooklyn Daily Times*, 5 January 1859.

E 2174
"The Fire Department," *Brooklyn Daily Times*, 6 January 1859.

E 2175
"Affairs at Albany," *Brooklyn Daily Times*, 7 January 1859.

E 2176
"Universal Suffrage," *Brooklyn Daily Times*, 7 January 1859.

E 2177
"New Publications [W. H. Thompson, *The Land and the Book;* Charles Dickens, *House To Let; Atlantic Monthly*]," *Brooklyn Daily Times*, 7 January 1859.

E 2178
"The Evergreens," *Brooklyn Daily Times*, 8 January 1859.

E 2179
"The Ferries," *Brooklyn Daily Times*, 8 January 1859.

E 2180
"The Coroners," *Brooklyn Daily Times*, 10 January 1859.

E 2181
"The Common Council," *Brooklyn Daily Times*, 11 January 1859.

E 2182
"Ferry Rights," *Brooklyn Daily Times*, 12 January 1859.

E 2183
"The County Buildings," *Brooklyn Daily Times*, 13 January 1859.

E 2184
"The Freedom of the Press," *Brooklyn Daily Times*, 14 January 1859.

E 2185
"The Ferry Meeting," *Brooklyn Daily Times*, 15 January 1859.

E 2186
"Godey's Lady's Book," *Brooklyn Daily Times*, 15 January 1859.

E 2187
"The Ferries," *Brooklyn Daily Times*, 17 January 1859.

E 2188
"Lectures and Lecturers," *Brooklyn Daily Times*, 19 January 1859.

Reprinted in *ISL*, pp. 52–53.

E 2189
"The Ferries," *Brooklyn Daily Times*, 19 January 1859.

E 2190
[*Brooklyn Eagle* Quoted in the London *Times*], *Brooklyn Daily Times*, 19 January 1859.

E 2191
"The County Buildings," *Brooklyn Daily Times*, 20 January 1859.

E 2192
"Ferry Matters—Another Postponement," *Brooklyn Daily Times*, 20 January 1859.

E 2193
"The Stationery Contract," *Brooklyn Daily Times*, 21 January 1859.

E 2194
"Congress and Commons," *Brooklyn Daily Times*, 21 January 1859.

E 2195
"The Expenses of Buchanan's Administration," *Brooklyn Daily Times*, 21 January 1859.

Listed in *ISL*.

E 2196
"A Registry Law," *Brooklyn Daily Times*, 22 January 1859.

Listed in *ISL*.

E 2197
"Gerard Stuyvesant," *Brooklyn Daily Times*, 22 January 1859.

E 2198
"Unequal Taxation," *Brooklyn Daily Times*, 24 January 1859.

E 2199
"The Stationery Contract," *Brooklyn Daily Times*, 24 January 1859.

E 2200
"Change of Name," *Brooklyn Daily Times*, 24 January 1859.

E 2201
"New Publications [Edward Bulwer Lytton, *What Will He Do With It?*; *The Comedies of Terence*, trans. Henry Thomas Riley; Holme Lee, *Sylvan Holt's Daughter*; *Harper's Monthly Magazine*; *Atlantic Monthly Magazine*]," *Brooklyn Daily Times*, 24 January 1859.

Partially reprinted in *ISL*, pp. 68–69 (Terence).

E 2202
"The Common Council," *Brooklyn Daily Times*, 25 January 1859.

E 2203
"The Common Council and the Ridgewood Water Works," *Brooklyn Daily Times*, 26 January 1859.

E 2204
"Counterfeit Bank Bills," *Brooklyn Daily Times*, 26 January 1859.

E 2205
"The Health of the City," *Brooklyn Daily Times*, 26 January 1859.

E 2206
"Public Readings," *Brooklyn Daily Times*, 26 January 1859.

E 2207
"Our Municipal Government," *Brooklyn Daily Times*, 27 January 1859.

E 2208
"The State Canals," *Brooklyn Daily Times*, 27 January 1859.

E 2209
"The Ferry Meeting," *Brooklyn Daily Times*, 28 January 1859.

E 2210
"Monument to the Revolutionary Martyrs Who Perished in Wallabout Bay," *Brooklyn Daily Times*, 28 January 1859.

Listed in *ISL*.

E 2211
"The Judiciary," *Brooklyn Daily Times*, 29 January 1859.

E 2212
"Carlyle," *Brooklyn Daily Times*, 29 January 1859.

Listed in *ISL*.

E 2213
"The Next Mayor," *Brooklyn Daily Times*, 31 January 1859.

E 2214
"Free Ferries," *Brooklyn Daily Times*, 31 January 1859.

E 2215
"Eastern District Park," *Brooklyn Daily Times*, 31 January 1859.

E 2216
"Brooklyn Mercantile Library," *Brooklyn Daily Times*, 2 February 1859.

E 2217
"The 15th Ward Park," *Brooklyn Daily Times*, 2 February 1859.

E 2218
"Williamsburgh Local Improvements," *Brooklyn Daily Times*, 2 February 1859.

E 2219
"The County Buildings," *Brooklyn Daily Times*, 4 February 1859.

E 2220
"The 15th Ward Cemetery," *Brooklyn Daily Times*, 4 February 1859.

E 2221
"How the City May Save Money," *Brooklyn Daily Times,* 5 February 1859.

E 2222
"The County Buildings," *Brooklyn Daily Times,* 7 February 1859.

E 2223
"New Publications [Thomas J. Page, *La Plata: The Argentine Confederation, and Paraguay; The Land of Norlaw: A Scottish Story; The House: A Pocket Manual of Rural Architecture*]," *Brooklyn Daily Times,* 7 February 1859.

E 2224
"The Way the Money Goes," *Brooklyn Daily Times,* 9 February 1859.

E 2225
"The Ferry Proprietors," *Brooklyn Daily Times,* 10 February 1859.

E 2226
"The Late W. H. Prescott, the Historian," *Brooklyn Daily Times,* 10 February 1859.

E 2227
"Detection and Punishment of Crime," *Brooklyn Daily Times,* 11 February 1859.

E 2228
"The Normal School," *Brooklyn Daily Times,* 11 February 1859.

Listed in *ISL*.

E 2229
"Normal School Anniversary," *Brooklyn Daily Times,* 11 February 1859.

E 2230
"Churlishness and Clannishness," *Brooklyn Daily Times,* 12 February 1859.

Reprinted in *ISL*, pp. 75–76 (dated '1858').

E 2231
"Grand Street," *Brooklyn Daily Times,* 12 February 1859.

E 2232
"The Ferries," *Brooklyn Daily Times,* 12 February 1859.

E 2233
"The Long Island Railroad Bill," *Brooklyn Daily Times,* 14 February 1859.

E 2234
"The Plagiarised Health Report," *Brooklyn Daily Times,* 15 February 1859.

E 2235
"Book Notices [James Hungerford, *The Old Plantation, and What I Gathered There;* Miss Pardoe, *Episodes of French History During the Consulate and Empire; Godey's Lady's Book*]," *Brooklyn Daily Times,* 16 February 1859.

E 2236
[Politics in the Board of Education], *Brooklyn Daily Times,* 16 February 1859.

E 2237
" 'Editorial Aristocracy,' " *Brooklyn Daily Times,* 16 February 1859.

E 2238
"The Future of Grand Street," *Brooklyn Daily Times,* 18 February 1859.

E 2239
"The Location of Quarantine," *Brooklyn Daily Times,* 19 February 1859.

E 2240
"The Evergreens Cemetery," *Brooklyn Daily Times,* 21 February 1859.

E 2241
"Public Drinking Fountains," *Brooklyn Daily Times,* 21 February 1859.

E 2242
"The Common Council," *Brooklyn Daily Times,* 22 February 1859.

E 2243
"The Ferries," *Brooklyn Daily Times,* 23 February 1859.

E 2244
"The Water Works," *Brooklyn Daily Times,* 23 February 1859.

E 2245
"Another 'Ex-Parte Council,' " *Brooklyn Daily Times,* 23 February 1859.

E 2246
"Legal Decisions," *Brooklyn Daily Times,* 24 February 1859.

E 2247
"A Mercantile Library," *Brooklyn Daily Times*, 24 February 1859.

E 2248
"The Edinburgh Review," *Brooklyn Daily Times*, 24 February 1859.

E 2249
"The Public Library Movement," *Brooklyn Daily Times*, 25 February 1859.

Listed in *ISL*.

E 2250
"Our Twelfth Volume," *Brooklyn Daily Times*, 28 February 1859.

E 2251
"The Rights of People," *Brooklyn Daily Times*, 1 March 1859.

E 2252
"The School Books," *Brooklyn Daily Times*, 1 March 1859.

Listed in *ISL*.

E 2253
"The Sickles Case," *Brooklyn Daily Times*, 1 March 1859.

E 2254
"The Code and the Lawyers," *Brooklyn Daily Times*, 2 March 1859.

E 2255
"The Common Council," *Brooklyn Daily Times*, 2 March 1859.

E 2256
"The Law, the Duello, and Assassination," *Brooklyn Daily Times*, 3 March 1859.

E 2257
"Brooklyn Legislation at Albany," *Brooklyn Daily Times*, 4 March 1859.

E 2258
"Foreclosure Sales," *Brooklyn Daily Times*, 5 March 1859.

E 2259
"The Personality of the Press," *Brooklyn Daily Times*, 7 March 1859.

Listed in *ISL*.

E 2260
"Blackwood's Magazine," *Brooklyn Daily Times,* 7 March 1859.

E 2261
[Douglas or Defeat], *Brooklyn Daily Times,* 7 March 1859.

Reprinted in *ISL,* p. 99.

E 2262
"The Republican Nominations," *Brooklyn Daily Times,* 9 March 1859.

E 2263
[Sickles Case], *Brooklyn Daily Times,* 9 March 1859.

E 2264
"The Sewerage Commission," *Brooklyn Daily Times,* 10 March 1859.

E 2265
"Book Notices [*Matrimonial Brokerage in the Metropolis*]," *Brooklyn Daily Times,* 10 March 1859.

E 2266
"The Meetings Last Evening," *Brooklyn Daily Times,* 11 March 1859.

E 2267
"The Financial Position of the City," *Brooklyn Daily Times,* 12 March 1859.

E 2268
"Ald. Backhouse's Report," *Brooklyn Daily Times,* 12 March 1859.

E 2269
"The Water Commissioners' Defence," *Brooklyn Daily Times,* 14 March 1859.

E 2270
"Our Brooklyn Water Works—The Two or Three Final Facts After All," *Brooklyn Daily Times,* 15 March 1859.

E 2271
"Common Council," *Brooklyn Daily Times,* 15 March 1859.

E 2272
"The Quarrel Between the Water Commissioners and the Common Council," *Brooklyn Daily Times,* 16 March 1859.

E 2273
"The Day [St. Patrick's]," *Brooklyn Daily Times,* 17 March 1859.

E 2274
"Business Prospects, the Coming Season," *Brooklyn Daily Times,* 17 March 1859.

E 2275
"Mike Walsh," *Brooklyn Daily Times,* 18 March 1859.

E 2276
"Patents—America Ahead," *Brooklyn Daily Times,* 19 March 1859.

E 2277
"London Quarterly," *Brooklyn Daily Times,* 19 March 1859.

E 2278
"Did Gen. Nye Get That House and Lot?", *Brooklyn Daily Times,* 21 March 1859.

E 2279
"Book Notices: Madagascar—Curious Interview with a Queen," *Brooklyn Daily Times,* 21 March 1859.

E 2280
"The Water and Sewerage Bills," *Brooklyn Daily Times,* 22 March 1859.

E 2281
"Wonders Will Never Cease [Bayard Taylor]," *Brooklyn Daily Times,* 22 March 1859.

Reprinted in *ISL,* pp. 69–70.

E 2282
"The Mandeville Case," *Brooklyn Daily Times,* 23 March 1859.

E 2283
"The Rates of Taxation," *Brooklyn Daily Times,* 23 March 1859.

E 2284
"The Spring Election," *Brooklyn Daily Times,* 24 March 1859.

E 2285
"Grand Street," *Brooklyn Daily Times,* 24 March 1859.

E 2286
"Bayard Taylor," *Brooklyn Daily Times,* 24 March 1859.

E 2287
"The Police," *Brooklyn Daily Times,* 25 March 1859.

E 2288
"The Eastern District Fountain," *Brooklyn Daily Times,* 26 March 1859.

E 2289
"The Mayoralty," *Brooklyn Daily Times,* 28 March 1859.

E 2290
"Insurance Companies," *Brooklyn Daily Times,* 28 March 1859.

E 2291
"The North British Review," *Brooklyn Daily Times,* 28 March 1859.

E 2292
[Coming Election], *Brooklyn Daily Times,* 29 March 1859.

E 2293
"Female Health," *Brooklyn Daily Times,* 31 March 1859.

Reprinted in *ISL,* pp. 117–118.

E 2294
"The First of April," *Brooklyn Daily Times,* 1 April 1859.

E 2295
"The Election," *Brooklyn Daily Times,* 4 April 1859.

E 2296
"A Word to Eastern District Democrats," *Brooklyn Daily Times,* 4 April 1859.

E 2297
"Mr. Demas Strong and the Times," *Brooklyn Daily Times,* 5 April 1859.

E 2298
"Blackwood's Magazine," *Brooklyn Daily Times,* 5 April 1859.

E 2299
"The Election," *Brooklyn Daily Times,* 6 April 1859.

E 2300
"The Late Contest," *Brooklyn Daily Times*, 7 April 1859.

E 2301
"The Water Celebration," *Brooklyn Daily Times*, 8 April 1859.

E 2302
"The Brooklyn Water Works—Is the Reservoir a Failure?", *Brooklyn Daily Times*, 9 April 1859.

E 2303
"The Police Law—Another Expense Impending," *Brooklyn Daily Times*, 11 April 1859.

E 2304
"New Books [Victor Cousin, *Secret History of the French Court;* Walter Scott, *Waverley Novels;* B. Jaeger, *The Life of North American Insects*]," *Brooklyn Daily Times*, 11 April 1859.

E 2305
"The City and the Fire Department," *Brooklyn Daily Times*, 12 April 1859.

E 2306
"The Reservoir," *Brooklyn Daily Times*, 12 April 1859.

E 2307
"The Supply of Gas," *Brooklyn Daily Times*, 13 April 1859.

E 2308
"The Law of Libel," *Brooklyn Daily Times*, 13 April 1859.

E 2309
"New Books [Mrs. E. D. E. N. Southworth, *The Lady of the Isles; The Romance and Its Hero*]," *Brooklyn Daily Times*, 13 April 1859.

E 2310
"The Sensation Lawyer," *Brooklyn Daily Times*, 14 April 1859.

Listed in *ISL*.

E 2311
"The Sickles Tragedy," *Brooklyn Daily Times*, 14 April 1859.

E 2312
"Ventilation of Public Buildings," *Brooklyn Daily Times,* 15 April 1859.

E 2313
"The Relief of the Poor," *Brooklyn Daily Times,* 15 April 1859.

E 2314
"The Registry Law," *Brooklyn Daily Times,* 16 April 1859.

Listed in *ISL.*

E 2315
"The Celebration—The Water, &c.," *Brooklyn Daily Times,* 18 April 1859.

E 2316
"Politics in England," *Brooklyn Daily Times,* 19 April 1859.

E 2317
"Crinoline and Marriage," *Brooklyn Daily Times,* 20 April 1859.

E 2318
"The Common Council," *Brooklyn Daily Times,* 21 April 1859.

E 2319
"The Lee Avenue Church—Powers of a Consistory," *Brooklyn Daily Times,* 21 April 1859.

E 2320
"The Water Bill," *Brooklyn Daily Times,* 22 April 1859.

E 2321
"Moving Considerations," *Brooklyn Daily Times,* 23 April 1859.

Listed in *ISL.*

E 2322
"Examination Postponed," *Brooklyn Daily Times,* 23 April 1859.

E 2323
"The Celebration," *Brooklyn Daily Times,* 25 April 1859.

E 2324
"The Water Works and the Celebration," *Brooklyn Daily Times,* 26 April 1859.

E 2325
"The Celebration," *Brooklyn Daily Times*, 27 April 1859.

E 2326
"The Celebration," *Brooklyn Daily Times*, 28 April 1859.

E 2327
"The [*Brooklyn*] Star and Ourselves," *Brooklyn Daily Times*, 29 April 1859.

E 2328
"A Library at Last," *Brooklyn Daily Times*, 30 April 1859.

E 2329
"The Moral of the Water Celebration," *Brooklyn Daily Times*, 30 April 1859.

E 2330
"Moving Day," *Brooklyn Daily Times*, 2 May 1859.

E 2331
"The Ferries," *Brooklyn Daily Times*, 2 May 1859.

E 2332
"The Increase of Population," *Brooklyn Daily Times*, 3 May 1859.

E 2333
"Beecherolatry," *Brooklyn Daily Times*, 4 May 1859.

Reprinted in *ISL*, pp. 84–85.

E 2334
"Society and Individuals," *Brooklyn Daily Times*, 5 May 1859.

E 2335
"The Common Council," *Brooklyn Daily Times*, 6 May 1859.

E 2336
"The Mayor's Message," *Brooklyn Daily Times*, 7 May 1859.

E 2337
"The County and the City," *Brooklyn Daily Times*, 9 May 1859.

E 2338
"Book Notices [*Social and Domestic Religion*; Charles Reade, *Love Me Little, Love Me Long*; E. H. Chapin, *A Discourse on Shameful Life*; Walter Scott, *The Abbott* and *The Antiquary*]," *Brooklyn Daily Times*, 9 May 1859.

E 2339
"The Mayor, the Ordinances, and the Public Conveniences," *Brooklyn Daily Times*, 10 May 1859.

E 2340
"The Republicans and the Local Press," *Brooklyn Daily Times*, 11 May 1859.

E 2341
"About Humbug," *Brooklyn Daily Times*, 11 May 1859.

E 2342
"Drunking Dydrants," *Brooklyn Daily Times*, 11 May 1859.

E 2343
[Advertising Is Essential], *Brooklyn Daily Times*, 11 May 1859.

E 2344
"The Democratic Party, Locally," *Brooklyn Daily Times*, 12 May 1859.

E 2345
"The Republicans and the Newspapers," *Brooklyn Daily Times*, 12 May 1859.

E 2346
"Our Contemporaries," *Brooklyn Daily Times*, 13 May 1859.

E 2347
"Modes of Salutation," *Brooklyn Daily Times*, 13 May 1859.

E 2348
"The Police," *Brooklyn Daily Times*, 13 May 1859.

E 2349
"Publications [*Monthly Casket; Dinsmore's American Railroad and Steam Navigation Guide; Typographic Advertiser*]," *Brooklyn Daily Times*, 13 May 1859.

E 2350
"Trade Unions," *Brooklyn Daily Times*, 14 May 1859.

E 2351
"Causes of Insanity," *Brooklyn Daily Times*, 16 May 1859.

Listed in *ISL*.

E 2352
"War in Europe," *Brooklyn Daily Times,* 16 May 1859.

E 2353
"Publications [*Edinburgh Review;* Charles Lever, *Gerald Fitzgerald*]," *Brooklyn Daily Times,* 16 May 1859.

E 2354
"The Collection of Taxes," *Brooklyn Daily Times,* 17 May 1859.

E 2355
"The Ferries and the Railroads," *Brooklyn Daily Times,* 18 May 1859.

E 2356
"The Truant Officers," *Brooklyn Daily Times,* 19 May 1859.

E 2357
"The Inebriate Asylum," *Brooklyn Daily Times,* 20 May 1859.

E 2358
"The Ferries," *Brooklyn Daily Times,* 20 May 1859.

E 2359
"Publications [Charles Dickens, *A Tale of Two Cities; Peterson's Waverley Novels; Godey's Lady's Book; Arthur's Home Magazine*]," *Brooklyn Daily Times,* 20 May 1859.

Partially reprinted in *ISL,* p. 70 (Dickens).

E 2360
"What Is a Fool? [Fanny Fern]," *Brooklyn Daily Times,* 20 May 1859.

E 2361
"Spasmodic Movements," *Brooklyn Daily Times,* 21 May 1859.

E 2362
"Hydropathy," *Brooklyn Daily Times,* 21 May 1859.

E 2363
"Three Incidents in Russian History," *Brooklyn Register,* 21 May 1859.

Reprinted in William White, "Some Uncollected Whitman Journalism," *Emerson Society Quarterly,* no. 33 (4th Quarter 1963), 84–90.

E 2364
"East Long Island," *Brooklyn Register,* 21 May 1859.

E 2365
"The War [Between Italy and Austria]," *Brooklyn Daily Times,* 23 May 1859.

Listed in *ISL.*

E 2366
"Mr. R. M. Demill and the South Seventh Street Ferry," *Brooklyn Daily Times,* 24 May 1859.

E 2367
"How to Be Healthy [D. H. Jacques, *Hints Towards Physical Perfection; or the Philosophy of Human Beauty*]," *Brooklyn Daily Times,* 24 May 1859.

E 2368
"Street Sketches.—The Chiffonier," *Brooklyn Daily Times,* 25 May 1859.

E 2369
[All Belief Governed by Circumstances], *Brooklyn Daily Times,* 25 May 1859.

E 2370
"The Mayor and the Aldermen—The Appointing and the Confirming Power," *Brooklyn Daily Times,* 26 May 1859.

E 2371
"The Austrian Butchers," *Brooklyn Daily Times,* 27 May 1859.

E 2372
"Accidents in the Streets.—Who's to Blame?", *Brooklyn Daily Times,* 27 May 1859.

E 2373
"Tracts and Their Authors," *Brooklyn Daily Times,* 27 May 1859.

E 2374
"The City Ordinances," *Brooklyn Daily Times,* 28 May 1859.

E 2375
"Facts About Water," *Brooklyn Daily Times,* 28 May 1859.

Listed in *ISL.*

E 2376
"Ferry Matters," *Brooklyn Daily Times*, 28 May 1859.

E 2377
"Sporting Matters," *Brooklyn Daily Times*, 30 May 1859.

E 2378
"The London Quarterly Review," *Brooklyn Daily Times*, 30 May 1859.

E 2379
"The Ferries," *Brooklyn Daily Times*, 31 May 1859.

E 2380
"The Common Council," *Brooklyn Daily Times*, 31 May 1859.

E 2381
"Renumbering and Renaming the Streets," *Brooklyn Daily Times*, 1 June 1859.

E 2382
"Drinking Hydrants," *Brooklyn Daily Times*, 1 June 1859.

E 2383
"The Fire Commissioners," *Brooklyn Daily Times*, 2 June 1859.

E 2384
"The Case of Ald. Deyton," *Brooklyn Daily Times*, 3 June 1859.

E 2385
"Street Music," *Brooklyn Daily Times*, 3 June 1859.

E 2386
"Criminal Statistics," *Brooklyn Daily Times*, 4 June 1859.

E 2387
"Re–naming the Streets," *Brooklyn Daily Times*, 4 June 1859.

E 2388
"The Tribulations of Flushing," *Brooklyn Daily Times*, 6 June 1859.

E 2389
[Lack of Street Lamps], *Brooklyn Daily Times*, 6 June 1859.

E 2390
"Franchises and Corporations," *Brooklyn Daily Times,* 7 June 1859.

E 2391
"The Public Schools," *Brooklyn Daily Times,* 8 June 1859.

Listed in *ISL.*

E 2392
"The Rival Ferries.—Which Will Sink?", *Brooklyn Daily Times,* 8 June 1859.

Listed in *ISL.*

E 2393
"The New Ferry," *Brooklyn Daily Times,* 9 June 1859.

Listed in *ISL.*

E 2394
"The 'Bertrams,' a Novel by Anthony Trollope," *Brooklyn Daily Times,* 9 June 1859.

E 2395
"The Ecomony of Sight," *Brooklyn Daily Times,* 10 June 1859.

Listed in *ISL.*

E 2396
"The St. Louis Breach of Promise of Marriage Case," *Brooklyn Daily Times,* 10 June 1859.

E 2397
"Lord Byron and the Maid of Athens," *Brooklyn Daily Times,* 10 June 1859.

E 2398
"Public School Teaching," *Brooklyn Daily Times,* 11 June 1859.

Listed in *ISL.*

E 2399
"Book Notices [Henry Alford, *The Greek Testament, with a . . . Revised Text;* Charles Kingsley, *The Good News of God;* Eliza W. Farnham, *My Early Days*]," *Brooklyn Daily Times,* 11 June 1859.

E 2400
"Shell Houses," *Brooklyn Daily Times*, 13 June 1859.

E 2401
"Strawberry Festivals," *Brooklyn Daily Times*, 13 June 1859.

E 2402
"Dr. J. H. Robinson and the New York Mercury," *Brooklyn Daily Times*, 13 June 1859.

E 2403
"The Common Council," *Brooklyn Daily Times*, 14 June 1859.

E 2404
"Strawberry Festival," *Brooklyn Daily Times*, 14 June 1859.

E 2405
"The Times," *Brooklyn Daily Times*, 15 June 1859.

E 2406
"More Gold," *Brooklyn Daily Times*, 15 June 1859.

Reprinted in *ISL*, p. 99. Not in White, *Journalism*.

E 2407
"Street Openings," *Brooklyn Daily Times*, 16 June 1859.

E 2408
"The Official Contract," *Brooklyn Daily Times*, 17 June 1859.

E 2409
[Egoism of the *Brooklyn Daily Eagle*], *Brooklyn Daily Times*, 17 June 1859.

E 2410
"Creditors' Rights," *Brooklyn Daily Times*, 18 June 1859.

E 2411
"The 13th Ward Bell Tower," *Brooklyn Daily Times*, 18 June 1859.

E 2412
"A Delicate Subject [Prostitution]," *Brooklyn Daily Times*, 20 June 1859.

Reprinted in *ISL*, pp. 119–120.

E 2413
"The First Great Battle," *Brooklyn Daily Times,* 20 June 1859.

E 2414
"The Common Council," *Brooklyn Daily Times,* 21 June 1859.

E 2415
"Unsound Churches," *Brooklyn Daily Times,* 21 June 1859.

E 2416
"Can All Marry?", *Brooklyn Daily Times,* 21 June 1859.

Reprinted in *ISL,* pp. 120–122 (dated '22 June').

E 2417
"The [Franco-Austrian] War," *Brooklyn Daily Times,* 22 June 1859.

E 2418
"The Ferry-Reduction of Fare," *Brooklyn Daily Times,* 23 June 1859.

E 2419
"Telegraph Between Brooklyn, Williamsburgh, and New York," *Brooklyn Daily Times,* 23 June 1859.

E 2420
"Prospect Hill Reservoir," *Brooklyn Daily Times,* 24 June 1859.

E 2421
"Shaking Hands and Making Affidavits," *Brooklyn Daily Times,* 25 June 1859.

E 2422
"Improvements in Our Ferries," *Brooklyn Daily Times,* 25 June 1859.

E 2423
"Literary Notices [N. F. Moore, *Ancient Mineralogy; Atlantic Monthly; Blackwood's Magazine*]," *Brooklyn Daily Times,* 25 June 1859.

E 2424
"A Central Park for Brooklyn," *Brooklyn Daily Times,* 27 June 1859.

E 2425
"The Atlantic Cable," *Brooklyn Daily Times,* 27 June 1859.

E 2426
"New Books [Miss Mulock, *John Halifax;* J. S. Edgar, *The War of the Roses;* Alexander von Humboldt, *Kosmos: A Description of the Universe*]," *Brooklyn Daily Times,* 27 June 1859.

E 2427
"Thomas Paine," *Brooklyn Daily Times,* 28 June 1859.

E 2428
"The Ferries," *Brooklyn Daily Times,* 28 June 1859.

E 2429
"Mine and Thine," *Brooklyn Daily Times,* 29 June 1859.

E 2430
"The Water Board," *Brooklyn Daily Times,* 29 June 1859.

E 2431
"The City Finances," *Brooklyn Daily Times,* 30 June 1859.

E 2432
"Naturalized Citizen and Foreign Powers," *Brooklyn Daily Times,* 30 June 1859.

E 2433
[At the Pewter Mug], *Brooklyn Daily Times,* 2 August 1859.

Reprinted in *ISL,* pp. 184–185, as of "possible Whitman authorship."

E 2434
"A Child's Reminiscence," *Saturday Press* (New York), 24 September 1859.

Poem. Revised as "A Word Out of the Sea" in *Leaves of Grass* (1860), pp. 269–277; as "Out of the Cradle Endlessly Rocking" in *Passage to India* (A 5), pp. 71–78. Reprinted in *A Child's Reminiscence* (A 29), pp. 11–18.

E 2435
"A Ballad of Long Island," *Brooklyn City News,* 24 December 1859.

Attributed by Herbert Bergman, "Walt Whitman: Self Advertiser," *Bulletin of the New York Public Library,* 74 (December 1970), 634–639.

E 2436
[William Hartshorne], *Brooklyn Daily Eagle,* 31 December 1859.

Reprinted in William White, "A Tribute to William Hartshorne: Unrecorded Whitman," *American Literature*, 42 (January 1971), 544–548.

E 2437
"All About a Mocking-Bird," *Saturday Press* (New York), 2, no. 1 (7 January 1860), 3.

Reprinted in *A Child's Reminiscence* (A 29), pp. 19–21.

E 2438
"Walt Whitman: *Leaves of Grass*," *Saturday Press* (New York), 2, no. 20 (7 January 1860).

Reprinted in *A Child's Reminiscence* (A 29), pp. 22–28.

E 2439
"You and Me and To-day," *Saturday Press* (New York), 14 January 1860.

Poem. Revised as "Chants Democratic. 7," in *Leaves of Grass* (1860), pp. 174–176; reprinted as "With Antecedents," *Leaves of Grass* (1867), pp. 182–184.

E 2440
"Bardic Symbols," *Atlantic Monthly Magazine*, 5 (April 1860), 445–447.

Poem. Revised as "Leaves of Grass. 1" in *Leaves of Grass* (1860), pp. 195–199; reprinted as "Elemental Drifts," *Leaves of Grass* (1867), pp. 331–334; as "As I Ebb'd With the Ocean of Life," *Leaves of Grass* (1881), pp. 202–204.

E 2441
"The Errand-Bearers (16th, 6th Month, Year 84 of The States)," *New York Times*, 27 June 1860.

Poem. Revised as "A Broadway Pageant (Reception Japanese Embassy, June 16, 1860)" in *Drum-Taps* (A 3), pp. 61–65; reprinted in *New York Citizen*, 5 September 1868; reprinted as "A Broadway Pageant" in *Leaves of Grass* (1881), pp. 193–196.

E 2442
"Longings from Home," *Southern Literary Messenger*, 31 (15 July 1860), 74.

Poem. Reprinted as "Longings for Home" in *Leaves of Grass* (1860), pp. 389–390; reprinted as "O Magnet-South" in *Leaves of Grass* (1881), pp. 359–360.

E 2443
"A Brooklynite Criticised," *Brooklyn City News*, 10 October 1860.

Reprinted in *Walt Whitman's Autograph Revision* (A 44), pp. 143–145.

E 2444

"Brooklyniana; A Series of Local Articles, on Past and Present. No. 1," *Brooklyn Daily Standard,* 3 June 1861.

Reprinted in *Brooklyn Weekly Standard,* 8 June 1861; *Brooklyn Standard,* 21 December 1861; *UPP,* II, 222–227.

E 2445

"Brooklyniana. No. 2," *Brooklyn Daily Standard,* 5 June 1861.

Reprinted in *Brooklyn Weekly Standard,* 8 June 1861; *Brooklyn Standard,* 28 December 1861; *UPP,* II, 227–230.

E 2446

"Brooklyniana. No. 3," *Brooklyn Daily Standard,* 12 June 1861.

Reprinted in *Brooklyn Standard,* 28 December 1861; *UPP,* II, 230–232.

E 2447

"Beat! Beat! Drums!", *Boston Daily Evening Transcript,* 24 September 1861.

Poem. Reprinted in *New York Leader,* 28 September 1861; *Harper's Weekly Magazine,* 28 September 1861; *Drum-Taps* (A 3), p. 38.

E 2448

"Little Bells Last Night," *New York Leader,* 12 October 1861.

Poem. Revised as "I Heard You Solemn Sweet Pipes of the Organ" in *Sequel to Drum-Taps* (A 3), p. 7.

E 2449

"Old Ireland," *New York Leader,* 2 November 1861.

Poem. Reprinted in *Drum-Taps* (A 3), p. 66.

E 2450

"Brooklyniana. No. 4," *Brooklyn Standard,* 28 December 1861.

Reprinted in *UPP,* II, 232–235.

E 2451

"Letters from a Travelling Bachelor, Number IV," *Brooklyn Standard,* 1862.

Reprinted in William White, "Some Uncollected Whitman Journalism," *Emerson Society Quarterly,* no. 33 (4th Quarter 1963), 84–90.

E 2452
"Brooklyniana. No. 5 [first part]," *Brooklyn Standard,* 4 January 1862.

Reprinted in *UPP,* II, 236–245.

E 2453
"Important Ecclesiastical Gathering at Jamaica, L.I.," *Brooklyn City News,* 9 January 1862.

E 2454
"Brooklyniana. No. 5 [second part] and No. 6," *Brooklyn Standard,* 11 January 1862.

Reprinted in *UPP,* II, 245–249.

E 2455
"Brooklyniana. No. 7," *Brooklyn Standard,* 18 January 1862.

Reprinted in *UPP,* II, 249–253.

E 2456
"Brooklyniana. No. 8," *Brooklyn Standard,* 25 January 1862.

Reprinted in *UPP,* II, 253–257.

E 2457
"Brooklyniana. No. 9," *Brooklyn Standard,* 1 February 1862.

Reprinted in *UPP,* II, 257–261.

E 2458
"Brooklyniana. No. 10," *Brooklyn Standard,* 8 February 1862.

Reprinted in *UPP,* II, 261–267.

E 2459
"Brooklyniana. No. 11," *Brooklyn Standard,* 15 February 1862.

Reprinted in *UPP,* II, 267–270.

E 2460
"Brooklyniana. No. 12," *Brooklyn Standard,* 22 February 1862.

Reprinted in *UPP,* II, 270–274.

E 2461
"Brooklyniana. No. 13," *Brooklyn Standard*, 1 March 1862.

Reprinted in *UPP*, II, 274–278.

E 2462
"Brooklyniana. No. 14," *Brooklyn Standard*, 8 March 1862.

Reprinted in *UPP*, II, 278–283.

E 2463
"Brooklyniana. No. 15," *Brooklyn Standard*, 15 March 1862.

Reprinted in *UPP*, II, 283–288.

E 2464
"City Photographs. I. The Broadway Hospital," *New York Leader*, 15 March 1862.

Reprinted in *Civil War*, pp. 24–29.

E 2465
"City Photographs. II. The Broadway Hospital," *New York Leader*, 22 March 1862.

Reprinted in *Civil War*, pp. 29–34.

E 2466
"Brooklyniana. No. 16," *Brooklyn Standard*, 29 March 1862.

Reprinted in *UPP*, II, 288–292.

E 2467
"City Photographs. III. The Broadway Hospital," *New York Leader*, 29 March 1862.

Reprinted in *Civil War*, pp. 34–39.

E 2468
"Brooklyniana. No. 17," *Brooklyn Standard*, 5 April 1862.

Reprinted in *UPP*, II, 292–296.

E 2469
"City Photographs. IV. The Broadway Hospital," *New York Leader*, 12 April 1862.

Reprinted in *Civil War*, pp. 40–47.

E 2470
"Brooklyniana. No. 18," *Brooklyn Standard*, 19 April 1862.

Reprinted in *UPP*, II, 296–300.

E 2471
"City Photographs. V. The Bowery," *New York Leader*, 19 April 1862.

Reprinted in *Civil War*, pp. 47–52.

E 2472
"City Photographs. VI. The Bowery," *New York Leader*, 3 May 1862.

Reprinted in *Civil War*, pp. 52–58.

E 2473
"City Photographs. VII. The Bowery," *New York Leader*, 17 May 1862.

Reprinted in *Civil War*, pp. 58–62.

E 2474
"Brooklyniana. No. 35," *Brooklyn Standard*, 30 August 1862.

Reprinted in *UPP*, II, 300–304.

E 2475
"Brooklyniana. No. 35—Continued," *Brooklyn Standard*, 6 September 1862.

Reprinted in *UPP*, II, 304–306.

E 2476
"Brooklyniana. No. 36," *Brooklyn Standard*, 20 September 1862.

Reprinted in *UPP*, II, 306–309.

E 2477
"Brooklyniana. No. 36—Continued," *Brooklyn Standard*, 27 September 1862.

Reprinted in *UPP*, II, 309–312.

E 2478
"An Old Landmark Gone. An Interesting Reminiscence of Old Times in Brooklyn," *Brooklyn Daily Eagle*, 9 October 1862.

Reprinted in Arthur Golden, "An Uncollected Whitman Article," *Bulletin of the New York Public Library*, 64 (July 1960), 358–360.

E 2479
"Brooklyniana. No. 37," *Brooklyn Standard*, 11 October 1862.

Reprinted in *UPP*, II, 312–316.

E 2480
"Brooklyniana. No. 38," *Brooklyn Standard*, 25 October 1862.

Reprinted in *UPP*, II, 316–318.

E 2481
"Brooklyniana. No. 39," *Brooklyn Standard*, 1 November 1862.

Reprinted in *UPP*, II, 319–321.

E 2482
"Our Brooklyn Boys in the War," *Brooklyn Daily Eagle*, 5 January 1863.

E 2483
"The Great Army of the Sick," *New York Times*, 26 February 1863.

Partially reprinted in *Memoranda During the War* (A 8), pp. 10–11; reprinted (partial) as "Patent-Office Hospital" in *Specimen Days* (A 11), pp. 30–31; as "The Great Army of the Wounded" in *The Wound Dresser* (A 15), pp. 1–10. See *PW92*, I, 39–40, 296–300.

E 2484
"Exemption from Military Service," *New York Times*, 15 March 1863.

Reprinted in Charles I. Glicksberg, "A Whitman Letter," *New York Times*, 1 May 1931, p. 26.

E 2485
"Life Among Fifty Thousand Soldiers," *Brooklyn Daily Eagle*, 19 March 1863.

Letter of 19 March 1863 to Nat and Fred Gray. Reprinted in *The Wound Dresser* (A 15), pp. 11–19; "Unpublished Letter of Walt Whitman," *New York Evening Post*, 7 September 1918, sec. 3, p. 1; *UPP*, II, 21–26.

E 2486
"Washington in the Hot Season," *New York Times*, 16 August 1863.

Reprinted (partial) in *Memoranda During the War* (A 8), pp. 21–24; in various places in *Specimen Days* (A 11). See *PW92*, I, 22–23, 57–63, 301–302.

E 2487
"From Washington. Military Anxieties . . . ," *Brooklyn Daily Union*, 22 September 1863.

Reprinted in *UPP*, II, 26–29.

E 2488
"Letter from Washington. Our National City . . . ," *New York Times*, 4 October 1863.

Reprinted in *UPP*, II, 29–36.

E 2489
"The Smithsonian," *Armory Square Hospital Gazette* (Washington), 13 January 1864.

Reprinted in Thomas Donaldson, *Walt Whitman* (D 29), in facsimile, following p. 140.

E 2490
"Fifty-First New-York City Veterans," *New York Times*, 29 October 1864.

Reprinted in *UPP*, II, 37–41.

E 2491
"Our Brooklyn Soldiers," *Brooklyn Daily Union*, 1 December 1864.

Possibly by Whitman; see *Notebooks*, II, 735.

E 2492
"Our Wounded and Sick Soldiers—Visits Among Army Hospitals, at Washington, on the Field, and Here in New York," *New York Times*, 11 December 1864.

Reprinted (partial) in *New York Weekly Graphic*, 14 February 1874, 28 February 1874, and 7 March 1874; in various places in *Memoranda During the War* (A 8); in various places in *Specimen Days* (A 11); as "Hospital Visits" in *The Wound Dresser* (A 15), pp. 21–46. See *PW92*, I, 22–23, 32–38, 44–45, 52–53, 56, 65–66, 72–74, 81–85, 97–98, 302–309.

E 2493
"What Stops the General Exchange of Prisoners of War?", *Brooklyn Daily Eagle*, 27 December 1864.

Reprinted as "[Prisoner of War Letter]," *New York Times*, 27 December 1864; in *Civil War*, pp. 178–180.

E 2494
"A Brooklyn Soldier and a Noble One," *Brooklyn Daily Union*, 19 January 1865.

Reprinted in Jerome M. Loving, " 'A Brooklyn Soldier and a Noble One': A *Brooklyn Daily Union* Article by Whitman," *Walt Whitman Review*, 20 (March 1974), 27–30.

E 2495
"The Soldiers," *New York Times*, 6 March 1865.

Reprinted (partial) in *New York Weekly Graphic*, 28 February 1874; in various places in *Memoranda During the War* (A 8); in various places in *Specimen Days* (A 11). See *PW92*, I, 23, 43–44, 85–89, 309.

E 2496
"News from Washington," *New York Times*, 12 March 1865, p. 5.

Reprinted in various places in *Memoranda During the War* (A 8); in various places in *Specimen Days* (A 11); W. T. Bandy, "An Unknown 'Washington' Letter by Walt Whitman," *Walt Whitman Quarterly Review*, 2, no. 3 (Winter 1984), 23–27.

E 2497
"Return of a Brooklyn Veteran. Campaigning for Four Years," *Brooklyn Daily Union*, 16 March 1865.

Reprinted in *Civil War*, pp. 86–89.

E 2498
"Passing Events," *Armory Square Hospital Gazette* (Washington), 20 May 1865.

Reprinted in Emory Holloway, "Whitman and the War's Finale," *Colophon*, 1, part 1 (February 1930), [7 pp.; unpaged].

E 2499
"Our Veterans Mustering Out," *Brooklyn Daily Union*, 5 August 1865.

Reprinted in Jerome M. Loving, " 'Our Veterans Mustering Out'—Another Newspaper Article by Whitman about His Soldier-Brother," *Yale University Library Gazette*, 49 (October 1974), 217–224.

E 2500
"O Captain! My Captain!", *Saturday Press* (New York), 4 November 1865.

Poem. Reprinted in *Sequel to Drum-Taps* (A 3), p. 13.

E 2501
Conway, Moncure D. "Walt Whitman," *Fortnightly Review*, 6 (15 October 1866), 538–548.

Letter of [September? 1866] to Moncure D. Conway (pp. 546–547). Reprinted in Whitman's *Poems,* ed. Rossetti (C 1; D 6), pp. 17–18.

E 2502
"A Carol of Harvest for 1867," *New York Weekly Tribune,* 21 August 1867, p. 8.

Poem. Revised in *Galaxy,* September 1867 (E 2503). Reprinted in *Tinsley's Magazine* (London), October 1867; revised as "The Return of the Heroes" in *Leaves of Grass* (1881), pp. 278–282.

E 2503
"A Carol of Harvest for 1867," *Galaxy,* 4 (September 1867), 605–609.

Revised from the *New York Weekly Tribune,* 21 August 1867 (E 2502).

E 2504
"Democracy," *Galaxy,* 4 (December 1867), 919–933.

Combined with "Personalism" (*Galaxy,* May 1868 [E 2505]) in *Democratic Vistas* (A 4); reprinted in *Specimen Days* (A 11), pp. 203–258.

E 2505
"Personalism," *Galaxy,* 5 (May 1868), 540–547.

Combined with "Democracy" (*Galaxy,* December 1867 [E 2504]) in *Democratic Vistas* (A 4); reprinted in *Specimen Days* (A 11), pp. 203–258.

E 2506
"Whispers of Heavenly Death," *Broadway* (London), 10 (October 1868), 180 (also n.s. 1, 21–22).

Poems (all later reprinted in *Passage to India* [A 5]): "Whispers of Heavenly Death" (p. 63), "Darest Thou Now O Soul" (p. 64), "A Noiseless Patient Spider" (p. 69), "At the Last Tenderly" (as "The Last Invocation," p. 69), "Pensive and Faltering" (p. 70).

E 2507
"Personal," *Sunday Morning Chronicle* (Washington), October 1868.

Reprinted in *Correspondence,* II, 64–65n.

E 2508
"Minor Topics," *New York Times,* 1 October 1868.

Submitted by Whitman; see *Correspondence,* II, 49–50. Reprinted in *Washington Star,* 2 October 1868.

E 2509
"Proud Music of the Sea-Storm," *Atlantic Monthly Magazine,* 23 (February 1869), 199–203.

Poem. Reprinted as "Proud Music of the Storm" in *Passage to India* (A 5), pp. 17–24.

E 2510
[On Whitman], *Washington Daily Morning Chronicle,* 9 May 1869.

Possibly by Whitman; reprinted in Emory Holloway, "Whitman as His Own Press-Agent," *American Mercury,* 18 (December 1929), 482–483.

E 2511
"The Singer in the Prison," *Saturday Evening Visitor* (Washington), 25 December 1869.

Poem. Reprinted in *Passage to India* (A 5), pp. 94–96.

E 2512
"Brother of All, With Generous Hand," *Galaxy,* 9 (January 1870), 75–76.

Poem. Revised as "Outlines for a Tomb: (G. P., Buried 1870)" in *Passage to India* (A 5), pp. 108–111.

E 2513
"Warble for Lilac-Time," *Galaxy,* 9 (May 1870), 686.

Poem. Reprinted in *New York Daily Graphic,* 12 May 1873; *Passage to India* (A 5), pp. 96–98.

E 2514
[Article], *Washington Evening Star,* 17 October 1870.

Manuscript facsimile. Reprinted in F. DeWolfe Miller, "Struggling Walt Whitman Had Press Agent's Skill," *Washington Sunday Star,* 30 July 1961, p. C-3.

E 2515
"O Star of France," *Galaxy,* 11 (June 1871), 817.

Poem. Reprinted in *As a Strong Bird on Pinions Free* (A 7), pp. 13–14.

E 2516
"The Fair of the American Institute. Walt Whitman's Poem" ["After All, Not to Create Only"], *New York Evening Post,* 7 September 1871, p. 2.

Poem. Also on 7 September: "The American Institute. Inauguration of the Fair. The Opening Exercises—Poem by Walt Whitman," *New York Commercial Advertiser,* p. 3; *Brooklyn Standard; Washington Daily Morning Chronicle.* Reprinted as "American Institute Fair," *New York Times,* 8 September 1871, p. 2; *New York Daily Tribune,* 8 September 1871; "Poetry and Ploughs . . . Barbaric Yaup [sic] from Whitman," *New York World,* 8 September 1871, p. 8; *Springfield Daily Republican,* 9 September 1871; *Washington Evening Star,* 7–8 September 1871. Reprinted as *After All, Not to Create Only* (A 6); as "Song of the Exposition" in "Centennial Songs" section of *Two Rivulets* (A 9), pp. 3–11.

E 2517
"The Mystic Trumpeter," *Kansas Magazine,* 1 (February 1872), 113–114.

Poem. Reprinted in *Washington Daily Morning Chronicle,* 7 February 1872; in translation by Csukássy József, *Fõvárosi Lapok* (Budapest), 19 January 1873, p. [61]; *As a Strong Bird on Pinions Free* (A 7), pp. 8–12.

E 2518
"Virginia—The West," *Kansas Magazine,* 1 (March 1872), 219.

Poem. Reprinted in *As a Strong Bird on Pinions Free* (A 7), p. 15.

E 2519
"An Aging Man of Genius Needing Help—An Appeal from Walt Whitman," *Washington Daily Morning Chronicle,* 26 April 1872.

Contributed by Whitman. Reprinted in Edwin H. Miller, "Walt Whitman and Louis Fitzgerald Tasistro," *Walt Whitman Review,* 7 (March 1961), 14–16.

E 2520
"Dartmouth College. The Exercises Marred by the Inclement Weather—Walt Whitman's Poem," *New York Herald,* 26 June 1872, p. 3.

Poem ("As a Strong Bird on Pinions Free"). Also on 26 June: as "Walt Whitman's Poem Today at Dartmouth College," *Washington Evening Star* (reprinted in William White, "Whitman at Dartmouth: 1872–1972," *Long-Islander,* 1 June 1972, sec. I, p. 5). Reprinted in *As a Strong Bird on Pinions Free* (A 7), pp. 1–7.

E 2521
"Band Music in Washington," *Washington Sunday Herald,* 20 October 1872.

Reprinted in Emory Holloway, "Whitman and Band Music," *Walt Whitman Review,* 6 (September 1960), 51–52.

E 2522
"A Tip-Top Caricature," *Washington Evening Star,* 22 November 1872, p. 1.

Prose manuscript facsimile. Reprinted in F. DeWolfe Miller, "Struggling Walt Whitman Had Press Agent's Skill," *Washington Sunday Star,* 30 July 1961, p. C-3.

E 2523
Hinton, Richard J. "Walt Whitman in Europe," *Kansas Magazine,* 1 (December 1872), 499–502.

Written by Whitman; see *Correspondence,* V, 295.

E 2524
"Nay, Tell Me Not To-day the Publish'd Shame: Winter of 1873, Congress in Session," *New York Daily Graphic,* 5 March 1873.

Poem. Reprinted in *Conservator,* 7 (October 1896), 121–122; *Leaves of Grass* (1897), pp. 426–427.

E 2525
"With All Thy Gifts," *New York Daily Graphic,* 6 March 1873.

Poem. Reprinted in the "Two Rivulets" section of *Two Rivulets* (A 9), p. 30.

E 2526
"The Singing Thrush," *New York Daily Graphic,* 15 March 1873.

Poem. Reprinted as "Wandering at Morn" in the "Two Rivulets" section of *Two Rivulets* (A 9), p. 28.

E 2527
"Spain," *New York Daily Graphic,* 24 March 1873.

Poem. Reprinted as "Spain, 1873–74" in the "Two Rivulets" section of *Two Rivulets* (A 9), p. 20.

E 2528
"Sea Captains, Young or Old," *New York Daily Graphic,* 4 April 1873.

Poem. Reprinted as "Song for All Seas, All Ships" in the "Centennial Songs" section of *Two Rivulets* (A 9), pp. 17–18.

E 2529
Anon. "Walt Whitman," *New York Times,* 20 August 1873, p. 5.

Undated letter to an unidentified correspondent (possibly Whitelaw Reid).

E 2530
"Halls of Gold and Lilac," *New York Daily Graphic,* 3 (24 November 1873), 157.

Reprinted in *UPP,* II, 42–49.

E 2531
"Silver and Salmon-Tint," *New York Daily Graphic,* 3 (29 November 1873), 189.

Reprinted in *UPP,* II, 49–53.

E 2532
" 'Tis But Ten Years Since [First Paper]," *New York Weekly Graphic,* 24 January 1874.

Reprinted (partial) in various places in *Memoranda During the War* (A 8); *New York Tribune,* 15 April 1879; in various places in *Specimen Days* (A 11). See *PW92,* I, 310–313; II, 757–758.

E 2533
"Song of the Redwood-Tree," *Harper's Monthly Magazine,* 48 (February 1874), 366–367.

Poem. Reprinted in the "Centennial Songs" section of *Two Rivulets* (A 9), pp. 12–15.

E 2534
" 'Tis But Ten Years Since [Second Paper]," *New York Weekly Graphic,* 7 February 1874.

Reprinted (partial) in various places in *Memoranda During the War* (A 8); in various places in *Specimen Days* (A 11). See *PW92,* I, 313–314; II, 757–758.

E 2535
" 'Tis But Ten Years Since [Third Paper]," *New York Weekly Graphic,* 14 February 1874.

Reprinted (partial) in various places in *Memoranda During the War* (A 8); in various places in *Specimen Days* (A 11). See *PW92,* I, 314–316; II, 757–758.

E 2536
" 'Tis But Ten Years Since [Fourth Paper]," *New York Weekly Graphic*, 21 February 1874.

Reprinted (partial) in various places in *Memoranda During the War* (A 8); in various places in *Specimen Days* (A 11); as "Army Hospitals and Cases" in *Century Magazine*, October 1888 (E 2714). See *PW92*, I, 316–318; II, 757–758.

E 2537
" 'Tis But Ten Years Since [Fifth Paper]," *New York Weekly Graphic*, 28 February 1874.

Reprinted (partial) in various places in *Memoranda During the War* (A 8); in various places in *Specimen Days* (A 11); as "Army Hospitals and Cases," *Century Magazine*, October 1888 (E 2714). See *PW92*, I, 318–319; II, 757–758.

E 2538
"Prayer of Columbus," *Harper's Monthly Magazine*, 48 (March 1874), 524–525.

Poem. Reprinted in the "Two Rivulets" section of *Two Rivulets* (A 9), pp. 21–23.

E 2539
" 'Tis But Ten Years Since [Sixth Paper]," *New York Weekly Graphic*, 7 March 1874.

Reprinted (partial) in various places in *Memoranda During the War* (A 8); in various places in *Specimen Days* (A 11); as "Army Hospitals and Cases," *Century Magazine*, October 1888 (E 2714). See *PW92*, I, 319–320; II, 757–758.

E 2540
"A Kiss to the Bride: Marriage of Nelly Grant, May 21, 1874," *New York Daily Graphic*, 21 May 1874.

Poem. Reprinted in *Leaves of Grass* (1897), p. 426.

E 2541
"Song of the Universal," *New York Daily Graphic*, 17 June 1874.

Poem. Also on 17 June in *New York Evening Post*. Reprinted in *Springfield Daily Republican*, 18 June 1874; *New York World*, 19 June 1874; *Camden New Republic*, 20 June 1874; "Centennial Songs" section of *Two Rivulets* (A 9), pp. 15–17.

E 2542
"An Old Man's Thought of School," *New York Daily Graphic*, 3 November 1874.

Poem. Revised in the "Two Rivulets" section of *Two Rivulets* (A 9), p. 29.

E 2543
"Death of a Fireman," *Camden New Republic*, 14 November 1874.

Reprinted (with other material) as "Three Young Men's Deaths" in *Cope's Tobacco Plant* (Liverpool), April 1879 (E 2567); *Specimen Days* (A 11), pp. 101–108.

E 2544
Anon. "Walt Whitman on Spooks," *New York Daily Graphic*, 19 December 1874, p. 357.

Letter of 16 December [1874] to the Editor of the *New York Daily Graphic*.

E 2545
"A Christmas Garland In Prose and Verse," *New York Daily Graphic*, 25 December 1874, p. 5.

Prose selections partially reprinted in various places in *Specimen Days* (A 11); reprinted in *UPP*, II, 53–58. See *PW92*, II, 758–763. Prose selections are "Genius—Victor Hugo—George Sand—Emerson," "A Thought on Culture," "Travel," "Friendship (the Real Article)," "Rulers Strictly Out of the Masses," "A Dialogue" (see "Ventures, on an Old Theme" in *PW92*, I, 294; II, 518), "It Remains a Question," "Has It Ever Occurred," "Of Poems of the Third and Fourth," "A Hint to Preachers and Authors," "Have Normal Belief," "In the Statesmanship," "Transportation, Mails, &c." Poetry selections are "The Ox-Tamer" (reprinted in the "Two Rivulets" section of *Two Rivulets* [A 9], pp. 77–78), "In the Wake Following" (reprinted as "After the Sea–Ship," in the "Two Rivulets" section of *Two Rivulets*, p. 32), "Come, Said My Soul" (reprinted in *New York Daily Tribune*, 19 February 1876; on title page of *Leaves of Grass* [1876]).

E 2546
Anon. "Notes and News," *Academy*, 7 (17 April 1875), 398.

Letter of [April? 1875] to William Michael Rossetti.

E 2547
Anon. "Notes and News," *Academy*, 7 (29 May 1875), 554.

Letter of 25 May 1875 to Edward Dowden.

E 2548
"Walt Whitman at the Poe Funeral—Conspicuous Absence of the Popular Poets," *Washington Star*, 18 November 1875, p. 2.

Reprinted (partial) as "Edgar Poe's Significance" in *Specimen Days* (A 11), pp. 156–158. Incorporated into "Edgar Poe's Significance," *Critic*, 3 June 1882 (E 2608).

E 2549
"Walt Whitman's Actual American Position," *West Jersey Press*, 26 January 1876.

Reprinted in *Walt Whitman's Workshop* (A 28), pp. 245–246.

E 2550
"Death of Lincoln," *New York Sun*, 12 February 1876.

Revised as "A Poet on the Platform," *New York Daily Tribune*, 15 April 1879 (E 2569); as "Death of Abraham Lincoln" in *Specimen Days* (A 11), pp. 306–315.

E 2551
"Walt Whitman's Poems," *New York Daily Tribune*, 19 February 1876, p. 4.

Prepublication review of *Leaves of Grass* (1876) and *Two Rivulets* (A 9) and first printing of poems. Attributed in Edwin Haviland Miller, "Walt Whitman's Correspondence with Whitelaw Reid, Editor of the New York *Tribune*," *Studies in Bibliography*, 8 (1956), 243–244. Poems: "Eidólons" (reprinted in "Two Rivulets" section of *Two Rivulets*, pp. 17–20), "After an Interval" (reprinted in *Leaves of Grass*, p. 369), "Out from Behind This Mask" (reprinted as "Out from Behind This Mask: To confront My Portrait, illustrating 'the *Wound–Dresser*,' in *Leaves of Grass*" in the "Two Rivulets" section of *Two Rivulets*, pp. 24–25; as "Out from Behind This Mask: [To Confront a Portrait]" in *Leaves of Grass* [1881], pp. 296–297), "The Beauty of the Ship" (reprinted in *Leaves of Grass*, p. 247), "Two Rivulets" (reprinted in the "Two Rivulets" section of *Two Rivulets*, p. 15), "To a Locomotive in Winter" (reprinted in the "Two Rivulets" section of *Two Rivulets*, pp. 25–26), "Or from that Sea of Time" (reprinted in the "Two Rivulets" section of *Two Rivulets*, p. 16), "Come, said my Soul" (reprinted on the title page of *Leaves of Grass*), "After an Interval" (reprinted in *Leaves of Grass*, p. 369), "When the Full-Grown Poet Came" (reprinted in *Leaves of Grass*, p. 359), "The Beauty of the Ship" (reprinted in *Leaves of Grass*, p. 247), "A Song by the Potomac" (retitled from "By Broad Potomac's Shore" in *As a Strong Bird on Pinions Free* [A 7], p. 16, and reprinted in that annex to *Two Rivulets*), "Ship of Democracy" (reprinted from the title poem in the annex *As a Strong Bird on Pinions Free* to *Two Rivulets*).

E 2552
[Review of *Leaves of Grass* and *Two Rivulets*], *Camden New Republic*, 11 March 1876.

Attributed by Charles I. Glicksberg, "Walt Whitman in New Jersey. Some Unpublished Manuscripts," *Proceedings of the New Jersey Historical Society*, 55 (January 1937), 42–46.

E 2553
[Walt Whitman], *West Jersey Press*, 15 March 1876.

Attributed by Charles I. Glicksberg, "Walt Whitman in New Jersey. Some Unpublished Manuscripts," *Proceedings of the New Jersey Historical Society*, 55 (January 1937), 42–46.

E 2554
"Walt Whitman on the American War," *Examiner* (London), 18 March 1876, pp. 317–318.

Reprinted in *Memoranda During the War* (A 8), pp. 65–66.

E 2555
"The Man–of–War–Bird," *Athenæum*, no. 2527 (1 April 1876), 463.

Poem. Reprinted as "Thou Who Hast Slept All Night Upon the Storm" in *Progress* (Philadelphia), 16 November 1878; as "To the Man-of-War-Bird" in *Leaves of Grass* (1881), pp. 204–205.

Note: Clippings of this poem are reported added to the *Centennial Edition* of *Leaves of Grass* (A 2.5.b$_2$); no copies have been located.

E 2556
"A Death Sonnet for Custer," *New York Daily Tribune*, 10 July 1876.

Poem. Reprinted as "From Far Dakotas Cañons" in *Leaves of Grass* (1881), pp. 366–367.

Note: Clippings of this poem are reported added to the *Centennial Edition* of *Leaves of Grass* (A 2.5.b$_2$); no copies have been located.

E 2557
[Death of Walter Whitman, the Poet's Nephew], *New York Daily Tribune*, 19 July 1876, p. 4.

Reprinted in *Philadelphia Public Ledger*, 20 July 1876. Attributed in Edwin Haviland Miller, "Walt Whitman's Correspondence with Whitelaw Reid, Editor of the New York *Tribune*," *Studies in Bibliography*, 8 (1956), 244–245.

E 2558
[Matlock, James Scovel]. "Walt Whitman. A Symposium in a Sick Room," *Camden Daily Post,* 18 November 1876.

Letter of 24 October 1876 to William J. Stillman.

E 2559
"Walt Whitman on Thomas Paine," *New York Daily Tribune,* 29 January 1877.

Reprinted with revisions as "In Memory of Thomas Paine" in *Specimen Days* (A 11), pp. 96–97.

E 2560
"Walt Whitman—He Visits New York After 5 Years Absence," *Camden Daily Post,* 29 March 1877.

E 2561
" 'The Old Gray' Under a Tree [On Herbert Gilchrist's Portrait of Whitman]," *Washington Star,* before 2 August 1877.

Reprinted in *Camden Daily Post,* 2 August 1877.

E 2562
"Walt Whitman for 1878," *West Jersey Press,* 16 January 1878, p. 1.

Possibly by Whitman; see William White, "Whitman or Whitmaniana?" *Emerson Society Quarterly,* no. 54 (1st Quarter 1969), 120–121 (reprinted on p. 121).

E 2563
"A Poet's Recreation," *New York Daily Tribune,* 4 July 1878.

Reprinted with other material as "Death of William Cullen Bryant" in *Specimen Days* (A 11), pp. 113–114. See *PW92,* I, 165–167, 329–330.

E 2564
"Gathering the Corn," *New York Daily Tribune,* 24 October 1878.

Reprinted in *Good-Bye My Fancy* (A 13), pp. 35–36.

E 2565
"Winter Sunshine: A Trip from Camden to the Coast," *Philadelphia Times,* 26 January 1879.

Reprinted (partial) in *Critic,* 29 January 1881 (E 2588); reprinted in several places in *Specimen Days* (A 11); in Herbert Bergman, "Walt Whitman on New Jersey: An Uncollected Essay," *Proceedings of the New Jersey Historical Soci-*

ety, 66 (October 1948), 139–154. See *PW92,* I, 118, 128–129, 136–138, 148, 158, 161, 330–338.

E 2566
"The First Spring Day on Chestnut Street," *Progress* (Philadelphia), 8 March 1879.

Reprinted in *Specimen Days* (A 11), pp. 128–129.

E 2567
"Three Young Men's Deaths," *Cope's Tobacco Plant* (Liverpool), 3 (April 1879), 318–319.

Letter of 28 July 1863 to Louisa Van Velsor Whitman and incorporates material from "Death of a Fireman," *Camden New Republic,* 14 November 1874 (E 2543). Reprinted in *Specimen Days* (A 11), pp. 106–108.

E 2568
"Only Crossing the Delaware," *Progress* (Philadelphia), 5 April 1879.

Reprinted with revisions as "Delaware River—Days and Nights" and "Scenes on Ferry and River—Last Winter's Nights" in *Specimen Days* (A 11), pp. 124–128.

E 2569
"A Poet on the Platform," *New York Daily Tribune,* 15 April 1879, p. 2.

Reprinted as "Death of Abraham Lincoln" in *Specimen Days* (A 11), pp. 306–315. Revision of "Death of Lincoln" in *New York Sun,* 12 February 1876 (E 2540).

E 2570
"Broadway Revisited," *New York Daily Tribune,* 10 May 1879.

Reprinted in three places in *Specimen Days* (A 11); partially reprinted as "New York—The Bay—The Old Name" in *Good-Bye My Fancy* (A 13), pp. 45–46. See *PW92,* I, 16–21, 338–339; II, 681–683.

E 2571
"Real Summer Openings," *New York Daily Tribune,* 17 May 1879.

Reprinted with revisions as "Up the Hudson to Ulster County" in *Specimen Days* (A 11), pp. 129–130. See *PW92,* I, 190–196, 339–341.

E 2572
"These May Afternoons," *New York Daily Tribune,* 24 May 1879.

Reprinted in five places in *Specimen Days* (A 11). See *PW92*, I, 196–202, 341–342.

E 2573
"Walt Whitman's Impressions of Denver and the West: What He Says of Its Present, Its People and Its Future," *Denver Daily Tribune*, 21[?] September 1879.

Incorporated into "Denver Impressions" in *Specimen Days* (A 11), pp. 146–147; printed from a manuscript in Rollo G. Silver, "Whitman Interviews Himself," *American Literature*, 10 (March 1938), 84–87. See *PW92*, I, 343–345 (see also I, 214–216).

E 2574
"A Poet's Western Trip," *Camden New Republic*, 15 November 1879.

Reprinted in *Washington Star*, 15 November 1879.

E 2575
[Burroughs, John]. "Nature and the Poets," *Scribner's Monthly Magazine*, 19 (December 1879), 285–295.

The section on Whitman (pp. 293–294) was contributed by him; see *Correspondence*, III, 163. Reprinted in Burroughs, *Pepacton* (D 9).

E 2576
"What Best I See in Thee," *Philadelphia Press*, 17 December 1879.

Poem. Reprinted in *Leaves of Grass* (1881), p. 368.

E 2577
"Cedar-Plums Like," *Philadelphia Press*, 1880.

Poem. Reprinted in *Specimen Days* (A 11), pp. 165–168.

E 2578
"A Riddle Song," *Tarrytown Sunnyside Press*, 3 April 1880.

Poem. Reprinted in *Forney's Progress*, 2 (17 April 1880), 508; *Leaves of Grass* (1881), pp. 362–363.

E 2579
[On "Death of Abraham Lincoln"], *Camden Daily Post*, 16 April 1880.

E 2580
"The Martyr President: The Good Gray Poet's Personal Recollections of Him," *Philadelphia Press*, 16 April 1880.

Incorporated into "Death of Abraham Lincoln" in *Specimen Days* (A 11), pp. 306–315.

E 2581
"The Prairie States," *Art Autograph*, May 1880, plate 8 (facsimile).

Poem. Reprinted in *Leaves of Grass* (1881), p. 310.

E 2582
"Emerson's Books, (the Shadows of Them)," *Literary World* (Boston), 11 (22 May 1880), 177–178.

Reprinted (partial) as "A Democratic Criticism" in *New York Daily Tribune*, 15 May 1882; reprinted in *Specimen Days* (A 11), pp. 319–322. See *PW92*, II, 514–518, 767–768.

E 2583
"Summer Days in Canada," *Camden Daily Post*, 22 June 1880.

Reprinted in *Philadelphia Press*, 22 June 1880; *London* (Ontario) *Advertiser*, 22 June 1880; in various places in *Specimen Days* (A 11). See *PW92*, I, 236–241, 345–346.

E 2584
[Trip on the St. Lawrence River], *Camden Daily Post*, 26 August 1880.

Reprinted in *Philadelphia Press*, 26 August 1880; as "Letter from Walt Whitman" in *London* (Ontario) *Advertiser*, 26 August 1880; in various places in *Specimen Days* (A 11). See *PW92*, I, 241–245, 346–347.

E 2585
"Home Again," *Camden Daily Post*, 30 September 1880.

Reprinted as "Walt Whitman Safe Home" in *London* (Ontario) *Advertiser*, 4 October 1880.

E 2586
"My Picture-Gallery," *American* (Philadelphia), 1 (30 October 1880), 39.

Poem. Reprinted in *Leaves of Grass* (1881), p. 310; incorporated into *Pictures* (A 26).

E 2587
"The Dalliance of the Eagles," *Cope's Tobacco Plant* (Liverpool), 2 (November 1880), 552.

Poem. Reprinted in *Leaves of Grass* (1881), p. 216.

E 2588
"How I Get Around at 60, and Take Notes [First Number]," *Critic*, 1 (29 January 1881), 2–3.

Includes material from "Winter Sunshine" in *Philadelphia Times*, 26 January 1879 (E 2565); reprinted in various places in *Specimen Days* (A 11).

E 2589
"The Poetry of the Future," *North American Review*, 132 (February 1881), 195–210.

Revised and reprinted as "Poetry To-day in America—Shakspere—The Future" in *Specimen Days* (A 11), pp. 288–301.

E 2590
"The Death of Carlyle," *Critic*, 1 (12 February 1881), 30

Reprinted as "The Dead Carlyle" in *Literary World* (Boston), 12 February 1881; reprinted in *Essays from "The Critic"* (D 11), pp. 31–37; as "Death of Thomas Carlyle" in *Specimen Days* (A 11), pp. 168–178.

E 2591
"Patroling Barnegat," *Harper's Monthly Magazine*, 62 (April 1881), 701.

Poem. Reprinted in *American* (Philadelphia), May 1881; *Leaves of Grass* (1881), pp. 208–209.

E 2592
"How I Get Around at 60, and Take Notes [Second Number]," *Critic*, 1 (9 April 1881), 88–89.

Reprinted in various places in *Specimen Days* (A 11). See *PW92*, I, 347.

E 2593
"How I Get Around at 60, and Take Notes [Third Number]," *Critic*, 1 (7 May 1881), 116–117.

Reprinted in various places in *Specimen Days* (A 11). See *PW92*, I, 347.

E 2594
"Bumble-Bees and Bird-Music," *American* (Philadelphia), 14 May 1881.

Reprinted in various places in *Specimen Days* (A 11). See *PW92*, I, 123–126, 146–147, 269–270, 352.

E 2595
"A Summer Invocation," *American* (Philadelphia), 2 (14 June 1881), 120.

Poem. Reprinted as "Thou Orb Aloft Full-Dazzling" in *Leaves of Grass* (1881), p. 352.

E 2596
"How I Get Around at 60, and Take Notes [Fourth Number]," *Critic,* 1 (16 July 1881), 184–185.

Reprinted in various places in *Specimen Days* (A 11). See *PW92,* I, 348.

E 2597
"A Week at West Hills," *New York Daily Tribune,* 4 August 1881.

Reprinted in various places in *Specimen Days* (A 11). See *PW92,* I, 4–8, 352–354.

E 2598
"City Notes in August," *New York Daily Tribune,* 15 August 1881.

Reprinted in various places in *Specimen Days* (A 11). See *PW92,* I, 273–276, 354–355.

E 2599
"Spirit That Form'd This Scene," *Critic,* 1 (10 September 1881), 246.

Reprinted as "Spirit That Form'd This Scene. Written in Platte Cañyon, Colorado" in *Leaves of Grass* (1881), p. 368.

E 2600
"The Sobbing of the Bells," *Boston Daily Globe,* 27 September 1881, p. 1.

Poem. Reprinted in Moses King, *The Poets' Tributes to Garfield* (D 10), p. 71; as "The Sobbing of the Bells. (Midnight, Sept. 19–20, 1881.)" in *Leaves of Grass* (1881), p. 378.

Note: The first page only, containing Whitman's poem, was reprinted on satin. *Location:* CtY.

E 2601
"A Poet's Supper to his Printer's and Proof-Readers," *Boston Daily Advertiser,* 17 October 1881, p. 8.

Listed as possibly by Whitman in Scott Giantvalley, *Walt Whitman, 1838–1939: A Reference Guide* (Boston: G. K. Hall, 1981), item 1881.36.

E 2602
"How I Still Get Around at 60, and Take Notes [Fifth Number]," *Critic,* 1 (3 December 1881), 330–331.

Reprinted in Alexander Ireland, *In Memoriam. Ralph Waldo Emerson.* (D 12), pp. 113–115; in three places in *Specimen Days* (A 11). See *PW92*, I, 348.

E 2603
"Death of Longfellow," *Critic*, 2 (8 April 1882), 101.

Reprinted in *Essays from "The Critic"* (D 11), pp. 41–45; revised in *Specimen Days* (A 11), pp. 193–194. See *PW92*, I, 284–286, 355.

E 2604
"By Emerson's Grave," *Critic*, 2 (6 May 1882), 123.

Reprinted in *Specimen Days* (A 11), p. 197.

E 2605
[A Defense of Walt Whitman], *Camden Daily Post*, 22 May 1882.

Reprinted as "Bits of Criticism: A Defense of Walt Whitman" in *Philadelphia Press*, 22 May 1882.

E 2606
"A Memorandum at a Venture," *North American Review*, 134 (June 1882), 546–550.

Reprinted in *Specimen Days* (A 11), pp. 302–306.

E 2607
"Starting Newspapers," *Camden Daily Courier*, 1 June 1882.

Reprinted as "Walt Whitman: His Several Ventures as a Journalist as Described by Himself," *New York World*, 11 June 1882; revised as "Starting Newspapers" in *Specimen Days* (A 11), pp. 194–196.

E 2608
"Edgar Poe's Significance," *Critic*, 2 (3 June 1882), 147.

Incorporates material from "Walt Whitman at the Poe Funeral," *Washington Star*, 18 November 1875 (E 2548). Reprinted in *Specimen Days* (A 11), pp. 156–158.

E 2609
[Letter], *Philadelphia Press*, 16 June 1882.

Letter of 23 May 1882 to James R. Osgood and Company.

E 2610
"To a Common Prostitute," *This World*, 3, no. 24 (17 June 1882), supplement, [1].

THE WORD—EXTRA

CENSORSHIP OF THE PRESS.—Att'y Gen. Marston, Oliver Stevens, Dist. Att'y of Suffolk Co., and Postmaster Tobey of Boston, say "Leaves of Grass" is obscene; we appeal the case from such narrow-minded judges, to Individual Citizens, & give them these interesting extracts from the "suppressed" book, now republished & for sale as advertised below :—

TO A COMMON PROSTITUTE.

1. Be composed—be at ease with me—I am Walt
   Whitman, liberal and lusty as Nature,
   Not till the sun excludes you, do I exclude you,
   Not till the waters refuse to glisten for you, and
   the leaves to rustle for you, do my words
   refuse to glisten and rustle for you.

2. My girl, I appoint with you an appointment—and
   I charge you that you make preparation to
   be worthy to meet me,   [till I come.
   And I charge you that you be patient and perfect

3. Till then, I salute you with a significant look,
   that you do not forget me.

1. A WOMAN waits for me—she contains all, nothing is lacking,
   Yet all were lacking, if sex were lacking, or if
   the moisture of the right man were lacking.

2. Sex contains all, [cies, results, promulgations,
   Bodies, Souls, meanings, proofs, purities, delica-
   Songs, commands, health, pride, the maternal
   mystery, the seminic milk,
   All hopes, benedictions, bestowals,   [earth,
   All the passions, loves, beauties, delights of the
   These are contained in sex, as parts of itself, and
   justifications of itself.

3. Without shame the man I like knows and avows
   the deliciousness of his sex,   [avows hers.
   Without shame the woman I like knows and

4. O I will fetch bully breeds of children yet !
   I will dismiss myself from impassive women,
   I will go stay with her who waits for me, and
   with those women that are warm blooded and
   sufficient for me;   [me,
   I see that they understand me, and do not deny
   I see that they are worthy of me—I will be the
   robust husband of those women.

5. They are not one jot less than I am,
   They are tanned in the face by shining suns and
   blowing winds,   .——[strength,
   Their flesh has the old divine suppleness and
   They know how to swim, row, ride, wrestle,
   shoot, run, strike, retreat, advance, resist,
   defend themselves,
   They are ultimate in their own right—they are
   calm, clear, well-possessed of themselves.

6. I draw you close to me, you women !
   I cannot let you go, I would do you good,
   I am for you, and you are for me, not only for
   our own sake, but for others' sakes;
   Enveloped in you sleep greater heroes & bards,
   They refuse to awake at the touch of any man
   but me.

7. It is I, you women—I make my way,
   I am stern, acrid, large, undissuadable—but I
   love, you,   [you,
   I do not hurt you any more than is necessary for
   I pour the stuff to start sons and daughters fit for
   These States—I press with slow, rude muscle,
   I brace myself effectually—I listen to no en-
   treaties.   [long accumulated within me.
   I dare not withdraw till I deposit what has so
   ... ugh you I drain the pent-up rivers of myself,
   In you I wrap a thousand onward years,
   On you I graft the grafts of the best-beloved of
   me and of America,
   The drops I distill upon you shall grow fierce and
   athletic girls, new artists, musicians, and
   singers,
   The babes I beget upon you are to beget babes in
   their turn,   [my love-spendings.
   I shall demand perfect men and women out of
   I shall expect them to interpenetrate with others,
   as I and you interpenetrate now,
   I shall count on the fruits of the gushing showers
   of them, as I count on the fruits of the gushing showers I give now,
   I shall look for loving crops from the birth, life,
   death, immortality, I plant so lovingly now.

E 2610 (*Note one*)

Poem (see *Leaves of Grass* [1860], p. 399). Also tipped in between pp. 6 and 7 of George Chainey, "Keep Off the Grass," *This World*, 3, no. 24 (17 June 1882), 3–9. Reprinted in "Editorial Notes," *The Word*, 11, no. 4 (August [1882]), [2].

Note one: Also printed in an undated broadside, *The Word—Extra,* measuring 12¼"×3¾", and headed "Censorship of the Press." *Locations:* MiU, NN-B.

Note two: This debate spilled over into *The Word* for November and December 1882, both of which issues reprint Whitman's letter of 23 May 1882 (E 2609) and related materials, and which in turn resulted in three broadsides (see *BAL*, IX, 98–99).

E 2611
[George Chainey]. "A New Joshua," *This World*, 3, no. 26 (1 July 1882), 2–4.

Letter of 26 June 1882 to Chainey (p. 4).

E 2612
"How I Still Get Around at 60, and Take Notes [Sixth Number]," *Critic*, 2 (15 July 1882), 185.

Reprinted as "Hours for the Soul" in *Specimen Days* (A 11), pp. 118–121.

E 2613
[Baxter, Sylvester]. "Whitman's New Book. The Prose Writings of the 'Good Grey Poet,'" *Boston Sunday Herald*, 15 October 1882, p. 9.

Letter of 20 December 1881 to [John Fitzgerald Lee].

E 2614
"Robert Burns," *Critic*, 2 (16 December 1882), 337.

Incoprorated into "Robert Burns as Poet and Person" in *North American Review*, November 1886 (E 2649).

E 2615
Anon. [Walt Whitman], *Critic*, 3 (13 January 1883), [ii].

Facsimile of four lines of manuscript poetry, beginning "Lo, where arise these peerless stars" from "Thou Mother with Thy Equal Brood" (*Leaves of Grass* [1881], pp. 346–351).

E 2616
"The Bible as Poetry," *Critic*, 3 (3 February 1883), 39–40.

Revised in *November Boughs* (A 12), pp. 43–46.

E 2617
"The Spanish Element in Our Nationality," *Philadelphia Press*, 5 August 1883.

Reprinted as "Walt Whitman on the Santa Fé Celebration" in *Critic*, 11 August 1883; reprinted in *November Boughs* (A 12), pp. 50–51.

E 2618
Anon. "Walt Whitman," *Long Islander*, 21 September 1883.

Letter of [before 21 September 1883] to the Editor.

E 2619
"Our Eminent Visitors (Past, Present, and Future)," *Critic*, 3 (17 November 1883), 459–460.

Revised in *November Boughs* (A 12), pp. 39–42; *Democratic Vistas, and Other Papers* (A 4.3), pp. 100–105.

E 2620
"A Backward Glance on My Own Road," *Critic*, 4 (5 January 1884), 1–2.

Revised in *Democratic Vistas, and Other Papers* (A 4.3), pp. 95–99; combined with "How I Made a Book," *Philadelphia Press*, 11 July 1886 (E 2647), and "My Book and I," *Lippincott's Magazine*, January 1887 (E 2651), as "A Backward Glance O'er Travel'd Roads" in *November Boughs* (A 12), pp. 5–18. See *PW92*, II, 711–732, 768–771.

E 2621
"Reminiscences of the Indian Bureau," *Baldwin's Monthly*, 28 (February 1884), 2.

Reprinted in *To-Day: The Monthly Magazine of Scientific Socialism* (London), 1 (May 1884), 340–342; as "An Indian Bureau Reminiscence" in *November Boughs* (A 12), pp. 73–75.

E 2622
Rolleston, T. R. "Wordsworth and Walt Whitman," *Camden Daily Post*, 13 February 1884.

Whitman helped with this translation by Traubel's father; see *Correspondence*, III, 349n.

E 2623
"With Husky-Haughty Lips, O Sea!," *Harper's Monthly Magazine*, 68 (March 1884), 607.

Poem. Reprinted in "Sands at Seventy" annex to *Leaves of Grass* (1888), p. 392.

E 2624
"A Fabulous Episode [Concerning Whitman and Henry Wadsworth Longfellow]," *Critic*, 4 (31 May 1884), 258.

See *Correspondence*, III, 370n.

E 2625
"Walt Whitman's Birthday," *Philadelphia Times*, 31 May 1884.

See *Correspondence*, III, 371n.

E 2626
"What Lurks behind Shakspeare's Historical Plays?", *Critic*, 5 (27 September 1884), 145.

Reprinted in *Democratic Vistas, and Other Papers* (A 4.3), pp. 109–112.

E 2627
"Red Jacket (from Aloft)," *Philadelphia Press*, 10 October 1884.

Poem. Reprinted in *Buffalo Historical Society Transactions* (D 14), p. 105; "Sands at Seventy" annex to *Leaves of Grass* (1888), p. 393.

E 2628
"If I Should Need to Name, O Western World," *Philadelphia Press*, 26 October 1884.

Poem. Reprinted as "Election Day, November, 1884" in the "Sands at Seventy" annex to *Leaves of Grass* (1888), p. 391.

E 2629
"The Dead Tenor," *Critic*, 5 (8 November 1884), 222.

Poem. Reprinted in the "Sands at Seventy" annex to *Leaves of Grass* (1888), p. 395.

E 2630
"A Poet's Prose: The Place Walt Whitman Thinks Gratitude Fills in a Fine Character," *Philadelphia Press*, 27 November 1884.

Reprinted as "The Place Gratitude Fills in a Fine Character," *November Boughs* (A 12), p. 108.

E 2631
"Chicago," *Toronto World*, 8 December 1884.

Poem. Signed "Walt Whitman." Reprinted in Herbert Bergman, " 'Chicago,' an Uncollected Poem, Possibly by Whitman," *Modern Language Notes*, 65 (November 1950), 478–481.

E 2632
[How *Leaves of Grass* Was Made], *New York Star*, 1885.

Incorporated into "How Leaves of Grass Was Made," *Frank Leslie's Popular Monthly*, June 1892 (E 2772).

E 2633
"Of That Blithe Throat of Thine," *Harper's Monthly Magazine*, 70 (January 1885), 264.

Poem. Reprinted in the "Sands at Seventy" annex to *Leaves of Grass* (1888), p. 394.

E 2634
"A Note on Water Works," *Brooklyn Daily Times*, 20 January 1885.

E 2635
"Ah, Not This Granite Dead and Cold," *Philadelphia Press*, 22 February 1885.

Poem. Reprinted as "Washington's Monument, February, 1885" in the "Sands at Seventy" annex to *Leaves of Grass* (1888), p. 393.

E 2636
"Authors at Home. VII. Walt Whitman at Camden," *Critic*, 6 (28 February 1885), 97–98.

Signed "George Selwyn." Reprinted in J. L. and J. B. Gilder, *Authors at Home* (D 16), pp. 335–342; as *Walt Whitman at Home* (A 16); in *UPP*, II, 58–62. See *Correspondence*, III, 387.

E 2637
"As One by One Withdraw the Lofty Actors," *Harper's Weekly Magazine*, 29 (16 May 1885), 310.

Poem. Reprinted as "Grant" in *Critic*, 7 (15 August 1885), 80; as "Death of General Grant" in the "Sands at Seventy" annex to *Leaves of Grass* (1888), pp. 392–393.

E 2638
Anon. "Walt Whitman," *New York Daily Graphic*, 31 May 1885, p. 4.

Letter of 21 May 1885 to the Editor of the *New York Daily Graphic* (facsimile).

E 2639
[Scovel, James]. "Walt Whitman. The Author of 'Leaves of Grass' at Home,"
Springfield Daily Republican, 16 June 1885, p. 7.

Letter of [17 March] 1876 to William Michael Rossetti. Whitman also contributed to the article; see *Correspondence,* III, 389n.

E 2640
"Fancies at Navesink," *Nineteenth Century,* 18 (August 1885), 234–237.

Poems (all reprinted in the "Sands at Seventy" annex to *Leaves of Grass*
[1888], pp. 390–391): "The Pilot in the Mist," "Had I the Choice," "You Tides
With Ceaseless Swell," "Last of the Ebb, and Daylight Waning," "And Yet Not
You Alone," "Proudly the Flood Comes In," "By That Long Scan of Waves,"
"Then Last of All."

E 2641
"The Voice of the Rain," *Outing,* 6 (August 1885), 570.

Poem. Reprinted in the "Sands at Seventy" annex to *Leaves of Grass* (1888), p.
399.

E 2642
"Booth and 'The Bowery,'" *New York Daily Tribune,* 16 August 1885.

Reprinted as "The Old Bowery" in *November Boughs* (A 12), pp. 87–92.

E 2643
[Letter], *Athenæum,* no. 3017 (22 August 1885), 241.

Letter of 1 August 1885 to Herbert Gilchrist. Reprinted in *New York Times,* 4
September 1885, p. 5.

E 2644
"Slang in America," *North American Review,* 141 (November 1885), 431–435.

Reprinted in *November Boughs* (A 12), pp. 68–72.

E 2645
"Some Diary Notes at Random," *Baldwin's Monthly,* 31 (December 1885), 8.

Reprinted in *November Boughs* (A 12), pp. 76–79.

E 2646
[Gilder, Jeannette]. "The Lounger," *Critic,* 9 (3 July 1886), 7.

Letter of 17 June 1886 to an unidentified correspondent.

E 2647
"How I Made a Book," *Philadelphia Press,* 11 July 1886.

Partially reprinted in *Frank Leslie's Popular Monthly,* June 1892 (E 2772). Reprinted in *Democratic Vistas, and Other Papers* (A 4.3), pp. 130–139. Combined with "My Book and I," *Lippincott's Magazine,* January 1887 (E 2651), and "A Backward Glance on My Own Road," *Critic,* 5 January 1884 (E 2620), as "A Backward Glance O'er Travel'd Roads" in *November Boughs* (A 12), pp. 5–18.

E 2648
"A Thought on Shakspere," *Critic,* 9 (14 August 1886), 73.

Reprinted in *Democratic Vistas, and Other Papers* (A 4.3), pp. 106–108; *November Boughs* (A 12), pp. 55–56.

E 2649
"Robert Burns as Poet and Person," *North American Review,* 143 (November 1886), 427–435.

Incorporates material from "Robert Burns" in *Critic,* 16 December 1882 (E 2614). Reprinted in *Democratic Vistas, and Other Papers* (A 4.3), pp. 113–114; *November Boughs* (A 12), pp. 57–64.

E 2650
"One who has been there." "Walt Whitman at Camden," *Pall Mall Gazette,* 23 December 1886, pp. 1–2.

Letters of 8 August 1885 (here dated "August 1886"), 2 August 1886, and 15 August 1886 to Mary Whitall Smith Costelloe (p. 2).

E 2651
"My Book and I," *Lippincott's Magazine,* 43 (January 1887), 121–127.

Partially reprinted in *Frank Leslie's Popular Monthly,* June 1892 (E 2772). Reprinted in *Democratic Vistas, and Other Papers* (A 4.3), pp. 84–94. Combined with "How I Made a Book," *Philadelphia Press,* 11 July 1886 (E 2647), and "A Backward Glance on My Own Road," *Critic,* 5 January 1884 (E 2620), as "A Backward Glance O'er Travel'd Roads" in *November Boughs* (A 12), pp. 5–18.

Note: The January 1887 issue of *Lippincott's* was issued in cloth and boards with this title page: 'SINFIRE. | BY | JULIAN HAWTHORNE, | AUTHOR OF "GARTH," "SEBASTIAN STROME," "ARCHIBALD MALMAISON," ETC. | [rule] | PHILADELPHIA: | J. B. LIPPINCOTT COMPANY.' (NRU).

E 2652

"Some War Memoranda—Jotted Down at the Time," *North American Review,* 144 (January 1887), 55–60.

Reprinted in *November Boughs* (A 12), pp. 80–85.

E 2653

"A Word About Tennyson," *Critic,* 10 (1 January 1887), 1–2.

Reprinted in *Democratic Vistas, and Other Papers* (A 4.3), pp. 115–129; *November Boughs* (A 12), pp. 65–67.

E 2654

"New Orleans in 1848: Walt Whitman Gossips of His Sojourn Here Years Ago as a Newspaper Writer: Notes of His Trip Up the Mississippi and to New York," *New Orleans Picayune,* 25 January 1887.

Reprinted in *November Boughs* (A 12), pp. 100–104; *New Orleans Picayune,* 25 January 1937. See *PW92,* II, 604–610, 773.

E 2655

Anon. "The Walt Whitman New Year's Gift," *Pall Mall Gazette,* 25 January 1887, p. 11.

Letter of 3 January 1887 to William T. Stead (and facsimile).

E 2656

"Father Taylor and Oratory," *Century Magazine,* 33 (February 1887), 583–584.

Reprinted as "Father Taylor (and Oratory)" in *November Boughs* (A 12), pp. 47–49.

E 2657

"Personal," *Philadelphia Press,* 1 February 1887.

Submitted by Whitman; see *Correspondence,* IV, 66.

E 2658

[On Tennyson], *Critic,* 10 (26 March 1887), 158.

Submitted by Whitman; see *Correspondence,* IV, 76–77n.

E 2659

"Five Thousand Poems," *Critic,* 10 (16 April 1887), 187.

Reprinted in *Democratic Vistas, and Other Papers* (A 4.3), pp. 140–141; *November Boughs* (A 12), p. 86.

E 2660
"Walt Whitman on Lincoln," *Critic*, 10 (23 April 1887), 206.

E 2661
Anon. "An Autograph of Whitman," *Brooklyn Times*, 21 May 1887.

Postcard of 20 April [1887] to Dr. John Johnston (facsimile).

E 2662
Anon. [Whitman's Birthday], *Camden Daily News*, 31 May 1887.

Partially reprinted in "Walt Whitman at Sixty-Eight," *Pall Mall Gazette*, 2 June 1887, p. 7.

E 2663
"The Dying Veteran," *McClure's Magazine*, June 1887.

Poem. Distributed by McClure's Syndicate, June 1887. Reprinted in *Pall Mall Gazette*, 9 July 1887; *Springfield Daily Republican*, 11 July 1887; "Sands at Seventy" annex to *Leaves of Grass* (1888), p. 400.

E 2664
[Whitman Society], *Camden Daily News*, 6 August 1887.

Submitted by Whitman; see *Correspondence*, IV, 113, 115.

E 2665
"From *Walt Whitman in America*," *Pall Mall Gazette*, 30 August 1887, p. 1.

Letter of 17 August 1887 to William T. Stead.

E 2666
"Shakspere–Bacon's Cipher," *Cosmopolitan*, 4 (October 1887), 142.

Poem. Reprinted in *Good-Bye My Fancy* (A 13), p. 10.

E 2667
"November Boughs," *Lippincott's Magazine*, 40 (November 1887), 722–723.

Poems (all reprinted in the "Sands at Seventy" annex to *Leaves of Grass* [1888]): "You Lingering Sparse Leaves of Me" (p. 402), "Going Somewhere" (p. 397), "After the Supper and Talk" (p. 404), "Not Meagre, Latent Boughs Alone" (p. 402).

E 2668
"Walt Whitman's Thanks," *New York World*, 24 November 1887.

Reprinted as "Thanks in Old Age," *Philadelphia Press,* 24 November 1887; *Springfield Republican,* 24 November 1887; in "Walt Whitman's Thanksgiving" in *New York World,* 23 November 1890 (E 2746); in the "Sands at Seventy" annex to *Leaves of Grass* (1888), p. 398.

E 2669
"Yonnondio," *Critic,* 11 (26 November 1887), 267.

Poem. Reprinted in the "Sands at Seventy" annex to *Leaves of Grass* (1888), p. 396.

E 2670
"Twilight," *Century Magazine,* 35 (December 1887), 264.

Poem. Reprinted in the "Sands at Seventy" annex to *Leaves of Grass* (1888), p. 401.

E 2671
"Walt Whitman's Praise [of Whittier]," *New York Herald,* 15 December 1887.

Reprinted in *Boston Daily Advertiser,* 17 December 1887; *Newburyport Daily Herald,* 17 December 1887.

E 2672
"As the Greek's Signal Flame," *New York Herald,* 15 December 1887.

Poem. Reprinted in *Boston Daily Advertiser,* 17 December 1887; *Munyon's Illustrated World,* January 1888; in the "Sands at Seventy" annex to *Leaves of Grass* (1888), p. 402.

E 2673
"Walt Whitman's Thanks," *London Literary World,* 6 January 1888.

Reprinted in *American Journal of Education and National Educator,* 9 March 1892.

E 2674
"To the Editor of the Herald: Please Wait [on President Cleveland's Free Trade Message]," *New York Herald,* 26 January 1888.

E 2675
"To Those Who've Fail'd," *New York Herald,* 27 January 1888.

Poem. Reprinted in the "Sands at Seventy" annex to *Leaves of Grass* (1888), p. 385.

E 2676
"Halcyon Days," *New York Herald,* 29 January 1888.

Poem. Reprinted in the "Sands at Seventy" annex to *Leaves of Grass* (1888), p. 388.

E 2677
"After the Dazzle of Day," *New York Herald,* 3 February 1888.

Poem. Reprinted in the "Sands at Seventy" annex to *Leaves of Grass* (1888), p. 388.

E 2678
"America," *New York Herald,* 11 February 1888.

Poem. Reprinted in the "Sands at Seventy" annex to *Leaves of Grass* (1888), p. 387.

E 2679
"Abraham Lincoln, Born Feb. 12, 1809," *New York Herald,* 12 February 1888.

Poem. Reprinted in the "Sands at Seventy" annex to *Leaves of Grass* (1888), p. 388.

E 2680
"True Conquerors," *New York Herald,* 15 February 1888.

Poem. Reprinted in the "Sands at Seventy" annex to *Leaves of Grass* (1888), p. 397.

E 2681
"Soon Shall the Winter's Foil Be Here," *New York Herald,* 21 February 1888.

Poem. Reprinted in the "Sands at Seventy" annex to *Leaves of Grass* (1888), p. 399.

E 2682
"The Dismantled Ship," *New York Herald,* 23 February 1888.

Poem. Reprinted in the "Sands at Seventy" annex to *Leaves of Grass* (1888), p. 403.

E 2683
"Old Salt Kossabone," *New York Herald,* 25 February 1888.

Poem. Reprinted in the "Sands at Seventy" annex to *Leaves of Grass* (1888), p. 395.

E 2684
"Mannahatta," *New York Herald*, 27 February 1888.

Poem. Reprinted in the "Sands at Seventy" annex to *Leaves of Grass* (1888), p. 385.

E 2685
"Paumanok," *New York Herald*, 29 February 1888.

Poem. Reprinted in the "Sands at Seventy" annex to *Leaves of Grass* (1888), p. 385.

E 2686
"From Montauk Point," *New York Herald*, 1 March 1888.

Poem. Reprinted in the "Sands at Seventy" annex to *Leaves of Grass* (1888), p. 385.

E 2687
"My Canary Bird," *New York Herald*, 2 March 1888.

Poem. Reprinted in the "Sands at Seventy" annex to *Leaves of Grass* (1888), p. 386.

E 2688
"A Prairie Sunset," *New York Herald*, 9 March 1888.

Poem. Reprinted in the "Sands at Seventy" annex to *Leaves of Grass* (1888), p. 400.

E 2689
"The Dead Emperor," *New York Herald*, 10 March 1888.

Poem. Reprinted in the "Sands at Seventy" annex to *Leaves of Grass* (1888), p. 402.

E 2690
"The First Dandelion," *New York Herald*, 12 March 1888.

Poem. Reprinted in the "Sands at Seventy" annex to *Leaves of Grass* (1888), p. 387.

E 2691
"The Wallabout Martyrs," *New York Herald*, 16 March 1888.

Poem. Reprinted in the "Sands at Seventy" annex to *Leaves of Grass* (1888), p. 387.

E 2692
"The Bravest Soldiers," *New York Herald*, 18 March 1888.

Poem. Reprinted in the "Sands at Seventy" annex to *Leaves of Grass* (1888), p. 386.

E 2693
"Orange Buds by Mail from Florida," *New York Herald*, 19 March 1888.

Poem. Reprinted in the "Sands at Seventy" annex to *Leaves of Grass* (1888), p. 401.

E 2694
"Continuities," *New York Herald*, 20 March 1888.

Poem. Reprinted in the "Sands at Seventy" annex to *Leaves of Grass* (1888), p. 396.

E 2695
"A Font of Type," *New York Herald*, 9 April 1888.

Poem. Reprinted in the "Sands at Seventy" annex to *Leaves of Grass* (1888), p. 386; (slightly different version) in John Russell Young, *Men and Memories* (D 37), p. 107.

E 2696
"Broadway," *New York Herald*, 10 April 1888.

Poem. Reprinted in the "Sands at Seventy" annex to *Leaves of Grass* (1888), p. 394.

E 2697
"Life," *New York Herald*, 15 April 1888.

Poem. Reprinted in the "Sands at Seventy" annex to *Leaves of Grass* (1888), p. 396.

E 2698
"The Final Lilt of Songs," *New York Herald*, 16 April 1888.

Poem. Reprinted as "To Get the Final Lilt of Songs" in the "Sands at Seventy" annex to *Leaves of Grass* (1888), p. 394.

E 2699
"To-day and Thee," *New York Herald*, 23 April 1888.

Poem. Reprinted in the "Sands at Seventy" annex to *Leaves of Grass* (1888), p. 388.

E 2700
"Queries to My Seventieth Year," *New York Herald,* 2 May 1888.

Poem. Reprinted in the "Sands at Seventy" annex to *Leaves of Grass* (1888), p. 387.

E 2701
"The United States to the Old World Critics," *New York Herald,* 8 May 1888.

Poem. Reprinted in the "Sands at Seventy" annex to *Leaves of Grass* (1888), p. 398.

E 2702
"Out of May's Shows Selected," *New York Herald,* 10 May 1888.

Poem. Reprinted in the "Sands at Seventy" annex to *Leaves of Grass* (1888), p. 388.

E 2703
"As I Sit Writing Here," *New York Herald,* 14 May 1888.

Poem. Reprinted in the "Sands at Seventy" annex to *Leaves of Grass* (1888), p. 386.

E 2704
"A Carol Closing Sixty-Nine," *New York Herald,* 21 May 1888.

Poem. Reprinted in the "Sands at Seventy" annex to *Leaves of Grass* (1888), p. 386.

E 2705
"Life and Death," *New York Herald,* 23 May 1888.

Poem. Reprinted in the "Sands at Seventy" annex to *Leaves of Grass* (1888), p. 398.

E 2706
"The Calming Thought of All," *New York Herald,* 27 May 1888.

Poem. Reprinted in the "Sands at Seventy" annex to *Leaves of Grass* (1888), p. 398.

E 2707
Anon. "Walt Whitman's Birthday," *New York Daily Graphic,* 2 June 1888, p. 105.

Letter of 25 May 1888 to V. S. C. (facsimile).

E 2708

"Twenty Years," *Pall Mall Gazette,* July 1888.

Poem. Reprinted in *Magazine of Art* (London), August 1888, p. 348; *Magazine of Art* (New York), September 1888; in the "Sands at Seventy" annex to *Leaves of Grass* (1888), p. 401.

E 2709

"Walt Whitman's Tribute [to General Sheriden]," *New York Herald,* 8 August 1888.

E 2710

"Over and Through the Burial Chant," *New York Herald,* 12 August 1888.

Poem. Reprinted as "Interpolation Sounds" in *Good-Bye My Fancy* (A 13), p. 11.

E 2711

"Old Age's Lambent Peaks," *Century Magazine,* 36 (September 1888), 735.

Poem. Reprinted in the "Sands at Seventy" annex to *Leaves of Grass* (1888), p. 404.

E 2712

[On Elias Hicks], *New York Herald,* 17 September 1888.

E 2713

[Habberton, John?]. "Walt Whitman's Words," *New York Herald,* 23 September 1888, p. 8.

The author was assisted by Whitman; see *Correspondence,* IV, 212.

E 2714

"Army Hospitals and Cases: Memoranda at the Time, 1863–66," *Century Magazine,* 36 (October 1888), 825–830.

Incorporates material from " 'Tis But Ten Years Since [Fourth-Sixth Papers]" in *New York Weekly Graphic,* 21, 28 February, 7 March 1874 (E 2536, E 2537, E 2539). Revised as "Last of the War Cases" in *November Boughs* (A 12), pp. 109–118.

E 2715

Anon. "The Good Gray Poet Still Cheerful," *New York Times,* 7 October 1888, p. 20.

Letter of 10 September 1888 to Karl Knortz.

E 2716
[Unassail'd Renown], *Critic,* 13 (24 November 1888), 251–253.

Reprinted in *Good-Bye My Fancy* (A 13), pp. 40–41.

E 2717
Anon. "Walt Whitman Mending," *Camden Daily Post,* 27 December 1888, p. 1.

See *Correspondence,* IV, 256; *WWWC,* III, 396–397.

E 2718
"To the Year 1889," *Critic,* 14 (5 January 1889), 7.

Poem. Reprinted as "To the Pending Year" in *Good-Bye My Fancy* (A 13), p. 10.

E 2719
"A Voice from Death," *New York World,* 7 June 1889, p. 1.

Poem. Reprinted in *Good-Bye My Fancy* (A 13), pp. 15–16.

E 2720
Garland, Hamlin. "Whitman at Seventy," *New York Herald,* 30 June 1889, p. 7.

Whitman made revisions in this; see Kenneth M. Price and Robert C. Leitz III, "The Uncollected Letters of Hamlin Garland to Walt Whitman," *Walt Whitman Quarterly Review,* 5, no. 3 (Winter 1988), 12.

E 2721
"Bravo, Paris Exposition!", *Harper's Weekly Magazine,* 33 (28 September 1889), 774.

Poem. Reprinted in *Good-Bye My Fancy* (A 13), p. 11.

E 2722
"My 71st Year," *Century Magazine,* 39 (November 1889), 31.

Poem. Reprinted in *Good-Bye My Fancy* (A 13), p. 8.

E 2723
"A Christmas Greeting," *McClure's Magazine,* 25 December 1889.

Poem. Reprinted in *Good-Bye My Fancy* (A 13), p. 13.

E 2724
Anon. [Paragraph on Whitman], *Camden Daily Post,* 26 December 1889.

See *Daybooks,* II, 543, 544n.

E 2725
"Old Age's Ship & Crafty Death's," *Century Magazine,* 39 (February 1890), 553.

Poem. Reprinted in *Good-Bye My Fancy* (A 13), p. 10.

E 2726
"Intestinal Agitation," *Pall Mall Gazette,* 8 February 1890.

Reprinted in *Good-Bye My Fancy* (A 13), p. 47.

E 2727
Anon. "Literary Notes, News, and Echoes," *Pall Mall Gazette,* 8 February 1890, p. 1.

Letter of 22 January 1890 to Ernest Rhys. Reprinted in *Good-Bye My Fancy* (A 13), p. 47.

E 2728
"Osceola," *Munyon's Illustrated World,* 6 (April 1890), 7.

Poem. Reprinted in *Good-Bye My Fancy,* (A 13), p. 15.

E 2729
Anon. "Walt Whitman Ill," *New York Times,* 6 April 1890, p. 1.

Submitted by Whitman.

E 2730
"Walt Whitman Tuesday Night," *Boston Evening Transcript,* 19 April 1890.

Reprinted in *Camden Daily Post,* 22 April 1890; as "Walt Whitman's Last 'Public,' " *Pall Mall Gazette,* 24 May 1890; *Good-Bye My Fancy* (A 13), pp. 47–49.

E 2731
Anon. [Facsimile of lines from "Song of Myself"], *Illustrated American,* 1 (19 April 1890), 207.

E 2732
"A Twilight Song for Unknown Buried Soldiers, North and South," *Century Magazine,* 40 (May 1890), 27.

Poem. Reprinted as "A Twilight Song" in *Good-Bye My Fancy* (A 13), p. 14.

E 2733
"For Queen Victoria's Birthday," *Philadelphia Public Ledger,* 22 May 1890.

Poem. Reprinted in *Critic,* 16 (24 May 1890), 262; *Pall Mall Gazette,* 24 May 1890; *Observer* (London), 25 May 1890; *Star* (London), 27 May 1890; *Home News* (London), 30 May 1890; *Good-Bye My Fancy* (A 13), p. 28.

E 2734
["Preface" to Daniel G. Brinton and Thomas Davidson, *Giordano Bruno, Philosopher and Martyr: Two Addresses*], *Critic,* 16 (31 May 1890), 270.

Reprinted in Brinton and Davidson, *Giordano Bruno* (D 18), p. iii; as "Inscription for a Little Book on Giordano Bruno" in *Good-Bye My Fancy* (A 13), p. 41.

E 2735
"Honors to the Poet. Walt Whitman's Friends Help Him Celebrate His Birthday," *Philadelphia Inquirer,* 1 June 1890, p. 1.

Reprinted as "Walt Whitman Honored" in *Camden Daily Post,* 2 June 1890, p. 3. See *Daybooks,* II, 557–559n.

E 2736
"Ingersoll's Speech," *Camden Daily Post,* 2 June 1890, p. 1.

Reprinted in *Good-Bye My Fancy* (A 13), pp. 49–50.

E 2737
"Old Brooklyn Days," *New York Morning Journal,* 3 August 1890.

Reprinted in *Good-Bye My Fancy* (A 13), pp. 50–51.

E 2738
Anon. "Literary Gossip," *Athenæum,* no. 3267 (7 June 1890), p. 739.

Letter of 22 May 1890 to H. Buxton Forman. Reprinted in *Home Journal* (New York), 13 June 1890.

E 2739
[On Charles Woodbury's *Conversations with Emerson*], *Camden Daily Post,* 12 August 1890.

Reprinted in "Some Personal and Old Age Memoranda" in *Lippincott's Magazine,* March 1891 (E 2755).

E 2740
"An Old Man's Rejoinder," *Critic,* 17 (16 August 1890), 85–86.

Reprinted in *Good-Bye My Fancy* (A 13), pp. 21–23.

E 2741
"A Talk with Whitman," *Philadelphia Times,* 25 August 1890.

E 2742
[Riley, William Harrison]. "John Ruskin," *Illustrated American,* 3 (30 August 1890), 347–352.

Letter of [18 March 1879] to William Harrison Riley (p. 351).

E 2743
"Shakespeare for America," *Poet-Lore,* 2 (15 September 1890), 492–493.

Reprinted as "Shakspere for America" in *Critic,* 17 (27 September 1890), 160; in *Good-Bye My Fancy* (A 13), pp. 39–40.

E 2744
"The Human Voice," *Munyon's Illustrated World* (Philadelphia), 6 (October 1890), 2.

Reprinted as "The Perfect Human Voice" in *Good-Bye My Fancy* (A 13), p. 39.

E 2745
"Old Poets," *North American Review,* 151 (November 1890), 610–614.

Reprinted from advance sheets in *Pall Mall Gazette,* 17 November 1890, p. 3; in *Good-Bye My Fancy* (A 13), pp. 24–28.

E 2746
Anon. "Walt Whitman's Thanksgiving," *New York Sunday World,* 23 November 1890, p. 26.

Letter to the paper of [18 November 1890] with reprinting of "Thanks in Old Age" (first published in *Philadelphia Press,* 24 November 1887 [E 2668]).

E 2747
[On *Good-Bye My Fancy*], *Critic,* 17 (29 November 1890), 282.

Submitted by Whitman.

E 2748
"To the Sun-Set Breeze," *Lippincott's Magazine,* 46 (December 1890), 861.

Poem. Reprinted in *Good-Bye My Fancy* (A 13), p. 12.

E 2749
"Thomas Jefferson Whitman: An Engineer's Obituary," *Engineering Record,* 13 December 1890.

Reprinted as "An Engineer's Obituary" in *Good-Bye My Fancy* (A 13), pp. 53–54.

E 2750
Beare, J. I. [Partial translation of "When Lilacs Last in the Dooryard Bloom'd" into Greek], *Kottabos* (Dublin), n.s. 1 (1891), 14–15.

Poem (titled "Euthenasia") on p. 14; translation on p. 15.

E 2751
"The Pallid Wreath," *Critic*, 18 (10 January 1891), 18.

Poem. Reprinted in *Good-Bye My Fancy* (A 13), p. 9.

E 2752
[Gilder, Jeannette]. "The Lounger," *Critic*, 18 (24 January 1891), 47.

Postcard of [16? January 1891] to the Editor of the *Critic*.

E 2753
Anon. "Photographs of the Month," *Review of Reviews*, 3 (February 1891), 163.

Facsimile of postcard of 6 January 1891 to William T. Stead. Quoted in M. M. Trumbull, [editorial paragraph], *Open Court*, 5 (7 May 1891), 280.

E 2754
"Old Age Echoes," *Lippincott's Magazine*, 47 (March 1891), 376.

Poems (all reprinted in *Good-Bye My Fancy* [A 13]): "Sounds of the Winter" (p. 13), "The Unexpress'd" (p. 19), "Sail Out For Good, Eidólon Yacht!" (p. 7), "After the Argument" (p. 44).

E 2755
"Some Personal and Old-Age Memoranda," *Lippincott's Magazine*, 47 (March 1891), 377–381.

Incorporates material from *Camden Daily Post*, 12 August 1890 (E 2739). Reprinted in *Critic*, 18 (28 February 1891), 115–116; as "Some Personal and Old-Age Jottings" in *Good-Bye My Fancy* (A 13), pp. 59–64.

E 2756
Traubel, Horace. "Walt Whitman: Poet and Philosopher and Man," *Lippincott's Magazine*, 47 (March 1891), 382–389.

"The Old Man Himself: A Postscript" (p. 389) is by Whitman. Reprinted in *UPP*, II, 62.

E 2757
"The Commonplace," *Munyon's Magazine*, 8 (March 1891), 117 (facsimile).

Poem. Printed in *Good-Bye My Fancy* (A 13), p. 17.

E 2758
"Have We a National Literature," *North American Review*, 152 (March 1891), 332–338.

Reprinted as "American National Literature: Is There Any Such Thing—or Can There Ever Be?" in *Good-Bye My Fancy* (A 13), pp. 29–34.

E 2759
"Ship Ahoy!", *Youth's Companion*, 44 (12 March 1891), 152.

Poem. Reprinted in *Good-Bye My Fancy* (A 13), p. 28.

E 2760
"Old Chants," *Truth* (New York), 10 (19 March 1891), 11.

Poem. Reprinted in *Good-Bye My Fancy* (A 13), pp. 12–13.

E 2761
"Out in the Open Again," *Camden Daily Post*, 16 April 1891.

Reprinted in *Good-Bye My Fancy* (A 13), p. 64.

E 2762
["On, On the Same, Ye Jocund Twain" and "Unseen Buds"], *Once a Week* (New York), 9 June 1891.

Poems. Reprinted in *Good-Bye My Fancy* (A 13), pp. 8, 19.

E 2763
"Walt Whitman's Last," *Lippincott's Magazine*, 48 (August 1891), 256.

Reprinted in *Complete Prose Works* (C 6.2), pp. 526–527.

E 2764
"Midnight Visitor [translated from the French of Murger]," *Critic*, 19 (17 October 1891), 201.

Reprinted in *Standard Recitations by Best Authors* (D 35), p. 37.

E 2765
Young, John Russell. "Men and Memories," *Philadelphia Evening Star*, 23 January 1892, p. 5.

Letter of 24 October 1891 to John Russell Young. Reprinted in Young, *Men and Memories* (D 37), p. 90.

E 2766
[Letter], *New York Evening Telegram,* 10 March 1892.

Letter of 6 February 1892 to Dr. John Johnston.

E 2767
Anon. "Walt Whitman Dead," *San Francisco Chronicle,* 27 March 1892, p. 14.

Letter of October 1891 to an unidentified correspondent.

E 2768
Anon. "A Hitherto Unpublished Poem by Walt Whitman," *Home Journal* (New York), 30 March 1892, p. 4.

Poem. Reprinted in *UPP,* I, 23–24; *Early Poems and Fiction,* p. 49. Listed as a doubtful attribution by Killis Campbell, "Miscellaneous Notes on Whitman," *University of Texas Studies in English,* 15 (8 July 1935), 116–117.

E 2769
"Death's Valley," *Harper's Monthly Magazine,* 84 (April 1892), 707–709.

Poem. Reprinted in *Leaves of Grass* (1897), p. 428.

E 2770
[Letter], *Brooklyn Times,* 2 April 1892.

Letter of 19 January 1885 to Charles M. Skinner. Reprinted in Stephen M. Ostrander, *A History of the City of Brooklyn and Kings County* (D 26), II, 90.

E 2771
R[hys, Ernest?]. "Recollections of Walt Whitman," *Illustrated London News,* 100 (2 April 1892), 418.

Letter of 8 February 1892 to John H. Johnston (partial facsimile; see also F 42).

E 2772
"How Leaves of Grass Was Made," *Frank Leslie's Popular Monthly,* 33 (June 1892), 731–735.

Incorporates material from "[How *Leaves of Grass* Was Made]" in *New York Star,* 1885 (E 2632), and "My Book and I" in *Lippincott's Magazine,* January 1887 (E 2651). Revised reprinting of "A Backward Glance O'er Travel'd Roads" from *November Boughs* (A 12), pp. 5–18.

E 2773
["A Thought of Columbus"], *Once A Week* (New York), 9, no. 13 (16 July 1892)
(facsimile).

Poem. Reprinted in Horace Traubel, "Walt Whitman's Last Poem," *Once A
Week* (New York), 9, no. 14 (16 July 1892), 3.

E 2774
Robinson, Charles. "The Confessions of an Autograph-Hunter," *Cosmopolitan*,
14 (January 1893), 305–313.

Lines from "Salut Au Monde!", sent in manuscript by Whitman, are quoted
(pp. 308–309).

E 2775
Traubel, Horace L., R. M. Bucke, and Thomas B. Harned. "Walt Whitman in
War-Time. Familiar Letters from the Capital," *Century Magazine*, 46 (October
1893), 840–850.

Letters written between 29 December 1862 and 17 June 1864 to his family,
"selected from a volume, now in preparation . . . bearing the title 'Hospital
Letters.' " Prepublication extracts from *Wound Dresser* (A 15).

E 2776
Kennedy, William Sloane. "The Friendship of Whitman and Emerson," *Poet-
Lore*, 7 (February 1895), 71–74.

Letter of 25 February 1887 to Kennedy (pp. 72–73).

E 2777
[Letter], *Detroit Sunday News-Tribune*, 5 April 1896.

Letter of 11 August 1885 to Percy Ives.

E 2778
Kennedy, William Sloane. "A Peep into Walt Whitman's Manuscripts,"
Conservator, 7 (June 1896), 53–55.

"Come, said my Soul." Poem.

E 2779
Traubel, Horace L. "Notes on the Text of 'Leaves of Grass.' IV," *Conservator*, 7
(January 1897), 171.

"Grand is the seen." Poem.

E 2780

Bucke, Richard Maurice. "Notes on the Text of 'Leaves of Grass.' V," *Conservator*, 7 (February 1897), 185–186.

Poetry fragments.

E 2781

Gilchrist, Grace. "Chats with Walt Whitman," *Temple Bar*, 113 (February 1898), 200–212.

Letters of 22 July [1877] and [28 July 1877] to Herbert Gilchrist. Reprinted in *Eclectic Magazine*, 130 (April 1898), 451–459.

Note: Letter of [28 July 1877] reprinted in the July 1927 *Bookman* (E 2823).

E 2782

Bucke, R. M. "Walt Whitman, Man and Poet," *National Magazine*, 8 (April 1898), 34–39.

Manuscript facsimile of "As at thy Portals also Death" (p. 37).

E 2783

Harned, Thomas B. "Whitman and Physique," *Walt Whitman Fellowship Papers*, 5, no. 8 (May 1899), 43–53.

Prose. Reprinted in *Conservator*, 10 (June, July 1899), 53–54, 68–70; *Letters Written . . . to His Mother* (A 18), pp. 107–132; *Complete Writings* (B 4), VIII, 261–274.

E 2784

Miller, Florence Hardiman. "Some Unpublished Letters of Walt Whitman's Written to a Soldier Boy," *Overland Monthly*, 43 (January 1904), 61–63.

Six letters written between 1864 and 1868 to an unidentified correspondent (one of [n.d.] in facsimile, p. 63).

E 2785

Traubel, Horace. "A Fragment of Whitman Manuscript," *Artsman*, 1 (March 1904), 195–199.

"Agitations, Dangers in America" (facsimile).

E 2786

Traubel, Horace. "An American Primer," *Atlantic Monthly Magazine*, 93 (April 1904), 460–470.

See *An American Primer* (A 19).

E 2787
Traubel, Horace. "The Good Gray Poet at Home: His Familiar Talks of Men, Letters and Events," *Saturday Evening Post*, 177 (13 May 1905), 1–2.

Prepublication extracts from *WWWC*, vol. 1 (D 46).

E 2788
Traubel, Horace. "The Good Gray Poet at Home: His Familiar Talks of Men, Letters and Events," *Saturday Evening Post*, 177 (3 June 1905), 8–9.

Prepublication extracts from *WWWC*, vol. 1 (D 46).

E 2789
Traubel, Horace. "The Good Gray Poet at Home: His Familiar Talks of Men, Letters and Events," *Saturday Evening Post*, 178 (19 August 1905), 14–15.

Prepublication extracts from *WWWC*, vol. 1 (D 46).

E 2790
Traubel, Horace. "With Walt Whitman in Camden," *Century Magazine*, 71 (November 1905), 82–98.

Prepublication extracts from *WWWC*, vol. 1 (D 46).

E 2791
Anon. "New Light on Walt Whitman. Extracts from Horace L. Traubel's Diary of Conversations and Opinions of 'the Good Gray Poet,' " *Philadelphia Public Ledger*, 21 January 1906, p. 4.

Prepublication extracts from *WWWC*, vol. 1 (D 46). Includes facsimile of "after the dazzle of Day."

E 2792
Traubel, Horace. "Talks with Walt Whitman," *American Magazine*, 64 (July 1907), 281–288.

Prepublication extracts from *WWWC*, vol. 1 (D 46).

E 2793
Traubel, Horace. "Whitman in Old Age, from Horace Traubel's Record," *Century Magazine*, 74 (September 1907), 740–55.

Prepublication extracts from *WWWC*, vol. 1 (D 46).

E 2794
Traubel, Horace. "Walt Whitman's Views," *Appleton's Magazine,* 10 (October 1907), 463–472.

Prepublication extracts from *WWWC,* vol. 2 (D 48).

E 2795
Traubel, Horace. "Whitman in Old Age: Third Paper from Horace Traubel's Record," *Century Magazine,* 74 (October 1907), 911–922.

Prepublication extracts from *WWWC,* vol. 2 (D 48). Includes letter of 15 April 1870 to Benton Wilson (p. 916).

E 2796
Anon. "Letters of Walt Whitman to His Mother and an Old Friend," *Putnam's Magazine,* 5 (November 1908), 163–169.

Ten letters written between 27 December 1871 and 21 April 1881 to Louisa Van Velsor Whitman and Abby H. Price.

Note: Letter of 29 March 1860 reprinted in the July 1928 *New England Quarterly* (E 2824).

E 2797
Anon. "Some Portraits and Autographs of Walt Whitman," *Century Magazine,* 81 (February 1911), 531–533.

The poem "Rise Lurid Stars" (facsimile, p. 532) and prose piece on Abraham Lincoln (facsimile, p. 533).

E 2798
Traubel, Horace. "With Walt Whitman in Camden," *Forum,* 46 (October 1911), 400–414.

Prepublication extracts from *WWWC,* vol. 3 (D 49).

E 2799
Traubel, Horace. "With Walt Whitman in Camden," *Forum,* 46 (November 1911), 589–600.

Prepublication extracts from *WWWC,* vol. 3 (D 49).

E 2800
Traubel, Horace. "Estimates of Well-Known Men," *Century Magazine,* 83 (December 1911), 250–256.

Prepublication extracts from *WWWC,* vol. 3 (D 49).

E 2801
Traubel, Horace. "With Walt Whitman in Camden," *Forum*, 46 (December 1911), 709–719.

Prepublication extracts from *WWWC*, vol. 3 (D 49).

E 2802
Traubel, Horace. "With Walt Whitman in Camden," *Forum*, 47 (January 1912), 78–89.

Prepublication extracts from *WWWC*, vol. 3 (D 49).

E 2803
Anon. "Walt Whitman," *Collector*, 26 (November 1912), 3–4.

Letters of 26 August 1865, 15 October 1865, and 20 September 1868 to Byron Sutherland.

E 2804
Traubel, Horace. "With Walt Whitman in Camden," *Forum*, 54 (July 1915), 77–85.

Prepublication extracts from *WWWC*, vol. 4 (published in 1953; see D 87).

E 2805
Traubel, Horace. "With Walt Whitman in Camden," *Forum*, 54 (August 1915), 187–199.

Prepublication extracts from *WWWC*, vol. 4 (published in 1953; see D 87).

E 2806
Traubel, Horace. "With Walt Whitman in Camden," *Forum*, 54 (September 1915), 318–327.

Prepublication extracts from *WWWC*, vol. 4 (published in 1953; see D 87).

E 2807
Traubel, Horace. "With Walt Whitman in Camden," *Seven Arts*, 2 (September 1917), 627–637.

Prepublication extracts from *WWWC*, vol. 4 (published in 1953; see D 87).

E 2808
Johnston, Alma Calder. "Personal Memories of Walt Whitman," *Bookman* (New York), 46 (December 1917), 404–413.

Letter of 4 March 1885 to Alma and John H. Johnston (p. 412).

E 2809
Harned, Thomas B. "The Good Gray Poet in Camden," *Modern School*, 6 (April–May 1919), 112–114.

Letter of 10 May 1889 to Thomas B. Harned (p. 113). Reprinted in "Walt Whitman's Personality," *Conservator*, 30 (June 1919), 54–55.

E 2810
Anon. "Unpublished Letters of Walt Whitman to John Burroughs," *Modern School*, 6 (April–May 1919), 126–127.

Letters of 2 July 1877, 24 September 1881, and 9 April 1887 to John Burroughs.

E 2811
Harned, Thomas Biggs. "Walt Whitman and His Publishers," *Brooklyn Daily Eagle*, 31 May 1919, Whitman sec., p. 4.

Facsimile of postcard of 24 May [1885] to John Burroughs.

E 2812
Anon. "A Walt Whitman Poem Written in Brooklyn," *Brooklyn Daily Eagle*, 31 May 1919, Whitman sec., p. 9.

Facsimile of "Thou vast Rondure, swimming in space." Reprinted in *GF*, 1, 260 (facsimile); Paul Marinaccio, "Long–Lost Whitman Poem Discovered in LI Basement," *Newsday* (Long Island), 12 October 1986, p. 2 (partial facsimile); Joann P. Krieg, "Holograph Manuscript of 'Thou Vast Rondure' Comes to Light on Long Island," *Walt Whitman Quarterly Review*, 5, no. 1 (Summer 1987), 32–35 (facsimile, back cover recto and verso).

E 2813
Price, Helen E. "Reminiscences of Walt Whitman," *New York Evening Post Book Review*, 31 May 1919, p. 2.

Letters of 27 October 1866 and [9 September 1873] to Abby H. Price.

E 2814
"Ned—A Phantasm," *Collector*, 33 (August–September 1920), 1.

Fiction. Reprinted in William White, " 'Ned—A Phantasm'—Uncollected Whitman," *Emerson Society Quarterly*, no. 47 (2d Quarter 1967), pt. 2, 100–101.

E 2815
Traubel, Horace. "Whitman on His Contemporaries," *American Mercury*, 2 (July 1924), 328–332.

Prepublication extracts from *WWWC*, vol. 4 (published in 1953; see D 87).

E 2816
Traubel, Horace. "Whitman on Himself," *American Mercury,* 3 (October 1924), 186–192.

Prepublication extracts from *WWWC,* vol. 4 (published in 1953; see D 87).

E 2817
Holloway, Emory. "A Whitman Manuscript," *American Mercury,* 3 (December 1924), 475–480.

Quotes from Notebook 4A (1854), including the poem "Love is the Cause of Causes" (pp. 475–478).

E 2818
Holloway, Emory. "Whitman's Embryonic Verse," *Southwest Review,* 10, no. 4 (July 1925), 28–40.

"Pictures." Poem. Revision of "My Picture-Gallery" *(Leaves of Grass* [1881], p. 310); reprinted as *Pictures* (A 26).

E 2819
Anon. "Notes on Rare Books," *New York Times Book Review,* 8 November 1925, p. 16.

Letter of 18 January 1872 to Edward Dowden (partial). Reprinted as "A Great Whitman Letter Brings a Small Price," *Biblio,* 5 (November–December 1925), 855–856.

E 2820
Catel, Jean. "Carnet de Notes de Walt Whitman," *L'Ane d'Or,* 5 (February–March 1926), 46–57.

Postcard of 5 January 1889 to Sylvester Baxter and letters of 23 December 1890, 8 April 1891, 29 April 1891, and 8–9 July 1891 to Dr. John Johnston.

Note: The postcard to Baxter is reprinted in Catel, *Walt Whitman, La Naissance de Poète* (D 67).

E 2821
"La Dix-Huitième Présidence!" [trans. Sylvia Beach and Adrienne Monnier], *Navire d'Argent,* March 1926.

See *The Eighteenth Presidency!* (A 27).

E 2822
Catel, Jean. "Walt Whitman pendant la Guerre de Sécession d'après documents inédits," *Revue Anglo-Américaine,* 3 (June 1926), 410–419.

Prose.

E 2823
Frend, Grace Gilchrist. "Walt Whitman as I Remember Him," *Bookman* (London), 72 (July 1927), 203–205.

Letters of 3–5 August 1878 and [28 July 1877] (facsimile) to Herbert Gilchrist (p. 204).

Note: Letter of [28 July 1877] is reprinted from the February 1898 *Temple Bar* (E 2781).

E 2824
Furness, Clifton Joseph. "Walt Whitman Looks at Boston," *New England Quarterly*, 1 (July 1928), 353–370.

Various manuscripts and letters of 29 March 1860 to Abby M. Price (pp. 358–359) and 1 April and 10 May 1860 to Thomas Jefferson Whitman (pp. 359–360).

Note: Letter of 29 March 1860 is reprinted from the November 1908 *Putnam's Magazine* (E 2796).

E 2825
Holloway, Emory. "Some New Whitman Letters," *American Mercury*, 16 (February 1929), 183–189.

Letters written between 1863 and 1865 to his family.

E 2826
Morley, Christopher. "The Bowling Green," *Saturday Review of Literature*, 5 (23 February 1929), 705.

Manuscript on Whitman's symptoms after his 1873 stroke.

E 2827
Furness, Clifton Joseph. "Walt Whitman's Politics," *American Mercury*, 16 (April 1929), 459–466.

Various manuscripts.

E 2828
Rodgers, Cleveland. "Walt Whitman Still an Outsider!", *Brooklyn Daily Eagle Sunday Magazine*, 25 May 1930, pp. 1–2.

Letter of 1 October 1861 to James Russell Lowell (facsimile).

E 2829
Anon. "Walt Whitman's Notes of His Western Trip," *Biblia* (Friends of the Princeton University Library), 1 (June 1930), 3.

Prose fragments.

E 2830
Hicks, Granville. "Letters to William Francis Channing," *American Literature,* 2 (November 1930), 294–298.

Letter of 27 September 1868 to William Francis Channing (pp. 297–298).

E 2831
Furness, Clifton Joseph. "Walt Whitman's Estimate of Shakespeare," *Harvard Studies and Notes in Philology and Literature,* 14 (1932), 1–33.

Various letters.

E 2832
G., N. L. "101 Books," *Dartmouth College Library Bulletin,* 1 (May 1932), 3–7.

Letter of 30 November 1868 to Ralph Waldo Emerson (p. 5).

E 2833
Birss, John Howard. "Whitman on Arnold: An Uncollected Comment," *Modern Language Notes,* 47 (May 1932), 316–317.

Reprints clipping from the "Herald." Not located in either the Boston or New York papers of that name.

E 2834
Holloway, Emory. "Walt Whitman's Visit to the Shakers," *Colophon,* 4, part 13 (February 1933), [12 pp., unpaged].

Prose notebook (with facsimile).

E 2835
Holloway, Emory. "Notes from a Whitman Student's Scrapbook," *American Scholar,* 2 (May 1933), 269–278.

Various manuscripts.

E 2836
Glicksberg, Charles I. "Walt Whitman and Heinrich Zschokke," *Notes and Queries,* 166 (2 June 1934), 382–384.

Prose.

E 2837
Glicksberg, Charles I. "Walt Whitman in 1862," *American Literature,* 6 (November 1934), 264–282.

Quotations from Whitman's 1862 notebook.

E 2838
Silver, Rollo G. "Seven Letters of Walt Whitman," *American Literature,* 7 (March 1935), 76–81.

Letters written between 20 July 1857 and 29 October 1891 to various corresondents.

E 2839
Metzdorf, Robert F. "A Whitman Letter," *Saturday Review of Literature,* 11 (6 April 1935), 598.

Letter 5 September 1863 to Nathaniel Bloom.

E 2840
Bernard, Edward G. "Some New Whitman Manuscript Notes," *American Literature,* 8 (March 1936), 59–63.

Various manuscripts.

E 2841
Traubel, Anne M. "Education in Our Schools," *Week-End* [Sunday supplement to *Brooklyn Daily Eagle*], 12 July 1936.

Prose.

E 2842
Silver, Rollo G. "Thirty-One Letters of Walt Whitman," *American Literature,* 8 (January 1937), 417–438.

Letters written between 8 March 1863 and 30 November 1890.

E 2843
Glicksberg, Charles I. "Walt Whitman in New Jersey. Some Unpublished Manuscripts," *Proceedings of the New Jersey Historical Society,* 55 (January 1937), 42–46.

Prose fragments.

E 2844
Alexander, Colin C. "A Note on Walt Whitman," *American Literature,* 9 (May 1937), 242–243.

Postcard of 14 January 1880 to John P. Usher (p. 243).

E 2845
Silver, Rollo G. "For the Bright Particular Star," *Colophon,* n.s. 2, no. 2 (Winter 1937), 197–216.

Various letters written between 4 March 1884 and 18 November 1890 to Mary Whitall Smith Costelloe and others.

Note: The letters of 20 July 1885 to Mary Whitall Smith Costelloe and 20 June 1890 to Robert Pearsall Smith are reprinted in Robert Allerton Parker, *The Transatlantic Smiths* (D 94), pp. 59–60, 53.

E 2846
McCusker, Honor. "Leaves of Grass," *More Books* (Boston Public Library), 13 (May 1938), 179–192.

Various letters and facsimile of the poem "Out from Behind this Mask" (p. 189).

E 2847
Coad, Oral Sumner. "A Walt Whitman Manuscript," *Journal of the Rutgers University Library,* 2 (December 1938), 6–10.

"Hush'd be the Camps Today" (and facsimile after p. 9). Poem.

E 2848
Catel, Jean. "Un inédit de Walt Whitman," *Études Anglaises,* 3 (October–December 1939), 359–360.

Prose.

E 2849
Naumberg, Edward, Jr. "A Collector Looks at Walt Whitman," *Princeton University Library Chronicle,* 3 (November 1941), 1–18.

Letters of [November 1890] and 18 March [1887] to Joseph B. Gilder, and prose fragments (pp. 5–6, 6–7, and in facsimile after p. 4).

E 2850
Coad, Oral S. "A Whitman Letter," *Journal of the Rutgers University Library,* 6 (December 1942), 29.

Letter of 2 May 1865 to Peter Eckler.

E 2851
Wecter, Dixon. "Walt Whitman as Civil Servant," *PMLA,* 58 (December 1943), 1094–1109.

Various letters.

E 2852
"Olybrius." "Whitman: Notes on Emerson," *Notes and Queries,* 186 (24 February 1944), 114.

Prose manuscript quoted from Goodspeed's Catalogue 373.

E 2853
Coad, Oral S. "Seven Whitman Letters," *Journal of the Rutgers University Library,* 8 (December 1944), 18–26.

Letters written between 24 May 1885 and 19 July 1891 to William Sloane Kennedy.

E 2854
Anon. "Unpublished Notes and Letters," *Wake,* 7 (Autumn 1948), 6–22.

Previously unpublished writings and letters (43 items), including the poem ["What the Sun"] (p. 18; reprinted in *Reader's Edition,* p. 653).

E 2855
Roos, Carl. "Walt Whitman's Letters to a Danish Friend," *Orbis Litterarum,* 7 (1949), 31–60.

Twenty-one letters written between 7 December 1871 and 24 December 1889 to Rudolf Schmidt.

E 2856
Hubach, Robert R. "An Uncollected Walt Whitman Letter," *Duke University Library Notes,* no. 23 (January 1950), 13.

Letter of 30 November 1890 to David L. Lezinsky.

E 2857
Grier, Edward F. "Walt Whitman, the *Galaxy,* and *Democratic Vistas,*" *American Literature,* 23 (November 1951), 332–350.

Eleven letters written between 7 August 1867 and 15 November 1869 to William Conant Church and Francis P. Church.

E 2858
Harding, Walter. "A Sheaf of Whitman Letters," *Studies in Bibliography,* 5 (1952), 203–210.

Fourteen letters written between 20 January 1860 and 30 September 1889.

E 2859
Bowers, Fredson. "Whitman's Manuscripts for the Original 'Calamus' Poems," *Studies in Bibliography*, 6 (1953), 257–265.

"Live Oak, with Moss." Poem. Incorporated into *Whitman's Manuscripts* (A 37).

E 2860
Hoeltje, Hubert H. "Whitman's Letter to Robert Carter," *American Literature*, 25 (November 1953), 360–362.

Letter of 7 May 1875 (p. 361).

E 2861
Bowers, Fredson. "The Manuscript of Whitman's 'Passage to India,' " *Modern Philology*, 51 (November 1953), 102–117.

Poem and letter of 15 March 1870 to Andrew and Thomas Rome (pp. 102–103).

E 2862
Bergman, Herbert. "Whitman and Tennyson," *Studies in Philology*, 51 (July 1954), 492–504.

Prose.

E 2863
Bowers, Fredson. "The Manuscript of Walt Whitman's 'A Carol of Harvest, for 1867,' " *Modern Philology*, 52 (August 1954), 29–51.

Poem.

E 2864
[Holloway, Emory]. "Walt Whitman and John Burroughs," *Nocturne* (Brooklyn College), 7 (Spring 1955), 10–11.

Letters of 18–20 June [1872] and 25 January [1879] to John Burroughs (in facsimile).

E 2865
McElderry, B. R., Jr. "Hamlin Garland's View of Whitman," *Personalist*, 36 (Autumn 1955), 369–378.

Postcard of 25 October 1889 to Hamlin Garland (pp. 373–374).

E 2866
White, William. "Walt Whitman on New England Writers: An Uncollected Fragment," *New England Quarterly*, 27 (September 1955), 395–396.

Prose.

E 2867
Cameron, Kenneth Walter. "Three Ungathered Whitman Manuscripts," *Emerson Society Quarterly*, no. 1 (4th Quarter 1955), 8–9.

Postcard of 23 April [1876] to William Michael Rossetti (p. 9; facsimile, p. 8); postcard of 14 November 1882 to Franklin Benjamin Sanborn (p. 9); letter of 13 January 1892 to Franklin Benjamin Sanborn (p. 9).

E 2868
Miller, Edwin Haviland. "Walt Whitman's Correspondence with Whitelaw Reid, Editor of the New York *Tribune*," *Studies in Bibliography*, 8 (1956), 242–249.

Eleven letters written between 5 December 1874 and 23 May 1882 to Whitelaw Reid.

E 2869
Bowers, Fredson. "The Manuscripts of Whitman's 'Song of the Redwood-Tree,'" *Papers of the Bibliographical Society of America*, 50 (1st Quarter 1956), 53–85.

Poem.

E 2870
Anon. "Whitman's Commonplace Book—31 May 1889–2 December 1891," *Walt Whitman Newsletter*, 2 (March–June 1956), 6.

Prose (facsimile).

E 2871
Blodgett, Harold W. "Toward the Second Edition of *Leaves of Grass*: An Unpublished Whitman Notebook, 1855–1856," *Walt Whitman Newsletter*, 2 (December 1956), 35–53, 55.

Facsimile on p. 55. See *An 1855–1856 Notebook* (A 38).

E 2872
Shelley, Fred. "From the Library," *Proceedings of the New Jersey Historical Society*, 75 (1957), 218–219.

Letters of 20 February 1867 to Llewellyn Avery, Jr., and 19 December 1867 to G. A. Tracy, and postcard of 15 September 1887 to Willard Carey.

E 2873
Asselineau, Roger. "Un Inédit de Walt Whitman: 'Taine's History of English Literature,'" *Études Anglaises,* 10 (April–June 1957), 128–138.

Prose (pp. 131–138).

E 2874
Bowers, Fredson. "The Earliest Manuscript of Whitman's 'Passage to India' and Its Notebook," *Bulletin of the New York Public Library,* 61 (July 1957), 319–352.

Prose and poetry.

E 2875
Hollis, C. Carroll. "Whitman and the American Idiom," *Quarterly Journal of Speech,* 43 (December 1957), 408–420.

Various manuscripts.

E 2876
White, William. "Sir Edmund Gosse on Walt Whitman," *Victorian Studies,* 1 (December 1957), 180–182.

Letter of 31 December 1884 to Edmund Gosse (p. 182).

E 2877
Anon. "From a Whitman Diary," *Walt Whitman Newsletter,* 3 (December 1957), 67.

Prose (entry of 25 February 1863, facsimile).

E 2878
Feinberg, Charles E. "A Whitman Collector Destroys a Whitman Myth," *Papers of the Bibliographical Society of America,* 52 (2d Quarter 1958), 73–92.

Facsimiles of receipts written by Whitman (pp. 77, 80).

E 2879
White, William. "Logan Pearsall Smith on Walt Whitman: A Correction and Some Unpublished Letters," *Walt Whitman Newsletter,* 4 (June 1958), 87–90.

Six postcards and letters written between 1 December 1883 and 22 January 1890 to Mary Whitall Smith Costelloe and Robert Pearsall Smith.

E 2880
Anon. " 'Kentucky': An Unpublished Poem," *Walt Whitman Newsletter,* 4 (June 1958), 99.

Partial facsimile. See *Kentucky* (A 39).

E 2881
Anon. "Sketch for the 1856 Spine," *Walt Whitman Newsletter,* 4 (September 1958), 99.

Facsimile. Reprinted in C. Carroll Hollis, "Whitman's Sketches for the Spine of the 1856 Edition," *Walt Whitman Quarterly Review,* 4, nos. 2–3 (Fall–Winter 1986), 75–76 (facsimile, back cover verso).

E 2882
[White, William, and James E. Miller, Jr.]. " 'Kentucky': Unpublished Poetic Fragments by Walt Whitman," *Prairie Schooner,* 32 (Fall 1958), 172–178.

Printed text and type facsimile. See *Kentucky* (A 39).

E 2883
Cameron, Kenneth Walter. "Rough Draft of Whitman's *By Emerson's Grave,"* *Emerson Society Quarterly,* no. 13 (4th Quarter 1958), 32–34.

Prose (partial facsimile, p. 33).

E 2884
Asselineau, Roger. "Walt Whitman to Gabriel Sarrazin: Four Unpublished Pieces," *Walt Whitman Newsletter,* 5 (March 1959), 8–11.

Letter of 5 September 1890 (p. 10), and postcards of 4 May 1889 (p. 9), 31 December 1890 (p. 11), and 26 June 1891 (p. 11).

E 2885
Asselineau, Roger. "Three Uncollected 'Leaves of Grass,' " *Huntington Library Quarterly,* 22 (May 1959), 255–259.

Poems (all reprinted in *Reader's Edition*): "To the Future" (p. 657), "Inscription, to precede Leaves of Grass, when finished" (pp. 668–669), "While the schools and the teachers are teaching" (p. 669).

E 2886
Anon. "Whitman's Last Words," *Walt Whitman Newsletter,* 5 (June 1959), 39.

Prose (facsimile). Reprinted from the 1959 Kindle Press edition (H 29).

E 2887
Anon. "Words from Walt Whitman," *Long-Islander,* 2 July 1959, sec. III, p. 1.

Facsimile of prose lines beginning "important points to recollect."

E 2888
Anon. " 'Spirit that Form'd this Scene,' " *Walt Whitman Newsletter,* 5 (September 1959), 58–59.

Poem (facsimile).

E 2889
White, William. " 'I am a Born Democrat': An Unpublished Whitman Fragment," *Notes and Queries,* 6 (December 1959), 454–455.

Prose.

E 2890
White, William. "Three Unpublished Whitman Fragments," *Walt Whitman Newsletter,* 5 (December 1959), 75–76.

Prose: "Recalles," "Grand Old Veteran Authors," and "I Am Not Afraid of Foreign Writers."

E 2891
Miller, Edwin Haviland. "New Letters of Walt Whitman," *Missouri Historical Society Bulletin,* 16 (January 1960), 99–113.

Various letters.

E 2892
Feinberg, Charles E. "Percy Ives, Detroit and Walt Whitman," *Detroit Historical Society Bulletin,* 16 (February 1960), 4–11.

Letter of 7 September 1881 to Percy and Lewis Ives (p. 6) and postcard of 26 October 1891 to Elisa S. Leggett (p. 10).

E 2893
Hollis, C. Carroll. "Whitman on 'Periphrastic' Literature . . . Speculations on an Unpublished Ms. Fragment," *Fresco* (University of Detroit), 10 (Winter–Spring 1960), 5–13.

Prose.

Note: Revised in the Winter 1990 *Walt Whitman Quarterly Review* (E 3021).

E 2894
Anon. "A Letter to Grant," *Walt Whitman Review,* 6 (March 1960), 19.

Draft of letter [of 27 February 1874] to Ulysses S. Grant (facsimile). Reprinted in William White, "Walt Whitman to U. S. Grant: An Unknown Exchange," *Prairie Schooner*, 34 (Summer 1961), 120–122; White, "Whitman to U. S. Grant: An Addendum," *Walt Whitman Review*, 13 (June 1967), 60–61.

E 2895
Anon. [Facsimile of "Paumanok"], *Long-Islander*, 26 May 1960, sec. 3, p. 1.

Poem.

E 2896
Miller, Edwin H. "Whitman's Correspondence with Edwin Booth," *Walt Whitman Review*, 6 (September 1960), 49–50.

Letters of 21 August (p. 49) and 3 September 1884 (p. 50).

E 2897
Anon. ["Criticism"], *Literary Review*, 4 (Autumn 1960), 49–59.

Prose (pp. 49–58 and in facsimile). See *Criticism* (A 22).

E 2898
Anon. "An Unpublished Whitman Poem Is Found in a California Attic," *New York Times*, 22 November 1960, sec. L, p. 27.

"Wood Odors." Poem. Reprinted in Rena V. Grant, "Wood Odors," *Harper's Magazine*, 221 (December 1960), 43; *Reader's Edition*, pp. 674–675.

E 2899
Anon. "Whitman Designs His Tomb," *Walt Whitman Review*, 6 (December 1960), 79.

Sketch (facsimile). Reprinted in William White, [Whitman's Design for His Own Tomb], *Long-Islander*, 13 June 1974, sec. 3, p. 5B (facsimile).

E 2900
White, William. "Whitman's Prose," *Harper's Magazine*, 222 (March 1961), 6, 8.

"Sunday Morning in the Woods." Prose.

E 2901
Grant, Rena V. "The Livesey-Whitman Manuscripts," *Walt Whitman Review*, 7 (March 1961), 3–14.

Prose.

E 2902
Anon. " 'Sunday Morning': An Unpublished MS," *Walt Whitman Review,* 7 (March 1961), 19.

Poem (facsimile).

E 2903
Miller, Edwin Haviland. "Whitman's 16.4 Diary," *American Book Collector,* 11, no. 2 (May 1961), 21–24.

Notebook of 1868–1870 (facsimile, pp. 23–24).

E 2904
White, William. "Walt Whitman in 'Ideals of Life,' " *American Book Collector,* 11, no. 2 (May 1961), 30–31.

Letter of 15 March 1891 to Wallace Wood (p. 31).

E 2905
Wyllie, John Cook. "The Barrett Collection of Walt Whitman," *American Book Collector,* 11, no. 2 (May 1961), 32–33.

Draft letter of 17 January 1863 to Ralph Waldo Emerson (facsimile, p. 32).

E 2906
McLeod, A. L. "Walt Whitman in Australia," *Walt Whitman Review,* 7 (June 1961), 23–35.

Ten letters written between July 1890 and 1 November 1891 to Bernard O'Dowd.

Note: Reprinted in A. L. McLeod, *Walt Whitman in Australia and New Zealand* (D 98).

E 2907
Anon. "Notes for a Letter to O'Dowd," *Walt Whitman Review,* 7 (June 1961), 39.

Facsimile.

E 2908
Sewell, Richard H. "Walt Whitman, John P. Hale, and the Free Democracy: An Unpublished Letter," *New England Quarterly,* 34 (June 1961), 239–242.

Letter of 14 August [1852] to John P. Hale.

E 2909
White, William. "Whitman on Newspaper Practices in the 1870s," *Journalism Quarterly,* 37 (Summer 1961), 438–439.

Prose manuscript of October 1876.

E 2910
White, William. "Trial Lines for the 1855 *Leaves?*", *Walt Whitman Review,* 7 (September 1961), [60].

Poetry.

E 2911
Golden, Arthur. "A Note on a Whitman Holograph Poem," *Papers of the Bibliographical Society of America,* 55 (3d Quarter 1961), 233–236.

"O brood continental" (see *"Apostrophe"*).

E 2912
White, William. "Walt Whitman, 'Western Nicknames': An Unpublished Note," *American Speech,* 36 (December 1961), 296–298.

"Western Nicknames." Prose.

E 2913
White, William. "$400 for the *Brooklyn Freeman?*", *Walt Whitman Review,* 7 (December 1961): back cover verso.

Facsimile of signed receipt written by Whitman.

E 2914
White, William. "An Unpublished Notebook: Walt Whitman in Washington in 1863," *American Book Collector,* 12, no. 5 (January 1962), 8–13.

Notebook of 1863 (facsimile, pp. 9–13).

E 2915
White, William. "Whitman as Short Story Writer: Two Unpublished Manuscripts," *Notes and Queries,* 9 (March 1962), 87–89.

Fragments of "Antoinette the Courtesan" or "The Fate of Antoinette."

E 2916
Anon. "O'Dowd to Whitman—Whitman to O'Dowd," *Overland* (Melbourne, Australia), no. 23 (April 1962), 8–18.

Letter of 15 March 1891 (p. 17). The other letters are reprinted from the June 1961 *Walt Whitman Review* (E 2906).

E 2917
White, William. "Walt Whitman on French Cookery," *Accent on Home Economics* (Wayne State University), no. 10 (Spring 1962), [1–4].

Prose.

E 2918
Anon. "What Is Poetry? An Early Draft," *Walt Whitman Review*, 8 (September 1962), [72].

Prose (facsimile).

E 2919
White, William. "Whitman's Copy of Epictetus," *Walt Whitman Review*, 8 (December 1962), 95–[96].

Prose (facsimile).

E 2920
White, William. " 'Nationalism': Unpublished Whitman?", *American Notes and Queries*, 1 (January 1963), 67–68.

Prose.

E 2921
White, William. "Whitman's First 'Literary' Letter," *American Literature*, 35 (March 1963), 83–85.

Letter of 17 June 1850 to Moses S. and Alfred E. Beach (pp. 84–85). Printed in facsimile in the 30 May 1963 *Long-Islander*.

E 2922
White, William. [Unpublished title page of *Leaves of Grass*], *Long-Islander*, 30 May 1963, sec. II, p. 8.

Facsimile.

E 2923
White, William. "An Unpublished Whitman Notebook for 'Lilacs,' " *Modern Language Quarterly*, 24 (June 1963), 177–180.

Prose.

E 2924
White, William. "Whitman on American Poets: An Uncollected Piece," *English Language Notes,* 1 (September 1963), 42–43.

Reprints a clipping from "Advertiser July 1st 1885." Not located in *Boston Daily Advertiser.*

E 2925
White, William. "Preface to *Democratic Vistas,*" *Walt Whitman Review,* 9 (September 1963), 71–[72].

Prose (facsimile).

E 2926
Anon. [Eight Poems], *Quarterly Review of Literature,* 13, nos. 1–2 (1964), 4–8.

Poems (all reprinted in *Reader's Edition*): "To the Poor" (p. 677), "My Own Poems" (p. 680), "To What You Said" (p. 681), "I Stand and Look" (p. 679), "Reminiscences, '64" (p. 682), "Champagne in Ice" (pp. 684–685), "Sunrise" (p. 686), "America to the Old World Bards" (p. 688).

E 2927
Anon. "Notes from the Rare Books Room—No. 15," *Occasional Notes* (University of Colorado Library), 4 (May 1964), 2–3.

Letter of 2 September 1889 to William Ingram (facsimile, p. 2).

E 2928
Anon. [Facsimile of "Going Somewhere"], *Long-Islander,* 28 May 1964, sec. 3, p. 1.

Poem.

E 2929
Anon. "Hegel—To Introduce. Whitman A.MS.," *Walt Whitman Review,* 10 (June 1964), 48.

Prose (facsimile).

E 2930
Miller, Edwin Haviland. "A Whitman Letter to Hiram J. Ramsdell," *Walt Whitman Review,* 10 (December 1964), 97–98.

Letter of 19 July 1867 (pp. 97–98).

E 2931
White, William. "MS of 'How I Get Around,'" *Walt Whitman Review,* 10 (December 1964), 103–104.

Prose (facsimile).

E 2932
Skipp, Francis E. "Whitman's 'Lucifer': A Footnote to 'The Sleepers,'" *Walt Whitman Review,* 11 (June 1965), 52–53.

"Sleepchasings" (p. 53). Poem.

E 2933
Golden, Arthur. "A Recovered Whitman Fair Copy of a 'Drum-Taps' Poem, and a 'Sequel to Drum-Taps' Fragment," *Papers of the Bibliographical Society of America,* 59 (4th Quarter 1965), 439–441.

Poems: "Come Up from the Fields Father" and "To the Leaven'd Soil They Trod."

E 2934
White, William. "Whitman's *Democratic Vistas:* An Unpublished Self-Review?" *American Book Collector,* 16, no. 4 (December 1965), 21.

"Preface to Dem[ocratic]. Vistas." Prose.

E 2935
Monteiro, George. "A New Whitman Letter," *Walt Whitman Review,* 11 (December 1965), 102–103.

Letter of 20 October 1866 to Theodore F. Dwight (p. 103).

E 2936
Broderick, John C. "An Unpublished Whitman Letter and Other Manuscripts," *American Literature,* 37 (January 1966), 475–478.

Letter of 23 August 1867 to William Conant Church and Francis P. Church (p. 476)

E 2937
White, William. "Author at Work: Whitman's *Specimen Days,*" *Manuscripts,* 18, no. 3 (Summer 1966), 26–28.

"The First Frost—Mems" (pp. 27–28). Prose.

E 2938
White, William. "Whitman's Commonplace Book," *Walt Whitman Review,* 12 (June 1966), 47–[48].

Prose (facsimile of entries for 9 April–11 May 1882, p. [48]).

E 2939
White, William. "A Nation's Poems: An Unpublished Fragment," *Walt Whitman Review,* 12 (December 1966), 103–[104].

Prose (facsimile, p. [104]).

E 2940
Miller, Edwin Haviland. "A New Whitman Letter to Josiah Child," *Walt Whitman Review,* 13 (March 1967), 32–33.

Letter of 8 December 1881 (p. 32–33).

E 2941
White, William. " 'Words': Whitman's Dictionary Notebook," *Walt Whitman Review,* 13 (September 1967), 103–[104].

Prose (facsimile, p. [104]).

E 2942
Anon. "The Engel Collection," *Columbia University Forum,* 10 (Winter 1967), 6–7.

Letter of 21 July 1870 to Moncure D. Conway (facsimile, p. 6) and Whitman's copy of his letter of 21 July 1855 to Ralph Waldo Emerson (facsimile, p. 7).

E 2943
Anon. "Walt Whitman's Blue Book," *Walt Whitman Review,* 13 (December 1967), 129–[130].

"Starting from fish-shaped Paumanok" (facsimile, p. [130]). Poem.

E 2944
Golden, Samuel A. "Whitman to Mrs. Vine Coburn: Three Letters," *Walt Whitman Review,* 15 (March 1969), 59–60.

Postcards of 9 February, 18 February, and 7 March 1882 (p. 60).

E 2945
White, William. "Walt Whitman: An Unpublished Autobiographical Note," *Notes and Queries,* n.s. 16 (June 1969), 221–222.

Prose.

E 2946
White, William. "Whitman on Himself: An Unrecorded Piece," *Papers on Language and Literature,* 6 (Spring 1970), 202–205.

Proof of "Foreign Criticisms of an American Poet" (pp. 202–204).

E 2947
White, William. "Some New Whitman Items," *Prairie Schooner,* 44 (Spring 1970), 47–55.

Suggests the possibility of "Remember me!" (written in an autograph album in 1837) being by Whitman (p. 48). Letter of 13 October 1891 to Samuel G. Stanley (pp. 51–52); postcards of 17 February 1887 and 1 August 1876 to John Burroughs (pp. 53, 54); letters of 29 July 1890 to John Addington Symonds (p. 54) and 6 November 1882 to W. Hale White (p. 55).

E 2948
Freedman, Florence B. "A Whitman Letter to Josiah Child," *Walt Whitman Review,* 16 (June 1970), 55–57.

Letter of 9 June 1879.

E 2949
White, William. "Two New Letters to R. Spence Watson," *Walt Whitman Review,* 16 (December 1970), 122.

Postcards of 30 August and 9 September 1876.

E 2950
White, William. " 'My Legacy' in Process," *Walt Whitman Review,* 16 (December 1970), 127–[128].

Poem (facsimile, p. [128]).

E 2951
White, William. "Billy Duckett: Whitman Rogue," *American Book Collector,* 21, no. 5 (February 1971), 20–23.

Prose (p. 20).

E 2952
Cole, John Y. "Of Copyright, Men & a National Library," *Quarterly Journal of the Library of Congress*, 28 (April 1971), 114–136.

Letter of 22 July 1876 to Ainsworth Rand Spofford (facsimile, p. 131).

E 2953
Preuschen, Karl Adalbert. "Walt Whitman's Undelivered Oration 'The Dead in This War,'" *Études Anglaises*, 24 (April–June 1971), 147–151.

"The Dead in this War" (prose; p. 148) and "Reminiscences 64" (poem; p. 151).

E 2954
White, William. " 'Is There a Port of Destination?' ", *Walt Whitman Review*, 17 (June 1971), 69–[70].

Prose (facsimile, p. [70]).

E 2955
White, William. "Two More Unpublished Whitman Letters," *American Notes and Queries*, 10 (September 1971), 3–4.

Letters of 12 February 1887 (p. 3) and 23 June 1891 (p. 3) to John H. Johnston.

E 2956
White, William. "Unpublished Whitman Prose," *American Notes and Queries*, 10 (October 1971), 27.

Prose.

E 2957
White, William. "Portraits from Life," *Walt Whitman Review*, 17 (December 1971), 145–[146].

Prose (facsimile, p. [146]).

E 2958
White, William. "An Unpublished Whitman Poem," *Walt Whitman Review*, 18 (March 1972), [36].

"Let musings flood thee" (facsimile). Poem.

E 2959
White, William. " 'Queries to My Seventieth Year': An Early Draft," *Walt Whitman Review*, 18 (September 1972), 109–[110].

Poem (facsimile, p. [110]).

E 2960
White, William. "Whitman on Hartmann's 'Society': An Unpublished (?) Walt Whitman Piece," *Sadakichi Hartmann Newsletter,* 3, no. 2 (Fall 1972), 8.

Prose.

E 2961
Shephard, Esther. "The Inside Front and Back Covers of Whitman's Earliest Known Notebook: Some Observations on Photocopy and Verbal Descriptions," *PMLA,* 87 (October 1972), 1119–1122.

Facsimile of the inside covers of an 1840s notebook (pp. 1121–1222).

E 2962
White, William. "Unrecorded Whitman Letter to H. H. Furness," *Walt Whitman Review,* 18 (December 1972), 141–[142].

Letter of 26 January 1881 to Horace Howard Furness (facsimile, p. [142]).

E 2963
Broderick, John C. "Walt Whitman's Earliest Letter," *Quarterly Journal of the Library of Congress,* 30 (January 1973), 44–47.

Letter of 30 March 1841 to an unidentified correspondent.

E 2964
White, William. "Unknown Letter to W. S. Huntington," *Walt Whitman Review,* 19 (June 1973), [73].

Letter of 5 March 1870 (facsimile).

E 2965
White, William. "A New Whitman Letter to *The Century,*" *Walt Whitman Review,* 19 (September 1973), [118].

Letter of 25 July 1886 to the editor of the *Century* (facsimile).

E 2966
White, William. " 'What is Greatest': Unpublished Whitman?", *Walt Whitman Review,* 20 (March 1974), 37–[38].

Prose (facsimile, p. [38]).

E 2967
Stibitz, E. Earle. "Walt Whitman Answers a Collector," *ICarbS,* 1 (Spring–Summer 1974), 141–144.

Letter of 17 October 1871 to an unidentified correspondent.

E 2968
White, William. "Whitman on Carlyle: A New Letter," *Walt Whitman Review,*
20 (June 1974), [74].

Letter of 30 August 1886 to G. Oscar Gridley (facsimile).

E 2969
Anon. [Facsimile of letter], *Long-Islander,* 13 June 1974, sec. 3, p. 5B.

Facsimile of letter of 25 March 1874 to J. C. Mann.

E 2970
Batten, Charles L., Jr. "Unpublished Whitman Letter to Dr. Bucke," *Walt
Whitman Review,* 20 (September 1974), 115–116.

Postcard of 21 March 1891 (p. 116).

E 2971
White, William. "Whitman to Roden Noel: A New Letter," *Walt Whitman
Review,* 20 (September 1974), 117–[118].

Postcard of 29 June 1886 (facsimile, p. [118]).

E 2972
White, William. "A New Whitman Letter to J. Q. A. Ward," *Walt Whitman
Review,* 21 (September 1975), 131–[132].

Letter of 8 June 1876 (facsimile, p. [132]).

E 2973
White, William. "Whitman to J. A. Symonds: Unpublished," *Walt Whitman
Review,* 21 (December 1975), [168].

Letter of 7 November [1881] (facsimile).

E 2974
White, William. "A New Whitman Letter to Mary Whitall Costelloe," *Walt
Whitman Review,* 22 (March 1976), 42–43.

Letter of 2 March 1890.

E 2975
White, William. " 'The Last Meaning': Unpublished Whitman?", *Walt Whitman Review,* 22 (September 1976), [134].

Poetry (facsimile).

E 2976
White, William. "An Unknown Whitman MS on the 1855 *Leaves*," *Walt Whitman Review*, 22 (December 1976), 172, [174].

Letter of 31 March 1885 to an unidentified correspondent (facsimile, p. [174]).

E 2977
Del Greco, Robert. "A New Whitman Letter to Talcott Williams," *Walt Whitman Review*, 23 (March 1977), 52–53.

Letter of 2 December 1890 (p. 53).

E 2978
White, William. "A New Whitman Letter to Deborah Browning," *Walt Whitman Review*, 23 (September 1977), 143–[144].

Postcard of 19 April 1887 (facsimile, p. [144]).

E 2979
De Marco, Sergio. "A Manuscript by Walt Whitman in the University of California Library," *Studi dell'Instituto Linguistico*, 1 (1978), 121–134.

Prose.

E 2980
White, William. "Unpublished Whitman Notes to Himself," *Walt Whitman Review*, 24 (March 1978), 41–[42].

Prose (facsimile, p. [42]).

E 2981
White, William. "*Daybook* Notes Left Over," *Walt Whitman Review*, 24 (June 1978), 91–[92].

Prose (facsimile, p. [92]).

E 2982
White, William. "A New Post Card to Samuel Hollyer," *Walt Whitman Review*, 24 (September 1978), 133–[134].

Postcard of 5 August 1888 (facsimile, p. [134]).

E 2983
White, William. "Whitman Sells Burroughs' *Notes:* An Unpublished Letter," *Walt Whitman Review*, 25 (June 1979), 83–[84].

Letter of 1 August 1877 to an unidentified correspondent (facsimile, p. [84]).

E 2984
White, William. "Unknown Whitman Letter to Mrs. Colquitt," *Walt Whitman Review,* 25 (December 1979), [182].

Postcard of 18 July 1890 (facsimile).

E 2985
White, William. " 'Some Late Occurences, Facts, in Boston': Unpublished Whitman Prose," *Walt Whitman Review,* 26 (1980), supplement, 75–78.

Prose and letter of 29 June [1882] to Talcott Williams.

E 2986
Eitner, Walter H. "Some Further Autograph Notes of Whitman's 1879 Western Trip," *Walt Whitman Review,* 26 (March 1980), 18–22.

Prose.

E 2987
White, William. "Unpublished Whitman Fragment (1890) to McKay," *Walt Whitman Review,* 26 (March 1980), [40].

Prose (facsimile).

E 2988
White, William. "Whitman to Eldridge: The Full Version," *Walt Whitman Review,* 26 (June 1980), 79–[80].

Letter of 20 July 1889 to Charles W. Eldridge (facsimile, p. [80]).

E 2989
Bauerle, Richard F. "Whitman's Index to His Scrapbook: A 'Map' of His 'Language World,' " *Walt Whitman Review,* 26 (December 1980), 158–162, 165–[166].

Prose (facsimile, pp. 165–[166]).

E 2990
White, William. " 'The Body at Its Best': A Whitman Fragment," *Walt Whitman Review,* 27 (March 1981), [48].

Prose (facsimile).

E 2991
White, William. "An Unpublished Whitman Letter to *The Critic,*" *Walt Whitman Review,* 27 (June 1981), [92].

Postcard of 25 November 1890 to the editor of the *Critic* (facsimile).

E 2992
White, William. "Whitman to P. J. O'Shea: Unpublished," *Walt Whitman Review*, 27 (September 1981), 139–[140].

Letter of 13 December 1886 (facsimile, p. [140]).

E 2993
White, William. "A Whitman Letter to Josiah Child," *Walt Whitman Review*, 28 (March 1982), 39–[40].

Letter of 27 June 1879 (facsimile, p. [40]).

E 2994
Dalgarno, E., and K. Streibich. "Miracle Enough: The History of Whitman's Farewell Poem," *Walt Whitman Review*, 28 (June–December 1982), 72–76, [110].

"Sail Out for Good, Eidólon Yacht!" (facsimile, p. [110]). Poem.

E 2995
White, William. "Whitman to Hezekiah Butterworth: Unpublished," *Walt Whitman Review*, 28 (June–December 1982), 108.

Letter of 2 January 1891 (facsimile).

E 2996
Folsom, Ed. "The Mystical Ornithologist and the Iowa Tufthunter: Two Unpublished Whitman Letters and Some Identifications," *Walt Whitman Quarterly Review*, 1, no. 1 (June 1983), 18–29.

Letters of 11 February 1884 to Thomas G. Gentry (p. 18; facsimile, p. 20) and 12 June 1884 to Charles Aldrich (p. 23; facsimile, p. 24).

Note: The letter to Aldich is reprinted in facsimile in Ed Folsom, "Walt Whitman at Iowa," *Books at Iowa*, 34 (November 1983), 19.

E 2997
White, William. "A New Whitman Letter to the Philadelphia *Record*," *Walt Whitman Quarterly Review*, 1, no. 1 (June 1983), 52.

Letter of 19 January 1884 to the editor of the *Philadelphia Record* (facsimile only, back cover verso).

E 2998
Westbrook, Wayne W. "The Case of Dr. Bowen: An Unknown Whitman Letter Recommending an Army Doctor," *Walt Whitman Quarterly Review*, 1, no. 2 (September 1983), 26–29.

Letter of 4 March 1868 to W. O. Baldwin (p. 27).

E 2999
White, William. "Whitman to Jeannette Gilder: Unpublished," *Walt Whitman Quarterly Review*, 1, no. 2 (September 1983), 47.

Letter of 9 April 1881 (facsimile only, back cover verso).

E 3000
White, William. "An Uncollected Whitman Letter to Alexander Black," *Walt Whitman Quarterly Review*, 1, no. 3 (September 1983), 63.

Letter of 12 May 1891 (facsimile only, back cover verso).

Note: Text first published in Black's *The Latest Thing and Other Things*, and in partial facsimile in his *Time and Chance* (D 57).

E 3001
Price, Kenneth M. "Whitman on Emerson: New Light on the 1856 Open Letter," *American Literature,* 56 (March 1984), 83–89.

Prose manuscript on Emerson (pp. 84–86).

E 3002
White, William. "An Unpublished Whitman Card to J. H. Johnston," *Walt Whitman Quarterly Review,* 1, no. 4 (March 1984), 49.

Postcard of 27 March 1884 (facsimile, back cover verso).

E 3003
White, William. "Another Whitman Letter to Jeannette Gilder," *Walt Whitman Quarterly Review*, 2, no. 1 (Summer 1984), 51.

Letter of 21 November 1881 (facsimile, back cover verso).

E 3004
White, William. "New: A Letter from Walt to Louisa Whitman," *Walt Whitman Quarterly Review*, 2, no. 2 (Fall 1984), 57.

Letter of 30 April 1887 (facsimile, back cover verso).

E 3005
White, William. "An Unknown Whitman Letter to an Unknown Editor about an Unknown Piece," *Walt Whitman Quarterly Review*, 2, no. 3 (Winter 1984), 35.

Letter of 9 August 1875 to an unidentified correspondent (facsimile, back cover verso).

E 3006
White, William. "Unpublished Prose MS: Idea for a Whitman Poemet," *Walt Whitman Quarterly Review*, 2, no. 4 (Spring 1985), 50.

Prose (facsimile, back cover verso).

E 3007
Perlman, James. "An Unpublished Whitman Letter to John and Ursula Burroughs," *Walt Whitman Quarterly Review*, 3, no. 1 (Summer 1985), 48.

Letter of 26 June [1878] (facsimile, back cover verso).

E 3008
Price, Kenneth M. "Whitman's Solutions to 'The Problem of the Blacks,'" *Resources for American Literary Study*, 15 (Autumn 1985), 205–208.

Poem (p. 205).

E 3009
Szathmary, Louis. "The Culinary Walt Whitman," *Walt Whitman Quarterly Review*, 3, no. 2 (Fall 1985), 28–33.

Letter of 31 October 1889 to Louisa Whitman (facsimile, back cover verso).

E 3010
Golden, Arthur. "Uncollected Whitman Material in the Folger Shakespeare Library," *Papers of the Bibliographical Society of America*, 79 (4th Quarter 1985), 529–539.

Letter of [14 January 1876] to Edward Dowden (p. 538).

E 3011
White, William. "Whitman: Unrecorded Notes on Health," *Walt Whitman Quarterly Review*, 3, no. 3 (Winter 1986), 44.

Prose (facsimile, back cover verso).

E 3012
White, William. " 'Morbid Adhesiveness—To Be Kept Down': Unpublished MS," *Walt Whitman Quarterly Review*, 4, no. 1 (Summer 1986), 49.

Prose (facsimile, back cover verso).

E 3013
Golden, Arthur. "Nine Early Whitman Letters, 1840–1841," *American Literature*, 58 (October 1986), 342–360.

Letters written between July 1840 and late 1841 to Abraham Paul Leech.

E 3014
Dedmond, Francis B. " 'Here among Soldiers in Hospital': An Unpublished
Letter from Walt Whitman to Lucia Jane Russell Briggs," *New England Quar-
terly,* 59 (December 1986), 544–548.

Letter of 26 April 1864 (pp. 547–548).

E 3015
Folsom, Ed. "Holograph Page of Whitman's 'Abraham Lincoln,' " *Walt Whitman Quarterly Review,* 5, no. 3 (Winter 1988), 47–48.

Prose (p. 47; facsimile, back cover verso).

E 3016
Engell, John. "Walt and Sir Walter or the Bard and the Bart: Balladeers," *Walt
Whitman Quarterly Review,* 5, no. 4 (Spring 1988), 1–15.

Whitman's holograph table of contents and title page for Sir Walter Scott's
Complete Poems (facsimiles, facing p. 1, back cover verso).

E 3017
Golden, Arthur. "A Recovered Harry Stafford Letter to Walt Whitman," *Walt
Whitman Quarterly Review,* 5, no. 4 (Spring 1988), 40–43.

Holograph list of poetry (p. 41).

E 3018
Golden, Arthur. "The Text of a Whitman Lincoln Lecture Reading: Anacreon's
'The Midnight Visitor,' " *Walt Whitman Quarterly Review,* 6 (Fall 1988), 91–94.

Prose (p. 92; facsimile, back cover verso).

E 3019
Diehl, Paul. " 'A Noiseless Patient Spider': Whitman's Beauty—Blood and
Brain," *Walt Whitman Quarterly Review,* 6 (Winter 1989), 117–132.

Poem (facsimile, p. 124).

E 3020
Sill, Geoffrey M. " 'You Tides with Ceaseless Swell': A Reading of the Manuscript," *Walt Whitman Quarterly Review,* 6 (Spring 1989), 189–197.

Poem (p. 190; facsimile, back cover verso).

E 3021
Hollis, C. Carroll. "Whitman on 'Periphrastic' Literature," *Walt Whitman Quarterly Review,* 7 (Winter 1990), 131–140.

Prose (facsimile on recto and verso of back cover). Revision of his article in the Winter–Spring 1960 *Fresco* (E 2893).

E 3022
Miller, Edwin Haviland. "The Correspondence of Walt Whitman: A Second Supplement with a Revised Calendar of Letters Written to Whitman," *Walt Whitman Quarterly Review*, 8, nos. 3–4 (Winter–Spring 1991), 1–106.

Prints 46 letters written between 30 July 1840 and 12 May 1891, pp. 9–42.

Note: Simultaneously published in book form; see D 111.

UNDATED MATERIALS

E 3023
"Is there any Hope?", *New York Sunday Dispatch,* n.d.

Reprinted in William White, "Some Uncollected Whitman Journalism," *Emerson Society Quarterly,* no. 33 (4th Quarter 1963), 84–90.

E 3024
"Lingrave's Temptation," clipping in Feinberg Collection, DLC.

Fiction. Reprinted in *Specimen Days* (A 11), pp. 366–368; *Early Poems and Fiction,* pp. 331–334.

E 3025
"The People and John Quincy Adams," *New Orleans Daily Crescent,* n.d.

Page proof. See *The People and John Quincy Adams* (A 40).

E 3026
"Public and Private Edifices," *New York Sunday Dispatch,* n.d.

Reprinted in William White, "Some Uncollected Whitman Journalism," *Emerson Society Quarterly,* no. 33 (4th Quarter 1963), 84–90.

F. Proof Copies, Circulars, and Broadsides

Material prepared by Whitman, usually for private circulation, listed chronologically. Proofs actually used in the publication process of Whitman's works, when located, are listed under the appropriate Section A entry.

It is likely that more of these "proofs" exist, since Whitman used the form to ensure accuracy in transmitting copy to periodicals for publication as well as for distributing to friends. As William H. Garrison recalled, "Each bit when it left his hands in manuscript was sent to a quaint old printing-establishment [Henry Curtz] . . . where it was set up in type. It was then returned to the author, who made such corrections as seemed to him desirable, and after this a revised and re-corrected copy was struck off and sent out as the matter to be used *punctatim et literatim*" ("Walt Whitman," *Lippincott's Magazine,* 49 [May 1892], 623–626). The slips were cut into sheets of varying sizes, rarely with parallel sides, and the measurements given below are approximate.

A number of items listed in *BAL* are omitted here as being beyond the scope of this section (see IX, 69–88, for more information).

F 1

AFTER THE SUPPER AND TALK. | *(To prelude some added Poems at the end of a Volume.)* | [18 lines of verse] | [flush right] WALT [WHITMAN.]

Broadside, printed on recto only. 9¹¹⁄₁₆″ × 15⁵⁄₁₆″ (DLC); 6⅝″ × 6″ (TxU); 6¼″ × 5⅞″ (ViU). *Locations:* DLC, TxU, ViU.

Note one: A galley proof, measuring 4¹³⁄₁₆″ × 6″, has the following corrections made by Whitman:

    line 3   done,] done.
    line 9   him,] him.
    line 16   Farewells,] Farewells.
    line 18   lost for aye] lost, for, aye

In addition, Whitman has written on it "30 copies." *Location:* DLC.

Note two: See *Lippincott's Magazine,* November 1887 (E 2667).

Note three: *BAL* dates this "1885" (IX, 71); see *Daybooks,* p. 349.

F 2

[boldface] AFTER TWENTY YEARS | [22 lines of verse] | [flush right] WALT WHITMAN.

AFTER THE SUPPER AND TALK.

(To prelude some added Poems at end of a Volume.)

After the supper and talk—after the day is done,
As a friend from friends his final withdrawal prolonging,
Good-bye and Good-bye with emotional lips repeating,
(So hard for his hand to release those hands—no more will they meet,
No more for communion of sorrow and joy, of old and young,
A far-stretching journey awaits him, to return no more,)
Shunning, postponing severance—seeking to ward off the last word ever so little,
E'en at the exit-door turning—charges superfluous calling back—
    e'en as he descends the steps,
Something to eke out a minute additional—shadows of nightfall deepening,
Farewells, messages lessening—dimmer the forthgoer's visage and form,
Soon to be lost for aye in the darkness—loth, O so loth to depart!
Garrulous to the very last.

WALT...

AFTER TWENTY YEARS.

Down on the ancient wharf, the sand, I sit, with a new-comer chatting:
He shipp'd as green-hand boy, and sail'd away, (took some sudden, vehement notion;)
Since, twenty years and more have circled round and round,
While he the globe was circling round and round,—and now returns:
How changed the place—all the old land-marks gone—the parents dead;
(Yes, he comes back *to lay in port for good—to settle*—has a well-fill'd purse—no spot will do but this;)
The little boat that scull'd him from the sloop, now held in leash I see,
I hear the slapping waves, the restless keel, the rocking in the sand,
I see the sailor kit, the canvas bag, the great box bound with brass,
I scan the face all berry-brown and bearded—the stout-strong frame,
Dress'd in its russet suit of good Scotch cloth:
(Then what the told-out story of those twenty years? what of the future?)

WALT WHITMAN.

Broadside, printed on recto only. 7½" × 6" (TxU); 7⅜" × 6" (DLC); 7¼" × 5¹⁵⁄₁₆" (DLC). *Locations:* DLC (2), TxU.

Note: See "Twenty Years," *Pall Mall Gazette,* July 1888; *Magazine of Art* (London), August 1888; *Magazine of Art* (New York), September 1888 (E 2708).

F 3
[boldface] AH, NOT THIS GRANITE DEAD AND COLD. | [19 lines of verse] | [flush right] WALT WHITMAN. | *February, 1885.*

Broadside, printed on recto only. 9½" × 6". *Location:* DLC (2).

Note one: A galley proof, measuring 9½" × 5⅞", has the following corrections made by Whitman:

   line 5   Thou,   ]   Thou
   line 12   legitimate, continued ever,   ]   legitimate, over,
   line 13   line,   ]   fine,

Location: DLC.

Note two: See *Philadelphia Press,* 22 February 1885 (E 2635).

F 4
AN AMERICAN POET AT LAST! *WALT WHITMAN'S "Leaves of Grass"* . . .

Broadside, printed on recto only. 8⅜" × 3⅞". See *BAL,* IX, 71. *Location:* DLC.

Note: *BAL* dates this 41-line "advertisement for *Leaves of Grass*," which is "presumably by Whitman," as "1855" (IX, 71).

F 5
AS A STRONG BIRD ON PINIONS FREE. COMMENCEMENT POEM, DARTMOUTH COLLEGE, N.H., JUNE 26, 1872, ON INVITATION PUB-LIC LITERARY SOCIETIES . . .

Only located copy "has been cut up and pasted onto 5 cards, possibly as a reading copy" (see *BAL,* IX, 71). *Location:* DLC.

Note: See *As a Strong Bird on Pinions Free* (A 7).

F 6
Two states have been noted, priority undetermined:

First state:

[two lines and roman numerals in boldface] AS ONE BY ONE WITHDRAW THE | LOFTY ACTORS. | I. | [13 lines of verse] | II. | [five lines of verse] | [flush right] WALT WHITMAN.

Broadside, printed on recto only. 6¹¹⁄₁₆″ × 6″ (DLC); 6⅝″ × 6¼″ (DLC); 6⅝″ × 6¹⁄₁₆″ (DLC); 6⁹⁄₁₆″ × 5⅞″ (DLC); 6½″ × 6⅛″ (RPB). *Locations:* DLC (4), RPB.

Second state:

[two lines and roman numerals in boldface] AS . . . | II. | [five lines of verse]

8¹¹⁄₁₆″ × 5¹⁵⁄₁₆″ (DLC); 8¹¹⁄₁₆″ × 6¹⁄₁₆″ (DLC, signed by Whitman); 8⅝″ × 6″ (NN-B, TxU [2]). *Locations:* DLC (2), NN-B, TxU (2).

Note: See *Harper's Weekly Magazine,* 16 May 1885 (E 2637).

AS ONE BY ONE WITHDRAW THE LOFTY ACTORS.

I.

As one by one withdraw the lofty actors
From that great play on history's stage eterne,
That lurid, partial act of war and peace—of old and new
        contending,
Fought out through wrath, fears, dark dismays, and many a
        long suspense;
All past—and since, in countless graves receding, mellowing,
Victor's and vanquish'd—Lincoln's and Lee's—now thou with
        them,
Man of the mighty days—and equal to the days!
Thou from the prairies!—tangled and many-vein'd and hard
        has been thy part,
To admiration has it been enacted!

II.

And still shall be;—resume again, thou hero heart!
Strengthen to firmest day O rosy dawn of hope!
Thou dirge I started first, to joyful shout reverse!—and thou,
        O grave,
Wait long and long!

F 6, second state

F 7

[boldface] AS THE GREEK'S SIGNAL FLAME. | [*For Whittier's 80th birthday, December 17th,* 1887.] | [eight lines of verse] | [flush right] WALT WHITMAN.

Broadside, printed on recto only. 4¾″ × 6″. *Locations:* DLC (3), NN-R, PHC.

Note: See *New York Herald,* 15 December 1887 (E 2672).

F 8

AT THE COMPLIMENTARY DINNER, CAMDEN, NEW JERSEY, MAY 31, 1889. WALT WHITMAN SAID: . . .

AS THE GREEK'S SIGNAL FLAME.

[For Whittier's **80th** *birth-day, December 17th,* **1887**.]

As the Greek's signal flame, by antique records told,
(Tally of many a hard-strain'd battle, struggle, year — trium-
     phant only at the last,)
Rose from the hill-top, like applause and glory,
Welcoming in fame some special veteran, hero,
With rosy tinge reddening the land he'd served,
So I aloft from Mannahatta's ship-fringed shore,
Lift high a kindled brand for thee, Old Poet.

                      WALT WHITMAN.

F 7

Broadside, printed on recto only. 4½″ × 5⅞″. See *BAL,* IX, 72. *Locations:* CtY, DLC.

Note: See *Camden's Compliment to Walt Whitman* (D 17).

F 9

AUTOBIOGRAPHIC NOTE. *From an old "remembrance copy."* | [54 lines of prose]

Single sheet (6⅜″ × 9⅜″) printed on both sides; Whitman's own advertisement for his books is printed on the verso. *Locations:* BL, CtY, DLC, JM, MB, MBU, NcU, ViU.

Note one: See *Camden's Compliment to Walt Whitman* (D 17).

Note two: Reprinted, along with the front of the advertising flier for Whitman's lecture on Lincoln (see H 35), on pp. 2–3 as a four-page keepsake distributed on the occasion of an address by Charles E. Feinberg on 31 May 1962. *Location:* JM.

F 10

Two sheets: (1) '[boldface] A Backward Glance on My Own Road. | [120 lines of prose]' and (2) '[82 lines of prose] | [flush right] WALT WHITMAN.'

Broadsides, printed on rectos only. (1) 17⅞″ × 6⅛″ and (2) 12¼″ × 6⅛″ (TxU); (1) 17⅞″ × 6⅛″ and (2) 11⅞″ × 6⅛″ (NN-B). *Locations:* NN-B, TxU.

Note one: See *Critic,* 5 January 1884 (E 2620).

Note two: Whitman noted on 10 January 1884 that "slips" of this had been "rec'd" (*Correspondence,* III, 362).

F 9 (recto)

AUTOBIOGRAPHIC NOTE. *From an old "remembrance copy."*

Was born May 31, 1819, in my father's farm-house, at West Hills, L. I.,
New York State. My parents' folks mostly farmers and sailors—on my
father's side, of English—on my mother's, (Van Velsor's,) from Hollandic
immigration. There was, first and last, a large family of children; (I was
the second.) We moved to Brooklyn while I was still a little one in frocks
—and there in B. I grew up out of the frocks—then, as child and boy, went
to the public schools—then to work in a printing office.

When only sixteen or seventeen years old, and for two years afterward, I
went to teaching country schools down in Queens and Suffolk counties, Long
Island, and "boarded round." Then, returning to New York, worked as
printer and writer, (with an occasional shy at "poetry.")

1848-'9.—About this time went off on a leisurely journey and working expedition (my brother Jeff with me,) through all the Middle States, and down
the Ohio and Mississippi rivers. Lived a while in New Orleans, and worked
there. (Have lived quite a good deal in the Southern States.) After a time,
plodded back northward, up the Mississippi, the Missouri, &c., and around
to, and by way of the great lakes, Michigan, Huron and Erie, to Niagara
Falls and lower Canada—finally returning through Central New York, and
down the Hudson.

1851-'54.—Occupied in house-building in Brooklyn. (For a little of the
first part of that time in printing a daily and weekly paper.)

1855.—Lost my dear father, this year, by death. . . . Commenced putting
Leaves of Grass to press, for good—after many Ms. doings and undoings—(I
had great trouble in leaving out the stuck "poetical" touches—but succeeded
at last.)

1862.—In December of this year went down to the field of War in Virginia.
My brother George reported badly wounded in the Fredericksburgh fight.
(For 1863 and '64, see *Specimen Days.*)

1865 to '71.—Had a place as clerk (till well on in '73) in the Attorney
General's Office, Washington.

(New York and Brooklyn seem more like *home*, as I was born near, and
brought up in them, and lived, man and boy, for 30 years. But I lived some
years in Washington, and have visited, and partially lived, in most of the
Western and Eastern cities.)

1873.—This year lost, by death, my dear, dear mother—and, just before, my
sister Martha—(the two best and sweetest women I have ever seen or known,
or ever expect to see.)

Same year, a sudden climax and prostration from paralysis. Had been
simmering inside for several years; broke out during those times temporarily
and then went over. But now at once a serious attack, beyond cure. Dr. Drinkard,
my Washington physician, (and a first rate one,) said it was the result of too
extreme bodily and emotional strain continued at Washington and "down in
front," in 1863, '4 and '5. I think if a heartier, stronger, healthier physique
ever lived, from 1840 to '70. My greatest call (Quaker) to go around and do
what I could among the suffering and sick and wounded was that I seem'd
to be *so strong and well.* (I considered myself invulnerable.) Quit work at
Washington, and moved to Camden, New Jersey—where I have lived since,
and now. (September, 1888,) write these lines.

(A long stretch of illness, or half-illness, with some lulls. During these
latter, have revised and printed over all my books—into'd out "November
Boughs"—and at intervals travelled to the Prairie States, the Rocky Mountains, Canada, to New York, to my birthplace in Long Island, and to Boston.
But physical disability and the war-paralysis above alluded to have settled
upon me more and more, the last year or so.)

W. W.

(4)

F 9 (verso)

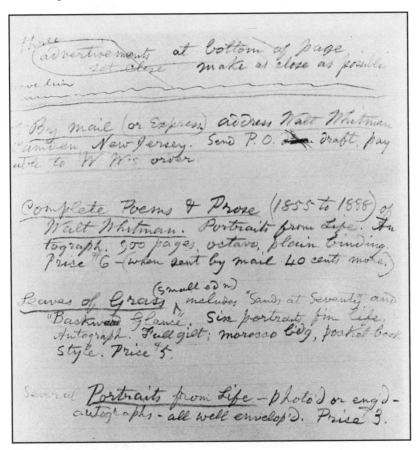

Whitman's notes for F 9 (verso)

F 11

THE BIBLE AS POETRY . . .

Broadside, printed on recto only. 24″ × 6″. See *BAL*, IX, 72. *Location:* CtY.

Note one: See *Critic*, 3 February 1883 (E 2616).

Note two: Whitman wrote on 25 January 1883, "I would like 50 copies . . . printed on heavier paper, with the 'Critic' imprint left off" (*Correspondence*, III, 322).

F 12

[boldface] BRAVO, PARIS EXHIBITION! | [10 lines of verse] | [flush right] WALT WHITMAN.'

A Backward Glance on My Own Road.

It is probably best at once to give warning, (even more specific than in the head-line,) that the following paragraphs have my ' Leaves of Grass,' and some of its reasons and aims, for their radiating centre. Altogether, they form a backward glimpse along my own road and journey the last thirty years.

Many consider the expression of poetry and art to come under certain inflexible standards, set patterns, fixed and immovable, like iron castings. To the highest sense, nothing of the sort. As, in the theatre of to-day, ' each new actor of real merit (for Hamlet or any eminent rôle) recreates the persons of the older drama, sending traditions to the winds, and producing a new character on the stage,' the adaptation, development, incarnation, of his own traits, idiosyncrasy, and environment—' there being not merely one good way of representing a great part, but as many ways as there are great actors '—so in constructing poems. Another illustration would be that for delineating purposes, the melange of existence is but an eternal font of type, and may be set up to any text, however different—with room and welcome, at whatever time, for new compositors.

The chief trait of any given poet is always the spirit he brings to the observation of humanity and nature—the mood out of which he contemplates his subjects. What kind of temper, and what amount of faith, reports these things? Up to how recent a date is the song carried? What the equipment, and special raciness of the singer—what his tinge of coloring? The last value of artistic expressers, past and present—the Greek æsthetes, Shakspeare, or, in our own day, Tennyson, Victor Hugo, Carlyle, Emerson—is certainly involved in such questions.

In connection, the profoundest service that poems or any other writings can do for their reader, is, (not to merely satisfy the intellect, or supply something polished and interesting, nor even to depict great passions, or persons, or events, but) to fill him with vigorous and clean manliness, religiousness, and give him *good heart* as a radical possession and habit. The educated world seems to have been growing more and more ennuied for ages, leaving to our time the inheritance of it all. Fortunately, there is the original inexhaustible fund of cheeriness, normally resident in the race, forever eligible to be appealed to and relied on.

I should say real American poetry—nay, within any high sense, American literature—is something yet to be. So far, the aims and stress of the book-making business here—the miscellaneous and fashionable parts of it, the majority—seem entirely adjusted (like American society life,) to certain fine-drawn, surface, imported ways and examples, having no deep root or hold in our soil. I hardly know a volume emanating American nativity, manliness, from its centre. It is true, the numberless issues of our day and land (the leading monthlies are the best,) as they continue feeding the insatiable public appetite, convey the kind of provender temporarily wanted—and with certain magnificently copious mass results. But as surely as childhood and youth pass to maturity, all that now exists after going on for a while will meet with a grand revulsion—nay, its very self works steadily toward that revulsion.

What a comment it is on our era of literary fulfilment, with the splendid day-rise of science, and resuscitation of history, that its chief religious and poetical works are not its own, but have been furnished by far-back ages, out of their darkness and ignorance—or, at most, twilight ! What is there in those works that so imperiously and scornfully dominates all our advancement, boasted civilization, and culture?

The intellect of to-day is stupendous and keen, backed by stores of accumulated erudition—but in a most important phase the antique seems to have had the advantage of us. Unconsciously, it possessed and exploited that something there was and is in Nature immeasurably beyond, and even altogether ignoring, what we call the artistic, the beautiful, the literary, and even the moral, the good. Not easy to put one's finger on, or name in a word, this something, invisibly permeating the old poems, religion-sources and art. If I were asked to suggest it in such single word, I should write (at the risk of being quite misunderstood at first, at any rate) the word physiological.

I have never wondered why so many men and women balk at ' Leaves of Grass.' None should try it till ready to accept (unfortunately for me, not one in a hundred, or in several hundred, is ready) that utterance from full-grown human personality, as of a tree growing in itself, or any other objective result of the universe, from its own laws, oblivious of conformity—an expression, faithful exclusively to its own ideal and receptivity, however egotistical or enormous (' All is mine, for I have it in me,' sings the old Chant of Jupiter)—not mainly indeed with any of the usual purposes of poems, or of literature, but just as much (indeed far more) with other aims and purposes. These will only be learned by the study of the book itself—will be arrived at, if at all, by indirections—and even at best, the task no easy one. The physiological point of view will almost always have to dominate in the reader as it does in the book—only now and then the psychological [or intellectual, and very seldom indeed the merely æsthetic.

Then I wished above all things to arrest the actual moment, our years, the existing, and dwell on the present—to view all else through the present. What the past has sent forth in its incalculable volume and variety, is of course on record. What the next generation, or the next, may furnish, I know not. But for indications of the individuality and physiognomy, of the present, in America, my two books are candidates. And though it may not appear at first look, I am more and more fond of thinking, and indeed am quite decided for myself, that they have for their nerve-centre the Secession War of 1860-65.

Then the volumes (for reasons well conned over before I took the first step) were intended to be most decided, serious, *bonâ fide* expressions of an identical individual personality—*egotism*, if you choose, for I shall not quarrel about the word. They proceed out of, and revolve around, one's-self, myself, an identity, and declaredly make that self the nucleus of the whole utterance. After all is said, it is only a concrete special personality that can finally satisfy and vitalize the student of verse, heroism, or religion—abstractions will do neither. (Carlyle said, ' There is no grand poem in the world but is at bottom a biography—the life of a man.')

The principal contrast and unlikeness of the personality behind every page of ' Leaves of Grass,' compared with the personality-sources of established poems, is undoubtedly the different relative *attitude* toward God, toward the universe, toward humanity, and still more (by reflection, confession, assumption, etc.), the attitude of the ego, the one chanting or talking toward himself. Whether my friends claim it for me or not, I feel certain that in respect to pictorial talent, description, dramatic situations, and especially in verbal melody and all the conventional technique of poetry, not only the divine work already alluded to, but dozens more, transcend (some of them immeasurably transcend) all I have done, or could do. But it seemed to me the time had arrived to reflect those same old themes and things in the lights thrown on them by the advent of America and Democracy—that such illustration, as far as its statement is concerned, is now and here a chief demand of imaginative literature—and that the New World is the most fitting place for its trial, its attempt in original song. Not to carry out, in the approved style, some choice plot or fancy, not to portray the passions, or the beautiful, or love, or fine thoughts, or incidents, or aspirations, or courtesies (all of which has been done overwhelmingly and well, probably never to be excelled.) But while, in such æsthetic presentation of objects, passions, plots, thoughts, etc., our lands and days do not want, and probably will never have, anything better than they already possess from the bequests of the past, it still remains to be said that there is even toward all these a subjective and democratic point of view appropriate to ourselves alone, and to our new genius and environments, different from anything hitherto—and that such point of view toward all current life and art is for us the only means of their assimilation consistent with the modern and scientific spirit, in our Western World.

The word I should put primarily as indicating the character of my own poems would be the word Suggestiveness. I round and finish little or nothing ; I could not, consistently with my scheme. If ' Leaves of Grass ' satisfies those who, to use a phrase of Margaret Fuller's, ' expect suggestions only and not fulfilments,' I shall be quite content.

That I have not been accepted during my own time—that the largely prevailing range of criticism on my book has been either mockery or denunciation—and that I, as its author, have been the marked object of two or three (to me pretty serious) official buffetings—is probably no more than I ought to have expected. I had my choice when I commenced. I bid neither for soft eulogies, big money returns, nor the approbation of existing schools and conventions. As now fulfilled after thirty years, the best of the achievement is, that I have had my say entirely my own way, and put it unerringly on record—the value thereof to be decided by time. In calculating that decision, Dr. Bucke and William O'Connor are far more definite and peremptory than I am. I consider the whole thing experimental—as indeed, in a very large sense, I consider the American Republic itself, to be.

There is always an invisible background to a high-intentioned book—the palimpsest on which every page is written. Apply this to my volume. The facts of these thirty-eight or forty empires soldered in one—fifty or sixty millions of equals, with their lives, their passions, their future—these incalculable areas and seething multitudes around us, and of which we are inseparable parts ! Think, in comparison, of the petty environage and limited area of the poets of past or present Europe, no matter how great their genius. To which I should add what Herder taught to the young Goethe, that really great poetry is always (like the Homeric or Biblical canticles) the result of the national spirit, and not the privilege of a polished and cultivated few.

No one will get at my verses who insists upon viewing them as a literary performance, or attempt at such performance, or as aiming mainly toward art or æstheticism. I hope to go on record for something different—something better, if I may dare to say so. That America necessitates for her poetry entirely new standards of measurement is such a point with me, that I never tire of dwelling on it. Think of the absence and ignorance, in all cases hitherto, of the vast ensemble, multitudinousness, vitality, and the unprecedented stimulants of to-day and here. It almost seems as if a poetry with anything like cosmic features were never possible before. It is certain that a poetry of democracy and absolute faith, for the use of the modern, never was.

I think the best and largest songs yet remain to be sung.

WALT WHITMAN.

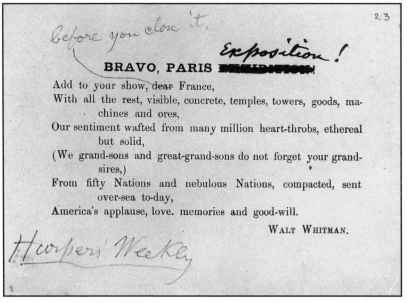

F 12

Broadside, printed on recto only. 9″ × 6″ (NNC); 9″ × 5⅞″ (DLC, marked as received from Whitman, 30 September 1889); 4½″ × 6″ (DLC [2], NjP, TxU); 4½″ × 5⅞″ (DLC). *Locations:* DLC (4), NNC, NjP, TxU.

Note one: All located copies have the following revisions in Whitman's hand:

line 1 EXPOSITION!] EXHIBITION!
line 2 before you close it,] dear

Note two: See *Harper's Weekly Magazine,* 28 September 1889 (E 2721).

F 13
BY EMERSON'S GRAVE . . .

Broadside, printed on recto only. 4¹⁵⁄₁₆″ × 4⁷⁄₁₆″. See *BAL,* IX, 72. *Location:* DLC.

Note: See *Critic,* 6 May 1882 (E 2604).

F 14
Two states have been noted, priority undetermined:

First state:

[boldface] A CAROL CLOSING SIXTY-NINE. | [12 lines of verse] | [flush right] WALT WHITMAN.

A CAROL CLOSING SIXTY-NINE.

A carol closing sixty-nine — a *resume* — a repetition,
My lines in joy and hope continuing on the same,
Of ye, O God, Life, Nature, Freedom, Poetry;
Of you, my Land — your rivers, prairies, States — you, mot-
    tled Flag I love,
Your aggregate retain'd entire — Of north, south, east and
    west, your items all;
Of me myself — the jocund heart yet beating in my breast,
The body wreck'd, old, poor and paralyzed — the strange in-
    ertia falling pall-like round me;
The burning fires down in my sluggish blood not yet extinct,
The undiminish'd faith — the groups of loving friends,

WALT WHITMAN.

F 14, first state

Broadside, printed on recto only. 4¹⁵⁄₁₆″ × 6″ (TxU); 4¹³⁄₁₆″ × 6″ (DLC). *Loca-tions:* DLC, TxU.

Second state:

[boldface] A CAROL CLOSING SIXTY-NINE. | [12 lines of verse] | [flush right]

3¾″ × 5½″. *Location:* DLC.

Note one: See *New York Herald*, 21 May 1888 (E 2704).

Note two: Originally printed on a single sheet with "Old Age's Lambent Peaks" and "To Get the Final Lilt of Songs" (see F 53).

F 15
[boldface] A CHRISTMAS GREETING | *From a Northern Star-Group to a Southern.* | [14 lines of verse] | [flush right] WALT WHITMAN.

Broadside, printed on recto only. 5⁵⁄₁₆″ × 7¼″ (DLC [2]); 5¼″ × 7¼″ (DLC). *Locations:* DLC (3).

Note one: A galley proof, measuring 5⁵⁄₁₆″ × 7⁵⁄₁₆″, has the following correc-tions made by Whitman:

line 1   GREETING] GREETING.
line 7   impedimentas] impediments,
line 8   aim,] cism,
line 9   faith;)] faith[?])
line 10   reaching arm,] r[?]aching aim,

line 12   thou, learning   ]   thou learning
line 14   sky,   ]   sky.
line 15   Crown,)   ]   crown.)

Location: DLC.

Note: See *McClure's Magazine,* 25 December 1889 (E 2723).

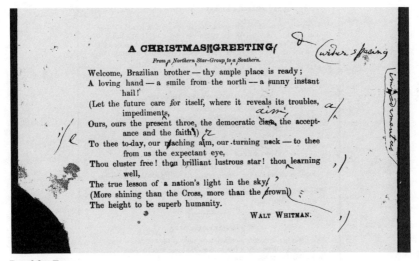

Proof for F 15

F 16

... COL. INGERSOLL'S LECTURE "LIBERTY AND LITERATURE."
WALT WHITMAN, WHEN CALL'D FOR, ROSE AND SAID: ...

Broadside, printed on recto only. 5½″ × 5 ³⁄₁₆″. See *BAL,* IX, 73, where this is
dated "1890." *Location:* DLC.

Note: See Robert G. Ingersoll, *Liberty in Literature* (D 19).

F 17

[boldface] THE DALLIANCE OF THE EAGLES. | BY WALT WHITMAN. |
[14 lines of verse] | [rule] | [ornate boldface] Ah, little knows the Laborer. |
[three lines of verse] | [rule] | [ornate boldface] Hast never come to thee an
hour? | [five lines of verse] | [rule] | [ornate boldface] My Picture-Gallery. |
[seven lines of verse]

Broadside, printed on recto only. 9½″ × 6¼″ (RPB); 9⁷⁄₁₆″ × 6″ (DLC); 8½″ ×
5¾″ (TxU). The second poem is from "Song of the Exposition"; the third poem
is from "By the Roadside"; the fourth poem is from "Autumn Rivulets." *Locations:* DLC, RPB, TxU.

THE DALLIANCE OF THE EAGLES.

BY WALT WHITMAN.

Skirting the river road, (my languid forenoon walk, my rest,)
Skyward, in air, a sudden muffled sound—the dalliance of the
　　eagles!
The rushing amorous contact there in space together!
The clinching, interlocking claws—a living, fierce, gyrating
　　wheel,
Four beating wings—two beaks;—A swirling mass, tight grap-
　　pling,
In tumbling, holding, clustering loops, comes downward falling,
Till o'er the river pois'd, the twain yet one, a moment's lull,
A motionless, still balance in the air—then parting, talons loosing,
Upward again, on slow-firm pinions slanting, their separate, di-
　　verse flight,
She hers, he his, pursuing.

Ah, little knows the Laborer.

Ah, little knows the laborer,
How near his work is holding him to God,
The Perfect Laborer of Time, Space, All.

Hast never come to thee an hour?

Hast never come to thee an hour,
A sudden gleam divine, precipitating, bursting all these bubbles,
　　fashions, wealth?
These eager business aims—books, politics, art, amours,
To utter nothingness?

My Picture-Gallery.

In a little house keep I pictures suspended—it is not a fix'd house,
It is round—it is only a few inches from one side to the other:
Yet behold! it has room for all the shows of the world—all
　　memories:
Here the tableaus of life, and here the groupings of death;
Here, do you know this? this is Cicerone himself,
With finger rais'd, he points to the prodigal pictures.

F 17

Note one: A galley proof, measuring 10⅛″ × 7⁵⁄₁₆″, has the following correction made by Whitman:

　　line 9　beaks;—A　]　beaks—a

In addition, Whitman has written on it "take ten (10) impressions like this."
Location: DLC.

Note two: See *Cope's Tobacco Plant* (Liverpool), November 1880 (E 2587).

F 18
[boldface] THE DEAD CARLYLE. | [53 lines of prose, signed 'WALT WHIT-
MAN.'] | [rule]'.

Broadside, printed on recto only. 9½″ × 3¾″ (NcD, RPB); 9¼″ × 3¾″ (TxU).
Locations: NcD, RPB, TxU.

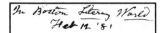

THE DEAD CARLYLE.

NOT for his merely literary merit, (though that was great)—not as "maker of books," but as launching into the self-compla-cent atmosphere of our days a rasping, question-ing, dislocating agitation and shock, is the man's final value. It is time the English-speak-ing peoples had some true idea about the verte-ber of genius, namely power. As if they must always have it cut and biased to the fashion, like a lady's cloak!

What a needed service he performs! How he shakes our comfortable reading circles with a touch of the old Hebraic anger and prophecy—and indeed it is just the same. Not Isaiah him-self more scornful, more threatening: "The crown of pride, the drunkards of Ephraim, shall be trodden under feet: And the glorious beauty which is on the head of the fat valley shall be a fading flower." (The word prophecy is much misused; it is narrowed to prediction merely. That is not the main sense of the Hebrew word translated prophet; it means one whose mind bubbles up and pours forth as a fountain, from inner, divine spontaneities revealing God. Pre-diction is a very minor part of prophecy. The great matter is to reveal and outpour the God-like suggestions pressing for birth in the soul. This is briefly the doctrine of the Friends or Quakers.)

Then the simplicity and amid ostensible frailty the towering strength of the man—a hardy oak knot, you could never wear out—an old farmer dressed in brown clothes, and not handsome—his very foibles fascinating. Who cares that he wrote about Dr. Francia and "Shooting Niag-ara,"—and "the Nigger Question,"—and didn't at all admire our United States? (I doubt if he ever thought or said half as bad words about us as we deserve.)

The way to test how much he has left us all were to consider, or try to consider, for a moment the array of British thought, the result-ant and *ensemble* of the last fifty years, as exist-ing to-day, *but with Carlyle left out*. It would be like an army with no artillery. The show were still a gay and rich one—Byron, Scott, Tenny-son, and many more—horsemen and rapid in-fantry, and banners flying—but the last heavy roar so dear to the car of the trained soldier, and that settles fate and victory, would be lacking. His mantle is unfallen. We certainly have no one left like him. I doubt if any nation of the world has. WALT WHITMAN.

F 18

Note: See *Literary World*, 12 February 1881 (E 2590).

F 19

From the CRITIC—*New York, Nov. 8, '84.* | [boldface] The Dead Tenor. | [20 lines of verse] | [flush right] WALT WHITMAN.

Broadside, printed on recto only. 9½" × 6¹⁄₁₆" (NN-B, NcD); 9½" × 6" (DLC); 9⅜" × 6" (DLC); 8⅛" × 6" (DLC). *Locations:* DLC (3), NN-B, NcD.

Note one: A galley proof, measuring 8⅜" × 5⅞", has the following corrections made by Whitman:

line 1   *From the* CRITIC—*New York, Nov. 8, '84.*   ]   [not present]
line 4   inimitable,   ]   inimitable
line 15   *naro's,*   ]   *nuro's,*
line 19   dead tenor,   ]   Italian,

From the CRITIC—*New York, Nov.* 8, '84.

The Dead Tenor.

As down the stage again,
With Spanish hat and plumes, and gait inimitable,
Back from the fading lessons of the past, I'd call, I'd tell and
    own,
How much from thee! the revelation of the singing voice from
    thee!
(So firm—so liquid-soft—again that tremulous, manly timbre!
The perfect singing voice—deepest of all to me the lesson—trial
    and test of all:)
How through those strains distill'd—how the rapt ears, the soul
    of me, absorbing
Fernando's heart, *Manrico's* passionate call, *Ernani's*, sweet *Gen-
    naro's,*
I fold thenceforth, or seek to fold, within my chants transmuting,
Freedom's and Love's and Faith's unloos'd cantabile,
(As perfume's, color's, sunlight's correlation:)
From these, for these, with these a hurried line, dead tenor,
A wafted autumn leaf, dropt in the closing grave, the shovell'd
    earth,
To memory of thee.

                                 WALT WHITMAN.

F 19

In addition, Whitman has dated it 4 November 1884. *Location:* DLC.

Note two: An uncorrected proof is at DLC.

Note three: See *Critic,* 8 November 1884 (E 2629).

F 20

DEATH OF CARLYLE. | [105 lines of prose] | [flush right] WALT WHITMAN.

Broadside, printed on recto only. 16¼″ × 5⅜″. *Location:* MBU.

Note one: See *Critic,* 12 February 1881 (E 2590).

Note two: On 6 February 1881, Whitman ordered "fifty impressions" of this
(*Correspondence,* III, 210).

F 21

From the New Republic, Camden, N.J. Nov. 14th. '74. | [boldface] Death of a
Fireman. | [short rule] | [49 lines of prose] | [flush right] WALT WHITMAN. |
[rule with dot in center]

From the New Republic, Camden, N. J. Nov. 14th. '74.

Death of a Fireman.

WILLIAM ALCOTT, aged 26 years.—Last Monday afternoon his widow, mother, relatives, mates of the Fire Department, and his other friends, (I was one, only lately it is true, but our love grew fast and close, the days and nights of those eight weeks by the chair of rapid decline, and the bed of death,) gathered to the funeral of this young man, who had grown up, and, was well-known in Camden. With nothing special, perhaps, to record, I would give a word or two to his memory? He seemed to me not an inappropriate specimen in character and elements, of that bulk of the average good American race that ebbs and flows perennially beneath this skim of eructations on the surface. Always very quiet in manner, neat in person and dress, good-temper—punctual and industrious at his work, at the house cor. Fifth and Arch sts., till he could work no longer—he just lived his steady square, unobtrusive life, in its own humble sphere, doubtless, unconscious of itself. (Though I think there were currents of emotion and intellect undeveloped beneath, far deeper than his acquaintances ever suspected —or than he himself ever did.) He was no talker. His troubles, when he had any, he kept to himself. As there was nothing querulous about him in life he made no complaints during his last sickness. He was one of those persons that while his associates never thought of attributing any particular talent or grace to him, yet all insensibly, really, liked Billy Alcott.

I, too, loved him. At last, after being with him quite a good deal—after hours and days of panting for breath, much of the time unconscious, (for though the consumption that had been lurking in his system, once thoroughly started, made rapid progress, there was still great vitality in him, and indeed for four or five days he lay dying, before the close,) late on Wednesday night, Nov. 4th, where we surrounded his bed in silence, there came a lull— a longer drawn breath, a pause, a faint sigh— another—a weaker breath, another sigh—a pause again and just a tremble— and the face of the poor wasted young man fell gently over, in death, on my hand, on the pillow.
—WALT WHITMAN.

F 21

Broadside, printed on recto only. 7½″ × 3⅛″ (NN-B); 5⅝″ × 2⅜″ (NcD). *Locations:* NN-B, NcD.

Note: See *Camden New Republic,* 14 November 1874 (E 2543).

F 22

DEATH'S VALLEY. (TO ACCOMPANY A PICTURE BY REQUEST.) . . .

Broadside, printed on recto only. 13 ½″ × 9¾″. See *BAL,* IX, 73, where it is dated "1889." *Location:* Pepper & Stern Rare Books.

Note: See *Harper's Monthly Magazine,* April 1892 (E 2769).

F 23

Walt Whitman's New Volume of Poems. | [ornate rule] | [boldface] DRUM TAPS. | To be issued immediately in a small handsome volume, good | paper and print. | The following is the | TABLE OF CONTENTS: | [two 24-line columns

Walt Whitman's New Volume of Poems.

DRUM TAPS.

To be issued immediately in a small handsome volume, good paper and print. The following is the

TABLE OF CONTENTS:

Drum-Taps.
Song of the Banner at Day-Break.
1861.
The Centenarian's Story.
Pioneers! O Pioneers!
The Dresser.
Rise O Days from your fathomless deeps!
Come up from the fields, father.
Beat! beat! drums!
Vigil strange I kept on the field one night.
A march in the ranks hard-prest, and the road unknown.
Shut not your doors to me, proud libraries.
A sight in camp in the day-break grey and dim.
By the bivouac's fitful flame.
Give me the splendid silent sun.
City of Ships.
Spirit with muttering voice.
Year of meteors.
A battle, (sighs, sounds, &c.)
Angry cloth, I see there leaping.
Flag of stars! thick-spangled bunting.
Lo, the camps of the tents of green.

As I lay with my head in your lap, camerado.
I dream, I dream, I dream.
As toilsome I wander'd Virginia's woods.
As I in vision surfaces piercing.
From Paumanok starting I fly like a bird.
Turn O libertad!
You foes that in conflict have overcome me.
A soldier returns, he will soon be home.
Quicksand years that whirl me I know not whither.
Over sea-hither from Niplon.
Beginning my studies.
When I heard the learn'd astronomer.
Aboard at a ship's helm.
Race of weapon'd men.
Out of the rolling ocean, the crowd.
I heard you solemn sweet pipes of the organ.
Cavalry crossing a ford.
Weave in, weave in, my hardy life.
I saw the old General at bay.
World take good notice.
The bivouac halt.
Pensive on her dead gazing.
Reconciliation.
Not youth pertains to me.

Also, will soon be issued, a new edition of

LEAVES OF GRASS,

Entirely revised and much changed from the last edition of 1860-61.

Whitman's draft for F 23

with a vertical line between them] | [ornate rule] | Also, will soon be issued, a new edition of | [boldface] LEAVES OF GRASS, | Entirely revised and much changed from the last edition of 1860–61.

Broadside, printed on recto only. 9⅝″ × 7⅝″; 9¾″ × 7⅝″ (both CtY). *Locations:* CtY (2).

Note: The manuscript of this advertising placard is at CtY and contains a notation ("Mr Romes Statement") that "only about 50 were printed for use in the bookstores as placards."

F 24

[boldface] THE DYING VETERAN. | [*A Long Island incident—early part of the present century.*] | [22 lines of verse] | [flush right] WALT WHITMAN.

THE DYING VETERAN.

[*A Long Island incident—early part of the present century.*]

Amid these days of order, ease, prosperity,
Amid the current songs of beauty, peace, decorum,
I cast a reminiscence—(likely 'twill offend you,
I heard it in my boyhood;)—More than a generation since,
A queer old savage man, a fighter under Washington himsel
Large, brave, cleanly, hot-blooded, no talker, rather spiritual
    istic,
(Had fought in the ranks—fought well—had been all throug
    the Revolutionary war,)
Lay dying—sons, daughters, church-deacons, lovingly tendin
    him,
Sharping their sense, their ears, toward his murmuring, hal
    caught words:
"Let me return again to my war-days,
To the sights and scenes—to forming the line of battle,
To the scouts ahead reconnoitering,
To the cannons, the grim artillery,
To the galloping aids, carrying orders,
To the wounded, the fallen, the heat, the suspense,
The perfume strong, the smoke, the deafening noise;
Away with your life of peace!—your joys of peace!
Give me my old wild battle-life again!"

WALT WHITMAN.

F 24

Broadside, printed on recto only. 6¾″ × 6″ (DLC); 5⅛″ × 4⅝″ (MoHi). *Locations:* DLC, MoHi.

Note one: See *McClure's Magazine,* June 1887 (E 2663).

Note two: Whitman mentions "slip copies" on 13 July 1887 (*Correspondence,* IV, 108).

F 25

AN ENGINEER'S OBITUARY. (FROM THE ENGINEERING RECORD, N.Y., DEC. 13, 1890.) . . .

Broadside, printed on recto only. 10⅛″ × 4⅛″. See *BAL,* IX, 74. *Location:* DLC.

Note one: See "Thomas Jefferson Whitman," *Engineering Record,* 13 December 1890 (E 2749).

Note two: Whitman mentions "slips" on 13 December 1890 (*Correspondence,* V, 131).

F 26

[at right] From the American Phrenological Journal. | [boldface] AN ENGLISH AND AN AMERICAN POET. | [208 lines of prose and verse]

Broadside, printed on recto only. 24″ × 5″ (NN-B); 20 ¾″ × 5″ (RPB). *Locations:* NN-B, RPB.

Note one: Not from the same setting of type used in the advertising supplement to the 1855 *Leaves of Grass.*

Note two: See *American Phrenological Journal,* October 1855 (E 1180).

F 27

ETHIOPIA SALUTING THE COLORS. | [rule with dotted line] | BY WALT WHITMAN. | 1. | [four lines of verse] | 2. | [three lines of verse] | 3. | [three lines of verse] | 4. | [four lines of verse] | 5. | [five lines of verse]

Broadside, printed on recto only. 8″ × 4¼″. *Location:* TxU.

Note: Originally printed on a single sheet with "Fables" and "Sparkles from the Wheel" (see F 74).

F 28

FABLES. | [rule with dotted line] | BY WALT WHITMAN. | [rule with dotted line] | [15 lines of verse]

Broadside, printed on recto only. 8¾″ × 4⅞″. *Location:* TxU.

Note: Originally printed on a single sheet with "Ethiopia Saluting the Colors" and "Sparkles from the Wheel" (see F 74).

Ethiopia Saluting the Colors.

By WALT WHITMAN.

1.

Who are you, dusky woman, so ancient, hardly human,
With your woolly-white and turban'd head, and bare
   bony feet?
Why, rising by the roadside here, do you the soldiers greet?

2.

('T is while our army lines Carolina's sand and pines,
Forth from thy hovel door, thou, Ethiopia, com'st to me,
As, under doughty Sherman, I march toward the sea.)

3.

Me, master, years a hundred since from my parents sunder'd,
A little child, they caught me as the savage beast is caught;
Then hither me, across the sea, the cruel slaver brought.

4.

No further does she say, but lingering all the day,
Her high-borne turban'd head she wags, and rolls her
   darkling eye,
And curtseys to the colors, to the soldiers moving by.

5.

What is it, fateful woman—so blear, hardly human?
Why wag your head, with turban bound—yellow, red and
   green?
Are the things so strange and marvellous, you see or have
   seen?

F 27

Fables.

By WALT WHITMAN.

Not you alone, O Truths of the world!
But Fables—the splendid fables!
The far darting beams of the spirit!—the unloos'd dreams!
The deep diving fables—the mythical bibles and legends;
The daring plots of the poets—the elder and newer re-
   ligions;
—O you temples fairer than lilies, pour'd over by the rising
   sun!
O you fables, spurning the known, eluding the hold of the
   known, mounting to heaven!
You lofty and dazzling towers, pinnacled, red as roses,
   burnish'd with gold!
Towers of fables immortal, fashion'd from mortal dreams!
You too I welcome, and fully, the same as the rest;
You too with joy I sing.

F 28

F 29

Two states have been noted, priority undetermined:

First state:

[boldface] FANCIES AT NAVESINK. | [ornate boldface] The Pilot in the mist. | [10 lines of verse] | [ornate boldface] Had I the choice. | [12 lines of verse] | [ornate boldface] You Tides with ceaseless swell. | [13 lines of verse] | [ornate boldface] Last of Ebb, and daylight waning. | [24 lines of verse] | [ornate boldface] Proudly the Flood comes in. | [nine lines of verse] | [ornate boldface] By that long scan of Waves. | [14 lines of verse] | [ornate boldface] Then last of all. | [five lines of verse] | [flush right] WALT WHITMAN. | [one line of prose]

Broadside, printed on recto only. 19″ × 6″ (CtY, DLC [3], NjP, RPB); 19″ × 5¹⁄₁₆″ (CaOTU). *Locations:* CaOTU, CtY, DLC (3), NjP, RPB.

Second state:

[boldface] FANCIES . . . | [ornate boldface] Then last of all. | [five lines of verse] | [one line of prose]

19″ × 6″ (DLC); 18⅜″ × 6⅛″ (CtY, signed by Whitman). *Locations:* CtY, DLC.

Note: See *Nineteenth Century,* August 1885 (E 2640).

F 30

FIFTY-FIRST NEW-YORK CITY VETERANS . . .

Two sheets, printed on rectos only, pasted together. 34¼″ × 5⁹⁄₁₆″. See *BAL,* IX, 75. *Location:* DLC.

Note: See *New York Times,* 29 October 1864 (E 2490).

F 31

FIVE THOUSAND POEMS . . .

Broadside, printed on recto only. 9⅛″ × 5¾″. See *BAL,* IX, 75, where two states are identified:

First state:

The text immediately follows the title.

Second state:

'[THE CRITIC, New York, April 16, 1887.]' is printed between the title and the text.

Locations: DLC (both).

Note one: See *Critic,* 16 April 1887 (E 2659).

Note two: Whitman mentions "8 or 10 proof-slips" on 14 February 1887 (*Correspondence,* IV, 68).

FANCIES AT NAVESINK.

The Pilot in the mist.

Steaming the northern rapids—(an old St. Lawrence reminis-
    cence,
A sudden memory-flash comes back, I know not why,
Here waiting for the sunrise, gazing from this hill;*)
Again 'tis just at morning—a heavy haze contends with day-
    break,
Again the trembling, laboring vessel veers me—I press through
    foam-dash'd rocks that almost touch me,
Again I mark where aft the small thin Indian helmsman
Looms in the mist, with brow elate and governing hand.

Had I the choice.

Had I the choice to tally greatest bards,
To limn their portraits, stately, beautiful, and emulate at will,
Homer with all his wars and warriors—Hector, Achilles, Ajax,
Or Shakspere's woe-entangled Hamlet, Lear, Othello—Tenny-
    son's fair ladies,
Metre or wit the best, or choice conceit to wield in perfect
    rhyme, delight of singers;
These, these, O sea, all these I'd gladly barter,
Would you the undulation of one wave, its trick to me
    transfer,
Or breathe one breath of yours upon my verse,
And leave its odor there.

You Tides with ceaseless swell.

You tides with ceaseless swell! you power that does this
    work!
You unseen force, centripetal, centrifugal, through space's
    spread,
Rapport of sun, moon, earth, and all the constellations!
What are the messages by you from distant stars to us? what
    Sirius'? what Capella's?
What central heart—and you the pulse—vivifies all? what
    boundless aggregate of all?
What subtle indirection and significance in you? what clue
    to all in you? what fluid, vast identity,
Holding the universe with all its parts as one—as sailing in
    a ship?

Last of Ebb, and daylight waning.

Last of ebb, and daylight waning,
Scented sea-cool landward making, smells of sedge and salt
    incoming,
With many a half-caught voice sent up from the eddies,
Many a muffled confession—many a sob and whisper'd word,
As of speakers far or hid.

How they sweep down and out! how they mutter!
Poets unnamed—artists greatest of any, with cherish'd lost
    designs,
Love's unresponse—a chorus of age's complaints—hope's last
    words,
Some suicide's despairing cry, *Away to the boundless waste, and
    never again return.*

On to oblivion then!
On, on, and do your part, ye burying, ebbing tide!
On for your time, ye furious debouché!

And yet not you alone, twilight and burying ebb,
Nor you, ye lost designs alone—nor failures, aspirations;
I know, divine deceitful ones, your glamour's seeming,
Duly by you, by you alone, the tide and light again—duly
    the hinges turning,
Duly the needed discord-parts offsetting, blending,
Weaving from you, from Sleep, Night, Death itself,
The rhythmus of Birth eternal.

Proudly the Flood comes in.

Proudly the flood comes in, shouting, foaming, advancing,
Long it holds at the high, with bosom broad outswelling,
All throbs, dilates—the farms, woods, streets of cities—work-
    men at work,
Mainsails, topsails, jibs, appear in the offing—steamers' pen-
    nants of smoke—and under the forenoon sun,
Freighted with human lives, gaily the outward bound, gaily
    the inward bound,
Flaunting from many a spar the flag I love.

By that long scan of Waves.

By that long scan of waves, myself call'd back, resumed upon
    myself,
In every crest some undulating light or shade—some retro-
    spect,
Joys, travels, studies, silent panoramas—scenes ephemeral,
The long past war, the battles, hospital sights, the wounded
    and the dead,
Myself through every by-gone phase—my idle youth—old age
    at hand,
My three-score years of life summ'd up, and more, and past,
By any grand ideal tried, intentionless, the whole a nothing,
And haply yet some drop within God's scheme's ensemble—
    some wave, or part of wave,
Like one of yours, ye multitudinous ocean.

Then last of all.

Then last of all, caught from these shores, this hill,
Of you O tides, the mystic human meaning:
Only by law of you, your swell and ebb, enclosing me the
    same,
The brain that shapes, the voice that chants this song.

WALT WHITMAN.

* Navesink—a sea-side mountain, lower entrance of New-York bay.

F 29, first state

F 32

FOR QUEEN VICTORIA'S BIRTHDAY. | [two lines of prose in italics] | [six lines of verse] | [flush right] WALT WHITMAN. | [16 lines of prose]

Broadside, printed on recto only. 9⅝″ × 5¹⁵⁄₁₆″ (DLC, marked received from Whitman, 25 May 1890); 9½″ × 6″ (NNC, TxU); 7¾″ × 6″ (ViU). *Locations:* DLC, NNC, TxU, ViU.

Note one: A galley proof, measuring 9½″ × 6″, has the following correction made by Whitman:

   line 14   national   ]   natural

In addition, Whitman has written on it "correct & give me this evening 30 slips on good paper." *Location:* DLC.

Note two: See *Philadelphia Public Ledger,* 22 May 1890; *Critic,* 24 May 1890 (E 2733).

FOR QUEEN VICTORIA'S BIRTHDAY.

An American arbutus bunch, to be put in a little vase, on the royal breakfast table, May 24th, 1890.

Lady, accept a birth-day thought — haply an idle gift and
      token,
Right from the scented soil's May-utterance here,
(Smelling of countless blessings, prayers, and old-time thanks),
A bunch of white and pink arbutus, silent, spicy, shy,
From Hudson's, Delaware's, or Potomac's woody banks.
                                        WALT WHITMAN.

NOTE.—Very little, as we Americans stand this day, with our sixty-five or seventy millions of population, an immense surplus in the treasury, and all that actual power or reserved power (land and sea) so dear to nations — very little I say do we realize that curious crawling national shudder when the "Trent affair" promised to bring upon us a war with Great Britain—followed unquestionably as that war would have, by recognition of the Southern Confederacy from all the leading European nations. It is now certain that all this then inevitable train of calamity hung on arrogant and peremptory phrases in the prepared and written missive of the British Minister, to America, which the Queen (and Prince Albert latent) positively and promptly cancelled; and which her firm attitude did alone actually erase and leave out, against all the other official prestige and Court of St. James's. On such minor and personal incidents (so to call them), often depend the great growths and turns of civilization. This moment of a woman and a queen surely swung the grandest oscillation of modern history's pendulum. Many sayings and doings of that period, from foreign potentates and powers, might well be drop'd in oblivion by America — but never *this,* if I could have my way.   W. W.

   F 32

Note three: On 10 May 1890, Whitman sent "five slips" to England to send "around to the London papers, to be used if they think proper" (*Correspondence,* V, 45–46).

F 33

[boldface] "GOING SOMEWHERE." | [15 lines of verse] | [flush right] WALT WHITMAN.

"GOING SOMEWHERE."

My science-friend, my noblest woman-friend,
(Now buried in an English grave—and this a memory-leaf for
     her dear sake,)
Ended our talk—" The sum, concluding all we know of old or
     modern learning, intuitions deep,
" Of all Geologies—Histories—of all Astronomy—of Evolution,
     Metaphysics all,
" Is, that we all are onward, onward, speeding slowly, surely
     bettering,
" Life, life an endless march, an endless army, (no halt, but
     it is duly over,)
" The world, the race, the soul, in space and time the uni-
     verses,
" All wisely bound as is befitting them—all surely going
     somewhere."

WALT WHITMAN.

F 33

Broadside, printed on recto only. 6⅜" × 6" (DLC); 6⅜" × 5⅞" (NN-B, TxU); 6¼" × 6" (PU); 6⅛" × 6" (DLC). *Locations:* DLC (2), NN-B, PU, TxU.

Note one: A galley proof, measuring 6" × 6¼", has the following corrections made by Whitman:

line 5   sum,] sum
line 6   learning, intuitions] learning—intuitions

In addition, Whitman has written on it "let me have 30 impressions." *Location:* DLC.

Note two: See *Lippincott's Magazine*, November 1887 (E 2667).

F 34

HALCYON DAYS. | [12 lines of verse] | [flush right] WALT WHITMAN.

Broadside, printed on recto only. 7" × 6" (DLC); 6¾" × 6" (DLC); 6" × 6¹/₁₆" (DLC); 5½" × 6" (DLC, NcD, TxU [2]). *Locations:* DLC (4), NcD, TxU (2).

Note: See *New York Herald*, 29 January 1888 (E 2676).

F 35

Two sheets: (1) '*From the North American Review, March*, 1891. | HAVE WE A NATIONAL LITERATURE? | BY WALT WHITMAN. | [short rule] | [118 lines of prose]' and (2) '[125 lines of prose] | [flush right] WALT WHITMAN.'.

Broadsides, printed on rectos only. Both 24" × 6⅜". *Location:* BBo.

HALCYON DAYS.

Not from successful love alone,
Nor wealth, nor honored middle age, nor victories of politics
    or war,
But as life wanes, and all the turbulent passions calm,
As gorgeous, vapory, silent hues cover the evening sky,
As an indescribable softness, fulness, rest, suffuse the spirit
      and frame, like freshier, balmier air,
As the days take on a mellower light, and the apple at
      last hangs really finished and indolent-ripe on the
      tree,
Then for the teeming quietest, happiest days of all!
The brooding and blissful halcyon days!

                        WALT WHITMAN.

F 34

Note one: A set at NcD has the sheets measuring 22¾″ × 6 ⅜″ and 20⅝″ × 6⅜″, with 61 lines on the second sheet.

Note two: See *North American Review*, March 1891 (E 2758).

Note three: On 4 March 1891, Whitman noted that he was expecting "printed slips" of this (*Correspondence*, V, 173).

F 36

Two sheets: (1) '[boldface] HOW I GET AROUND AT SIXTY AND TAKE NOTES. | (No. 2.) | [127 lines of prose]' and (2) '[20 lines of prose] | [five lines of verse] | [two lines of prose] | [flush right] WALT WHITMAN.'

Broadsides, printed on rectos only, pasted together to form one long galley. (1) 24″ × 6¼″; (2) 5″ × 6⅛″. *Location:* NN-R.

Note one: See *Critic*, 9 April 1881 (E 2592).

Note two: On 9 April and on 21 November 1881, Whitman wrote about "slips" of this (*Walt Whitman Quarterly Review*, 1, no. 2 [September 1983], back cover verso; 2, no. 1 [Summer 1984], back cover verso).

F 37

ITALIAN MUSIC IN DAKOTA . . .

Broadside, printed on recto only. 6¹/₁₆″ × 5¹³/₁₆″. See *BAL*, IX, 76, where it is dated "not before 1879." *Location:* DLC.

Note one: See *Leaves of Grass* (1881), p. 309.

F 38

[Letter to William Michael Rossetti]. [London: n.p., 1876].

Broadside, printed on recto only. 10½″ × 8″. Letter of 17 March 1876. *Location:* JM.

Note one: Rossetti printed and distributed copies of this letter as a circular. It was completed on 20 May, with a second circular of "like form" being done on 1 June (see *Selected Letters of William Michael Rossetti,* ed. Roger W. Peattie

---

CAMDEN, NEW JERSEY,
U. S. AMERICA.

March 17th, 1876.

431 STEVENS STREET,
COR WEST.

W. M. ROSSETTI.

Dear Friend,— Yours of the 28th Feb. received, and indeed welcomed and appreciated. I am jogging along still about the same in physical condition—still certainly no worse, and I sometimes lately suspect rather better, or at any rate more adjusted to the situation—Even begin to think of making some move, some change of base &c. : the doctors have been advising it for over two years, but I haven't felt to do it yet. My paralysis does not lift—I cannot walk any distance—I still have this baffling, obstinate, apparently chronic affection of the stomachic apparatus and liver : yet (as told in former letters) I get out of doors a little every day—write and read in moderation—appetite sufficiently good (eat only very plain food, but always did that)—digestion tolerable— and spirits unflagging. As said above, I have told you most of this before, but suppose you might like to know it all again, up to date. Of course, and pretty darkly colouring the whole, are bad spells, prostrations, *some pretty grave ones,* intervals—and I have resigned myself to the certainty of permanent incapacitation from solid work : but things may continue at least in this half-and-half way for months—even years.

My books are out, the new edition ; a set of which, immediately on receiving your letter of 28th, I have sent you (by Mail, March 15), and I suppose you have before this received them.

My dear friend, your offers of help, and those of my other British friends, I think I fully appreciate, in the right spirit, welcome and acceptive—leaving the matter altogether in your and their hands—and to your and their convenience, discretion, leisure, and nicety. Though poor now, even to penury, *I have not so far been deprived of any physical thing I need or wish whatever, and I feel confident I shall not in the future.* During my employment of seven years or more in Washington after the war (1865—72) I regularly saved a great part of my wages: and, though the sum has now become about exhausted by my expenses of the last three years, there are already beginning at present welcome dribbles hitherward from the sales of my new edition, which I just job and sell, myself (as the book-agents here for three years in New York have successively, deliberately, badly cheated me), and shall continue to dispose of the books myself. And *that* is the way I should prefer to glean my support. In that way I cheerfully accept all the aid my friends find it convenient to proffer.   •   *   *   •

To repeat a little, and without undertaking details, understand, dear friend, for yourself and all, that I heartily and most affectionately thank my British friends, and that I accept their sympathetic generosity in the same spirit in which I believe (nay, *know*) it is offered—that though poor *I am not in want*—that I maintain good heart and cheer ; and that by far the most satisfaction to me (and I think it can be done, and believe it will be) will be to live, as long as possible, on *the sales, by myself, of my own works,* and perhaps, if practicable, by further writings for the press.

WALT WHITMAN.

    •   •   •   •   I am prohibited from writing too much, and I must make this candid statement of the situation serve for all my dear friends over there.

[University Park: Pennsylvania State University Press, 1990], p. 339; Thomas Donaldson, *Walt Whitman* [D 29], p. 26). On 31 December 1876, Whitman wrote that Rossetti "had some copies printed as a sort of circular" (*Correspondence*, III, 72).

Note two: The letter was reprinted in *Specimen Days* (A 11), pp. 315–316.

F 39
[Letter to Herbert Gilchrist]. [London: n.p., 1885].

F 39

SEPTEMBER] [1885.

WALT WHITMAN.

A Subscription list is being formed in England with a view to presenting a free-will offering to the American Poet Walt Whitman. The poet is in his sixty-seventh year, and has, since his enforced retirement some years ago from official work in Washington, owing to an attack of paralysis, maintained himself precariously by the sale of his works in poetry and prose, and by occasional contributions to magazines.

Mr. Herbert H. Gilchrist, 12 Well Road, Hampstead, London, N.W., acts as *Honorary Secretary* to this scheme ; Mr. W. M. Rossetti, 5 Endsleigh Gardens, Euston Square, London, N.W., as *Treasurer*.

SUBSCRIPTIONS.

	£	s.	d.		£	s.	d.
John Addington Symonds	5	0	0	Professor Dowden	2	2	0
J. S. Mann	1	1	0	Charles Rowley, Jun.	2	2	0
Miss E. M. Abdy-Williams	2	0	0	W. A. Turner	2	2	0
A Friend	5	0	0	Henry Boddington, Jun.	1	0	0
George Saintsbury	2	2	0	C. Sheldon	1	1	0
Mrs. H. M. Thompson	2	2	0	H. J. Falk	1	1	0
Charles Aldrich	1	0	0				
A. Bolles Lee	0	8	6				
Havelock and Louie Ellis	0	5	0				
Mrs. Gilchrist	2	2	0				
W. M. Rossetti	2	0	0				
Mrs. Rossetti	2	0	0				
John Wallace	1	1	0				
John Fraser	1	1	0				
G. R. Rogerson	1	1	0				
Miss Hamilton	1	0	0				
G. T. Glover	5	0	0				

The Secretary had thought it desirable, before proceeding further, to ascertain what Walt Whitman's wishes would be in regard to accepting such a free-will offering, and had accordingly written to him and received the following answer.

[P.T.O.

F 39

Single sheet folded to make four pages; printed on pp. 1–2, with facsimile of Whitman's letter to Gilchrist of 1 August 1885 on p. 2. 10½″ × 8¼″. Intended as a subscription list "with a view to presenting a free-will offering" to Whitman, dated September 1885. *Location:* NcD.

F 40

[Letter to William Michael Rossetti]. [Liverpool: John Fraser, 1886].

Single sheet, folded to make four pages; printed on pp. 1, 3, with facsimile of
Whitman's letter to Rossetti of 30 May 1886 on p. 1. 10½″ × 8″ (NcD); 8⅜″ ×
7½″ (NN-B). *Locations:* NN-B, NcD.

F 41

[Letter to Dr. Johnston]. [N.p.: n.p., 1891].

Two states have been noted, priority assumed:

First state:

F 40

Cambridge
R. Colles   19. 6
                                                               2.
                                                               £74 19 8

Name	£	s	d		Name	£	s	d
W. B.	1	1	0		R. G. Fulton	5	0	0
Miss Gerstenberg	2	2	0		T. G. Leathes	1	0	0
Miss Amy Levy	0	5	0		New College, Oxford :—Collected by A.			
Oliver Elton, Oxford	1	1	0		H. Hawkins	0	10	0
Shadworth H. Hodgson	5	5	0		P. M. Wallace	0	5	0
Henry James	5	0	0		D. S. MacColl	0	5	0
Charles Pratt	1	1	0		G. Whale	1	1	0
Mrs. Pratt	0	5	0		R. R. Meade-King	5	0	0
A. Crompton	5	0	0		Mrs. Reinagle	3	0	0
R. B. C.	5	0	0		R. G Fulton and others in Oxford Uni-			
L. A. J.	0	5	0		versity	6	0	0
Miss Pease, [Annual]	1	0	0		Miss Emma Phipson	2	0	0
J. Johnston, M.D.	1	0	0		Miss Violet Paget	1	0	0
Oscar Gridley	3	0	0		A Friend	5	0	0
T. H. C.	1	1	0		Mrs. Fleming Jenkin	2	2	0
G. H. M.	1	1	0		Clement Templeton	1	1	0
H. G. Dakyns	5	0	0		John Addington Symonds	5	0	0
G. C. Macaulay	2	2	0		J. S. Mann	1	1	0
Ernest Myers	1	1	0		Miss E. M. Abdy-Williams	2	0	0
R. Louis Stevenson	1	1	0		A Friend	5	0	0
R. Hannah	3	0	0		George Saintsbury	2	2	0
A. Sidgwick	1	0	0		Mr. and Mrs. William Herford	2	2	0
An Englishwoman [Annual]	3	0	0		Charles Aldrich	1	0	0
Helen Zimmern	0	5	0		A. Bolles Lee	0	8	6
Leonard M. Brown [Annual]	5	0	0		Mrs. Gilchrist	2	2	0
Mr. and Mrs. Frank Darwin	1	0	0		W. M. Rossetti	2	0	0
Michael Sadler	1	1	0		Mrs. Rossetti	2	0	0
L. G. Fry	2	2	0		John Wallace	1	1	0
Mrs. Cowden Clarke	0	8	4		G. R. Rogerson	1	1	0
Miss Novello	0	8	4		Miss Hamilton	1	0	0
H. J. Falk	1	1	0		G. T. Glover	5	0	0
John Fraser	1	1	0		Professor Dowden ...annual	2	2	0
Some Members of the Manchester Literary					Charles Rowley, Jun.	2	2	0
Club	3	3	0		W. A. Turner	2	2	0
J. Fitzgerald Molloy	1	0	0		Henry Boddington, Jun.	1'	0	0
J. R. Williamson	0	10	6		C. Sheldon	1	1	0
G. M. G.	2	0	0		Mrs. Riley	1	1	0
L. W.	0	5	0		E. R. Pease	2	2	0
J. G. Dow	0	8	6		Rev. Lewis Campbell	3	0	0
The Honble. Roden Noel	0	10	0		W. H. Coffin	1	1	0
Aldrich	1	0	0		Henry Holmes	2	2	0
Havelock and Louie Ellis	0	5	0		John Todhunter, M.D.	2	0	0
G. R. Benson and others in Oxford Uni-								
versity	4	0	0					
	£74	19	8			£159	6	2

FINIS.

I contributed
Printed by John Fraser
of Liverpool.

Herbert H Salahorie
Hon: Sec:

F 40

Broadside, printed on recto only, on orange paper. 6⅛″ × 8 ⅛″. Clipping from the 7 May 1891 *Boston Evening Transcript* is pasted on the middle left side. Letter of 1 June 1891. *Location:* TxU.

Second state:

6⅛″ × 8⅛″. Clipping is typeset with the text. *Location:* PU.

Note: This was printed by Johnston at Whitman's request (see *Correspondence*, V, 205–206).

F 42
[Letter to John H. Johnston]. [N.p.: n.p., 1892].

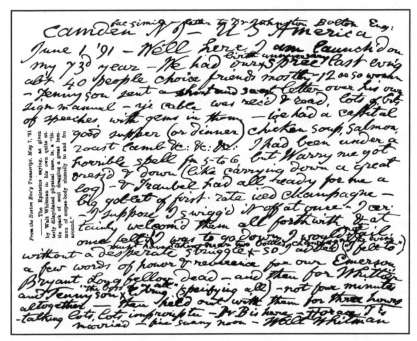

F 41, second state

Broadsides, printed on rectos only, on yellow paper, pasted together to form a single sheet. (1) 6⅝" × 8⅜" and (2) 3½" × 8½" (NN-B); (1) 6½" X 8¼" and (2) 3¾" × 8¼" (BBo, BMR, TxU). A printed advertisement for *Leaves of Grass* (written by Whitman) is pasted to the middle right side of the first sheet. The letter is dated 6–7 February 1892. *Locations:* BBo, BMR, NN-B, TxU.

Note one: In a printed broadside "Extract from Letter" from Traubel to John H. Johnston of 8 February 1892, the former states: 'W[hitman]. asked me this ev'g to give you this counsel.—"If entirely convenient, *fac-simile* the letter of February 6th, and send it copiously to European and American Friends and friends anywhere" ' (BBo, DLC).

Note two: For the background to this—called Whitman's "last words"—see Elizabeth Leavitt Keller, *Walt Whitman in Mickle Street* (New York: Mitchell Kennerley, 1921), pp. 168–171. In an earlier version, she stated that "fifty copies" were made ("Walt Whitman: The Last Phase," *Putnam's Magazine,* 6 [June 1909], 331–337).

Note three: See *New York Evening Telegram,* 10 March 1892 (E 2766).

Note four: A different facsimile is reproduced in J. Johnston and J. W. Wallace, *Visits to Walt Whitman* (D 51), after p. 234.

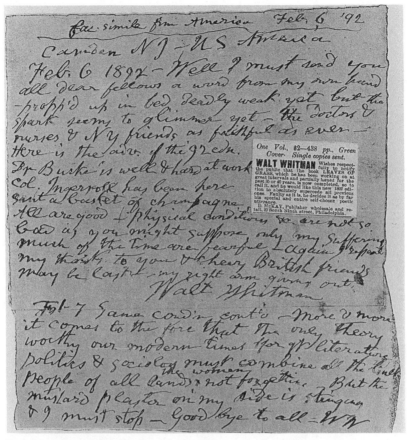

F 42 *(Note four)*

F 43
From the New Republic Camden, N.J[.], March 11, 187[6] . . . Literature. Walt Whitman's Works, 1876 Edition . . .

Broadside, printed on recto only. 8⅝″ × 3¼″. See *BAL*, IX, 76. *Location:* DLC.

Note: See *Camden New Republic,* 11 March 1876 (E 2552).

F 44
[first column] *(From the North American Review.)* | MEMORANDUM AT A VENTURE. | [short rule] | [two lines from F. J. Millet] | [92 lines of prose] | [second column] [107 lines of prose] | [flush right] WALT WHITMAN.

Broadside, printed on recto only. 16½″ × 9⁷/₁₆″. *Locations:* BL, CSt, DLC, JM, MBU, NNC, NcD, NcU, NjP, PU, TxU.

(From the North American Review.)

A MEMORANDUM AT A VENTURE.

"All is proper to be expressed, provided our aim is only high enough."
—*J. F. Millet.*

SHALL the mention of such topics as I have briefly but plainly and resolutely broached in the "Children of Adam" section of "Leaves of Grass" be admitted in poetry and literature? Ought not the innovation to be put down by opinion and criticism? and, if those fail, by the District Attorney? True, I could not construct a poem which declaredly took, as never before, the complete human identity, physical, moral, emotional, and intellectual (giving precedence and compass in a certain sense to the first), nor fulfil that *bona fide* candor and entirety of treatment which was a part of my purpose, without comprehending this section also. But I would entrench myself more deeply and widely than that. And while I do not ask any man to indorse my theory, I confess myself anxious that what I sought to write and express, and the ground I built on, shall be at least partially understood from its own platform. The best way seems to me to confront the question with entire frankness.

There are, generally speaking, two points of view, two conditions of the world's attitude toward these matters; the first, the conventional one of good folks and good print everywhere, repressing any direct statement of them, and making allusions only at second or third hand (as the Greeks did of death, which, in Hellenic social culture, was not mentioned point blank, but by euphemisms). In the civilization of to-day, this condition—without stopping to elaborate the arguments and facts, which are many and varied and perplexing—has led to states of ignorance, repressal, and covered-over disease and depletion, forming certainly a main factor in the world's woe. A non-scientific, non-æsthetic, and eminently non-religious condition, bequeathed to us from the past (its origins diverse, one of them the far-back lessons of benevolent and wise men to restrain the prevalent coarseness and animality of the tribal ages, with Puritanism, or perhaps Protestantism itself for another, and still another specified in the latter part of this memorandum), to it is probably due most of the ill births, inefficient maturity, snickering pruriency, and of that human pathologic evil and morbidity which is, in my opinion, the keel and reason-why of every evil and morbidity. Its scent, as of something sneaking, furtive, mephitic, seems to lingeringly pervade all modern literature, conversation, and manners.

The second point of view, and by far the largest—as the world in working-day dress vastly exceeds the world in parlor toilette—is the one of common life, from the oldest times down, and especially in England (see the earlier chapters of "Taine's English Literature," and see Shakespeare almost anywhere), and which our age to-day inherits from riant stock, in the wit, or what passes for wit, of masculine circles, and in erotic stories and talk, to excite, express, and dwell on, that merely sensual voluptuousness which, according to Victor Hugo, is the most universal trait of all ages, all lands. This second condition, however bad, is at any rate like a disease which comes to the surface, and therefore less dangerous than a concealed one.

The time seems to me to have arrived, and America to be the place, for a new departure—a third point of view. The same freedom and faith and earnestness which, after centuries of denial, struggle, repression, and martyrdom, the present day brings to the treatment of politics and religion, must work out a plan and standard on this subject, not so much for what is called society, as for thoughtfulest men and women, and thoughtfulest literature. The same spirit that marks the physiological author and demonstrator on these topics in his important field I have thought necessary to be exemplified, for once, in another certainly not less important field.

In the present memorandum I only venture to indicate that plan and view—decided upon more than twenty years ago, for my own literary action, and formulated tangibly in my printed poems (as Bacon says an abstract thought or theory is of no moment unless it leads to a deed or work done, exemplifying it in the concrete)—that the sexual passion in itself, while normal and unperverted, is inherently legitimate, creditable, not necessarily an improper theme for poet, as confessedly not for scientist—that, with reference to the whole construction, organism, and intentions of "Leaves of Grass," anything short of confronting that theme, and making myself clear upon it, as the enclosing basis of everything (as the sanity of everything was to be the atmosphere of the poems), I should beg the question in its most momentous aspect, and the superstructure that followed, pretensive as it might assume to be, would all rest on a poor foundation, or no foundation at all. In short, as the assumption of the sanity of birth, Nature and humanity is the key to any true theory of life and the universe—at any rate, the only theory out of which I wrote—it is, and must inevitably be, the only key to "Leaves of Grass," and every part of it.

That (and not a vain consistency or weak pride, as a late "Springfield Republican" charges) is the reason that I have stood out for these particular verses uncompromisingly for over twenty years, and maintain them to this day. *That* is what I felt in my inmost brain and heart when I only answered Emerson's vehement arguments with silence, under the old elms of Boston Common.

Indeed, might not every physiologist and every good physician pray for the redeeming of this subject from its hitherto relegation to the tongues and pens of blackguards, and boldly putting it for once at least, if no more, in the demesne of poetry and sanity—as something not in itself gross or impure, but entirely consistent with highest manhood and womanhood, and indispensable to both? Might not only every wife and every mother—not only every babe that comes into the world, if that were possible—not only all marriage, the foundation and *sine qua non* of the civilized state—bless and thank the showing, or taking for granted, that motherhood, fatherhood, sexuality, and all that belongs to them, can be asserted, where it comes to question, openly, joyously, proudly, "without shame or the need of shame," from the highest artistic and sociologic considerations—but, with reverence be it written, on such attempt to justify the base and start of the whole divine scheme in humanity, might not the Creative Power itself deign a smile of approval?

To the movement for the eligibility and entrance of women amid new spheres of business, politics, and the suffrage, the current, prurient, conventional treatment of sex is the main formidable obstacle. The rising tide of "woman's rights," swelling, and every year advancing farther and farther, recoils from it with dismay. There will in my opinion be no general progress in such eligibility till a sensible, philosophic, democratic method is substituted.

The whole question—which strikes far, very far, deeper than most people have supposed (and doubtless, too, something is to be said on all sides), is peculiarly an important one in art—is first an ethic, and then still more an æsthetic one. I condense from a paper read not long since at Cheltenham, England, before the "Social Science Congress," to the Art Department, by P. H. Rathbone, of Liverpool, on the "Undraped Figure in Art," and the discussion that followed:

"When coward Europe suffered the unclean Turk to soil the sacred shores of Greece by his polluting presence, civilization and morality received a blow from which they have never entirely recovered, and the trail of the serpent has been over European art and European society ever since. The Turk regarded and regards women as animals without soul, toys to be played with or broken at pleasure, and to be hidden, partly from shame, but chiefly for the purpose of stimulating exhausted passion. Such is the unholy origin of the objection to the nude as a fit subject for art; it is purely Asiatic, and though not introduced for the first time in the fifteenth century, is yet to be traced to the source of all impurity—the East. Although the source of the prejudice is thoroughly unhealthy and impure, yet it is now shared by many pure-minded and honest, if somewhat uneducated, people. But I am prepared to maintain that it is necessary for the future of English art and of English morality that the right of the nude to a place in our galleries should be boldly asserted; it must, however, be the nude as represented by thoroughly trained artists, and with a pure and noble ethic purpose. The human form, male and female, is the type and standard of all beauty of form and proportion, and it is necessary to be thoroughly familiar with it in order safely to judge of all beauty which consists of form and proportion. To women it is most necessary that they should become thoroughly imbued with the knowledge of the ideal female form, in order that they should recognize the perfection of it at once, and without effort, and so far as possible avoid deviations from the ideal. Had this been the case in times past, we should not have had to deplore the distortions effected by tight lacing (cheers), which destroyed the figure and ruined the health of so many of the last generation. Nor should we have had the scandalous dresses alike of society and the stage. The extreme development of the low dresses which obtained some years ago, when the stays crushed up the breasts into suggestive prominence, would surely have been checked had the eye of the public been properly educated by familiarity with the exquisite beauty of line of a well-shaped bust. (Cheers.) I might show how thorough acquaintance with the ideal nude foot would probably have much modified the foot-torturing boots and high heels, which wring the foot out of all beauty of line, and throw the body forward into an awkward and ungainly attitude. (Cheers.)

"It is argued that the effect of nude representation of women upon young men is unwholesome, but it would not be so if such works were admitted without question into our galleries, and became thoroughly familiar to them. On the contrary, it would do much to clear away from healthy-hearted lads one of their sorest trials—that prurient curiosity which is bred of prudish concealment. Where there is mystery there is the suggestion of evil, and to go to a theater, where you have only to look at the stalls to see one-half of the female form, and to the stage to see the other half undraped, is far more pregnant with evil imaginings than the least objectionable of totally undraped figures. (Cheers.) In French art there have been questionable nude figures exhibited; but the fault was not that they were nude, but that they were the portraits of ugly, immodest women."

Some discussion followed. There was a general concurrence in the principle contended for by the reader of the paper. Sir Walter Stirling maintained that the perfect male figure, rather than the female, was the model of beauty. After a few remarks from Rev. Mr. Roberts and Colonel Oldfield, the Chairman regretted that no opponent of nude figures had taken part in the discussion. He agreed with Sir Walter Stirling as to the male figure being the most perfect model of proportion. He joined in defending the exhibition of nude figures, but thought considerable supervision should be exercised over such exhibitions.

No, it is not the picture or nude statue or text, with clear aim, that is indecent; it is the beholder's own thought, inference, distorted construction. True modesty is one of the most precious of attributes, even virtues, but in nothing is there more pretense, more falsity, than the needless assumption of it. Through precept and consciousness, man has long enough realized how bad he is. I would not so much disturb or demolish that conviction, only to resume and keep unerringly with it the spinal meaning of the Scriptural text, God overlooked all that He had made (including the apex of the whole,—humanity,—with its elements, passions, appetites), and pronounced it *very good.*

Does not anything short of that third point of view, when you come to think of it profoundly and with amplitude, impugn Creation from the outset? In fact, however overlaid or unaware of itself, does not the conviction involved in it perennially exist at the center of all society, and of the sexes, and of marriage? Is it not really an intuition of the human race? For, old as the world is, and beyond statement as are the countless and splendid results of its culture and evolution, perhaps the best and earliest and purest intuitions of the human race have yet to be developed.

WALT WHITMAN.

F 44

Note one: See *North American Review*, June 1882 (E 2606).

Note two: On 8 April 1882, Whitman paid for "200 impressions," which he acknowledged receiving ("proof-impressions") on 17 May (*Daybooks*, II, 287; *Correspondence*, III, 279).

F 45

[boldface] MY 71st YEAR. | [nine lines of verse] | [flush right] WALT WHITMAN.

Broadside, printed on recto only. 4½" × 6" (NNC, RPB); 4½" × 5⅞" (CtY, DLC [3]); 4" × 5⅞" (DLC). *Locations:* CtY, DLC (4), NNC, RPB.

Note one: A galley proof on yellow paper, measuring 7½" × 8", has the following corrections made by Whitman:

line 1	71st	]	71ST
line 6	long,	]	long
line 8	twilight,	]	twilight
line 10	Officer	]	Ofilcer

Whitman marked line 5 to be changed from 'me,' to 'me, the war of '63 and '4.', but the correction was not made; Whitman subsequently wrote it in by hand on all located copies of the revised printing. In addition, Whitman has written on it "20 copies" and dated it November 1889. *Location:* DLC.

Note two: See *Century Magazine,* November 1889 (E 2722).

Note three: On 1 November 1889, Whitman noted that "slips" for this had been "sent" (*Daybooks,* II, 539).

F 46

THE NEW POET. *WALT WHITMAN dashes full grown . . .*

Broadside, printed on recto only. 10¾" × 4⅜". See *BAL,* IX, 77, where it is described as a 66-line "advertisement for *Leaves of Grass,* 1855, with blank space at foot for a bookseller to add name and address," and dated "1855." *Location:* DLC.

F 47

NOT MEAGRE, LATENT BOUGHS ALONE. | [nine lines of verse] | [flush right] WALT WHITMAN.

Broadside, printed on recto only. 4¹³⁄₁₆" × 6" (DLC); 4¾" × 6" (TxU); 4½" × 6" (ViU). *Locations:* DLC, TxU, ViU.

Note: See *Lippincott's Magazine,* November 1887 (E 2667).

F 48

NOVEMBER BOUGHS. YOU LINGERING SPARSE LEAVES OF ME . . . "GOING SOMEWHERE." . . . AFTER THE SUPPER AND TALK . . . NOT MEAGRE, LATENT BOUGHS ALONE . . .

Broadside, printed on recto only. 9" × 5⅞". See *BAL,* IX, 77. *Locations:* CtY, DLC.

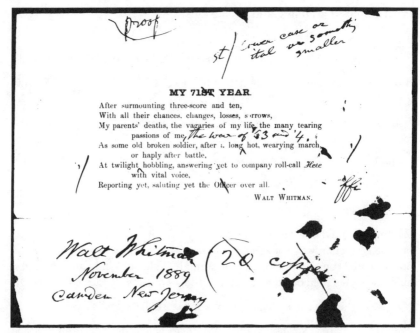

Proof for F 45

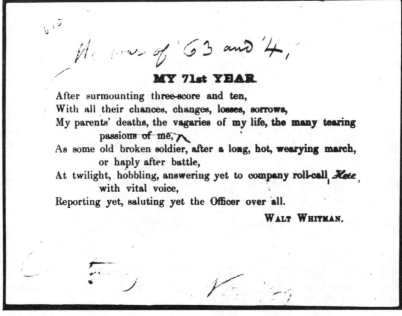

F 45

NOT MEAGRE, LATENT BOUGHS ALONE.

Not meagre, latent boughs alone, O songs! (scaly and bare,
    like eagles' talons,)
But haply for some sunny day, (who knows?) some future
    spring, some summer — bursting forth,
To blossoms, verdant leaves, or sheltering shade—to nourishing
    fruit,
Apples and grapes—and stalwart limbs of trees emerging --
    the fresh, free, open air,
And love and faith, like scented roses blooming.

WALT WHITMAN.

F 47

Note: See *Lippincott's Magazine*, November 1887 (E 2667).

F 49

Two states have been noted:

First state:

[boldface] Of that Blithe Throat of Thine. | [three lines of prose] | [13 lines of verse] | [flush right] WALT WHITMAN.

Broadside, printed on recto only. 9¾″ × 6″ (DLC [2], NcD, TxU); 9¼″ × 6″ (DLC). *Locations:* DLC (3), NN-B, NcD, TxU.

Second state:

[boldface] Of that . . . | [13 lines of verse]

9⅞″ × 6″ (DLC, signed by Whitman; ViU); 9¾″ × 6″ (DLC); 9½″ × 6″ (DLC); 9¼″ × 6″ (DLC). *Locations:* DLC (4), ViU.

Note one: A first galley proof, measuring 8″ × 5¾″, has the following corrections made by Whitman:

line 1	Blithe]	blithe
line 1	Thine.]	thine.
line 5	blank,]	blank
line 6	chilling]	chilliug
line 7	drifts,]	drifts.
line 8	chill,]	chill
line 10	cold,		cold.
lines 10–11	[no space between]]	[one-line space between]
line 11	my]	(my

Of that Blithe Throat of Thine.

[More than 83 degrees north—about a good day's steaming distance to the Pole by one of our fast oceaners in clear water—Greely heard the song of a single snow-bird merrily sounding over the desolation.]

Of that blithe throat of thine from arctic bleak and blank,
I'll mind the lesson, solitary bird—let me too welcome chilling
    drifts,
E'en the profoundest chill, as now—a torpid pulse, a brain un-
    nerv'd,
Old age land-lock'd within its winter bay—(cold, cold, O cold!)
These snowy hairs, my feeble arm, my frozen feet,
For them thy faith, thy rule I take, and grave it to the last;
Not summer's zones alone—not chants of youth, or south's warm
    tides alone,
But held by sluggish floes, pack'd in the northern ice, the cumulus
    of years,
These with gay heart I also sing.

F 49, second state

    line 12   faith,   ]   faith [see *Note two*]
    line 15   pack'd   ]   pack'

In addition, Whitman has dated it 17 October 1884. *Location:* DLC.

Note two: A second galley proof, measuring 8″ × 5¾″, has the following corrections made by Whitman:

    line 2   day's   ]   days'
    line 12   faith,   ]   faith
    line 13   youth,   ]   youth

In addition, Whitman has written on it "take 50 impressions," 20 with his name and 30 without, in that order. *Location:* DLC.

Note three: See *Harper's Monthly Magazine,* January 1885 (E 2633).

F 50

OLD AGE ECHOES. SOUND *[sic]* OF THE WINTER . . . THE UNEX-PRESS'D . . . AFTER THE ARGUMENT . . .

Broadside, printed on recto only. 11¼″ × 6½″. See *BAL,* IX, 77, where it is dated "1889." *Location:* DLC.

Note one: See *Lippincott's Magazine,* March 1891 (E 2754).

Note two: Whitman mentions "slips sent" on 1 November 1889, and a "slip copy" on 9 February 1890 (*Daybooks,* II, 539; *Correspondence,* V, 26).

F 51

(*From Lippincott's Magazine, March, 1891.*) | *OLD AGE ECHOES.* | BY WALT WHITMAN. | SOUNDS OF THE WINTER. | [seven lines of verse] | THE UNEXPRESS'D. | [12 lines of verse] | SAIL OUT FOR GOOD, EIDÓLON

(*From Lippincott's Magazine, March*, 1891.)

OLD AGE ECHOES.

BY WALT WHITMAN.

SOUNDS OF THE WINTER.

SOUNDS of the winter too,
   Sunshine upon the mountains—many a distant strain
From cheery railroad train—from nearer field, barn, house,
The whispering air—even the mute crops, garner'd apples, corn,
Children's and women's tones—rhythm of many a farmer, and of flail,
An old man's garrulous lips among the rest—*Think not we give out yet,*
Forth from these snowy hairs we too keep up the lilt.

THE UNEXPRESS'D.

How dare one say it?
After the cycles, poems, singers, plays,
Vaunted Ionia's, India's—Homer, Shakespeare—the long, long times'
    thick dotted roads, areas,
The shining clusters and the Milky Ways of stars—Nature's pulses
    reap'd,
All retrospective passions, heroes, war, love, adoration,
All ages' plummets dropt to their utmost depths,
All human lives, throats, wishes, brains—all experiences' utterance;
After the countless songs, or long or short, all tongues, all lands,
Still something not yet told in poesy's voice or print—something lacking,
(Who knows? the best yet unexpress'd and lacking).

SAIL OUT FOR GOOD, EIDÓLON YACHT!

Heave the anchor short!
Raise the main-sail and jib—steer forth,
O little white-hull'd sloop, now speed on really deep waters,
(I will not call it our concluding voyage,
But outset and sure entrance to the truest, best, maturest;)
Depart, depart from solid earth—no more returning to these shores,
Now on for aye our infinite free venture wending,
Spurning all yet tried ports, seas, hawsers, densities, gravitation,
Sail out for good, eidólon yacht of me!

AFTER THE ARGUMENT.

A group of little children with their ways and chatter flow in,
Like welcome rippling water o'er my heated nerves and flesh.

F 51

YACHT! | [nine lines of verse] | AFTER THE ARGUMENT. | [two lines of verse]

Broadside, printed on recto only. 17½″ × 6½″ (DLC); 10″ × 6⅝″ (IDeKN, TxU); 9¾″ × 6⅝″ (DLC). *Locations:* DLC (2), IDeKN, TxU.

Note one: See *Lippincott's Magazine,* March 1891 (E 2754).

Note two: On 5 December 1890, Whitman asked for "a printed slip of the pieces you have, so I can make a nice flush page" (*Correspondence,* V, 128).

F 52

[boldface] OLD-AGE RECITATIVES. | By WALT WHITMAN. | [ornate boldface] Sail out for good, Eidolon Yacht! | [10 lines of verse] | *My task* | [five lines of verse] | *L. of G's Purport.* | [four lines of verse] | *Death dogs my steps.* | [four lines of verse] | *For us two, reader dear.* | [two lines of verse] | [ornate boldface] Grand is the seen. | [10 lines of verse]

Broadside, printed on recto only. 10½″ × 6″ (DLC [2]); 10⅜″ × 6″ (TxU); 9½″ × 6″ (TxU). *Locations:* DLC (2), TxU (2).

Note: BAL reports an "early copy" of this sheet with Whitman's corrections (IX, 78).

F 53

[boldface] OLD AGE'S LAMBENT PEAKS. | [12 lines of verse] | [flush right] WALT WHITMAN. | [boldface] A CAROL CLOSING SIXTY-NINE. | [12 lines of verse] | [flush right] WALT WHITMAN. | [boldface] TO GET THE FINAL LILT OF SONGS. | [eight lines of verse] | [flush right] WALT WHITMAN.

Broadside, printed on recto only. 13¾″ × 5¹⁵⁄₁₆″ (DLC); 13½″ × 6″ (DLC); 13″ × 6″ (NcD); 12¹⁵⁄₁₆″ × 6″ (TxU). *Locations:* DLC (2), NcD, TxU.

Note one: A galley proof, measuring 13″ × 5⅞″, has the following corrections made by Whitman:

line 6	different, changing] different [?]hanging
line 6	twilight,] twilight
lines 9–10	situa- | tions] situa- | tions,
line 16	*resume*] resume
line 17	same,] same.
line 18	ye,] ye
line 19	you,] you
line 20	love,] love

OLD-AGE RECITATIVES.

By Walt Whitman.

Sail out for good, Eidolon Yacht!

Heave the anchor short!
Raise main-sail and jib—steer forth,
O little white-hull'd sloop, now speed on really deep waters,
(I will not call it our concluding voyage,
But outset and sure entrance to the truest, best, maturest;)
Depart, depart from solid earth — no more returning to these
    shores,
Now on for aye our infinite free venture wending,
Spurning all yet tried ports, seas. hawsers, densities, gravitation,
Sail out for good, eidólon yacht of me!

My task

Begun in ripen'd youth and steadily pursued,
Wandering, peering, dallying with all — war, peace, day and
    night absorbing,
Never even for one brief hour abandoning my task,
I end it here in poverty, sickness, and old age.

L. of G's Purport.

Not to exclude or demarcate, or pick out evils from their
    formidable masses (even to expose them,)
But add, fuse, complete, extend — and celebrate the immortal
    and the good.

Death dogs my steps.

I sing of life, yet mind me well of death :
To-day shadowy Death dogs my steps, and has for years —my
    seated shape,
Draws sometimes closer to me, as face to face.

For us two, reader dear.

Simple, spontaneous, curious, two souls interchanging,
With the original testimony for us continued on to the last.

Grand is the seen.

Grand is the seen, the light, to me — grand are the sky and
    stars,
Grand is the earth, and grand are lasting time and space,
And grand their laws, so multiform, puzzling, evolutionary;
But grander far the unseen soul of me, comprehending, en-
    dowing all those.
Lighting the light, the sky and stars, delving the earth, sailing
    the sea,
More evolutionary, vast, puzzling, O my soul!
More multiform far — more lasting thou than they.

F 52

line 25	falling] falliug
line 26	extinct,] extinct.
line 34	shifting-delicate] shiftlng-delicate
lines 34–35	pride and | doubt—to] pride—to
line 37	age,] age

In addition, Whitman has written on it "20 impressions," after which his name
was to be removed and "5 impressions more" made. *Location:* DLC.

OLD AGE'S LAMBENT PEAKS.

The touch of flame — the illuminating fire — the loftiest look
 at last,
O'er city, passion, sea — o'er prairie, mountain, wood — the
 earth itself;
The airy, different, changing hues of all, in falling twilight,
Objects and groups, bearings, faces, reminiscences;
The calmer sight — the golden setting, clear and broad:
So much i' the atmosphere, the points of view, the situa-
 tions whence we scan,
Bro't out by them alone — so much (perhaps the best) un-
 reck'd before;
The lights indeed from them — old age's lambent peaks.

WALT WHITMAN.

A CAROL CLOSING SIXTY-NINE.

A carol closing sixty-nine — a *resume* — a repetition,
My lines in joy and hope continuing on the same,
Of ye, O God, Life, Nature, Freedom, Poetry;
Of you, my Land — your rivers, prairies, States — you, mot-
 tled Flag I love,
Your aggregate retain'd entire — Of north, south, east and
 west, your items all;
Of me myself — the jocund heart yet beating in my breast,
The body wreck'd, old, poor and paralyzed — the strange in-
 ertia falling pall-like round me;
The burning fires down in my sluggish blood not yet extinct,
The undiminish'd faith — the groups of loving friends.

WALT WHITMAN.

TO GET THE FINAL LILT OF SONGS.

To get the final lilt of songs,
To penetrate the inmost lore of poets — to know the mighty
 ones,
Job, Homer, Eschylus, Dante, Shakspere, Tennyson, Emerson;
To diagnose the shifting-delicate tints of love and pride and
 doubt — to truly understand,
To encompass these, the last keen faculty and entrance-price,
Old age, and what it brings from all its past experiences.

WALT WHITMAN.

F 53

Note two: An uncorrected galley proof, measuring 13½″ × 6″, is at DLC.

Note three: Whitman mentioned a "printed slip" of "Old Age's Lambent Peaks" on 3 September 1888 (*Correspondence*, IV, 205).

Note four: See "Old Age's Lambent Peaks," *Century Magazine*, September 1888 (E 2711).

Note five: The printed sheets were sometimes cut up to make three separate items. A copy of "Old Age's Lambent Peaks," measuring 5″ × 6⅛″, is at DLC; for the other two, see F 14 and F 82.

F 54
[boldface] OLD AGE'S SHIP & CRAFTY DEATH'S. | [10 lines of verse] | [flush right] WALT WHITMAN.

Broadside, printed on recto only. 4⅞″ × 6″ (DLC [4]); 4¾″ × 5⅜″ (DLC). *Locations:* DLC (5).

Note one: All located copies have the following correction written in by Whitman:

  line 8   Crowd extra top-gallants   ]   Crowd top-gallant

Note two: See *Century Magazine*, February 1890 (E 2725).

Note three: Whitman mentions a "slip copy" on 5 February 1890 (*Correspondence*, V, 24).

F 55
[boldface] OLD CHANTS | [29 lines of verse]

Broadside, printed on recto only. 8⁹⁄₁₆″ × 6″ (NNPM); 8½″ × 6″ (DLC). *Locations:* DLC, NNPM.

Note: See *Truth* (New York), 19 March 1891 (E 2760).

F 56
[boldface] An Old Man's Rejoinder | [From *The Critic*, New York, Aug. 16, 1890.] | [132 lines of prose] | [flush right] WALT WHITMAN. | [short rule]

Broadside, printed on recto only. 19⅜″ × 5¼″. *Location:* NNPM.

Note one: See *Critic*, 16 August 1890 (E 2740).

Note two: Whitman mentions "20 slips" on 4 August 1890 (*Daybooks*, II, 564).

F 57

Two sheets: (1) (*From the North American Review for November, 1890.*) |
OLD POETS | BY WALT WHITMAN. | [rule] | [86 lines of prose]' and (2) '[89
lines of prose] | [flush right] WALT WHITMAN.'

Broadsides, printed on rectos only. (1) 19⅞" × 6"; (2) 19⅞" × 6¼". *Location:* NNPM.

Note one: See *North American Review,* November 1890 (E 2745).

Note two: Whitman mentions a "printed slip" on 1 November 1890 (*Correspondence,* V, 110).

F 58

ON JOURNEYS THROUGH THE STATES . . .

Broadside, printed on recto only. 8¾" × 6½". See *BAL,* IX, 79, where it is dated
"1871?" *Location:* DLC.

Note one: See *Passage to India* (A 5), p. 112.

F 59

[boldface] ON, ON THE SAME, YE YOCUND TWAIN! | [25 lines of verse] |
[flush right] WALT WHITMAN.

Broadside, printed on recto only. 9⁵⁄₁₆" × 6" (TxU); 9 ½" × 6" (DLC [2]).
Locations: DLC (2), TxU.

Note: A first galley proof, measuring 9½" × 6", has the following corrections
made by Whitman:

    line 1   SAME,] SAME.
    line 1   TWAIN!] TRAIN!
    line 2   twain!] train!
    line 3   mid-age] mid-age,
    line 4   motley-tongues] motley tongues
    line 4   flame,] flame [see *Note two*]
    line 7   alone,] alone.
    line 8   crucial] crucical [see *Note two*]
    line 8   (America's,] (America's
    line 10 *ecclaircissement*] *ecclai[?]ssement* [see *Note two*]
    line 10 past,] past
    line 11 ancient, medieval,] ancient medieval
    line 12 wars, defeats—] wars dcfeats— [see *Note two*]
    line 17 And] and
    line 18 age,] age.
    line 19 (My] My

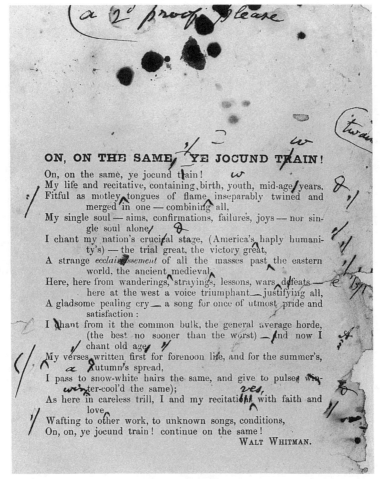

Proof for F 59

line 20	autumn's] Autumn's
lines 21–22	pulses | winter-cool'd] pulses win- | ter-cool'd
line 23	recitatives] recitations
line 24	love,] love

In addition, Whitman has written on it "a 2^d proof please." *Location:* TxU.

Note two: A second galley proof, measuring 9½″ × 6″, has the following corrections made by Whitman:

line 4	flame,] flame;
line 8	crucial] cruical
line 10	*eclaircissement*] *ecdaircissement*

ON, ON THE SAME, YE JOCUND TWAIN!

On, on the same, ye jocund twain!
My life and recitative, containing birth, youth, mid-age years,
Fitful as motley-tongues of flame, inseparably twined and
    merged in one — combining all,
My single soul — aims, confirmations, failures, joys — nor sin-
    gle soul alone,
I chant my nation's crucial stage, (America's, haply humani-
    ty's) — the trial great, the victory great,
A strange *eclaircissement* of all the masses past, the eastern
    world, the ancient, medieval,
Here, here from wanderings, strayings, lessons, wars, defeats —
    here at the west a voice triumphant — justifying all,
A gladsome pealing cry — a song for once of utmost pride and
    satisfaction ;
I chant from it the common bulk, the general average horde,
    (the best no sooner than the worst) — And now I
    chant old age,
(My verses, written first for forenoon life, and for the summer's,
    autumn's spread,
I pass to snow-white hairs the same, and give to pulses
    winter-cool'd the same);
As here in careless trill, I and my recitatives, with faith and
    love,
Wafting to other work, to unknown songs, conditions,
On, on, ye jocund twain! continue on the same!

                                 WALT WHITMAN.

F 59

    line 12   wars, defeats—] wars defeats—
    line 15   satisfaction;] satisfaction:

In addition, Whitman has written on it "give me 30 slips." *Location:* DLC.

Note: See *Once a Week* (New York), 9 June 1891 (E 2762).

F 60
ONLY CROSSING THE DELAWARE . . .

Broadside, printed on recto only. 19⅝″ × 8⅜″. See *BAL*, IX, 79. *Location:* DLC.

Note: See *Progress* (Philadelphia), 5 April 1879 (E 2568).

F 61
OUR WOUNDED AND SICK SOLDIERS. VISITS AMONG ARMY HOSPI-
TALS, AT WASHINGTON, ON THE FIELD, AND HERE IN NEW-YORK . . .

Five leaves, printed on rectos only, each measuring 24 ½″ × 5⅛″. See *BAL*, IX, 79. *Location:* DLC.

Note one: See *New York Times*, 11 December 1864 (E 2492).

F 62

[boldface] PATROLING BARNEGAT. | BY WALT WHITMAN. | [14 lines of verse]

F 62

Broadside, printed on recto only. 5⅞″ × 6¼″. Inscribed as received from Whitman 3 June 1880. *Location:* NcD.

Note one: See *Harper's Monthly Magazine*, April 1881 (E 2591).

Note two: Whitman enclosed a copy of this with a letter of 17 March 1881 (*Correspondence*, III, 219n).

F 63

[From the NORTH AMERICAN REVIEW.] | THE POETRY OF THE FUTURE. | [rule] | [32 lines of prose]

[195]–210. Head title. Stitched. Laid paper with vertical chain lines 1⅛″ apart. [1–4]¹ [5]⁴. 8⅝″ × 5⅝″. *Locations:* PU, ViU.

Note one: See *North American Review,* February 1881 (E 2589).

Note two: In the *North American Review,* the first four leaves (8 pp.) are the second half the gathering of eights that includes the end of the preceding article; the next four leaves (8 pp.) are a gathering of four.

F 64

[first column] [boldface] Preface. | [45 lines of prose] | [rule] | [eight lines of prose] | [second column] [59 lines of prose] | [flush right] WALT WHITMAN.

Broadside, printed on recto only. 12⅛″ × 7⅝″. Inscribed by Bucke: "Reached me from W. W. 27th Sept. in letter dated 24th & 25th September." *Location:* NcD.

Note one: A corrected galley proof, measuring 12″ × 9¾″, is at CtY.

Note two: See "Preface" to William Douglas O'Connor, *Three Tales* (D 22).

Note three: Whitman sent "printed slips" of this to a friend (Bucke?) on 25 September 1890 (*Correspondence,* V, 93).

F 65

[first column] PROUD MUSIC OF THE SEA–STORM. | [rule with dot in center] | BY WALT WHITMAN. | [rule with dot in center] | 1. | [21 lines of verse] | 2. | [12 lines of verse] | 3. | [nine lines of verse] | 4. | [28 lines of verse] | 5. | [10 lines of verse] [second column] 6. | [20 lines of verse] | 7. | [six lines of verse] | 8. | [33 lines of verse] | 9. | [five lines of verse] | 10. | [16 lines of verse] [third column] [14 lines of verse] | 11. | [10 lines of verse] | 12. | [nine lines of verse] | 13. | [nine lines of verse] | 14. | [13 lines of verse] | 15. | [33 lines of verse]

Broadside, printed on recto only. 21¼″ × 13¾″ (TxU); 21¼″ × 13½″ (DLC [2]). On the back in Bucke's hand: "He [Whitman] sent me the poems from time to time as they got published—say 1870 to 1885" (TxU). *Locations:* DLC (2), TxU.

Note one: See *Atlantic Monthly Magazine,* February 1869 (E 2509).

Note two: On 25 November 1868, Whitman placed an order to "print 20 copies" of this, and on the 30th he sent one to Emerson (*Correspondence,* VI, 6; II, 72).

Preface.

A hasty memorandum, not particularly for Preface to the following tales, but to put on record my respect and affection for as sane, beautiful, cute, tolerant, loving, candid and free and fair-intention'd a nature as ever vivified our race.

In Boston, 1860, I first met WILLIAM DOUGLAS O'CONNOR.* As I saw and knew him then, in his 29th year, and for twenty-five further years, he was a gallant, handsome, gay-hearted, fine-voiced, glowing-eyed man; lithe-moving on his feet, of healthy and magnetic atmosphere and presence, and the most welcome company in the world. He was a thorough-going anti-slavery believer, speaker and writer, (doctrinaire,) and though I took a fancy to him from the first, I remember I fear'd his ardent abolitionism — was afraid it would probably keep us apart. (I was a decided and out-spoken anti-slavery believer myself, then and always; but shy'd from the extremists, the red-hot fellows of those times.) O'C. was then correcting the proofs of *Harrington*, an eloquent and fiery novel he had written, and which was printed just before the commencement of the Secession War. He was already married, the father of two fine little children, and was personally and intellectually the most attractive man I had ever met. Last of '62 I found myself led towards the war-field—went to Washington City — (to become absorb'd in the armies, and in the big hospitals, and to get work in one of the Departments.)—and there I met and resumed friendship, and found warm hospitality from O'C. and his noble New England wife. They had just lost by death their little child-boy, Philip; and O'C. was yet feeling serious about it. The youngster had been vaccinated against the threatening of small-pox which alarm'd the city; but somehow it led to worse results than it was intended to ward off—or at any rate O'C. thought that proved the cause of the boy's death. He had one child left, a fine bright little daughter, and a great comfort to her parents. (Dear Jeannie!

* Born Jan. 2d, 1832. When grown, lived several years in Boston, and edited journals and magazines there—went about 1861 to Washington, D. C., and became a U. S. clerk, first in the Light-House Bureau and then in the U. S. Life-Saving Service, in which branch he was Assistant Superintendent for many years—sicken'd in 1887—died there at Washington May 9th, 1889.

She grew up a most accomplish'd and superior young woman — declined in health, and died about 1881.)

On through to '73 I saw and talk'd with O'C. almost daily. I had soon got employment, first for a short time in the Indian Bureau (in the Interior Department,) and then for a long while in the Attorney General's Office. The Secession War, with its tide of varying fortunes, excitements — President Lincoln and the daily sight of him — the doings in Congress and at the State Capitals — the news from the fields and campaigns, and from foreign governments — with a hundred matters, occurrences, personalities, — (Greeley, Wendell Phillips, the parties, the Abolitionists, &c.)— were the subjects of our talk and discussion. I am not sure from what I heard then, but O'C. was cut out for a first-class orator or public speaker or forensic advocate. No audience or jury could have stood out against him. He had a power and sharp-cut faculty of statement and persuasiveness beyond any man's else. I know it well, for I have felt it many a time. If not as orator, his forte was as critic, newer, deeper than any; also, as literary author. One of his traits was that while he knew all, and welcomed all sorts of great *genre* literature, all lands and times, from all writers and artists, and not only tolerated each, and defended every attack'd literary person with a skill and heart-catholicism that I never saw equal'd — invariably advocated or excused them — he kept an idiosyncrasy and identity of his own very mark'd, and without special tinge or color from any source. He always applauded the masters, whence and whoever. I remember his special defences of Byron, Burns, Poe, Rabelais, Victor Hugo, George Sand, and others. There was always a little touch of pensive cadence in his superb voice; and I think there was something of the same sadness in his temperament and nature. Perhaps, too, in his literary structure. But he was a very buoyant, jovial, good-natured companion.

So much for a hasty melanged reminiscence and note of William O'Connor, my dear, dear friend, and staunch, (probably my staunchest) literary believer and champion from the first and throughout without halt or demur, for twenty-five years. No better friend—none more reliable through this life of one's ups and downs. On the occurrence of the latter he would be sure to make his appearance on the scene, eager, hopeful, full of fight like a perfect knight of chivalry. For he was a born sample of the flower and symbol of olden time first-class knighthood here in the 19th century. Thrice blessed be his memory!

WALT WHITMAN.

Reached me from W. W. 27th Sept. in letter dated 24th & 25th Sept Rus3

*Atlantic Monthly
February.*

PROUD MUSIC OF THE SEA-STORM.

BY WALT WHITMAN.

I.

Proud music of the sea-storm!
Blast that careers so free, whistling across the
  prairies!
Strong hum of forest tree-tops! Wind of the
  mountains!
Personified dim shapes! you hidden orchestras!
You serenades of phantoms, with instruments alert,
Blending, with Nature's rhythmus, all the tongues
  of nations;
You chords left as by vast composers! you choruses!
You formless, free, religious dances! you from the
  Orient!
You undertone of rippling waters, rivers, pouring
  cataracts;
You sounds from distant guns, with galloping
  cavalry!
Echos of camps, with all the different bugle-calls!
Trooping tumultuous, filling the midnight late,
  bending me powerless,
Entering my lonesome slumber-chamber — Why
  have you seized me?

2.

Come forward, O my Soul, and let the rest retire;
Listen — lose not — it is toward thee they tend;
Parting the midnight, entering my slumber-chamber,
For thee they sing and dance, O Soul.

A festival song!
The duet of the bridegroom and the bride — a
  marriage-march,
With joyous voices — lips of love, and hearts of
  lovers, fill'd to the brim with love;
The red flush'd cheeks, and perfumes — the cortege
  swarming, full of friendly faces, young and old,
To flutes' clear notes and sounding harps' cantabile.

3.

Now loud approaching drums!
Victoria! see'st thou in powder-smoke the banners
  torn but flying? the rout of the baffled?
Hearest those shouts of a conquering army?

(Ah, Soul, the sobs of women — the wounded
  groaning in agony,
The hiss and crackle of flames — the blacken'd
  ruins — the embers of cities,
The dirge and desolation of mankind.)

4.

Now the great organ sounds,
Tremulous — while underneath, (as the hid foot-
  holds of the earth,
On which arising, rest, and leaping forth, depend,
All shapes of beauty, grace and strength — all hues
  we know,
Green blades of grass, and warbling birds — children
  that gambol and play — the clouds of heaven
  above,)
The strong base stands, and its pulsations intermits
  not,
Bathing, supporting, merging all the rest — mater-
  nity of all the rest;
And with it every instrument in multitudes,
The players playing — all the world's musicians,
The solemn hymns and masses, rousing adoration,
All passionate love-chants, sorrowful appeals,
The measureless sweet vocalists of ages,
And for their solvent setting, Earth's own diapason,
Of winds and woods and mighty ocean waves;
A new composite orchestra — binder of years and
  climes — ten-fold renewer,
As of the far-back days the poets tell — the
  Paradiso,
The straying thence, the separation long, but now
  the wandering done,
The journey done, the Journeyman come home,
And Man and Art, with Nature fused again.

5.

Tutti! for Earth and Heaven!
The Almighty Leader now for me, for once, has
  signal'd with his wand.

The manly strophe of the husbands of the world,
And all the wives responding.

The tongues of violins!
(I think O tongues, ye tell this heart, that cannot
  tell itself;
This brooding, yearning heart, that cannot tell
  itself.)

6.

Ah, from a little child,
Thou knowest, Soul, how to me all sounds became
  music;
My mother's voice, in lullaby or hymn;
(The voice — O tender voices — memory's loving
  voices!
Last miracle of all — O dearest mother's, sister's,
  voices;)
The rain, the growing corn, the breeze among the
  long-leav'd corn,
The measur'd sea-wave beating on the sand,
The twittering bird, the hawk's sharp scream,
The wild-fowl's notes at night, as flying low,
  migrating north or south,
The psalm in the country church, or mid the
  clustering trees,
The fiddler in the tavern — the glee, the long-strung
  sailor-song,
The lowing cattle, bleating sheep — the crowing
  cock at dawn.

7.

Now airs antique and medieval fill me!
I see and hear old harpers with their harps, at
  Welsh festivals;
I hear the minnesingers, and their lays of love,
I hear the minstrels, gleemen, troubadours, of the
  feudal ages.

8.

Above, below, all songs of current lands,
The German airs of friendship, wine and love,
The plaintive Irish ballads, merry jigs and dances
  — English warbles,
Chansons of France, Scotch tunes — and over all,
Italia's peerless compositions.

Across the stage, with pallor on her face, yet lurid
  passion,
Stalks Norma, brandishing the dagger in her hand.

I see poor crazed Lucia's eyes' unnatural gleam;
Her hair down her back falls loose and dishevell'd.

I see where Ernani, walking the bridal garden,
Amid perfumes of night-roses, radiant, holding his
  bride by the hand,
Hears the infernal call, the death-pledge of the
  horn.

To crossing swords, and grey hairs bared to heaven,
The clear, electric base and baritone of the world,
The trombone duo — Libertad for ever!

From Spanish chestnut trees' dense shade,
By old and heavy convent walls, a wailing song,
Song of lost love — the torch of youth and life
  quench'd in despair,
Song of the dying swan — Fernando's heart is
  breaking.

Awaking from her woes at last, retriev'd Amina
  sings;
Copious as stars, and glad as morning light, the
  torrents of her joy.

(The teeming lady comes!
The lustrous orb — Venus contralto — the bloom-
  ing mother,
Sister of loftiest gods — Alboni's self I hear.)

9.

I hear those odes, symphonies, operas;
I hear in the *William Tell*, the music of an arous'd
  and angry people;
I hear Meyerbeer's *Huguenots*, the *Prophet*, or *Robert*;
Gounod's *Faust*, or Mozart's *Don Juan.*

10.

I hear the dance-music of all nations,
The waltz, (some delicious measure, lapsing, bathing me in bliss;)
The bolero, to tinkling guitars and clattering
  castanets.

I see religious dances old and new,
I hear the sound of the Hebrew lyre,
I see the Crusaders marching, bearing the cross on
  high, to the martial clang of cymbals;
I hear dervishes monotonously chanting, inter-
  spersed with frantic shouts, as they spin
  around, turning always towards Mecca;
I see the rapt religious dances of the Persians and
  the Arabs;
Again at Eleusis, home of Ceres, I see the modern
  Greeks dancing,

I hear them clapping their hands, as they bend
  their bodies,
I hear the metrical shuffling of their feet.

I see again the wild old Corybantian dance, the
  performers wounding each other;
I see the Roman youth, to the shrill sound of
  flageolets, throwing and catching their weapons,
As they fall on their knees, and rise again.

I hear from the Mussulman mosque the muezzin
  calling;
I see the worshipers within, (nor form, nor sermon,
  argument, nor word,
But rhapsodes, silent, devout — rais'd, glowing
  heads — extatic faces.)

11.

The instruments, chants, of far-off climes resume
  themselves,
The Egyptian harp of many strings,
The primitive chants of the Nile boatmen;
The sacred imperial hymns of China,
To the delicate sounds of the king, (the stricken
  wood and stone;)
Or to Hindu flutes, and the fretting twang of the
  Vina,
A band of bayaderes.

12.

Now Asia, Africa leave me — Europe, seizing,
  inflates me;
To organs huge, and bands, I hear as from vast
  concourses of voices,
Luther's strong hymn, *Eine feste Burg ist unser Gott*;
Rossini's *Stabat Mater dolorosa*;
Or, floating in some high cathedral dim, with
  gorgeous color'd windows,
The passionate *Agnus Dei*, or *Gloria in Excelsis.*

13.

Mighty maestros!
And you, sweet singers of old lands — Soprani!
  Tenori!
To you a new bard, carolling free in the west,
Obeisant, sends his love.

Such led me thee, O Soul!
(All senses, shows and objects lead to thee,
But now it seems to me, soon I leave o'er all the
  rest.)

14.

I hear the annual singing of the children in St.
  Paul's Cathedral;
Or, under the high roof of some colossal hall, the
  symphonies, oratorios of Beethoven, Handel,
  or Haydn;
The *Creation*, in billows of godhood laves me.

Give me to hold all sounds, (I, madly struggling,
  cry,)
Fill me with all the voices of the universe,
Endow me with their throbbings — Nature's also,
The tempests, waters, winds — operas and chants
  — marches and dances,
Utter — pour in — for I would take them all.

15.

Then I woke softly,
And pausing, questioning awhile the music of my
  dream,
And questioning all those reminiscences — the
  tempest on the sea,
And all the songs of sopranos and tenors,
And those rapt oriental dances, of religious fervor,
And the sweet varied instruments, and the diapason
  of organs,
And all the artless plaints of love, and grief and
  death,
I said to my silent, curious Soul, out of the bed of
  the slumber-chamber,
Come, for I have found the clue I sought so long,
Let us go forth refresh'd amid the day,
Cheerfully tallying life, walking the world, the real,
Nourish'd henceforth by our celestial dream.

And I said, moreover,
Haply, what thou hast heard, O Soul, was not the
  sound of winds,
Nor dream of stormy waves, nor sea-hawk's flapping
  wings, nor harsh scream,
Nor vocalism of sun-bright Italy,
Nor German organ majestic — nor vast concourse
  of voices — nor layers of harmonies;
Nor strophes of husbands and wives — nor sound
  of marching soldiers,
Nor flutes, nor harps, nor the different bugle-calls
  of camps;
But, to a new rhythmus fitted for thee,
Poems, vaguely wafted in night air, uncaught,
  unwritten,
Which, let us go forth in the bold day, and write.

F 66

A Riddle Song. | BY WALT WHITMAN. | [41 lines of verse]

Broadside, printed on recto only. 10⅝″ × 6″; 9½″ × 5½″. *Locations:* DLC (2).

Note one: A galley proof, measuring 10⅛″ × 8¼″, has the following corrections made by Whitman:

line 7   world,] world
line 9   miss;] miss,
line 11 owner;] owner:

A Riddle Song.

BY WALT WHITMAN.

That which eludes this verse, and any verse,
Unheard by sharpest ear—unform'd in clearest eye, or cunning-
    est mind,
Nor lore, nor fame, nor happiness, nor wealth,
And yet the pulse of every heart and life throughout the world,
    incessantly;
Which you and I, and all, pursuing ever, ever miss,
Open, but still a secret---the real of the real---an illusion;
Costless, vouchsafed to each, yet never man the owner,
Which poets vainly seek to put in rhyme---historians in prose;
Which sculptor never chisel'd yet, nor painter painted;
Which vocalist never sung, nor orator nor actor ever utter'd;
Invoking here and now, I challenge for my song.

Indifferently, 'mid public, private haunts---in solitude,
Behind the mountain and the wood,
Companion of the city's busiest streets---through the assemblage,
It, and its radiations, constantly glide.

In looks of fair, unconscious babes,
Or strangely in the coffin'd dead,
Or show of breaking dawn, or stars by night,
As some dissolving delicate film of dreams,
Hiding, yet lingering.

Two little breaths of words comprising it;
Two words---yet all, from first to last comprised in it.

How ardently for it!
How many ships have sail'd and sunk for it!
How many travelers started from their homes, and ne'er return'd!
How much of genius boldly staked, and lost, for it!
What countless stores of beauty, love, ventured for it!
How all superbest deeds since time began, are traceable to
    it, and shall be to the end!
How all heroic martyrdoms to it!
How, justified by it, the horrors, evils, battles of the earth!
How the bright, fascinating, lambent flames of it, in every age
    and land, have drawn men's eyes;
(Rich as a sunset on the Norway coast---the sky, the islands,
    and the cliffs; .
Or midnight's silent glowing Northern lights, unreachable.)

Haply, God's riddle it---so vague, and yet so certain;
The Soul for it---and all the visible Universe for it;
And Heaven at last for it.

Proof for F 66

line 25   words,   ]   words
line 26   last,   ]   last
line 32   Time began,   ]   time began.

Location: DLC.

Note two: A partial copy, with 30 lines of verse, is at TxU.

Note three: See *Forney's Progress,* 17 April 1880 (E 2578).

F 67
[*From the* POET–LORE, *September 15, 1890.*] | SHAKESPEARE FOR AMER-
ICA. | [25 lines of prose] | [flush right] *Walt Whitman.*

[*From the* POET-LORE, *September 15, 1890.*]

SHAKESPEARE FOR AMERICA.

TO THE EDITORS OF POET-LORE.—Let me send you a supple-
mentary word to that "view" of Shakespeare attributed to me,
published in your July number, and so courteously worded by
the reviewer (thanks! dear friend). But you have left out what,
perhaps, is the main point, as follows:

  "Even the one who at present reigns unquestioned,—of Shakspere,—for all he stands for so much in modern literature, he stands
entirely for the mighty æsthetic sceptres of the past, not for the
spiritual and democratic, the sceptres of the future." (See pp. 55–
58 in " November Boughs," and also some of my further notions on
Shakespeare.)

  The Old World (Europe and Asia) is the region of the poetry of
concrete and real things,—the past, the æsthetic, palaces, etiquette,
the literature of war and love, the mythological gods, and the myths
anyhow. But the New World (America) is the region of the future,
and its poetry must be spiritual and democratic. Evolution is not
the rule in Nature, in Politics, and Inventions only, but in Verse. I
know our age is greatly materialistic, but it is greatly spiritual, too,
and the future will be, too. Even what we moderns have come to
mean by *spirituality* (while including what the Hebraic utterers, and
mainly perhaps all the Greek and other old typical poets, and also
the later ones, meant) has so expanded and colored and vivified the
comprehension of the term, that it is quite a different one from the
past. Then science, the final critic of all, has the casting vote for
future poetry.

Walt Whitman.

Broadside, printed on recto only. 7¹⁵⁄₁₆″ × 5¹³⁄₁₆″. *Location:* NcD.

Note one: Whitman ordered "thirty (30) little printed slips" headed "*From the Critic, New York* (date here)" on 10 November 1890 (*Correspondence*, V, 115).

Note two: See *Poet-Lore*, 15 September 1890; *Critic*, 27 September 1890 (E 2743).

F 68

[boldface] SHAKSPERE–BACON'S CIPHER. | [flush right] (*A Hint to Scientists.*) | [nine lines of verse] | [flush right] WALT WHITMAN.

SHAKSPERE-BACON'S CIPHER.

(*A Hint to Scientists.*)

I doubt it not—then more, far more;
In each old song bequeath'd — in every noble page or text,
(Different — something unreck'd before — some unsuspected
        author,)
In every object, mountain, tree, and star — in every birth and
        life,
As part of each — finality of each — meaning, behind the os-
        tent,
The mystic cipher waits infolded.

WALT WHITMAN.

F 68

Broadside, printed on recto only. 6″ × 6⅜″ (DLC [2], TxU [2]); 6″ × 5¾″ (DLC); 4¾″ × 6½″ (DLC). *Locations:* DLC (4), TxU (2).

Note one: All located copies have 'anthor,)' in line 6 corrected to 'author,)' in Whitman's hand.

Note two: See *Cosmopolitan*, October 1887 (E 2666).

Note three: Whitman mentioned a "slip" of this on 5 December 1888 (*Correspondence*, IV, 243).

F 69

[first column] THE SINGER IN THE PRISON. | [rule with dot in center] | BY WALT WHITMAN. | [rule with dot in center] | 1. | [11 lines of verse] | 2. | [20 lines of verse] | 3. | THE HYMN. | [12 lines of verse] | [second column] [12 lines of verse] | 4. | [10 lines of verse] | 5. | [22 lines of verse]

Broadside, printed on recto only. 14″ × 10⅛″ (NN-B); 14″ × 10″ (DLC); 11¼″ × 8½″ (ViU). *Locations:* DLC, NN-B, ViU.

THE SINGER IN THE PRISON.

By Walt Whitman.

1.

O sight of shame, and pain, and dole !
O fearful thought—a convict Soul !

RANG the refrain along the hall, the prison,
Rose to the roof, the vaults of heaven above,
Pouring in floods of melody, in tones so pensive,
    sweet and strong, the like whereof was never
    heard,
Making the hearer's pulses stop for extasy and
    awed amazement,
Reaching the far-off sentry, and the armed guards,
    who ceas'd their pacing.

2.

O sight of pity, gloom, and dole !
O pardon me, a hapless Soul !

The sun was low in the west one winter day,
When down a narrow aisle amid the thieves and
    outlaws of the land,
(There by the hundreds seated, sear-faced murderers,
    wily counterfeiters,
All that dark, cankerous blotch, a nation's criminal
    mass,
Gather'd to Sunday church in prison walls — the
    keepers round,
Plenteous, well-arm'd, with watching, vigilant eyes,)
Calmly a Lady walk'd, holding a little innocent
    child by either hand,
Whom, seating on their stools beside her on the
    platform,
She, first preluding with the instrument, a low and
    musical prelude,
In voice surpassing all, sang forth a quaint old
    hymn.

3

THE HYMN.

A Soul, confined by bars and bands,
Cries, Help ! O help ! and wrings her hands ;
Blinded her eyes—bleeding her breast,
Nor pardon finds, nor balm of rest.

O sight of shame, and pain, and dole !
O fearful thought—a convict Soul !

Ceaseless, she paces to and fro ;
O heart-sick days ! O nights of wo !
Nor hand of friend, nor loving face ;
Nor favor comes, nor word of grace.

O sight of pity, gloom, and dole !
O pardon me, a hapless Soul !

It was not I that sinn'd the sin,
The ruthless Body dragg'd me in ;
Though long I strove courageously,
The Body was too much for me.

O Life ! no life, but bitter dole !
O burning, beaten, baffled Soul !

Dear prison'd Soul, bear up a space,
For soon or late the certain grace ;
To set thee free, and bear thee home,
The Heavenly Pardoner, Death shall come.

Convict no more — nor shame, nor dole !
Depart ! a God-enfranchis'd Soul !

4.

The singer ceased ;
One glance swept from her clear, calm eyes, o'er
    all those up-turn'd faces ;
Strange sea of prison faces — a thousand varied,
    crafty, brutal, seam'd and beauteous faces ;
Then rising, passing back along the narrow aisle
    between them,
While her gown touch'd them, rustling in the
    silence,
She vanish'd with her children in the dusk.

5.

While upon all, convicts and armed keepers, ere
    they stirr'd,
(Convict forgetting prison, keeper his loaded
    pistol,)
A hush and pause fell down, a wondrous minute,
With deep, half-stifled sobs, and sound of bad men
    bow'd, and moved to weeping,
And youth's convulsive breathings, memories of
    home,
The mother's voice in lullaby, the sister's care, the
    happy childhood,
The long-pent spirit rous'd to reminiscence ;
— A wondrous minute then — But after, in the
    solitary night, to many, many there,
Years after — even in the hour of death — the sad
    refrain — the tune, the voice, the words,
Resumed — the large, calm Lady walks the narrow
    aisle,
The wailing melody again — the singer in the
    prison sings :

O sight of shame, and pain, and dole !
O fearful thought — a convict Soul !

F 69

Note: See *Saturday Evening Visitor* (Washington), 25 December 1869 (E 2511).

F 70

THE SOLDIERS, &C. FROM AN OCCASIONAL CORRESPONDENT.
WASHINGTON, FEBRUARY, 1865 . . .

Broadside, printed on recto only. 20¾″ × 3¼″. See *BAL*, IX, 81. *Locations:* CU, CtY.

Note: See *New York Times*, 6 March 1865 (E 2495).

F 71

SONG OF THE REDWOOD-TREE . . .

Broadside, printed in double columns on recto only. 10″ × 15¹⁵⁄₁₆″. See *BAL*, IX, 81. *Location:* DLC.

Note: See *Harper's Monthly Magazine*, February 1874 (E 2533).

F 72

[boldface] SONG OF THE UNIVERSAL. | *BY WALT WHITMAN.* | Commencement Poem, Tuft's College, Mass., | June 17, 1874. | 1 | [10 lines of verse] | 2 | [20 lines of verse] | 3 | [10 Lines of verse] | 4 | [three lines of verse] | 5 | [16 lines of verse] | 6 | [nine lines of verse] | [flush right] NEW REPUBLIC PRINT.39 FEDERAL ST.CAMDEN, N.J.

Broadside, printed on recto only. 17″ × 5½″. *Locations:* CtY, NN-B.

Note: See *New York Daily Graphic*, 17 June 1874, and especially, among other reprintings, *Camden New Republic*, 20 June 1874 (E 2541).

F 73

Broadside, printed on recto only. Paper watermarked 'WESTLOCK'. 17″ × 11″ (NcD); 13⅜″ × 8½″ (TxU). Letter of 20 July 1883. *Locations:* NcD, TxU.

Note: See "The Spanish Element in Our Nationality," *Philadelphia Press*, 5 August 1883; *Critic*, 11 August 1883 (E 2617).

F 74

[first column] SPARKLES FROM THE WHEEL. | [rule with dot in center] | BY WALT WHITMAN. | [rule with dot in center] | 1. | [13 lines of verse] 2. | [14 lines of verse] [second column] ETHIOPIA SALUTING THE COLORS. | [rule with dot in center] | BY WALT WHITMAN. | [rule with dot in center] | 1. | [four lines of verse] | 2. | [three lines of verse] | 3. | [three lines of verse] | 4. | [four lines of verse] | 5. | [five lines of verse] [third column] FABLES. | [rule with dot in center] | BY WALT WHITMAN. | [rule with dot in center] | [15 lines of verse]

Broadside, printed on recto only. 8⅞″ × 14⅛″. *Location:* DLC.

Note: Apparently torn in thirds to make three separate slips; copies of "Ethiopia Saluting the Colors" and "Fables" have been located (see F 27 and F 28). A copy of "Sparkles from the Wheel" only is at TxU.

Your kind invitation to visit you and deliver a poem for the 333d Anniversary of founding Santa Fe has reached me so late, that I have to decline, with sincere regret. But I will say a few words off hand.

We Americans have yet to really learn our own antecedents, and sort them, to unify them. They will be found ampler than has been supposed, and in widely different sources. Thus far, impressed by New England writers and schoolmasters, we tacitly abandon ourselves to the notion that our United States have been fashioned from the British Islands only, and essentially form a second England only—which is a very great mistake. Many leading traits for our future National Personality, and some of the best ones, will certainly prove to have originated from other than British stock. As it is, the British and German, valuable as they are in the concrete, already threaten excess. Or rather, I should say, they have certainly reached that excess. To day, something outside of them, and to counterbalance them, is seriously needed.

The seething materialistic and business vortices of the United States, in their present devouring relations, controlling and belittling everything else, are, in my opinion, but a vast and indispensable stage in the New World's development, and are certainly to be followed by something entirely different—at least by immense modifications. Character, literature, a society worthy the name, are yet to be established, through a Nationality of noblest spiritual, heroic and democratic attributes—not one of which at present definitely exists—entirely different from the past, though unerringly founded on it. and to justify it.

To that composite American identity of the future, Spanish character will supply some of the most needed parts. No stock shows a grander historic retrospect—grander in religiousness and loyalty, or for patriotism, courage, decorum, gravity and honor. (It is time to dismiss utterly the illusion-compound, half raw-head-and-bloody-bones and half Mysteries-of-Udolpho, inherited from the English writers of the past two hundred years. It is time to realize—for it is certainly true—that there will not be found any more cruelty, tyranny, superstition, &c in the resumé of past Spanish history, than in the corresponding resumé of Anglo-Norman history. Nay, I thind there will not be found so much)

Then another point, relating to American ethnology, past and to come, I will here touch upon at a venture. As to our aboriginal or Indian population—the Aztec in the south, and many a tribe in the north and west—I know it seems to be agreed that they must gradually dwindle as time rolls on, and in a few generations more, leave only a reminiscence, a blank. But I am not at all clear about that. As America, from its many far-back sources and current supplies, develops, adapts, entwines, faithfully identifies its own—are we to see it cheerfully accepting and using all the contributions of foreign lands from the whole outside globe—and then rejecting the only ones distinctively its own—the autochthonic ones?

As to the Spanish stock of our Southwest, it is certain to me that we do not begin to appreciate the splendor and sterling value of its race element. Who knows but that element, like the course of some subterranean river, dipping invisibly for a hundred or two years, is now to emerge in broadest flow and permanent action?

If I might assume to do so, I would like to send you the most cordial, heartfelt, respectful congratulations of your American fellow-countrymen here. You have more friends in the Northern and Atlantic regions than you suppose, and they are deeply interested in the development of the great Southwestern interior, and in what your festival would arouse to public attention.

F 73

F 75

Two sheets: (1) '[10 lines in boldface] SUMMER DAYS IN CANADA. | [short rule] | Letter from Walt Whitman. | [short rule] | [five lines of prose] | [short rule] | [134 lines of prose]' and (2) '[141 lines of prose] | [flush right] W. W.'

Broadsides, printed on rectos only. (1) 16¼″ × 4¼″; (2) 16 ¼″ × 4¼″. *Location:* NcD.

Note one: See *London* (Ontario) *Advertiser,* 22 June 1880 (E 2583).

Note two: Whitman sent copies of this to various papers for their use on 17 June 1880 (*Correspondence,* III, 181).

SPARKLES FROM THE WHEEL.

By WALT WHITMAN.

1.

WHERE the city's ceaseless crowd moves on the live long
day,
Withdrawn, I join a group of children watching — I pause
aside with them.

By the curb, toward the edge of the flagging,
An old knife grinder works at his wheel, sharpening a
great knife ;
Bending over, he carefully holds it to the stone—by foot
and knee,
With measur'd tread, he turns rapidly—As he presses with
light but firm hand,
Forth issue, then, in copious golden jets,
Bright sparkles from the wheel.

2.

The scene, and all its belongings — how they seize and
affect me !
The sad, sharp-chinn'd old man, with worn clothes, and
broad shoulder-band of leather ;
Myself effusing and fluid —a phantom curiously floating —
now here absorb'd and arrested ;
The group, (an unminded point, set in a vast surrounding) ;
The attentive, quiet children ; the loud, proud, restive base
of the streets ;
The low, hoarse purr of the whiring stone — the light-
press'd blade,
Diffusing, dropping, sideways-darting, in tiny showers of
gold,
Bright sparkles from the wheel.

F 74

F 76

[boldface] THANKS IN OLD AGE. | [24 lines of verse] | [flush right] WALT
WHITMAN.

Broadside, printed on recto only. 9⅝″ × 6″ (DLC [2]); 9½″ × 6⅛″ (NcD); 9½″ ×
6″ (RPB); 9″ × 6″ (TxU). Whitman has written on the RPB copy: 'You are
welcome to this if you | can use it to print in paper | of Nov 24'. *Locations:* DLC (2), NcD, RPB, TxU.

Note: See *Philadelphia Press,* 24 November 1887 (E 2668).

F 77

[Untitled text beginning *'Some thirty-five years ago, in New York–City . . .'*]

THANKS IN OLD AGE.

Thanks in old age—thanks ere 1 go,
For health, the midday sun, the impalpable air — for life,
    mere life,
For precious ever-lingering memories, (of you my mother
    dear — you, father — you, brothers, sisters, friends,)
For all my days — not those of peace alone — the days of
    war the same,
For gentle words, caresses, gifts from foreign lands,
For shelter, wine and meat — for sweet appreciation,·
(You distant, dim unknown — or young, or old — countless,
    unspecified, beloved,
We never met, and ne'er shall meet — and yet our souls em-
    brace, long, close and long;)
For beings, groups, love, deeds, words, books — for colors,
    forms,
For all the brave strong men — devoted, hardy men — who've
    forward sprang in freedom's help, all years, all lands,
For braver, stronger, more devoted men — (a special laurel
    ere I go to life's war's chosen ones,
The cannoneers of song and thought — the great artillery-
    men — the foremost leaders, captains of the soul;)
As soldier from an ended war return'd — As traveler out of
    myriads, to the long procession retrospective,
Thanks — joyful thanks! — a soldier's, traveler's thanks.

                                        WALT· WHITMAN.

F 76

Broadside, printed in double columns on recto only. 11¾″ × 8⅞″. See *BAL*, IX, 81, where it is described as "reading copy" for Whitman's 28 January 1877 lecture in Philadelphia. *Location:* DLC.

Note: See "Walt Whitman on Thomas Paine," *New York Daily Tribune*, 29 January 1877 (E 2559).

F 78
[two lines in boldface] THOU VAST RONDURE, SWIMMING IN | SPACE. | [rule with dot in center] | BY WALT WHITMAN. | [rule with dot in center] | 1. | [12 lines of verse] | 2. | [14 lines of verse] | 3. | [16 lines of verse]

Broadside, printed on recto only. 12¾″ × 5¼″ (DLC, NN-B); 12½″ × 5¼″ (DLC). *Locations:* DLC (2), NN-B.

F 79
THOU WHO HAST SLEPT ALL NIGHT UPON THE STORM.—(THE MAN-OF-WAR BIRD.) . . .

Broadside, printed on recto only. 5¹⁵⁄₁₆″ × 4¼″. See *BAL*, IX, 82. *Location:* DLC.

Note one: See "The Man-of-War Bird," *Athenæum*, 1 April 1876 (E 2555).

Note two: Whitman sent a copy of this to Bucke on 23 October 1878 (*Correspondence*, VI, 18).

F 80

A THOUGHT ON SHAKSPEARE . . .

Broadside, printed on recto only. 14⅛″ × 5⅞″. See *BAL*, IX, 82. *Locations:* CtY, DLC.

Note one: See *Critic*, 14 August 1886 (E 2648).

Note two: Whitman mentions "the slips" of this on 24 August 1886 (*Correspondence*, IV, 45).

F 81

[boldface] PERSONAL. | [two lines to the right] U. S. AMERICA: | *Camden, N. Jersey, April,* 1876. | [flush left] *To the Foreign Reader, at outset:* | *[58 lines of prose, signed 'W. W.']* | *[thick rule]* | *[thick rule]*

Broadside, printed on recto only. 9″ × 5½″ (TxU); 9″ × 6¼″ (TxU). *Locations:* TxU (2).

Note: See *Notebooks*, IV, 1526.

F 82

[boldface] TO GET THE FINAL LILT OF SONGS. | [eight lines of verse] | [flush right] WALT WHITMAN.

Broadside, printed on recto only. 4½″ × 6″. *Location:* DLC.

Note one: See "The Final Lilt of Songs," *New York Herald,* 16 April 1888 (E 2698).

Note two: Whitman ordered a "little slip" on 18 April 1888 (*Correspondence*, IV, 164).

Note three: Originally printed on a single sheet with "A Carol Closing Sixty-Nine" and "Old Age's Lambent Peaks" (see F 53).

F 83

Two states have been noted, priority undetermined:

First state:

[boldface] TO THE SUN-SET BREEZE. | [27 lines of verse] | [flush right] WALT WHITMAN.

Broadside, printed on recto only. 8⅛″ × 6″ (DLC); 8″ × 6¹⁄₁₆″ (DLC, NcD, ViU); 8″ × 6″ (TxU [2]). *Locations:* DLC (2), NcD, TxU (2), ViU.

PERSONAL.

U. S. AMERICA :
Camden, N. Jersey, April, 1876.

To the Foreign Reader, at outset :

Though there is many another influence and chord in the intentions of the following Recitatives, the one that for the purpose of this reprint doubtless o'erdominates the rest is to suggest and help a deeper, stronger, (not now political, or business, or intellectual, but) heroic, artistic, and especially emotional, intertwining and affiliation of the Old and New Worlds.

Indeed, the peculiar glory of These United States I have come to see, or expect to see, not in their geographical or even republican greatness, nor wealth or products, nor military or naval power, nor special, eminent Names in any department, (to shine with, or outshine, foreign special names, in similar departments,)—but more and more in a vaster, sauer, more splendid COMRADESHIP, typifying the People everywhere, uniting closer and closer not only The American States, but all Nations, and all Humanity. (That, O Poets! is not *that* a theme, a Union, worth chanting, striving for? Why not fix our verses henceforth to the gauge of the round globe? the whole race?)

Perhaps the most illustrious culmination of the Modern and of Republicanism may prove to be a signal cluster of joyous, more exalted Bards of Adhesiveness, identically one in soul, but contributed by every nation, each after its distinctive kind. Let me dare here and now to start it. Let the diplomats, as ever, still deeply plan, seeking advantages, proposing treaties between governments, and to bind them, on paper: what I seek is different, simpler. I would inaugurate from America, for this purpose, new formulas, international poems. I have thought that the invisible root out of which the Poetry deepest in, and dearest to, humanity grows, is Friendship. I have thought that both in Patriotism and Song, (even amid their grandest shows, past,) we have adhered too long to petty limits, and that the time has come to enfold the world.

While the following pieces, then, were put forth and sounded especially for my own country, and address'd to democratic needs, I cannot evade the conviction that the substances and subtle ties behind them, and which they celebrate, (is it that the American character has enormous Pride and Self-assertion? ah, but underneath, living Goodwill and Sympathy, on which the others rest, are far more enormous,) belong equally to all countries. And the ambition to waken with them, and in their key, the latent echoes of every land, I here avow.

To begin, therefore, though nor envoy, nor ambassador, nor with any official right, nor commission'd by the President—with only Poet's right, as general simple friend of Man—the right of the Singer, admitted, all ranks, all times —I will not repress the impulse I feel, (what is it, after all, only one man facing another man, and giving him his hand?) to proffer here, for fittest outset to this Book, to share with the English, the Irish, the Scottish and the Welsh,—to highest and to lowest, of These Islands—(and why not, launch'd hence, to the mainland, to the Germanic peoples—to France, Spain, Italy, Holland—to Austro-Hungary—to every Scandinavian, every Russ?) the sister's salutation of America from over sea—the New World's greeting-word to all, and younger brother's love.   W. W.

F 81

Second state:

[boldface] TO THE . . . | [27 lines of verse]

8⅛″ × 6″ (DLC [4], two signed by Whitman); 8″ × 6″ (TxU, signed by Whitman. *Locations:* DLC (4), TxU.

TO THE SUN-SET BREEZE.

Ah, whispering, something again, unseen,
Where late this heated day thou enterest at my window, door,
Thou, laving, tempering all, cool-freshing, gently vitalizing
Me, old, alone, sick, weak-down, melted-worn with sweat;
Thou, nestling, folding close and firm yet soft, companion bet-
    ter than talk, book, art,
(Thou hast. O Nature! elements! utterance to my heart be-
    yond the rest — and this is of them.)
So sweet thy primitive taste to breathe within — thy soothing
    fingers on my face and hands,
Thou, messenger-magical strange bringer to body and spirit of
    me.
(Distances balk'd — occult medicines penetrating me from head
    to foot.)
I feel the sky, the prairies vast — I feel the mighty northern
    lakes,
I feel the ocean and the forest — somehow I feel the globe
    itself swift-swimming in space;
Thou blown from lips so loved, now gone — haply from end-
    less store, God-sent.
(For thou art spiritual, Godly, most of all known to my
    sense.)
Minister to speak to me, here and now, what word has never
    told, and cannot tell,
Art thou not universal concrete's distillation? Law's, all As-
    Astronomy's last refinement?
Hast thou no soul? Can I not know, identify thee?

                                    WALT WHITMAN.

F 83, first state

Note one: In some copies, the misprint in line 8 of 'e!ements!' has been changed by hand (probably Whitman's) to 'elements!'.

Note two: See *Lippincott's Magazine,* December 1890 (E 2748).

Note three: Whitman mentioned "a couple of slips" of this on 3 November 1890 (*Correspondence,* V, 113).

F 84
[boldface] TO THE YEAR 1889. | [nine lines of verse] | [flush right] WALT WHITMAN.

Broadside, printed on recto only. 4⅞″ × 6⅛″ (TxU); 4⅞″ × 6″ (DLC); 4¾″ × 6″ (TxU). *Locations:* DLC, TxU (2).

Note: See *Critic,* 5 January 1889 (E 2718).

F 85
[boldface] TWILIGHT. | [four lines of verse] | [flush right] WALT WHITMAN.

Broadside, printed on recto only. 4¾″ × 6″ (DLC); 4½″ × 3¼″ (MoHi). *Locations:* DLC, MoHi.

Note one: A copy printed on birch bark, measuring 4¾″ × 6¾″, and dated by Whitman June 1889, is at DLC.

Note two: See *Century Magazine,* December 1887 (E 2670).

TO THE YEAR 1889.

Have I no weapon-word for thee — some message brief and
      fierce ?
Have I fought out and done indeed the battle ? Is there no
      shot left,
For all thy affectations, lisps, scorns, manifold silliness ?
Nor for myself — my own rebellious self in · thee ?

Down, down, proud gorge ! — though choking thee ;
Thy bearded throat and high-borne forehead to the gutter ;
Crouch low thy neck to eleemosynary gifts.

                              WALT WHITMAN.

F 84

TWILIGHT.

The soft voluptuous opiate-shades.
The sun just gone, the eager light dispell'd — (I too will soon
      be gone. dispell'd,)
A haze -- nirwana — rest and night — oblivion.

                              WALT WHITMAN.

F 85

F 86

Two states have been noted, priority undetermined:

First state:

A TWILIGHT SONG. | [28 lines of verse] | [flush right] WALT WHITMAN.

Broadside, printed on recto only. 8″ × 7¼″ (DLC [2], NN-B); 8″ × 6⅞″ (TxU);
8″ × 6¹⁄₁₆″ (NcD); 7⅞″ × 6½″ (DLC). *Locations:* DLC (3), NN-B, NcD, TxU.

Second state:

A TWILIGHT SONG. | [28 lines of verse]

8⅛″ × 7¼″ (DLC); 8″ × 6¹⁄₁₆″ (ViU). *Locations:* DLC, ViU.

Note one: A galley proof, measuring 8″ × 7⅜″, has the following corrections
made by Whitman:

A TWILIGHT SONG.

As I sit in twilight late alone by the flickering oak-flame,
Musing on long-past war-scenes — of the countless buried un-
    known soldiers,
Of the vacant names, as unindented air's and sea's — the un-
    return'd,
The brief truce after battle, with grim burial-squads, and the
    deep-fill'd trenches
Of gather'd dead from all America, North, South, East, West,
    whence they came up,
From wooded Maine, New-England's farms, from fertile Penn-
    sylvania, Illinois, Ohio,
From the measureless West, Virginia, the South, the Caro-
    linas, Texas,
(Even here in my room-shadows and half-lights in the noise-
    less flickering flames,
Again I see the stalwart ranks on-filing, rising — I hear the
    rhythmic tramp of the armies;)
You million unwrit names all, all — you dark bequest from all
    the war,
A special verse for you — a flash of duty long neglected — your
    mystic roll strangely gather'd here,
Each name recall'd by me from out the darkness and death's
    ashes,
Henceforth to be, deep, deep within my heart recording, for
    many a future year,
Your mystic roll entire of unknown names, or North or
    South,
Embalm'd with love in this twilight song.

F 86, second state

A TWILIGHT SONG.

As I sit in twilight late alone by the flickering oak-flame,
Musing on long-past war-scenes — of the countless buried un-
known soldiers,
Of the vacant names, as unindented airs and seas — the unreturn'd,
The brief truce after battle, with grim burial-squads, and the
deep-fill'd trenches
Of gather'd dead from all America, North, South, East, West,
whence they came up,
From wooded Maine, New-England's farms, from fertile Penn-
sylvania, Illinois, Ohio,
From the measureless West, Virginia, the South, the Caro-
linas, Texas,
(Even here in my room-shadows and half-lights in the noise-
less flickering flames,
Again I see the stalwart ranks on-filing, rising — I hear the
rhythmic tramp of the armies;)
You million unwrit names all, all — you dark bequest from all
the war,
A special verse for you — a flash of duty long neglected — your
mystic roll strangely gather'd here,
Each name recall'd by me from out the darkness and death's
ashes,
Henceforth to be, deep, deep within my heart recording, for
many a future year,
Your mystic roll entire of unknown names, or North or
South,
Embalm'd in love in this twilight song.

                WALT WHITMAN.

*Which paper do you prefer? They are the
same in quality — this a little darkest, but supposed to be the best. They differ in size, and ~~this~~
cut, the size of specimens respectively*

Proof for F 86

line 5   air's and sea's—the   ]   airs and seas—the
line 7   battle,   ]   battle
line 18   armies;)   ]   armies:)
line 21   you—a   ]   you, a
line 29   with   ]   in

In addition, Whitman has written on it "pull 40 impressions" and make "ab't" 25 with his name and "the rest" without it. *Location:* DLC.

Note two: See "A Twilight Song for Unknown Buried Soldiers, North and South," *Century Magazine,* May 1890 (E 2732).

Note three: Whitman mentions "slips" of this on 1 April 1890 (*Correspondence,* V, 32).

F 87
Two states have been noted, priority undetermined:

First state:

[boldface] THE VOICE OF THE RAIN. | [16 lines of verse] | [flush right] WALT WHITMAN.

Broadside, printed on recto only. 6½″ × 6½″. *Locations:* DLC (2).

Second state:

[boldface] THE VOICE OF THE RAIN. | [16 lines of verse]

THE VOICE OF THE RAIN.

And who art thou? said I to the soft-falling shower,
Which, strange to tell, gave me an answer, as here translated:
I am the Poem of Earth, said the voice of the rain,
Eternal I rise impalpable out of the land and the bottomless
      sea,
Upward to heaven, whence, vaguely form'd, altogether changed,
      and yet the same,
I descend to lave the drouths, atomies, dust-layers of the
      globe,
And all that in them without me were seeds only, latent,
      unborn,
And forever, by day and night, I give back life to my own
      origin, and make pure and beautify it:
(For song, issuing from its birth-place, after fulfilment, wan-
      dering,
Reck'd or unreck'd, duly with love returns.)

F 87, second state

8⅝″ × 6½″ (TxU); 6⅝″ × 6½″ (DLC); 6 ½″ × 6½″ (TxU); 6½″ × 6″ (DLC). *Locations:* DLC (2), TxU (2).

Note one: A first galley proof, measuring 4¾″ × 6″, has the following corrections made by Whitman:

line 1	THE VOICE OF THE RAIN.] A RAIN ENIGMA.
line 4	the voice of the rain,] the rain,
line 5	rise impalpable] rise, impalpably
line 8	same,] same.
lines 11–12	And all . . . unborn,] [not present]
line 13	I give] give
line 15	(For] For
line 17	returns.)] returns.

Location: DLC.

Note two: *BAL* reproduces a second galley proof, with Whitman's corrections and instructions to print 20 copies with his name and 10 without his name (IX, 84).

Note three: See *Outing*, August 1885 (E 2641).

F 88
[at right] From the Brooklyn Daily Times. | *WALT WHITMAN, A BROOKLYN BOY.* | [73 lines of prose]

Broadside, printed on recto only. 9″ × 5⅝″ (RPB); 7 ¾″ × 6⅝″ (NN-B). *Locations:* NN-B, RPB.

Note one: See *Brooklyn Daily Times*, 29 September 1855 (E 1179).

Note two: Not from the same setting of type used in the advertising supplement to the 1855 *Leaves of Grass*.

F 89
WALT WHITMAN. *COMMONSENSE has at last found . . .*

Broadside, printed on recto only. 10⅞″ × 4¼″. See *BAL*, IX, 85, where this 68–line text is described as an "announcement of *Leaves of Grass*, 1855." *Location:* DLC.

F 90
From the West Jersey Press, Jan. 16, 1878. . . . Walt Whitman for 1878 . . .

Broadside, printed in double columns on recto only. 8½″ × 5⅞″. See *BAL*, IX, 86. *Location:* DLC.

Note: See *West Jersey Press*, 16 January 1878 (E 2562).

F 91
Two sheets: (1) '[at right] From the United States Review. | [boldface] WALT
WHITMAN AND HIS POEMS. | [193 lines of prose and verse]' and (2) '[80
lines of prose and verse]'

Broadsides, printed on rectos only. (1) 24⅛" × 5¼" and (2) 10⅛" × 6¼" (NN-
B); (1) 23½" × 5½" and (2) 10" × 6½" (RPB). *Locations:* NN-B, RPB.

Note: See *United States Review,* September 1855 (E 1178).

Note two: Not from the same setting of type used in the advertising supplement to the 1855 *Leaves of Grass.*

F 92
[flush right] *From the West Jersey Press March 15th,* 1876. | [boldface] Walt
Whitman. | [47 lines of prose]

Broadside, printed on recto only. 8¾" × 5⅝". *Location:* NN-B.

Note: See *West Jersey Press,* 15 March 1876 (E 2553).

F 93
[flush right] *From the West Jersey Press, Jan. 26th,* 1876. | [two lines in
boldface] Walt Whitman's Actual American | Position. | [102 lines of prose]

Broadside, printed on recto only. 13⅝" × 3⅞" (NN–B); 13⅝" × 3¾" (NcD).
Locations: NN-B, NcD.

Note: See *West Jersey Press,* 26 January 1876 (E 2549).

F 94
[all within a thick-thin double-rule frame] [script] Walt Whitman's | BOOKS |
[nine lines of prose] | [four short rules] | [one line of prose]

Broadside, printed on recto only. Paper or linen. 23½" × 29½" (NN-R, PU); 24" ×
29¾" (NcD). *Locations:* NN-R (both), NNC (linen), NcD (paper), PU (both).

Note: See William White, "A Walt Whitman Poster," *American Book Collector,* 10 (November 1959), 4–6.

F 95
WHAT LURKS BEHIND SHAKSPEARE'S HISTORICAL PLAYS? . . .

Broadside, printed on recto only. 15 ⅞" × 6⅛". See *BAL,* IX, 87. *Location:* DLC.

Note: See *Critic,* 27 September 1884 (E 2626).

From the *West Jersey Press, Jan. 26th,* 1876.

Walt Whitman's Actual American Position.

The Springfield *Republican* prints another long account of Walt Whitman, and an estimate of his reputation in England and America. The criticism is friendly, and probably correct in its foreign statement, but makes an entire mistake about the position of " Leaves of Grass," and its author in this country. Indeed we had better furnish some facts of the matter within our positive knowledge.

The real truth is that with the exception of a very few readers, (women equally with men,) Whitman's poems in their public reception have fallen still-born in this country. They have been met, and are met to-day, with the determined denial, disgust and scorn of orthodox American authors, publishers and editors, and, in a pecuniary and worldly sense, have certainly wrecked the life of their author.

From 1845 to 1855 Whitman, then in Brooklyn and New York cities, bade fair to be a good business man, and to make his mark and fortune in the usual way—owned several houses, was worth some money and "doing well." But, about the latter date, he suddenly abandoned all, and commenced writing poems—got possessed by the notion that he must make epics or lyrics, " fit for the New World ;" and that bee has buzzed in his head ever since, and buzzes there yet.

Accordingly, the outlines of " Leaves of Grass " were sent out twenty years ago, printed partly by his own hands; for the first two or three years arousing only a *howl* of criticism and the charge of obscenity Since then numerous additions and new issues have been quietly, resolutely fashioned and put forth by his ownself, as if the author were sublimely indifferent to publishers, to the reading public, and to the usual profits.

That he went down to the field, soon after the war of 1861 broke out, and spent the ensuing four years as a hard-working unpaid army nurse and practical missionary—that in the overstrained excitement and labors of those years were planted the seeds of the disease that now cripples him—that he got work in 1865 at Washington as a clerk in the Interior Department, but was turned out forthwith by Secretary Harlan declaredly for his being the author of the " Leaves"—that he received an appointment again, but after some years was again discharged—being taken ill—that he left Washington, and has now lived for a while in a sort of half-sick, half-well condition, here in Camden—and that he remains singularly hearty in spirit and good natured, though, as he himself grimly expressed it lately, " pretty well at the end of his rope "—are parts of his history we will merely mention.

And now, since that beginning, over twenty years have passed away, and Whitman has grown gray in the battle. Little or no impression, (at least ostensibly,) seems to have been made. Still he stands alone. No established publishing house will yet publish his books. Most of the stores will not even sell them. In fact, his works have never been really published at all. Worse still; for the last three years having left them in charge of book agents in New York city, who, taking advantage of the author's illness and helplessness, have, three of them, one after another, successively thievishly embezzled every dollar of the proceeds !

Repeated attempts to secure a small income by writing for the magazines during his illness have been utter failures. The *Atlantic* will not touch him. His offerings to *Scribner* are returned with insulting notes; the *Galaxy* the same. *Harper's* did print a couple of his pieces two years ago, but imperative orders from head-quarters have stopped anything further.

All the established American poets studiously ignore Whitman. The *omnium gatherums* of poetry, by Emerson, Bryant, Whittier, and by lesser authorities, professing to include everybody of any note, carefully leave him out. Again, of perhaps the finest general criticism abroad, the articles friendly to him—for instance from the *Westminster Review*, the *Revue des Deux Mondes*, and the *Gentleman's Magazine*, have been unnoticed ; while the scolding and cheap abuse of Peter Bayne is copied and circulated at once in the Boston *Living Age*.

We have now said enough to suggest the bleakness of the actual situation, so far. But the poet himself is more resolute and persevering than ever. " Old, poor and paralyzed," he has, for a twelvemonth past been occupying himself by preparing, largely with his own handiwork, here in Camden, a small edition of his complete works in two volumes, which he himself now sells, partly "to keep the wolf from the door " in old age—and partly to give before he dies, as absolute an expression as may be to his ideas. " Leaves of Grass " is mainly the same volume previously issued, but has some small new pieces, and gives two characteristic portraits. Of 'Two Rivulets,' he has printed the newer parts here in Camden.

Walt Whitman's artist feeling for deep shadows, streaked with just enough light to relieve them, might find no greater study than his own life.

F 93

F 96

WHAT THE NEW JERSEY RAILROADS DO . . .

Broadside, printed on recto only. 14¼″ × 4⅛″. See *BAL,* IX, 87–88. *Location:* DLC.

Note: See "Winter Sunshine. A Trip from Camden to the Coast," *Philadelphia Times,* 26 January 1879 (E 2565).

F 97

WHISPERS OF HEAVENLY DEATH | [short rule] | *By Walt Whitman* | [short rule] | 1. | [12 lines of verse] | [short rule] | 2. | [15 lines of verse] | [short rule] | 3. | [11 lines of verse] | [short rule] | 4. | [11 lines of verse] | [short rule] | 5. | [five lines of verse]

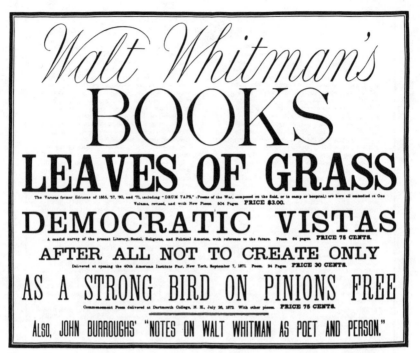

F 94

Broadside, printed on recto only. 19″ × 6″ (ViU); 18¾″ × 6″ (NN-B).
Locations: NN-B, ViU.

Note one: See *Broadway* (London), October 1868 (E 2506).

Note two: On 18 January 1868, Whitman sent a copy of this poem "in the
shape of a printed proof" (*Correspondence*, II, 13).

F 98
[ornate boldface lettering] With Husky-Haughty Lips, O Sea! | [29 lines of
verse] | [flush right] WALT WHITMAN.

Broadside, printed on recto only. 9⅞″ × 6″ (NN-B); 9¹³⁄₁₆″ × 6″ (JM, NcD); 8⅛″
× 6″ (RPB). The NcD copy is inscribed as received from Whitman November
1883 "before it was published." *Locations:* JM, NN-B, NcD, RPB.

Note one: A corrected galley proof, measuring 8¹⁄₁₆″ × 5 ¾″, is at CtY.

Note two: See *Harper's Monthly Magazine*, March 1884 (E 2623).

F 99
[boldface] A Word about Tennyson. | [*The Critic,* New-York, January 1, 1887.]
| [132 lines of prose, with extracts from Tennyson's poetry] | [flush right] WALT
WHITMAN. | [short rule]

WHISPERS OF HEAVENLY DEATH.

By *Walt Whitman.*

1.

Whispers of heavenly death, murmur'd I hear;
Labial gossip of night—sibilant chorals;
Footsteps gently ascending—mystical breezes, wafted soft and low;
Ripples of unseen rivers—tides of a current, flowing, forever flowing;
(Or is it the plashing of tears? the measureless waters of human tears?)

I see, just see, sk^ ward, great cloud-masses;
Mournfully, slowly they roll, silently swelling and mixing;
With, at times, a half-dimm'd, sadden'd, far-off star,
Appearing and disappearing.

Some parturition, rather—some solemn, immortal birth;
On the frontiers, to eyes impenetrable,
Some Soul is passing over.

2.

DAREST thou now, O Soul,
Walk out with me toward the Unknown Region,
Where neither ground is for the feet, nor any path to follow?

No map, there, nor guide,
Nor voice sounding, nor touch of human hand,
Nor face with blooming flesh, nor lips, nor eyes, are in that land.

I know it not, O Soul;
Nor dost thou—all is a blank before us;
All waits, undream'd of, in that region—that inaccessible land.

Till, when the ties loosen,
All but the ties eternal, Time and Space,
Nor darkness, gravitation, sense, nor any bounds, bound us.

Then we burst forth—we float,
In Time and Space, O Soul—prepared for them;
Equal, equipt at last—(O joy! O fruit of all!) them to fulfil, O Soul.

3.

A NOISELESS, patient spider,
I mark'd, where, on a little promontory, it stood, isolated;
Mark'd how, to explore the vacant, vast surrounding,
It launch'd forth filament, filament, filament, out of itself;
Ever unreeling them—ever tirelessly speeding them.

And you, O my Soul, where you stand,
Surrounded, surrounded, in measureless oceans of space,
Ceaselessly musing, venturing, throwing,—seeking the spheres, to connect them;
Till the bridge you will need, be form'd—till the ductile anchor hold;
Till the gossamer thread you fling, catch somewhere, O my Soul.

4.

AT the last, tenderly,
From the walls of the powerful, fortress'd house,
From the clasp of the knitted locks—from the keep of the well-closed doors,
Let me be wafted.

Let me glide noiselessly forth;
With the key of softness unlock the locks—with a whisper,
Set ope the doors, O Soul!

Tenderly! be not impatient!
(Strong is your hold, O mortal flesh!
Strong is your hold, O love.)

5.

PENSIVE and faltering,
The words, *the Dead*, I write;
For living are the Dead;
(Haply the only living, only real,
And I the apparition—I the spectre.)

With Husky-Haughty Lips, O Sea!

With husky-haughty lips, O Sea!
Where day and night I wend thy surf-beat shore,
Imaging to my sense thy varied strange suggestions,
Thy troops of white-maned racers racing to the goal,
Thy ample smiling face, dash'd with the sparkling dimples of
      the sun,
Thy brooding scowl and murk—thy unloos'd hurricanes,
Thy unsubduedness, caprices, wilfulness;
Great as thou art above the rest, thy many tears—a lack
      from all eternity in thy content,
(Naught but the greatest struggles, wrongs, defeats, could make
      thee greatest—no less could make thee,)
Thy lonely state—something thou ever seek'st and seek'st, yet
      never gain'st,
Surely some right withheld—some voice, in huge monotonous
      rage, of freedom-lover pent,
Some vast heart, like a planet's, chain'd and chafing in those
      breakers,
By lengthen'd swell, and spasm, and panting breath,
And rhythmic rasping of thy sands and waves,
And serpent hiss, and savage peals of laughter,
And undertones of distant lion roar,
(Sounding, appealing to the sky's deaf ear—but now, rapport
      for once,
A phantom in the night thy confidant for once,)
The first and last confession of the globe,
Outsurging, muttering from thy soul's abysms,
The tale of cosmic elemental passion,
Thou tellest to a kindred soul.

A Word about Tennyson.

[*The Critic*, New York, January 1, 1887.]

BEAUTIFUL as the song was, the original 'Locksley Hall' of half a century ago was essentially morbid, heart-broken, finding fault with everything, especially the fact of money's being made (as it ever must be, and perhaps should be) the paramount matter in worldly affairs.

Every door is barr'd with gold, and opens but to golden keys.

First, a father, having fallen in battle, his child (the singer)

Was left a trampled orphan, and a selfish uncle's ward.

Of course love ensues. The woman in the chant or monologue proves a false one ; and as far as appears the ideal of woman, in the poet's reflections, is a false one, at any rate for America. Woman is *not* 'the lesser man.' (The heart is not the brain.) The best of the piece of fifty years since is its concluding line :

For the mighty wind arises roaring seaward and I go.

Then for this current 1886-7, a just-out sequel, which (as an apparently authentic summary says) 'reviews the life of mankind during the past sixty years, and comes to the conclusion that its boasted progress is of doubtful credit to the world in general and to England in particular. A cynical vein of denunciation of democratic opinions and aspirations runs throughout the poem, in marked contrast with the spirit of the poet's youth.' Among the most striking lines of this sequel are the following :

Envy wears the mask of love, and, laughing sober fact to scorn,
Cries to weakest as to strongest, 'Ye are equals, equal-born.'
Equal-born ! Oh yes, if yonder hill be level with the flat.
Charm us, orator, till the lion look no larger than the cat,
Till the cat, through that mirage of overheated language, loom
Larger than the lion Demos-end in working its own doom,
Tumble nature heel over head, and, yelling with the yelling street,
Set the feet above the brain and swear the brain is in the feet,
Bring the old Dark Ages back, without the faith, without the hope
Beneath the State, the Church, the throne, and roll their ruins down the slope.

I should say that all this is a legitimate consequence of the tone and convictions of the earlier standards and points of view. Then some reflections, down to the hard-pan of this sort of thing.

The course of progressive politics (democracy) is so certain and resistless, not only in America but in Europe, that we can well afford the warning calls, threats, checks, neutralizings, in imaginative literature, or any department, of such deep-sounding and high-soaring voices as Carlyle's and Tennyson's. Nay, the blindness, excesses, of the prevalent tendency — the dangers of the urgent trends of our times—in my opinion, need such voices almost more than any. I should, too, call it a signal instance of democratic humanity's luck that it has such enemies to contend with—so candid, so fervid, so heroic. But why do I say enemy ? Upon the whole is not Tennyson—and was not Carlyle (like an honest and stern physician)—the true friend of our age ?

Let me assume to pass verdict, or perhaps momentary judgment, for the United States on this poet—a removed and distant position giving some advantages over a nigh one. What is Tennyson's service to his race, times, and especially to America ? First, I should say, his personal character. He is not to be mentioned as a rugged, evolutionary, aboriginal force—but (and a great lesson is in it) he has been consistent throughout with the native, personal, healthy, patriotic spinal element and promptings of himself. His moral line is loyal and conventional, but it is vital and genuine. He reflects the upper crust of his time, its pale cast of thought—even its *ennui*. Then the simile of my

friend John Burroughs is entirely true, 'his glove is a glove of silk, but the hand is a hand of iron.' He shows how one can be a royal laureate, quite elegant and 'aristocratic,' and a little queer and affected, and at the same time perfectly manly and natural. As to his non-democracy, it fits him well, and I like him the better for it. I guess we all like to have (I am sure I do) some one who presents those sides of a thought, or possibility, different from our own—different, and yet with a sort of home-likeness—a tartness and contradiction offsetting the theory as we view it, and construed from tastes and proclivities not at all our own.

To me, Tennyson shows more than any poet I know (perhaps has been a warning to me) how much there is in finest verbalism. There is such a latent charm in mere words, cunning collocations, and in the voice ringing them, which he has caught and brought out, beyond all others—as in the line,

And hollow, hollow, hollow, all delight,

in 'The Passing of Arthur,' and evidenced in 'The Lady of Shalott,' 'The Deserted House,' and many other pieces. Among the best (I often linger over them again and again) are 'Lucretius,' 'The Lotos Eaters,' and 'The Northern Farmer.' His mannerism is great, but it is a noble and welcome mannerism. His very best work, to me, is contained in the books of 'The Idyls of the King,' all of them, and all that has grown out of them. Though indeed we could spare nothing of Tennyson, however small or however peculiar—not 'Break, Break,' nor 'Flower in the Crannied Wall ' nor the old, eternally-told passion of 'Edward Gray:'

Love may come and love may go,
And fly like a bird from tree to tree
But I will love no more, no more
Till Ellen Adair come back to me.

Yes, Alfred Tennyson's is a superb character, and will help give illustriousness, through the long roll of time, to our Nineteenth Century. In its bunch of orbic names, shining like a constellation of stars, his will be one of the brightest. His very faults, doubts, swervings, doublings upon himself, have been typical of our age. We are like the voyagers of a ship, casting off for new seas, distant shores. We would still dwell in the old suffocating and dead haunts, remembering and magnifying their pleasant experiences only, and more than once impelled to jump ashore before it is too late, and stay where our fathers stayed, and live as they lived.

May-be I am non-literary and non-decorous (let me at least be human, and pay part of my debt) in this word about Tennyson. I want him to realize that here is a great and ardent Nation that absorbs his songs, and has a respect and affection for him personally, as almost for no other foreigner. I want this word to go to the old man at Farringford as conveying no more than the simple truth ; and that truth (a little Christmas gift) no slight one either. I have written impromptu, and shall let it all go at that. The readers of more than fifty millions of people in the New World not only owe to him some of their most agreeable and harmless and healthy hours, but he has entered into the formative influences of character here, not only in the Atlantic cities, but inland and far West, out in Missouri, in Kansas, and away in Oregon, in farmer's house and miner's cabin.

Best thanks, anyhow, to Alfred Tennyson—thanks and appreciation in America's name.

WALT WHITMAN.

F 99

Broadside, printed on recto only. 20¼″ × 6¾″. *Location:* TxU.

Note: See *Critic*, 1 January 1887 (E 2653).

F 100

[boldface] YONNONDIO | [two lines of prose] | [16 lines of verse] | [flush right] WALT WHITMAN.

Broadside, printed on recto only. 6¾″ × 5⅞″ (DLC); 6⅛″ × 6″ (DLC); 6″ × 6¼″ (TxU, ViU); 5⅞″ × 6¾″ (JM). *Locations:* DLC (2), JM, TxU, ViU.

Note: See *Critic*, 26 November 1887 (E 2669).

YONNONDIO.

[The sense of the word is *lament for the aborigines.* It is an Iroquois term; and has been used for a personal name.]

A song, a poem of itself — the word itself a dirge,
Amid the wilds, the rocks, the storm and wintry night;
To me such misty, strange tableaux the syllables calling up;
Yonnondio — I see, far in the west or north, a limitless ra-
          vine, with plains and mountains dark,
I see swarms of stalwart chieftains, medicine-men, and war-
          riors,
As flitting by like clouds of ghosts, they pass and are gone
          in the twilight,
(Race of the woods, the landscapes free, and the falls!
No picture, poem, statement, passing them to the future :)
Yonnondio! Yonnondio! —unlimn'd they disappear;
To-day gives place, and fades — the cities, farms, factories fade;
A muffled sonorous sound, a wailing word is borne through
          the air for a moment,
Then blank and gone and still, and utterly lost.

                                        WALT WHITMAN.

F 100

F 101

Two states have been noted, priority undetermined:

First state:

[boldface] YOU LINGERING SPARSE LEAVES | OF ME. | [seven lines of verse] | [flush right] WALT WHITMAN.

YOU LINGERING SPARSE LEAVES
OF ME.

You lingering sparse leaves of me on winter-nearing boughs,
And I some well-shorn tree of field or orchard-row ;
You tokens diminute and lorn—(not now the flush of May.
          nor July clover-bloom—no grain of August now ;)
You pallid banner-staves—you pennants valueless—you over-
          stay'd of time,
Yet my soul-dearest leaves—the faithfulest—hardiest—last.

                                        WALT WHITMAN.

F 101, first state

Broadside, printed on recto only. 6″ × 4½″ (ViU); 6″ × 4¾″ (DLC); 5″ × 6″ (TxU); 6½″ × 6″ (TxU); 4¾″ × 6″ (DLC, TxU); 6″ × 3¾″ (DLC). *Locations:* DLC (3), TxU (3), ViU.

Second state:

[boldface] YOU LINGERING SPARSE LEAVES | OF ME. | [seven lines of verse]

5″ × 6″. *Location:* DLC.

Note: See *Lippincott's Magazine,* November 1887 (E 2667).

FF. Supplement

Evidence from Whitman's *Correspondence, Daybooks,* and elsewhere points to the possibility of "proofs" of additional items, listed in this section.

FF 1
"A Carol of Harvest, for 1867."

"Six proof-impressions"; see 7 September 1867, *Correspondence*, I, 337.

FF 2
"Eidólons."

See 12 December 1876, *Correspondence*, III, 66.

FF 3
"Father Taylor (and Oratory)."

"Three slips"; see 15 July 1886, *Correspondence*, IV, 37.

FF 4
"How I Get Around at Sixty."

"Fair proof" mentioned for the fifth part, on Emerson; see 3 December 1881, *Correspondence*, III, 254.

FF 5
"How I Made a Book."

"100 proof sets in slips"; see 29 June 1886, *Correspondence*, VI, 33.

FF 6
"The Last of the Sacred Army."

A "Corrected Proof Sheet" is described at the William W. Cohen sale, American Art Association (1929), item 601; see *Whitman at Auction*, p. 163.

FF 7
"My Book and I."

"50 proofs"; see 2 July 1887, *Daybooks*, II, 390. CtY has a copy made up from loose pages from *Lippincott's*.

FF 8

"Our Eminent Visitors (Past, Present, and Future)."

"Proof slips"; see 23 November 1883, *Correspondence*, III, 355.

FF 9

"Preface" and "Additional Note" to *Specimen Days & Collect*.

"Printed slips"; see 8 June 1887, *Correspondence*, IV, 98.

FF 10

"Salut au Monde!"

William F. Gable sale, American Art Association (1924), item 1141; see *Whitman at Auction*, p. 109.

FF 11

"Spirit That Form'd This Scene."

"Five slip-impressions"; see 6 August 1881, *Correspondence*, III, 236.

FF 12

Whitman ordered "100 printed impressions" of his poetry and Traubel's article from the March 1891 *Lippincott's Magazine* (E 2756), which he received in late February; see 4 February and 28 February–1 March 1891, *Correspondence*, V, 161, 171, and *BAL,* IX, 86.

G. Reprinted Material in Books and Pamphlets

Reprinted prose, poetry, and letters by Whitman in books and pamphlets through 1892, the year of Whitman's death, arranged chronologically. All material in this section has had prior book publication. All material is signed unless otherwise noted.

G 1 ABBIE NOTT AND OTHER KNOTS
1856

ABBIE NOTT | AND | [gothic] Other`Knots. | BY | "KATINKA." | "It's a' a muddle." | DICKENS. | PHILADELPHIA: | J. B. LIPPINCOTT AND CO. | 1856.

By Catharine Brooks Yale.

"Preface" composed of three lines from "Song of Myself," p. [v]. See *Leaves of Grass* (1855).

Location: JM.

G 2 A HOUSEHOLD BOOK OF ENGLISH POETRY
1868

A HOUSEHOLD BOOK | OF | ENGLISH POETRY | SELECTED AND ARRANGED | [gothic] With Notes | BY | RICHARD CHENEVIX TRENCH, D.D. | ARCHBISHOP OF DUBLIN | LONDON | MACMILLAN AND CO. | 1868

"Come up from the Hills, Father," pp. 359–361. See A 3.

Location: AzU.

Note: The poem by Whitman is not included in the '*SECOND EDITION, REVISED*' published by Macmillan in London in 1870.

G 3 AMERIKANISCHE ANTHOLOGIE
1870

[all gothic] Amerikanische | Anthologie. | Aus dem Englischen | von | Adolph Strodtmann. | [rule] | Erster Theil: Dichtungen. | [ornate rule] | Leipzig. | Bibliographisches Institut.

929

Contains translations into German of:

"Weave in, My Hardy Life," p. 149. See A 3.
"Others May Praise What They Like," p. 149. See A 3.
"What Think You I Take My Pen in Hand?", p. 150. See *Leaves of Grass* (1867).
"Beat! Beat! Drums!", pp. 150–151. See A 3.
"Vigil Strange I Kept on the Field One Night," pp. 151–152. See A 3.
"As Toilsome I Wandered Virginia's Woods," pp. 152–153. See A 3.
"Reconciliation," p. 153. See A 3.
"Lo, Victress on the Peaks," pp. 153–154. See A 3.

Location: TNV.

Note: Bound in two-volumes-in-one format with '[all gothic] Amerikanische | Anthologie. | Aus dem Englischen | von | Adolph Strodtmann. | [rule] | Zweiter Theil: Novellen. | [ornate rule] | Leipzig. | Verlag des Bibliographischen Instituts.' (TNV).

G 4 AMERICAN INSTITUTE REPORT
1872

THIRTY-SECOND ANNUAL REPORT | OF THE | AMERICAN INSTI-TUTE | OF THE | CITY OF NEW YORK, | FOR THE | Year 1871–72. | [rule] | ALBANY: | THE ARGUS COMPANY, PRINTERS. | 1872.

"Addresses at the Exhibition of 1871" ("After All, Not to Create Only"), pp. 103–109. See A 6.

Location: Vi.

G 5 AMERICAN POEMS
1872

AMERICAN POEMS. | *SELECTED AND EDITED* | BY | WILLIAM MICHAEL ROSSETTI. | Nature and the Soul expressed, America and Freedom ex-pressed. | WHITMAN. | [publisher's device] | LONDON: | E. MOXON, SON, & CO., DOVER STREET, | AND | 1 AMEN CORNER, PATERNOSTER ROW.

"A Song," p. 247. See *Leaves of Grass* (1867).
"Envy," p. 248. See "When I Peruse the Conquer'd Fame," *Leaves of Grass* (1867).
"Parting Friends," p. 248. See "What Think You I Take My Pen in Hand?", *Leaves of Grass* (1867).
"Salut au Monde!" pp. 249–261. See *Leaves of Grass* (1860).

"Song of the Broad-Axe," pp. 261–273. See *Leaves of Grass* (1867).

"Crossing Brooklyn Ferry," pp. 273–280. See *Leaves of Grass* (1860).

"There Was a Child Went Forth," pp. 281–283. See *Leaves of Grass* (1871).

"To a Foiled European Revolutionnaire," pp. 283–285. See *Leaves of Grass* (1871).

"France, the 18th Year of These States," pp. 285–286. See *Leaves of Grass* (1860).

"To You" ["Whoever you are . . ."], pp. 286–288. See *Leaves of Grass* (1871).

"Years of the Modern," pp. 289–290. See *Leaves of Grass* (1871).

"To Think of Time," pp. 290–297. See A 5.

"A Dream," p. 297. See "Of Him I Love Day and Night," *Leaves of Grass* (1867).

"The Last Invocation," p. 298. See A 5.

"Sea-Shore Memories," pp. 298–305. See A 5.

"Tears," pp. 305–306. See A 5.

"Aboard, at a Ship's Helm," p. 306. See A 5.

"Who Learns My Lesson Complete?", pp. 307–308. See A 5.

"To One Shortly to Die," pp. 308–309. See *Leaves of Grass* (1860).

"Beat! Beat! Drums!", pp. 309–310. See A 3.

"Rise, O Days, from Your Fathomless Deeps," pp. 310–312. See A 3.

"A Letter from Camp" ["Come Up from the Fields, Father"], pp. 312–314. See A 3.

"Vigil on the Field," pp. 314–315. See A 3.

"A March in the Ranks," pp. 316–317. See A 3.

"A Sight in Camp," p. 317. See A 3.

"Manhattan Faces," pp. 318–319. See *Leaves of Grass* (1867).

"Reconciliation," p. 320. See A 3.

"In Midnight Sleep," p. 320. See A 5.

"Camps of Green," pp. 321–322. See A 3.

"The Mother of All," p. 322. See A 3.

"O Captain! My Captain!", pp. 323–333. See A 3.

No series or *Moxon's Popular Poets*.

Dedicated to Whitman "with Homage and Love."

Locations: BL, JM.

Note one: Reprinted, with Whitman's poems on the same pages: '[all within a single-rule red frame with maltese cross designs in each corner] *MOXON'S POPULAR POETS*. | [rule] | AMERICAN POEMS. | *SELECTED AND EDITED* | BY | WILLIAM MICHAEL ROSSETTI. | Nature and the Soul expressed, America and Freedom expressed. | WHITMAN. | LONDON: | WARD, LOCK, & CO., WARWICK HOUSE, | DORSET BUILDINGS, SALISBURY SQUARE, E.C.' (DLC).

Note two: Reprinted, with Whitman's poems on the same pages: 'AMERICAN POEMS. | [gothic] A Collection of Representative Verse. | *WITH SHORT BIO-GRAPHICAL SKETCHES OF THE | MOST CELEBRATED AMERICAN AU-THORS.* | [publisher's device] | LONDON: | WARD, LOCK, & CO., WARWICK HOUSE, | DORSET BUILDINGS, SALISBURY SQUARE, E.C.' (CtY).

Note three: Reprinted, with Whitman's poems on the same pages: 'AMERI-CAN . . . AND CO., | LONDON: WARWICK HOUSE, SALISBURY SQUARE, E.C. | NEW YORK: BOND STREET.' (CtY).

Note four: Reprinted, with Whitman's poems on the same pages: '[all within a single-rule red frame] AMERICAN POEMS. | *SELECTED AND EDITED* | BY | WILLIAM MICHAEL ROSSETTI. | Nature and the Soul expressed, America and Freedom expressed. | WHITMAN. | LONDON | JOHN WALKER & COMPANY, | 96 FARRINGDON STREET, E.C.' (NzD, PU).

G6 HUMOROUS POEMS
1872

HUMOROUS POEMS. | *SELECTED AND EDITED* | BY | WILLIAM MICHAEL ROSSETTI. | [four lines of verse] | BUTLER. | [one line of verse] | VICTOR HUGO. | [publisher's device] | LONDON: | E. MOXON, SON, & CO., DOVER STREET, | AND | 1 AMEN CORNER, PATERNOSTER ROW.

"A Boston Ballad. (1854.)," pp. 471–473. See *Leaves of Grass* (1871).

Locations: BL, DLC.

Note: Reprinted in *The People's Standard Library,* with Whitman's poems on the same pages: 'HUMOROUS POEMS | BY | ENGLISH AND AMERI-CAN WRITERS. | *CAREFULLY COMPILED AND EDITED, WITH | BRIEF BIOGRAPHIES OF THE AUTHORS.* | WARD, LOCK AND CO. | LONDON: WARWICK HOUSE, SALISBURY SQUARE, E.C. | NEW YORK: 10 BOND STREET.' (JM).

G7 THE POETS OF THE NINETEENTH CENTURY
1872

THE POETS | OF THE | NINETEENTH CENTURY. | SELECTED AND EDITED | BY THE | REV. ROBERT ARIS WILMOTT, | INCUMBENT OF BEARWOOD. | WITH ENGLISH AND AMERICAN ADDITIONS, | AR-RANGED BY | EVERT A. DUYCKINCK, | EDITOR OF THE CYCLOPEDIA OF AMERICAN LITERATURE. | ILLUSTRATED WITH ONE HUNDRED

AND FORTY-ONE ENGRAVINGS, | DRAWN BY EMINENT ARTISTS. | NEW YORK: | HARPER & BROTHERS, PUBLISHERS, | FRANKLIN SQUARE. | 1872.

"Proud Music of the Storm," pp. 661–667. See A 5.

Location: MB.

G 8 PUBLIC AND PARLOR READINGS
1872

PUBLIC AND PARLOR READINGS: | PROSE AND POETRY | FOR THE USE OF | READING CLUBS | AND FOR | PUBLIC AND SOCIAL ENTERTAINMENT. | [rule] | MISCLLANEOUS. | [rule] | EDITED BY | LEWIS B. MONROE. | [rule] | BOSTON: | LEE AND SHEPARD, PUBLISHERS. | NEW YORK: | LEE, SHEPARD, AND DILLINGHAM. | 1872.

"Come Up from the Fields, Father!", pp. 151–153. See A 3.

Location: MH.

G 9 A HAND-BOOK OF ENGLISH LITERATURE
1873

A HAND-BOOK | OF | ENGLISH LITERATURE. | INTENDED FOR THE | USE OF HIGH SCHOOLS, | AS WELL AS | A COMPANION AND GUIDE FOR PRIVATE STUDENTS, | AND FOR GENERAL READERS. | BY | FRANCIS H. UNDERWOOD, A.M. | [rule] | AMERICAN AUTHORS. | [rule] | BOSTON: | LEE AND SHEPARD, PUBLISHERS. | NEW YORK: | LEE, SHEPARD AND DILLINGHAM. | 1873.

Copyright 1872.

"Come Up from the Fields, Father," pp. 462–463. See A 3.
 "Dirge for Two Veterans," pp. 463–464. See A 3.

Location: JM.

G 10 A MANUAL OF AMERICAN LITERATURE
1873

A | MANUAL OF | AMERICAN LITERATURE: | [gothic] A Text-Book for Schools and Colleges. | BY | JOHN S. HART, LL.D. | PROFESSOR OF RHETORIC AND OF THE ENGLISH LANGUAGE AND LITERATURE IN

THE | COLLEGE OF NEW JERSEY, AND LATE PRINCIPAL OF THE NEW JERSEY | STATE NORMAL SCHOOL. | [floral design] | PHILADEL- PHIA: | ELDREDGE & BROTHER, | No. 17 North Seventh Street. | 1873.

From "After All, Not to Create Only," pp. 377–378. See A 6.

Location: JM.

G 11 THE POETS AND POETRY OF AMERICA
1873

[all within a single-rule frame] THE | POETS AND POETRY | OF | AMERICA. | BY RUFUS WILMOT GRISWOLD. | WITH ADDITIONS BY R. H. STOD- DARD. | [three lines of verse] | *BRYANT.* | [two lines of verse] | *HOFFMAN.* | [four lines of verse] | *AMERICAN PROSPECTS* —1763. | CAREFULLY REVISED, MUCH ENLARGED, AND CONTINUED TO THE PRESENT TIME. | [gothic] With Portraits, on Steel, from Original Pictures, | OF RICHARD H. DANA, WILLIAM C. BRYANT, JAMES G. PERCIVAL, HENRY W. LONG- FELLOW, | WILLIAM D. GALLAGHER, EDGAR A. POE, PHILIP PENDLE- TON COOKE, | JAMES RUSSELL LOWELL, AND BAYARD TAYLOR. | NEW YORK: | JAMES MILLER, PUBLISHER, 647 BROADWAY. | 1873

" 'Leaves of Grass.' 1871" ["Song of Myself"], pp. [626]–627. See *Leaves of Grass* (1871).

Location: MH.

Note: Reprinted, with Whitman's poems on the same pages: 'THE . . . JAMES MILLER, PUBLISHER, 779 BROADWAY' (LTF).

G 12 THE ROSE, THISTLE AND SHAMROCK
1874

THE | ROSE, THISTLE AND SHAMROCK. | [ornate rule] | A BOOK OF ENGLISH POETRY, | CHIEFLY MODERN. | SELECTED AND ARRANGED | BY | FERDINAND FREILIGRATH. | [rule] | FIFTH EDITION. | WITH IL- LUSTRATIONS. | [ornate rule] | STUTTGART. | EDWARD HALLBERGER.

"Come Up from the Fields, Father," pp. 150–151. See A 3.

Location: NcU.

Note: There is no Whitman contribution in earlier editions of this title.

G13 DANIEL DERONDA
1876

DANIEL DERONDA | BY | GEORGE ELIOT | VOL. I. [II.] [III.] [IV.] | WIL-
LIAM BLACKWOOD AND SONS | EDINBURGH AND LONDON |
MDCCCLXXVI

Epigraph from "Voices" beginning chapter 29 (II, 223). See *Leaves of Grass*
(*1871*).

Location: MH.

Note: American edition, with epigraph from Whitman on I, 332: 'DANIEL
DERONDA. | BY | GEORGE ELIOT. | VOL. I. [II.] | *HARPER'S LIBRARY
EDITION.* | *NEW YORK:* | *HARPER & BROTHERS, PUBLISHERS,* |
FRANKLIN SQUARE. | *1876.*' (*MH*).

G14 MIRIAM'S HERITAGE
1878

MIRIAM'S HERITAGE | [gothic] A Story of the Delaware River | BY ALMA
CALDER | [publisher's device] | NEW YORK | HARPER & BROTHERS,
PUBLISHERS | FRANKLIN SQUARE | 1878

Wrappers. *Harper's Library of American Fiction,*

Epigraphs from "Song of the Redwood Tree," p. 7 (see A 9); "Think of the
Soul," p. 24 (see *Leaves of Grass* [*1871*]), and "So Long!", p. 163 (see *Leaves
of Grass* [*1860*]).

Location: MB.

G15 MANY MOODS
1878

MANY MOODS | *A VOLUME OF VERSE* | BY | JOHN ADDINGTON SY-
MONDS | AUTHOR OF 'RENAISSANCE IN ITALY' 'STUDIES OF THE
GREEK POETS' ETC. | [rule] | *'The song is to the singer, and comes back most
to him'* | [rule] | LONDON | SMITH, ELDER, & CO., 15 WATERLOO PLACE
| 1878 | [*All rights reserved*]

The verse on the title page is from "Song of the Rolling Earth." See *Leaves of
Grass* (*1860*).

Location: ScGrwL.

G 16 POETRY OF AMERICA
1878

POETRY OF AMERICA | SELECTIONS FROM ONE HUNDRED AMERI-
CAN POETS | FROM 1776 TO 1876. | *WITH AN INTRODUCTORY REVIEW
OF COLONIAL* | *POETRY,* | AND SOME SPECIMENS OF NEGRO MEL-
ODY. | [rule] | BY W. J. LINTON. | [rule] | LONDON: GEORGE BELL &
SONS, YORK STREET, | COVENT GARDEN. | 1878.

"With Antecedents," pp. 199–201. See *Leaves of Grass* (1867).
  "Longings for Home," pp. 201–203. See *Leaves of Grass* (1860).
  "Pioneers! O Pioneers!", pp. 203–207. See A 3.
  "Quicksand Years," p. 207. See A 3.
  "The Dresser," pp. 207–210. See A 3.
  "Spirit Whose Work is Done," pp. 210–211. See A 3.
  "The City Dead-House," pp. 211–212. See *Leaves of Grass* (1867).
  "The Mystic Trumpeter," pp. 212–215. See A 7.

Location: MH.

G 17 POEMS OF PLACES. AMERICA. MIDDLE STATES.
1879

[all within a double-rule frame; outer frame is red with designs in each corner,
inner frame is black] [red] POEMS OF PLACES | [black] EDITED BY | HENRY
W. LONGFELLOW | [two lines of verse] | [flush right] CRABBE. | [two lines in
red] AMERICA. | MIDDLE STATES. | [black] [acorn device] | [red] BOSTON:
| [black] HOUGHTON, OSGOOD AND COMPANY. | [gothic] The Riverside
Press, Cambridge. | [red] 1879.

"The City of Ships," pp. 139–140. See A 3.

Location: TxU.

G 18 THE KANSAS MEMORIAL
1880

THE | KANSAS MEMORIAL, | A REPORT OF THE | Old Settlers' Meeting |
HELD AT | BISMARCK GROVE, KANSAS, | *September 15th and 16th, 1879.* |
[rule] | CHARLES S. GLEED, EDITOR. | [rule] | ILLUSTRATED. | [rule] |
KANSAS CITY, MO.: | PRESS OF RAMSEY, MILLETT & HUDSON. | 1880.

Copyright 1879.

"Not a grave of the murdered for Freedom," p. [4]. See "Europe, The 72d and 73d Years of These States," *Leaves of Grass* (1860).

Location: NcR.

Note: Also attributes to Whitman "Song of a Thousand Years" (pp. 15–16); according to *BAL,* this is by Henry Clay Work (IX, 42).

G 19 THE UNION OF AMERICAN POETRY AND ART
1880

THE UNION | OF | American Poetry and Art | A CHOICE COLLECTION OF | Poems by American Poets | SELECTED, ARRANGED, AND EDITED | BY | John James Piatt | With 300 Illustrations on Wood by Eminent American Artists. | CINCINNATI | W. E. DIBBLE, Publisher | 1880

"The City of Ships," p. 199. See A 3.

Location: MChB.

Note: Reprinted, with Whitman's poem on the same page: 'THE . . . CINCINNATI | W. E. DIBBLE & CO., Publishers | 1882 | Copyright, 1882, by W. E. Dibble' (MH).

G 20 HARPER'S CYCLOPÆDIA OF BRITISH AND AMERICAN POETRY
1881

HARPER'S CYCLOPÆDIA | OF | BRITISH AND AMERICAN | POETRY | EDITED BY | EPES SARGENT | NEW YORK | HARPER & BROTHERS, FRANKLIN SQUARE | 1881

"From 'The Mystic Trumpeter,' " p. 755. See A 7.
"Passages from 'Leaves of Grass,' " p. 756. See "Great are the Myths," *Leaves of Grass* (1867); "Miracles," *Leaves of Grass* (1867); "You Felons on Trial in Courts," *Leaves of Grass* (1867); "Night on the Prairies," A 5; "A Song of Joys" ["Poem of Joys"], *Leaves of Grass* (1860); "Song of the Rolling Earth" ["To the Sayers of Words"], *Leaves of Grass* (1860); "Song of the Open Road," *Leaves of Grass* (1867).

Location: OClW.

G 21 POEMS OF AMERICAN PATRIOTISM
1882

POEMS | OF | AMERICAN PATRIOTISM | CHOSEN BY | J. BRANDER MATTHEWS | NEW-YORK | CHARLES SCRIBNER'S SONS | 1882

"O Captain! My Captain!", pp. 268–269. See A 3.

Location: MH.

G 22 THE HOUSEHOLD BOOK OF POETRY
1883

[all within a single-rule frame] THE | HOUSEHOLD BOOK | OF | [red] PO-ETRY | [black] COLLECTED AND EDITED | BY | CHARLES A. DANA. | *A NEW EDITION—THOROUGHLY REVISED AND GREATLY ENLARGED.* | [gothic] With Illustrations. | NEW YORK: | [red] D. APPLETON AND COMPANY. | [black] LONDON: 16 LITTLE BRITAIN. | 1883.

Copyright 1882.

"Epigrams," pp. 1, 627.
  "A Sight in Camp in the Day-break Gray and Dim," p. 397. See A 3.
  "Vigil Strange I Kept on the Field," p. 397. See A 3.
  "An Old-Fashioned Sea-Fight," pp. 404–405. See "Song of Myself," section
    35, *Leaves of Grass* (1881).
  "Great are the Myths," pp. 634–635. See *Leaves of Grass* (1867).
  "The Mystic Trumpeter," pp. 669–670. See A 7.
  "Death Carol," p. 786. See "When Lilacs Last in the Dooryard Bloom'd," A 3.

Location: MH.

Note: Whitman's poems do not appear in the *'ELEVENTH EDITION—REVISED AND ENLARGED'* (New York and London: D. Appleton, 1881) or earlier editions.

G 23 THE LIFE AND PUBLIC SERVICES OF ULYSSES
       SIMPSON GRANT
       1885

THE | LIFE AND PUBLIC SERVICES | —OF— | [boldface] Ulysses Simpson Grant, | GENERAL OF THE | UNITED STATES ARMY, | AND TWICE | PRESIDENT OF THE UNITED STATES. | [rule] | —BY— | JAMES GRANT WILSON. | [rule] | [line of prose] | —Sir Walter Scott. | [line of prose] | —

VICTOR COUSIN. | [rule] | REVISED EDITION. | [ornate rule] | NEW YORK: | DE WITT, PUBLISHER, | No. 33 ROSE STREET.

Copyright 1885. Wrappers.

"What best I see in thee," p. 96. See *Leaves of Grass* (1881).

Location: RPB.

Note: Whitman's contribution is not present in the first edition: *The Life and Campaigns of Ulysses Simpson Grant* (New York: R. M. De Witt, 1868).

G24 BUGLE-ECHOES
1886

[all red] BUGLE-ECHOES | A COLLECTION OF | POEMS OF THE CIVIL WAR | [gothic] Northern and Southern | EDITED BY | FRANCIS F. BROWNE | [sepia engraving of cherub] | NEW YORK | WHITE, STOKES, & ALLEN | MDCCCLXXXVI

"Beat! Beat! Drums!", pp. 13–14. See A 3.
  "Come Up from the Fields, Father," pp. 133–135. See A 3.
  "Bivouac, on a Mountain Side," p. 241. See A 3.
  "Ethiopia Saluting the Colors," pp. 270–271. See *Leaves of Grass* (1871).
  "When Lilacs Last in the Dooryard Bloom'd," pp. 287–291. See A 3.
  "O Captain! My Captain!", pp. 291–292. See A 3.

Location: JM.

Note one: Reprinted, with Whitman's poems on the same pages: 'BUGLE-ECHOES | A COLLECTION OF THE | POETRY OF THE CIVIL WAR | [gothic] Northern and Southern | EDITED BY | FRANCIS F. BROWNE | *New and Revised Edition with Illustrations. Sold | by Subscription Only* | [engraving of book] | NEW YORK | WHITE, STOKES, & ALLEN | 1886' (PU).

Note two: A salesman's dummy copy has been noted, with "Beat! Beat! Drums!" only: 'BUGLE-ECHOES . . . [engraving of book] | RICHMOND, VA. | B. F. JOHNSON & CO. | 1886' (JM). No copies of the published book with this imprint have been located.

G25 CHILDREN OF THE POETS
1886

[all within a single-rule red frame] [gothic] The | [red ornate lettering] Children of the Poets | [black] *AN ANTHOLOGY* | FROM | [two lines in red] ENGLISH

AND AMERICAN WRITERS OF | THREE CENTURIES. | [black] *Edited, with Introduction* | BY | ERIC S. ROBERTSON. | [red acorn design] | [black] LONDON: | [red] Walter Scott, 24 Warwick Lane, Paternoster Row, | [black] AND NEWCASTLE-ON-TYNE. | 1886.

"There Was a Child Went Forth," pp. 168–171. See *Leaves of Grass* (1871).

Location: TxU.

G 26 REMINISCENCES OF ABRAHAM LINCOLN
1886

REMINISCENCES | OF | ABRAHAM LINCOLN | BY | DISTINGUISHED MEN OF HIS TIME | COMPILED AND EDITED BY | ALLEN THORNDIKE RICE | EDITOR OF THE NORTH AMERICAN REVIEW | NEW YORK | NORTH AMERICAN PUBLISHING COMPANY | 30 LAFAYETTE PLACE | 1886

Untitled essay, pp. 469–475. See A 8; A 11.

Location: JM.

Note one: English issue of the American sheets, with a cancel title leaf: 'REMINISCENCES . . . RICE | EDITOR OF THE 'NORTH AMERICAN REVIEW' | WILLIAM BLACKWOOD AND SONS | EDINBURGH AND LONDON | NORTH AMERICAN PUBLISHING COMPANY, NEW YORK | MDCCCLXXXVI | *All Rights reserved*' (ViU).

Note two: Reprinted: 'REMINISCENCES . . . REVIEW | EIGHTH EDITION | NEW YORK | PUBLISHED BY THE NORTH AMERICAN REVIEW | 3 EAST FOURTEENTH STREET | 1889' (TxU).

G 27 REPRESENTATIVE POEMS OF LIVING POETS
1886

REPRESENTATIVE POEMS | OF | LIVING POETS | AMERICAN AND ENGLISH | SELECTED BY THE POETS THEMSELVES | WITH AN INTRODUCTION BY | GEROGE PARSONS LATHROP | [rule] | CASSELL & COMPANY, LIMITED | 739 & 741 BROADWAY, NEW YORK | [rule] | 1886

Edited by Jeannette L. Gilder

"Eidólons," pp. 650–653. See A 9.
   "Patroling Barnegat," p. 653. See *Leaves of Grass* (1881).
   "The Ox-Tamer," pp. 653–654. See A 9.
   "Spirit that Form'd this Scene. Written in Platte Cañon, Colorado," p. 655.

See *Leaves of Grass* (1881).
"Ashes of Soldiers," pp. 655–657. See A 5.

Location: MH.

G 28 STANDARD RECITATIONS BY BEST AUTHORS
1886

[all within a double-rule frame with designs in each corner] No. 13 | [curved] STANDARD RECITATIONS | ——BY—— | BEST AUTHORS. | A CHOICE COL-LECTION OF | [ornate lettering] Beautiful Compositions | Carefully Compiled for | SCHOOL, LYCEUM, PARLOR, | AND OTHER ENTERTAINMENTS, | ——BY—— | *FRANCES P. SULLIVAN.* | [rule] | [at left] Issued Quarterly, September 1886. [at right] Subscription, 50 Cents per year. | [rule] | M. J. IVERS & CO., | PUBLISHERS, | 379 PEARL STREET, N. Y. | Entered at the Post Office, N. Y. as second class matter.

Wrappers.

"Walt Whitman's New Poem," p. 25. See "O Captain! My Captain!", A 3.

Location: MH.

G 29 THE TWO VOICES
1886

THE TWO VOICES | *POEMS OF THE MOUNTAINS* | *AND THE SEA* | SE-LECTED BY | JOHN W. CHADWICK | AUTHOR OF "A BOOK OF POEMS," "IN NAZARETH TOWN," ETC., ETC. | [two lines of verse] | —WORDSWORTH | TROY, N.Y. | H. B. NIMS & COMPANY | 1886.

"Those Who Have Failed," p. 93. See "Song of the Rolling Earth," *Leaves of Grass* (1881).
"Abraham Lincoln," pp. 95–96. See "O Captain! My Captain!", A 3.

Location: RPB.

Note: *BAL* reports a reprinting in [1886] by Joseph Knight, Boston (V, 321).

G 30 HALF-HOURS WITH THE BEST AMERICAN AUTHORS
1887

HALF-HOURS | WITH THE | BEST AMERICAN AUTHORS. | SELECTED AND ARRANGED BY | CHARLES MORRIS. | [rule] | VOL. II. | [rule] | PHILADELPHIA: | J. B. LIPPINCOTT COMPANY. | 1887.

"Song of the Redwood-Tree," pp. 489–494. See A 9.

Location: MH.

Note: Reprinted, with Whitman's contribution on the same pages: 'HALF-HOURS . . . COMPANY. | 1891.' (ScU).

G 31 SEA-MUSIC
1887

[all within a single-rule red frame] [red] SEA-MUSIC. | [black] AN ANTHOLOGY OF | POEMS AND PASSAGES DESCRIPTIVE OF THE SEA. | EDITED BY | [red] MRS. WILLIAM SHARP, | [black] *Editor of "Women's Voices," "Great Musical Composers," &c.* | *"For I have loved thee, Ocean!"* | BYRON. | LONDON: | [red] WALTER SCOTT, 24, WARWICK LANE, E.C. | [black] AND NEWCASTLE-ON-TYNE. | 1887.

Edited by Mrs. Elizabeth A. Sharp.

The Canterbury Poets.

"The World Below the Brine," p. 309. See A 5.
  "After the Sea–Ship," p. 310. See A 9.
  "From 'Out of the Cradle Endlessly Rocking,' " pp. 311–315. See A 5.

Location: MB.

Note one: Undated reprinting, with Whitman's poems on the same pages: '[all within a single-rule red frame] [red ornate initial capital] SEA-MUSIC. | AN ANTHO- | LOGY OF POEMS AND | PASSAGES DESCRIPTIVE OF | THE SEA. EDITED BY MRS. | WILLIAM SHARP. | *"For I have loved thee, Ocean!"* | BYRON. | LONDON | WALTER SCOTT, 24 WARWICK LANE | NEW YORK AND TORONTO: | W. J. GAGE & CO.' (ViU).

Note two: New edition in [1888], with Whitman's poems on pp. 465, 466, and 467–471: '[two lines in red] SONGS AND POEMS | OF THE SEA. | [black] *(SEA MUSIC.)* | EDITED BY | [red] MRS. WILLIAM SHARP, | [black] *Editor of "Women's Voices," "Great Musical Composers," etc.* | "Murmurs and scents of the infinite sea." | MATTHEW ARNOLD. | [ornate rule] | NEW YORK AND LONDON | WHITE AND ALLEN' (MB).

G 32 CHANTS OF LABOUR
1888

[drawing of man at seashore holding a banner with all but last three lines within banner] [ornate 'C'] CHANTS OF | [ornate 'L' and ':'] LABOUR: | A

SONG BOOK OF THE PEOPLE | : WITH MUSIC : | EDITED | BY | [ornate 'E'] Edward | [ornate 'C'] Carpenter | WITH | 2 | DESIGNS | BY | WALTER CRANE | 1888. | LONDON: SWAN SONNENSHEIN | & C⁰ .

"Love of Comrades," pp. 56–58. See "For You O Democracy," *Leaves of Grass* (1860).

Location: MH.

Note: The poem has been set to music.

G 33 THE GETTYSBURG SPEECH AND OTHER PAPERS
1888

[gothic] | The Riverside Literature Series. | [rule] | THE GETTYSBURG SPEECH | AND OTHER PAPERS | BY | ABRAHAM LINCOLN | AND | AN ESSAY ON LINCOLN | BY | JAMES RUSSELL LOWELL | *WITH INTRO-DUCTION AND NOTES* | [publisher's device] | HOUGHTON, MIFFLIN AND COMPANY | Boston: 4 Park Street; New York: 11 East Seventeenth Street | [gothic] The Riverside Press, Cambridge

Copyright 1888. Wrappers. *Riverside Literature Series,* no. 32, January 1888.

"O Captain! My Captain!" (three stanzas), p. 69. See A 3.

Location: MH.

Note one: Whitman received copies on 9 February 1888 (*Correspondence,* IV, 148).

Note two: BAL reports that "Whitman's contribution is not included in the first printing with dated title-page" (IX, 95).

Note three: New edition (copyright 1899) in wrappers, with Whitman's poem on p. 89: '[gothic] | The . . . LINCOLN | LOWELL'S ESSAY ON LINCOLN | AND | WHITMAN'S O CAPTAIN! MY CAPTAIN! | [publisher's device] | HOUGHTON MIFFLIN COMPANY | Boston: 4 Park Street; New York: 85 Fifth Avenue | Chicago: 378–388 Wabash Avenue | [gothic] The Riverside Press Cambridge' (MH).

G 34 POEMS OF WILD LIFE
1888

[all within a red single-rule frame] [red 'P'] POEMS OF WILD LIFE. | SE-LECTED AND EDITED | BY CHARLES G. D. ROBERTS, | M.A. | *Author of*

"Orion and other Poems," and "In | Divers Tones." Professor of English and | French Literature in King's College, | Windsor, Nova Scotia, Canada. | LONDON | WALTER SCOTT, 24 WARWICK LANE | TORONTO: W. J. GAGE AND CO. | 1888

The Canterbury Poets.

"Song of the Redwood Tree," pp. 221–226. See A 9.
    "From Far Dakota's Canons," pp. 226–227. See *Leaves of Grass* (1881).

Location: NcWsW.

G 35 HARPER'S FIFTH READER
1889

Harper's Educational Series | HARPER'S | FIFTH READER | AMERICAN AUTHORS | NEW YORK | HARPER & BROTHERS, FRANKLIN SQUARE

Edited by James Baldwin.

"O Captain! My Captain!", pp. 432–433. See A 3.

Location: MH.

Note: Reprinted, with Whitman's poem on the same pages: '*HARPER'S* . . . AUTHORS | NEW YORK [four-dot triangular design] CINCINNATI [four-dot triangular design] CHICAGO | AMERICAN BOOK COMPANY' (OCl).

G 36 A LIBRARY OF AMERICAN LITERATURE
1889

A LIBRARY OF | [red] AMERICAN LITERATURE | [black] FROM THE EARLIEST SETTLEMENT | TO THE PRESENT TIME | COMPILED AND EDITED BY | [two lines in red] EDMUND CLARENCE STEDMAN AND | ELLEN MACKAY HUTCHINSON | [black] IN TEN VOLUMES | VOL. VI | NEW–YORK | [red] CHARLES L. WEBSTER & COMPANY | [black] 1889

"Inscriptions," pp. 501–502. See "To Foreign Lands," *Leaves of Grass* (1871), and "I Hear American Singing"], *Leaves of Grass* (1867).
    "Starting from Paumanok," p. 502. See *Leaves of Grass* (1867).
    "From the 'Song of Myself,' " pp. 502–506. See *Leaves of Grass* (1881).
    "Youth, Day, Old Age and the Night," p. 506. See *Leaves of Grass* (1881).
    "From 'Out of the Cradle Endlessly Rocking,' " pp. 506–509. See A 5.
    "To the Man-of-War Bird," p. 509. See *Leaves of Grass* (1881).
    "Ethiopia Saluting the Colors," p. 510. See *Leaves of Grass* (1871).

"O Captain! My Captain!", pp. 510–511. See A 3.

"Old Ireland," p. 511. See A 3.

"Behold a Woman!", pp. 511–512. See "Faces," *Leaves of Grass* (1871).

"Spirit That Form'd This Scene. Written in Platte Cañon, Colorado," p. 512. See *Leaves of Grass* (1881).

"O Vast Rondure!", pp. 512–513. See "Passage to India," A 5.

"Whispers of Heavenly Death," p. 513. See A 5.

"Joy, Shipmate, Joy!", p. 513. See A 5.

Location: JM.

G 37 STANDARD RECITATIONS BY BEST AUTHORS
1889

[all within a double-rule frame with designs in each corner] No. 25 | [curved] STANDARD RECITATIONS | ——BY—— | BEST AUTHORS. | A CHOICE COLLECTION OF | [ornate lettering] Beautiful Compositions | Carefully Compiled for | SCHOOL, LYCEUM, PARLOR, | AND OTHER ENTERTAINMENTS, | ——BY—— | *FRANCES P. SULLIVAN.* | [rule] | [at left] Issued Quarterly, September 1889. [at right] Subscription, 50 Cents per year. | [rule] | M. J. IVERS & CO., | PUBLISHERS, | 379 PEARL STREET, N. Y. | Entered at the Post Office, N. Y. as second class matter.

Wrappers.

"Death Carol," p. 19. See "When Lilacs Last in the Dooryard Bloom'd," A 3.

Location: MH.

G 38 LOCAL AND NATIONAL POETS OF AMERICA
1890

[all within a single-rule frame] LOCAL AND NATIONAL | POETS OF AMERICA | WITH INTERESTING | BIOGRAPHICAL SKETCHES AND CHOICE SELECTIONS FROM | OVER ONE THOUSAND LIVING AMERICAN POETS. | *THE ONLY COMPLETE BIOGRAPHICAL DICTIONARY OF LOCAL AND NATIONAL | POETS OF AMERICA, CONTAINING NUMEROUS SELECTIONS* | [rule] | PROFUSELY ILLUSTRATED WITH OVER FIVE HUNDRED | LIFE-LIKE PORTRAITS. | [rule] | EDITED AND COMPILED UNDER THE SUPERVISION OF | THOS. W. HERRINGSHAW, | AUTHOR OF | "HOME OCCUPATIONS," "PROMINENT MEN AND WOMEN OF THE DAY," "AIDS TO | LITERARY SUCCESS," "MULIEROLOGY," ETC. | [rule] | "GREAT OAKS FROM LITTLE ACORNS GROW." | [rule] | CHICAGO, ILL.: | AMERICAN PUBLISHERS' ASSOCIATION. | 1890.

"What Am I After All," p. 193. See A 5.

   "Love," p. 193. See "The Mystic Trumpeter," A 7.

   "The World Below the Brine," p. 193. See A 5.

   "Life," p. 193. See "Sands at Seventy Annex," *Leaves of Grass* (1888).

   "Ethiopia Saluting the Colors," p. 194. See *Leaves of Grass* (1871).

   "Reconciliation," p. 194. See A 3. .

   'Failure," p. 194. See "Song of Myself," *Leaves of Grass* (1881).

   "Self," p. 194. See "Song of the Rolling Earth," *Leaves of Grass* (1881).

   "Animals," p. 194. See "Song of Myself," *Leaves of Grass* (1881).

   "Open Road," p. 194. See "Song of the Open Road," *Leaves of Grass* (1867).

Location: JM.

G 39 TESS OF THE D'URBERVILLES
1891

[large 'T' extending over two lines] TESS | OF THE D'URBERVILLES | *A PURE WOMAN | FAITHFULLY PRESENTED BY | THOMAS HARDY | IN THREE VOLUMES* | *VOL. I [II] [III]* | ' . . . Poor wounded name! My bosom as a bed | Shall lodge thee.'—W. Shakspeare. | O. M. | [publisher's device] | [two lines to the right] *ALL RIGHTS | RESERVED*

Copyright 1891. Published in London by James R. Osgood, McIlvaine, and Co.

Two-line quotation from Whitman, II, 46.

Location: NjP.

Note: These lines replaced lines from Swinburne that appeared in the serialization of the novel in England. The serial text was used for the first American (New York: Harpers, 1892) and "New and Revised Edition" (New York: Harper's, 1892), resulting in the Swinburne lines being used there as well (on pp. 140 and 173, respectively).

H. Separate Publication of Individual Poems and Prose Works

Separate book or pamphlet publication of individual poems or prose works from 1892, the year of Whitman's death, through 1991, arranged alphabetically. Includes first publication of fragmentary manuscript materials.

H 1
After all, not to destroy but inaugurate. [N.p.]: Horace Traubel and Albert Boni, 1913.

Broadside (7″ × 5″), printed on recto only. Nine lines of manuscript poetry from "Song of the Exposition" and facsimile signature. *Whitman Series 1*. *Locations:* MB, ViU.

H 2
After the Dazzle of Day. [New York: New York University Press, 1965].

Single leaf folded twice to make six pages. Advertising brochure for *The Collected Writings of Walt Whitman* (B 6), with facsimiles of manuscript poems "After the dazzle of Day" (p. [1]) and "Spirit that form'd this scene" (p. [3]). *Locations:* CU-B, CtY.

H 3
[As consequent from store of summer rains]. Northampton, Mass.: Gehenna Press, 1955.

Broadside (19″ × 19½″), printed on recto only. Printed in red and black. *Location:* NN-R.

H 4
As I Sit Writing Here. Long Island: Blackhole School of Poethnics, [n.d.].

Broadside (8½″ × 11″), printed on recto only. Five lines of verse. *Location:* RPB.

H 5
As If a Phantom Caress'd Me. Warren, Ohio: Fantome Press, [1978].

2 leaves; text on p. 3. Wrappers. Printed and illustrated by C. M. James. Limited to numbered 70 copies. Price, $3.95. *Locations:* MBU, RPB.

H 6.1.a–b
Assurances. Boston: [David] Godine, 1970.

949

Broadside (7¾″ × 9⅜″), printed on recto only. Prose. Unwatermarked paper with engraving of Whitman printed in blue or paper watermarked '[script] L A A' with engraving of Whitman printed in brown; priority undetermined. *Locations:* NcD (both).

H 7
As the time draws nigh. Grasse, France: Prometheus Press, 1983.

Unpaged (6 leaves); text of poem on pp. 6–7. Wrappers. Illustrated by Frederic Prokosch. Limited to five numbered copies, signed and hand-illustrated by Prokosch: one on Vellum Provence, numbered alpha; one on Guérimand, numbered beta; one on Les Aubiers, numbered gamma; one on Extra-Strong, numbered delta; one on Japon, numbered epsilon. Sold in a set with *The Dalliance of the Eagles, Proudly the Flood, Sounds of the Winter,* and *Weave in . . . . Location:* NcD (gamma).

H 8
Continuities. [San Francisco: Book Club of California, 1982].

Single leaf folded twice to make eight pages; printed on pp. 1, 4–5. Limited to 1,050 copies. *Location:* NjP.

H 9
The Dalliance of the Eagles. Grasse, France: Prometheus Press, 1983.

Unpaged (6 leaves); text of poem on pp. 6–7. Wrappers. Illustrated by Frederic Prokosch. Limited to five numbered copies, signed and hand-illustrated by Prokosch: one on Vellum Provence, numbered alpha; one on Guérimand, numbered beta; one on Les Aubiers, numbered gamma; one on Extra-Strong, numbered delta; one on Japon, numbered epsilon. Sold in a set with *As the time draws nigh, Proudly the Flood, Sounds of the Winter,* and *Weave in . . . . Location:* NcD (gamma).

H 10
The Dalliance of the Eagles. [St. Paul, Minn.: CIE/Media Central, n.d.].

Broadside (3½″ × 8¼″), printed on both sides with text on rectos. *Location:* RPB.

H 11
[Darest thou now o soul,]. [New York: Petrarch Press, 1986].

Unpaged (2 leaves); poem on p. 3. Wrappers. Printed December 1986. Limited to 300 numbered copies. Price, $30.00. *Locations:* JM, RPB.

H 12
Death of Abraham Lincoln. Chicago: Black Cat Press, 1962.

53 pp. Miniature book. Full leather. Note by Paul M. Angle. Lecture of 14 April 1879 reprinted from *Specimen Days*. Limited to 300 copies. Price, $10.00. *Locations:* JM, MBU.

H 13
An Excerpt from a Poem. New York: [n.p.], 1961.

5 leaves. Illustrated by Edward Colker. Listed in *NUC* (1956–1967; 122:215). *Not seen.*

H 14
[18-line manuscript facsimile, headed '*Five thousand Poems*—']. [Providence: Brown University, 1960].

Single leaf, folded twice to make eight pages; printed on pp. 1, 4–5, 8; facsimile of manuscript on p. 1. *Location:* CtY.

H 15
A Font of Type. Pittsburgh, Penn.: Laboratory Press, Carnegie Institute of Technology, 1927.

Broadside (12½″ × 7½″), printed on recto only. Designed, printed, and composed by Nelson P. Mitchell. *Location:* RPB.

H 16
A Font of Type. [N.p.]: Paul Johnston, 1928.

Unpaged (4 leaves), printed on p. 3 only. Wrappers. Limited to one copy. *Location:* PPT.

H 17
A Font of Type. [New York: Diamant Typographic Service, n.d.].

Single leaf folded once to make four pages; printed on pp. 1, 3–4. Printed by E. M. Diamant. Limited to 275 copies for "friends of the Graphic Arts, and 350 copies for the Typophiles." *Location:* RPB.

H 18
A Font of Type. [N.p.: n.p., n.d.].

Broadside (13¼″ × 16⅞″), printed on recto only. *Location:* NcD.

H 19
For one thing out of many . . . . [N.p.]: Horace Traubel and Albert Boni, 1913.

Broadside (7″ × 7½″), printed on recto only. 16 lines of manuscript prose with facsimile signature. *Whitman Series 5. Locations:* MB, ViU.

H 20
Good-Bye My Fancy! [N.p.: Charles E. Feinberg, 1969].

Broadside (15½″ × 11″), printed on recto only. Distributed to friends and subscribers of the *Walt Whitman Review. Locations:* NcD, RPB.

H 21
[11 lines of prose, beginning "Go on, my dear Americans," signed by Whitman]. [N.p.: n.p., 1907].

Broadside, printed on both sides: recto has manuscript facsimile above a monthly tear-off calendar for 1908; verso has Christmas greeting and information about the manuscript. Used as a Christmas keepsake by A. Edward Newton in 1907. Both sides facsimiled in George H. Sargent, *A Busted Bibliophile and His Books* (Boston: Little, Brown, 1928), pp. [44–45]; manuscript only facsimiled in Newton, *A Magnificent Farce and Other Diversions of a Book-Collector* (D 55), p. 39. *Location:* PP.

H 22
The great want of modern life . . . . [N.p]: Horace Traubel and Albert Boni, 1913.

Broadside (7″ × 7½″), printed on recto only. 13 lines of manuscript prose with facsimile signature. *Whitman Series 6. Locations:* MB, ViU.

H 23
'*I have never had more comforting words*'. [Syracuse, N.Y.: Syracuse University Library Associates, 1962].

Single leaf, folded horizontally approximately one-fourth from top. Facsimile of postcard of 13 November 1881 to the editor of the *Springfield Republican*. Limited to 250 numbered copies. *Locations:* CtY, IDeKN.

H 24.1.a–b
Walt Whitman's I Hear America Singing. [New York]: Delacorte Press/Seymour Lawrence, [1975].

Unpaged (16 leaves). Illustrated by Fernando Krahn. Listed in *Walt Whitman Review*, 22 (March 1976), 47. Copyright 21 March 1975; A624945. Deposit copies: cloth: DLC ('APR −3 1975'). Prices: cloth, $4.95; library binding,

$4.58. Reprinted with undated title page in 1976. *Locations:* DLC (1975), ScU (1975), RPB (1976).

H 25
I Hear America Singing. New York: Poet's Guild, [n.d.].

Broadside (7⅜″ × 4⅞″), printed on both sides. Simultaneously in *Unbound Anthology* and *Daughters of the American Revolution Series.* Price, 5¢. *Location:* RPB.

H 26
[17 lines of prose, beginning "I say we had best look our times and lands searchingly in the face . . ."]. [N.p.: Charles E. Feinberg, 1969].

Broadside (11″ × 8½″), printed on recto only. From *Democratic Vistas.* Distributed to friends and subscribers of the *Walt Whitman Review. Location:* CtY.

H 27
I Sing the Body Electric. [N.p.]: Interstate Graphic Corporation, 1949.

17 pp. *Brookhaven Book.* Limited to 400 numbered copies. *Location:* NNBMC.

H 28
I Sit and Look Out. [Marshall, Minn.]: Ox Head Press, 1984.

Unpaged (10 leaves). Miniature book. Wrappers. Folded paper slipcase. Printed May–July 1984. *Ox Head 21.* Limited to 150 copies. Price, $3.00. *Location:* JM.

H 29
Last Words. [New York: Kindle Press, 1959].

Single leaf folded once to make four pages; poem on p. 1. Note by Harold W. Blodgett. Seven lines of verse from an unpublished manuscript. DLC copy received 19 May 1959. *Locations:* DLC, RPB.

H 30
Letter to Nathan Hale, Jr. [N.p., n.p., n.d.].

Broadside (8¾″ × 8″), printed on both sides. Facsimile of letter of 14 June 1842. *Locations:* JM, PU.

Note: The copy at PU is annotated by Thomas Harned: "Original given to me by the Rev. Edward E. Hale in 1899."

H 30

H 31
[Facsimile of nine-line manuscript, beginning 'The most important | requisite now in the | United States is a']. [N.p.: Charles E. Feinberg, 1962].

Single leaf folded to make four pages; printed on pp. 1, 3–4. From a manuscript dated ca. 1867. Christmas card. *Locations:* CtY, RPB.

H 32.1.a
The Mystic Trumpeter. [Riverside, Conn.]: Hillacre Press, 1916.

Unpaged (4 leaves); poem on pp. 3–6. Cover title, imprinted with information that this is a new year's card from Frederick C. Bursch. *Locations:* CtY, NN-R.

H 32.1.b
[N.p.: n.p., n.d.].

The same as the first printing, but lacking the new year's card and press information. *Location:* RPB.

H 33
The Mystic Trumpeter. Northampton, Mass.: Apiary Press, MCMLXII.

Unpaged (10 leaves); text on pp. 6–8. Completed June 1962. Illustrated by Patricia Tobacco. Limited to 15 numbered copies, signed by the illustrator. *Location:* UU.

H 34

No dulcet rhyme, fitted for banquets of the night. [N.p.]: Horace Traubel and Albert Boni, 1913.

Broadside (7″ × 5″), printed on recto only. 10 lines of manuscript poetry with facsimile signature. *Whitman Series 3. Locations:* MB, ViU.

H 35

Walt Whitman on Abraham Lincoln. [Philadelphia]: Avil, [1886].

Single leaf, folded to make four pages, with "O Captain! My Captain!" printed on p. 3. Head title. Flier for Whitman's lecture on Lincoln. *Locations:* CtY, NN-B.

Note one: Reprinted with additional material and distributed on the occasion of an address by Charles E. Feinberg on 12 July 1959. *Location:* JM.

Note two: The front cover was reprinted, along with "Autobiographic Note. From an old 'remembrance copy' " and Whitman's advertisement for *Complete Poems & Prose, Leaves of Grass,* and *Portraits from Life,* and distributed on the occasion of an address by Charles E. Feinberg on 31 May 1962 (see F 9). *Location:* JM.

H 36

Captain! My Captain! Jamaica, N.Y.: Marion Press, [1931?].

Broadside (9″ × 6″), printed on recto only. *Location:* MWelC.

H 37

O Captain! My Captain! Baltimore: Enoch Pratt Free Library, MCMXXXIIII [*sic*].

Broadside (21¾″ × 16¾″), printed on recto only. Designed by Norman T. A. Munder. *Enoch Pratt Free Library Poetry Broadside. Location:* RPB.

H 38

O Captain! My Captain! San Francisco: Windsor Press, 1935.

Unpaged (2 leaves). Boards. Printed for Albert M. Bender by Cecil and James Johnson. Limited to 200 copies. *Location:* CSt, NcD.

H 39.1.a

[four lines to the right] First draft manuscript of O Captain! My Captain! | Written by Walt Whitman on the death of Abraham Lincoln | and now printed in memory of | John Fitzgerald Kennedy. 1917–1963

Single leaf, folded once to make four pages; printed on pp. 1–3; manuscript facsimile on p. 3. Christmas card. *Location:* CtY.

H 39.1.b
[eight lines in red, flush left] A KEEPSAKE TO CELEBRATE | The *SMALL EXHIBITION* of | *WALT WHITMAN MATERIALS* | from the collection of | Mr. Charles E. Feinberg | held at | THE GROLIER CLUB | February 5 – March 30, 1964 | [four lines in black, to the right] First draft manuscript of O Captain! My Captain! | Written by Walt Whitman on the death of Abraham Lincoln | and now printed in memory of | John Fitzgerald Kennedy. 1917–1963

Single leaf, folded once to make four pages; printed on pp. 1–3; manuscript facsimile on p. 3. *Locations:* JM, RPB.

H 39.1.c
[all in red, flush left] A KEEPSAKE TO CELEBRATE | The *SMALL EXHIBITION* of | *WALT WHITMAN MATERIALS* | from the collection of | Mr. Charles E. Feinberg | held at | THE GROLIER CLUB | February 5 – March 30, 1964

Location: RPB.

H 40
Oh Captain! My Captain! [Bushey Heath, Hertfordshire, England: Taurus Press, 1970].

Unpaged (5 leaves). Wrappers. Illustrated by Paul Peter Piech. *Taurus Poem No. 14.* Deposit copies: BO ('25JUN1970'), BE ('26 JN 70'). Limited to 300 numbered copies. Price, 2s.6d. *Locations:* BE, BO, JM, RPB.

H 41
O Captain! My Captain! [Brooklyn, N.Y.: August Becker Corporation, n.d.].

Unpaged (8 leaves); text on pp. 1, 4–5, 8. Dated by MH '[1928?]'. *Location:* MH.

H 42
O Captain! My Captain! Riverside, Conn.: Hillacre Press, [n.d.].

Broadside (13⅛″ × 10″), printed on recto only. *Hillacre Broadsides.* Limited to 100 copies. *Locations:* NN-R, TxU.

H 43

[p. 2] O CAPTAIN! MY CAPTAIN! | From the manuscript of Walt Whitman | in | The Pierpont Morgan Library | No other manuscript of this poem on the death | of Lincoln is known to exist. It was written | out by Whitman for S. Weir Mitchell in 1890.

Single leaf, folded once to make four pages; printed on pp. 1–3; manuscript facsimile on p. 3. *Location:* RPB.

H 44
O Captain! My Captain! New York: The Poet's Guild, [n.d.].

Broadside (7⅜″ × 4⅞″), printed on both sides. Simultaneously in *Unbound Anthology* and *Daughters of the American Revolution Series*. Price, 5¢. *Location:* RPB.

H 45
O Captain! My Captain! [N.p.]: E. S. Werner, [n.d.].

Listed in *CBI* (1902) for 25¢. *Not seen.*

H 46
One's-Self I Sing. [San Francisco: Andrew Hoyem, 1974].

Single leaf (poem partially printed on recto). *Location:* CU-SB.

H 47
O star of France (1870–1871). Paris: François Bernouard, [1921].

Unpaged (8 leaves). Wrappers. Illustrated by Combet-Descombes. Completed 12 January. Limited to 350 numbered copies. *Locations:* DLC, NNC.

H 48
Out of the Cradle Endlessly Rocking. New York: June House, 1926.

Unpaged (8 leaves). Boards. Unprinted dust jacket with printed paper label on spine. Printed July 1926. Copies inscribed by owners: TxU (9 February 1927). Limited to 180 copies. Price, $4.00. *Locations:* CtY, MB.

Note: A broadside advertising flier, printed on both sides, for *Pictures* (A 26) and this book, described as "Now Ready," is at CSt.

H 49
Out of the Cradle Endlessly Rocking. [Torence, Calif.: Labyrinth Editions, 1978].

Unpaged (10 leaves), printed on rectos only, with each leaf printed separately and enveloped in folded Japan paper. Burlap folding box or coarse linen binding. Afterword by James B. Hall. Designed and illustrated by Richard Bigus. Limited to 80 numbered copies, signed by Bigus: copies numbered 1–15 are enveloped in Unryu for $375; artist's proofs numbered 1–8 are enveloped in

Suzuki for $375; copies numbered 16–65 and artist's proofs numbered 9–15 are enveloped in Toshi for $325. *Locations:* BL, RPB, TxU.

Note: A folio broadside advertising flyer on Honsho paper is at TxU.

H 50.1.a
Poem describing A Perfect School. [New York: Simon de Vaulchier, 1923].

Broadside (20″ × 12″, NN-R; 17⅞″ × 10″, CSt; 17½″ × 10″, RPB), printed on recto only. Illustrations are handcolored. Illustrated by George Illian. Limited to 100 copies: copies numbered 1–10 are on Spanish handmade paper and are signed by the artist and printer; copies numbered 11–100 are on Chinese handmade paper and unsigned. Limitation information is on a slip pasted to the back of the broadside in CSt copy; handwritten at bottom of recto in RPB copy; not present in NN-R copy. *Locations:* CSt (Chinese), NN-R (Spanish), RPB (Chinese).

Note: Described as printed from unpublished manuscript ('Gymnastics, moral, mental and sentimental, on which magnificent men are formed').

H 50.1.b
[New York: Simon de Vaulchier, 1926?].

Broadside (16⅝″ × 9″), printed on recto only in black and orange, with illustrations handcolored in some copies. Watermarked 'EMCO Onion Skin'. Limited to 100 numbered copies, with information printed on bottom. *Locations:* NcD, NjP.

H 51
Poets to Come. Minneapolis: Holy Cow! Press, 1982.

Broadside (8″ × 10″), printed on recto only. *Location:* RPB.

H 52.1
This is What You Shall Do. [Lido Beach, N.Y.: John L. Davenport, 1955].

Single leaf, folded once to make four pages; printed on pp. 1 and 3 (poem on p. 1). From the preface to the 1855 *Leaves of Grass.* Illustrated by Jocelyn Taylor. *Locations:* TxU, ViU.

H 52.2.a
[Forest Hills, N.Y.]: Kindle Press, [1955].

Broadside (21″ × 13″), printed on recto only. *Location:* NN-R.

H 52.2.b
[New York]: Kurt H. Volk, 1955.

Broadside (21″ × 13″), printed on recto only. *Location:* NN-R.

H 53
Preface to the 1855 Edition of Leaves of Grass. Santa Rosa, Cal.: Santa Rosa Junior College, 1976.

23 pp. Wrappers. Introduction by John Whitman Bigby. 200 *Series, no. 1.* Copies inscribed by owners: PGlB (21 December 1975). *Location:* PGlB.

H 54
This is what you shall do. St. Louis: Ronart Press, [1979].

Broadside (11″ × 8½″), printed on recto only. Limited to 100 copies. *Location:* MoU.

H 55.1.a
American Bard. [Santa Cruz, Calif.]: Lime Kiln Press, 1981.

35 pp. Prose preface to the 1855 *Leaves of Grass* arranged in verse and illustrated by William Everson. Introduction by James D. Hart. Limited to 115 numbered copies signed by Everson, of which 100 are for sale. Price: $450.00. *Locations:* CSt, ViU.

Note: A four-page advertising flier is at CSt and RPB.

H 55.1.b
New York: Viking, [1982].

Unpaged (20 leaves). Reduced facsimile printing. Dust jacket. Deposit copies: DLC for CIP ('JAN 25 1982'), DLC for CIP ('FEB 3 1982'), BE ('26 MR 1985'). Price, $12.95. *Locations:* BE, DLC (2), JM.

H 56
This is What You Shall Do. [Browerville, Minn.]: Ox Head Press, 1988.

4 pp. Wrappers. Limited to 200 copies. *Minnesota Miniatures, Prototype Edition. Location:* CU–SC.

H 57
This is What You Shall Do. Port Jefferson, Long Island: Black Hole School of Poethnics, [n.d.].

Broadside (11″ × 8½″), printed on recto only. *Location:* RPB.

H 58
Proud Music of the Storm. [San Francisco: Press of H. S. Crocker, 1949].

Single leaf folded once to make four pages, with text of poem on p. 2. Calligraphy by Jim McDonald. *Location:* TxU.

H 59
Proudly the Flood. Grasse, France: Prometheus Press, 1983.

Unpaged (6 leaves); text of poem on pp. 6–7. Wrappers. Illustrated by Frederic Prokosch. Limited to five numbered copies, signed and hand-illustrated by Prokosch: one on Vellum Provence, numbered alpha; one on Guérimand, numbered beta; one on Les Aubiers, numbered gamma; one on Extra-Strong, numbered delta; one on Japon, numbered epsilon. Sold in a set with *As the time draws nigh, The Dalliance of the Eagles, Sounds of the Winter,* and *Weave in . . . . Location:* NcD (beta).

H 60
Rise Lurid Stars. New Haven: M[atthew]. B[ruccoli]. and M[ichael]. L[azare]., 1953.

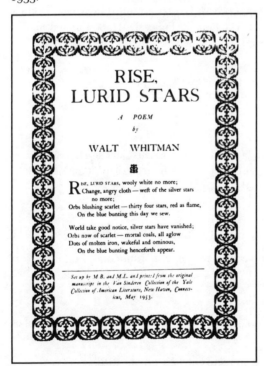

H 60

Broadside (13" × 10"), printed on recto only. Completed May 1953. Fewer than ten copies. Not for sale. *Locations:* Collection of Matthew J. Bruccoli, ViU.

H 61
Salut au Monde! New York: Random House, MCMXXX.

Unpaged (13 leaves). Unprinted dust jacket. Boxed. Illustrations by Vojtech Preissig. Printed in Czechoslovakia. *New Fine Books Series Number 1.* Published June 1931. Limited to 390 numbered copies signed by the artist, of which 360 are for sale. Price, $7.50. Listed in the *English Catalogue* as an importation by Simpkin for 31s.6d. *Locations:* JM, ScU.

H 62
Liberty Poem for Asia, Africa, Europe, America, Australia, Cuba & the Archipelagoes of the Sea. Jerome, Ariz.: Rampart Press, MCMLIX.

Broadside (22" × 13¾"), printed on recto only. From "Salut au Monde!" Printed by John and Barbara Beecher. Limited to 250 copies. *Locations:* MBU, NcD.

H 63.1.a
The Sleepers. Paris: François Bernouard, [1919].

Unpaged (18 leaves). Wrappers. Illustrated by Marcel Gaillard. Printed 26 December 1919. Copies inscribed by owners: RPB (19 April 1921, which contains a note that the book was "not out till March 1921"). Limited to 250 numbered copies. *Locations:* RPB, TxU.

H 63.1.b₁
[Folcroft, Penn.]: Folcroft Library Editions, 1973.

Facsimile reprinting. Deposit copies: DLC for CIP ('27 JUN 1973'). *Locations:* DLC, ScU.

H 63.1.b₂
[Norwood, Penn.]: Norwood Editions, 1978.

Title leaf is inserted. Price, $10.00. *Location:* ScCleU.

H 64
Song for All Seas, All Ships. New York: Poet's Guild, [n.d.].

Broadside (7⅜" × 4⅞"), printed on both sides. *Unbound Anthology.* Price, 5¢. *Location:* RPB.

H65.1.a
Song of Myself. East Aurora, N.Y.: Roycrofters, MDCCCCIV.

70 pp. Printed on Japan vellum. Three-quarter or full leather. Boxed. Completed February 1904. Limited to 100 numbered copies unsigned and with hand-colored title page and colophon; or uncolored and signed by Elbert Hubbard; or with hand colored title page and colophon, and signed by Hubbard. *Locations:* NN-R, RPB, TxU.

H65.1.b
East Aurora, N.Y.: Roycrofters, MDCCCCIV.

Printed on laid paper. Boards or limp suede. Boxed. Completed February 1904. Prices: boards, $10.00; leather, $25.00. *Locations:* JM, ScU.

Note: According to Paul McKenna (*A History and Bibliography of the Roycroft Printing Shop* [North Tonawanda, N.Y.: Tona Graphics, 1986], p. 117), available on Dickinson handmade paper, Whatman paper, and 100 copies on Japan vellum.

H66
Song of Myself. [Weimar: Utopia-Verlag, 1923].

81 pp. Boards. Printed fall 1923. Limited to 200 numbered copies. *Locations:* CtY, NjCW.

H67
Part one of the first edition of Leaves of Grass as published for Walt Whitman in 1855 and which is now called Song of Myself. New York: Powgen Press for Wm. R. Scott, [1936].

[50] pp., double columns. Dust jacket. Illustrated by Joseph A. Low. Printed September 1936. *American Renaissance Series,* boxed, with five other volumes. Price, $1.25. *Locations:* JM (all), RPB (all).

H68
Song of Myself from Leaves of Grass. New York: Greystone, [1951].

130 pp. Boards. Illustrated by Magda Barcinsky Cregg. *Castle Books. Location:* DGW.

H69
"*Song of Myself.*" [Philadelphia]: Masterbooks, [1973].

[1–4] [13] 14–56 pp. Facsimile reprinting from the 1855 *Leaves of Grass.* Cover title in newspaper format. *Masterbooks 1.* Deposit copy: BO ('4FEB1974'). *Locations:* BO, MBU, RPB.

H 70

["The spotted hawk swoops by and accuses me, he complains of my gab and my loitering"]. Lincoln, Mass.: Penmaen Press, 1974.

Broadside (18¾" × 12"), printed on recto only. From "Song of Myself." Engraving of Whitman by Stephen Harvard. Printed by John March. Limited to 300 copies, numbered and signed by Harvard. Price, $7.50. *Locations:* NjP, RPB.

H 71

I think I could turn and live with animals, they are so placid and self-contain'd. [London]: Poetry Bookshop, [n.d.].

Broadside (17½" × 7⅜"), printed on recto only. From "Song of Myself." Illustrated by John Nash. *New Broadside, No. 8. Locations:* CaOTU, DLC, RPB.

Note: The copy at CaOTU is dated '[1924?]'.

H 72

Song of the Broad–Axe. Philadelphia: Centaur Press, MCMXXIV.

Unpaged (29 leaves). Boards. Dust jacket. Illustrated by Wharton H. Esherick. Published Autumn 1924. Copies inscribed by owners: TxU (25 December 1924). Limited to 400 numbered copies, of which 375 are for sale. Price, $7.50. Listed in the *English Catalogue* for March 1926 as an importation by Simpkin at 31s.6d. *Locations:*   JM, TxU.

H 73

Song of the Open Road. London: St. Catherine Press, [1912].

31 pp. Cloth or suede over flexible boards. *Arden Books.* Deposit copies: BL ('5 MAR 12'), BC ('11 AP 1912'), BO ('15 4 1912'). Listed in the *English Catalogue* for September 1918 at 6d. *Locations:*   BC, BL, BO, CtY (2).

H 74

Song of the Open Road. [New York: Associated American Artists, 1933].

Unpaged (17 leaves), printed on rectos only; accompanied by 14 illustrations, signed by the artist. Full leather or unbound sheets in a paper folder. Illustrated by Lewis C. Daniel. NN-R copy received 29 March 1933. Limited to 100 numbered copies, signed by the artist. Price, $100.00. *Locations:*   NN-R, NcD.

Note one: An advertising flier of a single sheet folded twice to make six pages, stating that the book comes in a wooden portfolio, is at DLC.

Note two: An advertising flier of a single sheet folded twice to make eight pages (printed on pp. 1, 4, 5, and 8 only) in wrappers, stating that the book is bound in half leather and the price is $150.00, is at NN-R.

H 75
The Open Road. [Boston: Alfred C. Bartlett, n.d.].

Single leaf folded once to make four pages. Inscribed copies: OKentU (25 January 1915). *Location:* OKentU.

H 76
Song of the Redwood Tree. Mills College, Calif.: Eucalyptus Press, 1934.

Unpaged (13 leaves), printed on rectos only, except for an illustration on p. 10. Boards. Introduction by Aurelia Henry Reinhardt. Printed November 1934. Limited to 250 numbered copies. *Locations:* JM, ScU.

H 77
Song of the Redwood Tree. Bohemian Grove, Calif.: Friends of the Silverado Squatters, MCMLIV.

Unpaged (6 leaves). Wrappers. Printed by the Grabhorn Press in August 1954. Limited to 400 copies. *Location:* NzD.

H 78
Sounds of the Winter. Grasse, France: Prometheus Press, 1983.

Unpaged (6 leaves); text of poem on pp. 6–7. Wrappers. Illustrated by Frederic Prokosch. Limited to five numbered copies, signed and hand-illustrated by Prokosch: one on Vellum Provence, numbered alpha; one on Guérimand, numbered beta; one on Les Aubiers, numbered gamma; one on Extra-Strong, numbered delta; one on Japon, numbered epsilon. Sold in a set with *As the time draws nigh, The Dalliance of the Eagles, Proudly the Flood,* and *Weave in* . . . . *Location:* NcD (beta).

H 79
As in a swoon. [N.p.]: Horace Traubel and Albert Boni, 1913.

Broadside (7″ × 5″), printed on recto only. Seven lines of manuscript poetry from "Starting from Paumanok" and facsimile signature. *Whitman Series 4. Locations:* MB, ViU.

H 80
Tear Down and Build Over Again   an essay on Historic Preservation. [Huntington, N.Y.]: Town of Huntington, 1980.

8 pp. Wrappers. *Location:* NHem.

H 81

Assimilations. London: Arnold Fairbanks, 1908.

16 pp. Wrappers. "There Was a Child Went Forth." *Location:* CaOONL.

H 82.1.a–b

There Was a Child Went Forth. New York and London: Harper & Brothers, [1943].

Unpaged (16 leaves). Dust jacket. Illustrated by Zhenya Gay. Printed by Arthur and Edna Rushmore at the Golden Hind Press, Madison, N.J. Copyright page: '10–3 | *FIRST EDITION* | *H-S*'; publisher's code indicates August 1943 printing. Copyright A177567; received, 6 November 1943; renewed, 12 February 1971; R500259. Published 12 November 1943. NjCW copy received December 1943. Price, $1.50. Sold as an importation in Canada by Musson at $2.00. *Locations:* JM, NjCW. Reprinted with undated title page and copyright page reading: '10–3 | *SECOND EDITION* | *C-T*'; publisher's code indicates March 1944 printing. *Location:* TxU.

H 83.1.a–b

There Was a Child Went Forth. [Northampton, Mass.: Gehenna Press, 1968].

Unpaged (12 leaves), printed on rectos only. Boards. Boxed. Illustrations by Gillian Tyler. Limited to 100 numbered copies on Nideggon paper, signed by the illustrator. *Location:* JM. Reprinted with undated title page and limited to 100 unnumbered copies on Mead's Suede Book paper in 1968. Boxed. Price, $25.00. *Locations:* MBU, NNC.

Note: Numbered copies have an additional printed line in the colophon: 'This is number ' (p. [23]). The colophon is on an integral leaf.

H 84

There Was a Child Went Forth. [N.p.: Charles E. Feinberg, 1969].

Broadside (12" × 9"), printed on recto only. Distributed to friends and subscribers of the *Walt Whitman Review*. *Location:* CtY.

H 85

Thoughts Under an Oak—A Dream. [Liverpool]: Cracked Bell Press, 1979.

Unpaged (8 leaves), printed on alternating rectos and versos. From *Specimen Days*, 2 June 1878. Wrappers. Printed at the Press of Eric Salisbury. Deposit copy: BL ('21 APR 82'). Limited to 16 copies. Not for sale. *Locations:* BL, NzD.

H 86

To a Foil'd European Revolutionnaire. Berkeley Heights, N.J.: Oriole Press, 1955.

Unpaged (5 leaves), printed on rectos only. Wrappers. Printed December 1955. Limited to 52 copies for private distribution. *Locations:* MB, RPB.

H 87

To a Pupil. New York: Poet's Guild, [n.d.].

Broadside (7⅜" × 4⅞"), printed on both sides. *Unbound Anthology.* Price, 5¢. *Location:* RPB.

H 88

To Him That Was Crucified. [N.p.]: Cornelia and Waller Barrett, 1958.

Broadside (20¾" × 14¼"), printed on recto only. Printed by the Thistle Press, New York. Enclosed with etching of Whitman. Not for sale. *Locations:* JM, ViU.

H 89.1.a

To the Man-of-War Bird. [San Francisco: Lawton Kennedy, 1962].

Single leaf, folded twice to make eight pages; text on p. 5. *Adventures in American Literature,* no. 2. Page 1 headed in red '[gothic] A Christmas Greeting | Irving W. Robbins, Jr.'. *Locations:* NN-R, RPB.

H 89.1.b

[San Francisco: Lawton Kennedy, n.d.].

Page 1 is headed in red 'A KEEPSAKE | *From Irving W. Robbins, Jr.*'. Presentation copy: NNC (from Robbins, April 1968). *Locations:* NNC, NN-R.

H 90

To You. [London]: Gaberbocchus, [n.d.].

Single leaf folded to make four pages; printed on pp. 1–3. *Location:* ICarbS.

H 91

The Voice of America. San Francisco: H. S. Crocker, 1919.

Broadside (19¼" × 14", RPB; 18" × 13", BL), printed on recto only. "Spain. 1873–4." *Locations:* BL, RPB.

H 92

We Have Frequently Printed the Word Democracy. Brookline, Mass.: David R. Godine, [1972].

Broadside (30½″ × 22″), printed on recto only. From *Specimen Days*. Price, $1.00. *Locations:* NN-R, NcD.

H 93
Weave in . . . . Grasse, France: Prometheus Press, 1983.

Unpaged (6 leaves); text of poem on pp. 6–7. Wrappers. Illustrated by Frederic Prokosch. Limited to five numbered copies, signed and hand-illustrated by Prokosch: one on Vellum Provence, numbered alpha; one on Guérimand, numbered beta; one on Les Aubiers, numbered gamma; one on Extra-Strong, numbered delta; one on Japon, numbered epsilon. Sold in a set with *As the time draws nigh, The Dalliance of the Eagles, Proudly the Flood,* and *Sounds of the Winter. Location:* NcD (delta).

H 94
Well here I am in a grand old hotel, the finest in town. [Philadelphia: n.p., 1935].

Broadside (10⅝″ × 7″), printed on recto only. *Alpress Broadsides,* no. 1. Edited by Frank Ankenbrand, Jr. Limited to 300 numbered copies. Letter of 15[−17] April 1881 to the Staffords. *Location:* IU.

H 95
[*When Lilacs Last in the Dooryard Bloom'd*]. [London: Edward Arnold, 1900].

18 pp.; no title page. Printed on vellum. Vellum over boards; spine: 'WALT WHITMAN'S HYMN ON THE DEATH OF LINCOLN'. Illustrated by C. R. Ashbee. Printed by Essex House Press. Reviewed in *New York Times Saturday Review,* 24 August 1901, p. 598. Deposit copies: BL ('20 JY 1901'), BE ('29 JUL 1901'). For limitation, see *Note one* below. *Locations:* BE, BL, CtY, DLC, TxU, ViU.

Note one: The printed colophon states that the book is limited to 125 copies with hand-colored illustrations and capitals (BL, TxU), but in some copies '135' is written over a cancelled '125' (CtY, DLC, ViU).

Note two: Unnumbered copies, with a stated limitation of 125, are at BE and TxU (marked as the press' file copy).

Note three: A proof copy, printed on paper and bound in cloth, with illustrations not colored, and with a stated limitation of 125, is at JM.

H 96
When Lilacs Last In the Dooryard Bloom'd. Stanford University, Calif.: Stanford University Press, [1940].

14 pp. Boards or wrappers. DLC copy received 26 August 1940. Limited to 100 copies. *Locations:* DLC, NcD.

H 97
Come, Lovely and Soothing Death. New York: Poet's Guild, [n.d.].

Broadside (7⅜" × 4⅞"), printed on both sides. From "When Lilacs Last in the Dooryard Bloom'd." *Unbound Anthology.* Price, 5¢. *Location:* RPB.

H 98
While behind all firm and erect as ever. [N.p.]: Horace Traubel and Albert Boni, 1913.

Broadside (7" × 5"), printed on recto only. Eight lines of manuscript poetry with facsimile signature. *Whitman Series 2. Locations:* MB, ViU.

H 99
The Whole Present System. Boston: David Godine, [1972].

Broadside (30½" × 22"), printed on recto only. Prose from *Specimen Days.* Price, $1.00. *Location:* NcD.

H 100
"The World Below the Brine" A Poem from the Sea-Drift Section of Walt Whitman's Leaves of Grass 1892 Edition. [Berkeley, Calif.: Hart Press, 1940].

Unpaged (4 leaves); text printed on p. 3 only. Wrappers. Limited to 25 copies. *Locations:* NcD, RPB.

I. Compiler's Notes

Lists references to possible publications by Whitman that have not been dealt with elsewhere in the bibliography, arranged chronologically.

I1
Long Island Patriot, 1831–1832.

Whitman wrote "sentimental bits" for this newspaper when he worked for it (see *Specimen Days* [A 11], p. 195). No file is known to exist.

I2
Long Island Star, 1832–1833.

Whitman worked for this paper and contributed articles to it. No file is known to exist.

I3
New York Mirror, 1833.

Whitman contributed "a piece or two" to this paper (see *Specimen Days* [A 11], p. 195). No file is known to exist.

I4
Long-Islander, 5 June 1838–May 1839.

Whitman edited and "did most of the work [him]self" on this paper (see *Specimen Days* [A 11], p. 195). No file is known to exist.

I5
New York Statesman, 1843.

Whitman edited this paper for a few months and contributed articles to it. No file is known to exist.

I6
New York Democrat, 17 or 18 July 1844–16 October 1844.

Whitman worked for this paper and contributed articles to it. No file is known to exist.

971

I 7
New Mirror (New York), 1844.

Whitman contributed articles to this paper. No file is known to exist.

I 8
"A Jig in Prose," *Brooklyn Daily Eagle,* 11 January 1848.

"It is tempting to think" that Whitman wrote this piece; see Thomas L. Brasher, "A Whitman parody of 'The Raven'?", *Poe Newsletter,* 1 (October 1968), 30–31.

I 9
Brooklyn Freeman, November 1848–10 September 1849.

Whitman edited this paper and contributed articles to it. No file is known to exist.

I 10
Brooklyn Salesman, 1849?

Whitman contributed articles to this paper. No file is known to exist.

I 11
Daily News (New York), 19 December 1849–23 February 1850.

Whitman contributed articles to this paper. No file is known to exist.

I 12
[flush right] *From Putnam's Monthly, for September.* | [63 lines of prose]

Broadside (11½"×5⅜"), printed on recto only. Contains instructions for inserting extracts (not present here). This is Charles Eliot Norton's review of *Leaves of Grass* in the September 1855 *Putnam's Monthly Magazine. Location:* RPB.

I 13
"Wounded," *Brooklyn Standard,* 16 August 1862.

Signed "Walt Whitman." Poem. Reprinted from *Continental Monthly,* August 1862, where it appeared unsigned; attributed to Henry P. Leland in the index. For reasons why this is not by Whitman, see *NYD,* pp. 183–185.

I 14
O'Connor, William Douglas. *The Good Gray Poet. A Vindication.* New York: Bunce and Huntington, 1866.

There has been continuing debate about the possible amount and substance of Whitman's participation in this work. Most scholars now feel that Whitman's involvement was minimal; see, for an argument that Whitman played a major role in the book, Nathan Resnick, *Walt Whitman and the Authorship of* The Good Gray Poet (Brooklyn: Long Island University Press, 1948), and, arguing to the contrary, E. H. Eby, "Did Walt Whitman Write *The Good Gray Poet?*", *Modern Language Quarterly,* 11 (December 1950), 445–449; W. Gordon Milne, "William Douglas O'Connor and the Authorship of *The Good Gray Poet,*" *American Literature,* 25 (March 1953), 31–42; Jerome Loving, *Walt Whitman's Champion: William Douglas O'Connor* (College Station: Texas A&M University Press, 1978): "there is no convincing argument that Whitman participated in its composition" (p. 69); and Florence Bernstein Freedman, *William Douglas O'Connor: Whitman's Chosen Knight* (Athens: Ohio University Press, 1985).

I 15
"Oration of James Speed Upon the Inauguration of the Bust of Abraham Lincoln at Louisville, Kentucky, February 12, 1867," *Louisville Journal,* 13 February 1867.

Whitman may have ghostwritten this piece; see Margaret B. Collins, "Walt Whitman: Ghost Writer for James Speed? or 'None Goes His Way Alone,' " *Filson Club History Quarterly,* 37 (October 1963), 305–324.

I 16
[first column] *From the "West Jersey Press," May 24th, 1876.* | [boldface] Walt Whitman. | THE TRUE REMINISCENCE OF HIS WRITINGS. | [106 lines of prose] | [second column] [81 lines of prose] | [34 lines of verse]

Broadside (12"×6¼"), printed on recto only. Double columns. This item is an interview with Whitman. *Location:* NcD.

I 17
Treasures from the Poetic World, ed. Frank McAlpine. Philadelphia and Chicago: Elliott & Beezley, 1884.

Copyright 1882. Attributes "The Two Mysteries" to Whitman, pp. 42–43. This piece is actually by Mary Mapes Dodge; see "The Authorship of 'The Two Mysteries'. A Correction," *Arena,* 33 (March 1905), 318. Reprinted as *Popular Poetic Pearls, and Biographies of Poets* (Philadelphia, Chicago, Cincinnati: Elliott & Beezley, 1885), and by the same firm in 1886 and 1888. *Locations:* TNV (1884), FWpR (1885), TU (1886), GAuA (1888).

I 18
[four lines boldface] WALT WHITMAN'S LECTURE. | [short rule] | The Poet Gives His Graphic Description of | the Assassination of Lincoln. | [151 lines of prose] | [boldface short rule]

From the "West Jersey Press," May 24th, 1876.

Walt Whitman.

THE TRUE REMINISCENCE OF HIS WRITINGS.

At latest accounts the row in London about Walt Whitman had been turned into one of those petty side-squabbles too common among authors. Robert Buchanan, Scotchman, poet, and writer of the enthusiastic Whitmanite letter in the *London Daily News* of March 13th, cannot, it seems, be endured on any terms by the Rev. M. D. Conway, who, though also sailing under the Whitman flag, is so determined to have R. B.'s hair—nay, his heart's blood—that he goes for the Scotchman, letter, intentions, facts and all, and will not suffer the least shred of them to remain. Even W. W. himself must sink, rather than be floated by R. B. The substance of Conway's precious theory being, (as ventilated to his correspondents, and in the press of England and America,) that "the old gray" has *l'argent* in his pocket, needs neither literary defence or personal help—that children generally cry for his works throughout the United States—and that the eloquent call of R. B., instead of righteous anger and true benevolence, is a case of exaggerated bunkum and "false pretences."

Taking up the discussion in this country, and adding more or less faint praise or open superciliousness to it, Dr. Holland in *Scribner's*, G. W. Curtis in *Harper's Monthly*, Bayard Taylor in the *Tribune*, with somebody in *Appleton's*, the *Graphic*, and various Philadelphia, Boston and other journals, after buffeting R. B. to their heart's content, decidedly agree that on the question of the courtesy of treatment, from the trade and public, accorded to W. W. through his career of twenty years past in America, there has never been the least particle of "prejudice," ill-disposition, or lack of fair and open field about it.

As this is no affair of "whining," though the *Tribune* calls it so, but of verity and facts—what are the facts? They themselves are not perhaps of so much moment, (for what is the bulk of life but similar experiences, each after its sort?) but important to illustrate the pivotal truth that W. W. for twenty-five years, against the doubts, denials, almost unanimous remonstrances, convictions (until lately) of the world, of relatives, of the publishing and critical powers—with failure of each successive issue—has nevertheless steadily adhered, and actively labored forward in both life and books, to the strict accomplishment and formulation, in deed and print, of *his own ideal*. Truly, if the man were not, among his other qualities, the most phlegmatic, self-set and egotistical

of twenty years. Down to the present time, and to this hour, not one leading author of the United States (Whitman says grimly he is "getting to be rather proud of it") is friendly in either a personal or professional mode to *Leaves of Grass* or W. W. himself. Will it not prove a pretty page of the history of our literature a couple of decades hence, that in 1874-5 Emerson, Bryant and Whittier each make great Omnibus-gatherings of all the current poets and poetry—putting in such as Nora Perry and Charles Gayler—and carefully leaving Walt Whitman out? Not a magazine in America—not a single well-established literary journal—will to-day, on the usual terms, accept and issue his productions. Not a publisher will bring out his books, (which to this hour have never been really *published* at all.) There has been, in fact, something sublime in the unyielding *set* against them. To the vehement appeal of a well-known legal gentleman (J. H. A.) in Washington, for replacing Whitman, in 1865, Mr. Secretary Harlan, before referred to, as vehemently answered, "if the President of the United States ordered the author of *Leaves of Grass* reinstated in my department, I would resign sooner than do it." It is quite certain that this fairly represented, (perhaps still represents) the large majority feeling.

True, on one side, or in a little corner of this large majority feeling, Walt Whitman possesses a small, yet real fighting minority, of determined friends, absolute ones, literary and personal, British and American, O'Connor, Burroughs, Dowden, Rosetti, Joaquin Miller, the two Swintons, Mrs. Gilchrist, and especially Robert Buchanan—friends who, in their appreciation and affection, have done him far more good than they can ever know, and the thought of whom now in age, illness, and the neighborhood of death, is to him a daily, nightly, freshening memory and perfume.

But we see our article already eking itself too far. With regard to the poverty question, about which there have been such opposite stories, let Mr. Conway and the other gentlemen not be uneasy. No "pretences" yet given forth are half as dark and effective as the actual facts. Whitman, never worth property or lucre of any. Whitman, never worth property his money in certain ways, when he has any, (he has always of his moderate means given to the poor, sick, old and maimed, at least *thrice* the amount he has expended personally on his own wants) is now in the fourth year of a prostrating illness, with unintermitted daily expenses, shut off all that time from employment and income. Can any one doubt what the present state of the case is? what the future prospect? Fortunately yet, and with cheerful heart as ever, he is not only of simplest and most unexpensive personal habits, but of the mould that finds in age, pain, and any storms of penury, still ampler fields for the spirit, in the grandeur of sustaining and confronting them. "Walt Whitman," said lately one who knows him well, "takes the whole of his varied experiences and episodes, past and present, more as some of beings, and secretly one of the haughtiest, he would have gone under long ago. And there will never be contributed to the history of literature a more curious chapter than that which truly describes what has been called "the terrible parturition" of these poems.

About 1856, Whitman personally printed and put forth the first edition (1000 copies) of *Leaves of Grass.* It fell still-born from the press. Not twenty copies—not ten—were sold. Presentation ones were mostly sent back—some of them with insulting notes. (Apparently carried off his feet, however, R. W. Emerson made *salaam* to the book, and very lowly too; but he soon reacted, and got back into position; his praise created no impression, and was really of little consequence.)

The second enlarged edition, in the agency of a N. Y. Broadway firm, was hardly out before it was thrown up in terror and disgust, and the author notified by the firm that they would have nothing to do with such a book, and the bargain was cancelled. The third, fourth and fifth editions, (Whitman growing worse every time) fared no better. No copies worth mentioning were sold, of any issue. Criticism throughout was little more than a howl. Laughter and derision were occasionally shaded by the fierce charge of obsceneness. The London *Critic* called for "the executioner's whip," "Beastly" was the reiterated and remarkably original epithet of the *Saturday Review,* (which it still sticks to.) The *N. Y. Criterion Examiner* called it "a gathering of muck." The *Christian Examiner* called it "a crazy outbreak of conceit and vulgarity."

So things continued along to the war—one long stream of sputter or storm—book and poet, as far as noticed at all, derided, lampooned, yelped at. Of social and business results, coming home to the writer, one or two representative incidents of the train must suffice. Zealous, down among the war-fields and hospitals in 1863 and '64, Whitman gets a government clerkship, to serve as fulcrum in and around Washington for his army labors. When lo! the Hon. James Harlan, high cabinet officer, soon and summarily ejects him, openly and exclusively for being the author of *Leaves of Grass* The good of that day applaud this ignominious ejectment, and the newspapers think it a first-class joke.

About the same time another high representative cabinet officer (S. P. C.) answers to an earnest appeal from a Massachusetts man, one of Whitman's personal friends (J. T. T.) that he, the cabinet officer, must peremptorily refuse, as he could not and would not place gentlemen, the clerks of the Treasury Department, in the position of being forced to associate daily with such a person as the writer of *Leaves of Grass.*

But what is the use of multiplying these reminiscences? They could be accumulated to any extent, are well enough known, and are strictly representative

play, not acted around his own central figure, but a part of that great strange 'comedy human' which he yet, as all his life, loves so well to stand aside and observe."

As said, these facts and reminiscences are mainly important for showing that underneath all the escapades, and excessive emotional susceptibilities of the author of *Leaves of Grass,* his life and book are the most signal example on record of perseverance in and iron resolution and adherence to, *his and its own ideal.* For twenty years *has* he been a continuous target for slang, slur, insults, gas-promises, disappointments, caricature—without a publisher, and without a public—working away with composed and cheerful heart, as it were, in the darkness. Now, is the dawn glimmering—or not? His own lines to Lincoln, *dead* as soon as triumphant, (lines perhaps chanted by some young disciple, conning the voyage of W's life and poetry, and asking, Is *his* ship, too, at last coming in?) possess to-day a terrible appositeness:

O Captain! my Captain! our fearful trip is done;
The ship has weather'd every rack, the prize we sought is won;
The port is near, the bells I hear, the people all exulting,
While follow eyes the steady keel, the vessel grim and daring;
    But O heart! heart! heart!
      O the bleeding drops of red,
        Where on the deck my Captain lies,
          Fallen cold and dead.

O Captain! my Captain! rise up and hear the bells;
Rise up—for you the flag is flung—for you the bugle trills;
For you bouquets and ribbon'd wreaths—for you the shores a-crowding;
For you they call, the swaying mass, their eager faces turning;
    Here Captain! dear father!
      This arm beneath your head!
        It is some dream that on the deck,
          You've fallen cold and dead.

My Captain does not answer, his lips are pale and still;
My father does not feel my arm, he has no pulse nor will;
The ship is anchor'd safe and sound, its voyage closed and done;
From fearful trip, the victor ship, comes in with object won;
    Exult, O shores, and ring, O bells!
      But I, with mournful tread,
        Walk the deck my Captain lies,
          Fallen cold and dead.

Broadside (15¾"×6¼"), printed on recto only. Notation in Whitman's hand for *Philadelphia Press*, 16 April 1886. This item is a report of a lecture by Whitman. *Location:* RPB.

I 19
"A Death–Bouquet," *Philadelphia Press*, 2 February 1890.

According to *PW92*, this was sent to the *New York Sun* on 8 January and paid for, but the editor "failed to find this piece in either the Philadelphia or the New York paper" (*PW92*, II, 671n).

I 20
"Lines on Duluth," *Duluth Daily News*, 30 March 1892.

This poem was reprinted in the *New Orleans Item*, 4 April 1892; *UPP*, I, 30–31; and (partial) in *Early Poems and Fiction*, p. 52 (where it is called "certainly spurious" [p. 51n]). See also Thomas Ollive Mabbott, " 'Whitman's' Lines on Duluth," *American Literature*, 3 (November 1931), 316–317.

I 21
"Isle of La Belle Rivière," *Cincinnati Post*, 30 April 1892.

This poem was reprinted in *UPP*, I, 24–25, and *Early Poems and Fiction*, p. 50 (where it is called "a journalistic hoax" [p. 51n]). See also William White, "Walt Whitman's Short Stories: Some Comments and a Bibliography," *Papers of the Bibliographical Society of America*, 52 (4th Quarter 1958), 300–306.

I 22
Leaves of Grass. Chicago: Charles H. Kerr, [n.d.].

Cited in T. [Horace Traubel], "Whitman Editions," *Conservator*, 16 (December 1905), 157. Traubel's letterbook contains correspondence with Kerr in 1905 about the latter's plans to reprint the 1860 edition of *Leaves of Grass* (DLC). There is no evidence that this edition was published.

I 23
Corson, Hiram. *Spirit Messages*. Rochester, N.Y.: Austin, 1911.

"Spirit Messages" from Whitman, pp. 67–72, 229–236. Reprinted with the same title by the Christopher Publishing House of Boston in 1919. *Locations:* CRivL (1911), JM (1919).

I 24
A Lecture given by Walt Whitman before the Brooklyn Art Union on March 31, 1851 and Reported in the Brooklyn Daily Advertiser of April 3, 1851 and Notes. [Toronto: Henry S. Saunders, 1913].

20-page carbon typescript, limited to seven numbered copies, signed by Saunders. *Location:* NzD.

Note: Also prepared as 'A Lecture given by Walt Whitman before the Brooklyn Art Union on March 31st, 1851 and Reported in the Brooklyn Daily Advertiser of April 3, 1851 And Notes.', a 17-page carbon typescript, limited to nine numbered copies, signed by Saunders. *Location:* NNC.

I 25

Beginning in 1928, the Whitman scholar Rollo G. Silver printed lines from Whitman and distributed them as Christmas cards. None of these cards contains first appearance material. Listed below are those cards located; unless otherwise indicated, all the cards are a single sheet of paper folded twice to make eight pages, printed on one side of each page only.

1928	*Song of the Universal* (poem), wrappers, limited to 99 numbered copies (JM).
1929–1930	See *Note one.*
1931	*To Him That Was Crucified* (poem) (JM).
1932–1939	See *Note one.*
1940	See *Note two.*
1941	["Not a grave of the murder'd for freedom but grows"] (poem) (JM).
1942	["O star of France"] (poem) (JM).
1943	["I see the European headsman"] (poem) (JM).
1944	["The battle rages with many a loud alarm and"] (poem), broadside (JM).
1945	["O I see flashing that this America is only you and me"] (poem), broadside (JM).
1946	["The Four Years' War is over—and"] (prose), broadside (JM).
1947	*When I Heard the Learn'd Astronomer* (poem) (JM).
1948	*This Moment Yearning and Thoughtful* (poem) (JM).
1949	*Continuities* (poem) (JM).
1950	*Soon Shall the Winter's Foil Be Here* (poem), single leaf folded once to make four pages (JM).
1951	*On the Beach at Night* (poem), single leaf folded once to make four pages (ViU).
1952	["Here is the test of wisdom"] (poem), broadside (RPB).
1953	["Sail, sail thy best, ship of Democracy"] (poem) (JM).
1954	['And I say to mankind, Be not curious about God'] (poem), single leaf folded once to make four pages (JM).
1955	["There is something that comes to one now and perpetually"] (poem) (JM).
1956	["I do not think seventy years is the time of a man or a woman"] (poem), single leaf folded once to make four pages (JM).

1957	["The sum of all known reverence I add up in you whoever you are"] (poem) (JM).
1958	*O Me! O Life!* (poem), broadside (JM).
1959	*The Base of All Metaphysics* (poem) (JM).
1960	["Ever upon this stage"] (poem) (JM).
1961	["Know'st thou the excellent joys of youth?"] (poem) (RPB).
1962	["All you continentals of Asia, Africa, Europe"] (poem) (JM).
1963	*The Boston of To-day* (prose) (JM).
1964	["Never were such sharp questions ask'd as this day"] (poem), single leaf folded once to make four pages (JM).
1965	["Give me the splendid silent sun with all his beams full-dazzling"] (poem), single leaf folded once to make four pages (ViU).
1966	*Unseen Buds* (poem) (JM).
1967	["Whoever you are! you are he or she for"] (poem) (RPB).
1968	["I have said that the soul is not more than the body"] (poem) (JM).
1969	["What do you think endures"] (poem), single leaf folded once to make four pages (JM).
1970	["I say we had best look our times and lands searchingly"] (prose) (JM).
1971	*To a President* [and] ["The protectionists are fond of flashing to the public"] (poem; prose) (JM).
1972	["Political democracy, as it exists and practically works"] (prose), single leaf folded once to make four pages (JM).
1973	["It is the fashion among dillettants and fops"] (prose), single leaf folded once to make four pages (JM).
1974	*Origins of Attempted Secession* (prose), broadside (JM).
1975	["Are those really Congressmen? are those the great"] (poem), broadside (JM).
1976	["I learn'd one thing conclusively—that beneath all the"] (prose), broadside (JM).
1977	*Halcyon Days* (poem), broadside (JM).
1978	["All, all for immortality"] (poem), broadside (JM).
1979	*A Noiseless Patient Spider* (poem), broadside (RPB).
1980	*Ah Poverties, Wincings, and Sulky Retreats* (poem), broadside (JM).
1981	["When the psalm sings instead of the singer"] (poem), broadside (JM).
1982	["I think I could turn and live with the animals, they"] (poem), broadside (JM).
1983	*Not seen.*
1984	["Democracy, in silence, biding its time, ponders its own ideals, not of literature"] (prose), broadside (JM).

1985   ["O while I live to be the ruler of life, not a slave"] (poem),
              broadside (JM). This is the last card issued.

Note one: John Cook Wyllie of the University of Virgina wrote to Silver, 5
February 1957, asking about the gaps in the series of Christmas messages.
Silver replied that for the period between 1928 and 1931, "I was at college and
in 29 & 30 spent the money on wimmin"; in answer to the query "What of
those 20s & 30s?" Silver writes, "orchids coonskins bootleggers"; and concerning the gap between 1931 and 1940, Silver states, "31–40—lean, very lean,
years" (ViU).

Note two: In 1940, Silver's Christmas greeting was a non-Whitman item,
From Deor's Lament (ViU).

I 26
Trimble, Annie E. *Walt Whitman and Mental Science. An Interview.* [Mel-
bourne, Australia: Specialty Press, n.d.].

15 pp. Wrappers. An "interview" with Whitman quoting extensively from his
works. CaOTU copy received 8 June 1939. CSt copy dated '1911'. Limited to
200 numbered copies signed by the author. *Locations:* CSt, CaOTU.

I 27
White, William. "Walt Whitman's 'Elegy': An Early Poem?", *Notes and Queries,* n.s. 9 (June 1962), 227–228.

Questions whether this poem, in Whitman's hand, is actually by him.

I 28
Leaves of Grass and Selected Prose. Cleveland: World, [1967].

Wrappers. Edited by E. Fred Carlisle. Listed in *BIP* (1967) at $1.95. According
to Professor Carlisle, the book was canceled in page proof and not published
(letter to Myerson, 2 March 1987).

I 29
To Love Free: The Greatest Romantic Poems of Walt Whitman. [N.p.]: April
House, [1972].

Edited by Edward Scott [pseud. Webster Schott]. Listed in published copyright
catalogue: 1 December 1972; A 402491 ('1 v.'). No evidence can be found to
indicate that this book was actually published.

I 30
A Marriage of True Minds: Walt Whitman to Dora, comp. and ed. Dilys Gold.
London: Regency, [1990].

"Spirit Messages" from Whitman. *Location:* JM.

131

Titles published by Folcroft (Folcroft, Penn.), Norwood (Folcroft, Penn.), and Richard West (Philadelphia).

Books published under these imprints appear to be from the same publisher. Typically, one facsimile reprinting is repackaged with inserted title leaves bearing each of the three imprints.

Appendixes / Indexes

Appendix

Principal Works about Whitman

Allen, Gay Wilson. *The New Walt Whitman Handbook*. New York: New York University Press, 1975.

———. *A Reader's Guide to Walt Whitman*. New York: Farrar, Straus and Giroux, 1970.

———. *The Solitary Singer: A Critical Biography of Walt Whitman*. New York: Macmillan, 1955; rev. ed., New York: New York University Press, 1967; rev. ed., Chicago: University of Chicago Press, 1985.

———. *Walt Whitman*. New York: Grove Press, 1961.

———, ed. *Walt Whitman Abroad: Critical Essays from Germany, France, Scandinavia, Russia, Italy, Spain, and Latin America, Israel, Japan, and India*. Syracuse: Syracuse University Press, 1955.

———. *Walt Whitman as Man, Poet and Legend*. Carbondale: Southern Illinois University Press, 1961.

———. *Walt Whitman Handbook*. Chicago: Packard, 1946.

Arvin, Newton. *Whitman*. New York: Macmillan, 1938.

Aspiz, Harold. *Walt Whitman and the Body Beautiful*. Urbana: University of Illinois Press, 1980.

Asselineau, Roger. *The Evolution of Walt Whitman: The Creation of a Book*. Cambridge: Harvard University Press, 1962.

———. *The Evolution of Walt Whitman: The Creation of a Poet*. Cambridge: Harvard University Press, 1960.

———, and William White, eds. *Walt Whitman in Europe Today: A Collection of Essays*. Detroit: Wayne State University Press, 1972.

Bailey, John. *Walt Whitman*. New York: Macmillan, 1926.

Barrus, Clara. *Whitman and Burroughs: Comrades*. Boston: Houghton Mifflin, 1931.

Bazalgette, Leon. *Walt Whitman,* trans. Ellen FitzGerald. Garden City, N.Y.: Doubleday, Page, 1920.

Beaver, Joseph. *Walt Whitman: Poet of Science*. New York: King's Crown Press, 1951.

Binns, Henry Bryan. *A Life of Walt Whitman*. London: Methuen, 1905.

Black, Stephen A. *Walt Whitman's Journey into Chaos*. New Brunswick: Rutgers University Press, 1975.

Blodgett, Harold. *Walt Whitman in England*. Ithaca: Cornell University Press, 1934.

983

Born, Helen. *Whitman's Ideal Democracy*. Boston: Everett Press, 1902.

Brasher, Thomas L. *Whitman as Editor of the* Brooklyn Daily Eagle. Detroit: Wayne State University Press, 1970.

Briggs, Arthur E. *Walt Whitman: Thinker and Artist*. New York: Philosophical Library, 1952.

Bucke, Richard Maurice. *Cosmic Consciousness*. New York: E. P. Dutton, 1923.

———. *Richard Maurice Bucke, Medical Mystic: Letters of Dr. Bucke to Walt Whitman and His Friends*, ed. Artem Lozynsky. Detroit: Wayne State University Press, 1977.

———. *Walt Whitman*. Philadelphia: David McKay, 1883.

Burroughs, John. *Notes on Walt Whitman as Poet and Person*. New York: American News Company, 1867.

———. *Whitman: A Study*. Boston: Houghton, Mifflin, 1896.

Byers, Thomas B. *What I Cannot Say: Self, Word, and World in Whitman, Stevens,and Merwin*. Urbana: University of Illinois Press, 1989.

Cady, Edwin H., and Louis J. Budd, eds. *On Whitman: The Best from* American Literature. Durham: Duke University Press, 1987.

Canby, Henry Seidel. *Walt Whitman: An American*. Boston: Houghton Mifflin, 1943.

Carlisle, E. Fred. *The Uncertain Self: Whitman's Drama of Identity*. East Lansing: Michigan State University Press, 1973.

Carpenter, Edward. *Days with Walt Whitman*. London: George Allen, 1906.

———. *Some Friends of Walt Whitman: A Study in Sex-Psychology*. London: n.p., 1924.

Carpenter, George Rice. *Walt Whitman*. New York: Macmillan, 1909.

Catel, Jean. *Walt Whitman: La Naissance du Poète*. Paris: Editions Rieder, 1929.

Cavitch, David. *My Soul and I: The Inner Life of Walt Whitman*. Boston: Beacon Press, 1985.

Chari, V. K. *Walt Whitman in the Light of Vedantic Mysticism: An Interpretation*. Lincoln: University of Nebraska Press, 1965.

Chase, Richard. *Walt Whitman*. Minneapolis: University of Minnesota Press, 1961.

———. *Walt Whitman Reconsidered*. New York: William Slaone, 1955.

Clark, Leadie M. *Walt Whitman's Conception of the American Common Man*. New York: Philosophical Library, 1955.

Clarke, William. *Walt Whitman*. London: Swan Sonnenschein, 1892.

Crawley, Thomas Edward. *The Structure of* Leaves of Grass. Austin: University of Texas Press, 1970.

De Selincourt, Basil. *Walt Whitman: A Critical Study*. London: Martin Secker, 1914.

Donaldson, Thomas. *Walt Whitman, the Man*. New York: Francis P. Harper, 1896.

Duffey, Bernard. *Poetry in America: Expression and Its Values in the Times of Bryant, Whitman, and Pound*. Durham: Duke University Press, 1978.

Dutton, Geoffrey. *Whitman*. New York: Grove Press, 1961.

Eby, Edwin Harold. *A Concordance to Walt Whitman's "Leaves of Grass" and Selected Prose Writings*, 5 parts. Seattle: University of Washington Press, 1949–1955.

Eitner, Walter H. *Walt Whitman's Western Jaunt*. Lawrence: Regents Press of Kansas, 1981.

Elliot, Charles N., ed. *Walt Whitman as Man, Poet and Friend*. Boston: Richard G. Badger, 1915.

Erkkila, Betsy. *Walt Whitman Among the French: Poet and Myth*. Princeton: Princeton University Press, 1980.

———. *Whitman: The Political Poet*. New York: Oxford University Press, 1989.

Faner, Robert D. *Walt Whitman and Opera*. Philadelphia: University of Pennsylvania Press, 1951.

Faussett, Hugh I'Anson. *Walt Whitman: Poet of Democracy*. New Haven: Yale University Press, 1942.

Francis, Gloria A., and Artem Lozynsky, eds. *Whitman at Auction, 1899–1972*. Detroit: Gale, 1978.

Freedman, Florence Bernstein. *William Douglas O'Connor: Walt Whitman's Chosen Knight*. Athens: Ohio University Press, 1985.

Gardner, Thomas. *Discovering Ourselves in Whitman: The Contemporary American Long Poem*. Urbana: University of Illinois Press, 1989.

Gay, William. *Walt Whitman: His Relation to Science and Philosophy*. Melbourne, Australia: Firth and M'Cutcheon, 1895.

Giantvalley, Scott. *Walt Whitman, 1838–1939: A Reference Guide*. Boston: G. K. Hall, 1981.

Grant, Douglas. *Walt Whitman and His English Admirers*. Leeds: Leeds University Press, 1962.

Greenspan, Ezra. *Walt Whitman and the American Reader*. Cambridge, England: Cambridge University Press, 1990.

Guthrie, William N. *Walt Whitman: Camden Sage*. Cincinnati: Robert Clarke, 1897.

Hayes, Will. *Walt Whitman: The Prophet of the New Era*. London: C. W. Daniel, 1921.

Hayman, Ronald. *Arguing with Walt Whitman*. London: Covent Garden Press, 1971.

Hindus, Milton, ed. Leaves of Grass: *One Hundred Years After*. Stanford: Stanford University Press, 1955.

Hindus, Milton, ed. *Walt Whitman: The Critical Heritage*. London: Routledge and Kegan Paul, 1971.

Hollis, C. Carroll. *Language and Style in* Leaves of Grass. Baton Rouge: Louisiana State University Press, 1983.

Holloway, Emory. *Free and Lonesome Heart: The Secret of Walt Whitman.* New York: Vantage Press, 1960.

———. *Whitman: An Interpretation in Narrative.* New York: Alfred A. Knopf, 1926.

Hutchinson, George B. *The Ecstatic Whitman: Literary Shamanism & the Crisis of the Union.* Columbus: Ohio State University Press, 1986.

Ignoffo, Matthew F. *What the War Did to Whitman.* New York: Vantage Press, 1975.

Johnston, John. *Notes of a Visit to Walt Whitman, etc., in July, 1890.* Bolton: T. Brimelow, 1890; rev. ed., *Diary Notes of a Visit to Walt Whitman and Some of His Friends* (Manchester: Labour Press, 1898); rev. ed., with J. W. Wallace, *Visits to Walt Whitman in 1890–1891* (London: George Allen, 1917).

Kaplan, Justin. *Walt Whitman: A Life.* New York: Simon and Schuster, 1980.

Keller, Elizabeth Leavitt. *Walt Whitman in Mickle Street.* New York: Mitchell Kennerley, 1921.

Kennedy, William Sloane. *The Fight of a Book for the World.* West Yarmouth, Mass.: Stonecroft Press, 1926.

———. *Reminiscences of Walt Whitman.* London: Alexander Gardner, 1896.

Killingsworth, M. Jimmie. *Whitman's Poetry of the Body: Sexuality, Politics, and the Text.* Chapel Hill: University of North Carolina Press, 1989.

Knox, George, and Henry Lawton, eds. *The Whitman-Hartmann Controversy.* Bern: Herbert Lang, 1976.

Krieg, Joann P., ed. *Walt Whitman: Here and Now.* Westport, Conn.: Greenwood Press, 1985.

Kuebrich, David. *Minor Prophecy: Walt Whitman's New American Religion.* Bloomington: Indiana University Press, 1990.

Kummings, Donald D. *Walt Whitman, 1940–1975: A Reference Guide.* Boston: G. K. Hall, 1982.

Larson, Kerry C. *Whitman's Drama of Consensus.* Chicago: University of Chicago Press, 1988.

Law-Robertson, Harry. *Walt Whitman in Deutschland.* Giessen: Munchowsche Universitats, 1935.

Lewis, R. W. B., ed. *The Presence of Walt Whitman.* New York: Columbia University Press, 1962.

Long, Haniel. *Walt Whitman and the Springs of Courage.* Sante Fe, N.M.: Writers' Editions, 1938.

Loving, Jerome M. *Emerson, Whitman, and the American Muse.* Chapel Hill: University of North Carolina Press, 1982.

———. *Walt Whitman's Champion: William Douglas O'Connor.* College Station: Texas A&M University Press, 1978.

Marki, Ivan. *The Trial of the Poet: An Interpretation of the First Edition of Leaves of Grass.* New York: Columbia University Press, 1976.

Masters, Edgar Lee. *Whitman*. New York: Scribners, 1937.

Matthiessen, F. O. *American Renaissance: Art and Expression in the Age of Emerson and Whitman*. New York: Oxford University Press, 1941.

McLeod, A. L. *Walt Whitman in Australia and New Zealand: A Record of His Reception*. Sydney, Australia: Wentworth Press, 1964. Mimeographed.

Mendelson, Maurice. *Life and Work of Walt Whitman: A Soviet View*. Moscow: Progress Publishers, 1976.

Metzger, Charles R. *Thoreau and Whitman: A Study of Their Aesthetics*. Seattle: University of Washington Press, 1961.

Middlebrook, Diane Wood. *Walt Whitman and Wallace Stevens*. Ithaca: Cornell University Press, 1974.

Miller, Edwin Haviland. *Walt Whitman's Poetry: A Psychological Journey*. Boston: Houghton Mifflin, 1968.

———. *Walt Whitman's "Song of Myself": A Mosaic of Interpretations*. Iowa City: University of Iowa Press, 1989.

Miller, Edwin Haviland, ed. *The Artistic Legacy of Walt Whitman: A Tribute to Gay Wilson* Allen. New York: New York University Press, 1970.

Miller, Edwin Haviland, ed. *A Century of Whitman Criticism*. Bloomington: Indiana University Press, 1969.

Miller, James E., Jr. *A Critical Guide to* Leaves of Grass. Chicago: University of Chicago Press, 1955.

———. *The American Quest for a Supreme Fiction: Whitman's Legacy in the Personal Epic*. Chicago: University of Chicago Press, 1979.

———. *Walt Whitman*. New York: Twayne, 1962; rev. ed., Boston: G. K. Hall, 1990.

Moon, Michael. *Disseminating Whitman: Revision and Coporeality in* Leaves of Grass. Cambridge: Harvard University Press, 1991.

Morris, Harrison S. *Walt Whitman: A Brief Biography with Reminiscences*. Cambridge: Harvard University Press, 1929.

Musgrove, S. *T. S. Eliot and Whitman*. Wellington: New Zealand University Press, 1952.

Myerson, Joel, ed. *Whitman in His Own Time: A Biographical Chronicle of His Life, Drawn from Recollections, Memoirs, and Interviews by Friends and Associates*. Detroit: Omnigraphics, 1991.

Nambiar, O. K. *Walt Whitman and Yoga*. Bangalore, India: Jeevan Publications, 1966.

O'Connor, William Douglas. *The Good Gray Poet: A Vindication*. New York: Bunce and Huntington, 1866.

Pearce, Roy Harvey. *The Continuity of American Poetry*. Princeton: Princeton University Press, 1961.

Perlman, Jim, Ed Folsom, and Dan Campion, eds. *Walt Whitman: The Measure of His Song*. Minneapolis: Holy Cow! Press, 1981.

Perry, Bliss. *Walt Whitman*. Boston: Houghton Mifflin, 1906; rev. ed., 1908.

Platt, Isaac Hull. *Walt Whitman*. Boston: Small, Maynard, 1904.

Price, Kenneth M. *Whitman and Tradition: The Poet in His Century*. New Haven: Yale University Press, 1990.

Pucciana, Oreste F. *The Literary Reputation of Walt Whitman in France*. New York: Garland, 1987.

Rajasekharaiah, T. R. *The Roots of* Leaves of Grass: *Eastern Sources of Walt Whitman's Poetry*. Rutherford, N.J.: Fairleigh Dickinson University Press, 1970.

Rivers, W. C. *Walt Whitman's Anomaly*. London: George Allen, 1913.

Rogers, Cameron. *The Magnificent Idler: The Story of Walt Whitman*. Garden City, N.Y.: Doubleday, Page, 1926.

Rubin, Joseph Jay. *The Historic Whitman*. University Park: Pennsylvania State University Press, 1973.

Salska, Agnieszka. *Walt Whitman and Emily Dickinson: Poetry of the Central Consciousness*. Philadelphia: University of Pennsylvania Press, 1985.

Schyberg, Frederik. *Walt Whitman,* trans. Evie Allison Allen. New York: Columbia University Press, 1951.

Shephard, Esther. *Walt Whitman's Pose*. New York: Harcourt, Brace, 1938.

Smuts, Jan Christian. *Walt Whitman: A Study of the Evolution of a Personality,* ed. Alan L. McLeod. Detroit: Wayne State University Press, 1973.

Snyder, John. *The Dear Love of Man: Tragic and Lyric Communion in Walt Whitman*. The Hague: Mouton, 1975.

Stovall, Floyd. *The Foreground of* Leaves of Grass. Charlottesville: University Press of Virginia, 1974.

Symonds, John Addington. *Walt Whitman: A Study*. London: George Routledge, 1893.

Thomas, M. Wynn. *The Lunar Light of Whitman's Poetry*. Cambridge: Harvard University Press, 1987.

Thomson, James. *Walt Whitman*. London: Bertram Dobell, 1910.

Traubel, Horace L., Richard Maurice Bucke, and Thomas B. Harned, eds., *In Re Walt Whitman*. Philadelphia: David McKay, 1893.

Triggs, Oscar L. *Browning and Whitman: A Study in Democracy*. Chicago: University of Chicago Press, 1893.

Trimble, W. H. *Walt Whitman and* Leaves of Grass. London: Watts, 1905.

Walker, Jeffrey. *Bardic Ethos and the American Epic Poem: Whitman, Pound, Crane, Williams, Olson*. Baton Rouge: Louisiana State University Press, 1989.

Warren, James Perrin. *Walt Whitman's Language Experiment*. University Park: Pennsylvania State University Press, 1990.

Waskow, Howard. *Whitman: Explorations in Form*. Chicago: University of Chicago Press, 1966.

Whitman, George Washington. *Civil War Letters of George Washington Whitman,* ed. Jerome M. Loving. Durham: Duke University Press, 1975.

Whitman, Iris Lilian. *Whitman and Spain*. New York: Instituto de Las Espanas, 1927.

Whitman, Martha Mitchell. *Mattie: The Letters of Martha Mitchell Whitman*, ed. Randall H. Waldron. New York: New York University Press, 1977.

Whitman, Thomas Jefferson. *Dear Brother Walt: The Letters of Thomas Jefferson Whitman*, ed. Dennis Berthold and Kenneth Price. Kent: Kent State University Press, 1984.

Willard, Charles B. *Whitman's American Fame*. Providence: Brown University Press, 1950.

Winwar, Frances. *American Giant: Walt Whitman and His Times*. New York: Harpers, 1941.

Woodress, James, ed. *Critical Essays on Walt Whitman*. Boston: G. K. Hall, 1983.

Zweig, Paul. *Walt Whitman: The Making of the Poet*. New York: Basic Books, 1984.

Index to the Poems in
Leaves of Grass

The following index lists by title all poems that appeared in *Leaves of Grass* during Whitman's lifetime, their first newspaper or magazine appearance (if any), which edition(s) and on what page(s) they appeared, and cross-references to revisions that appeared under other titles. Included in this index are all annexes that Whitman added to *Leaves of Grass*. Poems that were not collected in *Leaves of Grass* or that were published after Whitman's death are not listed; information on them may be obtained by using the general index to this volume. Minor variations among the titles of poems are not noted.

The following abbreviations are used:

55	*Leaves of Grass* (1855)
56	*Leaves of Grass* (1856)
60	*Leaves of Grass* (1860)
67	*Leaves of Grass* (1867)
67[SBP]	"Songs Before Parting" annex to *Leaves of Grass* (1867)
71	*Leaves of Grass* (1871)
71[PI]	*Passage to India* (1871), used as an annex to *Leaves of Grass* (1871)
72[PI]	*Passage to India* (1871), used an an annex to *Leaves of Grass* (1872), and as an annex to *Two Rivulets* (1876)
76[ASB]	*As a Strong Bird on Pinions Free, and Other Poems* (1871), used as an annex to *Two Rivulets* (1876)
76[CE]	*Leaves of Grass. With Portraits and Intercalations* (1876), the *Centennial Edition*
76[CS]	"Centennial Songs" section of *Two Rivulets* (1876)
76[TE]	*Leaves of Grass. With Portraits from Life* (1876), the trade edition
76[TR]	"Two Rivulets" section of *Two Rivulets* (1876)
81	*Leaves of Grass* (1881–1882)
82[Camden]	*Leaves of Grass* (Camden, 1882)
88[SS]	"Sands at Seventy" annex to *Leaves of Grass* (1888)
91	*Leaves of Grass* (1891–92)
91[GBF]	*Good-Bye My Fancy* (1891) annex to *Leaves of Grass* (1891–92)

991

AA	*Art Autograph*
AMM	*Atlantic Monthly Magazine*
Am	*American* (Philadelphia)
Ath	*Atheæum*
B	*Broadway*
BDET	*Boston Daily Evening Transcript*
BDG	*Boston Daily Globe*
CM	*Century Magazine*
CPP	*Complete Poems & Prose* (1888)
CPP[NB]	*November Boughs* (1888) annex to *Complete Poems & Prose* (1888)
CPP[SD]	*Specimen Days* (1882) annex to *Complete Poems & Prose* (1888)
CTP	*Cope's Tobacco Plant* (Liverpool)
Co	*Cosmopolitan*
Cr	*Critic*
DT	*Drum-Taps* (1865). Also as an annex to *Leaves of Grass* (1867)
DTS	*Sequel to Drum-Taps* (1866). Also as an annex to *Leaves of Grass* (1867)
FP	*Forney's Progress*
G	*Galaxy*
HMM	*Harper's Monthly Magazine*
HWM	*Harper's Weekly Magazine*
KM	*Kansas Magazine*
LM	*Lippincott's Magazine*
MIW	*Munyon's Illustrated World*
McM	*McClure's Magazine*
MuM	*Munyon's Magazine*
NC	*Nineteenth Century*
NODC	*New Orleans Daily Crescent*
NYDG	*New York Daily Graphic*
NYDT	*New York Daily Tribune*
NYEP	*New York Evening Post*
NYH	*New York Herald*
NYL	*New York Leader*
NYW	*New York World*
NYWT	*New York Weekly Tribune*
O	*Outing*
PMG	*Pall Mall Gazette*
PP	*Philadelphia Press*
SEV	*Saturday Evening Visitor* (Washington)
SLM	*Southern Literary Messenger*

SP   *Saturday Press* (New York)
T   *Truth* (New York)

Index

Pittsburgh Series in Bibliography